Handbook of Research in Second Language Teaching and Learning
Volume II

This landmark volume provides a broad-based, comprehensive, state-of-the-art overview of current knowledge and research into second language teaching and learning. All authors are leading authorities in their areas of expertise. Fifty-seven chapters, all completely new for *Volume II*, are organized in eight thematic sections:

- Social Contexts in Research on Second Language Teaching and Learning
- Second Language Research Methods
- Second Language Research and Applied Linguistics
- Research in Second Language Processes and Development
- Methods and Instruction in Second Language Teaching
- Second Language Assessment
- Ideology, Identity, Culture, and Critical Pedagogy in Second Language Teaching and Learning
- Language Planning and Policy

Changes in *Volume II*:

- Captures new and ongoing developments, research, and trends that have evolved in the key areas of second language teaching and learning
- Surveys prominent areas of research that were not covered in *Volume I*
- Includes new authors from Asia, Australia, Europe, and North America to broaden the *Handbook*'s international scope

The *Handbook of Research in Second Language Teaching and Learning, Volume II* is primarily oriented toward ESL and EFL teachers, teacher trainers, teacher trainees, graduate students, and faculty in MA-TESL and applied linguistics programs, as well as curriculum and material developers.

Eli Hinkel, Professor, Seattle University, has taught ESL and applied linguistics, as well as trained teachers, for more than 30 years.

ESL & Applied Linguistics Professional Series
Eli Hinkel, Series Editor

Handbook of Research in Second Language Teaching and Learning

Volume II

Edited by
Eli Hinkel
Seattle University

Routledge
Taylor & Francis Group

NEW YORK AND LONDON

First published 2011
by Routledge
711 Third Avenue, New York, NY 10017

Simultaneously published in the UK
by Routledge
2 Park Square, Milton Park, Abingdon, Oxon OX14 4RN

Routledge is an imprint of the Taylor & Francis Group, an informa business

© 2011 Taylor & Francis

The right of Eli Hinkel to be identified as the author of the editorial material, and of the authors for their individual chapters, has been asserted in accordance with sections 77 and 78 of the Copyright, Designs and Patents Act 1988.

Typeset in Minion by Swales & Willis Ltd, Exeter, Devon
Printed and bound in the United States of America on acid-free paper by Edwards Brothers, Inc.

Library of Congress Cataloging in Publication Data
Handbook of research in second language teaching and learning / edited by Eli Hinkel.
  p. cm.
  Includes bibliographical references and index.
  1. Second language acquisition. 2. Language and languages—Study and teaching.
  3. English language—Study and teaching—Foreign speakers. I. Hinkel, Eli.
  P118.2.H359 2005
  418—dc22

ISBN13: 978–0–415–99871–0 (hbk)
ISBN13: 978–0–415–99872–7 (pbk)
ISBN13: 978–0–203–83650–7 (ebk)

Contents

Preface

"And how many hours a day did you do lessons?" said Alice, in a hurry to change the subject.
"Ten hours the first day," said the Mock Turtle: "nine the next, and so on."
"What a curious plan!" exclaimed Alice.
"That's the reason they're called lessons," the Gryphon remarked:
"because they lessen from day to day."

Lewis Carroll, Alice's Adventures in Wonderland

Overview

The quickening pace of globalization and the increasing influence of English as lingua franca world-wide has brought to the foreground the importance of research in second (L2) and foreign (FL) language teaching and learning. As was the case with Volume I of the *Handbook in Second Language Teaching and Learning,* the evolving complexities of human societies, political structures, and the expanding range of needs in L2 and FL learning and teaching call for novel perspectives on L2 research. In addition, however, the appearance of Volume II attests to the fact that the rapid changes in the discipline of L2 and FL teaching and research make practically any state-of-the-art overview dated even before it is published.

The overarching purpose of Volume II of the *Handbook* is to revisit, review, supplement, and complement Volume I. Several chapters in this book present entirely new perspectives and update the research in the subdisciplines that deal with the essential areas of investigation in L2 teaching and learning. That is, Volume II is not a second edition of Volume I, but it is a whole new book that covers new territories and research venues. As with Volume I, the content of Volume II continues to strive to remain comprehensive and inclusive, as much as possible within the scope of one book. The lineup of chapter authors also adheres to the original strategy of selecting leading authorities in their disciplinary areas. It is important to note, however, that this compendium of articles on research in second language teaching and learning, just like any other of its kind, does not aspire to cover the entire enormous range of variables that directly or indirectly impact L2 teaching and learning. In combination, though, both Volumes I and II have a better chance of presenting more thoroughly essential study areas in the field of language teaching and learning.

A collection of state-of-the-art overviews of what is known, important, advantageous, relevant, influential, fruitful, theoretical, practical, or controversial and contradictory in L2 teaching and learning may have little choice but exclude a number of research areas. This obvious constraint applies equally to both Volumes I and II of the *Handbook.* In part due to its comparatively short history as a discipline, research on second language teaching and learning has been a dynamic field, where new venues and perspectives continuously evolve and develop. The growth of new knowledge about the how and the what of L2 teaching and learning is certain to continue along its path of disciplinary maturation.

Like Volume I, Volume II seeks to bring together a comprehensive, state-of-the-art overview of current research into social contexts of L2 teaching and learning, research methods, contributions of applied linguistics to second language research, research into L2 processes and development, teaching methods and instruction, second language assessment (but less so testing, as was the case in Volume I), the place of ideology in second language education, second culture and a learner's identity, as well as critical L2 literacy, and language rights, policy, and planning.

The new features of the book are highlighted below, followed by those features that have endured the test of time and are therefore retained in Volume II.

New Directions, Contents, Chapters, and Authors in Volume II

The content changes in Volume II accomplish three goals:

1. survey the prominent areas of research that were not addressed or received less attention than they should have in Volume I due to space limitations
2. capture new and ongoing developments, research, and trends that have evolved in the key mainstay areas of L2 teaching and learning, to supplement their coverage in Volume I, e.g. the teaching of second language learners in school, teaching English as an International Language and as a Foreign Language in Europe, central and evolving directions in second language research methods, the contexts of language socialization, as well as the foundational language skills, such as speaking, listening, reading, writing, grammar, and vocabulary
3. present novel perspectives on research domains that have become particularly prominent in the past several years, since the publication of Volume I, e.g. English as an International Language, World Englishes, or the teaching of English within new European migratory realities

The author and chapter changes have the goal of bringing to the foreground additional innovative and expert perspectives on the foundational subdisciplines in L2 teaching and learning. As in Volume I, all authors in Volume II are leading authorities in their areas of expertise. Volume II includes 57 chapters with 17 returning and 40 new authors.

- One of the important changes in Volume II is an inclusion of new authors from Asia, Australia, Europe, and North America to expand to the book's international scope.
- Some authors whose names are synonymous with their areas of expertise and who are the pre-eminent figures in their subdisciplines have been invited back to contribute to Volume II. Nonetheless, all chapters are completely new and will not significantly overlap content in those domains published in Volume I.
- Some authors with world-class reputations and diverse research interests have chosen to work on chapters on topic areas different from those in their Volume I chapters.
- The Guest Editor of the Language Policy and Planning section, Richard Baldauf, University of Queensland, continues to edit this section in Volume II. The new overview of Language Policy and Planning includes all new chapters on current and broad-based areas, fundamentally different from those in Volume I.
- Carol Chapelle, Iowa State University, is the new Guest Editor of the Second Language Assessment

section. The new section focuses predominantly on assessment in various facets in L2 teaching and learning, and in this regard, bears little resemblance to the Testing section in Volume I. The assessment of, for instance, language ability, learning in the classroom, and social and political contexts of language assessment pick up on the thematic threads addressed in earlier chapters of the book.

Revisited Research Themes in L2 Teaching and Learning

The selection of the topics and areas of research for inclusion are based on several criteria, similar to those noted in Volume I. Like Volume I, Volume II of the *Handbook* seeks to provide state of the art overview of what is known and of what requires further study in a broad array of domains of second language teaching and learning. To this end, the far-ranging areas of research requisite in a comprehensive survey have remained largely unaltered:

- social contexts in research on second language teaching and learning
- second language research methods
- second language research and applied linguistics
- research in second language processes and development
- methods and instruction in second language teaching
- second language assessment
- ideology, identity, culture, and critical literacy in L2 teaching and learning
- language planning and policy

The main reason for some similarity of the research areas in Volume I and II is that it seems impossible for a handbook on L2 teaching and learning to proceed without the disciplinary essentials, such as research in the social contexts where second languages are taught and learned, methods for conducting academic studies, investigations of prevalent pedagogical approaches, or the current state of language assessment. However, within these broad-scope disciplinary foundations, the contents of the two volumes diverge substantially.

Both volumes of the *Handbook* are geared to all types of second and foreign language professionals: researchers and researchers-in-training, advanced and not-so-advanced graduate students, faculty in teacher training, teacher education, and applied linguistics programs, practicing, novice, and pre-service teachers, teacher trainers, curriculum designers, and material developers, or others who are still merely considering joining the profession.

The Organization of the Book

Part I, Social Contexts in Research on Second Language Teaching and Learning, begins with the research in many social contexts of learning and types of L2 learners and users that have different language learning needs and goals. The ten chapters in this section of the book focus on the populations and individuals who seek to learn and teach a second and foreign language in various locations, institutions, and political and educational systems, and with broad-ranging objectives for achieving different L2/FL proficiencies in order to accomplish their educational, vocational, personal, academic, professional, career, and communicative objectives.

Methods for research in second language teaching and learning are the focus of the second part of the book—**Part II, Second Language Research Methods**. Each of the five themes discussed in these chapters address divergent approaches to gathering, analyzing, and interpreting data, associated with L2 research.

The areas of applied linguistics that deal directly with research in L2 teaching and learning are presented in **Part III, Second Language Research and Applied Linguistics**. These seven chapters treat a number of broad domains of research such as the application and applicability of Second Language Acquisition (SLA) research, discourse analysis, the contexts of language socialization, L2 pragmatics, sociocultural theory and cognitive linguistics, conversational analysis and its relevance in language teaching and learning, and the role of corpus analyses in all manner of language pedagogy.

The ten chapters in **Part IV, Research in Second Language Processes and Development**, address the foundational elements of L2 teaching and learning. The study of the ecology and semiotic of language learning portrays an overarching perspective on the entire enterprise of language teaching and learning. The research into cognitive aptitudes that enable one to learn a language largely speaks to the strengths and limitations of the human condition, as do the studies of the Critical Periods in language learning that continue to remain hypotheses after many decades of research. Interactional competence and its attendant skills are similarly intertwined with the development of the essential L2 skills, such as speaking, listening, literacy and biliteracy, reading, grammar, and writing. At its core, L2 teaching and learning is fundamentally a very human undertaking, with all its advantages and flaws, and this essential theme largely undergirds the contents of chapters in Part IV.

The nine chapters in **Part V, Methods and Instruction in Second Language Teaching,** attempt to deal only with a few prominent exemplars widely adopted in various geographic locations and social contexts around the world. For example, the communicative method has been slowly changing how foreign languages, including English, are taught in many countries. However, the continued prevalence of traditional instructional methods also accords it a pride of place in various regions around the globe. The corrective feedback movement undertakes to research how this feature of language instruction has steadily gained importance in L2 pedagogy. In the past decade, content-based language teaching has become central in a range of teaching contexts and at various levels of schooling, such as elementary and secondary, including both majority- and minority-language learners. Research in written discourse and the applications of its findings to teaching L2 writing is probably one of the more robust areas in the academy today, and no handbook on second language anything can proceed without an overview of the current state of affairs in this discipline. The same can said about the proliferation of technology in language instruction in and out of school, as well as the expansion of techniques and innovative applications in Computer Assisted Language Learning. The chapter on L2 learner strategies highlights of strategies for language learning across all methods and approaches.

The six chapters in **Part VI, Second Language Assessment,** underscore the vexing complexity of language testing and assessment, as it is closely tied to L2 learning, learning processes, and inferential measurements of L2 competence, proficiency, and skill. Thus, the chapters in Part VI present brief overviews of the socio-political contexts of language assessment, considerations of validity and the history of testing, research methods, testing of language for specific purposes, and classroom-centered language assessment.

The topics of **Ideology, Identity, Culture, and Critical Pedagogy** are examined in **Part VII**. Research into the connections between language learning and ideology in language education, as well as learners' and teachers' identities, and intercultural communication in language education shows that these play a pivotal role in how languages are taught and learned around the world. The importance of critical literacy in the modern-day and technological society cannot be underestimated, as it undergrids the learner's path in contemporary educational and professional endeavors.

The six chapters in **Part VIII, Language Planning and Policy** present an overview of the important directions in the research of language policy and planning, and the impact of these on minority language rights. The introductory chapter outlines a number of general key issues and terms and a general framework for the types of activities that define the field. The next five chapters discuss the classic activity types and focus on the important recent research specifically geared toward language teaching and learning.

The Structure of the Chapters

In this volume, the principles for selecting and structuring chapters have largely remained the same as they were in Volume I. Based on the survey of professional associations and organizations around the globe, followed by a similar review of research themes at professional meetings, the areas of relevance and currency were relatively easy to identify. An examination of research articles published during the past decade in over 30 academic journals served as the foundation for selecting the relevant topics for the book as a whole. The purpose of the chapters is to highlight the major findings and advancements in various regions around the world.

Nonetheless, despite the great diversity of the field, research, and disciplinary perspectives, every effort has been made to make the chapters consistent in style, tone, and the depth of material coverage. For this purpose, all contributors were requested construct their chapters along a similar outline:

- An explanation of how the topic discussed in the chapter fits into a larger picture of the domain of L2 research
- Important developments, trends, and traditions in the discipline, as well as current controversies and the reasons that they have arisen
- A detailed examination of the current research findings presented in the chapter
- A section on conclusions and/or future research directions
- A substantial list of references that can assist interested readers in backtracking seminal and relevant works

Each chapter represents a stand alone examination of research in a specific L2 subdomain, yet, the book as a whole seeks to reflect the major trends in the current investigations into the people and the contexts where and how second and foreign languages are taught and learned.

Acknowledgements

I owe a debt of gratitude to my friends and colleagues whose guidance, assistance, and advice were vital. I am sincerely and deeply grateful to them for giving generously of their knowledge, experience, and time (in alphabetical order):

Carol Chapelle, Iowa State University
Nancy Hornberger, University of Pennsylvania
Elliot Judd, University of Illinois, Chicago
Robert B. Kaplan, University of Southern California
Sandra Lee McKay, San Francisco State University
Teresa Pica, University of Pennsylvania
Merrill Swain, Ontario Institute of Studies in Education

Naomi Silverman, Senior Commissioning Editor at Routledge, has been a wise, supportive, foresightful, and steadfast friend and colleague. Both volumes of the *Handbook* were Naomi's idea, and they simply wouldn't have happened without her initiative and enthusiasm for this ongoing project.

More than a dozen reviewers and graduate students read various drafts of all chapters and provided thorough, thoughtful, and detailed comments. Their work was instrumental in the development of individual chapters and, by extension, the volume as a whole. My heartfelt thanks to them: the book could not have proceeded without their knowledge, expertise, and devotion to the cause. My appreciation also goes to the two reviewers of the first volume of the *Handbook*, and their suggestions for revisions and changes in Volume II were very helpful.

My devoted comrade and sole member of the in-house IT department, Rodney Hill, created and maintained logistics software employed in making this second tome a reality. His pain and suffering remain immeasurable and untold.

Eli Hinkel, Seattle University

I

Social Contexts in Research on Second Language Teaching and Learning

1
Dual Language Education

Donna Christian

Introduction

As this handbook clearly demonstrates, the field of second language teaching and learning encompasses diverse goals, contexts, and traditions. New languages are learned in the community or in school, by children and adults, and for primarily oral communication purposes, literacy, or both. In the service of second language teaching and learning that occurs in school, dual language education occupies an important, if currently small, space that attends to the maintenance and development of the native language along with the second. The approach emphasizes bilingualism as an outcome when a new language is learned and fosters "additive bilingualism" (Lambert, 1984) as a foundational concept. Research shows that the model can be effective for second language learning while conveying other benefits as well.

In dual language education programs, the second language is not taught as a subject. Rather, it is used as a medium of instruction in an educational setting, and, with appropriate instructional techniques and materials, students learn curricular content as well as a new language. The native language of the students is also nurtured, and it is expected that the students will move toward bilingualism and biliteracy as a result of participating in this type of program. Thus, dual language education serves the goal of second language teaching and learning, but situates that goal in the broader context of bilingualism.

In this chapter, *dual language education* refers to programs, primarily for students in preschool, elementary, and secondary levels of schooling, which provide literacy and content area instruction to all students through two languages (their native language and a new language). The programs seek to develop bilingualism and biliteracy in the two languages, grade-level academic achievement, and multicultural competence for all students (Howard, Sugarman, Christian, Lindholm-Leary, & Rogers, 2007). Students learn subject matter content such as science and social studies through their second language, they develop oral proficiency and literacy skills in that language, and they gain understanding of its cultural connections. Thus, second language learning is embedded in grade-appropriate academic instruction, and language learning is an important, but not the only, goal for the programs.

Dual language classrooms may be linguistically homogeneous or may include speakers of both languages of instruction. The variations in student populations characterize four major types of dual language programs that will be discussed in later sections:

1. developmental bilingual programs, where all students are native speakers of the minority language that is one of the languages of instruction;
2. foreign language immersion programs, or "one-way" immersion, where all of the students are native speakers of the majority language and are learning another language;
3. heritage language immersion programs, where all of the students are from the language minority community, though they may have little or no actual proficiency in the heritage language; and
4. two-way immersion programs, where approximately half of the students are native speakers of the minority language and half are native speakers of the majority language, and all receive instruction through, and learn, both languages.

The distinctions drawn here follow that of Howard, Olague and Rogers (2003), who use the image of an umbrella to portray dual language education and these four types of programs (see Figure 1.1). This categorization has also been adopted by the National Dual Language Consortium (http://www. dual-language.org/) to define the Consortium's scope. The programs vary to meet the needs of different student groups but all operate within an additive bilingual paradigm.

The purpose of this chapter is to provide an overview of dual language education, an approach to second language learning and teaching that aims for bilingualism and biliteracy for students in diverse sociolinguistic settings. After some discussion of definitions and terms to set the stage, later sections will briefly outline the context and rationale for the approach, the major types of programs (along with the appropriate conditions and necessary resources for their success), and what we know

Figure 1.1 Dual language umbrella

Source: Howard, Olague, and Rogers (2003, p. 3).

about those programs. The chapter will conclude with some suggestions for future directions in research and practice.

Definitions

As Brisk (2005) points out, terms such as *bilingual* and *multilingual* are often confused, due to a failure to distinguish their meaning when applied to individuals, communities, educational programs, or national societies. Individuals (in our case, students) can be referred to as bilingual (or multilingual) if they know and can use more than one language. Their abilities in two (or more) languages typically vary according to the degree of fluency they have for different purposes in different contexts (or registers). In other words, an individual may be very fluent in one language for conversing with family members, and more able in another language to read a science text. There is also a strong link to identity for individuals whose language knowledge gives them a "sense of belonging that derives from linking one's own identity to the community of speakers of the language" (Cummins, 2008). At the community or national level, a society may be considered bilingual or multilingual if more than one language is regularly used by its members, but not all individual members may be bilingual.

In education, a *bilingual* program (simply stated) is one in which two languages are used for instruction. The label should not be used (but often is) for a program that serves language minority students using only their second language, such as a program for native Chinese speakers that uses only English. In such cases, the program is labeled according to the characteristics of its students rather than according to its pedagogy. In the United States, the term *bilingual* has become highly politicized, particularly in the context of *bilingual education* and has come to symbolize particular political stances (for or against the practice) rather than simply defining a type of educational programming.

A few other terms will be useful to define for the discussion to follow. *Native* language refers to the first language learned by a child, the one used in the family and community. A *second* language is learned after the native language (acknowledging that some children acquire two or more languages from early childhood, so the implied sequence may not apply in all cases). In dual language programs, one language is typically the *majority language* of the broader society (English in the United States or Japanese in Japan) and the *partner* language in the program (the other language used in instruction) may be a local community language (such as Spanish or Navajo in some communities in the United States) or another language not used in the students' home communities (such as English in Japan). Finally, a *heritage* language is a community language other than the majority language to which community members have a linguistic or cultural connection (for example, Cantonese for the children of immigrants from Hong Kong living in San Francisco) (Valdes, 2001). In some cases, partner languages in dual language programs are heritage languages in the local community.

The Context

Dual language education builds on research, history, and traditions of bilingual, foreign language, and heritage language education, as well as the global reality of multilingualism in education. Tucker (2001, p. 332) reminds us of the pervasiveness of multilingualism around the world and the fact that personal histories involving multiple languages, including at school, are the norm rather than the exception. He observes:

> There are many more bilingual or multilingual individuals in the world than there are monolingual … In many parts of the world, … approaches to education that involve the use of two or more languages constitute the normal everyday experience … The use of multiple languages

in education may be attributed to, or be a reflection of, numerous factors such as the linguistic heterogeneity of a country or region …; specific social or religious attitudes …; or the desire to promote national identity. In addition, innovative language education programs are often implemented to promote proficiency in international language(s) of wider communication together with proficiency in national and regional languages.

Despite the commonality of multilingualism, however, there is a long history of tension around language issues that spills over into education. Although many nations around the world promote early language learning for speakers of the majority language (Pufahl, Rhodes, & Christian, 2000), indigenous and immigrant language minorities do not typically have access to extended support for their native languages (Dutcher, 2004). Language education policies in various countries are complicated by colonial histories, political changes, and ideological factors (Brisk, 2005).

The tension of language and culture diversity manifests itself in disputes over the value of bilingual forms of education for students from minority (immigrant and indigenous) communities, as well as a general lack of support for learning languages other than the majority language. In the United States, Crawford (2004, p. 287) attributes the opposition to bilingual education to "the fear that it will enhance loyalty to minority tongues and retard the process of linguistic assimilation." At least partly as a result of this attitude, most programs designed for English language learners in the United States have taken a remedial approach, aiming to develop English skills as quickly as possible so students can join so-called "regular" English-medium classroom instruction. Most programs offer only monolingual English instruction, and, among bilingual offerings, the most common model is *transitional bilingual education*, where the students' native language is used to provide access to the subject matter for a limited time while the students learn enough English to transition to all-English instruction. Little or no attention is paid to preserving skills in the native language. The additive approach, developmental bilingual education, provides an enriched, rather than remedial, orientation, but is less common.

Foreign language teaching for majority language speakers has a somewhat different profile. In many places in the world, learning additional languages is required as part of the core curriculum in schooling, from the early years on (Pufahl, Rhodes, & Christian, 2000), but in the United States, the interest in developing competence in additional languages for English speakers is a relatively low priority in education overall. A 2008 survey of foreign language education in the United States found a decrease in the number of elementary schools offering foreign languages over a ten-year period, from 31% of schools to 25% (Rhodes & Pufahl, 2009). There have been occasional peaks of concern when international threats or competition enter the public awareness, but overall, fostering bilingualism in students by adding languages other than English has not been a mainstream education priority.

The third building block for dual language education relates to heritage languages (Brinton, Kagan, & Bauckus, 2008; Peyton, Ranard, & McGinnis, 2001). Programs in private (religious) schools and communities that support the preservation of heritage languages (of both indigenous and immigrant communities) are not new, but this goal is not widely addressed in schools in general. In the past, it was more common; Fishman (2001) notes the prevalence of heritage language schools in the late nineteenth and early twentieth centuries, stimulated by the vitality of immigrant communities (for example, nearly 4,000 German heritage schools existed at the turn of the twentieth century in the United States). However, the dominant expectation is that immigrant and indigenous community members will transition to the majority language as they assimilate, and maintaining the heritage language would be a private matter. Some communities, however, took the challenge and developed programs to maintain and/or revitalize the heritage language, sometimes involving the local schools. The programs vary greatly in intensity—from weekly language classes such as "Saturday schools" to full immersion in the language for schooling. Immersion pedagogy has been used in efforts to revitalize a declining language by making it the medium of instruction in the classroom, following the foreign language model. Good examples are found in indigenous communities, exemplified by programs for Hawaiian (Yamauchi & Wilhelm, 2001) and Māori (Benton, 2001).

Finally, the remaining section of the dual language education umbrella is occupied by two-way immersion education (originally known as "two-way bilingual education," among other labels), which emerged in the late 1980s in the United States as a viable model for educating, and integrating, language minority and majority students (Lindholm-Leary, 2001). Two-way immersion programs combine elements of bilingual education with foreign language immersion pedagogy, integrating students from two language backgrounds. At the time they gained recognition, interest in them came from a convergence of factors, including research on effective programs for educating language minority students and the successes being experienced in immersion education for native English speakers. The approach was not new (several schools, including the Coral Way Bilingual Elementary School in Miami, had been using the model for 20 or more years), but the number of programs and diversity of locations grew in the United States (to over 300 programs in 28 states in 2009 (Center for Applied Linguistics, 2009)).

The Rationale for Dual Language Education

As comprehensive educational programs, dual language approaches need a firm footing in educational effectiveness as well as second language learning pedagogy. Thus, overall academic achievement of participating students is relevant along with their second language development, and it has been important to build a literature that demonstrates that academic progress is not impeded (but may in fact be enhanced) by additive bilingualism and other features of a dual language program.

There is considerable evidence that learning through the native language has advantages for language minority students. It facilitates the development of literacy skills in the native language and in English (August & Shanahan, 2006) and it can enhance cognitive and social development (Hakuta, 1986; Cummins, 1995). It allows students to gain important content knowledge that in turn will make instruction in the majority language more comprehensible. Although schools have traditionally viewed the native language of minority students as an obstacle to overcome, findings from schools where an additive approach is taken, where the students' native languages are highly valued and their knowledge is considered a resource rather than a problem, have demonstrated the benefits of such an approach (Lindholm-Leary, 2001; Thomas & Collier, 2002).

At the same time, it is important for language majority students to have an opportunity to learn another language. Research has demonstrated that these students, who come to school with proficiency in the majority language of the wider society, benefit from an immersion experience for language learning and do not suffer academically when instruction is provided via a second language, with appropriate supports (Genesee, 1987; Johnson & Swain, 1997; Fortune & Tedick, 2008). Thus, dual language education for academic learning appears to be effective for both minority and majority language speakers.

The dual language approach also incorporates effective language teaching methods. In these classrooms, students learn their second language primarily through content (with support). Teachers shelter content instruction for second language learners, supporting comprehension and incorporating specific strategies to promote language development (Echevarria, Short, & Powers, 2006). They focus on form when appropriate, using meaningful contexts to support language learning and incorporate language objectives into curriculum planning. Evidence from research on various forms of dual language education indicates that second language learning goals are typically met for students in these programs (Howard, Christian, & Genesee, 2004; Lindholm-Leary, 2001; Genesee, 1987; Thomas & Collier, 2002).

Naturally, dual language programs, as with all educational programs, depend on high quality implementation to realize their promise of effectiveness for students. Lindholm-Leary (2007, p. 6) notes a high degree of consistency between characteristics of effective schools in general and features of exemplary dual language programs (adapted for the unique language demands). Local context is also an important influence on success, in that "[w]hat works in one community or with a particular population of students or teachers may not work as effectively in another community or with another population" (Lindholm-Leary, 2007, p. 7). These factors affect the success of any individual dual language program. However, the conceptual foundations of dual language education point to its suitability as an approach to second language teaching and learning, and studies of programs in action have borne out that promise.

The Implementation of Dual Language Education

As mentioned above, *dual language education* is a type of bilingual education where the goal is to maintain both languages over the long term. In order to pursue that goal, there are several key features that must be in place:

- Subject matter is taught in the partner language for a substantial portion of the instructional time—at least 50% of the time in elementary school and two or more courses at the secondary level.
- Additive bilingualism and biliteracy are fostered throughout the program.
- Teachers are fully proficient in the languages in which they teach (preferably bilingual in the two program languages), technically qualified to teach the relevant subject matter, and trained in teaching content through a learner's second language (sheltered instruction).
- Grade-level content standards and curricula are followed.
- Participation in the program is expected to be sustained at least through the elementary grades, and preferably through secondary schooling.
- Attention is paid to interactions of language and culture, and cross-cultural awareness and competence are developed.

In other words, dual language education conforms to local curriculum standards, but the curriculum is delivered through two languages, with special attention to second language development and content learning through a second language.

Programs are often characterized by the ratio of time of instruction in each of the languages, at least in the elementary school years (Christian, 1996). Table 1.1 depicts the prototypical language

Table 1.1 Sample Pattern of Instructional Time in Partner Language by Grade Level in Dual Language Education: Two Models

Grade level	% of instruction in partner language	
	90/10 model	50/50 model
K	90%	50%
1	90%	50%
2	85%	50%
3	80%	50%
4	60%	50%
5	60%	50%
6	50%	50%

allocation sequence in two basic patterns. In one pattern, the "50/50" model, the percentage of instruction in each language is roughly equal from the beginning. In foreign language immersion contexts, this model has been referred to as "partial immersion." At the other end of the continuum, the "90/10" model, the partner language is used in the early years for nearly all of the instruction, and the societal language (English in the US) is gradually increased as a medium of instruction until in the upper elementary grades the proportion of instruction is roughly 50/50. In the foreign language context, this has been referred to as "total immersion." In practice, programs are found at all points on a continuum between these two proportions, as might be expected.

Above the elementary school years, there are a variety of program designs, most of which seek to preserve and develop the target language skills through subject matter instruction and/or advanced language courses (Montone & Loeb, 2000). Secondary programs are often constrained by available resources and scheduling issues, and the student population rising from the elementary grades (or entering with comparable language proficiency) is often small in number. The schools generally offer an idiosyncratic set of content (such as science, mathematics, and social studies) and language arts courses in the target language, depending on the availability of teachers and the number of students who would enroll.

In the following sections, the major types of dual language education will be discussed. Three major intersecting dimensions provide a framework for categorizing the programs: their goals, the sociolinguistic status of the languages of instruction, and the profile of the students being instructed. There are always multiple ways of categorizing educational approaches (see Genesee (1999) for a discussion of program alternatives for language learners) and these program types are more like points on a continuum with overlapping edges. Table 1.2 summarizes the basic features of each model.

Developmental Bilingual Education

When students in a program are all minority language speakers who are learning the majority language, the dual language approach is known as developmental bilingual education (also called maintenance bilingual education and one-way immersion by some). This approach emerged in the 1970s and 1980s in the United States, as an alternative to transitional bilingual education that would foster native language maintenance (Crawford, 2004). Instead of the transitional program's subtractive orientation (a quick transition to English with no effort to maintain the native language), developmental bilingual programs aim for additive bilingualism; instead of the transitional focus on remediation, they offer an enrichment program.

Table 1.2 Dual Language Education Program Types

Program type	Language goals	Status of languages	Student population	Examples
Developmental bilingual	Bilingualism	Minority/majority	Language minority	Spanish–English bilingual
Heritage language immersion	Bilingualism—revitalization	Minority/majority	Heritage language minority	Hawaiian immersion (US); Catalan immersion (Catalonia)
Foreign language immersion	Bilingualism	Majority/international	Language majority	French immersion (Canada/US); English immersion (Japan)
Two-way immersion	Bilingualism	Minority/majority	Language minority/majority	Spanish–English, Korean–English (US)

Research on this approach, including several large studies that compared it to other programs for language minority students, indicates that it facilitates both English language and academic learning (Ramirez, 1992; Thomas & Collier, 2002). Most of the research has involved native speakers of Spanish, reflecting the demographic predominance of this group in language minority communities in the United States. Thomas and Collier's (2002) longitudinal examination of the effectiveness of various program models across five school districts showed that, when the students reached high school, language minority students who participated in developmental bilingual programs in elementary school outperformed students who received instruction only in English. Their conclusion from this study and other research they have conducted was that the strongest predictor of achievement in the second language (English) was the extent of schooling in the native language experienced by a student. In other words, maintenance of the native language can play a role in second language learning as well as content mastery for language minority students. Recent reviews of research targeting literacy development in second language learners have also found that oral proficiency and literacy in the native language benefits the acquisition of literacy in the second language (August & Shanahan, 2006).

Developmental bilingual programs are most well known in the United States, but have been implemented elsewhere, such as in the Slovak Republic for Hungarian-speaking communities (Gersten, 2001) and in the Basque Country (Cenoz, 1998). In many ways, they resemble heritage language programs (see next section), in that the language of instruction is the heritage language of the students in the classroom, and an objective of instruction is to maintain and develop that language along with the majority language.

Studies of this approach in other countries show similar results to those in the United States. Cenoz (1998), for example, reports that Basque-speaking students in Basque–Spanish developmental bilingual programs have a higher level of proficiency in Basque than students in programs where Basque is not the medium of instruction and show no significant differences in Spanish language proficiency (the majority language) or academic performance when compared with students in other types of programs. Thus, Basque speakers progress in learning the second language, Spanish, by participating in a developmental bilingual program. Cenoz (1998) also observes that students in Basque-medium programs outperform others in the learning of English, a foreign language in this context, their third language.

Heritage Language Immersion Programs

In heritage dual language programs, the students all come from a home that has strong cultural and linguistic ancestral ties with the heritage language, which is a minority language in the broader society (Hornberger & Wang, 2008). When they enter school, the students may be dominant in the heritage language or in the majority language, but they share this linguistic/cultural affiliation. In cases where the language has receded in use in the community as a whole, the school program may be part of a revitalization effort to develop a community of proficient speakers and to give students an opportunity to acquire the indigenous language that is a fundamental part of their cultural heritage.

Heritage language programs take many forms (Saturday schools, language courses for heritage learners, etc.), but the immersion model embodies the goals of dual language education, to develop bilingualism and biliteracy in the students. There have not been large-scale studies of heritage immersion education, but a number of individual programs have been documented.

A classic example is the Hawaiian Language Immersion program, a bilingual program in Hawaiian and English that spans preschool, elementary, and secondary grade levels (Yamauchi & Wilhelm, 2001; Slaughter, 1997). This program was established in the 1980s in response to a grassroots effort by parents and Hawaiian language educators, seeking an opportunity for their children to be educated through the medium of Hawaiian in order to preserve and maintain the Hawaiian language and culture. (The Hawaiian language was used widely through the nineteenth century in the schools, but it lost ground to English after Hawaii became part of the United States in 1898 and there was concern that it would become extinct (Slaughter, 1997).) The model selected was total immersion, with Hawaiian used exclusively through grade 5, and English introduced for part of the day after that. Most students are Hawaiian or of Hawaiian descent, but they enter school with little or no proficiency in the language. According to Slaughter (1997), a program evaluation that followed a group of students through grade 6 showed that they had gained fluency in their second language, Hawaiian, and were reading at appropriate levels. Further, their performance on English achievement tests (reading, writing, mathematics) was similar to comparable groups of students in non-immersion programs. In addition to language goals, a key component of many heritage immersion programs is cultural, and the Hawaiian immersion program carefully integrates Hawaiian history, culture, and values into instruction (Yamauchi & Wilhelm, 2001).

The Hawaiian program was in part inspired by similar efforts in New Zealand for the Māori language (Benton, 2001), although immersion education in Māori is much less extensive. Most Māori-medium instruction is offered at elementary schools, with some extending the experience into secondary school. Benton (2001) describes a high school partial immersion program where, in the first two years, students receive about half of their instruction through Māori (mathematics, social studies, science, and some electives). As with the Hawaiian schools, culture and identity are emphasized as well as language.

Foreign Language Immersion Programs

Foreign language immersion programs serve primarily students from majority language backgrounds, teaching them a second language by immersing them in the language as a medium of instruction, with the explicit aim of developing bilingualism. This feature distinguishes modern immersion education from the pervasive practice throughout history where the medium of instruction was a foreign language to most or all students (Latin in Europe, for example, or colonial languages in Africa and Asia). In those "submersion" situations, the native language of the students played little or no role in their academic development (Swain & Johnson, 1997). In today's immersion education, the native language of the students is supported and developed along with the second language, moving toward bilingualism and biliteracy. The partner language is typically chosen for its global status, although it may be a language used in the country, even locally (such as Spanish immersion for English speakers in the United States). In *total* immersion programs, the allocation of languages of instruction is similar to the 90/10 model described earlier (see Table 1.1). The partner language is used for instruction most of the time in the early grades, and the amount of instruction through the native language increases in subsequent years until a balance of the two languages is achieved.[1] *Partial* immersion programs follow the 50/50 model (Table 1.1), where the time spent in the two languages is roughly equal from the beginning.

The modern immersion program model emerged in Canada in the 1960s, when parents in English-speaking communities in the province of Quebec sought ways to improve opportunities for their children to learn French, the majority language of the province, in school. They wanted a program that would provide the native English-speaking students with higher levels of proficiency in French, giving them the ability to work and communicate in the language, and proposed a *total immersion* experience as an alternative. The model that was developed involved all-French instruction in kindergarten and grade 1, with English literacy introduced in grade 2, and, by grade 6, equal amounts of French and English instruction. The success of that effort (known as the St Lambert program; see Lambert & Tucker (1972)) and the increasing value associated with proficiency in French led to the implementation of the model in many schools around Canada. In 1997, Swain and Johnson (1997, p. 3) estimated that about 300,000 students (7% of the total) were involved in some form of French immersion education.

There have been many studies of immersion in Canada (1,000 by 1991, according to Cummins (1991)). In a summary of early studies, Genesee (1987) found that immersion students in the upper elementary grades "are most likely to perform as well as FC [native-speaking French control] on tests of comprehension, including both reading and listening" and demonstrate "high levels of functional proficiency" in oral language, though they do not possess native-like proficiency. At the same time, their English language skills were comparable to those of English speakers not in the immersion program. Later studies have refined the portrait of second language results obtained in immersion (Harley, 1992; Lyster, 2004), noting in particular the need for attention to certain areas where native-like proficiency does not readily develop.

The Canadian immersion model quickly spread to other countries, and the model was extended to situations where the partner language was not a societal language, such as French in Australia (Swain & Johnson, 1997). In the United States, immersion programs began with Spanish immersion in the early 1970s, followed soon by French and German, and currently schools also offer immersion in Japanese, Mandarin, Italian, Ojibwe, Diné, and others (Lenker & Rhodes, 2007). In other areas of the world, immersion provided opportunities to learn international languages such as English (in Germany, Hungary, Japan, and elsewhere) and regional or minority languages (such as Swedish in Finland and Catalan in Catalonia).

For example, the indigenous heritage language, Catalan, in Catalonia (in Spain, France, and elsewhere), was repressed over several centuries and declined in use, but its community members retained a strong identity with it, even if they had little proficiency. Once political circumstances allowed the open use of Catalan again, the language was given limited official status, and students were required to learn both Catalan and Spanish (Artigal, 1997). Catalan-medium instruction at elementary levels became the norm. However, there were groups of Spanish-speaking residents who had moved into Catalonia for employment, and a Catalan-immersion program was designed to meet their needs. Although limited research exists on this program, several studies point to higher skills in Catalan for students in immersion compared to non-immersion students (Artigal, 1997).

Immersion in major international languages is more common around the world, such as English immersion in Japan. At the Katoh Gakuen, a private school in Japan, an English immersion program is offered from preschool through secondary grades, with half to two-thirds of instruction in English (Bostwick, 2001). Program evaluations have shown students have the productive and receptive second language skills needed for participation in English-medium classes. Further, on national standardized tests, students in the program performed as well as non-immersion students on subject matter assessments in Japanese.

Two-Way Immersion Programs

Finally, two-way immersion in many ways combines features of the three program types described in the previous sections. It is distinguished by the student population: while the other models involve students from a single language background, two-way immersion classrooms integrate balanced (ideally) numbers of speakers from two different language communities, the majority language and a minority language spoken locally. Like developmental bilingual programs, they provide for native language maintenance and growth for language minority students; like heritage immersion programs, they support the language of the heritage community from which the language minority students come; and like foreign language immersion programs, they give majority language students an opportunity to become proficient in an additional language.

Two-way immersion is increasingly popular in the United States and is not yet widely practiced elsewhere. Most programs in the US operate in Spanish and English, for demographic reasons, but others pair English with Cantonese, French, Korean, Mandarin, Japanese, and Navajo; most are offered in the elementary grades, but there are increasing numbers with continuations to the secondary level (Center for Applied Linguistics, 2009). As in other dual language programs, there are major variations by language allocation: the "90/10" design in which most instruction in the primary grades is provided in the minority language, with a gradual increase in English instruction through the upper elementary grades, when a balance is reached; and "50/50," in which instruction at all grade levels is divided equally across the languages.

Alicia Chacón International School in El Paso, Texas, on the Texas–Mexico border, illustrates a type of 90/10 two-way immersion program (Calderón & Minaya-Rowe, 2003; Howard, 2002), with a twist. Most of the students are Latino, but they have different levels of English and Spanish proficiency, and some students enter school with some degree of bilingualism. This whole school program (many two-way programs are strands within a school) extends from kindergarten through 8th grade. All students learn mathematics, language arts, and science in Spanish, and social studies and language development/language arts in English. Emergent literacy in kindergarten through 2nd grade for all students is taught in Spanish, and instruction in English literacy begins in 3rd grade. Electives and other courses in both languages are added in upper grades, such as fine arts and technology. In addition (the "twist"), students study a third language (Japanese, Russian, Chinese, or German), making the program design closer to 80/10/10 in kindergarten through 2nd grade (for Spanish, English, and the third language), transitioning to 45/45/10 in 5th through 8th grade (Calderón & Minaya-Rowe, 2003).

The Francis Scott Key Elementary School in Arlington, Virginia, is an example of another two-way immersion design (Christian, Montone, Lindholm, & Carranza, 1997; Howard & Sugarman, 2007). Most of the students are Latino or White, but some other ethnicities are represented as well, including African American and Asian groups. Beginning as a strand within a school in 1986, it developed into a whole-school program after some years of operation. Students receive approximately half of their instruction in English and half in Spanish from kindergarten through 5th grade, and the language allocation is by teacher and content area. Typically, students spend the morning receiving instruction through one language and the afternoon through the other, in some cases changing teachers mid-day. As the program matured, a secondary continuation was established in a middle school and later in a high school, and other elementary school sites were opened as well. Thus, students in this district may choose to pursue two-way immersion from kindergarten through 12th grade.

Among dual language programs, the defining characteristic of two-way immersion—integration of students from the two language backgrounds—brings with it the promise of certain advantages for second language learning and teaching. In these classrooms, the teacher is not the only proficient model of the second language. There are many peer models as well, and it is expected that "authentic, meaningful interaction among speakers of the two languages" (Genesee, 1999, p. 37) will lead to better language learning, by increasing exposure to fluent, age-appropriate language in meaningful situations, such as cooperative group work in subject matter classes. While the research base is not extensive, some studies "do appear to confirm the scaffolding role of native speakers for their second language learning peers" in selected areas (de Jong & Howard, 2009, p. 85). In addition to the language learning benefits, the integration of the two language groups "contributes to the development of positive intergroup relationships between language minority students and language majority students" (de Jong & Howard, 2009, p. 85) and avoids the often-criticized segregation of language minority students in bilingual education.

Research on language outcomes supports the expectation of linguistic benefits from two-way immersion in general and second language learning for both groups in particular. In a review of language and literacy outcomes in two-way immersion, Howard, Sugarman and Christian (2003, p. 20) find that studies show that,

> on average, both native English speakers and English language learners in TWI [two-way immersion] programs achieve the goal of developing bilingualism and biliteracy. The English language learners, however, tend to develop more balanced abilities in the two languages than the native English speakers.

In a longitudinal study of Spanish and English oral language development in 11 two-way immersion programs across the United States, Howard, Christian and Genesee (2004) found that the native Spanish speakers scored well in English on an oral proficiency assessment in both 3rd and 5th grade, comparable with native English speakers, with low levels of individual variation (indicating that most students were at the advanced levels). In Spanish, the native English speakers performed at the advanced level on the assessment, but less well than the native Spanish speakers, and with a good deal of individual variation.

Lindholm-Leary (2001) presents language, literacy, and academic achievement results for a group of 16 two-way immersion programs (along with comparisons to several transitional bilingual programs), looking at outcomes and influences of demographic factors, especially characteristics of student participants. Overall, the study found that most students were rated proficient in both languages by the upper elementary grades. However, program and school differences had some effects. For English speakers, those in 90/10 programs developed higher proficiency in Spanish than those in 50/50 programs, indicating that the greater emphasis on Spanish instruction in the early grades appears to make a difference. The native Spanish speakers did not show a difference in English proficiency according to the program type (the 90/10 participants scored similarly in English to those in 50/50 programs), but their performance in Spanish was affected, with those in 90/10 programs showing higher proficiency.

Thus, research indicates that two-way immersion provides an effective environment for second language learning, at least for learning Spanish and English. Though not the focus here, there is also a body of evidence that bilingual proficiency and biliteracy are positively related to academic achievement (Lindholm-Leary & Howard, 2008; Genesee, Lindholm-Leary, Saunders, & Christian, 2006; Lindholm & Aclan, 1991).

Second Language Learning and Teaching in Dual Language Education

A primary goal of all dual language education is high levels of proficiency in a second (or additional) language. Across program types, then, second language learning and teaching is a common and important theme. This leads to some implications for practice, which will be briefly discussed in this section.

Instruction in dual language education must always respond to, and keep in mind, the goals of bilingualism, biliteracy, and multicultural competence. As a general education program, learning the grade-level core curriculum is critical as well, and students must have access to subject matter content through a language they are in the process of learning. As a result, language teaching is integrated with content teaching, in ways that give language learners at different proficiency levels the opportunity to develop their language skills and learn content concepts at the same time, such as in sheltered instruction. To promote learning of a new language, attention should be paid to input, opportunities for interaction and output, and the needs of individuals. In addition, the sociolinguistic context for language learning cannot be ignored.

Language learners need interesting, relevant, and comprehensible input in order to develop their language skills, and the content focus in dual language education is an advantage in that regard.

In a school setting, an approach such as sheltered instruction (Echevarria, Vogt, & Short, 2007) involves setting language and content objectives for curriculum units, so that particular language skills are attended to while meaningful content is being discussed (such as features of past tense in a history lesson or comparatives in a science lab). Since two languages are used for instruction, there is also a question of how they should be allocated (i.e., can they be mixed within a lesson?). There is some evidence that monolingual lesson implementation is the better choice, in order to allow sustained periods of immersion in each language (Howard, Sugarman, Christian, Lindholm-Leary, & Rogers, 2007), but others argue that some mixing (or code switching) is more sociolinguistically authentic.

In recent years, attention has turned to the desirability of incorporating some form-focused instruction in dual language programs (and more generally in all forms of language instruction). This awareness was sparked by studies of English speakers in French immersion in Canada who had experienced communicative language teaching (with little or no attention to language form or structure) and who did not accurately use certain grammatical distinctions, such as noun gender, even though they had been in immersion for many years (Harley, 1998). Although more research is needed concerning method and amount of attention to language form, dual language programs are encouraged to incorporate specific linguistic structures into academic content and language arts instruction to facilitate the acquisition of forms that are not readily acquired otherwise (Lyster, 2007).

Second language learning also calls for diverse opportunities for oral and written production (Swain, 1985). In the school context, this means that classrooms need to incorporate student-centered activities in addition to teacher-centered instruction and provide both structured and unstructured contexts for second language use (Lindholm-Leary, 2007). It would seem like two-way immersion classes would be ideal from this perspective, since peers would include native speakers of the language being acquired. However, Saunders and O'Brien (2006) found in a review of research on oral language development that simply having the opportunity to work in small groups with native speakers will not necessarily benefit language development. In order to gain the benefit, teachers need to design the task and train the native speakers in strategies that will promote language development. In general, then, it cannot be expected that the context of immersion in a second language will be sufficient for the development of high levels of proficiency; specific intentional strategies must be added by dual language educators to enhance language learning.

Finally, the actual use of the second language is also a factor in successful language learning. When two languages are available, and one is "easier" than the other because it is better known, it is natural for students to prefer that language. In immersion classrooms, there is a need for a "strong language policy … that encourages students to use the instructional language and discourages students from speaking the non-instructional language" (Lindholm-Leary, 2007, p. 14). The sociolinguistic status of the languages also plays an important role in this choice. When a majority language is paired with a minority language, students and teachers may favor the higher status language. De Jong and Howard (2009) examine the integration of students from two language backgrounds in two-way immersion programs. Although integration is intended to be an advantage for second language learning for all students, they find that this advantage may fail to materialize, especially in the minority language, in part due to the students' language choices. Once students have adequate proficiency in the majority language (here, English), the tendency is for all students to use that language more (Palmer, 2009). For example, Potowski (2007) examined language use in 5th and 8th grade classrooms in a Spanish–English two-way immersion program and found that English was preferred in both social contexts in school as well as peer–peer classroom interactions, such as in group work. Like Carranza (1995) and others, Potowski found that "the presence of students for whom Spanish was an L1 does not guarantee overall higher quantities of student Spanish use" (2007, p. 64). Programs can successfully address these issues, though, as demonstrated in four cases profiled by Howard and Sugarman (2007), in which the administrators and teachers found ways to equalize language and student status differences, including by ensuring active use of the minority language and promoting its value in and out of the classroom.

In sum, there is evidence that dual language education is a promising model for promoting second language learning in school. However, there are challenges presented by the educational and sociolinguistic context that must be addressed to optimize that promise.

Conclusion and Future Directions

Dual language education has taken its place among school-based programs for second language learning and teaching. It situates language learning in a comprehensive educational program, where its goals of bilingualism and biliteracy are accompanied by goals of strong academic achievement and cross-cultural appreciation and understanding. Although we have learned a good deal about this approach from research and experience in its short recent history, it remains a fairly new educational model, with many issues that call for further exploration in order to improve language and other outcomes. Several areas for future research with particular relevance for second language learning will be briefly touched on here. For an extensive account of research needs in dual language education, see Parkes and Ruth (2009).

Program Models and Variations

The preceding discussion has described the major types of dual language education (related to student population) and the primary variation based on allocation of languages of instruction (90/10 and 50/50). In practice, program features vary widely, and it is important to continue to investigate the consequences of implementation choices and how they might relate to local contexts to optimize student language learning. For example, some programs distribute their languages of instruction by time (alternate days, alternate weeks, or within a day), while others use subjects or teachers. Do these differences matter?

Biliteracy Development

Despite tremendous attention and research on the topic of reading, there is relatively little investigation of biliteracy development (and how it differs from literacy development in one language), and this is a central issue in dual language education (Parkes & Ruth, 2009). From an instructional point of view, the choices reside in timing and language choice. Literacy may be taught concurrently in both languages of instruction or sequentially, with initial literacy in one language only. Some programs choose sequential instruction, using the native language of each student for initial literacy, while others use the same language for all. For English speakers in Spanish foreign language immersion, for example, initial literacy might be in English or Spanish. Eventually, literacy is developed in both languages of instruction (the biliteracy goal), but research is needed on the effects of program variations for initial and later literacy for students from different language backgrounds and what the long-term effects are of these alternatives. It would also be important to learn more about what students can be expected to achieve at different grade levels, related to their language background and literacy experiences in school.

Time and Articulation across Educational Levels

Language learning in school requires long sequences of instruction and native language support for students to achieve bilingualism. As mentioned earlier, the bulk of dual language education occurs at the elementary grades, and articulation with secondary (and post-secondary) levels of education is not common. As a language learning question, investigation is needed to determine what amount and type of instruction will maintain and develop the bilingualism gained in dual language programs at the elementary level as the students move through higher levels of education. Given the dual language principle of learning language through content, can traditional language-focused instruction at the secondary level be effective for students who come from dual language programs?

Peer Interaction

As peer interaction is an important site for language learning, providing opportunities for meaningful interactions and output, much more needs to be known about how it can best support learning. There are many factors that affect participation and choice of language. For example, can grouping practices or activity types affect the quality of participation for different students? Can the shift to a preference for the majority language by all students as they move to higher grade levels be counteracted?

Students with Special Needs

A key question faced by dual language programs is whether or not all students can be educated well in them. In particular for our purposes here, the issue is whether there are any background factors, individual cognitive traits, or other characteristics that would suggest that a student would not succeed in a dual language program. There is research that indicates that children with language impairments can acquire more than one language (Genesee, Paradis, & Crago, 2004), and students with other special needs, including physical disabilities, have participated in dual language education. This is another important area for investigation.

Dual language education has the potential to be an effective way to promote language learning along with academic achievement for all students. It can address the desire of families and communities to revitalize a heritage language in danger of being lost; it can give children from majority language backgrounds the chance to learn a new language and engage the wider world; it can help students from language minority communities learn and achieve in the majority language while maintaining the many benefits of continuing to grow in their native language. And, in the form of two-way immersion, the approach can bring students from different communities together to learn each others' languages and gain an understanding of each others' cultures. There is still much to learn about dual language education, but it has taken its place in education around the world as an effective model for second language learning and teaching that can do much more.

Note

1. It should be noted that the role of native language differs in foreign language immersion programs and developmental bilingual programs. In foreign language immersion, the second language is the primary medium of instruction in the early years; in developmental bilingual programs, the native language is. This difference in roles reflects the sociolinguistic reality of the status differences between majority and minority languages in a society. For majority language speakers, early total immersion in a second language does not have negative effects on native language development; for minority language speakers, total immersion in a second language can lead to native language attrition ("subtractive bilingualism") since that language is not as strongly supported outside the classroom. See Tucker (1979) for a fuller discussion of the issues involved.

Bibliography

Artigal, J. M. (1997). The Catalan immersion program. In R. K. Johnson, & M. Swain (Eds.), *Immersion education: International perspectives* (pp. 133–150). Cambridge: Cambridge University Press.

August, D., & Shanahan, T. (2006). *Developing literacy in second language learners: Report of the National Literacy Panel on Language Minority Children and Youth.* Mahwah, NJ: Lawrence Erlbaum Publishers & Center for Applied Linguistics.

Benton, R. (2001). Balancing tradition and modernity: A natural approach to Māori language revitalization in a New Zealand secondary school. In D. Christian, & F. Genesee (Eds.), *Bilingual education* (pp. 95–108). Alexandria, VA: TESOL.

Bostwick, M. (2001). English immersion in a Japanese school. In D. Christian, & F. Genesee (Eds.), *Bilingual education* (pp. 125–137). Alexandria, VA: TESOL.

Brinton, D. M., Kagan, O., & Bauckus, S. (Eds.). (2008). *Heritage language education: A new field emerging.* New York: Routledge.

Brisk, M. (2005). Bilingual education. In E. Hinkel (Ed.), *Handbook of research in second language teaching and learning* (pp. 7–24). Mahwah, NJ: Lawrence Erlbaum Associates, Inc.

Calderón, M., & Minaya-Rowe, L. (2003). *Designing and implementing two-way bilingual programs: A step by step guide for administrators, teachers, and parents.* Thousand Oaks, CA: Corwin Press.

Carranza, I. (1995). Multilevel analysis of two-way immersion discourse. In J. Alatis, C. Straehle, B. Gallengerger, & M. Ronkin (Eds.), *Georgetown University Round Table on Language and Linguistics* (pp. 169–187). Washington, DC: Georgetown University Press.

Cenoz, J. (1998). Multilingual education in the Basque country. In J. Cenoz, & F. Genesee (Eds.), *Beyond bilingualism: Multilingualism and multilingual education* (pp. 175–191). Clevedon: Multilingual Matters.

Center for Applied Linguistics. (2009). *Directory of Two-Way Bilingual Immersion Programs in the U.S.* Retrieved June 2009, from http://www.cal.org/twi/directory/

Christian, D. (1996). Two-way bilingual education: Students learning through two languages. *Modern Language Journal, 80* (1), 66–76.

Christian, D., Montone, C., Lindholm, K., & Carranza, I. (1997). *Profiles in two-way immersion education.* McHenry, IL: Center for Applied Linguistics and Delta Systems.

Crawford, J. (2004). *Educating English learners: Language diversity in the classroom.* Los Angeles: Bilingual Education Services, Inc.

Cummins, J. (1991). The politics of paranoia: Reflections on the bilingual education debate. In O. Garcia (Ed.), *Bilingual education: Focusschrift in honour of Joshua A. Fishman* (pp. 183–199). Amsterdam: John Benjamins.

Cummins, J. (1995). Canadian French immersion programs: A comparison with Swedish immersion programs in Finland. In M. Buss, & C. Lauren (Eds.), *Language immersion: Teaching and second language acquisition* (pp. 7–20). Vaasa, Finland: Univerity of Vaasa.

Cummins, J. (2008). Foreword to special issue on multilingualism and minority languages. *AILA Review, 21,* 1–3.

de Jong, E., & Howard, E. (2009). Integration in two-way immersion education: Equalising linguistic benefits for all students. *International Journal of Bilingual Education and Bilingualism, 12* (1), 81–99.

Dutcher, N. (2004). *Expanding educational opportunity in linguistically diverse societies.* Washington, DC: Center for Applied Linguistics.

Echevarria, J., Short, D., & Powers, K. (2006). School reform and standards-based education: An instructional model for English language learners. *Journal of Educational Research, 99* (4), 195–210.

Echevarria, J., Vogt, M. E., & Short, D. J. (2007). *Making content comprehensible for English learners: The SIOP model* (3rd ed.). Boston: Allyn and Bacon.

Fishman, J. A. (2001). 300-plus years of heritage language education in the United States. In J. K. Peyton, D. A. Ranard, & S. McGinnis (Eds.), *Heritage languages in America: Preserving a national resource* (pp. 81–97). McHenry, IL: Center for Applied Linguistics and Delta Systems.

Fortune, T. W., & Tedick, D. J. (Eds.). (2008). *Pathways to multilingualism: Evolving perspectives on immersion education.* Clevedon: Multilingual Matters.

Genesee, F. (1987). *Learning through two languages: Studies of immersion and bilingual education.* Cambridge, MA: Newbury House.

Genesee, F. (1999). *Program alternatives for linguistically diverse students.* Santa Cruz, CA and Washington, DC: Center for Research on Education, Diversity & Excellence.

Genesee, F., Lindholm-Leary, K., Saunders, W., & Christian, D. (2006). *Educating English language learners: A synthesis of research evidence.* Cambridge: Cambridge University Press.

Genesee, F., Paradis, J., & Crago, M. B. (2004). *Dual language development & disorders: A handbook on bilingualism & second language learning.* Baltimore: Paul H. Brookes Publishing Company.

Gersten, B. F. (2001). A bilingual Hungarian/Slovak school in the Slovak Republic. In D. Christian, & F. Genesee (Eds.), *Bilingual education* (pp. 69–80). Alexandria, VA: TESOL, Inc.

Hakuta, K. (1986). *Mirror of language: The debate on bilingualism.* New York: Basic Books.

Harley, B. (1992). Patterns of second language development in French immersion. *Journal of French Language Studies, 2,* 159–184.

Harley, B. (1998). The role of focus-on-form in child second language acquisition. In C. Doughty, & J. Williams (Eds.), *Focus on form in classroom second language acquisition* (pp. 156–174). Cambridge: Cambridge University Press.

Hornberger, N. H., & Wang, S. C. (2008). Who are our heritage language learners? In D. Brinton, O. Kagan, & S. Bauckus (Eds.), *Heritage language education: A new field emerging* (pp. 3–38). New York: Routledge.

Howard, E. R. (2002). The Alicia Chacon International School: Portrait of an exemplary two-way immersion program. *NABE News, 25* (6), pp. 19–22, 42–43.

Howard, E. R., & Sugarman, J. (2007). *Realizing the vision of two-way immersion: Fostering effective programs and classrooms.* McHenry, IL: Center for Applied Linguistics and Delta Systems.

Howard, E. R., Christian, D., & Genesee, F. (2004). *The development of bilingualism and biliteracy from grade 3 to 5: A summary of findings from the CAL/CREDE study of two-way immersion education (Research Report No. 13).* Santa Cruz, CA and Washington, DC: Center for Research on Education, Diversity & Excellence.

Howard, E. R., Olague, N., & Rogers, D. (2003). *The dual language program planner: A guide for designing and implementing dual language programs.* Santa Cruz, CA and Washington, DC : Center for Research on Education, Diversity & Excellence.

Howard, E. R., Sugarman, J., & Christian, D. (2003). *Trends in two-way immersion education: A review of the research.* Baltimore, MD: Center for Research on the Education of Students Placed At Risk.

Howard, E. R., Sugarman, J., Christian, D., Lindholm-Leary, K. J., & Rogers, D. (2007). *Guiding principles for dual language education* (2nd ed.). Washington, DC: Center for Applied Linguistics.

Johnson, R. K., & Swain, M. (Eds.). (1997). *Immersion education: International Perspectives.* Cambridge: Cambridge University Press.

Lambert, W. E. (1984). An overview of issues in immersion education. In *Studies on immersion education: A collection for US educators* (pp. 8–30). Sacramento, CA: California State Department of Education.

Lambert, W. E., & Tucker, G. R. (1972). *The bilingual education of children: The St. Lambert experiment.* Rowley, MA: Newbury House.

Lenker, A., & Rhodes, N. (2007). Foreign language immersion programs: Features and trends over 35 years. *The ACIE Newsletter, 10* (2), pp. 1–8.

Lindholm, K. J., & Aclan, Z. (1991). Bilingual proficiency as a bridge to academic achievement: Results from bilingual/immersion programs. *Journal of Education, 173,* 99–113.

Lindholm-Leary, K. J. (2001). *Dual language education.* Clevedon: Multilingual Matters Ltd.

Lindholm-Leary, K. J. (2007). Effective features of dual language education programs: A review of research and best practices. In E. R. Howard, J. Sugarman, D. Christian, K. J. Lindholm-Leary, & D. Rogers, *Guiding principles for dual language education* (pp. 5–50). Washington, DC: Center for Applied Linguistics.

Lindholm-Leary, K. J., & Howard, E. R. (2008). Language development and academic achievement in two-way immersion programs. In T. W. Fortune, & D. J. Tedick (Eds.), *Pathways to multilingualism: Evolving perspectives on immersion education* (pp. 177–200). Clevedon: Multilingual Matters.

Lyster, R. (2004). Research on form-focused instruction in immersion classrooms: Implications for theory and practice. *Journal of French Language Studies, 14,* 321–341.

Lyster, R. (2007). *Learning and teaching languages through content: A counterbalanced approach.* Amsterdam: John Benjamins.

Montone, C., & Loeb, M. (2000). *Implementing two-way immersion programs in secondary schools.* Santa Cruz, CA and Washington, DC: Center for Research on Education, Diversity & Excellence.

Palmer, D. (2009). Middle-class English speakers in a two-way immersion bilingual classroom: "Everybody should be listening to Jonathan right now ...". *TESOL Quarterly, 43* (2), 177–202.

Parkes, J., & Ruth, T. (2009). *Urgent research questions and issues in dual language education.* Albuquerque, NM: Dual Language Education of New Mexico.

Peyton, J. K., Ranard, D. A., & McGinnis, S. (Eds.). (2001). *Heritage languages in America: Preserving a national resource.* McHenry, IL: Center for Applied Linguistics and Delta Systems.

Potowski, K. (2007). *Language and identity in a dual immersion school.* Clevedon: Multilingual Matters.

Pufahl, I., Rhodes, N. C., & Christian, D. (2000). *Foreign language teaching: What the U.S. can learn from other countries.* Washington, DC: Center for Applied Linguistics.

Ramirez, J. D. (1992). Longitudinal study of structured English immersion strategy, early-exit and late-exit transitional bilingual education programs for language minority children. *Bilingual Research Journal, 16,* 1–62.

Rhodes, N. C., & Pufahl, I. (2009). *Foreign language teaching in U.S. schools: Results of a national survey.* Washington, DC: Center for Applied Linguistics.

Saunders, W., & O'Brien, G. (2006). Oral language. In F. Genesee, K. Lindholm-Leary, W. Saunders, & D. Christian (Eds.), *Educating English language learners: A synthesis of research evidence* (pp. 14–63). Cambridge: Cambridge University Press.

Slaughter, H. (1997). Indigenous language immersion in Hawai'i. In R. K. Johnson, & M. Swain (Eds.), *Immersion education: International perspectives* (pp. 105–129). Cambridge: Cambridge University Press.

Swain, M. (1985). Communicative competence: Some roles of comprehensible input and comprehensible output in its development. In S. M. Gass, & C. G. Madden (Eds.), *Input in second language acquisition.* Rowley, MA: Newbury House.

Swain, M., & Johnson, R. K. (1997). Immersion education: a category within bilingual education. In R. K. Johnson, & M. Swain (Eds.), *Immersion education: International perspectives* (pp. 1–18). Cambridge: Cambridge University Press.

Thomas, W. P., & Collier, V. (2002). *A national study of school effectiveness for language minority students' long-term academic achievement.* Santa Cruz, CA and Washington, DC: Center for Research on Education, Diversity & Excellence.

Tucker, G. R. (1979). Implications of Canadian research for U.S. bilingual education: Setting the record straight. *NABE News, 3,* 1, 4, 5–7.

Tucker, G. R. (2001). A global perspective on bilingualism and bilingual education. In J. Alatis, & A. Tan (Eds.), *Georgetown University Round Table on Languages and Linguistics, 1999* (pp. 332–340). Washington, DC: Georgetown University Press.

Valdes, G. (2001). Heritage language students: Profiles and possibilities. In J. K. Peyton, D. A. Ranard, & S. McGinnis (Eds.), *Heritage languages in America: Preserving a national resource* (pp. 37–77). McHenry, IL: Center for Applied Linguistics and Delta Systems.

Yamauchi, L. A., & Wilhelm, P. (2001). E Ola Ka Hawai' I Kona 'Olelo: Hawaiians live in their language. In D. Christian, & F. Genesee (Eds.), *Bilingual education.* Alexandria, VA: TESOL.

2

Teacher Education and Teacher Development

Amy B. M. Tsui

Review Focus

This chapter provides an overview of the establishment of second language (L2) teacher education and teacher development as a field of inquiry, namely, the issues that the field has been grappling with, the recent trends, and the questions that researchers have yet to address. The term L2 is used in this chapter to refer to English as a second, foreign, or additional language in multilingual contexts. Studies are reviewed in relation to research in the fields of applied linguistics and teacher learning within the general education literature.

Important Developments and Trends

Emergence of L2 Teacher Education as a Field of Inquiry

L2 teaching, as a number of researchers have pointed out, has, until relatively recently, been considered a largely skills-based profession involving the acquisition of practical skills in the classroom but requiring little or no knowledge base. Early work on L2 teaching in the 1960s focused mainly on methods that would bring about effective L2 learning. Subsequently, in the 1970s and 1980s, the discussion was broadened from *methods*, which were largely constituted by prescriptive techniques, to *approaches*, which were underpinned by teaching philosophies that could be applied in different ways in the classroom (Rodgers, 2001). The increasing attention paid to the need to learn L2 worldwide, particularly in the 1960s, led to rapid developments in the field of L2 teaching and learning and the emergence of applied linguistics as a field of inquiry with a focus on how theories of language, language development, and language use can be applied in solving problems in the real world, both inside and outside of the classroom.[1] Areas of study in applied linguistics have hitherto become the knowledge base of L2 teacher education, with the core curriculum of L2 teacher education programs typically consisting of courses on linguistic analysis, sociolinguistics, and psycholinguistics, in particular theories of second language acquisition (SLA).

However, the emergence of L2 teacher education and development as *a field of inquiry* is much more recent than the emergence of applied linguistics. The first book-length publication devoted to L2 teacher education did not appear until 1990, when Richards and Nunan (1990) edited a collection of papers addressing issues relating to L2 teacher education, including the conceptual basis of L2 teacher education program designs, the practicum and models of supervision, observations of teaching, reflective teaching, and action research. Prior to that, the focus had been on equipping teachers with practical classroom skills through teacher training courses, which were typically short and offered by teacher training agencies. Even though, at the time, many of the published research articles on L2 learning concluded with implications for L2 teaching, very few were focused on L2 teacher education and professional development (Burns & Richards, 2009), and the few that were, were atheoretical in orientation (Freeman, 1989; Richards, 1987). Hence, the publication of Richards and Nunan (1990) was significant in that it established L2 teacher education as a field of inquiry and named it as such. The studies reported in the volume were underpinned by theories of teaching and supported by empirical evidence. The publication of the volume marked the point at which the concept of skills-oriented teacher training was replaced by cognitive-oriented teacher education (Larsen-Freeman, 1983) and, as the editors pointed out, also marked the point at which there was a move towards "less dependence on linguistics and language theory as a source of discipline for second language teacher education, and more of an attempt to integrate sound, educationally based approaches" (Richards & Nunan, 1990, p. xii).

Theoretical Underpinning and Knowledge Base of L2 Teacher Education

When establishing a field of inquiry, the question that needs to be addressed is: "What are the conceptual and theoretical bases that frame the research in this field?" As mentioned previously, between the 1960s and 1980s, research informed by linguistic and applied linguistic theories, especially SLA, was drawn on for teacher development purposes. The late 1980s saw the beginning of the search for conceptual and theoretical bases outside of linguistics and applied linguistics to guide empirical studies and to theorize research findings in L2 teacher education. The consolidated bibliography in Richards and Nunan (1990) consists of a number of influential studies in the field of general teacher education, although the bulk of the references were still from applied linguistics research. The research studies reported in the volume covered action research, critical reflection, practicum supervision, teacher knowledge, and teacher learning.

By the mid-1990s, it became clear that the research agenda of L2 teacher education had been shaped by those in general teacher education and underpinned by its theories. This can be seen from the increasing number of publications in L2 teacher education addressing issues of concern in general teacher education, among which were a major edited volume focusing on L2 teacher learning (Freeman & Richards, 1996), as well as another volume on teacher cognition (Woods, 1996). It is perhaps indicative of the shift in the theoretical bases of inquiry that in Freeman and Richards (1996), all of the suggestions for further reading recommended by the editors came from general education and teacher education literature. Similarly, the paradigm shift in perspectives of learning in educational research from a behaviorist view in the 1960s and 1970s, to a cognitivist view in the 1980s, and a sociocultural perspective in the 1990s, has also impacted on L2 teacher education research. Early research in L2 teacher education focused on the cognitive processes of teachers in the classroom and what they tell us about teacher learning, whereas in the past decade or so there have been an increased number of studies examining the situated nature of teachers' action and knowledge. In Lave's words, the focus has shifted to the teacher as "the whole person in action, acting with the setting of that activity" (1988, p. 17).

The shift in the disciplinary base of L2 teacher education was made explicit when Freeman and Johnson (1998) called for a reconceptualization of the knowledge base of L2 teacher education and a broader epistemological view of L2 teacher education. Freeman and Johnson defined the scope of the field by stating that "language teacher education is primarily concerned with teachers as learners of language teaching rather than with students as learners of language. Thus teacher education focuses on teacher-learners … as distinct from language learners" (1998, p. 407). This new focus, according to Freeman and Johnson, includes not only the what but also the who, the where, and the how of teaching. It entails an understanding of not only what teachers need to know in order to be effective but also teachers' conceptions and beliefs about teaching, their learning processes, their contexts of teaching, and their pedagogical practices. Freeman and Johnson were critical of the centrality given to second language learners and SLA in the field and the disconnection between SLA research and teaching knowledge. They proposed a tripartite framework that they claimed would ultimately redefine L2 teacher educators as professionals. First, "the core of the new knowledge base must focus on the activity of teaching itself; it should center on the teacher who does it, the contexts in which it is done, and the pedagogy by which it is done." Second, "this knowledge should include forms of knowledge representation that document teacher learning within the social, cultural, and institutional contexts in which it occurs." Third, "the knowledge base of language teacher education needs to account for the teacher as a learner of teaching, the social context of schools and schooling within which teacher-learning and teaching occur, and the activities of both language teaching, and language learning" (1998, p. 397).

Richards (1998) also defined the scope of L2 teacher education by posing a number of questions that the field should address pertaining to the following:

1. the knowledge base of teachers, the beliefs and principles that teachers hold, and how these impact on teaching;
2. the professional development of teachers and the influence of experience on their development; and
3. the impact of teacher education on teachers' classroom practices.

Richards' proposed focus and dimensions of inquiry largely converged with those proposed by Freeman and Johnson. However, more prominence was given to subject matter knowledge in Richards' conception of the knowledge base of L2 teacher education, which, he proposed, was constituted of the following six domains of content and knowledge (Richards, 1998, p. xiv):

- general theories of teaching;
- teaching skills;
- communication skills;
- subject matter knowledge;
- pedagogical reasoning and decision-making; and
- contextual knowledge.

Richards defined subject matter knowledge for L2 teachers as "what second language teachers need to know about their subject—the specialized concepts, theories, and disciplinary knowledge that constitute the theoretical basis for the field of second language teaching" (1998, p. 8). Richards, Li, and Tang (1998) maintained that "without a thorough knowledge of the content of teaching, teachers will have difficulty turning content into appropriate plans for teaching. They have insufficiently developed pedagogical content knowledge to be able to make content comprehensible to others" (1998, p. 99). Richards (1998) further pointed out that the question of how teachers draw on subject matter knowledge in their teaching practices had been under-explored.

The redrawing of the intellectual boundaries of L2 teacher education proposed by Freeman and Johnson (1998) has not gone unchallenged, however. Researchers working in the applied linguistics tradition have argued that central to the field are two aspects of teacher knowledge: knowledge of the subject matter and the way in which learners learn the target language, namely, knowledge of language systems, applied linguistics, and SLA. Hence, the emphasis on teachers' professional learning seems to have detracted from the focus on the target language. Tarone and Allwright (2005) pointed out that Freeman and Johnson's (1998) conceptual framework lacked a key element, namely, the second language learner, and stated that "the lack of a clear role for the learner ... [was] very troubling" (2005, p. 18). They proposed that the framework for teachers' knowledge base should include "a clear understanding of learners, who they are, why they learn, what they need to learn, what motivates them, and how a teacher goes about negotiating the teaching/learning activities with them," adding that "the management of learning ... can only be accomplished by the learners and the teacher together" (p. 18). Furthermore, Tarone and Allwright maintained that SLA is an important component of the knowledge base of L2 teachers because most of the research findings of SLA are directly relevant to teachers when they make decisions in classroom processes and curriculum planning. Acknowledging that some SLA research findings are not immediately usable to teachers, Tarone and Allwright suggested that, instead of marginalizing SLA in L2 teacher education, there should be a fundamental shift away from presenting SLA research to teachers as a product of researchers to encouraging teachers to collaborate on SLA research with researchers in order to better understand how L2 learners learn.

The knowledge base of L2 teacher education will continue to be contentious. However, the very fact that L2 teacher education is cross-disciplinary in nature suggests that the field has much to gain from a synergy between language and language learning theories and general educational theories.

Major Research Strands

Freeman (2009) has defined the scope of L2 teacher education in the last fifty years as encompassing three dimensions: "substance, engagement and outcomes" (p. 11). He has pointed out that the definition of the *substance* of the field has shifted from knowledge and skills to social activity, and that the processes in which teachers are expected to *engage* have shifted from application of professional input in contexts of teaching to a complex interplay between context, teaching, and learning. The measuring, or judgment, of *outcomes* of teacher education activities or program designs is a highly controversial area that has drawn a great deal of attention from policy makers.

Most of the research studies on L2 teacher education pertain to the first two dimensions: substance and engagement. The third dimension, outcomes, is perhaps the least developed and researched. The little research that has been published on the assessment of teachers' learning outcomes has been mostly conceptual and discursive, with little or no empirical evidence. The most recently published volume on the assessment of teachers' learning outcomes, *The Cambridge Guide to Second Language Teacher Education* edited by Burns and Richards (2009), is one of the few with a whole section devoted to standards and assessment in L2 teacher education. The paucity of research could be due to the fact that evaluation or assessment of outcomes of teacher education cannot be easily established, and extrapolations of teacher quality from such outcomes are problematic. The discussions and debates surrounding the first two dimensions, substance and engagement, have been summarized by Freeman (2009) as the widening of the scope to include not just what teachers need to learn but also increasingly how they would learn it. The what and the how are, in my view, closely linked, and it is the interplay between the two that characterizes the nature of the research in the field of L2 teacher education and teacher development. In the ensuing discussion, I shall outline the major themes that fall under the dimensions of substance and engagement, noting that they are closely interlinked.

Teacher Cognition

The investigation of the *hidden* side of teaching to illuminate teaching behaviors and classroom processes became a focus of educational research in the late 1960s and early 1970s. These processes, referred to as "teacher thinking" at the time, were seen as constituting the psychological context of teaching in which the curriculum was interpreted and acted on (Calderhead, 1987). Early studies of teacher thinking focused on teachers' planning thoughts, their classroom decision-making processes, and their implicit theories. An information-processing model, which was the predominant model of learning used in educational research at the time, was adopted for analysis. Findings of these investigations revealed that teacher cognition was highly complex and that teachers' classroom decision-making processes only constituted part of teachers' mental lives. It was argued that other dimensions, such as teachers' beliefs, attitudes, and knowledge were important in shaping their classroom practices. In particular, teacher beliefs were considered to play an important role (Pajares, 1992). Subsequently the broader term *teacher cognition* was used. The cognitive processing model was also challenged for its decontextualized and fragmented approach to cognition. It was pointed out that teacher cognition must be understood within the teachers' immediate and wider contexts of work, their personal biographies, and experiences. Studies of teacher cognition also turned to sociocultural theories of learning as their analytical framework. (For a detailed review of the literature on teacher thinking, see Clark & Peterson, 1986.)

The term teacher cognition has been defined in different ways, and different researchers have used different terms to refer to similar mental constructs. Some researchers have defined teacher cognition as referring to teacher thinking and beliefs, as distinct from teacher knowledge. However, a number of researchers have pointed out that teacher thinking, beliefs, and knowledge are interwoven, and that it is not easy to tease them out in empirical investigations. For example, Woods (1996) argued that beliefs, assumptions, and knowledge, which he referred to as BAK, were networks of interrelated propositions (see also Borg, 2006; Verloop, Van Driel, & Meijer, 2001). More recently, values and the ethical disposition of teachers have been considered to be integral to teacher knowledge (Scarino, 2005). In any case, the number of studies focused on teacher cognition is large and influential enough to constitute a distinct research strand in the teacher education literature (see Borg, 2006 for a thorough review of literature on teacher cognition).

Studies of L2 teachers' cognitive processes began in the early 1990s, with the bulk of the work appearing after the mid-1990s (Borg, 2006). Generally speaking, work on teacher cognition comes under two strands, one pertaining to the general cognitive processes of L2 teachers and the other specifically focusing on L2 teaching (mostly on the teaching of grammar). The latter strand will be discussed in more detail under a separate section on teacher knowledge. These studies are indicative of the research paradigm shift in L2 teacher education from the identification of effective teaching behaviors to an understanding of the unobservable aspects of teaching from the participant's perspective, rather than from the researcher's perspective.

Studies of L2 teachers' non-subject specific cognitive processes have been conducted among both pre-service and in-service teachers on the following aspects:

1. teachers' planning thoughts and classroom-decision making (see, for example, Bailey, 1996; Johnson, 1992a; Nunan, 1992; Richards, 1996, 1998; Smith, 1996; Tsang, 2004; Woods, 1996);
2. teacher beliefs, sources of influence, and the ways in which they shape classroom practices and decisions (see, for example, Almarza, 1996; Farrell, 1999; Numrich, 1996; Richards & Pennington, 1998; Tsui, 2003; Urmston, 2003);
3. the relationship between teacher cognition and classroom practices, for example, whether and why teachers depart from or modify their lesson plans (Bailey, 1996; Richards, 1998; Smith, 1996), and whether teachers' articulated beliefs were borne out in their classroom practices (Breen, Hird, Milton, Oliver, & Thwaite, 2001); and
4. the impact of teacher education on teacher cognition change (see, for example, Almarza, 1996; Singh & Richards, 2006).

The findings of these studies largely confirmed the findings in the general teacher education literature. Prospective and practicing L2 teachers' pedagogical philosophies, classroom practices, and decisions were shaped by their prior L2 learning experience. Certain pedagogical strategies, such as error correction and the incorporation of a cultural component, were adopted or avoided because of positive or negative learning experiences (see, for example, Bailey, Bergthold, Braunstein, Fleischman, Holbrook et al., 1996; Freeman, 1992; Golombek, 1998; Johnson, 1994; Numrich, 1996). Similarly, teachers' teaching experiences also impacted on teacher cognition. Some studies found that teaching experiences were cited most frequently as the sources of teachers' teaching ideas. Context of work was found to be another source of influence on teacher cognition. Many of these studies pointed out that teachers were unable to put their beliefs into practice because of contextual constraints, such as a prescribed curriculum, a lack of resources, or the school culture (see, for example, Breen et al., 2001; Crookes & Arakaki, 1999; Johnson, 1996; Poynor, 2005; Richards & Pennington, 1998).

Although research findings on the impact of learning and teaching experiences and context on teacher cognition converged with those in the general education research, findings on the impact of teacher education programs were more divergent. Some studies on L2 teacher cognition provided evidence of change in cognition and practice (see, for example, Peacock, 2001; Richards, Ho, & Giblin, 1996). Other studies, however, found that cognitive changes did not bring about behavioral changes in the classroom, and, conversely, behavioral changes did not necessarily entail changes in cognition (see, for example, Almarza, 1996; Freeman, 1993). What these studies also showed was that teacher education was only one source of influence, and that different student-teachers responded to teacher education courses in different ways. It is important, therefore, for teacher educators to identify these questions and help student-teachers to relate the courses to their own contexts and experiences so that they can formulate their own personal theory of teaching (Richards et al., 1996). Moreover, these studies indicated that although in some cases teachers' beliefs converged with their classroom practices, in others, there were discrepancies. Such discrepancies were found to be the result of the interaction between teachers' prior pedagogical beliefs and their perception of the immediate context, notably their response to students.

Borg (2006), in his review of research on L2 teachers' non-subject specific cognition, suggests that the study of the systemic nature of teacher cognition should be explored further. He maintains that what is least understood is "how different elements in teachers' cognitive systems interact and which of these elements, for example, are core and which are peripheral" (p. 272). Teacher cognition has been described as a network, as a continuum, or as clusters of beliefs with some being core beliefs and others peripheral. Research has shown that teachers often seem to hold conflicting beliefs. This is not surprising, given that teacher cognition not only shapes but is also shaped by classroom practices and the contexts in which teachers work (Shavelson & Stern, 1981). For example, Wu (2006) found that in different contexts, and depending on the different experiences teachers had had with students, teachers articulated different beliefs with regard to grammar teaching and the role of grammar in communicative language teaching. Teacher cognition is evolving and fluid. Reconciling conflicting beliefs and practices lies at the center of learning to teach and applies not only to novice teachers but also to experienced teachers. It appears, therefore, that exploring the systemic nature of teacher cognition may not be a fruitful undertaking. In light of the discrepancies between articulated beliefs and classroom practices revealed in empirical research, it is perhaps more useful to gain deeper insights into the situated nature of teacher cognition and the ways in which cognitive conflicts impede or facilitate teachers' professional growth.

Teacher Knowledge

The systematic study and explicit articulation of teacher knowledge, which took center stage in the teacher education literature in the 1980s and early 1990s, made an important impact on L2 teacher education research. The studies undertaken at this time generally pertained to the nature of teacher knowledge and teacher knowledge domains.

The Nature of Teacher Knowledge

Much of the work on the nature of teacher knowledge was initially inspired by Schön (1983, 1987). In his highly influential volume, *The Reflective Practitioner* (1983), Schön heavily criticized the widely accepted model of professional knowledge, in which professions such as medicine and law were classified as "major" professions (because their practices were considered to be based on specialized, firmly bounded, scientific, and standardized knowledge), and professions such as nursing, social work, and teaching were classified as "minor" professions (because they were considered to lack such a knowledge base) (Glazer, 1974). Schön argued that what professionals do in practice is not *knowing* and *acting* as two distinct processes, but an integrated process of "knowing-in-action." This form of knowledge, according to Schön, is specialized, tacit, and situated, and just as legitimate as the form of knowledge in the major professions. Schön's work provided the theoretical basis for legitimating teaching as a professional activity and set in train a large number of systematic studies on the specialized knowledge held by teachers across disciplines. It also generated heated discussion about the nature of teacher knowledge. For example, Elbaz (1983) and Connelly and Clandinin (1985) argued for the personal and practical nature of the knowledge held by teachers. This delineation of teacher knowledge, however, was challenged by Shulman (1986) as being somewhat truncated. Shulman drew attention to the fact that a missing paradigm in teacher knowledge research at the time was teachers' knowledge of the subject matter they teach. He argued for three basic knowledge domains of teacher knowledge: pedagogic knowledge, content knowledge (i.e., knowledge of the subject matter that the teacher is teaching), and pedagogic content knowledge (i.e., the effective representation of content knowledge to students). Subsequently, he broadened the knowledge domains to include knowledge of learners, context, and the curriculum. Shulman's work made a strong impact on the study of teacher knowledge, and a number of studies were conducted on the knowledge of teachers across a number of school subjects (see, for example, Brophy, 1991; Grossman, 1990).

Investigations of the nature of L2 teacher knowledge have been conducted through teacher interviews focusing on their planning thoughts, interactive classroom decision-making, and their reflections on their teaching. The findings of these studies converged with those in the general teacher education literature, namely, that teachers have implicit theories of teaching that guide their pedagogical actions and that are typically personal and oriented to the situation in which they operate. These theories, as Elbaz (1983) points out, encompass their firsthand experience of students' learning styles, interests, needs, strengths and difficulties, and a repertoire of pedagogical skills. They often take the form of principles and maxims, formulated over time, that reflect their own beliefs about language, language teaching, effective teaching, the teacher's role, and the teacher–student relationship (see, for example, Breen et al., 2001; Burns, 1996; Johnson, 1992b; Richards, 1996, 1998).

Teacher Knowledge Domains: Subject Matter Knowledge and Teacher Language Awareness

Prior to the 1990s, teachers' knowledge about language was neglected in L2 teacher education research. Within the scope of L2 teacher education, although discussions of L2 teacher knowledge often included teachers' beliefs about language and language teaching, the focus had not been on teachers' subject matter knowledge, that is, teachers' knowledge of the underlying systems of language (including phonological, lexical, grammatical, and discoursal features of L2), and their meta-linguistic knowledge. It was not until the late 1990s that more attention was given to this area. The research focus of this area, however, has been mostly on teachers' declarative knowledge of grammar, their beliefs about grammar teaching, and their procedural knowledge about grammar (i.e., how their knowledge of grammar is effectively represented to learners in the classroom) (Borg, 2003). The latter has also been referred to as "teacher language awareness" (TLA) (Andrews, 2007). Studies of L2 teachers' explicit, or declarative, knowledge of grammar have been conducted on native-speakers (NS) and non-native speakers (NNS) of the target language. Andrews' study on prospective and practicing NS and NNS L2 teachers showed that the latter scored substantially higher than the former in a test on knowledge of grammar and grammar terminology (Andrews, 1999). This tallied with research studies conducted on prospective L2 teachers' KAL (knowledge about language) in the UK, which showed a very low level of meta-linguistic knowledge (Chandler, Robinson, & Noyes, 1988; Williamson & Hardman, 1995; Wray, 1993) among NS teachers. These findings were a cause for concern, as teachers' KAL was considered to be essential for effective language teaching. This concern resonated with Shulman's concern for the neglect of teachers' subject matter knowledge in teacher education research. In the course of investigating the operationalization of KAL in the classroom, researchers found that teachers' subject matter knowledge was inextricably bound up with their beliefs about grammar and grammar teaching. Andrews (2007), therefore, used the term *subject matter cognition* in preference to subject matter knowledge, arguing that "while subject matter knowledge may constitute the core of TLA, any teacher's knowledge is inevitably bound up with beliefs about subject matter and, for example, how it should or can be taught and learnt in a given context" (p. 70).

A number of studies have been conducted on teachers' knowledge and beliefs about grammar, grammar teaching, and the impact of these on their actual classroom practices (see Borg, 2006, for a detailed summary of relevant studies). The findings showed that teachers' beliefs about grammar and grammar teaching may or may not be borne out in their classroom practices. For example, teachers were found to engage in explicit grammar instruction not because they believed that it could enhance L2 learning but because they believed that students wanted it (Borg, 1998); teachers who believed in minimizing explicit error correction frequently corrected student errors in the classroom (Ng & Farrell, 2003). In line with the findings reported in the general teacher education literature, these studies showed that teachers' subject matter cognition and classroom practices were shaped by their personal biographies and their specific contexts of work. What is perhaps most interesting and important is Andrew's empirical study, which showed that whereas the target group of seventeen L2 teachers performed reasonably well (mean score of 71%) on a sixty-item language awareness test on their explicit knowledge of grammar and grammatical terminology, they did poorly (mean score of 43%) on a test that required them to explain their corrections of errors in fifteen sentences, a typical classroom task. Borg (2006) maintains that these findings suggest that developing a "pedagogically oriented understanding of grammar among teachers" is more valuable than developing grammatical knowledge that is divorced from pedagogical concerns (p. 124). This endorses Shulman's position that pedagogical content knowledge lies at the heart of teacher knowledge. However, it does not mean that subject matter knowledge should be relegated to secondary importance. Indeed, Andrews' study showed that teachers who lacked subject matter knowledge were not able to engage with the subject matter adequately and effectively in the classroom, even though they had a certain degree of language awareness (i.e., they were aware of the language needs of the learners) (Andrews, 2001, 2007).

So far, the bulk of the work on L2 teachers' subject matter knowledge pertained to grammar knowledge. Other aspects of the language system and language skills remain largely neglected. Only a few studies deal with teacher cognition in L2 writing (see, for example, Burns, 1992; Shi & Cummings, 1995; Tsui, 1996). More research needs to be conducted on all aspects of L2 subject matter knowledge. More importantly, the relationship between L2 teachers' subject matter knowledge and pedagogical content knowledge is currently under-explored.

Teacher Learning and Teachers' Professional Development

Understanding how teachers learn to teach, their professional development trajectories, and the contributing factors behind their professional development lies at the core of teacher education (Johnson, 2009). Research in this area belongs to the *engagement* dimension in the scope of L2 teacher education (Freeman, 2009), namely, the process of professional learning in which teachers are engaged. As Freeman points out, the term *teacher-learner* signifies that teachers are learners of teaching throughout their career. The voluminous body of research on teacher knowledge, teacher cognition, and teachers' professional development has provided rich input for facilitating and scaffolding teachers' professional learning in teacher education programs. Courses such as reflective teaching, classroom research, and action research are now standard courses in many L2 teacher education and teacher development programs.

The first volume devoted to L2 teacher learning appeared in 1996 (Freeman & Richards, 1996). The aim of the volume, according to the editors, was to examine more closely and deeply "how teachers come to know what they know and do what they do in their work" (p. ix). Since then, other volumes on teacher learning have been published (see, for example, Burns, 1999; Richards, 1998). In this section, I shall focus on three research strands on teacher learning that are prevalent and important: teachers as reflective practitioners, teachers as researchers, and the development of teachers' expertise in teaching.

Teachers as Reflective Practitioners

The concept of reflective action as integral to teachers' work was first proposed by John Dewey, who argued that teachers are not just passive curriculum implementers but that they can also play an active role in curriculum design and educational reform (Dewey, 1933). The notion of teachers' engagement in reflective action was further developed by Schön, who proposed that teachers are not "technical experts" but "reflective practitioners" (1983, p. 332). Through processes of reflection and reframing, Schön argued, teachers often came to a new understanding of their professional practice. Reflective practice has been drawn on by teacher educators as a mediational tool for teachers' professional learning (Burton, 2009; Zeichner & Liston, 1996).

In L2 teacher education, reflective teaching has been an essential element in teacher education programs, and writing reflective journals has become almost a standard requirement. A number of studies have reported on how teachers came to a better understanding of their work through reflective practice. For example, Bailey and her teacher-learners reported on how writing autobiographies of their language learning experiences, and subsequent journal entries, helped them to reflect on the ways in which their development as teachers was influenced by the critical incidents in their learning and teaching histories, as well as a host of other factors that shaped their teaching philosophies and practices (Bailey et al., 1996). Knezevic and Scholl (1996) reported on their experience as teacher-learners on an MA Teaching program, during which they reflected on their experience of team-teaching a Spanish class by telling stories about their decision-making processes during lesson planning and while teaching the lesson itself. The significance of this kind of engagement is captured in their reflections on the stories that they authored together. They wrote:

> Because we have reflected on common experiences using our shared professional discourse … teaching concepts that began as words—and as symbolic representations of ideas—have

become anchored in personal experience. In this approach to learning, moments or stories from practice have been attached to issues and concepts. With these vivid examples in place, we grasped their meanings and constructed our own interpretations of these teaching ideas. Consequently, this knowledge has become available to us as a resource for use in the future.

(Knezevic & Scholl, 1996, p. 94)

One of the concerns in engaging teachers in reflective practice is how they can move beyond descriptive accounts of their work (Jarvis, 1992) to reflect on their practice critically. To achieve this, teachers need to move beyond technically oriented improvement of classroom skills to address the issues that are fundamental to their development as responsible and autonomous professionals and to see their actions in relation to the purposes of education (Bartlett, 1990; see also Burton, 2009).

For example, Richards and Ho (1998), in their study of the reflective journals written by thirty-two teachers on an MA course over a ten-week period, found that there was little change in the degree of critical reflectivity in the teachers' journal entries over time, although most teachers found that writing journals helped them to become more aware of their own actions and to better understand themselves as teachers. Richards and Ho concluded that more scaffolding was needed to help teachers to write reflectively and reflect critically. A number of publications provided detailed guidelines for teachers to engage in reflective teaching by collecting data on their own teaching, examining their own attitudes and beliefs about teaching, and reflecting on how they might improve their teaching (see, for example, Bartlett, 1990; Richards & Lockhart, 1994). Descriptions and analysis of cases of reflective practice, often with practical suggestions for adaptation, were also published (see, for example, Burton, 2001–2006; Farrell, 2007). What teachers seemed to find particularly useful was sharing reflective writings and engaging in collaborative reflections (see, for example, Burns, 1999).

Teachers as Researchers

The notion of "teacher as researcher" was developed in the late 1960s and early 1970s through Stenhouse's (1975) highly influential work on curriculum research and development, in which he proposed that curriculum development should involve testing educational theories through application in practice, hence the term *action research*. Stenhouse further maintained that, in order to be more effective, action research typically should be undertaken by teachers, rather than by researchers. A large number of studies on action research conducted by teachers were published, especially during the 1980s. The concept of action research developed from a somewhat linear and fixed sequence of planning, action, observation, and reflection (Kemmis & McTaggart, 1988) to a dynamic and cyclical model that allowed for feedback, modification, and re-trial. Action research has been commonly used as a mediational tool for teacher learning and for improving teachers' professional practice (Gore & Zeichner, 1991).

Since the early 1990s, there has been a growing number of studies on action research in L2 teacher education (see, for example, Burns, 1999; Crookes, 1993; Edge, 2001; Gebhard, 2005; Wallace, 1998). Many of the studies were conducted in the context of a teacher education program, in which student-teachers were required to conduct an action research project as partial fulfilment of the program requirements. Based on such experience, a number of studies have pointed out that teachers need to be equipped with certain skills and knowledge about how pedagogical research can and should be conducted, and that they need to learn these skills by actually engaging in action research (Nunan, 1990). For example, Wallace (1996) reported on the use of an action research project in a teacher preparation undergraduate program aimed at getting student-teachers to reflect on their professional action, to articulate their reflective practice, and to synthesize formal knowledge with experiential knowledge. Based on the problems that emerged from their action research projects, Wallace suggested that student teachers should be equipped with the skills and knowledge to conduct action research and be guided on how reflections could be structured. Pennington (1996) outlined the input and support that was provided to student-teachers on an MA program to help them conduct action research on process writing, and the findings of her study suggested that engaging in reflection in a meaningful way is a precondition for teacher change to take place. Moreover, a number of guides and handbooks on conducting action research were published for teachers. For example, Nunan (1990) contained detailed guidelines on the stages for conducting action research, as well as check-lists and worksheets for teachers to use for conducting lesson observation; Burns (1999) provided a comprehensive introduction to the conceptual and practical aspects of conducting action research. Burns (2009) summarized the purposes of action research in L2 teacher education as follows:

1. to address specific issues in teaching or learning situations;
2. to investigate curriculum innovation and the change processes;
3. to facilitate teachers' professional development;
4. to enhance teachers' knowledge of conducting research and to equip them with research skills;
5. to enhance the development of their personal practical theories; and
6. to provide a vehicle for reducing the gap between research and practice.

To the extent that action research, when properly conducted, engages teachers in problematizing and researching their own practice, making sense of the data they collect, and theorizing the findings, it is a powerful mediational tool for teacher learning (Burns, 2009).

Teaching Expertise

The study of teaching expertise has been inspired by the work of cognitive psychologists on expert practitioners in other fields (e.g., chess masters, doctors, radiologists, and physicists). It has been motivated by the need to understand the special form of knowledge held by teachers and to demonstrate that experts in teaching possess skills and knowledge that are as complex and sophisticated as those possessed by experts in other professions (Berliner, 1994). Studies on teaching expertise burgeoned in the 1980s and early 1990s.

Early studies of teaching expertise adopted an information-processing approach (often quasi-laboratory in nature), using simulated pedagogical tasks to examine teachers' cognitive processes in pedagogical decision-making (Carter, Cushing, Sabers, Stein, & Berliner, 1988). Typically, the characteristics of expert teachers were investigated through expert–novice comparisons, and by examining their cognitive processes in planning and conducting lessons, and the quality of their reflections (see Berliner, 1994, for a detailed summary; see also Johnson, 2005; Tsui, 2005, 2009 for an overview). These early studies showed that expert teachers, no less than experts in other highly regarded professions, demonstrated similar characteristics: Expert teachers have a complex but integrated and coherently structured knowledge base; they are capable of recognizing patterns very quickly and interpreting them in meaningful ways; they have better improvisational skills than novice teachers and are able to handle complex tasks with apparent automaticity and effortlessness; they are able to justify their classroom actions in a principled manner; and they have better self-monitoring and meta-cognitive skills than novice teachers. Studies of the subject matter knowledge and pedagogical content knowledge of expert and novice teachers found that, compared to novice teachers, expert teachers have a more coherent overview of the curriculum, a better understanding of the different ways of structuring the curriculum, a better grasp of the critical points in the content that students need to master, and are better able to represent these points effectively to students. More recent studies of teacher expertise have adopted a sociocultural approach to studying teachers as "the whole person in action, acting with the settings of that activity" (Lave, 1988, p. 17). Many of these studies were conducted in naturalistic rather than quasi-laboratory settings (Leinhardt, 1989; Smith & Strahan, 2004; Turner-Bisset, 2001; for a brief overview of the major research methodologies adopted, see Johnson, 2005).

The above studies, irrespective of their research approach, were criticized by Bereiter and Scardamalia (1993) for taking a static view of expertise. Bereiter and Scardamalia proposed an alternative conception of expertise as a process. Since then, several studies have been conducted on teachers' development of expertise over time (see, for example, Bullough & Baughman, 1995, 1997; Tsui, 2003). The different conceptions of expertise have yielded different characterizations. Whereas the conception of expertise as a state characterizes expert performance as effortless, efficient, and automatic, the conception of expertise as a process characterizes expertise as a process of continuous search for excellence, in which practitioners work "at the edge of their competence" (Bereiter & Scardamalia, 1993, p. 34; see Tsui, 2003 for a more detailed discussion).

In L2 teacher education research, studies have been done on highly skilled L2 teachers, though the focus was not on teaching expertise. A number of studies have examined the cognition and practices of experienced teachers (Borg, 2006; Breen et al., 2001; Woods, 1996) through investigating their pedagogical decisions and their personal practical knowledge (see Golombek, 2009 for an overview). Comparisons have been made between experienced and inexperienced teachers (see, for example, Richards et al., 1998; see also K. Johnson, 2005). The findings of these studies were congruent with those in general teacher education research. For example, experienced L2 teachers focused more on subject matter (i.e., language) than novice teachers, who paid more attention to classroom management (Nunan, 1992); were better able to respond to students' needs and improvise than novice teachers (Richards, 1998); had a deeper understanding of subject matter knowledge; were better able to present subject matter knowledge more appropriately and from the students' perspective; and were better able to integrate language learning with other curricular goals (Richards et al., 1998).

More recently, studies have been undertaken with a specific focus on expertise in L2 teaching and drawing on conceptual frameworks used in expertise studies. The first book-length investigation of L2 teaching expertise was Tsui (2003), which compares an expert teacher, two experienced teachers, and one novice teacher and examines their cognitive processes in managing learning in the classroom, as well as the knowledge and beliefs that underpinned these processes (including the teaching of four language skills, grammar, and vocabulary). In this study, the development of expertise of the expert teacher showed that teacher learning is a process in which the teacher constantly engages in exploration and experimentation of new ideas, problematizing what appears to be unproblematic in her own teaching, and looking for and responding to new challenges. Tsui concludes by pointing out the relevance of research on teaching expertise to teacher learning as follows: first, expert teachers' ways of thinking and ways of learning can serve as a reference for both novice and experienced non-expert teachers to think about their work as teachers and how they learn to teach; second, case studies of expert teachers can help to raise experienced teachers' awareness of their own actions and to make their implicit theories of teaching explicit; third, understanding the critical differences between expert and non-expert teachers can help teacher educators, mentors, and school leaders to identify the emerging characteristics of expertise in young teachers early on, so that they can be supported as well as challenged at appropriate phases of their professional development.

Teacher Identity

Teacher identity is an emerging theme in general teacher education as well as L2 teacher education. It has become increasingly important in the field of teacher education because of the centrality given to teacher identity formation as an integral part of teacher learning. Identity formation involves not only acquiring the competence that is valued by the community (i.e., acquiring the knowledge and skills of teaching) but also being able to engage in and contribute to the construction of meanings that are important to the community as a competent member of that community. Thus, identity is not just *relational* (i.e., how one talks or thinks about oneself, or how others talk or think about one), it is also *experiential* (i.e., it is formed from one's lived experience). Wenger's theory of learning as social participation and the concept of legitimate peripheral participation proposed by Lave and Wenger (1991) have been drawn on by many studies in general teacher education research to illuminate the professional development of teachers from peripheral to full participation and to distinguish between different trajectories of participation (see Tsui, Edwards, & Lopez-Real, 2009 for a detailed discussion).

Research on teacher identity in the general teacher education literature clusters around three major themes (Tsui, 2007). The first theme is the multi-dimensionality of professional identity and the relationships between these dimensions. Although there seems to be a general agreement that professional identities are multi-dimensional, there are opposing views with regard to whether striving for harmony and coherence of the multiple identities should be part of teacher learning (Beijaard, Meijer, & Verloop, 2004; Mishler, 1999), or whether the construction of identity is a "continuing site of struggle" between conflicting identities (Lampert, 1985; MacLure, 1993; Samuel & Stephens, 2000). The second theme relates to the personal and social dimensions of identity formation. Most studies emphasize the personal dimension, focusing on self-reflection on who one is and what one wants to become (Antonek, McCormick, & Donato, 1997). However, a number of researchers have pointed out the importance of the professional landscape, which is part of the broader sociocultural and sociopolitical landscape, in shaping teacher identity (Duff & Uchida, 1997; He, 2002a, 2002b, 2002c; Reynolds, 1996). The third theme relates to the relationship between agency and structure in identity formation. Whereas some researchers have stressed the importance of agency (i.e., the capacity of an individual to act on the world) over social structure and argued that the choices that teachers make constitute their professional identities (Coldron & Smith, 1999), others have argued that teachers' active location in social space can be undermined by policies or institutions that require conformity, and that it is the interaction between the two that shapes teachers' identities (Moore, Edwards, Halpin, & George, 2002).

In L2 teacher education, L2 teacher identity has only recently begun to draw interest from researchers (see, for example, Duff & Uchida, 1997; Johnson, 2003; Singh & Richards, 2006; Tsui, 2007; Varghese, 2006; Varghese, Morgan, Johnston, & Johnson, 2005). It is considered a critical component in the sociocultural and sociopolitical landscape of the L2 classroom and in L2 teachers' professional development (Burns & Richards, 2009). Identity has been defined in many different ways (see Miller, 2009 for a summary). Most definitions state identity as relational (i.e., identity pertains to perception of oneself in relation to others and others' perception in relation to oneself) (e.g., Duff & Uchida, 1997; Johnson, 2003; Norton, 2000). Others define identity as discursively constructed and context bound (Morgan, 2004), and as formed in the process of enacting one's role (Burns & Richards, 2009; Gee, 2000; Miller, 2009; Varghese et al. 2005). Wenger's theory of identity formation is perhaps the most powerful, in that it cogently argues for identity formation being relational and experiential, as well as social and personal. This theory also helps us to understand how different forms and trajectories of participation in the community's core practice can shape the identities formed by teachers. For example, Tsui and Edwards (2009) found that L2 teachers developed different identities in different schools depending on the extent to which opportunities were provided to them to participate in core activities (e.g., including having a cup of coffee in the common room) and the extent to which they responded to these opportunities.

Distinctive to research on L2 teacher identity is the fact that a very large number of L2 teachers are NNS of the target language. In the context of the hegemony of the English language worldwide, and the supremacy of the NS variety of English, the identity of teachers who are NNS of English as competent members of the community of TESL (teaching of English as a second language) is often characterized by conflict and struggle (e.g., Varghese et al., 2005; see also Tsui, 2007). Given that the rapid spread of English entails an ever-increasing number of English teachers who are NNS of English, this is a research theme where further work is much needed (see also Burns & Richards, 2009).

Issues for Future Research

L2 teacher education is a relatively new field of inquiry with a history of approximately only two decades. It has broadened from relying on linguistics, applied linguistics, and SLA research as its theoretical bases for scholarly inquiry to general education theories. This has resulted in new and refreshing insights for researchers and practitioners. In reviewing the literature in this field, it is apparent that studies in language-based disciplines and L2 teacher education have not been as closely linked as they should be, and that there remain areas that need to be strengthened and gaps that need to be filled. I shall briefly outline these areas as issues for future research.

Pedagogic Content Knowledge of L2 Teachers

Despite the emphasis given to the centrality of pedagogic content knowledge, few studies have focused on the ways in which L2 teachers are able to effectively represent subject matter knowledge to students, the difficulties students have in understanding how the language works, and how they could be helped. The work of Andrews (2007) is an important addition to the literature. More work of this nature is needed, as well as more work on other aspects of the language systems, including phonetics, lexis, and discourse. As the discussion on teachers' subject matter knowledge has shown, pedagogic content knowledge and pedagogical reasoning involve a sound knowledge of the language systems. In research literature on learning and learning theory (inspired by the work of Stevenson & Stigler, 1992), much attention has been given to how teachers engage with the object of learning. In recent years, lesson study research has become increasingly influential. This research strand has been inspired by Fernandez and Yoshida's (1999) work on mathematics teaching in Japan, in which teachers collaboratively planned and taught a lesson to deal with students' conceptions and misconceptions of the subject matter being taught. L2 teacher education has much to benefit from lesson study research, which now encompasses a number of disciplines.

Teacher and Learner Knowledge and Beliefs

A number of studies have been done on learner and teacher beliefs. However, so far these studies have largely been conducted separately, and the interrelationship between learner and teacher beliefs has been under-researched (Kiely, 2001). Kiely's work shows that the student's response to the teacher has a powerful impact on the latter and that it can lead to resistance, reflection, and/or reframing on the part of the teacher (see also Platt & Troudi, 1997). The few studies that have elicited data from both teachers and students show that there is a gap between the two sets of beliefs. For example, Schulz's (1996, 2001) comparison between the attitudes to grammar teaching and corrective feedback of L2 teachers and learners found that although the overwhelming majority of the students welcomed correction of the errors they made in class, less than half of the teachers agreed that they should correct students' errors. Similar gaps were found to exist between students' and teachers' beliefs about the formal study of grammar, with students attaching more importance to it than teachers. Identifying the gaps in teacher and student perceptions is just the beginning; more important is the impact of such gaps on student learning and how these gaps can be bridged.

Student Learning

To date, research on L2 teacher education has been focused on the teacher, which is to be expected as the teacher is at the center of field of inquiry. However, as Tarone and Allwright (2005) pointed out, claims made about teacher knowledge, pedagogical practices, and teacher change have so far made little reference to learners (i.e., whether teacher knowledge, pedagogical practices, and teacher change bring about better student learning and what supporting evidence there is for this improvement). Whereas much attention has been paid to teachers' voice, students' voice has largely remained silent. Although it is problematic to draw causal relationships between teacher learning and student learning, as Freeman and Johnson (2005) have cogently argued, it is equally problematic if learners' learning is left unconsidered. After all, the ultimate goal of L2 teacher education is to enhance the quality of student learning.

Note

1 It should be noted that the term *applied linguistics* appeared in the 1940s in the subtitle of *Language Learning* published by Michigan University. The scope of applied linguistics, however, was at that time much more narrowly defined and largely focused on linguistics.

References

Almarza, G. G. (1996). Student foreign language teachers' growth. In D. Freeman & J. Richards (Eds.), *Teacher learning in language teaching* (pp. 50–78). Cambridge: Cambridge University Press.

Andrews, S. (1999). 'All these like little name things': a comparative study of language teachers' explicit knowledge of grammar and grammatical terminology. *Language Awareness, 8,* 143–159.

Andrews, S. (2001). The language awareness of the L2 teacher: Its impact upon pedagogical practice. *Language Awareness, 10,* 75–90.

Andrews, S. (2007). *Teacher language awareness.* New York: Cambridge University Press.

Antonek, J. L., McCormick, D. E., & Donato, R. (1997). The student teacher portfolio as autobiography: Developing a professional identity. *Modern Language Journal, 81,* 15–27.

Bailey, K., Bergthold, B., Braunstein, B., Fleischman, N. J., Holbrook, M. P., Tuman, J., Waissbluth, X. & Zamboo, L. (1996). The language learner's autobiography: Examining the "apprenticeship of observation." In D. Freeman & J. Richards (Eds.), *Teacher learning in language teaching* (pp. 11–29). Cambridge: Cambridge University Press.

Bailey, K. M. (1996). The best laid plans: teachers' in-class decisions to depart from their lesson plans. In K. M. Bailey & N. David (Eds.), *Voices from the language classroom* (pp. 15–40). Cambridge: Cambridge University Press.

Bartlett, L. (1990). Second language teacher education. In J. Richards & D. Nunan (Eds.), *Teacher development through reflective teaching* (pp. 202–214). New York: Cambridge University Press.

Beijaard, D., Meijer, P. C., & Verloop, N. (2004). Reconsidering research on teachers' professional identity. *Teaching and Teacher Education, 20*(2), 107–128.

Bereiter, C., & Scardamalia, M. (1993). *Surpassing ourselves: An inquiry into the nature and implications of expertise.* Chicago: Open Court.

Berliner, D. C. (1994). The wonder of exemplary performances. In J. N. Margieri & C. C. Block (Eds.), *Creating powerful thinking in teachers and students' diverse perspectives* (pp. 161–186). Fort Worth, TX: Harcourt Brace College.

Borg, S. (1998). Studying teacher cognition in second language grammar teaching. *System, 27,* 19–31.

Borg, S. (2003). Teacher cognition in grammar teaching: A literature review. *Language Awareness, 3*(2), 61–71.

Borg, S. (2006). *Teacher cognition and language education.* New York: Continuum.

Breen, M., Hird, P. B., Milton, M., Oliver, R., & Thwaite, A. (2001). Making sense of language teaching: teachers' principles and classroom practices. *Applied Linguistics, 22*(4), 470–501.

Brophy, J. (1991). Introduction to volume 2. In J. Brophy (Ed.), *Advances in research on teaching* (Vol. 2) (pp. ix–xvi). London: JAI Press.

Bullough, R. V., & Baughman, K. (1995). Changing contexts and expertise in teaching: First year teacher after seven years. *Teaching and Teacher Education, 11*(2), 461–478.

Bullough, R. V., & Baughman, K. (1997). *First-year teacher eight years later: An inquiry into teacher development.* New York: Teachers College Press.

Burns, A. (1992). Teacher beliefs and their influence on classroom practice. *Prospect, 7*, 56–66.

Burns, A. (1996). Starting all over again: From teaching adults to teaching beginners. In D. Freeman & J. Richards (Eds.), *Teacher learning in language teaching* (pp. 154–177). Cambridge: Cambridge University Press.

Burns, A. (1999). *Collaborative action research for English language teachers*. Cambridge: Cambridge University Press.

Burns, A. (2009). Action research in second language teacher education. In A. Burns & J. Richards (Eds.), *The Cambridge guide to second language teacher education* (pp. 289–297). New York: Cambridge University Press.

Burns, A., & Richards, J. (2009). Second language teacher education. In A. Burns & J. Richards (Eds.), *The Cambridge guide to second language teacher education* (pp. 1–8). New York: Cambridge University Press.

Burton, J. (Ed.). (2001–2006). *Case studies of TESOL practice series*. Alexandria, VA: TESOL Publications, Inc.

Burton, J. (2009). The scope of second language teacher education. In A. Burns & J. Richards (Eds.), *The Cambridge guide to second language teacher education* (pp. 298–308). New York: Cambridge University Press.

Calderhead, J. (Ed.). (1987). *Exploring teachers' thinking*. London: Cassell.

Carter, K., Cushing, K., Sabers, D., Stein, P., & Berliner, D. (1988). Expert–novice differences in perceiving and processing visual classroom information. *Journal of Teacher Education, 39*(3), 25–31.

Chandler, P., Robinson, W. P., & Noyes, P. (1988). The level of linguistic knowledge and awareness among student training to be primary teachers. *Language and Education, 2*, 161–173.

Clark, C. M., & Peterson, P. L. (1986). Teachers' thought processes. In M. C. Wittrock (Ed.), *Handbook of research on teaching* (pp. 255–296). New York: Macmillan.

Coldron, J., & Smith, R. (1999). Active location in teachers' construction of their professional identities. *Journal of Curriculum Studies, 31*, 711–726.

Connelly, F. M., & Clandinin, D. J. (1985). Personal practical knowledge and the modes of knowledge: Relevance for teaching and learning. In E. Eisner (Ed.), *Learning and teaching the ways of knowing* (Vol. 84 Yearbook of the National Society for the Study of Education, Part II) (pp. 174–198). Chicago: University of Chicago Press.

Crookes, G. (1993). Action research for second language teachers: Going beyond teacher research. *Applied Linguistics, 14*(2), 130–144.

Crookes, G., & Arakaki, L. (1999). Teaching idea sources and work conditions in an ESL program. *TESOL Journal, 8*(15–19).

Dewey, J. (1933). *How we think*. Buffalo, NY: Prometheus Books.

Duff, P., & Uchida, Y. (1997). The negotiation of teachers' sociocultural identities and practices in postsecondary EFL classrooms. *TESOL Quarterly, 31*(3), 451–461.

Edge, J. (2001). *Action research*. Alexandria, VA: TESOL.

Elbaz, F. (1983). *Teacher thinking: A study of practical knowledge*. London: Croom Helm.

Farrell, T. (1999). The reflective assignment: Unlocking pre-service teachers' beliefs on grammar teaching. *RELC Journal, 30*, 1–17.

Farrell, T. (2007). *Reflective language teaching: From research to practice*. London: Continuum.

Fernandez, C., & Yoshida, M. (1999). *Lesson study: A Japanese approach to improving mathematics teaching and learning*. Mahwah, NJ: Lawrence Erlbaum Associates.

Freeman, D. (1989). Teacher training, development, and decision making model: A model of teaching and related strategies for language teacher education. *TESOL Quarterly, 23*, 27–45.

Freeman, D. (1992). Language teacher education: Emerging discourse, and change in classroom practice. In J. Flowerdew, M. Brock, & S. Hsia (Eds.), *Perspectives on language teacher education* (pp. 1–21). Hong Kong: City Polytechnic of Hong Kong.

Freeman, D. (1993). Renaming experience/reconstructing practice: Developing new understandings of teaching. *Teaching and Teacher Education, 9*, 485–497.

Freeman, D. (2009). The scope of second language teacher education. In A. Burns & J. Richards (Eds.), *The Cambridge guide to second language teacher education* (pp. 11–19). New York: Cambridge University Press.

Freeman, D., & Johnson, K. (1998). Re-conceptualizing the knowledge-base of language teacher education. *TESOL Quarterly, 32*(3), 397–417.

Freeman, D., & Johnson, K. E. (2005). Toward linking teacher knowledge and student learning. In D. Tedick (Ed.), *Second language teacher education: International perspectives* (pp. 73–96). Mahwah, NJ: Lawrence Erlbaum Associates.

Freeman, D., & Richards, J. (Eds.) (1996). *Teacher learning in language teaching*. Cambridge: Cambridge University Press.

Gebhard, J. G. (2005). Awareness of teaching through action research: Examples, benefits and limitations. *JALT Journal, 27*(1), 53–69.

Gee, J. (2000). Identity as an analytic lens for research in education. In W. Secada (Ed.), *Review of research in education 25* (pp. 99–125). Washington, DC: American Educational Research Association.

Glazer, N. (1974). Schools of the minor professions. *Minerva*, pp. 346–364.

Golombek, P. R. (1998). A study of language teachers' personal practical knowledge. *TESOL Quarterly, 32*(3), 447–464.

Golombek, P. R. (2009). Personal practical knowledge in L2 teacher education. In A. Burns & J. Richards (Eds.), *The Cambridge guide to second language teacher education* (pp. 155–162). New York: Cambridge University Press.

Gore, J., & Zeichner, K. M. (1991). Action research and reflective teaching. *Teaching and Teacher Education, 7*(2), 119–136.

Grossman, P. (1990). *The making of a teacher.* New York: Teachers College Press.

He, M. F. (2002a). A narrative inquiry of cross-cultural lives: Lives in China. *Journal of Curriculum Studies, 34,* 301–321.

He, M. F. (2002b). A narrative inquiry of cross-cultural lives: Lives in Canada. *Journal of Curriculum Studies, 34,* 323–342.

He, M. F. (2002c). A narrative inquiry of cross-cultural lives: Lives in the North American academy. *Journal of Curriculum Studies, 34,* 513–533.

Jarvis, J. (1992). Using diaries for teacher reflection on in-service courses. *ELT Journal, 46*(2), 133–143.

Johnson, K. (Ed.). (2005). *Expertise in second language learning and teaching.* Basingstoke: Palgrave Macmillan.

Johnson, K. E. (1992a). The instructional decisions of pre-service English as a second language teacher: New directions for teacher preparation programs. In J. Flowerdew, M. Brock, & S. Hsia (Eds.), *Perspectives on second language teacher education* (pp. 115–134). Hong Kong: City Polytechnic of Hong Kong.

Johnson, K. E. (1992b). The relationship between teachers' beliefs and practices during literacy instruction for non-native speakers of English. *Journal of Reading Behavior, 24,* 83–108.

Johnson, K. E. (1994). The emerging beliefs and instructional practices of preservice English as second language teachers. *Teaching and Teacher Education, 10*(4), 439–452.

Johnson, K. E. (1996). The vision versus reality: The tensions of the TESOL practicum. In D. Freeman & J. Richards (Eds.), *Teacher learning in language teaching* (pp. 30–49). Cambridge: Cambridge University Press.

Johnson, K. E. (2003). 'Every experience is a moving force': Identity and growth through mentoring. *Teaching and Teacher Education, 19,* 787–800.

Johnson, K. E. (2009). *Second language teacher education: A sociocultural perspective.* New York: Routledge.

Kemmis, S., & McTaggart, R. (1988). *The action research planner.* Rowley, MA: Newbury House.

Kiely, R. (2001). Classroom evaluation—values, interests and teacher development. *Language Teaching Research, 5*(3), 241–261.

Knezevic, A., & Scholl, M. (1996). Learning to teach together: Teaching to learn together. In D. Freeman & J. Richards (Eds.), *Teacher learning in language teaching* (pp. 79–96). Cambridge: Cambridge University Press.

Lampert, M. (1985). How do teachers manage to teach? Perspectives on problems in practice. *Harvard Educational Review, 55*(2), 178–194.

Larsen-Freeman, D. (1983). Training teachers or educating a teacher. In J. E. Alatis, H. H. Stern, & P. Strevens (Eds.), *Georgetown University round table on language and linguistics* (pp. 264–274). Washington, DC: Georgetown University Press.

Lave, J. (1988). *Cognition in practice: Mind, mathematics, and culture in everyday life.* Cambridge: Cambridge University Press.

Lave, J., & Wenger, E. (1991). *Situated learning: Legitimate peripheral participation.* Cambridge: Cambridge University Press.

Leinhardt, G. (1989). A contrast of novice and expert competence in mathematics lessons. In J. Lowyck & C. M. Clark (Eds.), *Teacher thinking and professional action* (pp. 75–98). Leuven: Leuven University Press.

MacLure, M. (1993). Arguing for yourself: Identity as an organizing principle in teachers' jobs and lives. *British Educational Research Journal, 19,* 311–322.

Miller, J. (2009). Teacher identity. In A. Burns & J. Richards (Eds.), *The Cambridge guide to second language teacher education* (pp. 172–181). New York: Cambridge University Press.

Mishler, E. G. (1999). *Storylines: Craft artists' narratives of identity.* Cambridge, MA: Harvard University Press.

Moore, A., Edwards, G., Halpin, D., & George, R. (2002). Compliance, resistance and pragmatism: The (re)construction of schoolteacher identities in a period of intensive educational reform. *British Educational Research Journal, 28,* 551–565.

Morgan, B. (2004). Teacher identity as pedagogy: Towards a field-internal conceptualization in bilingual and second language education. In J. Brutt-Griffler & M. Varghese (Eds.), *Re-writing bilingualism and the bilingual educator's knowledge base* (pp. 80–96). Clevedon: Multilingual Matters.

Ng, J., & Farrell, T. (2003). Do teachers' beliefs of grammar teaching match their classroom practices? A Singapore case study. In D. Deterding, A. Brown, & E. L. Low (Eds.), *English in Singapore: Research on grammar* (pp. 128–137). Singapore: McGraw Hill.

Norton, B. (2000). *Identity and language learning: Gender, ethnicity and educational change.* London: Longman.

Numrich, C. (1996). On becoming a language teacher: Insights from diary studies. *TESOL Quarterly, 30*(1), 131–153.

Nunan, D. (1990). Action research in the language classroom. In J. Richards & D. Nunan (Eds.), *Second language teacher education* (pp. 62–81). New York: Cambridge University Press.

Nunan, D. (1992). The teacher as decision-maker. In J. Flowerdew, M. Brock, & S. Hsia (Eds.), *Perspectives on second language teacher education* (pp. 135–165). Hong Kong: City Polytechnic of Hong Kong.

Pajares, M. F. (1992). Teachers' beliefs and educational research: Cleaning up a messy construct. *Review of Educational Research, 62*(3), 307–332.

Peacock, M. (2001). Pre-service ESL teachers' beliefs about second language learning: A longitudinal study. *System, 29*, 177–195.

Pennington, M. (1996). When input becomes intake: Tracing the sources of teachers' attitude change. In D. Freeman & J. Richards (Eds.), *Teacher learning in language teaching* (pp. 320–350). Cambridge: Cambridge University Press.

Platt, E., & Troudi, S. (1997). Mary and her teachers: A Grebo-speaking child's place in the mainstream classroom. *Modern Language Journal, 78*, 497–511.

Poynor, L. (2005). A conscious and deliberate intervention: The influence of language teacher education. In D. Tedick (Ed.), *Second language teacher education: International perspectives* (pp. 157–176). Mahwah, NJ: Lawrence Erlbaum Associates.

Reynolds, C. (1996). Cultural scripts for teachers: Identities and their relation to workplace landscapes. In M. Kompf, W. R. Bond, D. Dworet, & R. T. Boak (Eds.), *Changing research and practice: Teachers' professionalism, identities and knowledge* (pp. 69–77). London: Falmer Press.

Richards, J. (1987). The dilemma of teacher preparation in TESOL. *TESOL Quarterly, 22*, 9–27.

Richards, J. (1996). Teachers' maxims in language teaching. *TESOL Quarterly, 30*, 281–296.

Richards, J. (1998). *Beyond training*. New York: Cambridge University Press.

Richards, J., & Ho, B. (1998). Reflective thinking through journal writing. In J. Richards (Ed.), *Beyond training* (pp. 153–170). Cambridge: Cambridge University Press.

Richards, J., Ho, B., & Giblin, K. (1996). Learning how to teach in the RSA Cert. In D. Freeman & J. Richards (Eds.), *Teacher learning in language teaching* (pp. 242–259). Cambridge: Cambridge University Press.

Richards, J., Li, B., & Tang, A. (1998). Exploring pedagogical reasoning skills. In J. Richards (Ed.), *Beyond training* (pp. 86–102). New York: Cambridge University Press.

Richards, J., & Nunan, D. (Eds.) (1990). *Second language teacher education*. New York: Cambridge University Press.

Richards, J., & Pennington, M. (1998). The first year of teaching. In J. Richards (Ed.), *Beyond training* (pp. 173–190). New York: Cambridge University Press.

Richards, J. C., & Lockhart, C. (1994). *Reflective teaching in second language classrooms*. New York: Cambridge University Press.

Rodgers, T. S. (Producer). (2001). Language teaching methodology. *CAL: Digests*. Podcast retrieved from www.cal.org/resources/digest/rodgers.html (accessed July 7, 2001).

Samuel, M., & Stephens, D. (2000). Critical dialogues with self: Developing teacher identities and roles-a case study of South African student teachers. *International Journal of Educational Research, 33*, 475–491.

Scarino, A. (2005). Introspection and retrospection as windows on teacher knowledge, values and ethical dispositions. In D. Tedick (Ed.), *Second language teacher education: International perspectives* (pp. 33–52). Mahwah, NJ: Lawrence Erlbaum Associates.

Schön, D. A. (1983). *The reflective practitioner: How professionals think in action*. New York: Basic Books.

Schön, D. A. (1987). *Educating the reflective practitioner: Toward a new design for teaching and learning in the professions* (1st ed.). San Francisco: Jossey-Bass.

Schulz, R. A. (1996). Focus on form in the foreign language classroom: Students' and teachers' views on error correction and the role of grammar. *Foreign Language Annals, 29*, 343–364.

Schulz, R. A. (2001). Cultural differences in student and teacher perceptions concerning the role of grammar teaching and corrective feedback: USA-Columbia. *Modern Language Journal, 85*, 244–258.

Shavelson, R. J., & Stern, P. (1981). Research on teachers' pedagogical thoughts, judgements, decisions, and behaviour. *Review of Educational Research, 51*(4), 455–498.

Shi, L., & Cummings, A. (1995). Teachers' conceptions of second language writing instructions: Five case studies. *Journal of Second Language Writing, 4*, 87–111.

Shulman, L. (1986). Those who understand knowledge growth in teaching. *Educational Researcher, 15*(2), 4–14.

Singh, G., & Richards, J. (2006). Teaching and learning in the language teacher education course room. *RELC Journal, 37*(2), 149–175.

Smith, D. B. (1996). Teacher decision making in the adult ESL classroom. In D. Freeman & J. Richards (Eds.), *Teacher learning in language teaching* (pp. 197–216). Cambridge: Cambridge University Press.

Smith, T. W., & Strahan, D. (2004). Toward a prototype of expertise in teaching: A descriptive case study. *Journal of Teacher Education, 55*(4), 357–371.

Stenhouse, L. (1975). *An introduction to curriculum research and development*. London: Heineman.

Stevenson, H. W., & Stigler, J. W. (1992). *The learning gap*. New York: Simon and Schuster.

Tarone, E., & Allwright, R. (2005). Second language teacher learning and student second language learning: Shaping the knowledge-base. In D. Tedick (Ed.), *Second language teacher education: International perspectives* (pp. 5–24). Mahwah, NJ: Lawrence Erlbaum Associates.

Tsang, W. K. (2004). Teachers' personal practical knowledge and interactive decisions. *Language Teaching Research*, 8(2), 163–198.

Tsui, A. B. M. (1996). Learning how to teach writing. In J. Richards & D. Freeman (Eds.), *Teacher learning in language teaching* (pp. 97–124). Cambridge: Cambridge University Press.

Tsui, A. B. M. (2003). *Understanding expertise in teaching*. New York: Cambridge University Press.

Tsui, A. B. M. (2005). Expertise in teaching: Perspectives and issues. In K. Johnson (Ed.), *Expertise in second language learning and teaching* (pp. 167–189). New York: Palgrave Macmillan.

Tsui, A. B. M. (2007). The complexities of identity formation: A narrative inquiry of an EFL teacher. *TESOL Quarterly*, 41(4), 657–680.

Tsui, A. B. M. (2009). Teaching expertise: Approaches, perspectives and characterizations. In A. Burns & J. C. Richards (Eds.), *The Cambridge guide to second language teacher education* (pp. 190–197). Cambridge: Cambridge University Press.

Tsui, A. B. M., & Edwards, G. (2009). On becoming a member of a community of practice. *Learning in school–university partnership: Sociocultural perspectives.* (pp. 47–68). New York: Routledge.

Tsui, A. B. M., Edwards, G., & Lopez-Real, F. (with contributions from Kwan, T., Law, D., Stimpson, P., Tang, R., and Wong, A.) (2009). *Learning in school–university partnership: Sociocultural perspectives.* New York: Routledge.

Turner-Bisset, R. (2001). *Expert teaching: Knowledge and pedagogy to lead the profession.* London: David Fulton Publishers.

Urmston, A. (2003). Learning to teach English in Hong Kong: The opinions of teachers in training. *Language and Education*, 17(2), 112–126.

Varghese, M. (2006). Bilingual teachers-in-the-making. *Journal of Multilingual and Multicultural Development*, 27(3), 211–224.

Varghese, M., Morgan, B., Johnston, B., & Johnson, K. (2005). Theorizing language teacher identity: Three perspectives and beyond. *Journal of Language, Identity and Education*, 4, 21–44.

Verloop, N., Van Driel, J., & Meijer, P. C. (2001). Teacher knowledge and the knowledge base of teaching. *International Journal of Educational Research*, 35, 441–461.

Wallace, M. (1996). Structured reflection: The role of the professional project. In D. Freeman & J. Richards (Eds.), *Teacher learning in language teaching* (pp. 281–294). Cambridge: Cambridge University Press.

Wallace, M. (1998). *Action research for language teachers.* Cambridge: Cambridge University Press.

Williamson, J., & Hardman, F. (1995). Time for refilling the bath? A study of primary student-teachers' grammatical knowledge. *Language and Education*, 9, 117–134.

Woods, D. (1996). *Teacher cognition in language teaching.* New York: Cambridge University Press.

Wray, D. (1993). Student-teachers' knowledge and beliefs about language. In N. Bennett & C. Carre (Eds.), *Learning to teach* (pp. 51–72). London: Routledge.

Wu, K. Y. (2006). Teacher beliefs and grammar teaching practices: Case studies of four ESL teachers. Unpublished thesis (Ph. D.), University of Hong Kong,.

Zeichner, K. M., & Liston, D. P. (1996). *Reflective teaching: An introduction.* Mahwah, NJ: Lawrence Erlbaum Associates.

3

Learning to Write in the Second Language: K-5

María Estela Brisk

Research and the teaching of writing have evolved over time. From a focus on product where the expectation was that children had to be "corrected" until they achieved adult-like writing performance, to an emphasis on process where children are expected to experiment on their way to achieving adult-like proficiency. More recently, there has been an interest in genre "largely a response to changing views of discourse and of learning to write which incorporate better understandings of how language is structured to achieve social purposes in particular contexts of use" (Hyland, 2007, p. 148). Genre research focuses on students' products as evidence of the children's linguistic, communicative, and cognitive knowledge (Fang, 1999). These products are not prescribed but are the result of the interaction between contextual and linguistic input.

The purpose of this chapter is to explore the development of writing of elementary age bilingual learners[1] in their second language (L2).[2] Fitzgerald (2006) summarized in great detail the existing research on L2 writing and concluded that the evidence indicates that development of writing in young L2 writers does not differ much from writing development of native speakers of English. In this chapter, the existing research will be framed within two theories to analyze what L2 writers need to develop to be successful, particularly in school contexts. By framing the existing research in these theories, the chapter will show what is known and what teachers need to develop through instruction.

The research on L2 writing by children in elementary grades is framed within a theoretical model that is based on systemic functional linguistics (SFL) (Halliday, 1994) and Walters' (2005) model of bilingualism (see Figure 3.1). Texts, or the language produced orally or in writing, exist in the context of culture and are further embedded in the context of situation. Language users make choices in producing texts that are influenced by extralinguistic and linguistic input. The extralinguistic level includes register, medium, and purpose or genre. At the linguistic level, language users choose from lexical, grammatical, and orthographic knowledge (Butt, Fahey, Feez, Spinks, & Yallop, 2000). Walters (2005) proposes a model of language production by bilinguals that includes a sociopragmatic component, similar to the extralinguistic component of the SFL model, and a psycholinguistic component, similar to the linguistic component of the SFL model. These two components interact in the intentional component, which specifies the pragmatic intentions and the information to be conveyed, comparable to what SFL calls genre or purpose. In addition, Walters proposes that bilinguals are influenced by language choice and affective modules at every aspect of language production. The language choice module "selects, regulates, and retrieves information from a speaker's two languages during

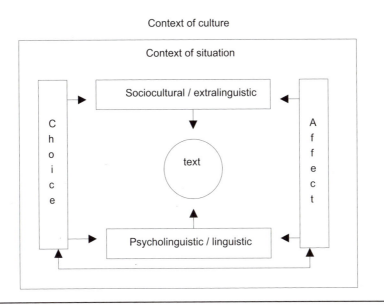

Figure 3.1 Theoretical framework

the entire course of language production" (p. 92). The affective module "is designed to select, regulate, and retrieve emotion-based information from other components of language processing" (p. 94).

The combination of these two theories helps create a framework that takes an in-depth look at the second language in the context of bilingualism. SFL provides a clear and complete theoretical picture of the choices children need to make if they want to "use linguistic codes to construct contextually appropriate and coherent text" (Fang, 1999, p. 180). Bilingual learners trying to write in the second language struggle with what they want to say. SFL provides teachers with the tools to analyze language and determine what bilingual students need to learn to express what they want to say in ways that will be understood and accepted by the culture (Schleppegrell & Go, 2007).

Within the SFL framework, learning to write means making the appropriate choices to convey meaning given the context of the specific situation, which exists within the context of a culture. As children develop writing they realize that they have power in language. They can "manipulate language for the best effect" (Urzua, 1987, p. 295). Writing in a US school means that children need to know the culturally appropriate patterns expected in the school. Different situational contexts call for different language choices based on the topic addressed (*field*), the relationship between the writer and readers (*tenor*), and the channel of communication being used, written or multimodal (*mode*). Together they constitute the linguistic *register*. An important aspect of schooling is familiarizing students with the academic registers of various content areas. Children also need to understand the features of the *medium*, such as books, letters, poems, or PowerPoints, each requiring certain organization and features. Another essential aspect of writing influencing language choices is the purpose, such as story telling, giving instructions, providing organized information, and persuading. These various purposes are realized in text types or *genres*, such as recounts, fictional narratives, procedures, reports, explanations, and expositions. Each of these genres has a specific culturally defined structural organization and language expectations (Butt et al., 2000). Writing also requires knowledge of vocabulary, grammar, spelling, and conventions. All these choices present challenges to children developing writing.

The research in L2 writing is discussed in this chapter in relation to language choice, affect, context of culture, context of situation, register, medium, and genre. The concepts as defined by the theories will be further explained in each subsection. To conclude, the chapter summarizes the way in which combining SFL with Walters' model provides a useful framework for understanding L2 writing and the needs of bilingual learners.

Language Choice

Bilinguals have access to more than one language and, according to Walters' theory (2005), they make choices at all levels of the production process. These choices are influenced by social factors, such as demographics and language status; interpersonal factors, such as setting, audience, topic, and attitudes; and individual factors, such as identity, language preference, language proficiency, and motivation (Walters, 2005). Even very young bilingual children are aware that they have more than one language and that they are different. For example, an emergent Chinese–English bilingual writer used invented spelling in both Chinese and English that looked like the characters or letters of each language (Buckwalter & Lo, 2002).

Children are not confused between the languages, although when they access language, they may switch to a different language or access native language (L1) data when writing in their second (L2). Code-switching is the alternate use of two languages (Mackey, 1968). Code-switching in written language is not as common as in oral language (Edelsky, 1986). Young writers switch because they do not have access to a term in the other language, or they do it on purpose to enhance the text. In a two-way program, both English and Spanish speakers writing in their native language would code-switch to the second language when writing about cultural aspects of that second language (Gort, 2006). Children may choose the language depending on the specific purpose and audience. For example, a 5th grader, who wrote mostly in Spanish, switched to English to pass secret notes to her English-speaking classmates (Laman & Van Sluys, 2008). Code-switching can occur across modes. Lo and Hyland (2007) noticed that when their students were given more freedom in the choice of topic they became very engaged and sometimes could not think how to write in English. They would give the sentence or phrase orally in Chinese for the teachers to translate so they could write it in English.

Sometimes the choice of language is defined by the classroom context. In a two-way program, students went from writing in one of the languages to writing in both. Only one 5th grader switched to writing only in English. In general, students felt more confident writing in their dominant language. They used more words, better spelling, more complexity, and better developed ideas (García & Colón, 1995). Teachers may encourage students to use their native language or may restrict writing to the second language. Even when encouraged to write in their native language, within a year (as their proficiency in English developed) students had switched to writing in English (Graves, Valles, & Rueda, 2000). On other occasions, bilingual students code-switched to English when writing in their native language. Often they encounter new concepts in the new culture for which they do not have terms in their native language, or they just get used to using these terms in English (Barrett-Pugh & Rohl, 2001; Gort 2006).

Children sometimes write texts in both languages, one being an approximate translation of the other. For example, a 1st grade Hebrew speaker divided the page in two, writing in Hebrew and English alongside each other. She wanted to share the notebook with her classmates, as well as teach them words in Hebrew (Lahman & Van Luys, 2008). Another child liked writing bilingual books, as her English was not as good as her Spanish; the Spanish version was simpler to facilitate writing the English version (Homza, 1995).

When L2 writers do not have access to linguistic information in L2, they resort to using L1 data to write in English. Accessing L1 as a resource may have different results in what is produced in the L2. Positive influence of L1 may not be apparent to the naked eye, but research has shown correlation between native language writing ability and performance in writing in English as a second language, even when the native language uses a different script (Cummins, 1991). Length of utterances, spelling (Davis, Carlisle, & Beeman, 1999), concept of print (Buckwalter & Lo, 2002), and productivity (Carlisle & Beeman, 2001) showed positive transfer. This positive influence is more evident when English is in the early stages of development, and when the native language literacy is strong (Lanauze & Snow, 1989).

Sometimes L1 influences L2 products, especially grammatical structures and spelling, resulting in non-native like language. First grade Spanish-speakers applied Spanish sentence structure to their English writing (Gort, 2006). They also omitted the subject, a common feature of Spanish grammar (Simpson, 2004). Khmer-speaking students in Australia, when writing in English, had difficulty with a number of grammatical morphemes due to Khmer influence. The fact that Khmer does not change words to indicate plural and past tense, it does not use articles, and uses prepositions differently influenced the inaccurate production of past tense, plural, articles, and prepositions when writing in English (Barrett-Pugh & Rohl, 2001). L1 can also influence spelling. L2 writers apply L1 phonology when spelling in English (Gort, 2006). Rather than view these L1-based choices negatively, educators must take the perspective that "what a young writer knows about writing in the first language forms the basis of new hypotheses rather than interferes with writing in another language" (Edelsky, 1982, p. 227).

To some degree, L1 influence may be related to the linguistic environment. Among students who are learning English in an environment where their L1 is widely used, the influence of L1 may be greater. Elementary students in Hong Kong wrote sentences that were a direct translation from Chinese to English (Lo & Hyland, 2007). These children were exposed to English only in school, and were otherwise immersed in Cantonese in all other contexts. The writing of Chinese children in school in the US, for the most part, showed little influence of Chinese in their English, with the exception of one child's writings that reflected a Chinese rhetorical structure. He concluded a report on computer games with a moral, a typical feature of Chinese rhetorical style (McCarthey, Guo, & Cummins, 2005). These children were surrounded by English while Chinese was only used at home. However, other research has also found evidence of the influence of L1 on L2 writing within English-speaking societies. Age of acquisition, level of proficiency, specific aspects of language, educational experiences, and register may explain the degree of this influence.

Affect

Emotions affect language production, impacting the individual's social identity. For example, an individual may fail at appearing humorous because humor is difficult to produce in a second language. Sometimes affect works in conjunction with choice, as when an author chooses to code-switch to reflect their cultural identity.

Affect impacts genre choice. Writers associate certain genres with one of their languages and others with the other. Walters (2005) argues that "the only apparent way to become an accomplished writer in two languages at the same time is to divide one's writing along genre lines" (p. 107).

Affect also impacts topic choice. Children reveal their feelings through writing and try to address their problems through it. Boys dislike writing personal recounts, but they will address personal struggles through fictional narratives (Newkirk, 2000). For example, a big student routinely bullied a small-built Puerto Rican 5th grader. His victim wrote a story about both visiting Puerto Rico and going horseback riding. The big boy fell from the horse in the story and died.

Context of Culture

According to SFL theory all texts exist in the context of culture (Butt et al., 2000). Learning to write in English as a second language means also learning how to function in a new culture. How writing is taught and the performance expectations in different cultures vary. For example, the process approach to teaching writing prevalent in the United States confuses Vietnamese children who like to write correctly from the start. They do not understand the notion of writing drafts and then revising (Dien, 2004). Culture defines all aspects of the language choices, including topic, relationship with the audience, specific features of the language of written text, as well as structural organization of texts and language features of various genres.

Cultural differences are salient in the uses of genres, the structural organization of texts, and expected language features given the genre. These culturally different styles are more of a challenge for students who have already started their schooling in their country of origin. It is also difficult for parents who try to understand these new rhetorical styles expected in schools. Recount or narrative genres are difficult because narratives are deeply rooted in culture and shared with children at home from an early age, either through reading or oral story telling (McCabe & Bliss, 2003; Perez, 2004). These narrative styles are transferred to personal recounts and fictional narratives produced by students. Personal recounts or narratives, widely used in writing instruction in elementary schools in the United States, create some tensions either because students use their own cultural organizational patterns (unacceptable to teachers), or because in certain cultures it is not considered appropriate to write about close personal matters in school (Dien, 2004).

Persuasive writing also varies across cultures. Indirection and starting a persuasive essay with a universal truth, rather than a thesis or claim are features of Chinese writing. Arabic persuasive writing supports reasons appealing to emotions, rather than with facts (Connor, 2002; Hinkel, 2002; Matalene, 1985). For many students just expressing an opinion is very difficult. In many cultures only adults express opinions, and children remain silent (Matalene, 1985).

Matsuda (1997) warns against stereotyping rhetorical practices of bilingual writers. He maintains that the construction of text structures by such writers is a dynamic process influenced by their cultural background, personal experiences, and instruction. The influence of the two languages is mutual. For young writers, who often learn the patterns of the American culture, the influence of L2 on L1 structural organization of text can be more pronounced. McCarthey et al. (2005) report that by the second year in the United States students' Chinese writing increasingly reflected US norms.

Aspects of the register are influenced by culture. For example, in American writing making the text clear is the writer's responsibility; the writer elaborates on the text to make interpretation accessible to the reader. Japanese consider it an insult to the reader to be too specific; implying the reader is incapable of understanding or inferring from the text (Hinds, 1987). Communal cultures are used to taking a "we" rather than the "I" perspective, common in American personal recounts (Matalene, 1985; Maguire & Graves, 2001). Children often start their narratives introducing the whole family, and then go on telling the story from the "we" perspective. For example, a Spanish-speaking 3rd grader wrote, "I was going to New York City. … There was 18 people in two cars. … We got there all ready. We saw a lot of buildings. We went in the hotel. We checked out for 3 hotel rooms …." Such cultural perspectives may have an impact on perception of students' writings. For example, the student samples posted on the internet of the Massachusetts state test illustrating the highest scores of the 4th grade long composition are all written in the first person singular. Those illustrating the lowest scores are written in the first person plural.

The topic of the text can be influenced by culture. Some students find it difficult to write about something that they have learned in another language, or that they associate with a particular culture. For example, Arabic students found it difficult to write about Ramadan in English or smoking in Arabic, topics they associated with the opposite culture (Bou-Zeneiddine, 1994). Chinese students found it difficult writing about a topic of their own creation, as opposed to something connected to history or a tradition (Matalene, 1985).

It is important not to stereotype cultural patterns because bilingual students may be raised in a bicultural environment and be accustomed to American cultural ways, or because they are very young and have not attended school and are learning many of the features of written text for the first time in the second language (Lisle & Mano, 1997). For example, a Somalian 2nd grader, much to her teacher's dismay, wrote elaborate personal recounts reflecting her own culture's narrative style. In school she was taught how to write reports, and (much to her teacher's surprise) was quick to apply the text structure expected in schools.

Context of Situation

Children develop writing in the second language in the context of different situations. The context of situation affects writing development of bilingual learners on four levels: societal, school, home, and specific writing task. Countries vary in their support for the various languages their inhabitants speak. Social, political, cultural, and economic factors impact the attitude toward languages (Baker, 2006; Brisk, Burgos, & Hamerla, 2004). Bilingual children in the United States learn to write in a context where their bilingualism encounters limited social and political support. Lack of support for heritage languages[3] influences school and home practices. In addition to attitude toward bilingualism, writing development in schools is influenced by the pressure to learn academic English and succeed in high-stakes tests.

Schools and families respond to political pressures to favor one or the other language. Some students in the United States attend bilingual programs where they develop full literacy in two languages (Lindholm-Leary, 2001). Most students develop literacy in English with the heritage language only used initially in the case of transitional bilingual education programs (Brisk, 2006). Some families promote heritage language literacy at home and others do not (McCarthey et al., 2005; Smith, 2006). However, research has shown that regardless of the efforts that families or schools may carry out to support heritage languages, the attitudes and practices of the larger environment prevail in children's bilingual development. Thus, children in the United States are more likely to develop English to a higher level (Caldas & Caron-Caldas, 2002). Moreover, writing in the heritage language is often strongly influenced by English. Code-switching to English is common (Gort, 2006), and text structure of genres follows the English norms (Barrett-Pugh & Rohl, 2001; McCarthey et al., 2005).

Research points out that biliteracy is not only possible but also may be desirable. Strong writing ability in the native language supports writing development in the second language (Barrett-Pugh & Rohl, 2001; Carlisle & Beeman, 2000; Cummins, 1991). For students receiving writing instruction in both languages, early development appears first in their dominant language, and later is transferred to their second language (Gort, 2006). Development in each language will depend on the features of the language itself, the influence of one language on the other, and instruction. For example, Khmer bilingual students attending a bilingual program in Australia found the Khmer writing system difficult and took longer to develop. The syntactic structure of Khmer influenced English syntax resulting in verb tense and person errors, as well as prepositions and articles. In turn, English text organization influenced Khmer narrative writing. Despite these difficulties students develop writing in both languages. By the end of the third year in the program, students could write in both languages considering purpose and audience, with control over most essential elements (Barrett-Pugh & Rohl, 2001). Simpson (2004) reports on 1st graders in Ecuador being instructed only in English, but encouraged to write in both languages. Their writing products were comparable in quality in some aspects, but showed fewer errors and more formulaic style in English, the language of instruction.

Another impact of bilingualism is metalinguistic awareness. Children negotiating two or more languages notice and talk about differences between the languages (Barratt-Pugh & Rohl, 2001;

Dagenais & Day, 2000). This ability to talk about language is an important aspect of understanding language and can help development (Swain, 2005).

Instruction is an important contextual factor on L2 writing development (Brisk & Harrington, 2007; Samway, 2006). Balanced literacy instruction, with native oral language support, helped Portuguese-speaking kindergarten students develop reading and writing in English (Araujo, 2002). Some effective strategies include using cooperative and interactive instruction (Gutierrez, 1994), mentoring and scaffolding, as opposed to highly controlled writing (Huss, 1995), and using peer support groups (Prater and Bermúdez, 1993; Urzua, 1987). Allowing the use of native language for planning and interacting was found more helpful in improving students' attitudes toward school (Fitzgerald, 2006) and comprehension of concepts (Garrett, Griffiths, James, & Scholfield, 1994; Huss, 1995), rather than directly in improving English writing. Explicit instruction using the SFL framework greatly helps students develop L2 writing for authentic purposes (Brisk & Zisselsberger, forthcoming; Gebhard, Harman, & Seger, 2007). Analyzing the context of high-stakes tests informed by SFL helped students in two 4th grade classrooms understand that they were producing text to impress a person they didn't know with their language and writing skills. Their narratives became lengthy and interesting, with varied vocabulary and figurative language, descriptive adjectivals, and numerous adverbials showing place, time, and manner.

Register

Register is language variation relative to context. Thompson (2004, p. 40) explains this relationship below:

> There are three main dimensions of variation which characterize any register: what is being talked about (this is called the "*field*"); the people involved in the communication and the relationship between them (the "*tenor*"); and how the language is functioning in the interaction: for example, whether it is written or spoken (the "*mode*").

Thus the field or topic, tenor, and mode help shape the language choices writers make when producing text.

Field

Knowledge, choice, and language demands of the field or topic are important in development and teaching of writing. Knowledge of the topic is essential to being able to write about it. In addition, L2 writers need the language to express their knowledge. Teachers claim that students do not know what to write about due to lack of background knowledge. Escamilla (2006) argues that bilingual students have rich background knowledge, but teachers do not tap into it for writing. Even if students express rich ideas, their value may be lost to teachers because they hide behind numerous spelling and mechanical errors (Hernández, 2001). Peer-conferencing helps students with choosing and developing the topic (Prater & Bermúdez, 1993). In classrooms where writing development is combined with content areas, content knowledge must be developed to give L2 writers the knowledge and technical language needed for writing. A group of 5th grade teachers who had asked students to write persuasive pieces in connection to their social studies units found that students had difficulty building evidence without strong knowledge of content.

The research on supporting L2 learners with the choice of topic, addresses the kinds of topics fostered in classrooms and the importance of who makes topic choices. Drawing on students' personal experiences and knowledge is considered a key source for writing content (Cummins, 2005; Moll,

1992). Bilingual students should be exposed to writing other topics because writing is an important medium for learning new topics. Huss (1995) found that when six-year-old Punjabi children in England were given the choice, they wrote on a greater variety of topics than when the teachers assigned topics. However, in a 5th grade class, the student who had the greatest difficulty with writing, when given a choice, wrote over and over again about his personal experiences with video games. The teacher switched from just letting the students write about whatever they chose, to developing writing activities with different purposes (i.e. genres), such as writing a class cookbook with family favorite recipes, creating an ad for their science invention, and writing a letter to the judge, siding with the wolf or the three little pigs after reading *The True Story of the Three Little Pigs* (Scieszka, 1989). The students' products changed not only in topic but also in quality. The evidence suggests that bilingual students should be allowed to choose topics that draw on personal experience, but they should also be exposed to new topics and different genres.

Topic choice produces language demands. To use language in order to create intended meaning, young L2 writers need vocabulary and grammatical knowledge. Research on L2 acquisition underscores the importance of vocabulary development (Páez & Rinaldi, 2006; Proctor, August, Carlo, & Snow, 2006). L2 writers must also learn how to form clauses with noun groups, verb groups, and adverbials. In writing, clauses are often combined into coordinate or compound sentences to pack information. Sentences and paragraphs are linked with rhetorical connectors that help relate the meaning between various sections of the text (Derewianka, 1998).

Grammar, Bae (2001) argues, is a global writing quality "because without adequate competency in grammar it is unlikely that learners can produce writing with quality and text length reasonable enough to communicate ideas" (p. 76). Children in elementary school use mostly simple sentences, making the writing monotonous and also lacking clarity by not showing relationships. These children can use compound and complex sentences orally, but very few appear in their writing (Hernández, 2001). As they grow older, they try to express more complex thoughts but have difficulty using the appropriate syntax (Barratt-Pugh & Rohl, 2001). A common problem in clauses is the subject–verb agreement (Simpson, 2004).

Sentences include participants and processes. Participants are introduced through nouns. Adjectives are used to describe these participants. Most children use very few adjectives. In a 161-word personal recount, a 3rd grader used only six adjectives. As children develop, these noun describers increase (Schleppegrell & Go, 2007). The position of the adjective may be problematic for L2 writers. In a number of languages, including Vietnamese, Khmer, and Spanish, the adjective goes after the noun. For this reason, Schleppegrell and Go (2007) argue that adjectival phrases, which go after the noun in English too, may be easier to use for L2 writers. The 3rd grader mentioned above created a phrase in order to place the adjectives in second place, resulting in an awkward construction (*I saw badges from polices and firefighters*).

Processes are expressed through verbs. Development of verb groups includes appropriate use of verb tenses and variation in the types of verbs such as action (*run, climb*), saying (*say, question*), sensing (*think, heard, love*), relational (*have, be*), or existential (*there is*) verbs. Young L2 writers when telling a story often use the present and past interchangeably. Formation of the past, especially with irregular past, is problematic. L2 writers tend to use mostly action and relational verbs, especially *to be*, and they often repeat the same verb. When using saying verbs it is always *say*. For example the 161-word personal narrative mentioned above included 12 action verbs (five *to go*), nine relational (eight *to be*), three sensing (all three *to see*), and one saying. Variety of verbs as well as the use of modals is a sign of development (Schleppegrell & Go, 2007). Verbs are further described through adverbs and adverbial phrases or clauses indicating place, time, manner, cause, accompaniment, and others (Butt et al., 2000; Derewianka, 1998). The personal narrative mentioned above included 11 adverbs and adverbial phrases only indicating time and place.

Grammatical morphemes are one of the greatest challenges for L2 learners, and can persist even when students have become very proficient in English (Genesee, Paradis, & Crago, 2004; Menyuk & Brisk, 2005). Such errors as past tense (*Then we went in side the house and sleep; He never ever did told me ...*), third person singular (*because water expand*), plurals (*Don't worry if you have childrens*), prepositions (*He died in July, 26*), determiners (*The Dennis was helping the Helen*) (Bae, 2001, p. 73). As well as, omission of the verb to be (both copula *Cortes want to famous* and auxiliary *Rosa parks married to Raymond parks*), possessive (*We went to the house of my ant's*) (Gort, 2006, p. 329), relative pronouns (*man play a piano* instead of *man who plays piano*) (Schleppegrell & Go, 2007, p. 532), pronouns (no distinction between *she, her* in Khmer and Korean; *She mom gives* for *Mom gives her*) (Bae, 2001, p. 73; Barratt-Pugh & Rohl, 2001), and contractions (*his going to*).

Tenor

From a very young age children are socialized on how to use language with different audiences. Bilingual children also develop the ability to choose the appropriate language given the audience (Laman & Van Sluys, 2008). Developing a sense of audience in writing is harder because the audience is not often present. Urzua (1987) found that peer-conferencing helped students understand that the purpose of writing is "to communicate something important to an audience" (p. 285). Understanding of audience background knowledge impacts the content and coherence of the writing. The writer needs to gage the level of detail that must be included in developing the piece so that it makes sense. In a personal recount of his early life, a 3rd grader wrote about his pre-school in California and about entering the W.R., his present school, in kindergarten. However, he neglected to include that by then he had moved to Massachusetts. It made sense for his immediate audience, that was familiar with the whereabouts of this school, but it would not have made sense to other audiences. Awareness of the audience had an impact on efforts made by the children to revise their writing. Before this awareness, Urzua (1987) reports that revision meant recopying to make the writing neater, but not to improve it. When writing in the second language bilinguals must understand that they need to be comprehensible to readers from a different culture. Although developing a sense of audience is difficult to achieve in writing, Martínez, Orellana, Pacheco, and Carbone (2008) argue that bilingual students' translation practice in their daily lives helps develop skills in adjusting language to different audiences and purposes. Researchers gave 6th grade bilingual students the challenge of writing a persuasive piece in their L2 for two different audiences. These students carefully constructed their argument for a more formal audience, but they were more casual when writing to their friends. They also chose different reasons and evidence, grammatical structures, and vocabulary.

The interpersonal function, or tenor, not only focuses on audience but also on the language users and the identity or voice they choose to reflect through their language choices. Bilingual writers may or may not choose to reflect their cultural and/or linguistic background in their language, or the evidence may be very subtle (Walters, 2005). Voice is "the imprint of ourselves on our writing" (Graves, 1983, p. 227). Voice reflects the identity that writers want to present to readers. Development of voice comes with interest in the topic and confidence in writing. As students in Urzua's study (1987) grew confident, they made decisions on how to improve their writing, accepting or ignoring peers' comments relative to what the writers thought sounded appropriate. Different genres call for different voice (Schleppegrell, 2006). A writer may reflect humor through a personal recount, authoritativeness through a report, and pathos through a persuasive piece. In their journal narratives, bilingual children showed great skill in reflecting their individual self. They used "*I* to describe an action, feeling, or point of view … *we* to describe a shared value, membership in a group activity, or a member of a community,… and *she, he,* and *they* to adopt a more distant stance as a persona" (Maguire & Graves, 2001, p. 588).

Mode

A text can be oral, written, or multimodal. In developing written language among L2 learners, the role of oral language has been a source of controversy. Earlier L2 methodologies encouraged the development of oral language before teaching literacy. Hudelson's (1984) and Edelsky's (1982) research demonstrated that L2 students enhanced their L2 development through reading and writing, and that there was no need to wait for full oral proficiency to introduce literacy. Reading can have an important impact on writing (Davis et al., 1999). Bernhardt (1991) concluded that both knowledge of the second language and literacy knowledge acquired through either language were essential for literacy development. Therefore oral language is important in as much as it helps develop the second language, but it is not a pre-condition for learning to write.

The mode or textual function also refers to how writers construct their messages in a way that all the parts fit smoothly as the text unfolds. In written text, mode includes text coherence, cohesion, and structure, as well as knowledge of the writing system, spelling, and conventions. Each presents a challenge to L2 writers.

Coherence refers to the text making sense, and there is cohesion when the text hangs together. Bae (2001) found that in the writing of early elementary children there was high correlation between coherence, content, and grammar. In turn, all of them correlated with text length and fluency. Coherence and content appeared to be related to maturity since 2nd graders demonstrated greater ability than 1st graders. In addition, coherence is supported by appropriate text structure defined by the genre and medium. Different genres require different organizational structures, as will be shown later. Organization of text also depends on the medium.

"At the more micro-level, the flow of information in the text is controlled by the choice of theme" (Derewianka, 1998, p. 104). The theme in SFL is the first constituent of the clause and the point of departure of the message. It places the clause within the context of the whole text (Thompson, 2004). What follows the theme is the rheme, or information about the theme. Young writers also need to include this theme to orient the reader. Hernández (2001) found that some students start by introducing the theme, and others start directly with the specific information. She found this to be a different skill from grammar and spelling. One of the students in her study had been identified as a low writer because of issues of grammar and spelling, yet her organizational skills were more developed than several of the other students, even those deemed to be better writers.

Cohesive ties impact text coherence. There are five types of cohesive links: reference, conjunctions, ellipsis, substitution, and lexical ties (Bae, 2001). The conjunction *and* and temporal connectives are prevalent in narratives (Maguire & Graves, 2001). In a study of 1st and 2nd graders, Bae (2001) found that referential and lexical links were the cohesive devises most used by children and accounted for almost two-thirds of the variance in coherence. Bae infers that acquisition of reference markers and of vocabulary are critical for length and quality of writing.

The other types of cohesive links, such as ellipsis, substitution, and conjunctions had no real impact on coherence. Ellipsis and substitution were barely used, while conjunctions (especially *and*) were used more often, but did not contribute to the overall quality of the writing. Overuse of *and* also changed with maturity, as 2nd graders used a greater variety of conjunctions. L2 writers tend to overuse such rhetorical connectors (Hinkel, 2002). Reynolds (2002) distinguished between links more typical of oral language (*and, then, when*), and those more common in written language (*because, so, therefore, thus*). He found that native speakers of English used more of the former when writing familiar topics and more of the latter when writing on school-related topics. L2 writers used more connectors overall regardless of topic, and there was not much difference in the amount between the two types in both kinds of topics.

Children had other difficulties with cohesive ties such as unclear references, problems with determiners, unnatural use of conjunctions, and others. For L2 learners, the greatest source of cohesive errors were the determiners either because *the* and *a* were misused or omitted (Bae, 2001).

To create text, L2 writers need to know the writing, spelling, and convention system of English. These features can be very different in the languages of bilingual learners. Barrett-Pugh and Rohl (2001) studied Cambodian children learning to write in Khmer and English. These children had to learn to write in two different scripts with different conventions. Initially there were difficulties in both languages because of the nature of the languages themselves, or because of differences between the languages. Eventually, some of the children became quite good at writing in both scripts, using the appropriate conventions. When scripts are similar writers may use the system of their L1 to spell English. First grade Spanish speakers used their sound system to spell in English (*Frayday* for *Friday*, *clous* for *clothes*, and *si* for *see*) (Gort, 2006, p. 339). Children also spelled *tipp* for *type* because in Spanish the name of the vowel is also the sound (Hernández, 2001). Children who use the name of the letter as a strategy, rather than place of articulation and voice–voiceless distinction are worse spellers. The voice–voiceless distinction is hard for native speakers of Spanish and needs to be taught (Ferroli & Shanahan, 1993). The fact that English is a deep orthography language with no one-to-one correspondence between sound and symbol causes spelling problems, such as not using double consonants, *droped* for *dropped* (Hernández, 2001), or knowing the vowel combination for *meat, feet,* and *priest,* since all sound the same. Spelling errors are the most prevalent errors in the writing of young children. When spelling is not automatic then children resort to invented spelling in order to pay attention to the message itself (Simpson, 2004). Although spelling and conventions improve over time (Davis et al., 1999; Maguire & Graves, 2001) as students' writing increased in length and complexity so did the spelling errors (Carlisle, 1989). Orthographic processing, or the understanding of writing conventions of the language, and correct and incorrect spelling of words remained a problem for both good and poor adolescent trilingual writers in all their languages (Abu-Rabia & Siegel, 2003).

Medium

Writers use different media for their texts, such as letters, poems, storybooks, informational books, memos, and others, each of which have their own norms to organize text. Some features of the medium can be culture specific. For example, American letters go straight to the point, while in other cultures the writer tries to first establish relations with the addressee.

Different media offer different opportunities for expression to L2 writers. Journals that lend themselves to writing personal recounts, "serve not only to incorporate the student's native language and sociocultural experiences but also to nurture the acquisition of communicative competencies in English" (Garcáa & Colón, 1995, p. 40). They can also facilitate the students' ability to develop their own voice and identity (Maguire & Graves, 2001). However, using only journals tends to limit the variety of genres in which students write, since journals contain mostly personal or fictional narratives. Individual writers have shown preference for different media. A young Dakota girl liked writing cards while the boys disliked the task (Franklin & Thompson, 1994). McPhail (2009) noticed that most 1st grade boys preferred comic book writing while girls enjoyed writing in their personal journals. He warns against stereotyping across gender lines.

Sometimes teaching to write in a particular medium can help children read in that medium. When teaching report writing, two 3rd grade teachers taught their bilingual learners how to include information in quotes, boxes, and diagrams imitating the structure of informational texts used in the classroom. These teachers commented that in the past when reading these types of texts, their students would skip the information contained in such features and only read the straight text. Thus, exposure to writing in a variety of media will help students develop a variety of aspects of writing that they need to succeed in American schools.

Genre

"Comparable texts which achieve the same general social purpose, and which therefore draw on the same relatively stable structural pattern, are said to belong to the same *genre*" (Butt et al., 2000, p. 214). Genre or purpose, which Walters (2005) calls intentional component, is the bridge between social and psycholinguistic information the language user taps into to create utterances or written script (Walters, 2005). Each culture develops patterns of text structures called genres in SFL theory. Genres refer solely to purpose, such as to tell stories, give instructions, organize information, or persuade. It does not include such things as letters, poetry, or comic books, which are considered media. A letter may be written in any of the genres, and as such it will follow the text structure of the chosen genre, as well as the features of a letter. Bilingual learners attending school in the United States are required to write in a variety of genres. For example, the prompts found in the Massachusetts Comprehensive Assessment System (MCAS) for grades 3, 4, and 5 demand personal and procedural recounts, procedure, reports, explanations, exposition (persuasive), and historical accounts. Although students are not required to write fictional narratives and historical recounts, these genres are found in the texts students must read, in order to respond to writing prompts. L2 learners need to learn the structural organization of text and language features expected in these different genres. Recognizing the demands of a genre correlated with overall quality and length of pieces in 4th and 6th graders (Carlisle, 1989).

Various forms of recounts and fictional narratives start with an orientation identifying the main participants, location, and time of the narrative. This is followed by a series of events, and often ends with some type of conclusion. Reports start with a general statement, followed by subtopics, and conclude with a statement usually connected to the initial statement. Persuasive pieces usually start with a thesis or claim, followed by reasons or arguments, each supported by evidence, and end with a conclusion. (For a good description of the organizational structure of various genres see Butt et al., 2000.) These organizational structures present challenges to children developing writing. Success in using such aspects of narrative text structure as a good orientation at the beginning and a successful conclusion was important for making the text comprehensible to the reader, and improved with grade level. However, writing an explicit ending was less successful than writing an introduction with all the typical elements of narratives (Bae, 2001). Young writers developing reports had more difficulty with both the introduction and conclusion. Fourth graders writing persuasive pieces struggled with stating convincing evidence (Bermúdez & Prater, 1994). By 6th grade, students showed the ability to make appropriate changes in the content and language of persuasive pieces when directed to different audiences (Martínez et al., 2008). Instruction supports this development. A 5th grade Spanish-speaking student, wrote, "Come live in Jamestown because *people are friendly*" using an opinion instead of a proven fact as her evidence. Extensive analysis of persuasive pieces including TV and newspaper advertisements helped the students realize what constitutes evidence. Later this student revised her piece to read, "Also, we have such great friends. Most important, the young girl named Pocahontas. She is a girl that helps us hunt animals and give us food when we are working very hard. We are also friends with other natives."

Children prefer writing in different genres. A Dakota 1st grade girl preferred personal and fictional narratives where the main participants were the children in her class. Other students in that class showed little interest in personal narratives and preferred fantasies, war stories, and adventure stories (Franklin & Thompson, 1994). This preference often divides along gender lines with boys mostly choosing fictional narratives and girls choosing personal recounts or narratives. Differences across gender lines were also apparent in the quality of persuasive writing samples of Hispanic 4th graders. Essays written by female writers "show a greater degree of elaboration and a clearer attempt to express the writer's point of view than those written by male Hispanic students, regardless of proficiency level" (Bermúdez & Prater, 1994, p. 53).

Although McPhail's (2009) research confirmed trends along gender lines, he also found individual differences that went against the gender preferred choices. Writing in the preferred genre correlated with better writing. Thus exposure to different genres is essential to give all children a chance to excel.

Genres have different language demands. (For specific details see Butt et al., 2000 and Derewianka, 1990.) For example, the students in 3rd–5th grade were required to write lab reports. Each component of the report is a different genre demanding a different verb tense. These reports start with a prediction (future), followed by a procedure (imperative), then comes the procedural recount (past), and finally a report (present), an explanation (present), or an argument (present). For example, Carlos, a 3rd grader, used the appropriate tenses. He responded to the question, "Which container will show the most evaporation in one week?" *I think the flat lid is going to evaporate first …* After observing the experiment, Carlos wrote his procedural recount, *The flat lid Evaporated because it got more surface Area.*

Participants tend to differ with genre. Personal recounts are written in the first person. In procedures usually no person is named, and most other genres are written in the third person, although occasionally fictional narratives are also written in the first person. Students have difficulty writing in the third person. For example, at the beginning of the year, Natacha wrote an uncoached piece about her grandmother. Her first three sentences were in the third person, but quickly transitioned to the first person. "Abuelita is a kind and helpful person …. She promised me that she will bring me to Puerto Rico …. I was sad when I heard that abuelita passed away." Her 5th grade teacher in a unit on historical recounts used several lessons to instruct about third person. Natacha started her piece about Christopher Columbus, "Have you heard of an explorer named Christopher Columbus? He was born in the year 1451. He was born in Genoa."[4] and went on to write the rest of the piece in third person.

Different genres may require different types of adjectives to describe the nouns. In persuasive pieces opinion adjectives are found in the thesis statement, while factual adjectives are found in the evidence. Carmen, a 5th grader, wrote in an advertisement to accompany her scientific invention "People should buy the everlasting clone machine for different good (opinion) reasons. If you live alone in your house and your really sick, the everlasting clone mashine will bring you a small (factual) touch screen."

Through exposure by reading texts in the various genres and abundant writing, L2 learners develop their ability to write in these various genres, acquiring different aspects gradually.

Conclusion

This chapter illustrates what bilingual learners need to master to successfully write in their second language in the context of school. The SFL framework was used because it helps to account explicitly for the extralinguistic and linguistic demands of the task. SFL is also a theory that supports bilingual learners because it places text relative to the culture and situation, giving a legitimate place in the linguistic landscape to students' languages and language varieties. At the same time, SFL gives teachers tools to unpack English in order to enhance their instruction by explicitly telling students how the language functions. Unfortunately, the limited teacher preparation on language (Fillmore & Snow, 2002) makes it very hard for teachers to tease out language in children's writing to understand their competence and needs. Pacing the introduction of SFL theory helps teachers absorb knowledge about language in order to impact their writing instruction (Gebhard, Demers, & Castillo-Rosenthal, 2008).

The components of choice and affect from the Walters' model (2005) add two important forces in the reality of bilingual language practice. Bilinguals have access to linguistic and sociocultural information that comes from their languages and varied cultural experiences. These constantly inform language use, even in a predominantly monolingual environment often encountered in schools. Moreover, research on L2 development should always be embedded in the context of bilingualism.

Supporting bilingual learners to develop writing in their second language produces tension among educators. Efforts to teach the code students need to succeed in school may give the perception that this knowledge will silence students' own ways of using language. Taking a bilingual integrative perspective (Taylor, 1987) makes both possible. Integrated bilinguals seek to function in their new culture without abandoning their heritage culture. Educators are well served by the tools provided by SFL and bilingualism "to make the linguistic expectations of schooling explicit to students" (Schleppegrell, 2004, p. 3) while considering that these students bring a wealth of cultural and linguistic knowledge to learning in the second language.

Notes

1. Bilingual learners know more than one language to different degrees. Some may be just in the process of acquiring a second language. The term bilingual rather than second language learner or English language learner is used to denote the full range of language abilities of these students.
2. Much of the content of this chapter is based on existing research on elementary L2 writing. In addition, I have used knowledge gained through my research using SFL theory to encourage teachers to teach writing in mainstream classrooms with large percentages of bilingual learners of a variety of language groups. I have disseminated this work through conferences and publications are forthcoming.
3. The term heritage language is used because with young children of culturally and linguistic diverse family, this is not always their first language, or their only first language.
4. I have strongly discouraged teachers to tell children to start texts with a question, a habit that has been disseminated in Writers' Workshop. Upon analysis of a number of published historical recounts, I showed teachers that none starts with a question.

References

Abu-Rabia, S., & Siegel, L.S. (2003). Reading skills in three orthographies: The case of trilingual Arabic–Hebrew–English-speaking Arab children. *Reading and Writing: An Interdisciplinary Journal, 16,* 611–634.

Araujo, L. (2002). The literacy development of kindergarten English language learners. *Journal of Research in Childhood Education, 16,* 232–247.

Bae, J. (2001). Cohesion and coherence in children's written English: Immersion and English-only classes. *Issues in Applied Linguistics,* 12(1), 51–88.

Baker, C. (2006). *Foundations of bilingual education and bilingualism* (4th ed.). Clevedon: Multilingual Matters.

Barratt-Pugh, C., & Rohl, M. (2001). Learning in two languages: A bilingual program in Western Australia. *The Reading Teacher,* 54(7), 664–676.

Bermúdez, A.B., & Prater, D. L. (1994). Examining the effects of gender and second language proficiency on Hispanic writers' persuasive discourse. *Bilingual Research Journal,* 18(3 & 4), 47–62.

Bernhardt, E. B. (1991). A psycholinguistic perspective on second language literacy. *AILA Review, 8,* 31–44.

Bou-Zeneiddine, A. (1994). The effect of pre-writing discussion language, Arabic/English on six adult students' writing in English. Unpublished doctoral dissertation, Boston University.

Brisk, M. E. (2006). *Bilingual education: From compensatory to quality schooling* (2nd ed.). Mahwah, NJ: Lawrence Erlbaum Associates.

Brisk, M. E., Burgos, A., & Hamerla, S. (2004). *Situational context of education: A window into the world of bilingual learners.* Mahwah, NJ: Lawrence Erlbaum Associates.

Brisk, M. E., & Harrington, M. M. (2007). *Literacy and bilingualism: A handbook for all teachers. Second Edition.* Mahwah, NJ: Lawrence Erlbaum Associates.

Brisk, M. E., & Zisselsberger, M. (forthcoming). "We've let them in on the secret": Using SFL theory to improve the teaching of writing to bilingual learners. In T. Lucas (Ed.), *Envisioning possibilities: Preparing all teachers to teach English language learners,* New York: Routledge/Lawrence Erlbaum.

Buckwalter, J. K., & Lo, Y. G. (2002). Emergent biliteracy in Chinese and English. *Journal of Second Language Writing, 11,* 269–293.

Butt, D., Fahey, R., Feez, S., Spinks, S., & Yallop, C. (2000). *Using functional grammar: An explorer's guide*. Sydney: National Centre for English Language Teaching and Research, Macquarie University.

Caldas, S., & Caron-Caldas, S. (2002). A sociolinguistic analysis of the language preferences of adolescent bilinguals: Sifting allegiances and developing identities. *Applied Linguistics, 23,* 490–514.

Carlisle, J. F., & Beeman, M. M. (2000). The effects of language instruction on the reading and writing of first-grade Hispanic children. *Scientific Studies of Reading, 4,* 331–353.

Carlisle, R. (1989). The writing of angle and Hispanic elementary school students in bilingual, submersion, and regular programs. *Studies in Second Language Acquisition, 11,* 257–280.

Connor, U. (2002). New directions in contrastive rhetoric. *TESOL Quarterly, 36,* 493–510.

Cummins, J. (1991). Interdependence of first- and second-language proficiency in bilingual children. In E. Bialystok (Ed.), *Language processing in bilingual children* (pp. 70–89). New York: Cambridge University Press.

Cummins, J. (2005). A proposal for action: Strategies for recognizing heritage language competence as a learning resource with the mainstream classroom. *The Modern Language Journal, 89,* 585–592.

Dagenais, D., & Day, E. (1998). Classroom language experiences of trilingual children in French immersion. *Canadian Modern Language Review, 54*(3), 376–393.

Davis, L. H., Carlisle, J. F., & Beeman, M. M. (1999). Hispanic children's writing in English and Spanish when English is the language of instruction. *National Reading Conference Yearbook, 48,* 238–248.

Derewianka, B. (1990). *Exploring how texts work*. Rozelle, Australia: Primary English Teaching Association.

Derewianka, B. (1998). *A grammar companion: For primary teachers*. Newtown, Australia: Primary English Teaching Association.

Dien, T. T. (2004). Language and literacy in Vietnamese American communities. In B. Pérez (Ed.), *Sociocultral context of language and literacy* (pp. 137–177) (2nd ed.). Mahwah, NJ: Lawrence Erlbaum.

Edelsky, C. (1982). Writing in a bilingual program: The relation of L1 and L2 texts. *TESOL Quarterly, 16*(2), 211–228.

Edelsky, C. (1986). *Writing in a bilingual program: Habia una vez*. Norwood, NJ: Ablex.

Escamilla, K. (2006). Semilingualism applied to the literacy behaviors of Spanish-speaking emerging bilinguals: bi-illiteracy or emerging biliteracy? *Teachers College Record, 108,* 2329–2353.

Fang, Z. (1999). Expanding the vista of emergent writing research: Implications for early childhood educators. *Early Childhood Education Journal, 26,* 179–182.

Ferroli, L., & Shanahan, T. (1993). Voicing in Spanish to English knowledge transfer. *Yearbook of the National Reading Conference, 42,* 413–418.

Fillmore, L. W., & Snow, C. E. (2002). What teachers need to know about language. In C. T. Adger, C. E. Snow, and D. Christian (Eds.), *What teachers need to know about language* (pp. 7–54). McHenry, IL: Delta Systems.

Fitzgerald, J. (2006). Multilingual writing in preschool through 12th grade: The last 15 years. In C. A. MacArthur, S. Graham, and J. Fitzgerald (Eds.), *Handbook of writing research* (pp. 337–354). New York: The Guilford Press.

Franklin, E. & Thompson, J. (1994). Describing students' collected works: Understanding American Indian children. *TESOL Quarterly, 28,* 489–506.

García, E., & Colón, M. (1995). Interactive journals in bilingual classrooms: An analysis of language "transition." *Discourse Processes, 19,* 39–56.

Garrett, P., Griffiths, Y., James, C., & Scholfield, P. (1994). Use of mother-tongue in second language classrooms: An experimental investigation of the effects on the attitudes and writing performance of bilingual UK school children. *Multilingual and Multicultural Development, 15,* 371–383.

Gebhard, M., Demers, J., & Castillo-Rosenthal, Z. (2008). Teachers as critical text analysts: L2 literacies and teachers' work in the context of high-stakes school reform. *Journal of Second Language Writing, 17,* 274–291.

Gebhard, M., Harman, R., & Seger, W. (2007). Reclaiming recess: Learning the language of persuasion. *Language Arts, 84,* 419–430.

Genessee, F., Paradis, J., & Crago, M. B. (2004). *Dual language development and disorders: A handbook on bilingualism & second language learning*. Baltimore: Paul Brookes.

Gort, M. (2006). Strategic codeswitching, interliteracy, and other phenomena of emergent bilingual writing: Lessons from first grade dual language classrooms. *Journal of Early Childhood Literacy, 6,* 323–354.

Graves, A. W., Valles, E. C., & Rueda, R. (2000). Variations in interactive writing instruction: A study in four bilingual special education settings. *Learning Disabilities Research & Practice, 15*(1), 1–9.

Graves, D. H. (1983). *Writing: Teachers and children at work*. Portsmouth, NH: Heinemann.

Gutierrez, K. D. (1994). How talk, context, and script shape contexts for learning: A cross-case comparison of journal writing. *Linguistics and Education, 5,* 335–365.

Halliday, M. A. K. (1994). *An introduction to functional grammar* (2nd ed.). London: Edward Arnold.

Hernández, A. C. (2001). The expected and unexpected literacy outcomes of bilingual students. *Bilingual Research Journal, 25*(3), 251–276.

Hinds, J. (1987). Reader versus writer responsibility: A new typology. In U. Connor & R. B. Kaplan (Eds.), *Writing across languages: Analysis of L2 text* (pp. 141–152). Reading, MA: Addison-Wesley.

Hinkel, E. (2002). *Second language writers' text.* Mahwah, NJ: Lawrence Erlbaum Associates.

Homza, A. (1995). Developing biliteracy in a bilingual first-grade writing workshop. *Dissertation Abstracts International*, 53(12), 2148. (UMI No. 95–33133).

Hudelson, S. (1984). "Kan yu ret an rayt en ingles": Children become literate in English as a second language. *TESOL Quarterly*, 18, 221–238.

Huss, R. L. (1995). Young children becoming literate in English as a second language. *TESOL Quarterly*, 29, 767–774.

Hyland, K. (2007). Genre pedagogy: Language, literacy and L2 writing instruction. *Journal of Second Language Writing*, 16, 148–164.

Laman, T. T. & Van Sluys, K. (2008). Being and becoming: Multilingual writers' practices. *Language Arts*, 85, 265–274.

Lanauze, M., & Snow, C. (1989). The relation between first- and second-language writing skills: Evidence from Puerto Rican elementary school children in bilingual programs. *Linguistics an Education*, 1, 323–339.

Lindholm-Leary, (2001). *Dual language education.* Clevedon: Multilingual Matters.

Lisle, B. and Mano, S. (1997). Embracing a multicultural rhetoric. In C. Severino, J. C. Guerra, & J. E. Butler (Eds.), *Writing in multicultural settings* (pp. 12–26). New York: The Modern Language Association of America.

Lo, J., & Hyland, F. (2007). Enhancing students' engagement and motivation in writing: The case of primary students in Hong Kong. *Journal of Second Language Writing*, 16, 219–237.

McCabe, A., & Bliss, L. S. (2003). *Patterns of narrative discourse: A multicultural, life span approach.* Boston: Allyn and Bacon.

McCarthey, S. J., Guo, Y. H., & Cummins, S. (2005). Understanding changes in elementary Mandarin students' L1 and L2 writing. *Journal of Second Language Writing*, 14, 71–104.Mackey, W. (1968). The description of bilingualism. In J. A. Fishman (Ed.), *Readings in the sociology of language* (pp. 554–584). The Hague: Mouton.

McPhail, G. (2009). The bad boy and the writing curriculum. In M. Cochran-Smith, & S. Lytle (Eds.), *Inquiry as stance. Practitioner research for the next generation* (pp. 193–212). New York: Teachers College Press.

Maguire, M., & Graves, B. (2001). Speaking personalities in primary school childrens L2 writing. *TESOL Quarterly*, 35(4), 561–593.

Martínez, R. A., Orellana, M. F., Pacheco, M., & Carbone. P. (2008). Found in translation: Connecting translating experiences to academic writing. *Language Arts*, 85, 421–441.

Matalene, C. (1985). Contrastive rhetoric: An American writing teacher in China. *College English*, 47, 789–808.

Matsuda, P. K. (1997). Contrastive rhetoric in context: A dynamic model of L2 writing. *Journal of Second Language Writing*, 6(1), 45–60.

Menyuk, P., & Brisk, M.E. (2005). *Language development and education: Children with varying language experience.* Basingstoke: Palgrave Macmillan.

Moll, L. (1992) Literacy research in community and classrooms: A sociocultural approach. In R. Beach, J. Green, M. Kamil, & T. Shanahan (Eds.), *Multidisciplinary perspectives on literacy research* (pp. 211–244). Urbana, IL: National Council of Teachers of English.

Newkirk, T. (2000). Misreading masculinity: Speculations on the great gender gap in writing. *Language Arts*, 77, 294–300.

Páez, M., & Rinaldi, C. (2006). Predicting English word reading skills for Spanish-speaking students in first grade. *Topics in Language Disorders*, 26, 338–350.

Perez, B. (2004). *Sociocultural context of language and literacy* (2nd ed.). Mahwah, NJ: Lawrence Erlbaum.

Prater, D., & Bermúdez, A. (1993). Using peer response groups with limited English proficient writers. *Bilingual Research Journal*, 17, 99–116.

Proctor, C. P., August, D., Carlo, M., & Snow, C. (2006). The intriguing role of Spanish language vocabulary knowledge in predicting English reading comprehension. *Journal of Educational Psychology*, 98(1), 150–169.

Reynolds, D. W. (2002). Learning to make things happen in different ways: Causality in the writing of middle-grade English language learners. *Journal of Second Language Writing*, 11, 311–328.

Samway, K. D. (2006). *When English language learners write: Connecting research to practice, K-8.* Portsmouth, NH: Heinemann.

Schleppegrell, M. J. (2004). *The language of schooling: A functional linguistics perspective.* Mahwah, NJ: Lawrence Erlbaum.

Schleppegrell, M. J. (2006). The challenges of academic language in school subjects. In I. Lindberg, & K. Sandwall (Eds.), *Språket och kunskapen: att lära på sitt andraspråk i skola och högskola* (pp. 47–69). Göteborg, Sweden: Göteborgs universitet institutet för svenska som andraspråk.

Schleppegrell, M. J., & Go, A. (2007). Analyzing the writing of English learners: A functional approach. *Language Arts*, 84(6), 529–538.

Scieszka, Jon (1989). *The true story of the three little pigs.* New York: Penguin Group.

Simpson, J. M. (2004). A look at early childhood writing in English and Spanish in a bilingual school in Ecuador. *Bilingual Education and Bilingualism*, 7(5), 432–448.

Smith, J. (2006). Immigrant Latino parents' perspective of parent engagement. Unpublished Doctoral dissertation, Boston College. UMI No. 3238841.

Swain, M. (2005). The output hypothesis; Theory and research. In E. Hinkel (Ed.), *Handbook of research in second language teaching and learning* (pp. 471–483). Mahwah, NJ: Lawrence Erlbaum Associates.

Taylor, Donald M. (1987). Social psychological barriers to effective childhood bilingualism. In P. Hornel, M. Palij, & D. Aaronson (Eds.), *Childhood bilingualism: Aspects of linguistic, cognitive and social development* (pp. 183–195). Hillsdale, NJ: Lawrence Erlbaum Associates.

Thompson, G. (2004). *Introducing functional grammar. Second edition.* London: Arnold.

Urzua, C. (1987). "You stopped too soon": Second language children composing and revising. *TESOL Quarterly, 21*(2), 279–297.

Walters, J. (2005). *Bilingualism: The sociopragmatic-psycholinguistic interface.* Mahwah, NJ: Lawrence Erlbaum Associates.

4
Social Practice and Register
Language as a Means of Learning

Bernard A. Mohan

Education is the socialisation of learners into the social practices of the community. Language is the major means of this socialisation. For learners learning through the medium of their second language (L2), such language socialisation is often problematic, particularly with respect to the development of academic discourse and academic achievement. This chapter will show how a systemic functional linguistics approach based on register illuminates how language functions as a means of learning and of assessment in the social practices of schooling of L2 learners, and how register provides tools to trace learning as a continuous dialectic between system and process, theory and practice. It will use four case studies to illustrate these themes in depth with discourse data.

Linguistic research on language and learning has done little to study social practice as a large unit of linguistic meaning. In the last century, L2 research on a structuralist model of language typically analysed items of language below the sentence. More recently, more L2 research has worked with models of language that recognise the text as a unit of meaning and analysis. However, there is a still a lack of linguistic research on social practice.

Reviewing issues of advanced literacy development of L2 learners, Schleppegrell and Colombi (2002, pp. 6–12) identify two major theoretical orientations towards literacy that have guided recent research. *Literacy as a social activity* highlights the socialisation of the individual into social practices through participation in communities of practice (Lave & Wenger, 1991) "including the subject-matter and disciplinary communities into which students begin to be socialised at the secondary and post-secondary levels". Strongly influenced by Vygotsky, this orientation emphasises "the interactional construction of meaning in particular ... social contexts where learning (and literacy development) emerge within specific cultural practices". This orientation holds that human thinking should be studied as socioculturally situated in social practices and that social practices can be explored through the general theme of the theory and practice of knowing and doing (see Martin, Nelson & Tobach, 1995, p. 2). For discussion of the sociocultural "turn" in L2 learning research, see Zuengler and Miller (2006). For a review of social practice in social theory see Reckwitz (2002).

According to Schleppegrell and Colombi (2002, pp. 6–12), *literacy as linguistic activity* "highlights the way that language as a semiotic tool interacts with social contexts in making meaning", and "the theory of language that is currently informing much of the work on literacy as linguistic activity is M. A. K. Halliday's systemic functional linguistic (SFL) theory. SFL uses the notion of linguistic 'register' to illuminate the relationship between language and context". This orientation "focuses on

57

the active role that grammatical and lexical choices play in realising advanced literacy contexts". To study social practices as units of linguistic meaning one needs to link these two orientations. This chapter will do so by relating social practice and register. For a very stimulating critical discourse analysis of social practice using register, see Van Leeuwen (2008).

Linguistic research on social practices is urgently needed. A recent review of research on teaching immigrant English language learners (ELLs) in the content areas in the US (Janzen, 2008) finds that these students have a high risk of academic failure, and notes that content areas require academic literacy rather than simply a basic knowledge of the language. This points to an urgent need to support and assess the learning of language and meaning in academic content tasks and practices. Janzen states that "studies based on SFL represent the most compelling perspective on content area instruction, doubtless because they start from an extensively developed stance on the nature of language in general" (p. 1015).

There is a very large potential payoff in developing the formative classroom assessment (assessment for learning) of language and meaning in academic content practices. A synthesis of more than 4,000 research studies shows that formative assessment for learning practices can *double* the rate of student learning (William, 2007/2008). Very few of these studies have addressed the role of language in formative assessment, but Leung and Mohan (2004), in a study of ELLs in content classrooms, have shown how formative assessment is a discourse process where meaningful language is both the object of assessment and the means of assessment.

How does SFL offer a "compelling perspective" on the learning of language and meaning in academic content practices? To address the sociocultural "turn", models of language and learning are needed that see language as meaning making in social context. Structuralist views of language that exclude meaning and reduce language to rules of language form foreclose the possibility of researching how the learner makes meaning. Such views treat learning subject matter in the content classroom as something independent of language and make it impossible to research language as a means of learning.

By contrast, SFL

> is oriented to the description of language as *a resource for meaning* rather than as a system of rules. It is oriented, in other words, to speakers' meaning potential (what they can mean) … SFL is concerned with *texts*, rather than sentences, as the basic unit through which meaning is negotiated. It treats grammar, in other words, as the realisation of discourse.
>
> (Halliday & Martin, 1993, p. 22)

Furthermore, SFL deals with relations between text and context. With regard to language assessment, for example, all of this implies that it is not enough simply to assess how a learner makes rule-based errors. Rather, one must assess how the learner makes meaning with language resources in discourse in context.

SFL provides a theory of language as a means of learning (see Painter, 1999, Ch. 2). "The distinctive characteristic of human learning is that it is a process of making meaning, a semiotic process, and the prototypical form of human semiotic is language" (Halliday, 1993, p. 93). Knowledge, and culture more generally, is seen as meaning, a resource for understanding and acting on the world. In addition, since "language is not only the primary means by which a person learns but also the primary evidence we have for judging what that person has learnt" (Halliday, 1998, p. 1), SFL points towards a theory of assessment as a linguistic process. Halliday's work describes how the young child learns the language system and culture system simultaneously through processes of conversation in the family, in a language socialisation process. With both the language system and the culture system there is a dialectic of learning between system and process, knowing and doing, theory and practice. When the child enters the school, education uses a more explicit dialectic by reflection on language, learning and meaning/content. For a detailed description of this complex dialectic of learning, see Painter (1999, Ch. 7).

Table 4.1 compares how scholars in different social sciences characterise the theory/practice dimension of a social practice (i.e. what participants in a community of practice know and what participants do). The ethnographer Spradley (1980) uses the terms "cultural knowledge" and "cultural behaviour", and relates them to qualitative research methods. Cultural knowledge is typically elicited by interview; information on cultural behaviour is typically gathered by participation or observation. To analyse social practices in classrooms, for instance, one could interview the participants and observe what happens in classrooms. The sociologist Goffman (1974) uses the terms "frame" and "action strip" and emphasises how a social practice has a coherent frame of meaning. Halliday, as a linguist who studies language in context, divides context into the wider "context of culture" of cultural knowledge and the "context of situation", the more immediate situation of actual language use. Since context of culture refers to the culture as a whole, the theory of a social practice is a subsystem of the context of culture, a domain of cultural knowledge.

For Halliday (1999, p. 8) a domain of cultural knowledge is a semiotic system, and the "register" of that domain is the meaning system that realises or encodes the domain in language. The register is a "meaning potential" that enables members of a community of practice to interpret and produce the texts of the social practice. Thus the register of a social practice is the linguistic means by which the members interact and jointly construct their shared experience. A register, then, is a system of meanings:

> We can refer to a "mathematics register", in the sense of the meanings that belong to the language of mathematics … and that language must express if it is used for mathematical purposes … we should not think of a mathematical register as consisting solely of terminology, or of the development of a register as simply a process of adding new words.
>
> (Halliday, 1978, p. 195)

Register is instantiated in a text in a context of situation. A text is an instance of a register. Context of situation is described through three variables that influence the use of language: "field" is concerned with the social activity being pursued and the topic or content being talked about (first order field and second order field); "tenor" is the relationships between the people involved; and "mode" is the medium and role of language in the situation. These three variables are related to three areas of meaning: ideational, which represents experience; interpersonal, which creates interaction between people; and textual, which constructs connected and coherent discourse.

I will now review four cases of social practices in education and describe them from a register perspective.

Magnetism: Social Practice as Reflection, Action and a Framework of Meanings

This section will use data of young L2 learners learning about magnetism, considered as a social practice. I will first illustrate how a social practice draws upon the discourse of action and the dis-

Table 4.1 Social Practice: Ethnography, Sociology, and Functional Linguistics

SOCIAL PRACTICE	Ethnography	Sociology	Linguistics
	Spradley (1980)	Goffman (1974)	Halliday (1999)
THEORY	Cultural Knowledge	Frame	Context of Culture
PRACTICE	Cultural Behaviour	Action Strip	Context of Situation

course of reflection in a theory–practice relation. Then I will illustrate social practice as a framework of ideational meanings.

There is a basic distinction between the discourse of doing a social practice (action discourse), whose primary function is to operate the social practice, and the discourse of talking about the social practice (reflection discourse), whose primary function is to construct and maintain knowledge of the social practice. Researching the difference between action discourse and reflection discourse is not the same as researching the theory–practice relation between them. Mohan (1969) showed how the reflection discourse of teaching about a card game was linguistically very different from the action discourse of playing a card game, by contrasting the two kinds of text. It was not the same thing, and not the same type of register study, to then use these texts to show how teaching about the card game helped a learner to play the game and interpret what was said and done in it.

The difference contrast and the theory–practice relation between action discourse and reflection discourse can be illustrated by magnetism data from Gibbons (2002, p. 40), as shown below.

(A1) (spoken by three 10-year-old students, with accompanying action) This ... no, it doesn't go ... try that.

(A2) (spoken by one student about the action, after the event) We tried a pin ... some iron filings ... the magnet didn't attract the pin.

(A3) (written by the same student) We discovered that *a magnet attracts some kinds of metal.* It attracted the iron filings, but not the pin.

(A4) (taken from a child's encyclopaedia). A magnet ... is able to pick up, or attract, a piece of steel or iron because its magnetic field flows into the steel or iron, turning it into a temporary magnet. Magnetic attraction occurs only between ferrous materials.

Considered from a difference perspective, (A1–4) are contrasting kinds of text. A1 is "action discourse": it is the discourse of doing an experiment. A2 is "specific reflection discourse" that talks about past events. A3 is "reflection discourse" that partly generalises about past events. A4 is "general reflection discourse" that talks about generalised knowledge.

Considered from a theory-practice perspective, (A1–3) are "locally" related texts in a series, showing a learner doing an experiment, making sense of an experiment and working towards a scientific explanation of it. The learner is moving from doing to knowing, practice to theory. The more elaborate explanation of A4 suggests the path of future development.

Table 4.2 is a basic model of action discourse and reflection discourse in a social practice. This model suggests how register can be extended to relate action texts and reflection texts to the context of the social practice as a whole. This positions us to trace the movement between action and reflection, practice and theory in a social practice, as when the learner in (A1–3) moves from practice towards theory.

Table 4.2 A Basic Model of Social Practice and Discourse

SOCIAL PRACTICE	DISCOURSE	Examples
Magnetism		
THEORY	General Reflection	Explanation of Experiment (A3 and A4)
	Specific Reflection	Recount of Experiment (A2)
PRACTICE	Action	Experimental Task (A1)

I will now use a study of young L2 learners learning a unit on magnetism to illustrate social practice as a framework of ideational meanings. Ideational meaning constructs our knowledge of the world from our experience. It provides language resources to make sense of three main realms of experience: the identification and classification of things in terms of qualities or processes; the representation of events and activity sequences; and human consciousness, including mental and verbal processes. These three main realms correspond to three main types of transitivity: processes of being and having, processes of doing and happening, and processes of sensing and saying, and are also reflected in lexical relations, conjunctive relations and in the structure of nominal and verbal groups (see Painter 1999, p. 74). In my analysis I also make use of specific and generic reference (see Painter 1999, p. 100). In the data below, processes of being are in bold, processes of doing are in italics, and processes of sensing (including saying) are underlined. I have done a very basic analysis to show the great importance of pursuing ideational analysis in depth as Painter (1999) has done.

Mohan (1986, 2007) views a social practice as having a coherent "frame of meaning", a gestalt that includes all three realms of ideational meaning in a theory–practice dynamic. He summarises this claim in a "knowledge framework" heuristic that includes "knowledge structures" of ideational meaning. Of course, the process of a social practice also includes interpersonal meaning and textual meaning, but a focus on ideational meaning allows one to concentrate on a single strand of meaning.

Mohan and Slater (2005) describe a Western Canadian grade 1 and grade 2 (combined) ESL (English as a second language) science class studying a unit on magnetism. In the teaching and learning phase of the unit, the children learned a simple "theory" of magnetism in experiments with bar magnets, whose poles were marked. Then, in the final phase of the unit, the teacher aimed to assess the children's understanding of magnetism by having them extend their "frame of meaning" (meaning potential) to the new case of ring magnets, whose poles were not marked and which looked very different.

The core of the "theory" of magnetism that the children were learning was the "rule of magnetism": north and south poles attract, south and north attract, north and north repel, south and south repel. Science theory discourse includes two types of patterns (Halliday, 1998): taxonomies of technical terms (e.g. a magnet has two poles, north and south) and sequences of reasoning (e.g. causal explanations such as north attracts south, or north repels north). Also, scientists <u>enquire</u> (human consciousness) into science research questions, linking together taxonomies and causal explanations. Similarly, teachers guide learners to <u>enquire</u> into science questions and link taxonomies and explanations together, e.g. Teacher: I <u>want</u> you <u>thinking</u> about (Enquiry) what things (Taxonomy) are *attracted* to the magnets (Cause–effect explanation).

In science practice (e.g. experiments) taxonomies or classifications are related to descriptions of specific things, principles are related to sequences of happenings, and enquiry values are related to choices/decisions in interpreting experimental data. In the experiments, these learners were expected to relate specific magnets to classifications/taxonomies of magnets, to explain sequences of magnetic attraction and repulsion in terms of cause–effect principles, and to choose answers by interpreting evidence in a "scientific" way (see Table 4.3). The three columns of Table 4.3, from left to right, correspond to the three main realms of experience: the identification and classification of things, the representation of events and activity sequences, and human consciousness. The rows of Table 4.3, from top to bottom, move from theory toward practice. There is a theory–practice relation between Classification, Principles and Evaluation on the one hand and Description, Sequence and Choice on the other. Theory involves generic reference and practice involves specific reference. Theory is talked about in general reflection and practice is talked about in specific reflection.

At the beginning of the magnetism unit, the students relied on their "commonsense" theories to explain magnetic attraction as with Janie who thought that attraction depended on the size of the

Table 4.3 A Knowledge Framework Heuristic for the Magnetism Unit

Classification	Principles	Evaluation
"Magnets have north and south poles" "This is north"	"If south and south, repel" "Why (do you say that)?" "It repelled"	T. asks: "How do you know"/ T. asks: "What is it/ what happened/ why?"
Description	**Sequence**	**Choice**

object (" the key's small"). They would later replace these commonsense theories with the scientific meanings of magnetism. Note how the teacher responds to Abby's trial with a key ("Hey it doesn't" —action discourse), and connects practice and theory by pressing for an explanation of why the key isn't attracted (reflection discourse). This opens the way for Janie's theory that size is significant to be challenged by hands-on experimentation.

Teacher: I want you <u>thinking</u> about what things are *attracted* to the magnets … and why. What **is** similar about all these things?
Abby: (trying a magnet on a key) Hey it *doesn't* [sc. attract].
Teacher: It *doesn't*. Why *doesn't* the key… what do you <u>think</u> Janie?
Janie: It *doesn't*. That key**'s** small.

The children then learned about the theory of magnetism through a series of 10 experiments where the teacher helped them develop the scientific concepts along with hands-on experiences. The teacher took special care to teach key meanings (e.g. attract, north pole, south pole, repel). The experiments included finding whether magnetism passes through paper, wood, plastic, making a magnet from a nail, making a compass, using iron filings to show lines of magnetic force, exploring attracting and repelling. The students did the experiments in small groups at identical stations. Each student then wrote up the experiment in their "Magnet Book". At the end of each experiment the teacher brought the class together to reflect on the action of the experiment in a process of teacher-guided reporting (see Gibbons, 2003; Gardner, 2004).

At the end of the unit, using the unfamiliar case of ring magnets, the teacher formatively assessed student understanding of the meaning potential of the magnetism register: ring magnets have poles on their top and bottom. The teacher placed one ring magnet over another with poles opposite so that it appeared to "float" and asked students to explain it. Students quickly applied their new, technical model of magnetism to the problem at hand:

Teacher: So … what *happened* here?
Students: It *repelled*.
Teacher: They're *repelling*. Right. … I'm *turning* it over. What …
Student: *Attract*.
[…]
Teacher: Okay. So <u>tell</u> me about these [ring] magnets? Do they **have** a north and south?
Students: Yeah …
Teacher: How do we <u>know</u>?
Jack: Because we <u>tried it out</u>.
Teacher: And? What did we <u>discover</u>?
Jack: Because if you *turn* it around it won't *attract* and if you *turn* it around [sc. again] it'll *attract*.

Here Jack has correctly reasoned that the ring magnets have north and south poles. When asked to give the reason for his claim, he uses the causal relations of attract and repel to argue that the ring magnet must have opposite poles on its top and bottom. In other words, he has shown understanding of the frame of magnetism meanings by using it to correctly interpret the unfamiliar case of ring magnets.

Thus there was evidence that the children had learned a simple theory that was an example of a framework of meanings of a social practice, and it was possible to use the linguistic analysis of ideational meanings to examine the evidence. It is also possible to use the analysis of ideational meaning to trace the development of the framework of meanings in a theory–practice dialectic.

In this section I aimed to show how:

1. The social practice of magnetism has a frame of meanings that is realised in its register, particularly but not exclusively in three realms of ideational meanings.
2. The theory and practice of magnetism are manifested in part through the reflection discourse and action discourse of teacher and students.
3. Language is a means of learning. Learning magnetism involves learning the register of magnetism i.e. developing the resources for making meaning in magnetism. Formative assessment involves assessing meaning making in magnetism.
4. Magnetism register meanings and their realisations in lexis and grammar are learned in a theory–practice dialectic which is manifested in part in the interaction between reflection discourse about magnetism and action discourse in magnetism experiments.

Academic Language Socialisation of Learners Through Participation in an Online Community of Practice

Online discussion in a graduate course is an advanced case of the use of academic discourse in content tasks. It is a social practice that is becoming increasingly widespread. Mohan and Luo (2005) studied online discussion (OD) as a social practice in a graduate language education course that included both English language learners and native speakers, and that was both classroom-based and also online. In the original, non-computer version of the course, the instructor assigned textbook readings and journal articles, gave lectures, and guided classroom discussion (CD) of them. In its online version, the teacher arranged for the students to discuss their views on the assigned reading in an OD forum or bulletin board, supported by WebCT, a distance learning system. Students were familiar with CD but OD was an unfamiliar practice. As a result, students were co-constructing the social practice and its register together for the first time. One intriguing finding was that ELL students strongly preferred OD to CD as a form of academic language socialisation.

The grade 1/2 children in the previous study were engaging in academic discussion while they were talking about magnetism, and the research focus was on the social practice of magnetism, an example of *learning a subject area*. The graduate students in this study were engaging in online academic discussion while talking about applied linguistics, and the research focus will be on the social practice of OD, an example of a *process* of learning a subject area.

I noted above how "Literacy as a social activity" highlights socialisation into social practices through participation in communities of practice. The OD data reveals the academic language socialisation of learners through participation in an academic community of practice. I will explore how this academic community of practice uses a register to theorise and talk about their practice. A first step will be to see how the OD data fit the model of social practice and register, with respect to action and reflection discourse and a frame of meaning.

Data collection for this social practice followed standard qualitative research procedures of recording observation of the practice and interviewing participants about the practice: the OD data of the class were collected over a semester and students were qualitatively interviewed about their experience with OD.

Action Discourse

B1. Actual OD

Student A: Hi, I would also <u>like</u> to share my point of view about the article by Carter. I do <u>agree</u> with Natasha that teachers should **be** aware of the educational background of their learners.

Specific Reflection

B2. Interview about OD

Student B: ... at the beginning, I **was** a little bit reluctant. I didn't <u>want</u> to <u>participate</u> [in OD].

General Reflection

B3. Interview about OD

Student C: [OD] *improves* English, especially the writing skills.

Student A is engaging in OD. Students B and C are talking about/reflecting on OD (which is what the interviewer is requesting them to do, of course). (B1) is an example of action discourse of OD and (B2) and (B3) are examples of reflection discourse of OD. Any investigation of a social practice using observation and interview is likely to collect action discourse and reflection discourse. This may seem obvious, but the natural correspondence between these two methods of data collection and these two kinds of discourse is important for the correspondence between social practice and register, so action and reflection discourse need to be defined in linguistic terms. I need to make it clear that action discourse relates to action *as defined by the social practice*, which is not necessarily physical action. Similarly, reflection discourse is reflection relevant to the social practice. In addition, the action discourse (doing OD) and the reflection discourse (talking about OD) must relate to the same social practice i.e. Students B and C are talking about what Student A is engaging in. I base the distinction between action discourse (doing OD) and reflection discourse (talking about OD) on the SFL distinction between field of discourse as the social activity being pursued (first order field) versus field as the topic or content being talked about (second order field) (see Halliday & Matthiessen, 1999, pp. 320ff.). Note that action and reflection are often defined in a different way in SFL (see Eggins, 2004, p. 91). Note also the additional complexity that actual OD normally talks about some topic, and may talk reflexively about OD itself. One benefit of connecting these two kinds of qualitative data and two kinds of discourse is that register offers a theory and analysis for "triangulating" interview data and observation data that is language use.

Turning to the issue of a frame of meaning, student reflections on OD showed that they were constructing a frame that included and related all three realms of ideational meaning. In the examples that follow I have marked ideational processes. I have also capitalised some of the technical terms that are important parts of the register of the student reflections.

> BEING "... [OD] should **be** somehow between CASUAL and ACADEMIC writing."
> DOING "[OD] *improves* English, especially the writing skills."

FEELING and SAYING "... ESL students, to a certain extent, would feel more comfortable and less inhibited communicating their ideas [in OD]."

The L2 students' reflections on OD were the result of their shared conversations with each other during the course. They saw OD very positively, viewed it as academic language socialisation, broadly speaking, and were developing a way of talking about OD (a register of OD) that explained how it helped their language development.

CD was difficult for L2 students because they had to compose their thoughts immediately in real time. OD was asynchronous and therefore easier because L2 students could take time to prepare their messages. Here a student contrasts these two types of discussion, describing how OD enables L2 students to express their ideas while CD inhibits students from expressing their ideas:

[OD] can *provide* every student a private talking space to express his/her very idea about everything. Just as Julian mentioned in his message, many students **are** shy to actively talk during class [CD] because they **are** not sufficiently **armed** by perfect English grammar or pronunciation etc. Through the [online] bulletin board everybody can freely express their personal ideas, besides, they can *go* to bulletin board whenever they want, and they can *do* some small preparation for the message that they will *post.*

L2 students felt that participation in OD improved their reading and writing competence: "From the point of view of L2 learners, like Natasha, Yun and May, I can see my reading and writing competence *progressing* through *posting* exchanges [in OD]."

Using the language of community of practice theory as a metalanguage, L2 students talked about OD as interacting in a community and stressed that the community should be supportive: "Most importantly, to me, online discussion **is** a SUPPORTIVE COMMUNITY. I think this **is** very, very important to students ... I feel online COMMUNITY **is** very SUPPORTIVE, to *share*, to **be** INTERACTIVE with one another."

One student gave an explanation of how less proficient ESL students would develop their meaning making by being scaffolded in a dialectical process by more proficient students in the supportive OD community:

[OD] *provides* more chances for those LESS PROFICIENT ESL students to CONSTRUCT MEANINGS with adequate length of time, especially when they **are** too shy or lacking confidence of expressing themselves in public. They will find [OD] as a SUPPORTIVE COMMUNITY where they can be *SCAFFOLDED* by the other MORE PROFICIENT students and *develop* their LANGUAGE COMPETENCE as time *goes* by.

Thus the L2 students had developed a register frame of meanings that viewed OD as a different type of discussion than CD (classification), saw OD as promoting language development (causal principle), and valued OD as providing a dialectical process of scaffolding by a supportive community (evaluation).

Students manifested a strong concern about the quality of academic discourse in OD and did so in ways that corresponded surprisingly closely with the register distinction between mode, field and tenor, though they did not use those terms.

OD was a change in mode of discourse from spoken CD to written OD. But should it be writing that was close to speaking? The students took different perspectives on whether online writing should be "formal" or more "casual" (to use their terms):

Student D: I think FORMAL writing [in OD] means HIGH QUALITY DISCUSSION.

Student E: I personally think [OD] should be somehow between CASUAL and ACADEMIC writing.

Students also had different views on the field of OD: should it be restricted to academic topics? Two contrasting views were:

Student F: As for the personal topics in online discussions in the academic setting, I don't accept them at all. *For me, ACADEMIC is ACADEMIC and PERSONAL is PERSONAL.*
Student G: I don't like boring, dry stuff. I hope to write for myself, not for school.

Finally, students disagreed about the tenor of OD: how far should participants support or disagree with each other. When one student asserted the importance of OD as a supportive community, it was pointed out by another participant that this made it more difficult for students to express academic disagreements straightforwardly.

Thus students in their interviews articulated a frame that emphasised scaffolding for developing language competence and included concerns, and differences of opinion, about the quality of academic discourse in OD. But they did not analyse the specifics of academic discourse or say how scaffolding specifically improved the quality of academic discourse. This raised a fundamental question: was there any evidence in OD *interaction* of scaffolding that addressed the quality of academic discourse in detail? In other words, was the students' practice ahead of their theory in this respect? The following OD example shows a native speaker scaffolding an L2 student by functionally recasting (see Mohan & Beckett, 2003) a causal statement about factors affecting language acquisition into a more academic and scientific form. Note the nominalisation of "access" to "accessibility" and the switch from "because" to "seems to play an integral role". These are features of grammatical metaphor in academic discourse (see Halliday, 1998).

Student H (ESL):   Learning environment is crucial for language learning. ESL students have more chance to expose to the language. <u>Everyday, they can access to English-speaking mass media easily.</u> However, in the context of EFL, English becomes a Forgotten Language (EFL) to students <u>because they do not have any access to the language.</u>
Student I (native speaker):   From your previous message it seems that a students' learning environment is key to language acquisition, but <u>the accessibility of the language</u> also <u>seems to play an integral role.</u>

Thus specific scaffolding of academic discourse quality was occurring in OD practice, but it was not recognised in the students' theory of OD. It could begin to be recognised if the community discussed register analyses of examples such as Student I's functional recast. Hence there is an opportunity for L2 learners to incorporate explicit accounts of academic discourse development into their theories of language development in social practices, if they are to form part of communities of practice that aim to be supportive more knowingly. To put this in terms of formative assessment: scaffolding in the example above is a form of formative assessment; since this community engages in practices of functional assessment of academic discourse, it has an opportunity to work towards recognising its own practice and theorising the functional assessment of academic discourse development.

In this discussion of the register analysis of OD, I have aimed to show how register analysis helped to analyse the community's theory, raising questions that it then examined through an analysis of the community's practice, which in its turn was a resource for extending the community's theory. On a more general level I have aimed to show how register can offer a linguistic analysis of the language data that are gathered by qualitative methods that combine the use of interviews and observations, and thereby contribute further depth to findings.

Cooperative Learning: Dilemmas of Choice in a Social Practice

Like the previous study of OD, the following study of cooperative learning is an investigation of the social practice of a process of learning. Cooperative learning is an educational practice widely used and recommended not only for learning academic content but also for learning academic discussion and argument:

> Cooperative learning refers to a variety of teaching methods in which students work in small groups to help one another learn academic content. In cooperative classrooms, students are expected to help each other, *to discuss and argue with each other, to assess each other's current knowledge and fill in gaps in each other's understanding.*
>
> (Slavin, 1995, p. 2, emphasis added)

Cooperative learning in the L2 classroom aims for at least three goals: learning of academic content, learning the academic discourse of the second language, maintaining knowledge of academic discourse in the L1.

Cummins' "Dual Iceberg" model (Cummins, 1992) suggests how these aims might be achieved together. The model holds that academic language proficiency underlies both L1 and L2, and that if it is already developed in the L1, given adequate exposure and motivation it will transfer to the L2, and gain the surface features of the L2.

As noted above, choices/decisions are an element in our linguistic analysis of social practices, along with evaluation. In the study below, certain choices made in cooperative learning (e.g. to cooperate or not, to use L1 or L2, to use L2 for academic discussion etc.) are talked about in interviews and are acted out in cooperative interactions. These turned out to be difficult choices.

In work on the concept of ideological dilemmas (Billig, Condor, Edwards, Gane, Middleton & Radley, 1988), dilemmas are difficult choices/decisions that contain contrary themes, involve tensions and contradictions, and often require the consideration of incompatible wants. Dilemmas may not be easily resolved, but they can be managed (Tracy, 1997). Billig et al. (1988) believe that existence of dilemmas provides essential seeds for productive thought about managing them.

Liang and Mohan (2003) describe a study conducted at a secondary school in Western Canada that used cooperative learning as a main instructional strategy. The learners selected were Chinese immigrant students from the ESL programme. Forty-nine students were individually interviewed to solicit their opinions about cooperative learning goals. One hundred and twenty students were observed and recorded in cooperative learning tasks, resulting in 30 hours of audiotapes.

Liang and Mohan (2003) examined cooperative learning in relation to the three goals mentioned above, using the interview data. They then compared the results with the observation data of cooperative learning interactions, and investigated the quality of the learners' academic discourse in L1 and L2, using an analysis of Halliday's ideational and interpersonal functions, which was based on Staab (1986) who built on a body of quantitative studies of L1 discourse stimulated by Halliday's early work. This analysis was appropriate for making quantitative comparisons between L1 and L2.

Results indicated that students regarded the groupwork aspect of cooperative learning as dilemmatic. In the interviews, they expressed likes and dislikes about working in groups. Working in groups produced more ideas, but it was hard to get consensus; groups shared the workload, but some members would not do their job; group members could help each other, but one could not demonstrate individual ability. Observation of cooperative groups gave evidence of cooperation (helping others with content knowledge and helping others with English language) but also showed the reverse of cooperation (getting the job done quickly rather than sharing understanding of the task, dividing the work between individuals rather than constructing it jointly, telling others the answer rather than helping them to work it out). Poor cooperation of these kinds is likely to mean poor cooperative learning of both academic language and content. Some of these ambivalences may arise from differences between the school culture of the Canadian high school and the Chinese educational cultures the students came from, where learning with others typically occurred outside class time, and group membership was long term rather than short term.

The choice between using Chinese and using English was dilemmatic for the students, and the students expressed discomfort with the choices they made. In the interviews, students expressed mixed feelings about L1 and L2 use in cooperative work. There was peer pressure for them to speak L1, but they wanted to speak less Chinese and more English, which would advance their academic goals and satisfy the expectations of their parents, who typically did not want them to use Chinese in the classroom. The evidence of their interactions resonated with this. In the cooperative groups students spoke Chinese 54% of the time and English 46% of the time.

There were also dilemmas connected with using L1 for academic language vs. developing academic language in L2. In the interviews students commented that they were under time pressure to complete the group task in class. If they aimed at getting the job done, then they would not spend much time struggling with academic language in L2. As a student said: "When I have a problem, I want to learn something quickly, I will ask my friend in Chinese. Like I don't need to translate it in English and tell them and they speak English to me."

One might expect therefore expect that Chinese would largely be used for ideational purposes in the cooperative groups, but for 45% of the time it was used interpersonal purposes, such as chatting about school life and social life. English, by contrast, was used 82% of the time for ideational purposes. However, when ideational use was divided further into informing (which was less demanding) and reasoning (which was more demanding), reasoning occurred considerably more in Chinese (28%) than in English (15%). A likely explanation for this pattern was found when further observations showed that Chinese was used for the more difficult discussions that demanded reasoning in the earlier stages of a task, and that English was used in the easier final stages of writing up the English answer to the task (and also for memorising questions and answers for tests in English). As a student commented: "We write [the answer] in English, but discuss in Mandarin. It's faster, more convenient, easier to understand, and better."

With respect to framing, note how this student summarises a general pattern of <u>choice</u> and lists reasons why Mandarin is the preferred choice for discussion. These reasons use the language of <u>evaluation</u> or appraisal (see Martin & Rose, 2007, pp. 25ff.) as in *convenient, easier, better*. He also very succinctly contrasts the different ways (<u>classification</u>) that students use English and Mandarin in the earlier and later stages (<u>time sequence</u>) of a cooperative learning task.

The time spent reasoning is even less when it is calculated as a percentage of total interaction. Reasoning was 15% of total interaction in Chinese and 12% of total interaction in English. This result provides only weak support for Slavin's expectation that students in cooperative learning will engage in academic discourse and "discuss and argue with each other" (though it must be pointed out that I know of no comparable studies using the same measure). Thus the result suggests that researchers and practitioners need to give more attention to conditions favouring increased reasoning in cooperative learning. One possible approach might be to design cooperative tasks that require answers to be *justified by reasoning*, rather in the way that students in mathematics are often expected to give the reasoning for their answers. However, there is little in the interview data to suggest that these students see the development of reasoning, much less the *bilingual* development of reasoning, as an important goal for their language development. Consequently, this approach should be complemented by drawing on Beckett and Slater's research strategies (discussed later) in order to help students to recognise and value their use of reasoning discourse and to help them foster it strategically using both of their languages (for a discussion of parallels between academic discourse in English and Chinese, see Mohan, Slater, Kobayashi, Luo, Kobayashi & Ji, 2006). There is an urgent need for research into possible fostering strategies.

To sum up, these bilingual students face a knot of dilemmas surrounding three main goals of cooperative learning, and a quantity problem with reasoning in academic discourse. The present dilemmas offer a deeper understanding of the ways that students work with these goals in their context of educational cultures and social values. They may give rise to new insights about and changes in cooperative learning if there is an increased attention to reasoning in discourse and an active effort to foster it bilingually.

From a register point of view this investigation of cooperative learning is centrally a study of the relation between the "choices discussed" in the interviews and "choices made" in the cooperative interactions.

The Theory–Practice Dialectic: Reflection Revising Theory

The OD study above showed ESL graduate students appreciating OD as a form of academic language socialisation and holding a community of practice theory that explained and justified the academic language socialisation process. But what if learners have a different theory of language and learning? What if they reject academic language socialisation opportunities because of this? What would it take to change their minds?

This section will report on research on project-based learning for L2 learners, on how learners may reject its opportunities for academic language socialisation, and on how researchers have attempted to change minds by engaging learners in action research.

In the OD study and the cooperative learning study the research focus was on the social practice of a *process of learning*. This study will focus on the social practice of *action research on a process of learning*, where students research and reframe their process of learning.

Beckett and Slater (2005) state that project-based instruction for L2 learners is a valuable way to promote the simultaneous acquisition of academic language, content, academic culture and academic skills, but they add an important proviso: "provided that students in academic ESL classes can see the value of learning through projects, which the literature notes has not consistently been the case".

Beckett (1999) studied secondary school ESL students engaged in project work, an appropriate choice in an ESL programme that was explicitly aimed at facilitating the discourse socialisation of ESL students into local academic and social cultures. In a typical project, for example, students chose a social issue that was interesting to them, researched the issue by surveying the media, designed a research study, conducted an interview survey, analysed the results and reported their findings in an oral class presentation. But she found that only 18% of the students were in favour of project-based instruction. The majority perceived it negatively, stating that the project distracted them from learning what they felt they needed to know to advance their education, particularly English grammar and vocabulary. Thus they believed that only learning of the "language code" would advance their education. This view or theory interfered with their needed entry into the academic culture of the school and was problematic. For a more comprehensive literature review of this issue, see Beckett (2002).

One possible approach to this issue is action research (AR) where students examine their own learning process. While there are varying definitions of AR, "one common thread is that participants in a given social situation/classroom are themselves centrally involved in a systematic process of enquiry arising from their own practical concerns" (Burns, 2005, p. 241). The AR tradition locates AR in relation to the study of the social practices of education and a theory–practice dialectic. An early advocate of AR was John Dewey (1904) who argued for "the centrality of educational practices as the source of data and the ultimate test of validity of research findings" (Burns, 2005, p. 242). Carr and Kemmis (1986, p. 44) describe how Kurt Lewin, an influential figure in AR, regarded "theory and practice as dialectically related, with theory being developed and tested on by application in and reflection upon practice". Carr and Kemmis (1986, p. 162) mirror this dialectic in their widely quoted definition of AR:

> Action research [AR] is simply a form of self-reflective enquiry undertaken by participants in order to improve the rationality and justice of their own practices, their understanding of these practices and the situations in which the practices are carried out.

Since AR examines the social practices of education and their theory–practice dialectic, it can be studied from a register perspective if it uses verbal data. I am not aware of any research which has yet done so.

Taking an AR approach, Beckett and Slater (2005) developed a tool they termed "The Project Framework" to raise ESL students' awareness of how academic language, content and culture learning develop simultaneously through projects. It thus aimed at the intentional language socialisation of students into new ways of thinking about language and language learning. It had two key components: the planning graphic and the project diary. The planning graphic helped students categorise target academic language, content and academic thinking skills relevant to the curriculum and student goals. It could be co-constructed with the students or used to guide the students to develop their own project-specific goals. It was intended to raise students' awareness that all components of the project lead towards the goal of becoming academically literate in their new L2 environment. It aimed to describe the components in ways that the students would understand. The project diary outlined a format for students to summarise weekly the academic language, content and academic skills they had been using, and what they were able to accomplish.

Beckett and Slater carried out research with this tool in three classes of Japanese students in a 14-week, content-based, undergraduate course called Language and Language Learning, offered in the second term of a 10-month exchange programme at a Canadian university. The students were not familiar with a content-based academic discourse socialisation approach. The students worked in small groups to choose, develop and present a term project. The study involved 57 students and their teacher. The data source for the study included the course syllabus, lesson plans, the teacher's reflections, the students' weekly portfolios of their research projects, their end-of-term reflections, and interviews with 22 students. All students used the "Project Framework" on a weekly basis to record their learning experiences.

At the end of the course, all students felt that they had learned a considerable amount about their chosen topics as well as the language and academic skills needed to demonstrate their knowledge. A large majority emphasised that the planning graphic and the project diary helped them to see what and how much they learned. Analyses of the interview and reflection data showed that the majority of the students (79%) clearly acknowledged an understanding of an academic language socialisation approach to ESL learning. That is, they saw how they learned language, subject matter content and academic skills simultaneously. One student stated this very simply when she wrote in her reflection about her learning:

A: I learned that] I could study not only English, but also other subject. In other words, I could kill two birds with one stone. I understand that there is a connection between the two.

Other students were proud of combining language, content and academic skills in their term paper:

B: I can't believe I wrote my paper —15 pages. I never wrote a long paper like this before. Not even in Japanese.

A third student reflected on her progress from initial scepticism to understanding with the help of the teacher and the research process. She makes a clear distinction between the way she learned English in Japan and the new way that she has learned:

C: I learned English by going to conversations class, essay writing, and ... So, I didn't believe her [the teacher] when she said we can learn English this way, too. She explained it in class and showed it to us by the visual [the Framework]. She told us to learn to speak when talking to the librarian and presentation, learn to write when we take notes and write report. I did that and I understand she taught us the new way. Now, I know how to learn English another way.

With regard to framing, student C contrasts two different ways of learning English (<u>classification</u>) in which the learner does different <u>actions</u> (e.g. go to conversation class vs. talk to the librarian and make presentations). She initially <u>evaluates</u> the new way negatively ("I didn"t believe her") but now accepts it ("now, I know how to learn English another way").

L2 learners who hold a "language code" view of language and learning and do not recognise the learning potential of their own language use are likely to fail to take advantage of possibilities for academic discourse socialisation. These Japanese students were able to move to an academic discourse socialisation view by engaging in a dialectical action research process where they systematically described their experiences of learning of language, content and academic skills in such a way as to begin to appreciate their functional, contextual relationships. In effect, they changed the criteria for their formative self-assessment of their own language learning. Future qualitative register research could build on Beckett and Slater's approach, aiming to identify learners' initial assumptions, examine their meaning-making processes and portray the theory–practice dialectic in detail. It could also explore the possibilities that their approach creates for more effective formative assessment. At a more general level, their work suggests how a register perspective could enrich AR by providing a linguistic perspective on its dialectical processes.

Conclusion

I have aimed to show how an SFL approach to register provides a metalanguage and analytical tools to examine the role of language as a means of learning in social practices. The study of social practices as units of linguistic meaning can provide a link between "social" and "linguistic" approaches to literacy, can speak to the needs of L2 learners who must develop academic discourse in content areas, and can point towards forms of formative assessment that take greater account of meaning-making by learners.

A social practice is a semiotic and semantic unit. With regard to the frame of meaning or "theory" of a social practice, I have described how field and ideational meaning offer a way to sketch central elements of the frame and open up the possibility of tracing how the learner's frame of meaning develops as it interacts with the learner's experiences in a theory–practice dialectic. Future work on social practices will need to account for the role of interpersonal and textual meaning (see Painter, 1999, pp. 318ff.).

The texts of a social practice include action discourse and reflection discourse. I have illustrated how register can help provide a linguistic account of relations between the social practice and its "ecology" of texts, by linking action discourse in the practice and reflection discourse about the practice, most obviously through field of discourse and mode of discourse. Movement between reflection discourse and action discourse offers a way of tracing a theory–practice dialectic of learning.

The study of magnetism as a social practice illustrated a frame of ideational meaning in detail, and indicated a theory–practice dialectic in the movement in discourse between magnetism "theory" and engagement in experiments. As a register study of the development of academic discourse in a "content" classroom, it exemplified how "content" was in fact register meanings learned through meaning-making i.e. through language as a means of learning. It was also possible to see how a register perspective could research formative assessment as the assessment of meaning-making.

The study of OD showed L2 graduate students recognising and valuing OD as a process of academic language socialisation. As a qualitative study of a social practice using observation and interview data, it naturally provided action and reflection discourse (OD interactions and reflection about OD), with register analysis to support triangulation between the two kinds of data. Register analysis of the interviews showed a frame of meaning that explained OD as a supportive community but did not explain academic discourse scaffolding. In a "triangulating" move, register analysis of OD interaction showed active academic discourse scaffolding, revealing a need to expand the frame to recognise and value it.

The study of bilingual cooperative learning showed L2 learners as agents in a social practice facing choices that were dilemmatic. Choice is an element of the frame of meaning of a social practice, and was here explored through reflections on choices and through actions chosen. Interviews showed how the goals of bilingual cooperative learning posed a complex knot of dilemmas for students, leading to tensions in decision-making and bringing to light problems of balancing these goals. These dilemmas offer a deeper understanding of the ways that students work with these goals and their reasons for doing so. Analysis of cooperative interactions showed a low level of reasoning in both languages. A possible way forward would be to give increased attention to reasoning in both languages along with an active effort to foster reasoning bilingually. This would ask students to view cooperative learning goals in a new way, which might be problematic for them.

In their study of project-based language-learning (PBL), Beckett and Slater addressed the problem of students rejecting opportunities to develop academic discourse because of the value they placed on "language code" learning. Slater and Beckett therefore helped learners revise their "frame" through a dialectical AR process where learners analysed their learning experiences for relevant elements of language, content and academic skills. More generally, their work suggests how a register perspective could enrich AR to the extent that it examines the social practices of education and their theory–practice dialectic from a functional linguistic point of view.

I have aimed to relate these four studies to each other. In the first study, the research focus was on the social practice of magnetism, an example of learning a subject area. In the second, it was on the social practice of OD, an example of a process of learning a subject area. In the third it was on the social practice of cooperative learning, a further example of a process of learning, but one that was dilemmatic. In the fourth, it was on the social practice of AR, an example of research on a process of learning. As Beckett and Slater's work shows, if students do not want what they need, this third level of social practice cannot be ignored, so all three levels of social practice have to be considered in the study of academic language socialisation. Corresponding to these three levels are three levels of formative assessment. In the first study, the teacher formatively assessed the learners' meaning-making in magnetism. In the second study, the students formatively assessed each other's meaning-making in OD, as they provided scaffolding in a supportive community. In the third study, the students formatively assessed their own use of Chinese and English, and might be open to assess it in a different way, as bilingual reasoning. In the fourth, the students systematically formatively assessed their own meaning-making in their AR. Future research from a register perspective on formative assessment in social practices may therefore yield considerable dividends for L2 learners' academic language socialisation.

References

Beckett, G. H. (1999). Project-based instruction in a Canadian secondary school's ESL classes: Goals and evaluations. Unpublished PhD thesis, University of British Columbia.

Beckett, G. H. (2002). Teacher and student evaluations of project-based instruction. *TESL Canada Journal, 19*(2), 52–66.

Beckett, G., & Slater T. (2005). The Project Framework: a tool for language, content, and skills integration. *ELT Journal, 59*, 108–116.

Billig, M., Condor, S., Edwards, D., Gane, M., Middleton, D. & Radley, A. (1988). *Ideological dilemmas: A social psychology of everyday thinking*. Newbury Park, CA: SAGE Publications Inc.

Burns, A. (2005) Action research. In E. Hinkel (Ed.), *Handbook of second language teaching and learning* (pp. 241–256). Mahwah, NJ: Erlbaum.

Carr, W., & Kemmis, S. (1986). *Becoming critical: Knowing through action research*. London: Falmer.

Cummins, J. (1992). Language proficiency, bilingualism, and academic achievement. In P. A. Richard-Amato & M. A. Snow (Eds.), *The multicultural classroom: Readings for content-area teachers* (pp. 16–26). White Plains, NY: Longman.

Dewey, J. (1904) *The relation of theory to practice in education*. Chicago: University of Chicago Press.

Eggins, S. (2004) *An introduction to systemic functional linguistics*. London and New York: Continuum.

Gardner, S. (2004). Four critical features of teacher-guided reporting (TGR) in infant science and literacy contexts, *Language and Education, 18*(5), 361–378.

Gibbons, P. (2002) *Scaffolding language, scaffolding learning*. Portsmouth, NH: Heinemann.

Gibbons, P. (2003) Mediating language learning: Teacher interactions with ESL students in a content-based classroom. *TESOL Quarterly, 27*(2), 247–273.

Goffman, E. (1974). *Frame analysis: An essay on the organisation of experience*. New York: Harper and Row.

Halliday, M. A. K. (1978). *Language as social semiotic*. London: Edward Arnold.

Halliday, M. A. K. (1993). Towards a language-based theory of learning. *Linguistics and Education, 5*, 93–116

Halliday, M. A. K. (1998). Language and the enhancement of learning. Paper presented at the Language in Learning Symposium held at Brisbane College of Advanced Education, Brisbane.

Halliday, M. A. K. (1999). The notion of "context" in language education. In M. Ghadessy (Ed.), *Text and context in functional linguistics* (pp. 1–24). Amsterdam and Philadelphia: John Benjamins.

Halliday, M. A. K., & Martin, J. R. (1993). *Writing science: Literacy and discursive power*. Pittsburgh, PA: The University of Pittsburgh Press.

Halliday, M. A. K., & Matthiessen, C. M. I. M. (1999). *Construing experience through meaning*. London: Cassell.

Janzen, J. (2008). Teaching English language learners in the content-areas. *Review of Educational Research, 78* (4), 1010–1038.

Lave, J., & Wenger, E. (1991). *Situated Learning: Legitimate peripheral participation*. Cambridge: Cambridge University Press.

Leung, C., & Mohan, B. (2004). Teacher formative assessment and talk in classroom contexts —assessment *as* discourse and assessment *of* discourse. *Language Testing, 20*(3), 335–359.

Liang, X., & Mohan, B. (2003). Dilemmas of cooperative learning and academic proficiency in two languages. *Journal of English for Academic Purposes, 2*(1), 35–51.

Martin, J. R., & Rose, D. (2007). *Working with discourse* (2nd ed.). London and New York: Continuum.

Martin, L., Nelson, K. & Tobach, E. (Eds.) (1995). *Sociocultural psychology: Theory and practice of doing and knowing*. Cambridge: Cambridge University Press.

Mohan, B. (1969). Language and situation. Unpublished PhD thesis, University of London.

Mohan, B. (1986). *Language and content*. Reading, MA: Addison-Wesley.

Mohan, B. (2007). Knowledge structures in social practices. In J. Cummins & C. Davison (Eds.), *The international handbook of English language teaching* (pp 303–316). New York: Springer.

Mohan, B., & Beckett, G. H. (2003). A functional approach to research on content-based language learning: Recasts in causal explanations. *Modern Language Journal, 87*(iii), 421–432.

Mohan, B., & Luo, L. (2005). A systemic functional linguistics perspective on CALL. In J. Egbert & G. Petrie (Eds.) *Research perspectives in CALL* (pp. 87–96). Mahwah, NJ: Erlbaum.

Mohan, B., & Slater, T. (2005). A functional perspective on the critical theory/practice relation in teaching language and science. *Linguistics and Education, 16*, 151–172.

Mohan, B., Slater, T., Kobayashi, E., Luo, L., Kobayashi, M. & Ji, K. (2006). Multimodal scientific representations across languages and cultures? In W. Bowcher & T. Royce (Eds.) *Multimodal discourse* (pp. 275–298). Hillsdale, NJ: Erlbaum.

Painter, C. (1999). *Learning through language in early childhood*. London: Continuum.

Reckwitz, A. (2002). Toward a theory of social practices: A development in culturalist theorizing. *European Journal of Social Theory, 5*(2), 245–265.

Schleppegrell, M., & Colombi, M. (Eds.) (2002). *Developing advanced literacy in first and second languages*. Mahwah, NJ: Erlbaum.

Slavin, R. E. (1995). *Cooperative learning: Theory, research, and practice* (2nd ed.). Toronto: Allyn and Bacon.

Staab, C. F. (1986). Eliciting the language of forecasting and reasoning in elementary school classrooms. *The Alberta Journal of Educational Research*, *32*(2), 109–126.

Spradley, J. (1980). *Participant observation*. New York: Holt, Rinehart, Winston.

Tracy, K. (1997). *Colloquium: Dilemmas of academic discourse*. Norwood, NJ: Ablex Publishing Corporation.

Van Leeuwen, T. (2008). *Discourse and practice*. New York: Oxford University Press.

William, D. (2007/2008). Changing classroom practice. *Educational Leadership*, *65*(4), 36–42.

Zuengler, J., & Miller, E. (2006). Cognitive and sociocultural perspectives: two parallel SLA worlds? *TESOL Quarterly*, *40*(1), 35–58.

5
Vocational ESL

Denise E. Murray

Adult immigrants and refugees,[1] who have limited, if any, English language proficiency, as well as needing English to function in their everyday lives, may need English for the workplace or for further study. As Auerbach and Burgess (1985) demonstrate, meeting learners'[2] survival needs (often called life skills) does not empower them to take responsibility for their lives as contributing members of their new society. For many, their need to eventually participate in the workforce is critical to their physical, emotional, and psychological welfare. There has therefore been a strand in adult English as a second language (ESL) that has focused on preparing learners for the workplace. This chapter will discuss the range of vocational ESL in the English-dominant countries of Australia, Canada, Great Britain, New Zealand, and the United States. It situates the discussion in the area of adult ESL, that is, programs for immigrants and refugees, as opposed to intensive English programs for international students (see Murray, 2005a for a discussion of adult ESL) or vocational programs in non-English-dominant countries such as Germany or Thailand. Adult ESL encompasses a variety of programs to teach immigrants and refugees—English, citizenship, and work-related content.

Situating Vocational ESL

As well as being situated in the adult ESL arena, vocational ESL can be considered to be a form of content-based instruction (CBI). CBI is an approach to curriculum design used in a variety of settings from schools to universities to adult education (Brinton & Master, 1997; Brinton, Snow, & Wesche, 1989; Chamot, 1995; Crandall, 1995; Kasper, 1999; Mohan, 1986; Mohan, Leung, & Davison, 2001; Snow & Brinton, 1997; Williams, 2004). CBI can be defined as "the integration of content learning with language teaching aims. More specifically, it refers to the concurrent study of language and subject matter, with the form and sequence of language presentation dictated by content" (Brinton, Snow, & Wesche 1989, p. vii).

In CBI, form follows content. In other words, the curriculum is designed around specific content and syntax, functions, and vocabulary result from the content. Brinton, Snow, and Wesche (1989) describe three models of CBI—theme-based, sheltered content instruction, and adjunct language instruction. Theme-based courses are organized around topics of interest to learners. Sheltered approaches are used primarily in high schools, although they are also found in community colleges and universities. In these courses, required content is delivered to second language learners using activities and techniques that make the content accessible to them. Usually the instructor is an expert in the content area. In adjunct courses learners are enrolled in two linked courses—one in their required content area, the other in English, requiring coordination between the two instructors. Any of these models can be used for vocational ESL.

Vocational ESL differs from English for specific purposes (ESP), another form of CBI, in that ESP tends to be used more in English as a foreign language (EFL) settings (Johns, 1992; Master, 1997) and its research focus is grounded in linguistic analysis, discourse studies, pragmatics, and discourse communities (Johns, 1992). ESP may also be linked to one skill because the particular learners only need, for example, to read scientific texts. English for science and technology (EST) and English for academic purposes (EAP) have dominated the research literature on ESP.

Within this framing within adult ESL, vocational ESL can take a variety of forms—pre-vocational, vocation-specific, and generic field, all of which are discussed in detail below. Wong (1992) refers to these as general VESL, occupation-specific VESL, and occupational-cluster VESL. It can also take place in a variety of settings—adult ESL schools, community colleges, technical colleges, community centers, and the workplace itself. Since workplace ESL was addressed in the first *Handbook* (Roberts, 2005), I will not address it here, even though it can be considered a subset of vocational ESL. Some researchers in the US (Cunningham Florez, 1998) distinguish between workplace instruction and workforce training, the former referring to instruction that takes place in the workplace, with the curriculum determined by specific worker needs derived from a work-task needs analysis. Usually such instruction is funded by the employer and employees sometimes may even be able to attend during work hours. Workforce training, on the other hand, includes employment skills such as effective communication or problem solving as part of the content of the ESL curriculum. Additionally, in the US, vocational ESL has often been referred to as VESL, and usually refers to non-professional occupations, such as maids in hotels or electronics assembly workers, although some use it more broadly. However, because vocational education for the general population (usually referred to as voc ed) is perceived negatively in the US, VESL, too is often perceived as only for those with limited skills, education, or even intelligence. In California, the governor, Arnold Schwarzenegger, who himself went to a vocational school in his homeland Austria, has called for a renaming and refocusing of vocational education programs as career technical education (Schwartzenegger, 2005). I have chosen vocational ESL as it is both transparent and more universal than alternate terms.

Program Types

Pre-Vocational Programs

Pre-vocational content is usually preparation for the workplace, often called job-readiness, and may be modules within a general ESL class or a stand-alone course. Content includes skills such as those defined in Canada by the Office of Literacy and Essential Skills—reading, document use, numeracy, writing, oral communication, working with others, thinking, computer use, and continuous learning (Office of Literacy and Essential Skills, 2007). Other countries use slightly different terminology, but all seem to agree that essential workplace skills include working as a team and problem solving.

The US has historically included employment skills as part of the federal act that enables adult education. However, until the 1990s, this was mostly to help adults acquire basic educational skills so they could obtain work, engage in job training programs, or gain a high school equivalency certificate. In the 1990s, the federal government sought to streamline federal programs, which, in the adult education area, resulted in the SCANS Commission (Secretary [of Labor]'s Commission on Achieving Necessary Skills), consisting of business and education leaders. They issued a major report (US Department of Labor, 1991), which has provided the basis for grants, research, and adult ESL instruction. Their report identified five workplace competencies and three foundation skills as essential for workplace performance by all workers, the competencies being resource management, information management, social interaction, systems behavior and performance skills, and technology utilization. The underlying foundational skills are basic skills, higher order intellectual skills, and motivational or character traits. The SCANS skills were included as part of the Workforce Investment Act (WIA) and the Personal Responsibility and Work Opportunity Reconciliation Act of 1996, also known as the Welfare Reform Act. In the UK, the competencies include key skills (effective communication, application of numbers, and use of information technology) and wider key skills (working with others, improving own learning and performance, and problem solving) (Leitch, 2006). Neither the Canadian, the SCANS, nor the UK lists include workplace culture, which is an issue raised in the literature—issues such as punctuality, time sheets, benefits, or occupational health and safety (Wong, 1992).

What differentiates Canada (see Folinsbee, 2007a for a review of the Canadian context) and the US from Australia, New Zealand, and the UK is that the latter have centralized adult education systems with national vocational and literacy strategies, even though in Australia provision is at the state level and states may provide additional programs from their own funds. In Canada and the US, in contrast, vocational education is primarily devolved to the provinces/states so that there are diverse provincial/state and territorial policies and provisions, despite the federal government being involved in some aspects of adult education, including literacy. Thus, adult education in Canada and the US is supported by both provincial/state and federal funds. Further, Canada is more like Australia in that adult literacy education and initial English language instruction for adult immigrants occur in different policy jurisdictions, with immigrant English falling under immigration and adult literacy and vocational programs under education. This is one of the strengths of the Canadian and Australian systems since initial immigrant language instruction is a dedicated part of settlement provision. Initial ESL for adult immigrants in Australia falls under the Department of Immigration and Citizenship; in Canada, under Citizenship and Immigration Canada. In addition to providing initial language instruction for newcomers with limited English proficiency, in 2003 Canada instituted a new federally funded program, Enhanced Language Training (ELT) for skilled stream immigrants to facilitate entry into the workplace of professionals and trades people, including job-specific language training, usually in the workplace. In Canada, in 2007, the federal Office of Literacy and Essential Skills changed priorities to workplace literacy, rather than community and family literacy. This resulted in a trend towards preparation for employment in Canada.

In contrast to Canada's and Australia's long histories of immigration, it was the growing number of guest workers in Europe in the 1970s that led to the development of programs for these workers, such as Jupp and Hodlin's *Industrial English* (1975). More recently, in the UK, the Skills for Life Strategy was developed in 2001, in response to a report to government that one in five adults had difficulties with literacy and numeracy (Moser, 1999). The strategy included standards for literacy, English to speakers of other languages (ESOL), and numeracy. An additional report in 2006 focused on employability skills (Leitch, 2006), which helped to keep employment at the forefront of the strategy. Unlike the SCANS skills set, this is a strategy whose goals are to engage potential learners and create a high quality infrastructure to raise standards. This infrastructure of standards, assessments, national core curricula, teacher qualifications, targets, and national inspections for quality assurance of provision has led to rates of literacy, numeracy, and English proficiency among immigrants and refugees increasing, as well as their progress into employment.

Vocation-Specific Programs

In the US, VESL "programs combine the ideas of coenrollment and curricular integration. Their goal is to help students with fairly low English levels make the transition to occupational/vocational programs" (Chisman & Crandall, 2007). For immigrants with low levels of English, VESL programs offer an alternative pathway to further education as they do not require that learners pass the high school equivalency exam and obtain a General Educational Development (GED) certification. Chisman and Crandall's definition is, however, a limited version of the possibilities of vocation specific courses.

As with other forms of CBI, (content) vocation specific courses include those that prepare learners for future study in a specific vocational course. They may also include adjunct courses where ESL and a vocational subject are team taught by an ESL instructor and a vocational education instructor. In both cases, an ESL professional relates the language learning to the vocabulary, terminology, and context of the skills training. While several VESL textbooks exist that can provide this language learning experience, when the courses are team taught, usually both instructors meet together to develop curricula and often the ESL professional attends the skills training classes. In some adjunct cases, the focus is on the skills training, with the ESL provided as support, with no specific language qualification being attained. However, there are also classes where the learner is achieving both language and skills credits (see Murray, 2007 for examples of this model).

Although vocation-specific programs are not held in the workplace, many providers work closely with related employers, who may advise on curriculum, provide equipment, and even work experience or internships.

Generic Field Programs

This type of course covers more than one occupation, but covers an area of employment with many similarities, such as hospitality or health care. Thus, such courses are mostly stand-alone language courses. However, in some systems (such as Technical and Further Education—TAFE—in Australia) where training programs may include generic courses such as occupational health and safety, or keyboard skills, adjunct programs are still possible.

Research Foci

Research on VESL is not coherent, largely because in some places it is subsumed under all vocational education and in others vocational second language learner issues are only addressed within the broader research agenda of ESL. Additionally, much of the research is descriptive and not generalizable to other contexts, and mostly conducted by outsiders rather than practitioners. In Australia, the National Centre for Vocational Education Research (NCVER) conducts a coordinated research program on vocational and technical post-secondary education—both private and public. Their work, therefore, also includes programs and classes that include second language learners.[3] In parallel, the Adult Migrant English Program (AMEP) Research Centre[4] has conducted research on immigrants and refugees for two decades. Some of their work has involved vocational programs, especially in the era prior to adoption of a national curriculum framework in the early 1990s. In the US, in the Research Agenda for Adult ESL Van Duzer, Kreeft Peyton, and Comings (1998), list pre-employment ESL, workplace ESL, and vocational ESL (VESL) separately, but do not differentiate among them—they leave such delineation to future research. In 1997, the National Centre for Adult Learning and Literacy, which included work on literacy for native speakers and also second language learners, was defunded. In Canada, the National Adult Literacy Database also hosts research and information on workplace literacy and skills, funded by the Office of Literacy and Essential Skills. The difficulty in defining VESL is further exacerbated because of the conflation of adult literacy and VESL at both policy and program levels. This conflation has impacted on provision of ESL to immigrants and refugees. As Lowes (2004, p. 18) notes for Australia, but equally applies to Canada, and New Zealand, who have also adopted an economic imperative for such provision:

In targeting the disadvantaged, English communication difficulties were lumped together, obscuring the needs of the clientele. Rationalisation thus reduced the components of the programs to their lowest common denominator, in this case literacy in English as well as reducing Commonwealth responsibility and resourcing for this specific service for people of non-English speaking background.

I would argue that this partly covers the situations in the US and UK, the difference being that the UK has only recently paid attention to ESL for immigrants, refugees, and asylum seekers, while the US has always had very limited federal responsibility for such provision. Because the literature conflates ESL and literacy, I shall refer to both specific VESL research and research that was more generally on vocational programs that included ESOL learners.

Despite this lack of coherence, three approaches to researching VESL can be found—policy, professionalism, and program evaluation.

Policy

Policy research on the education and training of immigrants focuses on how to ensure that immigrants become fully participating members of the host society and is often commissioned by government to specifically influence future policy decisions. Two strands are evident in this agenda—promoting citizenship and English language proficiency. The former has taken precedence most recently, with Australia and the UK both introducing a citizenship test, and the US revising theirs, and Australia even changing the department's name to include citizenship in the title. The underlying policy concern has been that citizenship demonstrates the newcomers' commitment to their new country and its democratic principles. Research tends to be limited to statistics on uptake of citizenship, how to promote it, and how to develop assessment instruments.

English language proficiency is promoted because research shows that higher levels of English language proficiency result in higher participation rates in the labor force and higher levels are especially essential for skilled occupations[5] (Boyd, DeVries, & Simkin, 1994; Burnley, Murphy, & Fagan, 1997; Chiswick, Cohen, & Zach, 1997; Chiswick, Lee, & Miller, 2003; Richardson, Miller-Lewis, Ngo, & Ilsley, 2002; Richardson & Lester, 2004; Wooden, 1994). A recent US study, for example, found that immigrants with high skills but limited English proficiency were twice as likely to work in unskilled jobs as those with English proficiency (Batalova, Fix, & Creticos, 2008). Batalova, Fix, and Creticos (2008) argue that "high-quality instruction that deploys anytime-anywhere learning and that places greater emphasis on immigrants' English needs in the context of work is needed" (p. 3). Such policy research, however, is a two-edged sword—if governments want a skilled workforce, and research shows that education and English language proficiency are key determiners of immigrant success in the workplace, then changes to immigration policy ensue, as discussed below. Canada introduced a points system for choosing skilled immigrants in 1967, Australia in 1989, New Zealand in 1991 and the UK in 2001, with employment skills and language included as desired characteristics. Australia later allocated additional points for international students completing post-graduate studies in Australia in desirable fields such as accounting. The UK in 2006 decided that graduates from the world's top 50 business schools who wanted to immigrate to the UK would automatically receive the highest number of points (Papademetriou, 2007). In Canada, the revision of the Immigration and Refugee Protection Act in 2002 placed greater emphasis on language proficiency and education (Richardson & Lester, 2004). Thus, research on immigrants' outcomes, especially economic outcomes, has driven changes to immigration policy.

Australia (Richardson et al., 2002), Canada (Statistics Canada, 2001, 2003), New Zealand (Department of Labour, 2009), and the United States (Jasso, Massey, Rosenzweig, & Smith, in press;

Princeton University, 2003) all conduct longitudinal studies of immigrants, which, of course, include English-speaking immigrants. These surveys are designed to both evaluate settlement programs and inform future policy-making. However, they include all immigrants, but not all disaggregate for those for whom English is not a first language.

Despite making this differentiation, the Australian survey asks about previous English classes, both AMEP and others, and bases findings about the benefits of such programs on learners' responses. It has been shown that learners are not able to differentiate among the different English classes they may have taken, let alone the type of program (general English, vocational English)—for example, in the AMEP, in TAFE, or in community-based programs. Therefore, it is not feasible to draw conclusions about the benefits of any *particular* course or program. Until data are tied to databases of the AMEP, TAFE etc. it will not be possible to determine which courses resulted in improved workforce participation, or even which courses students preferred. In addition, because these surveys all rely on self-report data, it is not possible to be certain whether respondents applied different cultural interpretations to questions, even when provided in their own language. For example, prior to entry to Australia, immigrants and refugees are asked to self-report their English level. This is voluntary, so some do not report. Others, concerned that lack of English might hinder their application being accepted, over-estimate their proficiency and, when tested by the AMEP on arrival, are found to have much lower proficiency (Murray & Lloyd, 2007).

The New Zealand survey provides details of immigrants' profiles six months after arrival, with a focus on skills and resources, labor market participation, and economic and social integration. The results strongly support selection policies that value immigrants with the language, skills, and qualifications that complement the needs of the New Zealand labor force (Department of Labour, 2009).

As a result, policy work on VESL tends to revolve around a nation's need for an educated workforce and the consequences of an unprepared workforce. It ties education to global competitiveness, positions learners in terms of their deficit in a time of crisis, and decries an education system that is failing to meet the challenges of globalization. While largely referring to high school graduates (whether second language learners or not), the findings of this research also drive VESL provision. ESL learners have to find their place in this same environment. A recent report in the US provides an insight into the policy trend across all English-dominant countries (National Center on Education and the Economy, 2007, p. 8):

> Strong skills in English, mathematics, technology, and science, as well as literature, history, and the arts will be essential for many; beyond this, candidates will have to be comfortable with ideas and abstractions, good at both analysis and synthesis, creative and innovative, self-disciplined and well organized, able to learn very quickly and work well as a member of a team and have the flexibility to adapt quickly to frequent changes in the labor market as the shifts in the economy become ever faster and more dramatic.

Interestingly, although the focus was on how to improve US workers, the Commission conducted field research in Australia, Canada, England, and New Zealand (among other countries) to provide a comparative analysis. What is striking about the report is that, although it addressed all aspects of the education system, no attention was paid to immigration, to those who arrive in the US in high school with limited English or arrive as adults with limited English.

In Australia, a recent report on the future demand for labor specifically noted that by 2020, Australia would need an additional 500,00 (note Australia's population is only 21 million) vocationally educated workers because of the high numbers of people exiting the labor force with those skills (largely because of the aging population), and the expected growth in skilled jobs if Australia is to remain globally competitive (Richardson and Teese quoted in McDonald & Temple, 2008). Because of similar research predictions in the past, Australia (and Canada) encourages the inflow of human capital in the form of skilled immigrants, as well as supporting immigrants joining families already in the country, and refugees. Over the past decade, the skilled stream has constituted a larger proportion than the other streams and the skills focused on have been determined by labor shortages (Richardson & Lester, 2004). Richardson and Lester's comparison of labor outcomes, in terms of job satisfaction and income, between Australia and Canada, shows that Australia experienced superior outcomes because the skilled immigrants to Australia were more highly educated and had higher levels of English language proficiency, even though more than half of the immigrants came as skilled workers. Policy research such as this results in changes in criteria for accepting immigrants. Since English language proficiency is one of the criteria for skilled immigration, the primary visa holder is not part of the VESL cohort; however, spouses and teenage children often are, with the remainder of potential clients coming from the refugee and family immigration streams. In the US, in contrast, immigrants have less education relative to the average of the established population in the United States than they do in Australia (Garnaut, 2003).

Professionalism

Crandall (1993) differentiates between professionalism and professionalization. The former, she among others (Burton, 1998; Hargreaves, 1997) defines as professional growth. Professionalization, on the other hand, refers to development of the field of teaching English to speakers of other languages (TESOL) as a recognized profession. She therefore makes the claim that, while the field may lack professionalization (compared with medicine or law, for example), its practitioners are professionals because of their professionalism. A number of themes emerge within the general framework of professionalism—teacher qualifications, forms of professional development, and professional development opportunities.

Teacher Qualifications

Researchers and others agree that VESL (along with other adult ESL) teachers need appropriate training. In the US, for example, the 1998 Adult Education and Family Literacy Act provides resources to improve the quality of instructional staff. Despite this, many adult educators lack training in the teaching of adults (as opposed to children and young people).

As mentioned earlier, ESL is often conflated with adult literacy programs. Where this occurs, qualifications of ESL educators is seriously compromised, as noted in a comparative study of six English-dominant nations—the five I refer to in this chapter, as well as the Republic of Ireland (McKenna & Fitzpatrick, 2004, p. 7):

> Where the literacy instructors are professionally qualified, they have frequently been recruited from the school sector and may not have experience in teaching adults, specialist English as a second language, or adult literacy and numeracy, in the context of vocational education and training and the workplace.

Canadian researchers (Folinsbee, 2007b; Millar, 1997) have noted that often ESL instructors are not trained in teaching literacy, while literacy instructors are not trained in second language development or cross-cultural awareness. Both groups identified the need for additional training as part of their initial qualifications. There is, of course, a concern that neither group would have sufficient training to be effective with second language learners and not all second language learners need literacy education as they may be literate in the first language.

Forms of Professional Development

The importance of professional development is recognized throughout the literature. But the question not always answered is "what form of professional development?" Wallace (1994) identifies three types of professional education that are applicable to professional development, namely, the craft model, the applied science model, and the reflective model. In the craft model, expertise lies with an experienced teacher, who models and guides the novice. The applied science model is the most common form of training, often called the transmission model, in which empirical research findings are transmitted to teachers who apply the findings. The reflective model, in contrast, combines both received knowledge and experiential knowledge for the teacher to practice, reflect on, adjust practice, reflect again, and so on. Action research (see, for example, Chapter 15, this volume) and continuing cooperative development (Edge, 2002) are the two most widely known examples of reflective professional development. Melles (1999) found that "[a]nother tangible effect has been the contribution of teacher research to legitimating the local knowledge teachers have developed as valid research knowledge" (p. 8). In so doing, he contends, it empowered ESL within vocational institutions. A number of researchers (for example, Schaetzel, Peyton, & Burt, 2007; Smith & Gillepsie, 2007; Wigglesworth & Murray, 2007) have also found that professional development that is ongoing, systematic, and of high quality results in greater improvement in teaching than do one-day workshops with little or no follow-up or conference presentations.

Professional Development Opportunities

Crandall (1993) makes the point that part-time and casual instructors rarely are provided opportunities for professional development, unless they engage in it at their own expense, a finding supported by an extensive study of professional development in the vocational education sector in Australia (Harris, Simons, Hill, Smith, Pearce, & Blakeley et al., 2001).

Program Evaluation

There has been no large scale program of evaluation of vocational programs. However, a number of studies have examined the outcomes of programs. Many of these have used self-report data, such as interviews with or questionnaires for learners, teachers, and program administrators. Consequently, measures of successful outcomes have been inconsistent across studies. However, a number of trends can be found in the literature.

One measure of program success can be student achievement. This has been the primary methodology for evaluating vocational programs within the VET sector in Australia, through the National Reporting System (NRS). The NRS, funded jointly by the Australian National Training Authority (ANTA), and the then Department of Employment, Education and Training, was designed to report to government on "the outcomes of adult English language,[6] literacy and numeracy provision, in the VET system, in labour market programs and in the adult community education sector" (ANTA, 1996). However,

> It has long been used in other ways as well—as a means of evaluating the content and emphasis of adult basic education curricula, as a framework for the development of curriculum and assessment materials, and in the consideration of the language, literacy and numeracy requirements of training packages.
>
> (Perkins, 2005, p. 6)

Because vocational ESL falls within the vocational education and training (VET) sector as well as the AMEP, there is another reporting system, used by the AMEP, where program evaluation is based on retention of students, outcomes as measure by assessment of student learning, how many potential clients are reached, as well as periodic external program reviews and client satisfaction surveys. Since none of these separate out VESL from other general English courses, one cannot draw conclusions about the efficacy of VESL within either the VET or AMEP sectors.

The US also has an NRS for adult education outcomes, which are reported to Congress (US Department of Education, 2007). While they disaggregate data on English literacy from data on English language acquisition, results reported are numbers of clients served, and number of clients moving to the next level. There is no indication of type of program (e.g., general English, VESL, or citizenship).

Another measure of program success is persistence. In a study of three different VESL classes (Sticht, 2005), persistence was found to be directly related to learners' reasons for taking the VESL course. The National Research and Development Centre (NRDC) for Adult Literacy and Numeracy Learner Study in the UK (NRDC, 2008) examined the Skills for Life strategy to determine participation, retention, achievement, progression, and impact. While the study involved literacy, ESOL, and numeracy learners, it disaggregated the results to provide a clear picture of ESOL learners. Over the period 2000–2005, enrolments had more than doubled and achievements had risen. One aspect of progression was learners' moving on to higher level courses, a vocational course, getting a job, or workplace promotion. ESOL learners progressed at a similar rate to literacy and numeracy learners, with 63% of ESOL learners "moving on." When interviewed about their reasons for taking the ESOL classes, the vast majority said they wanted to learn English to be able to find employment, sometimes after taking a vocational course or certificate. They were highly motivated to receive some form of qualification (e.g., a certificate), a finding confirmed by other researchers (Miralles, 2004; Murray, 2005b, 2007). Miralles and Murray also found that learners wanted a clear pathway to employment, but often did not understand what that pathway was or how to find the information. In fact, the immigrants and refugees in their studies had little awareness of VET opportunities in their new country. Further, for learners who were aware of VET programs, their preference was for a vocational program with integrated English language support and work experience.

As well as exploring issues for learners, the NRDC Learner Study examined providers' opinions of the Skills for Life strategy. They found that the profile of basic skills had been raised, which "had led to greater national awareness of literacy, ESOL and numeracy needs and an increased focus on the need to embed literacy, ESOL and numeracy within other courses, particularly vocational training" (NRDC, 2008, p. 45).

Since learners' goals in taking a VESL course are to gain employment, one would assume that their satisfaction would be related to obtaining a job. The literature is scant in this area as very few studies have followed learners past their VESL course/program. Some studies show that levels of satisfaction are related to how closely the vocational class fits the learners' purposes. McDonald (1997) found that a very specific electronics assembly course had the highest satisfaction rating and employment levels and was the most closely linked to actual jobs while Murray (2007) found that learners were satisfied with general certificates such as first aid or computer applications as they were components of these particular learners' goals. In Australia, almost all occupations requiring a VET certification require a first aid certificate. Others were satisfied with taking the drivers' license course because this was often a prerequisite for many jobs, such as delivery. Similarly, many of the vocational courses learners proposed to take once they had reached the requisite English proficiency required computer skills. The courses that learners found most engaging and led to high satisfaction and persistence were team-taught courses where learners achieved both a language certification and credit towards a VET certificate. In her study, Murray (2007) found that, even though learners in one adjunct course were achieving ESL certification and course credits towards a vocational certificate in information technology, many had no intention of completing the certificate program in information technology. They had chosen this adjunct course because they knew that whatever job they got in Australia, they would most likely need computer skills.

Some learners take the VESL course as preliminary to undertaking a vocational skill program. Therefore, another measure of success could be successful completion of such training. In interviews with students currently enrolled in vocational training, Murray (2007) found that these learners believed they were well prepared for the course, having taken VESL previously. One particular program included an innovative method for learners to determine whether they were indeed ready for vocational training. As an alternative to work experience that was part of the VESL course, students could take study experience, where they audited a course in the training program they intended to enroll in and could judge for themselves their readiness for mainstream classes.

An issue often raised about CBI and therefore VESL, is whether content is learned to the detriment of language learning. Both McDonald and Murray's studies demonstrate that "content-based instruction can lead to equally high gain in general literacy skills as well as job related skills" (McDonald, 1997, p. 5).

Future Directions for Research

As a result of the overview above, future research needs to take different theoretical approaches, as well as use a variety of research methodologies and measurements.

Theoretical Approaches

A 2002–2004 study in Australia (Chappell, Rhodes, Solomon, Tennant, & Yates, 2003; Solomon, 2007), while not focusing on ESL specifically, but vocational training more generally, provides a new way of looking at all vocational programs for adults. They problematize such instruction and ask what pedagogical practices help prepare adult learners for the workplace, why "authentic" and "real-world" labels entice both learners and educators into believing they have the holy grail for preparing learners for the workplace. Their findings thus far indicate that simulations are just as "unreal" as other pedagogical activities. They further question the whole enterprise of integrating work and learning in line with the current economic imperative for learning—how are learners and workers being constructed? Such a direction is also vital for policy research that seeks to examine the effects of low English language levels on workforce participation. Current research referred to above primarily uses an economic model but, more recently, many researchers have been calling for investigations that include social capital as part of expected and desirable outcomes (see, for example, Hartley & Horne, 2006).

Another direction, especially important for VESL is the decoupling of ESL from adult literacy. By grouping these two client groups together, there is no clear picture of either groups' needs, achievements, or preferences. So, for example, the extensive UK study on basic skills and its effect on employability provides no information about second language learners, even though they were included in the data (Bynner, McIntosh, Vignoles, Dearden, Reed, & van Reenan, 2001). Similarly, the comparative study of 14 Organisation for Economic Co-operation and Development (OECD) countries by Canadian researchers (Coulombe, Tremblay, & Marchand, 2004) does not disaggregate for ESL/native speaker literacy.

A further important focus is professional development, one that is also related to the issue of differentiating between literacy and language education. There is a dearth of research in the area of teacher qualifications and professional development, even though much of the literature and the standards promulgated by professional bodies, such as TESOL (TESOL, 2008) and the UK government, emphasize the importance of appropriate, effective professional development.

Research Methodologies and Measurements

Different methodologies need to be used, in addition to case studies and other small-scale qualitative studies. Without longitudinal studies, the full impact of a program on learners' lives is not visible. Learners in several studies referred to above indicated they wanted clear pathways through ESL, vocational training, and on to employment. It is therefore important to follow learner pathways to determine patterns, barriers, and opportunities. Although Australia, Canada, New Zealand, and the United States have conducted longitudinal studies, they are based on self-report data, and so are unreliable regarding the impact of vocational programs on learners' future workforce participation. Without comparative studies that clearly indicate program components and outcomes and participant characteristics, there is no certainty about best practice for which particular clients. McKay's (2007, p. 5) report, for example, indicates that successful programs not only teach vocational language, but also use a case management approach

> providing a range of supports to help them overcome their barriers to successful integration in the workplace, while at the same time working closely with employers who provide input to the curriculum and skills development and ultimately provide employment for the trainees.

Without large, multi-site studies, the range of learners is not represented, and there is no comparison of different programs and their outcomes. How should outcomes be measured? As mentioned above, income is not the only measure of learner (and program) success. So, a more rigorous, but inclusive theory of outcomes is needed, as well as the development of instruments to measure the different components of outcome in order to provide adult immigrants with learning experiences they need to become fully participating members of their new country.

Notes

1 Terminology varies across countries. Australia and New Zealand refer to immigrants as migrants. I have used the term immigrants throughout, except when citing Australian and New Zealand sources. I use refugee here to include both those coming through the United Nations High Commissioner for Refugees (UNHCR), asylum seekers, and humanitarian entrants whose status has been determined by the host country rather than the UNHCR.

2 Again, terminology varies. I will primarily use learners, although occasionally clients, the preferred term in Australia.

3 Their research reports are available free on their website: http://www.ncver.edu.au (accessed July 12, 2010).

4 Prior to 2000, the AMEP Research Centre was housed within the National Centre for Language Teaching and Research (NCELTR).

5 I do not wish to imply that English language proficiency is only valuable because of potential workforce participation. Research clearly shows that immigrants with low levels of English language proficiency experience more health problems and psychological stress, and are less likely to seek help in these areas (Carrington, McIntosh, & Walmsley, 2007). However, the current focus of governments on economic progress as a major indicator of a successful society drives the impetus to equate successful immigration with workforce participation.

6 Within the VET sector in Australia, language is used for ESL learners, literacy for those for whom English is a first language.

References

ANTA. (1996). *National reporting system professional development kit.* Melbourne: ANTA.

Auerbach, E. R., & Burgess, D. (1985). The hidden curriculum of survival ESL. *TESOL Quarterly, 19*(3), 475–495.

Batalova, J., Fix, M., & Creticos, P. A. (2008). *Uneven progress: The employment pathways of skilled immigrants in the United States.* Retrieved May 28, 2009, from http://www.migrationpolicy.org/pubs/BrainWasteOct08.pdf.

Boyd, M., DeVries, J., & Simkin, K. (1994). Language, economic status and integration. In H. Adelman, A. Borowski, M. Burstein & L. Foster (Eds.), *Immigration and refugee policy: Australia and Canada compared. Volume 1 & II* (pp. 549–577). Melbourne: Melbourne University Press.

Brinton, D. M., & Master, P. (Eds.) (1997). *New ways in content-based instruction.* Alexandria, VA: Teachers of English to Speakers of Other Languages.

Brinton, D. M., Snow, M. A., & Wesche, M. B. (1989). *Content-based second language instruction.* New York: Newbury House.

Burnley, I. H., Murphy, P., & Fagan, R. (1997). *Immigration and Australian cities.* Sydney: Federation Press.

Burton, J. (1998). Professionalism in language teaching. *Prospect, 13*(3), 24–34.

Bynner, J., McIntosh, S., Vignoles, A., Dearden, L., Reed, H., & van Reenan, J. (2001). *Improving adult basic skills: Benefits to the individuals and to society (research brief no. 251).* London: DfEE.

Carrington, K., McIntosh, A., & Walmsley, J. (2007). *The social costs and benefits of migration into Australia.* Retrieved June 20, 2009, from http://www.immi.gov.au/media/publications/research/social-costs-benefits/.

Chamot, A. (1995). Implementing the Cognitive Academic Language Learning Approach: CALLA in Arlington, Virginia. *Bilingual Research Journal, 19*(2), 221–247.

Chappell, C. S., Rhodes, C. H., Solomon, N. V., Tennant, M. C., & Yates, L. S. (2003). *Reconstructing the lifelong learner: Pedagogy and identity in individual, organisational and social change.* London: Routledge.

Chisman, F. P., & Crandall, J. (2007). *Passing the torch: Strategies for innovation in community college ESL.* New York: Council for Advancement of Adult Literacy.

Chiswick, B. R., Cohen, Y., & Zach, T. (1997). The labour market status of immigrants: Effects of the unemployment rate at arrival and duration of residence. *Industrial and Labour Relations Review, 50*(2), 289–303.

Chiswick, B. R., Lee, Y., & Miller, P. W. (2003). Schooling, literacy, numeracy and labour market success. *The Economic Record, 79*(245), 165–181.

Coulombe, S., Tremblay, J.-F., & Marchand, S. (2004). *Literacy scores, human capital and growth across fourteen OECD countries.* Ottawa: Statistics Canada and Human Resources and Skills Development Canada.

Crandall, J. (1993). Professionalism and professionalization of adult ESL literacy. *TESOL Quarterly, 27*(3), 497–515.

Crandall, J. (1995). *ESL through content-area instruction.* McHenry, IL: Delta Systems.Cunningham Florez, M. (1998). Concepts and terms in adult ESL [electronic version]. Retrieved June 20, 2009, from http://www.cal.org/caela/esl_resources/digests/termsQA.html.

Department of Labour. (2009). *New faces, new futures: New Zealand.* Retrieved June 24, 2009, from http://www.immigration.govt.nz/NR/rdonlyres/8981E7D8-E9E8-4BA5-B53B-0D781274A289/0/Introduction.pdf.

Edge, J. (2002). *Continuing cooperative development: A discourse framework for individuals as colleagues.* Ann Arbor, MI: University of Michigan.

Folinsbee, S. (2007a). *International workforce literacy review—Canada.* Retrieved June 24, 2009, from http://dol.govt.nz/PDFs/upskilling-2007-canada.pdf.

Folinsbee, S. (2007b). *Linkages: Connecting literacy and English as a second language.* Retrieved June 20, 2009, from http://library.nald.ca/research/item/6915.

Garnaut, R. (2003). *Migration to Australia and comparisons with the United States: Who benefits?* Retrieved June 20, 2009, from http://www.immi.gov.au/media/publications/pdf/mig_aust_us_compare.pdf.

Hargreaves, A. (1997). The four ages of professionalism and professional learning. *Unicorn, 23*(2), 86–114.

Harris, R., Simons, M., Hill, D., Smith, E., Pearce, R., Blakeley, J., Choy, S., & Snewin, D. (2001). *The changing role of staff development for teachers and trainers in vocational education and training.* Retrieved June 7, 2002, from http://www.ncver.edu.au/research/proj/nr8018.pdf.

Hartley, R., & Horne, J. (2006). *Social and economic benefits of improved adult literacy: Towards a better understanding.* Adelaide: NCVER.

Jasso, G., Massey, D. S., Rosenzweig, M. R., & Smith, J. P. (in press). The U.S. New Immigrant Survey: Overview and preliminary results based on the new-immigrant cohorts of 1996 and 2003. In B. Morgan & B. Nicholson (Eds.), *Immigration research and statistics service workshop on longitudinal surveys and cross-cultural survey design: Workshop proceedings* (pp. 29–46). London: Crown Publishing.

Johns, A. (1992). What is the relationship between content-based instruction and English for specific purposes? *The CATESOL Journal, 5*(1), 71–75.

Jupp, T. C., & Hodlin, S. (1975). *Industrial English: An example of the theory and practice in functional language teaching.* London: Heinemann.

Kasper, L. F. (1999). *Content-based college ESL instruction: An overview.* Mahwah, NJ: Lawrence Erlbaum Associates , Inc.

Leitch, S. (2006). *The Leitch review of skills: Prosperity for all in the global economy—world class skills.* Norwich: HMSO.

Lowes, D. (2004). Australian politics and the AMEP. *TESOL in Context, 13*(2), 16–20.

McDonald, B. (1997). The impact of content-based instruction: Three studies. *Focus on Basics, 1*(D), 1–6.

McDonald, P., & Temple, J. (2008). *Demographic and labour supply futures for Australia.* Retrieved June 23, 2009, from http://www.immi.gov.au/media/publications/research/_pdf/demo-labour-supply.pdf.

McKay, A. (2007). An investigation of strategies and programs that assist refugees and migrants into employment. A report to the Winston Churchill Trust of Australia. Unpublished manuscript.

McKenna, R., & Fitzpatrick, L. (2004). *Building sustainable adult literacy provision: A review of international trends in adult literacy policy and programs.* Retrieved June 20, 2009, from http://www.ncver.edu.au/research/proj/nr2L07.pdf.

Master, P. (1997). ESP teacher education in the USA. In R. Howard & G. Brown (Eds.), *Teacher education for LSP* (pp. 22–40). Clevedon: Multilingual Matters.

Melles, G. (1999). Negotiating curriculum constraints in ESOL through teacher research. Paper presented at the AAIR Conference 1.

Millar, D. (1997). *Second language students in Canadian literacy programs: Current issues and concerns.* Retrieved June 28, 2009, from http://www.nald.ca/library/research/slsinclp/cover.htm.

Miralles, J. (2004). *A fair go: Factors impacting on vocational education and training participation and completion in selected ethnic communities.* Retrieved June 7, 2005, from http://www.ncver.edu.au/research/proj/nr2L22/Miralles.pdf.

Mohan, B. A. (1986). *Language and content.* Reading, MA: Addison-Wesley Publishing Company.

Mohan, B. A., Leung, C., & Davison, C. (Eds.) (2001). *English as a second language in the mainstream.* Harlow: Longman.

Moser, S. C. (1999). *A fresh start: Improving literacy and numeracy.* London: DfEE.

Murray, D. E. (2005a). ESL in adult education. In E. Hinkel (Ed.), *Handbook of research in second language teaching and learning.* Mahwah, NJ: Lawrence Erlbaum Associates.

Murray, D. E. (2005b). *Vocational training and the AMEP* (Teaching issues no. 5). Sydney: AMEP Research Centre

Murray, D. E. (2007). *Vocational content for the certificates in spoken and written English.* Sydney: NCELTR.

Murray, D. E., & Lloyd, R. (2007). *Uptake of AMEP provision by youth from Africa: Opportunities and barriers.* Sydney: NCELTR.

National Center on Education and the Economy. (2007). *Tough choices or tough times: The report of the New Commission on the Skills of the American Workforce: executive summary.* San Francisco: Jossey-Bass.

NRDC. (2008). *The learner study: The impact of the Skills for Life Strategy on adult literacy, language and numeracy learners.* London: NRDC.

Office of Literacy and Essential Skills. (2007). Workplace skills: Essential skills [electronic version]. Retrieved May 25, 2009, from http://www.nald.ca/fulltext/sticht/31jan05/31jan05.pdf.

Papademetriou, D. G. (2007). *Selecting economic stream immigrants through points systems.* Retrieved June 30, 09, from http://www.migrationinformation.org/Feature/display.cfm?ID=602.

Perkins, K. (2005). *Reframe, rename, revitalise: Future directions for the language, literacy and numeracy National Reporting System.* Retrieved June 25, 2009, from http://www.ncver.edu.au/research/proj/nr3L09.pdf.

Princeton University. (2003). *The new immigrant study.* Retrieved June, 30, 2009, from http://nis.princeton.edu/nis_2003_questionaires.html.

Richardson, S., & Lester, L. (2004). *A comparison of Australian and Canadian immigration policies and labour market outcomes.* Retrieved June 20, 2009, from http://www.immi.gov.au/media/publications/pdf/comparison_immigration_policies.pdf.

Richardson, S., Miller-Lewis, L., Ngo, P., & Ilsley, D. (2002). *Life in a new land: The experience of migrants in Wave 1 of LSIA 1 and LSIA 2.* Retrieved June 20, 2009, from http://www.immi.gov.au/media/publications/multicultural/lsia/title.pdf.

Roberts, C. (2005). English in the workplace. In E. Hinkel (Ed.), *Handbook of research in second language teaching and learning* (pp. 117–135). Mahwah, NJ: Lawrence Erlbaum Associates, Inc.

Schaetzel, K., Peyton, J. K., & Burt, M. (2007). *Professional development for adult ESL practitioners: Building capacity.* Retrieved June 30, 2009, from http://cal.org/caela/esl_resources/briefs/profdev.html.

Schwartzenegger, A. (2005). Governor makes major investment in vocational education with new law [electronic version]. Retrieved May 26, 2009, from http://gov.ca.gov/index.php?/press-release/1393/.

Smith, C., & Gillepsie, M. (2007). Research on professional development and teacher change: Implications for Adult Basic Education. *Review of Adult Learning and Literacy, 7,* 205–244.

Snow, M. A., & Brinton, D. M. (1997). *The content-based classroom.* White Plains, NY: Longman.

Solomon, N. V. (2007). Reality bit(e)s: Bringing the "real" world of working to educational classrooms. In M. Osborne, M. Houston, & N. Toman (Eds.), *Researching the pedagogy of lifelong learning* (pp. 115–126). London: Routledge.

Statistics Canada. (2001). *Longitudinal survey of immigrants to Canada.* Retrieved June 25, 2009, from http://www.statcan.gc.ca/survey-enquete/household-menages/lsic-elic/immigr-eng.htm.

Statistics Canada. (2003). *Longitudinal survey of immigrants to Canada: Progress and challenges of new immigrants in the workforce.* Retrieved June 25, 2009, from http://www.statcan.gc.ca/pub/89-615-x/89-615-x2005001-eng.pdf.

Sticht, T. (2005). Persistence in English as a second language (ESL) programs: Research using the method of natural variations [electronic version]. Retrieved May 25, 2009, from http://www.nald.ca/fulltext/sticht/31jan05/31jan05.pdf.

TESOL. (2008). *Standards for ESL/EFL teachers of adults.* Retrieved June 30, 2009, from http://www.tesol.org/s_tesol/seccss.asp?CID=1974&DID=12056.

US Department of Education. (2007). *Adult education annual report to Congress 2004–05.* Retrieved June 19, 2009, from http://www.nrsweb.org/reports/documents/AEFLACongressionalReportFY04-05.pdf.

US Department of Labor. (1991). What work requires of schools: A SCANS report for America 2000 Washington, DC: US Department of Labor (ERIC No. ED 332 054).

Van Duzer, C., Kreeft Peyton, J., & Comings, J. (1998). *A research agenda for adult ESL.* Washington, DC: Center for Applied Linguistics.

Wallace, M. (1994). *Training foreign language teachers: A reflective approach.* Cambridge: Cambridge University Press.

Wigglesworth, G., & Murray, D. E. (2007). Opening doors: Teachers learning through collaborative research. *Prospect, 22*(1), 19–36.

Williams, A. (2004). *Fact-sheet—Enhancing language teaching with content.* Sydney: AMEP Research Centre.

Wong, K. (1992). What do VESL and content-based instruction have in common? *The CATESOL Journal, 5*(1), 97–101.

Wooden, M. (1994). The labour market experience of immigrants. In M. Wooden, R. Holton, G. Hugo, & J. Sloan (Eds.), *Australian immigration: A survey of the issues.* Canberra: Australian Government Publication Service.

6
English for Academic Purposes

Liz Hamp-Lyons

What Is EAP?

English for academic purposes (EAP) has emerged out of the broader field of English for specific purposes (ESP), defined by its focus on teaching English specifically to facilitate learners' study or research through the medium of English (Flowerdew & Peacock, 2001, p. 8; Hyland & Hamp-Lyons, 2002, p. 1). EAP is differentiated from ESP by this focus on academic contexts, but among the applied linguistics and English language teaching fields more widely the view of EAP as a sub-discipline within ESP still holds. Indeed, both these views are valid, as the histories of ESP and EAP do not distinguish between a view of them as parent to child, or as sister fields. It is not unusual to find articles with an EAP focus in the pages of the *English for Specific Purposes Journal*, but EAP work also appears in all the applied linguistics and English language teaching (ELT) journals from time to time. Differentiation depends more on the interests and concerns of the researcher than on the kind of data being discussed. In the "Aims and Scope" statement of the *Journal of English for Academic Purposes* (*JEAP*), published in the front matter of every issue and on the website (www.elsevier.com/locate/JEAP), Hyland and Hamp-Lyons define the scope of EAP as "the linguistic, sociolinguistic and psycholinguistic description of English *as it occurs in the contexts of academic study and scholarly exchange itself*".

Similarly, it is possible, indeed reasonable, to view EAP as a branch within education, or at least within language education: this is a view I hold myself. EAP teachers take pride in their expertise in classroom teaching, their responsiveness to students' needs through curriculum planning and materials development, through individualization of support to students and through context-aware educational management. But EAP is an eclectic and pragmatic discipline: a wide range of linguistic, applied linguistic and educational topics can be considered from the perspective of English for academic purposes, or drawn in methodologically to inform EAP. These include classroom language, teaching methodology, teacher education, assessment of language, needs analysis, materials development and evaluation, discourse analysis, acquisition studies in EAP contexts, research writing and speaking at all academic levels, the sociopolitics of English in academic uses and language planning—and this list is sure to be incomplete.

Drawing on the wisdom of our own discipline, we can turn to the work of John Swales, the British language teacher, applied linguist and academic advisor par excellence, who has worked around the world in EAP and ESP contexts, but at the University of Michigan for the past almost 30 years, to help us think about whether EAP, or ESP, or indeed any aspect of (applied) linguistics, is a discipline or sub-discipline in its own right. Swales' seminal book *Genre Analysis* (1990) teaches us the complexity that lies behind defining a single genre, let alone an entire discipline. But it also offers us a valuable way of organizing our thinking about disciplinarity: the concept of a *discourse community*. Swales defines discourse communities as

> sociorhetorical networks that form in order to work towards sets of common goals. One of the characteristics that established members of these discourse communities possess is familiarity with the particular genres that are used in the communicative furtherance of those common goals.
>
> (Swales, 1990, p. 9)

More recently this discourse communities view has been embraced and expanded as EAP has grown ever more complex with the identification of more and more goals. But few applied linguists inhabit only one discourse community. Work centrally located in or relevant to EAP can be found across a wide range of journals apart from *JEAP* and the *ESP Journal*, including *TESOL Quarterly, Applied Linguistics, Language Learning* as well as regional journals such as the *RELC Journal* and *Asia TEFL Journal*. Quite naturally, interest in English for academic purposes exists wherever English teachers are teaching English to learners within or in preparation for their academic studies.

The Early Years

In the 1950s and 1960s, Britain began to receive increasing numbers of international students funded by the British Council as part of the government policy of aid to developing countries. At the same time Britain was responding to the rapid growth in many countries of English as a common language for business and science, and there was an explosion of need for English teachers to deliver language teaching in-country at fairly low levels. ESP seemed the answer in the second context, while EAP seemed the answer for the minority of these language learners who progressed to study in Britain. Given this parallel history and close relationship it is not surprising that for many years EAP was seen by many as a sub-set of ESP (Strevens, 1977). Issues of audience—or customers—may have seemed the only reason for differentiating ESP and EAP early on, but as time went by other explanations for different trajectories emerged.

As Swales (2000) has described, ESP had seemed "eminently manageable to early LSP practitioners, who were often working in underprivileged environments and who were also having to administer programs, develop teaching materials, and do a fair amount of teaching" (p. 60). Swales points out that this 'manageable' new discipline grew from the work of Halliday, McIntosh and Strevens (1964), during the period when applied linguistics, and indeed English language teaching (or, in the US, "TESOL") were growing, self-defining and consolidating through the creation of professional bodies. ESP was part of that brave new world: Halliday, McIntosh and Strevens (1964) saw the critical first step as being linguistic description in order to establish language learning needs, from which decisions about curriculum and materials could be made: that is, their purposes were practical. However, it is worth noting that these three pioneers were themselves imbued in the academic tradition. Michael Halliday of course went on to become possibly the most well-known applied linguist of the English language, developing the theory of systemic-functional grammar in which he continues to research, write and lecture; Angus McIntosh was in 1964 already approaching retirement as Forbes Professor of English Language and General Linguistics at the University of Edinburgh, and was a medievalist and historian of language; only Peter Strevens had at that stage a real focus on language teaching, and his period at the University of Edinburgh, working with McIntosh and Halliday, was important in the founding of the School of Applied Linguistics. From this starting point, we might consider that the floating of the ideas behind ESP was more aspirational than actual.

The genesis of EAP seems to have been quite different. In the first issue of the *JEAP*, Bob Jordan describes the beginnings of what eventually became the field of EAP in Britain:

> In the 1960s, language support that was provided to international students tended to be on an ad hoc, part-time basis. As problems occurred or developed during studies, some kind of part-time help may have become available, often linked to ELT teacher-training courses in Departments of Education. This sometimes led to the development of short courses, e.g. four weeks at the beginning of the students' studies. Birmingham University appears to have been the first to be seriously concerned about the needs of overseas students. Vera Adamson, who had joined the University in 1958, was appointed in 1962 to advise overseas students and to start induction courses. This involved analyzing students' problems, developing some teaching materials as well as teaching part-time, and trying to devise an analytical test.
>
> (Jordan, 2002, p. 70)

This grass roots, practical response to an immediate problem characterised the beginnings of EAP. But it also made EAP a "poor relation" in academic environments and slowed the recognition of EAP as a field in its own right, as might be seen in the history of the two fields' journals. The *ESP Journal* began in 1980, and had a small hiatus before John Swales and Ann Johns began editing it in 1985: in 2010 it is in its twenty-ninth volume. *JEAP* is by contrast in its ninth volume, having begun publishing in 2002. It is interesting that Hewings, as recently as 2002, still feels able to analyse trends in "ESP" and mention EAP only in passing (Hewings, 2002).

Three Decades of Growth and Developing Tradition

Two developments characterise the period from the early 1970s to around the end of the century. These will now be discussed.

Supporting International Students

First, in response to the increasing demand from international applicants for access to universities in English-speaking countries, which began largely through the British Council in Britain, and through USIS in the US universities, there was steady growth in EAP support to international students. As Jordan (2002) reports, in the early years attention outside the classroom itself focused on students' needs, and this is both typical of any response to an emerging market, and entirely appropriate for a group of young and enthusiastic teachers encountering a new educational problem (Candlin, Kirkwood & Moore, 1975; Robinson, 1988). Consequently, much attention in EAP in those early years centred on two very practical areas: needs analysis and materials development.

Needs Analysis

Carkin (2005) in her overview of EAP, says that "[n]eeds assessment of the diverse learners in EAP underlies syllabus design, materials development, text selection, learning goals and tasks, and, ultimately, evaluation of students and course or program success" (p. 87). Important needs analyses were conducted in the 1970s and 1980s by, for example, Bridgeman and Carlson (1983); Johns (1981); Hutchinson and Waters (1987); and Munby (1978). Needs analysis became an near-inevitable first step in developing English language provision in a new situation (e.g. Zughoul & Hussein, 1985). Coleman (1988) problematised Munby's and similar needs models as discounting learners as people, and as assuming that identifying needs necessarily leads to satisfying them; Coleman suggested a more complex model. As time has gone by, needs analysis work has become more tightly focused and sophisticated, and has embraced a wider range of data collection and analytic methods (Holliday, 1995; Ferris & Tagg, 1996) as well as focusing on specific countries or sociopolitical contexts (Chia, Johnson, Chia & Olive, 1998; Dushku, 1998).

Materials Development

Allied with the focus on needs was a concern to develop appropriate materials. While discipline-specific materials were the main trend in the early years (e.g. the Nucleus series edited by Bates and Dudley-Evans, and the Focus series edited by Widdowson), in EAP materials intended to provide basic preparation for good study habits became popular and successful in the late 1970s and 1980s (e.g. Wallace, 1980; Williams, 1982; Salimbene, 1985). A Google search will quickly show that "study skills" materials and texts are now a major business around the world. As time has gone by, materials to help students with more advanced study, in particular research paper writing, have become prominent (Hamp-Lyons & Courter, 1984; Menasche, 1984; Weissburg & Buker, 1990; Swales & Feak, 2004/1994; Cooley & Lewkowitz, 2003; Paltridge & Starfield, 2007). But also, a sign of increasing sophistication in the field is the predominance of in-house development targeting EAP materials to the language levels, cultural backgrounds, etc. of the student groups being received into the particular institution.

English as the Language of Knowledge Exchange

The second significant development in EAP in its first 30 years or so has been the gradual growth of English as the leading language for the dissemination of academic knowledge. This development has come from outside EAP, as most disciplines have progressively switched from publishing in journals in their own language to publishing in journals in English. This is part of the globalisation trend in English (Swales, 1997; Crystal, 1997; Salager-Meyer, 2008). But along with this trend has come growth in attention to what Hyland and Hamp-Lyons (2002) referred to as "advanced EAP" such as English for research publication purposes (e.g. Swales & Feak, 2001; Prior's body of work with the language of graduate students (Prior, 1998); a special issue of *JEAP* (7, 2) on English for research publication purposes). An extension of this area has been the development of programmes within universities, and consultancies specifically aimed at supporting non-native academics in their efforts to publish in international, English-medium journals (e.g. Cargill & O'Connor (2006) on working with Chinese scientists; Sengupta, Forey & Hamp-Lyons (1999) on the development of such a programme at the Hong Kong Polytechnic University). Research into the publication genres themselves was pioneered by Swales (1981), and is a consistent thread of EAP research, for example by Swales and Najjar (1987), Hopkins and Dudley-Evans (1988), Peacock (2002), Sionis (1995), Flowerdew (1999), Mišak, Marušić and Marušić (2005), and Van Bonn and Swales (2007). Thus, we can also see that the expansion of "English for academic publication" as a lingua franca has benefits for international scholarly communication (Tardy, 2004) despite persistent concerns that the expanding use of English is having negative effects on scholarly publishing in other languages (Salager-Meyer, 2008) and in fuelling 'diaspora scholarship' (Welch & Zhen, 2008; Altbach, 2002).

The Current Situation

Practice and Pedagogy

In the past ten years or so EAP has become a larger field, but also more patchwork and fragmented, at least from the point of view of programme delivery. The ad hoc, small-scale, quick fix attitude that typified the modest beginnings of EAP teaching still pertains, and "study skills", "academic writing for international students", "seminar skills" and various other labels remain not only as the legacy of the field of EAP but also as appropriate titles for active curricula. Nevertheless, at the same time we can see a more mature approach to EAP practice emerging. A pattern seems to be becoming established whereby the usual teaching solutions in English first language contexts within universities, where (as is usually the case these days) a large proportion of students, particularly graduate students, are international students and non-native speakers of English, are for English language teachers to start from EAP solutions based on formal or informal needs analysis, but with some move towards ESP solutions in specific cases, such as, for example, designing and delivering in-programme language support for law students, or agricultural engineers. EAP teachers are more qualified and more committed than ever; at least in Britain, Australia, New Zealand and the US, EAP programmes and centres are firmly established and stable, allowing curriculum and programme development to flourish.

Research and Scholarship

The appearance on the scene in 2002 of the *JEAP* was a clear indication that EAP had come of age as an independent academic field, closely allied with ESP but with an identity and community of its own. *JEAP* was indeed a twenty-first century development. While the first issue had retrospective articles (all 2002 in References) by Ann Johns and John Swales, and by Bob Jordan, it also had articles very much of their time at the start of a new century by Suresh Canagarajah on the roles and relationships of multilingual writers in the academic community, and by George Braine on non-native graduate students specifically; it also had a very much forward-looking article by Mark Warschauer on the effects of new forms of information and communication technologies on curriculum and pedagogy in academic writing courses, where "students are still expected to master fairly traditional forms of academic writing, including essays, compositions, and, perhaps eventually, theses, dissertations, and scholarly articles" (2002, p. 45). The journal is not restricted to reports of empirical research; in fact it seeks a mix of research and practice, but nevertheless the bulk of papers, nor surprisingly, are from university staff in research-line posts. That such posts exist is itself a testimony to the maturity of the field and of its increasing acceptance in university systems. But *JEAP* is not the only journal by far that publishes EAP research and scholarship, as can be seen in the References to this chapter.

With the increase in published work on EAP, it has become possible to see the strands in the field that are continuing and strengthening in this first decade of a new century, and to see where new developments lie.

EAP and "Discourse Communities"

As Hyland and Hamp-Lyons (2002, p. 6) suggest,

> it is difficult to imagine EAP without some notion of community. It is central to our understanding of the ways individuals acquire and deploy the specialized discourse competencies that allow them to legitimate their professional identities and to effectively participate as group members.

This discourse community has been strengthened by the existence of its own journal, which forms a shared discursive space. The discourse community approach has been validated and strengthened by the socio-cultural direction of academic research in the twenty-first century (discussed later): it has fostered research that couples more traditional EAP textual analysis with the practices that surround their use, and with research drawing on ethnographic and action research methodologies in addition to discourse studies (e.g. Swales, 1998). Swales' (2009) look back on "an educational life" permeates his personal reminiscences not only with people and places, but also with the interconnections between these and his thinking about ESP, EAP, the needs of students, the peculiarities of educational institutions, and above all his desire to solve problems: through all of this we find the notion of a community of idea exchange, of adapting to contexts to come up with solutions and new principles. Swales' lifelong body of academic work is permeated with notions of his community as founded in discourse. The concept of "discourse communities" has become an important organising principle in EAP research, enabling scholars to look at the genres and communicative conventions of academic disciplines both linguistically and pedagogically, to unpack what marks a particular discourse community, and to use this understanding in teaching and in materials (see, for example, Hyland, 2002b, 2004).

At the same time, the discourse community concept also enables researchers to identify differences as well as patterns, between disciplines, within disciplines over time, across national research traditions and so on. Discourse communities are not fixed and static, and have no agreed-upon procedures, conventions or even values. Discourse communities are built by their members, and membership is always in flux (Becher, 1989). But we now know that becoming an effective scholar means joining an academic discourse community, and we know many of the processes that this "apprenticeship" entails: the work by Belcher (1994) is exemplary in this area, and the considerable work in this area in Australasia through HERDSA (Higher Education Research and Development Society of Australasia) is particularly of note (see, for example, Robinson-Pant, 2009; Tynan & Garbett, 2008; Woodward-Kron, 2007). And yet, the movement from researching to teaching community-building and membership skills is only beginning. To this end, it is essential to investigate claims about academic genres, patterns or behaviours. Supervisors as well as graduate students have learned much from Swales and Feak's (2001) guide to *English in today's research world*, which unpacks the conventional structures of research writing, opening a world of access for novice writers of research through English while maintaining a necessary hedging about the universality of particular structures and behaviours. Paltridge (2002) conducted an important study of whether published advice on how to organise a PhD thesis or Master's dissertation coincides with what happens, and is acceptable, in practice: he found that there is a much wider variation in structures of theses and dissertations than would be expected from reading the guidebooks available (at that time). Paltridge has continued work in this direction (2005) taking us "behind the scenes" of scholarly publication. A better understanding of what signals "membership" in an academic community enables supervisors to be more creative with their students in permitting moves away from the so-called traditional scientific method; it also, of course, provides valuable directions for materials development for dissertation writing courses.

EAP and Disciplinary Variation

The concept of disciplinary variation is the point where EAP sits uneasily next to ESP. Where is the boundary line between two things being "similar" or "comparable", and them being decidedly "different"? Hyland and Hamp-Lyons (2002, p. viii) followed Dudley-Evans and St John (1998) in suggesting that EAP operates within a world where "the fundamental concern is the acquisition of knowledge by individuals", finding this focus on the individual helpful, since ESP and sub-fields such as English for business, English for nursing, etc. focus not on the learner as an individual but on a transactional world where the focus is on the text or the activity.

Excellent work has been done on disciplinary variation: see, for example, Conrad (1996), Berkenkotter and Huckin (1995), Bloor (1998) and Woodward-Kron (2008). While some have argued that by focusing on the differences in genres and discourse behaviours between disciplines, we make life more difficult for novice members of the academy (e.g. Spack, 1988), the current position is predominantly an understanding that while at the early levels of undergraduate study we can identify a common core of essential skills, this will not take students very far into their studies of their disciplines beyond the first year of university. In many situations the "academic literacies" position, as exemplified by the work of Lea and Street (1999) and Ivanič (1998) is a reasonable solution to specific contextual problems students encounter in the early stages; but as Johns (1995, p. 55) argues "[s]tudents must … adjust somewhat to each academic discipline they encounter". Hyland (2002a, p. 385) argues the strong case for specificity, that we must "teach … the literacy skills which are appropriate to the purposes and understandings of particular academic and professional communities". An excellent example of this principle in practice is found in the work of Rose, Rose, Farrington and Page (2007). My own would be the middle position: by looking in our academic research across as well as within disciplines we are much better able to understand how academic language and interaction work *within* disciplines, and to begin to understand which differences are significant, and why. We need to use linguistic tools to achieve this middle of the road perspective (see, for example, Hyland, 2008a; Silver, 2003). However, as Ken Hyland and I lamented (2002) EAP has inherited some of ESP's tendency to work *for* rather than *with* subject specialists, a weakness that seems not to have changed in the past eight years.

Genre Analysis in EAP

As the field of EAP has developed, the emphasis has swung gradually away from practical problem solving and implementation research and genre analytic studies have become dominant. We can see that genre analysis has proved a very fertile ground for EAP researchers. Early work looked at highly visible and obviously important aspects of academic genres: Swales' early EAP work was with research article introductions (1981), and his explication of "move analysis" (1990) has been used, adapted, defended and critiqued by many of his students and other EAP researchers. Much valuable work has been published in this area; for example, on journal results sections (Basturkmen, 2009) and acknowledgement sections (Giannoni, 1998), article submission letters (Swales, 1996), academic book reviews (Motta-Roth, 1998), academic recommendation letters (Precht, 1998) and research grant applications (Connor & Mauranen, 1999). Genre analysis studies have also researched the genres of advanced study, e.g. Bunton (1999, 2005) and Thompson (2005), following earlier work by Dudley-Evans in particular (Hopkins & Dudley-Evans, 1988). This research is increasingly going beyond textual genre analysis to look at phenomenological aspects of dissertation writing (Kwan, 2009; Li, 2006).

EAP Assessment

It will not surprise anyone that I should comment that EAP assessment seems to be the least-developed area of the field. A very few very big tests (TOEFL—the Test of English as a Foreign Language, IELTS—the International English Language Testing System, TOEIC—Test of English for International Communication) and, to some extent, the smaller, university-based tests (such as MELAB—Michigan English Language Battery, DELA/DELNA—Diagnostic English Language [New Zealand] Assessment and OTESL—Ontario Test of English as a Second Language) have become well-established for use in EAP contexts. A new test, the Pearson Test of English—Academic, has recently come on the scene. But the big tests, despite publicity claims, do not do well at solving placement questions within EAP programmes. Creativity in assessment for purposes such as placing students into EAP course provision according to their specific needs, informing departments whether their rising seniors are adequately equipped with the language/knowledge creation skills called for in senior thesis writing and advanced exams, and academic language skills assessment for movement from undergraduate to graduate education—these are all apparent needs, and yet little if any work has been done in these areas. We might expect, and wish, that universities would take up the demand in this regard, but there is little sign of this. Michigan's own EAP course placement system gets little publicity; the DELA in Australia and DELNA in New Zealand are growing in popularity, they have been researched and some publications are available (Knoch, 2009); but despite calls for locally-derived and properly validated EAP assessments (Jacoby & McNamara, 1999) there is little evidence that this is occurring.

New Media and Technologies

In the lifetime of EAP, the key cultural change worldwide has been the emergence of new media and means of communication. The letter has practically gone out of existence in developed countries. No one posts hard copies of journal article submissions to the Editor's office any more. We live with e-mail, mobile telephony, text messaging, Skype and so on. New genres emerge as a result of these technological developments. It is surprising to me that in our scholarly journals we see so little in the way of colour graphics, active weblinks, papers submitted (and published) as a series of Powerpoint slides, etc. Similarly, we and our students are also increasingly required to negotiate and understand complex interactions between verbal and non-verbal features of academic texts (Kress, 1998). The new technology has thoroughly permeated the lecture theatre, but research on academic listening has always been sorely under-represented in EAP (but see Flowerdew, 1994; Salehzadeh, 2005). It is time for us to understand much better than we do what our students face when they engage in the *academic literacy* event of lecture listening.

One valuable development for the EAP classroom has been the use of corpora and concordances, through computer systems, to allow EAP students to conduct their own mini research projects. Students have access to a corpus (ideally a locally-developed one, such as the Hong Kong Corpus of Spoken English at the Hong Kong Polytechnic University: http://langbank.engl.polyu.edu.hk/HKCSE/) and set their own, small, research questions and explore the corpus to find an answer. The activities of software handling, data manipulation, not to mention basic computer familiarisation, is valuable and motivating in its own right, as well as providing students with a hands-on exercise in figuring out how language works.

Corpus-Based Research in EAP

There is considerable attention to the application of corpus linguistic methods to the analysis of EAP spoken and written discourse, and academic language corpora have become a key tool of genre analysts in the past ten years. Hyland's work has been increasingly informed by corpora, as shown by, for example, his entertaining and valuable corpus analysis of Swales' own writing by comparison with a set of others' texts (2008b), and his somewhat more distanced but equally engaging study of academics as "humble servants of the discipline" (2001). Thompson's (2001) work on the macrostructures, citation practices and uses of modal verbs would hardly have been feasible before the advent of corpus technology. Bruce's (2008) study of genre structures in the methods sections of research articles is a good example of corpus-based work at the more micro-level.

There are now a number of excellent corpora: MICASE (Michigan Corpus of Academic Spoken English) was developed by Rita Simpson and colleagues at the University of Michigan and comprises 1,848,364 words of English academic context transcripts, and is freely accessible: see http://quod. lib.umich.edu/m/micase/; Hilary Nesi and Paul Thompson developed the British Academic Spoken

English (BASE) corpus (2000–2005: see Thompson & Nesi, 2001), comprising lectures and seminars in British universities: see http://www.reading.ac.uk/AcaDepts/ll/base_corpus/; Nesi, Gardner, Thompson and Wickens (2008) developed the British Corpus of Academic Written English (BAWE): the BAWE corpus contains 2,761 pieces of student writing, ranging in length from about 500 words to about 5,000 words, at four levels of assessed proficiency, distributed across four broad disciplinary areas, and is available free of charge to non-commercial researchers: http://www2.warwick.ac.uk/fac/soc/al/research/collect/bawe/; Doug Biber and a team at Northern Arizona University (NAU) developed the Longman/Lancaster English Language Corpus and have drawn on it for a wide range of linguistic analyses, including several relevant to EAP, in particular Biber (2006) and Biber and Conrad (2009): see http://www.pearsonlongman.com/dictionaries/corpus/lancaster.html; the NAU team also created the TOEFL 2000 Spoken and Written Academic Language (T2K-SWAL) corpus, comprising data from US universities, which contributed to the design of the TOEFL iBT (internet-based TOEFL). Another well-known British corpus, CANCODE (Cambridge and Nottingham Corpus of Discourse in English), has been used to great effect for a number of publications by Michael McCarthy and Ron Carter (e.g. Carter & McCarthy, 2006; Carter, Hughes & McCarthy, 1998; McCarthy & Carter, 1994), but this corpus is for commercial use and is only available to contracted Cambridge authors. The above list is by no means exclusive and other corpora have been developed in many places, but mostly drawn from textbooks, or from casual conversation. We can expect the development of specific academic corpora to proceed apace as the technology behind corpus development has become so user-friendly.

EAP: Case Study and Ethnography

On perhaps the other end of a continuum of research methods that are used in EAP research from corpus-based work lies the case study. Belcher's (1994) acclaimed study of student–supervisor/mentor relationships is an example within the EAP mainstream. Prior's (1998) series of case studies describe in depth the lived experiences of graduate seminars, combining analysis of classroom talk, students' texts and professors' written responses with reporting of students' representations of their writing and its contexts, professors' interpretations of their tasks and their students, and a close understanding of the institutional context. Prior's work reveals that the processes of academic enculturation are much more complex and multi-faceted than the field had hitherto imagined.

Contrastive Rhetoric

One area of research of continuing interest to EAP is contrastive rhetoric, first associated with Kaplan (1966, 2000) and in academic writing with Connor (1996), but consistently occurring in articles and theses in EAP (e.g., Van Bonn & Swales, 2007; Yakhontova, 2006), and in an excellent collection by Duszak (1997) focusing on developments in Eastern Europe and employing newer perspectives on text and discourse such as attitudes and values and interpersonal meaning. In its use of count and corpus methods as well as qualitative analyses of texts and discourse events, contrastive rhetoric may be seen to lie between the extremes of the research methodological continuum.

"Academic Literacy" and/in EAP

For some time, the term "academic literacy" was mainly associated with the US composition literature, and rather narrowly referred to school reading and writing. In the 1990s we saw this perception change as more researchers and teachers became aware of how much other than text itself is bound up in becoming "literate" in the sense of preparedness to use language to learn and experience knowledge (Johns, 1997). Fairclough (1992) and Ivanič (1998) interrogated the conventions and power structures of universities and other academic institutions, in keeping with Foucault's (1977) critique of modernity, and Freire's (1993/1970) and Giroux's (1981) critical pedagogy; scholars such as Tang and John (1999) explored learner identities, in what has been a fairly thin thread of research focusing on the learner in EAP. Nowadays the term "academic literacy" is often revised as "academic litera*cies*", referring to the whole complex set of skills, not only those relating to reading and writing, which we know are essential underpinnings of success in academic life, starting from the earliest years (Brice Heath, 1983).

Future Directions

There is no real distinction between past and present: as in any community, outside of war or catastrophe, time moves at different speeds for different people, the old, the young, the breadwinners, the child-bearers, the teachers, the learners. In the academic community fields seem static for a time, then explode with activity. A seminal discovery or academic paper can set alight a whole body of scholars. In an earlier book chapter overviewing EAP (Hamp-Lyons, 2001), I made several predictions that have not yet, to my sight, come true. I predicted that there would be growing work on EAP at pre-tertiary levels, but I do not (yet?) see this happening, despite an issue of *JEAP* on "Academic English in the secondary schools", edited by Ann Snow and Ann Johns, with articles by Hammond, Slater and Mohan, Zwiers, Bunch, Schleppegrell and de Oliviera, and Kramer-Dalh, Teo and Chia. In contrast, my prediction of the growth in research into the English language skills of nonnative English speaking academics, especially those teaching and researching in non-English language countries such as Hong Kong and Singapore, has turned out to be correct and we now see a steady flow of work in that area, well-represented by John Flowerdew and Yongyan Li (e.g., 2009), and two *JEAP* special issues, 4(4) edited by Sima Sengupta (on "advanced academic literacy") and 7(2) edited by Margaret Cargill and Sally Burgess (based on a conference on English for research for publication purposes). My third prediction in 2001, that there would be controversy and debate over the relationship between EAP and research into academic literacies because of their different sociopolitical and philosophical underpinnings, has taken place but more in conferences and on discussion lists than in the pages of journals, and researchers from differing positions have found enough common ground to work and publish together, I think because, as I argued at the time, "the different movements share a common desire to provide appropriate and effective education" (Hamp-Lyons, 2001: 129).

In attempting to look into the future, I try to identify some of those sparks that seem likely to set groups or sub-communities on fire with enthusiasm, and some that I feel deserve to receive more attention and enthusiasm than they currently do.

Socio-Cultural Theories

EAP as a teaching profession and as a research community is becoming increasingly aware that we cannot explain text, discourse or genre behaviour without including in our consideration the social contexts within which text is created, students learn, and people see the need for English. The reasons that young people learn English now are quite different from the reasons students were learning English in the 1960s. English is different; the world is different—and our teaching and research must keep pace with these changes. As Hyland (2000) argued, it has become important to examine the ideological impact of expert discourses, in terms of equity (or otherwise) of the access non-native and novice members of academic communities (including EAP's own academic community) have to prestigious genres such as publication in international journals, and indeed of access to reading those journals. Academic publishing has begun to address these inequities with initiatives such as HINARI (Health InterNetwork Access to Research Initiative) and AGORA (Access to Global Online Networks in Agriculture) to enable researchers in undeveloped and developing countries free or greatly-reduced journal subscription costs. Even though *JEAP* and most other social science journals are encompassed by the expanded terms of HINARI and AGORA, as a journal editor I see daily the ways that inequality of access to the most up-to-date information keeps some would-be published academic authors on the periphery of participation in our discourse (Flowerdew & Li, 2009; Hamp-Lyons, 2009; Wen & Gao, 2007). We now accept that many differences in, for example, the distribution of particular features in texts, variations in text and genre uses, are as likely to reflect the socio-cultural context of the writer as they are to signal weaknesses in language command. A socio-cultural view of English as used in/for academic purposes has led to the legitimate inclusion of studies of, for example, the gatekeeping role of journal editors and the social consequences of such gatekeeping practices.

Multiple Literacies

Hyon (1996) takes a broader look at the position of genre as a construct in our studies of academic discourses, embracing not only "Swalesian" ESP genre analysis but also "North American" new rhetoric studies, and Hallidayan (primarily Australian, at that time) systemic-functional linguistic approaches. In the years since Hyon's work the use of systemic-functional analysis in genre studies reaching the mainstream international journals has grown tremendously. Developing from the work of Michael Halliday (Halliday, 1984; Halliday & Hasan, 1989) this approach has attracted a significant following in Australia and represents a linguistically-driven approach to much the same problems as Swales in his practical way addressed as he faced his classrooms of early learners of English in the Sudan. Authors such as Woodward-Kron (2008), De Oliviera and Pagano (2006) and Hood and Forey (2005) have utilised systemic-functional linguistic analyses to valuable effect in EAP.

Swales (2000) suggested that the field should begin to look at systems or repertoires of genres, and Bazerman (2002) suggested that Swales may be leaving behind his "strong theory" of genres, as he is the "strong" theory of moves. Such a shift would be wholly in line with the movement towards more socially-oriented educational theory and research, discussed below, and would bring "Swalesian" genre analysis closer to the Hallidayan "genre literacy" movement associated primarily with Australian educators such as Cope and Kalantzis (1993) and Christie and Martin (2005).

Critical EAP

In our editorial for the first issue of *JEAP* Ken Hyland and I commented that even though they arise from "quite different sociopolitical contexts, proponents of academic literacy and those of EAP share a common desire to provide appropriate and effective education". This somewhat lukewarm embrace of shared goals has become more enthusiastic, as work in this area increasingly becomes mainstream. When we wrote our editorial, Benesch's (2001) book, *Critical English for Academic Purposes,* had just been published. Since then the *JEAP* has published a trickle rather than a flood of papers taking a critical stance, and more have appeared in other journals (Abasi, Akbari & Graves, 2006; Morgan & Ramanathan, 2005). But in 2009 an entire issue of *JEAP* (8,(3)) on critical EAP facilitated the exploration of the duality put forward by Benesch (2001) of students' needs *and* rights. In a contribution to the 2009 issue, Morgan concludes that "the presence and circulation of critical texts, particularly when published by reputable journals and academic presses, not only inspires transformative work, it also counters narrow and prejudicial claims made in support of the status quo" (Morgan, 2009,

p. 96). If Morgan is correct, and if the other excellent papers in the issue have the intended effect, we may expect to see more "critical" exploration in the EAP literature. As Luke (2004) reminds us, literacies *are* education, and education has material consequences.

This discussion returns me to an issue raised in the 2002 editorial: is EAP a pragmatic or a critical discipline? Is our role to ensure that students develop academic literacy skills to facilitate their effective participation in academic communities, or rather, should we (as Benesch, 2009, describes) interrogate our theoretical, pedagogic and even political assumptions and values in the forum of our classrooms in order to provide learners with ways of considering their own academic sociopolitical status quo?

Professional Development for EAP

If these three movements described above represent areas to feel excited and encouraged about, the final one I deal with is more a matter of concern than a cause for celebration or satisfaction. The provision of professional education and training for EAP teachers lags behind the vast expansion in the need for teachers of EAP. Not only private language schools, but also some professional university-based EAP programmes employ minimally qualified teachers, and teachers with specific training in EAP are rare. Teaching those who are using English for their studies differs from teaching English to those who are learning for general purposes only. At the same time, many—probably most—of the teachers of EAP around the world are not native speakers of English. The needs of these non-native teachers are different from those of native speakers, and recognition of these needs has led to the development of new kinds of EAP materials, often with considerable support for participants (see, for example, Hyland, 2006). But progress in materials development has not been matched by progress in developing and delivering professional training courses for future teachers of EAP, and a great need still remains in this area.

The British Association of Lecturers in EAP (BALEAP: http://www.baleap.org.uk/) was founded in 1972 (as SELMOUS—Special English Language Materials for Overseas University Students: see Jordan, 1997) and has become a major professional and educational focus for those working in EAP in the UK. BALEAP (n.d.) has developed a set of "Core Competencies" for teachers of EAP (http://www.baleap.org.uk/teap/teap-competency-framework.pdf) that provides a foundation for asserting the special skills that teaching EAP call upon, and this document is an invaluable resource to help those designing professional training programmes intended to prepare teachers for teaching English for academic purposes/in academic contexts. But it seems that professional EAP organisations have not spread far around the world. Excellent work is being done in various branches of EAP in, for example, Spain, New Zealand and Canada but there often seems to be a gap between advanced research into the written, spoken and public language of academics and novice/aspiring academics, and the development and delivery of special courses for students needing further preparation for academic study in English. A Google search brought up only three universities running teacher professional education qualification programmes in EAP, and all three were in the United Kingdom. A valuable contribution is made by the series of small, tightly-focused "PIMs"—Professional Issues Meetings run by BALEAP—around UK, which advance areas of new ideas and provide considerable encouragement to those who attend, but these reach only a tiny number of the EAP teachers worldwide. In some countries, notably Spain and Brazil, there are active communities of EAP practitioners and scholars who get together at least annually, and in some other countries (e.g. Malaysia) EAP is served by ESP organisations. These local or regional home-grown professional communities can be a great asset to established as well as novice EAP teachers and researchers. It is to be hoped that they will grow and spread around the world as EAP continues to become a more fully-acknowledged area of expertise in teaching and in research.

Conclusion

I have not been able to discuss EAP at the level of the secondary and primary school, although great work has been and is being in that area, notably in Australia (e.g. Christie, 1995). Similarly, I have barely addressed classroom issues at all. Instead, I would like to spare a few words to make the point that teaching English to non-native users of English for their use in succeeding in English-medium academic settings is now a multi-million dollar enterprise, not merely around the world, but often within just a single country. Non-native international students bring in millions of dollars or pounds to universities in "centre" countries. But for us, the teachers and the scholars, EAP is not about profit. It is about those college and university students in many countries, who are struggling to learn enough English, and the right English, to succeed in mastering their subjects through the medium of English in their textbooks, lectures, study groups and so on. Equally, for countries that are trying to lift themselves out of poverty or to become actors on the stage of knowledge exchange, the annual expenditure on young people who can go overseas and learn essential skills and bring them back to use at home is not undertaken lightly.

We have, then, an important role to play. It becomes clearer to me each day—and still more so through the process of preparing this necessarily cursory view of the field—that EAP as a discipline, as a research activity and as an orientation to daily problem-solving in teaching, materials development and curriculum planning, is proving itself a highly robust and adaptable, expansive field, able to make a tremendous contribution to understanding of the varied ways language is used in academic communities.

References

Abasi, A. R., Akbari, N. & Graves, B. (2006). Discourse appropriation, construction of identities, and the complex issue of plagiarism: ESL students writing in graduate school. *Journal of Second Language Writing, 15,* 102–117.

Altbach, P. (2002). Centers and peripheries in the academic profession: The special challenges of developing countries. In P. Altbach (Ed.), *The decline of the guru: The academic profession in developing and middle-income countries* (pp. 1–21). New York: Palgrave.

BALEAP (n.d.). Core competencies: http://www.baleap.org.uk/teap/teap-competency-framework.pdf.

Basturkmen, H. (2009). Commenting on results in published research articles and masters dissertations in Language Teaching. *Journal of English for Academic Purposes, 8*(4), 241–251.

Bazerman, C. (2002). Rhetorical research for reflective practice: A multi-layered narrative. Paper presented at the Research and Practice in Professional Discourse Colloquium, City University of Hong Kong, November.

Becher, T. (1989). *Academic tribes and territories: Intellectual inquiry and the cultures of disciplines.* Milton Keynes: SRHE/Oxford.

Belcher, D. (1994). The apprenticeship approach to advanced academic literacy: Graduate students and their mentors. *English for Specific Purposes, 13*(1), 23–34.

Benesch, S. (2001). *Critical English for academic purposes: Theory, politics and practice.* Mahwah, NJ: Erlbaum.

Benesch, S. (2009). Theorizing and practicing critical English for academic purposes. *Journal of English for Academic Purposes, 8*(2), 81–85.

Berkenkotter, C., & Huckin, T. (1995). *Genre knowledge in disciplinary communication: Cognition/culture and power.* Hillsdale, NJ: Lawrence Erlbaum Associates.

Biber, D. (2006). *University language: A corpus-based study of spoken and written registers.* Amsterdam: John Benjamins.

Biber, D., & Conrad, S. (2009). *Register and genre variation.* Cambridge: Cambridge University Press.

Bloor, M. (1998). Variations in the methods sections of research articles across disciplines: the case of fast and slow text. In P. Thompson (Ed.), *Issues in EAP writing, research and instruction* (pp. 84–106). Reading: CALS, The University of Reading.

Braine, G. (2002). Academic literacy and the nonnative speaker graduate student. *Journal of English for Academic Purposes, 1*(1), 59–68.

Brice Heath, S. (1983). *Ways with words: Language, life and work in communities and classrooms.* Cambridge: Cambridge University Press.

Bridgeman, B., & Carlson, S. (1983). *Survey of academic writing tasks required of graduate and undergraduate foreign students.* TOEFL Research Report No. 15. Princeton, NJ: Educational Testing Service.

Bruce, I. (2008). Cognitive genre structures in methods sections of research articles: A corpus study. *Journal of English for Academic Purposes, 7*(1), 38–54.

Bunton, D. (1999). The use of higher level metatext in Ph.D. theses. *English for Specific Purposes, 18*, S41–56.

Bunton, D. (2005). The structure of PhD conclusion chapters. *Journal of English for Academic Purposes, 4*(3), 407–433.

Canagarajah, S. (2002). Multilingual writers and the academic community: Towards a critical relationship. *Journal of English for Academic Purposes, 1*(1), 29–44.

Candlin, C. N., Kirkwood, J. M. & Moore, H. M. (1975). Developing study skills in English. In ETIC, *English for academic study: problems and perspectives* (pp. 50–69). London: The British Council.

Cargill, M. & O'Connor, P. (2006). Developing Chinese scientists' skills for publishing in English: Evaluating collaborating-colleague workshops based on genre analysis. *Journal of English for Academic Purposes,* **5(3), 207–221.**

Carkin, S. (2005). English for academic purposes. In E. Hinkel (Ed.), *Handbook of research in second language teaching and learning* (pp. 85–98). Hillsdale, NJ: Lawrence Erlbaum Associates.

Carter, R. A., Hughes, R. & McCarthy, M. J. (1998). Telling tails: Grammar, the spoken language and materials development. In B. Tomlinson (Ed.), *Materials development in L2 teaching* (pp. 76–86). Cambridge: Cambridge University Press.

Carter, R. A., & McCarthy, M. J. (2006) *Cambridge grammar of English*. Cambridge: Cambridge University Press.

Chia, H-u., Johnson, R., Chia, H.-l. & Olive, F. (1998). English for College Students in Taiwan: A study of perceptions of English needs in a medical context. *English for Specific Purposes, 18*(2), 107–119.

Christie, F. (1995). Pedagogic discourse in the primary school. *Linguistics and Education, 7*(3), 221–242.

Christie, F. & Martin J. R. (2005). *Genre and institutions: Social processes in the workplace and school.* London: Continuum.

Coleman, H. (1988). Analyzing needs in large organizations. *English for Specific Purposes, 7*(3), 155–169.

Connor, U. (1996). *Contrastive rhetoric: Cross-cultural aspects of second-language writing.* New York: Cambridge University Press.

Connor, U. & Mauranen, A. (1996). Linguistic analysis of grant proposals: European Union research grants. *English for Specific Purposes, 18*(1), 47–62.

Conrad, S. (1996). Academic discourse in two disciplines: Professional writing and student development in biology and history. Unpublished PhD dissertation, Northern Arizona University.

Cooley, L., & Lewkowitz, J. (2003). *Dissertation writing in practice: Turning ideas into text.* Hong Kong: Hong Kong University Press.

Cope, B., & Kalantzis, M. (Eds.) (1993). *The powers of literacy: A genre approach to teaching writing.* London: Falmer Press.

Crystal, D. (1997). *English as a global language.* Cambridge: Cambridge University Press.

De Oliviera, J. M. & Pagano, A.S. (2006). The research article and the science popularization article: A probabilistic functional grammar perspective on direct discourse representation. *Discourse Studies, 8*: 627–646.

Dudley-Evans, T. & St John, M. (1998). *Developments in English for specific purposes.* Cambridge: Cambridge University Press.

Dushku, S. (1998). ELT in Albania: Project evaluation and change. *System, 26*(3), 369–388.

Duszak, A. (Ed.) (1997). *Culture and styles of academic discourse.* Berlin: Mouton de Gruyter.

Fairclough, N. (1992). *Discourse and social change.* Cambridge: Polity.

Ferris, D., & Tagg, T. (1996). Academic listening/speaking tasks for ESL students: Problems, suggestions and implications. *TESOL Quarterly, 30*(2), 297–320.

Flowerdew, J. (Ed.) (1994). *Academic listening.* Cambridge: Cambridge University Press.

Flowerdew, J. (1999). Writing for scholarly publication in English: The case of Hong Kong. *Journal of Second Language Writing, 8*(2),123–145.

Flowerdew, J., & Li, Y-y. (2009). English or Chinese? The trade-off between local and international publication among Chinese academics in the humanities and social sciences. *Journal of Second Language Writing, 18*(1), 1–16.

Flowerdew, J., & Peacock, M. (2001). Issues in EAP: A preliminary perspective. In J. Flowerdew & M. Peacock, (Eds.), *Research perspectives on English for Academic Purposes* (pp. 8–24). Cambridge: Cambridge University Press.

Foucault, M. (1977). *Discipline and punish: The birth of the prison.* Paris: Gallimard.

Freire, P. (1993/1970). *Pedagogy of the oppressed.* London: Continuum.

Giannoni, D. S. (1998). The genre of journal acknowledgements: Findings of a cross-disciplinary investigation. *Linguistica e Fililogia, 6*, 61–84.

Giroux, H. (1981). *Ideology, Culture and the Process of Schooling.* Philadelphia: Temple University Press/Falmer Press.

Halliday, M. A. K. (1984). *An introduction to functional grammar.* Cambridge, MA: Harvard University Press.

Halliday, M. A. K., & Hasan, R. (1989). *Language, context, and text.* Oxford: Oxford University Press.

Halliday, M. A. K., Strevens, P. & McIntosh, A. (1964). *The linguistic sciences and language teaching.* London: Longman.

Hamp-Lyons, L. (2001). English for academic purposes. In R. Carter & D. Nunan (Eds.), *The Cambridge TESOL Guide* (pp. 126–130). Cambridge: Cambridge University Press.

Hamp-Lyons, L. (2009). Equity, access and … plagiarism? *TESOL Quarterly, 43*(4), 690–693.

Hamp-Lyons, L., & Courter, K. (1984). *Research matters.* Rowley, MS: Newbury House.

Hewings, M. (2002). A history of ESP through English for specific purposes. *English for Specific Purposes World: Online Journal for Teachers, 3.* Accessed 18/8/2009, http://esp-world.info.

Holliday, A. (1995). Analysing language needs within an institutional context: An ethnographic approach. *English for Specific Purposes, 14*(2), 115–126.

Hood, S., & Forey, G. (2005). Introducing a conference paper: Getting interpersonal with your audience. *Journal of English for Academic Purposes, 4*(4), 291–306.

Hopkins, A., & Dudley-Evans, T. (1988). A genre-based investigation of the discussion sections in articles and dissertations. *English for Specific Purposes, 7,* 113–121.

Hutchinson, T., & Waters, A. (1987). *English for specific purposes: A learning centered approach.* Cambridge: Cambridge University Press.

Hyland, K. (2000). *Disciplinary discourses: Social interactions in academic writing.* London: Longman.

Hyland, K. (2001). Humble servants of the discipline? Self-mention in research articles. *English for Specific Purposes, 20*(3), 207–226.

Hyland, K. (2002a). Specificity revisited: How far should we go? *English for Specific Purposes, 21*(4), 385–395.

Hyland, K. (2002b). *Teaching and researching writing.* London: Longman/Pearson.

Hyland, K. (2004). *Genre and second language writing.* Ann Arbor: University of Michigan Press.

Hyland, K. (2006). Genre pedagogy: Language, literacy and L2 writing instruction. *Journal of Second Language Writing, 16*(3), 148–164.

Hyland, K. (2008a). Academic clusters: Text patterning in published and postgraduate writing. *International Journal of Applied Linguistics, 18*(1), 41–62.

Hyland, K. (2008b). 'Small bits of textual material': A discourse analysis of Swales' writing. *English for Specific Purposes, 27*(2), 143–160.

Hyland, K., & Hamp-Lyons, L. (2002). EAP: Issues and directions. *Journal of English for Academic Purposes, 1,* 1–12.

Hyon, S. (1996). Genre in three traditions: Implications for ESL. *TESOL Quarterly, 30*(4), 693–722.

Ivanič, R. (1998). *Writing and identity: The discoursal construction of identity in academic writing.* Amsterdam: John Benjamins.

Jacoby, S., & McNamara, T. (1999). Locating competence. *English for Specific Purposes, 18*(3), 213–241.

Johns, A. M. (1981). Necessary English: A faculty survey. *TESOL Quarterly, 15,* 51–57.

Johns, A. M. (1995). Teaching classroom and authentic genres: Initiating students into academic cultures and discourses. In D. Belcher & G. Braine (Eds.), *Academic writing in a second language* (pp. 277–291). New York: Ablex.

Johns, A. M. (1997). *Text, role and context: developing academic literacies.* Cambridge: Cambridge University Press.

Johns, A. M., & Swales, J. M. (2002). Literacy and disciplinary practices: Opening and closing perspectives. *Journal of English for Academic Purposes 1*(1), 13–28.

Jordan, B. (1997). *English for academic purposes: A guide and resource book for teachers.* Cambridge: Cambridge University Press.Jordan, B. (2002). The growth of EAP in Britain. *Journal of English for Academic Purposes, 1*(1), 69–78.

Kaplan, R. B. (1966). Cultural thought patterns in intercultural education. *Language Learning, 16*(1), 1–20.

Kaplan, R. B. (2000). Contrastive rhetoric and discourse analysis: Who writes what to whom? When? In what circumstances? In S. Sarangi & M. Coulthard (Eds.), *Discourse and social life* (pp. 82–102). Harrow: Longman.

Knoch, U. (2009). The development and validation of a rating scale for diagnostic writing assessment. *Language Testing, 26*(2), 275–304.

Kress, G. (1998). Visual and verbal modes of representation in electronically mediated communication: The potentials of new forms of text. In I. J. Lave & E. Wenger, (1991). *Situated learning: Legitimate peripheral participation.* Cambridge: Cambridge University Press.

Kwan, B. C. (2009). Reading in preparation for writing a PhD thesis: Case studies of experiences. *Journal of English for Academic Purposes, 8*(3), 180–191.

Lea, M., & Street, B. (1999). Writing as academic literacies: understanding textual practices in higher education. In C.N. Candlin & K. Hyland (Eds.), *Writing: Texts, processes and practices* (pp. 62–81). London: Longman.

Li, Y. (2006). A doctoral student of physics writing for publication: A sociopolitically-oriented case study. *English for Specific Purposes, 24*(4), 456–478.

Luke, A. (2004). On the material consequences of literacy. *Language and Education, 18*(4), 331–335.

McCarthy, M. J., & Carter, R. A. (1994). *Language as discourse: Perspectives for language teaching.* Harlow: Longman.

Menasche, L. (1984). *Writing a research paper.* Ann Arbor: University of Michigan Press.

Mišak, A., Marušić, M. & Marušić, A. (2005). Manuscript editing as a way of teaching academic writing: Experience from a small scientific journal. *Journal of Second Language Writing, 14*(2), 122–131.

Morgan, B. (2009). Fostering transformative practitioners for critical EAP: Possibilities and challenges. *Journal of English for Academic Purposes, 8*(3), 86–99.

Morgan, B., & Ramanathan, V. (2005). Critical perspectives and language education: Global and local perspectives. *Annual Review of Applied Linguistics, 25*, 151–169.

Motta-Roth, D. (1998). Discourse analysis and academic book review: A study of text and disciplinary cultures. In I. Fortanet, S. Posteguillo, J. C. Palmer & J. L. Coll (Eds.), *Genre studies for academic purposes* (pp. 29–58). Valencia: Universitat Jaume 1.

Munby, J. (1978). *Communicative syllabus design.* Cambridge: Cambridge University Press.

Nesi, H., Gardner, S., Thompson, P. & Wickens, P. (2008). *An investigation of genres of assessed writing in British higher education.* Final report for the ESRC for project no. RES-000–23–0800. Contact: baweplus@warwick.ac.uk.

Paltridge, B. (2002). Thesis and dissertation writing: An examination of published advice and actual practice. *English for Specific Purposes, 21*, 125–143.

Paltridge, B. (2005). Writing for scholarly publication: Behind the scenes in language education. *English for Specific Purposes, 24*(1), 111–113.

Paltridge, B., & Starfield, S. (2007). *Thesis and dissertation writing in a second language.* London: Routledge.

Peacock, M. (2002). Communicative moves in the discussion section of research articles. *System, 30*(4), 479–497.

Precht, K. (1998). A cross-cultural comparison of letters of recommendation. *English for Specific Purposes, 17*(3), 241–265.

Prior, P. (1998) *Writing/disciplinarity: a sociohistoric account of literate activity in the academy.* Mahwah, NJ: Erlbaum.

Robinson, P. (Ed.) (1988). *Academic writing: Process and product.* ELT Document 129. Basingstoke: Modern English Publications.

Robinson-Pant, A. (2009). Changing academies: Exploring international PhD students' perspectives on "host" and "home" universities. *Higher Education Research and Development, 28*(4): 417–429.

Rose, D., Rose, M., Farrington, S. & Page, S. (2007). Scaffolding academic literacy with indigenous health sciences students: An evaluative study. *Journal of English for Academic Purposes, 7*(3), 165–179.

Salager-Meyer, F. (2008). Scientific publishing in peripheral (a.k.a. developing) countries: Challenges for the future. *Journal of English for Academic Purposes, 7*(2), 121–132.

Salehzadeh, J. (2005). *Academic listening strategies: A guide to understanding lectures.* Ann Arbor: University of Michigan Press.

Salimbene, S. (1985). *Strengthening your study skills: A guide for overseas students.* Rowley, MA: Newbury House.

Sengupta, S., Foey, G. & Hamp-Lyons, L. (1999). Supporting effective English communication within the context of teaching and research in a tertiary institute: Developing a genre model for consciousness raising. *English for Specific Purposes, 18*: S7–S22.

Silver, M. (2003). The stance of stance: A critical look at ways stance is expressed and modeled in academic discourse. *Journal of English for Academic Purposes, 2*(4), 359–374.

Sionis, C. (1995). Communication strategies in the writing of scientific research articles by non native users of English. *English for Specific Purposes, 14*(2), 99–114.

Spack, R. (1988). Initiating ESL students into the academic discourse community: How far should we go? *TESOL Quarterly, 22*(1), 29–52.

Strevens, P. (1977). *New orientations in the teaching of English.* Oxford: Oxford University Press.

Swales, J. (1981). Aspects of research article introductions. *Aston ESP Research Reports No. 1.* Birmingham: University of Aston.

Swales, J. (1990). *Genre Analysis: English in academic and research settings.* Cambridge: Cambridge University Press.

Swales, J. M. (1996). Occluded genres in the academy: The case of the submission letter. In E. Ventola & A. Mauranen (Eds.) *Academic writing: Intercultural and textual issues* (pp. 45–58). Amsterdam: J. Benjamins.

Swales, J. (1997). English as *Tyrannosaurus Rex. World Englishes, 16*, 373–382.

Swales, J. (1998). *Other floors, other voices: A textography of a small university building.* Mahwah, NJ: Erlbaum.

Swales, J. (2000). Languages for specific purposes. *Annual Review of Applied Linguistics, 20*, 59–76.Swales, J. (2009). *Incidents in an educational life: A memoir (of sorts).* Ann Arbor: University of Michigan Press.

Swales, J. M., & Feak, C. (2001). *English in today's research world: A writing guide.* Ann Arbor: University of Michigan Press.

Swales, J. M., & Feak, C. (2004/1994). *Academic writing for graduate students: Essential tasks and skills.* Ann Arbor: University of Michigan Press.

Swales, J. M., & Najjar, H. (1987). The writing of research article introductions. *Written Communication, 4*, 175–191.

Tang, S., & John, R. (1999). The "I" in identity: Exploring writer identity in student academic writing through the first person pronoun. *English for Specific Purposes, 18*, S23–40.

Tardy, C. (2004). The role of English in scientific communication: *Lingua franca* or *Tyrannosaurus rex? Journal of English for Academic Purposes, 3*(3), 247–269.

Thompson, P. (2001). A pedagogically motivated corpus-based examination of PhD theses: Macrostructure, citation practices and uses of modal verbs. Unpublished PhD thesis, University of Reading.

Thompson, P. (2005). Points of focus and position: Intertextual reference in PhD theses. *Journal of English for Academic Purposes, 4*, 307–323.

Thompson, P., & Nesi, H. (2001). The British Academic Spoken English (BASE) corpus project. *Language Teaching Research*, 5(3), 263–264.

Tynan, B., & Garbett, D. (2008). Negotiating the university research culture: Collaborative voices of new academics. *Higher Education Research and Development*, 26(4), 411–424.

Van Bonn, S., & Swales, J. (2007). English and French journal abstracts in the language sciences: Three exploratory studies. *Journal of English for Academic Purposes*, 6(2), 93–108.

Wallace, M. (1980). *Study skills in English*. Cambridge: Cambridge University Press.

Warschauer, M. (2002). Networking into academic discourse. *Journal of English for Academic Purposes*, 1(1), 45–58.

Welch, A.R., & Zhen, Z. (2008). Higher education and global talent flows: Brain drain, overseas Chinese intellectuals, and diasporic knowledge networks. *Higher Education Policy*, 21(4), 519–537.

Wen, X., & Gao, Y. (2007) Dual publication and academic inequality. *International Journal of Applied Linguistics*, 17(2), 221–225.

Weissburg, R., & Buker, S. (1990). *Writing up research: Experimental research report writing for students of English*. Englewood Cliffs, NJ: Prentice Hall Regents.

Williams, R. (1982). *Panorama*. London: Longman.

Woodward-Kron, R. (2007). Negotiating meaning and scaffolding learning: Writing support for non-English speaking background postgraduate students. *Higher Education Research and Development*, 26(3), 253–268.

Woodward-Kron, R. (2008). More than just jargon—the nature and role of specialist language in learning disciplinary knowledge. *Journal of English for Academic Purposes*, 7(4), 234–249.

Yakhontova, T. (2006). Cultural and disciplinary variation in academic discourse: The issue of influencing factors. *Journal of English for Academic Purposes*, 5(2), 153–167.

Zughoul, M. R., & Hussein, R. F. (1985). English for higher education in the Arab world: A case study of needs analysis at Yarmouk University. *The ESP Journal* 4(2), 132–152.

7

Research in English for Specific Purposes

Brian Paltridge and Sue Starfield

In the previous edition of this handbook, Peter Master (2005) summarises publication trends in the journal *English for Specific Purposes*. As he points out, research that takes a text/discourse analytic perspective on English for specific purposes (ESP) has dominated the journal since its early days. The very first volume of the journal contained an article by Elaine Tarone and colleagues (Tarone, Dwyer, Gillette & Icke, 1981) on the use of the passive in astrophysics journal articles. In this article, she and her colleagues, at the same time as John Swales (1981) in the UK, provide the first mention of the word genre in ESP research, and indeed the world of English language teaching research in general. Since those days genre-based studies have been an important part of ESP research, and they continue to be so (see Johns, 2008; Johns, Bawarshi, Coe, Hyland, Paltridge, Reiff & Tardy, 2006; Tardy, 2006; Tardy & Swales, 2008 for reviews of much of this work).

A further development in ESP research is the use of computers to carry out studies of specific purpose language use. Diane Belcher, in her (2006) review article, points to the potential of *corpus-based studies* for ESP research to provide a better "empirically based understanding of language used for specific purposes" (p. 142). Corpus-based studies have helped us gain a better idea of the nature of specific purpose language use some of which, in the words of Biber (1988), is often "surprising and contrary to popular expectation" (p. 178). Corpus studies have provided a convincing reply to Hutchinson and Waters's (1987) claim that there are no specific structures, functions or discourse structures that might be associated with specific purpose language use (see Flowerdew, 2011, for a review of corpus-based studies in ESP).

In his 2005 review, Master highlights the international character of ESP research. In 2008, authors who published in *English for Specific Purposes* were from the US, the UK, Hong Kong, Italy, Canada, Lebanon, Japan, France, South Africa, Taiwan, Australia, Brazil, Macao, China and Turkey. The title of Ann Johns and Tony Dudley-Evans's (1991) review article, "English for specific purposes: International in scope, specific in purpose", is as true now as it was then, if not even more so, especially with the increase in the use of *English as the lingua franca* of international research (Tardy, 2004) as well as the language of international communications and business (see Mauranen, 2011; Planken & Nickerson, 2011).

There has also been increased attention given in ESP research to *advanced academic literacies* and the multiple literacy requirements (Hyland, 2007) of ESP students' present and future lives. While in past years, much attention has been given to undergraduate literacies in the area of English for academic purposes (EAP) research, there is now increased attention being given to writing for research purposes (Casanave & Vandrick, 2003; Hyland, 2009a) and second language thesis and dissertation writing (see e.g. Casanave & Li, 2008; Swales, 1990, 2004; Paltridge & Starfield, 2007) both of which present major challenges to second language writers.

A further important issue that is being explored in ESP research is the notion of *identity*. ESP students' identities are both negotiated and develop as they increase their participation in particular communities of practice (Casanave, 2002). Students may do what they are asked to do, or they may decide to resist (Benesch, 1999, 2001). The ways in which they can do this and what this might imply, however, are complex, and not at all transparent to someone who is only just beginning to become a member of the particular group (see Block, 2010; Belcher & Lukkarila, 2011 for discussions of identity-oriented research).

Recent years have also seen an increase in the use of *ethnographic* techniques in ESP research as a way of trying to understand the complexities of ESP language use and the worlds in which our students need to use this language. In their 1981 paper, Tarone and her colleagues interviewed authors to try to get a better understanding of the linguistic observations they had made. Nickerson (2000) combined text analysis and questionnaires to investigate the genres and discourse strategies used by Dutch writers working in English in multinational corporations. Curry and Lillis (2004) employed text analysis, interviews, observations, document analysis, written correspondence, reviewers' and editors' comments to examine multilingual writers' experiences of getting published in English. Each of these studies aims, in its way, to get an inside view of the worlds in which our learners are wishing to participate (see Starfield, 2010, 2011).

ESP and Genre

The notion of genre is an important one in the area of ESP research. This is especially the case in the area of academic writing research. Genre analysis is described by Dudley-Evans and St John (1998) as "the study of the structural and linguistic regularities of particular genres or text types and the role they play within a discourse community" (p. xv). They suggest that the terms "discourse analysis" and "genre analysis" might best be seen as two overlapping terms with discourse analysis being an umbrella term that includes the examination of characteristic features of particular genres.

In ESP genre studies, the structuring of texts is typically described as being made up of a series of moves, each of which may contain one or more steps (see e.g. Swales, 1990, 2004). Although ESP genre studies have largely focused on macro-level textual descriptions and analyses of sentence- and clause-level choices within the context of particular genres, the origins of ESP genre analysis are, however, much broader than such interests might suggest. These influences are summarised by Swales (1990) who describes them as including variety studies, situation-specific skill and strategy studies, notional-functional approaches to language programme development, discourse analysis, sociolinguistics, composition studies, studies in the areas of cultural anthropology, and language and cognition.

ESP genre analysis, thus, draws from a range of different areas for the description of genres as "a means of achieving a communicative goal that has evolved in response to particular rhetorical needs" (Dudley-Evans, 1994, p. 219). Emphasis in ESP genre studies is placed on the way in which a text realises its communicative purpose and "the role of the genre within the discourse community that regularly uses it" (Dudley-Evans, 1994, p. 220). ESP genre studies, thus, go beyond description, to explanation so as to provide an understanding of why genres are shaped the way they are, and how they achieve their particular communicative goals (Bhatia, 1993, 2004).

ESP genre research has been increasingly influenced by research in the area of composition studies in US universities, and in what is often called the new rhetoric (Freedman & Medway, 1994). This work has been influenced, in particular, by a paper written by the speech communications specialist

Carolyn Miller (1984) titled "Genre as social action", which laid the ground for much of the genre-based research in this area. Swales (2004) draws on the work of Devitt (1997) in the new rhetoric in his discussions of genre, particularly in relation to the notions of choice and constraint in the learning and teaching of genres. As Devitt (2004) argues, conformity among genre users "is a fact of genre" (p. 86). Both constraint and choice, she argues, are necessary and positive components of genres. It is not necessarily the case that choice is good and constraint is bad. Both are important in the description and teaching of genres.

ESP genre research has also considered the ways in which the use of one genre assumes, or depends on, the use of a number of other related genres, or the systems of genres (Bazerman, 1994) of which the text is a part, An example of this is the academic essay, which often draws from, and cites, a number of other genres such as academic lectures, specialist academic texts and journal articles. Academic essays also interrelate closely with assignment guidelines, assessment criteria, tutorial discussions and tutor-student consultations (Paltridge, 2000). Tardy (2008) presents what she calls a systems-based view of genre that accounts for relations between oral/aural, written and visual genres and which draws on the intertextual and multimodal nature of many academic genres. Molle and Prior (2008) take up the topic of multimodal genre systems in their discussion of a genre-based needs analysis for a number of graduate courses at a large US university. They found that the texts the students were producing were routinely hybrid and multimodal, highlighting the importance of going beyond purely linguistic descriptions of texts to ones that account for the complexities of the texts students are required to produce, and the processes through which they produce them.

The special issue of *English for Specific Purposes* published in honour of John Swales in 2008 contains a number of articles that capture well current developments in ESP genre studies. Bhatia's (2008) article argues for analyses that consider both typical characteristics of professional genres and the nature of professional practices. Hyon (2008) examines what Swales (1996) has called an "out of sight", or occluded genre, retention, promotion and tenure reports that are written for faculty in US universities, locating these reports within the context of the university's retention, promotion and tenure "genre chain". Samraj and Monk (2008) examine what they term a "semi-occluded" genre, the statement of purpose that students need to write for admission to graduate school in the US. They look at both the discourse structures of the texts, in terms of moves and steps, as well as disciplinary variation within the texts. Giannoni's (2008a) study of editorials in English language journals is a corpus-based genre study that shows the value this approach can provide for understanding the linguistic features of particular genres. Dressen-Hammouda's (2008) study, the final paper in the collection, draws on work in the new rhetoric as well as ESP genre studies to examine the ways in which students acquire genre mastery as they move from being novices to disciplinary experts in their areas of study.

ESP and Corpus Studies

The past few years have seen the development of a number of corpora that have been an important resource for ESP researchers. These include the Michigan Corpus of Academic Spoken English (MICASE) (http://www.lsa.umich.edu/eli/micase/index.htm), the British Academic Spoken English (BASE Plus) corpus (http://www2.warwick.ac.uk/fac/soc/al/research/collect/base/), the British Academic Written English (BAWE Plus) corpus (http://www2.warwick.ac.uk/fac/soc/al/research/collect/bawe) and the TOEFL Spoken and Written Academic Language Corpus (Biber, 2006; Biber, Conrad, Reppen, Byrd & Helt, 2002). The MICASE is an open access corpus that contains data from a wide range of spoken academic genres as well as information on speaker attributes and characteristics of the speech events that are contained in the data. The BASE Plus corpus includes recordings of conference presentations, lectures and seminars, interviews with academic staff, as well as tagged transcripts of some of the data. The BAWE Plus corpus includes contextual information on the data such as the gender and year of study of the student who wrote the text, details of the course the assignment was set for and the grade that was awarded to the text. The TOEFL corpus contains examples of genres such as class sessions, office hour conversations, study group discussions, on-campus service encounters, text books, reading packs, university catalogues and brochures (see Nesi, Sharpling & Ganobcsik-Williams, 2004 for discussion of a corpus of academic writing developed at a single university).

Academic word lists have also been produced from these kinds of corpora. Coxhead's (2000) academic word list is an example of this. Her list is based on a large-scale analysis of a corpus of published written texts and is designed to help students in their academic reading. Hyland and Tse (2007) argue, however, against generic lists of this kind, pointing out that individual words occur and behave in different ways in different areas of study, and that to be of the most value, academic word lists need to be more local and discipline-specific. There clearly is a need, then, for more discipline-specific studies of vocabulary use in academic settings to help inform writing teachers of typical vocabulary patterns in the kinds of texts our students need to write.

Examples of discipline-specific corpus studies include Harwood's (2005, 2006) studies of personal pronoun use in academic writing, and Hyland's (2008) study of Swales' writing in the area of applied linguistics. Harwood (2005) carried out a corpus-based study of self-promotional "I" and "we" in academic writing across four academic disciplines. He then interviewed a group of political scientists about appropriate and inappropriate use of the pronouns "I" and "we" in academic writing and compared what they had to say with a corpus-based examination of patterns of pronoun use in their writing (Harwood, 2006). He found that views and practices of pronoun use varied substantially among the writers whose work he examined, suggesting that this could be, in part, due to different epistemologies operating within the discipline. Harwood argues for further studies that combine the strengths of both corpus and interview studies to try to get more of an inside, or "emic" view on academic discourse as his study has done.

Hyland's (2008) study examines John Swales' writing in 14 single-authored papers and most of the chapters in three of his books. He then compares his findings with a larger corpus of writing in the area of applied linguistics. He concludes that Swales' writing reveals both individuality and disciplinarity, arguing that the distinctiveness of Swales' voice in his writing "reveals both the breadth of options that are acceptable to community members and the freedom of established disciplinary celebrities to manipulate them" (p. 158) (see Hyland, 2004, 2009b; Hyland & Bondi, 2006 for further corpus-based studies of academic discourse across disciplines).

Corpus studies have also been carried out in areas other than EAP. Bhatia and Gotti's (2006) *Explorations in specialized genres*, Flowerdew and Gotti's (2006) *Studies in specialized discourse*, Bargiela-Chiappini and Nickerson's (1999) *Writing business: Genres, media and discourses*, and Trosberg's (2000) *Analysing professional discourses* contain examples of these studies. These studies have examined, for example, Nobel Prize lectures, taxation web-sites, anti-discrimination bills, legal counsel opinions, persuasive and expository press genres, real estate discourse, emails in multinational corporations, sales letters, business faxes, company reports and courtroom discourse.

Books such as McEnery, Xiao and Tono's (2005) *Corpus-based language studies* and Baker's (2006) *Using corpora in discourse analysis* provide advice on how to prepare and carry out corpus-based studies. Baker makes a number of important observations about corpus studies. The first of these is that corpus-based discourse analysis is not just a quantitative process but involves human choice and decision at every stage, from deciding on the research questions, through to interpreting and explaining the results. Corpus studies take researchers beyond frequencies to dispersion, revealing patterns of language use across texts. They, importantly, draw to our attention patterns of language that we meet everyday, but are not necessarily conscious of. Kandil and Belcher's (2011) study of web-based news reports on the Israeli/Palestinian conflict is an example of a study that does this. Kandil and Belcher draw together techniques from both corpus linguistics and critical discourse analysis to consider the ways in which the language of the texts both inscribes and promotes a particular world view, despite the genre's ostensibly "fact-reporting features".

There have, however, been criticisms of corpus studies. Flowerdew (2005) discusses these criticisms. One criticism is that corpus studies lead to atomised, bottom-up descriptions of language use. A further criticism is that corpus studies do not consider contextual aspects of texts. Harwood (2006) and Tribble (2002) counter these views by providing advice on how contextual features can be incorporated into corpus studies. One way of gaining contextual information for a corpus-based analysis is by the use of interviews and focus group discussions with users of the genre and consideration of the textual information revealed in the corpus component of the study in relation to this information. Harwood, for example, did this in his (2006) study as did Hyland (2004) in his *Disciplinary discourses*. The analysis can also be combined with other information that is available on the data such as the contextual information that accompanies the MICASE and BAWE corpora. A further approach is to read more widely on the topic of the study to see if this might help explain or provide insights on the analysis as well as, as Kandil and Belcher advocate, taking a step back from the texts and critically framing them (Cope & Kalantzis, 2000) by looking at the texts in relation to the social, cultural and political contexts in which they are located, and unpacking the views and assumptions that underlie the texts and what they are aiming to do.

ESP and English as a Lingua Franca

English is now well established as the lingua franca of worldwide communication. It is the language of international business, the language of international conferences, the language of international education and research, the language of the international communications network and the language of international travellers. Often, it is the native language of neither group of speakers but it is the language they will most likely use to communicate in these kinds of settings. This is a topic that is attracting considerable attention in ESP research.

The special issue of *English for Specific Purposes* edited by Catherine Nickerson on English as a lingua franca (ELF) in international business provides examples of research in this area. Her editorial (Nickerson, 2005) provides an extensive overview of research in this area as well as discussing implications of this research for the teaching of English for specific business purposes (ELBP). Nickerson points to a number of trends in research in this area. The first of these is a move from the examination of language in isolation to analyses that consider organisational and cultural factors that impact on how the text is written or spoken. The second is a move from a focus on language skills to strategies that are effective in business communication, regardless of whether the person using the language is a native speaker of English or not. Important work she refers to as illustrations of this include studies carried out by Charles (1996) into business negotiations, Planken's (2005) study of non-native speaker sales negotiations, Bargiela-Chiappini and Harris's (1997) examination of Italian and British business meetings, Rogerson-Revell's (1999) work on management meetings, Poncini's (2004) study of company meetings with their international distributors, and the use of emails and faxes in multinational corporations (Gimenez, 2002). Planken and Nickerson (2009) focus specifically on spoken discourse in business settings where English is used as a lingua franca, discussing what business English actually is, as well as the ways in which the use of business English is shaped by national and corporate cultures, company policies and also the level of proficiency in English of the people who are using the language.

The use of ELF in Europe is discussed by Seidlhofer (2007) who discusses the use of English both within and outside of the world of ESP. She, also, discusses the question of what ELF actually looks (and sounds) like, as well as considers the question of whether ELF can and should be taught. Tardy (2004) provides a detailed discussion of the role of English in international scientific communication, then presents a study in which she investigated international students' attitudes towards English and its role in scientific communication. Many of the students she interviewed felt disadvantaged in their use of English and were likely, she felt, to face difficulties publishing in English when they returned to their home countries.

Maley (2007) provides a critique of the concept of ELF, arguing that, while there is no disputing the legitimacy of ELF as a research area, for him it is statistically unproven and pragmatically inoperable. He proposes, as his way forward, the promotion of views that are tolerant of non-native speakers' use of English, arguing that native speaker versions of English are not the only legitimate ones, nor are they in any way superior to any other varieties. Non-native speakers, he argues, should move from apologising for their English "to a more robust, even assertive, pride in their use of English as badge of identity" (p. 66). There are, however, studies that are examining the actual characteristics of ELF, especially in academic settings, which are providing data-driven answers to some of Maley's concerns. An example of this is the English as a Lingua Franca in Academic Settings corpus, the ELFA corpus, which includes lectures, presentations, seminars, thesis defences and conference discussions by speakers from a wide range of linguistic backgrounds (Mauranen, 2011). All of these data are authentic and are based on complete samples of speech events in a range of disciplinary domains (http://www.tay.fi/laitokset/kielet/engf/research/elfa/). As Mauranen (2006) argues, projects such as this can provide insights into language use in ESP settings, outside of the classroom, without the construction of second language speakers as simply "learners".

ESP and Advanced Academic Literacies

While the study of academic texts such as the research article has been a traditional area of research within ESP, more recently there has been a growing interest in the acquisition of advanced academic literacy by non-native English speakers writing at a doctoral or postdoctoral level as well as by practising academics in environments where English is not the national language or the language of instruction. This focus seems attributable to the ever increasing globalisation of higher education (Flowerdew, 2008), the continued dominance of English as the language of scientific communication (Belcher, 2007; Giannoni, 2008b) and reflects the growing pressure on novice and established academics to publish in English language journals and to use English as the main language at international conferences (Curry & Lillis, 2004; Flowerdew, 1999a, 1999b; Li, 2006; Lillis & Curry, 2006). By broadening its focus beyond the written text to examine contexts of production and reception, the research draws our attention to the complex challenges many "off-network" writers face in part due to their location at the periphery and not at the centre (Belcher, 2007; Canagarjah, 2002; Curry & Lillis, 2004; Salager-Meyer, 2008). The challenges that these writers face are not solely linguistic as they attempt to balance the desire to gain international recognition through publication in English with choices that reflect their own value systems and ideologies that may reflect the desire to resist the global dominance of English (Duszak & Lewkowicz, 2008; Flowerdew, 2008). As Uzuner (2008) points out in a recent article that provides a useful synthesis of a number of these studies, the work of multilingual scholars who seek to publish in English is of significance in that global scholars have a unique contribution to make to academic disciplinary communities and their absence from international knowledge production and dissemination will impoverish scholarship. It is therefore important that the specific challenges they may face, both discursive and non-discursive (Canagarajah, 1996), be investigated and "made public so that the research field can identify ways to help these scholar maintain visibility … and contribute more to the core knowledge base" (Uzuner, 2008, p. 251).

Much of this research takes the form of case studies that use qualitative methods to provide a thicker description of the contexts in which individual academics are developing their advanced academic literacies. Li's case study (2006) of a doctoral student of physics in China attempting to publish in a prestigious English language "international" journal identifies the final published version as a "sociopolitical artifact" (p. 473) shaped by the multiple negotiations the student engaged in with many disciplinary insiders including his supervisors, journal editors and referees. Lillis and Curry's (2006) ethnographic study of eastern European psychology scholars reveals the widespread use of "literacy brokers" (editors, reviewers, academic peers, English-speaking friends and colleagues) who mediated the attempts by these scholars to publish in English language journals. Recently, autobiographical reflective pieces and autoethnographies are proving a rich source of data on the (ultimately) successful enculturation and academic discourse socialisation of multilingual academics and graduate students into English medium environments (Belcher & Connor, 2001; Casanave & Vandrick, 2003; Casanave & Li, 2008). Both methodologies confirm the very local, situated nature of academic discourse and the complex negotiations that enmesh the construction and negotiation of success in writing, publication or presentation as writers seek entry to the new academic discourse community, with a number of the studies adopting a community of practice framework (Cho, 2004; Englander, 2009; Casanave & Li; 2008; Curry & Lillis, 2004; Flowerdew, 2000; Li, 2006; Wenger, 1998).

This research offers several challenges to ESP practitioners in that they are challenged to reflect on the dominance of English in scientific communication and its effect on other languages and ways in which they can best "broker" the advanced academic writing needs of the writers they work with (Lillis & Curry, 2006; Li, 2006). Workshops based on genre analysis of the type advocated by Cargill and O'Connor (2006) are clearly of value to non-native speaking researchers; however the research reviewed in this section is significant for ESP practitioners in that it situates the linguistic challenges faced by periphery scholars within more complex sociopolitical contexts and identifies the complex identity negotiations (see following section of this chapter) they need to engage in as they seek not only publication but also "acceptance in an English-only research world" (Belcher, 2007, p. 1).

ESP and Identity

It is interesting to note that in earlier ESP work (e.g. Dudley-Evans & St John, 1998), there is little discussion of the topic of identity; the focus is on identifying learner needs in relation to a fairly narrowly defined target situation (including personal information, language learning needs, subjective needs, lacks). Benesch (2001, p. 107) argues, however, for an expanded notion of context in EAP that "include[s] social issues and identities", and is shaped by gender, class race and power relations.

Through drawing the field's attention to issues of learners' rights and desires, Benesch's work, along with Norton's work on learner identity, investment and imagined community (see Norton, 2000; Kanno & Norton, 2003), has fostered a growing interest in recent years in issues of identity within the broad field of ESP. Belcher and Lukkarila (2011) suggest that this research provides ESP with richer conceptualisations of the learner, of the multiple roles learners may play in multiple contexts, how they are positioned and position themselves in shifting power relationships and how they envision their own legitimate, peripheral as well as more central participation in current and imagined future communities.

Most work to date has been within the subfield of EAP across the spectrum of undergraduate, postgraduate and advanced academic literacies and has looked at identity construction, negotiation and representation in both written and spoken academic discourse. Studies that have an academic discourse socialisation/enculturation framework may also include a more or less explicit focus on identity (Dressen-Hammouda, 2008; Duff, 2008; Morita, 2000, 2004; Zappa-Hollman, 2007) as they study "newcomers" (novices) seeking to participate in established disciplinary communities (e.g. Flowerdew, 2000; Li, 2005, 2006). As Duff (2008, p. 112) points out, studies that adopt as their theoretical framework notions of identity, participation and communities of practice, and that examine participants' desire for/uptake or rejection of new "subject positions within those communities contrast markedly with the earlier emphasis on the less contextualized acquisition of linguistic skills and knowledge". These newcomers are frequently non-native speakers of English and a number of the studies discuss their struggles to appropriate an identity of success in contexts in which they are being discursively positioned as second language speakers of English, as non-legitimate speaker/writers (Liu, 2004) or, in extreme cases, as "plagiarisers" (Ouellette, 2008; Starfield, 2002). Morita (2004, p. 599) points out that as academic communities are increasingly internationalised, viewing non-native speakers of English as simply linguistic or cultural minorities may no longer be useful. Within a communities of practice framework, "native-speaking students or even instructors are not simply the dominant group, target, or norm, but groups of peripheral participants who also need to be socialized into increasingly heterogeneous communities".

With its focus on meaning as negotiated within specific contexts, the advanced academic literacies research discussed above together with the influence of the work of Clark and Ivanič (1997) and Ivanič (1998) on writer identity and Hyland (2005) on stance and engagement, in particular, have shown not only that academic discourse is not impersonal but that "writers are social and political beings who are participating in complex literate activities and who have lives and histories that impinge upon their writing practices" (Casanave, 2003, p. 94). The constitution of the writerly self in academic writing has recently become a focus of interest, itself influenced by insights from postmodernist thinking about the constitutive nature of discourse in shaping the self in discourse. Starfield (2002, 2004) and Starfield and Ravelli (2006) draw on Ivanič's conceptualisation of writer identity as a complex negotiation of self between three "strands" of writer identity that come into play during the writing process: an autobiographical self, a discoursal or textual self created in the process of writing and an authorial self whose voice is more or less authoritative. In academic writing, these three elements interact with the institutionally available subject positions as the writer negotiates a writerly identity that aligns to a greater or lesser extent with disciplinary conventions. Starfield and Ravelli (2006, p. 226) argue that even "apparently trivial features of the [doctoral] thesis, the title pages, the table of contents and their typography are ... already sites of identity negotiation where the writer begins to align him or herself with a research tradition".

Phan Le Ha (2009) develops these views on identity, voice and investment from a critical perspective to write about both her own development as a bilingual academic writer and the struggles of one of her PhD students to negotiate the perceived norms of academic discourse and find a "voice" through which he feels able to represent himself in his writing.

Voice and writer identity are used somewhat interchangeably in the literature though there has been some debate over whether voice refers to an individual writer's voice or to Bhaktinian views of voice as social (Helms-Park & Stapleton, 2003; Matsuda & Tardy, 2007; Stapleton & Helms-Park, 2008; Ouellette, 2008). Ouellette's study of a student identified as having plagiarised, draws on this same body of work to argue, through a close study of her written texts and journals, that "Annie's" apparent plagiarism needs to be understood through the lens of her developing writer identity as she struggles with linguistic and discursive requirements. A study by Abasi and Akbari (2008) also adopted a critical academic literacies perspective to examine graduate students' attempts to appropriate authoritative identities in their writing. Of interest to EAP practitioners is the ways in which the academic context and task demands positioned the students to resort to plagiarism as they struggled to appear "legitimate" in the new context.

In a novel study, Matsuda and Tardy (2007) look at writer identity from the perspective of the ways in which manuscript reviewers construct identities for the writers whose articles they are reading through their attention to textual and rhetorical features of the manuscript.

Studies that examine identity work within business communication still draw largely on face theory for their conceptualisation of identity rather than on the more poststructuralist conceptions outlined above. Planken's (2005) examination of rapport management in ELF sales negotiations shows how experienced negotiators effectively emphasise their professional commonalities with their interlocutors, thus maintaining and reinforcing their professional identities and promoting solidarity, which the novice negotiators are less successful at accomplishing. A study of discourse strategies in email negotiation in a business context (Jensen, 2009) is one of the few to examine identity negotiation in ELF using a theoretical framework other than "face" theory, and in a non-EAP context. The study draws on Hyland's use of stance and engagement to examine how social relations and identities were constructed and negotiated through a series of email exchanges.

What clearly emerges from this brief review of the literature on identity and should be of concern to the field is the extent to which non-native writers and speakers of English feel stigmatised by the various discourses of the academy that tend to position them in stereotypical ways (Flowerdew, 2008; Phan Le Ha, 2009). Belcher and Lukkarila's (2011) suggested reconceptualisation of the learner appears an avenue worthy of pursuit by EAP and the wider ESP field.

ESP and Ethnographic Approaches

In a review article that looks back to the origins of language for specific purposes teaching in the 1960s, Swales (2000, p. 59) comments that for early LSP (languages for specific purposes) practitioners, research was "basically textual or transcriptal". Making a clear distinction between then and the contemporary period, Swales (2000, p. 60) concludes that in the 1960s there was little need for practitioners to have either "[e]xpert content knowledge of the fields or professions they were trying to serve; real understanding of the rhetorical evolution of the discourses central to those fields or professions" or what he refers to as "advanced anthropological training in 'fly on the wall' ethnography". Implicitly he seems to be arguing that all of these capabilities are now required of the ESP/LSP practitioner. Extending the contrast further, he states that these early practitioners "were well equipped to carry out relatively 'thin' descriptions of their target discourses" (p. 60). The use of the word "thin" in this context can be interpreted as a reference to Clifford Geertz's (1975) now well-known characterization of ethnography as requiring "thick description". To what extent though can ESP research be characterised as having adopted ethnographic research methods and methodologies?

The so-called "social turn" in applied linguistic research—the desire to develop in-depth understandings of language learning and teaching events in the specific (and frequently unequal) social contexts within which they are taking place—has certainly promoted a greater problematisation of the notion of "context", always a focus of ESP research. As pointed out earlier in this chapter, there is a growing body of research within ESP that seeks to deepen and broaden our understandings of the diverse contexts and communities in which English is being learned and taught, particularly from the emic (insider) perspectives of the various participants. Ethnographic research methods, with their combination of longer-term observation and the collection of diverse forms of data, provide understandings of participants' perspectives and meaning-making practices within the complex sociocultural worlds they inhabit that more traditional needs analyses may not have succeeded in capturing.

Some needs analyses studies have adopted ethnographic methods to move beyond survey methods to explore in greater depth the communities that learners and teachers inhabit or will inhabit (e.g. Giminez, 2001; Holme & Chaluaiseang, 2006; Northcott & Brown, 2006). Northcott's (2001) study of several MBA classrooms employs ethnographic methods to provide just such a thick description of these learning and teaching contexts, fleshing out the specific context of the interactive lectures both first and second language students are attending to identify areas of potential difficulty for her students. Such in-depth studies, relying on multiple data sources, appear relatively rare in the literature. Cheng and Mok's (2008) study of land surveyors in Hong Kong that aimed to describe the discursive competence of these professionals included six days of intensive observation in a consultancy firm's offices in an attempt to gain something of a fly on the wall perspective. None of these studies, apart from Jackson's (2002, 2004) however, seem to involve the sustained engagement over time that Lillis (2008) sees as central to ethnography. It has to be acknowledged, however, that the type of engagement required by sustained ethnographic observation and triangulation can be severely constrained by the resources available to ESP practitioners and researchers. Clearly though, the richness of the types of data collected and the unique perspectives afforded through such approaches make them worthy of greater adoption.

Academic socialisation studies such as those referred to earlier in this chapter typically adopt an ethnographic/observational approach as they study student enculturation processes/participation in new communities over time and are able to provide data from multiple sources to enrich analyses of language learning and identity negotiation in specific contexts (see for example Zappa-Holman, 2007; Morita, 2000; Vickers, 2007).

In their review of recent research on writing, Juzwik, Curcic, Wolbers, Moxley, Dimling and Shankland (2006) found that research focused on context and social practices of writing dominates writing research at the beginning of the twenty-first century. While this may not be the case for ESP research with the strong growth of corpus-based research and the continuation of genre-based research, it would be fair to say that there is a growing trend towards methodologies that are more qualitative within EAP and business communication studies and a realisation that genre studies and even corpora studies (see Flowerdew, 2005) can benefit from greater exploration of sociocultural contexts and participants' perspectives.

Attempting to develop a framework to investigate academic writing that would provide "thicker" contexts—something more than a traditional piece of discourse analysis, while at the same time less than a full-blown ethnography, Swales (1998a, 1998b) developed a modified version of ethnography that he called "textography": an approach to genre analysis that combines elements of text analysis with ethnographic techniques such as interviews, observations and document analysis. Paltridge (2008) describes three quite different textographic projects: a study of the production of the exegesis (a written text that accompanies a visual project submitted as the research component of a student's art and design Master's degree) at a New Zealand university; a textography of the writing component of the two main Chinese university college English tests that was carried out with a group of English language teachers at a large research university in China; and an advanced-level academic writing course in which students are encouraged to become "textographers" of their own disciplinary contexts in order to uncover the institutional and audience expectations for their academic writing as well as unpack the values and requirements they need to negotiate in order to achieve their academic goals.

Dressen-Hammouda's (2008; Dressen, 2003) work can be seen to bridge academic discourse socialisation research and more traditional genre studies. Her "situated genre analysis" of the development of a novice geologist's writing about fieldwork draws on a range of data sources including a genre-based study of the linguistic and rhetorical devices geologists use to talk about their fieldwork in the research article; a sociohistorical analysis of their field practices; an ethnography-oriented study of their current field practices; and an interview-based textography of modern field writing practices to understand the multiple and complex "semiotic resources" a student needs to master in order to begin writing like a specialist. It brings home to us how important situated attention to the local communicative practices of specific communities is for understanding the choices writers are making.

Starfield's (2001, 2002, 2004) ethnographic studies of black South African second language students from apartheid schools at a formerly whites-only university triangulate a range of data sources including extensive observation, in-depth interviews with students and their teachers, collection and analysis of student essays and the analysis of other documentation to produce an account of not only how students from these backgrounds struggle to become successful within this highly unequal context but also of how their teachers too are positioned by the discourses of apartheid. She draws on these data to outline a critique of the notion of discourse community as used in some EAP research.

Lillis (2008) makes a series of interesting distinctions between "method" and "methodology" in studies of academic writing that employ ethnographic approaches to deepen understanding of the relationships between texts and their contexts of production and reception. Many of the ESP/EAP studies of academic writing would be characterised as "ethnography as method" or "talk around text" as they primarily use interviews and text collection to provide more contextual data (e.g. Flowerdew, 2000; Li, 2006). "Ethnography as methodology" would involve a more sustained engagement over time with context and participants and the collection of data from multiple sources. Her own extensive studies (see Curry & Lillis, 2004; Lillis & Curry, 2006) of professional academic writers in a number of national contexts in Europe would be an example of this latter approach.

Conclusion and Future Directions

In a recent book, Pennycook (2007, pp. 5–6) critically reflects on the interconnectedness of globalisation and the material and symbolic power of English as it is appropriated by the diverse communities that speak it:

> English is closely tied to processes of globalization: a language of threat, desire, destruction and opportunity. … English is a translocal language, a language of fluidity and fixity that moves across, while becoming embedded in, the materiality of localities and social relations. English is bound up with transcultural flows, a language of imagined communities and refashioning identities.

The early proponents of ESP to some extent anticipated and understood this seemingly insatiable desire for English. What they understood less, located as they were in the main at the centre and products of the centre, was English's ability to become the property of many and to be changed in the process. This chapter has drawn attention to the diversity of location and authorship of those researching, writing and teaching ESP. While research in ESP has remained close to its earlier textualist or transcriptal roots, in broadening and deepening notions of context and the learner and adopting more qualitative research approaches to explore contexts and communities and the ways in which texts and talk are situated and used within communities of practice, the field of ESP has started to focus its attention on the "translocal" character of English. As Pennycook advises us, English has the power to reshape learner and teacher identities in ways that may have unexpected consequences.

Yongyan Li's (2005, 2006) ethnographically-oriented case studies of novice Chinese scientists negotiating publication put "flesh on the bones" of Pennycook's somewhat abstract notions, embodying a number of the themes discussed in this chapter. For the Chinese novice scientists for whom publication in an "international" (i.e. English language) journal is a prerequisite to graduation (Li, 2006), English is potentially a language of threat, desire, destruction and opportunity. Methodologically, her study, while perhaps not a "fly on the wall" investigation, provides rich description of her site and collects data through questionnaires, interviews and observation. Of particular interest are her motivations for the study: her own lived experience of the pressure to publish in English as an academic in China and her work as a teacher of EAP in that context. Her own successful journal publication therefore "add[s] [her] own voice to authoritative conversations in [the] field, and thus help change the field and its practices" (Casanave, 2002, cited in Li, 2006, p. 475).

In a recent article, Bhatia (2008, p. 171) proposes a "complex and dynamic multiperspective and multidimensional analytical framework" that would enrich genre studies by integrating ethnographic perspectives with textual, cognitive, socio-critical and institutional ones to help ESP researchers and practitioners "bridge the gap between the ideal world of classroom and the real world of professional practice". The field of ESP can only benefit from work that brings multiple perspectives to bear in its investigations of learners, their learning needs, the communities they inhabit or desire to inhabit, and the texts and genres they need to successfully access and author. While corpus studies and genre theory are providing us with greater empirically-based understandings of how language is used for specific purposes, we still know relatively little about the relationships between these understandings and learning and teaching. An Cheng's (2006) call for researchers to "conceptualiz[e] learning and to examin[e] how learners, as complex and instantiated agents, operate in the ESP genre-based pedagogical contexts" is embodied in his detailed case studies that draw on multiple data sources such as learners' genre-analysis tasks, writing tasks, classroom interaction data, curriculum materials, learners' literacy autobiographies and ethnographic interviews that help bridge the space between genre theory and description and ESP genre-based pedagogies (see Cheng, 2007, 2008).

Nowhere are the contradictory pulls of threat, desire, destruction and opportunity that English embodies more clearly seen than in the emergent global community of English lingua franca speakers as "non-native speakers" begin to reshape English for their own purposes. Research in this area is bound to grow rapidly and the field has only begun to consider its pedagogical implications. Again corpus studies are providing useful empirical data on which to base pedagogical decisions but practitioners and researchers will need to not lose sight of the individual learners whose multiple purposes are shaping and being shaped by the power of English.

References

Abasi, A. R., & Akbari, N. (2008). Are we encouraging patchwriting? Reconsidering the role of the pedagogical context in ESL student writers' transgressive intertextuality. *English for Specific Purposes, 27*, 267–284.

Baker, P. (2006). *Using corpora in discourse analysis*. London: Continuum.

Bargiela-Chiappini, F., & Nickerson, C. (Eds.) (1999). *Writing business: Genres, media and discourses*. London: Longman.

Bargiela-Chiappini, F., & Harris, S. (1997). *Managing language: The discourse of corporate meetings*. Amsterdam: John Benjamins.

Bazerman, C. (1994). Systems of genres and the enactment of social intentions. In A. Freedman & P. Medway (Eds.), *Genre and the new rhetoric* (pp. 97–101). London: Taylor and Francis.

Belcher, D. (2006). English for specific purposes: Teaching to perceived needs and imagined futures in worlds of work, study, and everyday life. *TESOL Quarterly, 40*, 133–156.

Belcher, D. (2007). Seeking acceptance in an English-only research world. *Journal of Second Language Writing, 16*, 1–22.

Belcher, D., & Connor, U. (Eds.) (2001). *Reflections on multiliterate lives*. Clevedon: Multilingual Matters.

Belcher, D., & Lukkarila, L. (2011). Identity in ESP context: Putting the learner front and center in needs. In D. Belcher, A. M. Johns & B. Paltridge (Eds.), *New directions for ESP Research*. Ann Arbor: University of Michigan Press.

Benesch, S. (1999). Rights analysis: Studying power relations in an academic setting. *English for Specific Purposes, 18*, 313–327.

Benesch, S. (2001). *Critical English for academic purposes: Theory, politics and practice*. Mahwah, NJ: Lawrence Erlbaum.

Bhatia, V. K. (1993). *Analysing genre: Language use in professional settings*. London: Longman.

Bhatia, V. K. (2004). *Worlds of written discourse: A genre-based view*. London: Continuum.

Bhatia, V. K. (2008). Genre analysis, ESP and professional practice. *English for Specific Purposes, 27*, 161–174.

Bhatia, V. K., & Gotti, M. (Eds.) (2006). *Explorations in specialized genres*. Bern: Peter Lang.

Biber, D. (1988). *Variation across speech and writing.* Cambridge: Cambridge University Press.

Biber, D. (2006). *University language. A corpus-based study of spoken and written registers.* Amsterdam: John Benjamins.

Biber, D., Conrad, S., Reppen, R., Byrd, P. & Helt, M. (2002). Speaking and writing in the university: a multidimensional comparison. *TESOL Quarterly, 36,* 9–48.

Block, D. (2010). Researching identity. In B. Paltridge & A. Phakiti. (Eds.), *Continuum companion to research methods in applied linguistics* (pp. 337–349). London: Continuum.

Canagarajah, S. (1996). "Nondiscursive" requirements in academic publishing, material resources of periphery scholars and the politics of knowledge production. *Written Communication, 13,* 435–472.

Canagarajah, S. (2002). *A geopolitics of academic writing.* Pittsburgh: University of Pittsburgh Press.

Cargill, M., & O'Connor, P. (2006). Developing Chinese scientists' skills for publishing in English: Evaluating collaborating-colleague workshops based on genre analysis. *Journal of English for Academic Purposes, 5,* 207–221.

Casanave, C. P. (2002). *Writing games: Multicultural case studies of academic literacy practices in higher education.* Mahwah: NJ: Laurence Erlbaum.

Casanave, C. P. (2003). Looking ahead to more sociopolitically-oriented case study research in L2 writing scholarship (But should it be called "post-process"?) *Journal of Second Language Writing, 12,* 85–102.

Casanave, C. P., & Li, X. (Eds.) (2008). *Learning the literacy practices of graduate school: Insiders' reflections on academic enculturation.* Ann Arbor: University of Michigan Press.

Casanave, C. P., & Vandrick, S. (Eds.) (2003). *Writing for scholarly publication. Behind the scenes in language education.* Mahwah, NJ: Lawrence Erlbaum.

Charles, M. (1996). Business negotiations: Interdependence between discourse and the business relationship. *English for Specific Purposes, 15,* 19–36.

Cheng, A. (2006). Understanding learners and learning in ESP genre-based writing instruction. *English for Specific Purposes, 25*(1), 76–89.

Cheng, A. (2007). Transferring generic features and recontextualizing genre awareness: Understanding writing performance in the ESP genre-based literacy framework. *English for Specific Purposes, 26,* 287–307.

Cheng, A. (2008). Individualized engagement with genre in academic literacy tasks. *English for Specific Purposes, 27,* 387–411.

Cheng, W., & Mok, E. (2008). Discourse processes and products: Land surveyors in Hong Kong. *English for Specific Purposes, 27,* 57–73.

Cho, S. (2004). Challenges of entering discourse communities through publishing in English. *Journal of Language, Identity, and Education, 3,* 47–72.

Clark, R., & Ivanič, R. (1997). *The politics of writing.* London: Routledge.

Cope, B., & Kalantzis, M. (2000). Introduction: Multiliteracies: The beginnings of an idea. In B. Cope & M. Kalantzis (Eds.), *Multiliteracies: Literacy learning and the design of social futures* (pp. 3–8). London: Routledge.

Coxhead, A. (2000). A new academic word list. *TESOL Quarterly, 34,* 213–238.

Curry, M. J., & Lillis, T. (2004). Multilingual scholars and the imperative to publish in English: Negotiating interests, demands, and rewards. *TESOL Quarterly, 38,* 663–688.

Devitt, A. (1997). Genre as a language standard. In W. Bishop & H. Ostrum (Eds.), *Genre and writing* (pp. 45–55). Portsmouth, NH: Boynton/Cook.

Devitt, A. (2004). *Writing genres.* Carbondale, IL: Southern Illinois University Press.

Dressen, D. (2003). Geologists' implicit persuasive strategies and the construction of evaluative evidence. *Journal of English for Academic Purposes, 2,* 273–290.

Dressen-Hammouda, D. (2008). From novice to disciplinary expert: Disciplinary identity and genre mastery. *English for Specific Purposes, 27,* 233–252.

Dudley-Evans, T. (1994). Genre analysis: An approach to text analysis for ESP. In M. Coulthard (Ed.), *Advances in written text analysis* (pp. 219–228). London: Routledge.

Dudley-Evans, T., & St John, M. (1998). *Developments in English for Specific Purposes.* Cambridge: Cambridge University Press.

Duff, P. (2008). Language socialization, participation and identity: Ethnographic approaches. In M. Martin-Jones, A.-M. de Mejia & N. Hornberger (Eds.), *Encyclopaedia of language and education* (Vol. 3: Discourse and Education) (pp. 107–119). New York: Springer.

Duszak, A., & Lewkowicz, J. (2008). Publishing academic texts in English: A Polish perspective. *Journal of English for Academic Purposes, 7,* 108–120.

Englander, K. (2009). Transformation of the identities of non-native English speaking scientists as a consequence of the social construction of revision. *Journal of Language, Identity, and Education, 8,* 35–53.

Flowerdew, J. (1999a). Problems in writing for scholarly publication in English: The case of Hong Kong. *Journal of Second Language Writing, 8,* 243–264.

Flowerdew, J. (1999b). Writing for scholarly publication in English: The case of Hong Kong. *Journal of Second Language Writing, 8*, 123–145.

Flowerdew, J. (2000). Discourse community, legitimate peripheral participation and the non-native English-speaking scholar. *TESOL Quarterly, 34*, 127–150.

Flowerdew, J. (2008). Scholarly writers who use English as an additional language: What can Goffman's "Stigma" tell us? *Journal of English for Academic Purposes, 7*, 77–86.

Flowerdew, J., & Gotti, M. (Eds.) (2006). *Studies in specialized discourse*. Bern: Peter Lang.

Flowerdew, L. (2005). An integration of corpus-based and genre-based approaches to text analysis in EAP/ESP: Countering criticisms against corpus-based methodologies. *English for Specific Purposes, 24*, 321–332.

Flowerdew, L. (2011). ESP and corpus studies. In D. Belcher, A. M. Johns & B. Paltridge (Eds.), *New directions in ESP research*. Ann Arbor: University of Michigan Press.

Freedman, A., & Medway, P. (Eds.) (1994). *Genre and the new rhetoric*. London: Taylor and Francis.

Geertz, C. (1975). *The interpretation of cultures*. London: Hutchinson.

Giannoni, D. S. (2008a). Popularizing features in English journal editorials. *English for Specific Purposes, 27*, 212–232.

Giannoni, D. S. (2008b). Medical writing at the periphery: The case of Italian journal editorials. *Journal of English for Academic Purposes, 7*, 97–107.

Gimenez, J. C. (2001). Ethnographic observations in cross-cultural business negotiations between non-native speakers of English: An exploratory study. *English for Specific Purposes, 20*, 169–193

Gimenez, J. C. (2002). New media and conflicting realities in multinational corporate communication: A case study. *International Review of Applied Linguistics in Language Teaching, 40*, 323–344.

Harwood, N. (2005). "Nowhere has anyone attempted … In this article I aim to do just that": A corpus-based study of self-promotional *I* and *we* in academic writing across four disciplines. *Journal of Pragmatics, 37*, 1207–1231.

Harwood, N. (2006). (In)appropriate personal pronoun use in political science: A qualitative study and a proposed heuristic for future research. *Written Communication, 23*, 424–450.

Helms-Park, R., & Stapleton, P. (2003). Questioning the importance of individualized voice in undergraduate L2 argumentative writing: An empirical study with pedagogical implications. *Journal of Second Language Writing, 12*, 245–265.

Holme, R., & Chalauisaeng, B. (2006). The learner as needs analyst: The use of participatory appraisal in the EAP reading classroom. *English for Specific Purposes, 25*, 403–419.

Hutchinson, T., & Waters, A. (1987). *English for specific purposes: A learning centred approach*. Cambridge: Cambridge University Press.

Hyland, K. (2004). *Disciplinary discourses: Social interactions in academic writing* (2nd ed.). Ann Arbor: The University of Michigan Press.

Hyland, K. (2005). Stance and engagement: A model of interaction in academic discourse. *Discourse Studies, 7*, 172–192.

Hyland, K. (2007). English for specific purposes: Some influences and impacts. In J. Cummins & C. Davison (Eds.), *The international handbook of English language teaching* (Vol. 1) (pp. 391–402). Norwell, MA: Springer Publications.

Hyland, K. (2008). Small bits of textual material: A discourse analysis of Swales' writing. *English for Specific Purposes, 27*, 143–160.

Hyland, K. (2009a). English for academic professional purposes: Writing for scholarly publication. In D. Belcher (Ed.), *English for specific purposes in theory and practice* (pp. 83–105). Ann Arbor: University of Michigan Press.

Hyland, K. (2009b). *Academic discourse: English in a global context*. London: Continuum.

Hyland, K., & Bondi, M. (Eds.) (2006). *Academic discourses across disciplines*. Bern: Peter Lang.

Hyland, K., & Tse, P. (2007). Is there an "academic" vocabulary? *TESOL Quarterly, 41*, 235–254.

Hyon, S. (2008). Convention and inventiveness in an occluded academic genre: A case study of retention–promotion–tenure reports. *English for Specific Purposes, 27*, 175–192.

Ivanič, R. (1998). *Writing and identity: The discoursal construction of identity in academic writing*. Philadelphia: John Benjamins.

Jackson, J. (2002). The L2 case discussion in business: An ethnographic investigation. In J. Flowerdew (Ed.), *Academic discourse*. (pp. 268–286). London: Longman.

Jackson, J. (2004). Case-based teaching in a bilingual context: Perceptions of business faculty in Hong Kong. *English for Specific Purposes, 23*(3), 213–232.

Jensen, A. (2009). Discourse strategies in professional e-mail negotiation: A case study. *English for Specific Purposes, 28*, 4–18.

Johns, A. M. (2008). Genre awareness for the novice student: An on-going quest. *Language Teaching, 41*, 237–252.

Johns, A. M., & Dudley-Evans, T. (1991). English for specific purposes: International in scope, specific in purpose. *TESOL Quarterly, 25*, 297–314.

Johns, A. M., Bawarshi, A., Coe, R. M., Hyland, K., Paltridge, B., Reiff, M. J. & Tardy, C. (2006). Crossing the boundaries of genre studies: Commentaries by experts. *Journal of Second Language Writing, 15*, 234–249.

Juzwik, M. M., Curcic, S., Wolbers, K., Moxley, K. D., Dimling, L. M. & Shankland, R. K. (2006). Writing into the 21st century: An overview of research on writing, 1999 to 2004. *Written Communication, 23*, 451–476.

Kandil, M., & Belcher, D., (2011). ESP and critical discourse analysis: Understanding the power of genres of power. In D. Belcher, A. Johns & B. Paltridge (Eds.), *New directions in ESP research*. Ann Arbor: University of Michigan Press.

Kanno, Y. & Norton, B. (2003) Imagined communities and educational possibilities: Introduction. *Journal of Language, Identity and Education, 2*, 241–249.

Li, Y. (2005). Multidimensional enculturation: The case of an EFL Chinese doctoral student. *Journal of Asian Pacific Communication, 15*, 53–70.

Li, Y. (2006). A doctoral student of physics writing for publication: A socio-politically oriented case study. *English for Specific Purposes, 25*, 456–478.

Lillis, T. (2008). Ethnography as method, methodology, and "deep theorizing": Closing the gap between text and context in academic writing research. *Written Communication, 25*, 353–388.

Lillis, T., & Curry, M. J. (2006). Professional academic writing by multilingual scholars. *Written Communication, 23*, 3–35.

Liu, J. (2004). Co-constructing academic discourse from the periphery: Chinese applied linguists' centripetal participation in scholarly publication. *Asian Journal of English Language Teaching, 14*, 1–22.

McEnery, A., Xiao, R. & Tono, Y. (2005). *Corpus-based language studies*. London: Longman.

Maley, A. (2007). EIL or ELF: cup half-full or half-empty? In *Proceedings of the 12th English in Southeast Asia conference: Trends and directions* (pp. 62–70). School of Liberal Arts, King Mongkut's University of Technology, Bangkok, Thailand.

Master, P. (2005). Research in English for Specific Purposes. In E. Hinkel (Ed.), *Handbook of research in second language teaching and learning* (pp. 99–115). Mahwah, NJ: Lawrence Erlbaum.

Matsuda, P. K., & Tardy, C. M. (2007). Voice in academic writing: The rhetorical construction of author identity in blind manuscript review. *English for Specific Purposes, 26*, 235–249.

Mauranen, A. (2006). A rich domain of ELF: The ELFA corpus of academic discourse. *Nordic Journal of English Studies, 5*, 145–159.

Mauranen, A. (2011). English as a lingua franca in ESP. In D Belcher, A. M. Johns & B. Paltridge (Eds.), *New directions in ESP research*. Ann Arbor: University of Michigan Press.

Miller, C. R. (1984). Genre as social action. *Quarterly Journal of Speech, 70*, 151–167.

Molle, D., & Prior, P. (2008). Multimodal genre systems in EAP writing pedagogy: Reflecting on a needs analysis. *TESOL Quarterly, 42*, 541–566.

Morita, N. (2000). Discourse socialization through oral classroom activities in a TESL graduate program. *TESOL Quarterly, 34*, 279–310.

Morita, N. (2004). Negotiating participation and identity in second language academic communities, *TESOL Quarterly, 38*, 573–604.

Nesi, H., Sharpling, G. & Ganobcsik-Williams, L. (2004). Student papers across the curriculum: Designing and developing a corpus of British student writing. *Computers and Composition, 21*, 439–450.

Nickerson, C. (2000). *Playing the corporate game: An investigation of the genres and discourse strategies in English used by Dutch writers working in multinational corporations*. Amsterdam: Adophi.

Nickerson, C. (2005). Editorial: English as a lingua franca in international business contexts. *English for Specific Purposes, 24*, 367–380.

Norton, B. (2000). *Identity and language learning*. London: Longman.

Northcott, J. (2001). Towards an ethnography of the MBA classroom: A consideration of the role of interactive lecturing styles within the context of one MBA programme. *English for Specific Purposes, 20*, 15–37.

Northcott, J., & Brown, G. (2006). Legal translator training: partnership between teachers of English for legal purposes and legal specialists. *English for Specific Purposes, 25*, 358–375.

Ouellete, M. (2008). Weaving strands of writer identity: Self as author and the NNES "plagiarist". *Journal of Second Language Writing, 17*, 255–273.

Paltridge, B. (2000). Systems of genres and the EAP classroom. *TESOL Matters, 1*, 12.

Paltridge, B. (2008). Textographies and the researching and teaching of writing. *IBÉRICA, 15*, 9–24.

Paltridge, B., & Starfield, S. (2007). *Thesis and dissertation writing in a second language*. London: Routledge.

Pennycook, A. (2007). *Global Englishes and transcultural flows*. London: Routledge.

Phan Le Ha. (2009). Strategic, passionate, but academic: Am I allowed in my writing? *Journal of English for Academic Purposes, 8*, 134–146.

Planken, B. (2005). Managing rapport in lingua franca sales negotiations: A comparison of professional and aspiring negotiators. *English for Specific Purposes, 24*, 381–400.

Planken, B., & Nickerson, C. (2009). English for specific business purposes: Intercultural issues and the use of business English as a lingua franca. In D. Belcher (Ed.), *English for specific purposes in theory and practice* (pp. 127–142). Ann Arbor: University of Michigan Press.

Poncini, G. (2004). *Discursive strategies in multicultural business meetings*. Frankfurt: Peter Lang.

Rogerson-Revell, P. (1999). Meeting talk: A stylistic approach to teaching meeting skills. In M. Hewings & C. Nickerson (Eds.), *Business English: Research into practice* (pp. 55–72). London: Longman.

Salager-Meyer, F. (2008). Scientific publishing in developing countries: Challenges for the future. *Journal of English for Academic Purposes*, 7, 121–132.

Samraj, B., & Monk, L. (2008). The statement of purpose in graduate program applications: Genre structure and disciplinary variation. *English for Specific Purposes*, 27, 193–211.

Seidlhofer. B. (2007). Common property: English as a lingua franca in Europe. In J. Cummins & C. Davison (Eds.), *The international handbook of English language teaching* (Vol. 1) (pp. 137–153). Norwell, MA: Springer Publications.

Stapleton, P., & Helms-Park, R. (2008). A response to Matsuda and Tardy's "Voice in academic writing: the rhetorical construction of author identity in blind manuscript review". *English for Specific Purposes*, 27, 94–99.

Starfield, S. (2001). "I'll go with the group": Rethinking discourse community in EAP. In J. Flowerdew & M. Peacock (Eds.), *Handbook of research on English for academic purposes* (pp. 132–147). Cambridge: Cambridge University Press.

Starfield, S. (2002). "I'm a second-language English speaker": Negotiating writer identity and authority in Sociology One. *Journal of Language, Identity, and Education*, 1, 121–140.

Starfield, S. (2004). Wordpower: Negotiating success in a first-year sociology essay. In L. J. Ravelli & R. A. Ellis (Eds.), *Analysing academic writing: Contextualised frameworks* (pp. 66–83). London: Continuum.

Starfield, S. (2010). Ethnographies. In B. Paltridge & A. Phakiti. (Eds.), *Continuum companion to research methods in applied linguistics* (pp. 50–65). London: Continuum.

Starfield, S. (2011). ESP and critical ethnography. In D Belcher, A. M. Johns & B. Paltridge (Eds.), *New directions in ESP research*. Ann Arbor: University of Michigan Press.

Starfield, S., & Ravelli, L. J. (2006). "The writing of this thesis was a process that I could not explore with the positivistic detachment of the classical sociologist": Self and structure in New Humanities research theses. *Journal of English for Academic Purposes*, 5, 222–243.

Swales, J. M. (1981). Aspects of article introductions. *Aston ESP Research Reports, No 1*. Language Studies Unit, the University of Aston at Birmingham.

Swales, J. M. (1990). *Genre analysis: English in academic and research settings*. Cambridge: Cambridge University Press.

Swales, J. M. (1996). Occluded genres in the academy: The case of the submission letter. In E. Ventola & A. Mauranen (Eds.), *Academic writing: Intercultural and textual issues* (pp. 45–58). Amsterdam and Philadelphia: John Benjamins.

Swales, J. M. (1998a). Textography: Toward a contextualization of written academic discourse. *Research on Language and Social Interaction*, 31: 109–121.

Swales, J. M. (1998b). *Other floors, other voices: A textography of a small university building*. Mahwah, NJ: Laurence Erlbaum.

Swales, J. M. (2000). Languages for specific purposes. *Annual Review of Applied Linguistics*, 20, 59–76.

Swales, J. M. (2004). *Research genres: Explorations and applications*. Cambridge: Cambridge University Press.

Tardy, C. (2004). The role of English in scientific communication: Lingua franca or Tyrannosaurus rex? *Journal of English for Academic Purposes*, 3, 247–269.

Tardy, C. (2006). Researching first and second language genre learning: A comparative review and a look ahead. *Journal of Second Language Writing*, 15, 79–101.

Tardy, C. (2008). Multimodality and the teaching of advanced academic writing: A genre systems perspective on speaking-writing connections. In A. Hirvela & D. Belcher (Eds.), *The oral/literate connection: Perspectives on L2 speaking, writing, and other media interactions* (pp. 191–208). Ann Arbor: University of Michigan Press.

Tardy, C., & Swales, J. M. (2008). Form, text organization, genre, coherence, and cohesion. In C. Bazerman (Ed.), *Handbook of research on writing. History, society, school, individual, text* (pp. 565–581). New York: Lawrence Erlbaum.

Tarone, E., Dwyer, S., Gillette, S. & Icke, V. (1981). On the use of the passive in two astrophysics journal papers. *English for Specific Purposes*, 1, 123–140.

Tribble, C. (2002). Corpora and corpus analysis: New windows on academic writing. In J. Flowerdew (Ed.), *Academic discourse* (pp. 131–149). London: Longman.

Trosberg, A. (Ed.) (2000). *Analysing professional discourses*. Amsterdam: John Benjamins.

Uzuner, S. (2008). Multilingual scholars' participation in core/global academic communities: A literature review, *Journal of English for Academic Purposes*, 7, 250–263.

Vickers. C. H. (2007). Second language socialization through team interaction among electrical and computer Engineering students. *The Modern Language Journal*, 91(iv), 621–640.

Wenger, E. (1998). *Communities of practice: Learning, meaning and identity*. Cambridge: Cambridge University Press.

Zappa-Hollman, S. (2007). Academic presentations across post-secondary contexts: The discourse socialization of non-native English speakers. *The Canadian Modern Language Review/La Revue Canadienne des Langues Vivantes*, 63, 455–485.

8
English as an International Lingua Franca Pedagogy

Sandra Lee McKay

This chapter begins by distinguishing major approaches to the current spread of English and discusses how the approach taken in this chapter differs. The chapter then summarizes existing research on various aspects of English language teaching (ELT) including:

- imagined communities and ELT;
- English learning and identity; and
- inequality of access in English language learning.

The third section describes future challenges and research agendas in ELT pedagogy while the closing section sets forth principles that should inform ELT pedagogy.

Globalization and the Use of English

Perhaps no other term has been as widely used and abused during the twenty-first century as the term *globalization*. For some, globalization has leveled the playing field, making it possible for everyone to have equal access to a global market and information exchange. This view of globalization forms the basis for Friedman's (2005) popular book, *The World Is Flat*, in which he argues that today the world is flat, allowing individuals to stay in their own locale while participating in a globally linked economic and information system. Others (e.g., Barber, 1996), however, see globalization as the cause of a loss of cultural and linguistic diversity, which, rather than leveling the playing field, has contributed to greater disparity between the rich and the poor.

Giddens (1990) defines globalization as "the intensification of world wide social relations which link distant localities in such a way that local happenings are shaped by events occurring many miles away and vice versa" (p. 64). In my discussion of globalization, I will view globalization as a reformulation of social space in which the global and local are constantly interacting with one another; in addition, I will argue that neither one should be afforded a dominant position. Canagarajah (2005, p. xiv) makes a similar point when he argues for the need to balance local and global concerns. As he puts it:

The local shouldn't be of secondary relation or subsidiary status to the dominant discourses and institutions from powerful communities, whereby the global is simply applied, translated, or contextualized to the local. Making a space for the local doesn't mean merely "adding" another component or subfield to the paradigms that already dominate many fields. It means radically reexamining our disciplines to orientate to language, identity, knowledge and social relations from a totally different perspective. A local grounding should become the primary and critical force in the construction of contextually relevant knowledge if we are to develop more plural discourses.

Currently, more and more books and articles are addressing the topic of globalization and English teaching (e.g., Block & Cameron, 2002; Canagarajah, 2005; Crystal, 1997; McKay, 2002; McKay & Bokhorst-Heng, 2008; Pennycook, 2007; Phillipson, 1992). In this chapter, I examine various perspectives of the global spread of English and its influence on English teaching. In sorting through these perspectives, it is helpful to consider Pennycook's (2003) categorization of current attitudes toward the spread of English. The first is what he calls the *homogeny position*, which views the spread of English as leading to a homogenization of world culture. For some, this homogenization is viewed favorably and almost triumphantly. Crystal (1997), for example, cites various statistics to document the pervasiveness of English today and tends to view this pervasiveness as a positive characteristic of globalization. Others, however, see homogenization as essentially a negative feature of globalization, reflecting imperialism and colonization (Phillipson, 1992), and leading to the loss of other languages (Nettle & Romaine, 2000). What is lacking in this perspective is an account of the agency of individuals to react to imperialism and language loss, a point raised by Brutt-Griffler (2002), Canagarajah (2005) and Pennycook (1998, 2007).

The second position delineated by Pennycook (2003) is the *heterogeny position* in which individuals such as Braj Kachru describe the features of World Englishes as a sign of the pluricentricism that has been brought about by globalization. The goal of the World Englishes paradigm has been to describe the manner in which English has become localized, creating different varieties of English around the world. For Pennycook (2003, p. 8), there is a major shortcoming in this perspective. As he puts it:

> While the homogeny argument tends to ignore all these local appropriations and adaptations, this heterogeny argument tends to ignore the broader political context of the spread of English. Indeed there is a constant insistence on the neutrality of English, a position that avoids all the crucial concerns around both the global and local politics of the language. Furthermore, by focusing on the standardization of local versions of English, the world Englishes paradigm shifts the locus of control but not its nature, and by so doing ignores power and struggle in language.

In the end, Pennycook (2003) argues that the ultimate effect of globalization on the use of English is neither homogenization nor heterogenization; rather it is "a fluid mixture of cultural heritage … and popular culture …, of change and tradition, of border crossing and ethnic affiliation, of global appropriation and local contextualization" (p. 10). This, he contends, is what the new global order is about.

It is essential to consider the various perspectives outlined above since the effect of globalization on language teaching can only be critically examined if one considers the manner in which the discourses surrounding English teaching frame the topic of globalization. I agree with Fairclough (2006) that it is important to distinguish the actual process of globalization from the discourses of globalization. As Fairclough puts it:

> (a) there are real processes of (e.g. economic) globalization, independently of whether people recognize them or not, and of how they represent them; (b) but as soon as we begin to reflect

upon and discuss these real processes, we *have* to represent them, and the ways in which we represent them inevitably draw upon certain discourses rather than others. So we might say that the problem turns into that of how we decide *which* discourses to draw upon in reflecting upon and discussing these real processes—how we determine whether and to what extent particular discourses provide us with representations which are adequate for these purposes.

(Fairclough, 2006, p. 5; emphasis in the original)

My purpose then in describing various discourses that surround the topic of globalization and language teaching is to better assess which discourses are more adequate for representing and assessing the relationship between globalization and language teaching. We turn now to an examination of current approaches to the global use of English.

Defining Present-Day English Use

World Englishes

The terminology used to describe present-day English reflects the different approaches to English use offered by professionals in the field. One of the most prevalent perspectives aims to describe the phonological, grammatical, lexical and pragmatic features of the current use of English as a factor of geographical region. This perspective is typically referred to as *World Englishes*. The term *World Englishes* is based on Kachru's (1986) early description of institutionalized varieties of English. Kachru distinguishes three major types of users of English: (1) native users of English for whom English is the first language in almost all functions; (2) nonnative users of English who use an institutionalized second-language (L2) variety of English; and (3) nonnative users of English who consider English as a foreign language and use it in highly restricted domains. Kachru refers to speakers in the first group as members of the Inner Circle, the second group as members of the Outer Circle and the last group as members of the Expanding Circle. Kachru argues that speakers in the Outer Circle have an institutionalized variety of English, which he describes in the following manner:

> The institutionalized second-language varieties have a long history of acculturation in new cultural and geographical contexts; they have a large range of functions in the local educational, administrative, and legal system. The result of such uses is that such varieties have developed nativized discourse and style types and functionally determined sublanguages (registers) and are used as a linguistic vehicle for creative writing.

(Kachru, 1986, p. 19)

According to Kachru, World Englishes have developed largely in former British colonies where English is used in many domains on a daily basis and has been influenced by local languages and cultures. Whereas Kachru's model was instrumental in initially recognizing the validity of varieties of English, the spread of English has brought with it far more complexity in use than can be captured by the model.

Presently there are a growing number of standardized varieties of English—not just in Kachru's Outer Circle countries, but also as Lowenberg (2002) documents, in many Expanding Circle nations as well. According to Lowenberg (2002, p. 431), in certain intranational and regional domains of language use (for example, across Europe), English actually functions as a second language, and often develops nativized norms. In addition, these processes of nativization have resulted in not just the development of different varieties of Standard English between countries, but also varieties of English within countries (see, for example, Bamgbose, 1998). In addition there exists a variety of English proficiency levels within a specific social context.

This situation has led Pakir (1991), drawing on the varieties of English spoken in Singapore, to depict the use of English within Singapore and other countries as a factor of the formality of the context and the speakers' level of proficiency (see Figure 8.1). It places variation in Singapore English along two clines (influenced by Kachru's (1983) "cline of English bilingualism"): the *proficiency* cline and the *formality* cline, reflecting the *users* and *uses* of English. Pakir's model is represented through a series of expanding triangles, which represent the differing ranges of styles of English-speaking Singaporeans, with education and English proficiency offering an increasing range of choice. Those users of English with higher education are located at the top ends of both the formality and proficiency clines. They often are capable of the whole range of English expressions, and able to move along the whole length of the formality cline. Those at the base of the triangle have lower levels of proficiency, typically have lower levels of education and tend to come from a lower socio-economic background. They are more restricted in their movement along the formality cline, and can usually speak only the colloquial forms of Singapore English.

What World Englishes interpretations attempt to do is to develop a model that describes and legitimizes a pluricentric view of English, and one that moves away from any view of there being just one standard form against which all others are measured. As argued by Kachru (1983, 1992), English has "blended itself with the cultural and social complex" (1983, p. 139) of the country and has thereby become "culture-bound" (1983, p. 140) in it. Therefore, he argues, new Englishes cannot be characterized in terms of acquisitional inadequacy, or be judged by the norms of English in Inner Circle countries. World Englishes attempts to place all varieties of English on par with each other without any one being a reference point.

English as a Lingua Franca

Recently a good deal of attention has been focused on an analysis of interactions between L2 speakers of English, termed English as a lingua franca (ELF) talk. Firth (1996) provided one of the earliest definitions of ELF stating that ELF interactions are those in which English is used as "a 'contact language' between persons who share neither a common native tongue nor a common (national) culture, and for whom English is the chosen *foreign* language of communication" (p. 240; emphasis in original).

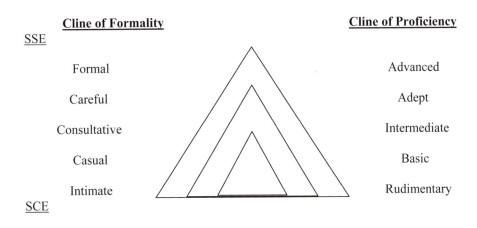

Figure 8.1 Pakir's expanding triangles of Singapore English

Source: Pakir (1991, p. 174).
Notes: SSE = Singapore Standard English; SCE = Singapore Colloquial English.

Such interactions occur frequently in Expanding Circle countries where English is used for business, political, academic and travel purposes.

Pragmatic Features

Some of the current research on ELF has focused on identifying the pragmatic features of ELF interactions, as was done in Firth's (1996) seminal article on ELF. Firth's data involved a collection of telephone calls from two Danish international trading companies involving Danish export managers and their international clients. As Firth points out, one of the major advantages of analyzing such discourse from a conversational analysis perspective rather than as "foreigner talk," "interlanguage talk" or "learner interaction" perspective is that the participant is viewed as "a *language user* whose real-world interactions are deserving of unprejudiced *description* rather … than as a person conceived *a priori* to be the possessor of incomplete or deficient communicative competence, putatively striving for the 'target' competence of an idealized 'native speaker'" (p. 241; emphasis in original). Firth contends that an unprejudiced description of ELF interactions clearly demonstrates that "lingua franca talk is not only meaningful, it is also '*normal*' and, indeed, '*ordinary*' (p. 242; emphasis in original).

Summarizing the findings of existing data on the pragmatic aspect of ELF interactions, Seidlhofer (2004, p. 218) provides the following generalizations regarding the pragmatics of ELF:

- Misunderstandings are not frequent in ELF interactions; when they do occur, they tend to be resolved either by topic change, or less often, by overt negotiation using communication strategies such as rephrasing and repetition.
- Interference from L1 [first language] interactional norms is very rare—a kind of suspension of expectations regarding norms seems to be in operation.
- As long as a certain threshold of understanding is obtained, interlocutors seem to adopt what Firth (1996) has termed the "let-it-pass principle," which gives the impression of ELF talk being overtly consensus-oriented, cooperative and mutually supportive, and thus fairly robust.

Grammatical Features

Current work in ELF research is also investigating the grammatical and phonological features of ELF interactions. Significant contributions to identifying the grammatical features of ELF are underway through the compilation of the Vienna–Oxford International Corpus of English (VOICE) now in progress at the University of Vienna under the supervision of Siedlhofer. The corpus includes face-to-face interactions among fairly fluent speakers of English from a wide range of L1 backgrounds in a variety of settings in which participants have various roles and relationships. At this point, an initial data analysis has highlighted particular grammatical items, which, though often emphasized in language classrooms, do not appear to cause problems in communicative success. These include:

- dropping the third person present tense *–s*;
- confusing the relative pronouns *who* and *which*;
- omitting the definite and indefinite articles where they are obligatory in ENL [English as a native language], and inserting them where they do not occur in ENL;
- failing to use correct tag questions (e.g., *isn't it?* or *no?* instead of *shouldn't they?*);
- inserting redundant prepositions, as in *We have to study about …*;
- overusing certain verbs of high semantic generality, such as *do, have, make, put, take*;
- replacing infinitive-constructions with *that*-clauses, as in *I want that*;
- overdoing explicitness (e.g., *black color* rather than just *black).*

(Seidlhofer, 2004, p. 220)

Phonological Features

Finally, research on ELF interactions has led to the identification of the phonological features of ELF interactions. Jenkins (2000), in her work on the phonology of English as an International Language, analyzed the interactions of six learners of English—two Japanese, three Swiss-German and one Swiss-French—all at the upper-intermediate to low-advanced level who were recorded as they practiced for the Cambridge Certificate in Advanced English speaking examinations. Some of these interactions were between interlocutors with the same L1, others were between speakers of different L1s. Using these data, Jenkins identified 40 occasions where there was a breakdown in communication due to pronunciation, lexis, grammar, world knowledge or ambiguity. All of the breakdowns in the data occurred between speakers of different L1 backgrounds. In addition, the vast majority of breakdowns (27) were due to pronunciation problems, with another eight due to lexis.

Based on her investigation, Jenkins (2000) delineates what she terms a phonological Lingua Franca Core, that is, phonological features that appear to be most crucial for intelligibility among L2 speakers of English. Based on her data (Jenkins, 2000, p. 132), the central features of this core appear to be the following:

1. most consonant sounds;
2. appropriate consonant cluster simplification;
3. vowel length distinction;
4. nuclear stress.

She argues that since these features have the greatest potential for causing breakdowns in communication between speakers of different L1 backgrounds, the pedagogical focus in ELT classrooms should be on the production of most consonant sounds, initial consonant clusters, vowel length and nuclear stress. Less attention needs to be given to word stress, rhythm and features of connected speech. While the World Englishes paradigm has highlighted the pluricentric nature of English standards, the ELF perspective has contributed to our understanding of some of the pragmatic, grammatical and phonological features of L2 speakers of English in contact with other L2 speakers.

English as an International Lingua Franca

Sharing Pennycook's perspective on the fluidity of current English use and standards, I will use English as an international lingual franca (EILF) as an umbrella term to characterize the use of English between any two L2 speakers of English, whether sharing the same culture or not, as well as between L2 and L1 speakers of English. Although it is valuable to define the features of local varieties of English as is done in the World Englishes and ELF paradigm, it is essential to describe the local linguistic ecology of interactions, as well as the social dimensions of particular interactions.

In many contexts there is a local lingua franca that affects and is affected by the role of English in the particular geographical and social context. For example, in many rural areas of Japan today, there are growing numbers of language minority migrant workers, mainly from Brazil, China, Thailand and Vietnam. The local lingua franca is, of course, Japanese. However, the current emphasis on English teaching in Japan has resulted in all children learning English rather than any of the minority languages spoken in the local area. It has also resulted in a commonly accepted assumption that the way to communicate with these migrants is through English or Japanese rather than other languages. Thus, while on the local level, bilingual speakers of Portuguese, Chinese, Thai and Vietnam are sorely needed, the second language that almost everyone is engaged in learning is English, primarily because it is seen as having more economic capital and international currency.

It is situations such as this that demonstrate the need to examine the local linguistic ecology in making any generalizations about the use of English in a particular social context. In fact in Japan today it is Japanese that serves as the local lingual franca even though many Japanese in their rhetoric and language policies seem to believe that English is the sole second language that should be learned. My approach to current English use then emphasizes the localized nature of interactions and the fluidity of present-day language use. Often in the local linguistic ecology English plays more of a symbolic role than an actual medium of communication. What exists today then is a "heterogeneous global English speech community, with a heterogeneous English and different modes of competence" (Canagarajah, 2006, p. 211).

Research Findings

With English being considered by many as a global language, individuals around the world are striving to learn English, leading to a large English teaching/learning industry. In summarizing current research on EILF, there are several areas in which researchers have gained important insights into the teaching and learning of English. These have to do with

- imagined communities and EILF;
- English learning and identity;
- inequality of access in English language learning; and
- standards and EILF pedagogy.

Imagined Communities as Incentives for English Learning

Back in 1986, in a book entitled, *The Alchemy of English*, Kachru (1986) argued that "knowing English is like possessing the fabled Aladdin's lamp, which permits one to open, as it were, the linguistic gates to international business, technology, science and travel. In short, English provides linguistic power" (p. 1). This belief in the power of English has resulted in many language learners imagining the various benefits that would come if they only learned English. Often these imagined communities are depicted in the narratives of language learners. Such narratives reinforce the belief of many English learners that if they invest in English learning, they will reap the benefits of social and intellectual mobility.

Recent research on English learning has documented some of these narratives of imagined communities. Niño-Murcia (2003) cites Peruvian narratives that recount the benefits of joining an imagined community of English speakers. Niño-Murcia examined the beliefs of English learners in Tupicocha, an agro-pastoral village of 1,543 inhabitants that is losing its population from emigration. While people over 40 generally do not express any interest in learning English, this is not true for the younger generation. Many of these young people want to learn English so that they can take distance-learning courses on the Internet; others want to learn English so that they can go to an English-speaking country and earn more money. For example, one respondent, Luz (age 25), when asked why she was studying English, responded that she wanted to learn English so she could go to the United States and earn a good salary. In her mind English proficiency was the key to both immigration and making money. Yet as Niño-Murcia (2003, p. 132) points out:

> Luz's illusions aside, English is in reality a very minimal factor in whether people are able to surmount the barrier. While the popular media contain vast amounts of false information about both English and the countries where it prevails, they give little or no accurate information about how in fact the immigration/illegal migration system works. It is the financial

requirements of the embassy, not the language factor at all, which actually sets limits on legal access to the USA.

Park and Abelmann (2004) offer a poignant account of the imagined communities Korean mothers want their children to belong to. Arguing that presently in South Korea there is "a veritable English language mania" (p. 646) brought on largely by the implementation of English learning in the elementary school in South Korea, Park and Abelmann investigated the aspirations of English learning of South Korean women of various economic classes. Regardless of economic class, all of the mothers yearned for their children to acquire English so that they would become cosmopolitan, living at home yet part of the world. While many of the upper-class women could afford to help their children become part of this world by giving them private English lessons or sending them abroad for their elementary education, this was not the case for less affluent families. The authors describe how less affluent mothers still imagine their children as part of this cosmopolitan world. As one less affluent mother put it, she "still dreams that her children might someday live abroad in a 'bigger world'—'even if they have to live abroad as beggars *(koij)*'" (p. 654). Like many less affluent mothers around the world, this mother imagines "her children on a broader stage, despite their likely lower status abroad" (p. 654).

The concept of an imagined community is one that has not gone unnoticed by ELT private schools. Evidence of this is the establishment of theme villages that depict an imagined environment. Seargeant (2005), for example, describes British Hill, a leisure language-learning complex that seeks to simulate an "authentic" English-speaking environment. In fact, the sales slogan "boasts that the complex is 'More English than England itself'" (p. 327). The village is staffed by native speakers recruited from Britain, Canada, Australia and New Zealand.

By hiring only native speakers and promoting native speaker competency, the village promotes a reality that is far different from the multilingual/multicultural Britain of today. In doing so,

> [t]he overall effect is to create an environment which is not necessarily truthful to the original upon which it is purportedly based but is instead an imagined idea with its own logic and reality. The authenticity upon which British Hills prides itself is not a representation of Britishness as it is currently constructed and enacted in mainstream British society. Instead, it is an image drawn from aspects of the popular imagination in Japan, from a tourist industry template … and also from local protocol for foreign language education.
>
> (Seargeant, 2005, p. 341)

In this context, authenticity becomes not the genuine item but a fake representation of a different reality. As Seargent (2005, p. 341) puts it:

> [S]imulation replaces reality, becomes its own reality. A place like British Hills is not merely representing Britishness but reconstructing it, thus presenting itself as a detailed realistic image of something that actually exists only within its own depiction. The use of the concept of authenticity is almost an irony of the process.

The theory underlying such villages is that learning can be enhanced by students actually imagining themselves in the role of a fluent speaker in an "authentic" environment.

Much has been learned then about how imagined communities can further reinforce Kachru's idea of English competency as a kind of Aladdin's lamp. These imagined communities can also be a powerful force in commercial aspects of language learning. Linked closely to language learners' imagined community of English speakers is the new identity that may potentially come from belonging to this community, either as an aspiration or as a reality. Indeed another area in which a great deal has been learned is the role of identity in language learning.

The Role of Identity in Language Learning

Examining the identity of L2 learners is a relatively recent interest in L2 acquisition research. In the past, major attention was devoted to interlanguage analysis, with little recognition given to learning processes, individual variables or the social context in which a second language is learned. However, recent work, informed by poststructuralist approaches and critical theory (e.g., McKay & Wong, 1996; Peirce, 1995; Rampton, 1995), has begun to examine how educational institutions can position students in particular ways. Work that is especially relevant to our discussion examines how school discourses can position English language learners within the educational context, and hence, give them a particular identity.

   One area that allows English learners to assume a new identity, challenging the identity often given to them as "deficient" learners, is cyber space. In fact recent research is documenting the many ways in which the Internet opens new opportunities for English learners. Lam's (2000) study documents how computer-mediated communication (CMC) allows language learners to assume a new identity, one that can enhance literacy skills. Lam's study was a case study of a Chinese immigrant teenager to the United States, named Almon. When Lam first began studying Almon, he had little confidence in writing in English, which he contended was always his worst subject. However, after designing his own home page and joining an electronic community interested in Japanese pop culture, he gained confidence in his literacy through his on-line exchanges with pen pals. Lam contends that the community Almon joined on the web allowed him to develop a new identity, one that gave him self-confidence. She concludes that,

> whereas classroom English appeared to contribute to Almon's sense of exclusion or marginalization (his inability to speak like a native), which paradoxically contradicts the school's mandate to prepare students for the workplace and civic involvement, the English he controlled on the Internet enabled him to develop a sense of belongingness and connectedness to a global English-speaking community. Almon was learning not only more English but also more relevant and appropriate English for the World Wide Web community he sought to become a part of.
>
> (Lam, 2000, p. 476)

Whereas before Almon joined the electronic community on Japanese pop culture he viewed English as his biggest problem believing that even in 10 years his English wouldn't be that good, his experience in the chat room and the friends he made changed his outlook. As he puts it:

> I've changed a lot in the last 2 months, actually. I have kind of changed my determination. I'm not as fearful, or afraid of the future, that I won't have a future. I'm not as afraid now ... When I was feeling *negative*, I felt the world doesn't belong to me, and it's hard to survive here. And I felt not many people understand me, or would. I didn't feel like I belong to this world ... But now I feel there's nothing much to be afraid of. It really depends on how you go about it. It's not like the world always has power over you. It was [names of a few chat mates and e-mail pen pals] who helped me to change and encouraged me. If I hadn't known them, perhaps I wouldn't have changed so much ... Yes maybe the *Internet* has changed me.
>
> (Interview, October 5, 1997 cited in Lam, 2000, p. 468)

Black (2006) finds similar benefits with the use of fanfiction by L2 learners. Fanfiction "is writing in which fans use media narratives and pop cultural icons as inspiration for creating their own texts"

(p. 172). While the majority of the fiction is in English there is a good deal of incorporation of other languages and culture. Based on a year of focused participant observation of one fanfiction website, Black (2005) found that many fan authors created linguistically hybrid texts in which they would ask other participants to help them incorporate aspects of the other participants' cultures into their texts. In so doing they often constructed a hybridized identity in their texts. Black also found that there was a great deal of peer review and proofreading that went on through the participants' interaction with one another. This occurred because frequently participants included an author's note in which they identified themselves as an English language learner who was trying to improve their composition skills. In light of the positive effect that pop culture and the World Wide Web can engender in learners' identity, confidence and literacy skills, one cannot help but agree with Lam (2000) that "TESOL in today's global, multicultural world needs a broad and critical conception of language and literacy that is responsive to students' relations to multiple target languages and cultural communities" (p. 478).

Inequality of Access in English Learning

As was pointed out in the case of the South Korean mothers, often less affluent families cannot afford special programs to support their children's English learning. Unfortunately, this economic divide in access to English is often reinforced by Ministries of Education themselves. China is a case in point. In 1976 Deng Xiaoping launched a national modernization program in which English education was seen as a key component: "English was recognized as an important tool for engaging in economic, commercial, technological and cultural exchange with the rest of the world and hence for facilitating the modernization process" (Hu, 2005, p. 8).

In 1978 the Ministry of Education issued the first unified primary and secondary curriculum for the era of modernization. This curriculum introduced foreign language learning at Primary 3. The directive also mandated that efforts in promoting English language proficiency were to be aimed at strengthening English language teaching in elite schools, which were expected to produce the English-proficient personnel needed to successfully undertake national modernization. In fact, in 1985 the Ministry of Education exempted poorly resourced schools from providing English instruction. In addition, the Ministry of Education gave several economically developed provinces and municipalities the autonomy to develop their own English curricula, syllabi and textbooks for primary and secondary education (Hu, 2005). These materials tended to be more innovative, learner-centered and communicative than earlier classroom texts and materials.

An economic divide in English learning is also evident in the current English education policies in Hong Kong where, in 1997, the Department of Education in Hong Kong announced a sweeping change in the medium of instruction in Hong Kong schools so that most schools were asked to adopt Chinese as the medium of instruction. At the same time, the government made an exemption for a minority of schools which had been operating successfully in English to continue using English as the medium of instruction (Choi, 2003). According to Choi (2003, p. 673) the policy that

> provided for the selection of the best primary school graduates for monolingual education, was designed to be a cost-effective way of training in English skills for those who had the economic and cultural capital to benefit from it. Meanwhile, the majority of students were barred from sufficient exposure to English, the language of power and wealth.

Choi contends that the policy was basically engineered by business interests right before the change over in 1997 and that its ultimate effect was to "perpetuate a form of linguistic imperialism" (2003, p. 673).

In order to justify the policy, the government extolled the benefits of mother-tongue education; however, many parents believed that what would be best for their children was for them to go to English-medium schools and potentially gain the economic capital they believed, rightly or wrongly, would come from proficiency in English. Many parents strove to get their children into the small number of English-medium schools, enrolled them in expensive international schools and even sent their children overseas to Anglophone countries to study, options that were available only to a small proportion of economically elite families. The Hong Kong language policy then had everal negative effects brought on by globalization and the spread of English: first it encouraged an economic divide in the learning of English; second, it minimized the value of using the mother tongue in education with its implicit suggestion that this option was in some ways less desirable; and finally, it promoted the idea of the desirability of an English-only classroom in the acquisition of English.

An economic divide in the teaching of English is also evident in South Korea where Park and Abelmann (2004, p. 646) argue that

> English has long been a class marker in South Korea: namely knowledge of and comfort with English has been a sign of educational opportunity, and for some of the experience of travel or study abroad and contact with foreigners in South Korea.

The size of the English language market in South Korea is estimated to be about $3,333 million dollars a year with another $833 million spent on study abroad programs. The private after-school education market is also booming, particularly after it was announced in 1995 that English would become an elementary school subject. Many Korean parents are sending their children to English language kindergartens, even though such schools are typically three times more expensive than ordinary kindergartens (Park, 2006). In addition, the number of Korean students studying abroad in English-speaking countries has increased more than tenfold in the past six years. In fact, the number of elementary students alone has increased from 212 in 1998 to 6,276 in 2004, marking a thirty-fold increase (Chung, 2006).

The current state of English education raises two critical issues. The first is how to convince parents and students of the value of having a bilingual/biliterate population. At the present time in many countries, parents, school administrators and teachers support an English-only agenda in the schools in the belief that this is best for their children. Often, a child's first language is viewed as a problem rather than a resource. The second issue is how to provide less advantaged children in the society with equal access to English so they can succeed in institutions of higher education.

Future Challenges and Research Agendas

The Question of Standards

A major concern in EILF pedagogy and research is the question of what standards of use and usage should be promoted in EILF classrooms. The spread of English has brought with it the development of many new varieties of English, which has led to much discussion regarding what standards should be promoted in the teaching of English. Implicit in discussions of variation are the notion of standards, a standard language and issues of power and identity that are built into such concepts. *Standard language* is the term generally used to refer to that variety of a language that is considered the norm. It is the variety regarded as the ideal for educational purposes, and usually used as a yardstick by which to measure other varieties. The related notion of *language standards* has to do with the language rules that inform the standard, and that are then taught in the schools.

The challenge that World Englishes present to the Standard English ideology is one of plurality—that there should be different standards for different contexts of use; that the definition of each Standard English should be endonormative (determined locally) rather than exonormative (determined by outside its context of use). However, if there are different forms of Standard English, the concern of mutual intelligibility emerges. The fact that some speakers of English use a variety of English that is quite different from a standard variety of English has led some to argue that the use of these varieties of English will lead to a lack of intelligibility among speakers of English. It is this fear that has led to a widespread debate over standards in the use of English.

The delineation of key features of ELF interactions has resulted in a good deal of consensus regarding what the pragmatics goals of an English as an international language (EIL) curricula should entail. Among these goals are the following:

1. Explicit attention should be given to introducing and practicing repair strategies, such as asking for clarification and repetition, rephrasing and allowing wait time.
2. A variety of conversational gambits or routines should be introduced and practiced, including such items as expressing agreement and disagreement, managing turn-taking and taking leave.
3. The curriculum should seek to promote students' understanding of how pragmatic norms can differ cross-culturally.
4. Students should be free to express their own pragmatic norms but to recognize that, to the extent these standards differ from the norms expected by their listener, there may be cross-cultural misunderstandings (McKay, 2005).

In her discussion on pragmatic competence in ELF, House (2003) argues that since ELF research suggests that the participants belong to a rather vague but existing community of ELF speakers, in which negotiation of meaning is paramount, it is inappropriate to teach the pragmatic norms of an Inner Circle country. Rather the curriculum should "focus on the learners' need to be flexibly competent in international communication through the medium of the English language in as broad a spectrum of topics, themes, and purposes as possible" (p. 149).

Whereas the delineation of pragmatic goals for ELF interactions has raised little controversy, this is not the case in regards to the grammatical goals of an ELF curriculum and to a lesser degree to phonological goals. Many agree that in terms of phonological emphasis, ELF classrooms should give primary attention to the Lingua Franca Core delineated by Jenkins. Prodromou (2006), for example, points out the difficulty of attaining native-like pronunciation, and thus believes it is reasonable to focus primarily on those phonological features that can impede communication. Likewise, Prodromou (2006) states that once it is clear which grammatical items do not impede comprehension, some educators may conclude these features need not be addressed in the English classroom. In terms of Seidlhofer's (2004) findings on the grammatical features of ELF interactions, this would suggest that ELF classes need not focus on items such as the deletion of the third person singular *-s* or the distinction between *who* and *which*. It is important to note, however, that Seidlhofer (2006, p. 44) herself makes no claim as to the pedagogical implications of her work. As she says:

I should also like to emphasize that I have never made any general pronouncements as to what should be taught and what shouldn't be—this is a complex pedagogic matter which will have to be decided by teachers for their particular contexts and their particular learners. … When doing empirical research into ELF I am doing this as a descriptive linguist, and it is not my task, and indeed impossible, to pre-empt any local pedagogic decisions.

Nevertheless some have assumed that her findings should be used as basis for deciding what should be taught in a grammar classroom, with ELF features rather than Standard English as the target. Some, however, take issue with this stance. Timmis (2002), for example, contends that many learners want to attain native-like grammatical proficiency and so it would be inappropriate not to teach the norms of a standard variety of English. He bases this conclusion on a survey he undertook of 400 students and 180 teachers on their pronunciation and grammatical goals. In terms of pronunciation, both students and teachers tended to want to attain native-like pronunciation. This tendency, however, was less prevalent among students from South Africa, Pakistan and India, suggesting that pronunciation goals may be context specific. In reference to grammatical goals, once again students and teachers preferred attaining native-speaker norms. Based on his survey results, Timmis (2002) argues that "while it is clearly inappropriate to foist native-speaker norms on students who neither want nor need them, it is scarcely more appropriate to offer students a target which does not meet their aspirations" (p. 249).

Kuo (2006) also argues for teaching native-speaker grammatical standards, pointing out that whereas English serves an important role in functional international interactions, English also is "the language for international, and in fact intra-national competition" (p. 219). For many learners of English, English is being learned as an important school subject to attain academic and professional goals. As such, learners need access to forms that will be used to determine their proficiency in English. Kuo (2006, p. 220) argues that it is

> because English is now used extensively for international and intercultural purposes that in order to ease or smooth the flow of conversation, to reduce the listener's burden of processing information, and to satisfy learners' need that stretch beyond merely international intelligibility, L2 learners should be allowed, if not encouraged, to follow a native-speaker phonological or grammatical model.

The debate regarding the teaching of standards continues today with some arguing for the promotion of a monolithic model of English while others support a pluricentric model. Those who argue for a monolithic model contend that native-speaker models should be promoted because they have been codified and have a degree of historical authority. The monolithic model is in keeping with one of the central tenets that Phillipson (1992) argues has traditionally informed English language teaching, namely, that the ideal teacher of English is a native-speaker. This perspective also lends support to the notion of the insider and outsider, the Self and the Other, since it is native speakers who are seen as the guardians of Standard English. On the other hand, those such as Kachru who support a pluricentric model of English contend that language contact necessarily leads to language change. They argue that the development of new varieties of English is a natural result of the spread of English. In many ways the debate reflects a tension between the global and the local brought about by the new social space of globalization. Whereas global space has brought exposure to English, local space has taken the language and modified it for the local context. What is important to add to the pluricentric perspective is that today language use is often not just English but a mix of a variety of languages that highlights the speaker's identity and proficiency. In such encounters, the question of standards needs to be highly contextualized.

A Tendency of Othering in EILF Pedagogy

A second area that presents a challenge for the ELT profession is the tendency toward *Othering* in EILF pedagogy. Othering refers to the ways in which the "discourse of a particular group defines other groups in opposition to itself; an Us and Them view that constructs an identity for the Other and, implicitly for the Self" (Palfreyman, 2005, pp. 213–214). In EILF pedagogy this discourse often positions English learners and bilingual teachers as deficient in comparison to native speakers. This discourse has led to the idealization of the so-called native speaker, as well as to a lack of recognition of the benefits of local bilingual teachers. It has also resulted in an unwillingness to recognize the right of English speakers outside Inner Circle countries to nativize the language for the local cultural context. Finally, the Self–Other discourse has at times positioned certain groups as incapable of participating in "modern" methods of language learning that typically involve group participation and "critical thinking."

Such Othering discourse regarding approaches to knowledge and learning styles is evident in a good deal of the discourse surrounding the implementation of communicative language teaching (CLT). Flowerdew (1998, p. 323), for example, discusses the use of group work and students' oral participation, central components of CLT, in reference to Chinese learners. She begins by asking:

> Why is it that when one poses a question to a group of Arab students the whole class is clamouring to answer, while a question addressed to a class of Chinese learners may elicit no response, followed by a stony silence or, as the Chinese say, "dead air"? Even if one nominates a particular student to reply in a class of Chinese learners, the question may still be met with a muffled reply and averted eyes. The answer lies, to some extent, in certain cultural and psychological factors deriving from Confucian philosophy.

Flowerdew goes on to discuss the use of group work with Chinese learners and argues that group work can be implemented with Chinese students if the group is viewed as a collective body that offers suggestions to one another not as individuals but as a group. Underlying her argument are the assumptions that group work in a classroom is admirable and conducive to language learning and that a particular group of learners, in this case Chinese students, are not open to group work and oral participation.

An Othering discourse is also evident in some discussions of critical thinking, a key component of a particular view of knowledge that is promoted in CLT. Atkinson (1997), for example, argues that critical thinking, while extremely difficult to define, is clearly a social practice and that some cultures promote such learning while others do not. He then goes on to compare "critical thinking and nonnative thinkers" (a powerful Othering discourse) arguing that "cross-cultural research into the early socialization and educational practices of non-European peoples" suggests that there are "three areas of potential discontinuity between cultural assumptions that may underlie critical thinking and modes of thought and expression prevalent among non-Western cultural groups" (p. 79). These involve notions of relations between individuals and society, differing norms of self-expression, and different perspective on the use of language as a means for learning. Underlying the discussion is a clear Othering between Westerners who engage in critical thinking and non-Westerners or "nonnative thinkers" whose social practice may not encourage critical thinking. At issue is exactly what is meant by critical thinking and if it is necessary for "nonnative thinkers" to engage in Western concepts of critical thinking in order to learn English.

One of the major ways in which global–local tensions manifest themselves in pedagogy is in the choice of the content of classroom materials. In many instances, the teaching of English is promoted as a way of developing international awareness and of helping the country to become part of a global economy. With this goal in mind, many texts approved by Ministries of Education promote global themes and a discussion of other cultures, particularly those of the Inner Circle. The appropriateness of such themes for the local context is generally not examined. Local teachers, however, aware of the interests and needs of their learners, may find such materials unsuitable for their students. A second issue that is evident in a good deal of ELT materials is a discourse of Othering in which those from

Western Inner Circle cultures are portrayed as having modern and desirable behavior while those from other cultures, who exhibit other ways of doing things, are seen as backward and lacking. Such polarization can inform classroom texts dealing with a variety of topics, ranging from gender issues to family relationships.

While some educational leaders explicitly reject the inclusion of Western culture in English teaching, many textbooks approved by official government bodies do in fact promote Western characters and values. Japan is a case in point. In an analysis of all 7th grade Ministry-approved texts, Matsuda (2002) found an Inner Circle emphasis in the textbooks' representation of users and uses of English. Of the 74 characters shown in the textbooks, Matsuda's analysis showed that most characters were from Japan (34), followed by Inner Circle country speakers (30) and the remaining from Outer and Expanding Circle countries (10). What was most telling, however, was who talked the most among these characters. Although there are more Japanese characters than Inner Circle characters, the Japanese speakers produce far fewer words than Inner Circle country speakers. In addition, those from Outer and Expanding Circle countries hardly speak at all. In a subtle way then these texts suggest that it is Inner Circle native speakers who have the right to use English.

The context of English uses portrayed in the textbooks is also revealing. According to Matsuda (2002), in terms of English being used intranationally in the textbooks, the majority of these cases are among Inner Circle English users. There is only one example of intranational use within an Outer Circle country, even though English is often used as a lingua franca in Outer Circle countries. In terms of international uses of English, the overwhelming majority of examples are between native speakers and nonnative speakers of English with only a few examples of English being used among nonnative speakers of English, even though L2–L2 interactions represent the majority of current interactions in English. Learners of English then are provided with few models of the present-day use of English.

Implications for Pedagogy

In view of the many diverse social and sociolinguistic contexts of EILF use, what principles should inform a socially sensitive EILF pedagogy? The following are what I believe are key principles.

Foreign and Second Language Curricula Should Be Relevant to the Local Linguistic Ecology

Earlier in the chapter it was noted that in many countries such as Japan the local linguistic ecology makes the value of English learning questionable. What is often needed is a knowledge of the local lingua franca, as well as a valuing of other local languages. Often students' time in situations where English has little relevancy and there is another local lingua franca would be better served in a language awareness class than in traditional English classrooms. In such classes students of all backgrounds could learn about the diversity of languages spoken today, the attitudes and values associated with them, and the variety of language use that exists in all languages.

EILF Professionals Should Strive to Alter Language Policies that Serve to Promote
English Learning Only Among the Elite of the Country

In many countries those with privilege are most likely to have access to English learning. It is often those who have both the economic resources and time for language learning who gain proficiency in English. To avoid English fluency contributing to a greater economic divide, educational leaders and planners need to establish policies that afford English access to learners of all economic backgrounds. In contexts in which gaining proficiency in English may threaten mother-tongue use and development, English programs should be established in such a way that the local language is fully supported.

EILF Curricula Should Include Examples of the Diversity of English Varieties Used Today

Recent research has documented the diversity of English use today, illustrating both the regularity of these varieties and the manner in which they are a source of personal and social identity. In light of this diversity, a socially sensitive EILF pedagogy needs to first of all afford equal status to all varieties of English and second, promote an awareness of variation in English use.

EILF Curricula Need to Exemplify L2–L2 Interactions

Given that the majority of English interactions today are among L2 speakers, EILF curricula need to include far more examples of L2–L2 English interactions. Including examples of actual L2–L2 interactions will hopefully create an awareness that one important value of English is that it allows individuals to communicate across a great variety of geographical and cultural boundaries and not merely with speakers from Inner Circle countries.

Full Recognition Needs to Be Given to the Other Languages Spoken by English Speakers

For too long a good deal of ELT pedagogy has been informed by an English-only discourse. Yet often bilingual speakers of English have a rich linguistic repertoire that they use to signal their personal identity and social relationships. Code-switching is an important means by which they do this. Encouraging code-switching in EILF classrooms is beneficial in that it will provide equal status to all of the languages learners speak and provide a context for students to investigate reasons for code-switching. And most importantly it allows for a well-planned use of the first language as a means of developing proficiency in English.

EILF Should Be Taught in a Way that Respects the Local Culture of Learning

In many instances globalization has led to the introduction of materials and methods that are not in keeping with the local culture of learning. When this occurs, local teachers may be placed in a situation in which their credibility as competent teachers is challenged because they do not know about some aspect of Western culture that appears in a textbook or they are encouraged to use group work when this is not in keeping with typical student roles.

In summary, it is clear that present-day globalization, migration and the spread of English have resulted in a great diversity of social and educational contexts in which English learning is taking place. Because English is an international language, effective pedagogical decisions and practices cannot be made without giving special attention to the many varied social contexts in which English is taught and learned. An appropriate EILF pedagogy is one that promotes English bilingualism for learners of all backgrounds, recognizes and validates the variety of Englishes that exists today, and teaches English in a manner that meets local language needs and respects the local culture of learning.

Note

An earlier version of this chapter appeared in Hornberger, N. H. & McKay, S. L. (Eds.) (2010) *Sociolinguistics and language education* (pp. 89–115). Bristol: Multilingual Matters.

138 · Sandra Lee McKay

References

Atkinson, D. (1997). A critical approach to critical thinking in TESOL. *TESOL Quarterly, 31*(1), 71–95.

Bamgbose, A. (1998). Torn between the norms: Innovations in World Englishes. *World Englishes, 17*(1), 1–14.

Barber, B. (1996). *Jihad vs. McWorld: How globalism and tribalism are reshaping the world*. New York: Ballantine Books.

Black, R. (2005). Access and affiliation: The literacy and composition practices of English-language learners in an online fan-fiction community. *Journal of Aloescent and Adult Literacy, 49*, 118–128.

Black, R. (2006). Language, culture and identity in online fiction. *E-Learning, 3*(2), 170–184.

Block, D., & Cameron, D. (Eds.) (2002). *Globalization and language teaching*. Mahwah, NJ: Lawrence Erlbaum Associates.

Brutt-Griffler, J. (2002). *World English: A study of its development*. Clevedon: Multilingual Matters.

Canagarajah, S. A. (Ed.) (2005). Introduction. In *Reclaiming the local in language policy and practice* (pp. xiii–xxx). Mahwah, NJ: Lawrence Erlbaum Associates.

Canagarajah, S. A. (2006). Negotiating the local in English as a lingua franca. *Annual Review of Applied Linguistics, 26*, 197–218.

Choi, P. K. (2003). "The best students will learn English": Ultra-utilitarianism and linguistic imperialism in post-1997 Hong Kong. *Journal of Education Policy, 28*(6), 673–694.

Chung, A. (2006). Children driven to learn English. *The Korea Times*. Retrieved Nov. 20, 2006, from http://search.hankooki.com/times/times.

Crystal, D. (1995). *The Cambridge encyclopedia of the English language*. Cambridge: Cambridge University Press.

Fairclough, N. (2006). *Language and globalization*. London: Routledge.

Firth, A. (1996). The discursive accomplishment of normality. On "lingua franca" English and conversation analysis. *Journal of Pragmatics, 26*, 237–259.

Flowerdew, L. (1998). A cultural perspective on group work. *ELT Journal, 52*(4), 323–329.

Friedman, T. (2005). *The world is flat*. New York: Farrar, Straus and Giroux.

Giddens, A. (1990). *The consequences of modernity*. Cambridge: Polity Press.

House, J. (2003). Teaching and learning pragmatic fluency in a foreign language: The case of English as a lingua franca. In A. Martinez Flor, E. Usó Juan & A. Fernández Guerra (Eds.), *Pragmatic competence and foreign language teaching* (pp. 133–159). Castelláo de la Plana, Spain: Publicacions de la Universitat Jaume I.

Hu, G. (2005). English language education in China: Policies, progress, and problems. *Language Policy, 4*, 5–24.

Jenkins, J. (2000). *The phonology of English as an international language*. Oxford: Oxford University Press.

Kachru, B. B. (1983). *The Indianization of English: The English language in India*. New York: Oxford University Press.

Kachru, B. B. (1986). *The alchemy of English*. Oxford: Pergamon Press.

Kachru, B. B. (1992). Models for nonnative Englishes. In B. B. Kachru (Ed.), *The other tongue: English across cultures* (2nd ed.) (pp. 48–74). Urbana, IL and Chicago: University of Illinois Press.

Kuo, I.-C. (2006). Addressing the issue of teaching as a lingua franca. *ELT Journal, 60*(3), 213–221.

Lam, W. S. (2000). L2 literacy and the design of the self: A case study of a teenager writing on the Internet. *TESOL Quarterly, 34*(3), 457–482.

Lowenberg, P. (2002). Assessing English proficiency in the Expanding Circle. *World Englishes, 21*(3), 431–435.

McKay, S. L., & Wong, S. C. (1996). Multiple discourses, multiple identities: Investment and agency in second-language learning among Chinese adolescent immigrant students. *Harvard Educational Review, 66*, 577–608.

McKay, S. L. (2002). *Teaching English as an international language: Rethinking goals and approaches*. Oxford: Oxford University Press.

McKay, S. L. (2005). Teaching the Pragmatics of English as an International Language. *Guidelines, 27*(2), 3–9.

McKay, S.L., & Bokhorst-Heng, W. (2008). *International English in its sociolinguistic contexts: Towards a socially sensitive pedagogy*. New York: Routledge.

Matsuda, A. (2002). Representation of users and uses of English in beginning Japanese EFL textbooks. *JALT Journal, 24*(2), 182–201.

Nettle, D., & Romaine, S. (2000). *Vanishing voices: The extinction of the world's languages*. Oxford: Oxford University Press.

Niño-Murcia, M. (2003). English is like the dollar: Hard currency ideology and the status of English in Peru. *World Englishes, 22*(2), 121–142.

Pakir, A. (1991). The range and depth of English-knowing bilinguals in Singapore. *World Englishes, 10*(2), 167–179.

Palfreyman, D. (2005). Othering in an English language program. *TESOL Quarterly, 39*(2), 211–233.

Park, C. (2006). Parents push early English learning. *The Korea Times*. Retrieved Nov. 20, 2006, from http://search.hankooki.com/times/times.

Park, S. J., & Abelmann, N. (2004). Class and cosmopolitan striving: Mother's management of English education in South Korea. *Anthropological Quarterly*, 645–672.

Peirce, B. (1995). Social identity, investment, and language learning. *TESOL Quarterly, 29*, 9–31.

Pennycook, A. (1998). *English and the discourses of colonialism.* London: Routledge.

Pennycook. A. (2003). Beyond homogeny and heterogeny: English as a global and worldly language. In C. Mair (Ed.), *The politics of English as a world language.* (pp. 3–17). Amsterdam: Rodopi.

Pennycook, A. (2007). *Gobal Englishes and transcultural flows.* London: Routledge.

Phillipson, R. (1992). *Linguistic imperialism.* Oxford: Oxford University Press.

Prodromou, L. (2006). Defining the "successful bilingual speaker" of English. In R. Rubdy & M. Saraceni (Eds.), *English in the world: Global rules, global roles* (pp. 51–70). London: Continuum.

Rampton, B. (1995). *Crossing: Language and ethnicity among adolescents.* New York: Longman.

Seargeant, P. (2005). "More English than England itself": The simulation of authenticity in foreign language practice in Japan. *International Journal of Applied Linguistics*, 15, 326–345

Seidlhofer, B. (2004). Research perspectives on teaching English as a lingua franca. *Annual Review of Applied Linguistics, 24*, 209–239.

Seidlhofer, B. (2006). English as a lingua franca in the expanding circle: What it isn't. In R. Rubdy & M. Saraceni (Eds.), *English in the world* (pp. 40–50). London: Continuum.

Timmis, I. (2002). Native-speaker norms and International English: A classroom view. *ELT Journal, 56*(3), 240–249.

9

Teaching English as a Foreign Language in Europe

Vivian Cook

Introduction

This chapter looks at two issues about the teaching of English as a foreign language (TEFL) that have been become increasingly important in a European context in recent years, namely the Common European Framework of Reference (CEFR) and English as lingua franca (ELF). Hence what is discussed does not necessarily apply to the majority of language teaching within any particular country but reflects broad tendencies. These two issues represent language teaching traditions that have been developed in Europe over many years and that have had a considerable impact on recent teaching of English to non-native speakers. Both are in some ways connected to second language acquisition (SLA) research, in others parallel developments.

Europe itself is not easy to pin down as a concept; the twenty-seven countries and twenty-three working languages of the European Union—the political association of states—are not the same as the forty-seven countries and two official languages plus two working languages of the Council of Europe, a cultural body that promotes the CEFR among other activities. The UK is ambivalent whether it is part of Europe; a possibly apocryphal English newspaper headline once announced "Fog in Channel; Continent Isolated". Language teaching policies and examination are primarily determined by national ministries, paying more or less heed to the policies of the European Union or the recommendations of the Council of Europe. Hence educational policies for language teaching in the UK are seldom fully in step with those in other European countries, for instance the removal of modern languages as a compulsory school subject after the age of fourteen.

A further preliminary is to tidy up the meaning of "foreign" in EFL. According to Howatt (2004) the distinction between "foreign" and "second" language teaching started in English language teaching in the 1950s. A typical European definition is provided by Klein (1986, p. 19):

> "[F]oreign language" is used to denote a language acquired in a milieu where it is normally not in use … A "second language" on the other hand, is one that becomes another tool of communication alongside the first language; it is typically acquired in a social environment in which it is actually spoken.

The distinction then embodies two distinct senses:

1. a social dimension according to whether a language meets the learner's current communicative need or not; and
2. a location dimension according to whether it is used in a native speaker milieu.

De Groot and van Hell (2005, p. 25) insist on a difference between European and North American use of the terms, where the North American definition does not include sense (2). Stern (1983, p. 10) puts it that "'foreign language' can be subjectively 'a language which is not my L1' or objectively 'a language which has no legal status within the national boundaries'"; in other words a definition that shifts between language as a mental individual property and language as a legal entity defined by law (Cook, in press a). A more neutral term provided by some is English as an additional language, describing children with a first language other than English.

A classic example of a second language then is Spanish learnt by a Japanese immigrant in Spain for immediate use in daily life versus Spanish learnt as a foreign language by a Japanese student in school in Japan with no use outside the classroom. Since the start of communicative language teaching, this distinction became in a sense deferred as all learners were thought to be aiming at eventual communicative use, hence it was more a matter of communication *now* in second language (L2) teaching versus communication *deferred* in foreign language teaching. Nor are the two European senses always compatible: waiters in London use Spanish as a lingua franca (Block, 2006), making it a second language in London in sense (1) despite its absence from the surrounding milieu in sense (2). A similar situation obtains for Italians in Toronto workplaces (Norton, 2000). To make matters more complicated, most teaching of foreign languages in Europe is actually referred to as modern language teaching, as opposed to teaching of the classical languages Greek and Latin. Indeed in the UK, modern language teaching of say French and foreign/L2 teaching of English have had different teaching traditions, career structures and teaching qualifications.

Cook (in press a) argues that the second/foreign distinction is past its sell-by date; it is rejected by probably most current SLA researchers, for example Myles and Mitchell (2004, p. 2); it is making a crude division into two types of learners and two types of situations, when a far more complex analysis of both is needed; it does not address perhaps the most common use of English today—non-native speakers in countries where it is not an official or indeed minority language using it to other non-native speakers, say Arabic businessmen communicating with Arabic businessmen in different countries through emails in English; a native speaker of English is not involved in 74% of tourist encounters using English (Graddol, 2006).

What is the position of English in Europe? Apart from its geographical definition, the scope of Europe varies from one context to another—the Eurovision song contest includes countries such as Israel and Azerbaijan. Europe has never exactly been a cultural, religious or political unity, indeed having had several internal wars in the twentieth century. Confining discussion to the European Union, the twenty-seven current member countries have twenty-three official languages, such as Italian and Latvian, and more than sixty indigenous regional or minority languages, such as Welsh and Kashubian. In terms of sheer number of languages, this is only the tip of the iceberg; on one set of calculations 438 languages are spoken in the EU (VALEUR, 2004–2007), on another 300 in London alone (Baker & Eversley, 2000). In European primary schools, English is the most widely taught second language except in Belgium and Luxembourg; in most European countries over 90% of secondary school children are taught English (EACE, 2008). To a large extent then second/foreign/modern language teaching in most of Europe means the teaching of English.

The CEFR

The crucial area in the applied linguistics of language teaching in the 1970s was undoubtedly syllabus design. Until then specifying what learners were supposed to learn had largely been a matter of describing the structures of the target language, say the present continuous tense *he is driving*, and the situations in which the language was used, say the railway station ticket office—the *structural* and *situational syllabuses* used in classic coursebooks such as *First things first* (Alexander, 1967). In the 1970s various alternative proposals were put forward to make the syllabus more relevant to teaching. Some suggested basing teaching on topics that people talked about such as food and jobs (Cook, 1975)—a *topic syllabus*; some advocated basing it on what the students wanted to do on a week to week basis (Breen, 1984)—a *process syllabus*; or on how students interact in conversational structure such as the sequence requesting/replying/thanking (Cook, 1978, 1980)—an *interactional syllabus*.

The most convincing alternative, which swept the world during the 1980s, was the *notional-functional syllabus* proposed by David Wilkins (1972) in a working paper for the Council of Europe. This set out the target for learning as a set of notions—ideas that the students could express such as time—and functions—purposes for using language such as asking directions. Such syllabuses became more and more elaborate, partly by ever-increasing lists of notions and functions, partly by tying in the structures and vocabulary, again in long lists (van Ek, 1975). The overall aim of the Council of Europe proposals was to get students through the *threshold level* (van Ek, 1975)—the take-off point for independent use of the second language in a country where it is in use. Language teaching then had the purpose of deferred L2 use. This view was instantiated in threshold level syllabuses for English (van Ek, 1975), French (Coste, Courtillon, Ferenczi, Martins-Baltar & Papo, 1976) and eventually for a further thirty-four languages. It was found necessary to add a lower level known as *Waystage* (Van Ek & Alexander, 1977). For a summary of the types of syllabus see Table 9.1.

Out of this background there emerged the *Common European framework of reference for languages*, usually cited in its print version (CEFR, 2001). Its avowed intention is to implement the Recommendation of the Council of Europe "to facilitate communication and interaction among Europeans of different mother tongues in order to promote European mobility, mutual understanding and co-operation, and overcome prejudice and discrimination" (p. 2), thoroughly worthy objectives with which it would be hard to disagree. This leads CEFR to the concept of "plurilingualism":

> Plurilingualism differs from multilingualism, which is the knowledge of a number of languages, or the co-existence of different languages in a given society. … the plurilingual approach emphasises the fact that as an individual person's experience of language in its cultural contexts expands, from the language of the home to that of society at large and then to the languages of other peoples (whether learnt at school or college, or by direct experience), he or she does not

Table 9.1 Types of Syllabus

Syllabus type	Description	Examples
Grammatical	Structural or phonological description and rules	The present perfect—*have* + past participle -*en*; the /p~b/ contrast
Situational	The context of situation in which language is used	Going to the dentist's, the station
Topical	The topics that people talk about in the language	The weather, football
Process	Whatever students request	Subject to students' requests
Interactional	The structured moves of conversation	Requesting/replying/thanking
Notional	The concepts that people express through language	Past time, possession
Functional	The reasons for which people use language	Complaining, stating

keep these languages and cultures in strictly separated mental compartments, but rather builds up a communicative competence to which all knowledge and experience of language contributes and in which languages interrelate and interact.

(CEFR, 2001, p. 4)

The CEFR is then the response to the recommendations of the Committee of Ministers of the Council of Europe: "To ensure, as far as possible, that all sections of their populations have access to effective means of acquiring a knowledge of the languages of other member states" (Council of Europe, 1982).

So the CEFR is not concerned with the many languages found within a single national border, whether indigenous say Finnish and Swedish in Finland or in local minority communities, say the different languages spoken in the communities of Berlin or Lisbon. It is concerned solely with

Table 9.2   Common Reference Levels: Global Scale

Description	Level	Specification
Proficient user	C2	Can understand with ease virtually everything heard or read. Can summarise information from different spoken and written sources, reconstructing arguments and accounts in a coherent presentation. Can express him/herself spontaneously, very fluently and precisely, differentiating finer shades of meaning even in more complex situations.
	C1	Can understand a wide range of demanding, longer texts, and recognise implicit meaning. Can express him/herself fluently and spontaneously without much obvious searching for expressions. Can use language flexibly and effectively for social, academic and professional purposes. Can produce clear, well-structured, detailed text on complex subjects, showing controlled use of organisational patterns, connectors and cohesive devices.
Independent user	B2	Can understand the main ideas of complex text on both concrete and abstract topics, including technical discussions in his/her field of specialisation. Can interact with a degree of fluency and spontaneity that makes regular interaction with native speakers quite possible without strain for either party. Can produce clear, detailed text on a wide range of subjects and explain a viewpoint on a topical issue giving the advantages disadvantages of various options.
	B1	Can understand the main points of clear standard input on familiar matters regularly encountered in work, school, leisure, etc. Can deal with most situations likely to arise whilst travelling in an area where the language is spoken. Can produce simple connected text on topics which are familiar or of personal interest. Can describe experiences and events, dreams, hopes and ambitions and briefly give reasons and explanations for opinions and plans.
Basic user	A2	Can understand sentences and frequently used expressions related to areas of most immediate relevance (e.g. very basic personal and family information, shopping, local geography, employment). Can communicate in simple and routine tasks requiring a simple and direct exchange of information on familiar and routine matters. Can describe in simple terms aspects of his/her background, immediate environment and matters in areas of immediate need.
	A1	Can understand and use familiar everyday expressions and very basic phrases aimed at the satisfaction of needs of a concrete type. Can introduce him/herself and others and can ask and answer questions about personal details such as where he/she lives, people he/she knows and things he/she has. Can interact in a simple way provided the other person talks slowly and clearly and is prepared to help.

languages across borders—the chance for citizens of one European country to communicate with the citizens of another, say Germans with Portuguese. Plurilingualism is the ability of an individual to function effectively in more than one European language. The emphasis is on being able to do things with the language: "It describes in a comprehensive way what language learners have to learn to do in order to use a language for communication and what knowledge and skills they have to develop so as to be able to act effectively" (CEFR, 2001, p. 1). It is not concerned with traditional educational advantages for learning another language, whether based on the improved cognition of the learners or on understanding the literature of a foreign language.

The bulk of the CEFR therefore describes what it means to be able to communicate in a second language. It is concerned with "communicative language competences" "which empower a person to act using specifically linguistic means" (2001, p. 9), made up of linguistic, sociolinguistic and pragmatic competences. In principle the CEFR applies to any of the languages of its member nations; various adaptations have been provided for different countries over the years. It establishes a series of levels, arising out of the earlier threshold level. Table 9.2 illustrates the levels at a global level.

The overall labels in Table 9.2 are basic user, independent user and proficient user, with two subdivisions at each level. These broad descriptions are split into understanding (listening and reading), speaking (spoken interaction and spoken production) and writing, and presented in various ways, such as in a self-assessment grid of "can-do" statements. For instance level A1 listening becomes: "I can understand familiar words and very basic phrases concerning myself, my family and immediate concrete surroundings when people speak slowly and clearly."

The specification of levels is in itself hardly novel—at Ealing Technical College in London in the 1960s like most people we used a five-way division: Beginners, Elementary, Intermediate, Cambridge Lower Certificate (now First Certificate) and Cambridge Proficiency. In the 1970s at North East London Polytechnic we used the FSI (Foreign Service Institute) levels of proficiency, now known as the ILR (Interagency Language Roundtable, 2009), which has four main levels 0, 1, 2, 3, with subdivisions of "+" at each level. Similarly the widely used IELTS (International English Language Testing System) Test has seven bands going from 3 to 9 (IELTS, 2009). What has distinguished the CEFR is its aim of specifying levels across different languages rather than for English alone.

The main achievement of the CEFR is probably the detail with which the different proficiency levels are spelled out through fifty-four sets of descriptors. For example the "domain" of "personal" has a subdivision of location:

- home: house, rooms, garden;
- own;

    - of family;
    - of friends;
    - of strangers;

- own space in hostel, hotel;
- the countryside, seaside.

While "Free time and entertainment" is subcategorised into:

4.1 leisure;
4.2 hobbies and interests;
4.3 radio and TV;
4.4 cinema, theatre, concert, etc.;
4.5 exhibitions, museums, etc.;

4.6 intellectual and artistic pursuits;

4.7 sports;

4.8 press.

In some ways the CEFR aims at a whole description of human existence, rather like Roget's Thesaurus; any situation, subject matter, social relationship, use of language, interaction strategy or whatever has to be enumerated somewhere within its framework.

The CEFR is now widely used within the educational systems of European countries (EACE, 2008). The Council of Europe (2008) recommends: "all tests, examinations and assessment procedures leading to officially recognised language qualifications take full account of the relevant aspects of language use and language competences as set out in the CEFR". It is directly linked to the national syllabuses in over half the countries of Europe, ranging from Greece to Finland, Slovenia to Spain. The UK national syllabus for primary schools claims "By age 11, they [i.e. children] should have the opportunity to reach a recognised level of competence on the Common European Framework and for that achievement to be recognised through a national scheme" (QCA, 2009). The languages ladder scheme in the UK relates its Breakthrough stage to CEFR A1 and its Mastery level to CEFR C2 (CILT, 2007):

> Syllabus designers, coursebook publishers and language test providers worldwide, including Cambridge ESOL, seek to align their exams to the CEFR for reasons of transparency and coherence; claims of alignment can also assist in marketing communications to try and gain a competitive edge.

> (Taylor & Jones, 2006)

Examinations are cross-referenced against the CEFR, though Figueras, North, Takala, Verhelst, and Van Avernaet (2005) caution that this is no simple matter. Hence Cambridge Proficiency is equated to CEFR C2 and First Certificate to B2 (Cambridge ESOL, 2009). From personal experience as a teacher of English at both levels, this considerably overstates the Proficiency level and leaves no room for improvement at university; many Newcastle MA students with first degrees in English are undoubtedly unable to "produce clear, well-structured detailed text on complex subjects, showing controlled use of organisational patterns, connectors and cohesive devices" (CEFR, 2001), as required for the C1 level.

It is now common for British-based EFL (English as a foreign language) coursebooks to state their aims in CEFR equivalents: *Just Right* (Harmer, 2004) claims to be CEFR B1, *Move* (Bowler & Parminter, 2007) to be A1–A2. Publisher's catalogues sell books on their CEFR levels inter alia: the Longman Pearson English catalogue shows a CEFR tag for each book (Pearson, 2009), even if sometimes this stretches from A1 to C1, as in the confidently titled *Total English* (Bygrave, Foley, Hall, Acklam, Crace, Clare & Wilson, n.d.), though indeed most Longman courses claim similar coverage.

The CEFR has spun off the *European Language Portfolio* (ELP) (Council of Europe, 2009), which allows people to present their language record to prospective employers etc. through a set of downloadable documents (CILT, 2007) and also to evaluate their own progress in learning a second language; the adult UK version is some forty pages long. The crucial component is the *Europass Language Passport* (http://www.coe.int/T/DG4/Portfolio/documents/Pass_2spr.pdf) on which the person assesses their own performance for each language they speak in terms of "can-do" statements related to the six CEFR levels under the broad headings understanding, speaking and writing. The scales are presented in the usual grid, of which Table 9.1 is the simple version. A number of ELPs have been developed in different countries using the CEFR descriptors "validated" by the Council of Europe. It is hard to know to what extent the ELP is at present used by students and employers; in

2008 1.6 million people downloaded the ELP documents (Europass, 2009), 20% of whom were Portuguese, 15% Italian, 10% Spanish and 7% Finnish. The Europass is compulsory in higher education in Poland (Ministry of National Education, Warsaw, 2007). However, some students find, compared to other ways of doing curricula vitae (CVs), the Europass is "too rigidly bureaucratic and 'like a form'" and "time-consuming in the self-assessment of language skills" (Gattoni, 2005).

The CEFR has exerted considerable and growing influence over the teaching of English in Europe, primarily at official governmental levels and in testing of students, seeping through to coursebooks and classroom teaching. It is, however, a strange beast. It appears almost anonymously as a quasi-governmental publication, written in a dense style all of its own, compounded of European bureau-cratese, academic jargon and invented terms, in the tradition of minutely numbered taxonomic lists such as Mackey (1965) or van Ek (1975), almost unreadable but giving an appearance of great organisation. To take some examples, the CEFR term *orthoepic competence* meaning "the study of the relationship between pronunciation and a system of writing or spelling" (OED, 2009) is certainly neither the preferred term in current writing systems research nor one used in everyday English speech; the CEFR's list of *intropunitive/extrapunitive/impunitive personality* are hardly current terms in applied linguistics; *plurilingual* and *multilingual* are given as synonyms in the OED rather than the opposing terms of the CEFR seen above.

The CEFR (2001) claims to be "developed through a process of scientific research and wide consultation". The sources it cites are usually itself, i.e. the work of the Council of Europe; Figueras et al. (2005, p. 265) claim that "the foundation of this quantification is empirical: the basic observations were the judgements of teachers". In other words it is not based on research in SLA, L2 teaching, linguistics, psychology or other academic discipline, even if it draws indirectly on concepts in these areas; its conceptual basis is unreferenced through academic sources. Due to its lack of academic references, it appears like Topsy to have sprung into being full-formed from the minds of its creators. Its research base is the checking of descriptors by a group of teachers, equivalent to the claim by advertisers of a washing powder that ten million housewives can't be wrong. In language teaching methodology it relates to traditional communicative language teaching, rather than to more recent developments. It rests on the authority of a group of experts recruited from prominent language teaching administrators. The simplicity of its basic approach with the six-level grid in Table 9.1 has been overlaid by a vast mass of publications, reports and manuals from the Council of Europe and national organisations, which have made it difficult to weave a way through the maze of mostly internet resources, as the references below soon show.

To some extent you have to take it on its own terms or leave it alone. As a checklist for teaching, it seems a reasonable way of designing a description of target language communicative competence; it is however curiously sanitised—no mention of toilets, police stations or politics, crucial as these may be to everyday living in another country. For practical purposes, because of the high regard given to it by official authorities in different countries, it can no longer be ignored, whatever one thinks of it. Traditionally language education has aimed at cultivating internal goals related to the social and cognitive development of the students as well as external goals related to their ability to communicate with other people though a second language (Cook, 2007a). The CEFR often refers to the other benefits that L2 learning brings: "it is a central objective of language education to promote the favourable development of the learner's whole personality and sense of identity in response to the enriching experience of otherness in language and culture" (2001, p. 1). Yet it is hard to see which parts of the reference scales in Table 9.1 refer to personal development. Intercultural awareness is spelled out in one brief paragraph (5.1.1.3), with no checklist of descriptors: intercultural skills have a brief paragraph (5.1.2.2) mostly concerned with the learner acting as a communicative intermediary. The CEFR comes across as utilitarian communicativism. What is needed, in the words of Mike Byram (2009, p. 212), is "a way of thinking about the purposes of foreign language education which is more than a simple focus on utility and gain together with the image of tourists speaking English wherever they go".

In particular its key opposition of plurilingualism with multilingualism is at odds with other recent trends, such as the lingua franca concept to be discussed in the next section. Languages are treated as discrete objective entities; plurilingualism is an additive language A + language B model rather than an integrative model where A + B yields a new possibility C made up of both languages interacting in the same mind, i.e. multi-competence (Cook, 2007b). The aim is to create citizens of country X who can speak the language of country Y, not a multilingual who combines citizenship of both in a way different from either; the idea of nation states and their national languages is paramount. It serves existing communities rather than creating a new community. Its concentration on the native speaker as the goal of language teaching is out of step with goals based on the successful L2 user, such as the Japanese national syllabus that aims at "Japanese with English abilities" (MEXT, 2003) or the Israeli curriculum that "does not take on the goal of producing near-native speakers of English, but rather speakers of Hebrew, Arabic or other languages who can function comfortably in English whenever it is appropriate" (English Curriculum for Israel, 2002). While there are hints of this in the CEFR, the overall impression is given that the successful learner speaks like a native speaker.

English as Lingua Franca

The other pan-European trend concerns the target and value of L2 learning. Is the goal to speak like a monolingual native speaker of that language or is it to become a successful L2 user who uses it in distinctive ways from native speakers? Inevitably this comes back to questions of politics: "That all education is imbued with social, political and moral values ought to be self-evident, even though contemporary terminology of 'skills' and 'competences' tries to hide this" (Byram, 2002). Some have argued that the native speakers' claims to be the only true speakers of the language gives them unjustifiable power over non-native speakers so that the best the learners can do is to become successful imitations of monolingual native speakers, perpetually doomed to an inferior position. Many or indeed most L2 students struggle with a feeling of inferiority; at worst none of them will meet the goal of passing for natives, at best a bare handful.

If you support a native speaker goal, you still have to decide *which* native speaker. In spoken language, many accents of English are spoken by native speakers both in the UK and round the world. English vocabulary varies from one place to another, what a Geordie calls a *bairn*, a Londoner calls a *child*; what a New Yorker calls a *cellphone*, an English person calls a *mobile*. In English grammar, there is still variation even if not so extreme; a black American speaker may leave out the copula *He great*; a Dublin speaker may distinguish singular *you* from plural *yiz*. Only in the written language and particularly in spelling is there a global consensus with limited variation according to British or American style in a few words like *color/colour* and *aluminum/aluminium*. The status of these different varieties has been a constant battle over the years, both for speakers of the non-prestige dialects in the UK and for speakers of mostly ex-Commonwealth countries against the prestige varieties in England. The discussion also skates over the issue that many speakers of English in England know more than one language or dialect; it is possible to talk of British Indian English, British Chinese English or London Jamaican English. Concentration on the dwindling monolingual section of the population obscures the multilingualism of people not only in England but also in virtually all the other countries of Europe.

It is virtually taken for granted that there is no question of teaching anything but the standard prestige version, labelled variously Oxford English, BBC English or standard English, accompanied by received pronunciation (RP). Yet the RP accent is spoken by about 3% of the population of England (Trudgill, 2001). RP-based English language teaching is open to the complaint EFL students often made to me in London: "Why does nobody speak like this outside the classroom?" Within Europe, unlike other areas of the world such as Sri Lanka (Canagarajah, 2005), the choice of which native speaker of English to aim at is hardly discussed, certainly not within the CEFR; a national standard language speaker is assumed to be the model for English students, usually from England, sometimes from the United States, even if the students are seldom likely to encounter one. The variety that is taught reflects the perceived structure of English society and now seems fairly dated in that RP accents, apart from media presenters, are rarely used in the modern spheres of business, celebrity culture or indeed politics.

Setting aside the debate about which kind of English to adopt as a teaching target, what about the peculiar status of English as a second language? According to De Swaan (2001), languages form a hierarchy. At the bottom come *peripheral* languages such as Welsh and Finnish, which are used by native speakers in fairly circumscribed localities for the full range of language functions—the term *local* may be preferred as it sounds less discriminatory. Next come *central* languages such as German in Germany used not only by native speakers but also by members of communities with other languages living in Germany such as Turkish or Sorbian; these languages are used for a range of function both for contacts between minority groups and the majority community and for contact between members of different minority communities. Next come *supercentral* languages such as Arabic and Japanese used across national boundaries for a limited range of functions, say Arabic for religion or Japanese for karate. Finally come *hypercentral* languages, which are used everywhere for a broad range of functions, of which there is currently only one example, English. Within Europe other languages have been used in supercentral ways, such as German in the Austro-Hungarian Empire or Russian in the old Soviet Union; Latin in the Middle Ages had a similar role across Europe for the functions of religion and scholarship. This hierarchy is discussed more fully in Cook (2009).

Virtually all L2 teaching in Europe ascends the hierarchy by teaching a language of a higher group than that of the students; hypercentral English is the most taught language in Europe, followed by the central languages German in northern and eastern Europe, French in southern Europe, and Russian in the Baltic states and Bulgaria (Eurydice, 2005). In conventional terms, the English language as spoken in, say, England or Canada is the goal, the language described in *A grammar of contemporary English* (Quirk, Greenbaum, Leech & Svartvik, 1972), the *Oxford English Dictionary* (OED, 2009) and *An Introduction to the Pronunciation of English* (Gimson, 1962). One goal of teaching English is indeed to teach this idealised abstract entity—the English language. In this case the matter of language target needs no further discussion. What the students end up with is a subset of native English, appropriate for their needs but in principle identical to whatever the native speaker possesses in that area. The target is no different from before, a national standard version of the language, even if it is described more comprehensively, say by the CEFR, and is taught by novel methods.

But is hypercentral English actually the same as this standard English language spoken by natives? For some years people have been claiming that English has escaped from the confines of English-speaking countries so that it is used primarily by those who do not have English as a native language and who do not need to converse with native speakers so much as with fellow non-native speakers; "World English (WE) belongs to everyone who speaks it, but it is nobody's mother tongue" (Rajagopalan, 2004, p. 111). Several varieties of English have been devised for particular international roles. One is for non-native speakers accessing English-speaking media. The Voice of America uses *Simple English* (VOA, 2009) and Wikipedia has a special section called *Simple English Wikipedia* (Wikipedia, 2009), both of which are partly based on the Basic English list of 850 words devised by Ogden (1937). Another is officially standardised forms of English used for jobs that stretch around the globe, whether *Standard Marine Communication Phrases* (IMO, 2001) or the "Simplified English" used in airplane maintenance manuals (Sarmento, 2005). These types of English are specific to international professions regardless of whether the users are native speakers of English or not. Indeed it has been claimed that some native speaker pilots do not speak aviation English as well as non-natives (Alderson, 2009). Crucially these simplified Englishes are constructed and maintained by one person or by an interested group; rather than emerging from the users, they are dictated by an authority, whether right or wrong, rather like the CEFR. Simplified Englishes are not the same as hypercentral English; they resemble supercentral languages in having a highly restricted set of speakers and a limited range of functions rather than the unlimited sets of hypercentral speakers and functions.

This international English over the years this has been variously called Global English, English as a world language, English as an international language and English as a medium of intercultural communication, with various overtones—sometimes these are confusingly used by those who deny the existence of a non-native-based variety to refer to the national native standard rather than to the hypercentral non-native variety. The term "lingua franca" implies a particular attitude to this variety as being both a non-native variety and one used for active communication: "a 'contact language' between persons who share neither a common native tongue nor a common (national) culture, and for whom English is the chosen *foreign* language of communication" (Firth, 1996). Approaches to ELF have explored both aspects of this definition: ELF as a variety of English and ELF as a form of communication, which can be called the product and the process approaches. To quote Cook (in press b): "Put in a nutshell, does an ELF learner acquire a specific form like 'When you will start practicing?' or do they acquire word order strategies that will yield this sentence among many others?"

To start with ELF as product; what are ELF's characteristics as a variety of English? As virtually all description of English varieties or of L2 acquisition of English has been based on native speakers, the nature of ELF has only recently started to emerge. Pioneer work by Jenkins (2007) looked at when EFL students had problems with pronunciation. She claimed on this basis that teachers could teach a "Lingua Franca Core" that concentrated on problems that non-natives had with comprehending each other rather than those that natives had with non-native speakers. This would imply inter alia concentrating on where to put the nuclear tone in the tone group rather than the choice of tone, i.e. the difference between *I love spinach, I love spinach* and *I love spinach,* emphasising extra vowel length before voiced consonants, say the different /ɪ/s in *bit* and *bid,* and not bothering with the voiced/voiceless "th" distinction /ð~θ/ as in *them/theme.* The phonology of ELF is different from that of native English, or at least is potentially so if teaching allows it.

The description of the syntactic characteristics of ELF is starting to emerge from projects such as the Vienna–Oxford International Corpus of English (VOICE, 2009) at the University of Vienna. This is based on a corpus of about one million words of spoken ELF interactions from 1,250 ELF speakers with approximately fifty different first languages collected from meetings, interviews etc., perhaps the first attempt to analyse this variety from a large set of data. It is of course early days in that the size is small, equivalent to the early Brown Corpus of English of the 1960s (Kucera & Francis, 1967) rather than the 100 million of the British National Corpus (2009) or the two billion words of English of the Oxford English Corpus (2009) derived from the web. The world-wide nature of ELF and its diversity demands even bigger corpora than native English; there may indeed be multiple ELFs, not just a single variety (Meirkord, 2004). VOICE is nevertheless a promising start, though one has to be cautious about extrapolating from it too far.

Box 9.1 shows some of the characteristics of the ELF of VOICE, based on Seidlhofer (2004). Some are already familiar to any EFL teacher in classroom use such as the omission of third person *-s, he go,* and highly erratic use of articles: *a research.* Others seem equally obvious as soon as they are pointed out, such as over-explicitness and redundant prepositions. But this is not of course a fair comparison. The VOICE data are collected from ordinary L2 use rather than the classroom. The classroom is for learning the language not for using it. While it would be surprising if some aspects did not carry over to the "real" world, the interesting thing is what ELF users do in their everyday functional

---

Box 9.1

Features of ELF Grammar

- "dropping" the third person -s;
- confusing the relative pronouns *who* and *which*;
- omitting definite *a/an* and indefinite *the* articles where they are obligatory in native speech, and inserting them where they do not occur in native speech;
- failing to use "correct" forms in tag questions, say using *isn't it?* or *no?* instead of *shouldn't they?*;
- inserting redundant prepositions, as in *We have to study about ...*;
- overusing certain verbs of high semantic generality, such as *do, have, make, put, take*;
- replacing infinitive *to* constructions with *that*-clauses, as in *I want that ...*;
- being over-explicit, as in *black colour* rather than just *black*.

---

communication where the communication matters to them rather than in the classroom where a mistake is a potential learning opportunity, not a failed deal.

The process ELF approach is exemplified by the extract shown in Box 9.2, taken from Firth (1991). Two businessmen are negotiating in English about a consignment of cheese, one an Egyptian, one a Dane. The recording is transcribed using conversational analysis conventions, e.g. capital letters mean extra loud as in *YES*; pauses are given in seconds in brackets (1.5), colons mean extra length *ha:d*.

Box 9.2

Sample of ELF

((ring))
1. B: allo
2. H: yes hello Michael Hansen melko dairies Denmark "calling (·) can I please speak to mister Akkad
3. (·)
4. B: "hello mister Michael
5. H: is it Barat?
6. B: ye: (h)s, how are you (·) si::r
7. H: well I'm OK, but you ha:d tu- have some uh problems with the: cheese
8. B: uuuuuuhhhhh ((one-second sound stretch))
9. H: the bad cheese (·) in the "customs
10. (0.5)
11. B: "one minute (0.4) mister Akkad will talk (·) w[ith (·) you
12. H: [ok "yes
13. (1.5)
14. A: YES (·) mister Hansen#
15. H: hello: mister Akkad (·).hh we haf some informations for you about the cheese (·)
16. with the "blowing
17. A: "yes mister Hansen

The pronunciation and grammar are clearly not those of native speech, as in *haf* (have) and *informations* (uncountable). Yet they understand each other well enough for the purposes of the conversation. The aim of the research is to look at how the interaction takes place between the participants. Partly this consists of learning on the wing, so to speak; the term *blowing* applied to cheese was unknown to A in a previous conversation but is now used fluently. Partly it is reformulating; *problems with the cheese* becomes *bad cheese in the customs* and then *with the blowing*. If there is a communication problem, the participants solve it between themselves with nobody explicitly discussing language or acting as the controlling expert. This is far from the teaching situations mostly described in ELF product research such as Jenkins (2007) or from the arbitrary abstract "tasks" of task-based learning with no point in the outside-world; according to Firth and Wagner (2007), it is "learning-in-action" in which community of practice is created "before our very eyes", "LFE [lingua franca English] is not a product located in the mind of the speaker; it is a form of social action" (Canagarajah, 2007). Note that these businessmen are already highly proficient at English and trusted to conduct such transactions by their companies. The English of the Danes comes from college or university courses, doubtless on conventional lines. Thus a fair proportion of their English skill comes from prior learning; the learning-in-action that takes place during business conversations is presumably either the interactional skills of, say, reformulating or job- or task-specific vocabulary such as *blowing*, probably unknown in this sense to all but cheesemongers. Indeed one assumes that native speaker businessmen to have to acquire these skills on the job.

We can then contrast the CEFR with the product view of ELF with regard to language teaching. The basis of the CEFR is the straightforward description of native speaker competence, albeit executed in a highly idiosyncratic doctrinaire fashion; the basis of ELF is the description of a new variety of English unrelated to native speakers. The aim of CEFR is to create plurilinguals who can adopt the language and culture of another European country; the aim of ELF qua product is to create speakers of a specific non-native variety who exist in a third space in between two cultures (Kramsch, 2009). Proposals for teaching and assessing the CEFR involve teaching this native variety and assessing how well the students do compared to this native standard, parallel to the UK Adult ESOL Core Curriculum (DfES, 2001) measuring success in terms of the standards for native speaker literacy (DfEE, 2001).

The process version of ELF denies the assumption of both CEFR and the product ELF view that a language description in whatever terms is appropriate for establishing the nature of non-native speech or as the foundation of teaching and assessment materials. If ELF consists of a set of processes that the user can employ in real-world tasks, the goal is effective use of these tasks measured by their real-world success—rather like the early uses of communication strategies research in language teaching (Tarone, 1981). The three present very different, probably incompatible, solutions to the issue of TEFL teaching: is Europe big enough to contain all of them?

Conclusions: Using Multi-Competence in Language Teaching

Much of the preceding discussion has been relying concepts drawn from the multi-competence perspective on SLA. This has developed over twenty years as a particular way of interpreting SLA that can be applied to issues of acquisition, use and teaching of second languages, for example in Ortega (2008) and Scott (2009).

Multi-competence is defined as "the knowledge of two languages in one mind". This knowledge is not the same as that of a monolingual native speaker, perhaps obviously in the second language as generations of research into transfer and ultimate attainment have demonstrated (Jarvis & Pavlenko, 2007), but also less obviously in the first language, as detailed in the various papers in Cook (2003). Indeed much current research has shown in addition that they do not "think" in the same ways as monolinguals (Cook & Bassetti, in press), affecting perception and categorisation among other aspects.

The starting point for SLA is then the recognition that people who know second languages are different from monolinguals. It is not that they know another language imperfectly; it is that they have a complex language knowledge of their own. Hence multi-competence research started to use the term *L2 user*, rather than *L2 learner*, as a recognition that they are achieving a state of their own rather than perpetually trying to achieve an unattainable native speaker goal. There may indeed be L2 learners who are not using the language apart from learning contexts in the classroom, say learners of English in China, but there are also vast numbers of L2 users who use it in their everyday lives whether as a central language, a language for the tourist industry or a language for flying (and indeed servicing) planes. The native speaker concept is a distraction from the reality of the distinctive nature of L2 users, as maintained by Grosjean (2008) among others.

From the point of view of multi-competence, both the CEFR and ELF miss the point. Learning another language is not just adding a new extension to your house but moving all the internal walls about. The CEFR pays no attention to the transformation that L2 learning makes to the learner, hence its overall utilitarianism compared to traditional humanistic language teaching. Product ELF similarly sees the learner as acquiring another language system, not developing a new whole system in which ELF plays its part in interaction with the other language systems in the mind. Process ELF shows how the learners interact using a set of strategies but it does not describe learning as such (partly because it denies any distinction between using and acquiring a language). Indeed if Danish businessmen can do as well as they seem to on the basis of conventional language teaching, there can't be very much wrong with it as a launching pad for ELF use.

We need then to develop the programmes incorporated in the CEFR and ELF towards this view of the independent L2 user. The target is not just someone who can go to another country and speak the language like a native, it is someone who can successfully use the second language for the purposes of their life and who has reaped the mental benefits of learning another language as well as its utilitarian use. The CEFR and ELF represent some steps towards this goal but there is still far to go to see language teaching that genuinely teaches second language for real-world L2 use.

References

Alderson, J. C. (2009). Air safety, language assessment policy, and policy implementation: the case of aviation English. *Annual Review of Applied Linguistics*, 29, 168–187.

Alexander, L. G. (1967). *First things first.* London: Longman.

Baker, P., & Eversley, J. (2000). *Multilingual capital.* London: Battlebridge.

Block, D. (2006). *Multilingual identities in a global city: London stories.* London: Palgrave.

Bowler, B., & Parminter, S. (2007). *Move.* Oxford: Macmillan.

Breen, M. P. (1984). Process syllabuses for the language classroom. In C. J. Brumfit (Ed.), *General English Syllabus Design, ELT Documents*, 118, 47–60.

British National Corpus (2009). http://www.natcorp.ox.ac.uk/.

Bygrave, J., Foley, M., Hall, D., Acklam, R., Crace, A., Clare, A. & Wilson, J. J. (n.d.). *Total English.* Harlow: Longman English.

Byram, M. (2002). Foreign language education political and moral education: an essay. *Language Learning Journal*, 26, 43–47.

Byram, M. (2009). Politics, policies and political action in foreign language education. In V. Cook & Li Wei (Eds.), *Contemporary applied linguistics* (pp. 193–214). London: Continuum.

Cambridge ESOL (2009). http://www.cambridgeesol.org/exams/exams-info/cefr.html.

Canagarajah, A. S. (2005). Reconstructing local knowledge, reconfiguring language studies. In A. S. Canagarajah (Ed.), *Reclaiming the local in language policy and practice* (pp. 3–24), Hillsdale, NJ: Lawrence Erlbaum Associates.

Canagarajah, A. S. (2007). Lingua Franca English, multilingual communities, and language acquisition. *The Modern Language Journal*, 91, 923–939.

CEFR (2001). *Common European Framework of Reference for Languages.* Cambridge: Cambridge University Press. Also available at http://www.coe.int/t/dg4/linguistic/CADRE_EN.asp.

CILT (Centre for Information on Language Teaching) (2007). http://www.cilt.org.uk/14to19/ladder/index.htm.

Cook, V. J. (1975). *English topics.* Oxford: Oxford University Press.

Cook, V. J. (1978). Some ways of organising language. *AudioVisual Language Journal, 16*(2), 89–94.

Cook, V. J. (1980). *People and places.* Oxford: Pergamon.

Cook, V. J. (Ed.) (2003). *Effects of the second language on the first.* Clevedon: Multilingual Matters.

Cook, V. J. (2007a). The goals of ELT: Reproducing native-speakers or promoting multi-competence among second language users? In J. Cummins & C. Davison (Eds.), *Handbook on English language teaching* (pp. 237–248). Dordrecht; Kluwer.

Cook, V. J. (2007b). Multi-competence: Black hole or wormhole for SLA research? In Z.-H. Han (Ed.), *Understanding second language process* (pp. 16–26), Clevedon: Multilingual Matters.

Cook, V. J. (2009). Language user groups and language teaching. In V. J. Cook & Li Wei (Eds.), *Contemporary applied linguistics: Volume 1 language teaching and learning* (pp. 54–74), London: Continuum.

Cook, V. J. (in press a). Prolegomena to second language learning. In P. Seedhouse & S. Walsh (Eds.), *Conceptualising language learning.* Palgrave MacMillan.

Cook, V. J. (in press b). ELF: Central or atypical second language acquisition? In D. Singleton & L. Aronin (Eds.), *A global perspective on multilingualism: Diversity, mobility and complexity.*

Cook, V. J., & Bassetti, B. (Eds.) (in press). *Bilingual cognition: Thinking in two languages.* Psychology Press.

Coste, D., Courtillon, J., Ferenczi, V., Martins-Baltar, M. & Papo, E. (1976). *Un niveau-seuil.* Paris: Hatier.

Council of Europe (1982). *Recommendation R (82) 18 of the committee of ministers.* https://wcd.coe.int/com.instranet.Inst raServlet?command=com.instranet.CmdBlobGet&InstranetImage=601630&SecMode=1&DocId=676400&Usage=2.

Council of Europe (2008). *Recommendation CM/Rec(2008)7 of the committee of ministers to member states on the use of the Council of Europe's Common European Framework of Reference for Languages (CEFR) and the promotion of plurilingualism.* Strasburg: Council of Europe.

Council of Europe (2009). *European language portfolio.* http://www.coe.int/t/dg4/linguistic/Portfolio_EN.asp.

De Groot, A. M. B., & van Hell. J. G. (2005). The learning of foreign language vocabulary. In J. Kroll & A. De Groot (Eds.) (2005). *Handbook of Bilingualism* (pp. 9–29). Oxford: Oxford University Press.

De Swaan, A. (2001). *Words of the world: The global language system.* Cambridge: Polity Press.

DfES (Department for Education and Skills) (2001). *The Adult ESOL core curriculum.* London: DfES.

DfEE (Department for Education and Employment) (2001). *The national literacy strategy.* London: DfEE.

EACE (Education, Audiovisual and Culture Agency) (2008). *Key data on teaching languages in Europe.* http://eacea.ec.europa. eu/ressources/eurydice/pdf/0_integral/095EN.pdf.

English Curriculum for Israel (2002). *English curriculum for all grades.* Jerusalem: Ministry of Education. http://www.education.gov.il/tochniyot_limudim/eng1.htm.

Europass (2009). http://www.coe.int/T/DG4/Portfolio/documents/Pass_2spr.pdf.

Eurydice (2005). *Key data on teaching languages at school in Europe.* Eurydice European Unit. http://www.eurydice.org.

Figueras, N., North, B., Takala, S. Verhelst, N. & Van Avernaet, P. (2005). Relating examinations to the Common European Framework: A manual. *Language Testing, 22*(3), 261–279.

Firth, A. (1991). Discourse at work: Negotiating by telex, fax, and phone. Ph.D. dissertation, Aalborg University.

Firth, A. (1996). The discursive accomplishment of normality: On conversation analysis and "lingua franca" English. *Journal of Pragmatics, 26,* 237–259.

Firth, A., & Wagner, J. (2007). Second/foreign language learning as a social accomplishment: elaborations on a "reconceptualised" SLA. *Modern Language Journal, 91,* 800–819.

Gattoni, C. (2005). Promoting employability and international competitiveness: Cultural, linguistic and technological issues in CV writing in English. *Proceedings of the Association for Business Communication 7th European Convention* (pp. 1–5).

Gimson, A. (1962). *An introduction to the pronunciation of English,* London: Edward Arnold.

Graddol, D. (2006). *English next.* London: The British Council. http://www.britishcouncil.org/files/documents/learning-research-english-next.pdf.

Grosjean, F. (2008). *Studying bilinguals.* Oxford: Oxford University Press.

Harmer, J. (2004), *Just right.* London: Marshall Cavendish.

Howatt, A. (2004). *A history of English language teaching* (2nd ed.). Oxford: Oxford University Press.

Interagency Language Roundtable (ILR) (2009). http://www.govtilr.org/.

IELTS (International English Language Testing System) (2009). http://www.cambridgeesol.org/teach/ielts/.

IMO (International Maritime Organisation) (2001). *Standard marine communication phrases (SMCP).* http://www.imo.org/Safety/index.asp?topic_id=357#top.

Jarvis, S., & Pavlenko, A. (2007). *Crosslinguistic influence in language and cognition.* Abingdon: Routledge.

Jenkins, J. (2007). *English as a lingua franca: Attitude and identity.* Oxford: Oxford University Press.

Klein, W. (1986). *Second language acquisition.* Cambridge: Cambridge University Press.

Kramsch, C. (2009). Third culture and language education. In V. Cook & Li Wei (Eds.) *Contemporary applied linguistics* (pp. 233–254), London: Continuum.

Kucera, H., & Francis, W.N. (1967). *Computational analysis of present-day American English.* Lebanon, NH: New England University Press.

Mackey, W. F. (1965). *Language teaching analysis.* London: Longman.

Meierkord, C. (2004). Syntactic variation in interactions. *English World-Wide, 25,* 1109–1132.

MEXT (Ministry of Education, Culture, Sports, Science and Technology, Japan) (2003). *Regarding the Establishment of an Action Plan to Cultivate "Japanese with English Abilities".* Tokyo: MEXT.

Ministry of National Education, Warsaw (2007). http://www.ihep.org/assets/files/gcfp-files/Lisbon_Poland_2007.pdf.

Myles, F., & Mitchell, R. (2004). *Second language learning theories* (2nd ed.). London: Edward Arnold.

Norton, B. (2000). *Identity in language learning.* London: Longman.

Ogden, C. K (1937). *Basic English: A general introduction with rules and grammar.* N. p.: Paul, Trench Trubner and Co.

Ortega, L. (2008). *Understanding second language acquisition.* London: Hodder Education.

Oxford English Corpus (2009). http://www.askoxford.com/oec/?view=uk.

OED (*Oxford English Dictionary*) (2009). On-line version, Oxford University Press. http://www.oed Grosjean (XXX).com/.

Pearson (2009). *Catalogue.* http://www.pearsonlongman.com/pdfs/ADULT_CATALOGUE_09.pdf.

QCA (Quality Control Authority) (2009). *Languages for All by 2010.* http://www.qca.org.uk/qca_14636.aspx.

Quirk, R., Greenbaum, S., Leech, G. & Svartvik, J. (1972). *A grammar of contemporary English.* London: Longman.

Rajagopalan, K. (2004). The concept of "World English" and its implications for ELT. *ELT Journal, 58*(2), 111–117.

Sarmento, S. (2005). A pragmatic account of aviation manuals. *English for Specific Purposes World, 4*(3). http://www.esp-world.info/Articles_11/apragmaticaccountofaviationmanuals%5B2%5D.htm.

Scott, V. (2009). *Double Talk.* Englewood Cliffs, NJ: Prentice-Hall.

Seidlhofer, B. (2004). Research perspectives on teaching English as a lingua franca. *Annual Review of Applied Linguistics, 24,* 209–239.

Stern, H. H. (1983). *Fundamental concepts of language teaching.* Oxford: Oxford University Press.

Tarone, E. (1981). Some thoughts on the notion of communication strategy. *TESOL Quarterly, 15,* 285–295.

Taylor, L., & Jones, N. (2006). Cambridge ESOL exams and the Common European Framework of Reference (CEFR). *Cambridge ESOL Research Notes, 24,* 2–5.

Trudgill, P. (2001). *Sociolinguistic variation and change.* Edinburgh: Edinburgh University Press.

VALEUR (Valuing All Languages in Europe) (2004–2007). European Centre for Modern Languages. 2nd medium-term programme. http://www.ecml.at/mtp2/VALEUR/html/Valeur_E_news.htm#March2007.

Van Ek, J. (1975). *Threshold level English.* Strasbourg: Council of Europe

Van Ek, J., & Alexander, L. G. (1977). *Waystage.* Strasbourg: Council of Europe

VOICE (Vienna–Oxford International Corpus of English) (2009). http://www.univie.ac.at/voice/page/publications.

VOA (Voice of America) (2009). *Simple English.* http://www.voanews.com/specialenglish/.

Wikipedia (2009). *Simple English Wikipedia.* http://simple.wikipedia.org/wiki/Main_Page.

Wilkins, D. A. (1972). The linguistic and situational content of the common core in a unit/credit system. In *Systems development in adult language learning* (pp. 129–145). Strasbourg: Council of Europe. Reprinted in J. Trim, R. Richterich, J. Van Ek & D. A. Wilkins, *Systems development in adult language learning.* Oxford: Pergamon, 1980.

10
World Englishes
*Contexts and Relevance for Language Education**

Yamuna Kachru

Introduction

The global spread of English has affected all domains of human activity from language in education to international relations. As a result, it is crucial to understand the role that English plays, the status that it has and the purposes it serves in different contexts—contexts that are different from where the language originated and assumed its present form or where the language spread and became the primary language of the majority population.

In order to study what English means and does, it may be useful to look at a particular construct suggested in B. Kachru (1985) according to which the English-using world can be divided into three concentric circles. This conceptualization is based not only on the historical context of English but also on the status of the language and its functions in the different regions of the world. The Inner Circle represents the traditional historical and sociolinguistic bases of English in the regions where it originated (e.g., England) and later spread and became the primary language of the majority population (including Ireland, Scotland and Wales in the UK, the USA, Australia, Canada and New Zealand).

The Outer Circle comprises the former colonies or spheres of influence of the UK and the USA, e.g., India, Kenya, Nigeria, the Philippines, Singapore, among others. There was no large-scale movement of English-speaking populations to the Outer Circle, instead, a small number of administrators, educators and missionaries were responsible for language spread among the indigenous population in these countries. Now, the nativized varieties of English in these countries have achieved the status of either an official language, or of an additional language widely used in education, administration, legal system, etc., though the indigenous languages continue to be used in many domains of activity. This change occurred over the past several centuries due to various sociocultural factors.

The Expanding Circle consists of countries that, though not directly colonized, gradually came under Western influence and where English is fast becoming a dominant additional language in academia, business and commerce, higher education, media and science and technology. Examples are the countries of the Arab world, Europe, Latin America and the Pacific, and China, Indonesia, Japan, Korea, Malaysia and Thailand. In these areas, English does not have an official status, but is widely taught and used for international communication.

The varieties of English used in all these Circles are referred to as *world Englishes* (WEs), the justification being that *Englishes* in the three Circles display variation in form, function, literary creativity and acculturation in the new contexts. The acculturation of the language is at all levels—phonology, lexicon, syntax, discourse and literary creativity.[1]

The aim of this chapter is to present a brief survey of the state of research on WEs from the point of view of teaching and learning of English in various regions of the world. The teaching of English across languages and cultures has serious implications for institutions involved in four domains of activity: (1) teacher training programs such as the Masters in Teaching English to Speakers of Other Languages (MATESOL) and teacher certification in TESOL; (2) professional organizations dedicated to the theoretical, methodological and pedagogical concerns of English language teaching (ELT) professionals; (3) journals dedicated to the same concerns; and (4) the vast English language textbook, reference book and language testing industry. I mention these in particular as they have the most significant impact on ELT practices across all the Circles.

The chapter begins with some background observations. It may be helpful to the readers to outline explicitly the perspective of researchers studying varieties of English around the world. That English has acquired both a *range* and a *depth* unparalleled in human history is uncontroversial. By *range* is meant the functional allocation of the language in intimate, social and professional domains by its users, and by *depth* is meant the penetration of the language in various strata of society across cultures and languages (B. Kachru, 1986a; B. Kachru & Nelson, 1996).

That English has developed a number of varieties in its diaspora is also beyond debate. Though there is still vigorous debate on the status of Outer and Expanding Circle varieties and how to characterize what is meant by "standard" in relation to varieties used in all the Circles, there is by now a healthy tradition of research in them (see, e.g., Bolton & B. Kachru, 2006, 2007; B. Kachru, 2005; Y. Kachru & Nelson, 2006; *World Englishes* journal issues *24*(2) (2005) for profiles of eight lesser known world Englishes, *24*(4) (2005) for Russian Englishes, and *26*(2) for Europe).[2] This research is motivated by the fact that these varieties are increasingly being employed to various degrees in educational and other domains in their respective regions.

There is, of course, debate on whether these varieties are on par with more established varieties such as American English or not. The debate on standards and varieties, as researchers in WEs believe, has just as much to do with attitudinal and ideological positions with regard to status of the varieties as to an unwillingness to face the linguistic and acquisitional realities (Sridhar, 1994). One clear evidence of attitudinal bias is provided by the instruments of testing proficiency in English developed in the UK and the USA and used around the world (see Davidson, 1994; Lowenberg, 1992, 1993, 2001) and the research paradigms of second language acquisition (SLA) of the last several decades prior to the end of the twentieth century.[3]

Following the background discussion, the research tradition is discussed in some detail. The relevance of research in WEs to linguistics in general and educational linguistics in particular in the context of teaching and learning of English across the world is considered. This relates to the debates that have been generated by researchers in sub-fields of English studies such as English as a lingua franca or global English(es) (see Seidlhofer, 2001, 2004, 2009; Jenkins, 2006, 2009; Murata & Jenkins, 2009), therefore, the relationship of WEs research to research within these approaches is explored. The educational status of English in various regions is reviewed and the interesting question of the future of English (Graddol, 1997) as a world language is examined. The chapter concludes with what all these developments entail for the teaching and learning of Englishes in the coming decades.

Emergence of Varieties in Diaspora

The diaspora of English, as B. Kachru suggests (1992c), is of two types. The first arose as a consequence of the migration of the English-speaking people and comprises Australia, North America and New Zealand. The second resulted from the diffusion of English among speakers of diverse groups of languages in Asia, Africa, the Caribbean and other parts of the world. These two diasporas have distinct historical, linguistic, sociological, pedagogical and ideological contexts.

The English language has undergone a number of linguistic processes—some similar, some quite different—in both types of diaspora. These processes were set in motion as a result of the physical context and patterns of settlement, for example, in the Inner Circle in North America and Australia. Populations from various parts of Europe, and later from other regions of the world, arrived and settled down next to each other in these countries of the Inner Circle. A composite language and culture grew out of this various population that gave the varieties of the first diaspora their characteristic structure. The evidence for this can be found, for instance, in the many features of African, Native American and Hispanic idioms, metaphors and discourse strategies that have become a part of American English. It is clear that varieties of Inner Circle English, such as American, Australian, Canadian and New Zealand, emerged because of the processes set in motion by language contact. The same factors are responsible for what occurred in the Outer Circle varieties such as Indian, Nigerian and Singaporean.

In the early twentieth century, American English gave rise to the same attitudinal prejudices that are now directed against the Outer Circle varieties, as is clear from the following quote from *New Statesman* (June 25, 1927) in Mencken (1936, p. 33):[4]

> [T]hat their [America's] huge hybrid population of which only a small minority are even racially Anglo-Saxons should use English as their chief medium of intercommunication is our misfortune, not our fault. They certainly threaten our language, but the only way in which we can effectively meet that threat is by assuming—in the words of the authors of "The King's English" [by H. W. and F. G. Fowler, Oxford, 1908] that "Americanisms are foreign words and should be so treated."

The only difference in the emergence of the two types of diaspora varieties is that in the case of the first, the language was brought in by a significant number of immigrants from the Mother country and adopted by other immigrants, initially mainly from Europe. In case of the second diaspora, the language was brought in, one might say, by a handful of users of English, not all of them English-speakers,[5] and transplanted in Africa, East, South and Southeast Asia and other so-called Anglophone regions of the world. This one difference, however, leads to very different historical, sociocultural and canonical contexts of development of varieties and their literatures in the second diaspora. Thus the claim that the three Circles model is a geographic model (Yano, 2009b) is simplistic and overlooks the details that crucially characterize the Circles.

Aims and Focus of Research

Researchers in WEs are interested in all aspects of the emergence, grammars, sociolinguistics, ideological issues, creative literatures and teaching and learning of WEs (see the collected papers in Bolton & B. Kachru, 2006; B. Kachru, 1986a, 1992a; B. Kachru, Y. Kachru & C. Nelson, 2006; Schneider, 1997; Smith, 1987; Smith & Forman, 1997; Thumboo, 2001). They have worked on the historical background of the dissemination of English in the world (e.g., Bamgboṣe, Banjo & Thomas, 1995; Bautista, 1997; B. Kachru 1983 and ff.; Pakir, 1991a, 1991b, 1992, 2001; K. Sridhar, 1989, among others). They are involved in studying the linguistic processes that are responsible for variety-specific characteristics as well as common features among varieties of the language in different regions of the world. These include phonological, lexical and grammatical processes, discourse strategies and textual properties (see, e.g., Bokamba, 1992; B. Kachru, 1983, 1986a, 2005; Y. Kachru & Nelson, 2006; Y, Kachru & Smith, 2008; Lowenberg, 1986, 1991; Mesthrie & Bhatt, 2008; Smith, 1987; Smith

& Forman, 1997; Thumboo, 2001). In addition, they are interested in investigating the sociocultural contexts of use of English, particularly in the second diaspora (see B. Kachru, 1986a, 1992a; Y. Kachru, 1993, 1995a, 1995b, 1997a; Nelson, 1992, K. Sridhar, 1991; Tawake, 1990, 1993; Valentine, 1988, 1991, 1995, 2001, 2006, among others). A great deal of attention is being paid to genres and styles in WEs (V. Bhatia, 2006) and the uses of English in the media, advertising, and commerce (see, e.g., Martin, 2006; T. Bhatia, 2006; Van Horn, 2006).

In view of the differing conventions of use and usage, intelligibility among the varieties is another topic that has been explored to some extent. Several studies have been conducted to determine if the claim regarding superior intelligibility of Inner Circle varieties can be sustained on the basis of empirical investigations (Frenck & Min, 2001; Smith, 1992; Smith & Christopher, 2001; Smith & Nelson, 1985; Smith & Rafiqzad, 1979). Another aspect of the intelligibility issue is that of the intelligibility of indigenized varieties in their native settings (see B. Kachru, 1992b; Sridhar, 1994; and Sridhar & Sridhar, 1986, 1992). As Sridhar (1994, p. 802) observes, accent, transfer from substratum languages, code-mixing and switching, etc. are enriching resources in stable multilingual communities with shared verbal repertoires. They are not an impediment to intelligibility; instead, they are as natural as style or register switching in monolingual communities. Researchers in English as lingua franca and global English(es) are also concerned with issues of intelligibility, but there the concern seems to be more with establishing norms for educational goals than with exploring the nature of the phenomenon and developing appropriate methodologies to study it (see Berns, 2008, for a critique of this approach).

Language contact and convergence in these regions have not only affected English, they have also had an impact on the local languages. Therefore, researchers in WEs are interested in looking at the two-way interaction between English and local languages to understand the effects of contact and convergence. The interface of contact and convergence has been termed "nativization" (of English) and "Englishization" (of local languages). Englishization of local languages has been discussed in studies such as Baik (2001), Hsu (1994a, 1994b, 2001), B. Kachru (1979) and Shim (1994).

Most users of English in these regions (i.e., Africa, Asia) are bilinguals, or even multilinguals (I will subsume "bilingual" under "multilingual" and will use "multilingual" to indicate both categories henceforth). A great deal of WE research focuses on the language use of multilinguals. For example, considerable work has been done on code repertoire of multilinguals and the phenomena of code-mixing and switching (Bautista, 1990, 1991; T. Bhatia & Ritchie, 1989, 1996; Bhatt, 1996; B. Kachru, 1978; Kamwangamalu, 1989; Kamwangamalu & Li, 1991; Pandey, 2001, among others).

It has been demonstrated beyond controversy that all Outer Circle varieties have a standard, or "acrolectal," form, which is mutually intelligible among all English-using populations. The characteristic features of the acrolectal forms within regions/national boundaries—whether they have been codified or not—are widely attested in highly literate domains of use, e.g., the domains of academia, creative literature, diplomacy, higher administration, media, etc., and have been looked at (e.g., Baumgardner, 1993; Bautista, 1997; B. Kachru, 1983; Llamazon, 1969; Pakir, 1991b and 2001; Rahman, 1990).

The teaching and learning of English in the Outer and Expanding circles is one sub-topic within the range of topics that WE research focuses on (Brown, 1993, 2001; Brown & Peterson, 1997; B. Kachru, 1995c, 1997b;Y. Kachru, 1985a, 1985b, 1997b). This research is informed by the findings of the fields of first and second language acquisition (FLA and SLA), ethnography of communication, literacy, psycholinguistic, multilingualism, neurolinguistics and other relevant fields. A large body of research is devoted to how fluent, proficient users of the varieties use them in administration, business, diplomacy, education, law, literary creativity, politics, religion and other spheres of human activity (see, e.g., papers in Baumgardner, 1996b; V. Bhatia, 1997; B. Kachru, 1992a; Pandharipande, 2001; Smith, 1987; Smith & Forman, 1997; Thumboo, 2001).

All institutionalized varieties have a body of literature that is useful for teaching language as well as the culture of the region. For readers across languages and cultures one resource for gaining familiarity with the varieties of English in the second diaspora is the literature created in them. Appreciation of literary creativity in WEs makes it hard to maintain prejudicial attitudes toward what is perceived as "non-standard" because it is unfamiliar. Some research has been devoted to classroom utilization of WE literatures for raising consciousness about the multicultural identity of WEs (see, e.g., Courtright, 2001; B. Kachru, 1986b, 1995a, 1995b, 2001, 2005; Nelson, 1992; Smith, 1992; Tawake, 1990, 1993; Thumboo, 1985, 1986, 1988, 1991, 1992; Thumbo & Says, 2007).

There is, of course, variation within regional varieties, such as South Asian English or West African English, and national varieties, such as Singaporean English, just as there is dialectal and diatypic variation within the English-speaking populations of Australia, Canada, New Zealand, the UK and the USA (McArthur, 1992). The basilectal, or pidgin-like forms, and the mesolectal, or colloquial forms, which may or may not be mixed with substratum language forms, are used for various purposes in the Outer and Expanding Circles, just as various speaker and speech types are used by Inner Circle speakers and writers. The focus of research, however, is not on just this variation and relating it to theories of acquisitional deficiency. Rather, the interest is in the functional allocation of the varieties within the English-using communities (see, e.g., Bamiro, 1991; B. Kachru, 1986a; Taiwo, 1976; Tay, 1993).

A great deal of attention is directed toward the communicative needs of the users that underlie the observed linguistic differences between the Outer and Expanding Circle varieties as compared to the Inner Circle ones (see, e.g., research in corpus linguistics; also the discussions in the sphere of literary creativity in Bolton & Kachru, 2006; Dissanayake, 1985, 1990; B. Kachru, 1992b, 1995a, 1995b; Y. Kachru, 1998b; Thumboo, 1985, 1986, 1992).

It is obvious from the research areas described above that the WEs paradigm is inclusive, in terms of topics that are investigated, and the subdisciplines of linguistics that have been found to be relevant to investigate the varieties and their properties.

The Relevance of WE as a Field of Research

The relevance and implications of WEs for linguistic theory are many as has been discussed since the 1960s. First, ways have to be found to build in variation instead of idealization of a linguistic system. Related to this, the whole idea of "native speaker" has to undergo drastic revision—linguists have to be able to think not in terms of *native* and *non-native speakers* of English, but of *native users* of different WEs. The notion of one standard language—the Queen's English, or American English—has to change; there are now multiple standard Englishes (Australian, Canadian, Caribbean, New Zealand, Indian, Nigerian, Philippine, Singaporean and others). Some of these have grammars and dictionaries; others are developing them. It is worth remembering that language is not dependent on grammars and dictionaries; "English" English existed long before it was codified in a dictionary or a grammar.

Another fascinating area of research for English studies is how the spread and use of English world-wide is changing the meaning potential of the language.[6] Just as once borrowing and adaptations from European (especially, first French, following the Norman conquest, and subsequently, the classical languages such as Greek and Latin) expanded the meaning potential of English, borrowings and adaptations from Asian and African languages, and languages of the Pacific (e.g., Māori) are changing the semantic range of English (Halliday, 2006).

To give one example, the English lexical item *religion* to capture the notion of *dharma* (Sanskrit) and *din* (Arabic), or *God* to translate *Brahman* (Sanskrit) and *Allah* (Arabic) has extended the meaning potential of these lexical items. The wide use of *karma, avatar(a)* and the phonologically adapted from *juggernaut* (from *jagannaath* "Lord of the universe," all from Sanskrit) have extended the meaning potential of English as they bring in new conceptual entities. A very interesting example of this phenomenon is the use of the Sanskrit greeting *namaste* "I bow to you" in some African American churches in the USA.[7] It is not only at the lexical level, but also at the level of total range of making meaning that English is expanding its meaning potential as it is used world-wide in contexts that are new to the language, e.g., in political, diplomatic, economic and commercial negotiations among speakers from the three Circles and in cultural exchanges, illustrated by the popularity of hip-hop world wide (Lee, 2006).

Research in SLA could benefit from reevaluating the usefulness of the concepts of native speaker, linguistic competence, transfer, interlanguage and fossilization in the context of acquisition of additional languages. The pronounced monolingual bias in SLA research has so far excluded a large population of multilingual speakers of languages from playing any role in such research in the multilingual contexts in which most people live. Current paradigms of research are hardly conducive to producing scientific knowledge of SLA constrained as they are by the "language myths of Europe." They inhibit generation of alternative perspectives on SLA that multilingual contexts provide (Y. Kachru, 1994). To take just one example, many languages of wider communication (LWC), including English (in the Outer Circle), modern standard Hindi (in India) and Swahili (in East Africa) are used essentially by populations who are almost exclusively multilinguals. They speak one language in their communities and another in educational, administrative, professional and other wider contexts where many communities may interact.[8] SLA theories at this point have hardly anything relevant to say about the acquisition of these LWCs (Y. Kachru, 1996), since they have a large number of speakers but no well-defined body of "ideal native speakers." The question naturally arises as to how we can afford to ignore such a wide-spread phenomenon and still claim to formulate "universal" theories.

Claims of universalism in linguistic and SLA theories at this point are meaningless. It is a greater pity since a wealth of data is available in Outer and Expanding Circle Englishes for the unbiased researcher to formulate adequate theories of human linguistic capacity in general and additional language acquisition in particular. As Sridhar (1994, p. 803) observes:

> What we need is a more functionally oriented and culturally authentic theory, one that is true to the ecology of multilingualism and views the multilingual's linguistic repertoire as a unified, complex, coherent, interconnected, interdependent, organic ecosystem, not unlike a tropical rain forest.

As B. Kachru (1990) points out, WEs provide the most extensive "laboratory" to date for applied linguistic and sociolinguistic research. Observation and analyses in this laboratory could bring important SLA concepts and claims into focus, and also bring serious gaps to light.

Lingua Franca and Global Englishes

It is useful at this point to consider the terminological debates regarding English as lingua franca, global English(es) and WEs. The term *lingua franca* has been used to characterize the global functions of the English language (e.g., James, 2000; McArthur, 2001; Seidlhofer, 2001) and there are attempts to define the core (e.g., Jenkins, 2000 is an attempt to do so in the area of the sound system) of this *lingua franca* English. There is also a characterization of lingua franca English as the language used by speakers of other languages when they get together to negotiate diplomatic or political issues in contexts such as those of the business of European Union. This definition excludes some users and uses of English. Besides, the label, lingua franca, does not capture the phenomenon of WEs for several reasons, as has been explained in many papers on this topic (e.g., B. Kachru, 1996, 2005; Phillipson, 2008; see also, Kahane & Kahane, 1979, 1986). Consider the case of English as used in the member states of the European Union. Euro-English (Cenoz & Jessner, 2000, p. viii; Modiano, 1996) is not just a language used for utilitarian purposes of business, commerce and tourism; it also serves as a medium of academic, cultural, diplomatic, legal, political and scientific-technological discourses. In view of its mathetic function (i.e., functions related to knowledge creation and dissemination), Euro-English is no more a lingua franca in the term's original sense than are South Asian, Singaporean or West African Englishes. In fact, all these Englishes, including Euro-English, exhibit internal variation as well, based on geographical and ethnic factors.

Recently, it has been claimed that lingua franca English or Englishes is a sub-field of research within the framework of WE research that concentrates exclusively on the communicative needs of people of different backgrounds coming together for conducting the business of the European Union, such as resolving issues between members of European Union, or negotiating wording of regulations, etc. (see Berns, 2009; Seidlhofer, 2009). The notion of a lingua franca English in Europe is thus analogous to lingua franca Englishes in Asia, Africa, Middle East, Latin America and other parts of the world (Yano, 2009a). These are all legitimate fields of sociolinguistic research, but trying to codify lingua franca Englishes for educational purposes seems to be of doubtful value in the long run, as Phillipson (2008) observes. These Englishes will continue to evolve as the membership of these regional groupings shift and reconfigure and the future of lingua franca Englishes will depend on the continuing usefulness of such regional groupings.

What has attracted researchers to the WEs perspective is that it strongly suggests, to quote McArthur (1993), "the democratization of attitudes to English everywhere on the globe" and "dissolves the trinity of ENL, ESL , EFL nations." Bolton (2006, p. 240) continues, in the same vein:

> [The WE perspective] has been characterized by an underlying philosophy that has argued for the importance of inclusivity and pluricentricity in approaches to the linguistics of English worldwide, and involves not merely the description of national and regional varieties, but many other related topics as well, including contact linguistics, creative writing, critical linguistics, discourse analysis, corpus linguistics, lexicography, pedagogy, pidgin and creole studies, and the sociology of language.

Global English(es) has been used in many different ways by many different experts in computers, media, sociology, politics, economics and other fields. Global Englishes in the plural has been used in the same way as WEs to indicate the global use of English in many recent publications. Global English in the singular, however, has come to designate the use of the language in the process of globalization, e.g., restricted to the economic domain (Halliday, 2006).

Future of WEs

The spread and functions of WEs are expanding; simultaneously, the domains of use of other contenders or languages of wider communication seem at this point to be shrinking (Phillipson, 2003, 2008). This is especially true of erstwhile European languages of wider communication such as French and Spanish in Africa and Southeast Asia, if we look at the favored language choice for a range of domains in these regions. The same is true of other languages, such as the Scandinavian languages and German, in certain domains in Europe (Phillipson, 2006). As far as various other LWCs are concerned (e.g., Arabic, Chinese and Hindi-Urdu), they are as yet providing no serious challenge to WEs.

We will look here at one candidate out of the three mentioned above, that is Chinese. Chinese is a dominant language in East and Southeast Asia for cultural and political, and increasingly, for economic reasons. China is making a concerted effort to encourage the teaching of Chinese (Mandarin) in its sphere of influence in Asia and increasingly, in Europe and the USA. Graddol estimates that the number of students of Mandarin world-wide will be 30 million within a decade or so (2006, p. 63), whereas the Office of Chinese Language Council International estimates that there are more than 40 million people learning Chinese world-wide now and the projection by the Ministry of Education of the Peoples' Republic is that by the year 2010, there will be approximately 100 million non-Chinese worldwide learning Chinese as a foreign language.[9] These figures do not come even close to the projected estimate of learners of English in the next decade or two (two billion; Graddol, 2006, p. 100). This number includes children who will start learning English in primary school, if the policies being instituted in almost all the nations of the world take effect as planned. It is worth noting that as China attempts to foster the teaching of Chinese in Asia and the West, more Chinese children and adults are learning English as well.

This means WEs will remain a highly valued medium of wider communication for the next few decades to come. There will be more blending and fusion of different Englishes in many domains. They will include the influence of African-American English in hip-hop and other genres of popular music (see, e.g., Lee, 2006; Moody, 2001; Moody & Matsumoto, 2003; Thompson, 2002; *World Englishes*, 25(2), 2006), and that of American English in several domains, including those of academia, business, commerce and finance. The influence of American English now is felt in Britain and other nations of Europe as well as South and Southeast Asia, China, Japan, Korea and Latin America (B. Kachru, Y. Kachru & C. Nelson, 2006; Hilgendorf, 1996; Matia, 2007; and Modiano, 1996 on Europe).

In view of these facts, a reasonable projection is to suggest that the depth and range of use of WEs will continue to grow at least for the foreseeable future with serious challenges to our current ideas in several domains of life, including those of national and cultural identity, and practices in English language teaching.

WEs and the Language Classroom

In any context of language learning and teaching, the issue of what to learn or to teach is bound to arise. In the case of ELT, the debate in recent decades has been about which English to aim for. For a majority of ELT experts in the Inner Circle as well as some members of Outer and Expanding Circle the competing standards are still British or American English. Other members of the Outer Circle, however, have started challenging the exocentric norms and rethinking the question of standards influenced by the WEs perspective (see Bamgboṣe, 1992; Gill & Pakir, 1999; B. Kachru, 1985, 1991; Pakir, 1991b, 1997; Sakai, 2005).

It is understandable as it is no longer believed that people in China or India or Japan or Nigeria learn English to interact with users of English from the Inner Circle, English is basically used by people of Outer and Expanding Circle interacting with each other within or outside their respective Circle. In an overwhelming majority of contexts, no one from the Inner Circle is either involved or even relevant.

The fear that development of multiple endocentric norms would result in a Tower of Babel is also losing credence. The American, Australian, British, Canadian and New Zealand norms differ significantly in some respects, yet the observed and documented differences present no barrier to mutual interaction. Moreover, as numerous English experts have documented, varieties within a small community of speakers such as England are not always mutually intelligible to each other.

In recent years the trend in intellectual fields related to language study has been toward a shift from communicator to message to receiver to context (Dissanayake, 1997; Pakir, 1997). Pluricentric languages such as Chinese, English, French and Spanish are likely to give rise to different norms in different geographical regions (Clyne, 1992). The sociolinguistic profile of WEs suggests that just as the Inner Circle shows a range of variation in its regional and social dialects, so do the Outer and Expanding Circles. And these varieties have functions within their sociocultural contexts. Therefore, it is neither possible nor desirable to impose any rigid linguistic norm on the entire world. Pakir (1997) describes the situation in Singapore; similar phenomena can be and have been documented for South Asia, Africa and other parts of the English using world (e.g., Bamiro, 1991; B. Kachru, 1986a; Owolabi, 1995).

The question naturally arises: if each region using English for its purposes develops its own variety of English, how can there be any mutual intelligibility among them? Research has shown that no particular variety is in a privileged position as far as mutual intelligibility is concerned. The more varieties one is exposed to, the more one learns how to accommodate the differences in accent, lexicogrammar and discoursal strategies (Smith, 1992). And it is becoming easier to get acquainted with more and more varieties of English through the media as the new century advances. The resources of internet and cable news are examples of two channels through which one can get exposure to almost all varieties of English.

Research studies in the fields of grammatical description (e.g., Baumgardner, 1993, 1996b; Bautista, 1997; Cheshire, 1991, B. Kachru, 1983; Lowenberg, 1984; Platt & Weber, 1979; Rahman, 1990; Simo-Bobda, 1994, among others) are documenting the phonological, lexical and grammatical features of WEs. Dictionary making has woken up to the usefulness of documenting the immense impact of language contact on the lexicon of English and there are several attempts at incorporating items from different regional Englishes into the mainstream dictionaries of Inner Circle varieties (*Encarta World English Dictionary*, 1999 had consultants for East Africa, Hong Kong, Hawaii, Malaysia-Singapore, South Africa, South Asia, UK Black English and US African-American English; *The Macquarie Dictionary*, 1997 has lexical items from South-East Asian Englishes, e.g., Malaysia, Singapore and the Philippines). Dictionaries and partial lexicons of different WEs are also being compiled and published for wider dissemination (e.g., Allison, 1996; Baumgardner, 1996a; Butler, 1997; Hawkins, 1984; B. Kachru, 1973, 1975; Lewis, 1991; Muthiah, 1991; Pakir, 1992; Rao, 1954, among others).

The international corpus of English (ICE) project, initiated in late 1980s (Greenbaum, 1990, 1991; Greenbaum & Nelson, 1996) will, it is projected, result in several descriptive studies of WEs on the basis of corpora gathered in 15 different countries from the three Circles (Nelson, 2004).

Studies on discourse conventions—spoken as well as written—are yielding valuable insights into how English is used as a medium of communicating different sociocultural practices (T. Bhatia, 1992; D'souza, 1988; Gumperz, 1982; Y. Kachru, 1987, 1991, 1993, 1995a, 1995b, 1996, 1997a, 1997b, 1998a, 1999, 2001a, 2001b, 2001c, 2003; Y. Kachru & Smith, 2008; Nwoye, 1992; Valentine, 1988, 1991).

Finally, English teachers are looking at literary works created in African, Indian, Singaporean and other varieties for making participants in their classes aware of the cultural meanings of WEs (Courtright, 2001; B. Kachru, 1986b; Tawake, 1990, 1993).

The survey above and studies such as B. Kachru (1997b) suggest that there are enough resources for imaginative use in the teaching or learning of WEs. For instance, Hannam University and Open Cyber University in Korea have introduced and are developing internet as a resource for teaching WEs to Korean learners of English (Jung & Min, 2002; Shim, 2002). Both sets of teachers are collecting materials from the websites of all the three Circles of English and preparing appropriate units for language teaching based on these materials.

There is, however, a great deal of work to be done before all those involved in ELT world-wide feel comfortable with the paradigm shift that teaching and learning WEs signals. Applied linguistics and ELT professionals have yet to take a principled stand and prepare themselves to incorporate the WEs perspective into their academic practices. These then will have an effect on the education policy makers and educational authorities will then be able to adopt an appropriate stance toward the teaching and learning of English.

One of the key areas to bring about a change in the current practices of ELT profession is that of EL teacher training. Almost no teacher training program in the Inner Circle at this point has a component of making trainees aware of world varieties of English (B. Kachru, 1997a; Vavrus, 1991). A pilot project started at Portland State University throws interesting light on what the consequences are when a serious component of world Englishes is introduced in a certificate or masters program of training teachers in English as a second language or TESOL (Brown & Peterson, 1997). The aim of the project was to see how the prior knowledge structures of trainees in such programs undergo modification as a result of their introduction to the key areas of research on WEs.

The findings of the project made it obvious that before and after the four-hour exposure to WEs concepts, the students had a very simplistic conceptual structure of the phenomenon. After the quarter long three-credit course, however, the trainees showed awareness of the three Circles of English and their three different historical and sociocultural contexts of development.

Many of the trainees come to the TESOL programs from language and literature departments as TESOL is not generally an undergraduate program. More language and literature departments, therefore, have to incorporate WE literatures (or, various Spanish, French, Portuguese or Chinese literatures, as the case may be) in their undergraduate curricula to sensitize students to the issues raised by LWCs. Universities in India have started including WE literatures in their undergraduate English literature curricula and several universities in the USA have made options available in "ethnic" literatures (e.g., African-American, African, Asian-American, Indian or South Asian). Awareness of differences resolves many issues of prejudice and resistance to variety and myths about standards and "ownership" of the language (Widdowson, 1994).

Conclusion

In conclusion, the WE research community is anticipating a paradigm shift in the teaching and learning of English in the Inner, Outer and Expanding Circles that will bridge the gap between sociolinguistic reality and prevailing myths about English, and the "native" speakers and "other" users of English. The emphasis is on inclusiveness of the global fellowship of the English-using populations.

It is encouraging to see the awareness of the complex issues of contexts, cultures, identities, etc. involved in the development of WEs in some recent work (Hinkel, 1999, 2005). This awareness is reflected in studies that deal with descriptions of English as an international language (e.g., Jenkins, 2000) and those that emphasize the communicative language teaching methodologies based on the relationship between context and communicative competence in particular social and cultural settings (e.g., Berns, 1990; Savignon, 2002).

Researchers in WEs are striving for adopting the perspective identified in the following quote (Davis, 2010):

> Philosophical inclusivity in linguistic description is not the only way in which the history of world Englishes may influence our present practice as linguists. It may be that inclusivity exists in language use at a more fundamental level, when pragmatic needs outweigh ideology sufficiently to give speakers the courage to take trans-lingual and trans-varietal communicational risks and the compassion to hear and create understanding from these attempts.

As language educators, we have to hope this will not be true of linguists only; language teachers and learners will also recognize the essential soundness of this perspective.

Notes

* This is a substantially revised and updated version, introducing several new topics, of my chapter in the first volume of this handbook. I am grateful to Larry E. Smith and Stanley Van Horn for their comments on an earlier version of this chapter.

1. For a succinct description of the conceptualization of WEs, see B. Kachru (1997b). See also B. Kachru and Nelson (1996). For acculturation of English in Asia and Africa, see the references cited in appropriate sections of this chapter, Bolton and Kachru (2006, 2007); B. Kachru (2005); and Y. Kachru and Nelson (2006).

2. *World Englishes* journal 24(2) contains profiles of Englishes in Costa Rica, Kenya, Macedonia, Mongolia, Poland, Puerto Rico, Russia and Turkey; 24(4) contains papers on various aspects of the nature, functions and teaching of English in Russia; and 26(2) contains papers on English in Norway, Macedonia, Germany , Finland, "Frenglish" in France, the Netherlands and Sweden. The topics covered range from English in media to youth culture and code-switching to cultural contexts of specific regions.

3. These issues have already been addressed in a number of studies and also briefly discussed in an earlier chapter in the first edition of the present volume (Y. Kachru, 2005). The relationship of research in WEs to research in SLA has also been discussed in Y. Kachru (2005) in some detail and hence need not be repeated here.

4. *New Statesman* was reacting to an International Conference in English that was held in London, but the call for it had come from the American side of the Atlantic.

5. Many of the agents of the spread of English in the former colonies came from various parts of the British Isles and Western Europe. Many English medium schools were and are still run by Belgian, Dutch and other missionary organizations all over the world. As Mesthrie (1992, p. 29) observes, the SAIE (South African Indian English) developed as a distinct variety as a result of several factors, including "the teaching of English by a French-speaking missionary to Tamil-speaking children via the medium of a Zulu-based pidgin."

6. In Halliday's framework, the central notion is "meaning potential" defined in terms of culture: what people can mean and can do. Biologically, all humans are alike in their capacity for language acquisition. However, we learn our first language(s) "in the context of behavioural settings where the norms of the culture are acted out and enunciated" (Halliday, 1978, p. 23). Language is thus the primary means of cultural transmission whereby social groups are integrated and the individual finds a personal and, subsequently, a social identity (Halliday, 1973). The context of culture defines the potential, or the range of possibilities, and the context of situation determines the actual, or the choice that takes place (Halliday, 1973). This is true of linguistic structure as well as rhetorical patterns. Language is not a set of isolated sentences, it is an interrelated set of texts in which meaning potential is actualized: people express meanings to realize some social goal.

7. Watch the sermon by Pastor Eddie D. Smith Sr where he explains the meaning of namaste as "The divinity in me bows to the divinity in you" and points out that if the African Americans use this greeting, they will not be able to commit acts of violence against each other easily: http://www.youtube.com/watch?v=izzNFCtFyyY&feature=related (accessed July 21, 2010).

8. In the Indian tradition, there was a distinction made between *sanskrit* (cultured, refined) and *prakrit* (natural, unsophisticated) forms of language beginning in the pre-Buddhist times (i.e., prior to 500 BC). In the Greek and Roman tradition (McArthur, 1998), Greek spoken by the upper class in Attica, including Athens, was the language of oratory and thus the focus of teaching oratory, the common dialects of the non-Attic populations was not highly valued. Cicero made a distinction between city usage, country usage and foreign usage, where the first had the most quality and prestige, the second less so, and the last one was "to be deplored" (McArthur, 1998, p. 163). In many parts of the Chinese-speaking world, a majority of the population speaks one of the dialects (e.g. Cantonese, Hokkien, Taiwanese) but learns and functions in Mandarin Chinese. In the Hindi belt of India, people speak one of the dialects of the Hindi region, e.g., Awadhi, Bhojpuri, Braj, Garhwali, Kumauni, Magahi, etc., at home and in their intimate domains, but are educated and function in the larger context in modern standard Hindi. Some of these so-called dialects of the Hindi area are mutually unintelligible and have very different grammars from each other and from Standard Hindi, and have developed hybrid varieties in their border regions where they are constantly in contact.

9. The source for the figure of 100 million learners of Chinese by 2010 is the following website: http://en.wikipedia.org/wiki/Confucius_Institute (accessed October 31, 2009)

References

Allison, Richard (Ed.) (1996). *Dictionary of Caribbean English usage.* Oxford: Oxford University Press.

Baik, Martin J. (2001). Aspects of Englishization of Korean discourse. In E. Thumboo (Ed.), *The Three circles of English* (pp. 181–193). Singapore: UniPress, The Center for the Arts, National University of Singapore.

Bamgboṣe, Ayọ (1992 [1982]). Standard Nigerian English: Issues of identification. In B. Kachru (Ed.), *The other tongue: English across cultures* (pp. 148–161). Urbana, IL: University of Illinois Press.

Bamgboṣe, Ayọ, Banjo, A., & Thomas, A. (1995). *New Englishes: A West African perspective.* Ibadan: Masuro.

Bamiro, E. O. (1991). Nigerian Englishes in Nigerian English literature. *World Englishes, 10*(1), 7–17.

Baumgardner, Robert J. (1993). *The English language in Pakistan.* Karachi: Oxford University Press.

Baumgardner, Robert J. (1996a). Innovations in Pakistani English political lexis. In R. J. Baumgardner (Ed.), *South Asian English: Structure, use and users* (pp. 175–188). Urbana, IL: University of Illinois Press.

Baumgardner, Robert J. (Ed.) (1996b). *South Asian English: Structure, use and users.* In the series English in the Global Context. Urbana, IL: University of Illinois Press.

Bautista, M. L. S. (1990). Tagalog–English code-switching revisited. *Philippine Journal of Linguistics, 21*(2), 15–29.

Bautista, M. L. S. (1991). Code-switching studies in the Philippines. *International Journal of the Sociology of Language,* 88, 19–32.

Bautista, M. L. S. (Ed.) (1997). *English is an Asian language: The Philippine context.* Sydney: Macquarie Library Pvt. Ltd. [First printing 1996.]

Berns, Margie (1990). *Contexts of competence: Social and cultural considerations in communicative language teaching.* New York: Plenum Press.

Berns, Margie (2008). World Englishes, English as a lingua franca, and intelligibility. *World Englishes, 27*(3/4), 327–334.

Berns, Margie (2009). Lingua franca: Form or functions? In T. Hoffmann & L. Siebers (Eds.), *World Englishes—Problems, properties and prospects* (pp. 369–371). Amsterdam: John Benjamins.

Bhatia, Tej K. (1992). Discorse functions and pragmatics of mixing: Advertising across cultures. *World Englishes, 11*(2/3), 195–215.

Bhatia, Tej K. (2006). World Englishes in global advertising. In B. Kachru, Y. Kachru & C. Nelson (Eds.), (pp. 601–619).

Bhatia, Tej K., & Ritchie, William C. (Eds.) (1989). *Code-mixing: English across languages.* Special issue of *World Englishes, 8*(3), 269–439.

Bhatia, Vijay K. (Guest Ed.) (1997). *Genre analysis and world Englishes.* Special issue of *World Englishes, 16*(3).

Bhatia, Vijay K. (2006). Genres and styles in World Englishes. In Braj B. Kachru, Yamuna Kachru & Cecil L. Nelson (Eds.) *The handbook of World Englishes* (pp. 386–401). Oxford: Blackwell.

Bhatt, Rakesh M. (Guest Ed.) (1996). Symposium on *Constraints on code-switching. World Englishes, 15*(3), 359–404.

Bokamba, Eyamba (1992). The Africanization of English. In B. Kachru (Ed.), *The other tongue: English across cultures* (pp. 125–147). Urbana, IL: University of Illinois Press.

Bolton, Kingsley (2006). World Englishes today. In B. Kachru, Y. Kachru & C. Nelson (Eds.), (pp. 240–269).

Bolton, Kingsley, & Braj B. Kachru (Eds.) (2006). *World Englishes: Critical concepts in linguistics* (6 vols). London: Routledge.

Bolton, Kingsley, & Braj B. Kachru (Eds.) (2007). *Origin and development of Asian Englishes: Critical concepts in linguistics* (5 vols). London: Routledge.

Brown, Kimberley (1993). World Englishes in TESOL programs: An infusion model of circular innovation. *World Englishes, 12*(1), 59–73.

Brown, Kimberley (2001). World Englishes and the classroom: Research and practice agendas for 2000. In E. Thumboo (Eds.), *The Three circles of English* (pp. 371–382). Singapore: UniPress, The Center for the Arts, National University of Singapore.

Brown, Kimberley, & Peterson, Jay (1997). Exploring conceptual frameworks: Framing a world Englishes paradigm. In L. E. Smith & M. L. Forman (Eds.), *World Englishes 2000* (pp. 32–47). Honolulu, HI: University of Hawai'i Press..

Butler, Susan (1997). World English in the Asian context: Why a dictionary is important. In L. E. Smith & M. L. Forman (Eds.), *World Englishes 2000* (pp. 90–125). Honolulu, HI: University of Hawai'i Press.

Cenoz, J., & Jessner, U. (2000). *English in Europe: The acquisition of a third language.* Clevedon and Buffalo: Multilingual Matters.

Cheshire, Jenny (Ed.) (1991). *English around the world: Sociolinguistic perspectives.* Cambridge: Cambridge University Press.

Clyne, Michael (1992). *Pluricentric languages: Differing norms in different nations.* Berlin/New York: Mouton de Gruyter.

Courtright, Marguerite S. (2001). Intelligibility and context in reader responses to contact literary texts. Ph.D. dissertation, University of Illinois at Urbana-Champaign.

Davidson, Fred (1994). The interlanguage metaphor and language assessment. *World Englishes, 13*(3), 377–386.

Davis, Daniel (2010). Presidential address: The inclusivity of world Englishes. *World Englishes, 29*(1) (in press).

Dissanayake, Wimal (1985). Towards a decolonized English: South Asian creativity in fiction. *World Englishes, 4*(2), 233–242.

Dissanayake, Wimal (1990). Self and modernism in Sri Lankan poetry in English. *World Englishes, 9*(2), 225–236.

Dissanayake, Wimal (1997). Cultural studies and world Englishes: Some topics for further exploration. In L. E. Smith & M. L. Forman (Eds.), *World Englishes 2000* (pp. 126–145). Honolulu, HI: University of Hawai'i Press.

D'souza, Jean (1988). Interactional strategies in South Asian languages: Their implications for teaching English internationally. *World Englishes, 7*(2), 159–171.

Frenck, Susan & Min, Sujung (2001). Culture, reader and textual intelligibility. In E. Thumboo (Ed.) *The Three circles of English* (pp. 19–34). Singapore: UniPress, The Center for the Arts, National University of Singapore.

Gill, Saran Kaur, & Pakir, Anne (Eds.) (1999). Symposium on standards, codification and world Englishes. *World Englishes, 18*(2), 159–274.

Graddol, David (1997). *The future of English.* London: The British Council.

Graddol, David (2006). *English next: Why global English may mean the end of "English as a Foreign Language".* British Council publication. [Revised. 2007.] http://www.britishcouncil.org/learning-research-englishnext.htm (accessed October 28, 2007).

Greenbaum, Sydney (1990). Standard English and the international corpus of English. *World Englishes, 9*(1), 79–83.

Greenbaum, Sydney (1991). ICE: The international corpus of English. *English Today, 28*(7.4), 3–7.

Greenbaum, Sydney, & Nelson, Gerald (Guest Eds.) (1996). *Studies on international corpus of English.* Special issues of *World Englishes, 15*(1), 1–124.

Gumperz, John J. (Ed.) (1982). *Language and social identity.* Cambridge: Cambridge University Press.

Halliday, M. A. K. (1973). *Explorations in the functions of language.* London: Arnold.

Halliday, M. A. K. (1978). *Language as social semiotic.* Baltimore, MD: University Park Press.

Halliday, M. A. K. (2006). Written language, standard language, global language. In B. Kachru, Y. Kachru & C. Nelson (Eds.), (pp. 349–365).

Hawkins, R. E. (1984). *Common Indian words in English.* Delhi: Oxford University Press.

Hilgendorf, Suzanne K. (1996). The impact of English in Germany. *English Today, 47*(12), 3–14.

Hinkel, Eli (Ed.) (1999). *Culture in second language teaching and learning.* Cambridge: Cambridge University Press.

Hinkel, Eli (Ed.) (2005). *Handbook of research in second language teaching and learning.* Mahwah, NJ: Lawrence Erlbaum.

Hoffmann, Thomas, & Siebers, Lucia (2009). *World Englishes—Problems, properties and prospects.* Amsterdam: John Benjamins.

Hsu, Jia-Ling (1994a). Language change in modern Chinese: Some aspects of Englishization. *World Englishes, 13*(2), 167–184.

Hsu, Jia-Ling (1994b). Language contact and convergence: Englishization of Mandarin Chinese in Taiwan. Ph.D. dissertation, University of Illinois at Urbana-Champaign, Urbana, Illinois.

Hsu, Jia-Ling (2001). The sources, adapted functions, and the public's subjective evaluation of the Englishization of Mandarin Chinese in Taiwan. In E. Thumboo (Ed.) *The three circles of English* (pp. 241–256). Singapore: UniPress, The Center for the Arts, National University of Singapore.

James, Allan (2000). English as a European lingua franca: Current realities and existing dichotomies. In J. Cenoz & U. Jessner (Eds.), *English in Europe: The acquisition of a third language* (pp. 22–38). Clevedon and Buffalo: Multilingual Matters.

Jenkins, Jennifer (2000). *World Englishes: A resource book for students.* London: Routledge.

Jenkins, Jennifer (2006). Currents perspectives on teaching world Englishes and English as a lingua franca. *TESOL Quarterly, 40*(11), 157–181.

Jenkins, Jennifer (2009). English as lingua franca: Interpretations and attitudes. In T. Hoffmann & L. Siebers (Eds.), *World Englishes—Problems, properties and prospects* (pp. 371–374). Amsterdam: John Benjamins.

Jung, Kyutae, & Min, Sujung (2002). Web-based world Englishes learning program. Paper presented at the ninth annual meeting of the International Association of World Englishes at the University of Illinois at Urbana-Champaign, October 18–20.

Kachru, Braj B. (1973). Toward a Lexicon of Indian English. In B. B. Kachru, R. B. Lees, S. Saporta, A. Pietrangeli & Y. Malkiel (Eds.), *Issues in linguistics: Papers in honor of Henry and Renee Kahane* (pp. 352–376). Urbana, IL: University of Illinois Press.

Kachru, Braj B. (1975). The New Englishes and old dictionaries: Directions in lexicographical research on non-native varieties of English. In Ladislav Zgusta (Ed.), *Theory and method in lexicography* (pp. 71–101). Chapel Hill, NC: Hornbeam Press.

Kachru, Braj B. (1978). Code-mixing as a communicative strategy in India. In James E. Alatis (Ed.), *International dimensions of bilingual education* (pp. 107–124). Washington DC: Georgetown University Press.

Kachru, Braj B. (1979). The Englishization of Hindi: language rivalry and language change. In I. Rauch & G. F. Carr (Eds.), *Linguistic method: Papers in honor of H. Penzl* (pp. 199–211). The Hague: Mouton.

Kachru, Braj B. (1983). *The Indianization of English: The English language in India.* Delhi: Oxford University Press.

Kachru, Braj B. (1985). Standards, codification and sociolinguistic realism: The English language in the Outer Circle. In Randolph Quirk & Henry Widdowson (Eds.), *English in the world, teaching and learning the language and literatures* (pp. 11–30). Cambridge: Cambridge University Press.

Kachru, Braj B. (1986a). *The alchemy of English: The spread, Functions and models of non-native Englishes.* London: Pergamon Press [South Asian Edition published by the Oxford University Press, New Delhi, 1989].

Kachru, Braj B. (1986b). Nonnative literatures in English as a resource for language teaching. In C. J. Brumfit & R. A. Carter (Eds.), *Literature and language teaching* (pp. 140–149). Oxford: Oxford University Press.

Kachru, Braj B. (1990). World Englishes and applied linguistics. *World Englishes, 9*(1), 3–20.

Kachru, Braj B. (1991). Liberation linguistics and the Quirk concern. *English Today, 7*(1), 1–13. [Reprinted in Tickoo, M. L. (Ed.) *Languages and standards: Issues, attitudes, case studies* (pp. 206–226). Singapore: SEAMEO Regional Language Center.]

Kachru, Braj B. (Ed.) (1992a). *The other tongue: English across cultures.* Urbana, IL: University of Illinois Press. [2nd edition; 1st edition 1982].

Kachru, Braj B. (1992b). Meaning in deviation: Toward understanding non-native literary texts. In B. Kachru (Ed.), *The other tongue: English across cultures* (pp. 301–326). Urbana, IL: University of Illinois Press.

Kachru, Braj B. (1992c). The second diaspora of English. In Tim William Machan & Charles T. Scott (Eds.), *English in its social contexts: Essays in historical sociolinguistics* (pp. 230–252). New York: Oxford University Press.

Kachru, Braj B. (1995a). The speaking tree: A medium of plural canons. In James A. Alatis (Ed.,) *Educational linguistics, cross-cultural communication, and global interdependence* (pp. 6–22) (Georgetown Round Table on Language and Linguistics 1994). Washington, DC: Georgetown University Press.

Kachru, Braj B. (1995b). Tanscultural creativity in world Englishes and literary canons. In B. Seidlhofer & G.Cook (Eds.), *Principle and practice in applied linguistics* (pp. 271–287). Oxford: Oxford University Press.

Kachru, Braj B. (1995c). Teaching world Englishes without myths. In Saran K. Gill , I. Abdul Aziz, H. Wong, Tg. T. M. M. Nor Rizan, D. A. H. Bahiyah, A. Hazita, S. Checketts & S. K. Lee (Eds.), *INTELEC '94: International English Language Education Conference, National and International Challenges and Responses* (pp. 1–19). Bangi, Malaysia: Pusat Bahasa Universiti Kebangsaan Malaysia.

Kachru, Braj B. (1996). English as a lingua franca. In H. Goebl, P. H. Nelde, Z. Stáry & W. Wölck (Eds.), *Contact linguistics: An international handbook of contemporary research* (pp. 906–913). Berlin and New York: Walter de Gruyter.

Kachru, Braj B. (1997a). Past-imperfect: The other side of English in Asia. In L. E. Smith & M. L. Forman (Eds.), *World Englishes 2000* (pp. 68–89). Honolulu: University of Hawaii Press.

Kachru, Braj B. (1997b). World Englishes 2000: Resources for research and teaching. In L. E. Smith & M. L. Forman (Eds.), *World Englishes 2000* (pp. 209–251). Honolulu: University of Hawaii Press.

Kachru, Braj B. (2001). World Englishes and culture wars. In C. K. Tong, A. Pakir, K. C. Ban and R. B. H. Goh (Eds.), *Ariels: Departures and returns—Essays for Edwin Thumboo* (pp. 391–414). Singapore: Oxford University Press.

Kachru, Braj B. (2005). *Asian Englishes: Beyond the canon.* Hong Kong: Hong Kong University Press. [South Asian ed. New Delhi: Oxford University Press.]

Kachru, Braj B., & Nelson, Cecil (1996). World Englishes. In Sandra Lee McKay & Nancy H. Hornberger (Eds.), *Sociolinguistics and language teaching.* Cambridge: Cambridge University Press.

Kachru, Braj B., Kachru, Yamuna & Nelson, Cecil L. (Eds.) (2006). *The handbook of World Englishes.* Oxford: Basil Blackwell.

Kachru, Yamuna (1985a). Discourse analysis, non-Native Englishes and second language acquisition research. *World Englishes,* 4(2), 223–232.

Kachru, Yamuna (1985b). Discourse strategies, pragmatics and ESL: Where are we going? *RELC Journal,* 16(2), 1–30.

Kachru, Yamuna (1987). Cross-cultural texts, discourse strategies and discourse interpretation. In L. E. Smith (Ed.), *Discourse across cultures: Strategies in world Englishes* (pp. 87–100). London: Prentice Hall International.

Kachru, Yamuna (Guest Ed.) (1991). *Symposium on speech acts in world Englishes. World Englishes,* 10(3), 299–306.

Kachru, Yamuna (1993). Social meaning and creativity in Indian English. In James E. Alatis (Ed.) *Language, communication and social meaning* (pp. 378–387) (Georgetown University Roundtable on Languages and Linguistics 1992). Washington, DC: Georgetown University Press.

Kachru, Yamuna (1994). Monolingual bias in SLA research. *TESOL Quarterly,* 28(4), 795–800.

Kachru, Yamuna (1995a). Cultural meaning and rhetorical styles: Toward a framework for contrastive rhetoric. In Barbara Seidlhofer and Guy Cook (Eds.), *Principles and practice in applied linguistics: Studies in honor of Henry G. Widdowson* (pp. 171–184). London: Oxford University Press.

Kachru, Yamuna (1995b). Lexical exponents of cultural contact: Speech act verbs in Hindi-English dictionaries. In B. B. Kachru, & Henry Kahane (Eds.), *Cultures, ideologies, and the dictionary: studies in honor of Ladislav Zgusta* (pp. 261–274). Tübingen: Max Niemeyer Verlag.

Kachru, Yamuna (1996). Culture, variation and languages of wider communication: The paradigm gap. In James E. Alatis, Carolyn A. Straehle, Maggie Ronkin & Brent Gallenberger (Eds.), *Linguistics, language acquisition, and language variation: Current trends and future prospects* (pp. 178–195) (Georgetown University Round Table on Languages and Linguistics 1996). Washington, DC: Georgetown University Press.

Kachru, Yamuna (1997a). Culture and argumentative writing in world Englishes. In L. E. Smith and M. L. Forman (Eds.), *World Englishes 2000* (pp. 48–67). Honolulu, HI: University of Hawai'i Press.

Kachru, Yamuna (1997b). Culture, variation and English language education. In Steve Cromwell , Peggy Rule & Toshiko Sugino (Eds.), *On JALT 96: Crossing Borders* (pp. 199–210). The Proceedings of the JALT 1996 Conference on Language Teaching and Learning, Tokyo.

Kachru, Yamuna (1998a). Culture and speech acts: Evidence from Indian and Singaporean English. *Studies in The Linguistic Sciences,* 28(1), 79–98.

Kachru, Yamuna (1998b). Context, creativity, style: Strategies in Raja Rao's novels. In Robert L. Hardgrave (Ed.), *Word as mantra: The art of Raja Rao* (pp. 88–107). New Delhi: Katha.

Kachru, Yamuna (1999). Culture, context and writing. In E. Hinkel (Ed.), *Culture in second language teaching and learning* (pp. 75–89). Cambridge: Cambridge University Press.

Kachru, Yamuna (2001a). Communicative styles in world Englishes. In Chee Kiong Tong, Anne Pakir, Kah Choon Ban & Robbie B. H. Goh (Eds.), *Ariels: Departures and returns—Essays for Edwin Thumboo* (pp. 267–284). Oxford: Oxford University Press.

Kachru, Yamuna (2001b). Discourse competence in world Englishes. In Edwin Thumboo (Ed.), *The three circles of English* (pp. 341–355). Singapore: UniPress, The Centre for the Arts, National University of Singapore.

Kachru, Yamuna (2001c). World Englishes and rhetoric across cultures. *Asian Englishes: An International Journal of the Sociolinguistics of English in Asia/Pacific,* Winter, 54–71.

Kachru, Yamuna (2003). Conventions of politeness in plural societies. In Rüdiger Ahrens, David Parker, Klaus Stierstorfer & Kowk-Kan Tam (Eds.), *Anglophone cultures in South-East Asia: Appropriations, continuities, contexts* (pp. 39–53). Heidelberg, Germany: University of Heidelberg Press.

Kachru, Yamuna (2005). Teaching and learning of world Englishes. In E. Hinkel (Ed.), *Handbook of research in second language teaching and learning* (pp. 155–173). Mahwah, NJ: Lawrence Erlbaum.

Kachru, Yamuna, & Nelson, Cecil L. (2006). *World Englishes in Asian contexts.* Hong Kong: Hong Kong University Press.

Kachru, Yamuna, & Smith, Larry E. (2008). *Cultures, contexts, and world Englishes.* New York: Routledge.

Kahane, H., & Kahane, R. (1979). Delcine and survival of Western prestige languages. *Language,* 55, 183–198.

Kahane, H., & Kahane, R. (1986). A typology of prestige language. *Language,* 62, 495–508. Kamwangamalu, Nkonko (1989). A selected bibliography of studies on code-mixing and code-switching (1970–1988). *World Englishes,* 8(3), 433–440.

Kamwangamalu, Nkonko, & Li, Charles L. (1991). Mixers and mixing: English across cultures. *World Englishes,* 10, 247–261.

Lee, Jamie S. (2006). *Crossing* and *crossers* in East Asian pop music: Korea and Japan. *World Englishes,* 25(2), 235–250.

Lewis, Ivor (1991). *Sahibs, Nabobs and Boxwallahs: A dictionary of the words of Anglo-India.* Delhi: Oxford University Press.

Llamazon, Teodoro A. (1969). *Standard Filipino English.* Manila: Ateneo University Press.

Lowenberg, Peter H. (1984). English in the Malay Archipelago: Nativization and its functions in a sociolinguistic area. Ph.D. dissertation, University of Illinois at Urbana-Champaign.

Lowenberg, Peter H. (1986). Non-native varieties of English: Nativization, norms, and implications. *Studies in Second Language Acquisition,* 8(1), 1–18.

Lowenberg, Peter H. (1991). Variation in Malaysian English: The pragmatics of languages in contact. In J. Cheshire (Ed.), *English around the world: Sociolinguistic perspectives* (pp. 364–375). Cambridge: Cambridge University Press.

Lowenberg, Peter H. (1992). Teaching English as a world language: Issues in assessing non-native proficiency. In B. Kachru (Ed.), *The other tongue: English across cultures* (pp. 108–121). Urbana, IL: University of Illinois Press.

Lowenberg, Peter H. (1993). Issues of validity in tests of English as a world language: Whose standards? *World Englishes,* 12(1), 95–106.

Lowenberg, Peter H. (2001). Creativity, context and testing. In E. Thumboo (Ed.), *The three circles of English* (pp. 383–400). Singapore: UniPress, The Center for the Arts, National University of Singapore.

McArthur, Tom (Ed.) (1992). *The Oxford companion to the English language.* Oxford: Oxford University Press.

McArthur, Tom (1993). The English language or the English languages? In W.F. Bolton & David Crystal (Eds.), *The Penguin History of Literature* (Vol. 10) (pp. 323–341). London: Penguin.

McArthur, Tom (1998). *The English languages.* Cambridge: Cambridge University Press.

McArthur, Tom (2001). World English and world Englishes: Trends, tensions, varieties, and standards. *Language Teaching,* 34, 1–20.

The Macquarie Dictionary (3rd ed., 1997). Sydney, Australia: The Macquarie Library, Macquarie University.

Martin, Elizabeth A. (2006). World Englishes in the media. In B. Kachru, Y. Kachru and C. Nelson (Eds.), (pp. 583–600).

Martin, Elizabeth A. (2007). "Frenglish" for sale: Multilingual discourses for addressing today's global consumer. *World Englishes, 26*(2), 170–190.

Mencken, A. L. (1936). *The American language.* New York: Alfred A. Knopf.

Mesthrie, Rajend (1992). *English in language shift: The history, structure and sociolinguistics of South African Indian English.* Cambridge: Cambridge University Press.

Mesthrie, Rajend, & Bhatt, Rakesh M. (2008). *World Englishes: The study of new linguistic varieties.* Cambridge: Cambridge University Press.

Modiano, M. (1996). The Americanization of Euro-English. *World Englishes, 15*(2), 207–215.

Murata, Kumiko, & Jenkins, Jennifer (2009). *Global Englishes in Asian contexts: Current and future debates.* New York: Palgrave Macmillan.

Muthiah, S. (1991). *Words in Indian English: A reader's guide.* Delhi: Harper Collins.

Nelson, Cecil L. (1992). My language, your culture, whose communicative competence? In B. Kachru (Ed.), (pp.327–339).

Nelson, Gerald (Guest Ed.) (2004). Special issue on international corpus of English. *World Englishes, 23*(2), 225–316.

Nwoye, O. G. (1992). Obituary announcements as communicative events in Nigerian English. *World Englishes, 11*(1), 15–27.

Owolabi, K. (Ed.) (1995). *Language in Nigeria: Essays in honor of Ayọ Bamgboṣe.* Ibadan: Group Publishers.

Pakir, Anne (1991a). The range and depth of English-knowing bilinguals in Singapore. *World Englishes, 10*(2), 167–179.

Pakir, Anne (1991b). The status of English and the question of "standard" in Singapore: A sociolinguistic perspective. In Makhan L. Tickoo (Ed.), *Languages and standards: Issues, attitudes, case studies* (pp. 109–130). Singapore: SEAMEO Regional Language Center.

Pakir, Anne (1992). *Words in a cultural context.* Proceedings of the Lexicography Workshop, Singapore: UniPress.

Pakir, Anne (1997). Standards and codification for world Englishes. In L. E. Smith & M. L. Forman (Eds.), *World Englishes 2000* (pp. 169–181). Honolulu: University of Hawaii Press.

Pakir, Anne (2001). Bilingualism in Southeast Asia and the evolution of a new English language ecology. In C. K. Tong , A. Pakir, K. C. Ban & B. H. K. Goh (Eds.), *Ariels: Departures and returns—Essays for Edwin Thumboo* (pp. 415–428). Singapore: Oxford University Press.

Pandey, Anita (2001). Code alteration and Englishization across cultures. In E. Thumboo (Ed.), *The three circles of English* (pp. 277–300). Singapore: UniPress, The Center for the Arts, National University of Singapore.

Pandharipande, Rajeshwari (2001). Constructing religious discourse in diaspora: American Hinduism. *Studies in the Linguistic Sciences, 31*(1), 231–252.

Phillipson, Robert (2003). *English only Europe? Challenging language policy.* London: Routledge.

Phillipson, Robert (2006). Figuring out the Englishisation of Europe. In Constant Leung & Jennifer Jenkins (Eds.), *Reconfiguring Europe: The contribution of applied linguistics* (pp. 65–86). London: Equinox, and British Association for Applied Linguistics.

Phillipson, Robert (2008). Lingua franca or lingua frankensteinia? English in European integration and globalization. *World Englishes, 27*(2), 250–267.

Platt, John, & Weber, H. (1979). *English in Singapore and Malaysia.* Kuala Lumpur: Oxford University Press.

Rao, G. Subba (1954). *Indian Words in English: A Study of Indo-British Cultural and Linguistic Relations.* Oxford: Clarendon Press.

Rahman, Tariq (1990) *Pakistani English: The linguistic description of a non-native variety of English.* NIPS Monograph Series III. Islamabad: National Institute of Pakistan Studies.

Sakai, Sanzo (2005) (Guest Ed.). Symposium on world Englishes in the Japanese context: Introduction. *World Englishes, 24*(3), 321–322.

Savignon, Sandra J. (Ed.) (2002). *Interpreting communicative language teaching: Contexts and concerns in teacher education.* New Haven, CT: Yale University Press.

Schneider, Edgar W. (Ed.) (1997). *English around the World: Studies in honor of Manfred Görlach* (2 vols). In the series Varieties of English around the World. Amsterdam: John Benjamins.

Seidlhofer, Barbara (2001). Closing a conceptual gap: The case for a description of English as a lingua franca. *International Journal of Applied Linguistics 11*, 133–158.

Seidlhofer, Barbara (2004). Research perspectives on teaching English as a lingua franca. *Annual Review of Applied Linguistics, 24*, 200–239.

Seidlhofer, Barbara (2009). World Englishes and English as a lingua franca: Two frameworks or one? In T. Hoffmann and L. Siebers (Eds.), *World Englishes—Problems, properties and prospects.* (pp. 376–379). Amsterdam: John Benjamins.

Shim, Rosa J. (1994). Englishized Korean: Structure, status and attitudes. *World Englishes, 13*(2), 233–244.

Shim, Rosa J. (2002). The internet as a resource of materials for teaching English as a world language. Paper presented at the American Association of Applied Linguistics Annual Conference, April 6, Salt Lake City, Utah.

Simo-Bobda, A. (1994). *Aspects of Cameroon English phonology*. Berne: Peter Lang.

Smith, Larry E. (1992). Spread of English and issues of intelligibility. In B. Kachru (Ed.) *The other tongue: English across cultures* (pp. 75–90). Urbana, IL: University of Illinois Press.

Smith, Larry E. (Ed.) (1987). *Discourse across cultures: Strategies in world Englishes*. London: Prentice Hall International.

Smith, Larry E., & Christopher, Elizabeth M. (2001). Why can't they understand me when I speak English so clearly? In E. Thumboo (Ed.), *The three circles of English* (pp. 91–100). Singapore: UniPress, The Center for the Arts, National University of Singapore.

Smith, Larry E., & Rafiqzad, Khalilulla (1979). English for cross-cultural communication: The question of intelligibility. *TESOL Quarterly*, 13, 371–380.

Smith, Larry E., & Nelson, Cecil E. (1985) International intelligibility of English: Directions and resources. *World Englishes*, 4(3), 333–342.

Smith, Larry E., & Forman, Michael L. (Eds.) (1997). *World Englishes 2000*. Honolulu, HI: University of Hawai'i Press.

Sridhar, Kamal K. (1989). *English in Indian bilingualism*. New Delhi: Manohar Publications.

Sridhar, Kamal K. (1991). Speech acts in an indigenized variety: Sociocultural values and language variation. In J. Cheshire (Ed.), *English around the world: Sociolinguistic perspectives* (pp. 308–318). Cambridge: Cambridge University Press.

Sridhar, Kamal K., & Sridhar, S. N. (1986). Bridging the paradigm gap: Second language acquisition theory and indigenized varieties of English. *World Englishes*, 5(1), 3–14. [Also in B. Kachru (Ed.) (1992). *The other tongue: English across cultures*. Urbana, IL: University of Illinois Press, pp. 91–107.]

Sridhar, S. N. (1994). A reality check for SLA theories. *TESOL Quarterly*, 28(4). 800–805.

Sridhar, S. N., & Sridhar, Kamal K. (1992). The empire speaks back: English as a non-native language. In P. Nelde (Ed.), *Plurilingua XIII: It's easy to mingle when you are bilingual* (pp. 187–198). Bonn: Dummler.

Taiwo, O. (1976). *Culture and the Nigerian novel*. New York: St Martin's Press.

Tawake, Sandra K. (1990). Culture and identity in literature of the South Pacific. *World Englishes*, 9(2), 205–213.

Tawake, Sandra K. (1993). Reading *The Bone People* cross-culturally. *World Englishes*, 12(3), 325–333.

Tay, Mary Wan Joo (1993). *The English language in Singapore: Issues and development*. Singapore: National University of Singapore, UniPress, Center for the Arts.

Thompson, Eric C. (2002). Rocking East and West: the USA in Malaysian music (an American remix). In Timothy J. Craig and Richard King (Eds.), *Global goes local: Popular culture in Asia* (pp. 58–79). Vancouver: University of British Columbia Press.

Thumboo, Edwin (1985). Twin perspectives and multi-ecosystems: Tradition for a commonwealth writer. *World Englishes*, 4(2), 213–221.

Thumboo, Edwin (1986). Language as power: Gabriel Okara's *The Voice* as a paradigm. *World Englishes*, 5(2–3), 249–264.

Thumboo, Edwin (1988). The literary dimension of the spread of English: Creativity in a second tongue. In Peter Lowenberg (Ed.), *Language spread and language policy: Issues, implications and case studies* (pp. 385–415). Washington DC: Georgetown University Press.

Thumboo, Edwin (1991). The pragmatics of meaning: Language as identity in new English literature. In Lawrence F. Bouton & Yamuna Kachru (Eds.), *Pragmatics and language learning* (Monograph Series, Vol. 2) (pp. 203–222). Urbana, IL: Division of English as an International Language, University of Illinois.

Thumboo, Edwin (1992). The literary dimension of the spread of English. In B. Kachru (Ed.), *The other tongue: English across cultures* (pp. 255–282). Urbana, IL: University of Illinois Press.

Thumboo, Edwin (Ed.) (2001). *The three circles of English*. Singapore: UniPress, The Center for the Arts, National University of Singapore.

Thumboo, Edwin, & Sayson, Rex I. (Eds.) (2007). *Writing Asia: The literatures in Englishes. Vol. 1: From the inside: Asia-Pacific literatures in Englishes*. Singapore: Ethos Books.

Valentine, Tamara M. (1988). Developing discourse types in non-native English: Strategies of gender in Hindi and Indian English. *World Englishes*, 7(2), 143–158.

Valentine, Tamara M. (1991). Getting the message across: Discourse markers in Indian English. *World Englishes*, 10(3), 325–334.

Valentine, Tamara M. (1995). Agreeing and disagreeing in Indian English discourse: Implications for language teaching. In Makhan L. Tickoo (Ed.), *Language and culture in multilingual societies: Viewpoints and visions* (pp. 227–250). Anthology Series 36. Singapore: SEAMEO Regional Language Center.

Valentine, Tamara M. (2001). Women and the other tongue. In E. Thumboo (Ed.), *The three circles of English* (pp. 143–158). Singapore: UniPress, The Center for the Arts, National University of Singapore.

Valentine, Tamara M. (2006). World Englishes and gender identities. In B. Kachru, Y. Kachru & C. Nelson (Eds.), (pp. 567–580).

Van Horn, Stanley Y. (2006). World Englishes and global commerce. In B. Kachru, Y. Kachru & C. Nelson (Eds.), (pp. 620–641).

Vavrus, Frances K. (1991). When paradigms clash: The role of institutionalized varieties in language teacher education. *World Englishes, 10*(2), 181–195.

Widdowson, Henry G. (1994). The ownership of English. *TESOL Quarterly, 26*(2), 337–389.

Yano, Yasukata (2009a). English as an international lingua franca: From societal to global. *World Englishes, 28*(2), 246–255.

Yano, Yasukata (2009b). The future of English: Beyond the Kachruvian Three Circle model. In Kumiko Murata and Jennifer Jenkins (Eds.), *Global Englishes in Asian contexts: Current and future debates* (pp. 208–226). Basingstoke: Palgrave Macmillan.

II
Second Language Research Methods

11
Approaches and Methods in Recent Qualitative Research

Linda Harklau

This chapter profiles trends in qualitative research on second language teaching and learning since 2003. It includes research studies in peer reviewed journals indexed in Linguistics and Language Behavior Abstracts that were characterized primarily or solely as qualitative. The review focuses on studies using naturalistic language data sources, often deemed a fundamental property of qualitative research (see, e.g., Belcher & Hirvela, 2005). It thus excludes studies characterized as experimental or quasi-experimental that featured control and treatment conditions, and that elicited data through questionnaires, language tests, or other instruments. Also excluded are studies that featured both quantitative and qualitative analysis of naturalistic linguistic data from corpuses since contextualization is often deemed an inherent characteristic of qualitative research (see, e.g., Belcher & Hirvela, 2005). It must be acknowledged, however, that such distinctions are not always clearcut.

Profile of Recent Research

With over 230 research reports in major publications over the past six years, qualitative work in second language acquisition (SLA) is clearly robust. It routinely appears in major international journals including *Applied Linguistics, Language Learning, Modern Language Journal*, and *TESOL Quarterly*. English remains by far the most studied target language in this work with over 110 studies identified. Other target languages included Spanish (10 studies identified), French (seven studies), German (seven studies), Japanese (five studies), Italian (three studies), Hebrew (two studies), Irish (two studies), Swedish (two studies), Bengali (one study), Chinese (one study), Danish (one study), Korean (one study), and Portuguese (one study). Studies in contexts involving multiple native and target languages (see, e.g., Masso & Tender, 2008; McDonough, 2006; Orsini-Jones, 2004; Stracke, 2007; Watzke, 2007) have been rare.

Second language learners at the college level have been the most studied group by far, with over 70 studies identified. Teachers of language learners and teacher education programs have also been a frequent focus of study in recent work (28 studies identified). Secondary schools, once relatively underexplored, were the subject of 21 studies in recent years. Less researched contexts include elementary or primary schools (14 studies); adult education (13 studies); preschools (three studies); and language programs and institutions as a whole (six studies). While the vast majority of qualitative research in the field has focused on school settings, other foci have included language contact and policy (four studies); family and home language learning and use (three studies); medical clinics (one study); personal conversations (two studies); academic and professional publishing (three studies); study abroad programs (one study); community language use (one study) and resources (one study); and chat rooms (one study). Recent qualitative research has rarely bridged multiple domains such as home and school or workplace and community (but see, e.g., Bongartz & Schneider, 2003; Gordon, 2004; Hawkins, 2005; Stroud & Wee, 2007).

The US has been overwhelmingly the most studied national context for this work, with over 70 studies identified. Other predominantly Anglophone nations are also well represented including Canada (13 studies); the UK (14 studies); Australia (seven studies); and New Zealand (four studies). Other qualitative studies have taken place in European countries including Germany (five studies), Spain (three studies), Sweden (three studies), France (two studies), Ireland (two studies), Turkey (two studies), Austria (one study), Denmark (one study), Estonia (one study), Italy (one study), and Switzerland (one study). A number of studies have also taken place in Pacific Rim nations including China (eight studies), Japan (seven studies), Singapore (three studies), Taiwan (two studies), Indonesia (one study), Korea (one study), Malaysia (one study), Thailand (one study), and Vietnam (one study). Research from other Asian countries, the Middle East, Africa, and South America remain rare, with only 10 studies identified. Research spanning multiple national contexts has likewise been rare (10 studies identified).

The overwhelming Anglophone and US-centric nature of recent qualitative research on SLA may be attributed in part to "nondiscursive" resources available to periphery scholars (Canagarajah, 1996), their relative unfamiliarity with qualitative research (see, e.g., Duong & Nguyen, 2006), and the overwhelming predominance of English in international academic publishing (Montgomery, 2004) combined with the heavy linguistic demands associated with qualitative analysis and writing (Belcher & Hirvela, 2005).

Methods of Data Collection

The most frequently used methods or techniques for gathering data in qualitative studies of SLA have included interviews, observations, audio- and videorecordings of interaction, and collection of print artifacts.

Interviews

Interviews have been by far the most commonly employed research method. Most research has referred to interviews generically without further specification (38 studies) or described interviews as "semi-structured" (39 studies). Other terms that have been used to describe interviewing techniques have included "structured," "unstructured," "open-ended," "in-depth," "long," "formal," "informal," "open format schedule," "text-based," "discourse-based," "literacy history," "reflective," and "intraview." Interviews have sometimes been repeated over time. Interviews have almost always been conducted face to face with researchers and participants, with surprisingly few studies making use of email interviews (five studies), phone interviews (four studies), or email follow-ups to face to face interviews (two studies). Focus groups and group interviews have also been used relatively rarely (17 studies). It has become standard in contemporary peer reviewed research to audiorecord and transcribe interviews. Transcription conventions, however, are rarely made explicit (but see Farrell & Kun, 2007; Kobayashi, 2003; Stroud & Wee, 2007). It can be surmised that most have followed what Stroud and Wee (2007, citing Johnstone, 2000), call "play script" style, omitting some linguistic detail such as overlaps and hesitation phenomena. Nevertheless, more explicitness might be useful since, as Ochs (1979) famously observed, transcription is theory. Frequently cited authorities on qualitative interview methods have included Holstein and Gubrium (1995), Mishler (1986), Rubin and Rubin (2005), and Seidman (2006).

Observations

A great number of recent qualitative studies on SLA have also used observations and fieldnotes. These have most often taken place in classrooms and other school locales and consisted of sustained engagement characterized as participant observation (31 studies). In 18 of these studies the participant-observer was also the instructor. Very few studies have explicitly been identified as longitudinal (see, e.g., Curry & Lillis, 2004; James, 2006; Lamb, 2007), even though "prolonged engagement" (Iddings, 2005) has long been considered one means of enhancing participant observation and qualitative research validity more generally. In other studies, observations have taken the form of briefer and more concentrated "site visits" (see, e.g., Gebhard, 2004; Pawan & Thomalla, 2005) or selective non-participatory observations of classes and other school environs (17 studies). Very few studies have used preset observation protocols or rubrics (but see Hawkins, 2005; Hickey, 2007). Participant observation conducted outside of school contexts has been rare. It has been used in settings including workplaces (Curry & Lillis, 2004; Gordon, 2004; Lear, 2005), homes (Bongartz & Schneider, 2003; Gordon, 2004; Hawkins, 2005), and communities (Gordon, 2004; Kramsch & Whiteside, 2008).

Recordings

Audiorecordings (24 studies) and videorecordings (32 studies) of classroom events have also been widely used in recent qualitative research on SLA. These have often focused on specific portions or sequences of classroom proceedings or on selected participants. One study of an online course used a video archive of web-based classroom interaction (Jauregi & Bañados, 2008). Only a handful of studies have featured videorecordings of interactions in contexts outside the classroom. These have included diverse settings including personal conversations, conversation partner sessions, foreign language "conversation tables," writing conferences, and police interrogations (see, e.g., Kang, 2005; Kramsch & Whiteside, 2008; Mori & Hayashi, 2006; Pavlenko, 2008; Young & Miller, 2004). Audiorecordings have likewise rarely been collected outside classrooms. Examples include peer tutoring sessions, audio journals by students, and conversations in learners' homes and communities (see, e.g., Bell, 2005; Bongartz & Schneider, 2003; Caldas, 2007; Kobayashi, 2003; Waring, 2005).

Written Artifacts

A number of qualitative researchers have also collected and analyzed textual data. Most commonly this has consisted of learner-produced texts documenting their subjective experience and perspectives such as diaries, journals, logs, blogs, essays, and opinion/reaction pieces, either on paper or online (21 studies). Other written artifacts have taken diverse forms including language learning autobiographies; teacher diaries and journals; student evaluations of classroom activities; email correspondence between learners and researchers and instructors; and records of learner interactions in public and course-based chat sessions and discussion groups (see, e.g., Belz & Müller-Hartmann, 2003; Chu, 2008; Coffey & Street, 2008; Fang & Warshauer, 2004; Fuchs, 2006; Li, 2007; McDonough, 2006; McDonough & Chaikitmongkol, 2007; Orsini-Jones, 2004; Pavlenko, 2008; Shin & Crookes, 2005; Tsui, 2007). Many studies included samples of student writing and other coursework both in classrooms (17 studies) and online (see, e.g., Fuchs, 2006; Jauregi & Bañados, 2008; Orsini-Jones, 2004). Other diverse textual data have included environmental print such as posters on walls; textbooks; samples of academic published writing; drafts of and correspondence about professional texts; and model and source texts (Curry & Lillis, 2004; Flowerdew & Li, 2007; Gibbons, 2003; Li, 2007; Schleppegrell, Achugar, & Oteíza, 2004). Finally, 22 studies collected online or print texts documenting the broad context of SLA including language policies, second language learner demographic profiles, and learning standards at the local or national level.

Supplementary Methods

Researchers have often supplemented primary methods of qualitative data collection with supplementary methods used to augment or bolster analysis. Surveys and questionnaires of learners, for example, were featured as supplementary method in 21 studies, while nine studies featured surveys of teachers and other study participants besides learners. Another supplementary method has included think aloud protocols or participants' elicited comments on their own or others' texts, recorded conversations, videorecorded classroom behavior, and other interactions (e.g., Bell, 2005; Gu, 2003; T.-h. He & Wang, 2009; Jenkins & Parra, 2003; Lazaraton & Ishihara, 2005). These were sometimes specifically referred to as stimulated recall protocols (e.g., de Courcy, 2003; Kang, 2005; Mullock, 2006). Other supplementary methods have taken diverse forms. Basturkmen, Loewen, and Ellis (2004), for example, elicited teacher comments on how they would react in particular classroom scenarios. Hawkins (2005) used sociograms in an elementary classroom. Payne (2006) used an index card sorting task to gauge participants' attitudes towards languages taught in one program. Several studies collected learner standardized test scores, pre- and post-test scores, or learner school transcripts (Ketchum, 2006; Kinginger, 2008; Pavlenko, 2008). A growing number of researchers in recent years have employed qualitative data archiving and analysis software (see Séror, 2005), including NUD*IST and Nvivo, HyperResearch, Atlas.ti, "textanalyzer," Filemaker Pro, and the CHILDES online database and analysis system (e.g., Chu, 2008; Edwards, Ran, & Li, 2007; Hickey, 2007; James, 2006; Kol & Schcolnik, 2008; Lear, 2005; Masso & Tender, 2008; Orsini-Jones, 2004; Simon-Maeda, 2004; Stracke, 2007; Taylor, 2006).

Methodological Frameworks

In the practice of qualitative research, discrete methods or techniques of qualitative data collection are expected to embedded in a broader methodology—a conceptual framework for investigation that entails underlying notions of knowledge (or *ontology*) and how one obtains knowledge (or *epistemology*). Recent qualitative research in SLA has tapped a broad array of such methodological frameworks. For the most part, these have fallen roughly into two groups. One has focused on the broad sociocultural and ecological contexts of language learning and teaching as captured in methods such as participant observation and interviews. The other group has emphasized the construction of social realities through discourse, relying primarily on audio- or videorecordings and texts.

Analyses of Sociocultural Context

Methodologies: Some SLA researchers have described their research simply as "*qualitative*" in the generic sense of "not quantitative" or appear to equate "qualitative" with preliminary or exploratory research (e.g., Mullock, 2006; Shin & Crookes, 2005). Many others have associated their methodology with a canon of qualitative methods texts including Merriam (1998), Miles and Huberman (1994), Denzin and Lincoln (2000), Lincoln and Guba (1985), Bogdan and Biklen (2007), Patton (2002), Creswell (2007), Marshall and Rossman (2006), and Spradley (1979, 1980). While such texts may be presented as neutral or generic presentation of qualitative methods, nonetheless it is important to note that they inevitably carry intellectual histories and particular philosophical and methodological leanings (Roberts, 2006). For example, Lincoln and Guba (1985) have identified an implicit "subtle realist" stance in many methods texts. Likewise, Miles and Huberman (1994) have been associated a with "transcendental realist" stance. Second language researchers following texts such as these have thus implicitly—and sometimes perhaps even unknowingly—adopt particular ontological and epistemological stances in their work. Also of concern is the frequent invocation of 20- or 30-year-old methods texts that seldom reflect seismic shifts in qualitative inquiry since the "crisis of representation" of the mid-1980s (see, e.g., Clifford, 1986; Marcus & Fischer, 1986).

Like the term *qualitative, case study* has often been used generically by second language researchers with little further explanation (27 studies). Widely cited authorities for this methodology have included Merriam (1998), Stake (1995, 2000), Yin (2009), Duff (2008), Patton (2002), and Creswell (2007). Other recent research has identified itself more specifically with terms such as "multiple case study," "embedded case study model," "sociopolitically-oriented qualitative case study," "self-reflective case study," "ethnographic case study," "exploratory case study," "interpretive case study," and "case history" (Belz & Müller-Hartmann, 2003; Casanave, 2003; Fang & Warshauer, 2004; Kinginger, 2008; Menard-Warwick, 2009; Morita, 2004; Payne, 2006; Wiltse, 2006). A few recent studies have followed a long tradition of longitudinal case studies (see Duff, 2008; Hakuta, 1986; Harklau, 2008) by documenting their own or their children's second language learning (Bongartz & Schneider, 2003; Caldas, 2007; Churchill, 2007). In an approach related to case study, 12 studies used "focal" participants within a broader study.

Grounded theory (Corbin & Strauss, 2008; Glaser & Strauss, 1967) has also been a popular methodological framework in recent qualitative research. It was cited explicitly in 10 studies, and identified implicitly in seven others by the use of terminology such as "open coding" or "constant comparative method" that are associated with grounded theory. Second language researchers invoking grounded theory have seldom explicitly indicated whether they their work is aligned philosophically with the social realist or social constructivist stances typically associated with this methodology (see Charmaz, 2006; Motha, 2006).

Ethnographic or *participant observation* methodology (17 studies) is another paradigm that has also been frequently invoked in recent qualitative studies in SLA. Typically studies have used the terms generically and have not followed the anthropological tradition of sustained engagement at a site (Roberts, 2006). Instead, they have borrowed methods—particularly observation and interviews—in a more circumscribed approach. Methodological touchstones most frequently invoked for this approach include Watson-Gegeo (1988), Holliday (2007), Miles and Huberman (1994), Spradley (1980), Merriam (2009), Wolcott (1999, 2005), Le Compte, Preissle, and Tesch (1993), Ramanathan and Atkinson (1999), Green and Bloome (1997), Agar (1996), and Cohen, Manion, and Morrison (2007).

A smaller number of researchers have identified a particular school or style of ethnography. For example, seven studies used the term "thick description," although it was sometimes not clear whether they aligned their approach philosophically with Geertz (1983, following Gilbert Ryles) and the interpretivist stance associated with the term. Likewise, it was not always apparent whether researchers citing Spradley (1980) subscribe to the methodological and theoretical premises of ethnoscience and cognitive anthropology with which he was affiliated (see, e.g., de Courcy, 2003; Wiltse, 2006). Other specific schools of ethnographic inquiry identified by SLA researchers include critical and critical feminist ethnography (see Carspecken & Walford, 2001; May, 1997; Thomas, 1993), and Holland's (1998) work on cultural models and construct of "figured worlds" (Coffey & Street, 2008; Menard-Warwick, 2008; Motha, 2006; Talmy, 2008).

Several researchers identified their work methodologically with forms of *practitioner inquiry.* These were variously called "teacher research," "action research," "practitioner research," or "practitioner study" (see, e.g., Allwright, 2005; Hruska, 2004; McDonough, 2006; Orsini-Jones, 2004; Taylor,

2006). Frequently cited methodological precedents for practitioner inquiry included Cochran-Smith and Lytle (2009), Carr and Kemmis (1986), Crookes (1993), Bailey and Nunan (1996), and Burns (1999). A handful of studies explored the dynamics of researcher–teacher collaborations (e.g., Hawkins & Legler, 2004; Stewart, 2006).

Less commonly invoked methodologies in recent research have included *phenomenology* (Andrew & Kearney, 2007; Churchill, 2007; de Courcy, 2003; Moustakas, 1994; Payne, 2006; Shedivy, 2004; Stracke, 2007; Van Manen, 1990; Willis, 1991), *hermeneutics* (Gadamer, 1982; Orland-Barak & Yinon, 2005), and *content analysis* (Bogdan & Biklen, 2007; Chu, 2008; Gebhard, 2004; Miles & Huberman, 1994).

While relatively few qualitative researchers in recent SLA scholarship have specifically identified an *epistemological or ontological stance* in their work, those who do vary widely in their stances, from "social realism" to "constructivism" and "social constructivism" to "social constructionism" to "interpretivism" to "poststructuralism" (see Andrew & Kearney, 2007; Belz & Müller-Hartmann, 2003; Burley & Pomphrey, 2003; de Courcy, 2003; Dooly, 2007; Fuchs, 2006; Golombek & Jordan, 2005; Gordon, 2004; Hruska, 2004; Jauregi & Bañados, 2008; Morita, 2006).

Characteristics of good research: A number of researchers using methodologies focusing broadly on sociocultural context have associated good qualitative research with the development of an "in-depth" and "complex" understanding of a phenomenon and a focus on second language learning as occurring in and through sociocultural context (e.g., Abrams, 2008; Fuchs, 2006; Hawkins, 2005; James, 2006; Kobayashi, 2003; Lamb, 2007; Lear, 2005; Morita, 2004). Some have pointed to the recursive and inductive nature of qualitative analysis as methodological strengths (see, e.g., James, 2006; Li, 2007; McDonough, 2006). Seventeen studies cited "member checks" (Lincoln & Guba, 1985) or participant verification of research findings as a means of enhancing research validity and credibility. Several indicators of research quality frequently cited in recent work are implicitly associated with post-positivist and realist stances. For example, several studies have asserted that themes "emerged" from the data (e.g., Edwards et al., 2007; McDonough, 2006). Others have claimed the goal of portraying "emic" or participants' own insider perspectives (see e.g., Churchill, 2007; Davis, 2005; Headland, Pike, & Harris, 1990; Kobayashi, 2003; Morita, 2004). Both the notion of emergent themes and emic perspectives are associated with realist orientations to research since they are difficult to reconcile with a postmodern stance on researcher subjectivities (Markee & Kasper, 2004). Likewise, "triangulation" (Denzin, 1978), the comparing of multiple sources in data analysis, is another technique frequently identified with enhancing research quality, and one that Holliday (2004) places in "a positivist tradition."

For the most part, recent scholarship indicates that the field seems to have accepted that different criteria apply to reliability and generalizability in qualitative research (Lazaraton, 2003). While a handful of researchers note measures taken to ensure reliability—primarily through coding with multiple raters (see, e.g., Andrew & Kearney, 2007; Basturkmen et al., 2004; Farrell & Kun, 2007; Gu, 2003; James, 2006; Mullock, 2006)—few address the issue explicitly. A number of evaluative criteria not typically addressed in quantitative approaches have been offered by qualitative researchers, including "trustworthiness," "verisimilitude," intersubjective validation, analytic generalization to a broader theory, transferability to other settings, aesthetic merit, and sociopolitical impact (see, e.g., Belcher & Hirvela, 2005; Casanave, 2003; Churchill, 2007; Iddings, 2005; Lazaraton, 2003; E. Lee & Maeda-Simon, 2006; Payne, 2006; Roberts, 2006; Simon-Maeda, 2004; Thorne, 2005; Watson-Gegeo, 2004; Yin, 2009).

Just as notable as the characteristics of good research that are addressed in recent work are the ones that are not. Few studies, for example, explicitly discuss the selection of sites and participants. Among those that do, approaches have been characterized variously as "purposive" or "purposeful" sampling, "maximum variation sampling," "criterion sampling," "opportunistic," "strategic," "convenience sampling," and "snowball" or "chaining" sampling (e.g., Davis, 2005; Flowerdew & Li, 2007; Iddings, 2005; Jia, Eslami, & Burlbaw, 2006; Masso & Tender, 2008; Pawan & Thomalla, 2005; Shedivy, 2004). Considering the implicit realist orientation of many recent qualitative studies, surprisingly few researchers explicitly note searches for discrepant or disconfirming data (but see, e.g., Kang, 2005; McDonough & Chaikitmongkol, 2007).

There has also been surprisingly little discussion of researcher conduct, particularly the effects of the presence of researchers and recording equipment on the nature of the data collected (but see, e.g., Kol & Schcolnik, 2008). Also absent in most studies is discussion of researcher role on the continuum from observer to full participant (but see, e.g., Kobayashi, 2003; Morita, 2004). The particular ethical demands of qualitative research have likewise rarely been addressed (but see Allwright, 2005; Kubanyiova, 2008; Ortega, 2005; Thorne, 2005). Finally, only a handful of studies have explicitly addressed how the researcher's background and perspective potentially influences research questions, methods, and findings (see, e.g., Davis, 2005; Iddings, 2005; E. Lee & Maeda-Simon, 2006; Morita, 2004; Motha, 2006), even though post-structuralist challenges to researchers' authority have rendered such reflexivity routine in the social sciences (Clifford, 1986; Rosaldo, 1989).

Analyses of Discourse and Interaction

Research traditions: By far the most frequently invoked methodology for the analysis of discourse and interaction in recent SLA studies has been *conversation analysis* and related traditions of *ethnomethodology, interactional sociolinguistics,* and *microethnography* or *microanalysis* (see Atkinson & Heritage, 1984; Erickson, 2004; Garfinkel, 1967; Garfinkel & Rawls, 2002; Gumperz, 1982a, 1982b; ten Have, 2007; Heller, 2001; Hruska, 2004; Jenkins & Parra, 2003; Markee, 2000; Maynard & Clayman, 2003; Menard-Warwick, 2008; Olson, 2007; Psathas, 1995; Richards & Seedhouse, 2007). Another methodology usually associated with a *language socialization* framework combines close analysis of discourse with broader ethnographic data (see Bayley & Schecter, 2003; Bongartz & Schneider, 2003; Duff & Hornberger, 2008; A. W. He, 2004; Schieffelin & Ochs, 1986; Talmy, 2008; Watson-Gegeo, 2004; Zuengler & Cole, 2005).

Another discourse analytic tradition frequently claimed by SLA researchers is *narrative analysis* and *life history* research. This methodology is particularly associated with learner autobiographical narratives (see Brockmeier & Carbaugh, 2001; Clandinin, 2007; Langellier & Peterson, 2004; Lyons & LaBoskey, 2002; Pavlenko, 2007; Polkinghorne, 1988). Work in this tradition has analyzed both the structure and content of participants' stories (see Burley & Pomphrey, 2003; Coffey & Street, 2008; Golombek & Jordan, 2005; Orland-Barak & Yinon, 2005; Simon-Maeda, 2004; Spradley, 1980; Tsui, 2007). Other researchers have identified a methodology associated with *systemic functional linguistics* or a "*genrebased*" methodology for analyzing the syntactic and lexical structure of texts (see Eggins, 2000; Flowerdew & Li, 2007; Halliday & Matthiessen, 2004; Haneda, 2004; Schleppegrell et al., 2004; Swales, 2004). Still others identify their methodolody as *critical discourse analysis* (see Dijk, 2008; Fairclough, 1995; Gebhard, 2004; Heller, 2001; Hruska, 2004; Menard-Warwick, 2008; Wodak & Meyer, 2001)

Characteristics of good research: Researchers working with conversation analysis and other discourse analytic methodologies typically cast the collection and analysis of naturalistic interactional data as paramount to the quality of research. In fact, some adherents argue that its absence in other forms of inquiry constitutes a major methodological weakness and threat to validity (see, e,g, Y.-A. Lee, 2006). Considerable recent discussion among scholars has focused on whether conversation analysis (CA) in SLA ("CA for SLA" as it is also known) should rely on the epistemological and methodological premises of its "pure" sociological variants and rely exclusively on the local context of interaction, or draw on broader sociocultural and ecological contexts as a supplementary interpretive frame (see A. W. He, 2004; Kramsch & Whiteside, 2008; Markee & Kasper, 2004; Seedhouse, 2007).

Some advocates of conversation analysis note similarities with other qualitative research methodologies. These include an interpretive and empirical orientation, an inductive and recursive analytic process, and emic characterization of socially situated interaction and learning (A. W. He, 2004; Markee & Kasper, 2004; Mori, 2004; Rampton, Roberts, Leung, & Harris, 2002). However, others distinguish between the notion of "emic" analysis in ethnography and other broad qualitative traditions—where it refers to discerning participants' subjective understandings of experience and the broader sociocultural structures and forces shaping those understandings—and CA's "radically emic" approach, where the focus is solely on observable talk and behavior in order to discern normative, intersubjective understandings of interaction.

Finally, it must be noted that methodologies do not always map neatly onto existing categories or names. For example, some recent qualitative studies have combined diverse research methodologies such as case study and practitioner inquiry (e.g. Abrams, 2008), ethnography and close analysis of discourse (e.g. Cekaite & Aronsson, 2005), or narrative analysis and ethnography (e.g. Coffey & Street, 2008). On the one hand, the resulting combinations can be felicitous and generative. On the other hand, they can also result in philosophical and methodological incompatibilities that are left unrecognized or unaddressed by researchers. Theories of SLA often do not map neatly onto particular research methodologies either. This may be most evident in the case of *sociocultural and cultural historical activity theory* and related constructs of community of practice and legitimate peripheral participation, where researchers have used widely diverse methodologies spanning discourse and sociocultural contextually-based traditions (see, e.g., Andrew & Kearney, 2007; Bongartz & Schneider, 2003; Dooly, 2007; A. G. Gutiérrez, 2008; X. Gutiérrez, 2008; Haneda, 2004; Kinginger, 2008; Lantolf, 2000; Lantolf & Thorne, 2006; Lave & Wenger, 1991; Olson, 2007; Wenger, 1998; Wertsch, Río, & Alvarez, 1995).

Future Directions

This and other recent reviews (e.g. Benson, Chik, Gao, Huang, & Wang, 2009) make it clear that qualitative approaches are well-represented in recent SLA research. However, this review also indicates that their use remains heavily concentrated in studies of English acquisition in university settings in Western nations. Qualitative research has yet to be widely applied in the study of other target languages and contexts.

SLA research includes an increasingly sophisticated and generative repertoire of qualitative methodologies, leading some to optimistically proclaim a new era in SLA that is more accepting of qualitative approaches and the diverse visions of knowledge and research underlying them (e.g. Holliday, 2004; Thorne, 2005; Watson-Gegeo, 2004). Yet there are cross-currents with considerable political and economic force behind them. These include government initiatives demanding greater research "rigor," typically interpreted as quantitative studies. Becker (2009), for example, notes that the US National Science Foundation's Sociology Section has routinely made statements and policies over the past decade disfavoring qualitative studies and promoting hypothesis-driven quantitative projects. Similarly in the UK, Roberts (2006) and Hammersley (2001) note the predominance of large-scale quantitative and experimental studies in government-funded research and policy. These currents may very well continue to undercut the status and influence—if not the quantity—of qualitative research on SLA.

This review has also shown countervailing centripetal and centrifugal trends in current qualitative research in the field. Qualitative methodologies continue to diversify, proliferate, and change. Not only are there major differences in approach and outlook between broad socioculturally-focused approaches such as ethnography and discourse-focused analyses such as conversation analysis, but also as much or more diversity within them. There is also considerable diversity in perspectives regarding the purposes and ends of qualitative research. For example, the creation and reception of TESOL Quarterly's Research Guidelines (Chapelle, Duff, Atkinson, Brown, Canagarajah, & Davis, 2003) illustrates the diversity of the field as well as fears that defining qualitative research approaches too finely might lead to prescriptive notions and stifle innovation (Shohamy, 2004). Researchers also vary in their opinions of whether qualitative research can or should be in dialog with quantitatively-oriented work. For example, scholars disagree over the extent to which conversation analysis can or should reflect an interpretivist stance privileging emic perspectives of participants versus a more positivistically and etically oriented "basic science" stance (see, e.g., Hall, 2007; A. W. He, 2004; Seedhouse, 2007). This debate is mirrored in the field more broadly, where some argue that differences between qualitative and quantitative research have been exaggerated on both sides (e.g. Belcher & Hirvela, 2005), while others see incommensurate worldviews that cannot, and perhaps should not, be bridged (Roberts, 2006; Zuengler & Miller, 2006). Instead these scholars advocate for tolerance for diversity of research perspectives.

Nevertheless, while methodologists and researchers continue to push at the boundaries of innovation and diversity in qualitative SLA research, at the same time there are centripetal forces promoting homogeneous, but largely implicit, understandings of qualitative research in our field. The default in current work tends toward constructionist or even objectivist stances regarding researcher subjectivities and research reporting. These stances are supported by the often unexamined and unelaborated endorsement of practices such as triangulation for analytic rigor. They are also supported by a canon of qualitative methods texts that have a homogenizing influence and may not elaborate fully on the range of contemporary qualitative research traditions available or the philosophical premises underlying them. Granted, as Scollon (2003) noted, it is not uncommon for research practitioners in the social sciences to "be rather vague" about the ontological and epistemological premises of their work and its intellectual history. Nevertheless, when examined as a whole, recent qualitative research in SLA suggests a need for the field to become more attuned to the multiplicity of qualitative research traditions and their underlying premises.

References

Abrams, Z. (2008). Alternative second language curricula for learners with disabilities: Two case studies. *Modern Language Journal, 92*, 414–430.

Agar, M. (1996). *The professional stranger: An informal introduction to ethnography* (2nd ed.). San Diego: Academic Press.

Allwright, D. (2005). Developing principles for practitioner research: The case of exploratory practice. *Modern Language Journal, 89*, 353–366.

Andrew, M., & Kearney, C. (2007). Practicing in and learning from community placements. *New Zealand Studies in Applied Linguistics, 13*(2), 31–45.

Atkinson, J. M., & Heritage, J. (1984). *Structures of social action: Studies in conversation analysis.* New York: Cambridge University Press.

Bailey, K. M., & Nunan, D. (1996). *Voices from the language classroom: Qualitative research in second language education.* New York: Cambridge University Press.

Basturkmen, H., Loewen, S., & Ellis, R. (2004). Teachers' stated beliefs about incidental focus on form and their classroom practices. *Applied Linguistics, 25*, 243–272.

Bayley, R., & Schecter, S. R. (2003). *Language socialization in bilingual and multilingual societies.* Buffalo: Multilingual Matters.

Becker, H. S. (2009). How to find out how to do qualitative research. Retrieved May 2, 2009, from http://home.earthlink.net/~hsbecker/articles/NSF.html.

Belcher, D., & Hirvela, A. (2005). Writing the qualitative dissertation: What motivates and sustains commitment to a fuzzy genre? *Journal of English for Academic Purposes, 4*, 187–205.

Bell, N. D. (2005). Exploring L2 language play as an aid to SLL: A case study of humour in NS-NNS interaction. *Applied Linguistics, 26*, 192–218.

Belz, J. A., & Müller-Hartmann, A. (2003). Teachers as intercultural learners: Negotiating German-American telecollaboration along the institutional fault line. *Modern Language Journal, 87*, 71–89.

Benson, P., Chik, A., Gao, X., Huang, J., & Wang, W. (2009). Qualitative research in language teaching and learning journals, 1997–2006. *Modern Language Journal, 93*, 79–90.

Bogdan, R., & Biklen, S. K. (2007). *Qualitative research for education: An introduction to theory and methods* (5th ed.). Boston: Pearson/Allyn and Bacon.

Bongartz, C., & Schneider, M. L. (2003). Linguistic development in social contexts: A study of two brothers learning German. *Modern Language Journal, 87*, 13–37.

Brockmeier, J., & Carbaugh, D. A. (2001). *Narrative and identity: Studies in autobiography, self and culture.* Philadelphia: John Benjamins.

Burley, S., & Pomphrey, C. (2003). Intercomprehension in language teacher education: A dialogue between English and modern languages. *Language Awareness, 12*, 247–255.

Burns, A. (1999). *Collaborative action research for English language teachers.* New York: Cambridge University Press.

Caldas, S. J. (2007). Changing bilingual self-perceptions from early adolescence to early adulthood: Empirical evidence from a mixed-methods case study. *Applied Linguistics, 29*, 290–311.

Canagarajah, A. S. (1996). "Nondiscursive" requirements in academic publishing, material resources of periphery scholars, and the politics of knowledge production. *Written Communication, 13*, 435–472.

Carr, W., & Kemmis, S. (1986). *Becoming critical: Education, knowledge, and action research.* Philadelphia: Falmer Press.

Carspecken, P. F., & Walford, G. (2001). *Critical ethnography and education.* New York: JAI.

Casanave, C. P. (2003). Looking ahead to more sociopolitically-oriented case study research in L2 writing scholarship (But should it be called "post-process"?). *Journal of Second Language Writing, 12*, 85–102.

Cekaite, A., & Aronsson, K. (2005). Language play, a collaborative resource in children's L2 learning. *Applied Linguistics, 26*, 169–191.

Chapelle, C. A., Duff, P. A., Atkinson, D., Brown, J. D., Canagarajah, S., Davis, K., Harklau, L., Jamieson, J., Markee, N., & Ross, S. (2003). Some guidelines for conducting quantiative and qualitative research in TESOL. *TESOL Quarterly, 37*, 157–178.

Charmaz, K. (2006). *Constructing grounded theory: A practical guide through qualitative analysis.* Thousand Oaks, CA: Sage.

Chu, C. Y. (2008). The discourse of an English teacher in a cyber writing course: Roles and autonomy. *Asian EFL Journal [online], 10*(1), Article 5.

Churchill, E. (2007). A dynamic systems account of learning a word: From ecology to form relations. *Applied Linguistics, 29*, 339–358.

Clandinin, D. J. (2007). *Handbook of narrative inquiry: Mapping a methodology.* Thousand Oaks, CA: Sage.

Clifford, J. (1986). Introduction: Partial truths. In J. Clifford & G. E. Marcus (Eds.), *Writing culture: The poetics and politics of ethnography* (pp. 1–26). Berkeley: University of California Press.

Cochran-Smith, M., & Lytle, S. L. (2009). *Inquiry as stance: Practitioner research for the next generation.* New York: Teachers College Press.

Coffey, S., & Street, B. (2008). Narrative and identity in the "Language Learning Project." *Modern Language Journal, 92*, 452–464.

Cohen, L., Manion, L., & Morrison, K. (2007). *Research methods in education* (6th ed.). New York: Routledge.

Corbin, J. M., & Strauss, A. (2008). *Basics of qualitative research: Techniques and procedures for developing grounded theory* (3rd ed.). Thousand Oaks, CA: Sage.

Creswell, J. W. (2007). *Qualitative inquiry & research design: Choosing among five approaches* (2nd ed.). Thousand Oaks, CA: Sage.

Crookes, G. (1993). Action research for second language teachers: Going beyond teacher research. *Applied Linguistics, 14*, 130–144.

Curry, M. J., & Lillis, T. (2004). Multilingual scholars and the imperative to publish in English: Negotiating interests, demands, and rewards. *TESOL Quarterly, 38*, 663–688.

Davis, J. N. (2005). Power, politics, and pecking order: Technological innovation as a site of collaboration, resistance, and accommodation. *Modern Language Journal, 89*, 161–176.

de Courcy, M. (2003). French takes over your mind: Private speech and making sense in immersion programs. *Journal of Educational Thought, 37*, 349–367.

Denzin, N. K. (1978). *Sociological methods: A sourcebook* (2d ed.). New York: McGraw-Hill.

Denzin, N. K., & Lincoln, Y. S. (2000). *Handbook of qualitative research* (2nd ed.). Thousand Oaks, CA: Sage.

Dijk, T. A. v. (2008). *Discourse and power.* New York: Palgrave Macmillan.

Dooly, M. (2007). Constructing differences: A qualitative analysis of teachers' perspectives on linguistic and cultural diversity. *Linguistics and Education, 18*, 142–166.

Duff, P. (2008). *Case study research in applied linguistics.* New York: Lawrence Erlbaum.

Duff, P., & Hornberger, N. H. (Eds.). (2008). *Language socialization. Volume 8. Encyclopedia of Language and Education* (2nd ed.). New York: Springer.

Duong, T. H. O., & Nguyen, T. H. (2006). Memorization and EFL students' strategies at university level in Vietnam. *TESL-EJ*, *10*(2), [online edition].

Edwards, V., Ran, A., & Li, D. (2007). Uneven playing field or falling standards?: Chinese students' competence in English. *Race Ethnicity and Education*, *10*, 387–400.

Eggins, S. (2000). *An introduction to systemic functional linguistics (illustrated)*. London: Pinter.

Erickson, F. (2004). *Talk and social theory: Ecologies of speaking and listening in everyday life*. Malden, MA: Polity Press.

Fairclough, N. (1995). *Critical discourse analysis: The critical study of language*. New York: Longman.

Fang, X., & Warshauer, M. (2004). Technology and curricular reform in China: A case study. *TESOL Quarterly*, *38*, 301–323.

Farrell, T. S. C., & Kun, S. T. K. (2007). Language policy, language teachers' beliefs, and classroom practices. *Applied Linguistics*, *29*, 381–403.

Flowerdew, J., & Li, Y. (2007). Language re-use among Chinese apprentice scientists writing for publication. *Applied Linguistics*, *28*, 440–465.

Fuchs, C. (2006). Exploring German preservice teachers' electronic and professional literacy skills. *ReCALL*, *18*, 174–192.

Gadamer, H. G. (1982). *Truth and method*. New York: Crossroad.

Garfinkel, H. (1967). *Studies in ethnomethodology*. Englewood Cliffs, NJ: Prentice-Hall.

Garfinkel, H., & Rawls, A. W. (2002). *Ethnomethodology's program: Working out Durkheim's aphorism*. Lanham, MD: Rowman & Littlefield.

Gebhard, M. (2004). Fast capitalism, school reform, and second language literacy practices. *Modern Language Journal*, *88*, 245–265.

Geertz, C. (1983). *Local knowledge*. New York: Basic Books.

Gibbons, P. (2003). Mediating language learning: Teacher interactions with ESL students in a content-based classroom. *TESOL Quarterly*, *37*, 247–273.

Glaser, B. G., & Strauss, A. L. (1967). *The discovery of grounded theory: Strategies for qualitative research*. New York: Aldine de Gruyter.

Golombek, P., & Jordan, S. R. (2005). Becoming "black lambs" not "parrots": A poststructuralist orientation to intelligibility and identity. *TESOL Quarterly*, *39*, 513–533.

Gordon, D. (2004). "I'm tired. You clean and cook." Shifting gender identities and second language socialization. *TESOL Quarterly*, *38*, 437–457.

Green, J., & Bloome, D. (1997). Ethnography and ethnographers of and in education: A situated perspective. In J. Flood, S. B. Heath & D. Lapp (Eds.), *Handbook of research on teaching literacy through the communicative and visual arts* (pp. 181–202). New York: Simon & Schuster Macmillan.

Gu, P. Y. (2003). Fine brush and freehand: The vocabulary-learning art of two successful Chinese EFL learners. *TESOL Quarterly*, *37*, 73–104.

Gumperz, J. J. (1982a). *Discourse strategies*. New York: Cambridge University Press.

Gumperz, J. J. (1982b). *Language and social identity*. New York: Cambridge University Press.

Gutiérrez, A. G. (2008). Microgenesis, *method* and *object*: A study of collaborative activity in a Spanish as a foreign language classroom. *Applied Linguistics*, *29*, 120–148.

Gutiérrez, X. (2008). What does metalinguistic activity in learners' interaction during a collaborative L2 writing task look like? *Modern Language Journal*, *92*(4), 519–537.

Hakuta, K. (1986). *Mirror of language: The debate on bilingualism*. New York: Basic Books.

Hall, J. K. (2007). Redressing the roles of correction and repair in research on second and foreign language learning. *Modern Language Journal*, *91*(4), 511–526.

Halliday, M. A. K., & Matthiessen, C. M. I. M. (2004). *An introduction to functional grammar* (3rd ed.). New York: Arnold.

Hammersley, M. (2001). On systematic reviews of research literatures: A "narrative" response to Evans and Benefield. *British Educational Research Journal*, *27*, 543–554.

Haneda, M. (2004). The joint construction of meaning in writing conferences. *Applied Linguistics*, *25*, 178–219.

Harklau, L. (2008). Developing longitudinal case studies of advanced language learners. In L. Ortega & H. Byrnes (Eds.), *Longitudinal study of advanced language capacities* (pp. 23–35). Mahwah, NJ: Erlbaum.

Have, P. ten (2007). *Doing conversation analysis* (2nd ed.). Los Angeles: Sage.

Hawkins, M. R. (2005). Becoming a student: Identity work and academic literacies in early schooling. *TESOL Quarterly*, *39*, 59–82.

Hawkins, M. R., & Legler, L. L. (2004). Reflections on the impact of teacher–researcher collaboration. *TESOL Quarterly*, *38*, 339–343.

He, A. W. (2004). CA for SLA: Arguments from the Chinese language classroom. *Modern Language Journal*, *88*, 568–582.

He, T.-h., & Wang, W.-l. (2009). Invented spelling of EFL young beginning writers and its relation with phonological awareness and grapheme-phoneme principles. *Journal of Second Language Writing*, *18*, 44–56.

Headland, T. N., Pike, K. L., & Harris, M. (1990). *Emics and etics: The insider/outsider debate*. Beverly Hills, CA: Sage.

Heller, M. (2001). Critique and sociolinguistic analysis of discourse. *Critique of Anthropology*, 21(2), 117–141.

Hickey, T. M. (2007). Children's language networks in minority language immersion: What goes in may not come out. *Language and Education*, 21(1), 46–65.

Holland, D. C. (1998). *Identity and agency in cultural worlds.* Cambridge, MA: Harvard University Press.

Holliday, A. (2004). Issues of validity in progressive paradigms of qualitative research. *TESOL Quarterly*, 38, 731–734.

Holliday, A. (2007). *Doing and writing qualitative research* (2nd ed.). Thousand Oaks, CA: Sage.

Holstein, J. A., & Gubrium, J. F. (1995). *The active interview.* Thousand Oaks, CA: Sage.

Hruska, B. (2004). Constructing gender in an English dominant kindergarten: Implications for second language learners. *TESOL Quarterly*, 38, 459–485.

Iddings, A. C. D. (2005). Linguistic access and participation: English language learners in an English-dominant community of practice. *Bilingual Research Journal*, 29(1), 165–183.

James, M. A. (2006). Transfer of learning from a university content-based EAP course. *TESOL Quarterly*, 40, 783–806.

Jauregi, K., & Bañados, E. (2008). Virtual interaction through video-web communication: A step towards enriching and internationalizing language learning programs. *ReCALL*, 20(2), 183–207.

Jenkins, S., & Parra, I. (2003). Multiple layers of meaning in an oral proficiency test: The complementary roles of nonverbal, paralinguistic, and verbal behaviors in assessment decisions. *Modern Language Journal*, 87, 90–107.

Jia, Y., Eslami, Z. R., & Burlbaw, L. M. (2006). ESL teachers' perceptions and factors influencing their use of classroom-based reading assessment. *Bilingual Research Journal*, 30, 407–430.

Johnstone, B. (2000). *Qualitative methods in sociolinguistics.* New York: Oxford University Press.

Kang, S.-J. (2005). Dynamic emergence of situational willingness to communicate in a second language. *System*, 33, 277–292.

Ketchum, E. M. (2006). The cultural baggage of second language reading: An approach to understanding the practices and perspectives of a nonnative product. *Foreign Language Annals*, 39(1), 22–42.

Kinginger, C. (2008). Language learning in study abroad: Case studies of Americans in France. *Modern Language Journal*, 92(s1), [online edition].

Kobayashi, M. (2003). The role of peer support in ESL students' accomplishment of oral academic tasks. *Canadian Modern Language Review*, 59, 337–368.

Kol, S., & Schcolnik, M. (2008). Asynchronous forums in EAP: Assessment issues. *Language Learning and Technology*, 12(2), 49–70.

Kramsch, C., & Whiteside, A. (2008). Language ecology in multilingual settings. Towards a theory of symbolic competence. *Applied Linguistics*, 29, 645–671.

Kubanyiova, M. (2008). Rethinking research ethics in contemporary applied linguistics: The tension between macroethical and microethical perspectives in situated research. *Modern Language Journal*, 92, 503–518.

Lamb, M. (2007). The impact of school on EFL learning motivation: An Indonesian case study. *TESOL Quarterly*, 41, 757–780.

Langellier, K., & Peterson, E. E. (2004). *Storytelling in daily life: Performing narrative.* Philadelphia: Temple University Press.

Lantolf, J. P. (Ed.) (2000). *Sociocultural theory and second language learning.* New York: Oxford University Press.

Lantolf, J. P., & Thorne, S. L. (2006). *Sociocultural theory and the genesis of second language development.* New York: Oxford University Press.

Lave, J., & Wenger, E. (1991). *Situated learning: legitimate peripheral participation.* Cambridge, New York: Cambridge University Press.

Lazaraton, A. (2003). Evaluative criteria for qualitative research in applied linguistics: Whose criteria and whose research? *Modern Language Journal*, 87, 1–12.

Lazaraton, A., & Ishihara, N. (2005). Understanding second language teacher practice using microanalysis and self-reflection: A collaborative case study. *Modern Language Journal*, 89, 529–542.

Lear, D. W. (2005). Spanish for working medical professionals: Linguistic needs. *Foreign Language Annals*, 38, 223–235.

LeCompte, M. D., Preissle, J., & Tesch, R. (1993). *Ethnography and qualitative design in educational research* (2nd ed.). San Diego: Academic Press.

Lee, E., & Maeda-Simon, A. (2006). Racialized research identities in ESL/EFL research. *TESOL Quarterly*, 40, 573–594.

Lee, Y.-A. (2006). Respecifying display questions: Interactional resources for language teaching. *TESOL Quarterly*, 40, 691–713.

Li, Y. (2007). Apprentice scholarly writing in a community of practice: An intraview of an NNES graduate student writing a research article. *TESOL Quarterly*, 41, 55–79.

Lincoln, Y. S., & Guba, E. G. (1985). *Naturalistic inquiry.* Beverly Hills, CA: Sage.

Lyons, N., & LaBoskey, V. K. (2002). *Narrative inquiry in practice: Advancing the knowledge of teaching.* New York: Teachers College Press.

Marcus, G., & Fischer, R. (1986). A crisis of representation in the human sciences. In G. Marcus & R. Fischer (Eds.), *Anthropology as cultural critique: An experimental moment in the human sciences* (pp. 7–16). Chicago: University of Chicago Press.

Markee, N. (2000). *Conversation analysis*. Mahwah, NJ: Lawrence Erlbaum.

Markee, N., & Kasper, G. (2004). Classroom talks: An introduction. *Modern Language Journal, 88,* 491–500.

Marshall, C., & Rossman, G. B. (2006). *Designing qualitative research* (4th ed.). Thousand Oaks, CA: Sage.

Masso, A., & Tender, T. (2008). About the linguistic constitution of social space: The case of Estonia. *Trames, 12(62/57)*(2), 151–182.

May, S. (1997). Critical ethnography. In N. H. Hornberger & D. Corson (Eds.), *Encyclopedia of language and education. Volume 8. Research methods in language and education* (pp. 149–171). Dortrecht: Kluwer.

Maynard, D. W., & Clayman, S. E. (2003). Ethnomethodology and conversation analysis. In L. T. Reynolds & N. J. Herman-Kinney (Eds.), *Handbook of symbolic interactionism* (pp. 173–202). Walnut Creek, CA: AltaMira Press.

McDonough, K. (2006). Action research and the professional development of graduate teaching assistants. *Modern Language Journal, 90,* 33–47.

McDonough, K., & Chaikitmongkol, W. (2007). Teachers' and learners' reactions to a task-based EFL course in Thailand. *TESOL Quarterly, 41,* 107–132.

Menard-Warwick, J. (2008). '"Because she made beds. Every day." Social positioning, classroom discourse, and language learning. *Applied Linguistics, 29,* 267–289.

Menard-Warwick, J. (2009). Co-constructing representations of culture in ESL and EFL classrooms: Discursive faultlines in Chile and California. *Modern Language Journal, 93,* 30–45.

Merriam, S. B. (1998). *Qualitative research and case study applications in education* (2nd ed.). San Francisco: Jossey-Bass.

Merriam, S. B. (2009). *Qualitative research: A guide to design and implementation*. San Francisco: Jossey-Bass.

Miles, M. B., & Huberman, A. M. (1994). *Qualitative data analysis: An expanded sourcebook* (2nd ed.). Thousand Oaks, CA: Sage.

Mishler, E. G. (1986). *Research interviewing: Context and narrative*. Cambridge, MA: Harvard University Press.

Montgomery, S. (2004). Of towers, walls, and fields: Perspectives on language in science. *Science, 303,* 1333–1335.

Mori, J. (2004). Negotiating sequential boundaries and learning opportunities: A case from a Japanese language classroom. *Modern Language Journal, 88,* 536–550.

Mori, J., & Hayashi, M. (2006). The achievement of intersubjectivity through embodied completions: A study of interactions between first and second language speakers. *Applied Linguistics, 27,* 195–219.

Morita, N. (2004). Negotiating participation and identity in second language academic communities. *TESOL Quarterly, 38,* 573–603.

Morita, N. (2006). The author replies … Studying power, agency, and transformation in classroom settings. *TESOL Quarterly, 40,* 435–437.

Motha, S. (2006). Racializing ESOL teacher identities in U.S. K-12 public schools. *TESOL Quarterly, 40,* 495–518.

Moustakas, C. E. (1994). *Phenomenological research methods*. Thousand Oaks, CA: Sage.

Mullock, B. (2006). The pedagogical knowledge base of four TESOL teachers. *Modern Language Journal, 90,* 48–66.

Ochs, E. (1979). Transcription as theory. In E. Ochs & B. B. Schiefflin (Eds.), *Developmental pragmatics* (pp. 43–72). New York: Academic Press.

Olson, K. (2007). Lost opportunities to learn: The effects of education policy on primary language instruction for English learners. *Linguistics and Education, 18,* 121–141.

Orland-Barak, L., & Yinon, H. (2005). Different but similar: Student teachers' perspectives on the use of L1 in Arab and Jewish EFL classroom settings. *Language, Culture, and Curriculum, 18*(1), 91–113.

Orsini-Jones, M. (2004). Supporting a course in new literacies and skills for linguists with a Virtual Learning Environment: Results from a staff/student collaborative action-research project at Coventry University. *ReCALL, 16*(1), 189–209.

Ortega, L. (2005). For what and for whom is our research? The ethical as transformative lens in instructed SLA. *Modern Language Journal, 89,* 427–443.

Patton, M. Q. (2002). *Qualitative research and evaluation methods* (3rd ed.). Thousand Oaks, CA: Sage.

Pavlenko, A. (2007). Autobiographic narratives as data in applied linguistics. *Applied Linguistics, 28*(2), 163–188.

Pavlenko, A. (2008). "I'm very not about the law part": Nonnative speakers of English and the Miranda warnings. *TESOL Quarterly, 42,* 1–30.

Pawan, F., & Thomalla, T. G. (2005). Making the invisible visible: A responsive evaluation study of ESL and Spanish language services for immigrants in a small rural county in Indiana. *TESOL Quarterly, 39,* 683–705.

Payne, M. (2006). Foreign language planning in England: The pupil perspective. *Current Issues in Language Planning, 7*(2&3), 189–213.

Polkinghorne, D. (1988). *Narrative knowing and the human sciences*. Albany, NY: State University of New York Press.

Psathas, G. (1995). *Conversation analysis: The study of talk-in-interaction*. Thousand Oaks, CA: Sage.

Ramanathan, V., & Atkinson, D. (1999). Ethnographic approaches and methods in L2 writing research: A critical guide and review. *Applied Linguistics, 20,* 44–70.

Rampton, B., Roberts, C., Leung, C., & Harris, R. (2002). Methodology in the analysis of classroom discourse. *Applied Linguistics, 23,* 373–392.

Richards, K., & Seedhouse, P. (2007). *Applying conversation analysis.* New York: Palgrave Macmillan.

Roberts, C. (2006). Figures in a landscape: Some methodological issues in adult ESOL research. *Linguistics and Education, 17,* 6–23.

Rosaldo, R. (1989). *Culture & truth: The remaking of social analysis.* Boston: Beacon Press.

Rubin, H. J., & Rubin, I. (2005). *Qualitative interviewing: The art of hearing data* (2nd ed.). Thousand Oaks, CA: Sage.

Schieffelin, B. B., & Ochs, E. (1986). *Language socialization across cultures.* New York: Cambridge University Press.

Schleppegrell, M. J., Achugar, M., & Oteíza, T. (2004). The grammar of history: Enhancing content-based instruction through a functional focus on language. *TESOL Quarterly, 38,* 67–93.

Scollon, R. (2003). The dialogist in a positivist world: Theory in the social sciences and the humanities at the end of the twentieth century. *Social Semiotics, 13*(1), 71–88.

Seedhouse, P. (2007). On ethnomethodological CA and "linguistic CA": A reply to Hall. *Modern Language Journal, 91,* 527–533.

Seidman, I. (2006). *Interviewing as qualitative research: A guide for researchers in education and the social sciences* (3rd ed.). New York: Teachers College Press.

Séror, J. (2005). Computers and qualitative data analysis: Paper, pens, and highlighters vs. screen, mouse, and keyboard. *TESOL Quarterly, 39,* 321–328.

Shedivy, S. L. (2004). Factors that lead some students to continue the study of foreign language past the usual 2 years in high school. *System, 32,* 103–119.

Shin, H., & Crookes, G. (2005). Exploring the possibilities for EFL critical pedagogy in Korea: A two-part case study. *Critical Inquiry in Language Studies, 2*(2), 113–136.

Shohamy, E. (2004). Research guidelines in TESOL: Alternative perspectives. Reflections on research guidelines, categories, and responsibility. *TESOL Quarterly, 38,* 728–731.

Simon-Maeda, A. (2004). The complex construction of professional identities: Female EFL educators in Japan speak out. *TESOL Quarterly, 38,* 405–436.

Spradley, J. P. (1979). *The ethnographic interview.* New York: Holt, Rinehart and Winston.

Spradley, J. P. (1980). *Participant observation.* New York: Holt, Rinehart and Winston.

Stake, R. E. (1995). *The art of case study research: Perspectives on practice.* Thousand Oaks, CA: Sage.

Stake, R. E. (2000). Case studies. In N. K. Denzin & Y. S. Lincoln (Eds.), *Handbook of Qualitative Research* (2nd ed.) (pp. 435–454). Thousand Oaks, CA: Sage.

Stewart, T. (2006). Teacher–researcher collaboration or teachers' research? *TESOL Quarterly, 40,* 421–430.

Stracke, E. (2007). A road to understanding: A qualitative study into why learners drop out of a blended language learning (BLL) environment. *ReCALL, 19*(1), 57–78.

Stroud, C., & Wee, L. (2007). A pedagogical application of liminalities in social positioning: Identity and literacy in Singapore. *TESOL Quarterly, 41,* 33–54.

Swales, J. M. (2004). *Research genres: Explorations and applications.* New York: Cambridge University Press.

Talmy, S. (2008). The cultural productions of the ESL student at Tradewinds High: Contingency, multidirectionality, and identity in L2 socialization. *Applied Linguistics, 29,* 619–644.

Taylor, L. (2006). Wrestling with race: The implications of integrative antiracism education for immigrant ESL youth. *TESOL Quarterly, 40,* 519–544.

Thomas, J. (1993). *Doing critical ethnography.* Newbury Park, CA: Sage Publications.

Thorne, S. L. (2005). Epistemology, politics, and ethics in sociocultural theory. *Modern Language Journal, 89,* 393–409.

Tsui, A. B. M. (2007). Complexities of identity formation: A narrative inquiry of an EFL teacher. *TESOL Quarterly, 41,* 657–680.

Van Manen, M. (1990). *Researching lived experience: Human science for an action sensitive pedagogy.* Albany, NY: State University of New York Press.

Waring, H. Z. (2005). Peer tutoring in a graduate writing centre: Identity, expertise, and advice resisting. *Applied Linguistics, 26,* 141–168.

Watson-Gegeo, K. A. (1988). Ethnography in ESL: Defining the essentials. *TESOL Quarterly, 22,* 575–592.

Watson-Gegeo, K. A. (2004). Mind, language, and epistemology: Toward a language socialization paradigm for SLA. *Modern Language Journal, 88,* 331–350.

Watzke, J. L. (2007). Foreign language pedagogical knowledge: Toward a developmental theory of beginning teacher practices. *Modern Language Journal, 91,* 63–82.

Wenger, E. (1998). *Communities of practice: Learning, meaning, and identity.* New York: Cambridge University Press.

Wertsch, J. V., Río, P. d., & Alvarez, A. (1995). *Sociocultural studies of mind.* New York: Cambridge University Press.

Willis, G. (1991). Phenomenological inquiry: Life-world perceptions. In E. C. Short (Ed.), *Forms of curriculum inquiry* (pp. 173–186). Albany, NY: State University of New York Press.

Wiltse, L. (2006). "Like pulling teeth": Oral discourse practices in a culturally diverse language arts classroom. *Canadian Modern Language Review, 63,* 199–223.

Wodak, R., & Meyer, M. (2001). *Methods of critical discourse analysis.* London: Sage.

Wolcott, H. F. (1999). *Ethnography: A way of seeing.* Walnut Creek, CA: AltaMira Press.

Wolcott, H. F. (2005). *The art of fieldwork* (2nd ed.). Walnut Creek, CA: Altamira Press.

Yin, R. K. (2009). *Case study research: Design and methods* (4th ed.). Los Angeles: Sage.

Young, R. F., & Miller, E. R. (2004). Learning as changing participation: Discourse roles in ESL writing conferences. *Modern Language Journal, 88,* 519–535.

Zuengler, J., & Cole, K. (2005). Language socialization and second language learning. In E. Hinkel (Ed.), *Handbook of research in second language teaching and learning.* (Vol. 1) (pp. 301–316). Mahwah, NJ: Erlbaum.

Zuengler, J., & Miller, E. R. (2006). Cognitive and sociocultural perspectives: Two parallel SLA worlds? *TESOL Quarterly, 40,* 35–58.

12

Quantitative Research in Second Language Studies

James Dean Brown

Introduction

The purpose of this chapter is to examine where quantitative research in the field of second language studies (SLS) has come from, where it is today, and where it is likely to head in the future. To those ends, I will explore what *research* is, how quantitative research fits into that broad definition of research, and then zero in on SLS quantitative research by looking at what it is, what books have been written about it, and what guidelines are available for quantitative researchers in our field. I will then turn to what I call *research on research* in terms of what it is, how comparative reviews of quantitative research methods books can serve as research on research, and then turn to research on quantitative research methods in SLS. I will conclude by considering what the future may hold for quantitative research in SLS and by suggesting issues that future research on SLS research might profitably investigate.

What is Research?

Brown (1992a) reported the results of a survey of the TESOL (Teaching English to Speakers of Other Languages) membership. When asked to define *research*, the respondents produced a wide range of answers from brief, idealistic responses such as "the search for the truth" to longer, cynical responses like "something that profs at universities that grant *advanced* degrees do because they don't teach and need to publish." Generally, the respondents gave four types of definitions that (1) listed the types of research; (2) listed the topics of research; (3) covered the purpose of research; or (4) listed the steps in the research process.

   Given this variety of definitions for research, it may be quixotic to even attempt to find a single definition specific enough to be clear, yet general enough to include all options. Years ago, I discussed this topic with Donald Freeman; he defined research very eloquently as "any principled inquiry." I have since modified that definition somewhat to fit my views of SLS research. My definition is *any systematic and principled inquiry in second language studies*. I added *systematic* to Donald's definition because, to me, research is not only *principled*, but must also be well-organized, methodical, and precise (Brown, 2004a).

Where Does Quantitative Research Fit into this Broad Definition of Research?

Such a broad definition of research allows for the many types of investigations in SLS, but it could lead to substantial confusion if the differences among the many types of SLS research are not sorted out. I will briefly attempt to do so here, while gradually zeroing in on quantitative research. One major distinction is between primary research and secondary research (see Figure 12.1). *Primary research* is based on original, primary data, and *secondary research* is based on the writings of other researchers (the present chapter is an example of secondary research). Thus, primary and secondary research studies are largely distinguished by the strategies used to gather the information.

Primary research includes research that I have classified elsewhere (Brown, 2001a, 2004a) as qualitative, survey, and quantitative (as shown in Figure 12.1). This three-way distinction can be seen as a continuum with qualitative research on one end and quantitative research on the other. Survey research is situated in between because it typically draws on both the qualitative and quantitative research methods.

The qualitative–quantitative distinction has been widely discussed in SLS (see e.g., Grotjahn, 1987; Van Lier, 1988; Seliger & Shohamy, 1989; Larsen-Freeman & Long, 1991; Johnson, 1992; Nunan, 1992; McDonough & McDonough, 1997; Brown & Rodgers, 2002; and Brown, 2004a). In Figure 12.2, I have placed case studies, introspection, discourse analysis, interactional analysis, and classroom observations under qualitative research. Survey research includes both interviews and questionnaires. And quantitative research includes at least four categories: descriptive, exploratory, quasi-experimental, and experimental.

In Brown (2004a), I made much of this continuum by describing 12 research characteristics on which qualitative and quantitative research vary. These 12 characteristics essentially define the differences between qualitative and quantitative research in continua with the strictest versions of qualitative and quantitative research on the ends:

1. *Data type*: qualitative vs. quantitative.
2. *Data collection methods*: non-experimental vs. experimental.
3. *Data analysis procedures*: interpretive vs. statistical.
4. *Degree of intrusiveness*: non-intervention vs. high intervention.
5. *Degree of selectivity*: non-selective vs. highly selective.
6. *Variable description*: variable definition vs. variable operationalization.
7. *Theory generation*: hypothesis forming vs. hypothesis testing.
8. *Reasoning*: inductive vs. deductive.

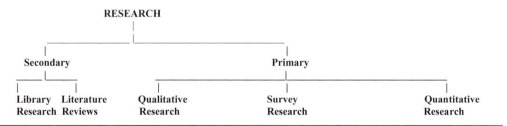

Figure 12.1 General research types

Figure 12.2 Primary research types

9. *Context*: natural vs. controlled.
10. *Time orientation*: longitudinal vs. cross-sectional.
11. *Participants*: small sample size vs. large sample size.
12. *Perspective*: emic vs. etic.

Similarly, I identified four differences in the standards against which qualitative and quantitative studies are compared in deciding if they are systematic and principled (for more details, see Brown, 2004a):

1. *Consistency*: dependability vs. reliability.
2. *Fidelity*: credibility vs. validity.
3. *Verifiability*: confirmability vs. replicability.
4. *Meaningfulness of results*: transferability vs. generalizability.

Quantitative Research

What is Quantitative Research?

I suppose in the simplest sense any study that counts things could be considered quantitative. So, *quantitative research* can be defined as any research that focuses on counting things and on understanding the patterns that emerge from those counts. In Figure 12.3, I have divided quantitative research into descriptive, exploratory, quasi-experimental, and experimental studies. These are not mutually exclusive categories, though some research papers will fall into only one, two, or three categories.

Descriptive studies are those that describe behaviors, outcomes, scores, etc. using statistics such as frequencies, percentages, descriptive statistics (including the mean, mode, median, midpoint, low, high, range, standard deviation, etc.). All quantitative studies should be at least descriptive, that is, researchers must think about and report descriptive statistics in any quantitative study because descriptive statistics provide the basis for understanding any other analyses that may follow.

Exploratory studies are those that examine relationships and correlations in the data. I list seven examples in Figure 12.3 of typical statistical analyses used in such studies, each of which can and has been given chapter and book length treatments elsewhere.

Quasi-experimental studies primarily differ from *true experimental studies* in that the latter are based on random samples from a population, while the former are not. Given that very little SLS research can be said to be based on random samples from a population (unless that population is defined very narrowly), most SLS research of this general type is quasi-experimental. Such studies are typically designed to understand differences in means or medians within and between groups with great concern for accurate p values (values that indicate the probability that the findings in the

Descriptive	Exploratory Analyses	Quasi-Experimental	Experimental
Descriptives	Correlation	t-test, z statistic, chi-square	t-test, z-statistic, chi-square
Frequencies	Regression & Multiple-regression	ANOVA	ANOVA
Cross-tabs	Discriminant function analysis & Logistic regression	MANOVA	MANOVA
	Factor analysis/Confirmatory factor analysis	Covariate versions of the above	Covariate versions of the above
	Structural equation modeling		
	Canonical correlation analysis		
	Implicational scaling & Cluster analysis		

Quantitative Research

Figure 12.3 Quantitative research types

particular study are due to chance alone). I give four examples in Figure 12.3, the *t*-test, *z* statistic, analysis of variance (ANOVA), and multivariate analysis of covariance (MANOVA), but ANOVA can come in many forms (e.g., one-way, two-way, and *n*-way designs) and include a number of important follow-up statistics (e.g., planned comparisons and post-hoc comparisons like Scheffé, Tukey, etc., eta squared or omega squared analyses, power analysis, and confidence intervals), with other features that must be dealt with differently such as repeated-measures designs and the use of covariates. Similarly, MANOVA can come in many forms (e.g., two-group Hotelling T, one-way, two-way, and *n*-way designs) and include all of the follow-up statistics and other features listed above for ANOVA. Clearly, the analyses in quasi-experimental studies are very complex, and probably because researchers have insufficient training, these are the studies that seem to most often be analyzed incorrectly by researchers in SLS. These statistical analyses typically require multiple-chapter or book length treatments.

What Books Cover Research Methods in SLS?

A number of books on research are available for language teachers to choose from (see Table 12.1). Some cover *classroom research* (Chaudron, 1988; Allwright & Bailey, 1991; Bailey & Nunan, 1997; Griffee & Nunan, 1997; Freeman, 1998), while others discuss *research and second language acquisition* (SLA) in more general terms (Cook, 1986; Kasper & Dahl, 1991; Larsen-Freeman & Long, 1991; Tarone, Gass, & Cohen, 1994; Schachter & Gass, 1996; Bachman & Cohen, 1998). Still other books explore the various research *options for SLS researchers* (Johnson, 1992; Nunan, 1992; McDonough & McDonough, 1997), and two cover *action research* (Wallace, 1998; Burns, 1999). Some books cover *qualitative research* pure and simple (Richards, 2003; Heigham & Croker, 2009), and four books focus more narrowly on single types of research: van Lier (1988) on ethnography; Gass, Sorace, and Selinker (1999) on SLA data analysis; Gass and Mackey (2000) on stimulated recall; and Duff (2008) on case study research. In addition, one book (Chalhoub-Deville, Chapelle, & Duff, 2006) focuses on the research issues of dependability and generalizability from a variety of perspectives. While it is true that a number of the books listed in this paragraph touch on quantitative research in one way or another, they are not designed specifically to teach quantitative research methods.

Books that do focus on teaching how to do quantitative SLS research are shown in Table 12.1. These include: Anshen (1978), Hatch and Farhady (1982), Butler (1985), Woods, Fletcher, and Hughes (1986), Seliger and Shohamy (1989), Hatch and Lazaraton (1991), Rietveld and van Hout (1993), Scholfield (1995), Wray, Trott, and Bloomer (1998), and Baayen (2008). For overviews of some of these books, see Hamp-Lyons (1989), Silver (1995), Brown (2004b), and Lazaraton (2005). In addition, Brown (1988) and Porte (2002) focus on quantitative research, but they do so in terms of critically reading that research rather than doing it. Brown (2001a) and Dörnyei (2003) also cover quantitative methods, but focus exclusively on questionnaire-based research. Still other books systematically present both qualitative and quantitative research methods (Brown & Rodgers, 2002; Mackey & Gass, 2005; Dörnyei, 2007). And, Norris and Ortega (2006a) is the only book to date in SLS on research synthesis and meta-analysis.

Are There Guidelines for Quantitative Researchers?

From the 1992 *TESOL Quarterly 26*(4) to the 2002 *TESOL Quarterly 36*(4), *Statistical Guidelines* were published in the *Information for Contributors* section at the back of each issue. Beginning in the 1994 *TESOL Quarterly 28*(4), *Qualitative Research Guidelines* were added. In the first issue of the 2003 *TESOL Quarterly*, TESOL presented revised guidelines for quantitative and qualitative research in TESOL. The quantitative portion of the revised guidelines appears in TESOL (2003). About one

Table 12.1 General Research Types

Type	1975–1979	1980–1984	1985–1989	1990–1994	1995–1999	2000–2004	2005–present
Classroom research			Chaudron (1988)	Allwright & Bailey (1991)	Bailey & Nunan (1997), Griffee & Nunan (1997), Freeman (1998)		
Research and SLA			Cook (1986)	Kasper & Dahl (1991), Larsen-Freeman & Long (1991), Tarone, Gass, & Cohen (1994)	Schachter & Gass (1996), Bachman & Cohen (1998)		
Options for SLS researchers							
Action research				Johnson (1992), Nunan (1992)	McDonough & McDonough (1998), Wallace (1998), Burns (1999)		
Qualitative research						Richards (2003)	Heigham & Croker (2009)
Single types of research			van Lier (1988) on ethnography		Gass, Sorace, & Selinker (1999) on SLA data analysis	Gass & Mackey (2000) on stimulated recall	Duff (2008) on case study research
Research issues							Chalhoub-Deville, Chapelle, & Duff (2006)
Quantitative research	Anshen (1978)	Hatch & Farhady (1982)		Hatch & Lazaraton (1991), Rietveld & van Hout (1993)	Scholfield (1995), Wray, Trott, & Bloomer (1998)		Baayen (2008)
Reading quantitative research			Brown (1988)				
Survey research methods						Brown (2001a), Dörnyei (2003)	
Qualitative/ quantitative						Brown & Rodgers (2002)	Mackey & Gass (2005), Dörnyei (2007)
Meta-analysis and research synthesis						Porte (2002)	Norris & Ortega (2006a)

year later, three articles appeared under the title "Research guidelines in TESOL: Alternative perspectives." Two of these articles (Bachman, 2004; and Shohamy, 2004) reflect in interesting ways on the revised research guidelines with particular reference to quantitative research.

Quantitative researchers in SLS have also leaned on guidelines from psychology (American Psychological Association, 1994, 2001) and articles responding to those guidelines (e.g., Vacha-Haase, Nilsson, Reetz, Lance, & Thompson, 2000; Wilkinson & Task Force on Statistical Inference, 1999).

Research on Research

What is Research on Research?

One sub-area of SLS examines how we do research in the field. I think of this as *research on research*. For example, there have been a number of published papers focused on qualitative research methods (e.g., Davis, 1992, 1995; Lazaraton, 1995; Brown, 2001a, 2005; Richards, 2009; and the multiple-book review in Tafaghodtari, 2009). A steady stream of papers has also been published over the years on quantitative research. Some articles promote critically reading statistical research (e.g., Brown, 1991a, 1992b, 1995). Still other articles explain and promote quantitative survey research methods (e.g., Baker, 1997, and Brown, 1997b, 1997e, 2000, 2009a). More focused articles take on specific issues in quantitative research such as designing statistical studies (Brown, 1997a), experimental research (Verhoeven, 1997), Likert scales (Busch, 1993; Turner, 1993; Brown, 2000), the generalizability of research results (Brown, 2006), correlation (Brown, 2001c, 2003), factor analysis and principle components analysis (Brown, 2001b, 2009b, 2009c), multiple t-tests and the Bonferroni adjustment (Siegel, 1990; Brown, 1990, 2008a), Cronbach alpha reliability (Brown, 2002), chi square and Yates' correction (Brown, 2004c), skewness and kurtosis (Brown, 1997c), as well as the cluster of issues surrounding sample size, power, statistical precision, effect size, and eta squared (Lazaraton, 1991; Crookes, 1991; Ellis, 2000; Brown, 2007a, 2007b, 2008b).

Comparative Reviews of Quantitative Methods Books

One fairly large category of articles that offers research on research is the group of articles that review books on quantitative research methods including at least: Hamp-Lyons (1989, 1990), Silver (1995), Brown (2004b), and Lazaraton (2005). Since these reviews compare a number of the quantitative research books in SLS, they provide a type of research on SLS research, so I will discuss each in a bit more depth.

In Part I of a two-part review, Hamp-Lyons (1989) describes and compares three quantitative research books by Brown (1988), Butler (1985), Woods, Fletcher, and Hughes (1986), and one language testing book. She describes each of the books in some detail, pointing out that Brown (1988) is designed for consumers of statistical studies, while the other two aim at "productive competence" (p. 128) in statistics. She briefly compares the books in terms of the common ground covered and ways they diverge.

Silver (1995) is more comprehensive in that she reviews five such books (Brown, 1988; Hatch & Lazaraton, 1991; Johnson, 1992; Nunan, 1992; Seliger & Shohamy, 1989). Her review "evaluates each text in terms of its stated purpose and audience, evaluates the strengths and weaknesses of each text for individual study, and discusses each book as a resource and reference for teachers" (pp. 263–264). She also provides a comparison of these five books in terms of their intended audience, their goals, their clarity and ease of access, their perspectives on research approaches, their scope of coverage, their comprehensiveness, as well as their usefulness for evaluating research and for preparing to do research (pp. 270–275).

Brown (2004b) is also relatively comprehensive, providing a comparative review of nine such books (Anshen, 1978; Hatch & Farhady, 1982; Butler, 1985; Woods, Fletcher, & Hughes, 1986; Seliger & Shohamy, 1989; Hatch & Lazaraton, 1991; Rietveld & van Hout, 1993; Brown, 2001a; Brown & Rodgers, 2002). This review concludes that 20 *conceptual topics in quantitative research* appear to be most essential for researchers in SLS and lists those conceptual topics (pp. 378–379, 382, 389–390). The review also concludes that certain *statistical topics* are apparently most important and lists those statistical topics as well (pp. 380–382, 390).

Lazaraton (2005) provides an historical review of some of the key books that cover quantitative research. Her literature review and Appendix A provide useful comparisons of 12 research books (Hatch & Farhady, 1982; Butler, 1985; Woods, Fletcher, & Hughes, 1986; Brown, 1988; Seliger & Shohamy, 1989; Hatch & Lazaraton, 1991; Johnson, 1992; Nunan, 1992; Scholfield, 1995; McDonough & McDonough, 1997; Wray et al., 1998; and Porte, 2002). She compares them in terms of eight features: their organizing principles; the degree to which they address research design issues; the statistics they cover; the amount of computer guidance; the existence of reader activities and an answer key; the degree to which they show how to format a research report; and other features. Her paper also reports on a study of the trends in research methods and statistics in four prominent journals, but that is discussed in the next section.

Research on Quantitative Research

I classify six articles that have appeared in the last 23 years as papers that explicitly present research on quantitative research. In one way or another, these papers are all examining trends and important issues in the quantitative research in SLS.

Henning (1986) reviews articles in *TESOL Quarterly* and *Language Learning* between 1970 and 1985 and tallies in five-year increments from 1970 to 1985 those articles that were quantitative, experimental, hypothesis testing, inferential, and multivariate and discusses the trends over that period. He also discusses what he called "promising quantitative research paradigms" (p. 701), including correlation, ANOVA, chi-square, path-analytic, latent-trait, factor analytic, and confirmatory factor analytic methods. He ends by arguing for the importance of using appropriate and valid data elicitation methods and by listing available resources for novice quantitative researchers (interestingly, all of these resources came from other fields except for Hatch & Farhady, 1982; see Table 12.1 to understand why).

Lazaraton, Riggenbach, and Ediger (1987) surveys 121 applied linguistics professionals about their knowledge of and attitudes toward quantitative research. The respondents indicate considerable dissatisfaction with their training in statistics and wide variation in their knowledge of the procedures and concepts of quantitative research. They also vary in their attitudes toward the usefulness of statistical research as well as the degree to which they feel they need to be informed about statistical procedures. The authors capture the value of their study when they write that it is "useful as a 'gauge' of literacy in research methodology and statistics in our field and as evidence that a need for such literacy exists" (p. 263).

Brown (1991a, reprinted in 1995) is Part I of a two-part series. While ostensibly offering strategies for reading statistical studies, Part I addresses important issues that readers (and researchers) should pay attention to: using the abstract to show the value of the study; organizing a research paper along conventional lines; using appropriate forms of statistical reasoning; relating the research to professional experience; and constantly expanding the reader's (researcher's) knowledge of statistics and research design. All of this is discussed with examples drawn from the next article (Brown, 1991b) in the same issue of *TESOL Quarterly*. Part II (Brown, 1992b) addresses other important issues in quantitative research: carefully thinking about the variables in a study and their relative roles; making sure the correct statistical tests are selected; checking all of the assumptions underlying each statistical analysis; thinking carefully about why each of the statistical analyses have been used; and using statistical tables effectively. Examples are drawn from contemporary volumes of *TESOL Quarterly*.

Lazaraton (2000) carefully examines data-based articles in four applied linguistics journals (*Language Learning, Modern Language Journal, Studies in Second Language Learning*, and *TESOL Quarterly*) over the seven-year period from 1991 to 1997. A total of 332 articles are analyzed, of which 88% were quantitative, 10% qualitative, and 2% partially qualitative.

Lazaraton concludes that "parametric statistical procedures still reign supreme" (p. 180) but stresses the importance of appropriately applying statistics by checking the underlying assumptions of each statistical test. She ends by writing that she hopes "to see more studies that combine qualitative and quantitative research methods" (p. 180).

Lazaraton (2005) appears to be a considerably expanded version of her 2000 article. This version provides a review of some of the key books and articles in the history of quantitative research (as discussed in the previous section). She then reports the results of a study of 524 empirical research articles that appeared in the same four journals covered in Lazaraton (2000), but for the years 1991 to 2001. She finds that 86% of the articles were quantitative, 13% qualitative, and 1% mixed methods. She also presents a table with side-by-side results for all four journals in each of the 11 years, as well as a table comparing all four journals in all 11 years, for different types of statistical analyses (descriptive, ANOVA, Pearson, *t*-test, regression, and chi-square). As in her 2000 article, she concludes by hoping that "more care would be taken in applying *all* statistical procedures appropriately as per their underlying assumptions" and that "we would see more studies that combine qualitative and quantitative research methods, since each highlights 'reality' in a different, yet complementary, way" (p. 219).

Loewen and Gass (2009) provide an annotated list of many of the articles and books on quantitative research methods. This article focuses on quantitative research methods as they relate to SLA research. Hence, the annotations provide an interesting view of quantitative research as seen from the SLA perspective. Because the annotated references are arranged chronologically, reading through them gives the reader a sense of how these books and articles are related historically, as well as how they became progressively more sophisticated over time.

Conclusion

What Does the Future Hold for Quantitative Research?

A number of quantitative researchers have argued in various places for careful evaluation of the assumptions underlying all statistical procedures (e.g., Brown, 1992b; Lazaraton, 2000, 2005; TESOL, 2003), for adequate maintenance of experiment-wise alpha (e.g., Brown, 1990; TESOL, 2003), and for the importance of reliable measurement to quantitative research (e.g., TESOL, 2003; Brown, 2004a). Since many quantitative researchers in SLS continue to ignore these issues, I hope the importance of checking assumptions, maintaining experiment-wise alpha, and reliable measurement will continue to be mentioned, argued for, and perhaps attended to by most SLS researchers in the years to come.

However, here, I am more interested in trying to determine new directions that quantitative research might head in the coming years. Glimmerings in the current literature on research and statistics in SLS as well as more pronounced trends in other fields may foreshadow things to come. I am no soothsayer, but based on what I am reading in SLS and in allied fields such as education and psychology, I can predict with a certain degree of confidence that the following issues will play a big part in the future of quantitative research in SLS: ethics; the inadequacy of alpha; power, effect size, and confidence intervals; mixed methods research; replication; and meta-analysis.

Ethics

First, ethical considerations in research have periodically surfaced in the literature (e.g., TESOL Research Committee, 1980; Dufon, 1993; Brown, 2004a). However, with the relatively recent and pervasive formation of human subjects committees at universities across the United States, most researchers at the tertiary level in the US are suddenly more concerned than ever about the ethics of quantitative research, and I predict that these trends will continue well into the future. For an early overview on this issue outside of our field, see Kimmel (1988). For the ethical guidelines provide in the field of psychology, see American Psychological Association (1953, 1982, 1992, 2002).

The Inadequacy of Alpha

Second, I believe that alpha will lose its luster in our field as it has in other disciplines. What this means is that the days of chasing a significant p value (what one colleague in psychology called "p-value envy") may soon be over, and with it the tendency in SLS to conduct small-sample studies that make it necessary to torture the data until they finally confess a significant t-value, chi-square, etc. I am not predicting that alpha and the resulting p values will disappear, but rather that researchers will come to understand that finding a significant p value is not enough; that is, p values are not an end, but just the beginning of further analyses that can help researchers better understand their "significant" results (as explained in the next sub-section).

Power, Effect Size, and Confidence Intervals

Third, as far back as I can remember, follow-up power, effect size, and confidence interval analyses have been available to help researchers understand and clarify the results of their studies. However, by and large, few researchers in SLS have reported and interpreted these potential additions to their statistical analyses. I predict that future research in SLS will move into alignment with educational and psychological research and that SLS journals will increasingly require that power, effect size, and confidence intervals be reported along with p values in all studies where they are appropriate. Certainly calls for reporting these statistics in our field began as far back as 1991 (e.g., see Lazaraton, 1991; Crookes, 1991; Ellis, 2000; Brown, 2007a, 2007b, 2008b). And, the guidelines for *TESOL Quarterly* have also been applying pressure in that direction:

> Provide the power of your study (calculate it using a standard reference such as Cohen, 1988, or a computer program) … Always supplement the reporting of an actual p value with a measure of effect magnitude (e.g., measures of strength of association or measures of effect size). Briefly contextualize the magnitude of the effect in theoretical and practical terms. Confidence intervals for the effect magnitudes of principal outcomes are recommended.
>
> (TESOL, 2003, pp. 160–161)

It is time for the researchers in SLS to wake up to the advantages that power, effects size, and confidence intervals have in terms of understanding and explaining statistical results.

Since little information (beyond what is found in the citations in the previous paragraph) is currently available on these topics in our field, researchers interested in being on the front edge of these issues in SLS may want to turn to other fields such as education and psychology where researchers have tackled these issues in earnest. Two books worth reading on these topics are Kline (2004) and Ziliak and McCloskey (2007). Some recent articles worth examining on *the vagaries of significance testing* can be found in: B. Thompson (1999); W. L. Thompson (2000); Mittag and Thompson (2000);

Vacha-Haase et al. (2000); Capraro and Capraro (2002); Gigerenzer, Krauss, and Vitouch (2004); and Hubbard and Armstrong (2006). The very fact that W. L. Thompson (2000) lists 326 citations on this topic indicates the importance of the significance-testing controversy in other fields. Recent articles on *effect size* include: Vacha-Haase et al. (2000); Capraro and Capraro (2002); Huberty (2002); B. Thompson (2002); Henson (2006); as well as Alhija and Levy (2009). For more information on *confidence intervals* see: Smithson (2001, 2004); Bird (2002); B. Thompson (2002); and Byrd (2007). And, of course, for information on *power analysis*, turn to the classic Cohen (1988) or to more recent articles on power statistics by Hoenig and Heisey (2001); Algina and Olejnik (2003); and Yuan and Maxwell (2005).

Mixed Methods Research

Fourth, I believe that, in coming years, increasing numbers of quantitative researchers in SLS will see the advantages of combining quantitative and qualitative research methods (as advocated by Chaudron, 1986, 2000; Lazaraton, 2000, 2005; Brown, 2004a) in such a way that they reinforce and cross-validate each other so that the whole is greater than the sum of its parts. Numerous definitions have surfaced for *mixed methods research*. Burke Johnson, Onwuegbuzie, and Turner (2007) review these definitions. The first and most central part of the definition they offer at the end of their article is:

> Mixed methods research is an intellectual and practical synthesis based on qualitative and quantitative research; it is the third methodological or research paradigm (along with qualitative and quantitative research). It recognizes the importance of traditional quantitative and qualitative research but also offers a powerful third paradigm choice that often will provide the most informative, complete, balanced, and useful research results.
>
> (Burke Johnson et al., 2007, p. 129)

From my point of view, those who can use both quantitative and qualitative methods and can use them to reinforce and cross-validate each other will be stronger researchers. For anyone interested in exploring the burgeoning area of mixed methods research, I would recommend any of the following books: Creswell and Plano Clark (2007); Greene (2007); Bergman (2008); Plano Clark and Creswell (2008); Cresswell (2009); and Teddlie and Tashakkori (2009).

Replication

Fifth, I believe that, in the coming years, the need for replication will finally get the recognition that it deserves. *Replication* is the "repetition of an experiment with different subjects, and frequently with a different experimenter and different location" (Yaremko, Harari, Harrison, & Lynn, 1988, p. 199). In SLS, at least the following have argued for more replications: Valdman (1988); Santos (1989); Polio and Gass (1997); *Language Teaching* Review Panel (2008); and *Language Teaching* (2009). That last reference differentiated among three types of replications (also see Hendrik, 1991):

> *Literal (or exact) replication* is the exact duplication of a previous methodologically sound study whereby the methods and conditions are repeated to confirm the original findings. *Approximate (or systematic) replication* involves the duplication of the methods of the original study as closely as possible but altering some non-major variable. *Constructive (or conceptual) replication* means beginning with a similar problem statement as the original study but creating a new means or design to verify the original findings.
>
> (*Language Teaching*, 2009, p. i; italics added)

To my knowledge, only one book on replication exists to date in the social sciences (Neuliep, 1991, is an edited collection of articles on replication).

Meta-Analysis

Sixth, SLS needs to wake up to the truth that individual studies are not very important, except insofar as they collectively lead to consensus-building in the field. I believe that accepting the need for consensus will inevitably lead us to do increasing numbers of meta-analytic research studies. *Meta-analysis* is a term that dates back to Glass (1976, p. 3; emphasis mine), where he defined it as follows:

> Meta-analysis refers to the analysis of analyses. I use it to refer to the *statistical analysis* of a large collection of analysis results from individual studies for the purpose of integrating the findings. It connotes a rigorous alternative to the casual, narrative discussions of research studies which typify our attempts to make sense of the rapidly expanding research literature.

In SLS, meta-analyses have been conducted on a number of topics in recent years (e.g., Norris & Ortega, 2000; Goldschneider & DeKeyser, 2001; Masgoret & Gardner, 2003; Rolstad, Mahoney, & Glass, 2005; Russell & Spada, 2006; Jeon & Kaya, 2006; Taylor, Stevens, & Asher, 2006; and Mackey & Goo, 2007). Norris and Ortega (2006a, 2006b, 2007) provide information, examples, and references that serve as an excellent introduction to doing meta-analysis. However, researchers interested in pursuing meta-analysis strategies may also wish to look outside the field at some of the following recent books: Hartung, Knapp, and Sinha (2008); Kulinskaya, Morgenthaler, and Staudte (2008); Littell, Corcoran, and Pillai (2008); Bernstein, Hedges, Higgins, and Rothstein (2009); or Cooper, Hedges, and Valentine (2009).

Suggestions for Future Research on Research

I would recommend that the current strands of research on quantitative research be continued and that several others be added. To those ends, research on the following or related topics would be useful:

1. Periodic reviews of the books available in SLS on quantitative research (such as those provided in Hamp-Lyons, 1989; Silver, 1995; Brown, 2004b, Lazaraton, 2005; and the present chapter).
2. Periodic replications of studies that survey the types of research (quantitative, qualitative, and mixed) published in SLS journals (such as those reported in Henning, 1986; Lazaraton, 2000, 2005) including at least the four journals covered by Lazaraton, but perhaps additional journals as well.
3. Periodic replications of the Lazaraton et al. (1987) survey research on what researchers know about quantitative research methods and their attitudes toward statistical analyses.
4. Periodic surveys of what is taught in quantitative research methodology courses in SLS, as well as the stakeholders' (students, teachers, textbook writers, etc.) perspectives on that content (similar to what Bailey & Brown, 1996; Brown & Bailey, 2008, did for language testing courses).
5. Periodic studies looking at the quality of published quantitative research studies (over time) in terms of experiment-wise control of alpha, reliability of measurement, checking of the assumptions, as well as the adequacy of the analyses and follow up analyses (such as power, effect size, confidence intervals, etc.).

6. Periodic studies of the degree to which readers of various journals and types of journals understand the different types of research studies that are published in those journals (recognizing that the responsibility for the quality of quantitative research in SLS is a two-way street and that it is important for the readership of our journals to be able to read such studies critically, as consumers).

References

Algina, J., & Olejnik, S. (2003). Conducting power analyses for Anova and Ancova in between-subjects designs. *Evaluation and Health Professsions, 26*(3), 288–314.

Alhija, F. F.-A., & Levy, A. (2009). Effect size reporting practices in published articles. *Educational and Psychological Measurement, 69*(2), 245–265.

Allwright, D., & Bailey, K. M. (1991). *Focus on the language classroom: An introduction to classroom research for language teachers.* Cambridge: Cambridge University Press.

American Psychological Association. (1953). *Ethical standards of psychologists.* Washington, DC: American Psychological Association.

American Psychological Association. (1982). *Ethical principles in the conduct of research with human participants.* Washington, DC: American Psychological Association.

American Psychological Association. (1992) Ethical principles of psychologists and code of conduct. *American Psychologist, 47*, 1597–1611.

American Psychological Association. (1994). *Publication manual of the American Psychological Association* (4th ed.). Washington, DC: American Psychological Association.

American Psychological Association. (2001). *Publication manual of the American Psychological Association* (5th ed.). Washington, DC: American Psychological Association.

American Psychological Association. (2002). Ethical principles of psychologists and code of conduct. *American Psychologist, 57*(12), 1060–1073.

Anshen, F. (1978). *Statistics for linguists.* Rowley, MA: Newbury House.

Baayen, R. H. (2008). *Analyzing linguistic data: A practical introduction to statistics using R.* Cambridge: Cambridge University Press.

Bachman, L. F. (2004). Linking observations to interpretations and uses in TESOL research. *TESOL Quarterly, 38*(4), 723–727.

Bachman, L. F., & Cohen, A. (Eds.) (1998). *Interfaces between second language acquisition and language testing research.* Cambridge: Cambridge University Press.

Bailey, K. M., & Brown, J. D. (1996). Language testing courses: What are they? In A. Cumming & R. Berwick (Eds.), *Validation in language testing* (pp. 236–256). Clevedon: Multilingual Matters.

Bailey, K. M., & Nunan, D. (Eds.) (1997). *Voices from the language classroom.* Cambridge: Cambridge University Press.

Baker, C. (1997). Survey methods in researching language and education. In N. H. Hornberger & C. Corson (Eds.), *Encyclopedia of language and education, Volume 8: Research methods in language and education* (pp. 35–46). Dordrecht: Kluwer Academic.

Bergman, M. (Ed.) (2008). *Advances in mixed methods research.* Thousand Oaks, CA: Sage.

Bernstein, M., Hedges, L. V., Higgins, J. P. T., & Rothstein, H. R. (2009). *Introduction to meta-analysis.* San Francisco: Wiley.

Bird, K. (2002). Confidence intervals for effect sizes in analysis of variance. *Educational and Psychological Measurement, 62*(2), 197–226.

Brown, J. D. (1988). *Understanding research in second language learning: A teacher's guide to statistics and research design.* Cambridge: Cambridge University Press.

Brown, J. D. (1990). The use of multiple *t*-tests in language research. *TESOL Quarterly, 24*(4), 770–773.

Brown, J. D. (1991a). Statistics as a foreign language: What to look for in reading statistical language studies—Part 1. *TESOL Quarterly, 25*(4), 569–586.

Brown, J. D. (1991b). Do English and ESL instructors rate writing samples differently? *TESOL Quarterly, 25*(4), 587–603.

Brown, J. D. (1992a). What is research? *TESOL Matters, 2*(5), 10.

Brown, J. D. (1992b). Statistics as a foreign language—Part 2: More things to look for in reading statistical language studies. *TESOL Quarterly, 26*(4), 629–664.

Brown, J. D. (1995). Statistics as a foreign language: What to look for in reading statistical language studies. In H. Douglas Brown & S. T. Gonzo (Eds.), *Readings in second language acquisition* (pp. 15–35). Englewood Cliffs, NJ: Prentice Hall. Reprinted and adapted by permission from the original article.

Brown, J. D. (1997a). Designing a language study. In D. Nunan & D. Griffee (Eds.), *Classroom teachers and classroom research* (pp. 109–121). Tokyo: Japan Association for Language Teaching (also available from ERIC: ED 415 696).

Brown, J. D. (1997b). Designing surveys for language programs. In D. Nunan & D. Griffee (Eds.), *Classroom teachers and classroom research* (pp. 55–70). Tokyo: Japan Association for Language Teaching (also available from ERIC: ED 415 700).

Brown, J. D. (1997c). Statistics corner: Questions and answers about language testing statistics: Skewness and kurtosis. *Shiken: JALT Testing & Evaluation SIG Newsletter, 1*(1), 16–18. Also retrieved from the World Wide Web at http://www.jalt.org/test/bro_1.htm.

Brown, J. D. (1997d). Statistics corner: Questions and answers about language testing statistics: Reliability of surveys. *Shiken: JALT Testing & Evaluation SIG Newsletter, 1*(2), 17–19. Also retrieved from the World Wide Web at http://www.jalt.org/test/bro_2.htm.

Brown, J. D. (2000). Statistics corner: Questions and answers about language testing statistics: What issues affect Likert-scale questionnaire formats? *Shiken: JALT Testing & Evaluation SIG Newsletter, 4*(1), 18–21. Also retrieved from the World Wide Web at http://www.jalt.org/test/bro_7.htm.

Brown, J. D. (2001a). *Using surveys in language programs.* Cambridge: Cambridge University Press.

Brown, J. D. (2001b). Statistics corner: Questions and answers about language testing statistics: What is an eigenvalue? *Shiken: JALT Testing & Evaluation SIG Newsletter, 5*(1), 13–16. Retrieved from the World Wide Web at http://www.jalt.org/test/bro_10.htm.

Brown, J. D. (2001c). Statistics corner: Questions and answers about language testing statistics: What is a point-biserial correlation coefficient? *Shiken: JALT Testing & Evaluation SIG Newsletter, 5*(3), 12–15. Also retrieved from the World Wide Web at http://www.jalt.org/test/bro_12.htm.

Brown, J. D. (2002). Statistics corner: Questions and answers about language testing statistics: The Cronbach alpha reliability estimate. *Shiken: JALT Testing & Evaluation SIG Newsletter, 6*(1), 14–16. Also retrieved from the World Wide Web at http://www.jalt.org/test/bro_13.htm.

Brown, J. D. (2003). Statistics corner: Questions and answers about language testing statistics: The coefficient of determination. *Shiken: JALT Testing & Evaluation SIG Newsletter, 7*(1), 14–16. Also retrieved from the World Wide Web at http://www.jalt.org/test/bro_16.htm.

Brown, J. D. (2004a). Research methods for applied linguistics: Scope, characteristics, and standards. In A. Davies & C. Elder (Eds.), *The handbook of applied linguistics* (pp. 476–500). Oxford: Blackwell.

Brown, J. D. (2004b). Resources on quantitative/statistical research for applied linguistics. *Second Language Research, 20*(4), 408–429.

Brown, J. D. (2004c). Statistics corner: Questions and answers about language testing statistics: Yates Correction. *Shiken: JALT Testing & Evaluation SIG Newsletter, 8*(1), 19–22. Also retrieved from the World Wide Web at http://www.jalt.org/test/bro_19.htm.

Brown, J. D. (2005). Statistics corner: Questions and answers about language testing statistics: Characteristics of sound qualitative research. *Shiken: JALT Testing & Evaluation SIG Newsletter, 9*(2), 31–33. Also retrieved from the World Wide Web at http://www.jalt.org/test/bro_22.htm.

Brown, J. D. (2006). Statistics corner: Questions and answers about language testing statistics: Generalizability from second language research samples. *Shiken: JALT Testing & Evaluation SIG Newsletter, 10*(2), 24–27. Also retrieved from the World Wide Web at http://www.jalt.org/test/bro_24.htm.

Brown, J. D. (2007a). Statistics corner: Questions and answers about language testing statistics: Sample size and power. *Shiken: JALT Testing & Evaluation SIG Newsletter, 11*(1), 31–35. Also retrieved from the World Wide Web at http://www.jalt.org/test/bro_25.htm.

Brown, J. D. (2007b). Statistics corner: Questions and answers about language testing statistics: Sample size and statistical precision. *Shiken: JALT Testing & Evaluation SIG Newsletter, 11*(2), 21–24. Also retrieved from the World Wide Web at http://www.jalt.org/test/bro_26.htm.

Brown, J. D. (2008a). Statistics corner: Questions and answers about language testing statistics: The Bonferroni adjustment. *Shiken: JALT Testing & Evaluation SIG Newsletter, 12*(1), 23–28. Also retrieved from the World Wide Web at http://www.jalt.org/test/bro_27.htm.

Brown, J. D. (2008b). Statistics corner: Questions and answers about language testing statistics: Effect size and eta squared. *Shiken: JALT Testing & Evaluation SIG Newsletter, 12*(2), 36–41. Also retrieved from the World Wide Web at http://www.jalt.org/test/bro_28.htm.

Brown, J. D. (2009a). Using open-response questionnaires in qualitative language research. In J. Heigham & R. Croker (Eds.), *Qualitative research in applied linguistics: A practical introduction* (pp. 200–219). Basingstoke: Palgrave Macmillan.

Brown, J. D. (2009b). Statistics corner: Questions and answers about language testing statistics: Principal components analysis and exploratory factor analysis—Definitions, differences, and choices. *Shiken: JALT Testing & Evaluation SIG Newsletter, 13*(1), 26–30. Also retrieved from the World Wide Web at http://www.jalt.org/test/bro_29.htm.

Brown, J. D. (2009c). Statistics corner: Questions and answers about language testing statistics: Choosing the right number of components or factors in PCA and EFA. *Shiken: JALT Testing & Evaluation SIG Newsletter, 13*(2), 19–23. Also retrieved from the World Wide Web at http://www.jalt.org/test/bro_30.htm.

Brown, J. D., & Bailey, K. M. (2008). Language testing courses: What are they in 2007? *Language Testing, 25*(3), 349–383.

Brown, J. D., & Rodgers, T. (2002). *Doing second language research.* Oxford: Oxford University Press.

Burke Johnson, R., Onwuegbuzie, A. J., & Turner, L. A. (2007). Toward a definition of mixed methods research. *Journal of Mixed Methods research, 1*(2), 112–133.

Burns, A. (1999). *Collaborative action research for English language teachers.* Cambridge: Cambridge University Press.

Busch, M. (1993). Using Likert scales: A researcher comments. *TESOL Quarterly, 27*(4), 733–736.

Butler, C. (1985). *Statistics in linguistics.* Oxford: Blackwell.

Byrd, J. K. (2007). A call for statistical reform in EAQ. *Educational Administration Quarterly, 43*(3), 381–391.

Capraro, R. M., & Capraro, M. M. (2002). Treatments of effect sizes and statistical significance tests in textbooks. *Educational and Psychological Measurement, 62*(5), 771–782.

Chalhoub-Deville, M., Chapelle, C., & Duff, P. (Eds.) (2006). *Inference and generalizability in applied linguistics: Multiple perspectives.* Amsterdam: John Benjamins.

Chaudron, C. (1986). The interaction of quantitative and qualitative approaches to research: A view of the second language classroom. *TESOL Quarterly, 20*(4), 709–717.

Chaudron, C. (1988). *Second language classrooms: Research on teaching and learning.* Cambridge: Cambridge University Press.

Chaudron, C. (2000). Contrasting approaches to classroom research: Qualitative and quantitative analysis of language use and learning. *Second Language Studies, 19*(1), 1–56.

Cohen, J. (1988). *Statistical power analysis for the behavioral sciences.* Hillsdale, NJ: Erlbaum.

Cook, V. (Ed.) (1986). *Experimental approaches to second language learning.* Oxford: Pergamon Press.

Cooper, H., Hedges, L. V., & Valentine, J. C. (2009). *The handbook of research synthesis and meta-analysis.* Thousand Oaks, CA: Sage.

Cresswell, J. W. (2009). *Research design: Qualitative, quantitative, and mixed methods approaches.* Thousand Oaks, CA: Sage.

Creswell, J. W., & Plano Clark, V. L. (2007). *Designing and conducting mixed methods research.* Thousand Oaks, CA: Sage.

Crookes, G. (1991). Power, effect size, and second language research: Another researcher comments … *TESOL Quarterly, 25*(4), 762–765.

Davis, K. A. (1992). Validity and reliability in qualitative research on *second language acquisition* and teaching: Another research comments. *TESOL Quarterly, 26*(3), 605–608.

Davis, K. A. (1995). Qualitative theory and methods in applied linguistics research. *TESOL Quarterly, 29*(3), 427–453.

Dörnyei, Z. (2003). *Questionnaires in second language research: Construction, administration, and processing.* Mahwah, NJ: Lawrence Erlbaum Associates.

Dörnyei, Z. (2007). *Research methods in applied linguistics.* Oxford: Oxford University Press.

Duff, P. A. (2008). *Case study research in applied linguistics.* New York: Lawrence Erlbaum Associates.

Dufon, M. (1993). Ethics in TESOL research. *TESOL Quarterly, 27*(1), 157–160.

Ellis, N. (2000). Editor's statement: Statistical reporting of effect sizes. *Language Learning, 50*(1), xi–xii.

Freeman, D. (1998). *Doing teacher research: From inquiry to understanding.* Boston, MA: Heinle & Heinle.

Gass, S., & Mackey, A. (2000). *Stimulated recall methodology in second language research.* Mahwah, NJ: Lawrence Erlbaum Associates.

Gass, S., Sorace, A., & Selinker, L. (1999). *Second language learning data analysis* (2nd ed.). Mahwah, NJ: Lawrence Erlbaum Associates.

Gigerenzer, G., Krauss, S., & Vitouch, O. (2004). The null ritual: What you always wanted to know about significance testing but were afraid to ask. In D. Kaplan (Ed.), *The Sage handbook of quantitative methodology for the social sciences* (pp. 391–408). Thousand Oaks, CA: Sage.

Glass, G. V. (1976). Primary, secondary, and meta-analysis. *Educational Researcher, 5*, 3–8.

Goldschneider, J., & DeKeyser, R. M. (2001). Explaining the "natural order of L2 morpheme acquisition" in English: A meta-analysis of multiple determinants. *Language Learning, 51*, 1–50.

Greene, J. C. (2007). *Mixed methods in social inquiry.* San Francisco: Wiley.

Griffee, D. T., & Nunan, D. (Eds.) (1997). *Classroom teachers and classroom research.* Tokyo: JALT.

Grotjahn, R. (1987). On the methodological basis of introspective methods. In C. Færch & G. Kasper (Eds.), *Introspection in second language research.* Clevedon: Multilingual Matters.

Hamp-Lyons, L. (1989). Recent publications on statistics, language testing and quantitative research methods: I. *TESOL Quarterly, 23*(1), 127–132.

Hamp-Lyons, L. (1990). Recent publications on statistics, language testing and quantitative research methods: II. *TESOL Quarterly, 24*(2), 293–300.

Hartung, J., Knapp, G., & Sinha, B. K. (2008). *Statistical meta-analysis with applications*. San Francisco: Wiley.

Hatch, E., & Farhady, H. (1982). *Research design and statistics for applied linguistics*. Rowley, MA: Newbury House.

Hatch, E., & Lazaraton, A. (1991). *The research manual: Design and statistics for applied linguistics*. Rowley, MA: Newbury House.

Heigham, J., & Croker, R. (Eds.) (2009). *Qualitative research in applied linguistics: A practical introduction*. New York: Palgrave Macmillan.

Hendrik, C. (1991). Replications, strict replications, and conceptual replications: Are they important? In J. W. Neuliep (Ed.), *Replication research in the social sciences* (pp. 41–49). Newbury Park, CA: Sage.

Henning, G. (1986). Quantitative methods in language acquisition research. *TESOL Quarterly, 20*(4), 701–708.

Henson, R. K. (2006). Effect-size measures and meta-analytic thinking in counseling psychology research. *The Counseling Psychologist, 34*(5), 601–629.

Hoenig, J. M., & Heisey, D. M. (2001). The abuse of power: The pervasive fallacy of power calculation for data analysis. *American Statistician, 55*, 19–24.

Hubbard, R., & Armstrong, J. S. (2006). Why we don't really know what statistical significance means: Implications for educators. *Journal of Marketing Education, 28*(2), 114–120.

Huberty, C. J. (2002). A history of effect size indices. *Educational and Psychological Measurement, 62*(2), 227–240.

Jeon, E., & Kaya, T. (2006). Effects of L2 instruction on interlanguage pragmatic development: A meta-analysis. In J. Norris & L. Ortega (Eds.), *Synthesizing research on language learning and teaching* (pp. 165–211). Philadelphia: John Benjamins.

Johnson, D. M. (1992). *Approaches to research in second language learning*. New York: Longman.

Kasper, G., & Dahl, M. (1991) *Research methods in interlanguage pragmatics (NFLRC Technical Report #1)*. Honoluolu, HI: National Foreign Language Resource Center, University of Hawaii Press.

Kimmel, A. J. (1988). *Ethics and values in applied social research*. Newbury Park, CA: Sage.

Kline, R. B. (2004). *Beyond significance testing: Reforming data analysis methods in behavioral research*. Washington, DC: American Psychological Association.

Kulinskaya, E., Morgenthaler, S., & Staudte, R. G. (2008). *Meta analysis: A guide to calibrating and combining statistical evidence*. San Francisco: Wiley.

Language Teaching Review Panel. (2008). Replication studies in language learning and teaching: Questions and answers. *Language Teaching, 41*(1), 1–14.

Language Teaching (2009). Call for papers: Replication research studies. *Language Teaching, 42*(2), i.

Larsen-Freeman, D., & Long, M. H. (1991). *An introduction to second language acquisition research*. London: Longman.

Lazaraton, A. (1991). Power, effect size, and second language research: A researcher comments. *TESOL Quarterly, 25*(4), 759–762.

Lazaraton, A. (1995). Qualitative research in applied linguistics: A progress report. *TESOL Quarterly, 29*, 455–472.

Lazaraton, A. (2000). Current trends in research methodology and statistics in applied linguistics. *TESOL Quarterly, 34*(1), 175–181.

Lazaraton, A. (2005). Quantitative research methods. In E. Hinkel (Ed.), *Handbook of research in second language teaching and learning* (pp. 209–224). New York: Routledge.

Lazaraton, A., Riggenbach, H., & Ediger, A. (1987). Forming a linguists' literacy in research methodology and statistics. *TESOL Quarterly, 21*(2), 263–267.

Littell, J. H., Corcoran, J., & Pillai, V. (2008). *Systematic reviews and meta-analysis*. Oxford: Oxford University Press.

Loewen, S., & Gass, S. (2009). Research timeline: The use of statistics in L2 acquisition research. *Language Teaching, 42*(2), 181–196.

McDonough, J., & McDonough, S. H. (1997). *Research methods for English language teachers*. London: Edward Arnold.

Mackey, A., & Gass, S. (2005). *Second language research: Methodology & design*. Mahwah, NJ: Lawrence Erlbaum Associates.

Mackey, A., & Goo, J. (2007). Interaction research in SLA: A meta-analysis and research synthesis. In A. Mackey (Ed.), *Conversational interaction in second language acquisition: A series of empirical studies* (pp. 407–452). Oxford: Oxford University Press.

Masgoret, A.-M., & Gardner, R. C. (2003). Attitudes, motivation, and second language learning: A meta-analysis of studies conducted by Gardner and associates. *Language Learning, 53*, 123–163.

Mittag, K., & Thompson, B. (2000). A national survey of AERA members' perceptions of statistical significance tests and other statistical issues. *Educational Researcher, 29*(4), 14–20.

Neuliep, J. W. (Ed.) (1991). *Replication research in the social sciences*. Newbury Park, CA: Sage.

Norris, J. M., & Ortega, L. (2000). Effectiveness of L2 instruction: A research synthesis and quantitative meta-analysis. *Language Learning, 50*, 417–528.

Norris, J. M., & Ortega, L. (Eds.) (2006a). *Synthesizing research on language learning and teaching*. Amsterdam: John Benjamins.

Norris, J. M., & Ortega, L. (2006b). The value and practice of research synthesis for language learning and teaching. In J. M. Norris & L. Ortega (Eds.), *Synthesizing research on language learning and teaching* (pp. 3–50). Philadelphia: John Benjamins.

Norris, J. M., & Ortega, L. (2007). The future of research synthesis in applied linguistics: Beyond art or science. *TESOL Quarterly, 41*(4), 805–815.

Nunan, D. (1992). *Research methods in language learning.* Cambridge: Cambridge University Press.

Plano Clark, V. L., & Creswell, J. W. (Eds.) (2008). *The mixed methods reader.* Thousand Oaks, CA: Sage.

Polio, C., & Gass, S. (1997). Replication and reporting: A commentary. *Studies in Second Language Acquisition, 19,* 499–508.

Porte, G. K. (2002). *Appraising research in second language learning: A practical approach to critical analysis of quantitative research.* Amsterdam: John Benjamins.

Richards, K. (2003). *Qualitative inquiry in TESOL.* Basingstoke: Palgrave Macmillan.

Richards, K. (2009). Trends in qualitative research in language teaching since 2000. *Language Teaching, 42*(2), 147–180.

Rietveld, T., & van Hout, R. (1993). *Statistical techniques for the study of language and language behaviour.* Berlin: Mouton de Gruyter.

Rolstad, K., Mahoney, K., & Glass, G. (2005). Weighing the evidence: A meta-analysis of bilingual education in Arizona. *Bilingual Research Journal, 29,* 43–67.

Russell, J., & Spada, N. (2006). The effectiveness of corrective feedback for the acquisition of L2 grammar: A meta-analysis of the research. In J. M. Norris & L. Ortega (Eds.), *Synthesizing research on language learning and teaching* (pp. 133–164). Philadelphia: John Benjamins.

Santos, T. (1989). Replication in applied linguistics research. *TESOL Quarterly, 23*(4), 699–702.

Schachter, J., & Gass, S. (Eds.) (1996). *Second language classroom research: Issues and opportunities.* Mahwah, NJ: Lawrence Erlbaum Associates.

Scholfield, P. (1995). *Quantifying language: A researcher's guide to gathering language data and reducing it to figures.* Clevedon: Multilingual Matters.

Seliger, H. W., & Shohamy, E. (1989). *Second language research methods.* Oxford: Oxford University Press.

Shohamy, E. (2004). Reflections on research guidelines, categories, and responsibility. *TESOL Quarterly, 38*(4), 728–731.

Siegel, A. F. (1990). Multiple *t* tests: Some practical considerations. *TESOL Quarterly, 24*(4), 773–775.

Silver, R. E. (1995). A comparative review: Research methods and approaches. *Linguistics and Education, 7*(3), 263–275.

Smithson, M. (2001). Correct confidence intervals for various regression effect sizes and parameters: The importance of non-central distributions in computing intervals. *Educational and Psychological Measurement, 61*(4), 605–632.

Smithson, M. J. (2004). Confidence intervals. In M. Lewis-Beck, A. Bryman, & T. Futing Liao (Eds.), *Encyclopedia of social science research methods* (pp. 168–169). Belmont, CA: Sage.

Tafaghodtari, M. (2009). Qualitative inquiry: New alternatives for the applied linguist. *Language Teaching, 42*(2), 272–282.

Tarone, E., Gass S., & Cohen, A. D. (Eds.) (1994). *Research methodology in second-language acquisition.* Hillsdale, NJ: Lawrence Erlbaum Associates.

Taylor, A., Stevens, J., & Asher, W. (2006). The effects of explicit reading strategy training on L2 reading comprehension: A meta-analysis. In J. M. Norris & L. Ortega (Eds.), *Synthesizing research on second language learning and teaching* (pp. 3–50). Philadelphia: John Benjamins.

Teddlie, C., & Tashakkori, A. (2009). *Foundations of mixed methods research: Integrating quantitative and qualitative approaches to social and behavioral sciences.* Thousand Oaks, CA: Sage.

TESOL. (2003). Quantitative research guidelines. *TESOL Quarterly, 37*(1), 159–163.

TESOL Research Committee. (1980). Guidelines for ethical research in ESL. *TESOL Quarterly, 14*(3), 383–388.

Thompson, B. (1999). Journal editorial policies regarding statistical significance tests: Heat is to fire as *p* is to importance. *Educational Psychology Review, 11,* 157–169.

Thompson, B. (2002). What future quantitative social science research could look like: Confidence intervals for effect sizes. *Educational Researcher, 31*(3), 25–32.

Thompson, W. L. (2000). *326 articles/books questioning the indiscriminate use of statistical hypothesis tests in observational studies.* Retrieved from the World Wide Web at http://www.cnr.colostate.edu/~anderson/thompson1.html.

Turner, J. (1993). Using Likert scales: Another researcher comments. *TESOL Quarterly, 27*(4), 736–739.

Vacha-Haase, T., Nilsson, J., Reetz, D., Lance, T., & Thompson, B. (2000). Reporting practices and APA editorial policies regarding statistical significance and effect size. *Theory and Psychology, 10,* 413–425.

Valdman, A. (1988). Replication study. *Studies in Second Language Acquisition, 15*(4), 505.

van Lier, L. (1988). *The classroom and the language learner: Ethnography and second language classroom research.* London: Longman.

Verhoeven, L. (1997). Experimental methods in researching language and education. In N. H. Hornberger & C. Corson (Eds.), *Encyclopedia of language and education, Volume 8: Research methods in language and education* (pp. 79–87). Dordrecht: Kluwer Academic.

Wallace, M. J. (1998). *Action research for language teachers.* Cambridge: Cambridge University Press.

Wilkinson, L. & the Task Force on Statistical Inference. (1999). Statistical methods in psychology journals: Guidelines and explanations. *American Psychologist, 54*(8), 594–604.

Woods, A., Fletcher, P., & Hughes, A. (1986). *Statistics in language studies.* Cambridge: Cambridge University Press.

Wray, A., Trott, K., & Bloomer, A. (1998). *Projects in linguistics: A practical guide to researching language.* London: Edward Arnold.

Yaremko, R. M., Harari, H., Harrison, R. C., & Lynn, E. (1988). *Handbook of research and quantitative methods in psychology.* Mahwah, NJ: Lawrence Erlbaum Associates.

Yuan, K.-H., & Maxwell, S. (2005). On post hoc power in testing mean differences. *Journal of Educational and Behavioral Statistics, 30*(2), 141–167.

Ziliak, S., & McCloskey, D. N. (2007). *The cult of statistical significance: How the standard error costs us jobs, justice, and lives (economics, cognition, and society).* Ann Arbor: University of Michigan Press.

13
Case Study

Keith Richards

Introduction

Unusually, I should like to begin with a footnote:

> Wolcott calls his study an ethnography, but it is at the same time a case study, under the definitions discussed in this chapter.

(van Lier, 2005, p. 206)

In doing so, I pick up where van Lier left off in his chapter in the first volume of this book. My contribution will complement rather than build on his excellent overview of the contribution that case studies have made to an understanding of second language acquisition, focusing instead on core methodological challenges in case study research and the distinctive contribution it can make to the broader field of language teaching. I shall get my only quibble out of the way quickly by suggesting at the outset that van Lier's perfectly legitimate footnote reflects a widespread terminological laxity that leaves experienced practitioners unmoved but has for too long been a source of unnecessary confusion on the part of novice researchers. The discussion that follows will use this as a point of departure for addressing what I take to be the most important methodological issues facing case study researchers.

The main thrust of my argument in this chapter is that the nature of case study research throws up distinctive methodological issues and that the key to resolving these lies in preliminary decisions about the nature of the particular case study to be developed. The chapter begins by identifying the essential characteristics of any case study before moving on to consider issues of sample selection, approaches to data collection, analysis and representation, and the generalisation debate. It concludes with an overview of recent research in language teaching and learning and identifies possible lines of development.

The chapter aims to provide a clear statement of what constitutes a case study, a point of methodological orientation for those who wish to undertake case study research, and a practical guide to recent work published in language teaching and learning. It is not designed as a brief general introduction because a number of very good basic guides to case study research are already available (e.g. Baxter & Jack, 2008; Hood, 2009; Yin, 2009), while Duff's outstanding treatment (2008) is an essential resource for anyone with a serious interest in case studies in applied linguistics.

Basic Considerations

The Case Versus the Case Study

The beguiling simplicity of the term "case study" has seduced many a novice researcher. The intellectual heft of labels such as "ethnomethodology" and "phenomenological hermeneutics" serves as a warning against lightweight assumptions: nobody ventures into their territory without taking a deep breath and a dictionary. A "case study", however, offers such comforting familiarity that by the time the novice begins to ask just what it is that *counts* as one, the many lines of response have already tangled themselves into an impossible knot. More than twenty-five different definitions (VanWynsberghe & Khan, 2007, p. 81) may line up impressively on the page of a doctoral thesis, but conceptually they are all of a tangle. And since case study can be understood either as a set of procedures common to different types of research or as a distinct approach in itself (Scott & Usher, 1999, p. 87), the potential for confusion is intimidating.

Before going further, therefore, I should like to propose a crude test for whether something counts as a case study in the sense of this being its primary label rather than some incidental description loosely applied. It is based on the fact that a case study must involve a focus on a unit or units and that these are in some sense fundamental. It should therefore always make sense to ask what the relevant unit is a unit *of*—what is the bigger category to which it belongs? So if this is a case study of an individual learner's development, then this particular learner is seen in some sense as a member (though, as I shall show later, not necessarily representative) of a larger class of learners. The perspective involved is therefore a dual one that seeks to understand the nature of a particular unit both in itself and as a case of something larger.

The distinction between a *case* (a descriptive term that might be applied within any research tradition) and a *case study* (the label for a particular tradition) is both clear and practical, but unfortunately it does not reflect general usage, which tends to be rather lax. Nevertheless, it serves the important purpose of enabling the researcher to make properly informed decisions at the methodological level. It might be essential in an ethnographic project, for example, to establish an *emic* (or insider) perspective, but this is by no means necessary in case study research; and while case studies rarely, if ever, involve intervention in order to bring about change, this is the fundamental requirement of all action research: working within tradition entails a commitment to that tradition's methodological tenets. The fact that there is no core data collection method associated with case study, in the way that observation features in ethnography or the interview in life history, merely reflects the wide range of case study types available to the researcher. These are best approached via a consideration of the defining characteristics of case study research.

Essential Characteristics of a Case Study

"The torment of the case study begins with its definitional penumbra" (Gerring 2007, p. 65). Anyone who has had to wrestle with the challenge of pinning down the essential nature of case studies will have sympathy with Gerring's position: the porous nature of case study research means that it takes on the distinct colouring of the researcher's broader orientation and this makes it difficult to identify commonalities. Nevertheless, these do exist and in what follows I seek to pin them down, ignoring the peripheral problems of "definitional penumbra". Readers seeking more extensive collections of definitions can find these in Bassey (1999, pp. 22–27), VanWynsberghe and Khan (2007, pp. 81–83) or Duff (2008, pp. 21–23).

Case Studies Are Bounded

Nearly all definitions of case studies include a reference to their boundedness, either explicitly or implicitly, and Merriam (1988, p. 9) considers this a "deciding factor". Gerring (2007, p. 33) offers perhaps the most succinct definition: "Case study research, by definition, is focused on a single, relatively bounded unit." From a methodological perspective, it is worth noting that the size of the unit is not at issue. Studies range from of focus on individual teachers or learners to the educational policy of whole countries, while the extent of the data collection involved can be staggering: Yin's chapter on the *Yankee City* study (2004, pp. 33–46) points to interviews with almost an entire community of 17,000 people as well as observations, documentary analysis, etc. Methodological challenges, though, are more likely to arise from contextual issues.

Case Studies Are Contextualised

There are two, interrelated, aspects of context that the case study researcher must address: the *situated context* with which all qualitative researchers must grapple, and what might be called the *axial context* within which a particular case is configured. The first is reflected in definitions of the sort offered by Dyson and Genishi (2005, pp. 119–120): "A case, be it a community, a classroom, or a program, is not a separate entity but a located one, existent in some particular geographic, political, and cultural space and time."

Qualitative researchers are familiar with the demands of working with socially embedded phenomena and the need to relate these interpretively to the broader contexts in which they occur. In this respect, case study is no different from other forms of social research in terms of its methodological and conceptual demands it makes. However, because all case studies are cases *of* something, they imply a different sort of contextualisation, reflected in Walton's definition (1992, p. 121): "An 'instance' is just that and goes no further. A 'case' implies a family; it alleges that the particular is a case of something else. Implicit in the idea of the case is a claim."

The essential issue in what I have termed the axial context is the extent to which a single case can throw light on features of the larger class of cases to which it belongs, and here the main methodological challenge may lie in resisting a natural temptation to appeal to representativeness or typicality. An antidote to this condition is available in the form of Small's systematic demolition of a hypothetical case involving an "average" neighbourhood (2009, pp. 15–18) as part of his paper on the logic of case selection. His essential point is that no "sample" of a single unit can satisfy the criteria for an adequate representative sample, so this is not the way in which researchers should approach case selection. This is consistent with the position of other writers in the field (e.g. Stake, 1995, p. 4; George & Bennett, 2004, pp. 30–31) who deny that sampling or the search for a "representative" case is relevant to case study.

The relationship between a particular case and its larger family need not depend on notions of typicality or representativeness, which may serve only to distract the researcher's attention from more important considerations. Instead, a useful starting point for addressing the issue of case selection is Stake's distinction between *intrinsic* and *instrumental* studies (1995, pp. 3–4). In the former, the starting point is not the need to learn about other cases or particular phenomenon, rather the interest derives from a need to learn about that particular case because it raises questions that need to be answered, represents a troubling conundrum or stands out as distinctly unusual. This is not to say that the findings will not have broader relevance: it is just that the researcher does not choose the case with this in mind and the discussion of case selection will focus on the intrinsic interest of the case. Instrumental case studies, on the other hand, arise because the researcher wishes to understand a broader issue or investigate a particular phenomenon (the case is not the primary focus of interest).

Here, the case will be selected for its value in terms of throwing light on this and the discussion of case selection will be framed in terms of its potential contribution.

In practical terms, there seem to be two overriding considerations in justifying single case selection: the potential explanatory power of the relevant case (Scott & Usher, 1999, p. 86) and the transparency with which the basis for the choice is presented. It is perhaps also worth adding that, as Platt (1988, pp. 13–15) points out, where cases are chosen from within particular settings the reader's trust will derive from evidence of the researcher's familiarity with these.

Cases Are Studied in Their Natural Context

It is a fundamental tenet of case study research that the phenomenon being researched should be studied in its natural context. This straightforward requirement brings with it two important considerations: that the data collection methods chosen should do justice to the richness and complexity of the natural context and that due consideration should be given to ethical issues. The former has received more than adequate attention in the literature and will be considered under the next point, but to my knowledge the latter has been largely neglected, with Duff's well-judged discussion (2008, pp. 144–151) being an admirable exception. Rather than review the ethical landscape here, I should like instead to point to a particular ethical challenge in case study research that, to my knowledge, has not so far been recognised: the elusiveness of anonymity.

Anonymity has long been recognised as problematic in qualitative inquiry (e.g. Nespor, 2000), where richness of description renders the changing of names and places largely redundant, and in his treatment of the topic Walford (2005) advances cogent arguments for rejecting it in certain circumstances. What is most disturbing in Walford's paper is its illustration of how easy it is to identify particular cases, which leads him to the conclusion that "giving anonymity through pseudonyms to sites and people often does not work" (2005, p. 88). Researchers in the field of language education will be only too aware of how small and interconnected this world can seem, and anyone developing the sort of richly detailed description of settings that case study demands should bear in mind that in so doing they may be undermining their participants' rights to privacy. There is no easy solution to this problem but it underlines the need for particular sensitivity to ethical issues and a realistic appraisal of the extent to which anonymity can be promised.

Case Studies Draw on Multiple Data Sources

In order to do justice to the complexity of the natural context, case studies typically draw on multiple data sources. However, the assumption that this implies an exclusively qualitative orientation is misleading, even though many case study researchers seem to take this for granted. Sjoberg, Williams, Vaughan and Sjoberg (1991, p. 6) even go so far as to make qualitative methods effectively a necessary condition for research of this kind, while others simply list data collection methods that are essentially qualitative: Bassey (1999, p. 81), for example, lists asking questions, observing events and reading documents; Yin (1997) lists documentation, archival records, interviews, direct observation, participant observation and physical artefacts as data sources; and Stake (1995) says that he will pay little attention to quantitative case studies.

While qualitative research is particularly well suited to developing the sort of rich description and interpretive penetration that is most suited to bringing a case to life, there is no a priori reason for refusing to consider a quantitative dimension, and as mixed method research gathers strength it is likely that this will feature more and more. In fact, Yin declares in the latest edition of his standard work that one of his aims is to devote greater attention to mixing quantitative and qualitative data (2009, p. x), while Duff (2008, p. 42) explicitly calls for more and better work of this kind in applied linguistics.

Design and Procedure

Types of Case Study

One of the most puzzling aspects for anyone approaching case study research for the first time is the plethora of ways in which the territory has been divided up, and I admit to having no definitive map to offer. Instead, this section sets out to identify those categories that seem to me to be relevant to practical decisions that researchers need to make. To this end I divide relevant categorisations into three types: number of cases, orientation and case type.

Number

The most straightforward distinction is that between the *single case* and the *multiple case*. Procedurally, the distinction is an important one because while the aim of the former is to understand a rare or unique event or reveal something of importance (or, more contentiously, to test theory), multiple-case designs follow a logic of replication where the researcher predicts either similar or contradictory findings (for a summary, see Yin, 2009, pp. 53–59). It is important here to distinguish between individual cases and embedded units. For example, in a study of dropout among beginners involving five schools (each a case), one of the sources of data might be interviews with secretaries (each an embedded unit) about the way in which admissions are handled. The temptation might then be to pool the results of these interviews in order to form a general picture. But this would involve ignoring the local context and failing to interpret the data in terms of each particular school, which is essential in order to make the sort of comparison between cases (schools) that is essential for replication. In fact, any attempt to pool data across embedded units effectively shifts the approach to one in which the separate schools are being treated as embedded units in a single case.

Orientation

The core distinction here is that between *intrinsic* and *instrumental* case study, which was discussed in the previous section.

Type

The third way of thinking about a case study is in terms of its nature, and here three types of study feature prominently in the literature, with most writers drawing on Yin's categorisation: *exploratory*, *descriptive* and *explanatory*. There are other categorisations, but these follow broadly the same lines. Although in his most recent treatment of the subject Yin (2009, pp. 3–23) avoids such a neat labelling, opting for a more nuanced discussion, these terms remain common currency and offer a way of thinking about what a proposed case study is setting out to do.

An *exploratory case study* is designed to define parameters, refine research questions, test procedures, etc. prior to the main study (and hence might be regarded as a form of pilot study), so, although it is a category in its own right, it is perhaps best regarded as a special case. The *descriptive case study* represents a very straightforward approach where the aim is to deliver as complete a description as possible of the relevant phenomenon in its context, while the *explanatory case study* seeks to explain how events happen, often linking cause and effect. Both Merriam (1988) and Bassey (1999), working from an educational perspective, also include the *evaluative case study* in their list and there seems no reason to exclude this. It might be subsumed under explanatory but, as Merriam points out, it includes an element of the descriptive study and the role of the researcher's judgement looms large.

I have excluded the collective case study from this section because it seems to me to be potentially confusing and procedurally unnecessary. It is confusing because it appears very similar to the multiple case study and while some writers (e.g. Hood, 2009) treat these as identical, others (e.g. Hancock & Algozzine, 2006) limit collective case studies to those that contribute to theory. It therefore seems to be procedurally more straightforward to work with the simpler distinctions of intrinsic/instrumental, single/multiple and (exploratory)/descriptive/explanatory/evaluative, which combine to produce a useful (though not rigid) descriptive set.

Procedures

In this section I summarise the stages in case study research, highlighting those features that seem to me to be distinctive. This means that areas common to other forms of research will not receive detailed consideration. The section follows what I take to be standard stages in the design and execution of a research project: planning and design, data collection and analysis.

Planning and Design

The elements in this stage have already been discussed within the context of a broader consideration of the distinctive characteristics of a case study. These can be summarised as follows:

1. Consider the aim of the research and the research question(s) that derive from this. This leads naturally into decisions about the nature of the unit or case to be studied. "No issue", claims Yin (2003, p. 114), "is more important than defining the unit of analysis."
2. Identify the relevant phenomenon (or phenomena) to be studied (the focus of the case) and when developing the study be prepared if necessary to extend the boundaries of the case for the sake of explanatory breadth. The process of deciding the boundaries of the case will involve deciding what will be excluded, in order to ensure that if expansion is necessary it falls within manageable parameters.
3. Consider any theoretical or conceptual dimensions. Some writers (e.g. Hammersley, Gomm & Foster, 2000) emphasise the importance of this in case study research but the depth of engagement will vary from project to project.
4. Decide on the nature of case: Will it be exploratory? Will it be single or multiple, intrinsic or instrumental? Will the focus be broadly descriptive, explanatory or evaluative?
5. Decide why this case or these cases represent(s) an acceptable selection in terms of the aims of the case study. This is not a matter of satisfying statistical requirements, but rather a requirement to consider carefully the characteristics of the case(s) that make it (them) worthy of study. Stake's distinction between intrinsic and instrumental case studies may be helpful here.
6. Pay particular attention to ethical issues, especially those relating to anonymity.
7. Consider not only qualitative approaches, but also the potential of mixed methods.

Data Collection and Analysis

Stake (1995, p. xii) refers to the "palette of methods" employed in case study research, but for those familiar with fieldwork these are unlikely to present new challenges. Data collection methods such as interviews and observation have been well covered in the research literature (for introductions, see Kvale, 2009 for interviews and Emerson, Fretz & Shaw, 2001 for observation), and researchers in applied linguistics are likely to have experience with audio and video recording, though these tend to be neglected as data sources by most writers on case study. Documents and archival records might be less familiar, but Yin (2009, pp. 101–106) provides a very useful brief overview, Hodder (2000) a more detailed introduction, and Prior (2003) an extensive treatment. For projects including both qualitative and quantitative approaches, Dörnyei (2007) offers an outstanding introduction.

Triangulation of data involves drawing together different sources in order to develop a robust "fix" on the case while at the same time allowing for the subtle nuances of interpretation and insight that multiple perspectives can provide (for useful brief introductions, see Duff, 2008, pp. 143–144 and Yin, 2009, pp. 114–118). Rather than elaborate on this, I should like instead to draw attention to three distinctive procedures that ultimately feed into a rich data set and facilitate effective triangulation in case study research, where the quantity and variety of data can easily lead to data overload:

> *Protocol*: All research requires careful planning, but Yin's case study protocol (2009, pp. 79–82) calls for something more: a specification of all the relevant aspects of the project that can then be used to inform other procedures. It provides not just an overview of the project (objectives, issues, etc.) and data collection procedures (sources, contacts, plan, etc.), but also case study questions and a sketch of how the final report might be approached (orientation, format, etc.). This serves not only as a way of checking that all the necessary preparations have been made but also as a map of the research territory to be covered and a reference point for changes of plan, developments, reconfigurations, etc.
>
> *Database*: Yin is categorical in his insistence that the lack of a formal database is a "major shortcoming" of case study research (2009, p. 119) and proposes case study notes (interviews, observations, etc.), documents, tabular materials and narratives as core elements (in the case of language teaching, transcripts should also be added). While all fieldwork relies on a database of some sort, it is perhaps fair to say that particular attention needs to be paid to this in case study research, which lends considerable weight to the argument for using appropriate computer software (e.g. NVivo).
>
> *Journal*: It is generally regarded as good practice to keep a research journal and the incidental benefits of this for the researcher can be considerable (Borg, 2001). However, the more complex the situation and the more likely it is to evolve in terms of extent and focus, the greater the need for the researcher to reflect on the developing process and consider emerging analytical options. Bassey (1999, pp. 70–71), for example, draws particular attention to the need for analytical statements throughout the research process as means of getting to grips with the data.

Good journal-keeping and intelligent use of computer software can take a researcher a long way towards an effective analysis, but the process of developing and organising relevant categories, bringing these to bear on the research questions and making illuminating connections with theory is perhaps the most demanding aspect of qualitative research (see Richards, 2003, pp. 354–373 for a brief overview of considerations, approaches and techniques) and the wide range of options within case study complicates matters further. Yin's observation (2004, p. 205) that a "case study is often the unfolding of events over time, and a detailed chronological rendition can represent a basic analytic strategy" offers a useful option, especially for longitudinal studies; nevertheless, case study analysis generally calls for sensitive and rigorous organisation and interpretation of data in terms of substance, concept and theme in order to capture the complexities of the relevant situation without sacrificing clarity of insight. Any attempt to reduce this to simple formulae would be obstructive and misleading, but taken together Duff (2008, pp. 153–160) and Yin (2009, pp. 127–162) make a powerful combination that does justice to the relevant issues and processes involved.

Representation

The Art of Seeing

There is, I think, something special about the representation of a case study, the essential quality of which is captured in Hancock and Algozzine's insistence that it should be "richly descriptive" (2006, p. 16) and Peattie's (2001) emphasis on density rather than mere "summing up" as a guiding principle. These are more stringent demands than they may seem at first sight and, given the limitations of length imposed by journals or editors, they may represent an ideal. Nevertheless, they are essential points of orientation in the writing up process and Gillham is probably not exaggerating when he claims that the "meticulous description of a case can have an impact greater than almost any other form of research report" (2000, p. 101).

The issue of structure is addressed in the next section, but the test of a good case study lies in its substance. Any case study worth its salt will have generated a considerable data set and the temptation is naturally to capture as much of this as possible. However, representation should not pursue the chimera of completeness, but rather aim for a unified representation of the object of study—which is something very different. As a way of understanding what this involves, I offer the following description of the visual process by a researcher in that area:

> Like the narrowness of our window-on-the-world, the modularity of visual perception is counter-intuitive. We experience our perceptions as single, homogeneous wholes. But, as with much else in perception, this is misleading. Perception is actually a set of distinct, heterogeneous processes, operating in parallel, which are somehow linked together to give an illusion of homogeneity.
>
> (Latto, 1995, p. 80)

As with vision, case study representation is the product of a number of different processes brought together to create the sense of a unified whole. There is no deception in this: just as people depend on the eye to present very selective information about the world that they then experience as complete and whole, so the reader of a case study relies on the writer to select aspects of the relevant case that, taken together, constitute an adequately complete and accessible representation. Like the visual systems, this needs to be "exceptionally well focused" (Latto, 1995, p. 71) in order to provide the reader with adequate access for the purposes of understanding and assessment.

There are no simple recipes for achieving this or for deciding what level of detail is appropriate. However, I would suggest that what might be called *interpretive synecdoche* plays an important part in achieving adequate representation through selective presentation. This involves selecting and presenting in fine detail some part of an embedded unit or feature to stand for the whole. The resulting description then provides the reader not only with an impression of the relevant unit but also with a sense of its significance to the case as a whole. This might involve, for example, presenting a broad picture of the institutional context and then selecting a particular feature (or features) for detailed description in order to convey a sense of the whole. Narrative vignettes illustrating core events or procedures might serve a similar purpose, as would the detailed description of an individual participant as representative of a particular group.

If carefully chosen and effectively delineated, such descriptions can provide a more telling picture than detailed tables or lists and can be deployed as part of a carefully structured report, though the ways in which they are used and the extent to which they feature will depend on the nature of the case.

Issues of Structure

The organisation and writing up of a report will inevitably reflect considerations relating to purpose and audience, and a report for a sponsor seeking practical recommendations and advice will differ significantly from an academic paper addressing theoretical issues or contributing to the ongoing investigation of a particular phenomenon. However, the format will also reflect whether the case is a single case or a multiple case (or part of a larger, mixed methods study) and whether it is essentially exploratory, descriptive or explanatory. Yin, who provides a useful discussion of the implications of these decisions (2009, pp. 170–179), identifies a number of possible structures including linear-analytic, comparative and chronological.

Most writers adopt a similar approach, sometimes suggesting other possibilities. Bassey (1999, pp. 84–90), for example, uses "structured reporting" for Yin's "linear analytic", adding narrative and descriptive as further options, but he also suggests that fictional representations can be very effective as a means of maintaining anonymity while opening up different perspectives. Fictional letters, for example, might represent different viewpoints. While more radical perspectives on case study design have been proposed (see, for example, the approach based on complexity theory offered by Anderson, Crabtree, Steele & McDonald, 2005), most conventional descriptions include a reference to narrative. While all would agree with Flyvbjerg (2006, p. 237) that "[g]ood narratives typically approach the complexities and contradictions of real life", not all would concur that case studies often "contain a substantial element of narrative" or agree with Hood's (2009) claim that a case study can be looked at as a good story. In fact, one of the criteria Yin (2009) uses for categorising approaches to writing case study reports is whether or not they include a narrative element at all. More important is a strong sense of the case itself, a feeling that it has been in some sense *inhabited* by the writer and although narrative might usefully contribute to this end, it is not a necessary element.

Making Claims

Unless a case study is *purely* descriptive (in which case there is an implicit claim to authenticity), it will include claims that might range from practical recommendations to the refinement of theory. While the link between evidence and claim remains fundamental, the way that this is articulated will depend to a considerable extent on the writer's paradigmatic orientation. The debate among proponents of "positivist" and "interpretive" perspectives has a long history and seems thankfully to be quietly slipping into the background as more pragmatic perspectives gain ground (Bryman, 2006), but anyone wanting a sense of how this bears on case study will find Duff's brief overview (2008, pp. 175–179) very accessible. More problematic, for novice researchers at least, is the issue of generalisability.

The roots of this go back to early challenges to claims made on the basis of a single case and, though these rightly belong in the past, they cast a long shadow: "[T]he most frequently cited shortcoming of all is the case study's presumed lack of generalisability. It is this vexing issue that perpetually hovers, like an ominous cloud over any case study" (Snow & Anderson, 1991, p. 164).

Part of the problem may arise from the different attempts that have been made to substitute something else in place of generalisability, which have served only to muddy the waters. Responses tend to fall into three groups: those that attempt to reconceptualise generalisation, such as Stake's "naturalistic generalisation" (2000, p. 22), Bassey's case for "fuzzy generalisation" (1999, pp. 51–54) or Flyvbjerg's argument for falsification (2006, pp. 225–226); those that insist that connection with theory is what broadens the relevance of case studies (e.g. Yin, 1997, p. 239); and those based on the idea that "[t]he real business of case study is particularisation, not generalisation" (Stake, 1995, p. 8). However, despite these and numerous efforts to come to grips with the underlying issues (e.g. Donmoyer, 1990), attempts to reformulate the concept of generalisation in a way that will work for case studies have not found general favour (see Gomm, Hammersley & Foster, 2000). It is therefore hard to avoid the conclusion reached by Khan and Wynsberghe (2008, p. 25): "It is far easier, and more epistemologically sound, simply to give up on the idea of generalisation."

Instead of seeking to justify outcomes of case study in terms of whether they can be generalised, it is probably more productive to examine the relevant case as carefully as possible in order to decide what sort of contribution it might make to understanding and how this might best be represented. Rather than seeking to work within an inappropriate trajectory from "representative sample" to "generalisable findings", it is more productive to think in terms of using "strategic selection" of a case to generate "illustrative outcomes" that draw strength from the rich particularity of individual cases. The impact of such outcomes might then be felt in the strength of their resonance with other researchers or professionals, the success of the practical recommendations they make, or the nature of their contribution to the development of theory.

Illustrative Examples

Some Examples of Case Studies

The riches available the field of language teaching and learning are striking in their variety, ranging in scope from studies of single teachers (Assaf, 2008) or lessons (Akcan, 2005) to a whole country (Baker, 2008) and in focus from a single phenomenon (Basturkmen, Loewen & Ellis, 2004) to the complexities of identity construction (Her, 2005). However, even the most modest overview must overcome the challenge of deciding what is to count as a case study.

A characteristic shared by the terms "ethnography" and "case study" is that researchers make remarkably free with their use, so that the appearance of "case study" in a title is no guarantee that what follows will manifest any of the definitional features identified above. For example, it is very hard to see how genre analysis of reports (Hyon, 2008) or discourse analysis of emails (Jensen, 2009) can count as case studies, or how 558 students drawn from eleven Japanese universities with only the learning of English in common can represent a case (McKenzie, 2008). By contrast, although Haworth (2008) does not describe her study of eight teachers at four primary schools as a case study, it meets all the relevant criteria.

There are also borderline cases where the decision is more difficult. Gan's (2009) study of the impact of preparing for the IELTS test, which draws on the experiences of 146 students from twenty-three programmes, seems to fall into the same category as McKenzie's project, but these are drawn from a single institution and only the lack of a strong sense of context and a failure to use the interview data collected make the author's use of the term "case study" problematic. Chen's (2008) paper could easily count as a case study, but the author does not describe it as such and it lacks a strong sense of local or personal context, so I have excluded it. Some papers in the selection that follows might therefore be open to challenge, but I think the set as a whole is defensible. I have chosen my examples with an eye to methodological issues, with a view to representing the variety of what is available and in the hope of conveying a sense of what is distinctive about case study research. In addition, these are all papers that I have found stimulating, revelatory or provocative in some way.

Studies of teacher identity have proved invaluable in revealing hidden tensions and contradictions in professional activity. Haworth's (2008) examination of contextual tensions that emerge where class teachers encounter English as an additional language students is an excellent example of this, as is Assaf's (2008) richly contextualised study of a single teacher trying to resolve tensions between her beliefs about the importance of nurturing "real readers" and the need for her English language learners to pass tests required by the local school district.

Case studies of teacher identity have also opened up new perspectives on the profession itself. Menard-Warwick's (2008) study of the bicultural identity of two transnational teachers, for example, problematises traditional categorisations and suggests new areas for research, while Zheng and Adamson's (2003) impressively revealing study of a single "traditional" Chinese teacher not only challenges current stereotypes but also adds weight to Flyvbjerg's (2006) claim for the value of case study as falsification. Similarly, Bruna, Vann and Escudero's (2007) use of a combination interviews and analysis of classroom discourse to explore pedagogic tensions between language and content teaching within a single teacher's class is a good illustration of how case study can connect with theory.

Whether studies of individuals based only on interviews count as case studies is debatable and such work could categorised as life histories or narrative studies, but it would be a pity to exclude it on that basis. One consequence would be to miss the invaluable contributions to an understanding of teachers' lives and professional experience made by researchers such as Tsui (e.g. 2007) or Hayes (e.g. 2008, 2009). It would also exclude work such as Chik's revealing study of bilingual identity formation in students returning to Hong Kong (2008) and perhaps any case study based entirely on interviews, such as Burden's (2009) investigation of teacher perspectives on end-of-course teacher evaluation.

From a more methodologically mainstream perspective, the relationship between case and phenomenon is well illustrated in studies that relate classroom features to teacher beliefs. Basturkmen et al.'s (2004) case study of three teachers in New Zealand, comparing focus on form in the classroom with their stated beliefs, draws on a range of data collection methods and offers an excellent example of how quantitative and qualitative data can be integrated to powerful effect, while Farrell and Lim (2005) employ a more limited range of qualitative methods to compare the beliefs and practices relating to grammar teaching of two primary school teachers in Singapore. Some studies focus on teacher beliefs more generally, and Zeng and Murphy's (2007) study of the beliefs of six overseas English as a foreign language (EFL) teachers in China is particularly interesting for its use of cross-case analysis.

It is also interesting to compare how the same classroom activity can be approached in very different ways. Akcan's (2005) treatment of a read aloud activity in terms of how this can support oral second language use takes the reader through a typical day, describing the reading aloud phase of a lesson in detail, with transcripts of lesson exchanges interspersed with comments from interviews. Torres-Guzman, Kumar and Eng (2009), however, base their analysis primarily on transcripts of classroom interaction.

Other areas of particular interest include studies of student experiences, which seem to be increasing in range and depth. Lamb's (2007) mixed method study of motivation among Indonesian adolescents, for example, covers a period of twenty months and includes some excellent learner vignettes, while Payne's (2007) study of pupil voice in foreign-language planning suggests interesting possibilities. Case study research into aspects teacher development also continues to broaden out, embracing teacher research (Jones, 2004), support in teaching practice (Farrell, 2008), teacher study groups (Huang, 2007) and curriculum development (Sharkey, 2004). Finally, an unexpected area where case studies are making a contribution is computer-mediated communication (CMC). The range of possible approaches here is evident in a comparison of Shamsudin and Nesi (2006) with Shin (2006), the latter more ethnographic and descriptive in approach, the former interventionist in orientation.

Looking Forward

A constant challenge in writing up case studies is how evidence is to be deployed and which aspects are to be foregrounded. In her 2004 paper, for example, Jackson uses student diaries and interviews to good effect, while in a later paper, drawing on quantitative data, she admits that "only a small sample of the qualitative data can be provided" (2008, p. 352). In both cases the research is described as ethnographic, but this is reflected more fully in the earlier paper. Similarly, while Her (2005) uses ethnographic methods to collect data, her presentation benefits from a decision to focus on narrative elements to explore the nature of identity construction, and Menard-Warwick's (2008) selection of two from a group of eight participants allows her to present these cases in greater depth and detail than would otherwise have been possible. More generally, anyone seeking a model of how data from a wide range of sources can be integrated and deployed to excellent effect will find Hyland (2000) or Sharkey (2004) invaluable.

Despite many examples of good practice, there is still a tendency to sacrifice discussion of methodological issues to extended literature reviews and/or discussion sections. If Gerring is right to claim that case study "survives in a curious methodological limbo" (2007, p. 7), this merely underlines the need to give serious attention to developing a clear picture of the approach used, couched in terms of core case study issues. Discussions of research methodology amounting to little more than a lightly sketched paragraph (e.g. Jones, 2004) are clearly inadequate, and it is surprising how often no discussion of case selection is offered. Wall is a notable exception and her deliberate choice of a non-representative case, a "best-case scenario" (2008, p. 61), is a shining example of thinking from the perspective of the case rather than employing more abstract sampling notions.

While there is no easy solution to the challenges of representing an extensive data set, there are signs that developments in multimedia may offer a way forward. Nearly thirty years ago Stenhouse (1980) proposed the establishment of a national archive of case studies and his call is picked up by Walker (2002) in a thought-provoking discussion of case records and multimedia. The potential of the internet as a repository for case study reports has also been recognised (e.g. Bassey, 1999, pp. 54–55) and the online database ("4C") described by Khan and VanWynsberghe (2008) provides a valuable resource (with an associated online tutorial) for researchers wishing to perform cross-case analysis.

The growth of the technological dimension in case study research can be confidently predicted, as can the continued expansion of areas in language teaching where case study research is applied, but methodological innovation is a different matter. There is little evidence, for example, that the lead given by Kennedy (2000) in the use of autoethnography has been taken up. However, it is likely that that mixed methods approaches will grow in prominence and experimentation with multiple researcher perspectives seems to be opening up interesting possibilities, exemplified in Lazaraton and Ishihara's (2005) collaborative case study and the "three-take approach" in Barnard and Torres-Guzman's collection (2009).

Conclusion

"Case study" is not a convenient umbrella term for eclectic approaches that fail to fit neatly into any other research tradition, it is a distinctive form of inquiry that "remains one of the most challenging of all social science endeavours" (Yin, 2009, p. 1). This consideration, and the methodological rigour it implies, should underlie any approach to case study, however modest.

Working from the assumption that the criteria for sound research of whatever kind have already been met, I should like to highlight three impressions that good quality case study research conveys to its readers. The first is a sense that the case itself has been *inhabited* by the writer. By this I mean that there is evidence that the writer has engaged with the nature of the case itself and its boundaries, showing an understanding of, and sensitivity to, the relevant context. The second impression is that the writer has given careful thought to how the case can best be *represented* to the reader, which implies that careful thought has been given to the selection, display and integration of examples from the data set. Finally, it must be clear how the case is *connected* to wider issues, whether as an intrinsically interesting example of a larger set, as the basis for practical recommendations or in terms of its contribution to the development of theory.

These are not formulae for constructing successful case studies but reflections of the intensive engagement that characterises serious case study research. Ultimately questions of definition, which is where this chapter began, transmute into more serious concerns about the nature of a particular case, and it is this sense of significant particularity that makes case study research uniquely powerful.

Acknowledgements

I should like to thank Xiaozhou Zhou and Hugo Santiago Sanchez for their very careful and helpful reading of the draft of this chapter.

References

Akcan, S. (2005). Supporting oral second language use: A learning experience in a first grade German immersion class. *Early Childhood Education Journal*, *32*(6), 359–364.

Anderson, R. A., Crabtree, B. F., Steele, D. J. & McDonald Jr, R. R. (2005). Case study research: The view from complexity science. *Qualitative Health Research*, *15*(5), 669–685.

Assaf, L. C. (2008). Professional identity of a reading teacher: responding to high-stakes testing pressures. *Teachers and Teaching: Theory and Practice*, *14*(3), 239–252.

Barnard, R., & Torres-Guzman, M. E. (Eds.) (2009). *Creating classroom communities of learning: International case studies and perspectives*. Bristol: Multilingual Matters.

Baker, W. (2008). A critical examination of ELT in Thailand: The role of cultural awareness. *RELC Journal*, *39*(1), 131–146.

Bassey, M. (1999). *Case study research in educational settings*. Buckingham: Open University Press.

Basturkmen, H., Loewen, S., & Ellis, R. (2004). Teachers' stated beliefs about incidental focus on form and their classroom practices. *Applied Linguistics*, *25*(2), 243–272.

Baxter, P., & Jack, S. (2008). Qualitative case study methodology: Study design and implementation for novice researchers. *The Qualitative Review*, *13*(4), 544–559. Available at http://www.nova.edu/ssss/QR/QR13-4/baxter.pdf (accessed 5 April 2009).

Borg, S. (2001). The research journal: A tool for promoting and understanding researcher development. *Language Teaching Research*, *5*(2), 156–177.

Bruna, K. R., Vann, R., & Escudero, M. P. (2007). What's language got to do with it?: A case study of academic language instruction in a high school "English Learner Science" class. *Journal of English for Academic Purposes*, *6*(1), 36–54.

Bryman, A. (2006). Paradigm peace and the implications for quality. *International Journal of Social Research Methodology*, *9*(2), 111–126.

Burden, P. (2009). A case study into teacher perceptions of the introduction of student evaluation of teaching surveys (SETs) in Japanese tertiary education. *Asian EFL Journal*, *11*(1), 126–149. Available at http://www.asian-efl-journal.com/March_09_pb.php (accessed 7 April 2009).

Chen, Y.-M. (2008). Learning to self-assess oral performance in English: A longitudinal case study. *Language Teaching Research*, *12*(2), 235–262.

Chik, A. (2008). Native English-speaking students in Hong Kong EFL classrooms: A case study. *Innovation in Language Learning and Teaching*, *2*(1), 18–32.

Donmoyer, R. (1990). Generalisability and the single-case study. In E. W. Eisner & A. Peshkin (Eds.), *Qualitative inquiry in education: The continuing debate* (pp. 175–200). New York: Teachers College Press.

Dörnyei, Z. (2007). *Research methods in applied linguistics*. Oxford: Oxford University Press.

Duff, P. A. (2008). *Case study research in applied linguistics*. New York: Lawrence Erlbaum.

Dyson, A. H., & Genishi, C. (2005). *On the case: Approaches to language and literacy research*. New York: Teachers College Press.

Emerson, R. M., Fretz, R. I., & Shaw, L. L. (2001). Participant observation and fieldnotes. In P. A. Atkinson, A. J. Coffee, S. Delamont, J. Lofland & L. H. Lofland (Eds.), *Handbook of ethnography* (pp. 352–368). London: Sage.

Farrell, T. S. C. (2008). "Here's the book, go teach the class": ELT practicum support. *RELC Journal*, *39*(2), 226–241.

Farrell, T. S. C., & Lim, P. C. P. (2005). Conceptions of grammar teaching: a case study of teachers' beliefs and classroom practice. *TESL-EJ*, *9*(2). Available at http://tesl-ej.org/ej34/a9.pdf (accessed 6 April 2009).

Flyvbjerg, B. (2006). Five misunderstandings about case-study research. *Qualitative Inquiry*, *12*(2), 219–245.

Gan, Z. (2009). IELTS preparation course and student IELTS performance: A case study in Hong Kong. *RELC Journal*, *40*(1), 23–41.

George, A. L., & Bennett, A. (2004). *Case studies and theory development in the social sciences*. Cambridge, MA: MIT Press.

Gerring, J. (2007). *Case study research: Principles and practices*. Cambridge: Cambridge University Press.

Gillham, B. (2000). *Case study research methods*. London: Continuum.

Gomm, R., Hammersley, M. & Foster, P. (2000). Case study and generalisation. In R. Gomm, M. Hammersley & P. Foster (Eds.), *Case study methods: Key issues, key texts* (pp. 98–115). London: Sage.

Hammersley, M., Gomm, R. & Foster, P. (2000). Case study and theory. In R. Gomm, M. Hammersley & P. Foster (Eds.), *Case study methods: Key issues, key texts* (pp. 234–258). London: Sage.

Hancock, D. R., & Algozzine, B. (2006). *Doing case study research: A practical guide for beginning researchers*. New York: Teachers College Press.

Haworth, P. (2008). Crossing borders to teach English language learners. *Teachers and Teaching: theory and practice*, 14(5–6), 411–430.

Hayes, D. (2008). Becoming a teacher of English in Thailand. *Language Teaching Research*, 12(4), 471–494.

Hayes, D. (2009). Learning language, learning teaching: Episodes from the life of a teacher of English in Thailand. *RELC Journal*, 40(1), 83–101.

Her, Y. (2005). Identity construction in literacy practices in L2: A case study of three Korean graduate students in a TESOL programme. *Second Language Studies*, 23(2), 102–137.

Hodder, I. (2000). The interpretation of documents and material culture. In N. K. Denzin & Y. S. Lincoln (Eds.), *Handbook of qualitative research* (pp. 703–715). Thousand Oaks, CA: Sage.

Hood, M. (2009). Case studies. In J. Heigham & R. A. Croker (Eds.), *Qualitative research in applied linguistics* (pp. 66–90). Basingstoke: Palgrave Macmillan.

Huang, Y.-C. (2007). How teachers develop their professional knowledge in English study group [*sic*] in Taiwan. *Educational Research and Review*, 2(3), 36–45. Available at http://www.academicjournals.org/ERR/PDF/pdf%202007/Mar/Huang.pdf (accessed 9 April 2009).

Hyland, F. (2000). ESL writers and feedback: Giving more autonomy to students. *Language Teaching Research*, 4(1), 33–54.

Hyon, S. (2008). Convention and inventiveness in an occluded academic genre: A case study of retention–promotion–tenure reports. *English for Specific Purposes*, 27(2), 175–192.

Jackson, J. (2004). Language and cultural immersion: An ethnographic case study. *RELC Journal*, 35(3), 261–279.

Jackson, J. (2008). Globalisation, internationalisation, and short-term stays abroad. *International Journal of Intercultural Relations*, 32(4), 349–358.

Jensen, A. (2009). Discourse strategies in professional e-mail negotiation: A case study. *English for Specific Purposes*, 28(1), 4–18.

Jones, J. F. (2004). The many benefits of a research component in English language teacher education: A case study. *Prospect*, 19(2), 25–38.

Kennedy, M. M. (2000) Learning to teach in a different culture. *Teachers and Teaching: theory and practice*, 6(1), 75–100.

Khan, S., & VanWynsberghe, R. (2008). Cultivating the under-mined: Cross-case analysis as knowledge mobilization. *Forum: Qualitative Social Research*, 9(1), Art. 34. Available at http://www.qualitative-research.net/index.php/fqs/article/view/334/730 (accessed 12 May 2009).

Kvale, S. (2009). *InterViews: Learning the craft of qualitative research interviewing* (2nd ed.). Thousand Oaks, CA: Sage.

Lamb, M. (2007). The impact of school on EFL learning motivation: An Indonesian case study. *TESOL Quarterly*, 41(4), 757–780.

Latto, R. (1995). The brain of the beholder. In R. Gregory, J. Harris, P. Heard & D. Rose (Eds.), *The artful eye* (pp. 66–94). Oxford: Oxford University Press.

Lazaraton, A., & Ishihara, N. (2005). Understanding second language teacher practice using microanalysis and self-reflection: A collaborative case study. *The Modern Language Journal*, 89(4), 529–542.

Lier, L. van (2005). Case study. In E. Hinkel (Ed.), *Handbook of research in second language teaching and learning* (pp. 195–208). Mahwah, NJ: Lawrence Erlbaum.

McKenzie, R. M. (2008). Social factors and non-native attitudes towards varieties of spoken English: A Japanese case study. *International Journal of Applied Linguistics*, 16(1), 63–88.

Merriam, S. B. (1988). *Case study research in education: A qualitative approach*. San Francisco, CA: Josey-Bass.

Menard-Warwick, J. (2008). The cultural and intercultural identities of transnational English teachers: Two case studies from the Americas. *TESOL Quarterly*, 42(4), 617–640.

Nespor, J. (2000). Anonymity and place in qualitative inquiry. *Qualitative Inquiry*, 6(4), 546–69.

Payne, M. (2007). Foreign language planning: Pupil choice and pupil voice. *Cambridge Journal of Education*, 37(1), 89–109.

Peattie, L. (2001). Theorizing planning: Some comments on Flyvbjerg's *Rationality and Power*. *International Planning Studies*, 6(3), 257–262.

Platt, J. (1988). What can case studies do? *Studies in Qualitative Methodology*, 1, 1–23.

Prior, L. (2003). *Using documents in social research*. London: Sage.

Richards, K. (2003). *Qualitative inquiry in TESOL*. Basingstoke: Palgrave Macmillan.

Scott, D., & Usher, R. (1999). *Researching education: Data, methods and theory in educational enquiry*. London: Continuum.

Shamsudin, S., & Nesi, H. (2006). Computer-mediated communication in English for Specific Purposes: A case study with computer science students at Universiti Teknologi Malaysia. *Computer Assisted Language Learning, 19*(4–5), 317–339.

Sharkey, J. (2004). ESOL teachers' knowledge of context as critical mediator in curriculum development. *TESOL Quarterly, 38*(2), 279–299.

Shin, D.-S. (2006). ESL students' computer-mediated communication practices: Context configuration. *Language Learning and Technology, 10*(3), 65–84. Available at http://llt.msu.edu/vol10num3/pdf/shin.pdf (accessed 26 July 2009).

Sjoberg, G., Williams, N., Vaughan, T. R. & Sjoberg, A. F. (1991). The case study approach in social research: Basic methodological issues. In J. R. Feagin, A. M. Orum & G. Sjoberg (Eds.), *A case for the case study* (pp. 27–79). Chapel Hill, NC: University of North Carolina Press.

Small, M. L. (2009). How many cases do I need? On science and the logic of case selection in field-based research. *Ethnography, 10*(1), 5–38.

Snow, D. A., & Anderson, L. (1991). Researching the homeless: The characteristic features and virtues of the case study. In J. R. Feagin, A. M. Orum & G. Sjoberg (Eds.), *A case for the case study* (pp. 148–173). Chapel Hill, NC: University of North Carolina Press.

Stake, R. E. (1995). *The art of case study research.* Thousand Oaks, CA: Sage.

Stake, R. E. (2000). The case study method in social inquiry. In R. Gomm, M. Hammersley & P. Foster (Eds.), *Case study methods: Key issues, key texts* (pp. 19–26). London: Sage.

Stenhouse, L. (1980). The study of samples and the study of cases. *British Educational Research Journal, 6*(1), 1–6.

Torres-Guzman, M. E., Kumar, V. & Eng, W. B. (2009). Negotiating appropriateness in the second language within a dual language education classroom setting. In R. Barnard & M. E. Torres-Guzman (Eds.), *Creating classroom communities of learning: International case studies and perspectives* (pp. 70–87). Bristol: Multilingual Matters.

Tsui, A. B. M. (2007). Complexities of identity formation: A narrative inquiry of an EFL teacher. *TESOL Quarterly, 41*(4), 657–680.

VanWynsberghe, R., & Khan, S. (2007). Redefining case study. *International Journal of Qualitative Methods, 6*(2), 80–94. Available at http://ejournals.library.ualberta.ca/index.php/IJQM/article/view/542/2495 (accessed 26 July 2009).

Walford, G. (2005). Research ethical guidelines and anonymity. *International Journal of Research & Method in Education, 28*(1), 83–93.

Walker, R. (2002). Case study, case records and multimedia. *Cambridge Journal of Education, 32*(1), 109–127.

Wall, U. (2008). A needs assessment interview: The professional development needs of non-native speaking EFL teachers in Thailand. *Innovation in Language Learning and Teaching, 2*(1), 47–64.

Walton, J. (1992). Making the theoretical case. In C. C. Ragin & H. S. Becker (Eds.), *What is a case? Exploring the foundations of social inquiry* (pp. 121–137). Cambridge: Cambridge University Press.

Yin, R. K. (1997). The abridged version of case study research: Design and method. In L. Bickman & D. J. Rog (Eds.), *Handbook of applied social research methods* (pp. 229–259). Thousand Oaks, CA: Sage.

Yin, R. K (2003). *Applications of case study research* (2nd ed.). Thousand Oaks: Sage.

Yin, R. K. (2004). *The case study anthology.* Thousand Oaks, CA: Sage.

Yin, R. K. (2009). *Case study research: Design and methods* (4th ed.). Thousand Oaks, CA: Sage.

Zeng, Z., & Murphy, E. (2007). Tensions in the language learning experiences and beliefs of Chinese teachers of English as a Foreign Language. *TESL-EJ, 10*(4). Available at http://tesl-ej.org/ej40/a1.pdf (accessed 6 April 2009).

Zheng, X., & Adamson, B. (2003). The pedagogy of a secondary school teacher of English in the People's Republic of China: Challenging the stereotypes. *RELC Journal, 34*(3), 323–337.

14
Shifting Sands
The Evolving Story of "Voice" in Qualitative Research

David Nunan and Julie Choi

We are in a new age where messy, uncertain, multivoiced texts, cultural criticism, and new experimental works will become more common, as will more reflexive forms of fieldwork, analysis, and intertextual representation … It is true that, as the poet said, the center no longer holds. We can reflect on what should be at the new center. Thus we have come full circle.

(Denzin & Lincoln, 2005, p. 26)

Introduction

In her chapter on ethnography in the *Handbook of Research in Second Language Teaching and Learning*, Harklau (2005) wrote: "[T]here is an ongoing tension in the second language research community between codifying what constitutes 'good' ethnography and yet honoring diverse scholarly traditions and perspectives" (p. 187). In this contribution, we would like to take Harklau's quote as the point of departure for summarizing the story of qualitative research in second language learning and teaching as it has evolved over the last 40 years. There are many similar reviews out there in the academic marketplace. What we hope in this piece is to give it a slightly different stamp by foregrounding the construct of "voice" in the representation of scholarly work.

By "voice" we are referring to the centrality of the human story to qualitative research in terms of *what* the story is and *how* the story is told. "Traditional" research admitted a limited number of voices. Typically, the researcher was an invisible "I". In this piece we shall explore some of the ways in which making the "I" visible, that is, part of the research story, challenged and transformed not only the nature of the research report, but the ways in which research can be defined.

In a recent review of the harrowing film *United 93*, a narrative reconstruction of the hijacking and subsequent destruction of United Airlines flight 93 on September 11, 2001, the author Garner (2006) writes:

I have a rule of thumb for judging the value of a piece of art. Does it give me energy, or take energy away. When I staggered out of *United 93*, this rule had lost traction. I realised I had spent most of the screening crouching forward half out of my seat, with my hand clamped around my jaw. Something in me had been violently shifted off centre. … I'm [left with] the same old haunting question: why do stories matter so terribly to us that we will offer ourselves up to, and later be grateful for an experience that we know is going to fill us with grief and despair?

The argument we present in this chapter is that voice has been relatively underrepresented in the qualitative research literature, but is now coming into focus.

In his book on educational research, which is tellingly entitled *The Educational Imagination*, Eisner (1985a, pp. 32–40) identifies six characteristics of qualitative research. These are that it is (1) field-focused, (2) constructed so that the researcher is an instrument, (3) interpretive in nature, (4) expressive in language, (5) highly detailed and (6) persuasive. We will go into the nature of qualitative research in greater detail in the body of this chapter. However, we would like to draw attention to this list at the outset of the chapter. We particularly like Eisner's argument that qualitative research is, or should be expressive, detailed and persuasive; characteristics that are a direct slap in the face to adherents of the psycho-statistical paradigm with their claims to objectivity. (The psycho-statistical paradigm sets out to establish generalizable relationships between variables through formal experimentation.) Eisner's list also speaks to the importance of ethics in research.

Before dealing directly with the issues of voice foregrounded above, we need to sketch in the trends that led to the emergence of voice, and that, in fact, made this emergence possible. We do this in the next section by summarizing historical phases in the evolution of qualitative research.

Historical Phases in Qualitative Research

In their introduction to the discipline and practice of qualitative research, Denzin and Lincoln (2005, p. 3) describe eight historical moments. They characterize these as follows:

> [T]he *traditional* (1900–1950); the *modernist*, or golden age (1950–1970); *blurred genres* (1970–1986); *crisis of representation* (1986–1990); the *postmodern*, a period of experimental and new ethnographies (1990–1995); *postexperimental inquiry* (1995–2000); the *methodologically contested present* (2000–2004); and the *fractured future*, which is now (2005–). The future, the eighth moment, confronts the methodological backlash associated with the evidence-based social movement.

In this section, we borrow this notion of historical moments to trace the emergence of voice and to set it within the context of the qualitative paradigm.

The 1960s–1970s

The battle for qualitative research to be legitimized in educational research came into focus in the 1960s and 1970s, a time when quantitative research dominated the agenda. If qualitative research were accorded a role at all, it was as a ground clearing operation, a precursor to more "hard-nosed" rigorous experimental studies. As Denzin and Lincoln (2005) note, "the positivist and postpositivist traditions linger like long shadows over the qualitative research project. Historically, qualitative research was defined within the postpositivist paradigm, where qualitative researchers attempted to do good positivist research with less rigorous methods and procedures" (p. 11).

In language education, several expensive, large-scale experimental studies were carried out to investigate the efficacy of different kinds of instructional methods. These studies were inconclusive, which led to considerable dissatisfaction with the psycho-statistical paradigm in its "pure" form (Scherer & Wertheimer, 1984). Critics pointed out that the work was what they called "black box" research, because the researchers never actually looked inside the classroom for qualitative data on what was actually going on. When they added a qualitative observational dimension to their experimental investigation into the relative merits of cognitive code learning versus audiolingualism, they discovered that their (and presumably other) studies was inconclusive, because at the level of classroom action, teaching practices were indistinguishable across treatment sites.

At the same time, in the United Kingdom, battle lines were being drawn between experimental scientists and a group of educational researchers who were beginning to explore an alternative paradigm predicated on a search for insight rather than truth. Employing methods such as illuminative evaluation and action research, they questioned what they called the "agricultural-botanical" model of research that saw human beings as little more than botanical specimens to be manipulated and experimented upon in the same way as botanists experiment on strains of wheat (see, for example, Stenhouse, 1983).

Experimental researchers countered by pointing out the vulnerability of qualitative research when it came to validity and reliability. How, they asked, could descriptive and interpretive studies carried out in particularized contexts possibly guard against threats to internal validity? How could the results possibly be generalizable? Furthermore,

> Because of the quantity of data yielded in these studies, it is impossible to include anything but a small amount of the data in a published account of the research. This makes it difficult for outsiders to analyze the data themselves (and thereby establish the internal reliability of the study) or to replicate the study (thereby establishing its external reliability).
>
> (Nunan, 1992, p. 58)

An additional, but related point is made by Benson, Chik, Gao, Huang and Wang, (2009, p. 86). In a survey of qualitative research published over the last ten years, they found that certain types of data were privileged over other types. While multiple methods might have been used, it were the "hard", "quotable" data that tended to be privileged at the expense of more "subjective" data such as observational field notes.

These criticisms led to a certain amount of defensiveness. LeCompte and Goetz (1982) produced a detailed and considered analysis of issues of reliability and validity in qualitative research. They admit that, given the contextualized nature of the research, it may, in comparison with laboratory experiments, "baffle attempts at replication". However, external reliability can be strengthened if the researcher is explicit about five key aspects of the research: the status of the researcher within the research process, the choice of informants, the social situations and conditions, the analytic constructs and premises, and the methods of data collection and analysis.

Having dealt with reliability, LeCompte and Goetz turn to the issue of validity. Internal validity has to do with the extent to which researchers are actually measuring what they purport to be measuring, while external validity has to do with generalizability. Formal experiments are explicitly designed to deal with threats to validity and reliability. Tightly controlling the conditions under which the experiment takes place increases the confidence with which researchers can claim that it is the independent variable (for example, method of teaching grammar) in a study that is affecting the dependent variable (grammatical knowledge as measured by a test of grammar) and not some other variable (skill of the teacher or cognitive style of the learner). Positivists argue that qualitative research is particularly vulnerable when it comes to internal validity because there is no attempt to control variables and consequently it is difficult, if not impossible, to make claims about relationships between variables. Interestingly, LeCompte and Goetz argue that naturalistic research, particularly ethnography, can lay claim to high internal validity because of the data collection and analysis techniques employed.

> First, the ethnographer's common practice of living among participants and collecting data from long periods provides opportunities for continual data analysis and comparison to refine constructs and ensure the match between scientific categories and participant reality. Second, informant interviewing, a major ethnographic data source, necessarily is phrased more closely

to the empirical categories of participants and is formed less abstractly than instruments used in other research. Third, participant observation, the ethnographer's second key source of data, is conducted in natural settings that affects the reality of the life experiences of participants more accurately than do contrived setting. Finally, ethnographic analysis incorporates a process of researcher self-monitoring … that exposes all phases of the research activity to continual questioning and reevaluation.

(LeCompte & Goetz, 1982, p. 43)

Underlying this battle for legitimacy, it is possible to detect a degree of defensiveness. Qualitative researchers are trying hard to play by the rules of the game established by the positivists. They are attempting to inhabit the same playing field, and also share common methodological ground, seeing research as a systematic process of enquiry involving question formation, data collection, interpretation and analysis and publication (Nunan, 1992). They also agree that reliability and validity are key aspects to the research enterprise, although they differ in the criteria and methods that are applied to defending research in terms of these key constructs. Both traditions also largely agree on the nature of academic "voice" i.e. rhetorical conventions, although in the case of qualitative research, this was to change by the 1980s. In quantitative research, on the one hand, the researcher strives to remain "invisible", maintaining the stance of the objective outsider. In qualitative research on the other hand, researchers are insiders—very much part of the research process. The objective pronoun "one" is exchanged for the subjective pronoun "I". The active voice creeps in. Contractions make an occasional appearance. Consider the way that Heath (1983), who studied language development and use in children from rural communities in the United States, positions herself. In this quote, she places herself squarely in the centre of the research context.

I spend many hours cooking, chopping wood, gardening, sewing, and minding children by the rules of the community. For example, in the early years of interaction in the communities, audio and video recordings were unfamiliar to community residents; therefore I did no taping of any kind then. By the mid-1970s, cassette players were becoming popular gifts, and community members used them to record music, church services, and sometimes special performances in the community. When such recordings became a common community-initiated practice, I audiotaped, but only in accordance with community practices. Often, I was able to write in a field notebook while minding children, tending food, or watching television with families; otherwise, I wrote fieldnotes as soon as possible afterwards when I left the community on an errand or to go to school. In the classrooms, I often audiotaped, we sometimes videotaped; and both teachers and I took fieldnotes as a matter of course on many days of each year.

(Heath, 1983, pp. 8–9)

If the metaphor for quantitative educational research was an agricultural one based on the "hard sciences", qualitative educational researchers embraced anthropology. Particularly potent techniques appropriated from anthropology included the use of diaries and narrative inquiry.

The 1980s

Narrative inquiry and storytelling as forms of research became increasingly prominent in the 1980s (Denny, 1978; Stenhouse, 1983). Narratives are fundamental to the human condition. To our knowledge, no cultures exist without narratives. Some cultures, such as those of Australian Aborigines, do not have a written form of language. In these cultures, oral narratives are the vehicles that carry the culture. In his article, "Life as Narrative", Bruner (2004, p. 692) argues that narrative is a fundamental way of what he calls "world making":

> We seem to have no other way of describing "lived time" save in the form of a narrative. Which is not to say that there are not other temporal forms that can be imposed on the experience of time, but none of them succeeds in capturing the sense of lived time: not clock or calendrical time forms, not serial or cyclical orders, not any of these.

Numerous other scholars have made a similar point. Polkinghorne (1995) for instance, argues that the increased interest in narrative in a range of social sciences stems from the fact that narrative "is the linguistic form uniquely suited for displaying human existence as situated action" (p. 5).

Narratives or (auto)biographies focus on the description and analysis of social phenomena as they are experienced within the context of individual lives. Benson (2005) coined the term "(auto)biography" to indicate that "in the context of second language learning research, the data are as a rule first-person (autobiographical) accounts of experience that are analysed either by the subject of the research (autobiographically) or by another researcher (biographically)" (p. 21).

Narratives are important in all forms of qualitative research, from ethnographies to case study. Case studies, which are the investigation of a "bounded instance" (Stake, 1988; van Lier, 2005; Duff, 2008), are generally more limited in scope than an ethnography, and do not always set behavior within a cultural context:

> Denny (1978) draws a distinction between ethnography, case study, and "story telling". While an ethnography is a complete account of a particular culture, case studies examine a facet or particular aspect of the culture or subculture under investigation. Despite this more limited reach of case studies, many case studies share certain characteristics with ethnographies. Both attempt to provide a portrait of what is going on in a particular setting. Additionally, according to Denny, they must be more than objective accounts of the culture being portrayed—they must encapsulate a point of view (in other words, they must go beyond description). Finally, they must provide sufficient data for the reader to draw conclusions other than those presented directly by the writer.
>
> (Nunan, 1992, p. 77)

Chik (2004) argues that the biographical approach puts people at the centre of the research process, providing a means by which researchers can facilitate an individual's recreation of their past, present and future from an insider's perspective. According to Chik, "[t]he particular advantage of this method is the empowerment of the interviewees through highlighting the most important aspects of their life history" (p. 5).

Benson (personal communication) makes the point that consideration needs to be given to the question of who is speaking for whom in qualitative research. In much research, the researcher acts as a ventriloquist: the real voice is that of the learner, but it is refracted through the voice of the researcher. He goes on to argue that researchers are often incautious in their claims to know and represent what their informants really think. In his view, this strengthens the case for autobiography and autoethnography because while they lay themselves open to the charge of subjectivity, they are at least trustworthy. (See Ellis, 2004 and Pavlenko & Lantolf, 2000 for issues related to first person narratives and trustworthiness.)

Until recently, the use of narrative, (auto)biography or "storytelling" has been overlooked in language learning research. However, it has a considerable, if somewhat controversial, history in general education research. Denny, one of the early proponents of the approach, champions its use in the following way:

> Storytelling is an attempt to employ ancient conceptualizations … focused on directly observable referents. We now have Newtonians in educational research—no Einsteins—car-

rying on 4th decimal place ethnography before getting the rudimentary realities in place. This much I propose for general agreement: without good documentation, good storytelling, we'll never get good educational theory, which we desperately need. … I claim story telling can contribute to our understanding of problems in education and teachers can help. Folks are forever calling for and proposing nifty solutions to problems never understood. Storytelling is unlikely to help in the creation or evaluation of educational remedies, but can facilitate problem definition. Problem definition compared to problem solving is an underdeveloped field in education.

(Denny, 1978, p. 3)

Goodson and Walker (1988) also emphasize the essentially practical nature of storytelling in educational research: "Storytelling seems to offer a kind of intermediate technology of research adapted to the study of practical problems in realistic time scales without the prospect of ten years' initiation among dwindling (and probably best left) tribes of Primitives" (p. 29).

Stories provide insights into the human condition that can only be glimpsed in the rear view mirror of regular research. Lawrence Stenhouse, one of the founders of qualitative approaches to curriculum research and development, suggests that even fictionalized accounts can carry greater force than quantitative research. In the following extract, he draws a contrast between quantitative survey research and fiction, arguing that a fictionalized voice can create a "texture of reality":

There is a need to capture in the presentation of the research the texture of reality which makes judgment possible for an audience. This cannot be achieved in the reduced, attenuated accounts of events which support quantification. The contrast is between the breakdown of questionnaire responses of 472 married women respondents who have had affairs with men other than their husbands and the novel *Madam Bovary*. The novel relies heavily on that appeal to judgment which is appraisal of credibility in the light of the reader's experience. You cannot base much appeal to judgment on the statistics of survey; the portrayal relies almost entirely upon appeal to judgment.

(Stenhouse, 1983, p. 24)

The issue of fictionalizing narrative accounts is controversial. Angrosino, cited in Ellis (2004), argues that the techniques of fiction "allowed him to get to the truth of his participants' experience without risking revealing the identity of any specific character or place" (Ellis, 2004: 125).

Bell (2002) points out that narrative research is based on the human need to impose meaning on what might otherwise be perceived as random experiences, and that we do this by imposing a story line on these experiences. However, she makes the telling point that narrative enquiry is more than just telling stories. The narrative is the starting point. However, for the researcher, it is the point of departure rather than the destination. The researcher draws on the narrative to generate insights and assumptions about constructs and phenomena (such as motivation, identity and anxiety) that are illustrated by the story. She goes on to point out that

narrative inquiry involves working with people's consciously told stories, recognizing that these rest on deeper stories of which people are often unaware. Participants construct stories that support their interpretation of themselves, excluding experiences and events that undermine the identities they currently claim. Whether or not they believe the stories they tell is relatively unimportant because the inquiry goes beyond the specific stories to explore the assumptions inherent in the shaping of those stories.

(Bell, 2002, p. 209)

Pavlenko (2002) draws a distinction between Bell's approach and her own, which she calls narrative study. She suggests that while narrative enquiry represents an ethnographic approach to eliciting understanding, narrative study focuses on narrative construction from a variety of perspectives. She points out that narratives are highly specific to biographical variables such as race, ethnicity, class, gender and sexuality, and that the audience for whom the narrative is constructed will also influence what gets told. Rather than viewing any given narrative account as a factual statement of past events, it is important to look behind the narrative and to "examine whose stories are being heard and why, and whose stories are still missing, being misunderstood, or being misinterpreted" (Pavlenko, 2002) p. 216).

Lieblich, Tuval-Mashiach and Zilber (1998, pp. 2–3) suggest that narrative research

> refers to any study that uses or analyzes narrative materials. The data can be collected as a story (a life story provided in an interview or a literary work) or in a different manner (field notes of an anthropologist who writes up his or her observations as a narrative or in personal letters). It can be the object of the research or a means for the study of another question. It may be used for comparison among groups, to learn about a social phenomenon or historical period, or to explore a personality.

While narrative enquiry has a healthy research tradition going back many years in general education, in recent years, it has attracted the attention of researchers in applied linguistics and language education (Benson & Nunan, 2004). Narratives enable people to construct a meaningful story about themselves over time. As Hardy (1968) attests: "We dream in narrative, daydream in narrative, remember, anticipate, hope, despair, plan, revise, criticize, gossip, learn, hate and love by narrative" (p. 5).

The opportunity for learners to tell their own stories, and the control that they have over those stories, is empowering. It changes the learner's role within the research process. Learners are no longer individuals who have research done to them. They are collaborators in an ongoing, interpretive process. These realizations then invite what we call, "the narrative turn, a concern for storytelling, for composing ethnographies in new ways" (Denzin & Lincoln, 2005, p. 3).

Diaries/Diary Studies

In general, diaries are focused on looking "more closely at what we have done, what we do, and what we can do—both individually and collaboratively" (Holly, 1989, p. 5). For second language research purposes, diaries have been commonly used to look into areas of for instance, competitiveness and anxiety, the role of materials, teaching methods etc. (see Bailey, 1983, 1991; Bailey & Ochsner, 1983; Nunan & Bailey, 2008, pp. 294–296). Over the past decade, as noted by Pavlenko (2007, p. 163), we are particularly seeing an increase in "language memoirs, linguistic autobiographies, learners' journals and diaries [which] have become a popular means of data collection in applied linguistics". As a result, autobiographical and autoethnographical studies are also prominently coming into focus.

The popularity of the usage of diaries is not surprising seeing "they are transformative as they shift the power relationship between the researchers and the participants, and between teachers and learners, making the object of the inquiry into the subject and granting the subject both agency and voice" (Pavlenko, 2007, p. 180). A note of caution is warranted here. As we noted earlier, there is a difference between the voice of the researcher and that of the researched. We therefore need to be clear about *whose* voice is being represented. In autobiographical narratives and autoethnography, the researcher and the researched are one and the same, and the researcher is representing her own voice. In research in which the researcher and the researched are not one and the same, the power to represent remains with the researcher.

Kubota (2005) states, in using the diary as data, the researcher can present it as a "self-reflexive interrogation of one's attitude" so that it may be a step towards "critically examining the pervasiveness of cultural essentialism and dichotomies" (p. 324). As researchers engage in self-reflexivity, they also open doors to numerous moral and ethical responsibilities and questions such as: Is the text fact or fiction? Is there a truth? Whose story is it? Whose truth do I represent? Is this legitimate data? Many of these questions have been in circulation for over two decades in the *blurred genres* moment. However in our present period, as Finlay and Gough (2003) note "a new 'self-other' consciousness—where the boundaries between the researcher and the researched is blurred—[has come] to the fore" (p. 5).

The 1990s–Present

The defensiveness apparent in the writing of many qualitative researchers in the 1970s and 1980s has been largely replaced by a new assertiveness. From the 1990s through to the present, qualitative researchers have decided to leave the quantitative playing field, stake out their own terrain and create their own sets of rules and operating principles. We now look at how this terrain is taking shape. Before we discuss the issues surrounding "voice", let us take a look at an emerging approach (or framework) that has come to the fore under the general rubric of "doing ethnography".

Autoethnography

The term "autoethnography" has only recently gained currency in Education, but has, in fact, been around since the 1970's. Today, the approach (or framework) is used in disciplines as diverse as Anthropology, Social Sciences, Humanities, Psychology, Applied Communications, Nursing, Occupational Therapy, Journalism and Life History Research. Sociologist Carolyn Ellis (2004) refers to autoethnography as "writing about the personal and its relationship to culture. It is an autobiographical genre of writing and research that displays multiple layers of consciousness" (p. 37). Although the inquiries come from personal stories, the narratives reach out to social, historical and philosophical contexts to gain a wider significance, academically and personally "making the personal political" (Holman Jones, 2005, p. 763). In second language teaching and learning, autoethnographic research looks into issues related to subjectivity, language, culture, gender, class, race and identity through the researcher's personal stories. A number of reflexive accounts are already present in academic journals, books and theses (see Cummings, 1996; Pennycook, 2004; Choi, 2006; Santana 1999).

Writing styles in autoethnographic research are central as the research is often concerned with the ways the researcher perceives his or her experiences and the world. Texts can appear as

> short stories, poetry, fiction, novels, photographic essays, personal essays, journals, fragmented and layered writing, and social science prose. In these texts, concrete action, dialogue, emotion, embodiment, spirituality, and self-consciousness are featured, appearing as relational and institutional stories affected by history, social structure, and culture, which themselves are dialectically revealed through action, feeling, thought, and language.
>
> (Ellis & Bochner, 2000, p. 739)

Because the data are (usually) gathered and analyzed by the Self, we are reminded of the power researchers have in the multiple interpretations of the data and the shifting outcome of the study—issues that have been hotly debated during the *crisis of representation* moment. An increasing number of books published since the late 1980s such as *The Vulnerable Observer: Anthropology That Breaks Your Heart* (Behar, 1996), *Tales of the Field* (1988), *Writing the New Ethnography* (Goodall, 2000), *The*

Ethnographic I: A Methodological Novel about Autoethnography (Ellis, 2004), *Narratives and Fictions in Educational Research* (Clough, 2002), *Representation and the Text: Reframing the Narrative Voice* (Tierney & Lincoln, 1997), *Reflexive Methodology: New Vistas for Qualitative Research* (Alvesson & Skoldberg, 2000) and *Writing Qualitative Inquiry: Self, Stories and Academic Life* (Goodall, 2008) interrogate postmodern issues of writing, theorizing and judging qualitative research.

Conference streams dedicated to New Ethnographies and Critical Creativity (ACSPRI, 2008) for example, inform us of the importance of practising reflexivity and the use of the "self" in conducting (ethnographic) research. In the *methodologically contested present* and the *fractured future* moments we are in today, it is not surprising then that researchers are continuing to experiment, defend and critically examine the strengths and weaknesses and the multiple uses of the first person "I" when we compose these types of research (see Ramanathan, 2005; Pennycook, 2005; Canagarajah, 2005; Nelson, 2005). While the attacks by positivists have not ceased, changes in qualitative research have taken place and are continuing to be developed. There is a new assertiveness on the part of qualitative researchers.

As Finlay (2002, p. 531) notes,

> as qualitative researchers, we now accept that the researcher is a central figure who actively constructs the collection, selection and interpretation of data. We appreciate that research is co-constituted—a joint product of the participants, researcher and their relationship. We realize that meanings are negotiated within particular social contexts so that another researcher will unfold a different story. We no longer seek to abolish the researcher's presence—instead, 'subjectivity in research is transformed from a problem to an opportunity.'

Reflexivity and Voice

As we crafted this chapter, tracing the emergence of narrative enquiry and voice in qualitative research, it became clear that the construct of reflexivity was central to the story we were trying to tell. When we trawled the literature for definitions and perspectives on reflexivity and its relationship to voice and to reflection, we discovered multiple perspectives, points of view and even skirmishes between those who had chosen to offer a characterization of the construct. Finlay and Gough (2003) draw a contrast between reflection and reflexivity, suggesting that, "[r]eflection can be defined as 'thinking about' something after the event. Reflexivity, in contrast, involves a more immediate, dynamic and continuing self-awareness" (p. ix).

This notion of reflexivity as a more immediate, dynamic construct in which the writer shuttles between the data and the explicit positioning of him/herself in relation to the data is reflected in numerous other efforts to pin the construct down. Linde (1993, p. 122) for instance, states,

> reflexivity in narrative is created by the separation of the narrator to observe, reflect, and correct the self that is being created. The act of narrating itself requires self-regard and editing, since, a distance in time and standpoint necessarily separates the actions being narrated from the act of narration.

Gadamer (1989, p. 383) captures the interrogation between the narrative and the narrator by deploying a conversational metaphor:

> [T]he way one word follows another, with the conversation taking its own twists and reaching its own conclusion, may well be conducted in some way, but the partners conversing are far less the leaders of it than the led. No one knows in advance what will "come out" of a conversation.

Following this line of thought, the twists and turns the researcher encounters during his/her journey (the research questions, choice of methods, approaches and analysis, historical background, the context, the readings, the people who are involved and influence the study) will bring about unique issues and ways of thinking about reflexivity.

Callaway (1992, p. 33) opens yet another facet on the construct, arguing that reflexivity opens the way

> to a more radical consciousness of self in facing the political dimensions of fieldwork and constructing knowledge. Other factors intersecting with gender—such as nationality, race, ethnicity, class, and age—also affect the anthropologist's field interactions and textual strategies. Reflexivity becomes a continuing mode of self-analysis and political awareness.

Studies and debates on *how* to write about representing our Selves and our subjects through our texts still continue to develop (see Richardson, 2000, 2001, 2006; St Pierre, 2002; Piirto, 2002; Ellis, 2002; Tierney, 2002; Brodkey, 1996). Writing genres such as narrative writing, fiction writing, non-fiction writing, creative non-fiction writing, ficto-critical writing as well as areas of new journalism are no longer just subjects for creative writers (see Muecke, 2002; Cheney, 2001; Wolfe, 1975). They are tools and pathways for all researchers involved in qualitative research. Ultimately,

> how we write and speak in the world does shape who we become, because communication—as we preach in every basic course—is how we engage life, behave in our relationships, make the world meaningful, and do our jobs. It determines the stories we tell as the way we tell them, the way we share with the world our choices of better ways to live.
>
> (Goodall, 2004, p. 189)

The possibilities of the ways in which we can write, the technology available for researchers to share their works and the conversations we can have across disciplines are exciting and valuable. However, we must also remember that these possibilities do not come without dangers, caveats and limitations. Richardson (1994, p. 523) concludes that

> although we are freer to present our texts in a variety of forms to diverse audiences, we have different constraints arising from self-consciousness about claims to authorship, authority, truth, validity, and reliability. Self-reflexivity unmasks complex political/ideological agendas hidden in our writing. Truth claims are less easily validated now; desires to speak "for" others are suspect. The greater freedom to experiment with textual form, however, does not guarantee a better product. The opportunities for writing worthy texts—books and articles that are a "good read"—are multiple, exciting and demanding. But the work is harder. The guarantees are fewer. There is a lot more for us to think about.

As we stated at the beginning of this chapter, by "voice" we are referring to the centrality of the human story to qualitative research in terms of *what* the story is and *how* the story is told. In this process, the writer is a central part of the story, a visible presence in the narrative. This presence is marked linguistically by the use of stylistic devices such as the first person pronoun (*The Ethnographic I*, as Carolyn Ellis, 2004) puts it), and a preference for the active rather than passive voice. Such devices, however, do not constitute "voice". They are epiphemomena. Voice is less about stylistics than the positioning of the writer within the text. This can only be done by taking a reflective stance, which is why we have argued for a concatenation of reflexivity and voice. One enables the other. We have a slightly different perspective from authors such as Pillow (2008) who characterize reflexivity as a research method. For the purposes of this chapter, we see it, as we have indicated above, as a stance taken by the writer towards the research as it unfolds. In this sense, it is qualitatively different from diaries, observational records, interviews and so on.

Multiple Voices: On Judging the Quality of Educational Research

In her 2004 book, Yates addresses the issue of judging educational research in relation to the rules of the game in specific contexts and genres (i.e. in academic theses", academic journals, commissioned research, book publishing etc.). Before we can even consider what we mean by "good", however, we need to understand the "politically charged space" we are in and what qualitative research means in this period (Denzin & Lincoln, 2005, p. 20). Answering the question "what does good educational research look like?" (the title of Yates' book) is a political act. As researchers in a postmodern world, we do not speak with one voice, and the "rules of the game" we embrace; indeed, selecting the game itself entails ideological stance and political choice.

Years before this view was fashionable, Elliot Eisner (1985a, 1985b) argued that case for connoisseurship in judging the value of educational research. We come to appreciate the quality of a piece of educational research in the same way as we develop an appreciation of literature, art and fine wine. Eisner was not being elitist. He accepted that one person's meat would be another's poison. What he was trying to do was to transcend the reductionism and prescriptivism that dominated a great deal of the debate at the time on the establishment of criteria for judging the quality of educational research.

Over a decade later Clough (2002) questioned whether it was possible or even desirable to assign criteria, stating that "this is not to say that there are no criteria and no rules; there are—as Richardson (1994) asserts—multiple and complex criteria, but it is not possible in the postmodern turn to offer prescription" (p. 8). So what we seem to be facing now as Brew (2001) has pointed out, is the possibility that "[a]cademic research is in crisis … Research, it seems, has lost its authority to define for society what knowledge is and how to get it" (opening page, no page number). So how do we make our narrative accounts count?

Notable scholars in fields of Social Sciences and Applied Communication, for instance, are making calls for more creative and reflexive ways of gathering data, writing academic theses and questioning the criteria for judging an academic piece of work (see Conle, 2000; Etherington, 2004; Piirto, 2002; Goodall, 2008; Tierney & Lincoln, 1997; Pavlenko, 2007). These arguments do not call for academic writing to be dropped. They are opening up and celebrating different ways of writing so that all voices (the underprivileged, minority voices etc.) may be heard through our research. In his eloquently crafted paper "The preface as exegesis", Krauth (2002) argues for the writing of prefaces in academic theses. He states, "[e]xegetic activity provides opportunity for postgraduate writers to 'speak twice' about the literary nerves of their work, about the creative mechanisms driving it, and about the personal and cultural orientations that inform and frame and guide it" (p. 17). However, even with all these studies and suggestions, there are no easy answers to the questions on how we can make our narrative accounts count in the *fractured future*. "Today, more than ever, lack of self-consciousness and lack of reflexivity about the genres [researchers] must work within is likely to work to the disadvantage of the neophyte researcher" (Yates, 2004, p. 211).

Instead of trying to find quick and easy answers, Yates suggests what is really important is to think about

who is judging research in particular areas, how they came to be there, what might be influencing them, [and] what signs are they going on when they make their judgments … We need to discuss the conditions we work in, and to recognize that judgments are not free-floating abstract things, but practices performed in particular contexts, with particular histories and relationships, and using particular materials, frequently specifically textual materials.

(Yates, 2004, pp. 211–212)

In considering the issues of quality, connoisseurship, appeals to judgement and the multiplicity of voices that are emerging in the educational marketplace, trust looms large:

We have a dialogue going now. It is about how we make judgments, how we can trust each other and the things we write. It is about creating certainty when life is about ambiguity. It is about what Karl Weick called creating "a little cognitive economy, and some peace of mind." We are not ready either to close down the conversation or to say farewell to criteria quite yet.

(Lincoln, 2002, p. 343)

Conclusion

In this chapter, we set out to summarize the story of qualitative research in second language learning and teaching as it has evolved over the last 40 years. While there are many similar reviews in books and journals, we hoped to give this piece a slightly different orientation by tracing the emergence of "voice" in qualitative research. We chose to view the evolution of qualitative research through the lens of voice because it speaks strongly to our own current research interests and concerns.

We took a rather unadventurous historical route because it seemed the most fitting way to frame the concerns and themes that were important to us. Although we felt that we had a reasonable grasp on issues to do with culture, identity, narrative enquiry, reflexivity and so on, we were surprised, on revisiting familiar literature and turning up new perspectives and accounts, at just how richly layered is work that portrays these key constructs and their evolution. As Denzin and Lincoln (2005, p. 7) have pointed out, qualitative research is interdisciplinary, transdisciplinary and sometimes counter-disciplinary, multiparadigmatic and multimethodological. It is hardly surprising then that perspectives and portrayals are complex and contentious.

In early discussions with volume editor Eli Hinkel, we were warned that "this will be a challenging chapter to pull off". How right she was! However, we take comfort in the fact that the issue of voice in qualitative research is part of an evolving conversation. Following Holman-Jones (2005, p. 783),

[w]e want to close by asking you to keep this conversation going in your texts, contexts and praxes. We want you to take this conversation into the next turn, crisis, and moment in qualitative research and to move your work, "without hesitation or encumbrance from the personal to the political".

Acknowledgement

We would like to acknowledge the valuable comments made by Phil Benson on an earlier draft of this chapter.

References

ACSPRI. (2008). ACSPRI Social Science Methodology Conference, 7th–10th December, the University of Sydney, Australia.

Alvesson, M., & Skoldberg, K. (2000). *Reflexive methodology: New vistas for qualitative research*. London: Sage Publications.

Bailey, K. M. (1983). Competitiveness and anxiety in adult second language learning: Looking at and through the diary studies. In H. W. Seliger & M. H. Long (Eds.), *Classroom oriented research in second language acquisition* (pp. 67–102). Rowley, MA: Newbury House Publishers.

Bailey, K. M. (1991). Diary studies of classroom language learning: The doubting game and the believing game. In E. Sadtono (Ed.), *Language acquisition and the second/foreign language classroom* (pp. 60–102). Singapore: SEAMEO Regional Language Center.

Bailey, K. M., & Ochsner, R. (1983). A methodological review of the diary studies: Windmill tilting or social science? In M. Long, K. Bailey & S. Peck (Eds.), *Second language acquisition studies* (pp. 188–198). Rowley, MA: Newbury House Publishers.

Behar, R. (1996). *The vulnerable observer: Anthropology that breaks your heart.* Boston: Beacon Press.

Bell, J. (2002). Narrative inquiry: More than just telling stories. *TESOL Quarterly, 36*(2), 207–213.

Benson, P. (2005). (Auto)biography and learner diversity. In P. Benson & D. Nunan (Eds.), *Learners stories: Difference and diversity in language learning* (pp. 4–21). Cambridge: Cambridge University Press.

Benson, P., & Nunan, D. (Eds.) (2004). *Learners' stories: Difference and diversity in language learning.* Cambridge: Cambridge University Press.

Benson, P., Chik, A., Gao, X., Huang, J. & Wang, W. (2009). Qualitative research in language teaching and learning journals, 1997–2006. *Modern Language Journal, 93*(i), 79–90.

Brew, A. (2001). *The nature of research.* New York: RoutledgeFalmer.

Brodkey, L. (1996). *Writing permitted in designated areas only.* Minneapolis: University of Minnesota Press.

Bruner, J. (2004). Life as narrative. *Social Research, 71*(3), 691–710.

Callaway, H. (1992). Ethnography and experience: Gender implications in fieldwork and texts. In J. Okely & H. Callaway (Eds.), *Anthropology and autobiography* (pp. 29–49). New York: Routledge.

Canagarajah, S. (2005). Rhetoricizing reflexivity. *Journal of Language, Identity and Education, 4*(4), 309–315.

Cheney, T. (1987). *Writing creative nonfiction: Fiction techniques for crafting great nonfiction.* Berkeley, CA andToronto: Ten Speed Press.

Chik, A. (2004). How experience shapes individual differences among second language learners: A biographical study of Hong Kong learners in five age groups. Unpublished Detailed Scheme of Research. Hong Kong: English Centre, the University of Hong Kong.

Choi, J. (2006). A narrative analysis of second language acquisition and identity formation. Unpublished thesis, Anaheim University, Anaheim, California.

Clough, P. (2002). *Narratives and fiction in educational research.* Buckingham: Open University Press.

Conle, C. (2000). Thesis as narrative or "what is the inquiry in narrative inquiry?". *Curriculum Inquiry, 30*(2), 189–214.

Cummings, M. C. (1996). Sardo revisited: Voice, faith, and multiple repeaters. In K. Bailey & D. Nunan (Eds.), *Voices from the language classroom* (pp. 224–235). Cambridge: Cambridge University Press.

Denny, T. (1978). Story-telling and educational understanding. In L. Bartlett, S. Kemmis & G. Gillard (Eds.), *Perspectives on case study* (pp. 1–24). Geelong: Deakin University Press.

Denzin, N., & Lincoln, Y. (2005). Introduction: The discipline and practice of qualitative research. In N. Denzin & Y. Lincoln (Eds.), *The Sage handbook of qualitative research* (3rd ed.) (pp. 1–32). Thousand Oaks, CA: Sage Publications.

Duff, P. A. (2008). *Case study research in applied linguistics.* New York: Lawrence Erlbaum Associates.

Eisner, E. W. (1985a). *The educational imagination: On the design and evaluation of school programs* (2nd ed.). New York and London: Collier Macmillan.

Eisner, E. W. (1985b) *The art of educational evaluation: A personal view.* London: Falmer Press.

Ellis, C. (2002). Being real: Moving inward toward social change. *International Journal of Qualitative Studies in Education, 15*(4), 399–406.

Ellis, C. (2004). *The ethnographic I: A methodological novel about autoethnography.* Walnut Creek, CA: Alta Mira Press.

Ellis, C., & Bochner, A. P. (2000). Autoethnography, personal narrative, reflexivity: Researcher as subject. In N. K. Denzin (Ed.), *The Sage handbook of qualitative research* (2nd ed.) (pp. 733–768). Thousand Oaks, CA: Sage Publications.

Etherington, K. (2004). *Becoming a reflexive researcher: Using our selves in research.* London: Jessica Kingsley.

Finlay, L. (2002). "Outing" the researcher: the provenance, principles and practice of reflexivity. *Qualitative Health Research, 12*(3), 531–545.

Finlay, L., & Gough, B. (Eds.) (2003). *Reflexivity: A practical guide for researchers in health and social sciences.* Oxford: Blackwell Science.

Gadamer, H. (1989). *Truth and method.* London: Sheed & Ward.

Garner, H. (2006). The rules of engagement: Paul Greengrass's "United 93". *The Monthly.* Retrieved 22 February 2009, from http://www.themonthly.com.au/tm/node/271.

Goodall, H. L. (2000). *Writing the new ethnography.* Walnut Creek, CA : Alta Mira Press.

Goodall, H. L. (2004). Commentary. *Journal of Applied Communication Research, 32*(3), 185–194.

Goodall, H. L. (2008). *Writing qualitative inquiry: Self, stories and academic life.* Tucson, AZ: University of Arizona Press.

Goodson, I., & Walker, R. (1988). Putting life into educational research. In R. Sherman & R. Webb (Eds.), *Qualitative research in education: Focus and methods* (pp. 110–122). London: RoutledgeFalmer.

Hardy, B. (1968). Toward a poetics of fiction. *Novel*, *2*, 5–14.

Harklau, L. (2005). Ethnography and ethnographic research on second language teaching and learning. In E. Hinkel (Ed.), *Handbook of research in second language learning and teaching*, (pp. 179–194). Mahwah, NJ: Lawrence Erlbaum.

Heath, S. B. (1983). *Ways with words: Language, life, and work in communities and classrooms.* Cambridge: Cambridge University Press.

Holly, M. (1989). *Writing to grow: Keeping a personal-professional journal.* Portsmouth: Heinemann.

Holman-Jones, S. (2005). Autoethnography: Making the personal political. In N. Denzin & Y. Lincoln (Eds.), *The Sage handbook of qualitative research* (pp.763–791). Thousand Oaks, CA: Sage Publications.

Krauth, N. (2002). The preface as exegesis. *TEXT*, *6*(1).

Kubota, R. (2005). Book review: *Onna rashiku (Like a woman): The diary of a language learner in Japan* by Karen Ogulnick. *Journal of Language, Identity & Education*, *4*(4), 321–325.

LeCompte, M., & Goetz, J. (1982). Problems of reliability and validity in educational research. *Review of Educational Research*, *52*(2), 31–60.

Lieblich, A., Tuval-Mashiach, R., & Zilber, T. (1998). *Narrative research: Reading, analysis, and interpretation.* Thousand Oaks, CA: Sage Publications.

Lincoln, Y. (2002). Emerging criteria for quality in qualitative and interpretive research. In N. Denzin & Y. Lincoln (Eds.), *The qualitative inquiry reader* (pp. 327–346). Thousand Oaks, CA: Sage Publications.

Linde, C. (1993). *Life stories: The creation of coherence.* New York: Oxford University Press.

Muecke, S. (2002). The fall: Fictocritical writing. *Parallax*, *8*(4), 108–112.

Nelson, C. (2005). Crafting researcher subjectivity in ways that enact theory. *Journal of Language, Identity & Education*, *4*(4), 315–320.

Nunan, D. (1992). *Research methods in language learning.* Cambridge: Cambridge University Press.

Nunan, D., & Bailey, K. (2008). *Exploring second language classroom research.* Boston: Heinle, Cengage Learning.

Pavlenko, A. (2002). Narrative study: Whose story is it anyway? *TESOL Quarterly*, *36*(2), 213–218.

Pavlenko, A. (2007). Autobiographic narratives as data in applied linguistics. *Applied Linguistics*, *28*(2), 163–188.

Pavlenko, A., & Lantolf, J. (2000). Second language learning as participation and the (re)construction of selves. In J. Lantolf (Ed.), *Sociocultural theory and second language learning* (pp. 155–178). Oxford: Oxford University Press.

Pennycook, A. (2004). Critical moments in TESOL praxicum. In B. Norton & K. Toohey (Eds.), *Critical pedagogies and language learning* (pp. 327–345). Cambridge: Cambridge University Press.

Pennycook, A. (2005). Performing the personal. *Journal of Language, Identity & Education*, *4*(4), 297–304.

Pillow, W. (2008). Confession, catharsis, or cure? Rethinking the uses of reflexivity as methodological power in qualitative research. *International Journal of Qualitative Studies in Education*, *16*(2), 175–196.

Piirto, J. (2002). The unreliable narrator, or the difference between writing prose in literature and in social science: A commentary on Tierney's article. *International Journal of Qualitative Studies in Education*, *15*(4), 407–415.

Polkinghorne, D. (1995). Narrative configuration in qualitative analysis. In J. Hatch & R. Wisniewski (Eds.), *Life history and narrative* (pp. 5–23). London: Falmer.

Ramanathan, V. (2005). Some impossibilities around researcher location: Tensions around divergent audiences, languages, social stratifications. *Journal of Language, Identity & Education*, *4*(4), 293–297.

Richardson, L. (1994). Writing: A method of inquiry. In N. Denzin & Y. Lincoln, (Eds.), *Handbook of qualitative research* (pp. 516–529). London: Sage.

Richardson, L. (2000). Writing: A method of inquiry. In N. K. Denzin & Y. S. Lincoln (Eds.), *The Sage handbook of qualitative research* (2nd ed.) (pp. 923–948). Thousand Oaks, CA: Sage.

Richardson, L. (2001). Getting personal: Writing-stories. *International Journal of Qualitative Studies in Education*, *14*(1), 33–38.

Richardson, L. (2006). Skirting a pleated text: De-disciplining an academic life. In S. N. Hesse-Biber & P. L. Leavy (Eds.), *Emergent methods in social research* (pp. 1–11). Thousand Oaks, CA: Sage Publications.

St Pierre, E. A. (2002). Circling the text: Nomadic writing practices. In N. K. Denzin & Y. S. Lincoln (Eds.), *The qualitative inquiry reader* (pp. 51–69). Thousand Oaks, CA: Sage Publications.

Santana, J. (1999). Americanization: A Dominican immigrant's autobiographical study of cultural and linguistic learning. Unpublished doctoral dissertation, School of Education, New York University.

Scherer, G., & Wertheimer, M. (1984). *A psycholinguistic experiment in foreign language teaching.* New York: McGraw-Hill.

Stake, R. (1988). Case study methods in educational research: seeking sweet water. In R. M. Jaeger (Ed.), *Complementary methods for research in education* (pp. 253–265). Washington, DC: American Educational Research Association.

Stenhouse, L. (1983). Case study in educational research and evaluation. In L. Bartlett, S. Kemmis & G. Gillard (Eds.), *Case study: An overview* (pp. 11–54). Geelong: Deakin University Press.

Tierney, W. (2002). Get real. *International Journal of Qualitative Studies in Education*, *15*(4), 385–398.

Tierney, W. G., & Lincoln, Y. S. (Eds.) (1997). *Representation and the text: Reframing the narrative voice.* New York: State University of New York Press.

van Lier, L. (2005). Case study. In E. Hinkel (Ed.), *Handbook of research in second language learning and teaching* (p. 195–208). Mahwah, NJ: Lawrence Erlbaum.

Van Maanen, J. (1988). *Tales of the field*. London: University of Chicago.

Wolfe, T. (1975). *The new journalism*. New York: Picador Books.

Yates, L. (2004). *What does good education research look like?: Situating a field and its practices*. Maidenhead: Open University Press.

15

Action Research in the Field of Second Language Teaching and Learning

Anne Burns

Introduction

The concept of action research has developed rapidly in the field of applied linguistics and second language teaching from the end of the 1980s, influenced in no small part by the "teacher as researcher" movement in the field of education (see Cochran Smith & Lytle, 1999), as well as more general shifts in orientation toward qualitative and ethnographic research. Since then in these fields, as in other educational sectors, action research has come to be seen as a means for teacher practitioners to be engaged in self-reflective and investigative approaches to understanding and researching their working environments. This chapter first outlines briefly the nature, purpose and focus of action research and then places its development within its historical contexts. The position of action research in relation to major research paradigms is also discussed. A consideration of developments and trends within the fields of language teaching and research as well as the different positions and controversies that have arisen then follows. The chapter ends by outlining some implications and directions for the future.

The Nature, Purpose, and Focus of Action Research

Stringer (1999, p. 17) defines action research as

a collaborative approach to inquiry or investigation that provides people with the means to take systematic action to resolve specific problems. This approach to research favors consensual and participatory procedures that enable people (a) to investigate systematically their problems and issues, (b) to formulate powerful and sophisticated accounts of their situations, and (c) to devise plans to deal with the problems at hand. Community-based action research focuses on methods and techniques of inquiry that take into account people's history, culture, interactional practices, and emotional lives. Although it makes use of techniques and strategies commonly applied in the behavioral and social science it is a more user-friendly approach to investigation than most.

The user-friendliness that Stringer refers to is a key factor likely to have contributed to the ever increasing popularity and attractiveness of action research for practitioners in the field of education, including applied linguistics and the teaching of English to speakers of other languages (TESOL). There seem to be few preparatory and in-service programs for language teachers, or policy recommendations for language teacher professional development, that do not now advocate some form of introduction to practitioner inquiry, usually through action research. Nolen and Vander Putten (2007) suggest that educators "see it as a practical yet systematic research method to investigate their own teaching and their students' learning in and outside the classroom" (p. 401).

Methodologically, Kemmis and McTaggart (2005, p. 563) stress that action research should be envisaged, not as a linear procedure, but as a cyclical and spiraling process achieved through:

- planning a change;
- acting and observing the process and consequences of the change;
- reflecting on these processes and consequences;
- replanning;
- acting and observing again;
- reflecting again and so on ….

Their four phase model of action research—Plan, Act, Observe, Reflect—has become something of a classic representation of educational action research, despite criticisms that it assumes too fixed a sequence of self-contained stages and that it glosses over the complexity and "messiness" of the actual research processes involved (e.g. Ebbutt, 1985; Elliott, 1991). Hopkins (1994, p. 55), for example, argues that such models "cannot mirror reality" and at best, can only provide a starting point; he warns that they should not be allowed to constrict the researcher's "freedom of action." Similarly, Somekh (1993) argues that educational action research is "chameleon-like" and intrinsically flexible "not merely in terms of being eclectic in research methods, but more fundamentally in needing to adapt to the social and political situation in which it is employed" (p. 29).

In terms of its essential characteristics Grundy and Kemmis (1981, cited in Grundy, 1988) consider that three minimal requirements underpin action research:

These requirements incorporate the goals of improvement and involvement which characterize any action research project. The conditions which are set out there as individually necessary and jointly sufficient for action research to exist are:

1. the project takes as its subject-matter a social practice, regarding it as a strategic action susceptible to improvement;
2. the project proceeds through a spiral of cycles of planning, acting, observing and reflecting, with each of these activities being systematically and self-critically implemented and inter-related; and
3. the project involves those responsible for the practice in each of the moments of the activity, widening participation in the project gradually to include others affected by the practice and maintaining collaborative control of the process.

(Grundy, 1988, p. 353)

In sum, it can be said that the essential purpose of educational action research is to investigate a social environment (the classroom, school, school district or other localized entity) in which researchers (teacher practitioners, students, administrators, teacher educators and academic researchers may all potentially participate) perceive a situation where a gap exists between the "actual" and the "ideal." Through a collaborative, systematic and cyclical research process participants in that situation work towards meaningful change, employing deliberate intervention through strategic action, and systematic data collection and analysis. The outcomes of the process are focused on ongoing, critically reflective practice, deepening understanding, interpretation and theorization of the educational, social and/or policy environments in which the work unfolds (see Burns, 2010 for a detailed introduction to undertaking action research in the language teaching field).

The Development of Action Research

Greenwood and Levin (2007) note that the history of action research (see also McTaggart, 1991) is one of diverse, sometimes separate, strands of thinking influenced by broad twentieth-century democratic social movements. One "fundamental building block" (p. 18) was that of industrial democracy, embodied in the work of the social psychologist Kurt Lewin in the USA during the Second World War, on how to conceptualize and promote social change through experimentation and strategic intervention in a natural, holistic, social and material situation in order to achieve a specific goal. In Lewin's words:

> The research needed for social practice can best be characterized as research for social management or social engineering. It is a type of action-research, a comparative research on the conditions and effects of various forms of social action, and research leading to social action. Research that produces nothing but books will not suffice.
>
> (Lewin, 1946, reproduced in Lewin, 1948, pp. 202–203)

Lewin conceptualized social change as a three-way process: *unfreezing* (dismantling existing structures); *changing* (changing the structures); *freezing* (re-stabilizing the structure). He also developed the concept of T-groups (groups led by a facilitator who acts as an authority figure but does not take control) through his work on Group Dynamics, "identifying factors and forces important for the development, conflict and cooperation in groups" (Greenwood & Levin, 2007, p. 16). Lewin's work was significant in shifting the focus of research from the more abstract and decontextualized theorization of experimental scientific research to pragmatic, real-world problematization, redefining the role of the researcher, and creating new criteria for judging the quality of research. The foundational premises of Lewin's work were taken up in the UK by the Tavistock Institute in London (e.g. Trist & Bamforth, 1951) and subsequently in Norway by the Industrial Democracy Project (Emery & Thorsrud, 1976) and further developed and modified for application in organizational industrial contexts. Action research is now widely used as an approach to research in business, management and other organizational fields (see, for example, Eden & Huxman, 2005).

A second strand of development occurred through liberal-democratizing and civil rights movements in "liberationist" and ex-colonial situations of poverty and political oppression. Freire's educational literacy and "conscientization" campaigns with disempowered rural communities in Brazil (e.g. Freire, 1970) and Fals Borda's promotions of community action through adult education and group cooperatives in Colombia (e.g. Fals Borda, 1969) are prominent examples. This form of action research has also found a place among disenfranchised groups in wealthy countries such as the USA, for example through work in rural Appalachian communities, deindustrialized areas and urban slums (e.g. Horton, 1990). These activities are essentially political activist and community building initiatives aimed at equalizing power relationships and redistributing resources.

In addition, Human Inquiry and Cooperative Inquiry approaches emerged from 1977 through the work of the New Paradigm Group in the UK, which sought to promote alternatives to conventional social science methods and to "to better justice for the humanity of the participants" (Greenwood & Levin, 2007, p. 32). Participation is a crucial tenet for protagonists of this form of action research: major aims were to do research *with* and not *on* people, to foreground participatory forms of action research (PAR), and to convert participants with the main sources of knowledge of the social situation into *insiders* rather than *outsiders* (see Heron, 1996; Reason & Bradbury, 2001).

In its applications within educational contexts an early antecedent of action research was the work of John Dewey (e.g. 1916) who saw practice as central to sources of data collection and tests of the validity of educational theory. Early work with teachers by Corey (e.g. 1953) and Taba and Noel (1957) was challenged by criticisms that action research was unscientific with the result that burgeoning moves in this direction were temporarily halted in the US. In the 1960s and 1970s, mainly under the influence of Lawrence Stenhouse's initiatives in the Humanities Curriculum Project (1967–1972) in the UK and influenced by developments in curriculum theory, the teacher–researcher movement gained ground. The Ford Teaching Project and the Classroom (now Collaborative) Action Research Network (CARN, http://www.did.stu.mmu.ac.uk/carnnew/) were further developments during this period. A further impetus was added to the field of action research through the work of Kemmis, McTaggart, Carr, Grundy and others at Deakin University in Australia. Their approach was based on concepts of a more "emancipatory" educational action research than those that had previously manifested themselves. They advocated engagement in action research in relation to the social, political and economic conditions that mediated existing practices and their meanings. They drew on the theories of Jürgen Habermas "who commits participants in critical social science to actions and critique *together*" (McTaggart, 1991, p. 30, emphasis in original). Their approach emphasized the collective, collaborative and "communitarian" (p. 31) dimensions of action research.

Thus, it is possible to depict educational action research in terms of broad movements or "generations" of theoretical development with their own underlying assumptions and world views (see McKernan, 1996, Burns 2005a, 2007 for more detailed discussion): *technical-scientific* (a technically motivated, step-wise activity seeking basic improvements to practice), *practical-deliberative* (a solution-oriented approach oriented to morally problematic situations) and *critical-emancipatory* (an emancipatory approach embedded in critical theory and addressing broader socially constituted educational structures at the local level). Denzin and Lincoln (2005, p. 560) identify a more recent fourth generation of what could be called *social-participatory* action research emerging "in the connection between critical-emancipatory action research and participatory action research that has developed in the context of social movements in the developing world" and influenced by the work of Freire, Fals Borda and others. They argue that two key themes in fourth generation action research are "theoretical arguments for more 'actionist' approaches and the need for participatory action research to make links with broader social movements" (p. 560). MacNaughton (2001, p. 210) claims that fourth generation action research embodies "educational transformation and emancipation by working with others to change existing social practices and by using critical reflection and social criticism as key research processes. It is therefore collaborative, change-orientated and overtly political."

In terms of action research movements in the language teaching field, Crookes argued in 1993 that critical-emancipatory approaches were uncommon and thus, generational change, if it was occurring at all, was still in its infancy. And indeed in many versions of second language action research much emphasis seems to have been placed on classroom "problem-solving" (e.g. Nunan, 1993; Wallace, 1998) rather than critical "problematization" taking account of broader socio-political concerns. However, there is evidence that the situation is slowly changing; critical-emancipatory and participatory approaches that highlight sociocultural and transformational change are beginning to infuse second language action research (see Auerbach, 1992, 1996; Tuffs, 1995; Crookes & Lehner, 1998, Edge, 2001a; Toohey & Waterstone, 2004; McGee, 2008, Mugford, 2008; Denos, Toohey, Neilson & Waterstone, 2009; Grey, 2009).

Action Research in Research Context

A question that is frequently asked by practitioners new to action research is where its methodologies are located vis-à-vis quantitative (positivist/scientific) and qualitative (interpretive/hermeneutic) research approaches more broadly, and indeed, the question of how to "place" action research is one that continues to challenge commentators. Action research is often categorized as qualitative research, since it is widely accepted that its emphasis on "practice, participation/collaboration, reflection, interpretation, and, often, emancipation, puts it squarely in opposition to positivist social research" (Hitchcock & Hughes, 1995, p. 29). However, the positioning of action research is more complex than this would suggest, and, for various reasons, some would argue that it could be seen as a "third paradigm" (see Burns, 2005b).

Positivist research, based on longer-standing traditions of Cartesian logical positivism, became particularly dominant from the early nineteenth century in the natural sciences, where researchers set out to establish universal scientific theories or laws. Positivism is based on principles of objective reality, independent measurement and replicability, statistically quantifiable and verifiable data, the proving or disproving of hypotheses, and the minimization of researcher or other variable effects that might prejudice results. Dörnyei (2007, p. 31) explains that in the social sciences "this hegemony only started to change in the 1970s as a result of the challenges of qualitative research, leading to a restructuring of research methodology". He notes that in the newly developing discipline of applied linguistics, quantitative research became prevalent in the period 1970–1985, spurred by the publication of several books on research methods, a landmark volume being Hatch and Farhady (1982), followed by the influential Hatch and Lazaraton (1991). A very gradual orientation toward more (but not predominant) qualitative research in the field of applied linguistics is an even more recent development than in other social science disciplines. Some evidence for this shift was documented by Lazaraton (1995, 2000) who researched the relative numbers of quantitative and qualitative journal articles published in four leading journals and found a small increase in the publication of qualitative research over seven years. However, a more recent survey by Benson, Chik, Gao, Huang and Wang (2009) of ten major journals shows that 22% of the total number were qualitative, and that over the 10-year period of the survey the numbers published each year were relatively stable. In general, advocates of educational action research consider action research to be the antithesis of a positivist approach (see, for example, Winter, 1989; Altrichter, Posch & Somekh, 1993; Kincheloe, 1991; Burnaford, Fischer & Hobson, 2001).

Qualitative, or interpretive, research with its focus on socially engendered theorization and analysis adopts a very different worldview from social research employing a statistical scientific base. Dörnyei (2007) notes that qualitative research is difficult to define because of the lack of clearly delineated theories, methods and practices. Moreover, the boundaries of qualitative research are fragmented as "researchers bring their own worldviews, paradigms, or sets of beliefs to the research project and these inform the conduct and writing of the qualitative study" (Creswell, 2007, p. 15). Thus, it is usually the case that researchers use emergent approaches and procedures shaped by their own experiences and needs in conducting the research (see also Holliday, 2002; Richards, 2003). Moreover, varied philosophical parameters are employed including phenomenology, ethnography, grounded theory, social-constructivism and critical theory. Creswell (2007, pp. 37–39) notes that qualitative studies can, nevertheless, be characterized by various common features: natural settings, the researcher as a key research instrument, multiple data sources, inductive data analysis, the importance of participants' meanings, emergent design, selection of a theoretical lens, interpretive inquiry and holistic accounts. Qualitative approaches are used when a research issue is complex and needs to be explored rather than measured. However, despite its interpretive, emergent and multiple designs, qualitative research still values an objectified stance on the part of the researcher in the collection, analysis and reporting of the research and typically the interpolation of the researcher into the operations of the research site is discouraged. Thus, although action research is often viewed as fitting into an exploratory, qualitative paradigm, its deliberate intervention into the social situation and its collaborative, practical, and participatory orientations distinguish it from simply being labelled as qualitative research.

Researchers such as Lather (1992) and McNiff, Lomax and Whitehead (2003) argue that action research is driven neither by the epistemologies of quantitative nor qualitative research. In line with Carr and Kemmis (1983), they consider that the essence of action research lies within the notion of *praxis*. Aristotle used this term to denote the process by which people might change the social, ethical or political conditions they face by acting upon them. Praxis is contrasted with *theoria*, or sciences and activities aimed at producing knowledge for its own sake. Aristotle considered both to be necessary to advance the human condition. Praxis is a cornerstone of action research as it is concerned with a mutually reinforcing and ongoing process where knowledge is derived from practice and practice reinforces knowledge. McTaggart (1991) stresses that social practices in action research should be understood through Habermas's notion of "communicative action", where "technical actions should be distinguished from social practices which involve a notion of *praxis* (theoretically informed practice)" (p. 49). Moreover, the notion of researcher objectivity, in the sense that it applies to quantitative and qualitative approaches, is inappropriate in action research. Action research participants are inevitably involved centrally and actively in intervening to change an unresolved status quo in a research process that, for them, has personal high stakes.

Thus as McNiff, Lomax and Whitehead (2003, p. 15) stress, it is a misconception that quantitative methods have no place, or that researchers "cannot use statistics in action research." Similarly, McKay (2006) argues that "action research cannot easily be placed on a qualitative/quantitative continuum because the amount of control and structure used in action research studies can vary greatly" (p. 29). Research methodologies and data collection techniques from both qualitative and qualitative paradigms are employable in action research, depending on whether a small number of cases is to be studied through in-depth exploratory analysis or a more extensive population through statistical procedures where variables may need to be controlled (see Burns, 2009).

A study that illustrates the effective use of a quantitative action research design is O'Gara (2008). O'Gara conducted action research in his own school in Italy, to evaluate the impact of drama methods on children's learning of certain verb tenses in Year 4 classes. Arguing that much of the research on drama as a tool for language learning falls within a qualitative paradigm, he adopted a quantitative approach involving an experimental and control group. One group of students was taught through drama methods while the other group received traditional instruction. He hypothesized that there would be no significant difference between the two methods. The two groups were assessed pre- and post-instruction and data were collected using a two-tailed *t*-test for two independent samples with equal variance to examine whether either method was more effective. The results of the study provided statistically reliable evidence for the effectiveness of teaching tenses through drama and therefore the null hypothesis was rejected. O'Gara also notes that he collected qualitative data, which were not yet analyzed. He concludes his study by recommending the analysis of these data to round out the study further and to examine to what extent they would support his quantitative findings. This kind of study suggests the viability of using either, or both, quantitative and qualitative methodologies to conduct action research. The point of the use of particular approaches is the extent to which they deepen meanings and understandings of practice.

Developments and Trends in Action Research in the Field of Second Language Education

Since the late 1980s, publications promoting and exemplifying action research in second language teaching and learning have increased exponentially, if sporadically. Interest in action research from this time grew from a confluence of various disciplinary, theoretical and research influences. While the growth of action research through the next decade remained relatively slow at an international level, it has burgeoned from the late 1990s, so that numerous published examples now exist. In the late 1980s, action research had been permeating the broader educational field for some time, as outlined above and as noted by van Lier (1988) and Nunan (1989) among others, as had interest in the quantitative and ethnographic study and analysis of naturalistic classrooms through observation and interaction analysis (Allwright, 1988; Chaudron, 1988; van Lier, 1988). Advances in learner-centered and process-oriented curriculum theory (e.g. Breen & Candlin, 1980; Yalden, 1983) as well as the growth of the concept of the classroom as socially situated context for language learning (e.g. Breen, 1985) and the teacher as curriculum negotiator (Connelly & Clandinin, 1988) also contributed to constructing the base for second language action research. Calls for teachers to be co-participants in classroom-centered research became inevitable and were mounting (Jarvis, 1983; Long, 1983, Allwright, 1988, Allwright & Bailey, 1991).

Such calls were complemented by the idea that, rather than envisaging the initial "training" of teachers as a sufficient basis for future practice, teachers should be involved in a lifelong process of professional "education" (Larsen-Freeman, 1983; Richards, 1987), which would equip them for reflexive and self-critical expansion of their skills and knowledge (Schön, 1983, 1987; Shulman, 1987; Richards & Lockhart, 1994; Zeichner & Liston, 1996). The publication of volumes edited by Richards and Nunan (1990) on teacher education and by Wallace (1991) on teachers as reflective practitioners served to cement such ideas as the basis for language teacher professional development up to the present time (see Burns & Richards, 2009a). They were closely followed by other works highlighting the related concepts of teacher learning (Freeman & Richards, 1996), teacher knowledge (Freeman, 1996; Freeman & Johnson, 1998), teacher beliefs and cognition (Burns, 1992; Woods, 1996; Borg, 1998) and teacher narrative (Golombek, 1998). Thus the seedbeds for the growth of action research were becoming firmly established throughout the 1990s.

While volumes on how second language teachers could conduct action research were few and far between for over a decade from the late 1980s (an exception is Nunan, 1989), the end of the 1990s saw a small surge of publications. Although differing somewhat in orientation from individualized to collaborative forms of action research, Wallace (1998), Freeman (1998) and Burns (1999) all offered practical advice to teachers about investigating their own educational contexts. Rather surprisingly however, it is still the case that volumes for practitioners on the processes of conducting action research per se are still scarce in the field of language teaching (but see Burns, 2010). More common during the period from the late 1990s, although even these are still limited in this field, have been volumes assisting classroom practitioners with skills for engaging with research methods in general (McDonough & McDonough, 1997; Brown & Rodgers, 2002; Mackey & Gass, 2005; Perry, 2005; Nunan & Bailey, 2009; Paltridge & Phakiti, 2010), quantitative research (Porte, 2002), qualitative research (Holliday, 2002; Heigham & Croker, 2009), qualitative TESOL-oriented research (Richards, 2003) and classroom-based research (McKay, 2006).

One of the early publications to provide actual examples of action research conducted by language teachers was Edge and Richards (1993). Their volume was the product of presentations made at the first Teachers Develop Teachers Research (TDTR) conference, a joint initiative of the International Association for Teachers of English as a Foreign Language (IATEFL) Teacher Development and the Research Special Interest Groups, which was "the brainchild of Julian Edge" (personal communication, Keith Richards, July 20, 2009) and held at Aston University in 1992. The deliberately ambiguous title of the conference was seen as a way of reclaiming "the difficult term 'research' to characterize a teacher's personal investigations" and to "broaden the base of people who might be attracted" (Edge & Richards, 1993, p. 6). The volume had considerable impact at the time as it served to document the progress of English language teaching (ELT) action research, and other TDTR conferences where teachers could present their action research followed (e.g. Field, Graham, Griffiths & Head, 1997). These conferences served to highlight during this period that action research was having an impact on teachers in numerous locations internationally, including Australia, Austria, Brazil, Estonia, Hong Kong, Holland, Israel, the Philippines Oman, Poland, Spain and the United Kingdom. A few years later Roberts (1998) noted the spread of action research in formal courses, for example in Spain (James, 1996) and China (Thorne & Quiang, 1996) and in curriculum and teacher development initiatives, for example in India (e.g. Mathew & Eapen, 1996), Australia (e.g. Burns & Hood, 1995), Hong Kong (e.g. Pennington, 1996) and Japan (e.g. Sano, 1996). More recent major projects utilizing principles of reflection, exploration and action include the Teacher Knowledge Project in the US (Freeman, 2000) and the School-Based Language Assessment Project in Hong Kong (Davison, 2007).

Richards (1998) took an action research orientation in a collection published by TESOL International of short accounts of contextualized classroom situations where teachers identified issues, outlined their responses or solutions to them and reflected upon their practices. Teacher-written descriptions were accompanied by "meta-commentaries" from language teacher educators around the world. A further valuable set of accounts for practitioner researchers was provided by Edge (2001b). This volume, part of the Case Studies Series published by TESOL International, drew together examples from highly varied international locations and sectors including primary education in Slovenia (Rogers, 2001), secondary instruction in France (Nicol, 2001), adult learning in the UK (Adams, 2001), undergraduate writing classes in Japan (Cowie, 2001), teacher education in Brazil (Santana-Williamson, 2001) and teacher–researcher collaboration in Thailand (Maneekhao & Watson Todd, 2001). It provided a rich collection that reflected the scope and potentialities for application of action research at this time. Other sources of models for teacher researchers and teacher educators have proliferated into the 2000s. Among the volumes produced are the *Teachers' Voices* series from Australia (e.g. Burns & Hood 1995; Burns & de Silva Joyce, 2005), accounts from Hong Kong teachers (Tinker Sachs, 2002), classroom examples mainly from teachers in the Asian region (Hadley, 2003) and reports written as part of BA courses in Oman (Borg, 2006a, 2008) and in the United Arab Emirates (Warne, 2006; Gallagher & Bashir-Ali, 2007).

The professional association, TESOL International, has done much to support the publication of action research and a major series, edited by Farrell, entitled *Language Teacher Research in …* has recently served to expand the range of illustrative examples. Each book in this six-volume series offers a collection of research studies carried out by language practitioners in various parts of the world, Asia (Farrell, 2006), Europe (Borg, 2006b), the Americas (McGarrell, 2007), the Middle East (Coombe & Barlow, 2007), Australia and New Zealand (Burns & Burton, 2008) and Africa (Makalela, 2009). The series is marked by its goals to "document how individual teachers at all levels of practice systematically reflect on their own practice" (p. vii) and to "encourage an inquiry stance towards language teaching" (p. viii) (see series editor's preface, Farrell, 2006). Apart from the volumes now available to practitioner researchers, articles on action research are increasingly accepted by journals, particularly those that focus on links between theory and practice. Recent examples, beyond those noted in the chapter published in the first volume of this handbook (Burns, 2005a), focus on incorporating blog projects in the English as a foreign language (EFL) classroom in Japan (Pinkman, 2005), investigating non-native teacher study groups in the USA (Yeh, 2005), facilitating collaborative action research for Indonesian high school teachers (Burns & Rochantiningsih, 2006), introducing critical literacy at secondary level in Hong Kong (Wong, Chan & Firkins, 2006), teaching cultural sensitivity in the French foreign language classroom (Durocher, 2007), increasing junior high school student independence in Argentina (Blásquez, 2007), supporting primary school teachers ongoing professional development in Hong Kong (Poon, 2008) and socializing teachers to the teaching of English language learners in the UAE (Sowa, 2009).

Issues and Controversies Surrounding Action Research in Language Teaching

Numerous debates and controversies have continually accompanied the development of action research in the second language field. One of the most prominent has been the capacity of teachers to undertake research since, it is argued, they are trained to teach and not to research. Such arguments were put forward early by Brumfit and Mitchell (1989), and more recently by Jarvis (2002a, 2002b), for example. A dimension of this argument is the question of whether practitioner research can meet adequate scientific research standards. Mackey and Gass (2005), while acknowledging the point that action research is an evolving and independent genre with its own features and standards (see also Freeman, 1998; Wharton, 2007), comment that nevertheless, "if action research is intended to inform a wide research community, it will need to meet the basic standards for publication and presentation" (p. 219). Opinions on the matter of how action research should be evaluated differ, however, with some arguing that the same standards as for other research should pertain (e.g. Nunan, 1997), and others suggesting that sustainability and not scientific rigor is paramount (e.g. Allwright, 1997). McDonough (2006) supports as a relevant framework the validity criteria associated with qualitative research put forward by authors such as Anderson, Herr and Nihlen (1994) and Jacobson (1998), while Marshall and Rossman (2006) suggest that usefulness and built-in relevance to participants may be more important that traditional methodological rigor. In short, there is still some way to go to reach agreement on the most relevant and reliable standards for reporting action research.

A further angle on this debate has been in respect of the unreasonable demands that action research places on teachers. Posing the question "Is action research a 'natural' activity for teachers?," Johnson (1994) took issue with prevailing arguments that defined action research as a process with which practitioners feel "comfortable." She suggested that inquiry-based and teacher-as-researcher approaches where teachers could utilize the narrative forms they typically employ to explore and understand their work were more natural practices for many teachers. In a similar vein, Allwright argues that action research forces teachers to adopt "research skills taken from the academic repertoire" (Allwright, 2005, p. 355). From the early 1990s, when he commenced working in Brazil with teachers at the Rio de Janeiro Cultura Inglesa, Allwright has been a particularly strong critic of action research (see Allwright & Bailey, 1991; Allwright, 1993, 2003, 2005; Allwright & Hanks, 2009), arguing that it is essentially "parasitical" on the lives of teachers and learners, as it leads to practitioner burnout, is unsustainable beyond the life of a professional development course, requires expert support and generally results in a technicist, rather than an "understanding" stance toward practitioner inquiry. Instead he proposed the concept of exploratory teaching (Allwright & Bailey, 1991; Allwright, 1993). Exploratory teaching is now termed exploratory practice (EP), which Allwright states he gets "close to clarifying" in this description:

> Exploratory Practice offers an epistemologically and ethically motivated framework for conducting practitioner research in the field of language education. It does not offer a technical framework in itself, but it does make practical suggestions and there is a considerable and growing published literature of examples of EP work in a wide variety of settings around the world.
>
> (Allwright, 2005, p. 361)

While, since its inception, EP has moved from a set of ethical design criteria, to "a temporary reversion to a technicist approach" involving a set of eight practical steps, Allwright's most recent proposals for EP focus on six principles and two practical suggestions. These consist of:

Principle 1: Put quality first
Principle 2: Work primarily to understand classroom life
Principle 3: Involve everybody

Principle 4: Work to bring people together
Principle 5: Work also for mutual development
Principle 6: Make the work a continuous enterprise
Suggestion 1: Minimize the extra effort of all sorts for all concerned
Suggestion 2: Integrate the "work for understanding" into the existing life of the classroom.

(Allwright, 2005, p. 360)

Although EP may offer a justifiable alternative to action research, it is not necessarily straightforward to discern the fundamental differences between the central tenets of action research and Allwright's notion of practitioner research, either epistemologically or ethically. For example, the following "four things action research is not" (from Kemmis & McTaggart, 1988, pp. 21–22 and abbreviated in the interests of space) might well be mapped on to the principles suggested above:

1. It is *not* the usual things teachers do when they think about their teaching. Action research is more systematic and collaborative in collecting evidence on which to base rigorous group reflection. [*Principle 1, Principle 4, Suggestion 2*]
2. It is *not* simply problem-solving … It does not start from a view of "problems" as pathologies. It is motivated by a quest to improve and understand the world by changing it and learning how to improve it from the effects of the changes made. [*Principle 5, Principle 6*]
3. It is *not* research done on other people. Action research is research done by particular people on their own work, to help them improve what they do, including how they work with and for others. Action research is research that treats people as autonomous responsible agents who participate actively in making their own histories and conditions of life, by knowing what they are doing, and as collaboratively potent in the construction of their collective history and conditions of life …. [*Principle 2, Principle 3*]
4. It is *not* the scientific method applied to teaching. There is not just one view of the scientific method; there are many …. Action research also concerns the "subject" (the researcher) him or herself …. Action research is a systematically evolving, a living process, changing both the researcher and the situations in which he or she acts …. [*Principle 1, Principle 6, Suggestion 1*]

It is arguable that the two approaches should be seen, not as mutually exclusive or in opposition to each other (this would indeed be unfortunate), but as complementary dimensions on a continuum of options for practitioner reflexivity, intended to expand their personal or professional development and understanding (see also Griffiths & Tann, 1992). Moreover, it could be seen as equally restraining for would-be teacher researchers to have to confine their aspirations to "exploratory practice," as it is for them to be required to equip themselves with "the repertoires of academic researchers."

Doubts about the viability of action research are also raised by Dörnyei (2007) who declares that although it is "a noble idea, it just does not seem to work in practice" (p. 191). Alluding to action research as "controversial" (p. 177) and "an enigma" (p. 191), he bases his objections on the notion that "the most important tenet" is "the link between the researcher and teaching," the fact that "there is one big problem with action research: there is too little of it," and that as far as he is personally concerned he has "still to meet a teacher who has been voluntarily involved in an action research project." In addition, echoing Allwright, he claims that action research is a top-down movement, predominantly imposed from above by researchers, who are unwilling themselves to conduct action research (cf. Bartels, 2005), on teachers. While it may be true, as he argues, that action research is time-consuming (as is any research), there are few incentives for teachers and professional support is required, there is also counter-evidence that teachers are prepared to devote time to learning about research (e.g. McDonough, 2006), that the increasing professionalism of the language teaching field requires a knowledge of research and how to conduct it (e.g. Leung, 2009) and that collaborative and supportive initiatives between researchers and teachers are becoming more widespread across the world (e.g. School for International Training, 2003; Perrett, 2003; Murphey & Sato, 2005; Atay, 2006; Torres Jaramillo & Mongui Sánchez, 2008; Locke, 2009). It would be unfortunate if such analyses of the current status of action research only serve to widen rather than to narrow the breach between researchers and practitioners, to reinforce the concept that applied linguistic and second language acquisition (SLA) research is either irrelevant or forbidden territory for teachers (see Ellis, 2010, for an interesting discussion of the complexities of practitioner contributions to SLA research), or to consign teachers to being "mechanical operators of pedagogical procedures" (Leung, 2009, p. 55) on the basis that they cannot learn to equip themselves to investigate their practices. In this respect, Stewart's (2006, p. 427) observation is apt:

> Today, the second language field is struggling to produce [a] TESOL knowledge base. For this to happen, practitioner participation is essential, and support is needed from university-based educators. The teacher–researcher distinction has a potential to disable effective collaboration by establishing artificial and divisive barriers from the start. Although collaboration between teachers is essential, the danger is that the dichotomy inherent in distinct role labels might unintentionally privilege technical knowledge over practical or social knowledge. This would be highly detrimental to the development of a new knowledge base in TESOL that better fits our field.

These various positions notwithstanding, estimating how widespread action research actually is among teachers is difficult. A decade ago, Rainey (2000) suggested that action research might be in decline. The survey she conducted, involving the responses of 228 surveys from teachers from 10 countries, indicated that 75.5% of her respondents had never heard of action research. Of those who had (55 responses), 75.9% claimed to have done action research, although the responses of 57.4% of these indicated they were not very active researchers. Lack of time, training and adequate support were identified as major inhibitors (see Burns, 2005b for more detailed analysis of Rainey's research). A more recent 2008 survey of 413 teachers internationally by the British Council (see http://www.teachingenglish.org.uk/talk/polls/action-research) suggests a somewhat more optimistic picture with 54% of respondents claiming that they do action research either "a lot" (33%) or "sometimes" (21%). As in Rainey's research, the accompanying comments posted on the website suggest positive attitudes among those familiar with conducting action research, but also the need for more time, training and support, as well as recognition for undertaking research and access to appropriate publication venues (in this respect the Language Teacher Research section of the new *TESOL Journal* initiated from 2009 should offer more opportunities, see http://www.tesol.org/s_tesol/seccss.asp?CID=1997&DID=12258). Borg (2009) investigated to what extent teachers engage with research, both reading and doing it. He found that, for the 505 teachers from 13 countries whom he surveyed, the concept of research is ambiguous, with many associating the characteristics of research predominantly with conventional scientific and experimental approaches. On the other hand, research topics in which teachers were interested, such as collecting course feedback from students or observing colleagues, were closely related to classroom practice and professional development. Lack of time, knowledge and access to materials, as well as institutional barriers were major inhibitors. Borg suggests that more reliable guidance and support is needed for teachers attracted to research and that volumes on research methods need to go beyond generic advice to address the more specific kinds of questions that practitioners pose. He also argues that the field of ELT needs to recognize and understand these factors in order to make teacher research engagement a more feasible activity.

Future Directions and Challenges

Despite the criticisms and doubts that have dogged the progress of action research into the language teaching field, it appears that action research is here to stay, at least as far as the immediate future is concerned. Various commentators have taken a firm stance on the role and position of action research in the second language field. Edge (2001a) posits: "I see the TESOL field as committed to a mode of operation for which the umbrella title, action research, is appropriate … Of course, perspectives and foci vary, but the broad sweep of the movement is undeniable" (p. 6). Richards (2003) enthuses about action research as a way for novices to enter the research field: "The most powerful form of research for the beginning researcher in TESOL is action research" (p. 236). Larsen-Freeman and Cameron (2008) see action research as compatible with the "turn" in applied linguistics towards complexity system theory as "action research is also concerned with possibility rather than prediction, and with the study of systems" (p. 244), while Norton, Pennycook and Ramanathan, in their editors' preface to Denos et al. (2009) go so far as to declare that action research has "come of age in second language scholarship" (p. ix).

Nevertheless, there is a need to be cautious, as Breen (2007) suggests, that action research does not come to reify "vernacular wisdom" or to position teachers as "guardians of pedagogies that somehow lack the capacity for evolution" (p. 1074). In this respect, one danger for practitioners engaging in action research is its cooption by school systems or bureaucratic agencies intent on simplistically confirming so-called educational "reform." Thus, among current challenges is the need, as already noted, to expand perspectives that connect to critical explorations of social justice, politics, power, identity, diversity or gender. The productive localism of action research may become a weakness rather than a strength if it also fails to incorporate initiatives that can bring about more fundamental contributions to the theory and practice of language teaching (cf. Brydon-Miller, Greenwood & Maguire, 2003).

Another major challenge, and one that has received minimal attention in action research in the second language field as in others, concerns ethical practices. With the expansion of critical and reflective orientations to teacher education, teachers and teacher educators will need more understanding of the complex ethical issues inscribed in approaches that operate under the umbrella of practitioner investigation. Nolen and Vander Putten (2007) draw attention to several issues related to ethical positioning in action research that may not be present in more traditional research. Among the key aspects are confidentiality, consent, power relations and participant roles. Confidentiality becomes of particular importance in localized situations where participant identity may be easily uncovered, as do questions of participant autonomy where complex power relations exist, particularly in teacher–student relationships. As the authors note "freedom to participate or decline is not likely to be clearly definable" (p. 403) and making decisions to participate may also be beyond the maturity of learner participants, especially where they are dependent in teacher researchers for their learning experiences and grades. In addition, teacher–student relationships must continue regardless of the scope and duration of the explorations. Moreover, action research may incur conflicted positions and roles where participants are acting not just as researchers but also as "change agents." There is the potential in such a situation for the primary objective, that of student learning, to be obscured. Among their key recommendations, Nolen and Vander Putten draw attention to the central role that professional organizations should play in advancing ethical statements for practitioner research, but note that at present few associations have such posts on their websites.

Finally, despite the gains in the deployment of qualitative and action research in the field of applied linguistics and second language teaching, as Lazaraton notes (2005) parametric and quantitative studies still "reign supreme" (p. 219). Her imputation that "perhaps the next frontier in applied linguistics research should be developing alternatives to parametric statistics for small-scale research studies that involved limited amounts of dependent data" (p. 219) could be aptly applied in respect of action research. In the "third decade" of the action research movement in the second language field, advocates will need to be vigilant to the criticisms, issues and challenges raised in this chapter, to evaluate why and how action research has achieved its current prominence in this field, and to consider carefully how to "sustain and expand it with integrity" (Brydon-Miller et al., 2003, p. 25).

References

Adams, K. (2001). Minding the gap! Noticing in real time. In Edge, J. (Ed.), *Action research* (pp. 105–116). Alexandria, VA: TESOL.

Allwright, D. (1988). *Observation in the language classroom.* London: Longman.

Allwright, D. (1993). Integrating "research" and "pedagogy": Appropriate criteria and practical possibilities. In J. Edge & K. Richards (Eds.), *Teachers develop teachers research,* (pp. 125–135). Oxford: Heinemann.

Allwright, D. (1997). Quality and sustainability in teacher-research. *TESOL Quarterly, 31*(2), 368–370.

Allwright, D. (2003). Exploratory practice: Rethinking practitioner research in language teaching. *Language Teaching Research, 7,* 113–141.

Allwright, D. (2005). Developing principles for practitioner research: The case for exploratory practice. *The Modern Language Journal, 89*(3), 353–366.

Allwright, D., & Bailey, K. M. (1991). *Focus on the language classroom.* New York: Cambridge University Press.

Allwright, D., & Hanks, J. (2009). *The developing language learner.* Basingstoke: Palgrave Macmillan.

Altrichter, H., Posch, P. & Somekh, B. (1993). *Teachers investigate their work. An introduction to the methods of action research.* Abingdon: Routledge.

Anderson, G., Herr, K. & Nihlen, A. (1994). *Studying your own school: An educator's guide to qualitative practitioner research.* Thousand Oaks, CA: Corwin Press.

Atay, D. (2006). Teachers' professional development: Partnerships in research. *TESL_EJ, 10*(2), http://tesl-ej.org/ej38/a8.html (retrieved July 9, 2009).

Auerbach, E. (1992). *Making meaning making change: Participatory curriculum development for adult literacy.* Washington, DC: Centre for Applied Linguistics.

Auerbach, E. (1996). *From the community, to the community: A guidebook for participatory literacy training.* Mahwah, NJ: Lawrence Erlbaum Associates.

Bartels, N. (2005). *Applied linguistics and language teacher education.* New York: Springer.

Benson, P, Chik, A., Gao, X., Huang, J. & Wang, W. (2009). Qualitative research in language teaching and learning journals, 1997–2006. *The Modern Language Journal, 93*(1), 79–90.

Blásquez, B. A. (2007). Reflection as a necessary condition for action research. *English Teaching Forum, 1,* 26–34.

Borg, S. (1998). Teachers' pedagogical systems and grammar teaching: A qualitative study. *TESOL Quarterly, 32*(1), 9–38.

Borg, S. (2006a). *Classroom research in English language teaching in Oman.* Muscat: Sultanate of Oman, Ministry of Education.

Borg, S. (Ed.) (2006b). *Language teacher research in Europe.* Alexandria, VA: TESOL.

Borg, S. (2008). *Investigating English language teaching and learning in Oman.* Muscat: Sultanate of Oman, Ministry of Education.

Borg, S. (2009). English language teachers' conceptions of research *Applied Linguistics, 29*(3), 456–482.

Breen, M. P. (1985). The social context for language learning—a neglected situation? *Studies in Second Language Acquisition, 7,* 135–158.

Breen, M. P. (2007). Appropriating uncertainty: ELT professional development in the new century. In Cummins, J. & C. Davison (Eds.), *International handbook of English language teaching. Part II* (pp. 1067–1084). New York: Springer.

Breen, M. P., & Candlin, C. N. (1980). The essentials of a communicative curriculum in language teaching. *Applied Linguistics, 1*(2), 89–112.

Brown, J. D., & Rodgers, T. S. (2002). *Doing second language research.* Oxford: Oxford University Press.

Brumfit, C., & Mitchell, R. (1989). The language classroom as a focus for research. In C. Brumfit & R. Mitchell (Eds.), *Research in the language classroom* (pp. 3–15). ELT Documents 133. London: Modern English Publications and the British Council.

Brydon-Miller, M., Greenwood, D. & Maguire, P. (2003). Why action research? *Action Research, 1*(1), 9–28.

Burnaford, G., Fischer, J. & Hobson, D. (Eds.) (2001). *Teachers doing research.* Mahwah, NJ: Lawrence Erlbaum Associates.

Burns, A. (1992). Teacher beliefs and their influence on classroom practice. *Prospect, 7*(3), 56–66.

Burns, A. (1999). *Collaborative action research for English language teachers.* New York: Cambridge University Press.

Burns, A. (2005a). Action research. In E. Hinkel (Ed.), *Handbook of research in second language teaching and learning* (pp. 241–256). Mahwah, NJ: Lawrence Erlbaum Associates.

Burns, A. (2005b). Action research: An evolving paradigm? *Language Teaching, 38*(2), 57–74.

Burns, A. (2007). Action research: Contributions and future directions in ELT. In J. Cummins & C. Davison (Eds.), *International handbook of English language teaching. Part II* (pp. 987–1002). New York: Springer.

Burns, A. (2010). *Doing action research in English language teaching. A guide for practitioners.* New York: Routledge.

Burns. A., & Burton, J. (Eds.) (2008). *Language teacher research in Australia and New Zealand.* Alexandria, VA: TESOL.

Burns, A., & Hood, S. (Eds.) (1995). *Teachers' voices: Exploring course design in a changing curriculum.* Sydney: National Centre for English Language Teaching and Research.

Burns, A., & de Silva Joyce, H. (Eds.) (2005). *Teachers' voices 8: Explicitly supporting reading and writing in the classroom.* Sydney: National Centre for English Language Teaching and Research.

Burns, A., & Richards, J. C. (2009a). Introduction. In A. Burns & J. C. Richards (Eds.), *The Cambridge guide to second language teacher education* (pp. 1–8). New York: Cambridge University Press.

Burns, A., & Richards, J. C. (Eds.) (2009b). *The Cambridge guide to second language teacher education.* New York: Cambridge University Press.

Burns, A. & Rochsantiningsih, D. (2006). Conducting action research in Indonesia: Illustrations and implications. *Indonesian Journal of English Language Teaching, 2*(1), 21–35.

Carr, W., & Kemmis, S. (1983). *Becoming critical: Knowing through action research.* Geelong: Deakin University Press.

Chaudron, C. (1988). *Second language classrooms: Research on teaching and learning.*New York: Cambridge University Press.

Cochran-Smith, M., & Lytle, S. L. (1999). The teacher researcher movement: A decade later. *Educational Researcher, 28*(7), 15–25.

Connelly, F. M., & Clandinin, J. D. (1988). *Teachers as curriculum planners: Narratives of experience.* New York: Teachers College Press.

Coombe, C., & Barlow, L. (Eds.) (2007). *Language teacher research in the Middle East.* Alexandria, VA: TESOL.

Corey, S. (1953). *Action research to improve school practices.* New York: Columbia University Teachers College Press.

Cowie, N. (2001). An "it's not action research yet, but I'm getting there" approach to teaching writing. In Edge, J. (Ed.), *Action research* (pp. 21–32). Alexandria, VA: TESOL.

Creswell, J. (2007). *Qualitative inquiry and research design. Choosing among five approaches.* (2nd ed.). London: Sage.

Crookes, G. (1993). Action research for second language teachers: Going beyond teacher research. *Applied Linguistics, 14*(2), 130–144.

Crookes, G., & Lehner, A. (1998). Aspects of process in an ESL critical pedagogy teacher education course. *TESOL Quarterly, 32*(2), 319–328.

Davison, C. (2007). School-based English language assessment in Hong Kong: Action research as an agent of change. Paper presented at Board-sponsored session, 41st Annual TESOL Convention, Seattle, March 20–24.

Denos, C., Toohey, K., Neilson, K. & Waterstone, B. (2009). *Collaborative research in multicultural classrooms.* Bristol: Multilingual Matters.

Denzin, N. K., & Lincoln, Y. S. (Eds.) (2005). *The Sage handbook of qualitative research* (3rd ed.). Thousand Oaks, CA: Sage.

Dewey, J. (1916). *Democracy and education.* New York: The Free Press.

Dörnyei, Z. (2007). *Research methods in applied linguistics.* Oxford: Oxford University Press.

Durocher, D. O. (2007). Teaching sensitivity to cultural difference in the first-year foreign language classroom. *Foreign Language Annals, 40*(1), 143–160.

Ebbutt, D. (1985). Educational action research: Some general concerns and specific quibbles. In R. Burgess (Ed.), *Issues in Educational Research* (pp. 152–174). Lewes: Falmer Press.

Eden, C., & Huxman, C. (2005). Action research for management research. *British Journal of Management, 7*(1), 75–86.

Edge, J. (2001a). Attitude and access: Building a new teaching/learning community in TESOL. In Edge, J. (Ed.), *Action research* (pp. 1–12). Alexandria, VA: TESOL.

Edge, J. (Ed.) (2001b). *Action research.* Alexandria, VA: TESOL.

Edge, J., & Richards, K. (Eds.) (1993). *Teachers develop teachers research.* Oxford: Heinemann.

Elliott, J. (1991). *Action research for educational change.* Buckingham: Open University Press.

Ellis, R. (2010). Second language acquisition, teacher education and language pedagogy. *Language Teaching, 43*(2), 182–201.

Emery, F., & Thorsrud, E. (1976). *Democracy at work.* Leiden: Martinus Nojhoff.

Fals Borda, O. (1969). *Subversion and social change in Colombia.* New York: Colombia University Press.

Farrell, T. S. C. (Ed.) (2006). *Language teacher research in Asia.* Alexandria, VA: TESOL.

Field, J., Graham, A., Griffiths, E. & Head, K. (Eds.) (1997). *Teachers develop teachers research 2.* Whitstable: IATEFL.

Freeman, D. (1996). Redefining the relationships between research and what teachers know. In K. Bailey & D. Nunan (Eds.), *Voices from the language classroom* (pp. 88–115). Cambridge: Cambridge University Press.

Freeman, D. (1998). *Doing teacher research: From inquiry to understanding.* Boston: Heinle and Heinle Publishers.

Freeman, D. (2000). *First annual report of the Teacher Knowledge Project at the School for International Training to the Fund for the Improvement of Post-Secondary Education.* Brattleboro, VT: SIT.

Freeman, D., & Johnson, K. E. (1998) Reconceptualizing the knowledge-base of language teacher education. *TESOL Quarterly, 32*(3), 397–417.

Freeman, D., & Richards, J. (Eds.) (1996). *Teacher learning in language teaching.* Cambridge: Cambridge University Press.

Freire, P. (1970). *Pedagogy of the oppressed.* New York: Herder & Herder.

Gallagher, K., & Bashir-Ali, K. (2007). *Action research and initial teacher education in the UAE.* Abu Dhabi: Higher Colleges of Technology Press.

Golombek, P. R. (1998). A study of language teachers' personal practical knowledge. *TESOL Quarterly, 32*(3), 447–464.

Greenwood, D., & Levin, M. (2007). *Introduction to action research. Social research for social change* (2nd ed.). Thousand Oaks, CA: Sage Publications.

Grey, M. (2009). Ethnographers of difference in a critical EAP community—becoming. *Journal of English for Academic Purposes, 8*(2), 121–131.

Griffiths, M., & Tann, S. (1992). Using reflective practice to link personal and public theories. *Journal of Education for Teaching, 18*(1), 69–84.

Grundy, S. (1988). The three modes of action research. In S. Kemmis & E. McTaggart (Eds,), *The action research reader* (3rd ed.) (pp. 321–335). Geelong: Deakin University Press.

Grundy, S., & Kemmis, S. (1981). Educational action research in Australia: The state of the art (an overview). In S. Kemmis, R. McTaggart, G. di Chiro, S. Henry, J. Mousley & I. Robottom (Eds.), *The action research reader* (pp. 277–285). Geelong: Deakin University Press.

Hadley, G. (Ed.) (2003). *Action research in action.* Singapore: RELC.

Hatch, E., & Farhady, H. (1982). *Research design and statistics for applied linguistics.* Rowley, MA: Newbury House.

Hatch, E., & Lazaraton, A. (1991). *The research manual: Design and statistics for applied linguistics.* Boston: Heinle and Heinle.

Heigham, J., & Croker, R. (Eds.). (2009). *An introduction to qualitative research in applied linguistics.* London: Palgrave Macmillan.

Heron, J. (1996). *Co-operative inquiry: Research into the human condition.* London: Sage.

Hitchcock, G., & Hughes, D. (1995). *Research and the teacher* (2nd ed.). London: Routledge.

Holliday, A. (2002). *Doing and writing qualitative research.* London: Sage.

Hopkins, D. (1994). *A teacher's guide to classroom research* (2nd ed.). Buckingham: Open University Press.

Horton, M. (with Kohl, J. and Kohl, H.) (1990). *The long haul: An autobiography.* New York: Doubleday.

Jacobson, W. (1998). Defining the quality of practitioner research. *Adult Education Quarterly, 48*, 125–138.

James, P. (1996). Collaborative teacher development/action research: A way forward. *APAC News, 27*, n.p.

Jarvis, G. (1983). Pedagogical knowledge for the second language teacher. In J. Alatis, H. H. Stern & P. Strevens (Eds.), *Applied linguistics and the preparation of teachers: Towards a rationale* (pp. 281–297). Washington, DC: Georgetown University Press.

Jarvis, S. (2002a). Research in TESOL Part I. *TESOL Research Interest Section Newsletter, 8*(3), 1–2.

Jarvis, S. (2002b). Research in TESOL Part II. *TESOL Research Interest Section Newsletter, 9*(1), 1–2.

Johnston. S. (1994). Is action research a "natural" process for teachers? *Educational Action Research, 2*(1), 39–48.

Kemmis, S., & McTaggart, R. (Eds.) (1988). The *action research planner* (3rd ed.). Geelong: Deakin University Press.

Kemmis, S., & McTaggart, R. (2005). Participatory action research: Communicative action and the public sphere. In N. K. Denzin & Y. S. Lincoln (Eds.), *The Sage handbook of qualitative research* (pp. 589–603). London: Sage.

Kincheloe, J. (1991). *Teachers as researchers: Qualitative inquiry as a path to empowerment.* London: Falmer.

Larsen-Freeman, D. (1983). Training teachers or educating a teacher? In J. E. Alatis, H. H. Stern & P. Strevens (Eds.), *Georgetown University Roundtable on language and linguistics* (pp. 264–274). Washington, DC: Georgetown University Press.

Larsen-Freeman, D., & Cameron, L. (2008). *Complex systems and applied linguistics.* Oxford: Oxford University Press.

Lather, P. (1992). Critical frames in educational research: Feminist and post-structural perspectives. *Qualitative Issues in Educational Research, 31*(2), 87–89.

Lazaraton, A. (1995). Qualitative research in applied linguistics: A progress report. *TESOL Quarterly, 29*(3), 455–472.

Lazaraton, A. (2000). Current trends in research methodology and statistics in applied linguistics. *TESOL Quarterly, 34*(1), 175–181.

Lazaraton, A. (2005). Quantitative research methods. In E. Hinkel (Ed.), *Handbook of research in second language teaching and learning*, (pp. 209–224). Mahwah, NJ: Lawrence Erlbaum Associates.

Leung, C. (2009). Second language teacher professionalism. In A. Burns & J. C. Richards (Eds.), *The Cambridge guide to second language teacher education* (pp. 49–58). New York: Cambridge University Press.

Lewin, K. (1948). *Resolving social conflicts: Selected papers on group dynamics.* New York: Harper & Row.

Locke, T. (2009). Teachers as action researchers: Some reflections on what it takes. Paper presented at the International Association for the Improvement of Mother Tongue Education Conference on Learning and Teaching Language and Literature (IAIMTE) Conference, Ontario Institute for Studies in Education, University of Toronto, June 23–26, http:// waikato.researchgateway.ac.nz/bitstream/10289/2697/1/Locke_teacher.pdf (retrieved July 29, 2009).

Long, M. (1983). Training the second language teacher as classroom researcher. In J. E. Alatis, H. H. Stern & P. Strevens (Eds.), *Applied linguistics and the preparation of teachers: Towards a rationale* (pp. 281–297). Washington, DC: Georgetown University Press.

McDonough, K. (2006). Action research and the professional development of graduate teaching assistants. *The Modern Language Journal, 90*(1), 33–47.

McDonough, J., & McDonough, S. (1997). *Research methods for English language teachers.* London: Arnold.

McGarrell, H. M. (Ed.) (2006). *Language teacher research in the Americas.* Alexandria, VA: TESOL.

McGee, A. (2008). Critical reflections of action research used for professional development in a Middle Eastern Gulf State. *Educational Action Research, 16*(2), 235–250.

McKay, S. L. (2006). *Researching second language classrooms.* Mahwah, NJ: Lawrence Erlbaum Associates.

Mackey, A., & Gass, S. (2005). *Second language research. Methodology and design.* Mahwah, NJ: Lawrence Erlbaum Associates.

McKernan, J (1996). *Curriculum action research. A handbook of methds and resources for the reflective practitioner* (2nd ed.). London: Kogan Page.

MacNaughton, G. (2001). Action research. In G. MacNaughton, S. A. Rolfe & I. Siraj-Blatchford (Eds.), *Doing early childhood research: International perspectives on theory and practice* (pp. 208–223). Sydney: Allen and Unwin.

McNiff, J., Lomax, P. & Whitehead, J. (2003). *You and your action research project* (2nd ed.). London: Routledge.

McTaggart, R. (1991). *Action research: A short modern history.* Geelong: Deakin University.

Makalela, L. (Ed.) (2009). *Language teacher research in Africa.* Alexandria, VA: TESOL.

Maneekhao, K., & Todd, R. W. (2001). Two kinds of becoming: The researcher's tale and the mentor's tale. In Edge, J. (Ed.), *Action research,* (pp. 57–68). Alexandria, VA: TESOL.

Marshall, C., & Rossman, G. B. (2006). *Designing qualitative research* (4th ed.). London: Sage.

Mathew, R., & Eapen, L. R. (Eds.) (1996). *The language curriculum dynamics of change. Teacher as researcher* (Vol. 2). Report of the International Seminar (August 1995). Hyderabad: CIEFL.

Mugford, G. (2008). Keeping a critical eye on "lexical friends": Cognates as critical pedagogy in pre-service teacher education. *Profile, 9*(Jan./June), 129–142.

Murphey, T., & Sato, K. (Eds.) (2005). *Communities of supportive professionals.* Alexandria, VA: TESOL.

Nicol, C. (2001). Beverage assassination and the making of appropriate requests. In Edge, J. (Ed.), *Action research* (pp. 93–104). Alexandria, VA: TESOL.

Nolen, A., & Vander Putten, J. (2007). Action research in education: Addressing gaps in educational principles and practices. *Educational Researcher, 36*(7), 401–407.

Nunan, D. (1989). *Understanding language classrooms.* London: Prentice Hall.

Nunan, D. (1993). Action research in language education. In J. Edge & K. Richards (Eds.), *Teachers develop teachers research* (pp. 39–50). Oxford: Heinemann.

Nunan, D. (1997). Developing standards for teacher-research in TESOL. *TESOL Quarterly, 31*(2), 365–367.

Nunan, D., & Bailey, K. M. (2009). *Exploring second language classroom research: A comprehensive guide.* Farmington Hills, MI: Cengage Learning.

O'Gara. P. (2008). To be or have not been: Learning language tenses through drama. *Issues in Educational Research, 18*(2), 156–165.

Paltridge, B., & Phakiti, A. (Eds.) (2010). *Continuum companion to research methods in applied linguistics.* London: Continuum.

Pennington, M. (1996). When input becomes intake. In D. Freeman & J. C. Richards (Eds.), *Teacher learning in language teaching* (pp. 320–348). New York: Cambridge University Press.

Perrett, G. (2003). Teacher development through action research. *Australian Journal of Teacher Education, 27*(2), 1–10.

Perry, F. L. (2005). *Research in applied linguistics. Becoming a discerning consumer.* Mahwah, NJ: Lawrence Erlbaum.

Pinkman, K. (2005). Using blogs in the foreign language classroom: Encouraging learner independence. *JALT CALL Journal, 1*(1), 12–24.

Poon, A. Y. K. (2008). How action research can complement formal language teacher education. *The Asia-Pacific Education Researcher, 17*(1), 43–62.

Porte, G. K. (2002). *Appraising research in second language learning.* Amsterdam: John Benjamins.

Rainey, I. (2000). Action research and the English as a foreign language practitioner: Time to take stock. *Educational Action Research, 8*(1), 65–91.

Reason, P., & Bradbury, H. (Eds.) (2001), *Handbook of action research.* London: Sage.

Richards, J. C. (1987). The dilemma of teacher education in TESOL. *TESOL Quarterly, 21*(2), 209–226.

Richards, J. C. (1998). *Teaching in action.* Alexandria, VA: TESOL.

Richards, J.C., & Lockhart, C. (1994). *Reflective teaching in second language classrooms.* New York: Cambridge University Press.

Richards, J. C., & Nunan, D. (1990). *Second language teacher education.* New York: Cambridge University Press,

Richards, K. (2003). *Qualitative inquiry in TESOL.* Basingstoke: Palgrave Macmillan.

Roberts, J. (1998). *Language teacher education.* London: Arnold.

Rogers, J. (2001). Process courting context: Action research meets learner education. In Edge, J. (Ed.), *Action research* (pp. 45–56). Alexandria, VA: TESOL.

Sano, M. (1996). Action research in writing class: How to develop writing proficiency in Japanese university students. *The Japan–Britain Association for English Language Teaching Journal, 1,* 1–20.

Santana-Williamson, E. (2001). Early reflections: Journaling a way into teaching. In Edge, J. (Ed.), *Action research* (pp. 33–44). Alexandria, VA: TESOL.

Schőn, D. (1983). *The reflective practitioner: How professionals think in action.* New York: Basic Books.

Schőn, D. (1987). *Educating the reflective practitioner.* San Francisco: Jossey-Bass.

School for International Training (2003). *The Teacher Knowledge Project—making teacher inquiry an integral part of professional development,* http://www.sit.edu/tkp/ (retrieved November 15, 2005).

Shulman, L. S. (1987). Knowledge and teaching: Foundations of the new reform. *Harvard Educational Review, 57*(1), 1–22.

Somekh, B. (1993). Quality in educational research—the contribution of classroom teachers. In J. Edge & K. Richards (Eds.), *Teachers develop teachers research* (pp. 26–38). Oxford: Heinemann.

Sowa, P. (2009). Understanding our learners and developing reflective practice: Conducting action research with English language learners. *Teaching and Teacher Education, 25*(8), 1026–1032.

Stewart, T. (2006). Teacher researcher collaboration or teachers' research? *TESOL Quarterly, 40*(2), 421–430.

Stringer, E. (1999). *Action research* (2nd ed.). London: Sage Publications.

Taba, H., & Noel, E. (1957). *Action research: A case study.* Washington, DC: Association for Supervision and Curriculum Development NEA.

Thorne, C., & Quiang, W. (1996). Action research in language teacher education. *ELT Journal, 50*(3), 254–262.

Tinker Sachs, G. (2002). *Action research in English language teaching.* Kowloon: City University of Hong Kong.

Toohey, K., & Waterstone, B (2004). Negotiating expertise in an action research community. In B. Norton & K. Toohey (Eds.), *Critical pedagogies and language learning* (pp. 291–310). New York: Cambridge University Press.

Torres Jaramillo, C., & Mongui Sánchez, R. (2008). Professional development schools: Establishing alliances to bridge the gap between universities and schools. *Profile, 10,* 181–194.

Trist, E., & Bamforth, K. W. (1951). Some social and psychological consequences of the longwall method of coal getting. *Human Relations, 4,* 3–38.

Tuffs, R. (1995). Language teaching in the post-Fordist era. *Language Qualifications in Europe, 23*(4), 491–501.

van Lier, L. (1988). *The classroom and the language learner.* London: Longman.

Wallace, M. (1991). *Training foreign language teachers: A reflective approach.* Cambridge: Cambridge University Press.

Wallace, M. J. (1998). *Action research for language teachers.* New York: Cambridge University Press.

Warne, A. (2006). *Action research in English language teaching in the UAE.* Abu Dhabi: Higher Colleges of Technology Press.

Wharton, S. (2007). Social identity and parallel text dynamics in the reporting of educational action research. *English for Specific Purposes Journal, 26*(4), 485–501.

Winter, R. (1989). *Learning from experience: Principles and practice in action-research.* Lewes: Falmer Press.

Wong, P.C., Chan, C. & Firkins, A. (2006). School-based critical literacy programme in a Hong Kong secondary school. *Hong Kong Teachers' Centre Journal, 5,* 129–139.

Woods, D. (1996). *Teacher cognition in language teaching: Beliefs, decision-making, and classroom practice.* New York: Cambridge University Press.

Yalden, J. (1983). *The communicative syllabus. Evolution, design, and implementation.* Oxford: Pergamon.

Yeh, H. (2005). Teacher study groups as a vehicle to strengthen EFL teachers' professional identity and voice. *Asian EFL Journal, 7*(4), http://www.asian-efl-journal.com/December_05_hc.php (retrieved July 29, 2009).

Zeichner, K., & Liston, D. (1996). *Reflective teaching: An introduction.* Mahwah, NJ: Lawrence Erlbaum Associates.

III
Second Language Research and Applied Linguistics

16
Second Language Acquisition Research
Applied and Applicable Orientations to Practical Questions and Concerns

Teresa Pica

Chapter Focus and Purpose

This chapter describes the relationship between second language acquisition (SLA) research and the field of applied linguistics across "applied" and "applicable" orientations. It focuses on applied studies designed to address practical questions and concerns and on applicable studies designed to address theoretical questions, but also relevant to applied questions and concerns. Three questions are addressed: Is there an optimal age to begin formal classroom second language (L2) study? Are there effective ways to integrate a yet to be acquired L2 with subject matter content? What are the contributions of a first language (L1) to classroom teaching and learning?

Disciplinary Contexts

SLA Research and Applied Linguistics

It is difficult to pinpoint exactly when the study of SLA and the field of applied linguistics got officially under way. What is quite evident, though, is that the field of applied linguistics came first. Thus, the journal now known simply as *Language Learning* began publication in 1948, with its original subtitle, *A Journal of Applied Linguistics*. Several decades later, a new journal, *Applied Linguistics*, was launched. It has maintained its original title and grown in readership since that time. The American Association for Applied Linguistics was founded in the 1970s, well over a decade after the International Association of Applied Linguistics (AILA), was already an active community in Europe, convening Congresses on a regular basis and declaring language learning and teaching, socio- and contrastive linguistics, as its principal lines of scholarship. One of the distinctive dimensions shared by these journals and organizations is that they reflect the ways in which the field of applied linguistics has broadened greatly in topics, issues, applications, and source disciplines over time, and has also sustained its role in addressing practical questions and concerns through application of a range of resources. This phenomenon is especially evident among applied linguists who specialize in SLA research. As they address practical questions about language learning and teaching, they design and implement new studies, and draw on theoretical studies from a broad range of related fields.

Applied linguists have worked on language teaching and learning long before the label "SLA" gained widespread use in the late 1960s, as new theories emerged about language, its acquisition, and use (see, for example, Corder, 1967; Ravem, 1968; Selinker, 1972). Initially, they looked to a structuralist model of language to guide their development of L2 learning materials. They would identify differences between sounds, grammatical features, and words between the L1 of the learner and the L2 to be learned. They also turned to behaviorist psychology for a theory of learning. Applying its principles of repetition and reinforcement, they would develop exercises and drills that centered on individual linguistic structures and thereby lead the learner to L2 habit formation.

As cognitive and nativist approaches to psychology took hold in the 1960s, and the study of child language grew in interest, applied linguists began to see that the learning of an L2 was much like the learning of an L1. Drawing on compelling evidence from the field of psycholinguistics that language acquisition was a creative, rule governed process, they went to work at understanding SLA processes and outcomes, doing so with resilience and forward thinking approaches. They identified systematic patterns in the errors that learners made and in their manipulation of sentence constituents and used them to develop typologies and classification schemes (Richards, 1974).

In other studies, applied linguists identified language forms and functions across academic, professional, and occupational fields, and used them to construct syllabi for specific purposes and content-based language needs (Munby, 1978; Widdowson, 1978). They examined situated language learning and teaching through classroom observation and research, and created new inventories and approaches for understanding teacher and student relationships in what had long been considered a 'black box" (Sinclair & Coulthard, 1975).

Around the same time, they were joined by scholars from disciplines such as sociolinguistics, anthropology, and psychology, from fields across the social sciences and humanities, and from professions and institutions of law, medicine, and business, who introduced research on questions about the efficacy of oral and written language in medical interviews, business transactions, religious texts, and courtroom procedures (DiPietro, 1982). Their importance and influence in defining the field of applied linguistics has continued to grow, and is evident in the vast number and range of publications, professional organizations, and research conferences available world wide.

Just as the field has come to broaden the scope of its research contexts, take on new questions, and reach out to new colleagues, it has taken on societal, educational, and professional questions that seek practical answers. To address these matters, they originate their own studies and refer to completed studies in their field. They also turn to theoretical and empirical work from related disciplines and fields as sources of research methods, current evidence, and recommendations for work to be done.

SLA Research as a Context for Applied and Applicable Studies: Development, Trends, Traditions, Controversies, and Recommendations

Is There an Optimal Age to Begin Formal Classroom L2 Study?

As explained and reviewed in Hyltenstam and Abrahamsson (2001a), questions on the optimal age for formal L2 or foreign language (FL) learning and instruction reflect practical concerns about schooling and theoretical issues about neurological development. These matters are widely different in origination, but have been brought together within the context of education as decisions are made about language policy and classroom practice.

Applied research has designed and implemented studies that confront concerns about age by examining and comparing the timing, duration, and intensity of instruction in the course of the learner's schooling. Learner needs, learning readiness, and resource availability are taken into account as well (Lightbown & Spada, 2006). Many applied studies have distinguished between English as a second language (ESL) contexts in which an L2 is the standard language of a community, country, or school, and English as a foreign language (EFL) contexts in which an L2 is a goal set by Ministries of Education, but is not used routinely. For children who must succeed academically and professionally in an ESL environment, it is essential that they begin the SLA process early in their schooling, as vital academic content and important socialization experiences are often available to them in the L2 only. In an EFL environment, there is less urgency to begin early, as academic content is likely to be widely available in learners' L1.

Despite these contextual distinctions, applied researchers consistently recommend meaning-based programs of L2 and FL enrichment, awareness, and communication throughout the early years. They emphasize that early learning of another language is more theoretically grounded and empirically supported by these experiences than formal study of linguistic structures and features, and analysis, practice, and application to rules (Isik, 2000; Nikolov & Krashen, 1997). Arguments have been made that young learners lack the cognitive skills for success in L2 programs of formal classroom study and should delay their participation until adolescence (August, Beck, Calderón, Francis, Lesaux, & Shanahan, 2006; Lightbown & Spada, 2006). Even among adolescent learners, meaning-based programs have been found to make the L2 available in ways that eliminate a great deal of the need for formal study of its more complex or non-salient features (August et al., 2006; Lightbown & Spada, 2006).

Applied Research

Research undertaken to address age-related questions about formal L2 or FL instruction has compared adults and children in terms of rate and difficulty of learning. Some studies have shown that young children learn languages slowly, with a good deal of effort due to limitations in their attention span and background knowledge. They require at least three to four years before they can attain functional use of a language (Marinova-Todd, Marshall, & Snow, 2000), and perform better when instruction is delivered slowly and monitored intensively (Singleton & Lengyel, 1995). Early formal instruction may therefore not be the optimal choice for them.

Somewhat older children, especially adolescents, often fare better than younger learners (Krashen, Scarcella, & Long, 1979; Munoz, 2006; Snow & Hoefnagel-Hoehle, 1978). This is revealed in their near native performance in pronunciation and grammar, and has been attributed to the level of cognitive development, academic background, and social experience they have been able to develop (Genesee, Lindholm-Leary, Saunders, & Christian, 2006). Learners whose maturation process is still under way might not be able to cope with the intensity and precision required for the complex learning processes of acquiring an L2 and learning to read and understand academic content at the same time.

Further support for an approach that originates with somewhat older children comes from studies carried out within school contexts. A large scale study of British children learning French as an FL over a five-year period revealed higher proficiency among learners who had initiated classroom study of French at age 11 than those who had initiated such study at eight (Burstall, 1975). These results suggested that older children are better second language learners than are younger ones in a school situation. Similar results have been reported by McLaughlin (1992) in studies of Danish and Swedish children learning English (see respectively, Florander & Jansen, 1968; Gorosch & Axelsson, 1964), and Swiss children learning French (Buehler, 1972).

Comparison research on children vs. adults has been more supportive with respect to the acquisition rate of L2 grammatical features by children. Features of input have been used to explain this finding. For example, Zdorenko and Paradis (2008) found that both children and adults whose L1 lacked articles omitted these features in their initial English learning, but the children overcame the omissions at a faster rate than adults. Although the basis for such results was not part of their study, one possibility, drawn from earlier applied research, was that the children had more access than the adults to opportunities for predictable, redundant input and contextualized interaction. This, in turn enhanced L2 comprehensibility and drew attention to its grammatical forms and operations (Hatch, 1977; Long, 1990).

The heavy emphasis on age in making decisions about school policy and practice has overlooked the abundant research on psychosocial factors such as learner personality and motivation that have been shown to impact language learning in school contexts (Ioup, Boustagui, El Tigi, & Moselle, 1994). A range of social, cognitive, and affective factors, especially those that bear on the ability to learn and apply SLA skills and strategies, is relevant to explaining why, for so many early L2 schooling is not necessarily better, and initiation of formal learning at a somewhat later time might be best. Such studies are far too numerous to include in this review chapter but are cited in many textbook topics such as 'Individual Differences" (R. Ellis, 2008; Gass & Selinker, 2007). As was emphasized earlier in this section, meaningful activities, grounded in comprehensible input and goal oriented interaction, transcend individual factors and have been shown to be far more predictable for success among all learners, young and old.

Applicable Research

Over the years that age-related questions have been advanced in the educational arena, applied linguistics has looked to theoretically grounded research in neurology, biology, and psychology as a source of answers. This theoretical foundation has provided important and suggestive insights into SLA processes and outcomes, but has had limited applicability to practical questions in education.

Much of the thinking on the age at which to launch L2 instruction has been based on the Critical Period Hypothesis (CPH) (Lenneberg, 1967), and the claim that there is a biologically determined period of activity for that part of the brain capable of learning a language with native speaker (NS) proficiency. Researchers share a good deal of consensus about the relevance of the CPH for L1 acquisition, but are less united in their views about its role in SLA (e.g., Marinova-Todd et al., 2000). Despite its theoretical importance and its contributions to the study of brain and mind, work on the CPH has been applied to educational questions, where its application is arguably inapplicable (Hyltenstam & Abrahamsson, 2001b). Indeed, much has been written about the development and maturation of the human brain, and the ways in which they account for a child's seemingly effortless ability to acquire language in their early years (Genesee, 1988; Long, 1990).

These phenomena provide only a portion of what is needed to inform education policy and practice. Still this work contributes to the knowledge base that teachers can apply to their analyses of students' errors and their decisions about their approaches to instruction and use of feedback. Long (1990) has shown that the effect of the critical period is mainly on phonological development, as pronunciation depends on neuromotor patterns that are acquired early in the L1 and are difficult to alter over time (Flege, Birdsong, Bialystok, MacKay, Sung, & Tsukaada, 2006). Pronunciation is therefore one aspect of language learning for which younger learners might be better equipped than their older schoolmates to benefit from classroom instruction.

Research has revealed ways in which even older learners can overcome this age-related, neurological challenge. Moyer (1999, 2004) has found that adults who devote a great deal of attention to their pronunciation are able to develop near native-like accents, especially with respect to pitch, stress, and intonation.

Some researchers have suggested that alternative instructional approaches (for example, computer-assisted and task-based) might also be effective for assisting adults, as they require learners to emphasize message comprehensibility (Sicola, 2008). Other researchers have shown that an emphasis on prosody might be a more effective focus for adults than segmental practice (Pennington, 1996). These and other applied studies have ushered in a re-consideration of the learner's age as a primary determinant in educational decisions.

As was noted above, children require at least three to four years before they can attain even a functional use of a language (Marinova-Todd et al., 2000), and do best when instruction is delivered slowly and monitored intensively (Singleton & Lengyl, 1995). Such time requirements raise caution as to the feasibility of undertaking formal L2 study in early schooling in light of the institutional commitment that must be made and the cognitive challenges that learners must bear. These concerns suggest the need for more comparative, descriptive, and outcomes studies of the younger and older learner, as well as of different types of program models. One possible model calls for the integration of L2 learning with content learning. It is described in the following section.

Are There Effective Ways to Integrate a Yet To Be Acquired L2 with Subject Matter Content?

Many students come to school, university, and employment settings with twofold needs—to learn an L2 or FL and to learn subject-specific content in that language. Often the need is based on the fact that the content is available only or primarily in the language to be learned. At other times, it is based on the need for efficiency: a student must move quickly through a course of study, and the integration of language and content instruction is considered an expedient approach. To meet the needs of such students, several program models have been developed and investigated. They are described briefly here.

One model of integration employs the L2 as an instrument for instruction in mathematics, science, and history, and in designing materials, activities, and strategies. It holds as its goal the achievement of both content learning and language learning. This format has enjoyed a great deal of success in French and English immersion programs in Canada (Swain, 1991). A variation on immersion is found in sheltered subject content instruction. In this approach, a teacher whose primary expertise is in a subject content area, but has been trained to make the content comprehensible to students, offers subject content instruction in an L2 or FL but uses explanations and demonstrations, and provides feedback on content and on L2 form (Brinton, Snow, & Wesche, 1989; Genesee, 1987; Met, 1991).

Many bilingual program models combine immersion and sheltered instruction, as students receive subject content instruction in their L1, then move to sheltered content instruction in the L2, and then on to the mainstream, where the L2 is used for the remainder of the subject content instruction (Freeman, Freeman, & Gonzalez, 1987). Other integrated programs follow an adjunct model, as students receive tutorial support in the language skills that are relevant to their content area in the academic mainstream. Yet others follow the theme-based or specific purpose models in which subject content is used as the foundation for L2 instruction, and topics from a subject area of interest or professional relevance are used to support their language development and literacy learning.

Applied Research

There is a great deal of research on approaches that address L2 learning as an outcome of content learning and on concurrent L2 and content learning. Research on programs that are time-intensive and extensive, such as French immersion, has revealed that learners are typically able to master content effectively, but have more difficulty with achieving native-like, L2 grammatical accuracy (Swain, 1991, 1996). Research on L2 skill development in the context of content integration has revealed positive results. Studies have shown that academic skills learned in an L1 can transfer to skills for the L2 (Turnbull, Lapkin, & Hart, 2001, and Turnbull, Hart, & Lapkin, 2003). In mathematics, Bournot-Trites and

Reeder (2001) have also found favorable results. Their research revealed that English L1 learners of French L2, who had received 80 percent of their instruction in French, performed significantly better on a standardized test administered in English than a control group who had received their mathematics instruction in equal amounts of English L1 and French L2. While literacy skills take longer to transfer across languages, these too appear to progress positively across the academic subject areas of immersion students.

Content mastery among immersion students has been revealed world wide, seen, for example, in the schooling of French immersion students in Australia (de Jabrun, 1997). Some researchers have noted that it is not the integration alone that is responsible for such positive results. They have identified other crucial variables, including psychosocial factors related to socioeconomic status, ethnicity, and aptitude, and academic factors such as initial, language-specific instruction (Genesee et al., 2006). Others have noted that the nature of the content and its compatibility with students' cognitive development play important roles. Thus, for example, Weber and Tardif (1991) and Pelletier (1998) found that students in early French immersion classrooms progressed well as they worked with highly contextualized materials and activities.

Time spent in immersion has also been revealed as a critical factor. As such 50 percent or more of students' school day appears to be a decent base level of support for positive L2 and content learning outcomes (Genesee, 1987). In addition, it is the integration of content and language itself that appears responsible, as studies that have compared this approach with language-only approaches have revealed positive results (Wesche, 1993). Literacy gains were particularly strong and content appeared to remain on a par with that learned through the L1.

As was noted above, the consistent success of content and language integration has been revealed at the content and skill level. L2 learning, particularly in the area of grammatical accuracy, has also been documented, but grammatical progress has been shown to lag behind progress in listening, reading, and oral communication skills. Harley (1993), for example, found that, even after many years of French immersion, students' production of verb contrasts for future, *imparfait*, and *passé compose* still exhibited English L2 transfer, thus distinguishing them from their NS French peers. Some of this phenomenon appeared to be due to the absence of L2 error correction, the content focus, and a classroom emphasis on discussion and lecture (Pica, 2001; Swain, 1985). Further explanation will depend on what is revealed in long-term studies to track the progression of content and L2 learning over time. It might be that L2 learning lags behind content learning initially, but over time, catches up with content learning so that both are accomplished.

Although many studies have been deemed long term, their data have been limited to several weeks or months of treatment at best (for example, Doughty & Varela, 1998; Iwashita, 1999). The usual design is to look for results of short-term treatment and follow up with delayed post testing long after the treatment is over. Many studies do not appear to use a comparison group. Others have looked at both NS and FL learner populations as comparison groups with L2 learners (see Genesee, Polich, & Stanley 1977; Sternfeld, 1988), while others have structured their comparisons solely between L2 learners and NSs (for example, Harley, 1993). Differences of L2 exposure across these populations have made them poor candidates for research on questions about SLA. Among comparative studies that have been carried out, it is the FL learner whose achievement is used as a basis for comparison (as in Ho, 1982; Sternfeld, 1989). The contrasts in motivation, time, and context make the two groups ill suited for comparison.

Several researchers have shown that form focused interventions within the content curriculum are an effective way to assist the learning of complex or low salience grammatical features such as pronouns, articles and determiners, and verb time and agreement markers, many of which are difficult to acquire through meaningful content alone (Day & Shapson, 1991; Doughty & Varela, 1998; Harley, 1993, 1998; Pica, Kang, & Sauro, 2006). Positive results for vocabulary learning have also been found in studies in which content specific words were taught directly (Gibbons, 2003). As many relevant studies have been implemented in controlled settings rather than in classrooms, they will be covered next, in the section on applicable research.

Another set of concerns, related to issues regarding the integration of content and language in the academic curriculum, has to do with the policies of the educational institutions which house content and language studies. There are concerns, for example, about the extent to which students are awarded language credit, or any credit at all, for their participation in content-based L2 courses. Most notably, in content-based and theme-based courses, the academic credit awarded to students is seen as providing entry-level status to a mainstream curriculum, and is not transferable for grade promotion or degree program completion (Pica, 2002). Another institutional concern relates to the background and training of professionals responsible for teaching L2 and content. Many language teachers are given responsibility for teaching both language and content, despite their lack of training in the latter area. Conversely, content teachers are often expected to provide language instruction, and find themselves overwhelmed by this process (Shah, 1999). These concerns warrant serious qualitative and descriptive analyses that would provide documentation as to their veracity and scale.

Further, there are concerns about the research findings that have been used to promote the interface of content and language as an optimal approach to L2 teaching and learning. These concerns pertain to the dimensions of language that have been used to identify L2 accomplishments, and to the characteristics of the students who have been included for control and comparison analysis. In a literature survey, Pica, Washburn, Evans, and Jo (1998) found that in nearly all of the 35 studies they reviewed, L2 learning was defined in terms of global features of L2 proficiency or basic subject-matter skills in comprehension of written and spoken texts. Students' internalization or use of specific features of L2 morphology and syntax was seldom investigated. Many studies that reported L2 learners' success often did so without reference to a control or comparison group. One, quite legitimate reason was because the studies themselves had been designed not to compare groups of learners, but to answer theoretical questions or address policy issues regarding L2 development (see for example, studies by Swain, 1991; Swain & Carroll, 1987).

Applicable Research

Most of the theoretical support for the integration of content and language has come from the fields of cognitive psychology and the study of SLA processes and outcomes. Much of it has been theoretical in its grounding and research design, but it has been highly applicable to decisions about education policy and practice. It is widely held that subject content instruction provides a context for meaningful communication and a springboard for language learning to occur (Met, 1991). As L2 scholars have argued, language form and meaning are not readily separable in language learning (for example, Lightbown & Spada, 2006). Subject content instruction provides meaningful comprehensible input (Krashen, 1985), and opportunities for learners to negotiate meaning (Long, 1996, 2006), which are known to enhance conditions in which students can access input, gain feedback in order to modify their output, and advance along the process of L2 learning.

Subject content instruction is also believed to be effective for students who require academic language competence, and fits very much within an information processing approach to learning. According to Anderson (1990, 1993) and O'Malley, Chamot, and Walker (1987) for example, language learners attend to language and content as information, and this in turn draws their attention to language features, forms, and constructions and their content embedded functional encodings. They gradually build their knowledge of a language until they can retrieve it automatically to understand and communicate meaningful messages. Such automatic behavior allows them to connect the linguistic system they have already internalized to individual features they are noticing anew. Little by little, they build their knowledge base. Other cognitive psychologists, working from connectionist perspectives (N. Ellis, 1994), also acknowledge these internal processes and have argued for their role in understanding L2 learning phenomena as well.

Challenges abound for acquiring L2 forms that appear infrequently in classroom input, lack perceptual prominence or communicative significance, or are too complex in function or operation to be mastered independently (Harley, 1993; Long, 1996, 2006). For learners of English, such forms include articles and determiners, pronouns, verb particles, endings and modals. Woven on to connected discourse, they seldom carry much semantic importance. However, their abundance in subject content makes mastery of such forms and their multiple functions a critical component of spoken and written competence. However, as long as grammatical accuracy remains a concern, current immersion and theme-based models need to be further improved. This is an area where basic, L2 research on form focused dimensions of SLA can be readily apply.

Many professional resources provide approaches that integrate L2 skills, strategies, and literacy across the subject content curriculum (see, for example, Brinton et al., 1989). These volumes serve as a foundation for learners to access subject content and acquire a good deal of the L2. The tackling of linguistic forms with limited salience in the content, however, has required further precision and sensitivity. Such forms need to be highlighted in ways that are likely to gain students' attention but do not interrupt their understanding of content meaning. Among the successful approaches are those that engage students in transactions with content texts in which needed forms are made more abundant and visually identifiable (Day & Shapson, 1991) and in content-focused exchanges in which errors of form are recast (Doughty & Varela 1998; Iwashita, 2003; Mackey, 2006; Mackey & Philp, 1998), negotiated (Mackey 2006; Mackey & MacDonough, 2000), or subject to collaboration (Ellis, Loewen, & Erlam, 2006; Swain & Lapkin 2001). These form-focused approaches are highly compatible with content teaching concerns, as they offer teachers a sense of anticipation that any number of difficult to learn L2 forms can be incorporated into meaning-based activities and implemented in a content focused classroom. Many have been conducted under researcher-controlled conditions, and beg for application to actual classroom contexts.

To enhance their authenticity and insure their long-term use, these activities must have enough variety to warrant sustained participation. With this in mind, Pica et al. (2006) developed a portfolio of collaborative, interactive, goal-oriented tasks and integrated them into the curriculum texts, topics, and assignments for a course on American culture and daily life. The tasks were design in keeping with the course emphasis on academic English. Thus task directions began with a purpose statement, i.e., that the task would help the students become "more accurate and precise" in their speaking and writing in areas such as reviewing, editing, organizing, and reporting information. In addition, the tasks were simple to implement for long-term application by the teacher, as the researchers could not be on hand on a daily basis. Teacher, researcher, and student involvement was ongoing in task design, piloting, and revision. Directions were reworded and revised frequently, based on numerous pilot runs. Results thus far learners' participation in tasks on difficult form and function relationships of article and pronoun reference have revealed greater awareness and accuracy in noticing and producing these features in time and over time.

This study and others such as that of Doughty and Varela (1998), Harley (1998), and Swain and Lapkin (2001) have expanded the role of the classroom as a more controlled SLA research environment than was previously thought. All used activities and tasks that were consistent with the curriculum, schedule, and format of the classrooms where the studies were implemented, and were therefore not intrusive to the work of teachers and students. The classroom, with a cohort of learners in place over time, offers a site worth considering, for its validity in informing questions on content and language integration as an aid to language learners in the academic arena. Task-based activities and classroom sites are rich resources for addressing policy and practice concerns about simultaneous learning of an L2 and the subject content it communicates.

What Are the Contributions of an L1 to Classroom Learning and Teaching?

Learning-Focused Questions

As was noted at the beginning of this chapter, questions and concerns about the impact of an L1 on L2 learning processes and teaching strategies have been a focus of the field of applied linguistics since its inception. Research has shown that the learner's L1 can be a valuable resource in SLA (Atkinson, 1999). It is believed to provide a foundation for learners to test hypotheses (Auerbach, 1993) and to seek help from L1 speakers who share their L1 (Storch & Wigglesworth, 2003; Swain & Lapkin, 2001). Practical realities and urgent problems continue to demand effective, immediate, and efficient solutions. In many countries, where a world language such as English or Chinese is a majority language, L2 populations have increased with remarkable rapidity, as adults recognize the need to speak a world language to transact fields such as science, technology, and business, and children are enrolled in settings where a ministry of education requires L2 proficiency as a goal of their schooling. In the US, policies have been put forth at federal, regional, and local levels. Despite recent studies on "what works," educators continue to seek effective and efficient pedagogical practices. The role of the students' L1 figures heavily into their selections.

Applied Research

Applied research has attempted to identify successful approaches to using the learner's L1 in L2 learning within the context of schooling. For most learners, success entails mastery of academic content, L2 forms and features, and literacy skills. Much of the research has been focused on learners of English. In a sequenced approach, learners are given initial language instruction in an L2 and content instruction in their L1. After several years, they are placed in classrooms where their academic content is taught through the L2. Early and follow up studies have revealed favorable results: academic content and literacy skills that have been acquired in the L1 are transferred to the L2 (Genesee, 1987; Genesee et al., 2006).

Collier (1992) has reported that dual language, two-way bilingual education, especially if initiated while learners are at elementary school levels, is a highly promising approach for their long-term academic success. Learners who speak languages that are considered majority and minority languages in the broader community, are taught academic content in both languages as well. Thus, both the L1 and the L2 are used for academic instruction. Research results have revealed that learners could maintain grade-level skills in their L1 at least through sixth grade and reach content proficiency in the L2 after four to five additional years. Many were able to maintain these gains when they reached the secondary level. When tested in the L2, they typically performed like NSs across all subject areas after four to seven years in the dual language program. This was not the case for students enrolled in programs that provided minimal, if any, academic instruction in the L1.

When L1 instructional support cannot be provided, several program characteristics have been found to make a difference in academic achievement for L2 learners. Children and adolescents, who need to work on cognitive, academic, and linguistic development throughout their schooling, have been found to be most successful in programs characterized by meaning-based L2 learning, problem-posing activities and strategies for solving them, teacher demonstrations of respect for students' home language and culture, and ongoing assessment through multiple measures (Collier, 1992; Genesee, 1994; Short, 1993, 1994). In addition, there is involvement among parents, faculty, and staff.

Applicable Research

The learner's L1 was long considered a problem that interfered with L2 learning. This perception was linked with the "Contrastive Analysis Hypothesis" that learners' L1 could predict ease or difficulty in SLA. L2 forms and features that were similar to the L1 would be easy to learn and L2 forms and features that were different from the L1 would be difficult to learn. Application of this theory to classroom practice meant drill and practice of the different L2 items, an approach that was consistent with behaviorist principles, which, as noted in the first section of this chapter, dominated learning theories at the time.

This approach to the L1 began to diminish in weight with theories advanced by Chomsky (1965) that language was a property of mind and language acquisition was a rule-driven, learner-focused process that was influenced by creative construction (Dulay & Burt, 1973, 1974). This spurred a need to undertake a new look at the L1 in SLA. Among the research efforts, studies revealed that many L2 forms had no L1 connections at the grammatical and semantic level, thus reducing the strength of the interference argument.

Over the years, research has revealed that the L1 plays a selective role in L2 learning at specific stages of development, especially for negation and question formation (Zobl, 1980). In English, consonant clusters (for example, -sk, -kt(ed), and -sks), are sensitive to L1 influence in final positions of words and syllables, as in *task, locked, and looks*. For English L2 learners, this can affect pronunciation and grammar, making *desk(s)* or *liked* more difficult to produce than *sky, score, scare*. As these vital endings are used to mark grammatical functions such as plural and regular past, students' performance in both pronunciation and grammar may appear much lower than the students' actual knowledge (Sato, 1986). Many studies have revealed that L1 and L2 differences are only one factor in ease and difficulty in SLA. Other factors are related to the complexity of the L2 form or feature itself (Hyltenstam, 1987). As such limited transparency of form and meaning makes L2 forms for grammatical gender more difficult than those for plurality; complexity of form and meaning relationships makes French *connaitre* and *savoir* more difficult to acquire than their single English counterpart, *know*.

Teacher-Focused Questions

There has been a great deal of interest in the teacher who speaks an L1 and teaches in an L2, and who is often called a non-native speaking teacher (NNST). This interest has been focused on English, and reflects the growing number of English language teachers world wide who are non-native English speakers. Much of the work so far has covered their qualifications and skills, perceptions of their abilities and effectiveness by their students, colleagues, the teachers themselves, and the researchers who study them at work in their classrooms. Questions and issues pertaining to NNSTs emanate from many directions and constituencies–the students they teach, the colleagues with whom they work, the educators who train them, and the administrators who hire them. Yet research on their teaching and its impact on students' learning has been slow in coming. Comparative studies with native speaking teachers (NSTs) or between trained and novice NNSTs have only recently begun to appear.

Applied Research

Canagarajah (2005) has reported that NNSTs comprise 80% of the English teachers world wide. Liu (1999) has noted that NNSTs constitute a near majority of Master's program trainees in ESL settings. Most are international students who plan to teach in their home countries (Polio, 1994) after they obtain their degrees. NNSTs have been studied in comparison to NSTs, with respect to their views of themselves and those of others. Much of this work has examined self and other perception and much of it has been applied to the understanding of their unique skills and special needs, and to explain employment needs and outcomes.

Medgyes (1994) and Árva and Medgyes' (2000) have described several strengths that NNSTs appear to bring to the classroom. They provide good models of language learning, are empathetic toward students' difficulties, and can teach them the strategies that were effective in their own language learning. Their bilingualism can also be applied strategically to explain difficult concepts, provide directions, and explain assignments. Noting the uniqueness of these areas to the NNST, Barratt and Kontra (2000) have applied them to arguments that raise awareness of the limitations of NSTs who work with non-native speakers (NNSs).

The majority of studies have been carried out in ESL contexts. They portray a picture of NNSTs as concerned about their linguistic accuracy (Kamhi-Stein, Aagard, Ching, Paik, & Sasser, 2004) and teaching effectiveness (Reves & Medgyes, 1994), with feelings of inadequacy in a good deal of their classroom performance (Braine, 2004; Modiano, 2004). Amin (2004) was able to trace this to their concerns about their English language performance, gender, and race. Canagarajah (2005) has noted the higher standard to which some NNSTs feel they are held. Those who are enrolled in degree programs are also keenly aware that they may be seen as inadequate, especially if they choose to work in L2 settings. Some report that they are prepared to address this in their professional life, by drawing on their strengths rather than limitations (Samimy & Brutt-Griffler, 1999). As researchers explore the professional contexts in which NNSTs work, they have identified numerous psychosocial factors that bear on their perceptions. These include the educational backgrounds of their students, for example; the higher the educational level, the more favorable attitude was perceived by the teachers.

Studies undertaken in EFL contexts have revealed that teachers' perceptions of themselves appear to vary by placement and experience, with secondary teachers more favorable toward their skills than primary teachers, and those who had studied or taught in EFL contexts more likely to support the role and contributions of the NNST for students in their home countries (Llurda, 2005). Participants in Bayyurt (2006) also noted the unique skills and attributes that NNSTs bring to their students in an EFL context. Other research has revealed that NSTs report favorable perceptions of NNSTs. Nemtchinova (2005) revealed that teachers who supervised and sponsored student NNSTs in their classrooms found them linguistically proficient and helpful to students. Some of the NSTs noted that, despite their competence, NNSTs indicated a lack of confidence.

Research on student perceptions of NNSTs has shown a great deal of acceptance and appreciation and can serve to reduce the widespread perception by program administrators that their students want only NSTs. Even students who had initial misgivings about NNSTs have been found to upgrade their opinions as they came to know their teachers and benefit from their teaching (Moussu, 2002, 2006). Most of their negative views had centered around the NNST's linguistic skills and cultural insights. Additional work on learner reports has revealed their perceptions that NNSTs offer unique attributes as role models, sources of motivation and empathy (Benke & Medgyes, 2005; Cheung & Braine, 2007; Lasagabaster & Sierra, 2002; Llurda, 2005; Pacek, 2005). When asked to choose, however, learners have tended to view a teacher more favorably if the teacher used an American-English accent rather than a foreign-accented variety, even though the latter variety was as understandable to them (Butler, 2007).

Studies of NNSTs provide a rich and revealing data base that can be made available to policy makers and program administrators who make hiring decisions. Many NNSTs report great difficulty in obtaining employment in ESL settings, and even in EFL settings, as program administrators appear to favor NSs. In university settings, intensive English programs with academic English curricula tend to hire NSs (Mahboob, Uhrig, Newman, & Hartford, 2004). Among the factors fostering this reluctance, researchers have cited NNSTs' accented English, pedagogical formality, emphasis on grammar, and lack of NNST self-confidence as concerns. At the same time, they have recognized the NNSTs' strengths in background knowledge of teaching techniques and curriculum, collegiality, and attitude toward students. Flynn and Gulikers (2001) found that the level of literacy skills and breadth of experience required often eliminates many applicants, both NNSTs and NSTs from securing teaching positions. Thus recent graduates of Master's programs are turned down for these reasons more so than their nativeness. In general, the research, which is small in scope, portrays administrators as reluctant to hire NNSTs, but drawing on their lack of experience rather than their non-nativeness as the basis for the hiring decision. Such attitudes warrant a broader dissemination of the results on this matter.

Applicable Research

Considerable attention has been given to characterizing and describing the "non-nativeness" that has been applied to address questions about NNSs in general and NNSTs' competence in particular. Over time, the work has grown from an emphasis on standard English to a recognition of its many varieties across and within ESL/EFL contexts, and its reflection of the diversity shared among all world languages.

Chomsky's (1965) theoretical claim that native speakers are the only reliable source of linguistic data in terms of judging sentence grammaticality has often been invoked to justify decisions about teacher qualifications for language teaching. As Chomsky's statement was made in the context of arguments about mental properties, it has had little, if any, application to the evaluation of teacher qualifications and decisions about hiring and promotion. Researchers such as Cook (2005), whose expertise extends across theoretical and applied linguistics, have pointed out the fallacies in the way that Chomsky's original intention has been misplaced. Along with others (Rampton, 1990), they have argued that coinage and application of the NNS label is itself misleading because it suggests that teachers can be separated into groups of "have" and "have-not."

Widely known characteristics of individuals whose language proficiency extends beyond their L1 have been applied to assessments of qualifications for effective teaching. Cook (2005), Kramsch (1997), and Phillipson (1992), for example, have pointed out the value of knowing more than one language and culture and the experience of having learned another language, often through classroom study. New terminology has also emerged, which can also be applied to teachers. These labels suggest strengths and skills such as "expert speaker" (Rampton, 1990). Research has uncovered characteristics of the learner's delegation of time and attention to L2 study that explain why many NNSs perform linguistically like NSs (for example, Davies, 1991, 2003; Moyer, 1999, 2004), even though they might have different judgments from them, for example, on sentence grammaticality (Coppietiers, 1987).

Much has also been written about the construct of World Englishes and indigenized varieties of English (Brutt-Griffler & Samimy, 2001; Higgins, 2003; Kachru, 1992). Some of it has been applied to promote the role of NNSTs as speakers of local varieties that have greater familiarity with their students and are more intelligible to them than NS varieties (Modiano, 2004). Much of the emphasis has been on describing the linguistic features of these varieties at lexical, grammatical, and sociolinguistic levels (Mesthrie, 2006). As the number of English NNS continues to increase world wide (Braine, 1999; Crystal, 2003; Graddol, 1999) and the demand for English language education looms large, it is inevitable that NNSTs will implement most English instruction through different varieties. As a result, issues surrounding the non-nativeness of teachers may diminish in their relevance and application to language education.

Research is still needed at applied and applicable levels, to address new and emergent concerns and research questions on SLA and L2 teaching. Information that goes beyond specification of teachers' grammar knowledge and communicative proficiency can be augmented through studies that examine credentials of practitioner training, knowledge, and skills, with a focus on those that correlate with successful learning outcomes. Outcomes criteria can come from SLA research on the sequences and processes of L2 development, so that learning progress can be tracked along the way to outcome attainment. Applied linguistics researchers could take the lead in translating this area of research into recommendations for teacher knowledge and practice, then communicating their findings to language program administrators and sharing them widely across the education arena. Both descriptive data and outcomes data are needed for such documentation. In order to pinpoint crucial differences between NSTs and NNSTs, classroom researchers need to describe their use of instructional moves, feedback practices, and management styles, and link them with inventories of what constitutes effective teaching (for example, Peacock, 2002; Richards, 1992), as well with documentation of their students' L2 development over time.

Conclusions and Future Directions

The questions and concerns and directional needs that were raised about the role of an L1 in the learning and teaching of another language are reminiscent of those covered in earlier sections of this chapter. As was noted, questions about optimal age for formal classroom L2 study and content and language sequencing and integration, require more comparative, descriptive, and outcomes directed research on learners, programs, and practices. There is clearly much more applied research to be designed and implemented, just as there are questions and contexts waiting for extant research results to be applied. Over the years, the field of applied linguistics has shown both resilience and growth in addressing practical questions and concerns, designing relevant research, and generating publications and presentations. These accomplishments hold promise for future work whose findings and applications are needed now, and will continue to arise in the days and years ahead.

References

Anderson, J. R. (1990). *Cognitive psychology and its implications* (3rd ed.). New York: W. H. Freeman.

Anderson, J. R. (1993). Problem solving and learning. *American Psychologist, 48*, 35–44.

Amin, N. (2004). Nativism, the native speaker construct, and minority immigrant women teachers of English as a second language. In L. Kamhi-Stein et al. (Eds.), *Learning and teaching from experience: Perspectives on nonnative English-speaking professionals* (pp. 61–90). Ann Arbor: University of Michigan Press.

Árva, V., & Medgyes, P. (2000). Native and non-native teachers in the classroom. *System, 28*, 355–372.

Atkinson, D. (1999). TESOL and culture. *TESOL Quarterly, 33*(4), 625–654.

Auerbach, E. (1993). Reexamining English only in the ESL classroom. *TESOL Quarterly, 27*, 9–32.

August, D., Beck, I. L., Calderón, M., Francis, D. J., Lesaux, N. K., & Shanahan, T. (2006). Instruction and professional development. In D. August & T. Shanahan (Eds.), *Developing reading and writing in second language learners. Lessons from the Report of the National Literacy Panel of Language-Minority Children and Youth*. New York: Routledge, the Center for Applied Linguistics and the International Reading Association.

Barratt, L., & Kontra, E. (2000). Native English-speaking teachers in cultures other than their own. *TESOL Journal, 9*(3), 19–23.

Bayyurt, Y. (2006). Non-native English language teachers' perspective on culture in English as a foreign language classroom. *Teacher Development, 10*(2), 233–247.

Benke, E., & Medgyes, P. (2005). Differences in teaching behaviour between native and non-native speaker teachers: As seen by the learners. In E. Llurda (Ed.), *Non-native language teachers: Perceptions, challenges, and contributions to the profession* (pp. 195–216). New York: Springer.

Bournot-Trites, M., & Reeder, K. (2001). Interdependence revisited: Mathematics achievement in an intensified French immersion program. *Canadian Modern Language Review, 58*(1), 27–43.

Braine, G. (Ed.) (1999). *Nonnative educators in English language teaching*. Mahwah, NJ: Lawrence Erlbaum.

Braine, G. (2004). The nonnative English-speaking professionals' movement and its research foundations. In L. Kamhi-Stein et al. (Eds.), *Learning and teaching from experience: Perspectives on nonnative English-speaking professionals* (pp. 9–24). Ann Arbor: University of Michigan Press.

Brinton, D., Snow, M. A., & Wesche, M. (1989). *Content-based second language instruction.* New York: Newbury House.

Brutt-Griffler, J., & Samimy, K. (2001). Transcending the nativeness paradigm. *World Englishes,* 20(1), 99–106.

Buehler, U. B. (1972). *Empirische and lernpsychologische Beitraege zur Wahl des Zeitpunktes fuer den Fremdsprachenunterrichtbeginn: Lernpsychologischinterpretierte Leistungsmessungen im Frage Franzoesischunterricht an Primaerschulen des Kantons Zuerich.* Zurich: Orell Fuessli.

Burstall, C. (1975). Factors affecting foreign language learning: a consideration of some relevant research findings. *Language Teaching and Linguistics Abstracts,* 8, 105–125.

Butler, Y. (2007). How are nonnative-English-speaking teachers perceived by young learners? *TESOL Quarterly,* 41, 731–755.

Canagarajah, A. S. (Ed.) (2005). *Reclaiming the local in language policy and practice.* Mahwah, NJ: Lawrence Erlbaum.

Cheung, Y. L., & Braine, G. (2007). The attitudes of university students towards non-native speakers English teachers in Hong Kong. *RELC Journal,* 38(3), 257–277.

Chomsky, N. (1965). *Aspects of the theory of syntax.* Cambridge, MA: MIT Press.

Collier, V. P. (1992). A synthesis of studies examining long-term language minority student data on academic achievement. *Bilingual Research Journal,* 16(1–2), 187–212.

Cook, V. (2005). Basing teaching on the L2 user. In E. Llurda (Ed.), *Non-native language teachers: Perceptions, challenges, and contributions to the profession* (pp. 47–61). New York: Springer.

Coppieters, R. (1987). Competence difference between native and near-native speakers. *Language,* 63, 544–573.

Corder, S. P. (1967). The significance of learners' errors. *International Review of Applied Linguistics,* 5, 161–169.

Crystal, D. (2003). *English as a global language* (2nd ed.). Cambridge: Cambridge University Press.

Davies, A. (1991). *The native speaker in applied linguistics.* Edinburgh: Edinburgh University Press.

Davies, A. (2003). The native speaker of World Englishes. *Journal of Pan-Pacific Association of Applied Linguistics,* 6(1), 43–60.

Day, E., & Shapson, S. (1991). Integrating formal and functional approaches to language teaching in French immersion: An experimental study. *Language Learning,* 41, 25–58. Republished, *Language Learning,* 51, 2001, 47–80.

de Jabrun, P. (1997). Academic achievement in late partial immersion French. *Babel,* 32(2), 20–23, 35, 37.

DiPietro, R. J. (Ed.) (1982). *Linguistics and the professions.* Norwood, NJ: Ablex Publishing Corp.

Doughty, C., & Varela, E. (1998). Communicative focus on form. In C. Doughty & J. Williams (Eds.), *Focus on form in second language classroom* (pp. 114–138). New York: Cambridge University Press.

Dulay, H., & Burt, M. (1973). Should we teach children syntax? *Language Learning,* 23, 245–258.

Dulay, H., & Burt, M. (1974). Natural sequences in second language acquisition. *Language Learning,* 24, 37–58.

Ellis, N. (1994). Vocabulary acquisition: The implicit ins and outs of explicit cognitive mediation. In N. Ellis (Ed.) *Implicit and explicit learning of languages* (pp. 211–282). London: Academic Press.

Ellis, R. (2008). *The study of second language acquisition.* London: Oxford University Press.

Ellis, R., Loewen, S., & Erlam, R. (2006). Implicit and explicit corrective feedback and the acquisition of L2 grammar. *Studies in Second Language Acquisition,* 28, 339–368.

Flege, J., Birdsong, D., Bialystok, E., Mackay, M., Sung, H., & Tsukadaa, K. (2006). Degree of foreign accent in English sentences produced by Korean children and adults. *Journal of Phonetics,* 34, 153–175.

Florander, J., & Jansen, M. (1968). *Skoleforsog i Engelsk 1959–1965.* Copenhagen: Danish Institute of Education.

Flynn, K., & Gulikers, G. (2001). Issues in hiring nonnative English-speaking professionals to teach English as a Second Language. *CATESOL Journal,* 13(1), 151–161.

Freeman, D., Freeman, Y., & Gonzalez, G. (1987). Success for LEP students: The Sunnyside sheltered English program. *TESOL Quarterly,* 21, 361–367.

Gass, S., & Selinker, L. (2007). *Second language acquisition: An introductory course.* Mahwah, NJ: Lawrence Erlbaum Associates.

Genesee, F. (1987). *Learning through two languages: Studies of immersion and bilingual education.* Cambridge, MA: Newbury House.

Genesee, F. (1988). Neuropsychology and second language acquisition. In Leslie Beebe (Ed.), *Issues on second language acquisition multiple perspectives* (pp. 81–112). New York: Newbury House/Harper and Row.

Genesee, F. (1994). Integrating language and content: Lessons from immersion. *Educational Practice,* Report 11.

Genesee, F., Lindholm-Leary, K., Saunders, W., & Christian, D. (2006). *Educating English language learners: A synthesis of research evidence.* New York: Cambridge University Press.

Genesee, F., Polich, E., & Stanley, M. (1977). An experimental French immersion program at the secondary school level 1969 to 1974. *Canadian Modern Language Review,* 33, 318–332.

Gibbons, P. (2003). Mediating language learning: Teacher interactions with ESL students in a content-based classroom. *TESOL Quarterly,* 37(2), 247–273.

Gorosch, M., & Axelsson, C. A. (1964). *English without a book: A bilingual experience in primary schools by audio-visual means.* Berlin: Comelsen Verlag.

Graddol, D. (1999). The decline of the native speaker. In D. Graddol & U. Meinhof (Eds.), *English in a changing world (AILA Review 13)* (pp. 57–68). Milton Keynes: Open University Press.

Harley, B. (1993). Instructional strategies and second language acquisition in early French immersion. *Studies in Second Language Acquisition, 15,* 245–260.

Harley, B. (1998). The role of focus-on-form tasks in promoting child L2 acquisition. In C. Doughty & J. Williams (Eds.), *Focus on form in classroom second language acquisition* (pp. 156–174). New York: Cambridge University Press.

Hatch, E. (1977). Optimal age or optimal learners? *UCLA Workpapers in TESOL, 11,* 45–56.

Higgins, C. (2003). "Ownership" of English in the Outer Circle: An alternative to the NS–NNS dichotomy. *TESOL Quarterly, 37*(4), 615–644.

Ho, K. K. (1982). Effect of language of instruction on physics achievement. *Journal of Research in Science Teaching, 19,* 761–767.

Hyltenstam, K. (1987). Markedness, language universals, language typology, and second language acquisition. In C. Pfaff (Ed.), First and second language acquisition process (pp. 55–78). Cambridge, MA: Newbury House.

Hyltenstam, K., & Abrahamsson, N. (2001a). Age and L2 learning: The hazards of matching practical "Implications" with theoretical "Facts" and S. H. Marinova-Todd, D. Bradford Marshall, & C. E. Snow, Missing the point: A response to Hyltenstam and Williamson. *TESOL Quarterly, 1,* 151–176.

Hyltenstam K., & Abrahamsson N. (2001b). Comments on Stefka H. Marinova-Todd, D. Bradford Marshall, & Catherine E. Snow's "Three misconceptions about age and L2 learning" and age and L2 learning: The hazards of matching practical "Implications" with theoretical "Facts." *TESOL Quarterly, 35,* 151–176.

Ioup, G., Boustagui, E., El Tigi, M., & Moselle, M. (1994). Reexamining the critical period hypothesis: A case study of successful adult SLA in a naturalistic environment. *Studies in Second Language Acquisition, 16,* 73–98.

Isik, A. (2000). The role of input in second language acquisition: More comprehensible input supported by grammar instruction or more grammar instruction? *ITL: Review of Applied Linguistics, 129–130,* 225–274.

Iwashita, N. (1999). The role of task-based conversation in the acquisition of Japanese grammar and vocabulary. Unpublished doctoral dissertation, University of Melbourne, Australia.

Iwashita, N. (2003). Negative feedback and positive evidence in task-based interaction. *Studies in Second Language Acquisition, 25,* 1–36.

Kachru, B. (Ed.) (1992). *The other tongue: English across cultures* (2nd ed.). Chicago, IL: University of Illinois Press.

Kamhi-Stein, L. D., Aagard, A., Ching, A., Paik, A., & Sasser, L. (2004). Teaching in K–12 programs: Perceptions of native and nonnative English-speaking practitioners. *The CATESOL Journal, 13*(1), 69–88.

Kramsch, C. (1997). The privilege of the non-native speaker. *PMLA, 3,* 359–369.

Krashen, S. (1985). *The input hypothesis: Issues and implications.* London: Longman.

Krashen, S, D., Scarcella R. C., & Long M. A. (1979). Age, rate and eventual attainment in second language acquisition. *TESOL Quarterly, 13,* 573–582.

Lasagabaster, D., & Sierra, J. M. (2002). University students' perceptions of native and non-native speaker teachers of English. *Language Awareness, 11*(2), 132–142.

Lenneberg, E. H. (1967). *The biological foundations of language.* New York: John Wiley and Sons.

Lightbown, P., & Spada, N. (2006). *How languages are learned* (3rd ed.). London: Oxford University Press.

Liu, J. (1999). From their own perspectives: The impact of non-native ESL professionals on their students. In G. Braine (Ed.), *Nonnative educators in English language teaching* (pp. 159–176). Mahwah, NJ: Lawrence Erlbaum.

Llurda, E. (Ed.) (2005). *Non-native language teachers: Perceptions, challenges, and contributions to the profession.* New York: Springer.

Long, M. H. (1990). Maturational constrains on language development. *Studies in Second Language Acquisition, 12,* 251–286.

Long, M. (1996). The role of the linguistic environment in second language acquisition. In W. C. Ritchie & T. K. Bhatia (Eds.), *Handbook of language acquisition* (Vol. 2: Second language acquisition) (pp. 413–468). New York: Academic Press.

Long, M. H. (2006). Recasts: The story so far. In M. Long (Ed.), *Problems in SLA* (pp. 75–116). Mahwah, NJ: Erlbaum.

Mackey, A. (2006). Feedback, noticing and instructed second language learning. *Applied Linguistics, 27,* 405–430.

Mackey, A., & McDonough, K. (2000). Communicative tasks, conversational interaction/ linguistic form. *Foreign Language Annals, 33,* 82–91.

Mackey, A., & Oliver, R. (2002). Interactional feedback and children's L2 development. *System, 30,* 459–477.

Mackey, A., & Philp, J. (1998). Conversational interaction and second language development: Recasts, responses, and red herrings? *The Modern Language Journal, 82,* 338–356.

McLaughlin, B. (1992). *Myths and misconceptions about second language learning.* ERIC Digest. National Center for Research on Cultural Diversity and Second Language Learning. December.

Mahboob, A., Uhrig, K., Newman, K., & Hartford, B. S. (2004). Children of a lesser English: Status of nonnative English speakers as college-level English as a Second Language teachers in the United States. In L. Kamhi-Stein et al. (Eds.), *Learning and teaching from experience: Perspectives on nonnative English-speaking professionals* (pp. 100–120). Ann Arbor: University of Michigan Press.

Marinova-Todd, S. H., Marshall, D. B., & Snow, C. E. (2000). Three misconceptions about age and L2 learning. *TESOL Quarterly*, 34, 9–34.

Medgyes, P. (1994). *The non-native teacher*. London: Macmillan.

Mesthrie, R. (2006). World Englishes and the multilingual history of English. *World Englishes*, 25(3/4), 381–390.

Met, M. (1991). Learning language through content: Learning content through language. *Foreign Language Annals*, 24(4), 281–295.

Modiano, Morita, N. (2004). Negotiating participation and identity in second language academic communities. *TESOL Quarterly*, 38(4), 573–603.

Moussu, L. (2002). English as a second language students' reactions to nonnative English-speaking teachers. Master's thesis, Brigham Young University, Provo, Utah (ERIC Document Reproduction Service No. ED468879).

Moussu, L. (2006). Native and nonnative English-speaking English as a second language teachers: Student attitudes, teacher self-perceptions, and Intensive English Program administrator beliefs and practices. Doctoral thesis, Purdue University, West Lafayette, Indiana (ERIC Document Reproduction Service No. ED492599).

Moyer, A. (1999). Ultimate attainment in L2 phonology: The critical factors of age, motivation, and instruction. *Studies in Second Language Acquisition*, 21, 81–108.

Moyer, A. (2004). *Age, accent, and experience in second language acquisition: An integrated approach to critical period inquiry*. Clevedon: Multilingual Matters.

Munby, J. (1978). *Communicative syllabus design*. Cambridge: Cambridge University Press.

Munoz, C. (Ed.) (2006). *Age and the rate of foreign language learning*. Clevedon: Multilingual Matters.

Nemtchinova, E. (2005). Host teachers' evaluations of nonnative-English-speaking teacher trainees—A perspective from the classroom. *TESOL Quarterly*, 39(2), 235–262.

Nikolov, M., & Krashen, S. (1997). Need we sacrifice accuracy for fluency? *System*, 25, 197–201. O'Malley, J., Chamot, A., & Walker, C. (1987). Some applications of cognitive theory to second language acquisition. *Studies in Second Language Acquisition*, 9, 287–306.

Pacek, D. (2005). "Personality not nationality": Foreign students' perceptions of a non-native speaker lecturer of English at a British university. In E. Llurda (Ed.), *Non-native language teachers: Perceptions, challenges, and contributions to the profession* (pp. 243–262). New York: Springer.

Peacock, M. (2002). The god teacher of English as a foreign language. *Perspectives*, Hong Kong Polytechnic, 30–45.

Pelletier, J. (1998). A comparison of children's understanding of school in regular English language and French immersion kindergartens. *The Canadian Modern Language Review*, 55(2), 239–259.

Pennington, M. C. (1996). *Phonology in English language teaching*. Essex: Addison Wesley Longman.

Phillipson, R. (1992). *Linguistic imperialism*. Oxford: Oxford University Press.

Pica, T. (2001). The content based curriculum: Does it provide an optimal or optional approach to language learning? In W. Renandya & N. Sunga (Eds.), *Language curriculum and instruction in multicultural societies* (pp. 145–174). Singapore: SEAMEO Regional Language Centre.

Pica, T. (2002). Subject matter content: How does it assist the interactional and linguistic needs of classroom language learners? *The Modern Language Journal*, 85, 1–19.

Pica, T., Kang, H., & Sauro, S. (2006). Information gap tasks: Their multiple roles and contributions to interaction research methodology. *Studies in Second Language Acquisition*, 28, 301–338.

Pica, T., Washburn, G., Evans, B., & Jo, V. (1998). *Negative feedback in content-based second language classroom interaction: How does it contribute to second language learning?* Annual Pacific Second Language Research Forum, Tokyo, Japan, January.

Polio, C. (1994). International students in North American TESOL programs. Presented at the 28th TESOL Conference, Baltimore, MA.

Rampton, M. B. H. (1990). Displacing the "native speaker": Expertise, affiliation, and inheritance. *ELT Journal*, 44(2), 97–101.

Ravem, R. (1968). Language acquisition in a second language environment. *International Review of Applied Linguistics*, 6, 165–185.

Reves, T., & Medgyes, P. (1994). The non-native English speaking EFL/ESL teacher's self image: An international survey. *System*, 22(3), 353–357.

Richards, J. (1974). *Error analysis*. London: Longman.

Richards, J. (1992). Theories of teaching in language teaching. *Perspectives*. Hong Kong Polytechnic, 30–45.

Samimy, K., & Brutt-Griffler, J. (1999). To be a native or non-native speaker: Perceptions of "non-native" students in a graduate TESOL program. In G. Braine (Ed.), *Nonnative educators in English language teaching* (pp. 127–144). Mahwah, NJ: Lawrence Erlbaum.

Sato, C. (1986). Conversation and interlanguage development: Rethinking the connection. In Richard Day (Ed.) *Talking to Learn* (pp. 23–48). Rowley, MA: Newbury House.

Selinker, L. (1972). Interlanguage. *International Review of Applied Linguistics, 10*, 209–231.

Shah, I. (1999). The sheltered classroom as an environment for second language acquisition. Ph.D. dissertation, University of Pennsylvania.

Short, D. (1993). Assessing integrated language and content instruction. *TESOL Quarterly, 27*(4), 627–656.

Short, D. (1994). Expanding middle school horizons: integrating language, culture, and social studies. *TESOL Quarterly, 28*(3), 581–608.

Sicola, L. (2008). *No, they won't "just sound like each other": NNS–NNS negotiated interaction and attention to phonological form on targeted L2 pronunciation tasks.* Frankfurt am Main: Duisburg Papers on Research in Language and Culture. Vol. 72.

Sinclair, J., & Coulthard, M. (1975). *Towards an analysis of discourse.* London: Oxford University Press.

Singleton, D., & Lengyel, Z. (1995). *The age factor in second language acquisition.* Clevedon: Multilingual Matters.

Snow, C. E., & Hoefnagel-Hoehle, M. (1978). The critical period for language acquisition: Evidence from second language learning. *Child Development*, 49, 1114–1118.

Sternfeld, S. (1988). The applicability of the immersion approach to college foreign language instruction. *Foreign Language Annals, 21*, 221–226.

Sternfeld, S. (1989). The University of Utah's Immersion/Multiliteracy Program: An example of an area studies approach to the design of first-year college foreign language instruction. *Foreign Language Annals, 22*, 341–352.

Storch, N., & Wigglesworth, G. (2003). Is there a role for the use of the L1 in and L2 setting? *TESOL Quarterly, 37*(4), 760–771.

Swain, M. (1985). Communicative competence: Some roles of comprehensible input and comprehensible output in its development. In S. Gass & C. Madden (Eds.), *Input in second language acquisition* (pp. 235–253). Rowley, MA: Newbury House.

Swain, M. (1991). French immersion and its offshoots: Getting two for one. In B. Freed (Ed.), *Foreign language acquisition and the classroom* (pp. 91–103). Lexington, MA: Heath.

Swain, M. (1996). Discovering successful second language teaching strategies and practices: From program evaluation to classroom experimentation. *Journal of Multilingual and Multicultural Development, 17*, 89–104.

Swain, M., & Lapkin, S. (2001). Focus on form through collaborative dialogue: Exploring task effects. In M. Bygate, P. Skehan, & M. Swain (Eds.), *Researching pedagogic tasks, second language learning, teaching and testing* (pp. 99–118). Harlow: Longman.

Swain, M., & Carroll, S. (1987). The immersion observation study. In B. Harley, P. Allen, J. Cummins, & M. Swain (Eds.), *The development of bilingual proficiency. Final Report* (Vol. II) (pp. 190–263). Toronto: The Institute for Studies in Education.

Turnbull, M., Hart, D. & Lapkin, S. (2003). Grade 6 French immersion students' performance on large-scale reading, writing and mathematics tests: Building explanations. *The Alberta Journal of Educational Research, 46*(1), 6–23.

Turnbull, M., Lapkin, S., & Hart, D. (2001). Grade Three immersion students' performance in literacy and mathematics: Province-wide results from Ontario (1998–99).*The Canadian Modern Language Review, 58*(1), 9–26.

Weber, S., & Tardif, C. (1991). Culture and meaning in French immersion kindergarten. In L. M. Malavé & G. Duquette (Eds.), *Language, culture and cognition* (pp. 93–109). Clevedon: Multilingual Matters.

Wesche, M. (1993). Discipline-based approaches to language study: Research issues and outcomes. In M. Krueger & F. Ryan (Eds.) *Language and content: Discipline- and content-based approaches to language study.* Lexington, MA: D. C. Heath.

Widdowson, H. (1978). *Explorations in the study of language.* Oxford: Oxford University Press.

Zdorenko, T., & Paradis, J. (2008). The acquisition of articles in child second language English: fluctuation, transfer or both? *Second Language Research, 24*, 227–250.

Zobl, H. (1980). The formal and developmental selectivity of L1 influence on L2 acquisition. *Language Learning, 30*, 43–57.

17

Constrained but Not Determined
Approaches to Discourse Analysis

Sandra Silberstein

The operations [of discourse analysis] make no use of any knowledge concerning the meaning of the morphemes or the intent or conditions of the author. They require only a knowledge of morpheme boundaries, including sentence junctures … and grammatical equivalences.

(Harris, 1952)

In fairly stark terms, Harris's epigraph captures what would become the tension between "formal linguistic" or "structural" approaches to language study and what has been termed more recently the "social turn." For Harris (an early teacher of Noam Chomsky), discourse was seen as an accretion of lower-level features. "Discourse analysis" implied the study of the operations of structures, without regard to meaning, "above the sentence." This separation of structure from meaning is unfamiliar in today's applied linguistics. Widdowson (2004) points out that a "text" can be smaller than a sentence insofar as, for example, the single letter *P*, designating a parking space, conveys a complete message.

Contemporary discourse analysis (DA) moves more easily across "levels" of text,[1] across disciplines and intellectual traditions, borrowing insights on language use (e.g., LeVine & Scollon, 2004; Schiffrin, Tannen, & Hamilton, 2001; Scollon & Scollon, 2004). For most contemporary discourse analysts the heart of DA is the interrelation between form and function in communication. Most succinctly, within both the social and critical turns in language study, which comprise the focus of this chapter, one finds discourse analysts from a variety of perspectives looking at the work that language (including language structure) does, at what is accomplished through language.

This chapter views contemporary approaches of discourse analysis relevant to language learning and teaching: approaches representing the "social turn," the "critical turn," and the "discursive turn" in corpus linguistics. It is not exhaustive in this regard; rather it examines and, to some extent, places into dialogue, several approaches that represent a current trend. The chapter argues that implicit in the theoretical marriage of form and function has been an over-arching ontological assumption that I term *constrained but not determined* (cf. Silberstein, 2008). Contemporary approaches to discourse have at their heart a sense that language use is constrained by structural, cognitive, and contextual factors; but the complexities of all three, along with the important element of human agency, assure that language use and acquisition are never determined.

The Social Turn

Research on second language teaching and learning often focuses on language in interaction. The approaches discussed in this section are conversation analysis (CA), a Vygotskyan-influenced socio-cultural approach, and discourse pragmatics. While their research agendas often address oral dis-course,[2] the latter two approaches theoretically extend to written texts as well. CA research focuses both on "naturally occurring"[3] talk in interaction and institutional (including classroom) interac-tion. Putting these approaches in conversation with each other, highlights issues of theory, research, and practice in language learning and teaching.

Conversation Analysis

Conversation analysis has become increasingly salient in the wake of Firth and Wagner's (1997) critique of second language research, arguing for a shift from etic (analyst-relevant/outsider) to emic (or participant-relevant) conceptualizations of second language acquisition (SLA) and critiquing what they saw as an imbalance between cognitive vs. social/contextual orientations to language. This section devotes particular attention to CA because of its role in galvanizing attention to these con-temporary issues.

CA grew out of a sociological approach developed by Harold Garfinkel (1967), which he called ethnomethodology: the study of the methodologies by which individuals create and make sense of their world. His students Harvey Sacks and Emanuel Schegloff with Gail Jefferson (Sacks, 1992; Sacks, Schegloff, & Jefferson, 1974; Schegloff & Sacks, 1973) turned an ethnomethodological lens onto conversation, asking how social beings display an ongoing shared sense of the social accom-plishment of talk in interaction. Wagner (1996b, p. 145) summarizes nicely:

> As an ethnomethodological enterprise, Conversation Analysis (CA) studies the methods by which members of a society ongoingly create orderly and meaningful social practices. Since the early 1970's an increasing number of studies have demonstrated that talk-in-interaction is a highly organized practice, that the participants in talk deploy formal procedures to make sense to each other in their social life and to instantiate social structure. Talk and social order are situ-ationally accomplished by the participants in regular, describable ways.

Of appeal to those of a more structuralist bent have been the normative practices displayed in structures such as adjacency pairs, the regularities of openings and closings, and the turn taking sys-tem overall. But Seedhouse (2007) notes the dangers of "linguistifying" CA. Particularly since 1997, the appeal for "poststructuralist" or "sociocultural" researchers has been CA's emic possibilities. Ironically, not unlike Harris, CA researchers make no a priori assumptions about the intentions or social identity of a speaker. Instead, researchers attend to features of talk oriented to by the speakers themselves.

In this focus, CA is radically contextualized, and context itself is seen as a local achievement. Central to CA is the concept of "recipient design" (Sacks et al., 1974): the ways in which talk dis-plays "an orientation and sensitivity to" (p. 727) recipients and to previous and projected future turns at talk. In conversation, there is always sequential relevance. This is not without its cognitive aspects. In projecting and displaying understandings, speakers create and maintain a shared world of understanding, termed in CA, *intersubjectivity*. But this is not an individual or purely biological phenomenon. Schegloff (1991) opts for "socially shared cognition." Shared understandings are pub-licly observable.

The possibility of intersubjectivity has implications for how one theorizes the goal of language learning. Even such structural/cognitive concepts as rules have been rendered radically contextual in CA. Rules are never deterministic. Rather, central to CA is the concept of *accountability*: that interactants assume shared knowledge of norms such that speakers will be held accountable for their violation ("What was he thinking?"). This, of course, can lead to intercultural awkwardness. If conversation turns on shared assumptions, what is obviously polite in one culture (e.g., overlapping speech) is accountably not inviting in another (cf. Tannen, 1984).

CA contributes insights for SLA while it simultaneously provides an epistemology and methodology. With respect to the former, insights range from the most tangible: what are the actual greetings/closings speakers accomplish versus the formulas found in language textbooks?[4] to more procedural understandings: how do learners orient to learning roles and activities to "actively use the microstructure of interactional language as a resource for acquisition" (Markee & Kasper, 2004, p. 496). Methodologically, CA contributes a kind of analytic discipline: if interactants themselves do not orient to a feature of/in language, on what basis can the analyst? In fact, recent research shows so-called native speaker/nonnative speaker (NS/NNS) dyads orienting to NS status only when the second language speaker invokes this identity (Ahn, forthcoming; also cf. Mori, 2007, discussing Hosoda, 2006; Kasper, 2004; Kurhila, 2001, 2005; and Wong, 2005). This should not be surprising as Firth (1996) argued that participants in lingua franca interactions show an aversion to focusing on the form of other's talk, overwhelmingly adopting the "default" position that talk that accomplishes its task is "normal" (p. 256). These studies respond nicely to Wagner's (1996a) critique of earlier research on conversational adjustments. Rather than judging NS/NNS interactions on the basis of an analyst-defined "normal information transfer," these more recent studies show how speakers create meaning in ongoing, recipiently designed interactions. Wagner summarizes that "communication is locally accomplished" (p. 273).

Recent volumes applying CA to SLA include: Gardner and Wagner, 2004; Lazaraton, 2002; Mackey, 2007; Markee, 2000; Richards & Seedhouse, 2005; Seedhouse, 2004. Classroom based studies appear in the special-topic issue of the *Modern Language Journal* edited by Markee and Kasper (2004).

A final dilemma in applying CA to interactions among speakers from multiple linguistic or cultural backgrounds especially is the fact that speakers may not always display their confusions. Not only can the analyst not assume that speakers will always orient to misapprehensions, but the speakers themselves may not be aware at the time what was happening. Speakers of different primary languages may only have a nagging sense that comprehension did not take place. Tannen (1984) demonstrates that speakers of the same language may not be conscious of the ethnic and cultural divides that lead to different experiences of talk in interaction. It is not atypical for those seeking to understand the workings of culture and/or power to join CA techniques with more multi-pronged, ethnographic approaches to discourse. For some analysts, one way to move toward an emic approach is to ask the participants themselves what they perceive to have transpired (an early example of this is Tannen, 1984). It is important then to distinguish between the use of CA as an overarching research paradigm and the strategic use of CA techniques along with other approaches. Issues of methodological purity are beyond the scope of this chapter.

Sociocultural Theory

Congruent with CA's understanding of language at the nexus of the interrelations of individuals and the social is the discourse-focused work based in Vygotsky-influenced sociocultural theory (e.g., Byrnes, 2006; Lantolf, 2000; Lantolf & Appel, 1994; Lantolf & Poehner, 2008; Lantolf & Thorne, 2006; Leontiev, 1981; Ohta, 2001; Vygotsky, 1997–1998; Wertsch, 1985.).[5] Aligning themselves with Firth and Wagner's critique, Lantolf and Johnson (2007) see sociocultural approaches extending Firth and Wagner's marriage of language learning and use and of the human to the social, to a marriage of the social and the psychological. Language learning constitutes a process by which norms of social interaction are internalized to eventually become cognitive resources of a fully independent language user. As Ohta (2001, p. 21) explains:

> *Social* and *cognitive* are all too often considered to be discrete categories, separated and isolated in an attempt to better understand their nature If considered developmentally, however the dialogic origins of cognition are evident because cognition itself is formed through social interaction. Thus one way to consider the social and the cognitive are as interpenetrated elements that cannot be isolated from the environments in which the learner finds him/herself.

This interpenetration of the social and the cognitive is reminiscent of CA's intersubjectivity.

Another dualism challenged by sociocultural approaches is the familiar language/culture dichotomy. Lantolf and Johnson (2007) evoke Agar's (1994) *languaculture* to argue for a reframing of language instruction. Recall that in CA, individuals learn to make appropriate utterances accountable to cultural norms. Similarly, in a sociocultural approach teachers are urged to focus on social activities which highlight languacultural resources:

> We would expect L2 [second language] teachers to spend less time explaining whether an utterance is right or wrong and more time exploring with learners how an utterance positions the speaker in relation to others and the cultural schema it evokes, how it may be understood and evaluated by others, and what is assumed to be shared knowledge and thus remains unarticulated. … We would expect L2 pedagogy to move learners from an abstract understanding of the concept under investigation to a concrete understanding as it plays out in practical activity in the everyday world.
>
> (Lantolf & Johnson, 2007, p. 886)

Like the other approaches that are the focus of this article, sociocultural approaches underscore the marriage of form and function and the work accomplished through language.

Lantolf and Johnson (2007, p. 881) advocate concept-based instruction:

> [G]rammatical mastery is not about typical uses of grammatical forms in particular contexts; it is about conceptually understanding how grammar can be deployed in the service of the meanings a speaker (or writer) wishes to (co)construct in a particular circumstance.

They endorse DiPietro's (1987) "strategic interaction" scenarios, classroom activities that, over time, encourage the development of fully internalized, unconscious discursive language strategies. They recommend that L2 teachers use discourse strategies, for example, "nonjudgmental listening, … that model alternative ways of thinking and talking … for students, … focus[ing] … not so much on what is being said, but on what is being accomplished in the activity of what is being said" (p. 888). In this way through social activities, meaning is co-constructed and, recalling Ohta, language is internalized and learned: "Internalization processes function to transform social interactive processes into the individual cognitive processes that we recognize as what it means for a person to 'know' a language" (p. 2). A similarity of conversation analysis and a sociocultural approach is the meticulous attention to the moment-by-moment unfolding of social interaction.

At the center of a sociocultural study of the discourses of teaching and learning is the notion of learner agency in both what is learned and how that learning is used to engage in social activities (e.g., Lantolf & Johnson, 2007). In this way, as in CA, learners' language use turns on strategic decisions based on internalization of norms, arguably parallel to CA's "accountability." Thus human consciousness for Vygotskyan sociocultural theory is not predictable or determined, but rather human behavior is "grounded in a historical epistemology" (Lantolf & Johnson, 2007, p. 888). Understanding learner behavior, then, arguably becomes similar to the task for the CA analyst: detailing the history of the discourse (the moment-by-moment recipient designs) and the epistemological (ethnomethodological) procedures that speakers display in accomplishing an interaction.

Pragmatics

Another locus of interactional discourse analysis is pragmatics. Building initially on the work on speech acts by Austin (1962), Searle (1969), and Grice (1975), pragmatics examines how particular acts are accomplished in interaction, focusing on speaker/writer meaning and listener/reader reception. Like the other approaches to language discussed here, pragmatics takes into account both the context and the production of meaning in interaction (Cutting, 2002). Kasper and Rose (2001) define pragmatics as "the study of communicative action in its sociocultural context" (p. 2). Like CA, pragmatics assumes that conversation is rational, that speakers follow shared norms for the use of language in interaction (Levinson, 1983). This is captured in Grice's (1975) "Cooperative Principle." When cooperation does not appear to be taking place, the flouting of maxims (quantity, quality, relevance, manner)[6] triggers *conversational implicature:* listeners come to assume/infer unstated meanings. The simple, oft-cited example is the Queen's statement that "It's cold in here," which the servant understands as an order, subsequently closing the window.[7] In this way, pragmatics studies how more is done/communicated than said (Yule, 1996).

Of course, pragmatics is not entirely parallel to CA. And actual practitioners of these different approaches to discourse analysis have different research investments. In a version of "where's the beef?," Kasper's (1997) response to Firth and Wagner reminded readers that the "A" in SLA stands for acquisition and suggested that the microanalytic tools of CA be incorporated into a language socialization approach to SLA. Nonetheless, there are potentially fruitful parallels between CA and pragmatics, including the role ascribed to the listener. As anyone who has accepted a grudging apology knows, in the end, the success of a speech act rests in how it is received. An apology is an apology when it counts as such for the (over)hearer. Many is the public career whose end was hastened when a public apology to a wife for sexual indiscretion proves inadequate for the overhearers. In that sense, a pragmatics perspective can be said to parallel CA's understanding of the mutual accomplishment of conversational/interactive work. In the United States in 2007, talk show host Don Imus was essentially required by the public to redo his apology for having made racist comments; public outcry and media attention indicated that the first apology, which among other things, took no responsibility was a sociopragmatic failure.

Research on pragmatics in SLA focuses on the development of pragmatic competence (Kasper & Roever, 2005). Pragmatic research has been especially fruitful in its examination of communication across cultures, particularly the gaffs that get speakers into trouble. Early work often focused on less-than-successful speech act realizations: pragmalinguistic and sociopragmatic "failures" (Leech, 1983; Thomas, 1983). Oversimplifying: the former refers to failures due to inappropriate choices of linguistic forms for particular intents; the latter to inappropriate behaviors given the social context (including the demographics, social status, and roles of the interlocutors). Arguably, the dualism separates linguistic from social knowledge. Kasper and Roever (2005) and Soler and Martínez-Flor (2009) note the importance of seeing the interaction between these.

The early work of the CCSARP (Cross-Cultural Study of Speech Act Realization Patterns) project (Blum-Kulka & Olshtain, 1984) studied the realization of a limited series of speech acts across cultures. As an example, early work showed that to count as an apology, across cultures different "offenses" required different pragmalinguistic strategies among the possible options of an expression of apology: excuse/explanation, acknowledgment of responsibility, offer of repair, and promise of forbearance ("This won't happen again") (Cohen & Olstain, 1981, 1991) Over the years, research has confirmed that students benefit from pragmatics instruction (Kasper & Roever, 2005; Rose & Kasper, 2001; Cohen & Olstain, 1991). Soler and Martínez-Flor (2009) note the utility of instruction in pragmatics in foreign language contexts, where students do not have the advantage of linguistic/cultural immersion.

Moving beyond earlier work that used more artificial research protocols (e.g., questionnaires and dialogue completion activities), Bardovi-Harlig and Hartford's (2005, p. 2) collection argues for the study of institutional talk,

> locating research in talk that native and nonnative speakers actually perform …. [By studying consequential talk,] native and nonnative differences can be understood in light of what pragmatic strategies seem to contribute to and which seem to impede the interlocutor's success at the institution.

Moreover, they argue, "institutional settings also afford researchers the opportunity to observe the acquisition of institutional rules themselves, which represent a microcosm of culture" (p. 1).

Note that Firth and Wagner (1997) and those working exclusively within a CA framework would not accept Bardovi-Harlig and Hartford's (2005) a priori orientation to NS status. This represents an important gulf between CA and other research traditions, including pragmatics. Kasper (1997, p. 309) argues for use of the NS designation:

> The constructs "nonnative speaker" and 'learner" focus upon the aspect that is *common* to the studied agents, and relevant to the global research context (or discourse universe) of L2 study generally and L2 acquisition (SLA) specifically …. These learner variables are *not* included in studies because they are relevant to the interlocutors in the ongoing interaction (to the extent that the data is interactional), but because the research has theoretically or empirically motivated reason to believe that such variables may influence L2 use and learning in some way.

What all of the approaches described in this section currently share is a focus on discourse jointly produced in social interaction. They focus research and teaching attention on the cognitive task of the learner in interaction, on the joint production of meaning, and, ultimately, on the relationship of form and function. Note, again, that while linguistic/cultural norms can constrain production and reception, these cannot be entirely predicted.

The Critical Turn

The approaches outlined above fall within the social turn in discourse analysis. A second turn has been the critical one, which contributes a different set of insights to second language teaching and learning. Contemporary approaches to DA increasingly focus on unequal access to linguistic and material resources and the discursive means by which hegemonic ideologies and power relations are sustained. To be clear, as this chapter moves into critical discourse analysis (CDA), the implication should not be taken that CA, sociocultural SLA, or pragmatics cannot have a critical edge. In fact there are many examples of just that. When CA focuses on issues such as who has the floor, whose topics are ratified, turn length, or any of a host of issues highlighting hierarchy, the work is critical. Similarly, when sociocultural research notes shifting roles, it is also noting shifting access to certain kinds of interactional (and potentially institutional) power. And when research studies pragmatic failure of language learners, especially within institutions or within gatekeeping interactions, it, too, has taken a critical turn. But these approaches needn't by definition do so. A critical perspective is what characterizes CDA, the focus of this section.

A complementary caveat is in order with respect to CDA. Following Kress, critical discourse analyst Ruth Wodak (2001) sees texts themselves as "the relevant units of language in communication" (p. 6). The fact that CDA sees its analytic unit as the "text," should not suggest that CDA works solely on written discourse; in fact, it works across all semiotic/representational systems, analyzing discourses of all kinds, including, and often, mediated texts. CDA takes a critical look at all language use, with an eye toward documenting the accomplishment of power relations (some would say "uncovering" power, but I dislike the implication that, as consumers of texts, we are all dupes should a CDA specialist not be at hand). If the focus of discourse analysis in general is the relation of form and function, CDA focuses on how that relationship instantiates particular social relations, specifically relations of power. It is sometimes referred to as an orientation. Van Dijk (2001) terms it "DA with an attitude" (p. 96).

Critical approaches to DA see language use as a form of social practice, an axiom of substantial consequence. As Fairclough and Wodak (1997) explain: "Describing discourse as social practice implies a dialectical relationship between a particular discursive event and situation(s), institution(s) and social structure(s) which frame it: the discursive event is shaped by them, but it also shapes them" (p. 26). The mutually constitutive nature of text and context, discursive and social structures, such that they are in fact indistinguishable, is a claim by critical theories in general that has been powerfully taken up by CDA. Fairclough and Wodak (1997) succinctly note "since discourse is so socially consequential, it gives rise to issues of power" (p. 258).

Fairclough and Wodak (1997, pp. 271–279) outline eight principles of CDA theory and method:

1. CDA addresses social problems;
2. power relations are discursive;
3. discourse constitutes society and culture;
4. discourse does ideological work;
5. discourse is historical;
6. the link between text and society is mediated;
7. discourse analysis is interpretative and explanatory;
8. discourse is a form of social action.

In the understanding that discourse analysis must focus on both microanalysis of texts and macroanalysis of social structures, critical discourse analysts (e.g., Caldes-Coulthard & Coulthard, 2006; Fairclough, 1995, 2003; Gee, 2004; Lazar, 2007; Locke, 2004; Rogers, 2004; van Dijk, 2001, 2008; Van Leeuven, 2008; Weiss & Wodak, 2003; Wodak & Chilton, 2005; Wodak & Meyer, 2001, 2009)[8] tend to rely on a multi-pronged approach. As well, different analysts bring different investments and foci to the task (Wodak, for example, utilizes her "discourse-historical approach," while van Dijk is more cognitive.) The linguistic aspects of CDA are most often located[9] in Halliday's systemic functional linguistics (SFL) (e.g., 2004) with its focus on the function of linguistic forms (cf. Young & Harrison, 2004). While SFL proves a powerful tool for microanalyses of language use, it is the discourse analyst who provides the critical edge. An example is the increasing use of nominalizations in English: the conversion of a verb into a noun-like word, and semantically of a process into an entity. In her introduction to Hallidayan linguistics, Eggins ([1994] 2004, pp. 95–96) provides the following example:

Text 1: Late Essays

Formal extensions of time are not granted as such// but if, through **misfortune** or bad **planning**, an assignment cannot be submitted on time,// it may be submitted within the next 14 days … If it is late because of some **unforeseen disability**// it will not be penalized// provided that (i) documentary evidence of the **disability** is attached to the essay and// (ii) the nature of the

disability and of the **evidence** is **acceptable** to the Late Essay Committee. Full **details** of **penalties** are provided in the "**Submission** of Essays and **Assignments**" document.

Text 2: Late Essays (unpacked)

We won't formally extend the time you have to do your assignments,// but if you can't hand your assignment in on time// because something has gone wrong// or because you didn't plan properly,// then you can submit it within the next 14 days … If it is late because something happened to disable you// and you couldn't have foreseen that that would happen,// then it will not be penalised,// provided that you attach a **document** which proves what happened to you to the essay and// the Late Essay Committee accepts// what you say// you had wrong with you// and the way you prove that to us. Look in the booklet about submitting essays and **assignments**// if you want to find out more about how we penalise you.

Eggins notes that while the clauses in the first text frequently begin with nominalization, those in the second begin with human actors. I provide schematically below Eggins' ([1994], 2004) description of the functions of nominalization:

- By turning verbs into nouns we can express logical relations
- Spoken language is concerned with human actors; written language is concerned with abstract ideas/reasons, linked by relational processes
- Although heavily nominalized language can sound pretentious and may make the meaning obscure, the real motivation for this grammatical process is a functional one: by nominalizing we are able to do things with the text that we cannot do in unnominalized text. Nominalization has two (main) textual advantages:

  ◦ First, it allows us to organize our text rhetorically …. By nominalizing actions and logical relations, we can organize our text not in terms of ourselves, but in terms of ideas, reasons, causes, etc. ….
  ◦ Second, nominalization allows us to pack in more lexical content per sentence.

In contrast, Fairclough (2003) gives a much more critical description of nominalization:

- Loss of semantic elements (tense and modality, so distinctions between *is, may be, should* are lost)
- Exclusion of participants (loss of agents)
- Becomes a resource for generalizing, for abstracting from particular events and series or sets of events (useful for scientific and governmental discourse)

  ◦ Such generalizations/abstractions can suppress difference
  ◦ Can obfuscate agency, and therefore responsibility and social divisions

Making clear the shift in meaning that nominalization can entail in discourse, Fairclough (2003, p. 13) first quotes from a text by Tony Blair: *The modern world is swept by change.* He unpacks this to include "the agents of processes, people who initiate processes or act upon other people or objects," newly rendering the sentence: *Multinational corporations in collaboration with governments are changing the world in a variety of ways.*

In the context of language teaching and learning, it is worth recollecting the call in sociocultural theory to teach grammar in terms of strategic decisions. In the case of nominalization, CDA implies pedagogical options. The language teacher can stop after noting that in scientific genres (e.g., Berkenkotter & Huckin, 1995; Bruce, 2008; Huckin & Olsen, 1991; Swales, 1990, 2004; Swales & Feak, 2004) nominalization allows both more lexical content per sentence (Eggins, 2004) and the generalizing/abstracting that makes it an "irreducible resource" (Fairclough, 2003, p. 144) in technical discourse. But teachers can also note nominalization's more political effects when processes with agents become agentless entities, naturally occurring givens, for example, today's "globalization."

Foundations of the current critical turn in DA can be found in a range of neo-Marxist, poststructuralist, and critical theories (e.g., Althusser, 1971; Bakhtin, 1981, 1986; Bourdieu, 1991; Derrida, 1997; Foucault, 1995, 2002; Gramsci, 1992; Williams, 1977). Silberstein, Doyle, Eastman, and Watkins (1998, pp. 12–13) explain how poststructuralism breaks down precisely the kinds of binaries now challenged in other approaches to language study, for example, a dualism of text and context:

> Although frequently and impatiently dismissed as "reducing" reality to textuality, Derrida's programmatic slogan, "il n'y a pas de hors-texte," might better be understood as both a claim that discourse is materially real in its production and its effects and a warning that, epistemologically, analysis in any case is never in a position to "decide" the difference between discursive and extradiscursive "reality."

Resonating with other approaches discussed here, a central project of CDA and its foundational theories are the material consequences of language use. We see this in Raymond Williams' (1977) critique of "vulgar Marxists," who argue for a reified model with an economic base that unidirectionally "determines" a superstructure of social relations. In its stead, Williams sees a dynamic set of relations and processes, limits and pressures; society is seen as a "constitutive process" (p. 29). Althusser (1971) theorizes how individuals come to internalize social relations (like Williams, he sees language use as material). Using Althusser's concept of *interpellation*, Butler (1997, p. 5) explains how the social subject is produced through discourse:

> The subordination of the subject takes place through language, as the effect of the authoritative voice that hails the individual . . . a policeman hails a passerby on the street, and the passerby turns and recognizes himself as the one who is hailed. In the exchange by which that recognition is proffered and accepted, interpellation—the discursive production of the social subject—takes place.

What makes a subject social is its integration within a set of taken-for-granted understandings (i.e., its interpellation within particular ideologies). From Gramsci, critical applied linguists take the concept of hegemony to capture a sense that the system of meanings and values (of signification) that constitutes ideology is far from neutral; rather "the whole lived social process [is] practically organized by specific and dominant meanings and values" (Williams, 1977, p. 109). Hegemony refers to the entire social process in which lived identities and relationships are saturated by these dominant ideologies. When language learners defer to "native speakers" for expertise in areas far beyond language, they are creating culturally and historically situated identities within a set of hegemonic power relations. When instructors rely solely on teacher-fronted activities they are arguably doing the same.

Foucault (1995, 2002) argues that power in the modern world inheres in complex constitutive relations configured in discursive formations (such as legal or diplomatic language—or the language and surveillance of educational institutions). For Foucault, understandings of "truth" are everywhere produced in the power relations of everyday life. Derrida's epistemological critique of the text and context binary thus turns into a critique of power. Through the Foucauldian lens, the production of disciplinary binaries (form/function, cognition/culture) would become one measure of the ubiquitous expansion of power relations (particularly if understandings of cultural and functional processes are marginalized, thus marginalizing learners and the worlds they inhabit).

Through Foucault's work, discourse analysts see discourse as a way of representing knowledge in a particular period. Discourse is understood to define and produce the objects of our knowledge. While all of the approaches discussed here are radically contextual, Foucault's contextualization is radically historical. Stuart Hall (2001, p. 74) explains how Foucault sees the historical production of knowledge through discourse using the figure of the "madman":

> It is only *within* a definite discursive formation that the object "madness" could appear at all as a meaningful or intelligible construct. It was "constituted by all that was said, in all the statements that named it, divided it up, described it, explained it, traced its development, indicated its various correlations, judged it, and possibly gave it speech by articulating in its name, discourses that were to be taken as its own" (1972:32). And it was only after a certain definition of "madness" was put into practice, that the appropriate subject—"the madman" as current medical and psychiatric knowledge defined "him"—could appear.

Through a Foucauldian lens, the figure of "the student," "the learner," the "nonnative speaker" comes into being through practical and analytic discourses that create a particular set of entailments for the figure sitting in a classroom, asking for directions on the street, operating within the laboratory. The production of knowledge and meaning occurs through discursive choices—in the contexts under discussion here, choices made by the researcher and the pedagogue. If nothing else, understanding the ontological power of these choices should encourage the continuation of the terminological debates that have flowered in recent years.

Finally, it should be underscored that, notwithstanding the powerful constitutive role of discourse assumed within critical approaches to language, social subjects are not theorized without agency. Returning to a sense of strategy familiar to the identity work of the more sociocultural approaches outlined above, Bourdieu (1991) extends the traditional concept of capital to include the social, political, and symbolic capital that individuals bring to interactions and/or work to attain. Within the discursive formations in which they operate, individuals use strategies to accomplish their ends, including their self-creations, through language. They do so, quite often, within power relations that critical theory works to critique.

New Directions: The Discursive Turn in Corpus Linguistics

An increasingly productive area of research has been the proliferation of work in corpus linguistics, influencing and influenced by both the social and critical turns. Associated initially with lexis and syntax (Bhatia, Flowerdew, & Jones, 2008a), corpus approaches are discussed at some length here because of the recent advent of extensive applications to discourse analysis (e.g., Baker, 2006; Bhatia, Flowerdew, & Jones, 2008b; Biber, Connor, & Upton, 2007; Hoey, Mahlberg, Stubbs, & Teubert, 2007). Corpus-based discourse analysis (CBDA), particularly with a focus on genre, echoes themes appearing throughout this chapter: a focus on language in use, nondeterministic constraints on human behavior, and the potential for a critical stance toward power relations.

Like the other approaches examined here, corpus linguistics is the study of language in use. Termed variously a *research domain* (McEnery, Xiao, & Tono, 2006), a *methodological innovation* (Lee, 2008), and a *technology* (Tardy & Swales, 2008), corpus research often analyzes large amounts of "real" text, in recent years as electronic corpora.[10] As McEnery et al. describe, an electronic "corpus is a collection of sampled texts, written or spoken in machine-readable form, which may be annotated with various forms of linguistic information" (2006, p. 4). Approaches to corpus linguistics can be categorized as either bottom-up or top-down (cf. Biber et al., 2007), reflecting different method-ological approaches to discourse structure and function. A bottom-up approach begins with lexical/grammatical patterns; Biber et al. (2007) note that it was "developed to address the methodological problem of how discourse patterns could be analyzed in a large corpus, with hundreds or thou-sands of texts" (p. 16). Functional analysis comes later, and serves "an interpretive role" (p. 17) as "discourse unit types emerge from the corpus patterns" (Upton & Cohen, 2009, p. 585). Based on linguistic criteria, discourse units are grouped into clusters, which are then interpreted as discourse unit types by looking at their typical functions in texts.

In contrast, a top-down approach, which generally uses smaller corpora because of the demands on the analyst, begins with functional/communicative purpose. The analyst creates a specialized cor-pus (for example, Biber et al., 2007, report research on biochemistry research articles and fundraising appeals), and develop a set of possible discourse unit types. An example of the contribution of this approach to discourse studies is Upton and Cohen's (2009) discussion of "birthmother" letters writ-ten by prospective adoptive parents to expectant mothers.

Methodologically, the study joins with work on genre, using Swales' (1981) "move analysis." Swales (e.g., 1990, 2004) defines genre on the basis of communicative purpose. Genres not only comprise texts structured in conventionalized ways, but they also serve particular functions, and do particular work. Bawarshi and Reiff (2010, p. 45) explain:

> By proposing that a genre "comprises a class of communicative events, the members of which share some set of communicative purposes" ... Swales [1990, p. 58] defines genres first and foremost as linguistic and rhetorical actions, involving the use of language to communicate something to someone at some time in some context for some purpose.

Martin (1997) sees genres functioning as "goal-oriented social processes through which social sub-jects in a given culture live their lives" (p. 43). Bawarshi and Reiff's summary of Swales shows its compatibility with top-down CBDA: "A genre, therefore, is a relatively stable class of linguistic and rhetorical 'events' which members of a discourse community have typified in order to respond to and achieve shared communicative goals" (p. 45). This simultaneous focus on typification and commu-nicative function creates compatibilities between some approaches to genre studies and top-down CBDA's search for textual and linguistic patterns that instantiate communicative functions.

Upton and Cohen (2009) apply CBDA to move analysis. Referencing Biber et al. (2007), they refer to the seven-step top-down approach they detail as the BCU (Biber, Connor, and Upton) Approach. Following Bhatia (1993), they identify birthmother letters as a "distinct genre" because the genre "has a specific communicative purpose, is identified and mutually understood by the community in which it is used, is usually highly structured, and is bound by 'constraints' that are readily noticed when broken" (p. 590). Another echo of earlier themes is the function of "constraint." The potential for "noticing" a violation can be thought of as similar to CA's *accountability*.

Upton and Cohen (2009) begin by determining the function of the genre, identifying possible move types (e.g., "detailing the couple's history before marriage"); they then segment the full text into moves, classify each move by move type, conduct a linguistic analysis of move features, describ-ing move types in terms of the linguistic features of the moves; finally they analyze the move structure of each text in terms of move types and describe the corpus of texts in terms of typical and alternate move structures. In the end they are able to provide examples of prototypical letters that reflect typi-cal organization structures for successful birthmother letters. The article provides some procedural detail.

This use of a relatively smaller corpus reflects current trends. Tardy and Swales (2008, p. 574) note

"In retrospect, the 20th century will probably be seen as the era of large, relatively undifferentiated corpora ... there are signs that the first decade of the new century will turn out to be the decade of fairly small, genre-specific or multigenre-specific corpora.

This parallels Swales' (1990) earlier observation regarding English for specific purposes (ESP) studies, noting that they were becoming both "narrower and deeper"—narrower in the sense that the foci were becoming more differentiated (moving from broad registers such as "scientific discourse" to more specific disciplines) and deeper as studies move beyond a sole focus on linguistic features to social purposes and effects.

This joint focus on linguistic features and on the social (combining quantitative and qualitative methodologies[11]) is not the only way in which CBDA has come to resonate with other approaches to DA. It does so as well in its attention to expectations and the unfolding nature of discourse. Papers in Hoey et al. (2007) argue that previous communicative events shape current ones. Within that volume, the most succinct interpretation of Hoey and Teubert is found in Sinclair (2007, p. 1): Hoey argues that "participants in an event adjust their expectations in light of that shared experience." Hoey terms *priming* the psychological link between experience and expectation. The corpus, then, becomes "a record both of the routine regular primings and the instances that go against the anticipated primings" (p. 2). Teubert argues that corpora provide evidence of meaning defined as "the accumulation of ... previous occurrences," not for an individual, but as the "available language experience of a society." As such, he argues "meaning is always provisional, always changing" (p. 2).

In their corpus approach to spoken discourse, O'Keeffe, McCarthy, and Carter (2007) maintain that the noncanonical grammatical usage they find bolsters those supporting a theory of "emergent" grammar, "where structure is not seen as a pre-ordained system through which discourse realises its communicative intent, but rather, the opposite: grammar is always 'deferred', temporarily negotiable, and is always emergent from the exigencies of discourse, moment by moment" (p. 136). Their description of the situated unfolding of interaction holds echoes of the recipient design detailed above: "What we find in spoken corpora is messy, variable, anomalous (at least in terms of conventional 'rules') and embedded in the moment-by-moment contingencies of face-to-face interaction" (p. 137). Perhaps nowhere more than in this messy variability is the nondetermined nature of communication more evident. O'Keeffe et al. take pedagogical implications from the corpus finding of "flexibility of form" in conversation: "The cognitive demands of speaking in real time are heavy enough, without having to stop to make everything conform to what we find in writing." At the same time, along with cognitive constraints are the linguistic constraints under which speakers are judged; seeming to respond to both, they suggest that second language students have constant exposure to "prefabricated chunks" (p. 137).

Pedagogical discussions of genre and corpus approaches also echo the critical concerns outlined earlier. Genre approaches to academic language (increasingly aided by CBDA) are implicated in issues of power and privilege. Hyland (2003) argues that "by making the genres of power visible and attainable through explicit instruction, genre pedagogies seek to demystify the kinds of writing that will enhance learners' career opportunities and provide access to a greater range of life choices" (p. 24). But others focus on the social relations of power instantiated in language use. Benesch (1993) argues that by adopting an accommodationist stance, English for academic purposes (EAP) reproduces the academic and societal contexts that work against the full participation of EAP students. Responding to that concern, Bawarshi and Reiff (2010, p. 53) endorse Pennycook's (1997) call for "critical pragmatism":

Such an approach argues that effective participation within a discourse community requires more than just the ability to follow genre conventions as these relate to communicative purposes; it requires the ability to know why genres and purposes exist, whose interests they serve and whose they exclude, what they make possible and what they obscure, and so on. This more critical approach to genre … shifts the focus from a pedagogy of cultural accommodation to what Pennycook [1997] calls a "pedagogy of cultural alternatives" ([p.] 264), whereby students can potentially adapt genre conventions in order to represent alternative purposes and/or their own cultural perspectives.

These ongoing debates are a reminder that technology does not absolve the analyst or practitioner from critical analysis (see also, Baker, 2009b). Nor does it replace the analyst at each stage of research. As Lee (2008, p. 94) observes:

> The pervasiveness of computers and electronic texts makes it easy to predict that more discourse analyses in the future will be corpus-based in one form or another, although the need for a human analyst, ethnographic knowledge of events and close textual readings will in no way be replaced because the nature of language is such that it is resistant to easy interpretations and automatized analyses.

At the same time, corpus linguists such as Lee note that corpus studies can provide easier access to verifiable results, confirm intuitions, and provide quantitative information about frequency and typicality (trends and preferences) that might not otherwise be discernible.

Within all of these approaches to language, and in their application to teaching and learning, the outcomes are never determined. Individuals may be constrained by (hegemonic) discursive formations and by limitations on their linguistic/cultural knowledge, but the results of these phenomena are never entirely predictable. Contemporary discourse-analytic approaches offer ways to explore the constitutive and contingent processes of language use and acquisition. Through their focus on form and function, social and critical trends in DA provide increasing opportunities for converging perspectives to collectively illuminate the processes by which language is discursively produced, understood, and acquired.

Notes

1. Schiffrin (1994) noted two paradigms within linguistics that can lead to varying definitions of discourse analysis. Formalist approaches tended to define discourse as a unit larger than the sentence. Those more aligned with functionalist approaches, contrastingly, focus on language use. These are sometimes framed in terms of text and context. Increasingly, approaches seek to capture both as a kind of "(con)text" (e.g., Kramsch, 1993). Even as early as the 1970s, Sacks et al. (1974) married structure and sequential context by noting the utterance as the building block of oral interaction. The utterance was often found to be much longer than a sentence and had a structural and psychological reality they found missing in the sentence. Schiffrin (1994) makes a similar argument. It is this marriage of the two approaches that is the focus here.
2. For a fuller discussion of approaches to spoken discourse, see Cameron (2001).
3. CA distinguishes between "naturally occurring" conversation among presumed equals and institutional discourses. However, it can be argued that most things humans do are "natural," and identities established through interaction can be more or less equal at any given moment.
4. See Eisenstein Ebsworth, Bodman and Carpenter (1995), for a study of openings; Grant and Starks (2001), for closings.
5. It would be possible to classify all of the approaches in this section as "sociocultural" (cf. Markee & Kasper, 2004), but for reasons I hope will become clear, I prefer to maintain the distinction among these.
6. *Quantity:* make your contribution as informative as is required for the current purposes of the exchange; *quality:* say only what is true (Lakoff); *relevance:* be relevant; *manner:* avoid obscurity, ambiguity, be succinct.
7. For many discourse analysts the closing of the window is textual.
8. Roger Fowler's (e.g., 1979) work in critical linguistics is seen as foundational. Also see the edited compendium by Toolan (2002).

9. Although Gee (2004) bases his linguistics in North American sources.
10. For earlier work on electronic corpora, see, Biber, Conrad, and Reppen (1998) and Stubbs (1996). Among more recent work not explicitly referenced here, see Baker (2009a) and Connor and Upton (2004).
11. There have been increased calls for combining large-scale corpus analysis with careful analysis of individuals (cf. Biber et al., 2007, p. 7).

References

Agar, M. (1994). *Language shock: Understanding the culture of conversation*. New York: William Morrow.

Ahn, Tae-youn. (forthcoming). Learner collaboration and identity construction in Korean–English language-exchange interactions. Unpublished doctoral dissertation, University of Washington, Seattle.

Althusser, L. (1971). *Lenin and philosophy and other essays* (Ben Brewster, trans.). New York: Monthly Review Press.

Austin, J. L. (1962). *How to do things with words*. Oxford: Oxford University Press.

Baker, P. (2006). *Using corpora in discourse analysis*. London: Continuum.

Baker, P. (Ed.) (2009a) *Contemporary approaches to corpus linguistics*. London: Continuum.

Baker, P. (2009b) Issues in teaching corpus-based (critical) discourse analysis. In L. Lombardo (Ed.), *Using corpora to learn about language and discourse* (pp. 73–98). Oxford: Peter Lang.

Bakhtin, M. M. (1981) *The dialogic imagination: Four essays* (M. Holquist, Ed., C. Emerson & M. Holquist, trans). Austin: University of Texas Press.

Bakhtin, M. M. (1986) *Speech genres and other late essays* (V.W. McGee, trans.). Austin: University of Texas Press.

Bardovi-Harlig, & Hartford, B. S. (Eds.) (2005). *Interlanguage pragmatics: Exploring institutional talk*. Mahwah, NJ: Lawrence Erlbaum.

Bawarshi, A., & Reiff, M. J. (2010). *Genre: An introduction to history, theory, research, and pedagogy*. West Lafayette, IN: Parlor Press.

Benesch, S. (1993). ESL, ideology, and the politics of pragmatism. *TESOL Quarterly*, *27*, 705–717.

Berkenkotter, C., & Huckin, T. N. (1995). *Genre knowledge in disciplinary communication: Cognition, culture, power*. Hillsdale, NJ: Lawrence Erlbaum.

Bhatia, V. K. (1993). *Analyzing genre: Language use in professional settings*. London: Longman.

Bhatia, V. K., Flowerdew, J., & Jones, R. H. (Eds.) (2008a). Approaches to discourse analysis. In *Advances in discourse studies*. London: Routledge.

Bhatia, V. K., Flowerdew, J., & Jones, R. H. (Eds.) (2008b). *Advances in discourse studies*. London: Routledge.

Biber, D., Connor, U., & Upton, T. A. (2007). *Discourse on the move: Using corpus analysis to describe discourse structure*. Amsterdam: John Benjamins.

Biber, D., Conrad, S., & Reppen, R. (1998). *Corpus linguistics: Investigating language structure and use*. Cambridge: Cambridge University Press.

Blum-Kulka, S., & Olshtain, E. (1984). Requests and apologies: A cross-cultural study of speech act realization patterns (CCSARP). *Applied Linguistics*, *5*, 196–213.

Bourdieu, P. (1991). *Language and symbolic power* (J. B. Thompson, Ed., G. Raymond & M. Adamson, trans.). Cambridge, MA: Harvard University Press.

Bruce, I. (2008). *Academic writing and genre: A systematic analysis*. London: Continuum.

Butler, J. (1997). *Excitable speech: A politics of the performative*. New York: Routledge.

Byrnes, H. (Ed.) (2006). *Advanced language learning: The contributions of Halliday and Vygotsky*. London: Continuum.

Caldes-Coulthard, C. R., & Coulthard, M. (Eds.) (2006). *Texts and practices: Readings in critical discourse analysis*. London: Routledge.

Cameron, D. (2001). *Working with spoken discourse*. Los Angeles: Sage.

Cohen, A., & Olshtain, E. (1981). Developing a measure of sociocultural competence: The case of apology. *Language Learning*, *31*, 113–134.

Cohen, A., & Olshtain, E. (1991). Teaching speech act behaviors to nonnative speakers. In M. Celce-Murcia (Ed.), *An introduction to teaching English as a second or foreign language* (2nd ed.) (pp. 154–165). Cambridge, MA: Harper & Row.

Connor, U., & Upton, T. A. (Eds.) (2004). *Applied corpus linguistics: A multidimensional perspective*. Amsterdam: Rodopi.

Cutting, J. (2002). *Pragmatics and discourse*. London: Routledge.

Derrida, J. (1997) *On grammatology* (corrected ed., G. C. Spivak, Trans.). Baltimore, MD: Johns Hopkins University Press.

DiPietro, R. J. (1987). *Strategic interaction*. Cambridge: Cambridge University Press.

Eisenstein Ebsworth, M., Bodman, J., & Carpenter. M. (1995). Cross-cultural realization of greetings in American English. In S. Gass & J. Neu (Eds.), *Speech acts across cultures: Challenges to communication in a second language* (pp. 89–108). New York: Mouton de Gruyter.

Eggins, S. (2004). *An introduction to systemic functional linguistics* (2nd ed.). New York: Continuum. (First ed. 1994.)

Fairclough, N. (1995). *Critical discourse analysis.* London: Longman.

Fairclough, N. (2003). *Analysing discourse: Textual analysis for social research.* London: Routledge.

Fairclough, N., & Wodak, R. (1997). Critical discourse analysis. In T. van Dijk (Ed.), *Discourse and interaction* (pp. 258–284). London: Sage.

Firth, A. (1996). The discursive accomplishment of normality: On "lingua franca" English and conversation analysis. *Journal of Pragmatics, 26,* 237–259.

Firth, A., & Wagner, J. (1997). On discourse, communication, and (some) fundamental concepts in SLA research. *Modern Language Journal, 81,* 285–300.

Foucault, M. (1972). *The archaeology of knowledge.* London: Tavistock.

Foucault, M. (1995). *Discipline and punish: The birth of the prison* (A. M. S. Smith, trans.). New York: Vintage.

Foucault, M. (2002). *The Archaeology of knowledge* (A. M. S. Smith, trans.). London: Routledge.

Fowler, R. (1979). *Language and control.* London: Routledge.

Gardner, R., & Wagner, J. (Eds.) (2004). *Second language conversations.* London: Continuum.

Garfinkel, H. (1967). *Studies in ethnomethodology.* Englewood Cliffs, NJ: Prentice-Hall.

Gee, J.P. (2004). Discourse analysis: What makes it critical? In R. Rogers (Ed.), *An introduction to critical discourse analysis in education* (pp. 19–50). Mahwah, NJ: Lawrence Erlbaum.

Gramsci, A. (1992). *Prison Notebooks.* New York: Columbia University Press.

Grant, L., & Starks, D. (2001). Screening appropriate teaching materials: Closings from textbooks and television soap operas. *International Review of Applied Linguistics and Language Teaching, 39,* 39–50.

Grice, P. (1975). Logic and conversation. In P. Cole & J. Morgan (Eds.), *Syntax and semantics: Vol. 3. Speech Acts* (pp. 41–58). New York: Academic Press.

Hall, S. (2001). Foucault: Power, knowledge and discourse. In M. Wetherell, S. Taylor, & S. J. Yates (Eds.), *Discourse theory and practice: A reader* (pp. 72–81). London: Sage.

Halliday, M. A. K. (2004). *An introduction to functional grammar* (3rd ed., rev. by C. M. I. M. Matthiessen). London: Arnold.

Harris, Z. (1952). Discourse Analysis. *Language, 28,* 1–30.

Hoey, M., Mahlber, M., Stubbs, M., & Teubert, W. (Eds.) (2007). *Text, discourse, and corpora: Theory and analysis.* London: Continuum.

Hosoda, Y. (2006). Repair and relevance of differential language expertise in second language conversation. *Applied Linguistics, 27,* 25–50.

Huckin, T. N., & Olsen, L. (1991). *Technical writing and professional communication: For nonnative speakers of English.* New York: McGraw-Hill.

Hyland, K. (2003). Genre-based pedagogies: A social response to process. *Journal of Second Language Writing, 12,* 17–29.

Kasper, G. (1997). "A" stands for acquisition: A response to Firth and Wagner. *Modern Language Journal, 81,* 307–312.

Kasper, G. (2004). Participant orientation in conversation-for-learning. *Modern Language Journal, 88,* 551–567.

Kasper, G., & Roever, C. (2005). Pragmatics in second language learning. In E. Hinkel (Ed.), *Handbook of research in second language learning and teaching* (pp. 317–334). Mahwah, NJ: Erlbaum.

Kasper, G., & Rose, K. R. (2001). Pragmatics and language teaching. In K. R. Rose & G. Kasper (Eds.), *Pragmatics and language teaching* (pp. 1–10). Cambridge: Cambridge University Press.

Kramsch, C. (1993). *Context and culture in language teaching.* Oxford: Oxford University Press.

Kurhila, S. (2001). Correction in talk between native and non-native speakers. *Journal of Pragmatics, 33,* 1083–1110.

Kurhila, S. (2005). Different orientations to grammatical correctness. In K. Richards & P. Seedhouse (Eds.), *Applying conversation analysis* (pp. 143–158). Basingstoke: Palgrave Macmillan.

Lantolf, J. P. (Ed.) (2000). *Sociocultural theory and second language learning.* New York: Oxford University Press.

Lantolf, J. P., & Appel, G. (Eds.) (1994). *Vygotskian approaches to second language research.* Norwood, NJ: Ablex.

Lantolf, J.P., & Johnson, K. E. (2007). Extending Firth and Wagner's (1997) ontological perspective to L2 classroom praxis and teacher education. *Modern Language Journal, 91,* 877–892.

Lantolf, J. P., & Poehner, M. E. (Eds.) (2008). *Sociocultural theory and the teaching of second languages.* London: Equinox.

Lantolf, J.P., & Thorne, S.L. (2006). *Sociocultural theory and the genesis of second language development.* Oxford: Oxford University Press.

Lazar, M. M. (Ed.) (2007). *Feminist critical discourse analysis: Studies in gender, power and ideology.* Basingstoke: Palgrave Macmillan.

Lazaraton, A. (2002). *A qualitative approach to the validation of oral language tests.* Cambridge: Cambridge University Press.

Lee, D. (2008). Corpora and discourse analysis: New ways of doing old things. In V. K. Bhatia, J. Flowerdew, & R. H. Jones (Eds.), *Advances in discourse studies* (pp. 86–99). London: Routledge.

Leech, G. (1983). *Principles of pragmatics.* London: Longman.

Leontiev, W. W. (1981). *Psychology and the language learning process.* London: Pergamon.

LeVine, P., & Scollon, R. (Eds) (2004). *Discourse and technology: Multimodal discourse analysis.* Washington, DC: Georgetown University Press.

Levinson, S. C. (1983). *Pragmatics.* Cambridge: Cambridge University Press.

Locke, T. (2004). *Critical discourse analysis.* London: Continuum.

McEnery, T., Xiao, R., & Tono, Y. (2006). *Corpus-based language studies.* London: Routledge.

Mackey, A. (Ed.) (2007). *Conversational interaction in second language acquisition: A collection of empirical studies.* Oxford: Oxford University Press.

Markee, N. (2000). *Conversation analysis,* Mahwah, NJ: Lawrence Earlbaum.

Markee, N., & Kasper, G. (2004) Classroom talks: An introduction. In Classroom talks [Special issue]. *Modern Language Journal, 88,* 491–499.

Martin, J. R. (1997). Analysing genre: Functional parameters. In F. Christie and J. R. Martin (Eds.), *Genres and institutions: Social processes in the workplace and school* (pp. 33–69). London: Cassell.

Mori, J. (2007). Border crossing? Exploring the intersection of second language acquisition, conversation analysis, and foreign language pedagogy. *Modern Language Journal, 91,* 849–862.

Ohta, A. (2001). *Second language acquisition processes in the classroom: Learning Japanese.* Mahwah, NJ: Lawrence Erlbaum.

O'Keeffe, A., McCarthy, M., & Carter, R. (2007). *From corpus to classroom: Language use and language teaching.* Cambridge: Cambridge University Press.

Pennycook, A. (1997). Vulgar pragmatism, critical pragmatism, and EAP. *English for Specific Purposes, 16,* 253–269.

Richards, K., & Seedhouse, P. (Eds.) (2005). *Applying conversation analysis.* Basingstoke: Palgrave Macmillan.

Rogers, R. (2004). *An introduction to critical discourse analysis in education.* Mahwah, NJ: Lawrence Erlbaum.

Rose, K.R., & Kasper, G. (Eds.) (2001). *Pragmatics in language teaching.* Cambridge: Cambridge University Press.

Sacks, H. (1992). *Lectures on conversation* (Vols. I & II) (G. Jefferson, Ed.). Cambridge, MA: Blackwell.

Sacks, H., Schegloff, E. A., & Jefferson, G. (1974). A simplest systematics for the organization of turn-taking for conversation. *Language, 50,* 696–735.

Schegloff, E. A. (1991). Conversation analysis and socially shared cognition. In L. Resnick, J. Levine, & S. Teasley (Eds.), *Perspectives on socially shared cognition* (pp. 150–171). Washington, DC: APA.

Schegloff, E.A., & Sacks, H. (1973). Opening up closings. *Semantica, 7,* 289–327.

Schiffrin, D. (1994). *Approaches to discourse.* Oxford: Blackwell.

Schiffrin, D., Tannen, D., & Hamilton, H. (Eds.) (2001). *The handbook of discourse analysis.* Malden, MA: Blackwell.

Scollon, R., & Scollon, S. W. (2004). *Nexus analysis: Discourse and the emerging internet.* London: Routledge.

Searle, J. (1969). *Speech acts: An essay in the philosophy of language.* Cambridge: Cambridge University Press.

Seedhouse, P. (2004). *The interactional architecture of the language classroom: A conversation analysis perspective.* Malden, MA: Blackwell.

Seedhouse, P. (2007). On ethnomethodological CA and "linguistic CA": A reply to Hall. *Modern Language Journal, 91,* 527–533.

Silberstein, S. (2008). "Theorizing" TESOL, *TESOL Quarterly, 42,* 299–302.

Silberstein, S., Doyle, A., Eastman, C. M. K., & Watkins, E. (1998). Talking peace, waging war: Mining the language of leadership. In J. H. O'Mealy and E. L. Lyons (Eds.), *Literary Studies East and West: Vol. 15. Language, linguistics, and leadership* (pp. 1–18). Honolulu: University of Hawaii East–West Center.

Sinclair, J. M. (2007). Introduction. In M. Hoey, M. Mahlberg, M. Stubbs, & W. Teubert (Eds.), *Text, discourse and corpora: Theory and Analysis* (pp. 1–5). London: Continuum.

Soler, A., & Martínez-Flor, A. (Eds.) (2009). *Investigating pragmatics in foreign language learning, teaching, and testing.* Bristol: Multilingual Matters.

Stubbs, M. (1996). *Text and corpus analysis.* Oxford: Blackwell.

Swales, J. M. (1981). *Aspects of article introductions.* Birmingham: University of Aston, The Language Studies Unit.

Swales, J. M. (1990). *Genre analysis: English in academic and research settings.* Cambridge: Cambridge University Press.

Swales, J. M. (2004). *Research genres: Explorations and applications.* Cambridge: Cambridge University Press.

Swales, J. M., & Feak, C. B. (2004). *Academic writing for graduate students: Essential tasks and skills* (2nd ed.). Ann Arbor: University of Michigan Press.

Tannen, D. (1984). *Conversational style: Analyzing talk among friends.* Norwood, NJ: Ablex.

Tardy, C., & Swales, J. (2008). Form, text organization, genre, coherence, and cohesion. In C. Bazerman (Ed.), *Handbook of research on writing: History, society, school, individual, text* (pp. 565–581). New York: Lawrence Erlbaum.

Thomas, J. (1983). Cross-cultural pragmatic failure. *Applied Linguistics, 4,* 91–112.

Toolan, M. (2002). *Critical discourse analysis: Critical concepts in linguistics* (Vols. I–IV). London: Routledge.

Upton, T. A., & Cohen, M. A. (2009). An approach to corpus-based discourse analysis: The move analysis as example. *Discourse Studies, 11,* 585–605.

van Dijk, T. A. (2001). Multidisciplinary CDA: A plea for diversity. In R. Wodak & M. Meyer (Eds.), *Methods of critical discourse analysis* (pp. 95–120). London: Sage.

van Dijk, T. A. (2008). *Discourse and power.* Basingstoke: Palgrave Macmillan.

Van Leeuven, T. (2008). *Discourse and practice: New tools for critical discourse analysis.* Oxford: Oxford University Press.

Vygotsky, L. S. (1997–1998). *The collected works of L. S. Vygotsky* (R. W. Rieber & A. S. Carton, Eds., N. Minick, trans.). New York: Plenum.

Wagner, J. (1996a). Foreign language acquisition through interaction: A critical review of research on conversational adjustments. *Journal of Pragmatics, 26,* 215–235.

Wagner, J. (1996b). Introduction. *Journal of Pragmatics, 26,* 145–146.

Weiss, G., & Wodak, R. (Eds.) (2003). *Critical discourse analysis: Theory and interdisciplinarity.* Basingstoke: Palgrave Macmillan.

Wertsch, J. V. (1985). *Vygotsky and the social formation of mind.* Cambridge, MA: Harvard University Press.

Widdowson, H. (2004). *Text, context, pretext: Critical issues in discourse analysis.* Malden, MA: Blackwell.

Williams, R. (1977). *Marxism and literature.* Oxford: Oxford University Press.

Wodak, R. (2001). What CDA is about: A summary of its history, important concepts and its developments. In R. Wodak & M. Meyer (Eds.), *Methods of critical discourse analysis* (pp. 1–13). London: Sage.

Wodak, R., & Chilton, P. (Ed.) (2005). *A new agenda in (critical) discourse analysis: Theory, methodology and interdisciplinarity.* Amsterdam: John Benjamins.

Wodak, R., & Meyer, M. (Eds.) (2009). *Methods of critical discourse analysis* (2nd ed.). London: Sage. (First ed. 2001.)

Wong, J. (2005). Sidestepping grammar. In K. Richards & P. Seedhouse (Eds.), *Applying conversation analysis* (pp. 159–194). Basingstoke: Palgrave Macmillan.

Young, L., & Harrison, C. (Eds.) (2004). *Systemic functional linguistics and critical discourse analysis: Studies in social change.* London: Continuum.

Yule, G. (1996). *Pragmatics.* Oxford: Oxford University Press.

18
Language Socialization in Multilingual and Second Language Contexts

Robert Bayley and Juliet Langman[1]

Introduction

Language socialization, the study of how children and older speakers are socialized by and through language into the practices of their own and other communities, developed as a distinct approach in the 1980s with studies such as Heath's (1983) work with African American and white working-class communities in the southern United States, Ochs' (1988) studies of language acquisition in Samoa, Schieffelin's (1990) work with the Kaluli in Papua New Guinea, and Watson-Gegeo's (1992; Watson-Gegeo & Gegeo, 1986) work in the Solomon Islands.[2] For the most part, the pioneering studies focused on the interactions between young children and caregivers during the period of primary language acquisition, most often in situations where only one language was involved (Reyes & Moll, 2008). As Kulick and Schieffelin (2004) note, in the 1980s, language socialization researchers were responding to what they regarded as two significant absences in psycholinguistic accounts of language acquisition and anthropological accounts of child socialization. The first absence concerns culture. Kulick and Schieffelin observe that scholars studying first language (L1) acquisition proceeded as though the practices they observed, for example the use of a simplified register in child-directed speech, were universal and essential to acquisition. The fact that participants in most studies were white middle-class children in developed countries was ignored. The second gap concerns the absence of language from classic studies of socialization such as Mead's (1930, 1954) work on growing up in Samoa and New Guinea. Kulick and Schieffelin argue that the language socialization paradigm

> addresses the lack of culture in language acquisition studies, and the absence of language in child socialization studies by insisting that in becoming competent members of the social groups, children are socialized through and they are socialized to use language.
>
> (Kulick & Schieffelin, 2004, p. 350)

They make strong claims that language is the central and crucial dimension of the process of socialization and that any study of socialization that fails to document the role of language is "fundamentally flawed" (p. 350).

Despite the emphasis on primary language acquisition in the early years, the study of language socialization is not limited to children's acquisition of a first language. Rather, language socialization extends throughout the lifespan. As Ochs notes, "language socialization research examines how language practices organize the lifespan process of becoming an active, competent participant in one or more communities" (1999, p. 230). Ochs goes on to state that communities can be "households, neighborhoods, peer groups, schools, workplaces, professions, religious organizations, recreational gatherings, and other institutions" (p. 230), and, of course, communities can involve the use of more than one language. In recent years, language socialization researchers have focused on a wide range of multilingual and second language (L2) communities including heritage language schools (He, 2003, 2008; He & Xiao, 2008; Jia, 2009), language minorities in North and South America (Baquedano-López, 2004; Guardado, 2008; Li, 2006; Luykx, 2005; Schecter & Bayley, 2002, 2004; Song, 2009; Zentella, 1997, 2005a), language minority children in Japan (Caltabiano, 2009), multicultural high school classrooms (Talmy, 2008), immigrants seeking employment (Duff, Wong, & Early, 2002), and scientific and engineering research groups (Vickers, 2007), to name just a few. In addition, Watson-Gegeo (2004) recently proposed an elaborated language socialization model for second language acquisition (SLA) research. She argued for a view of learning as highly contextualized or situated, a central conception that "linguistic and cultural knowledge are *constructed* through each other," and a view that language-acquiring children and adults "are active and selective agents in both processes" (Watson-Gegeo & Nielsen, 2003, p. 165, drawing on Schieffelin & Ochs, 1986).

Key for studies in the language socialization paradigm is careful attention to language forms and the examination of how forms are tied to contextually bound meanings and subjectivities. As Kulick and Schieffelin write: "A powerful contribution that the language socialization paradigm makes to an understanding of the production of subjects is its close attention to the linguistic forms that are used to socialize children and other novices into expected roles and behaviors" (2004, p. 360). This attention helps us to understand the *what* and the *how* of socialization into particular subjectivities and, when "problematic cases" are involved, allows for an analysis of why social change occurs. An important added dimension, recently highlighted by Kulick and Schieffelin (2004), is the focus on desire as a cognitive construct that explains the motivation for individuals' action to either socialize or not into the sets of practices that constitute normative behavior for particular individuals in particular communities.

It is clear, then, that language socialization research has developed far beyond its initial focus on primary language acquisition. In this chapter, we examine current and recent approaches to language socialization research, with emphasis on work in multilingual and L2 settings not covered in Garrett and Baquedano-López's (2002) and Zuengler and Cole's (2005) recent overviews. Given the amount of work that has been accomplished in recent years, our discussion of studies that illustrate both relatively smooth and problematic multilingual and L2 socialization is necessarily quite selective. Moreover, although we include studies of classroom socialization, both in minority classrooms as well as in classrooms with diverse student populations, we cast a wide net and attend as well to studies that concentrate on multilingual and L2 socialization at different life stages and in non-school settings as well as on the transmission of minority languages from one generation to the next.

The chapter is organized as follows. We first examine the theoretical and methodological underpinnings of language socialization research, with particular attention to recent developments. We then examine studies of language socialization in multilingual and L2 contexts, focusing first on studies that examine relatively unproblematic trajectories of L2 learning and later moving to consideration of recent studies that illuminate problematic cases and the ways in which individuals as agents navigate their socialization trajectories across multiple communities. Next we propose directions for future research that may serve to build a stronger understanding of how continuity and change in cultural contexts occur, and how multilingual/multicultural individuals experience and choose "resistance, the transgression of norms, incomplete reproduction or attainment of demonstrated norms, or the development of hybridized (syncretic) or multiple codes/practices, subject positions, and cultures" (Duff, 2008, p. 110). We conclude with a very brief summary of the advantages of a language socialization perspective for L2 research.

Theoretical and Methodological Issues

Traditionally, research in language acquisition, whether first or second, viewed acquisition as an individual cognitive phenomenon in which context played a relatively unimportant role. Among the more direct statements of this view in SLA is the following, from Michael Long's response to Firth and Wagner's (1997) call for a broader agenda for SLA research: "Given … that most SLA researchers are, in my view, correctly, endeavoring to understand a mental process and a changing mental representation of the L2, or interlanguage grammar, cognitive variables are for them inevitably and justifiably a central focus" (Long, 1997, p. 319). The following year, Long elaborated his perspective on the lack of importance of the social setting for understanding the process of SLA:

> Remove a learner from the social setting, and the L2 grammar does not change or disappear. Change the social setting altogether, e.g., from street to classroom, or from a foreign to a second language environment, and, as far as we know, the way the learner acquires does not change much either, as suggested, e.g., by comparisons of error types, developmental sequences, processing constraints, and other aspects of the acquisition process in and out of classrooms.
>
> (Long, 1998, p. 93)

As Tarone (2000) notes, Long's statement provides a useful set of hypotheses. However, these hypotheses need to be subjected to verification in a wide range of contexts, just as the hypotheses about, for example, the role of child-directed speech, or "motherese," in L1 acquisition needed to be examined in a wide range of contexts. We suggest that, just as language socialization research showed that many presumed universal aspects of L1 acquisition were in fact culture specific, research in multilingual and L2 socialization also demonstrates that context has a profound effect on the process of L2 acquisition and language development.

In contrast to the views put forward by Long and others in the cognitive tradition, researchers in language socialization, as indicated in the introduction to this chapter, view acquisition, whether first, second, or *n*th, more broadly. Language socialization researchers view language acquisition as a composite phenomenon of cognitive-linguistic and sociocultural factors (Ochs, 1988, 1999; Schieffelin & Ochs, 1986; Watson-Gegeo, 2004). Moreover, researchers working within a language socialization framework see both the context and content of interaction and the culturally sanctioned roles of the participants as major determinants of language forms and strategies used in given situations. In fact, in both L1 and L2 acquisition, the nature of the interactions in which learners engage as well as their positioning and self-positioning within those interactions influence the linguistic forms acquired, the extent to which they are acquired, and even which language is acquired (Bronson & Watson-Gegeo, 2008; Kulick, 1992; Ochs & Schieffelin, 1995). Bronson and Watson-Gegeo (2008), for example, describe the case of a Japanese student of English, Keiko, whose unconventional use of the English definite article would most likely be characterized by traditional SLA researchers as a case of fossilization. However, as revealed in an extensive qualitative study, Keiko had read widely in English and she had become aware that there were many English varieties. Her use of the definite article was connected to her sense of identity. As she wrote in her journal: "I have found that I can subvert and create a sort of 'my English' and style with following certain genres so that my articles can be read and understood" (Bronson & Watson-Gegeo, 2008, p. 51). We suggest that Keiko's decision about article use offers a counter example to Long's views concerning the role of the environment in acquisition. We also suggest that Keiko's learning provides an example of the agentive nature of language learning.

Casting the net more broadly, language socialization researchers who examine multilingual communities also rely on a careful analysis of the forms and functions of socializing interaction to consider both the reproduction of society as well as social change. As Kulick and Schieffelin (2004, p. 352) point out:

> By analyzing ways in which praxis comes to be acquired, and performativity actually operates in situated interactions, language socialization studies can document not only how and when practices are acquired, but also how and when they are acquired differently from what was intended, or not acquired at all. Hence, reproduction is not assumed, and unintended consequences of socializing practices, or change, can be documented and accounted for in empirically delineated social contexts.

Thus, we further suggest the case of Keiko highlights the idea that there are no predictable endpoints of the socialization process, and therefore of the language learning process.

As an approach that focuses on the nature of interactions between novices and more experienced members of a community, language socialization entails certain methodological requirements. First, as Ochs (1999) observes, the researcher's focus is not limited to the novice (or language acquirer). Rather, the focus includes all parties in the interaction. Moreover, although language socialization research has some similarities to conversation analysis in its attention to the details of interaction, it takes a broader perspective and attends as well to the overall sociocultural context in which socialization occurs. Kulick (1992), for example, shows how both local beliefs and modernization introduced by missionaries impact children's acquisition of Tok Pisin, a lingua franca, rather than the traditional language, in a small village in Papua New Guinea, resulting in broad social change.

Kulick and Schieffelin maintain that language socialization studies must fulfill three essential criteria: "They should be ethnographic in design, longitudinal in perspective, and they should demonstrate the acquisition (or not) of particular linguistic and cultural practices over time and across contexts" (2004, p. 350). We will use Zentella's (1997) study of Puerto Rican children in New York City, Schecter and Bayley's (2002) study of language use by Mexican background children in California and Texas, and Guardado's (2008) recent study of language socialization among Hispanic families in Vancouver to illustrate how these criteria may be satisfied.

First, all three studies are ethnographic, involving extensive participant observation in a wide range of settings. Zentella's (1997) work with the children of *el bloque* in a Manhattan *barrio* included extensive interviews and observations with a range of community residents as she followed the development of a group of young people from childhood through to early adulthood. Schecter and Bayley (2002) focused on language use—Spanish or English—in the home. In addition to interviewing parents and children in 40 families, they conducted case studies of eight families (four in each state) drawn from the larger sample. These case studies involved extensive observations of interactions among parents, focal children, siblings, and other relatives, as well as participation as observers in family trips to a border city in Mexico and various family events (e.g. picnics with relatives). Guardado (2008) conducted participant observations in homes, with a focus on three case study families, and in Hispanic community groups organized to facilitate language and cultural maintenance, including a co-educational scouting group, "El Grupo Scouts Vista," a heritage language program, "El Centro de Cultura," and an arts program, "La Casa Amistad."

Second, as might be inferred from the wide range of contexts and participants in the three exemplary studies, all are longitudinal. Zentella's (1997) study extended over 14 years and we witness the development of the focal participants from young girls to young women. Schecter and Bayley's (2002) data collection occupied less time, but still extended over two years, while Guardado's (2008) fieldwork, including initial ethnographic interviews with a broad range of families and participant observation with focal families and organizations, occupied a year and a half.

Third, all three studies demonstrate varying degrees of minority language maintenance, as well as how the interactions in which children participate at home and in schools and community settings either facilitate or impede the transmission of the minority language across generations. In addition, while all three studies attend, to a greater or lesser extent, to the details of interactions, all also focus on the larger sociohistorical and cultural contexts of the research settings and all use multiple data sources in their analysis including ethnographic interviews, field notes, recorded audio and video observations of a range of interactions, and writings produced by the focal children. Finally, all three studies adopt an emic perspective.

Recently Bronson and Watson-Gegeo (2008) expanded on the methodological specifications discussed by Kulick and Schieffelin (2004) and exemplified by the three studies discussed above. Noting the critical turn in a number of areas of research in language and culture, Bronson and Watson-Gegeo suggest that language socialization research must "at a minimum" draw on "criticalist" work such as Fairclough (2005) and van Dijk (1993) in ethnography, sociolinguistics, and discourse analysis; that is, language socialization work, which already focuses on the cultural context, should also focus on power. Kulick and Schieffelin (2004) also emphasize this point and propose that researchers continue to examine "how speakers encode desire in language, but also how that desire is articulated with different kinds of authority and power" (p. 362), arguing that "[o]nce we understand the structures through which this occurs, we are in a better position to also understand the ways in which those structures may be challenged, resisted, changed—or entrenched" (p. 362). The argument for focusing on power relationships that articulate desire has been made most forcefully by Zentella (1996, 2005b), who has argued for what she terms "anthropolitical linguistics," which she defines as "research that sees through the language smokescreen that obscures ideological, structural, and political impediments to equity" (2005b, p. 9). Just as the pioneering studies of L1 socialization that showed how children come to acquire language in many different ways helped to challenge the positioning of language and ethnic minority parents as deficient (Valdés, 1996), according to Zentella, language socialization research from an anthropolitical perspective can provide evidence to challenge ideologies that privilege one language or language variety over another or one way of interacting with the world over all other ways.

Finally, although Bronson and Watson-Gegeo (2008) recognize that researchers inevitably bring some *a priori* theory to a study, they maintain that language socialization methods "depend greatly on evolving theory and research questions 'grounded theory' style in the field site and through accumulating data and continuing analysis" (p. 50–51).

Language Socialization as Continuity

Considering the Trajectory

A number of studies in recent years focus on successful and relatively unproblematic trajectories of L2 socialization, continuing the tradition of L2 socialization work, by recording and reporting on the movement from novice to expert, through an examination of particular features of participation. Some of these studies, in addition, prompt us to consider the nature of the socialization trajectory in more detail, and from the perspective of the community and the learner in interaction with one another. Čekaitė's (2007) longitudinal study of a seven-year-old Kurdish girl's development of interactional competence in a Swedish as an L2 immersion program outlines the intersection of trajectories of learning with different positionalities or identities on the part of the learner. In particular, Čekaitė outlines the three stages the child, Kusi, moves through over the course of a year, from a silent member, to a noisy and often reprimanded student, and finally to a skillful interlocutor able to express disagreement and defend her position through normative practices appreciated by

the teacher. Through this study, Čekaitė suggests that we should expect neither unilinear development to full participation nor unidirectional development of a single unified learner identity. Rather,
we should consider socialization as a series of positionalities tied to the interactional practices the
learner is able to engage in, based in part of the learner's growing facility with employing new interactional strategies in specific contexts.

While Čekaitė (2007) focuses on the link between trajectories and language learning affordances,
Pease-Alvarez (2002) examines the effect of shifting perspectives on the L2 socialization trajectory.
Drawing on a study of language socialization of bilingual Spanish English speakers conducted over
a seven-year time span, she argues for moving beyond linear trajectories as the metaphor for understanding language socialization over time. This is because with time, desired trajectories of learning
change together with learners' perspectives on, for example, what counts as "success," what counts
as taking on a "good" identity, and what counts as being "well socialized." Tension between home,
school (or schools if there is a heritage school), and parents and their children in terms of what it
means to "have" a particular identity with a particular evaluative valence as "good" or "bad" shifts
over time, leading to learning trajectories that are neither unilinear nor unidirectional, nor necessarily situatable in a particular "socialization field" or community.

Focusing on the Cognitive

Moving from articles that consider the metaphor of the learning trajectory, to an explicit consideration of the socio-cognitive factors that determine L2 socialization, Vickers (2007) examines the
relatively smooth trajectory of L2 socialization for Ramelan, an advanced learner, in this case in the
context of science and engineering courses, arguing that access to the socializing moments is key. In
her study, she outlines four specific types of interactional events that supported Ramelan's movement from peripheral to core member of the engineering course activities:

> (a) access to observations of core members interacting; (b) scaffolding by core members both in
> the lab and in the team meetings; (c) ridicule by core members; (d) opportunities for successful
> design experiences and for chances to explain these design processes.
>
> (Vickers, 2007, p. 637)

Through these key sites for socialization, Vickers draws an explicit link between the social context
and cognitive development through the lens of activity types, thus explicitly linking language socialization work to activity theory as a key construct in a sociocultural learning theory:

> Activity in Leontiev's (1978) theory is not merely doing something, it is doing something that is
> motivated either by a biological need, such as hunger, or a culturally constructed need, such as
> the need to be literate in certain cultures.
>
> (Lantolf, 2000, p. 8)

Vickers further highlights one of the key events—"ridicule by core members"—as central to
successful socialization, thus linking her work to recommendations by Kulick and Schieffelin (2004)
to focus on issues of desire (or fear) as central cognitive forces determining trajectories. Through this
work, Vickers highlights L2 socialization as a social cognitive process that is situated "within particular social contexts and within particular activity types" (2007, p. 637).

These studies are representative of many others that outline successful trajectories of L2 socialization in the case of children as well as adults, in the case of beginning language learners, as well as
advanced language learners being socialized into new communities of practice. Vickers' study, in

particular, supports a call from Duff (2008, p. 117) that "we need to explore the advanced end of the language learning/performativity spectrum more. How does discourse socialization proceed in highly sophisticated professional or academic settings, such as physicists' laboratory discussions and conference presentation rehearsals (Jacoby and Gonzales, 1991)?"

Language Socialization as Change

Examining the Invisible

Numerous studies, heeding the call to examine "bad subjects" (Kulick & Schieffelin, 2004), resistance, or the development of hybridized or multiple practices (Duff, 2008), allow for a consideration of concepts that explain how socialization occurs in complex multi-sited, multilingual contexts. Recently authors have begun to examine the borders of language socialization practice by clarifying distinctions between implicit and explicit socialization and the parallel notion of visible and invisible practices of new socializing patterns. In a study of literacy instruction in a Chinese heritage school in the United States, Jia (2009) provides an example of a complex context where multiple socialization "ideals" are in conflict or competition with one another. In particular, Jia shows how a teacher's own socialization into literacy with a focus on values rather than developing literacy skills influences perspectives on literacy instruction in the heritage classroom in the US—a context quite different from the context in which the teacher developed those perspectives. From this work emerge questions about the extent to which long-established patterns of activity that "imagine" a norm to which one is socializing students can be disrupted in the face of counter socialization desires on the part of students and, in some cases, their parents. Questions raised include: Can we examine ways by which patterns of activity that do not match the new context in which they are being carried out become disrupted? When adding the notion of authority and power, we can add the question: Are these patterns subject to disruption? Who should decide whether and how they should be disrupted? This study also alludes to the multiple layers of community into which Chinese heritage language students are being socialized and the various forms of resistance that ensue.

Examining the notion of invisibility in a slightly different way, Iddings (2005) uses a community of practice approach to illustrate how students in an elementary classroom form two parallel linguistic communities that are not seen by the teacher: one of English language learners and the other of English dominant students. While for the teacher the classroom may constitute a single site, for students it constitutes a multi-sited context in which language socialization may or may not take place. As a consequence of the two parallel communities that do not interact, very little L2 socialization is taking place, as English language learners are not gaining access to the language, in spite of their physical proximity to it in the classroom.

Another kind of invisibility, silence, is explored by Morita (2004) in a study of academic discourse socialization of international first-year Asian female MA students in a Canadian university. Expanding on the key tool of participant observation to uncover socialization processes, Morita's study focuses on the "socially constructed nature of silence" (p. 575) and its significance in developing the subject position of a competent student in the academic classroom context. By examining silence, Morita draws more subjects into the research field of language socialization that, by focusing on routines and rituals of language use, often focuses on more verbal participants in communication. By examining silence and asking students to reflect on their reticence in class, Morita outlines a range of explanations, beyond broad identity categories of gender, culture, or language proficiency in English, to explain their silence as well as outlining how "students were actively negotiating their multiple roles and identities in the classroom even when they appeared passive or withdrawn" (p. 587). In particular in the case of Nanako, Morita outlines how in three different contexts,

Nanako's silence was reflective of a competent student identity jointly negotiated within the classroom. In this way, Morita's study also highlights the issues of agency and positionality in flux or in transformation across time and across different socializing groups or communities of practice that overlap with one another.

Creating Contexts for Success

Lam (2004) employs a multi-contextual approach to examine language socialization practices in the Internet. In this new context, individuals, in this case, English as a second language (ESL) learners, can create new identities not bound by the constraints of face-to-face contexts. Lam traces how two Chinese girls create a new identity as neither Chinese Americans nor Chinese immigrants within the medium of the chat room in which the girls "acquired a particular linguistic variety of English to construct ethnic identifications with other young people of Chinese descent around the world" (p. 59). In addition, Lam explicitly ties her study to power relationships in considering how use of language in one context—the Internet—is influenced by and in turn influences other contexts, in this case English in the national context of the US. In this way, Lam ties her study to critical considerations of global English and the interplay of global concerns practiced in locally situated contexts. In Lam's study, we see students seeking contexts in which L2 socialization practices will allow for a positive identity, rather than one in which they may be labeled as incompetent.

Resisting Socializing Norms

Shifting the lens to studies that report contested accounts of L2 socialization, Talmy (2008) examines the trajectories of L2 socialization of teenage learners in a high school ESL class in which students actively reject institutionally assigned, negative identities as permanent ESL students, and develop for themselves alternative local ESL identities. Talmy argues for a careful reexamination of the language socialization literature, arguing that the concepts of multidirectionality and contingency have always been a key part of this socially situated theory of learning. In particular, he suggests, that early language socialization literature, asserted "the contested, unpredictable, and reciprocal character of LS [language socialization]" (Talmy, 2008, p. 640), a practice that he demonstrates by "considering the ostensible socialization of older 'learners', who were generally uninvested, unwilling incumbents of a stigmatized identity category, studying an L2 in a multilingual, compulsory educational context (Talmy, 2008, p. 640). Talmy thus calls for

> analytic attention to the essential unpredictability, contestedness, and fluidity of socialization, as it is or is not achieved, in ways anticipated or not, in L1 and in L2, among younger and older "novices" and "experts", at earlier and later stages of the lifespan, across a range of monolingual, multilingual, "naturalistic", and institutional contexts.
>
> (Talmy, 2008, p. 640)

Talmy's work, as with several of the others outlined above, ties in with Kulick and Schieffelin's consideration of Althusser's "bad" subjects "who don't heed 'socially powerful, coercive calls to inhabit certain subject positions'" (2004, p. 355), and who may also be sources for change in community practices over time.

New Directions

In this section we outline three areas in which we see a need for further research in L2 and multilingual socialization: (1) reconsidering the concept of the expert; (2) expanding the conception of community to be multi-sited in essence; and (3) extending the focus of study across the lifespan.

Expanding the Concept of the Expert

We tend to think of language socialization as involving an expert and a novice. However, as language socialization clearly implies, and as a number of recent studies suggest, much language socialization takes place among peers, or among "beginners" from the perspective of a particular community of practice. Langman, Bayley, and Cacéda (forthcoming), for example, chronicle the ways in which "Manuel," an emergent bilingual seventh grader with limited experience in the US and limited knowledge of English, serves as a socializing agent by sharing the knowledge he possesses with a recent immigrant peer, Alfonso, to the "ways of doing school" in a new school culture. Through an examination of Manuel's discourse in Spanish during his English language science classroom lessons, we uncover the "hidden" expertise recent immigrants hold. Manuel, as all individuals, simultaneously practices multiple discourses and enacts multiple identities across time and space. These practices show how he is at one and the same time perceived as a *newcomer* or peripheral science student and as an *expert* or old-timer depending of the perspective of the interlocutor. Manuel takes on the role of an expert in a variety of ways: (1) by providing Spanish support to the teacher and other students on the one hand and (2) by guiding a newcomer, Alfonso, to life in a US classroom, on the other hand. In so doing, Manuel's knowledge about classroom and school culture, including knowledge about his peers' language and cultural identities, as well as practices that situate him as an immigrant in the US, position him as an expert. The multiplicity of identities is clear for many recent immigrants being socialized into monolingual classrooms in the US. While many studies examine how newcomers turn to their friends with a greater degree of English for support, we also see how Manuel provides Alfonso with support as he orients this newcomer to class, including how to use the linguistic resources at his disposal.

A need for increased focus on peer-to-peer socialization has been identified in other recent work. For example, Heath and Kramsch (2004) discuss how the changing world of youth has shifted from contexts in which adults socialize youth, to a world in which the major socializing influences that occur are from youth to youth. They discuss how this shift in societal practices of interaction and associated socialization presents difficulties in terms of the potential for narratives of possibility and probability to be articulated to youth.

If Heath and Kramsch are correct in their claim that increasingly, in the US at least, youth are socializing youth, we need to reconsider who counts as "expert" and "novice" in the particular community in which socialization is taking place. While Heath and Kramsch focus their discussion on non-institutional contexts (or at least non-traditional institutions such as youth groups), Langman et al. (forthcoming) and Talmy (2008) are examining how even within traditional institutions, such as schools, youth are socializing each other as much as the normatively recognized "experts," i.e., the teachers.

Refocusing on the Locus of Socialization: Multi-Sited Community Studies

Related to the need to think more deeply about the positions or identities of "expert" and "novice," is the need to consider the concept of the community, and what criteria might be central for conceptualizing a particular space and those in proximity within it as engaged in a single or multiple, overlapping or intersecting communities with different socializing agents and different socializing practices. If speakers' identities and subjectivities vary according to the site, the interlocutors, and the practices being engaged in, then to understand multiple language socialization—which all socialization is—we need more studies that move beyond a single site. Two recent studies begin to examine simultaneous multi-sited language socialization. Jia (2009) examines children in the heritage school and at home, while Guardado (2008) focuses on socialization in the home and within the community. Zentella (1997) also illustrates the socializing interactions of her participants in a range of contexts.

Pu (2008) focuses on the cross-pollination of literacy practices between the Chinese language heritage school, the US English language elementary school, and the bilingual home setting. We are now in a position to encourage studies of language socialization in a range of comparable contexts. For example, what is the situation of children and youth being socialized and socializing in multiple contexts in countries across the globe?

Language Socialization across the Lifespan

With the need to consider carefully the concept of community and how it is interpreted for individuals engaged in L2 socialization, is the need for more studies that span time and place. For example, we need more studies of adult immigrants, returnees, long-term border crossers who make their home in two countries, and are faced with L2 socialization in their first language, when for example, after long sojourns in a different country individuals return "home" to a community and context that has shifted over time. Kanno's (2003) work although not taking a language socialization approach, examines returnees, and from this we propose an area of study examining the nature of re-socialization in later life, a practice increasingly common in the current age of globalization.

Conclusions

In the last ten years, language socialization theory has advanced our understanding of the contexts and practices surrounding the socialization into new communities and new language practices. It is clear, however that there is more to do to build a strong link between the cognitive processes of the individual in community(ies) and the contextualizing sites and the practices therein which create the context for socialization. The anthropological perspective of language socialization allows for a number of advantages including the ability to build on comparative work, and the foregrounding of the emic perspective of those engaged in socialization. Through this perspective, we have seen the development of more work in multilingual communities, in particular immigrant communities in which practices in language socialization are varied and complex and deeply interconnected with desire differentially accorded power and authority within and beyond particular communities.

Returning to a more specific focus on SLA, the language socialization perspective has a well-developed methodology that allows us to explain a great deal about what the context does and does not do in the service of L2 learning. Of practical importance to the field of L2 teaching, moreover, language socialization studies provide teachers with clear and concrete examples of how learners' identities orient them to different perceptions of the classroom context. Such studies also illustrate how these perceptions affect learners' participation in practices that from the perspective of the teacher are seemingly normative. However, from the perspective of the learner, many practices are in fact problematic and thus contested, as we have suggested in the case of silence and particular interactional styles. That is, the language socialization approach provides teachers with guidelines for interpreting and considering learner practices, initially seen as non-responsive or resistant. With its emphasis on the culturally-specific nature of development, language socialization has a great deal to offer in explaining some fundamental questions in SLA, including for example, different rates and degrees of success. It also has much to say about what constitutes success.

Notes

1. Authors' names are listed alphabetically. Both authors contributed equally to this chapter.
2. See Schieffelin and Ochs (1986) for a review of early work in language socialization.

References

Baquedano-López, P. (2004). Traversing the center: The politics of language use in a Catholic religious education program for immigrant Mexican children. *Anthropology and Education Quarterly, 35,* 212–232.

Bronson, M. C., & Watson-Gegeo, K. A. (2008). The critical moment: Language socialization and the (re)visioning of first and second language learning. In P. A. Duff & N. H. Hornberger (Eds.), *Encyclopedia of language and education* (2nd ed., Vol. 8: *Language socialization*) (pp. 43–55). Norwell, MA: Springer.

Caltabiano, Y. M. (2009). Children's negotiation of multicultural identities and multiple languages in Japan: An ethnographic study of Cambodian, Peruvian, and Vietnamese families. Unpublished doctoral dissertation, University of California, Davis.

Čekaitė, A. (2007). A child's development of interactional competence in a Swedish L2 classroom. *Modern Language Journal, 91,* 45–62.

Duff, P. A. (2008). Language socialization, participation, and identity: Ethnographic approaches. In M. Martin Jones, A. M. De Mejia, & N. H. Hornberger (Eds.), *Encyclopedia of Language and Education* (2nd ed., Vol. 3: *Discourse and education*) (pp. 107–119). Norwell, MA: Springer.

Duff, P. A., Wong, P., & Early, M. (2002). Learning language for work and life: The linguistic socialization of immigrant Canadians seeking careers in healthcare. *Modern Language Journal, 57,* 397–422.

Fairclough, N. (2005). Critical discourse analysis. *Marges Linguistiques, 9,* 1–19.

Firth, J., & Wagner, J. (1997). On discourse, communication, and (some) fundamental concepts in SLA. *Modern Language Journal, 81,* 285–300.

Garrett, P., & Baquedano-López, P. (2002). Language socialization: Reproduction and continuity, transformation and change. *Annual Review of Anthropology, 31,* 339–361.

Guardado, J. M. (2008). Language socialization in Canadian Hispanic communities: Ideologies and practices. Unpublished doctoral dissertation, University of British Columbia.

He, A. W. (2003). Novices and their speech roles in Chinese heritage language classes. In R. Bayley & S. R. Schecter (Eds.), *Language socialization in bilingual and multilingual societies* (pp. 128–146). Clevedon: Multilingual Matters.

He, A. W. (2008). Heritage language learning and socialization. In P. A. Duff and N. H. Hornberger (Eds.), *Encyclopedia of language and education* (2nd ed., Vol. 8: *Language socialization*) (pp. 202–213). Norwell, MA: Springer.

He, A. W., & Xiao, Y. (Eds.) (2008). *Chinese as a heritage language: Fostering rooted world citizenry.* Honolulu: University of Hawai'i, National Foreign Language Resource Center.

Heath, S. B. (1983). *Ways with words: Language, life and work in communities and classrooms.* Cambridge: Cambridge University Press.

Heath, S. B., & Kramsch, C. (2004). Individuals, institutions and the uses of literacy: Shirley Brice Heath and Claire Kramsch in conversation. *Journal of Applied Linguistics, 1,* 75–91.

Iddings, A. (2005). Linguistic access and participation: English language learners in an English-dominant community of practice. *Bilingual Research Journal, 29,* 165–183.

Jacoby S., & Gonzales P. (1991). The constitution of expert-novice in scientific discourse. *Issues in Applied Linguistics, 2,* 149–181.

Jia, L. (2009). Contrasting models in literacy practice among heritage learners of Mandarin. *Journal of Asian Pacific Communication, 19,* 56–75.

Kanno, Y. (2003). *Negotiating bilingual and bicultural Identities: Japanese returnees betwixt two worlds.* Mahwah, NJ: Lawrence Erlbaum.

Kulick, D. (1992). *Language shift and cultural reproduction: Socialization, self, and syncretism in a Papua New Guinea village.* Cambridge: Cambridge University Press.

Kulick, D., & Schieffelin, B. B. (2004). Language socialization. In A. Duranti (Ed.), *The handbook of linguistic anthropology* (pp. 349–368). Oxford: Blackwell.

Lam, E. (2004). Second language socialization in a bilingual chat room: Global and local considerations. *Language Learning and Technology, 8*(3), 44–65.

Langman, J., Bayley, R., & Cacéda, C. (forthcoming). Second language socialization: Considering expert identities in classroom communities of practice.

Lantolf, J. (Ed.) (2000). *Sociocultural theory and second language learning.* Oxford: Oxford University Press.

Leontiev, A. N. (1978). *Activity, consciousness, and personality.* Hillsdale, NJ: Prentice-Hall.

Li, G. (2006). Biliteracy and trilingual practices in the home context: Case studies of Chinese-Canadian children. *Journal of Early Childhood Literacy, 6,* 355–381.

Long, M. (1997). Construct validity in SLA: A response to Firth and Wagner. *Modern Language Journal, 81,* 318–323.

Long, M. (1998). Breaking the siege. *University of Hawai'i Working Papers in ESL, 17,* 79–129.

Luykx, A. (2005). Children as socializing agents: Family language policy in situations of language shift. In J. Cohen, K. T.

McAlister, K. Rolstad, & J. MacSwan (Eds.), *ISB4: Proceedings of the 4th International Symposium on Bilingualism* (pp. 1407–1414). Somerville, MA: Cascadilla Press.

Mead, M. (1930). *Growing up in New Guinea.* Harmondsworth: Penguin.

Mead, M. (1954). *Coming of age in Samoa.* New York: Morrow.

Morita, N. (2004). Negotiating participation and identity in second language academic communities. *TESOL Quarterly, 38,* 573–603.

Ochs, E. (1988). *Culture and language development: Language acquisition and language socialization in a Samoan village.* Cambridge: Cambridge University Press.

Ochs, E. (1999). Socialization. *Journal of Linguistic Anthropology, 9,* 230–233.

Ochs, E., & Schieffelin, B. B. (1995). The impact of language socialization on grammatical development. In P. Fletcher & B. MacWhinney (Eds.), *The handbook of child language* (pp. 73–94). Oxford: Blackwell.

Pease-Alvarez, L. (2002). Moving beyond linear trajectories of language shift and bilingual language socialization. *Hispanic Journal of Behavioral Sciences, 24,* 114–137.

Pu, Chang. (2008). Chinese American children's bilingual and biliteracy development in heritage language and public schools. Unpublished doctoral dissertation, University of Texas at San Antonio.

Reyes, I., & Moll, L. C. (2008). Bilingual and biliteratre practices at home and school. In B. Spolsky & F. M. Hult (Eds.), *The handbook of educational linguistics* (pp. 147–160). Oxford: Blackwell.

Schecter, S. R., & Bayley, R. (2002). *Language as cultural practice: Mexicanos en el norte.* Mahwah, NJ: Lawrence Erlbaum.

Schecter, S. R., & Bayley, R. (2004). Language socialization in theory and practice. *International Journal of Qualitative Studies in Education, 17,* 606–625.

Schieffelin, B. B. (1990). *The give and take of everyday life: Language socialization of Kaluli children.* Cambridge: Cambridge University Press.

Schieffelin, B. B., & Ochs, E. (1986). Language socialization. *Annual Review of Anthropology, 15,* 163–191.

Song, J. (2009). Bilingual creativity and self-negotiation: Korean American children's language socialization into Korean address terms. In A. Reyes & A. Lo (Eds.), *Beyond yellow English: Toward a linguistic anthropology of Asian Pacific America* (pp. 213–232). Oxford: Oxford University Press.

Talmy, S. (2008). The cultural productions of the ESL student at Tradewinds High: Contingency, multidirectionality, and identity in L2 socialization. *Applied Linguistics, 29,* 619–644.

Tarone, E. (2000). Still wrestling with "context" in interlanguage theory. *Annual Review of Applied Linguistics, 20,* 182–198.

Valdés, G. (1996). *Con respeto: Bridging the distances between culturally diverse families and schools.* New York: Teachers College Press.

van Dijk, T. (1993) Principles of critical discourse analysis. *Discourse and Society, 4,* 249–283.

Vickers, C. H. (2007). Second language socialization through team interaction among electrical and computer engineering students. *Modern Language Journal, 91,* 621–640.

Watson-Gegeo, K. A. (1992). Thick explanation in the ethnographic study of child socialization: A longitudinal study of the problem of schooling for Kwara'ae (Solomon Islands) children. In W. A. Corsaro & P. J. Miller (Eds.), *Interpretive approaches to children's socialization* (pp. 51–66). San Francisco: Jossey-Bass.

Watson-Gegeo, K. A. (2004). Mind, language, and epistemology: Toward a language socialization paradigm for SLA. *Modern Language Journal, 88,* 331–350.

Watson-Gegeo, K. A., & Gegeo, D. (1986). Calling out and repeating routines in Kwara'ae children's language socialization. In B. B. Schieffelin & E. Ochs (Eds.), *Language socialization across cultures* (pp. 17–50). Cambridge: Cambridge University Press.

Watson-Gegeo, K. A., & Nielsen, S. (2003). Language socialization in SLA. In C. Doughty & M. Long (Eds.), *The handbook of second language acquisition* (pp. 155–177). Oxford: Blackwell.

Zentella, A. C. (1996). The "chiquitafication" of U.S. Latinos and their languages, or why we need an anthropolitical linguistics. *SALSA III: Proceedings of the Third Annual Symposium about Language and Society-Austin. Texas Linguistic Forum, 36,* 1–18.

Zentella, A. C. (1997). *Growing up bilingual: Puerto Rican children in New York.* Oxford: Blackwell.

Zentella, A. C. (2005a). *Building on strength: Language and literacy in Latino families and communities.* New York: Teachers College Press.

Zentella, A. C. (2005b). Premises, promises, and pitfalls of language socialization research in Latino communities. In A. C. Zentella (Ed.), *Building on strength: Language and literacy in Latino families and communities* (pp. 13–30). New York: Teachers College Press.

Zuengler, J., & Cole, K. (2005). Language socialization in second language learning. In E. Hinkel (Ed.), *Handbook of research in second language teaching and learning* (pp. 301–316). Mahwah, NJ: Lawrence Erlbaum.

19

Integrating Sociocultural Theory and Cognitive Linguistics in the Second Language Classroom

James P. Lantolf

Fauconnier and Turner (2002, p. 3) argue that if the twentieth century was "the age of the triumph of form," the twenty-first century is likely to be the century where meaning comes to the fore and perhaps even supercedes form as the major focus of interest in the social sciences. In the last century, for the most part, social sciences followed the model of the hard sciences on the assumption that by uncovering "deep hidden forms behind ostensible forms" it was possible to unlock the mysteries of the universe, including the world created and inhabited by humans (Fauconnier & Turner, 2002, p. 4). However, as Fauconnier and Turner (p. 4) argue, structuralism does not reveal the full picture of what it means to be a human being, because it leaves out the central role of meaning. In an especially forceful analogy the authors (pp. 4–5) recount the episode in the *Iliad* where Hector slays Patroclus mistaking him for Achilles because he is wearing his cousin's body armor. Fauconnier and Turner (p. 5) point out that

> having the armor is never having Achilles; having the form—and indeed even the intricate transformations of form (all those 1s and 0s [reference to computational models of phenomena ranging from hurricanes to human thinking]) is never having the meaning to which the form has been suited.

Despite structuralism's scientific hegemony during most of the past century, not all social sciences succumbed to its allure. Indeed, at least one psychological theory, established at the beginning of the twentieth century and one linguistic theory, which appeared in the final decades of the same century, brought meaning to center stage.

The foundation for the psychological theory, variously known as sociocultural theory, cultural psychology, and cultural-historical psychology, was laid down by the Russian psychologist L. S. Vygotsky between 1925 and 1934. The linguistic theory, cognitive linguistics, comprised of various sub-domains, including cognitive grammar, cognitive semantics, and metaphor theory, emerged between 1980 and the turn of the twenty-first century with the work of Lakoff and Johnson (1980), Langacker (1987) and Talmy (2000, 2001), among others. Sociocultural theory (henceforth, SCT) argues that human consciousness is mediated through semiotic processes, the most important of which is communicative activity (Vygotsky, 1987). One of the problems confronting SCT from the outset has been the lack of a coherent linguistic theory. Jones (2009), for example, argues that while

Vygotsky wrote extensively about language and in particular the linguistic sign, he did not operate with a fully developed theory of language and ended up borrowing heavily from Saussurian structuralism. While I agree with Jones's position on the lack of a fully developed theory of language, I strongly disagree with his assertion that Vygotsky relied on Saussure's theory of language.[1]

Cognitive linguistics (henceforth, CL), for its part, proposes that linguistic form "subserves meaning rather than being an end in itself" (Langacker, 2008, p. 8). Over the past decade, CL has begun to show intense interest in the educational implications of its theory of language (e.g., Pütz, Niemeier, & Dirven, 2001; Achard & Niemeier, 2004; De Knop & De Rycker, 2008). As interesting as its theoretical statements on language are, CL so far has failed to present a unified approach to the psychological processes that underlie development. Cadierno (2008), for example, relies on VanPatten's (1996) input processing model, while Niemeier and Reif (2008) suggest a more or less eclectic approach to instruction where students engage in a variety of activities, including drawing models of the relevant linguistic feature to be used as a "mental pillar" (p. 348) as they carried out exercises and tests.[2] Later in the chapter I will consider briefly some of the applied CL research.

The purpose of the present chapter is follow up on the proposal put forth by Lantolf and Thorne (2006) that SCT and CL, grounded as they are in meaning rather than structure, are highly compatible theories that can be integrated into a unified and effective approach to language development in the classroom setting. SCT provides the psychological framework that organizes development, while CL offers the linguistic framework, which provides the substance of what is to be learned. In making the case for integration, I will present an overview of each theory especially with regard to their relevance to educational practice. I will also discuss some pedagogical projects to illustrate the potential that integration has for enhancing second language (L2) pedagogy.

Sociocultural Theory and Artificial Development

Within second language acquisition (SLA) it is generally accepted that the psychological process of acquiring a second language is more or less universal. Long (2006, p. 145) succinctly describes the Universal Acquisition Hypothesis (henceforth, UAH) as follows:

> Remove a learner from the social setting and the L2 grammar does not change or disappear. Change the social setting altogether (e.g., from street to classroom), or from a foreign to a second language environment and, as far as we know, the way the learner acquires does not change much either (as suggested, e.g., by comparisons of error types, developmental sequences, processing constraints, and other aspects of the acquisition process in and out of classrooms); … An eight-hour flight from a foreign language to a second language environment does not alter a learner's brain after all, so why should one *expect* any basic differences [italics in original].

Robinson and Ellis (2008a) also support the UAH, when they point out that despite "cross-linguistic differences in how languages structure conceptual content for expression … the processes which give rise to them are shared by all language learners" (p. 494). The processes, according to Robinson and Ellis, are sensitive to type-token frequencies in the input and rely on "general cognitive mechanisms" much in the way children are assumed to acquire their first language (L1) (p. 494). To be sure, some researchers such as Tarone (2007) have challenged the UAH, arguing that changes in social context can result in differential developmental trajectories.[3] Nevertheless, the non-UAH perspective continues to be a minority view.

Vygotsky argued that development occurs through different processes in accordance with the characteristics of specific cultural activities. Here he is in agreement with the position supported by Tarone. However, he makes what I believe to be a stronger claim—one that clearly diverges from the UAH. Vygotsky specifically juxtaposes development through educational practice with development as it takes place in the everyday world. In the natural setting, he views development as an unconscious, "spontaneous" process, whereby children are mediated into their culture by parents and other members of their social group. Through mediation, by and large a communicative process, children engage in the appropriate activities (e.g., play, dining practices, religious practices, family gatherings, etc.) as defined by the culture and in so doing internalize the relevant ways of talking and thinking sanctioned by the community. Play is an especially important everyday developmental activity, because it is here that children begin the process of understanding language as a symbolic tool (Vygotsky, 1978). In play words are disconnected from the objects to which they normally refer in the child's daily life and are linked to imaginary objects.

Although I cannot be absolutely certain, I do believe that Vygotsky and his colleague A. R. Luria, who carried out a great deal of research on the development of language and cognition (e.g., Luria, 1982), would agree with the usage-based model of L1 acquisition proposed by Tomasello (2003). However, I do think they would have problems extending the model to the educational setting. To be more precise, for Vygotsky, Luria, and others who operate within their theory, if educational activity seeks to replicate those processes at work in everyday development, it fails to fulfill its unique function in the culturally organized development of the person. As Vygotsky put it:

> Education may be defined as the artificial development of the child. Education is the artificial mastery of natural processes of development. Education not only influences certain processes of development, but restructures all functions of behavior in a most essential manner.
>
> (Vygotsky, 1997, p. 88)

Vygotsky considered education to be a specific form of cultural activity that had important and unique developmental consequences. It is not just an undertaking whereby knowledge is obtained, but is an intentionally organized (i.e., artificial) activity that reorganizes mental behavior. In classic Piagetian psychology, education is only effective if students are developmentally ready to learn (Egan, 1983). Development itself is a smooth and sequential process that is impervious to instruction and in fact lays down a pathway for instruction to follow. On this view, instruction becomes a matter of timing, and if, as Ellis (2007, p. 91) suggests, it is "ill-timed and out of synchrony with development … it can be confusing; it can be easily forgotten; it can be dissociated from usage, lacking in transfer-appropriateness" and "it can be unmotivating." This perspective is reflected in SLA, for example, in Krashen's (1985) natural order hypothesis and Pienemann's (1998) processability theory.

Vygotsky (1987) reverses the Piagetian position and argues that effective instruction must precede and indeed lay down the path for development to follow. This viewpoint emerges from Vygotsky's core principle that development, understood as the ability to intentionally organize and control one's own mental functioning (including, memory, attention, perception, rational thinking) through culturally constructed symbolic mediation (Yaroshevsky, 1989). In other words, development is a socially regulated process in which social relationships are appropriated and internalized. This means that psychological processes are in their origin social. Furthermore, development is anything but smooth and sequential; instead it proceeds in fits and starts and is better characterized as a "revolutionary process" (Vygotsky, 1978).[4]

The social activity where learning and development come together to form a dialectically unified process where each feeds the other is captured by Vygotsky's (1978) concept of the *zone of proximal development* (henceforth, ZPD). The ZPD enables an individual to experience success in doing things that they cannot otherwise do alone. This spans the gamut from such seemingly simple acts as an infant learning to sit up with the help of his/her mother (see Fogel, 1991, p. 91) to procedures as complex as a student solving quadratic equations through collaborative participation with others.

It is in essence the process of simultaneously being who you are and becoming who you are not (see Holzman, 2009). Vygotsky describes the relationship between learning and development as one in which the former "awakens a variety of internal developmental processes that are able to operate only when the child is interacting with people in his environment and in cooperation with his peers" (Vygotsky, 1978, p. 90). According to Talyzina (1970, p. 155), mental development is "impossible without the influence of learning," and she continues, "the role of learning stands out with particular sharpness in the process whereby the principal forms of mental activity come into being."[5] What this means is that the environment (i.e., the social world) does not merely influence development; rather, it is its source (A. N. Leont'ev, 1981). This environment includes social relationships as well as the symbolic artifacts (e.g., conceptual knowledge emanating from scientific research) constructed by specific cultures as well as human culture as a whole. Cultural knowledge not only mediates thought processes, but its appropriation is itself mediated by cooperation with others in the ZPD.

The difference between development in the everyday world and in the educational world is that in the former it is by and large unconscious and incidental, whereas in the latter it is "ideally" at least conscious and intentional. This distinction, stressed repeatedly by Vygotsky, is profoundly important. If education were to replicate the process through which development occurred in the everyday world "it would be completely unnecessary" (Vygotsky, 1987, p. 212). In the next section I will discuss the broader significance of the distinction.

Spontaneous and Scientific Concepts and Developmental Education

Vygotsky proposed that the basic unit of formal instruction, which promotes artificial (i.e., intentionally organized and conscious) development, is the "scientific concept" (Vygotsky, 1987, p. 167). Scientific concepts "represent the generalizations of the experience of humankind that is fixed in science, understood in the broadest sense of the term to include both natural and social science as well as the humanities" (Karpov, 2003, p. 66). These concepts are explicit, and therefore accessible to conscious inspection, domain specific, and "aimed at selecting the essential characteristics of objects or events of a certain class and presenting these characteristics in the form of symbolic and graphic models" (Karpov, 2003, p. 71).

Scientific knowledge contrasts sharply with *spontaneous* knowledge formed during concrete practical experience largely on the basis of the "an immediate observable property of an object" (Kozulin, 1995, p. 123). Spontaneous knowledge is empirically based, usually, though not exclusively, inaccessible to conscious inspection, and requires lengthy periods of practical experience to develop. It is, however, at the heart of lived experience and is more than adequate for carrying out daily activities. Empirical knowledge, as Karpov (2003, pp. 69–71) points out, "may work if the common salient characteristics of objects or events reflect their significant, essential characteristics" but this type of knowledge is very often incomplete and fails to reflect the essential features of the object or event they refer to.

To illustrate the distinction between everyday empirically-based and abstract scientific knowledge, consider how the concept *circle* is understood in the two domains. Everyday knowledge of circle is a generalization usually arrived at by extracting the common geometric shape of objects such as wheels, pancakes, bracelets, coins, etc. The scientific concept of circle, on the other hand, is "a figure that appears as the result of a movement of a line with one free and one fixed end" (Kozulin, 1995, p. 124). The scientific definition, according to Kozulin, encompasses all possible circles and "requires no previous knowledge of round objects to understand" (p. 124).

Vygotsky (1987, p. 218) argued that scientific and spontaneous knowledge each had strengths and weaknesses. The strength of the latter is that it is saturated with personal experience and its use is automatic. Its weakness consists in the fact that it is tied to concrete empirical situations and is therefore not sufficiently abstract to be flexible so as to be easily extended to a wide array of circumstances.

Its automatic quality, which is part of its strength, is at the same time a weakness. The fact that spontaneous knowledge is not easily accessible to conscious inspection means that humans have less intentional control over it in order to make it serve particular needs. Before children come to school their language is largely automatic behavior and is not very visible to them. When they enter school and encounter literacy the language becomes visible and their awareness and control over it increases as they develop the capacity to produce and read written texts, the primary medium of education.

The strength of scientific knowledge resides in its visibility, rigor, and completeness, which imparts to learners greater "understanding, awareness, control and creativity" (Negueruela, 2008, p. 193). At the same time, its weakness is that it lacks rich personal experience because it is not connected to relevant practical activity. For scientific knowledge to be of value it must become proceduralized through connections to practical activity otherwise it gives rise to "verbalism"; that is, knowledge "detached from reality" (Vygotsky, 1987, p. 217). And as Ilyenkov (1974) notes, verbalism is "that chronic disease of school education." In the case of language education, the challenge is to connect scientific knowledge of language with practical communicative activity.[6]

The point I want to make here is that Vygotsky is proposing a vastly different approach to development through education, including language development, than what transpires in the everyday world. In his critique of inquiry-based pedagogy Karpov (2003, p. 75) asks, "why, when dealing with particular students, should we require them to reinvent this [knowledge accumulated by previous generations], even if such reinvention is guided by the teacher?" This is an especially important matter for concepts that are particularly complex and that would require a great deal of effort and time for learners to figure out on their own, even if their attention is directed to specific features of input. For example, given the amount of time students are in language classes, I seriously doubt that they would be able to work out on their own the subtleties of Spanish middle voice constructions as discussed by Maldonado (2008): *Adrián consiguió un empleo* (active) "Adrian got a job" vs. *Adrián se consiguió un empleo* (middle) "Adrian got himself a job." However, with an appropriately organized explanation (see Maldonado's chapter) coupled with appropriate communicative activities and mediation through the ZPD, they have a chance at gaining control over this fairly pervasive, yet complex, feature of the language.

Some may raise the hackneyed argument that active construction of one's own knowledge is better than passive reception of knowledge created by someone else. I do not believe that active construction and passive reception are the only two choices available. There is a third option—active reception. Clearly, the task of understanding and integrating new concepts into humans' cognitive system is an active process. Admittedly, it is different from "independently discovering solutions to new problems" (Ausubel, 1970, p. 201); nevertheless, it is an active process that involves thinking and cognitive integration. The danger for the student, and the challenge for the educator, is to avoid rote memorization of conceptual knowledge and the delusion that students have grasped the concept precisely rather than in a "vague and confused" manner through overt explication (Ausubel, 1970, p. 202). Negueruela (2003) documents the negative consequences of rote learning of grammatical rules of thumb (e.g., in Spanish "use imperfect verbal aspect to describe emotions and mental states"—a rule that is in fact inaccurate since perfective aspect can just as readily be used), which instills in learners a misguided assumption that they really understand how a particular feature of an L2 functions.

To summarize, the fundamental principle of Vygotsky's theory of educational development is the integration of systematic conceptual knowledge with concrete practical activity. While Vygotsky did not make any specific proposals for implementing his theory, his colleagues and students undertook the task of fleshing out and concretizing the general framework he outlined. Four researchers in particular are recognized as leaders in completing Vygotsky's educational project: Gal'perin (1967, 1970, 1979), Haenen (1996), Davydov (2004) and A. A. Leont'ev (1981). It is also important to acknowledge the contributions of Gal'perin's leading student, Talyzina (1970, 1973, 1981). In the next section, focus will be primarily on Gal'perin's theory, given that most of the work on L2 pedagogy is informed by his particular theoretical orientation (e.g., Negueruela, 2003; Yáñez-Prieto, 2008; Kabanova, 1985; Carpay, 1974; Thorne, Reinhardt, & Golombek, 2008; Lapkin, Swain, & Knouzi, 2008; van Parreren, 1975; Oboukhova, Porshnev, Porshneva, & Gaponova, 2002).[7]

Systemic-Theoretical Instruction

Gal'perin's theory of developmental education, Systemic-Theoretical Instruction (henceforth, STI), alternatively referred to as Concept-Based Instruction, is based on systematically organized instruction that begins with explicit presentation of conceptual knowledge and terminates with its automatization (i.e., internalization) in practice. Crucially important for the transition from explanation to internalization are two additional processes: materialization or visualization and verbalization of the conceptual knowledge. Verbalization, in turn, comprises two subphases: verbalization of the concept as such and verbalization of the concept as it relates to and guides one's performance in practical activity.

The initial phase, presentation of the concept, is carried out in two dimensions: the verbal-symbolic dimension and the concrete-material dimension. It is here that I believe CL makes its significant contribution to developmental education. For one thing, as I noted at the outset of the chapter, CL is a theory of language that foregrounds conceptual meaning and for another, its theoretical mechanism includes a visual depiction of linguistic concepts. Talyzina's (1981) research has shown that theoretical concepts are much more coherent and far better understood if they are materialized in age-appropriate forms that permit learners to visualize the concept rather than to only deal with it verbally. It turns out that materialization is also advantageous for adult learners (see Serrano-Lopez & Poehner, 2008). However, for adults conceptual knowledge can also be visualized as two-dimensional graphic figures similar to those used in CL. One advantage of graphic representations of conceptual knowledge is their portability. On the other hand, it is often not easy to depict movement, as in the case of verbal aspect in Spanish (e.g., the middle of an activity). It is worth exploring the feasibility of computer-based graphics to project movement, as in the case of motion events where manner and path of motion may be relevant to conceptual knowledge. The materialization of conceptual knowledge is referred to as a SCOBA (Schema for the Orienting Basis of Action). SCOBAs are used to systematize relevant knowledge in a holistic way and to avoid rote memorization of purely verbal formulations of the knowledge. Figure 19.1 from a STI project by Lee (in progress) illustrates a SCOBA for the English particle "out." The particular study aims to teach English as a second language (ESL) students at the university level phrasal verbs formed with "out," "over," and "up."

Following explication of a concept and presentation of its related SCOBA, learners are engaged in communicative activity (spoken or written) where the knowledge depicted in the SCOBA can be brought to bear in realizing learners' communicative intent. Negueruela (2003), for example, constructed a series of activities based on Di Pietro's (1987) Strategic Interaction approach—an approach that uses scenarios, or mini-dramas, to create dramatic tension in order to stimulate dialogue between interactants. Yáñez-Prieto (2008) used literature as a means for engaging students with L2 Spanish. In her study, students not only read a variety of literary texts, including prose and poetry, they also were asked to try to recreate experiences from their own lives in ways that deployed the language knowledge displayed in SCOBAs, for instance, verbal aspect, in accordance with the creative ways this same knowledge was exhibited in literary texts.

One particularly impressive activity featured in Yáñez-Prieto's study was to ask students to read a one-page short story written by the Argentinian author, Julio Cortázar, *Continuidad de los parques* ("Continuation of the parks") in which the author relates the events of the story exclusively through

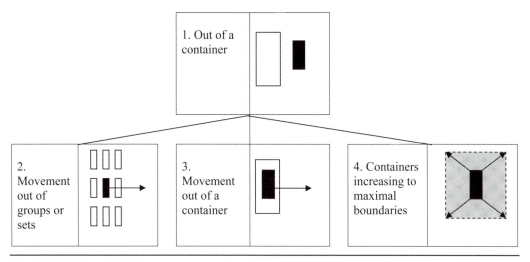

Figure 19.1 SCOBA for particle "out"

Lee (in progress).

imperfective aspect rather than the expected alternation between this aspect and perfective aspect. The story was compared to an excerpt from a Spanish television soap opera where aspect is used much as it would be in everyday discourse. The students then created a written text of their own where they were to relate an emotional experience from their life and where they were expected to use verbal aspect to convey their own communicative intentions in accordance with the meaning of aspect presented in the SCOBA (the SCOBA appears in an article by Lantolf, 2008) and as illustrated in the literary and everyday texts. One student (pseudonym, Emma) produced a story in which she intentionally shifted between imperfective and perfective aspect in order to create a sense of closeness and distance for relating different portions of her story. A portion of the story is quoted below:

> *Pero esa noche, mi papá no nos molestaba con sus preguntas y mi mama ni siquiera levantaba la vista de su plato. Esa noche, el silencio no era cómodo; era pesado y fuerte. Llenaba el cuarto, hundiendo a mi familia, y mis hermanas y yo cruzábamos miradas preocupadas. Algo no estaba bien.*
>
> (Yáñez-Prieto, 2008)

[But that night, my father did not bother (imperfective) us with his questions and my mother did not even raise (imperfective) her head from her plate. That night, the silence was (imperfective) not comfortable; it was (imperfective) heavy and strong. It filled (imperfective) the room, drowning my family, and my sisters and I exchanged (imperfective) worried glances. Something was (imperfective) not right.]

(Translation by Lantolf)

The event related in this part of the story deals with Emma's parents informing her and her sisters that their mother had been recently diagnosed with a serious illness. The fact that the author chose to use only imperfective aspect at this point, much in the way Cortázar does in his story, has the effect of drawing the reader into the story as if it were unfolding before one's eyes. In fact, when verbalizing her explanation of aspect use, Emma made this point clear:

> Although a lot of my paper could have been written in either imperfect or preterit, I tried to use each tense strategically to convey different meanings. For example, when I was talking about the

moments when we were in the dining room in silence, I used imperfect to depict everything as if the reader was there in the middle of the action, seeing everything as it was happening.

(Yáñez-Prieto, 2008)

To relate the next event in her story, Emma chose perfective aspect:

Descendí la escalera lentamente, sin sentir los escalones bajo los pies. Con cada paso hacia su cuarto mi corazón latió más alto. Cuando llegué a su cuarto, era oscuro y callado y mi mamá estaba en la cama, los ojos cerrados.

(Yáñez-Prieto, 2008)

[I went (perfective) down the stairs slowly, without feeling the steps below my feet. With each step toward her room my heart beat (perfective) louder. When I arrived (perfective) at her room, it was (imperfective) dark and quiet and my mother was (imperfective) in bed, her eyes closed.]

(Translation by Lantolf)

Emma stated that at this point in her story "when I went to my mom's room to see her after I found out that she was sick, I used preterit for all the verbs. This time I wanted to show each action as a complete act." Emma did not follow the usual rules of thumb in creating her story. Instead, she manipulated the concept in order to produce the appropriate emotional impact on the reader.

Once learners are accustomed to operating with a SCOBA, the next phase of the internalization process begins—bringing the knowledge depicted in the SCOBA to the "plane of audible speech" (Gal'perin, 1970, p. 148). This phase of the pedagogical process arises from SCT's principle that language (understood as communicative activity) not only mediates social activity but also mediates mental behavior. According to Vocate (1994) social communication entails linguistic exchanges between "I" and "You" but as mediation moves from the social to the psychological domain the role of "You" shifts to "Me." Thus, in psychological, or private communication, "I" decides what to pay attention to, what to think about, and formulates a plan for how to carry this out. "Me" interprets, critiques, monitors, and evaluates the actions of "I" (Vocate, 1994, p. 12), just as "You" (e.g., parent, teacher, peer, etc.) does in social communication. As Gal'perin (1970, p. 151) states, "words spoken aloud can be heard, as if they were those of another person, and their guiding power is even greater."

The following example, from Negueruela's (2003) study illustrates how self-talk unfolds in the service of development.[8] At the outset of course, one student self-explained aspect as follows:

[Preterit] is used a lot to report a story and to present completed events that have happened. Imperfect is used for description and to open a scene. It is like to say in English: "I was doing something" when … [something else happened].

(Negueruela, 2003, p. 358)

This definition, as Negueruela points out, does not explain the meaning of aspect but instead mentions some examples of its use. This is similar to a child defining what "uncle" means by naming his "uncle Harry."

In the eleventh week of the course, and following extensive communicative experience guided by the appropriate SCOBA, the same student offered the ensuing explanation:

[T]here is no real time that you cannot use either or … *pretérito* is used for definite actions in the past when you are giving emphasis to the fact that it is over or that it just began. Imperfect is used when talking about the middle or giving background, it sets the scene and shows that the action is in progress in the past.

(Negueruela, 2003, p. 359)

According to Negueruela, the second statement is a more coherent and accurate reflection of the concept. Above all, the student realizes that use of aspect is not linked to empirical triggers but is a matter of user choice with regard to the meanings one wishes to introduce into a communicative event. Some may wonder why STI emphasizes learner mastery of explicit conceptual knowledge rather than focus primarily on performance, especially since L2 studies have shown a lack of relationship between explicit knowledge and performance (e.g., Seliger, 1979, 1983). Negueruela (2008, p. 206) explains that concepts, unlike rules of thumb, function as (symbolic) tools for thinking in communicative situations and as such enable users to create the precise meanings they wish to manifest in spoken and written performance. They thus imbue users with greater communicative freedom and agency than learning that emanates exclusively from empirical experiences. This argument is powerfully attested in Markova's (1979) study mentioned earlier in the chapter.

Nergueruela (2003) and Yáñez-Prieto (2008) also asked their students to regularly explain their thinking for speaking (or writing) activity (see Slobin, 1996), as illustrated in Emma's explanation of aspect selection in her story. The purpose of this activity is not for teachers or researchers to gain access to learners' thinking process, although it certainly is something that helps both understand the developmental process; but it is for learners themselves to externalize and therefore confront their own thinking (in I–Me dialogue) and potentially modify it as necessary. The following examples are from one of the students in Negueruela's (2003, p. 430) study, where the student explains his use of aspect in an utterance produced during a scenario. The student carried out the activity in his dorm, while speaking into a tape recorder:

Fourth week of the semester:
El seis de junio fui a la escuela a mi dormitorio para comenzar mis clases. [On June 6th, I went to school to my dorm to begin my classes]
"I used preterit there because it's referring to a recalled point: '*el seis de junio*' and since '*fui*' is a non-cyclic verb, it's referring to the beginning of the action."
Eighth week of the semester:
Siempre había mucho para comer [There was always a lot to eat]
"Imperfect because it's emphasizing an ongoing action because I am saying '*siempre*', so I use imperfect cause it's a habitual action."

(Translations in square brackets are Lantolf's)

In the first example the student explains his use of perfective aspect (*fui*) based on the conceptual information provided by the instructor in which cyclic actions are distinguished from non-cyclic actions (in CL terminology, bounded and unbounded actions). However, in the second example the student falls back on the traditional rule for use of imperfective with ongoing events. The problem is that focus is on a state rather than an event. Hence, even though both performances are appropriate, the learner is still in the process of mastering the concept of aspect and must overcome the difficulty created by an earlier internalized rule of thumb, which keys on the adverb "always." There is no reason why someone could not use perfective aspect in the second example, although with a different meaning.

When asked to comment on their experience with STI, the students in both studies provided very interesting responses. With regard to SCOBAs, one of Negueruela's (2003, p. 261) students remarked that the charts are a grammar-figuring-out-guide that work better than the rules (like the rules for preterit and imperfect) that we had learned in Spanish 100. It was very helpful to see the concepts in a visual structure because the concept of grammar is a very structural concept, and being able to visualize it made it make much more sense.

This student oriented to the SCOBAs as expected and clearly appreciated the precision achieved through a visual depiction of conceptual knowledge.

With regard to verbalizations, most of the students remarked that at the outset it seemed somewhat odd to have to externalize their thinking into a tape recorder (the procedure used in Negueruela's study) when alone in their dorms. However, they recognized that the activity not only helped them improve their use of the language but it also enhanced their understanding of the concepts. The following excerpt illustrates this point quite well:

> The verbalizations and recordings have helped a lot because it's a more abstract way of thinking about it, so instead of saying "ok, this situation uses this particular rule, so I need to use this tense" I say "what is the point I'm trying to express here, and which tense best accomplishes that." I think I've learned how to effectively communicate my ideas better. I need to consider the aspect that I wish to emphasize and what the meaning is behind the words that I'm saying so that the verb tense helps people understand what I'm saying as much as the actual verb I use.
>
> (Negueruela, 2003, p. 253)

Perhaps the most insightful reaction of all was provided by one of Yáñez-Prieto's (2008, p. 378) students who remarked:

> It's kind of funny how you can have a grammar st … the gram … grammatical structure actually tell a story. I'd not really noticed that or seen that before. I mean, the words are telling the story and the grammar is telling the story, which is kind of weird. Yeah, I'd never seen that before. Interesting.

This comment, quite by chance, reflects a central claim of CL to the effect that "grammar itself is meaningful, just as lexical items are" (Langacker, 2008, p. 8). In the next section I consider in more detail the contribution that CL makes to an SCT-based approach to developmental L2 education.

Cognitive Linguistics: The Source of Conceptual Knowledge

According to Langacker (2008, p. 8), "when ordinary people speak and listen, it is not for the sheer pleasure of manipulating syntactic form—their concern is with the meanings expressed." For this reason, CL is a theory in which "grammar subserves meaning rather than being an end in itself" (p. 8). Most importantly, CL argues that conceptual knowledge is not only relevant for language but it also generalizes to other cognitive systems. For this reason, CL is particularly appealing to psychological theories of mind such as SCT.

As far as I can determine, work in applied CL began in earnest with the publication of Pütz et al.'s (2001) edited volume, although some sporadic publications had appeared prior to this work (e.g., Kövecses & Szabó, 1996). Three years later, a second edited volume appeared (Achard & Niemeier, 2004), which included a focus on foreign language instruction, and four years after this two more edited collections were published (De Knop & De Rycker, 2008 and Boers & Lindstromberg, 2008) along with a handbook on CL and SLA (Robinson & Ellis, 2008b). More or less coinciding with the appearance of Pütz et al.'s volume, journal articles began to accumulate in which focus was squarely on the applications of CL to language pedagogy. And in 2003 Rudzka-Ostyn produced a CL-based textbook intended for instruction on English phrasal verbs. As with the general field of CL, work in the applied area is divided between cognitive grammar with its focus on meaning-form mappings and cognitive semantics, which is interested in semantic domains (e.g., motion events) and figurative language (e.g., metaphor, metonymy). Although my concern here is with cognitive grammar, this is not to downplay the importance of semantics and figurative language in L2 learning. Indeed, I strongly agree with Danesi (2008), who argues that conceptual fluency (i.e., the ability to interpret and use figurative language) is a necessary, yet unfortunately overlooked, component of advanced language proficiency.

It is important to keep in mind that meaning in CL entails encyclopedic knowledge of the world and therefore the theory attempts to capture the important fact that people at the individual as well at the collective level "have the capacity to conceive and portray the same situation in alternate ways" (Langacker, 2008, p. 9). One of the interesting questions that CL can undertake to answer is one that I raised more than a decade ago: "to what extent can learners become cognitively like members of other cultures; that is, can [L2] adults learn to construct and see the world through culturally different eyes ?" (Lantolf, 1999, pp. 29–30). Thus, when speaking of motion events, speakers of languages such as Spanish, French, Turkish, and Korean exhibit a preference to foreground path of movement, whereas speakers of languages such as English, German, Russian, and Chinese, more often highlight the manner of movement, although any given speaker can decide to highlight either of the properties of motion events, especially when gesture is brought into the picture (see Choi & Lantolf, 2008).

As I said at the outset of this chapter, there does not seem to be general agreement among applied cognitive linguists on how best to bring CL knowledge to bear in the service of language learning. Langacker (2008), for instance, appears to favor a usage-based approach to learning on analogy with how people learn their native language in childhood. On this view, as with native speakers, mastery "will come about only gradually through long-term practice with the language" (p. 27). Moreover, Langacker does not commit to exposing learners to "theoretical concepts or explicit analysis" and even seems somewhat reluctant to include teachers among those who should be fully aware of CL notions and instead prefers to reserve this information for curriculum designers (p. 29).

Other researchers argue for providing learners with explicit CL-based explanations of target language features. I have already mentioned Cadierno's (2008) and Niemeier and Reif's (2008) work in this regard. However, in both cases the pedagogical recommendations offered are speculative in that neither publication reports on actual implementation of the proposed recommendation. On the other hand, a number of studies have investigated the effects of exposing students to CL-based explanations of target language features, and importantly, most of these have used visualizations to help learners comprehend the relevant concepts. Condon (2008) discusses the results of a fairly large-scale study involving 111 students of L2 English where focus was on phrasal verbs comprised with *in, out, up, down* (e.g., break in, point out, use up, settle down). The study used a pre-, immediate post- and delayed post-test design. Although the learners improved their to ability to appropriately interpret phrasal verbs, this ability was limited to those verbs whose meaning was explained and did not transfer to verbs the students had only encountered incidentally during instruction (p. 153). According to Condon (2008, p. 153), one of the reasons for lack of transfer may have been the "short, simplified statements" used during instruction, which the author believes may have made it difficult for students to interpret abstract phrasal verbs (e.g., "John turned down the offer"). This is an important point that speaks to STI's preference for using comprehensive explanations of conceptual knowledge.

Tyler (2008) reports on two dissertation projects that focused on teaching modal verbs to advanced learners of English enrolled in a US law school. The first study employed detailed explanations as well as visualizations, which presented students with "the root meanings of the modals and their metaphoric extension into the realm of reasoning and logical prediction" (p. 478). The students worked in pairs to determine if modals used in several written excerpts were appropriately used or not. Thus, it appears the students had some opportunity to verbalize, as called for in Gal'perin's theory; however, it is difficult to determine how focused and systematic it may have been. They were also allowed to refer to the visualizations if necessary during the pair work activity. The students receiving CL-based instruction as well as feedback on grammar improved significantly in their use of modals in writing legal texts compared to a control group, which read several legal documents that made extensive use of modals to hedge arguments (p. 480) and which received feedback on the content of their writing but did not receive specific instruction on modals. The second study followed six students in the same law school also learning English modals. Again the students received CL-based instruction and also engaged in pair work. All but one of the students improved markedly in their use of modals following instruction (one student already had a fairly well developed ability to use modals at the outset of the study). Tyler concludes that CL-based instruction produced better learning outcomes than did one that exposed students to "massive amounts of contextualized input" (p. 483).

Conclusion

In this chapter I have argued for the integration of SCT and CL in L2 pedagogy. Both theories understand meaning as emanating from culturally organized experiences (this includes bodily experiences as well) with the world. For SCT meaning is the key to mediation and therefore mental development and for CL meaning is the key to linguistic communication. Given that SCT pedagogy realized as STI requires exposing students to coherent theoretical knowledge and given that CL makes the commitment to uncovering this type of knowledge with regard to language, the theories mesh quite well. In my view the most important mechanism for connecting the theories is the SCOBA, which visualizes in material form the relevant conceptual knowledge. The challenge is to develop pedagogically functional SCOBAs without sacrificing theoretical coherence and validity.

It remains to be seen how precisely conceptual knowledge must be tuned to the proficiency level of learners. Instruction understood as mediation by concepts and by other individuals (in this case, teachers) allows for a fair amount of leeway with regard to what to teach and when to teach it. On the other hand, mediation itself must be adjusted in accordance with learner needs for support, which means that it must be sensitive to the ZPD. Everything else being equal, in a full-scale instructional program based on SCT–CL principles, beginning level students should require more and more explicit mediation than would more advanced students (see Poehner, 2008 on attuning mediation to learners' needs). On this account, beginning level learners in such a program organized around tasks or scenarios (as in Di Pietro's approach) may need access to specific concepts (e.g. modals, phrasal verbs, middle voice, verbal aspect, figurative language) and the concepts should not be withheld.

If conceptual knowledge is to be an essential component of language instruction then it is incumbent on teacher education programs to provide teachers with extensive and intensive preparation in applied CL (see Lantolf, 2009). Teacher education programs place strong emphasis on curriculum design, teaching methodologies, assessment practices, use of technology, and learning theory (including SLA research) at the expense of the language itself, other than stressing a teacher's communicative proficiency. In my view this is not sufficient preparation. Sophisticated knowledge of the target language cannot be left out of the picture. If it is, it is difficult to imagine how teachers can guide learners to develop sophisticated knowledge that allows them to use the new language in creative and agentive ways. This leads me to my final point.

Perhaps the most significant consequence of integrating SCT and CL is the flexibility and sense of agency that is likely to develop, simply because of the way in which language is understood in both theories. Taylor (2008, p. 54) notes that in CL "rules" do not have the same interpretation as they do in formal theories of language. A rule in CL "states a conventionalized pairing of semantic structure with a formal structure" and therefore "the ungrammaticality of a sentence is to be explained in terms of the oddness incongruity, or other kind of ill-formedness of the meaning that the sentence has, or would have, rather than in terms of the violation of some arbitrary rule of syntax." With this understanding of grammar, as Taylor (2008, p. 56) suggests, comes the possibility of "'breaking' rules, just in case a special, unusual, or even bizarre conceptualization is called for" as for instance when converting a count to a mass noun (e.g., "*After the accident, there was cat all over the road*" [italics in original]), or using stative verbs in the progressive ("*Meat is costing a lot these days*" [italics in original]) (p. 56 and p. 57). Vygotsky (1987, p. 252), for his part, makes a similar argument in distinguishing between the grammatical and psychological properties of utterances. The former relates to the conventional features of a language, while the latter corresponds to the individual intentions of the user. More often than not, according to Vygotsky, these two aspects are not aligned and what may appear to be an error from the perspective of grammar may not be from the perspective of psychology. The difference reflects Vygotsky's distinction between meaning and sense. The former corresponds to the stable aspects of language as reflected in community norms, while the latter relates to what an individual wishes to express in a concrete communicative circumstance. Markova (1979, p. 45) points out that for Vygotsky genuine understanding "consists in deciphering sense" where the user inserts emotional and evaluative information into an utterance that betrays its motive. Thus, while speakers may share meanings, they negotiate personal sense. This is ultimately what learners must master in a new language and my belief is that the integration of SCT and CL will make this possible.

Notes

1. Lantolf (forthcoming) challenges Jones's interpretation of Vygotsky's linguistics and shows clearly that his perspective on language is linked more closely to Sapir and meaning-based theories of language than it is to Saussure's orientation.
2. A bit later in the chapter, I will argue that drawings and other forms of visual representation of linguistic knowledge is an important component in the internalization process.
3. One could speculate that based on Robinson and Ellis's stance variations in social context might result in different type-to-ken frequencies in the input, which might account for differences in developmental sequences attested in Tarone's research. This would not necessarily invalidate the claim that learners still rely on the same general cognitive mechanisms as they undertake to induce the grammar (here I include lexical, discourse, pragmatic, semantic, and metaphorical knowledge along with traditional domains of grammar) of the new language.
4. For an account of L2 development as a revolutionary process see Lantolf and Aljaafreh (1995).
5. It is worth nothing that the Russian word *obuchenie*, which is often translated into English as "learning" means both learning and instruction. Thus, when Vygotsky and his colleagues talk about the dialectic unity of learning/instruction and development, they are clearly introducing the social nature of the process.
6. Markova (1979) discusses an extensive ten-year project carried out in the school system of Moscow that was designed to significantly enhance students understanding and control of their native language, Russian, through the integration of scientific knowledge and practical communicative, in this case, written, activities. One of the important outcomes of the project is that students developed a far greater ability to use their language in exceptionally creative ways—ways that exceeded how the language was conventionally used in particular pragmatic situations.
7. A recent study on ESL writing carried out by Ferreira adopts Davydov's theoretical perspective (see Ferreira & Lantolf, 2008).
8. Swain, Lapkin, Knouzi, Suzuki, and Brooks (2009) conducted a study in which they asked L2 learners to explain their understanding of the concept (middle voice in French) to each other rather than to themselves. It remains to be determined if the additional phase of "social explanation" results in more effective learning than eliminating this phase in the developmental process. In my view, even if social explanation is included self talk is still necessary, because of the theoretical principle that internalization must entail a self-dialogue phase.

References

Achard, M., & Niemeier, S. (Eds.) (2004). *Cognitive linguistics, second language acquisition and foreign language teaching.* Berlin: Mouton de Gruyter.

Ausubel, D. P. (1970). Reception learning and the rote-meaningful dimension. In E. Stones (Ed.), *Readings in educational psychology. Learning and teaching* (pp. 193–206). London: Methuen.

Boers, R., & Lindstromberg, S. (Eds.) (2008). *Cognitive linguistic approaches to teaching vocabulary and phraseology*. Berlin: Mouton de Gruyter.

Cadierno, T. (2008). Motion events in Danish and Spanish: A focus on form pedagogical approach. In S. De Knop & T. De Rycker (Eds.), *Cognitive approaches to pedagogical grammar* (pp. 259–294). Berlin: Mouton de Gruyter.

Carpay, J. A. M. (1974). Foreign language teaching and meaningful learning. A Soviet Russian point of view. *ITL Review of Applied Linguistics*, 25–26, 161–187.

Choi, S.-J., & Lantolf, J. P. (2008). The representation and embodiment of meaning in L2 communication: Motion events in speech and gesture in L2 Korean and L2 English speakers. *Studies in Second Language Acquisition*, 30, 191–224.

Condon, N. (2008). How cognitive linguistic motivations influence the learning of phrasal verbs. In R. Boers & S. Lindstromberg (Eds.), *Cognitive linguistic approaches to teaching vocabulary and phraseology* (pp. 133–158). Berlin: Mouton de Gruyter.

Danesi, M. (2008). Conceptual errors in second-language learning. In S. De Knop & T. De Rycker (Eds.), Cognitive approaches to pedagogical grammar (pp. 231–258). Berlin: Mouton de Gruyter.

Davydov, V. V. (2004). *Problems of developmental instruction. A theoretical and experimental psychological study*. Moscow: Academiya.

De Knop, S., & De Rycker, T. (Eds.) (2008). *Cognitive approaches to pedagogical grammar*. Berlin: Mouton de Gruyter.

Di Pietro, R. J. (1987). *Strategic interaction*. Cambridge: Cambridge University Press.

Egan, K. (1983). *Education and psychology: Plato, Piaget and scientific psychology*. New York: Teachers College Press.

Ellis, N. (2007). The associative-cognitive CREED. In B. VanPatten & J. Williams (Eds.), *Theories in second language acquisition. An Introduction* (pp. 77–98). Mahwah, NJ: Erlbaum.

Fauconnier, G., & Turner, M. (2002). *The way we think: Conceptual blending and the mind's hidden complexities*. New York: Basic Books.

Ferreira, M., & Lantolf, J. P. (2008). A concept-based approached to teaching. Writing through genre analysis. In J. P. Lantolf & M. E. Poehner (Eds.), *Sociocultural theory and the teaching of second languages* (pp. 285–320). London: Equinox.

Fogel, A. (1991). *Developing through relationships. Origins of communication, self, and culture*. Chicago: University of Chicago Press.

Gal'perin, P. Ya. (1967). On the notion of internalization. *Soviet Psychology*, 5, 28–33.

Gal'perin, P. Ya. (1970). An experimental study in the formation of mental actions. In E. Stones (Ed.), *Readings in educational psychology. Learning and teaching* (pp. 142–154). London: Methuen.

Gal'perin, P. Ya. (1979). The role of orientation in thought. *Soviet Psychology*, 18, 19–45.

Haenen, J. (1996). *Piotr Gal'perin: Psychologist in Vygotsky's footsteps*. New York: Nova Science Publishers.

Holzman, L. (2009). *Vygotsky at work and play*. London: Routledge.

Ilyenkov, E. V. (1974). Activity and knowledge. Available at http://www.marxists.org/archive/ilyenkov/works/activity/index.html.

Jones, P. (2009). From "external speech" to "inner speech" in Vygotsky: A critical appraisal and fresh perspectives. *Language & Communication*, 29, 166–181.

Kabanova. O. Ya. (1985). The teaching of foreign languages. *Instructional Science*, 14, 1–47.

Karpov, Y. V. (2003). Vygotsky's doctrine of scientific concepts: Its role for contemporary education. In A. Kozulin, B. Gindis, V. S. Ageyev, & S. Miller (Eds.), *Vygotsky's educational theory in cultural context* (pp. 39–64). Cambridge: Cambridge University Press.

Kövecses, Z., & Szabó, P. (1996). Idioms: A view from cognitive semantics. *Applied Linguistics*, 17, 326–335.

Kozulin, A. (1995). The learning process: Vygotsky's theory in the mirror of its interpretations. *School Psychology International*, 16, 117–129.

Krashen, S. D. (1985). *The input hypothesis: Issues and implications*. New York: Longman.

Lakoff, G., & Johnson, M. (1980). *Metaphors we live by*. Chicago: University of Chicago Press.

Langacker, R. W. (1987). *Foundations of cognitive grammar. Volume 1: Theoretical prerequisites*. Stanford, CA: Stanford University Press.

Langacker, R. W. (2008). The relevance of cognitive grammar for language pedagogy. In S. De Knop & T. De Rycker (Eds.), *Cognitive approaches to pedagogical grammar* (pp. 7–35). Berlin: Mouton de Gruyter.

Lantolf, J. P. (1999). Second culture acquisition: Cognitive considerations. In E. Hinkel (Ed.), *Culture in language teaching and learning* (pp. 28–42). Cambridge: Cambridge University Press.

Lantolf, J. P. (2008). Praxis and L2 classroom development. *ELIA: Estudios de Linguistica Inglesa Aplicada*, 8, 13–44.

Lantolf, J. P. (2009). Knowledge of a foreign language in teacher education. *The Modern Language Journal*, 93, 270–274.

Lantolf, J. P. (forthcoming). Challenging Jones's view of Vygotsky's linguistics.

Lantolf, J. P., & Aljaafreh, A. (1995). Second language learning in the zone of proximal development: A revolutionary experience. *International Journal of Educational Research, 23,* 619–632.

Lantolf, J. P., & Thorne, S. L. (2006). *Sociocultural theory and the genesis of second language development.* Oxford: Oxford University Press.

Lapkin, S., Swain, M., & Knouzi, I. (2008). French as a second language: University students learn the grammatical concept of voice: Study design, materials development and pilot data. In J. P. Lantolf & M. E. Poehner (Eds.), *Sociocultural theory and the teaching of second languages* (pp. 228–255). London: Equinox.

Lee, H. (in progress). A concept-based approach to second language teaching and learning: Cognitive linguistics-inspired instruction of English phrasal verbs. Ph.D. dissertation, The Pennsylvania State University. University Park, PA.

Leont'ev, A. A. (1981). *Psychology and the language learning process.* London: Pergamon.

Leont'ev, A. N. (1981). *Problems of the development of the mind.* Moscow: Progress.

Long, M. H. (2006). *Problems in second language acquisition.* Mahwah, NJ: Erlbaum.

Luria, A. R. (1982). *Language and cognition.* New York: John Wiley & Sons.

Maldonado, R. (2008). Spanish middle syntax: A usage-based proposal for grammar teaching. In S. De Knop & T. De Rycker (Eds.), *Cognitive approaches to pedagogical grammar* (pp. 155–196). Berlin: Mouton de Gruyter.

Markova, A. K. (1979). *The teaching and mastery of language.* White Plains, NY: M. E. Sharpe.

Neguervela, E. (2003). A sociocultural approach to the teaching and learning of second languages: Systemic-theoretical instruction and L2 development. Ph.D. dissertation, the Pennsylvania State University, University Park, PA.

Neguervela, E. (2008). Revolutionary pedagogies: Learning that leads (to) second language development. In J. P. Lantolf & M. E. Poehner (Eds.), *Sociocultural theory and the teaching of second languages* (pp. 189–227). London: Equinox.

Niemeier, S., & Reif, M. (2008). Applying cognitive grammar to tense-aspect teaching. In S. De Knop & T. De Rycker (Eds.), *Cognitive approaches to pedagogical grammar* (pp. 323–355). Berlin: Mouton de Gruyter.

Oboukhova, L. F., Porshnev, A. V., Porshneva, E. R., & Gaponova, S. A. (2002). *Konstruirovanie komp'uternoj obuchayushej programmy na osnove teorii P. I. Gal'pernina.* [Constructing a computer-based instructional program on the basis of P. Y. Galperin's theory]. *Voprosy Psikhologii, 5,* 103–114.

Pienemann, M. (1998). *Language processing and second language development. Processability theory.* Amsterdam: John Benjamins.

Poehner, M. E. (2008). *Dynamic assessment. A Vygotskian approach to understanding and promoting L2 development.* Berlin: Springer.

Pütz, M., Niemeier, S., & Dirven, R. (Eds.). (2001). *Applied cognitive linguistics II: Language pedagogy.* Berlin: Mouton de Gruyter.

Robinson, P., & Ellis, N. (2008a). Conclusion: Cognitive linguistics, second language acquisition and L2 instruction—issues for research. In P. Robinson & N. Ellis (Eds.), *Handbook of cognitive linguistics and second language acquisition* (pp. 489–545). New York: Routledge.

Robinson, P., & Ellis, N. (Eds.) (2008b). *Handbook of cognitive linguistics and second language acquisition.* New York: Routledge.

Rudzka-Ostyn, B. (2003). *Word power: Phrasal verbs and compounds.* Berlin: Mouton de Gruyter.

Seliger, H. W. (1979). On the nature and function of language rules in language teaching. *TESOL Quarterly, 13,* 359–369.

Seliger, H. W. (1983). The language learner as linguist: Of metaphors and realities. *Applied Linguistics, 4,* 179–191.

Serrano-Lopez, M., & Poehner, M. E. (2008). Materializing linguistic concepts through 3-D clay modeling: A tool-and-result approach to mediating L2 Spanish development. In J. P. Lantolf & M. E. Poehner (Eds.), *Sociocultural theory and the teaching of second languages* (pp. 321–350). London: Equinox.

Slobin, D. I. (1996). From "thought and language" to "thinking for speaking." In S. Gumperz & S. Levinson (Eds.), *Rethinking linguistic relativity* (pp. 70–96). Cambridge: Cambridge University Press.

Swain, M., Lapkin, S., Knouzi, I., Suzuki, W., & Brooks, L. (2009) Languaging: University students learn the grammatical concept of voice in French. *The Modern Language Journal, 93,* 5–29.

Talmy, L. (2000). *Toward a cognitive semantics. Volume I: Concept structuring systems.* Cambridge, MA: MIT Press.

Talmy, L. (2001). *Toward a cognitive semantics. Volume II: Typology and process in concept structuring.* Cambridge, MA: MIT Press.

Talyzina, N. F. (1970). The stage theory of the formation of mental operations. In E. Stones (Ed.), *Readings in educational psychology. Learning and teaching* (pp. 155–162). London: Methuen.

Talyzina, N. F. (1973). Psychological basis of programmed instruction. *Instructional Science, 2,* 243–280.

Talyzina, N. F. (1981). *The psychology of learning.* Moscow: Progress Press.

Tarone, E. (2007). Sociolinguistic approaches to second language acquisition research—1997–2007. *The Modern Language Journal, 91,* 837–848.

Taylor, J. R. (2008). Some pedagogical implications of cognitive linguistics. In S. De Knop & T. De Rycker (Eds.), *Cognitive approaches to pedagogical grammar* (pp. 37–66). Berlin: Mouton de Gruyter.

Thorne, S. L., Reinhardt, J. & Golombek, P. (2008). Mediation as objectification in the development of professional academic discourse: A corpus-informed curricular innovation. In J. P. Lantolf & M. E. Poehner (Eds.), *Sociocultural theory and the teaching of second languages* (pp. 256–284). London: Equinox.

Tomasello, M. (2003). *Constructing language. A usage-based theory of language acquisition.* Cambridge: Cambridge University Press.

Tyler, A. (2008). Cognitive linguistics and second language instruction. In P. Robinson & N. Ellis (Eds.), *Handbook of cognitive linguistics and second language acquisition* (pp. 456–488). New York: Routledge.

van Parreren, J. (1975). Grammatical knowledge and grammatical skill. In A. J. Van Essen & J. P. Menting (Eds.), *The context of foreign language learning* (pp. 28–36). Assen: van Gorcum & Company.

VanPatten, B. (1996). *Input processing and grammar instruction: Theory and research.* Norwood, NJ: Ablex.

Vocate, D. R. (1994). Self-talk and inner speech: Understanding the uniquely human aspects of intrapersonal communication. In D. R. Vocate (Ed.), *Intrapersonal communication. Different voices, different minds* (pp. 3–32). Hillsdale, NJ: Erlbaum.

Vygotsky, L. S. (1978). *Mind in society. The development of higher psychological processes.* Cambridge, MA: Harvard University Press.

Vygotsky, L. S. (1987). *The collected works of L. S. Vygotsky. Volume 1: Problems of general psychology. Including the volume Thinking and Speech.* New York: Plenum.

Vygotsky, L. S. (1997). *The collected works of L.S. Vygotsky. Volume 3. Problems of the theory and history of psychology.* New York: Plenum.

Yáñez-Prieto, C. M. (2008). On literature and the secret art of invisible words: Teaching literature through language. Unpublished doctoral dissertation, the Pennsylvania State University, PA.

Yaroshevsky, M. (1989). *Lev Vygotsky.* Moscow: Progress Press.

20
Second Language Pragmatics

Virginia LoCastro

Introduction

Second language (L2) pragmatics is a field of applied linguistics that pursues research on second language acquisition (SLA), specifically on language use in social contexts, and the development of the ability to comprehend and produce appropriate language in complex, social interactions. Further, it brings together applications of pragmatics research to L2 teaching and learning as well as to other professional and everyday contexts, from service encounters to interpersonal relationships, where communication in more than one language or in one language by speakers from different cultural backgrounds takes place. Tannen's book *That's Not What I Meant!* (1986), after all, was inspired by L2 pragmatics about intimate, male–female native and nonnative English speaker couples. This contribution to the current handbook focuses not only on SLA and development concerns, but also on cross-linguistic and intercultural communication across languages and cultures in a variety of environments, especially in situated naturally occurring, everyday talk but not excluding classroom contexts. This chapter draws on work from formal linguistics and various disciplines of applied linguistics that contribute research findings to further our understanding of comprehension and production of pragmatic meanings.

Further, the chapter moves beyond studies in which English is the default, target language. The continued virtual domination of research on English as the de facto target language for language learners is problematic for several reasons. First, it places all nonnative English speakers in a secondary, deficit position; there is a clear need for studies of how, for example, Turkish speakers learn the L2 pragmatics of German or French in a world where bilingualism is increasingly common, even in areas that were previously predominantly Anglophone. Second, baseline pragmatic data of under-represented languages is thus needed to inform the teaching and learning of languages from Arabic and Chinese to Pashto and Wolof. Third, the necessary change in attitude toward acceptance of difference and diversity requires greater awareness and understanding of intercultural communication so that styles and strategies of communication and enactments of pragmatic meaning become as much a part of everyday life as airline travel and improving one's computer skills. Educational institutions can benefit from L2 pragmatics research in the context of local social and gender groupings in their communities. Fourth, acquisition and development of pragmatic competence of languages other than English can inform theory-building efforts regarding SLA and L2 pragmatics.

The purpose, then, of this chapter is to explore and examine applied linguistics research over the last decade in a variety of subdisciplines that have the potential to expand the sometimes narrow range of L2 pragmatics to a more inclusive view that reflects the diversity of daily life today. This chapter takes up several areas (see below) of research that tend to be less recognized in order to address this call for a larger frame, beyond the almost de facto limitation of equating L2 pragmatics with cross-cultural studies of isolated speech acts and a perspective on politeness that views such behavior as static and ignores human agency. Research on phonological and prosodic features and cognitive linguistics are included, as well as theoretical frameworks that propose methodologies for data collection and analysis that increase understanding of the complexities of pragmatic competence. A section on politeness reviews recent developments in that important area of L2 pragmatics, bringing it more in line with research in other social sciences. Another section provides illustrative studies of corpus linguistics in which advances in technology facilitate the quest for natural language data to inform studies in a variety of contexts. Two sections on "Beyond Speech Acts" and "Non-English Target Languages" studies then cover what have become substantial bodies of L2 pragmatic literature. While speech act studies greatly advanced the field of L2 pragmatics since Austin's (1962) and Searle's (1969) seminal publications, recognition of the need to study longer texts beyond adjacency pairs has pushed researchers to work with speech act realization strategies, oral proficiency interviews, and intercultural workplace literacy programs. Research on acquisition of non-English target languages grounds L2 pragmatics more solidly, not only intellectually in contemporary social sciences but also politically, with an increasingly aware public that seeks greater equity and mutual respect in multilingual environments. The final section of the chapter looks at an old standby of L2 pragmatics, pragmatic transfer, which is often the frontline of intercultural communication and where it is most crucial that acceptance of diversity be mindfully enacted.

This goal of inclusiveness clearly entails a greater awareness of the range of resources utilized in interactional contexts of language use. Researchers and practitioners increasingly recognize complexity involved in developing L2 pragmatic ability, particularly since Larsen-Freeman's seminal article on chaos and complexity theory in 1997. Larsen-Freeman argues that a new emerging paradigm for studying complex nonlinear systems in physical sciences can shed light on SLA theory building and interpretation of research findings. In addition to incorporating both social and cognitive dimensions in SLA studies, Larsen-Freeman suggests caution with "false dichotomies," such as competence/performance and individual speaker/hearer, in favor of a more holistic perspective that avoids the separation of the acquisition of syntax from sociolinguistic approaches that see language structure as inherently tied to the social contexts in which it is used. In addition to this 1997 article, revisited in a special 2007 issue of the *Modern Language Journal*, is a companion article by Firth and Wagner (1997) in which they take a strong, critical stance vis-à-vis the view of the learner/user of L2 pragmatics as "a deficient communicator … striving to reach the 'target' competence of an idealized native speaker" (pp. 295–296). They claim research should focus on communication success and explicate it, rather than on instances or patterns of pragmatic failure. In order to increase understanding of learning, teaching, and using L2 pragmatics, studying interactions in "naturalistic, real-life encounters" (p. 766) is a basic requirement for progress whether the reader is interested in such areas as instructed SLA, intercultural communication, or academic literacy skills for international students. Thus the stance in favor of a broader view of SLA and L2 pragmatics has evolved over the last decade to address the inarguably complex issues of L2 pragmatics. This call by Larsen-Freeman (2007, p. 773) for a "larger frame," seconded by Firth and Wagner, is the starting point of this chapter.

The eight areas listed below contribute to our knowledge of how human beings comprehend and produce pragmatic meanings across languages, cultures, and social groups:

- phonological and prosodic features;
- cognitive linguistics;

- theoretical frameworks;
- politeness;
- corpus linguistics;
- beyond speech acts;
- non-English target languages;
- L2 pragmatic transfer.

Phonological and Prosodic Features

An area of research that has also been developing recently within applied linguistics with the potential to contribute to the knowledge base of L2 pragmatics involves phonological and prosodic features of spoken interactions. Anecdotal evidence and discussion in seminars, conferences, and dissertation defenses frequently cite the role of prosody in comprehending and signaling pragmatic meaning. However, despite the significant improvements in both software and hardware for collecting and processing naturally occurring data of high quality, a paucity of studies in this area remains. This section looks into some of the research that has been done in this important area.

One notable contribution is Wichmann's work. Her doctoral dissertation was published in 2000 as *Intonation in Text and Discourse* and assesses the function of intonation in discourse beyond tone groups, specifically the "beginnings, middles and ends" of extended units of spoken text. More recently (2004), an investigation into the use of the word *please* with requests provides a needed appraisal of the aspects of that ubiquitous word. Wichmann's study of *please* emphasizes the need to distinguish speaker-oriented from hearer-oriented talk to ascertain the felicity conditions required for the appropriate use of *please* and the accompanying prosodic contours. The meaning of *please* with requests is explicated, with supporting diachronic evidence, in such a way as to inform those concerned with L2 pragmatics, specifically the explicit teaching of pragmatic development. Wichmann's continuing research agenda on the function of *please* as an interpersonal, attitudinal marker will further contribute to the L2 pragmatics knowledge base, despite the fact that her work does not directly apply to SLA.

Another study on the role of intonation is Ramirez-Verdugo and Romero Trillo's (2005) work on English tag questions used by first language (L1) Spanish speakers, specifically the choice of tone and pitch. Two data sets were collected and compared: one of the Spanish learners' English production of tag questions in read alouds and spontaneous talk, and a second of L1 English speakers' production in the same contexts. The researchers found significant differences in tone and pitch in comparable speech contexts, results that may account for misunderstandings in cross-cultural interactions. Other related studies by Ramirez-Verdugo and Romero Trillo focus on such topics as nuclear pitch accent in native Spanish speaker and nonnative Spanish speaker utterances (Ramirez-Verdugo, 2006) and prosodic features in texts read aloud by native Spanish speakers and nonnative Spanish speakers (Romero Trillo & Llinares-Garcia, 2004).

A discouraging aspect of phonological and prosodic studies is that the efforts by researchers to arrive at samples of naturally occurring speech data require a considerable amount of time; according to Wichmann (2004, p. 1527), auditory analysis cannot be replaced by instrumental analysis alone, even with the few corpus databases that are available with accessible sound files (the London-Lund Corpus and the Spoken English Corpus). Wichmann explains that manually edited transcriptions have been criticized for being "too impressionistic" and "subjective" (2004, p. 1527). Consequently, she recommends that corpus analysis be complemented by a form of discourse analysis, such as conversation analysis, to arrive at a close textual analysis of naturally occurring spoken talk recorded in the field with the inevitable noise. Despite the limitations of working with corpora to increase understanding of the role of intonation and prosody, researchers are pursuing means to increase the validity and reliability of analysis of these features and their contributions to L2 pragmatics.

Cognitive Linguistics

This section considers contributions from cognitive linguistics (hereafter, CL). It provides evidence of the expansion of L2 pragmatics research into incorporating more complex theoretical frameworks and related explorations of more rigorous data collection and analysis procedures. More studies that are explicitly theory-driven are noticeable in the literature of general L2 pragmatics.

There is one salient feature of CL that links it strongly with pragmatics: CL takes a functional perspective on communication and language use. Pragmatics is ostensibly grounded in the same view of language use in that it seeks to explain how communication functions through linguistic forms and nonlinguistic means. In other words, rather than starting one's study from the point of view of linguistic forms, the functional perspective zeros in on what meaning an individual wants to convey and then how it is done with the resources available, typically in a natural language. L2 pragmatics essentially shares the same view and specializes in a variety of linguistic and nonlinguistic enactments across cultures, subcultures, and groups to make meaning. CL pushes the functional perspective to "further explain how language mutually interfaces with conceptual structure as this becomes established during child L1 development and as it becomes available for change during adult L2 language learning" (Ellis & Robinson, 2008, p. 4). CL argues that "the basic units of language representation are constructions, 'form-meaning mappings,'" that are the language knowledge of both "the child's L1 and the adult's L2 learner's mind" (Ellis & Robinson, 2008, p. 4). Ellis and Robinson outline six areas of inquiry in CL that are supported by seven areas of research, among them corpus linguistics, connectionist models of language, sociocultural theory, and chaos/complexity theory (2008, pp. 5–6). The link that brings together those areas of inquiry and the frameworks of investigation is the assumption that "language is learned from usage" (p. 5). The following explores that assumption.

Usage-based theories of language are based on the premise that languages are acquired through communication, specifically through repeated exposure to and production of linguistic forms that enact frequent communicative functions. Further, CL does not assume that a specific language module exists in the mind; there is no "autonomous cognitive facility" (Clark, 2008, p. 259). Rather, language is regarded as part of "interlocking networks of knowledge, including social and pragmatic knowledge" (Clark, 2008, p. 259). There is a clear trend in CL to combine various qualitative and quantitative methodologies as, for example, discourse analysis and corpus studies with a theoretical framework comprising sociocultural theory, in order to "explore the ways in which the systematic study of natural language usage can provide insights not only into the nature and specific organization of the linguistic system, but also into the interplay between linguistic, cognitive, and cultural phenomena" (Mittelberg, Farmer, & Waugh, 2007, p. 19). Usage-based studies are found in recent sociolinguistics literature that attempts to account for variation and potential language change of linguistic features from a cognitive perspective. For example, Clark (2008) investigated vocalic variation in L1 Scottish English, basing her argument regarding the source of the change on word frequency. The assumption is that frequency drives the cognitive schemas to become stronger and more entrenched in the neural networks in the brain. The greater the frequency or usage of a particular linguistic form such as a local vowel variable, the more likely that pronunciation will take hold in the community, especially if it correlates with creating or maintaining the identity of a local sociolinguistic group. This approach to language change thus incorporates a cognitive account of social facts and sociolinguistic variation. Note that Clark's work, which arguably concerns only variation in L1 Scottish English, can be viewed as of import to L2 pragmatics since it does look at phonological variation of different groups within the Scottish English speech community.

Although the potential of CL to inform L2 pragmatics research is clear, few studies currently exist that include work on more than one language. Waugh, Fonseca-Gerber, Vickers, and Eroz (2007) describe two studies, one carried out by Vickers (2004) and the other by Eroz (2003), which involve native English speakers (NESs) and nonnative English speakers (NNESs) in the US academic community. Vickers concentrated on how the two groups of participants interactively accommodated to each other as they performed a task; she was interested in how they might come to use a "shared interpretative frame," that is, "ways of knowing and of experiencing the world" (Waugh et al., 2007, p. 134). Eroz investigated whether or not international students in the US academic community interacted differently from Americans and, if so, whether their patterns of behavior had been transferred from classroom patterns in their home cultures. Vickers collected ethnographic data in addition to engaging in microanalyses of collected interactional talk. Eroz also triangulated sources of data; using a community of practice framework, he looked at classroom and nonclassroom interactional patterns using conversation analysis procedures for data analysis. In all, Eroz engaged in nine steps for data analysis and interpretation, reflecting the strong stance in Waugh et al. and others in favor of multiple empirical approaches. Waugh et al. conclude: "We are interested in the nature of human interaction through language in its social and cultural setting, and it is from that perspective that we can draw conclusions about, and provide insight into, cognition" (2007, p. 144).

Several other projects investigate cognitive processing of such features as speed of comprehension and/or production. Nguyen (2008) assessed L1 English learners of Vietnamese, specifically their production of syntactically complex structures of criticism in peer feedback sessions, hypothesizing that such structures, being more cognitively demanding, would result in greater cognitive difficulty. Nguyen's finding supports the Complexification Hypothesis regarding an acquisition order of L2 syntactic structures. Taguchi (2008a, 2008b) investigated the cognitive processing ability of L1 Japanese learners of English in the context of such variables as L2 pragmatic comprehension over time, the role of the amount of language contact, and participants' listening abilities and working memory capacities to develop a picture of their L2 pragmatic competence development.

Further, there have been some recent efforts to revise Sperber and Wilson's (1986) original conception of relevance theory (RT) to explore issues related to L2 pragmatics. Sroda (2000) proposes a mechanism of pragmatic enrichment to account for how L2 learners arrive at ostensible explicatures and implicatures for propositions, as well as for social relationships. Specifically, she studied pragmatic failure in naturally occurring data of L2 English language learners, thus moving RT into the field of L2 pragmatics. Moeschler (2004) also investigated L2 pragmatic failure and misunderstandings that he considers to be the result of inadequate understanding of the explicature of the utterances in question. What he labels a "cognitive approach" draws on RT; he explores how the effect of shared cultural knowledge affects the retrieval of the speaker's intended meaning. Thus his explanation of the cause of the inability to retrieve the intended meaning and implicatures of utterances in general is diverging world and situational knowledge. Both fit into the category of "higher level explicatures" (p. 60), which differ from "ordinary" explicatures. Moeschler's analysis of L2 French data thus suggests that there are several potential levels of pragmatic failure and the results of his study of L2 pragmatics point to the higher level explicatures of content and world knowledge as being more serious with regard to misunderstandings than basic or weaker level of explicatures. As with Sroda's study, Moeschler brings a revisited RT into the domain of L2 pragmatics research.

Another trend within this developing research agenda of including cognitive and social dimensions is increased attention to what are called "interfaces," specifically the syntax-pragmatic interface, to assess the role of formal linguistic resources, particularly morphosyntactic constituents, and pragmatics in L2 performance. One issue here is whether a threshold of grammatical competency is required before learners can benefit from explicit instruction in L2 pragmatics (Kasper & Rose, 2002; Bardovi-Harlig, 1999). Rothman (2004) studied the use of null or overt subject pronoun use in the L2 Spanish of L1 English learners. The results of his study indicate overuse of both overt and null subject pronouns, suggesting L1 transfer was not the origin of the L1 English learners' production, nor is the syntax-pragmatics interface the site of fossilization. Rothman's study uses a universal grammar approach, assessing the role of parameter resetting of the Overt Pronoun Constraint by Anglophone learners. In a related article (2008), Rothman claims that while intermediate learners may have knowledge of the preference in Spanish for the null subject, they do not yet know enough about the pragmatic meanings of the null vs. overt subject pronouns in the L2 to move toward mastery of this form-function instance of usage in L2 Spanish. In a related project, Montrul and Rodriguez-Louro (2006) address the question as to whether discourse-pragmatic properties are acquired simultaneously with syntactic properties by L2 learners of Spanish. In their study of null vs. overt subject pronoun use by L1 English learners, oral production task results indicated that while the intermediate and advanced learners' utterances were morphosyntactically accurate, the discourse-pragmatic dimensions of their production were inaccurate. The authors argue that full parameter resetting occurs at only very advanced stages, with transfer effects remaining with discourse-pragmatic properties.

Another study in the same interface framework regarding interface-conditioned behaviors is that of Gurel (2006), who investigated the acquisition of pragmatic and syntactic constraints of overt and null subject pronouns in Turkish by L1 English learners. Gurel based her study on the Binding Principle B within the Overt Pronoun Constraint as well as pragmatics constraints, i.e., the contrastive or emphatic function of overt subject pronouns in Turkish. Gurel found that there was evidence of L1 transfer effects in the L2 grammar of the English learners.

These studies represent a line of research within applied linguistics that seeks to understand the interaction of syntax and pragmatics in SLA. It suggests a need to bring together the theories of Chomsky's approach to language with pragmatics, previously viewed as a dimension of language production that came only after linguistic processing had occurred at the final stage. That linear view of language comprehension and production is no longer acceptable, and studies show the need to move beyond that now-dated model and incorporate recognition of pragmatic meaning as a contributing variable to linguistic processing. A full discussion of this inclusive approach to the study of language usage/use is beyond the scope of this chapter. It represents a powerful alternative to the Chomsky perspective on language and cognition that has ignored sociocultural dimensions. Readers are referred to Ellis and Robinson (2008) and Gonzalez-Marquez, Mittelberg, Coulson, and Spivey (2007), among others, for further exploration.

Theoretical Frameworks

Larsen-Freeman and Firth and Wagner are among an increasing and more vocal number of SLA researchers who part company with the dominant, exclusively universal grammar cognitive approach to language acquisition, a view that virtually denies the role of any aspect other than the mind and the internalization of the lexicogrammar of a language (Atkinson, Churchill, Nishino, & Okada, 2007). Continued focus on only this decontextualized view of human learning flies in the face of recent advances in neurolinguistics and brain research. Connectionism, to provide only one example, has challenged the existence of a discrete, modular-like entity, the language acquisition device (LAD), in the brain. Sacks's recent bestseller, *Musicophilia: Tales of Music and the Brain* (2008), has described for the general public multiple case studies of correlations between brain damage, recovery, and musical competence that change our understanding of the brain and calls into question the Universal Grammar approach to learning and language acquisition. One result of the more public challenging of the previously dominant agenda of many SLA researchers has been a movement away from the formal, decontextualized model of language acquisition and a search for more appropriate theoretical frameworks to inform studies and account for findings. A considerable literature of research projects based on sociocultural theory (Vygotsky, 1978) and language socialization is developing. Sociocultural theory, based on Vygotsky's model of L1 acquisition that includes social and cognitive dimensions, has contributed significantly to the debates on SLA as well. Further, language socialization focuses on the learning of language and culture in the context of community activities; the findings from Ochs's (1988) investigations into child–parent communicative practices in Western Samoa have informed research on language use and acquisition of L2 learners at any age and in a variety of activities within and outside classrooms. This chapter adds to this overview of current developments by focusing on two areas that have received less attention: conversation analysis and sociocognitive approaches.

Conversation Analysis

A theoretical perspective on meaning making and comprehension, conversation analysis (hereafter, CA) is a research methodology in applied linguistics that is gaining increased attention as a particularly useful tool for L2 pragmatics. Adopting CA reflects a general concern for methodologies that are more rigorous and that entail greater accountability by the analyst regarding data collection and analysis. CA has developed from its parent, ethnomethodology (EM) (McHoul, 2008). One issue in the controversy regarding CA vs. EM is to what extent context is relevant to the analysis of talk, and a second, according to McHoul, regards the relationship of CA to EM. He argues that the agenda of EM—i.e., to seek the social order in talk-in-interaction—is clearly implied in the multiple approaches within discourse analysis and pragmatics, and supports the stance that inclusion of whatever the analyst deems necessary to show relevance to participants in the instance of talk being studied is possible. The issue of the inclusion of text-external contextual features continues to play a significant role in the adoption of CA as an appropriate methodology for L2 pragmatics, a field that is inherently concerned with the sociocultural context of situated talk. The following studies illustrate the value of both traditional CA and a modified CA approach for data collection and interpretation.

According to Lazaraton (2002), orthodox or traditional CA states that the analyst should know nothing about the participants in a sample of talk; s/he must reduce the frame of reference to what can be discerned from the talk, particularly the sequences, turn-taking, and recurring patterns. Rather than seeking text-external explanations for evidence, such as is done in variationist sociolinguistics, attention is focused exclusively on the interactional moves in the data and the orientation of the participants to each other's talk. An example of traditional CA is Ishida (2006) on the use of modal expressions by Japanese as a L2 learner interacting with a native speaker of Japanese in a ten-minute conversation. CA demonstrated the range of interactional competence by means of a microgenetic analysis of local, situated talk between the learner and host family members. The affordances of social chat facilitated the L2 pragmatic development of the learner and her ability to use modal expressions such as *ne, ja nai*, and *-yoo*, and turn-taking, based on her conversational partner's modeling through contributions to the talk.

In a study that represents a transition away from traditional CA, Houck and Fujii (2006) investigated the use of delay in academic interactions with native English and nonnative English speakers in a discussion at an American university in Japan. The ethnicity of the participants plays a role in the data analysis. Delay sequences tend to occur when a speaker wants to put off a dispreferred response. Delays may be short vocalizations, pauses, and other forms of hesitation markers as well as silence. Houck and Fujii used CA-like techniques to locate delays in the sequences of the collected data of seven female NES and native Japanese speaker (NJS) pairs conversing in English. The goal of the study was to compare the findings with those of Pomerantz (1984) on agreement/disagreement with assessments of NESs only. In the context of the academic setting with advanced-level learners of English and graduate student peers, delay appeared to function in a more complex manner than its use in Pomerantz. The participants were engaged in expressing opinions; the Japanese speakers may have been seeking opportunities not only to express a "nonaligning point of view" (p. 49), but also to seek a more preferential opportunity in the sequence of talk to communicate their own opinions. Delay was a strategic move in their communication skills repertoire.

The requirement of CA analysis that the researcher not consider features outside the data being analyzed does result in increased awareness of, in particular, sequential evidence in the talk as well as of other features. However, it does not seem to be conducive to discovering the patterns of language use and functions used in everyday talk across multiple contexts. Consequently, studies in L2 pragmatics may claim to use a "conversation-analytic approach," thereby signaling a certain degree of hybridity in the data analysis with less attention to the rigor expected in conversation analysts trained by Schegloff (see, for example, Schegloff, 1996). There is a movement in the direction of inclusion of contextual variables outside of the text itself; indeed, Moerman (1988) advocates adoption of a "culturally contextualized conversation analysis (CCCA)" that affords close analysis of texts, e.g., with CA, along with an ethnography of communication of participants and their community (p. 123). The analyst must tread a fine line to avoid over-interpreting the data and imposing an interpretation, yet more attention to the participants can provide vital information that will open up the analysis to the complexity of human interactions (Waugh et al., 2007). CCCA gives a label to what has become noticeable in many recent studies in which multiple approaches to examining "culturally contextualized examples of authentic language use" (Waugh et al., 2007, p. 120) are investigated using a "rich, fine grained analysis derived from various empirical approaches" (p. 120). Linguistic, sociocultural, cognitive, historic, and ideological variables and features all need to be considered to increase understanding of the "complex ecological system" in which language is embedded (p. 120).

Exactly this type of study is exemplified by Collier's (2008) investigation of "Immigrant women's use of language in entrepreneurial contexts." Collier studies the communication strategies of a group of bilingual women entrepreneurs in Philadelphia, PA and Los Angeles, CA through surveys, interviews, observations, and audio recordings. Conversation and linguistic analysis were applied to case study data of four of these women, demonstrating how the women learned L2 interactional skills through small talk. The immigrant women primarily used conversational opportunities with their customers to get scaffolded help and expansions of their utterances, thereby becoming more proficient users of L2 English. The results of the study showed continued problems with grammar and lexical items while at the same time they acquired greater mastery of L2 pragmatics.

Walters (2007) has also attempted to apply CA in the context of second language pragmatics testing (SLPT), an area of interest for L2 pragmatics where the speech act theory base for assessment of pragmatic ability has proven to be too limited and an unreliable measure of testees' pragmatic competence in extended talk. CA presents a mismatch with psychometrics-based language testing. Walters followed two CA-trained testers using a more holistic rubric to evaluate testees' responses on an oral English as a second language (ESL) pragmatic exam. Although not statistically significant, the results of the study suggest a role for CA in developing improved SLPT.

The inclusion of nonverbal cues in conversation—gestures and eye gaze—makes Olsher's (2004) CA study particularly fruitful as an example of the interactional competence of NNEs at the novice level. Three students were videotaped while completing a map-making task in English at a Japanese college. The CA is informed by observations and ethnographic data. Olsher's analysis of the transcribed video data brought to light sequentially organized routines, including specifically the completion of turns at talk through embodied actions that were pragmatically accurate. The detailed analysis that CA affords brought to light evidence of the novice learners' abilities to enact interactional skills in order to work collaboratively in their L2, and to negotiate help with linguistic items without using metalanguage for grammatical items.

Sociocognitive Approach

This next study centers on one recent attempt to development a sociocognitive framework that brings together many aspects that have been discussed so far in this chapter. Atkinson et al. (2007) propose a sociocognitive approach to SLA in which a central tenet is that "L2 development takes place through … mind-body-world activities, of which cognitive internalization of input is only a part" (p. 169). The authors provide an analogy between language learning and improvisational dance or team sports where what goes on between or among participants is as important as "what goes in" and how it gets processed internally (p. 169). "A continuous ecological circuit" is the locus of the mind-body-world variables that interact "relationally and intergratively" (p. 170). In their view the social, the cognitive, and the physical all comprise the ecology in which "grammar and syntax might be construed as coordinate with, not superior to, the practices and resources of language development" (Schegloff, Ochs, & Thompson, 1996, p. 26). Although Atkinson et al. do not overtly claim application of their framework or of this quotation from Schegloff et al. to L2 pragmatics, that connection can be made, given the emphasis in their work on the social context of their SLA study.

This sociocognitive approach accounts for the data in these researchers' assessment of the role of alignment in SLA. Alignment labels the adaptation of language and nonverbal actions in real-time interactional discourse as the participants engage intersubjectively to achieve their communicative goals. An example of alignment would be the timing of listener behavior (LoCastro, 1987) whereby the listener uses back channel cues at socioculturally appropriate response moments in the real-time unfolding of conversation, basically signaling orientation to the speaker during turns at talk. If the cues are uttered according to the cultural norms or expectations of the local situation, the listener and speaker can be said to have achieved alignment. Atkinson et al. drew their primary data from a videotaped tutoring session of two junior high school Japanese students of English working on a grammar exercise sheet. The focus of the interaction is on one of the student's use of scaffolding, repetition, and other strategies to help the other student, who can be observed aligning her talk with the first student's efforts to help her. There is interactive evidence of the learners' using in particular the English structure "have you (ever) …" to formulate their experiences, thus supporting the researchers' stance that alignment of mind-body-world contributes to learning and presumably the acquisition of L2 pragmatics.

Politeness

Another reflection of the renewed interest in research methods; more rigorous, close analysis of data; and multiple approaches to the subjects of inquiry is the reconceptualization of politeness both at the theoretical level and at the methodological level. Earlier theories of politeness, in particular Brown and Levinson (1987) and Leech (1983) to name only two of the most influential, are now viewed as having been based on Anglocentric assumptions about face; static, fixed values regarding power, social distance, and weight of imposition; determinism regarding sociocultural contextual features; agentless social actors deemed to be rational; speaker-oriented theories; and exclusion of nonlinguistic resources to signal attention to the hearer (Kasper, 2006a). From a methodological perspective, most of the research has been based on elicited data in the form of discourse completion tests, role plays, or decontextualized speech acts. It is then reasonable that researchers such as Kasper (2006a) call for a change to viewing politeness as a "discursive phenomenon" (2006a, p. 243), coconstructed by participants in situated, local interactions in the course of the enactment of relational work.

Kasper (2006a) outlines several approaches to the current revision of politeness theory. This section focuses on that of Watts (2003) and Locher (2004), which emphasizes the role of relational work in human interaction. A key concept in Watts's model is "politic" behavior. This label designates verbal and nonverbal behavior that is appropriate or normative for a particular local, situated interaction and recognized by the participants as such in the course of their relational work. Any other behaviors that are either more or less than the expected behavior could be open to interpretation as (im)polite. In this view, the word *please* could simply be politic, i.e., what is expected, or polite, thereby communicating more than local participants would deem necessary, or impolite, where intonation could render a request like "Would you *please* remove your feet?"[1] "too much" and impolite. This view leads to Watts's insistence that no word or phrase is inherently polite or impolite. Labeling behavior as (im)polite occurs in the emerging discourse as the interactants attribute values to the conduct of the social actors: they establish the norms, the label of appropriacy for behaviors. The basis of their ability to do so derives from Bourdieu's (1990) concept of habitus. What is "outside" the habitus of the interactants gives rise to the inferences of (im)politeness. Clearly, if the habitus of one participant presents a mismatch with that of the other(s), misunderstanding may arise in inferring pragmatic meaning.

Locher and Watts (2005) discuss in particular the notion of "relational work" that participants engage in with others to coconstruct discourse, noting that politeness is only a small part of the interactional efforts of human beings in daily activities. They take on Goffman's (1967, 1981) conception of face as being much more than the narrow meaning attributed to it in Brown and Levinson's theory. A great deal of facework in human interactions does not necessarily entail a static attention to face threats and mitigation. Watts and Locher (2005) provide close, textual analyses of five extracts of conversation in which they participated as individuals to demonstrate the discursive construction of politic, polite, and impolite phenomena, using the term "relational work" to explain "cooperative communication" (p. 28). They claim "individuals evaluate certain utterances as polite against the background of their own habitus …. Politeness, like beauty, is in the eye of the beholder" (p. 29).

Much of the recent research on this more current view of (im)politeness did not involve L2 pragmatics or SLA. A special issue of *Pragmatics* (December 2008) presents ten contributions on "(Im)politeness in Spanish-speaking socio-cultural contexts." The articles report on a variety of issues on politeness across varieties of Spanish and are published in both Spanish and English versions. A more obviously L2 pragmatics study is Kasper's (2006b) investigation of the discourse of oral proficiency interviews (OPIs) in which the interviewer uses questions to obtain relevant responses so that the interviewee's language can be assessed. Both linguistic and pragmatic appropriacy are evaluated. All of the interviewees were native speakers of Japanese who worked for a Japanese company, and the interviewers were native speakers of different varieties of English. Kasper focused on "multiple questions," that is, questions repeated by the interviewers in the same turn, functioning as "proactive actions" to facilitate responses in potentially unclear instances in the interview. Specifically, the multiple requests would become more direct, thus risking being perceived as less polite or appropriate than the initial, more conventionally indirect requests. The findings allow a claim to be made that the subsequent or second request would be perceived by the interviewees as an "affiliative" practice, despite the directness; the participants oriented to the sequential organization made transparent in the CA analysis of the data, and processed the "politeness-implicative" use of the conversational resources (Kasper, 2006b, pp. 345–346).

LoCastro (2007) adopted the relational perspective to inform her study of an international teaching assistant's (ITA) classroom practices in an upper division undergraduate physics course at a large US public university. The study operationalized politic behavior as building and maintaining rapport by the ITA with his undergraduate students. Displaying respect and concern for students, one of the nine factors on the university's faculty evaluation instrument, was defined as the expected or politic behavior of the ITA. Through the relational work he enacted with the students Pedro was able to achieve this goal, as evidenced by the high evaluations he received at the end of the semester from the students. His nonnative speaker proficiency in English and classroom practices influenced by those of his country of origin did not negatively constrain his ability to display respect and concern for his students.

Corpus Linguistics

Corpus linguistics is yet another developing field in applied linguistics as more and more emphasis is placed on the need to base studies, language learning materials, and dictionaries on large bodies of data of naturally occurring spoken and written language usage/use. Corpora enable researchers to investigate a myriad of different phenomena, including pragmatic functions and linguistic enactments in large databases, thus providing results that may be viewed as more reliable, valid, and generalizable across populations without the lack of reliability that arises from the use of scholars' intuitions and created or self-reported data. Quantitative studies and statistical analyses are thus facilitated by means of computerized procedures for data collection and analysis, providing sources for triangulation and alternative views to qualitative, ethnographic-like studies that are common in L2 pragmatics. Consequently, this section reports on corpus studies. However, a caveat is in order. A review of the literature points to a noticeable increase in the use of term "corpus" for what are essentially data sets that are limited in terms of number of items or tokens and in the range of data included. Thus in my view it is necessary to distinguish between readily available corpora such as the London-Lund compiled at the Survey of English Usage at University College London and an individual researcher's "corpus" of classroom interactions collected in one classroom over a three-month period, to give one typical example. The words "corpus" and "corpus linguistics" have been appropriated for what have been previously labeled "data sets" or "databases." The amount and type of data in corpora in terms of number of items, concordancing capacities, and other details about the data collection varies considerably. Further, the availability of the smaller databases to other researchers is not assured.

A major contributor to the study of corpora of spoken language data and the value of such studies in L2 language teaching is McCarthy. His 1998 publication encompasses ten years of his work, in particular participating in the CANCODE (Cambridge–Nottingham Corpus of Discourse of English) corpus project. Chapters in the 1998 book demonstrate the variety of topics of his work, ranging from characteristics of genres to speech in everyday conversation. McCarthy has been interested in such features that can carry pragmatic meaning as discourse markers, turn taking, and information staging, and why these features matter in teaching second/foreign languages.

Some examples of recent studies, based on smaller, individual databases or corpora, that may be of particular interest to L2 pragmatics researchers are de Klerk's (2005) paper on *well* in Xhosa English, a variety of Black South African English; Belz and Vyatkina's (2005) report on a L2 pedagogical project using corpus data for the teaching of L1 German modal particles; and Hobenstein's (2005) use of corpus data of L1 Japanese and L1 German interactional expectations in academic expert discourse, for the purpose of studying transfer from German to Japanese or vice versa. Hyland (2002) investigated personal pronoun use, his operationalization of author identity, in sixty-four Hong Kong L2 English undergraduate theses using a corpus of research articles and interview data with the students and their supervisors. These studies are typical of smaller, corpus-based research projects that have been increasing in number since the late 1990s.

As for the larger corpora, the London-Lund Corpus is a well-known example of an available database and includes one million words of which 600,000 are "orthographically transcribed speech" (Wichmann, 2004, p. 1528). It also comprises a concordance of tagged items, which facilitates the search for particular features of spoken data (Nelson, Wallis, & Aarts, 2002). Wichmann utilized this corpus for her studies of *please*.

Another available corpus, the Michigan Corpus of Academic Spoken English (MICASE), provides baseline data for a study by Shimura (2005) on the use of *please* with the speech act of complaints by Japanese L2 speakers of English. MICASE includes academic spoken language from seminars, lectures, office hours, and service encounters from the University of Michigan campus environment that first began to be collected in 1997. As of 2005 it included 295,045 words and nineteen hours of transcribed data (Shimura, 2005, p. 64). In addition, Shimura collected L2 pragmatic data with a discourse completion test (DCT), administered at five university campuses in the Tokyo area of Japan. These data comprise the second corpus Shimura used in her analysis, which included a chi-square test to compare the two data sets, both hers and MICASE. Shimura examined three features in the use of *please* with complaints: (1) its part of a collocation; (2) its position in the utterance; and (3) the social distance between the speaker and addressee. Shimura concluded that L2 pragmatics can be studied by using electronic corpora; however, there are limitations or constraints. The researcher must be familiar with computers and programming specifically in order to recognize the fact that certain pragmatic variables, such as social distance, cannot be categorized instrumentally without the researcher doing a manual text analysis, entailing interpretation and subsequent tagging of items.

Another contribution is that of Aijmer and Simon-Vandenbergen (2006). They edited a collection of studies of pragmatic markers that includes contributions that work with translation and other corpora to investigate across languages functions of several pragmatic markers in natural discourse. The editors point out the value of comparable corpora (2006, p. 5), which are matched in terms of text type, subject matter, and function with a corresponding corpus in another language. This requirement of comparability is often ignored in studies such as that of Shimura (2005) above who, however, did acknowledge that the MICASE spoken database came from limited, academic settings whereas the DCT corpus included only written responses to the prompts.

Studies based on larger corpora include Wichmann (2000, 2004). She has been carrying out corpus-based studies on the functions of intonation in spoken discourse. Specifically, she has investigated discourse features such as the beginnings of new topics, closure of a topic, cohesive cues, global pitch markers, and prosodic units in conversation. In her 2004 article she focuses on the intonation of *please* with requests in NES talk. The corpora for these studies are the Spoken English Corpus (SEC) of the ICE GB Corpus, i.e., the British contribution to the International Corpus of English.

Stenstrom (2006) investigated the Spanish pragmatic markers *o sea* and *pues* and the English functional counterparts, *well* and *'cos*, using four corpora of adult and adolescent talk: COLAm, COLT, COR92, and BNC/spoken (2006, p. 155).[2] The goal of her study was to establish the equivalent forms in English, entailing first, a description of each form; second, its function at the discourse level; third, its pragmatic function; and fourth, the interactional function of the forms. This analytical framework consisted of a discourse-pragmatic-functional review of data from the corpus. The author looked at word frequencies in the corpora to contrast adolescent and adult speech.

Another contribution to Aijmer and Simon-Vandenbergen that draws on large corpora, Johansson (2006) utilizes the English–Norwegian Parallel Corpus (ENPC) and the Oslo Multilingual Corpus with English, Norwegian, and German. These corpora allow the researcher to study original and translated texts across the three languages, retrieving all instances of *well* and corresponding items in the other two languages. The author notes that some manual processing was necessary to eliminate *well* used in an adverbial function, for example, since discourse markers are not tagged in the corpora and are notoriously multifunctional. This disadvantage as well as other shortcomings are discussed, one being the lack of coding of prosodic features, an important variable in the interpretation of discourse markers such as *well*. Johansson sought to assess how *well* in an English text is translated in Norwegian and German, and the pragmatic forms that translate *well* in those two languages. In answering his research question as to the translation of *well*, Johansson concludes that the "many correspondences and the high degree of zero correspondence show that the translation of *well* is far from straightforward" (p. 135). Further, he claims that by using the corpora, the great range of variation and the problems of translation of *well* become transparent and facilitate more learning about complications.

A 2002 Festschrift publication in honor of Stenstrom presents fifteen contributions on language corpora studies (Brevik & Hasselgren, 2002). Stenstrom was instrumental in developing the COLT (Corpus of London Teenage Language) in 2000, an invaluable resource on spontaneous, spoken talk. The first chapter of the book by Aarts (2002) reviews issues of a corpus approach to linguistic analysis. The issues include: (1) types of linguistic data; (2) the nature and use of corpus data; (3) annotation of data; (4) spoken language research; and (5) other methodological concerns. One L2 pragmatic study in this volume is Hasund's (2002) investigation of the pragmatic marker *like* in English and *liksom* in Norwegian, both of which have increased in use in informal spoken language. Hasund utilized two comparable corpora, the English language part of the Bergen Corpus of London Teenage Language and the Oslo teenage language database of a Norwegian project, the Sprakkontaktoch Ungdomssprack I Norden (UNO) (p. 126). The objective was to assess the similarity of the two forms, in particular their pragmatic function as a cue of the speaker's epistemic stance toward the content or form of an utterance (p. 125). The results of the corpora analysis supported Hasund's earlier studies of three pragmatic functions of the two forms, all of which point to a similar epistemic stance on the part of the speaker. In addition, Hasund found a correlation in both languages between use and gender: both *like* and *liksom* are most frequently used by middle-class females, possibly to signal informality and in-group identity.

Beyond Speech Acts

Until recently speech acts analysis has dominated L2 pragmatics for several reasons. It is relatively easy to collect speech act data by means of DCTs, role plays, and other elicitation procedures. In addition, the type of data lends itself to quantitative as well as qualitative analysis, such as the use of statistical measures to assess percentages and levels of significance in the use of particular speech acts by different sociocultural populations. Further, researchers can carry out member checking and retrospective accounts to learn informants' rationales for using a particular speech act. However, once Hymes (1972) emphasized the importance of speech event data collection and Blum-Kulka, House and Kasper (1989) and others focused on analysis of speech act realization strategies, researchers expanded the domains of their studies.

This section focuses on the extension of analysis beyond speech acts to speech act realizations strategies and extended talk or discourse, particularly international discourse. This approach to L2 pragmatics is driven by interest in research sites where participants or interlocutors use different languages, potentially different cultural values and practices in the enactment of indirectness, politeness, illocutionary force indicating devices, and alignment moves. Simultaneously, in real time, they are attending or orienting to each other in the "moment-by-moment unfolding of the interaction" (Kasper, 2004, p. 124). In talk-in-interaction, the sociocultural features or aspects become more noticeable and the participants more involved in more complex behaviors, closer to actual, everyday requirements of human communication.

Kasper's (2004, 2006b) study of repeated questions in an OPI demonstrates more vividly than speech act analysis the effect of different types of questions to elicit talk from candidates for rating their language proficiency levels in the OPI. Such testing procedures for oral competencies, found in many standardized exams (see the TOEFL, TOEIC, IELTS), are important assessment instruments that can have consequences for the candidates in terms of graduate school admission and employment and promotion possibilities. The OPI rater elicits talk from a candidate; consequently, the syntactic form of the questions, which by itself communicates pragmatic meaning, is crucial in carrying out the task of the OPI. Kasper (2004, p. 130) offers examples from the data of the types of questions or solicits, exhibiting different levels of directness with one example for each type:

Direct questions (wh-)	What did you *do* in Indonesia?
Locution-derivable/direct	Please tell me about it.
Conventionally indirect	*Can* you tell me what you did over Golden Week?

At issue is the observance that repeated questions, using different pragmalinguistic structures, can result in different sociopragmatic meanings. Kasper is in particular interested in the pragmalinguistic form of the repeated elicitation by the interviewer that functions to repair a problem in hearing or understanding the initial question by the addressee. Here is a modified example from Kasper (2004, p. 126):

I: Can you tell me about what you did over Golden Week?
C: Pardon?
I: *Tell me* what you did *for Golden Week*, over Golden Week.
C: Yah, I worked as a assistant of cameraman and one day I met my parents in Okayama.

Although the form of the second elicitation differs from that of the first, both the interviewer and C accept it as functionally equivalent. The first is conventionally indirect in form, an ability question format, while the second is more direct: the grammatical form communicates its force (Kasper, 2004, p. 128). The pragmalinguistic modification enacts "downward interviewer accommodation" in a presumed attempt to modify the level of possible difficulty in sociopragmatic comprehension (Ross, 1995). Kasper argues that there is a pattern of repeated questions in the OPI context, as demonstrated in this example. The analysis supports the value of repeated questions in facilitating the assessment of the interviewee's proficiency level through the OPI.

In a data-based study comparing conversational routines and verbal rituals in French and Syrian service encounters, Traverso (2006) explains the inherent connection between the two interactional practices: conversational routines are most often used to carry out ritual acts, and while the core features of rituals are their symbolic value, conversational routines possess functional or pragmatic value rather than symbolic value. Ritual acts, for example, comprise thanking, responses to thanking, well-wishing, willingness to help customers, acceptance of the item ("God bless you") (p. 116). These acts function to communicate pragmatic meanings in the commercial context and, at the same time, constituting "a prominent feature of Arabic interaction" (p. 106). Conversational routines, which typically occur in French encounters at the opening of the speech event of purchasing items in a service encounter, function as greetings, elicitation of requests for an item, and then the customer's request. Thus while a routine in French may be interpreted solely as a conversational routine with pragmatic meaning of thanking in this situated context, the routine of accepting an item for purchase in Arabic conveys additional meanings of closeness, familiarity, and deference, thus ritualized meanings. The possible mismatch due to the overlap may be invisible to interlocutors in the course of an intercultural interaction. Traverso investigates the conversational routines used in verbal ritual acts and differences in Syrian and French data, collected in France and Syria, regarding the overlap. The findings from her comparison of the two culturally bound enactments of a transactional speech event do not support any significant differences between the two languages. However, a difference was noticeable in the organization of the transactional structure of the routine. Traverso provides data excerpts to illustrate a request and an acceptance sequence with the ritual acts. In Syrian commercial transactions there are two cultural values of affectivity communicated through expressions of "closeness and familiarity" and of deference, typically used when addressing a superior (p.119). Receipt or acceptance of a requested item in a shop becomes a ritual act in Syrian Arabic:

> Thus, whereas in the French corpus acknowledging a request is not more than a practical matter, dealt with by a functional act, in the Syrian corpus it becomes the occasion for stating a certain type of relationship and for assuring the co-participants of one's good will.
>
> (Traverso, 2006, p. 120)

Clear evidence of enlarging the frame is the recognition that L2 pragmatics is more than speech acts. There is a movement away from an almost exclusive focus on speech acts, particularly apologies, requests, refusals, and compliments, and formulaic language to a much broader view of language in use. Some examples of other linguistic resources that involve pragmatic meanings are topic marking (Hendriks, 2000), negation strategies (Bernini, 2000), referent introduction and maintenance (Turco, 2008), self-qualification (Geyer, 2007), discourse markers (Pellet, 2006), modal particles (Belz & Vyatkina, 2005), definiteness (Sleeman, 2004), and text organization (Ferraris, 2001). Further, many of these studies delve into complexities in signaling pragmatic meaning beyond the more commonplace comparisons of a speech act in learners' L2 production and the native speaker enactment of the same speech act. Belz and Vyatkina (2005), for example, examined the success of pedagogical intervention regarding German modal particle use in the context of electronically mediated collaboration between learners and native speaker "keypals." The learners were trained to assess their own emerging progress in the authentic interactions that involve completing a foreign language learning project.

Addressing macro, sociolinguistic dimensions, it has been several decades since research on interactional discourse and L2 pragmatic meanings has shown its applications to many domains of modern life, particularly in efforts to document biases and discrimination in discourse related to sexism, racism, and other forms of inequality. Gumperz's (1982) contribution to interactional sociolinguistics in which natural interactions formed the basis of his conceptualization of contextualization cues have been followed up and further developed by researchers such as Roberts and Sarangi (see, for example, their 2007 work on assessing medical students' interactions with patients). Demonstrations of mismatches in interactional, specifically institutional, discourse due to interlocutors' diverging culturally influenced beliefs and expectations have been invaluable in illustrating the sources of miscommunication. However, Shea (1994) challenged the limited, in his view, perspective of interactional sociolinguistics, and bases his argument that racial prejudice must be acknowledged as a source of mismatches in native speaker–nonnative speaker interactions in his microanalysis of native English speaker and native Japanese speakers of English conversational data. Clearly, culturally specific contextualization cues as well as the culturally loaded interpretations of inferences cannot be regarded as apolitical. Recent research discussed below acknowledges the need to move beyond native speaker dominant frames of interpretation of intercultural and intergroup encounters.

Workplace environments in particular have drawn the attention of researchers, undoubtedly due to the seriousness of the consequences of workplace discord, and the fact that stakeholders can play a vital role in addressing intolerance due to interactional mismatches and underlying beliefs associated with racism, sexism, and discrimination of all sorts.

One example, a workplace study at a cable manufacturing plant near Silicon Valley in California, illustrates the effect of interactional differences in language use and practice within the United States. As described by Katz (2000), with over 90 percent of the workforce Spanish-speaking and over half women, the predominately white, European or American male managers established a workplace literacy program to address the perceived lack of skills deemed necessary to promote employer–employee harmony and to increase profitability. The deficit-oriented assumptions of the management were that the workers needed to improve their language proficiency in English and their workplace literacy behaviors and knowledge of, for example, how to behave on the job. Katz argues that while the reasons for the lack of the program's literacy success are complex, a deeper understanding of communication on the part of all participants was required, entailing the adoption of the concept of discourses, defined by Gee (1999, p. 42) as "ways of being in the world, or forms of life which integrate words, acts, values, beliefs, attitudes, social identities, as well as gestures, glances, body positions and clothes." Essentially, the workplace program was flawed due to management assuming that language use could be treated as comprised of neutral, generalizable skills, used irrespective of contextual variables. Further, the managers believed the attempt at social engineering would work despite acknowledged cultural differences between them and the workers. The particular intercultural practice identified in Katz's study concerned the managers' preference for "workers who speak their minds, step forward with new ideas and ways to solve problems (part of team discourse) and show what they know by sharing that knowledge with co-workers" (p. 152). This ideology of desirable employees, however, contrasted radically with the Mexican origins of the workers, especially given that many of them came from the same small communities in Michoacan and formed a close-knit community in the country of sojourn, the United States. Moreover, their cultural practices concerning gender, power/status, and group loyalty diverged from those of their employers: they were reluctant to speak up, preferring to remain quiet and discreet in the workplace. Indeed, a specific example of misunderstandings concerns the employees' quiet, even silent, demeanors, perceived by management as acts of independence and challenges to the "involvement" metaphor they valued. Not only were the managers irritated, as Katz reports, by the workers' silence, but they also interpreted the silences as increasing social distance and a form of "pulling rank" (p. 160). Clearly, the strategy of the employees to use silence created a mismatch with the expectations and assumptions of the management, who were following a presumed American interpretation of the pragmatic meaning of silence. Katz states: "Transformation, as far as managers were concerned, was the duty of workers" (p. 160).

Schnurr, Marra, and Holmes (2007) carry out case studies of two "ethnicised" communities of practice in New Zealand, specifically Pakeha and Māori workplaces. Pakehua, white New Zealanders of mostly British European descent, have ways of conducting meetings in workplaces that reflect their predominance in the country: 80 percent of the population currently is Pakehua, with only 14 percent Māori (www.stats.govt.nz, 2005). The meeting openings under Pakehua leadership that involve dispensing with initial formalities to save time tend to be viewed as displays of impoliteness by Māori participants. In addition, the use of humor in the context of potentially disruptive challenges by subordinates to one member's efforts to get confirmation on solving an issue were also regarded with discomfort by Māoris, due to cultural differences. In their study Schnurr et al. use corpus data from the Wellington Language in the Workplace Project to learn how leaders enact their professional and ethnic identities while respecting local norms regarding polite behavior in the two ethnically different workplaces, or communities of practice. They focus on instances of unintentional impoliteness or inappropriate behavior in the context of two aspects of the organizational leaders' talk: meeting openings and challenging humor. Their findings suggest that the potential for causing offense is present in the informal meeting style, in particular the directness of Pakeha leaders in negotiating disagreements or behavior viewed as unacceptable, especially with other people present. This study provided research data to support efforts by leaders in the New Zealand workplaces to move toward developing discursive strategies and practices that would avoid alienating one group while still facilitating achievement of institutional goals.

Non-English Target Languages

One area of impressive growth in applied linguistics and L2 pragmatics studies has been where the target language or language of interaction are languages other than English. As of publication in 2002, Kasper and Rose state that research on the teaching of pragmatics has focused by far most frequently on English as the target language, followed by Japanese and then French. This step to include more target languages is important in moving toward recognition of the diversity in communities all over the world, but it also provides valuable information on baseline data for comparisons of enactment of pragmatic meaning, and opens up the research agenda to include studies by nonnative speakers of English of their own languages and cultures. In some cases in the literature reviewed in this chapter, English may be the L1 of the learners or speakers of, for example, Japanese as the L2. However, there are also studies of L1 Arabic speakers learning French, or L1 French speakers studying Italian. Eckerth, Schramm and Tschirner (2009) state that "recent political changes" have motivated researchers of L1 German to move away from a focus on their own subject matter to broaden their contributions to SLA learning, teaching, and applied linguistics in general. This trend is certainly welcomed since it dovetails with ideological changes in applied linguistics that challenge the issues of ownership of English by native speakers and the prioritization of native-speaker-only interactional norms in favor of greater equity in areas of employment, admission to tertiary level education, and publishing opportunities. The following reviews three areas of applied linguistics research that evidence the broadening of pragmatics concerns.

Studies of other target languages derive from the ongoing concern for promoting more successful acquisition of the ability to interact in the L2. Ishihara (2007) discusses a Web-based curriculum for instruction in Japanese pragmatics that prioritizes awareness raising about appropriate pragmatic use, the explicit teaching of information about pragmatics, and then exercises including journaling. Pellet's (2006) dissertation on the French discourse markers *donc* and *alors* and their core functional values contributes to the pragmatic development of learners of French as a L2. Without explicitly presenting this type of information on functional core values to teachers, materials developers, and testers, learners are then at a loss as to how to improve their pragmatic ability. A similar contribution is made by Ding (2006) regarding the distributional features of Chinese yes/no questions by L1 and L2 Chinese speakers; and Ferraris's (2001) study of causal connectives in L1 and L2 Italian provides another example. The literature on L2 pragmatics has seen a noticeable increase in particular in research on L2 Spanish, both peninsular and Latin American. Additionally, there is an increasing body of studies on the L1 pragmatics of Italian, Korean, Portuguese, Russian, Indonesian, Arabic, Turkish, and Quechua, potentially of use by learners of those languages as well as by reaearchers for theory building.

As governments (see, for instance, Jackson & Malone, 2009), international organizations, and corporations become increasingly aware of the need for language and cultural expertise in the critical languages, particularly of the Middle East, Africa, and the Asian subcontinent, there has been a virtual explosion of interest in the languages and sociocultural beliefs and practices of those parts of the world. Kleifgen and Bond (2009) have edited a collection of papers on "The languages of Africa and the disapora" that demonstrate the linguistic diversity of Africa and the diaspora communities found in such disparate cities as Tokyo, the Queens borough of New York City, and Minneapolis, Minnesota. Kleifgen (2009) emphasizes characteristics of these communities that are often ignored and overlooked that impact on educational opportunities. It is a fact that the verbal repertoires of speakers of African languages are likely to be complex since many, if not most, come from plurilingual, hybrid urban environments in Africa where their ways of speaking have been influenced by "multiple languages, varieties and mixtures, along with registers, modes and styles associated with them" (p. 7). Privileging European languages and monolingualism, at most bilingualism, a remnant of colonialism, must be done away with, particularly when it comes to developing L2 pragmatic competence across multiple cultural boundaries and communicative practices.

L2 Pragmatic Transfer

Since time immemorial, human beings have been aware that when talking with someone of a background different from their own, there was a greater potential for misunderstandings than if the people came from the same local speech community. This realization tends to not be available cognitively in the face of mismatches of expectations regarding unexamined everyday behavior, such as in mixed-sex/gender conversations—as Tannen (1986) discussed in the early popularization of her scholarly work, or in multilingual/multicultural classrooms. Due to the ubiquitous nature of common glitches in interactional discourse, particularly when the language being used is not the primary language of one or more of the speakers, L2 pragmatics has generated a large literature on studies of transfer from other languages of speakers to the target language or language of communication in the situated context. L2 pragmatic transfer studies have attempted to describe different manifestations of the phenomenon from the individual word or formulaic routines to speech acts and realization strategies, to turn-taking practices, to information structuring in extended texts. Scholars have also examined the causes of transfer. For example, Takahashi and Beebe (1987) proposed the "positive correlation hypothesis." Drawing on their empirical study, they advanced the generalization that negative transfer of form and meaning is more likely to occur with higher proficiency learners because they have the L2 morphosyntactic resources to utilize their L1 communicative knowledge and practices in the L2. However, this hypothesis has been challenged by Kasper and Rose (2002), who strongly suggest that more sophisticated research is needed to explore the conditions of pragmatic transfer in tandem with L2 learners' developmental stages and proficiency levels in addition to the effect of the learning environment (i.e. ESL or EFL).

Despite a paucity of research on the interactional consequences of L2 pragmatic transfer in naturally occurring contexts (see Tatsuki & Houck, 2010), there is massive anecdotal evidence of hesitations, discomfort, and outright misunderstandings. The anecdotes are the stuff of travel stories told at parties or in airports while waiting for connecting or delayed flights. Comparing greetings (Did you sleep well? *Vous avez bien dormi?*) or different expressions to say "good night" (*Que duermes bien con los angelitos*) can be humorous and informative. However, the number of research studies with valuable information that provide data-based generalizations is increasing.

DuFon (1999, cited in Kasper & Rose, 2002, p. 150) explains that the use of information questions with greetings in Indonesia caused her study-abroad informants to experience resistance. Here are some examples:

Dari mana?	Where are you (coming) from?
Sudah makan?	Have you eaten yet?
Sudah Mandi?	Have you had your bath yet?

The L1 English participants in her study processed these greetings as questions for information, despite the face that a ubiquitous American English greeting also asks, "Hi, how are you?"

Omar (1991) found another type of greeting posed problems for American students of Kiswahili, an African language and the main lingua franca in east Africa. Elaborated greetings found in that language include questions concerning the addressee's family members and general state of health and business in the context of linguistic resources, such as a large amount of turn-taking, repetition, and back channel cues. The informants in Omar's study were uncomfortable with such elaborated greetings even when they had achieved higher levels of proficiency in the language, and were thus presumably able to use the linguistic resources of Kiswahili to enact such greetings. Nevertheless, despite pragmalinguistic competence in terms of linguistic ability for elaborated greetings, the learners lacked sociopragmatic awareness of the role of these speech act realization strategies played in the Kiswahili community. Anecdotal evidence suggests that elaborated greetings are common in African cultures; that they are enacted in other, even European, languages; and that successful intercultural communication with Africans requires participation in greeting sequences, just as carrying out business in East Asia—e.g., Japan, Korea, China—entails preliminary getting-to-know-you talk at restaurants.

L2 transfer at the level of extended written texts caused Kaplan (1966) to write a seminal work on the subject that resulted in the development of a whole new field of applied linguistics, originally labeled "cross-cultural rhetoric" and more recently reconstructed as "intercultural rhetoric" (Connor, Nagelhout, & Rozycki, 2008). Although Kaplan's work was controversial due to assumptions he was presumably making regarding cultural differences in the information structures of academic essays and the cognitive capacities of the different cultural groups, recognition of culturally-based rhetorical practices cannot be avoided. The field of intercultural rhetoric has continued to draw attention and provide research studies due to very obvious examples of L1 transfer into L2 written texts, particularly observable in academic essays and dissertations written by international students. Clearly, intercultural rhetoric studies are needed on written text creation of academic discourse in a wide variety of first or primary languages. However, due to the high percentage of scholarly papers and research studies being published in international English-language journals, the research focus continues to be on transfer into English written discourse and writing instruction for members of the academic community in order to learn the skills necessary to complete graduate programs, present papers, and publish in English.

LoCastro (2008) carried out an ethnographic study of the academic writing skills of Mexican Spanish university students that looked at the role of the sociocultural context on their rhetorical skills, specifically at the preparation the informants had received through the local educational system, textbooks, and other materials. She also reported on classroom observations, interviews with teachers, and questionnaire and interview data with students. Of particular relevance for this chapter is the evidence of transfer from Mexican Spanish rhetorical practices in which the stated rationale for the example presented below is to communicate pragmatic meaning, specifically politeness. Just as researchers such as Scollon and Wong Scollon (1995) and Meyers (1989) claim that rhetorical styles of Chinese and native English speakers, respectively, are motivated by politeness concerns for the reader's face, so the graduate student writer gave the same interpretation of his rhetorical practices:

Al comparar el método comunicativo y participativo de la enseñanza de la matemática con el método de enseñanza tradicional, se encontró que el primero fue mas eficiente sobre el segundo debido a que el método tradicional tiene una estructura rígida en su forma de enseñanza y en donde se hace énfasis en procedimientos rutinarios, formulas y demostraciones carentes de significado para los estudiantes, este tipo de procedimientos es para la mayoría de los estudiantes estériles, aburridos y carentes de sentido, fuera de contexto y del ámbito cultural de los estudiantes, además la impartición de la clase se realiza a través de monólogos par parte del maestro con lo que la parte interactiva de la enseñanza se pierde.

(LoCastro, 2008, p. 204)

[Comparing the communicative and participative method of teaching mathematics with the traditional method, one finds that the first one is more effective than the second, due to the traditional method having a rigid structure in its form of teaching and where emphasis is put on routine procedures, formulas, and demonstrations devoid of meaningfulness for the students. For the majority of the students this type of procedure is sterile, boring, and devoid of meaning, without context, and outside the cultural context of the students, in addition to the fact that the class is realized through monologues by the teacher where the interactive dimension of teaching is lost.][3]

This sentence-long paragraph in Spanish exemplifies several features such as run-on sentences; additive clauses, appended with only commas or semi-colons to join them; loose coordination with few explicit cohesive markers; an extended sequential linking of ideas; and no explicit expression of the author's voice or stance. These characteristics comprise the high variety or the written code in Mexican Spanish, called *la lengua culta* (cultured language). This style is highly valued, viewed as more "polite" and as a signal of higher intelligence on the part of the writer. When Mexican Spanish writers create texts in English, many of the same features are transferred. Here is a sentence paragraph from an undergraduate student's paper:

> Other point that I think it was important and that at the same time got my attention is that nowadays the way of solving conflicts has a become more sophisticated, and I think this is because the rules have change, what I'm trying to say it that they are evolutionating as the way conflicts are evolutionating, and the people want more and more, because they have been suffering for so long that now they want to get all back and they don't realized that the people in the other side have been through the same situation and no one want to hear the same story.
>
> (LoCastro, 2004, [n.p.])

This example, written by a student with high proficiency in spoken English, has few serious grammatical or lexical errors. Yet the long, one-sentence paragraph with additive clauses strung together breaks the norms of academic writing in American English.

Another instance of L2 pragmatics transfer involves the lack of response to a question in an adjacency pair, i.e. silence. Although not commonly addressed in L2 pragmatics per se, Miller (1982) and Lebra (1987), both noted scholars of Japanese cultural practices, considered the role of silence and the positive value attached to silence in oral communication in Japan. Silence is the topic of Tannen and Saville-Troike's (1985) edited collection of articles across cultures; in Saville-Troike's (1985) contribution she presented a taxonomy of functions of silences. Note, however, that these contributions to the literature were not based on empirical studies.

Silence is unquestionably a linguistic resource to signal pragmatic inferences in interactional contexts. Many stereotypes or myths surround the role of silence in L2 classroom environments where it is often assumed that Asian students have lower L2 proficiency levels, are unwilling to participate, and/or are disinterested in learning as it is defined from a Western teacher's perspective. The cultural differences in privileging speech in the West contrasts with the deprivileging of talk in classrooms in Japan. These differences have been researched and discussed in numerous studies, mostly through the assessment of the values and practices of Japanese learners and Western teachers.

Nakane (2006) and Ellwood and Nakane (2009) engaged in empirical studies of silence in university settings in Australia with Japanese and Australian participants. Nakane (2006) focused on the enactment of politeness with regard to the use of speech and silence; she carried out participant interviews, classroom observations, and discourse analyses of collected classroom data. The findings all pointed to the use of silence by the Japanese participants as a face-saving strategy for the speaker, whereas the Australian informants used speech to deal with face-threatening situations such as not knowing the answer to the questions posed by the teacher. Nakane notes that although silence would be an unmarked, off-record strategy in the Japanese educational system, other cultural contexts may perceive lack of response as "rude" or "impolite." University instructors in the United States, UK, and Australia may lower the final grades of students who do not participate in classroom discussions. Nakane states: "Japanese students' face-saving silences did not appear to be perceived as such by Australian lecturers, but rather as threatening to the lecturer's face" (2006, p. 1832).

Nakane's study has limitations; one weakness entails not addressing the tension that arises between the Japanese informants' desire to protect their face needs, presumably from having to show they could not respond or not respond correctly, especially in their L2, and the lecturer's face needs to have students reply to elicitations in an interactive classroom teaching format. The tension or negative reaction on the part of the lecturer is compounded by the need to do extra interactional classroom "work" to conduct the class and encourage the participation of the Japanese students.

In Ellwood and Nakane (2009) the researchers took a more critical perspective in their analysis of interview data, collected on Japanese and Australian perspectives of speech and silence, again in university environments. Ellwood and Nakane's research found evidence that supports earlier studies with one additional finding: Japanese students expressed the desire to become more articulate in classroom activities. LoCastro (1997; Netsu & LoCastro, 1997) had found that students at the Japanese university where she was teaching expressed great interest in learning to express their opinions more actively, a speech act/event they viewed as typical of Americans. Ellwood and Nakane (2009, p. 219) noted related concerns of their informants regarding

> a number of factors to explain their struggle to overcome their silences …: the preference for teacher-nomination, difficulty with precision timing in turn-taking, the need to reflect before speaking, a fear of making mistakes, and a fear of standing out from others.

The informants suggested teachers could change their classroom practices to facilitate their participation.

The perspectives of Ellwood and Nakane's participants reveal deep cultural practices, such as the belief that it is impolite or reveals a lack of modesty to express one's opinions in class, which have a strong influence on actual classroom behaviors and rationales for L1 transfer in L2 pragmatic contexts. Their informants claim that Japanese cultural explanations lead to stereotyped views of all Japanese students in classrooms. However, as SLA research has shown (see Kasper & Rose, 2002), this point only goes so far since transfer from learners' primary language culture, whether it is pragmalinguistic forms or sociopragmatic dimensions of behavior, is ubiquitous and not easily overcome without awareness of and attention to the non-target instances (Schmidt, 1995) that may result in less than successful interactions across cultures. Furthermore, Ellwood and Nakane neglect to discuss one major issue: classroom environments cannot be separated from the sociocultural contexts in which they are embedded. In my view, research clearly needs to explore: (1) Westerners' levels of participation in educational contexts in which they are expected to use a second language; and (2) non-educational environments in Japan where status and age differences are less salient than observed in the ubiquitous hierarchy that predominates in classrooms throughout the world. The role of speech and silence in any sociocultural environment is complex.

The value of L2 pragmatics transfer research is twofold. First, with regard to academic writing skills, a non-deficit, critical perspective enables educators in particular to use informed teaching practices so that international students can develop their multilingual literacy skills and increase their cultural/symbolic capital. Research shows that L2 learners present degrees of resistance (LoCastro, 2000, 2001; Nakane, 2006; Ellwood & Nakane, 2009) to adoption of L2 pragmatic norms, seeking rather to establish L2 identities compatible with their own individual needs and aspirations. Second, awareness of L2 transfer in the use of linguistic resources and cultural, strategic, and discourse competencies enable service providers in communities with high migrant/immigrant populations to take on different communication styles in critical areas such as health literacy (Connor & Lopez-Yuñez, 2009), education, and financial literacy training.

In sum, beyond amusing anecdotes, L2 pragmatic transfer, which is ubiquitous and not easily examined, constitutes a serious area of research entailing real-world consequences. Raising awareness of the effects, such as stereotyping and discrimination against minority group members, is necessary before behaviors can be changed, and greater tolerance promoted and put into practice. L2 pragmatic transfer is thus a pervasive feature of intercultural communication. The ideal goals, given the diversity in the contemporary world, are awareness, understanding, and strategies to handle the differences, without blame attributed to any one cultural group.

Conclusion

This chapter has reviewed eight areas within applied linguistics that are providing major contributions to our knowledge of L2 pragmatics, whether the individuals or groups are in the process of learning a new language or are users of more than one language on an everyday basis in governments, businesses, or institutions throughout the world. All of these areas are likely to have greater influence on the development of the field and its role in L2 teaching, materials creation, assessment, and training programs locally, nationally, and internationally.

Notes

1. Italic indicates (a) stressed word(s).
2. COLAm: El Corpus de Lenguaje Adolescente de Madrid; COLT: The Bergen Corpus of London Teenage Language; COR92: El Corpus Oral de Referencía del Español; and BNC: The British National Corpus (Stenstrom, 2006, p. 155).
3. The author provides the functionally equivalent translation.

References

Aarts, J. (2002). Does corpus linguistics? Some old and new issues. In L. E. Brevik & A. Hasselgren (Eds.), *From the COLT's mouth … and others: Language studies in honor of Anna-Brita Stenstrom* (pp. 1–17). Amsterdam/New York: Rodopi.

Aijmer, K., & Simon-Vandenbergen, A. M. (Eds.) (2006). *Pragmatic markers in contrast.* Amsterdam: Elsevier.

Atkinson, D., Churchill, E., Nishino, T., & Okada, H. (2007). Alignment and interaction in a sociocognitive approach to second language acquisition. *The Modern Language Journal, 91*(ii), 171–188.

Austin, J. L. (1962). *How to do things with words* (2nd ed.). Cambridge, MA: Harvard University Press.

Bardovi-Harlig, L. (1999). Exploring the interlanguage of interlanguage pragmatics: A research agenda for acquisitional pragmatics. *Language Learning, 49*, 677–713.

Belz, J. A., & Vyatkina, N. (2005). Learner corpus analysis and the development of L2 pragmatic competence in networked intercultural language study: The case of German modal particles. *The Canadian Modern Language Review/La Revue canadienne des langues vivantes, 62*(1), 17–48.

Bernini, G. (2000). Negative items and negation strategies in nonnative Italian. *Studies in Second Language Acquisition, 22*(3), 399–440.

Blum-Kulka, S., House, J., & Kasper, G. (Eds.) (1989). *Cross-cultural pragmatics: Requests and apologies.* Norwood, NJ: Ablex.

Bourdieu, P. (1990). *The logic of practice.* Cambridge: Polity Press.

Brevik, L. E., & Hasselgren, A. (Eds.) (2002). *From the COLT's mouth … and others: Language studies in honor of Anna-Brita Stenstrom.* Amsterdam/New York: Rodopi.

Brown, P., & Levinson, S. (1987). *Politeness: Some universals in language usage.* Cambridge: Cambridge University Press.

Clark, L. (2008). Re-examining vocalic variation in Scottish English: a cognitive grammar approach. *Language, Variation and Change, 20*, 255–273.

Collier, S. (2008). Voices of power: Immigrant women's use of language in entrepreneurial contexts. *Dissertation Abstracts International A: The Humanities and Social Sciences, 68*(12), 4952.

Connor, U., & Lopez-Yuñez, A. (2009). Intercultural negotiation and health literacy. Paper presented at the American Association for Applied Linguistics Conferences, Washington, DC, March 29–April 1.

Connor, U., Nagelhout, E., & Rozycki, W. V. (Eds.) (2008). *Contrastive rhetoric: Reaching to intercultural rhetoric.* Amsterdam/Philadelphia: John Benjamins.

Ding, X. (2006). The distributional features and developing of Chinese yes-no questions used by elementary and intermediate foreign learners. *Shijie Hanyu Jiaoxue/Chinese Teaching in the World, 3*(July), 103–112.

DuFon, M. A. (1999). The acquisition of linguistic politeness in Indonesian as a second language by sojourners in a naturalistic context. Doctoral dissertation, University of Hawaii. Dissertation Abstracts International, 60, 3985.

Eckerth, J., Schramm, K., & Tschirner, E. (2009) Review of recent research (2002–2008) on applied linguistics and language teaching with specific reference to L2 German (part 1). *Language Teaching, 42*(1), 41–66.

Ellis, N. C., & Robinson, P. (2008). An introduction of cognitive linguistics, second language acquisition, and language instruction. In P. Robinson & N. C. Ellis (Eds.), *Handbook of cognitive linguistics and second language acquisition* (pp. 3–24). New York: Routledge.

Ellwood, C., & Nakane, I. (2009). Privileging of speech in EAP and mainstream university classrooms: A critical evaluation of participation. *TESOL Quarterly, 43*(2), 203–230.

Eroz, B. (2003). An ethnographic examination of international students in English composition classes: Cultural patterns, classroom dynamics, and adjustment difficulties. Unpublished doctoral dissertation. Tucson, AZ: University of Arizona.

Ferraris, S. (2001). Text organization in Italian L2 learner variation. *EUROSLA Yearbook 1*, 225–237.

Firth, A., & Wagner, J. (1997). On discourse, communication, and (some) fundamental concepts in SLA research. *The Modern Language Journal, 81*, 285–300. (Republished in *The Modern Language Journal, 91*, 2007, 757–772.)

Gee. J. P. (1999). *Social linguistics and literacies: Ideology in discourses*. London: Falmer.

Geyer, N. (2007). Self-qualification in L2 Japanese: An interface of pragmatic, grammatical, and discourse competencies. *Language Learning, 57*(3), 337–367.

Goffman, E. (1967). *Interaction ritual: Essays on face-to-face behavior*. Garden City, NY: Anchor Books.

Goffman, E. (1981). *Forms of talk*. Oxford: Blackwell.

Gonzalez-Marquez, M., Mittelberg, I., Coulson, S., & Spivey, M. J. (Eds.) (2007). *Methods in cognitive linguistics*. Amsterdam/Philadelphia: John Benjamins.

Gumperz, J. J. (1982). *Discourse strategies*. Cambridge: Cambridge University Press.

Gurel, A. (2006). L2 acquisition of pragmatic and syntactic constraints in the use of overt and null subject pronouns. In R. Slabakova, S. A. Montrul, & P. Prevost (Eds.), *Inquires in linguistic development: In honor of Lydia White* (pp. 259–282). Amsterdam: John Benjamins.

Hasund, I. K. (2002). Congratulations, like!—*Gradulerer, liksom!* Pragmatic particles in English and Norwegian. In L. E. Brevik & A. Hasselgren (Eds.), *From the COLT's mouth … and others: Language studies in honor of Anna-Brita Stenstrom* (pp. 125–140). Amsterdam/New York: Rodopi.

Hendriks, H. (2000). The acquisition of topic marking in L1 Chinese and L1 and L2 French. *Studies in Second Language Acquisition, 22*(3), 369–397.

Hobenstein, C. (2005). Interactional expectations and linguistic knowledge in academic expert discourse (Japanese/German). *International Journal of the Sociology of Language, 175–176*, 285–306.

Houck, N., & Fujii, S. (2006). Delay as an interactional response in native speaker–nonnative speaker academic interaction. In K. Bardovi-Harlig, C. Felix-Brasdefer, & A. S. Omar (Eds.), *Pragmatics and language learning, 11*, (pp. 29–54). Manoa, HI: National Foreign Language Resource Center, University of Hawaii at Manoa.

Hyland, K. (2002). Authority and invisibility: Authorial identity in academic writing. *Journal of Pragmatics, 34*(8), 1091–1112.

Hymes, D. (1972). On communicative competence. In J. Pride & J. Holmes (Eds.), *Sociolinguistics: Selected readings* (pp. 269–293). Harmondsworth: Penguin.

Ishida, M. (2006). Interactional competence and the use of modal expressions in decision-making activities. In K. Bardovi-Harlig, C. Felix-Brasdefer, & A. S. Omar (Eds.), *Pragmatics and language learning, 11*, (pp. 55–79). Honolulu, HI: National Foreign Language Research Center/University of Hawaii at Manoa.

Ishihara, N. (2007). Web-based curriculum for pragmatics instruction in Japanese as a foreign language: an explicit awareness-raising approach. *Language Awareness, 16*(1), 21–40.

Jackson, F. H., & Malone, M. E. (2009). Building the foreign language capacity we need: Toward a comprehensive strategy for a national language framework. CAL News, June 9, 2009, http://www.cal.org/about/calnews/archive/060909, PDF: http://www.cal.org/resources/languageframework.pdf.

Johansson, S. (2006). How well can *well* be translated? On the English discourse particle *well* and its correspondences in Norwegian and German. In K. Aijmer & A. M. Simon-Vandenbergen (Eds.), *Pragmatic markers in contrast* (pp. 115–138). Amsterdam: Elsevier.

Kaplan, R. B. (1966). Cultural thought patterns in intercultural education. *Language Learning, 16*(1), 1–20.

Kasper, G. (2004). Speech acts in (inter)action: Repeated questions. *Intercultural Pragmatics, 1*(1), 125–133.

Kasper, G. (2006a) Introduction. *Multilinga, 25*, 243–248.

Kasper, G. (2006b). When once is not enough: Politeness of multiple requests in oral proficiency interviews. *Multilingua, 25*, 323–350.

Kasper, G., & Rose, K. R. (2002). *Pragmatic development in a second language*. Oxford: Blackwell.

Katz, M. L. (2000). Workplace language teaching and the intercultural construction of ideologies of competence. *Canadian Modern Language Review, 57*(1), 144–172.

Kleifgen, J. A. (2009). Discourses of linguistic exceptionalism and linguistic diversity in education. In J. A.Kleifgen & G. C. Bond (Eds.), *The languages of Africa and the diaspora: Educating for language awareness* (pp. 1–21). Bristol: Multilingual Matters.

Kleifgen, J. A., & Bond, G. C. (Eds.) (2009). *The languages of Africa and the diaspora: Educating for language awareness*. Bristol: Multilingual Matters.

de Klerk, V. (2005). Procedural meanings in "well" in a corpus of *Xhosa* English. *Journal of Pragmatics, 38*(8), 1183–1205.

Larsen-Freeman, D. (1997). Chaos/complexity science and second language acquisition. *Applied Linguistics, 18*(2), 141–165.

Larsen-Freeman, D. (2007). Reflecting on the cognitive-social debate in second language acquisition. *The Modern Language Journal, 91*, 773–787.

Lazaraton, A. (2002). Quantitiative and qualitative approaches to discourse analysis. In M. McGroarty (Ed.), *Annual review of applied linguistics 22: Discourse and dialogue* (pp. 32–51). Cambridge: Cambridge University Press.

Lebra, T. S. (1987). The cultural significance of silence in Japanese communication. *Multilingua*, 6(4), 343–357.

Leech, G. (1983). *Principles of pragmatics*. London: Longman.

LoCastro, V. (1987). Aizuchi: A Japanese conversational routine. In L. E. Smith (Ed.), *Discourse across cultures: Strategies in world English* (pp. 101–113). New York: Prentice Hall.

LoCastro, V. (1997). Pedagogical intervention and pragmatic competence development. *Applied Language Learning*, 8(1), 75–109.

LoCastro, V. (2000). Evidence of accommodation to L2 pragmatic norms in peer review tasks of Japanese learners of English. *JALT Journal*, 22(2), 245–270.

LoCastro, V. (2001). Individual differences in second language acquisition: Attitudes, learner subjectivity, and L2 pragmatic norms. *System*, 29, 69–89.

LoCastro, V. (2004). Situated practices of Mexican learners' academic writing. Paper presented at TESOL 2004 Conference, Long Beach, CA, March 31–April 4.

LoCastro, V. (2007). Politeness in ITA/student discourse. Paper presented at the 17th International Conference on Pragmatics and Language Learning, University of Hawaii, March 26–28.

LoCastro, V. (2008). "Long sentences and floating commas": Mexican students' rhetorical practices and the sociocultural context. In U. Connor, E. Nagelhout, & W. V. Rozycki (Eds.), *Contrastive rhetoric: Reaching to intercultural rhetoric* (pp. 195–218). Amsterdam/Philadelphia: John Benjamins.

Locher, M. (2004). *Power and politeness in action: Disagreements in oral communication*. Berlin/New York: Mouton de Gruyter.

Locher, M. C., & Watts, R. J. (2005). Politeness theory and relational work. *Journal of Politeness Research*, 1, 9–33.

McCarthy, M. (1998). *Spoken language and applied linguistics*. Cambridge: Cambridge University Press.

McHoul, A. (2008). Questions of context in studies of talk and interaction–Ethnomethodology and conversation analysis. *Journal of Pragmatics*, 40, 823–826.

Meyers, G. (1989). The pragmatics of politeness in scientific articles. *Applied Linguistics*, 10(1), 1–35.

Miller, R. (1982). *Japan's modern myth: The language and beyond*. New York: Weatherhill.

Mittelberg, I., Farmer, T. A., & Waugh, L. R. (2007). They actually said that? An introduction to working with usage data through discourse and corpus analysis. In M. Gonzalez-Marquez, I. Mittelberg, S. Coulson, & M. J. Spivey (Eds.), *Methods in cognitive linguistics* (pp. 19–52). Amsterdam/Philadelphia: John Benjamins.

Moerman, M. (1988). *Talking cultures: Ethnography and conversation analysis*. Philadelphia, PA: University of Philadelphia Press.

Moeschler, J. (2004). Intercultural pragmatics: a cognitive approach. *Intercultural Pragmatics*, 1(1), 49–70.

Montrul, S., & Rodriguez-Louro, C. (2006). Beyond the syntax of the null subject parameter: A look at the discourse-pragmatic distribution of null and overt subjects by L2 learners of Spanish. In V. Torrens & L. Escobar (Eds.), *The acquisition of syntax in romance languages* (pp. 401–418). Amsterdams: John Benjamins.

Nakane, I. (2006). Silence and politeness in intercultural communication in university seminars. *Journal of Pragmatics*, 38, 1811–1835.

Netsu, M., & LoCastro, V. (1997). Point of view and opinion-giving in discussion tasks. In T. Fujimura, Y. Kato, M. Ahmed, & D. Fujimoto (Eds.), *Proceedings of the 8th Conference on Second Language Acquisition in Japan* 8 (pp. 136–153). Niigata: International University of Japan.

Nelson, G., Wallis, S., & Aarts, B. (2002). *Exploring natural language: Working with the British component of the International Corpus of English*. Amsterdam: John Benjamins.

Nguyen, T. T. M. (2008). Modifying L2 criticism: How learners do it? *Journal of Pragmatics*, 40(4), 768–791.

Ochs, E. (1988). *Culture and language development: Language acquisition and language socialization in a Samoan village*. Cambridge: Cambridge University Press.

Olsher, D. (2004). Collaborative group work in second and foreign language classrooms: Talk, embodiment, and sequential organization. *Dissertation Abstracts International A: The Humanities and Social Sciences*, 64(11), May, 4031-A-4032-A.

Omar, A. (1991). How learners greet in Kiswahili: A cross sectional survey. In L. F. Bouton & Y. Kachru (Eds.), *Pragmatics and language learning* (Vol. 2) (pp. 59–73). Urbana-Champaign, IL: Division of English as an International Language, University of Illinois.

Pellet, S. H. (2006). The development of competence in French interlanguage pragmatics: The case of the discourse marker *donc*. *Dissertation Abstracts International A: The Humanities and Social Sciences*, 67(04), 1315.

Pomerantz, A. (1984). Agreeing and disagreeing with assessments: Some features of preferred/dispreferred turn shapes. In J. M. Atkinson & J. Heritage (Eds.), *Structures of social action: Studies in conversation analysis* (pp. 57–101). Cambridge: Cambridge University Press.

Pragmatics (2008). (Im)politeness in Spanish-speaking socio-cultural contexts. Special issue of *Pragmatics*, 18(4), December, International Pragmatics Association.

Ramirez-Verdugo, D. (2006). Prosodic realization of focus in the discourse of Spanish learners and English native speakers. *Estudios Ingleses de la Universidad Complutense*, 14, 9–32.

Ramirez-Verdugo, D., & Romero Trillo, J. (2005). The pragmatic function of intonation in L2 discourse: English tag questions used by Spanish speakers. *Intercultural Pragmatics, 2*(2), 151–168.

Roberts, C., & Sarangi, S. (2007). Mapping and assessing medical students' interactional involvement styles with patients. In K. Spellman Miller & P. Thompson (Eds.), *Unity and diversity in language use* (pp. 99–117). London: Continuum.

Romero Trillo, J., & Llinares-Garcia, A. (2004). Prosodic competence in reading aloud: An acoustic corpus-based study of native and nonnative (Spanish) speakers of English. *Estudios Ingleses de la Universidad Complutense, 12*, 63–77.

Ross, S. (1995). Aspects of communicative accommodation in oral proficiency interview discourse. Unpublished Ph.D. dissertation, University of Hawaii at Manoa.

Rothman, J. (2008). How pragmatically odd! Interface delays and pronominal subject distribution in L2 Spanish. *Studies in Hispanic and Lusophone Linguistics, 1*(2), 317–339.

Rothman, J. (2009). Pragmatic deficits with syntactic consequences?: L2 pronominal subjects and the syntax-pragmatic interface. *Journal of Pragmatics, 41*(5), 951–973.

Sacks, O. (2008). *Musicophilia: Tales of music and the brain.* New York: Vintage Books.

Saville-Troike, M. (1985). The place of silence in an integrated theory of communication. In D. Tannen & M. Saville-Troike (Eds.), *Perspectives on silence* (pp. 3–18). Norwood, NJ: Ablex.

Schegloff, E. A. (1996). Turn organization: One intersection of grammar and interaction. In E. Ochs, E. A. Schegloff, & S. Thompson (Eds.), *Interaction and Grammar* (pp. 52–133). Cambridge: Cambridge University Press.

Schegloff, E. A., Ochs, E., & Thompson, E. (1996). Introduction. In E. Ochs, E. A. Schegloff, & S. Thompson (Eds.), *Interaction and Grammar* (pp. 1–51). Cambridge: Cambridge University Press.

Schmidt, R. (1995). Consciousness and foreign language learning: A tutorial on the role of attention and awareness in learning. In R. Schmidt (Ed.), *Attention and awareness in foreign language learning* (pp. 1–63). Honolulu: University of Hawaii, Second Language Teaching & Curriculum Center.

Schnurr, S., Marra, M., & Holmes, J. (2007). Being (im)polite in New Zealand workplaces: Māori and Pakehua leaders. *Journal of Pragmatics, 39*, 712–729.

Scollon, R., & Wong Scollon, S. (1995). *Intercultural communication.* Oxford: Blackwell.

Searle, J. R. (1969). *Speech acts: An essay in the philosophy of language.* Cambridge: Cambridge University Press.

Shea, D. P. (1994). Perspective and production: Structuring conversational participation across cultural borders. *Pragmatics, 4*(3), 357–389.

Shimura, M. (2005). *Please* in DCT complaint corpus and MICASE. *ICU Language Research Bulletin, 20*, 63–74.

Sleeman, P. (2004). The acquisition of definiteness distinctions by L2 learners of French. *Linguistics in the Netherlands, 21*, 158–168.

Sperber, D., & Wilson, D. (1986) *Relevance: Communication and cognition.* Oxford: Blackwell.

Sroda, M. S. (2000). Relevance theory and the markedness model of SLA: Cognitive approaches to pragmatics and second language acquisition. *Dissertation Abstracts International, A: The Humanities and Social Sciences, 61*(4), 1382-A.

Stenstrom, A. B. (2006). The Spanish discourse markers *o sea* and *pues* and their English correspondences. In K. Aijmer & A. M. Simon-Vandenbergen (Eds.), *Pragmatic markers in contrast* (pp. 155–172). Amsterdam: Elsevier.

Taguchi, N. (2008a). Cognition, language contact, and the development of pragmatic comprehension in a study-abroad context. *Language Learning, 58*(1), 33–71.

Taguchi, N. (2008b). The effect of working memory, semantic access, and listening abilities on the comprehension of conversational implicatures in L2 English. *Pragmatics & Cognition, 16*(3), 517–539.

Takahashi, T., & Beebe, L. (1987). The development of pragmatic competence by Japanese learners of English. *JALT Journal, 8*, 131–155.

Tannen, D. (1986). *That's not what I meant! How conversational style makes or breaks relationships.* New York: Ballantine Books.

Tannen, D., & Saville-Troike, M. (Eds.) (1985). *Perspectives on silence.* Norwood, NJ: Ablex.

Tatsuki, D., & Houck, N. (Eds.) (2010) Pragmatics: Teaching speech acts. Washington, DC: TESOL Publications.

Traverso, V. (2006). Aspects of polite behavior in French and Syrian service encounters: A data-based comparative study. *Journal of Politeness Research, 2*, 105–122.

Turco, G. (2008). Introduction and identification of a referent by French speaking learners of Italian L2. *AILE: Acquisition et Interaction en Langue Etrangere, 26*, (n.p.).

Vickers, C. (2004). Interactional accommodation and the construction of social roles among cultural diverse undergraduates. Unpublished doctoral dissertation, Tucson, AZ: University of Arizona.

Vygotsky, L. S. (1978). *Mind in society: The development of higher psychological process.* Cambridge, MA: Harvard University Press.

Walters, F. S. (2007). A conversation-analytic hermeneutic rating protocol to assess L2 oral pragmatic competence. *Language Testing, 24*(2), 155–183.

Watts, R. J. (2003). *Politeness.* Cambridge: Cambridge University Press.

Waugh, L. R., Fonseca-Gerger, B., Vickers, C., & Eroz, B. (2007). Multiple empirical approaches to a complex analysis of discourse. In M. Gonzalez-Marquez, I. Mittelberg, S. Coulson, & M. J. Spivey (Eds.), *Methods in cognitive linguistics* (pp. 120–148). Amsterdam/Philadelphia: John Benjamins.

Wichmann, A. (2000). *Intonation in text and discourse: Beginnings, middles and endings.* Harlow: Longman.

Wichmann, A. (2004). The intonation of *Please*-requests: A corpus-based study. *Journal of Pragmatics, 36*, 1521–1549.

21

Conversation Analytic Research into Language Teaching and Learning

Paul Seedhouse

Introduction

This article provides an overview of recent conversation analytic research in the area of language learning and teaching. Conversation analysis (CA) is a methodology for the analysis of naturally-occurring spoken interaction. It is a multi-disciplinary methodology that is now applied in a very wide range of professional and academic areas. CA research into language learning and teaching can be viewed as a subset of CA research into institutional talk, in which the organisation of the interaction is related to the institutional goal. Applications of CA reviewed here are closely associated with the concerns of applied linguistics. The research is also a subset of second language acquisition (SLA) research, one which is firmly located in the socio-cultural school of SLA. There are synergies with education, particularly in relation to assessment and teacher training and the study of learning processes, as well as with sociology, where CA originated. The main argument is that CA research in the area of language learning and teaching has grown exponentially over the last fifteen years. It has developed many useful applications and is used to uncover learning processes and to reconceptualise established constructs.

Space precludes a full account of CA methodology here, but these are available in ten Have (1999); Hutchby and Wooffitt (1998) and Seedhouse (2004). At the start I should make clear that there is a fundamental difference between the "CA mentality" and the "linguistic mentality" in relation to the status of language. CA's primary interest is in the social act, whereas a linguist's primary interest in normally in language. CA therefore does not treat language as an autonomous system independent of its use; rather, it treats "grammar and lexical choices as sets of resources which participants deploy, monitor, interpret and manipulate" (Schegloff, Koshik, Jacoby & Olsher, 2002, p. 15) in order to perform their social acts. According to Seedhouse (2004), one way of presenting the principles of CA is in relation to the questions that it asks. The essential question that must be asked at all stages of CA analysis of data is "Why that, in that way, right now?" This encapsulates the perspective of interaction as action (why that) that is expressed by means of linguistic forms (in that way) in a developing sequence (right now).

Applied linguistics, by definition, has always focused on applications. CA, by contrast, has only relatively recently begun to develop an applied dimension (Heritage, 1999; Richards & Seedhouse, 2005; ten Have, 1999). In his review of CA at century's end, Heritage argued that "[p]art of the claim of any framework worth its salt is that it can sustain 'applied' research of various kinds" (Heritage, 1999, p. 73). He indicated that this aspect might feature prominently in developments within the discipline, but warned that the concept of application is by no means straightforward. According to Richards (2005), the model of application that is most consistent with the nature of CA is that of description leading to informed action. Some of the studies cited below (Packett, 2005; Wong, 2005) exemplify the use of this model. The development of an applied dimension in CA and its fundamental concern with language as a form of social action suggest a natural link with applied linguistics. There is currently growing interest within the field of applied linguistics in CA methodology. This is evidenced by a growing number of publications in applied linguistics journals that use a CA methodology. Schegloff et al. (2002, p. 14) noted that "[a] small but increasing amount of CA and CA-informed research on talk in educational institutions directly addresses issues of interest to applied linguists". By 2009 it would be correct to say that CA and CA-informed studies are now commonly found in applied linguistics journals and have become much more of a mainstream phenomenon.

The study considers the latest CA and CA-informed research in the following areas: teaching languages for specific purposes; language proficiency assessment; competence; teacher training and development; language classroom interaction; teaching and learning activities; language teaching materials design; identity; non-native speaker (NNS) talk outside the classroom; and bilingual and multilingual code-switching. I consider how CA has been used for methodological critiques, to study learning processes and socially distributed cognition and I discuss issues of data presentation. A common theme in the research is that competence is co-constructed by the participants rather than being fixed and static. I conclude by considering possible future directions for research.

Teaching Languages for Specific Purposes (LSP and ESP)

The area of languages for specific purposes (LSP) can be informed by CA research on institutional or professional discourse. As Jacoby (1998, p. 1) points out, LSP teachers have to prepare students to carry out spoken professional communication in a second language (L2). However, the problem is that the LSP teacher sometimes has little idea of the type of spoken interaction that takes place in the target professional setting and the teaching coursebook often "doesn't reflect the communication reality in which (the students) actually have to function" (p. 1). If, then the teacher wishes to provide students with a curriculum based on the real-world target professional communication norms, practices, and its own discourse "culture", then s/he may need to research the professional setting. A fundamental aim in applying CA to the field of LSP is to attempt to describe and analyse spoken interaction in the target situation.

Bowles and Seedhouse's (2007a) collection proposes a theoretical and methodological framework for applying CA to LSP and includes several examples of practical applications. Seedhouse and Richards (2007) provide a framework for conceptualising the relationship between an instance of professional interaction and the institutional variety of interaction as a whole, i.e. how one can generalise from the particular. When LSP researchers collect data, they may employ the concepts of variety, sub-variety and micro-contexts. Any instance collected needs to be characterised as (1) belonging to a particular variety of institutional discourse that has particular characteristics, (2) belonging to a particular sub-variety of institutional discourse that has distinctive characteristics, and (3) a unique instance. By relating instances to varieties and sub-varieties in this way, researchers can build up a description of the characteristics of interaction in the institutional variety as a whole and in its sub-varieties. Bowles and Seedhouse (2007b) suggest a set of procedures for examining the data that comes out of the target speech community. This covers single case analysis, characterising the institutional nature of the interaction, key moves, conceptualising the relationship between the individual instance of interaction, the institutional sub-variety of interaction and the institutional variety of interaction of the extract. Bowles and Seedhouse then turn to the way in which the analysed data can be employed in the LSP classroom, including noticing the specific features and practices of talk and by comparing particular speech performances.

CA methodology has spawned studies in a wide variety of professional settings, as evidenced in collections such as Drew and Heritage (1992) and Richards and Seedhouse (2005). Settings covered by CA studies include legal hearings, news interviews, visits by health visitors, phone calls to emergency services and help lines, psychiatric interviews, airplane cockpit talk, mediation and counselling. In some professional settings, then, there is already a body of CA research that can be exploited by LSP teachers, health care being the most prominent. CA can also identify sequence organisations that may be vital to the institutional business and that may need to be understood or learnt by novices as part of their induction. An example of a concrete and direct application of CA findings to the English for specific purposes (ESP) classroom is provided by Packett (2005), who identifies an "insertion action" used by radio interviewers. Expert data and the learner data were then used by Packett as classroom materials to demonstrate to students the use of the device in interaction. Packett's paper serves as a model not only for CA-informed pedagogy, but also for CA research in LSP with the aim of linking sequences to the institutional goal. Future CA research in this area would seek to identify such institution-specific interactional patterns and employ them in teaching. Packett (2007) develops the concept of CA-informed pedagogy in LSP. He shows how CA can be used for raising the awareness of students of the specific features of broadcasting interviewing. Problems displayed by students in achieving the required footing are diagnosed. Formulations are identified as a means used by professionals to overcome such problems and these were taught to students as an intervention. Walsh and O'Keeffe (2007) also consider how CA and corpus linguistics can be combined for the purposes of LSP.

Language Proficiency Assessment

Language proficiency assessment is probably the area in which CA has had the greatest impact on practice so far, particularly in relation to the construct of competence. Previous CA-informed work in the area of oral proficiency interviews area by Young and He (1998) and Lazaraton (1997) examined language proficiency interviews (LPIs). Egbert points out that many "LPIs are implemented in imitation of natural conversation in order to evaluate a learner's conversational proficiency" (Egbert, 1998, p. 147). Young and He's collection demonstrates, however, a number of clear differences between LPIs and ordinary conversation. First, the systems of turn-taking and repair differ from ordinary conversation. Second, LPIs are examples of goal-oriented institutional discourse, in contrast to ordinary conversation. Third, LPIs constitute cross-cultural communication in which the participants may have very different understandings of the nature and purpose of the interaction. Egbert's (1998) study demonstrates that interviewers explain to students not only the organisation of repair they should use, but also the forms they should use to do so; the suggested forms are cumbersome and differ from those found in ordinary conversation. He's (1998) microanalysis reveals how a student's failure in an LPI is due to interactional as well as linguistic problems. Kasper and Ross (2001, p. 10) point out that their analysis of LPIs portrays candidates as "eminently skilful interlocutors", which contrasts with the general SLA view that clarification and confirmation checks are indices of NNS incompetence, whilst their 2003 paper analyses how repetition can be a source of miscommunication in LPIs. In the context of course placement interviews, Lazaraton (1997) notes that students initiated a particular sequence, namely self-deprecations of their English language ability. She further suggests that a student demonstration of or statement about poor English language ability constitutes grounds for acceptance onto courses. Interactional sequences are therefore linked to participant orientations and goals.

CA can be employed to monitor the reliability and validity of assessment. Lazaraton (2002) presents a book-length framework for the application of CA to the validation of LPIs. Her rationale is that CA is able to shed light on the assessment process itself; this can complement the use of traditional statistical methods of test validation which focus on product, i.e. scores. Brown (2003) analyses two LPIs involving the same candidate taking the same test with two different interviewers. The two interviewers were shown to ask different types of questions, provide different types of feedback and to structure sequences of topical talk in different ways. The candidate's communicative ability in the two interviews was rated differently by four raters. The study emphasises the need for interviewer training and standardisation of practices and critiques the robustness of the concept of communicative competence. Ross (2007) reports a case of the same candidate receiving a lower rating three months after the first test and relates this to the different interactional strategies employed by the different examiners. In relation to testing in ESP, Jacoby and McNamara (1999, p. 213) critique the "primarily linguistic orientation of traditional assessment procedures". They show that CA is able to locate what counts as communicative competence in specific professional contexts. CA research can clarify the advantages and disadvantages of assessment formats and inform the design of assessment tasks (Schegloff et al., 2002).

Kasper and Ross (2007) reveal the role of multiple questions by examiners in LPIs. They identify reactive repeated questions (in response to trouble) and proactive repetitions (in fragile environments). They demonstrate that an examiner's decision to employ, or not employ, repeated questions can influence candidate performance. Kasper (2006a) shows that examiners use multiple questions to mark topic change, facilitating the candidate's understanding of the question. Often the first question is formatted as an indirect request with a politeness marker, whilst the second question is more direct and unmitigated. Seedhouse and Egbert (2006) identify instances in which scripted LPI questions for examiners generate trouble, topic disjunction and poor recipient design. They identify instances in the data in which some examiners have used their initiative to modify the scripted questions in order to maintain topic flow and create good recipient design. This has implications for test design and examiner training. Walters (2007) reports on the development of a CA-based rating protocol for L2 pragmatics testing. Many of the CA studies of language proficiency assessment cited above uncover through microanalysis subtle and complex issues with implications for LPI design, policy and implementation.

Competence

A theme that runs through the above-mentioned studies of language teaching assessment is the contribution that CA can make to the study of competence. This has been accepted as fundamental to language learning and teaching interests since the 1970s, when communicative language teaching shifted attention to issues of communicative competence and how this might be developed through teaching. The communicative competence model proved highly successful in broadening the scope of classroom teaching and applied linguistics. However, it has, like all methods before or since, been based on a deficit model; the purpose of language teaching, it is generally assumed, is to help students develop linguistic knowledge and skills that will enable them to overcome current limitations and develop their communicative competence to the level of the teacher or native speaker (NS). Also, communicative competence has been a fixed and static construct; as Mondada and Pekarek Doehler (2004, p. 502) point out, the traditional notion of competence is of "a phenomenon that is isolated from socialization processes". CA offers a very different view of the nature of competence. Instead of working from the static assumption that competence is something that one has a fixed degree of at a point in time, CA presents competence as variable and co-constructed by participants in interaction. CA also provides a means of exploring the variable ways in which such competence is co-constructed in particular contexts by the participants involved:

Competence cannot be defined in purely individual terms as a series of potentialities located in the mind/brain of a lone individual, but needs to be conceived of as a plurality of capacities embedded and recognized in the context of particular activities.

(Mondada & Pekarek Doehler, 2004, pp. 502–503)

CA studies such as Carroll (2005) and Seedhouse (2004) portray how interactants with minimal linguistic resources can nonetheless employ these resources skilfully and innovatively in interaction in their L2.

There has been interest in how CA can be employed to investigate notions such as communicative competence and interactional competence. Lee (2006) suggests that, whereas communicative competence has traditionally been viewed as the goal of L2 teaching, it can also be viewed as a precondition of L2 teaching. Seedhouse (2004, p. 241) shows how CA can reveal the current state of a learner's competence and the level that a learner is able to achieve when assisted. Hellermann (2007, p. 85) defines interactional competence as "the "ability to co-construct appropriate linguistic forms, registers, and sequential routines in appropriate contexts in order to accomplish discursive practices". Cots and Nussbaum (2008) portray the construct of communicative competence as intricately linked to issues of language choice, identity and institutional affiliation amongst immigrant children in Catalonia. Such CA research, then, reinforces a shift away from a linguistic deficit model focused on individual performance towards a model in which communicative competence is seen to be co-constructed.

Teacher Training and Development

CA has very recently started to be employed as a tool for raising interactional awareness in language teacher training and development programmes; this is clearly an area ripe for development. Walsh (2006) combines CA analysis of classroom interaction with reflective practices to create a framework for teacher training and development. Walsh's Self-Evaluation of Teacher Talk (SETT) framework identifies different varieties or modes of discourse and the pedagogical aims and interactional characteristics of each. Walsh identifies features of a teacher's Classroom Interactional Competence or features that make the teaching/learning process more or less effective. These include maximizing interactional space, shaping learner contributions (e.g. scaffolding), effective use of eliciting, instructional idiolect and interactional awareness. The framework is intended to enable teachers to research and understand interaction in their own classrooms and to maximise learning opportunities. Lazaraton and Ishihara (2005) also promote the combination of microanalysis and teacher reflection, suggesting that "close examination of classroom discourse recorded precisely as it happens not only allows detailed analyses of classroom practices, but can also validate or provide counter evidence to the self reflection provided by the teacher" (p. 529).

Seedhouse (2008) suggests that a particular puzzle for trainee language teachers is how it is that experienced teachers manage to create a pedagogical focus, i.e. to get students to do what they want, in an apparently effortless manner. He examined an example of what trainee teachers sometimes do wrong and shows how and why the instructions which they give manage to confuse students. He compares an example of what experienced teachers typically do right and how they give instructions so that the students are able to carry out the required procedures. Seedhouse suggests that fine-grained CA analysis of transcripts can be combined with video to create a powerful induction tool into professional discourse for trainee or newly qualified L2 teachers.

Language Classroom Interaction

A number of studies have examined issues related to language classroom interaction from a CA perspective, revealing subtle interactional practices that transform our perceptions of L2 learners and teachers. Olsher (2004) demonstrates how L2 learners in small-group project work may complete sequential actions through gesture or embodied displays. Koshik (2002) reveals how teachers use the pedagogical practice of designedly incomplete utterances in order to initiate self-correction by learners. Carroll (2004, 2005) challenges the general perception of L2 novice learners as incompetent communicators, uncovering their ability to make creative communicative use of their minimal linguistic resources and use sophisticated conversational micro-adjustments. Novice learners can precision-time their entry into interaction, recycle turn-beginnings to solicit the gaze or attention of partners and use vowel-marking as a resource for forward-oriented repair. Mori (2002) traces how a task-as-workplan (discussion with NSs) is transformed into a task-in-process resembling a structured interview of question–answer exchanges. Markee (2000) portrays the progress of intersubjectivity during two tasks, one of which results in learner comprehension of the target item whilst the other does not. Markee (2005b) demonstrates how learners working in pairs on a task carefully disguise their social talk from the teacher and are able to instantly switch between on-task and off-task talk. Mortensen (in press a) reveals how students self-select for turns in classrooms or establish recipiency using resources such as in-breaths and body movements. Appel (2007, p. 282) examines how L2 classroom interaction can be seen as a form of performance and suggests that "verbal interaction in the language classroom can be seen as a reflexive mode of communication which uses some of the resources characteristic of performance to make language its special focus".

Seedhouse (2004) applies CA methodology to an extensive and varied database of language lessons from around the world and attempts to answer the question "How is L2 classroom interaction organised?" The main thesis developed in this monograph is that there is a reflexive relationship between pedagogy and interaction in the L2 classroom, and that this relationship is the foundation of its context-free architecture. This relationship means that, as the pedagogical focus varies, so the organisation of the interaction varies too. However, this also means that the L2 classroom has its own interactional organisation that transforms intended pedagogy into actual pedagogy. The overall organisation of L2 classroom interaction is then outlined. The concept of the rational design of institutional interaction is employed to identify the institutional goal as well as three interactional properties that derive directly from the goal. The basic sequence organisation of L2 classroom interaction is presented, together with an emic methodology for its analysis. Seedhouse stresses the dynamic nature of context by exemplifying how the institution of the L2 classroom is talked in and out of being by participants and how teachers create L2 classroom contexts and shift from one context to another. The monograph portrays the L2 classroom as a complex, fluid, dynamic and variable interactional environment and provides a concrete example of how CA methodology can be applied to an issue of interest to language teachers and applied linguists. In order to understand the relationship between interaction and the process of language learning, it is vital to understand how the interaction is organised.

CA studies of L2 classroom interaction have been undertaken in many countries around the world and have predominantly featured data from classrooms in which English has been the target language. However, a number of classroom studies have recently been published which feature a variety of target languages including French (Mondada & Pekarek Doehler, 2004; Seedhouse, 2004); German (Huth & Taleghani-Nikazm 2006; Kasper, 2004; Liebscher & Daley-O'Cain, 2003; Seedhouse, 2004); Danish (Mortensen, in press a); Chinese (He, 2004; Rylander, 2004); Japanese (Mori, 2002, 2004; Ohta, 2001). It is to be hoped that this trend will continue and that data from an increasing range of target languages will be published.

Teaching and Learning Activities

CA has been employed to provide evidence of what actually happens during particular language learning activities. In recent years, the range of activities covered has become very diverse, expanding the knowledge and evidence base. Bushnell (2009) reveals how language play emerges and is organised in a beginner's Japanese classroom. Piirainen-Marsh and Tainio (forthcoming) relate the interactional practices of collaborative video-game playing to language learning processes. Jung (2004) traces vocabulary learning of one learner during conversations over a three-month period. Mortensen (in press b) reveals the practice of "doing word explanation" or the joint production of vocabulary explanation by teacher and learners. Lazaraton (2004) produces a microanalysis of gesture and speech used by a teacher during vocabulary explanations and concludes that "classroom L2 learners receive considerable input in nonverbal form that may modify and make verbal input (more) comprehensible" (p. 111). Nguyen (2007) shows how a teacher builds rapport with learners and positive affect at the same time as managing the pedagogical element of the lesson. Lee (2008) focuses on yes–no questions in teacher-fronted English as a second language (ESL) lessons, whilst Hellermann (2006) investigates reading classes and Hellermann (2005) portrays the co-construction of a quiz game.

A number of articles have explored the mechanism of repair. Liebscher and Dailey-O'Cain (2003) suggest that the different types of repair initiations employed by teachers and learners are reflexively related to their respective roles as teachers and learners. Hosoda (2006) relates the employment of repair trajectories to level of language proficiency, showing that this became relevant when one participant invited repair by another and when intersubjectivity was threatened. Jung (2004) shows how a learner employs repair-initiation as a resource in production of vocabulary items. Koshik (2002) reveals how teachers use the pedagogical practice of designedly incomplete utterances in order to initiate self-correction by learners. Nakamura (2008) explores how repair is related to the management of talk. Waring (2008) and Wong and Waring (2008) investigate the role of positive feedback in language learning and teaching, arguing that this sometimes has the effect of curtailing opportunities for students to raise concerns and tracing its impact on learning through interaction.

Huth and Taleghani-Nikazm (2006) propose a model for applying the insights of CA to the explicit teaching of L2 pragmatics. They suggest using authentic conversations and contrasting sequences in L1 (first language) and L2. Audio and video materials are presented together with transcripts. L2 sequences are practised by the learners and then there is reflection related to cultural issues. The authors report on a study of how a CA-based unit was delivered and it is shown that learners were able to learn and employ a telephone-opening sequence typical of German. Kasper (2006b, p. 330) shows that issues of politeness and face are relevant to language proficiency interviews and points out that "politeness has barely figured at the margins of CA research, at least in name".

CA studies have impacted on issues related to language learning. Studies have critiqued the notion of "task" employed by the task-based approach to language teaching and learning. A number of CA works (Kasper, 2004; Mondada & Pekarek Doehler, 2004; Mori, 2002; Seedhouse, 2004, 2005a) demonstrate that there can be significant differences between the task-as-workplan and the task-in-process and reveal learners to be active agents, who transform tasks-as-workplans into tasks-in-process on a moment-by-moment basis. Mondada and Pekarek Doehler (2004, p. 505) therefore insist "that (tasks) cannot be understood as stable predefined entities". Seedhouse (2005a) suggests that this can create serious problems with validity in task-based research. What is purported to be measured/researched is conceptualised in terms of task-as-workplan, whereas what is actually measured/researched derives from the task-in-process. This threat to validity can only be overcome by switching the conceptual and methodological focus to task-in-process; CA can help to accomplish this shift. Jenks (2007) investigates the relationship between the participatory structures of tasks and floor management.

Language Teaching Materials Design

Language teaching materials frequently feature dialogues presented on audio or video together with a transcription. Issues relating to authenticity of dialogues are complex and have been hotly debated. However, in many countries around the world, materials writers continue (for a variety of reasons) to invent dialogues. CA is well positioned to portray the similarities and differences between invented dialogue and naturally-occurring or "authentic" interaction, both in terms of ordinary conversation and institutional interaction.

Wong (2002, 2007) compares real and invented telephone conversations. Wong (2002) identifies four sequence types that typically occur in American English telephone conversations, namely summons-answer, identification-recognition, greeting and *how are you*? Examining the presentation of thirty inauthentic phone conversations in ESL textbooks, Wong (2002, p. 37) finds that the above sequences are "absent, incomplete or problematic". Wong (2007) compared the closing sequences of eighty-one invented phone calls from language teaching materials with those of authentic phone calls and found a similar mismatch. Wong points out that social and interactional issues are involved in closing phone calls and that there may be cultural differences in procedures. Bernsten (2002) examined invented dialogues from twenty-two ESL textbooks to see whether pre-sequences occur in relation to invitations, offers and requests. Pre-sequences are very common and interactionally useful devices in talk-in-interaction. Bernsten found that the invented dialogues contained very few examples of pre-sequences.

Possible uses of insights from CA in materials design are indirect and direct. In an indirect approach, materials writers would choose authentic, naturally-occurring dialogues for coursebooks to illustrate phenomena such as pre-sequences uncovered by CA. A direct approach would actually teach conversational sequences and phenomena. Similarly, Mori (2005) reveals significant differences between the way a question word (*dooshite*) is used in beginner-level Japanese coursebooks and the way it is used in L1 talk. CA research findings, such as the above sequence types, can be fed into future language teaching materials design. The model used by Bernsten (2002) and Wong (2002, 2007) of comparing invented dialogues with what is known about naturally occurring interaction could be extensively applied to other aspects of conversation in future research.

Identity

Identity has recently become a major focus for research in the social sciences, including applied linguistics. A relatively new field is that of relating identity to interaction using CA or alternatively the closely related membership categorisation analysis (MCA). Also deriving from the work of Sacks, this explores how membership of particular categories (e.g. "teacher", "non-native speaker") is made relevant in talk through the use of membership categorisation devices (MCDs)). Richards (2006, p. 51) draws on MCA and "demonstrates how shifts in the orientation to different aspects of identity produce distinctively different interactional patterns in teacher-fronted talk". Richards proposes instead an approach to analysis which takes account of the dynamic nature of identity construction and its relationship to the development of ongoing talk. Dooly (2007) employs MCA to reveal how language teachers categorise learners according to their linguistic and cultural backgrounds. CA studies have furthered our understanding of how

[l]earners and teachers construct their identities in and through their talk … these identities are quite permeable and are deployed by members on a moment-by-moment basis as a resource for making particular types of learning behaviour relevant at a particular moment in a particular interaction.

(Markee & Kasper, 2004, p. 496)

An aspect of identity that is of vital interest in L2 learning and teaching is that of cultural identity, and a number of recent CA studies have explored how cultural identities are talked into being and transformed in cross-cultural communication. Mori (2003) demonstrates how interculturality is spoken into being or made relevant by the participants in the details of the interaction. Park (2007) reveals how the identities of NS and NNS are made relevant by participants in the course of activities such as word search and evaluation of competence. Seedhouse (1998) provides a discussion of how CA methodology can be applied to identity in the study of NS–NNS interaction. One cannot start from the assumption that the identities "native speaker" and "non-native speaker" are relevant to the talk. Seedhouse analyses an extract of NS–NNS talk; working from the details of the interaction, these identities are shown to be procedurally relevant to the linguistic forms used, to the topic of the talk and to the interactional moves made. For example, NS used minimalised, interlanguage forms when talking to the NNS and thereby talked into being the relevance of the identities NS and NNS.

NNS Talk Outside the Classroom

There has been much recent CA research into NNS talk outside the classroom. A section on such talk is included in this survey in recognition that language learning is not limited to the classroom. Also, many different varieties of NNS talk are being uncovered and analysed, challenging traditional language teaching conceptions of a single standard language, competence and correctness. It is problematic to categorise the varieties uncovered so far. I will use the following categories in this section: (1) NS–NNS talk; (2) NNS–NNS talk or lingua franca talk; (3) language learning talk outside the classroom. It should be recognised that such categories are porous and sometimes poorly defined.

NS–NNS Talk

Interest in the CA analysis of NS–NNS talk outside the classroom has developed in recent years, including Egbert(2005); Hosoda (2006); Kurhila (2006); Mori and Hayashi (2006); Seedhouse (1998); Wagner (1996); Wong (2000a, 2000b, 2005). It is important to understand the characteristics and organisation of such talk in that L2 learners may engage in it on leaving the classroom. Gardner and Wagner (2004) is a major collection of work in the area of NS–NNS talk. It features talk in a variety of social, professional and educational settings and presents analyses of talk using Danish, Finnish, Japanese, German, French and English as L2s. Mondada (2004) reveals some of the complexities of analysing plurilingual NS–NNS talk. She reveals how, in her corpus of video-conferencing meetings between surgeons in several different European countries, "the working language of the meeting is never decided once and for all, but is constantly renegotiated" (p. 31). For interactants (and hence for the analysis), NS and NNS categories may not be relevant; rather, they may present themselves as "experts", "seniors" or "juniors".

The CA study of NS–NNS interaction in non-pedagogic settings has broadened in recent years to include languages other than English, for example German (Egbert, 2005; Seedhouse, 1998; Wagner, 1996), Finnish (Kurhila, 2006), Danish (Brouwer, 2004) and Japanese (Hosoda, 2006).

NNS–NNS Talk or Lingua Franca Talk

The field has also broadened to include the CA study of interaction between NNS and NNS using English as *international lingua franca* talk (Firth, 1996, 2009; Firth & Wagner, 1997, 2007; Mondada, 2004; Wagner, 1996), and Finnish as *international lingua franca* talk (Mazeland & Zaman-Zadeh, 2004) as well as studies which compare the identical interactional phenomenon in NNS talk (Wong,

2000a) and in NS talk (Schegloff, 2000) in English. This is a variety of talk in which many L2 learners around the world engage ever more frequently.

Carroll's (2005) study demonstrates that a CA focus on sequence can sometimes reveal hitherto unnoticed aspects of the talk of NNSs. Japanese speakers of English as a foreign language (EFL) (particularly at the novice level) often add vowels to word-final consonants, for example: "Oldest child-u is-u (0.21) um:: twenty". Generally, English teachers have treated this as a pronunciation problem, resulting from negative transfer from the L1. Whilst not disputing these origins, Carroll's analysis of his data demonstrates that his subjects were employing vowel-marking as an interactional resource, particularly during forward-oriented repair or word search, as in the example below:

Extract 2

A: what-o what-o interesting-u (0.43) e:to schoo:l-u festival

(Carroll, 2005, p. 220)

According to Carroll, vowel-marking, in delaying the production of some *next-item-due*, serves to buy the speaker initiating the repair a little more time to achieve self-repair. Furthermore, vowel-marking alerts co-participants to the fact that a search is underway and to their possible role in resolving it. In terms of application, Carroll suggests that training students in the use of interactionally equivalent conversational micro-practices, such as the use of *uh* and *um* would be helpful. Furthermore, Carroll's microanalysis reveals a previously unimagined degree of interactional sophistication in the way these novice NNSs employ their limited resources.

Language Learning Talk Outside the Classroom

A number of studies have examined how L2 learners engage in talk and activities related to language learning but outside a formal teaching classroom. Piirainen-Marsh and Tainio (forthcoming) examine repetition as a language learning practice and as a resource in a computer game-playing activity. Firth and Wagner (2007) exemplify learning in a workplace setting. Koshik (2002) and Young and Miller (2004) look at talk during writing conferences. Mori (2003), Carroll (2005), Hauser (2005), Jung (2004), Kasper (2004), Mori and Hayashi (2006) and Nakamura (2008) examine small-group conversations arranged for language practice.

Bilingual and Multilingual Code-Switching

Recent years have seen a growth in the number of studies that have employed a CA approach to bilingual and multilingual interaction and to code-switching in particular (e.g. Mondada, 2004; Torras, 2005; Wei, 2002). Wei (2002) provides an overview of the CA approach to bilingual interaction, in which "particular attention is paid to the way in which individuals strategically use the codes in their bilingual repertoires to achieve specific interactional goals" (p. 159). Analyses must be demonstrably oriented to participant concerns and actions and aim to reveal the underlying procedural apparatus by which interactants themselves arrive at local interpretations of language choice.

Although there is a considerable literature on bilingual code-switching, relatively little CA research had been undertaken on code-switching in L2 classrooms until very recently. Code-switching as a methodical phenomenon in L2 classroom interaction is now starting to be researched using a CA methodology. Mori (2004, p. 537) shows "how code switching … serves as a resource for managing sequential boundaries, and at the same time, affects the ways in which their interactive activities are organized". Kasper (2004, p. 551) shows how "code switching worked as one device by which the novice requested a target language action format from the L2 expert". Liebscher and

Dailey-O'Cain (2005) conceptualise code-switching as a resource for effective bilingual communication. They found that learners in their classroom setting often employed code-switching "for discourse-related functions that contextualise the interactional meaning of their utterances" (Liebscher & Dailey-O'Cain, 2005, p. 234). Unamuno (2008) shows that language choice is related to the management and completion of assigned pairwork tasks. Nussbaum and Unamuno (2006) suggest that the ability to switch languages constitutes part of a child's sociolinguistic competence in the multilingual classroom setting of Catalonia. Üstünel and Seedhouse (2005) depict the relationship between pedagogical focus and language choice in the language teaching/learning environment of EFL at a Turkish university. The study presents the organisation of code-switching that is teacher-initiated and "teacher-induced". Transcripts of lessons were examined by relating incidence of code-switching to the pedagogical focus. An adapted version of the classic CA question (why that, right now?) was applied for interaction involving code-switching, namely *why that, in that language, right now?* The study demonstrates that code-switching in L2 classrooms is orderly and related to the evolution of pedagogical focus and sequence. Through their language choice, learners may display their alignment or misalignment with the teacher's pedagogical focus.

Methodological Critiques

CA has been used to critique existing methodological practices and epistemologies. Golato (2003) investigated responses to compliments in German using both discourse completion questionnaires and CA of naturally-occurring talk. There were some major differences between what people wrote that they would say (in the discourse completion questionnaires) and what they actually said. For example, a number of respondents wrote that they would say "*danke*" in response to a compliment, but such a response was not recorded at all in the spoken corpus. This has implications for both materials design and for research methodology. Hauser (2005) points out a number of problems involved in the coding of corrective recasts, arguing that coding decontextualises complex interactional data and obscures the emic perspective on interaction. Hauser argues strongly against the use of coding of interaction more generally since it depends on the stability of meaning, whereas the CA view is that meaning is negotiated in interaction.

Some CA studies have the broader aim of reconceptualising SLA. The late 1990s saw a CA-motivated debate on a proposed "re-conceptualisation" of SLA (Firth & Wagner, 1997, 1998; Markee, 1994, 2000, 2005a). Some of the criticisms which Firth and Wagner (1997, 1998) made of SLA are as follows: SLA had neglected the social and contextual aspects of language use and their contribution to SLA processes; SLA was becoming a "Hermetically sealed area of study" (1998, p. 92), which was losing contact with sociology, sociolinguistics and discourse analysis in favour of a psycholinguistic focus on the cognition of the individual; there was an etic rather than emic approach to fundamental concepts; the traditional SLA database was too narrow. Essentially the call was for a holistic approach that includes the social dimension and emic perspectives. A number of publications since that date have therefore tried to establish what CA might be able to contribute to the study of language learning.

At the time of writing there are a number of competing and sometimes conflicting conceptions of how CA may or may not be employed in language learning and teaching research. From a temporal perspective, this lack of clarity is not a matter of major concern. CA itself only emerged in the 1960s, had no connection with learning and in its genesis dealt exclusively with monolingual English data. It is only in the period since 2000 that publications have started to address the relationship between CA and language learning, for example the special issue of the *Modern Language Journal* in 2004 (Markee & Kasper, 2004). As Gass (2004, p. 598) points out, the different articles in the special issue approach the relationship between CA and learning in very different ways. The common ground is that all studies use microanalysis of transcripts of classroom interaction. Kasper (2004, p. 551) "explores some roles for CA as an approach to second and foreign language learning" whereas He (2004, p. 579) is quite clear that "CA is not a learning theory" and that "CA is not concerned with what is not observable" (p. 578). Hall (2004, p. 608) notes that the studies are not "successful in making a collective case for CA's potential as an approach to studies of language learning". Larsen-Freeman (2004, p. 607) suggests:

> Saying that something has been learned, saying what has been learned, when it has been learned, and the reason it has been learned are big challenges for all SLA researchers, cognitivists as well as those who practice CA. Yet these are the challenges which CA researchers must confront if they want to move CA to the center of the field.

Seedhouse (2005b) identifies three different approaches to the application of CA to the broad field of language learning and teaching; these are the ethnomethodological CA approach, the sociocultural theory approach to CA and linguistic CA.

Language Learning Processes

In this section I consider what CA may have to offer in relation to the broad field of study of L2 learning processes. I separate these into longitudinal and cross-sectional studies.

Longitudinal Studies of Learning

One area of CA research into language learning that is expected to grow considerably in coming years is that of longitudinal studies that document the development of interactional patterns in learners over time. Studies so far demonstrate the promise of this approach. Young and Miller (2004) conducted longitudinal observation of revision talk, noted that the participation framework changed over time and "demonstrate processes by which the student moved from peripheral to fuller participation" (p. 519). Hellermann (2006) traces the development of the interactional practices of two learners in an L2 literacy class over three terms of study. The investigation demonstrates how the learners (with different L1s) are socialised into classroom interaction practices and how their ability to participate in these practices evolves. Hellermann (2007) examines task openings by successful learners over a period of at least eighteen months. He proposes (2007, p. 91) that learning can be conceptualised as "the change in the use of resources and strategies for engaging in a particular aspect of social interaction". Brouwer and Wagner (2004, p. 44) examine the development over a period of two months of a Japanese learner of Danish:

> The differences between early and later encounters are found in the complexity of the emerging structures which build on earlier talk and topics and where increasing displays of understanding by both participants can be seen. Learning a second language, then, may be described in terms of increasing interactional complexity in language encounters rather than as the acquisition of formal elements.

They conclude that "instead of describing [the learner's] change in use of linguistic elements alone, one can explain her progress in terms of interactional resources and how they are employed in the interaction in collaboration with her conversation partner" (p. 45). Markee (2008) proposes a "learner behaviour tracking methodology" that is able to track longitudinal L2 development. This methodology tracks how the "learning object" occurs in interaction and also portrays the process of learning via interaction.

Cross-Sectional Accounts of Learning

A number of CA studies of learning are cross-sectional rather than longitudinal, that is, they analyse a single instance or a collection of instances or a case. Brouwer (2003) provides an example of how detailed CA examination of interactional data can increase our understanding of learning processes. Brouwer examines word search sequences between NSs and NNSs and develops a distinction between word search sequences that act as language learning opportunities and those that do not. Lazaraton (2004) produces a microanalysis of gesture and speech used by a teacher during vocabulary explanations and concludes that "classroom L2 learners receive considerable input in nonverbal form that may modify and make verbal input (more) comprehensible" (p. 111). Seedhouse (2004, p. 238) analyses a single instance of interaction in detail, showing the complex inputs of the teacher and employing a three-stage approach to the analysis of learning processes. Mondada and Pekarek-Doehler (2004) demonstrate how the accomplishment of a grammar exercise depends on learners following sequence and turn, social practices and a complex set of social and cultural competencies in addition to linguistic competence.

In all of the above studies, insights are provided into language learning as a process that is inextricably intertwined with interaction. Also, they avoid cognitivist accounts of learning. Whereas in cognitive, quantitative approaches to SLA, discrete syntactical or lexical items are extracted for quantitative treatment, these CA studies portray the learning of individual items as being related in complex ways to other features of interaction. However, there are a number of differences in the studies. Some are linked to specific learning theories (Brouwer & Wagner, 2004; Hellermann, 2007, 2008; Mondada & Pekarek-Doehler, 2004; Young & Miller, 2004) whereas others are not. Some of the studies reconceptualise language learning as a change in social participation patterns, whereas others show how a specific language item is learned via the process of interaction.

Socially Distributed Cognition

Linked to the study of learning processes is the study of socially distributed or socially shared cognition, in which there has been strong recent interest. Seedhouse (2004) argues that a part of what is meant by the cognitive state of a learner involved in L2 classroom interaction is inextricably entwined and engaged with the unique sequential, social and contextual environment in which s/he is engaged. It is argued that this part of the individual's cognitive state can be portrayed emically in situ, that is, in that unique sequential environment. Cognitive claims and displays are thus seen as interactionally occasioned and intertwined with the action(s) that participants are accomplishing at particular moments in the talk (Kasper, 2008, p. 66). Kasper (2009) explores the relationship between interactional organisations and socially distributed cognition, showing them to be mutually dependent as components of the architecture of intersubjectivity.

This is not to suggest that this provides anything like the whole picture, nor that the methods employed by SLA and psychology are not useful in portraying other aspects of the full picture in relation to cognition. Rather, CA is able to make a major contribution to the SLA project in terms of the portrayal of socially distributed cognition (Markee, 2000, p. 3). Ohta (2001) demonstrates how socially distributed cognition can work in the L2 classroom. Recasts are not necessarily just responses by the teacher to one learner. Ohta shows (by recording and transcribing the private talk of individually microphoned students in a classroom) that other students can use recasts in which they are not personally involved as negative evidence and display uptake in their private talk. These studies demonstrate that what can be called "language learning" is inextricably embedded in classroom interaction.

Data Presentation

An issue that is receiving increasing prominence is the question of what constitutes adequate primary data for CA studies. At the start of CA in the 1960s, the new technology of audio recording was the only one available and telephone conversation data were easily accessible. However, with the rise of video recording, it became possible to include non-verbal communication and gaze in transcripts as well as still photographs. CA aims to understand how social action is accomplished and claims that no detail of the interaction can be dismissed as insignificant. It is therefore argued (e.g. Zuengler, Ford & Fassnacht, 1998) that non-verbal communication and gaze are potentially important features of face-to-face interaction and should therefore be detailed in transcripts. Recent CA studies in the area of language learning that demonstrate the significance of non-verbal communication and gaze for our understanding of interaction include Carroll (2004); Lazaraton (2004); Mori (2003); Mori and Hayashi (2006); Olsher (2004); Zuengler et al. (1998). To exemplify the significance of this, Olsher (2004) identifies the practice of "embodied completion" in which a verbal turn of talk is designedly left incomplete and the turn may be completed with a gesture or other embodied action. The disadvantages of using extremely detailed non-verbal communication and gaze information are that they increase transcription time considerably and may sometimes render transcripts more difficult to read and less accessible to a general readership. However, the nature of data presented in CA studies has always been linked to technological developments and no doubt further developments will have an impact in this area. A number of studies (Carroll, 2005; Hosoda, 2006; Mori & Hayashi, 2006; Mortensen, in press a) employ frames from videos together with overlays such as arrows and graphics, which highlight the significance of non-verbal features.

Markee and Stansell (2007) argue that advances in electronic publishing technology mean that video and audio data can be combined with text and graphics in a single environment. These enable the incorporation of details of non-verbal communication into a written transcript. As journals increasingly move to electronic media, it seems likely that the normal presentation of data in CA studies will shift from written transcript to electronic presentation with transcript and graphics. Markee and Stansell (2007) argue that providing access to original recordings improves the accountability of analyses—previously, readers relied on the accuracy of transcripts.

Conclusion

There are a number of difficulties in attempting to compile a comprehensive review of the literature in this area. It is quite common for authors employing a CA methodology to make no mention of this in their title or abstract. Sometimes, CA is combined with other approaches. Also, the boundaries differentiating a CA study from a non-CA study are quite fuzzy and poorly defined. A number of studies are characterising themselves as "CA-informed" or "CA-inspired" or "microanalysis" as opposed to "purist" or "hard-core" CA. Publications (Tainio, 2007, in Finnish; Nussbaum & Unamuno, 2006, in French) and doctoral theses (Masats I Viladoms, 2008, in Catalan; Schwab aus Sindelfingen, 2007, in German) have started appearing in languages other than English in the field of CA and language learning and teaching. Unfortunately, these studies do not always become known in Anglophone circles.

Looking to possible future directions for CA research in the area of language learning and teaching, the current study suggests that it will examine a wider range of languages being learnt and taught, using a wider range of teaching practices and activities in a wider range of contexts. In some areas of language learning and teaching, the potential of CA has only recently started to be explored, particularly in relation to teacher training, LSP, materials design and code-switching. Another likely growth area is research into technology-based forms of communication, e.g. Webchat and Skype and their implications for language learning. Publications have started to appear in this area, e.g. Negretti (1999) and Jenks (2009). It is not yet clear, however, how many of the basic principles of CA can be applied to such a medium. A fundamental part of the system of talk that has been seriously neglected in recent CA research is "topic". This is surprising as this construct is vital in teaching L2 speaking and language proficiency tests evaluate the ability to develop a topic. Much of Sacks's early work was on topic and clearly this is an area ripe for research. A question still unresolved is whether and how the insights of CA can be employed in terms of practical L2 classroom teaching techniques. One approach might be very atomistic and mechanical: these are the rules of turn-taking and can be taught as such to students. As a teaching technique, this might be quite similar to grammar-translation teaching of the rules of syntax. At present, learners in "communicative" classrooms practice actually doing conversations in L2 through role plays, information gaps etc. There is no evidence as yet that teaching the rules of conversation to L2 learners would produce better results than having them practise doing it.

In this chapter, I have argued that CA has been employed in many different ways in this field. CA has been employed to investigate the use of various teaching and learning activities and to develop areas such as teacher training, testing, materials design and LSP. It has helped to develop our understanding of how constructs such as identity and competence are realised in interaction. CA has developed our understanding of talk in which NNSs engage inside and outside the classroom and of target varieties of interaction in LSP. It has been used as a tool for methodological critique. Perhaps its main contributions have been to provide us with a realistic idea of what actually happens in language learning talk and to enable a process account of language learning through interaction.

References

Appel, J. (2007). Language teaching in performance. *International Journal of Applied Linguistics, 17*(3), 277–293.

Bernsten, S. G. (2002). Using conversation analysis to evaluate pre-sequences in invitation, offer and request dialogues in ESL textbooks. Unpublished Master's thesis, University of Illinois, Urbana-Champaign, USA.

Bowles, H., & Seedhouse, P., (2007a). *Conversation analysis and LSP*. Berlin: Peter Lang.

Bowles, H., & Seedhouse, P. (2007b). Interactional competence and the LSP classroom. In H. Bowles & P. Seedhouse (Eds.), *Conversation analysis and LSP*, (pp. 305–329). Berlin: Peter Lang.

Brouwer, C. (2003). Word searches in NNS–NS interaction: Opportunities for language learning? *The Modern Language Journal, 87*(4), 534–545.

Brouwer, C. (2004). Doing pronunciation: A specific type of repair sequence. In R. Gardner & J. Wagner (Eds.), *Second language talk* (pp. 148–178). London: Continuum.

Brouwer, C. E., & Wagner, J. (2004). Developmental issues in second language conversation. *Journal of Applied Linguistics, 1*(1), 30–47.

Brown, A. (2003). Interviewer variation and the co-construction of speaking proficiency. *Language Testing, 20*(1), 1–25.

Bushnell, C. (2009). "Lego my keego!": An analysis of language play in a beginning Japanese as a foreign language classroom. *Applied Linguistics, 30*, 49–69.

Carroll, D. (2004). Restarts in novice turn-beginnings: Disfluencies or interactional achievements? In R. Gardner & J. Wagner (Eds.), *Second language talk* (pp. 318–345). London: Continuum.

Carroll, D. (2005). Vowel-marking as an interactional resource in Japanese novice ESL conversation. In K. Richards & P. Seedhouse (Eds.), *Applying conversation analysis* (pp. 214–234). Basingstoke: Palgrave Macmillan.

Cots, J., & Nussbaum, L. (2008). Communicative competence and institutional affiliation: Interactional processes of identity construction by immigrant students in Catalonia. *International Journal of Multilingualism, 5*(1), 17–40.

Dooly, M. (2007). Constructing differences: A qualitative analysis of teachers' perspectives on linguistic and cultural diversity. *Linguistics and Education, 18*, 142–166.

Drew, P., & Heritage, J. (Eds.) (1992). *Talk at work: Interaction in institutional settings*. Cambridge: Cambridge University Press.

Egbert, M. (1998). Miscommunication in language proficiency interviews of first-year German students: Comparison with natural conversation. In R. Young & A. He (Eds.), *Talking and testing: Discourse approaches to the assessment of oral proficiency* (pp. 147–169). Amsterdam: Benjamins.

Egbert, M. (2005). Discrimination due to non-native speech production? In K. Richards & P. Seedhouse (Eds.), *Applying conversation analysis* (pp. 174–196). Basingstoke: Palgrave Macmillan.

Firth, A. (1996). The discursive accomplishment of normality: On "lingua franca" English and conversation analysis. *Journal of Pragmatics, 26,* 237–259.

Firth, A. (2009). Doing *not* being a foreign language learner: English as a *lingua franca* in the workplace and (some) implications for SLA. *IRAL, 47,* 127–156.

Firth, A., & Wagner, J. (1997). On discourse, communication, and (some) fundamental concepts in SLA research. *The Modern Language Journal, 81,* 285–300.

Firth, A., & Wagner, J. (1998). SLA property: No trespassing! *The Modern Language Journal, 82,* 91–94.

Firth, A., & Wagner, J. (2007). Second/foreign language learning as a social accomplishment: Elaborations on a reconceptualized SLA. *The Modern Language Journal, 91,* 800–819.

Gardner, R., & Wagner, J. (Eds.) (2004). *Second language conversations.* London: Continuum.

Gass, S. M. (2004). Conversation analysis and input-interaction. *Modern Language Journal, 88,* 597–602.

Golato, A. (2003). Studying compliment responses: A comparison of DCTs and recordings of naturally occurring talk. *Applied Linguistics, 24*(1), 90–121.

Hall, J. K. (2004). Language learning as an interactional achievement. *Modern Language Journal, 88,* 607–612.

Hauser, E. (2005). Coding "corrective recasts": The maintenance of meaning and more fundamental problems. *Applied Linguistics, 26,* 293–316.

Have, P. ten (1999). *Doing conversation analysis: a practical guide.* London: Sage Publications.

He, A. (1998). Answering questions in language proficiency interviews: A case study. In R. Young & A. He (Eds.), *Talking and testing: Discourse approaches to the assessment of oral proficiency* (pp. 101–115). Amsterdam: Benjamins.

He, A. (2004). CA for SLA: Arguments from the Chinese language classroom. *Modern Language Journal, 88,* 568–582.

Hellermann, J. (2005). The sequential and prosodic co-construction of a "quiz game" activity in classroom talk. *Journal of Pragmatics, 38*(6), 919–944.

Hellermann, J. (2006). Classroom interactive practices for literacy. *Applied Linguistics, 27,* 377–404.

Hellermann, J. (2007). The development of practices for action in classroom dyadic interaction: Focus on task openings. *Modern Language Journal, 91*(1), 83–96.

Hellermann, J. (2008). *Social actions for classroom language learning.* Clevedon: Multilingual Matters.

Heritage, J. (1999). Conversation analysis at century's end: Practices of talk-in-interaction, their distributions and their outcomes. *Research on Language and Social Interaction, 31,* 69–76.

Hosoda, Y. (2006). Repair and relevance of differential language expertise in second language conversations. *Applied Linguistics, 27*(1), 25–50.

Hutchby, I., & Wooffitt, R. (1998). *Conversation analysis.* Cambridge: Polity Press.

Huth, T., & Taleghani-Nikazm, C. (2006). How can insights from conversation analysis be directly applied to teaching L2 pragmatics? *Language Teaching Research, 10,* (1), 53–79.

Jacoby, S. (1998). How can ESP practitioners tap into situated discourse research: And why should we? (Part 1). *English for Specific Purposes News, 7*(1 & 2), 1–10.

Jacoby, S., & Mcnamara, T. F. (1999). Locating competence. *English for Specific Purposes Journal, 18*(3), 213–241.

Jenks, C. J. (2007). Floor management in task-based interaction: The interactional role of participatory structures. *System, 35*(4), 609–622.

Jenks, C. J. (2009). Getting acquainted in Skypecasts: Aspects of social organization in online chat rooms. *International Journal of Applied Linguistics, 19,* (1), 26–46.

Jung, K. (2004). L2 vocabulary development through conversation: A conversation Analysis. *Second Language Studies, 23*(1), 27–66.

Kasper, G. (2004). Participant orientations in German conversation-for-learning. *The Modern Language Journal, 88,* 551–567.

Kasper, G. (2006a). When once is not enough: Politeness in multiple requests. *Multilingua, 25,* 323–349.

Kasper, G. (2006b). Beyond repair: Conversation analysis as an approach to SLA. *AILA Review, 19,* 83–99.

Kasper, G. (2008). Discourse and socially shared cognition. In J. Cenoz & N. H. Hornberger (Eds.), *Encyclopedia of language and education,* (2nd ed., Vol. 6: Knowledge about language) (pp. 59–78). New York: Springer Science+ Business Media, LLC.

Kasper, G. (2009). Locating cognition in second language interaction and learning: Inside the skull or in public view? *International Journal of Applied Linguistics, 47,* 11–36.

Kasper, G., & Ross, S. (2001). "Is drinking a hobby, I wonder": Other-initiated repair in language proficiency interviews. Paper presented at American Association for Applied Linguistics, St Louis, MS.

Kasper, G., & Ross, S. (2003). Repetition as a source of miscommunication in oral proficiency interviews. In J. House, G.

Kasper & S. Ross (Eds.), *Misunderstanding in social life. Discourse approaches to problematic talk* (pp. 82–106). Harlow: Longman/Pearson Education.

Kasper, G., & Ross, S. (2007). Multiple questions in oral proficiency interviews. *Journal of Pragmatics, 39*, 2045–2070.

Koshik, I. (2002). Designedly incomplete utterances: A pedagogical practice for eliciting knowledge displays in error correction sequences. *Research on Language and Social Interaction, 35*(3), 277–309.

Kurhila, S. (2006). *Second language interaction.* Amsterdam: John Benjamins.

Larsen-Freeman, D. (2004). CA for SLA? It all depends. *Modern Language Journal, 88*, 603–607.

Lazaraton, A. (1997). Preference organization in oral proficiency interviews: The case of language ability assessments. *Research on Language and Social Interaction, 30*(1), 53–72.

Lazaraton, A. (2002). *A qualitative approach to the validation of oral language tests.* Cambridge: Cambridge University Press.

Lazaraton, A. (2004). Gesture and speech in the vocabulary explanations of one ESL Teacher: A microanalytic inquiry. *Language Learning, 54*(1), 79–117.

Lazaraton, A., & Ishihara, N. (2005). Understanding second language teacher practice using microanalysis and self-reflection: A collaborative case study. *The Modern Language Journal, 89*(4), 529–542.

Lee, Y. A. (2006). Towards respecification of communicative competence: Condition of L2 instruction or its objective? *Applied Linguistics, 27*(3), 349–376.

Lee, Y. A. (2008). Yes–no questions in the third-turn position: Pedagogical discourse processes. *Discourse Processes, 45*, 237–262.

Liebscher, G., & Dailey-O'Cain, J. (2003). Conversational repair as a role-defining mechanism in classroom interaction. *Modern Language Journal, 87*, 374–390.

Liebscher, G., & Dailey-O'Cain, J. (2005). Learner code-switching in the content based foreign language classroom. *Modern Language Journal, 89*, 234–247.

Markee, N. (1994). Toward an ethnomedological respecification of SLA studies. In A. Cohen, S. Gass & E. Tarone, (Eds.), *Research methodology in second language acquisition* (pp. 89–116), Hillsdale, NJ: Erlbaum.

Markee, N. (2000). *Conversation analysis.* Mahwah, NJ: Lawrence Erlbaum.

Markee, N. (2005a). Conversation analysis for second language acquisition. In E. Hinkel (Ed.), *Handbook of research in second language teaching and learning.* Mahwah, NJ: Lawrence Erlbaum.

Markee, N. (2005b). The organization of off-task classroom talk in second language classrooms. In K. Richards & P. Seedhouse (Eds.), *Applying conversation analysis* (pp. 197–213). Basingstoke: Palgrave Macmillan.

Markee, N. (2008). Toward a learning behavior tracking methodology for CA-for-SLA. *Applied Linguistics, 29*, 404–427.

Markee, N., & Kasper, G. (2004). Classroom talks: An introduction. *Modern Language Journal, 88*, 491–500.

Markee, N., & Stansell, J. (2007). Using electronic publishing as a resource for increasing empirical and interpretive accountability in conversation analysis. *Annual Review of Applied Linguistics, 27*, 24–44.

Masats I Viladoms, M. D. (2008). El discurs dels aprenents d'anglès com a llengua estrangera: Una aproximació interactivista al process de construcció de tasques comunicatives. Unpublished doctoral thesis, Universitat Autònoma de Barcelona.

Mazeland, M., & Zaman-Zadeh, M. (2004). The logic of clarification: Some observations about word-clarification repairs in Finnish-as-a-lingua-franca interactions. In R. Gardner & J. Wagner (Eds.), *Second language talk* (pp. 208–246). London: Continuum.

Mondada, L. (2004). Ways of "doing being plurilingual" in international work meetings. In R. Gardner & J. Wagner (Eds.), *Second language talk* (pp. 27–60). London: Continuum.

Mondada, L., & Pekarek Doehler, S. (2004). Second language acquisition as situated practice: Task accomplishment in the French second language classroom. *Modern Language Journal, 88*, 501–518.

Mori, J. (2002). Task design, plan and development of talk-in-interaction: An analysis of a small group activity in a Japanese language classroom. *Applied Linguistics, 23*(3), 323–347.

Mori, J. (2003). Construction of interculturality: A study of initial encounters between Japanese and American students. *Research on Language and Social Interaction, 36*(2), 143–184.

Mori, J. (2004). Negotiating sequential boundaries and learning opportunities: A case from a Japanese language classroom. *Modern Language Journal, 88*, 536–550.

Mori, J. (2005). Why not why? The teaching of grammar, discourse, sociolinguistic and cross-cultural perspectives. *Japanese Language and Literature, 39*(2), 255–289.

Mori, J., & Hayashi, M. (2006). The achievement of intersubjectivity through embodied completions: A study of interactions between first and second language speakers. *Applied Linguistics, 27*, 195–219.

Mortensen, K. (in press a). Establishing recipiency in pre-beginning position in the second language classroom. *Discourse Processes.*

Mortensen, K. (in press b). Doing word explanation in interaction. In G. Pallotti, J. Wagner & G. Kasper (Eds.), *Second language learning and conversation analysis.* Honolulu: University of Hawaii Press.

Nakamura, I. (2008). Understanding how teacher and student talk with each other: An exploration of how "repair" displays the co-management of talk-in-interaction. *Language Teaching Research, 12,* 265–283.

Negretti, R. (1999). Web-based activities and SLA: A conversation analysis research approach. *Language Learning and Technology, 3*(1), 75–87.

Nguyen, H. T. (2007). Rapport building in language instruction: A microanalysis of the multiple resources in teacher talk. *Language and Education, 21*(4), 284–303.

Nussbaum, L., & Unamuno, V. (2006). La compétence sociolinguistique, pour quoi faire? *Bulletin Suisse de Linguistique Appliqué, 84,* 47–65.

Ohta, A. S. (2001). *Second language acquisition processes in the classroom.* Mahwah, NJ: Lawrence Erlbaum.

Olsher, D. (2004). Talk and gesture: The embodied completion of sequential actions in spoken interaction. In R. Gardner & J. Wagner (Eds.), *Second language talk* (pp. 346–380). London: Continuum.

Packett, A. (2005). Teaching patterns of interaction in English for specific purposes. In K. Richards & P. Seedhouse (Eds.), *Applying conversation analysis* (pp. 235–250). Basingstoke: Palgrave Macmillan.

Packett, A. (2007). Teaching institutional talk: A CA approach to broadcast interviewing. In H. Bowles & P. Seedhouse (Eds.), *Conversation analysis and LSP* (pp. 247–270). Berlin: Peter Lang.

Park, J.-E. (2007). Co-construction of nonnative speaker identity in cross-cultural interaction. *Applied Linguistics, 28*(3), 339–360.

Piirainen-Marsh, A., & Tainio, L. (forthcoming) Collaborative game-play as a site for participation and situated learning of a second language. *Scandinavian Journal of Educational Research.*

Richards, K. (2005). Introduction. In K. Richards & P. Seedhouse (Eds.), *Applying conversation analysis* (pp. 1–18). Basingstoke: Palgrave Macmillan.

Richards, K. (2006) "Being the teacher": Identity and classroom conversation. *Applied Linguistics, 27*(1), 51–77.

Richards, K., & Seedhouse, P. (Eds.) (2005). *Applying conversation analysis.* Basingstoke: Palgrave Macmillan.

Ross, S. (2007). A comparative task-in-interaction analysis of OPI backsliding. *Journal of Pragmatics, 39,* 2017–2044.

Rylander, J. (2004). Interaction in a Chinese as a foreign language classroom: A conversation analysis approach. *Second Language Studies, 23*(1), 67–144.

Schegloff, E. (2000). When "others" initiate repair. *Applied Linguistics, 21*(2), 205–243.

Schegloff, E. A., Koshik, I., Jacoby, S. & Olsher, D. (2002). Conversation analysis and applied linguistics. *Annual Review of Applied Linguistics, 22,* 3–31.

Schwab aus Sindelfingen, G. (2007). Schülerbeteiligung im Englischunterricht der Hauptschule. Unpublished doctoral thesis, Pädagogischen Hochschule Ludwigsburg.

Seedhouse, P. (1998). CA and the analysis of foreign language interaction: A reply to Wagner. *Journal of Pragmatics, 30,* 85–102.

Seedhouse, P. (2004). *The interactional architecture of the language classroom: A conversation analysis perspective.* Malden, MA: Blackwell.

Seedhouse, P. (2005a). Task as Research Construct. *Language Learning, 55*(3), 533–570.

Seedhouse, P. (2005b). Conversation analysis and language learning. *Language Teaching, 38*(4), 165–187.

Seedhouse, P. (2008). Learning to talk the talk: Conversation analysis as a tool for induction of trainee teachers. In S. Garton, & K. Richards (Eds.), *Professional encounters in TESOL* (pp. 42–57). Basingstoke: Palgrave Macmillan.

Seedhouse, P., & Egbert, M. (2006). The interactional organisation of the IELTS speaking test. *IELTS Research Reports, 6,* 161–206.

Seedhouse, P., & Richards, K. (2007). Describing and analysing institutional varieties of interaction. In H. Bowles & P. Seedhouse (Eds.), *Conversation analysis and languages for specific purposes* (pp. 17–36). Bern: Peter Lang.

Tainio, Liisa (Ed.) (2007). *Vuorovaikutusta luokkahuoneessa: näkökulmana keskustelunanalyysi* [*Interaction in the classroom: A conversation analytic perspective*]. Helsinki: Gaudeamus.

Torras, M. C. (2005). Social identity and language choice in bilingual service talk. In K. Richards & P. Seedhouse (Eds.), *Applying conversation analysis* (pp. 107–123). Basingstoke: Palgrave Macmillan.

Unamuno, V. (2008). Multilingual switch in peer classroom interaction. *Linguistics and Education, 19*(1), 1–19.

Üstünel, E., & Seedhouse, P. (2005). Why that, in that language, right now? Code-switching and pedagogical focus. *International Journal of Applied Linguistics, 15*(3), 302–325.

Wagner, J. (1996). Foreign language acquisition through interaction—a critical review of research on conversational adjustments. *Journal of Pragmatics, 26,* 215–236.

Walsh, S. (2006). *Investigating classroom discourse.* London: Routledge.

Walsh, S., & O'Keeffe, A. (2007). Applying CA to a modes analysis of higher education spoken academic discourse. In H. Bowles & P. Seedhouse (Eds.), *Conversation analysis and languages for specific purposes* (pp. 101–139). Bern: Peter Lang.

Walters, F. S. (2007). A conversation-analytic hermeneutic rating protocol to assess L2 oral pragmatic competence. *Language Testing, 24*(2), 155–183.

Waring, H. Z. (2008). Using explicit positive assessment in the language classroom: IRF, Feedback and learning opportunities. *Modern Language Journal, 92*(4), 577–594.

Wei, L. (2002). "What do you want me to say?" On the conversation analysis approach to bilingual interaction. *Language in Society, 31,* 159–180.

Wong, J. (2000a). Delayed next turn repair initiation in native/nonnative speaker English conversation. *Applied Linguistics, 21,* 244–267.

Wong, J. (2000b). The token "yeah" in nonnative speaker English conversation. *Research on Language and Social Interaction, 33*(1), 39–67.

Wong, J. (2002). "Applying" conversation analysis in applied linguistics: Evaluating dialogue in English as a second language textbooks. *International Review of Applied Linguistics, 40*(1), 37–60.

Wong, J. (2005). Sidestepping grammar. In K. Richards & P. Seedhouse (Eds.), *Applying conversation analysis* (pp. 159–173). Basingstoke: Palgrave Macmillan.

Wong, J. (2007). Answering my call: A look at telephone closings. In H. Bowles & P. Seedhouse (Eds.), *Conversation analysis and language for specific purposes,* (pp. 271–304), Bern: Peter Lang.

Wong, J., & Waring, H. (2008). "Very good" as a teacher response. *ELT Journal,* Oxford: Oxford University Press. [Advance access online version is available: ELT Journal 2008;doi;10.1093/elt/ccn042)]

Young, R. F., & He, A. (Eds.) (1998). *Talking and testing: Discourse approaches to the assessment of oral proficiency.* Amsterdam: Benjamins.

Young, R. F., & Miller, E. R. (2004). Learning as changing participation: Discourse roles in ESL writing conferences. *Modern Language Journal, 88,* 519–535.

Zuengler, J., Ford, C. & Fassnacht, C. (1998). Analyst eyes and camera eyes: Theoretical and technological considerations in "seeing" the details of classroom interaction. Technical Report. The National Research Center on English Learning and Achievement, the University at Albany, State University of New York. Available from http://cela.albany.edu/reports/zuengleranalyst11006.pdf.

22
What Corpora Can Offer in Language Teaching and Learning

Tony McEnery and Richard Xiao

Introduction

The corpus-based approach to linguistics and language education has gained prominence over the past four decades, particularly since the mid-1980s. This is because corpus analysis can be illuminating "in virtually all branches of linguistics or language learning" (Leech, 1997, p. 9; cf. also Biber, Conrad & Reppen, 1998, p. 11). One of the strengths of corpus data lies in its empirical nature, which pools together the intuitions of a great number of speakers and makes linguistic analysis more objective (McEnery & Wilson, 2001, p. 103). Unsurprisingly, corpora have been used extensively in nearly all branches of linguistics including, for example, lexicographic and lexical studies, grammatical studies, language variation studies, contrastive and translation studies, diachronic studies, semantics, pragmatics, stylistics, sociolinguistics, discourse analysis, forensic linguistics and language pedagogy. Corpora have passed into general usage in linguistics in spite of the fact that they still occasionally attract hostile criticism (e.g. Widdowson, 1990, 2000).[1]

The early 1990s saw an increasing interest in applying the findings of corpus-based research to language pedagogy. The upsurge of interest is evidenced by the eight well-received biennial international conferences on Teaching and Language Corpora (TaLC) held in Lancaster, Oxford, Graz, Bertinoro, Granada, Paris and Lisbon. This is also apparent when one looks at the published literature. In addition to a large number of journal articles, at least twenty-five authored or edited volumes have recently been produced on the topic of teaching and language corpora: Wichmann, Fligelstone, McEnery and Knowles (1997), Partington (1998), Bernardini (2000), Burnard and McEnery (2000), Kettemann and Marko (2002, 2006), Aston (2001), Ghadessy, Henry and Roseberry (2001), Hunston (2002), Granger, Hung and Petch-Tyson (2002), Connor and Upton (2002), Tan (2002), Sinclair (2003, 2004), Aston, Bernardini and Stewart (2004), Mishan (2005), Nesselhauf (2005), Römer (2005), Braun, Kohn and Mukherjee (2006), Gavioli (2006), Scott and Tribble (2006), Hidalgo, Quereda and Santana (2007), O'Keeffe, McCarthy and Carter (2007), Aijmer (2009) and Campoy, Gea-valor and Belles-Fortuno (2010). These works cover a wide range of issues related to using corpora in language pedagogy, e.g. corpus-based language descriptions, corpus analysis in the classroom and learner corpus research (cf. Keck, 2004).

In the opening chapter of *Teaching and Language Corpora* (Wichmann et al., 1997), Leech (1997) observed that a convergence between teaching and language corpora was apparent. That convergence has three focuses, as noted by Leech: the indirect use of corpora in teaching (reference publishing, materials development, and language testing), the direct use of corpora in teaching (teaching about, teaching to exploit, and exploiting to teach) and further teaching-oriented corpus development (languages for specific purposes (LSP) corpora, first language (L1) developmental corpora and second language (L2) learner corpora).

In the remainder of this chapter, we will explore the potential uses of corpora in language pedagogy in terms of Leech's three focuses of convergence. The chapter concludes by discussing the debate over the relevance of authenticity and frequency of corpora in language education as well as the future of corpus-based language pedagogy.

Indirect Use of Corpora

The use of corpora in language teaching and learning has been more indirect than direct. This is perhaps because the direct use of corpora in language pedagogy is restricted by a number of factors including, for example, the level and experience of learners, time constraints, curricular requirements, knowledge and skills required of teachers for corpus analysis and pedagogical mediation, and the access to resources, such as computers, and appropriate software tools and corpora, or a combination of these (see the concluding section for further discussion). This section explores how corpora have impacted on language pedagogy indirectly.

Reference Publishing

Corpora can be said to have revolutionized reference publishing (at least for English), be it a dictionary or a reference grammar, in such a way that dictionaries published since the 1990s are typically have used corpus data in one way or another so that "even people who have never heard of a corpus are using the product of corpus-based investigation" (Hunston, 2002, p. 96).

Corpora are useful in several ways for lexicographers. The greatest advantage of using corpora in lexicography lies in their machine-readable nature, which allows dictionary makers to extract all authentic, typical examples of the usage of a lexical item from a large body of text in a few seconds. The second advantage of the corpus-based approach, which is not readily available when using citation slips, is the frequency information and quantification of collocation that a corpus can readily provide (see the section "Syllabus Design and Materials Development" for further discussion of collocation). Some dictionaries, e.g. COBUILD (HarperCollins, 1995) and Longman, 1995, include such frequency information. Frequency data plays an even more important role in the so-called frequency dictionaries, which define core vocabulary to help learners of different modern languages, e.g. Davies (2005) for Spanish, Jones and Tschirner (2005) for German, Davies and de Oliveira Preto-Bay (2007) for Portuguese, Lonsdale and Bras (2009) for French, and Xiao, Rayson and McEnery (2009) for Chinese. Information of this sort is particularly useful for materials writers and language learners alike.

A further benefit of using corpora is related to corpus markup and annotation. Many available corpora (e.g. the British National Corpus, BNC) are encoded with textual (e.g. register, genre and domain) and sociolinguistic (e.g. user gender and age) metadata, which allows lexicographers to give a more accurate description of the usage of a lexical item. Corpus annotations such as part-of-speech tagging and word sense disambiguation also enable a more sensible grouping of words that are polysemous and homographs. Furthermore, a monitor corpus, which is constantly updated, allows lexicographers to track subtle change in the meaning and usage of a lexical item so as to keep their dictionaries up-to-date.

Last but not least, corpus evidence can complement or refute the intuitions of individual lexicographers, which are not always reliable (cf. Sinclair, 1991, p. 112; Atkins & Levin, 1995;

Murison-Bowie, 1996, p. 184) so that dictionary entries are more accurate. The above observations are line with Hunston (2002, p. 96), who summarizes the changes brought about by corpora to dictionaries and other reference books in terms of five "emphases": an emphasis on frequency, an emphasis on collocation and phraseology, an emphasis on variation, an emphasis on lexis in grammar, and an emphasis on authenticity.

It has been noted that non-corpus-based grammars can contain biases while corpora can help to improve grammatical descriptions (McEnery & Xiao, 2005). The *Longman Grammar of Spoken and Written English* (Biber, Johansson, Leech, Conrad & Finegan, 1999) can be considered as a new milestone in reference publishing following Quirk, Greenbaum, Leech and Svartvik's (1985) *A Comprehensive Grammar of the English Language*. Based entirely on the forty-million-word Longman Spoken and Written English Corpus, the book gives "a thorough description of English grammar, which is illustrated throughout with real corpus examples, and which gives equal attention to the ways speakers and writers actually use these linguistic resources" (Biber et al., 1999, p. 45). The new corpus-based grammar is unique in many different ways, for example, by taking account of register variations and exploring the differences between written and spoken grammars.

While lexical information forms, to some extent, an integral part of the grammatical description in Biber et al. (1999), it is the Collins COBUILD series (Sinclair, 1990, 1992; Francis, Hunston & Manning 1997, 1998), that focus on lexis in grammatical descriptions (the so-called "pattern grammar", Hunston & Francis, 2000). In fact, Sinclair and colleagues (1990) flatly reject the distinction between lexis and grammar. While pattern grammars focusing on the connection between pattern and meaning challenge the traditional distinction between lexis and grammar, they are undoubtedly useful in language learning as they provide "a resource for vocabulary building in which the word is treated as part of a phrase rather than in isolation" (Hunston, 2002, p. 106).

For language pedagogy the most important developments in lexicography relate to the learner dictionary. Yet corpus-based learner dictionaries have a quite short history. It was only in 1987 that the *Collins COBUILD English Language Dictionary* (Sinclair, 1987) was published as the first "fully corpus-based" dictionary. Yet the impact of this corpus-based dictionary was such that most other publishers in the English language teaching (ELT) market followed Collins' lead. By 1995, the new editions of major learner dictionaries such as the *Longman Dictionary of Contemporary English* (3rd edition) (Longman, 1995), the *Oxford Advanced Learner's Dictionary* (5th edition, Hornby & Crowther, 1999), and a newcomer, the *Cambridge International Dictionary of English* (Procter, 1995) all claimed to be based on corpus evidence in one way or another.

One of the important features of corpus-based learner dictionaries is their inclusion of quantitative data extracted from a corpus. Another important feature, which is also related to frequency information, is that such dictionaries typically select the vocabulary used from a controlled set when defining the entry for a word. Producing definitions in an L2 that language learners can understand is a problem; language learners may not have a very well developed L2 vocabulary. This makes it necessary and desirable for dictionary makers to limit the vocabulary they use when defining words in a dictionary. Nowadays, most learner dictionary makers prepare a list of defining words, usually ranging from 2,000 to 2,500 words, based on the frequency information extracted from corpora as well as on the lexicographers' experience of defining words.

As noted earlier, an important use of corpus data for lexicography is in the area of example selection so that nowadays most dictionaries of English use corpora as the source of their examples. In the case of learner dictionaries, however, there was a tradition of using examples invented by lexicographers, rather than authentic materials, in dictionary production, because they believed that foreign language learners have difficulty understanding authentic materials and therefore have to be presented with simple, rewritten examples in which the use of a given word is highlighted to show its syntactic and semantic properties. It was corpus-based learner dictionary work that challenged this received wisdom. The COBUILD (Collins Birmingham University International Language Database) project broke with tradition and used authentic data extracted from corpora to produce illustrative examples for a learner dictionary. The use of authentic examples in learner dictionaries is an area where corpus-based learner dictionaries have innovated.

Syllabus Design and Materials Development

While corpora have been used extensively to provide more accurate descriptions of language use, a number of scholars have also used corpus data directly to look critically at existing teaching English as a foreign language (TEFL) syllabuses and teaching materials. Mindt (1996), for example, finds that the use of grammatical structures in textbooks for teaching English differs considerably from the use of these structures in L1 English. He observes that one common failure of English textbooks is that they teach "a kind of school English which does not seem to exist outside the foreign language classroom" (Mindt, 1996, p. 232). As such, learners often find it difficult to communicate successfully with native speakers. A simple yet important role of corpora in language education is to provide more realistic examples of language usage that reflect the complexities and nuances of natural language.

In addition, however, corpora may provide data, especially frequency data, which may further alter what is taught. For example, on the basis of a comparison of the frequencies of modal verbs, future time expressions and conditional clauses in native English corpora and their grading in textbooks used widely in Germany, Mindt (1996) concludes that one problem with non-corpus-based syllabuses is that the order in which those items are taught in syllabuses "very often does not correspond to what one might reasonably expect from corpus data of spoken and written English", arguing that teaching syllabuses should be based on empirical evidence rather than tradition and intuition, with frequency of usage as a guide to priority for teaching (Mindt, 1996, pp. 245–246). While frequency is certainly not the only determinant of what to teach and in what order (see the concluding section for further discussion), it can indeed help to make learning more effective. For example, McCarthy, McCarten and Sandiford's (2005–2006) innovative *Touchstone* book series, which is based on the Cambridge International Corpus, aims to present the vocabulary, grammar and functions students encounter most often in real life.

Hunston (2002, p. 189) echoes Mindt, suggesting that "the experience of using corpora should lead to rather different views of syllabus design". The type of syllabus she discusses extensively is a "lexical syllabus", originally proposed by Sinclair and Renouf (1988) and outlined fully by Willis (1990) and embodied in Willis, Willis and Davids' (1988–1989) three-part *Collins COBUILD English Course*. According to Sinclair and Renouf (1988, p. 148), a lexical syllabus would focus on "(a) the commonest word forms in a language; (b) the central patterns of usage; (c) the combinations which they usually form".

While the term may occasionally be misinterpreted to indicate a syllabus consisting solely of vocabulary items, a lexical syllabus actually covers "all aspects of language, differing from a conventional syllabus only in that the central concept of organization is lexis" (Hunston, 2002, p. 189). Sinclair (2000, p. 191) would say that the grammar covered in a lexical syllabus is "lexical grammar", not "lexico-grammar", which attempts to "build a grammar and lexis on an equal basis". Indeed, as Murison-Bowie (1996, p. 185) observes,

in using corpora in a teaching context, it is frequently difficult to distinguish what is a lexical investigation and what is a syntactic one. One leads to the other, and this can be used to advantage in a teaching/learning context.

Sinclair and his colleagues' proposal for a lexical syllabus is echoed by Lewis (1993, 1997a, 1997b, 2000), who provides strong support for the lexical approach to language teaching.

A focus of the lexical approach to language pedagogy is teaching collocations (i.e. habitual co-occurrences of lexical items) and the related concept of prefabricated units. There is a consensus that collocational knowledge is important for developing L1/L2 language skills (e.g. Bahns, 1993; Zhang, 1993; Cowie, 1994; Herbst, 1996; Kita & Ogata, 1997; Partington, 1998; Hoey, 2000, 2004; Shei & Pain, 2000; Sripicharn, 2000; Altenberg & Granger, 2001; McEnery & Wilson, 2001; McAlpine & Myles, 2003; Nesselhauf, 2003). Hoey (2004), for example, posits that "learning a lexical item entails learning what it occurs with and what grammar it tends to have". Cowie (1994, p. 3168) argues that "native-like proficiency of a language depends crucially on knowledge of a stock of prefabricated units". Aston (1995) also notes that the use of prefabs can speed language processing in both comprehension and production, thus creating native-like fluency.

A powerful reason for the employment of collocations, as Partington (1998, p. 20) suggests, "lies in the way it facilitates communication processing on the part of hearer", because "language consisting of a relatively high number of fixed phrases is generally more predictable than that which is not" while "in real time language decoding, hearers need all the help they can get". As such, competence in a language undoubtedly involves collocational knowledge (cf. Herbst, 1996, p. 389).

Collocational knowledge indicates which lexical items co-occur frequently with others and how they combine within a sentence. Such knowledge is evidently more important than individual words themselves (cf. Kita & Ogata, 1997, p. 230) and is needed for effective sentence generation (cf. Smadja & McKeown, 1990). Zhang (1993), for example, finds that more proficient L2 writers use significantly more collocations, more accurately and in more variety than less proficient learners. Collocational error is a common type of error for learners (cf. McAlpine & Myles, 2003, p. 75). Gui and Yang (2002, p. 48) observe, on the basis of the one-million-word Chinese Learner English Corpus, that collocation error is one of the major error types for Chinese learners of English. Altenberg and Granger (2001) and Nesselhauf (2003) find that even advanced learners of English have considerable difficulties with collocation. One possible explanation is that learners are deficient in "automation of collocations" (Kjellmer, 1991). "As a result, learners need detailed information about common collocational patterns and idioms; fixed and semi-fixed lexical expressions and different degrees of variability; relative frequency and currency of particular patterns; and formality level" (McAlpine & Myles, 2003, p. 75).

Corpora are useful in this respect, not only because collocations can only reliably be measured quantitatively, but also because the key word in context (KWIC) view of corpus data exposes learners to a great deal of authentic data in a structured way. Our view is line with Kennedy (2003), who discusses the relationship between corpus data and the nature of language learning, focusing on the teaching of collocations. The author argues that second or foreign language learning is a process of learning "explicit knowledge" with awareness, which requires a great deal of exposure to language data.

In addition to the lexical focus, corpus-based teaching materials try to demonstrate how the target language is actually used in different contexts, as exemplified in Biber, Leech and Conrad's (2002) *Longman Student Grammar of Spoken and Written English*, which pays special attention to how English is used differently in various spoken and written registers.

Language Testing

Another emerging area of language pedagogy that has started to use the corpus-based approach is language testing. Alderson (1996) envisaged the following possible uses of corpora in this area: test construction, compilation and selection, test presentation, response capture, test scoring, and calculation and delivery of results. He concludes that "[t]he potential advantages of basing our tests on real language data, of making data-based judgments about candidates' abilities, knowledge and performance are clear enough. A crucial question is whether the possible advantages are born out in practice" (Alderson, 1996, pp. 258–259). The concern raised in Alderson's conclusion appears to have been addressed satisfactorily so that nowadays computer-based tests are recognized as being comparable to paper-based tests (e.g. computer-based versus paper-based TOEFL tests).

A number of corpus-based studies of language testing have been reported. For example, Coniam (1997) demonstrated how to use word frequency data extracted from corpora to generate cloze tests automatically. Kaszubski and Wojnowska (2003) presented a corpus-driven computer program, TestBuilder, for building sentence-based ELT exercises. The program can process raw corpora of plain texts or corpora annotated with part-of-speech information, using another linked computer program that assigns the part-of-speech category to each word in the corpus automatically in real time. The annotated data is used in turn as input for test material selection. Indeed, corpora have recently been used by major providers of test services for a number of purposes:

- as an archive of examination scripts;
- to develop test materials;
- to optimize test procedures;
- to improve the quality of test marking;
- to validate tests; and
- to standardize tests.

For example, the University of Cambridge Local Examinations Syndicate (UCLES) is active in both corpus development (e.g. Cambridge Learner Corpus, Cambridge Corpus of Spoken English, Business English Text Corpus, and Corpus of Young Learners English Speaking Tests) and the analysis of native English corpora and learner corpora. At UCLES, native English corpora such as the BNC are used "to investigate collocations, authentic stems and appropriate distractors which enable item writers to base their examination tasks on real texts" (Ball, 2001, p. 7);[2] the corpus-based approach is used to explore "the distinguishing features in the writing performance of EFL/ESL learners or users taking the Cambridge English examinations" and how to incorporate these into "a single scale of bands, that is, a common scale, describing different levels of L2 writing proficiency" (Hawkey, 2001, p. 9); corpora are also used for the purpose of speaking assessment (Ball & Wilson, 2002; Taylor, 2003) and to develop domain-specific (e.g. business English) wordlists for use in test materials (Ball, 2002; Horner & Strutt, 2004).

Teacher Development

For learners to benefit from the use of corpora, language teachers must first of all be equipped with a sound knowledge of the corpus-based approach. It is unsurprising then to discover that corpora have been used in training language teachers (e.g. Allan, 1999, 2002; Conrad, 1999; Seidlhofer, 2000, 2002; O'Keeffe & Farr, 2003). Allan (1999), for example, demonstrates how to use corpus data to raise the language awareness of English teachers in Hong Kong secondary schools. Conrad (1999) presents a corpus-based study of linking adverbials (e.g. *therefore* and *in other words*), on the basis of which she suggests that it is important for a language teacher to do more than using classroom concordancing and lexical or lexico-grammatical analyses if language teaching is to take full advantage of the corpus-based approach. Conrad's concern with teacher education is echoed by O'Keeffe and Farr (2003), who argue that corpus linguistics should be included in initial language teacher education so as to enhance teachers' research skills and language awareness.

Direct Use of Corpora

While indirect uses such as syllabus design and materials development are closely associated with what to teach, corpora have also provided valuable insights into how to teach. Of Leech's (1997) three focuses, direct uses of corpora include "teaching about", "teaching to exploit", and "exploiting to teach", with the latter two relating to how to use. Given a number of restricting factors as noted in the previous section, direct uses have so far been confined largely to learning at more advanced levels, for example, in tertiary education, whereas in general English language teaching (let alone to mention other foreign languages), especially in secondary education (see Braun, 2007 for a rare example of an empirical study of using corpora in secondary education), the direct use of corpora is "still conspicuously absent" (Kaltenböck & Mehlmauer-Larcher, 2005).

"Teaching about" means teaching corpus linguistics as an academic subject like other sub-disciplines of linguistics such as syntax and pragmatics. Corpus linguistics has now found its way into the curricula for linguistics and language related degree programmes at both postgraduate and undergraduate levels in many universities around the world. "Teaching to exploit" means providing students with "hands-on" know-how, as emphasized in McEnery, Xiao and Tono (2006), so that they can exploit corpora for their own purposes. Once the student has acquired the necessary knowledge and techniques of corpus-based language study, the learning activity may become student centred. "Exploiting to teach" means using a corpus-based approach to teaching language and linguistics courses (e.g. sociolinguistics and discourse analysis), which would otherwise be taught using non-corpus-based methods.

If the focuses of "teaching about" and "exploiting to teach" are viewed as being associated typically with students of linguistics and language programmes, "teaching to exploit" relates to students of all subjects which involve language study and learning, who are expected to benefit from the so-called data-driven learning (DDL) or "discovery learning".

The issue of how to use corpora in the language classroom has been discussed extensively in the literature. With the corpus-based approach to language pedagogy, the traditional "three Ps" (Presentation, Practice and Production) approach to teaching may not be entirely suitable. Instead, the more exploratory approach of "three Is" (Illustration, Interaction and Induction) may be more appropriate, where "illustration" means looking at real data, "interaction" means discussing and sharing opinions and observations, and "induction" means making one's own rule for a particular feature, which "will be refined and honed as more and more data is encountered" (see Carter & McCarthy, 1995, p. 155). This progressive induction approach is what Murison-Bowie (1996, p. 191) would call the interlanguage approach: namely, partial and incomplete generalizations are drawn from limited data as a stage on the way towards a fully satisfactory rule. While the "three Is" approach was originally proposed by Carter and McCarthy (1995) to teach spoken grammar, it may also apply to language education as a whole, in our view.

It is clear that the exploratory teaching approach focusing on "three Is" is in line with Johns' (1991) concept of "data-driven learning (DDL)". Johns was perhaps among the first to realize the potential of corpora for language learners (e.g. Higgins & Johns, 1984). In his opinion, "research is too serious to be left to the researchers" (Johns, 1991, p. 2). As such, he argues that the language learner should be encouraged to become "a research worker whose learning needs to be driven by access to linguistic data" (Johns, 1991, p. 2). John's web-based Kibbitzer (www.ling.lancs.ac.uk/corplang/Kibbitzers/Kibbitzers.chw) gives some very good examples of DDL.

DDL can be either teacher-directed or learner-led (i.e. discovery learning) to suit the needs of learners at different levels, but it is basically learner-centred. This autonomous learning process "gives the student the realistic expectation of breaking new ground as a 'researcher', doing something which is a unique and individual contribution" (Leech, 1997, p. 10). It is important to note, however, that the key to successful DDL, even if it is student-centred, is the appropriate level of teacher guidance or pedagogical mediation depending on the learners' age, experience and proficiency level, because "a corpus is not a simple object, and it is just as easy to derive nonsensical conclusions from the evidence as insightful ones" (Sinclair, 2004, p. 2). In this sense, it is even more important for language teachers to be equipped with the necessary training in corpus analysis.

Johns (1991) identifies three stages of inductive reasoning with corpora in the DDL approach: observation (of concordanced evidence), classification (of salient features) and generalization (of rules). The three stages roughly correspond to Carter and McCarthy's (1995) "three Is". The DDL approach is fundamentally different from the "three Ps" approach in that the former involves bottom-up induction whereas the latter involves top-down deduction. The direct use of corpora and concordancing in the language classroom has been discussed extensively in the literature (e.g. Tribble, 1991, 1997a, 1997b, 2000, 2003; Tribble & Jones, 1990, 1997; Flowerdew, 1993; Karpati, 1995; Kettemann, 1995, 1996; Wichmann, 1995; Woolls, 1998; Aston, 2001; Osborne, 2001, Braun, 2007), covering a wide range of issues including, for example, underlying theories, methods and techniques, and problems and solutions.

Teaching Oriented Corpora

Teaching-oriented corpora are particularly useful in teaching LSP (LSP corpora) and in research on L1 (developmental corpora) and L2 (learner corpora) language acquisition. Such corpora can be used directly or indirectly in language pedagogy as discussed in the previous sections.

LSP and Professional Communication

In addition to teaching English as a second or foreign language in general, a great deal of attention has been paid to domain-specific language use and professional communication (e.g. English for specific purposes and English for academic purpose). For example, Thurstun and Candlin (1997, 1998) explore the use of concordancing in teaching writing and vocabulary in academic English. Hyland (1999) compares the features of the specific genres of metadiscourse in introductory course books and research articles on the basis of a corpus consisting of extracts from twenty-one university textbooks for different disciplines and a similar corpus of research articles.

Likewise, Upton and Connor (2001) undertake a "move analysis" in the business English using a business learner corpus. The authors approach the cultural aspect of professional communication by comparing the "politeness strategies" used by learners from different cultural backgrounds. Thompson and Tribble (2001) examine citation practices in academic text. Koester (2002) argues, on the basis of an analysis of the performance of speech acts in workshop conversations, for a discourse approach to teaching communicative functions in spoken English. Yang and Allison (2003) study the organizational structure in research articles in applied linguistics. Carter and McCarthy (2004) explore, on the basis of the Cambridge and Nottingham Corpus of Discourse in English (CANCODE), a range of social contexts in which creative uses of language are manifested. Hinkel (2004) compares the use of tense, aspect and the passive in L1 and L2 academic texts.

Xiao (2003) reviews a number of case studies using specialized multilingual corpora to teach domain specific translation. Parallel concordancing is not only useful in translation teaching; it can also aid the so-called "reciprocal learning" (Johns, 1997), where two language learners from different L1 backgrounds are paired to help each other learn their language. Studies such as these demonstrate that LSP corpora are particularly useful in teaching LSP and professional communication.

Learner Corpora and Interlanguage Analysis

The creation and use of learner corpora in language pedagogy and interlanguage research has been welcomed as one of the most exciting recent developments in corpus-based language studies. If native speaker corpora of the target language provide a top-down approach to using corpora in language pedagogy, learner corpora provide a bottom-up approach to language teaching (Osborne, 2002).

A learner corpus, as opposed to a "developmental corpus" composed of data produced by children acquiring their mother tongue (L1), comprises written or spoken data produced by language learners who are acquiring a second or foreign language. Data of this type has particularly been useful in language pedagogy and second language acquisition (SLA) research, as demonstrated by the fruitful learner corpus studies published over the past decade (see Pravec, 2002; Keck, 2004; and Myles, 2005 for recent reviews). SLA research is primarily concerned with "the mental representations and developmental processes which shape and constrain second language (L2) productions" (Myles, 2005, p. 374).

Language acquisition occurs in the mind of the learner, which cannot be observed directly and must be studied from a psychological perspective. Nevertheless, if learner performance data is shaped and constrained by such a mental process, it at least provides indirect, observable and empirical evidence for the language acquisition process. Note that using product as evidence for process may not be less reliable; sometimes this is the only practical way of finding about process. Stubbs (2001) draws a parallel between corpora in corpus linguistics and rocks in geology, "which both assume a relation between process and product. By and large, the processes are invisible, and must be inferred from the products". Like geologists who study rocks because they are interested in geological processes to which they do not have direct access, SLA researchers can analyse learner performance data to infer the inaccessible mental process of SLA.

Learner corpora can also be used as an empirical basis that tests hypotheses generated using the psycholinguistic approach, and to enable the findings previously made on the basis of limited data of a small number of informants to be generalized. Additionally, learner corpora have widened the scope of SLA research so that, for example, interlanguage research nowadays treats learner performance data as a category in its own right rather than as decontextualised errors in traditional error analysis (cf. Granger, 1998, p. 6).

At the pre-conference workshop on learner corpora affiliated to the second International Symposium of Corpus Linguistics held at the University of Lancaster, the workshop organizers Tono and Meunier observed that learner corpora are no longer in their infancy but are going through their nominal teenage years—they are full of promise but not yet fully developed.

In language pedagogy, the implications of learner corpora have been explored for curriculum design, materials development and teaching methodology (cf. Keck, 2004, p. 99). The interface between L1 and L2 materials has been explored. Meunier (2002), for example, argues that frequency information obtained from native speaker corpora alone is not sufficient to inform curriculum and materials design. Rather, "it is important to strike a balance between frequency, difficulty and pedagogical relevance. That is exactly where learner corpus research comes into play to help weigh the importance of each of these" (Meunier, 2002, p. 123). Meunier also advocates the use of learner data in the classroom, suggesting that exercises such as comparing learner and native speaker data and analysing errors in learner language will help students to notice gaps between their interlanguage and the language they are learning.

Interlanguage studies based on learner corpora which have been undertaken so far focus on what Granger (2002) calls "Contrastive Interlanguage Analysis (CIA)", which compares learner data and the data produced by native speakers of the target language, or the learner's L1. The first type of comparison typically aims to evaluate the level of under- or overuse of particular linguistic features in learner language while the second type aims to uncover L1 interference or transfer. Corpus data produced by learners from different L1 backgrounds can also be compared against one another with the aim of uncovering common features of SLA process by discarding L1-specific peculiarities. In addition to CIA, learner corpora have also been used to investigate the order of acquisition of particular morphemes. Readers can refer to Granger et al. (2002) for recent work in the use of learner corpora, and read Granger (2003) for a more general discussion of the applications of learner corpora such as the International Corpus of Learner English (ICLE).

In addition to SLA research, learner corpora can also be used directly in classroom teaching. For example, Seidlhofer (2002) and Mukherjee and Rohrbach (2006) demonstrate how a "local learner corpus" containing students' own writings can be used directly for learning by coping with students' questions about their own or classmates' writings, or analysing and correcting errors in such familiar writings.

Conclusions

Before we close the discussion of using corpora in language pedagogy, it is appropriate to address some objections to the use of corpora in language learning and teaching. While frequency and authenticity are often considered two of the most important advantages of using corpora, they are also the locus of criticism from language pedagogy researchers. For example, Cook (1998, p. 61) argues that corpus data impoverishes language learning by giving undue prominence to what is simply frequent at the expense of rarer but more effective or salient expressions. Widdowson (1990, 2000) argues that corpus data is authentic only in a very limited sense in that it is de-contextualized (i.e. traces of texts rather than discourse) and must be re-contextualized in language teaching. On the other hand, it can be argued that

> using corpus data not only increases the chances of learners being confronted with relatively infrequent instances of language use, but also of their being able to see in what way such uses are atypical, in what contexts they do appear, and how they fit in with the pattern of more prototypical uses.
>
> (Osborne, 2001, p. 486)

This view is echoed by Goethals (2003, p. 424), who argues that "frequency ranking will be a parameter for sequencing and grading learning materials" because "frequency is a measure of *probability* of usefulness" and "high-frequency words constitute a core vocabulary that is useful above the incidental choice of text of one teacher or textbook author". Hunston (2002, pp. 194–195) observes that "items which are important though infrequent seem to be those that echo texts which have a high cultural value", though in many cases "cultural salience is not clearly at odds with frequency".

While frequency information is readily available from corpora, no corpus linguist has ever argued that the most frequent is most important. On the contrary, Kennedy (1998, p. 290) argues that frequency "should be only one of the criteria used to influence instruction" and that "the facts about language and language use which emerge from corpus analyses should never be allowed to become a burden for pedagogy". As such, raw frequency data is often adjusted for use in a syllabus, as reported in Renouf (1987, p. 168).

It would be inappropriate, therefore, for language teachers, syllabus designers and materials writers to ignore "compelling frequency evidence already available", as pointed out by Leech (1997, p. 16), who argues that: "Whatever the imperfections of the simple equation 'most frequent' = 'most important to learn', it is difficult to deny that frequency information becoming available from corpora has an important empirical input to language learning materials".

Kaltenböck and Mehlmauer-Larcher (2005, p. 78) downplay the role of frequency in language learning, arguing that "what is frequent in language will be picked up by learners automatically, precisely because it is frequent, and therefore does not have to be consciously learned". This is not true, however. Determiners such as *a* and *the* are certainly very frequent in English, yet they are difficult for Chinese learners of English because their mother tongue does not have such grammatical morphemes and does not maintain a count-mass noun distinction.

Clearly, frequency is not "automatically pedagogically useful" (Kaltenböck & Mehlmauer-Larcher, 2005, p. 78); decisions relating to teaching must also take account of overall teaching objectives, learners' concrete situations, cognitive salience, learnability, generative value and, of course, teachers' intuitions (cf. Kaltenböck & Mehlmauer-Larcher, 2005, p. 78). However, frequency can at least help syllabus designers, materials writers and teachers alike to make better-informed and more carefully motivated decisions (cf. Gavioli & Aston, 2001, p. 239).

If we leave objections to frequency data to one side, Widdowson (1990, 2000) also questions the use of authentic texts in language teaching. In his opinion, authenticity of language in the classroom is "an illusion" (1990, p. 44) because even though corpus data may be authentic in one sense, its authenticity of purpose is destroyed by its use with an unintended audience of language learners (see Murison-Bowie, 1996, p. 189). Widdowson (2003, p. 93) makes a distinction between "genuineness" and "authenticity", which are claimed to be the features of text as a product and discourse as a process respectively: corpora are genuine in that they comprise attested language use, but they are not authentic for language teaching because their contexts (as opposed to co-texts) have been deprived.

We will not be engaged in the debate here, but would like to draw readers' attention to Stubbs' (2001) metaphor of product versus process as cited in the section "Learner Corpora and Interlanguage Analysis". The implication of Widdowson's argument is that only language produced for imaginary situations in the classroom is "authentic". Even if we do follow Widdowson's genuineness-authenticity distinction, it is not clear why such imaginary situations are authentic because authenticity, as opposed to genuineness, would mean real communicative context. Situations conjured up for classroom teaching obviously do not take place in really communicative contexts; then how can they be authentic, if we choose to keep this distinction? When students learn and practise a shopping "discourse", they are actually by no means doing shopping! Furthermore, as argued by Fox (1987), invented examples often do not reflect nuances of usage. That is perhaps why, as Mindt (1996, p. 232) observes, students who have been taught "school English" cannot readily cope with English used by native speakers in real life. As such, Wichmann (1997, p. xvi) argues that in language teaching, "the preference for 'authentic' texts requires both learners and teachers to cope with language which the textbooks do not predict".

The discussions in the previous sections suggest that corpora appear to have played a more important role in helping to decide what to teach (indirect uses) than how to teach (direct uses). While indirect uses of corpora seem to be well established, direct uses of corpora in teaching are largely confined to advanced levels such as higher education. Corpus-based learning activities are nearly absent general teaching English as a foreign language (TEFL) classes at lower levels such as secondary education. Of the various causes for this absence mentioned earlier, perhaps the most important are the access to appropriate corpus resources and the necessary training of teachers, which we view as priorities for future tasks of corpus linguists if corpora are to be popularized to more general language teaching context.

While there are a wide range of existing corpora that are publicly available (see Xiao, 2008 for a recent survey), the majority of those resources have been developed "as tools for linguistic research and not with pedagogical goals in mind" (Braun, 2007). As Cook (1998, p. 57) suggests, "the leap from linguistics to pedagogy is […] far from straightforward". To bridge the gap between corpora and language pedagogy, the first step would involve creating corpora that are pedagogically motivated, in both design and content, to meet pedagogical needs and curricular requirements so that corpus-based learning activities become an integral part, rather than an additional option, of the overall language curriculum. Such pedagogically motivated corpora "should not only be more coherent than traditional corpora; they should, as far as possible, also be complementary to school curricula, to facilitate both the contextualisation process and the practical problems of integration" (Braun, 2007, p. 310). The design of such corpus-based learning activities must also take account of learners' age, experience and level as well as their integration into the overall curriculum.

Given the situation of learners (e.g. their age, level of language competence, level of expert knowledge and attitude towards learning autonomy) in general language education in relation to advanced learners in tertiary education, even such pedagogically motivated corpus-based learning activities must be mediated by teachers. This in turn raises the issue of the current state of teachers' knowledge and skills of corpus analysis and pedagogical mediation, which is another practical problem that has prevented direct use of corpora in language pedagogy. As Kaltenböck and Mehlmauer-Larcher (2005, p. 81) argue, "mediation by the teacher is a necessary prerequisite for successful application of computer corpora in language teaching and should therefore be given sufficient attention in teacher education courses" (cf. also O'Keeffe & Farr, 2003). However, as the integration of corpus studies in language teacher training is only a quite recent phenomenon (cf. Chambers, 2007), "it will therefore at least take more time, and perhaps a new generation of teachers, for corpora to find their way into the language classroom" (Braun, 2007, p. 308).

In conclusion, if these two tasks are accomplished, it is our view that corpora will not only revolutionize the teaching of subjects such as grammar in the twenty-first century as Conrad (2000) has predicated, they will also fundamentally change the ways we approach language education, including both what is taught and how it is taught. As Gavioli and Aston (2001) argue, corpora should not only be viewed as resources that help teachers to decide what to teach, they should also be viewed as resources from which learners may learn directly.

Notes

1. In this chapter, we will not be concerned with the debate over the use of corpus data in linguistic analysis and language education. Readers interested in the pros and cons of using corpus data should refer to Sinclair (1991), Widdowson (1991, 2000), de Beaugrande (2001) and Stubbs (2001). While Widdowson, Sinclair and de Beaugrande characterize two extreme attitudes towards corpora, there are many milder (positive or negative) reactions to corpus data between the two extremes. Readers can refer to Nelson (2000) for a good review.
2. "Stem" is a technical term in language testing that refers to "the top part of a multiple-choice item, usually a statement or question" (Fulcher & Davidson, 2007, p. 53). As a collection of attested language data, a corpus is a good resource for test writers as it can provide abundant authentic stems.

References

Aijmer, K. (2009). *Corpora and language teaching*. Amsterdam: John Benjamins.

Alderson, C. (1996). Do corpora have a role in language assessment? In J. Thomas & M. Short (Eds.), *Using corpora for language research* (pp. 248–259). London: Longman.

Allan, Q. (1999). Enhancing the language awareness of Hong Kong teachers through corpus data. *Journal of Technology and Teacher Education, 7*(1), 57–74.

Allan, Q. (2002). The TELEC secondary learner corpus: a resource for teacher development. In S. Granger, J. Hung & S. Petch-Tyson (Eds.), *Computer learner corpora, second language acquisition and foreign language teaching* (pp. 195–212). Amsterdam: John Benjamins.

Altenberg, B., & Granger, S. (2001). The grammatical and lexical patterning of MAKE in native and non-native student writing. *Applied Linguistics, 22*(2), 173–195.

Aston, G. (1995). Corpora in language pedagogy: matching theory and practice. In G. Cook & B. Seidlhofer (Eds.), *Principle and practice in applied linguistics: Studies in honour of H. G. Widdowson* (pp. 257–270). Oxford: Oxford University Press.

Aston, G. (Ed.) (2001). *Learning with corpora*. Houston, TX: Athelstan.

Aston , G., Bernardini, S. & Stewart, D. (Eds.) (2004). *Corpora and language learners*. Amsterdam: John Benjamins.

Atkins, B., & Levin, B. (1995). Building on a corpus: A linguistic and lexicographical look at some near-synonyms. *International Journal of Lexicography, 8*, 85–114.

Bahns, J. (1993). Lexical collocations: A contrastive view. *ELT Journal, 47*(1), 56–63.

Ball, F. (2001). Using corpora in language testing. *Research Notes, 6*, 6–8.

Ball, F. (2002). Developing wordlists for BEC. *Research Notes, 8*, 10–13.

Ball, F., & Wilson, J. (2002). Research projects relating to YLE speaking tests. *Research Notes, 7*, 8–10.

Bernardini, S. (2000). *Competence, capacity, corpora: A study in corpus-aided language learning*. Bologna: CLUEB.

Biber, D., Conrad, S. & Reppen, R. (1998). *Corpus linguistics: Investigating language structure and use*. Cambridge: Cambridge University Press.

Biber, D., Johansson S., Leech G., Conrad S. & Finegan, E. (1999). *Longman grammar of spoken and written English*. London: Longman.

Biber, D., Leech, G. & Conrad, S. (2002). *Longman student grammar of spoken and written English*. Harlow: Longman.

Braun, S. (2007). Integrating corpus work into secondary education: From data-driven learning to needs-driven corpora. *ReCALL, 19*(3), 307–328.

Braun, S., Kohn, K. & Mukherjee, J. (Eds.) (2006). *Corpus technology and language pedagogy*. Frankfurt: Peter Lang.

Burnard, L., & McEnery, A. (Eds.) (2000). *Rethinking language pedagogy from a corpus perspective*. Frankfurt: Peter Lang.

Campoy, M., Gea-valor, M. & Belles-Fortuno, B. (2010). *Corpus-based approaches to English language teaching*. London: Continuum.

Carter, R., & McCarthy, M. (1995). Grammar and the spoken language. *Applied Linguistics, 16*(2), 141–158.

Carter, R., & McCarthy, M. (2004). Talking, creating: interactional language, creativity, and context. *Applied Linguistics, 25*(1), 62–88.

Chambers, A. (2007). Popularising corpus consultation by language learners and teachers. In E. Hidalgo, L. Quereda & J. Santana (Eds.), *Corpora in the foreign language classroom: Selected papers from the sixth International Conference on Teaching and Language Corpora (TaLC 6)* (pp. 3–16). Amsterdam: Rodopi.

Coniam, D. (1997). A preliminary inquiry into using corpus word frequency data in the automatic generation of English language cloze tests. *CALICO Journal, 16*(2–4), 15–33.

Connor, U., & Upton, T. (Eds.) (2002). *Applied corpus linguistics: A multidimensional perspective*. Amsterdam: Rodopi.

Conrad, S. (1999). The importance of corpus-based research for language teachers. *System, 27*, 1–18.

Conrad, S. (2000). Will corpus linguistics revolutionize grammar teaching in the 21st century? *TESOL Quarterly, 34*, 548–560.

Cook, G. (1998). The uses of reality: A reply to Ronald Cater. *ELT Journal, 52*(1), 57–64.

Cowie, A. (1994). Phraseology. in R. Asher (Ed.), *The Encyclopaedia of language and linguistics* (Vol. 6) (pp. 3168–3171). Oxford: Pergamon Press Ltd.

Davies, M. (2005). *A frequency dictionary of Spanish*. London: Routledge.

Davies, M., & de Oliveira Preto-Bay, A. (2007). *A frequency dictionary of Portuguese*. London: Routledge.

de Beaugrande, R. (2001). Interpreting the discourse of H. G. Widdowson: A corpus-based critical discourse analysis. *Applied Linguistics, 22*(1), 104–121.

Flowerdew, J. (1993). Concordancing as a tool in course design. *System, 21*(3), 231–243.

Fox, G. (1987). The case for examples. In J. Sinclair (Ed.), *Looking up: An account of the COBUILD project* (pp. 137–149). London: HarperCollins.

Francis, G., Hunston, S. & Manning, E. (1997). *Collins COBUILD grammar patterns 1: Verbs*. London: HarperCollins.

Francis, G., Hunston, S. & Manning, E. (1998). *Collins COBUILD grammar patterns 2: Nouns and adjectives*. London: HarperCollins.

Fulcher, G., & Davidson, F. (2007). *Language testing and assessment: An advanced resource book*. London: Routledge.

Gavioli, L. (2006). *Exploring corpora for ESP learning*. Amsterdam: John Benjamins.

Gavioli, L., & Aston, G. (2001). Enriching reality: language corpora in language pedagogy. *ELT Journal, 55*(3), 238–246.

Ghadessy, M., Henry, A. & Roseberry, R. (Eds.) (2001). *Small corpus studies and ELT: Theory and practice*. Amsterdam: John Benjamins.

Goethals, M. (2003). E.E.T.: the European English Teaching vocabulary-list. In B. Lewandowska-Tomaszczyk (Ed.), *Practical Applications in language and computers* (pp. 417–427). Frankfurt: Peter Lang.

Granger, S. (1998). The computer learner corpus: a versatile new source of data for SLA research. In S. Granger (Ed.), *Learner English on computer* (pp. 3–18). London: Longman.

Granger, S. (2002). A bird's-eye view of learner corpus research. In S. Granger, J. Hung & S. Petch-Tyson (Eds.), *Computer learner corpora, second language acquisition and foreign language teaching* (pp. 3–33). Amsterdam: John Benjamins.

Granger, S. (2003). Practical applications of learner corpora. In B. Lewandowska-Tomaszczyk (Ed.), *Practical applications in language and computers* (pp. 291–302). Frankfurt: Peter Lang.

Granger, S., Hung, J. & Petch-Tyson, S. (Eds.) (2002). *Computer learner corpora, second language acquisition, and foreign language teaching.* Amsterdam: John Benjamins.

Gui, S., & Yang, H. (2002). *Zhongguo Xuexizhe Yingyu Yuliaoku* [*Chinese learner English corpus*]. Shanghai: Shanghai Foreign Language Education Press.

HarperCollins (1995). *Collins COBUILD English dictionary* (2nd ed.). London: Collins COBUILD.

Hawkey, R. (2001). *IIS student questionnaire.* Cambridge: UCLES.

Herbst, T. (1996). What are collocations: sandy beaches or false teeth? *English Studies, 4,* 379–393.

Hidalgo, E., Quereda, L. & Santana, J. (2007). *Corpora in the foreign language classroom: Selected papers from the sixth International Conference on Teaching and Language Corpora (TaLC 6).* Amsterdam: Rodopi.

Higgins, J., & Johns, T. (1984). *Computers in language learning.* Oxford: Oxford University Press.

Hinkel, E. (2004). Tense, aspect and the passive voice in L1 and L2 academic texts. *Language Teaching Research, 8*(1), 5–29.

Hoey, M. (2000). A world beyond collocation: new perspectives on vocabulary teaching. In M. Lewis (Ed.), *Teaching collocations* (pp. 224–245). Hove: Language Teaching Publications.

Hoey, M. (2004). Lexical priming and the properties of text. In A. Partington, J. Morley & L. Haarman (Eds.), *Corpora and discourse* (pp. 385–412). Bern: Peter Lang.

Hornby, A., & Crowther, J. (1999). *Oxford advanced learner's dictionary* (5th ed.). Oxford: Oxford University Press.

Horner, D., & Strutt, P. (2004). Analyzing domain-specific lexical categories: evidence from the BEC written corpus. *Research Notes, 15,* 6–8.

Hunston, S. (2002). *Corpora in applied linguistics.* Cambridge: Cambridge University Press.

Hunston, S., & Francis, G. (2000). *Pattern grammar: A corpus-driven approach to the lexical grammar of English.* Amsterdam: John Benjamins.

Hyland, K. (1999). Talking to students: Metadiscourse in introductory coursebooks. *English for Specific Purposes, 18*(1), 3–26.

Johns, T. (1991). "Should you be persuaded": Two samples of data-driven learning materials. In T. Johns and P. King (Eds.), *Classroom Concordancing ELR Journal, 4* (pp. 1–16). University of Birmingham.

Johns, T. (1997). Contexts: The background, development and trialling of a concordance-based CALL program. In A. Wichmann, S. Fligelstone, T. McEnery & G. Knowles (Eds.), *Teaching and language corpora* (pp. 100–115). Harlow: Longman.

Jones, R., & Tschirner, E. (2005). *A frequency dictionary of German.* London: Routledge.

Kaltenböck, G., & Mehlmauer-Larcher, B. (2005). Computer corpora and the language classroom: On the potential and limitations of computer corpora in language teaching. *ReCALL, 17,* 65–84.

Karpati, I. (1995). *Concordance in language learning and teaching.* Pecs: University of Pecs.

Kaszubski, P., & Wojnowska, A. (2003). Corpus-informed exercises for learners of English: The TestBuilder program. In E. Oleksy & B. Lewandowska-Tomaszczyk (Eds.), *Research and scholarship in integration processes: Poland–USA–EU* (pp. 337–354). Łódź: Łódź University Press.

Keck, C. (2004). Corpus linguistics and language teaching research: Bridging the gap. *Language Teaching Research, 8*(1), 83–109.

Kennedy, G. (1998). *An introduction to corpus linguistics.* Harlow: Longman.

Kennedy, G. (2003). Amplifier collocations in the British National Corpus: Implications for English language teaching. *TESOL Quarterly, 37*(3), 467–487.

Kettemann, B. (1995). On the use of concordancing in ELT. *TELL&CALL, 4,* 4–15.

Kettemann, B. (1996). Concordancing in English Language Teaching. In S. Botley, J. Glass, T. McEnery & A. Wilson (Eds.), *Proceedings of teaching and language corpora* (pp. 4–16). Lancaster: Lancaster University.

Kettemann, B., & Marko, G. (2002). *Teaching and learning by doing corpus Analysis.* Amsterdam: Rodopi.

Kettemann, B., & Marko, G. (Eds.) (2006). *Planning, gluing and painting corpora: Inside the applied corpus linguist's workshop.* Frankfurt: Peter Lang.

Kita, K., & Ogata, H. (1997). Collocations in language learning: Corpus-based automatic compilation of collocations and bilingual collocation concordancer. *Computer Assisted Language Learning, 10*(3), 229–238.

Kjellmer, G. (1991). A mint of phrases. In K. Aijmer & B. Altenberg (Eds.), *English corpus linguistics: Studies in honour of Jan Svartvik* (pp. 111–127). Harlow: Longman.

Koester, A. (2002). The performance of speech acts in workplace conversations and the teaching of communicative functions. *System, 30,* 167–184.

Leech, G. (1997). Teaching and language corpora: A convergence. In A. Wichmann, S. Fligelstone, T. McEnery & G. Knowles (Eds.), *Teaching and language corpora* (pp. 1–23). London: Longman.

Lewis, M. (1993). *The lexical approach: The state of ELT and the way forward.* Hove: Language Teaching Publications.

Lewis, M. (1997a). *Implementing the lexical approach: Putting theory into practice.* Hove: Language Teaching Publications.

Lewis, M. (1997b). Pedagogical implications of the lexical approach. In J. Coady & T. Huckin (Eds.), *Second language vocabulary acquisition: A rationale for pedagogy* (pp. 255–270). Cambridge: Cambridge University Press.

Lewis, M. (Ed.) (2000). *Teaching collocation: Further developments in the lexical approach.* Hove: Language Teaching Publications.

Longman (1995). *Longman Dictionary of Contemporary English* (3rd ed.). Harlow: Longman.

Lonsdale, D., & Bras, Y. (2009). *A frequency dictionary of French.* London: Routledge.

McAlpine, J., & Myles, J. (2003). Capturing phraseology in an online dictionary for advanced users of English as a second language: A response to user needs. *System, 31,* 71–84.

McCarthy, M., McCarten, J. & Sandiford, H. (2005–2006). *Touchstone* (Books 1–4). Cambridge. Cambridge University Press.

McEnery, A., & Xiao, R. (2005). Help or help to: What do corpora have to say? *English Studies, 86*(2), 161–187.

McEnery, T., & Wilson, A. (2001). *Corpus linguistics* (2nd ed.). Edinburgh: Edinburgh University Press.

McEnery, T., Xiao, R. & Tono, Y. (2006). *Corpus-based language studies: An advanced resource book.* London: Routledge.

Meunier, F. (2002). The pedagogical value of native and learner corpora in EFL grammar teaching. In S. Granger, J. Hung & S. Petch-Tyson (Eds.), *Computer learner corpora, second language acquisition and foreign language teaching* (pp. 119–142). Philadelphia: John Benjamins.

Mindt, D. (1996). English corpus linguistics and the foreign language teaching syllabus. In J. Thomas & M. Short (Eds.), *Using Corpora for language research* (pp. 232–247). Harlow: Longman.

Mishan, F. (2005). *Designing authenticity into language learning materials.* Chicago: Chicago University Press.

Mukherjee, J., & Rohrbach, J. (2006). Rethinking applied corpus linguistics from a language-pedagogical perspective: New departures in learner corpus research. In B. Kettemann & G. Marko (Eds.), *Planning, gluing and painting corpora: Inside the applied corpus linguist's workshop* (pp. 205–232). Frankfurt: Peter Lang.

Murison-Bowie, S. (1996). Linguistic corpora and language teaching. *Annual Review of Applied Linguistics, 16,* 182–199.

Myles, F. (2005). Interlanguage corpora and second language acquisition research. *Second Language Research, 21*(4), 373–391.

Nelson, M. (2000). A corpus-based study of business English and business English teaching materials. PhD thesis, the University of Manchester, Manchester. Accessed on 15 July 2010 at the URL http://users.utu.fi/micnel/thesis.html.

Nesselhauf, N. (2003). The use of collocations by advanced learners of English and some implications for teaching. *Applied Linguistics, 24*(2), 223–242.

Nesselhauf, N. (2005). *Collocations in a learner corpus.* Amsterdam: John Benjamins.

O'Keeffe, A., & Farr, F. (2003). Using language corpora in initial teacher education: pedagogic issues and practical applications. *TESOL Quarterly, 37*(3), 389–418.

O'Keeffe, A., McCarthy, M. & Carter, R (2007). *From corpus to classroom: Language use and language teaching.* Cambridge: Cambridge University Press.

Osborne, J. (2001). Integrating corpora into a language-learning syllabus. In B. Lewandowska-Tomaszczyk (Ed.), *PALC 2001: Practical applications in language corpora* (pp. 479–492). Frankfurt: Peter Lang.

Osborne, J. (2002). Top-down and bottom-up approaches to corpora in language teaching. In U. Connor and T. Upton (Eds.), *Applied corpus linguistics: A multidimensional perspective* (pp. 251–265). Amsterdam: Rodopi.

Partington, A. (1998). *Patterns and meanings: Using corpora for English language research and teaching.* Amsterdam: John Benjamins.

Pravec, N. (2002). Survey of learner corpora. *ICAME Journal, 26,* 81–114.

Procter, P. (1995) *Cambridge international dictionary of English.* Cambridge: Cambridge University Press.

Quirk, R., Greenbaum, S., Leech, G. & Svartvik, J. (1985). *A comprehensive grammar of the English language.* Harlow: Longman.

Renouf, A. (1987). Moving on. In J. Sinclair (Ed.), *Looking up: An account of the COBUILD project* (pp. 167–178). London: HarperCollins.

Römer, U. (2005). *Progressives, patterns, pedagogy: A corpus-driven approach to English progressive forms, functions, contexts and didactics.* Amsterdam: John Benjamins.

Scott, M., & Tribble, C. (2006). *Textual patterns: Key words and corpus analysis in language education.* Amsterdam: John Benjamins.

Seidlhofer, B. (2000). Operationalizing intertextuality: Using learner corpora for learning. In L. Burnard & T. McEnery (Eds.), *Rethinking language pedagogy from a corpus perspective* (pp. 207–224). New York: Peter Lang.

Seidlhofer, B. (2002). Pedagogy and local learner corpora: Working with learning driven data. In S. Granger, J. Hung & S. Petch-Tyson (Eds.), *Computer learner corpora, second language acquisition and foreign language teaching* (pp. 213–234). Philadelphia: John Benjamins.

Shei, C., & Pain, H. (2000). An ESL writer's collocational aid. *Computer Assisted Language Learning, 13*(2), 167–182.

Sinclair, J. (1987). *Collins COBUILD English language dictionary.* London: HarperCollins.

Sinclair, J. (1990). *Collins COBUILD English grammar.* London: HarperCollins.

Sinclair, J. (1991). *Corpus, concordance, collocation: Describing English language.* Oxford: Oxford University Press.

Sinclair, J. (1992). *Collins COBUILD English usage.* London: HarperCollins.

Sinclair, J. (2000). Lexical grammar. *Naujoji Metodologija, 24,* 191–203.

Sinclair, J. (2003). *Reading concordances.* Harlow: Longman.

Sinclair, J. (Ed.) (2004). *How to use corpora in language teaching.* Amsterdam: John Benjamins.

Sinclair, J., & Renouf, A. (1988). A lexical syllabus for language learning. In R. Carter & M. McCarthy (Eds.), *Vocabulary and language teaching* (pp. 140–158). Harlow: Longman.

Smadja, F., & McKeown, K. (1990). Automatically extracting and representing collocations for language generation. In B. Berwick (Ed.), *Proceedings of the 28th annual meeting of Association for Computational Linguistics* (pp. 252–259). Pittsburgh: University of Pittsburgh.

Sripicharn, P. (2000). Data-driven learning materials as a way to teach lexis in context. In C. Heffer, H. Sauntson & G. Fox (Eds.), *Words in context: A tribute to John Sinclair on his retirement* (pp. 169–178). Birmingham: University of Birmingham.

Stubbs, M. (2001). Texts, corpora, and problems of interpretation: A response to Widdowson. *Applied Linguistics, 22*(2), 149–172.

Tan, M. (2002). *Corpus studies in language education.* Bangkok: IELE Press.

Taylor, L. (2003). The Cambridge approach to speaking assessment. *Research Notes, 13,* 2–4.

Thompson, P., & Tribble, C. (2001). Looking at citations: Using corpora in English for academic purposes. *Language Learning & Technology, 5*(3), 91–105.

Thurstun, J., & Candlin, C. (1997). *Exploring academic English: A workbook for student essay writing.* Sydney: NCELTR.

Thurstun, J., & Candlin, C. (1998). Concordancing and the teaching of the vocabulary of academic English. *English for Specific Purposes, 17,* 267–280.

Tribble, C. (1991). Concordancing and an EAP writing program. *CAELL Journal, 1*(2), 10–15.

Tribble, C. (1997a). Corpora, concordances and ELT. In T. Boswood (Ed.), *New ways of using computers in language teaching.* Alexandria, VA: TESOL.

Tribble, C. (1997b). Improving corpora for ELT: Quick and dirty ways of developing corpora for language teaching. In B. Lewandowska-Tomaszczyk & P. Melia (Eds.), *Practical applications in language corpora—Proceedings of PALC '97* (pp. 107–117). Łódź: Łódź University Press.

Tribble, C. (2000). Practical uses for language corpora in ELT. In P. Brett & G. Motteram (Eds.), *A special interest in computers: Learning and teaching with information and communications technologies* (pp. 31–41). Kent: IATEFL.

Tribble, C. (2003). The text, the whole text … or why large published corpora aren't much use to language learners and teachers. In B. Lewandowska-Tomaszczyk (Ed.), *Practical applications in language and computers* (pp. 303–318). Frankfurt: Peter Lang.

Tribble, C., & Jones, G. (1990). *Concordances in the classroom: A resource book for teachers.* Harlow: Longman.

Tribble, C., & Jones, G. (1997). *Concordances in the classroom: Using corpora in language education.* Houston TX: Athelstan.

Upton, T., & Connor, U. (2001). Using computerized corpus analysis to investigate the text-linguistic discourse move of a genre. *English for Specific Purposes, 20,* 313–329.

Wichmann, A. (1995). Using concordances for the teaching of modern languages in higher education. *Language Learning Journal, 11,* 61–63.

Wichmann, A. (1997). General introduction. In A. Wichmann, S. Fligelstone, T. McEnery & G. Knowles (Eds.), *Teaching and language corpora* (pp. xvi–xvii). London: Longman.

Wichmann, A., Fligelstone, S., McEnery A. & Knowles, G. (Eds.) (1997). *Teaching and language corpora.* London: Longman.

Widdowson, H. (1990). *Aspects of language teaching.* Oxford: Oxford University Press.

Widdowson, H. (1991). The description and prescription of language. In J. Alatis (Ed.), *Georgetown University Round Table on Languages and Linguistics 1991,* (pp. 11–24). Washington, DC: Georgetown University Press.

Widdowson, H. (2000). The limitations of linguistics applied. *Applied Linguistics, 21*(1), 3–25.

Widdowson, H. (2003). *Defining issues in English language teaching.* Oxford: Oxford University Press.

Willis, D. (1990). *The lexical syllabus: A new approach to language teaching.* London: HarperCollins.

Willis, J., Willis, D. & Davids, J. (1988–1989). *Collins COBUILD English course* (Parts 1–3). London: HarperCollins.

Woolls, D. (1998). Multilingual parallel concordancing for pedagogical use. In *Teaching and language corpora* (pp. 222–227). Keble College, Oxford, 24–27 July.

Xiao, R. (2003). Use of parallel and comparable corpora in language study. *English Education in China, 1.* Accessed on 8 September 2010 at the URL http://pub.sinoss.net/portal/webgate/_CmdArticleList?QUERY=1126&JOURNALNO=1126&JournalID=1125.

Xiao, R. (2008). Well-known and influential corpora. In A. Lüdeling & M. Kyto (Eds.), *Corpus linguistics: An international handbook* (pp. 383–457). Berlin: Mouton de Gruyter.

Xiao, R., Rayson, P. & McEnery, T. (2009). *A frequency dictionary of Mandarin Chinese.* London: Routledge.

Yang, Y., & Allison, D. (2003). Research articles in applied linguistics: Moving from results to conclusions. *English for Specific Purposes, 22,* 365–385.

Zhang, X. (1993). *English collocations and their effect on the writing of native and non-native college freshmen.* PhD thesis, Indiana University of Pennsylvania.

IV
Research in Second Language Processes and Development

23

Language Learning
An Ecological-Semiotic Approach

Leo van Lier

In this chapter I will sketch the main principles of an ecological-semiotic approach to language, learning, and pedagogy. The ecological-semiotic approach (from now on I will use the shorthand term *ecology*, to avoid creating another acronym) described here is different from other ecological approaches to language and linguistics, such as ecolinguistics (Fill & Mühlhäusler, 2001), linguistic landscape (Shohamy & Gorter, 2008), translanguaging (Creese & Blackledge, 2010), and similar perspectives on language and linguistics that look at such issues as language contact, linguistic oppression, language death, linguistic landscaping, and other important ecological/linguistic interrelationships and connections. The ecology approach I describe here is on a social-cultural-historical scale that is consonant with these latter perspectives, but on the ontogenetic and microgenetic scales it rests on quite different theoretical and research foundations. In particular, ecological learning addresses issues such as perception, affordance, semiosis, and educational quality that do not receive central focus in ecolinguistics, to the best of my knowledge. In one sense one might say that ecology takes a more micro approach to the principles of ecology, and ecolinguistics a more macro approach. However, the micro–macro dichotomy is a rather crude delineation and might suggest that one can only focus either on the micro, or on the macro. In actual fact, all ecological approaches aim to transcend any one particular spatio-temporal scale and thus break down the micro–macro split. We can provisionally say that ecological approaches are concerned with situated cognition and agency. The situatedness (of both cognition and agency) can be drawn wide or narrow, as required by the phenomena in question.

The notion of scale in ecological theory may need some elaboration. The first thing to note is that *scale* is not the same as *level*. From an anthropocentric viewpoint, scales are perceptual, levels are organizational (from the perspective of a glacier, or a gazelle, neither scale nor level have any significance, although they are affected by both). Scales are spatio-temporal, perceptual systems that we employ in order to look at change in a particular domain; levels are hierarchical, conceptual systems that we postulate to try and explain what goes on within a particular scale. I will give first an example from the biological world, and then an example from the human educational world.

In biology, you might want to study the life of rabbits. How do you start? Another way to ask that question is, what is your focal scale? Is it the life cycle of one rabbit and its family, from birth to death, covering growing up, foraging, breeding, family life, digging warrens, and darting away when presumed predators loom near? Is it the physiological life of the rabbit with its digestive system, sensori-motor abilities, nesting habits, and so on? Or is it the cyclical occurrence of diseases such as rabbit myxomatosis, the cycles of overpopulation and starvation, periodic climatic changes, the effects of global warming, and so on? We can note that these three choices address different scales of time and space. Informally put, they are, in the order described, medium (in terms of length of time and demands of space), small, and large. We notice that within each scale, information from other (smaller or larger) scales can become relevant. For example, when there are so many rabbits in an ecosystem that there is insufficient food for all, the size of rabbit families will decrease. These are not direct causal reactions between one scale and the next one, but rather a cascading series of local events that set in motion a particular trend.

This is a relatively simple example of scales. What about the notion of level? Within each scale we can characterize certain types of events in terms of levels. Levels, as noted earlier, are conceptual constructions (or event structures), relating ecological facts. We note, for example, that foxes hunt and eat rabbits, parasites attack the rabbits as well in their intestines and other organs, and in addition human hunters try to shoot them or domesticate them. In turn, rabbits dig tunnels, chew through roots, eat carrots, and erode natural defenses against landslides. They may also compete with gophers, moles, and badgers for food and territory.

We might see these phenomena as part of a "food chain," or "battle for survival," but such levels of interaction in nature are not rigid hierarchies (see Capra, 1996), rather, they are interdependencies. Hierarchies are human constructions; levels are interdependencies on a particular scale.

Now, let's consider the relevance of ecological scales and levels, and turn our rabbits into school-age language learners. In their educational habitat they operates on the scale of the classroom, one of the ecosystems they are members of (Bronfenbrenner, 1979, 2005). They are also members of other ecosystems, such as the home, the school cafeteria, the playground. These are all on the same spatio-temporal scale. They may be bounded by walls, bells, bus routes, or routines, and these boundaries create conflicts and clashes sometimes.

However, above that scale, there is the larger scale of the school, which is bigger, long-term, and governed by budgets, annual cycles, trajectories across school years, tests, and promotions, among many other things, and perhaps greater distances between buildings. Above that scale there is the political scale of periodic reform efforts, grants, hiring and firing of principals and school board members, funding cycles, media reports, and so on. A couple of scales below we find what goes on in the student's head and body: I can't understand this; where do I go for information or assistance; I can't concentrate with all this noise; I am nervous about this test; and so on.

Given all these criss-crossing complexities, the different levels that cause conflict and struggle, and the different scales that cause abrupt or cyclical changes that any particular microsystem of learner–teacher or child–parent interaction would seem to be powerless against, how are we to research the processes and the possibilities of second language (L2) language teaching and learning?

In the following contribution I will try to offer an ecological way forward. I will use ten principles or characteristics that, in my view, provide a rationale, a foundation, and a research agenda. They first appeared in abbreviated form in van Lier (2004) and are further developed and substantiated in this chapter.

Relations

This section covers relations in language, in the world, and among language users. In ecology, the central focus of study is the notion of relation, rather than the notions of objects, subjects, and rules.

Ferdinand de Saussure's view of language was a relational one (1907/1983). He persuasively argued that the meaning of a word (its "value") could only be established by seeing it in its place among all other words in the system of language. As an example, the word "Knight" in chess can only be understood in comparison with the other pieces on the board (King, Queen, Bishop, and so on), and by its place and role in the game of chess, i.e., by what it *does*. Knowing that it has the shape of a horse's head, or that it may have a circle of green felt on the bottom, does not mean much. What is more, if in a particular chess set one of the knights is missing, we can take any object nearby, say a bottle cap or a random pebble, and agree that this object will be a knight. Its material properties are irrelevant so far as the game is concerned, so long as there is agreement that the bottle cap "counts as" (or "is") a knight.

In a similar way, a word just means what we (a certain speech community, or a particular set of interlocutors) say and agree that it means. This will be influenced by convention and habit, but it can just as easily be influenced by invention, the need of the moment, or playfulness. As an example, in a telephone conversation reported by Firth and Wagner (2007), between a Danish cheese exporter and an Egyptian importer, when the Egyptian complains that the cheese is stuck in customs and is "blowing," this word is jointly accepted by both as meaning that the cheese is going bad (p. 808).

As I have argued elsewhere (van Lier, 1996), language use is always contingent. Every utterance points analeptically and proleptically to preceding and following discourse, i.e., to the utterance(s) that came before, and those that may become relevant subsequently, partly because of being called forth, made relevant, or being foreshadowed by the present utterance. If I say, "yeah, right?" this clearly relates to something said (or done) before, but it also makes a next utterance or action relevant. This is discursive reflexivity. But the utterance is also contingent along another axis: it relates to the world in which we are active, and it relates to my mind, which signals my relation to that world (including the interlocutors, past, present, and future, but also cultural, historical, and physical events and artifacts). Utterances in language (and signs in semiotics) are therefore contingent in "before–after" and in "inside–outside" ways. Without such contingencies there would be no language, and without the study of such contingencies there can be no theory of language, or linguistics.

For ecological research, this implies a program that incorporates both micro and macro aspects of the life world (Lewin, 1943; Merleau-Ponty, 1962), thus addressing a persistent conundrum that has long bedeviled sociological and sociocultural research (Giddens, 1984; Turner, 1988; Engestrom, 1999). Instead of casting research foci in terms of an either–or choice of a macro or micro perspective, ecology envisions a multi-layered reality in which meanings and interpretations of meanings reverberate and resonate across multiples layers that may span many levels and scales (Lemke, 2002).

Examples of research frameworks attempting to deal with these puzzles include Engestrom's activity theory (1999), Bronfenbrenner's nested ecosystems (1979), Oyama's developmental systems theory (2000), among others. However, such attempts are best seen as preliminary heuristics for dealing with complexities that surpass any attempts at classification.

The second characteristic below, context, will elaborate on this, and my description of ecological scales and levels above also suggest some ways in which approaches from field biology can be informative.

Context

This section discusses how meaning only emerges in a particular context. One might equally say, context emerges along with meanings; in other words, context is an emergent system of those meanings that are assigned relevance by participants in a specific spatio-temporal event.

There is no such thing as a context that is separable from meaning, or meaning as separable from context (even dictionaries invoke contexts of use for the isolated terms that they list alphabetically). The context is not a corral or arena in which specific speech actions or events are enacted, rather, it is those complexes of actions and emergent facts, rituals and meanings that arise in and through the activities that unfold, in relation to the physical, social, and symbolic resources that are around and that are invoked. Put another way, context is not a container in which speech actions are performed, but an unbounded space of resonances that emanates from any all expressions of agency.

This means that context is a highly problematic entity. Several linguistic theories have attempted to ignore context, most notably structuralism (Bloomfield, 1933) and generative linguistics (Chomsky, 1965). However, in current theories of language, cognition, or education, we see all sorts of models that attempt to capture the context as an analytical template or etic grid of some sort. As mentioned in the previous section, examples include activity theory, nested ecosystems, and a variety of developmental systems theories. Diagrams used depict a range of different representations of the context: interlocking triangles in the case of activity theory, concentric circles for nested ecosystems (depicted as an "igloo" in van Lier, 2004, p. 209), a pyramid of contributing factors in MacIntyre et al.'s model of Willingness To Communicate (WTC; MacIntyre, Clément, Dörnyei, & Noels, 1998), among many others. All of these should be seen as useful heuristics, but also as potentially reductive tools that can suggest or even legislate what is deemed to be relevant or not (thus diminishing, compromising, or corrupting the illuminative power of emic inquiry). Whenever confronted with a model of context, a reasonable set of questions includes the following two: (1) What is highlighted in this model? (2) What is left out? After that, a more fundamental question asks what the theoretical assumptions or practical considerations might be that underlie the inclusion or exclusion of particular aspects of the context.

An alternative way of looking at context is one that does not attempt to establish a classification or a model consisting of various interacting components or modules. I'll give just three examples of such non-taxonomic approaches to context that fall within a more organic or ecological perspective: Vygotsky's (1987) sociocultural theory (SCT) context, Bakhtin's (1981) dialogical context, and Peirce's (1992/1998) semiotic context.

Vygotsky's context is a social-cultural-historical one. The focus is on tools, gradually transformed into signs, moving from the practical to the mental. The tools and signs mediate between subject and object, but without necessarily questioning the subject–object dichotomy. This is a Marxian perspective, one that highlights the role of labor and dialectical materialism. It is an important perspective, but one that is not complete, as political as well as socio-philosophical applications of Marxian ideas have shown repeatedly over the last century or so. It is interesting to consider the thought that Vygotsky's approach is often interpreted as a *dialectical* one, in which subjects' understandings are mediated by tools and signs used to resolve oppositions or differences (the tools are needed to resolve dissonances), whereas Bakhtin's approach is *dialogical*, implying not dichotomy, opposition, or difference, but resonance and polyphony, in a Rabelaisian, carnivalesque dance, rather than a Hegelian synthesizing, rational promenade. Bakhtin himself said, in his late essays, that dialectic is basically dialogue stripped from its essentials and de-personalized, but that it may return to dialogue "on a higher level" (1986, p. 162). What that higher level might look like is not clear. But we need to bear in mind, at the very least, that Bakhtin considered dialectic a rather poor substitute for dialogue, as a play that is predicated on opposites, rather than a dance that unfolds in converging and diverging movements. Vygotsky's work remains unfinished, cut of by his untimely death in 1934. He did not have the opportunity that Bakhtin did, in his late essays (Bakhtin died in 1975), to reflect on some of his major ideas.

An ecological perspective (and a Peircean semiotics, which is an ecological semiotics par excellence), aligns with Bakhtin, and refutes the subject–object split through the relational notion of affordance, and the triadic nature of the sign, which is not just the signifier pointing to a signified, but also an interpretant creating a new sign based on the connection between sign and object, in a constantly emergent process of semiosis or meaning-making, a never-ending dialogue in fact, between what is, what may have been, and what may come to be.

The ecological context is a physical as well as a social and symbolic one. The centrality of the physical world is not prominent in Marxian theory, since the latter emphasizes manufactured "material" (including cultural and historical) goods. However, the growth of signs into signs in Peircean semiotics is a never-ending, emergent process, and no distinction is made between or among the raw materials from which the signs arise in meaning-making action, whether they be physical, imagined, or manufactured. A cloud in the sky is a sign and an occasion for making meaning, just as surely as a word, a story, a hammer, or a rolling pin.

A crucial aspect of an ecological approach is the notion of *affordance*, which can be dynamically related to mediation or tool/sign use. Affordance ties perception and attention to activity, and relates the agent to the environment in purposeful ways.

Through the notion of affordance we can draw Vygotsky's view of development back into a semiotic (Peircean and Bakhtinian) sphere, since it is only through his nuanced analysis of the growth of perception and its role in the development of interfunctional sociocognitive systems that we can understand his vision of the development of consciousness and higher mental functioning. Referring to the increasing connection between immediate (i.e., direct, in Gibson's sense) and categorical perception (i.e., mediated), Vygotsky notes that "we can no longer separate the perception of the object as such from its meaning or sense" (1987, p. 299). The connection between perception and speech changes the course of the child's development, "if we view this perception through the prism of speech, if the child not only perceives but tells about what is perceived" (1987, p. 300).

Patterns, Systems

Language is not governed by rules, but by interrelated organizational forces. We have long seen language and language teaching as governed by rules: language is put (and held) together by rules, and we have to teach and learn it by focusing on those rules, because rules are what make language "regular' (in spite of all the exceptions that bedevil the language student).

Long ago, the notion of rule was problematized by the philosopher Ludwig Wittgenstein (1958). Following (or obeying, applying) a rule, in Wittgenstein's analysis, can only make sense in a community of language users, as an agreement or regular pattern of use, not as a characteristic of a formal linguistic system. Chomsky (1986), in a discussion of Saul Krippke's (1982) interpretation of Wittgenstein's arguments, suggested that, perhaps, "the best theory will depart from the model of rule following altogether in any standard sense of the notion of rule" (1986, p. 243). In later writing, Chomsky bemoaned the "huge proliferation of rule systems" (2002, p. 92) necessitated by generative grammar, a circumstance that led to the proposal of the minimalist program, in which the notion of grammatical rule has no status.

It appears that Wittgenstein's notion of "following rules," with its social and cultural connections, cannot be incorporated into a formal linguistic or philosophical system, an argument also made by Davidson (1986). In fact, distinguishing between "prior theory" and "passing theory," Davidson concludes that "there is no such thing as a language, not if a language is anything like what many philosophers and linguists have supposed. There is therefore no such thing to be learned, mastered or born with" (1986, p. 446). This argument is very similar to Hopper's (1998) notion of emergent grammar, in which a priori grammar is juxtaposed to emergent grammar, and the status of the former as a "prerequisite" for learning language is rejected as merely a byproduct of communication.

However, there is another ingredient in this argument, namely, that there is a difference between the "steady-state" knowledge of language that, in Chomskyan theorizing, a child acquires roughly by the age of eight, and the many years required to master the normative academic uses of language (which, incidentally, are exemplified in the many illustrative examples of sentences in generative grammar). When talking about foreign language teaching and academic language development,

Vygotsky (1987) already saw the fundamental difference between the language a child masters by the age of five, and the many long and hard years of study needed to master academic language and concepts that school students face, right up to and beyond the writing of a doctoral thesis. Those academic and professional uses of language do require conformity to elaborate, explicit, and often quite arcane sets of rules. But they are not linguistic rules (in the narrow sense of "linguistic"), they are rules of the academic game, or of other particular professional games. These are rules to be *followed*, since they are not intrinsic to the linguistic system as such.

Philosophers (e.g., Hospers, 1967) often distinguish between *rules* and *reasons* (see van Lier, 2004, for examples). Larsen-Freeman (2003) has proposed a similar distinction in the teaching and learning of grammar. So, instead of asking, what are the rules for using the preterit or the imperfect tense in Spanish, we might more usefully ask, what was a particular person's reason to use one or the other, in a given context? Similarly, capturing the English article system in terms of rules might seem a hopeless task for students whose first language (L1) does not have articles. Yet, speakers have various reasons for using definite, indefinite, or zero articles, and proponents of cognitive (Langacker, 2008), construction (Ellis & Collins, 2009), or concept-based (Negueruela, 2008) grammar are all searching for ways of illuminating the reasons why speakers make particular grammatical choices. For example, I might tell a friend, "I like to take the dog to the park at the weekend, and she likes to jump in the water when I throw a stick in the pond." What explains the uses of "the" and "a" here? The notion of rule would seem an obstacle, rather than a help, in this endeavor.

Emergence

Language development is not an accumulation of objects, but a process of transformation, growth, and reorganization. Vygotsky emphasized the notion of transformation, that is, he noted that new levels of learning cannot be directly derived from existing levels, and this is an emergentist view of learning. Recent studies in emergentism (MacWhinney, 1999) confirm the notion of transformation, and provide strong evidence supporting Vygotsky's observations. Here is a direct quote from Vygotsky on emergentism: "Throughout the child's development ... new systems constantly emerge within which perception acts. Within these systems, and only within these systems, perception acquires new characteristics that are not inherent to it outside that developmental system" (1987, p. 300). In ecological semiotics, every sign originates in a prior sign (through the interpretant), and leads to another sign that foregrounds iconic, indexical, or symbolic ingredients and then elaborates on them through a new interpretant, thus illustrating that semiosis is never finished but always remains en route, deferred, similar to Derrida's notion of *différance* (1998). The birth of signs can be said to be the notion of affordance (see above), which is the immediate result of organismic agency in an environment. There is nothing "deferred" in an affordance, since it is immediate, but it contains the potential to produce future meanings, i.e., focused actions. One can also call this the birth of language learning, if learning be construed as use-based, rather than as rule-based.

Quality

Language learning and educational experience are about quality, not just quantity; quality combines intellect and affect, and yields a higher level of consciousness (van Lier, 1996). The Norwegian philosopher Arne Naess, founder of deep ecology, famously pointed out that *standard of living* is not the same as *quality of life* (Naess, 1989, p. 29). While it would be foolish to deny that there is some connection between the two (for example, abject poverty and starvation are unlikely to enhance quality of life), it is important to note that a focus on quality comes before a focus on quantity (in other words, you do not automatically get to quality via quantity), a point that educational policy makers and politicians might do well to remember when they attempt to equate educational success with test scores.

Vygotsky remarks, in the context of literacy—and referring to the work of Maria Montessori—that "learning must be relevant to life." It should be based on raising "intrinsic needs" in a context in which the educational activities are "necessary and relevant for life" (1978, p. 118). This is essentially an ecological approach to learning, since it unites the usual atomistic measurements and separations into life skills, and postulates an organic vision of learning.

Value

Language education requires an overtly ethical and moral stance, embodying visions of self and identity. There is no denying the reality that teaching is a profoundly ethical and moral activity, both for the teacher and for the learner. A utilitarian or instrumentalist approach does not really teach language, it teaches tricks, or recipes.

A teacher may have a predetermined model of what the successful learner in his or her class should look like, have an idealized goal of promoting the optimal development of every learner, or attempt to instill the seeds of autonomous or lifelong learning, but whatever the case may be, moral and ethical choices are central to the day-to-day conduct of teaching and learning activities. Even a teacher who has basically given up on his or her students, and thinks that they are not going to "make it" anyway (so why bother?), has made a moral choice, which is the choice of abdication of responsibility.

An ecological approach, in line with SCT and the notions of prolepsis and scaffolding, i.e., future-oriented lesson designs and the communication of autonomy-supporting expectations (Deci & Flaste, 1995), believes in emergent and sustainable learning, rather than in the numerical outcomes of tests, which, for many students (and often their teachers, and the schools in which they study), are indictments of past failure without redemption. When learners (and schools) are categorized in terms of percentiles, and they fall below the "average," an accusatory finger is pointed at them, and far too often they fail, succumbing to the "Pygmalion Effect" (Rosenthal & Jacobson, 1966).

It is discouraging that, in a society that celebrates "the little engine that could," struggling learners and schools are confronted with ever-increasing hurdles, rather than with opportunities to show that "they can, too." The crucial question has been well put by Hersh (2006): do we measure what we value, or do we value what we measure? (cited in Warschauer & Matuchniak, 2010, p. 179). From an ecological perspective I can add that not everything that is important can be measured.

Critical Perspective

This section examines a critical perspective oriented toward understanding and actively improving humanity in a sustainable world. Continuing from the previous point, a critical perspective also examines institutional structures involved in education and argues for change and improvement from a clearly articulated ideological stance. A critical (and, inevitably, a political) edge has been the hallmark of most educational thinkers and reformers across the ages, including, in no particular order and with no pretense of comprehensiveness, Rousseau, Pestalozzi, Vygotsky, Montessori, Whitehead, Dewey, Freire, Stenhouse, and Bernstein.

Education can be oriented toward information or transformation. The former is quantifiable and measurable in industrially produced tests, since information can be commodified and accumulated; the latter is emergent, unpredictable, and always moving. Transformative education requires teaching students how to perceive, how to talk about what they perceive, and how to think clearly, in well-articulated argumentative and rhetorical patterns.

Variation

Variation in terms of social and regional varieties is both inevitable and interesting.

Under normal (non-colonial, non-imperialistic) conditions, languages are not threatened by contact with other languages, and they cannot be "improved" by isolation or by purification efforts. Indeed, such notions as improvement or protection have no linguistic or semiotic status.

L2 students tend to receive a version of the L2 that is homogeneous and unchanging. In its final state, it is "perfect." The words are perfect and the grammatical structures are perfect. The pronunciation is perfect too, as is the pragmatic appropriateness of every utterance within the context that it is spoken (or written). This all-round perfection is personified in the "native speaker." The ideal target of the learner is to use the language in a "native-like" manner. Anything that is different from that ideal is deviant, i.e., non-native. However, there is no linguistic support for such an unchanging ideal. Paikeday (1985), in a book-length discussion with many linguists, concluded that "the native speaker is dead."

If there is no native speaker, then there cannot be a definition of "native-like." The learner, in setting goals, will have to reflect carefully, not on what *level* s/he wants to reach, but rather on what *identity* s/he wishes to enact and embody.

Diversity

Students in our classes are not all of one kind, cut from the same cloth. At the end of our course, when we say goodbye to our students, we realize that they will pursue different careers, have different dreams, and will end up in many different situations. If we had any control in our classroom during the course, now that control ends, and we can only wonder what they will remember from all the things we did in our classes. And, recalling something Dick Allwright once told me, we may realize that perhaps the best thing we did was to create memorable occasions for language use and for learning opportunities.

The diversity of futures among our learners can be enhanced if we approach our classroom ecology from the perspective of multilingualism rather than monolingualism, which offers our students both cognitive and socio-economic advantages over a monolingual approach, as research has convincingly shown (for an overview, see Cook, 2002). Yet, in many settings, contact phenomena such as lingua franca and code alternation remain fringe or taboo topics, except perhaps for entertainment value. Assessments, grades, and certificates will be designed with an imagined "target" in mind, and this target is calibrated on a monolingual "ideal speaker" fiction. Students learn "the target language," a phrase that assumes there is such a thing, although a moment's reflection should suffice to realize that there is not. Every learner must imagine his or her destination, though this imagination may be thwarted, obstructed, and squashed by the commodified notion of the test score (beyond which there may be nothing).

Agency

Language is activity and process, not object. As a result it is in the world as well as in the head, and it is happening now, rather than being a finished product that can be described in a rulebook (i.e., a grammar book).

I define agency as *movement* (see Bohm, 1998, for a similar argument from the perspective of physics). This means physical, social, and intellectual movement. There are a number of preconditions to the possibility of movement. For example, physical movement may be hampered by material obstructions; social movement may be obstructed by "not getting a word in edgeways"; intellectual movement may be obstructed by habitus, indoctrination, fear, or lack of awareness. On the other side of the coin, agency may be enabled by perceptual learning, initiative taking, engaging in discourse, critical reflection, and many other processes that can be fostered in an ethical and moral education (see above).

It is clear that an ecological and semiotic stance on language learning is anchored in agency, as all of life is. Teaching, in its very essence, is promoting agency. Pedagogy is guiding this agency wisely.

Where Do We Go from Here?

I have given ten characteristics of an ecological-semiotic approach to language learning and teaching. I eschew any resemblance to the Ten Commandments, since I have no illusion that it is easy to fight the golden calf of educational tradition. However, as a teacher I find it immensely easier to fight than not to fight. I have also learned that this fight is a long and slow struggle, rather than an immediate violent revolution. In the final section of this chapter I will illustrate some ways in which an ecological approach might be enacted in educational settings.

Ecological-Semiotic Learning in Pedagogic Practice

What does a classroom, or any learning environment (see Heath, 2000; Rogoff, 1995 for non-traditional learning environments), look like when guided by ecological-semiotic practices? Barbara Rogoff presents an interesting picture of such a classroom (1995, p. 158), where small groups, pairs, and individual children, along with adults, are busy in various ways, standing, talking, sitting on the floor. Rogoff suggests that such classrooms can be examined using different "lenses": classroom/institutional, interpersonal, and personal. These three lenses coincide with three participation structures: Apprenticeship, Guided Participation, and Participatory Appropriation. Apprenticeship implies a long time scale of working with a master or a guild; Guided Participation refers to particular patterns of master–apprentice interaction, including modeling, scaffolding, and imitation; Participatory Appropriation refers to the moment-to-moment microgenesis of cognitive understandings resulting from interactional dynamics.

Participation in common events and pursuits does not have to lead to lockstep input-output practice or identical processes of information processing; instead it can lead to convergent and divergent work, sharing, self study exploration, and many other acts and sources of learning (in a carnivalesque dynamic, rather than rational dialectic one, as suggested earlier in this chapter (Bakhtin, 1981)).

Similar notions are proposed in the exploratory practice approach of Dick Allwright and colleagues (Gieve & Miller, 2009), in which the quality of education and the critical values are directly addressed. As Allwright notes:

> [T]he quality of classroom life is itself the most important matter, both for the long-term mental health of humanity (and the mental health of the language teacher!), and for the sake of encouraging people to be lifelong learners, rather than people resentful of having to spend years of their lives as "captive" learners, and therefore put of further learning for life.
>
> (Cited in Gieve & Miller, 2009, p. 20)

Ways of working suggested here, which seem to be more familiar from Kindergarten contexts than from high school or adult classes, are not always easy to implement, even if teachers and students are convinced of their value and effectiveness. We are more likely to see them on the fringes of the educational spectrum: the youth clubs and other non-traditional learning contexts by Heath (2000) and Rogoff (1995) among others, or in adult settings that are not constrained by high-stakes tests and enforced standards. As I have argued elsewhere (van Lier, 2006), arguing for or even showing the benefits of such action-based or project-based curricula (or as Allwright (2003) puts it, puzzle-based learning) is not enough to result in their large-scale adoption.

There are many excellent and penetrating analyses, e.g., by Bernstein (2000), Bourdieu (1991), and Foucault (1977), that show how educational practices are constrained by political, commercial, and ideological forces that by and large insure conformity, homogeneity, and the persistence of the status quo. This is not the place to delve into these, but I merely wish to remind the reader that, as noted above, the quality of education is not the same as the quantified results that schools are called upon to produce, often along models derived from business. The improvement of education is essentially a political struggle, not a pedagogical project, since sound principles of pedagogy have been well established for a long time.

Having thrown this bucket of ice-cold water on the ecological-semiotic enterprise, I nevertheless suggest that there are many ways in which teachers and schools can work toward implementing some (if not all) of its principles in the interstices of mandated test-driven programs, albeit perhaps in small, incremental steps. We may bang our head against the walls of educational obstacles, and live our work-life with a huge, never-ending headache, or we can find small spaces of light, lightness, and promise in between the heavy and dreary duties of standards and tests. The latter choice may lead us to helping students find that spark to ignite life-long language learning.

There are many examples of classrooms in which such work is manifested in a variety of ways. One such example is the work in CLIL (content and language integrated teaching) that is increasingly popular in several European countries and elsewhere. In such classrooms, a regular school subject (e.g., geography, mathematics) is taught through the medium of a foreign language, often using collaborative projects, portfolio assessment and other innovative strategies. Various models of content-based and project-based learning are also increasingly practiced, often as part of the learners' educational experiences, in the USA, Japan, Brazil, and in many other countries (Becket & Miller, 2006; Gieve & Miller; 2009; Jourdenais & Springer, 2005; Murphy, 2010; van Lier & Walqui, 2010). In Germany a similar approach goes by the name of *Handlungsorientierter Unterrricht* or action-oriented teaching (Finkbeiner, 2000).

Conclusion

I do not claim that the ecological approach outlined in this chapter brings radically new ideas to the table. As indicated in the various references cited, the ideas presented have a long history. However, they seem to be as often forgotten as they are remembered, so that a collection of reminders, framed in the coherent and consistent perspective of an ecology of learning, is useful. My purpose has been to show that this ecological perspective organizes a number of well-known ideas into a principled pedagogical stance, as well as a mandate for action, in interrelated, common-sense ways that are conducive to an organic way of thinking about language and learning. This way of thinking involves all ten (and maybe more) characteristics of an ecology of learning, and allows a thoughtful (reflective) educator to build a firm yet flexible foundation upon which to base a quality-oriented way of working.

Ecology refers to ways of being in the world. Our students are in the world, but, as language students, they are faced with new and often bewildering worlds, and it is the task of educators to help them construct their identity in it. For this to be possible, the things that happen in the classroom must be meaningfully (that is, in non-trivial ways) connected to the things that have happened, that are happening, or that may happen in the life of the students.

This task is never easy, neither for teachers nor for learners. Identity construction and, in the words of David Little, breaking down the barriers between learning "and the rest of living" (1991, p. 36) are long-term projects and struggles. Regardless of the difficulties, the ecological-semiotic perspective, as illustrated in the ten principles outlined here, firmly insists that the task must be done.

References

Allwright, D. (2003). Exploratory practice: Rethinking practitioner research in language teaching. *Language Teaching Research*, *7*(2), 113–141.

Bakhtin, M. (1981). *The dialogical imagination*. Austin, TX: University of Texas Press.

Bakhtin, M. (1986). *Speech genres and other late essays*. Austin, TX: University of Texas Press.

Beckett, G. H., & Miller, P. C. (Eds.) (2006). *Project-based second and foreign language education: Past, present and future*. Greenwich, CT: Information Age Publishing.

Bernstein, B. (2000). *Pedagogy, symbolic control and identity: Theory, research, critique (Revised Edition)*. Lanham, MD: Rowman & Littlefield Publishers, Inc.

Bloomfield, L. (1933). *Language*. Chicago: University of Chicago Press.

Bohm, D. (1998). *On creativity*. London: Routledge.

Bourdieu, P. (1991). *Language and symbolic power*. Cambridge, MA: Harvard University Press.

Bronfenbrenner, U. (1979). *The ecology of human development*. Cambridge, MA: Harvard University Press.

Bronfenbrenner, U. (2005). *Making human beings human: Bioecological perspectives on human development*. Thousand Oaks, CA: Sage Publications.

Capra, F. (1996). *The web of life: A new scientific understanding of living systems*. New York: Anchor Books.

Chomsky, N. (1965). *Aspects of a theory of syntax*. Cambridge, MA: MIT.

Chomsky, N. (1986). *Knowledge of language*. Cambridge, MA: MIT.

Cook, V. J. (Ed.) (2002). *Portraits of the L2 user*. Clevedon: Multilingual Matters.

Creese, A., & Blackledge, A. (2010). Translanguaging in the bilingual classroom: A pedagogy for learning and teaching? *The Modern Language Journal*, *94*(1).

Davidson, D. (1986). A nice derangement of epitaphs. In E. Lepore (Ed.), *Truth and interpretation: Perspectives on the philosophy of Donald Davidson* (pp. 433–446). Oxford: Basil Blackwell.

Deci, E., & Flaste, R. (1995). *Why we do what we do: The dynamics of personal autonomy*. New York: Putnam's Sons.

Derrida, J. (1998). *Of grammatology*. Baltimore and London: Johns Hopkins University Press.

Ellis, N., & Collins, L. (Eds.) (2009). Input and second language construction learning: Frequency, form, and function. Special issue of *The Modern Language Journal*, *93*(3).

Engeström, Y. (1999). Innovative learning in work teams: Analyzing cycles of knowledge creation in practice. In Y. Engeström, R. Miettinen, & R.-L.Punamäki (Eds.), *Perspectives on activity theory* (pp. 377–404). Cambridge: Cambridge University Press.

Fill, A., & Mühlhäusler, P. (Eds.) (2001). *The ecolinguistics reader: Language, ecology and environment*. London: Continuum.

Finkbeiner, C. (2000). Handlungsorientierter Unterricht [Holistic and action-oriented learning and teaching]. In M. Byram (Ed.), *Routledge encyclopedia of language teaching and learning* (pp. 255–257). London: Routledge.

Firth, A., & Wagner, J. (2007). Second/foreign language learning as a social accomplishment: Elaborations on a reconceptualized SLA. *Modern Language Journal* (Special focus issue on: The impact of the ideas of Firth and Wagner on SLA), *91*, 798–817.

Foucault, M. (1977). *Discipline and punish: The birth of the prison*. New York: Pantheon.

Giddens, A. (1984). *The constitution of society*. Berkeley, CA: University of California Press.

Gieve, S., & Miller, I. K. (Eds.) (2009). *Understanding the language classroom*. London: Palgrave Macmillan.

Heath, S. B. (2000). Seeing our way into learning. *Cambridge Journal of Education*, *30*, 121–132.

Hopper, P. H. (1998). Emergent grammar. In M. Tomasello (Ed.), *The new psychology of language: Cognitive and functional approaches to language structure* (pp. 155–175). Mahwah, NJ: Lawrence Erlbaum.

Hospers, J. (1967). *An introduction to philosophical analysis*. Englewood Cliffs, NJ: Prentice-Hall.

Jourdenais, R., & Springer, S. (Eds.) (2005). *Content, tasks and projects in the language classroom: 2004 conference proceedings* (pp. 13–21). Monterey, CA: Monterey Institute of International Studies.

Kripke, S. (1982). *Wittgenstein on rules and private language*. Cambridge, MA: Harvard University Press.

Langacker, R. W. (2008). *Cognitive grammar: A basic introduction*. Oxford: Oxford University Press.

Larsen-Freeman, D. (2003). *Teaching language: From grammar to grammaring*. Boston: Heinle.

Lemke, J. (2002). Language development and identity: Multiple timescales in the social ecology of learning. In C. Kramsch (Ed.), *Language acquisition and language socialization* (pp. 68–87). London: Continuum.

Lewin, K. (1943). Defining the "field at a given time." *Psychological Review*, *50*, 292–310.

Little, D. (1991). *Learner autonomy: Definitions, issues and problems*. Dublin: Authentik.

MacIntyre, P. D., Clément, R., Dörnyei, Z., & Noels, K. A. (1998). Conceptualizing willingness to communicate in a L2: A situational model of L2 confidence and affiliation. *The Modern Language Journal*, *82*(4), 545–562.

MacWhinney, B. (Ed.) (1999). *Emergence of language*. Mahwah, NJ: Erlbaum.

Merleau-Ponty, M. (1962). *The phenomenology of perception*. London: Routledge.

Murphy, T. (2010). The role of group dynamics in modeling L2 possible selves in the language classroom. Presentation at the AAAL 2010 Annual Conference, March 6–9, Atlanta, Georgia.

Naess, A. (1989). *Ecology, community and lifestyle.* Translated and edited by D. Rothenberg. Cambridge: Cambridge University Press.

Negueruela, E. (2008). Revolutionary pedagogies: Learning that leads development in the second language classroom. In J. P. Lantolf & M. Poehner (Eds.), *Sociocultural theory and second language teaching* (pp. 189–227). London: Equinox.

Oyama, S. (2000). *Evolution's eye: A systems view of the biology–culture divide.* Durham, NC: Duke University Press.

Paikeday, T. (1985). *The native speaker is dead.* Toronto: Paikeday Publishing.

Peirce, C. S. (1992/1998). *Selected philosophical writings* (Vols. 1 and 2). Bloomington, IN: Indiana University Press. [Vol. 1 edited by Nathan Houser and Christian Kloesel, 1992; Vol. 2 edited by The Peirce Edition Project, 1998.]

Rogoff, B. (1995). Observing sociocultural activity on three planes: Participatory appropriation, guided participation, and apprenticeship. In J. V. Wertsch, P. Del Rio, & A. Alvarez (Eds.), *Sociocultural studies of mind* (pp. 139–164). Cambridge: Cambridge University Press.

Rosenthal, R., & Jacobson, L. (1966). Teachers' expectancies: Determinates of pupils' IQ gains. *Psychological reports, 19,* 115–118.

Saussure, F. (de) (1907/1983). *Course in general linguistics.* La Salle, IL: Open Court.

Shohamy, E., & Gorter, D. (Eds.) (2008). *Linguistic landscape: Expanding the scenery.* London: Routledge.

Turner, J. (1988). *A theory of social interaction.* Stanford, CA: Stanford University Press.

van Lier, L. (1996). *Interaction in the language curriculum: Awareness, autonomy and authenticity.* London: Longman.

van Lier, L. (2004). *The ecology and semiotics of language learning: A sociocultural perspective.* Boston: Springer.

van Lier, L. (2006). Foreword. In G. H. Beckett & P. C. Miller (Eds.), *Project-based second and foreign language education: Past, present and future* (pp. xi–xvi). Greenwich, CT: Information Age Publishing.

van Lier, L., & Walqui, A. (2010). *Scaffolding the academic success of adolescent English language learners: A pedagogy of promise.* San Francisco: WestEd.

Vygotsky, L. S. (1978). *Mind in society.* Cambridge: Cambridge University Press.

Vygotsky, L. S. (1987). Thinking and speech. Translated by N. Minick. In *The Collected Works of L. S. Vygotsky* (Vol. 1: Problems of general psychology) (pp. 39–285). New York: Plenum Press.

Warschauer, M., & Matuchniak, T. (2010). New technology and digital worlds: Analyzing evidence of equity in access, use, and outcomes. *Review of Research in Education, 34,* 179–225.

Wittgenstein, L. (1958). *Philosophical investigations* (2nd ed.). Oxford: Blackwell.

24

Cognitive Aptitudes for Second Language Learning

Robert DeKeyser and Joel Koeth

Aptitude is of obvious practical importance to the enterprise of language learning and teaching. No language teaching professional would doubt that a learner's aptitude is an important predictor of success and that teachers should take their students' aptitude into account when deciding on the kind of instruction to be provided. In some cases aptitude carries even more weight because learners are required to take an aptitude test to be accepted into certain training programs. The role of aptitude is also of theoretical importance because it shows what is involved in the learning process and thereby indirectly reveals something about the nature of that process. The concept of aptitude, then, is of crucial importance to just about every area of applied linguistics, from psycholinguistic research on learning processes to a variety of pedagogical and administrative considerations.

The term "aptitude" requires some clarification, however. In educational psychology it is used with the technical meaning of all characteristics that the learner brings to the learning process, whether these characteristics be cognitive, affective, conative (motivational) or even in the form of previous knowledge (see e.g. Cronbach, 2002; Cronbach & Snow, 1977). This is also the sense in which the term "aptitude" is used in a name such as the "Scholastic Aptitude Test" (SAT): such a test does not measure any specific psychological construct, but rather the whole background that a student brings to college: from intelligence in the broadest sense, to more specific forms of intelligence, to motivation to do well on a test, ability to concentrate, test-taking strategies, specific and general knowledge. In other areas, however, and in applied linguistics in particular, researchers tend to use the term aptitude in a sense that is more restricted in two ways: limited to cognitive aspects (for affective individual differences see especially Dewaele, 2009; for conative ones see especially Dörnyei & Ushioda, 2009), and limited to more or less stable characteristics of an individual, largely the result of genetics and early experience, and not easily modified by specific learning experiences such as a recently taken foreign language course. John Carroll, for example, in his manual for the Modern Language Aptitude Test (MLAT; Carroll & Sapon, 1959) argued that MLAT test scores were not significantly influenced by previous foreign language course work (for a different, more dynamic/interactive point of view, see Dörnyei, 2009).

Even restricting the use of "aptitude" in these two ways, however, one still does not have a pure, theoretically motivated construct. Just as intelligence testing still relies on (adaptations of) tests that were developed a century ago under the time pressure of the First World War, with predictive validity being a much more important concern than construct validity, language aptitude tests such as the MLAT (Carroll & Sapon, 1959), and soon thereafter the Pimsleur Language Aptitude Battery (PLAB;

Pimsleur, 1966), the Defense Language Aptitude Battery (DLAB; Petersen & Al-Haik, 1976) and so on, were developed under the pressures of the Second World War and the Cold War, again striving for maximal predictive validity, with little concern at the time about theoretical motivation (see e.g. Carroll, 1981).

Meanwhile another half century has gone by, and the theoretical constructs that psychologists posit today as being important as components of aptitude for first (L1) or second language (L2) learning and processing are not even directly represented on aptitude tests such as the MLAT, PLAB and DLAB, which are still in fairly wide use today. No convincing alternatives (i.e. tests with equal or higher predictive power and at the same time better theoretical foundation) have been developed—even though some new tests have been designed and are beginning to be used such as the CANAL-F test (Grigorenko, Sternberg & Ehrman, 2000) and the LLAMA test (Meara, 2005), and one ambitious project is underway to develop a test battery with good theoretical motivation and high predictive validity, i.e. the Hi-LAB project at the University of Maryland (see Doughty, Campbell, Mislevy, Bunting, Bowles & Koeth, forthcoming). What has become clear, however, is that there is no unitary construct of aptitude (i.e., aptitude is not one indivisible "thing"; it is just an encompassing term for many "things"), and that even just in the cognitive domain, one can only speak of cognitive *aptitudes*, in the plural, for learning a second language. Any aptitude test, then, will have to include a number of components that measure these various aptitude constructs.

Multiple Aptitudes

What are the constructs/components then that just about any cognitive psychologist would agree are important ingredients of L2 learning aptitude? Nobody would doubt that analytical ability (closely related to verbal aptitude and even general intelligence), memory (including various aspects) and phonetic sensitivity are among the most important. The obvious involvement of these components of aptitude is undoubtedly what led them to be included in some form or another in all existing tests anyway. Beyond these few components it becomes harder to reach consensus. Even from a merely predictive point of view, the value of including certain constructs in a test battery may depend on the kinds of learners, languages, levels of knowledge required and learning contexts. When tests such as the PLAB and the MLAT were developed, the target population consisted primarily of adolescents and young adults learning Indo-European languages at a relatively low level in a traditional classroom. Would the same predictive validity be found for middle-aged learners changing careers, for languages that are known to be very hard (in part because they are very far removed from the native language, such as Chinese or Arabic for English speakers), for highly advanced levels of language learning, for learning in much more communicative classrooms or even for untutored learning? Research that could answer all these questions simply does not exist yet, let alone that anyone would be able to predict learning when a number of these factors are combined (the above-mentioned Hi-LAB project is meant to address these issues, among others). Yet, for a variety of reasons, from global trade issues to national security concerns, to attempts at a less ethnocentric form of liberal education, a larger percentage of students are now studying more "exotic" languages, and for some of the same reasons a higher level of proficiency is required, especially in the receptive skills and sometimes in speaking.

Somewhat paradoxically, this situation is bringing researchers with more immediate concerns of predictive validity closer to those more interested in the fundamental issues of what psychological mechanisms are involved in L2 learning. Indeed, with such a wide variety of target populations to be considered, one cannot afford to go on a fishing expedition to try out what kinds of tests are most predictive of what, and the most practical way to go about designing better tests seems to be taking a step back to reflect on what processes are involved in different kinds of people learning different languages at different levels under different conditions. As research on these issues has taken off only recently, no solid empirical findings exist yet (the Hi-LAB project is about to enter the validation stage at the time of writing). A number of well-founded hypotheses exist, however; they are guiding some of the current research and are likely to lead to radically new aptitude tests in the near future. Some of these are:

1. Various aspects of working memory (WM) are important for all forms of language learning and processing and must therefore be represented on any aptitude test. The emphasis on WM is probably the most important innovation in thinking about language learning aptitude of the last few decades, both in terms of its potential contribution to predictive validity and in terms of integrating aptitude research better with contemporary cognitive psychology and psycholinguistics, and is therefore treated in a separate section below.

2. The need for advanced learning implies long-term practice in the target language environment, with more potential involvement of implicit learning processes, and hence the importance of testing aptitude for implicit learning. Little research exists on individual differences in implicit learning, but some educational psychologists have started to research this issue (Woltz, 2003); given the interest in the field of second language acquisition (SLA) in implicit learning, including this kind of aptitude also seems a priority.

3. The need for more advanced levels of learning combined with the learning of more difficult, less commonly taught, and sometimes even poorly documented languages requires that tests be predictive of untutored learning. This increases the importance of the ability for analytic induction, whether implicit or explicit.

4. The need for advanced learning (including of the receptive skills) gives new importance to subtleties of pragmatics (e.g. forms of address, ways of holding or yielding the floor or ways of adapting the "tone" of a request to the social status of the addressee), and therefore to the need to determine aptitude for learning these elements of pragmatics, whether the learning process be implicit or explicit.

5. The need for untutored learning implies inductive learning in the target environment, which may not only put more of a burden on analytical skills but also on social skills, personality characteristics or forms of aptitude not traditionally considered part of intelligence or sometimes not even cognitive (e.g. social intelligence (Goleman, 2006), emotional intelligence (Goleman, 1996) or cognitive styles such as field independence or tolerance of ambiguity (Kozhevnikov, 2007; Price, 2004; for applications in SLA, see e.g. Ehrman, 1996; Ehrman & Oxford, 1995; Hokanson, 2000; Johnson, Prior & Artuso, 2000; Littlemore, 2001)).

6. Learning a language to the highest levels not only requires broad cognitive, affective and conative aptitudes, but also a number of narrow components. Learning all aspects of pronunciation, segmental as well as non-segmental, requires phonetic sensitivity and perhaps a certain level of musical ability (e.g. Slevc & Miyake, 2006); learning how to infer non-referential meaning (irritation, irony, discomfort, embarrassment, subtle rebuke, subtle language correction) from interaction with native speakers requires social sensitivity/intelligence and not just WM or analytical ability; minimizing interference from L1 (or L3, L4 …) requires aspects of WM that go far beyond storage.

At the same time, however, three very important points should be kept in mind. First of all, it should not be lost from sight that any broad "aptitude" concept, whether language learning aptitude or something even broader like verbal intelligence or general intelligence tends to be a good predictor of L2 learning under a variety of circumstances, whether in more communicative classrooms (Ranta, 2002) or informal learning by adult immigrants (Abrahamsson & Hyltenstam, 2008; DeKeyser, 2000; DeKeyser, Alfi-Shabtay & Ravid, in press; cf. also Skehan, 1989, 1998, 2002).

Second, where more specialized aptitudes are concerned, these do not only interact with the learning context, but also with other aptitudes. Richard Snow (1987) was one of the first to study the interaction of aptitudes, in other words their combined effect on educational achievement; he coined important combinations of aptitudes "aptitude complexes." His work has been continued in educational psychology by researchers such as Ackerman (2003) and applied in the field of SLA by Skehan (1989, 1998, 2002) and Robinson (2002, 2005).

Certain combinations of aptitudes may be particularly important for certain stages of the learning process or for certain learning tasks. Skehan (1998, 2002), for instance, argues that phonemic coding ability and WM are more important at the input stage (for noticing), grammatical sensitivity and inductive ability at the "patterning" stage (for pattern identification, complexification and integration), and various aspects of memory again at the output stage (for retrieval of patterns/rules from long-term memory and holding them in working memory, and eventually storing them in memory in forms that are more easily accessible, often called "procedural knowledge"[1]); Robinson (2001, 2002) suggests how perceptual speed and pattern recognition abilities contribute to the capacity for "noticing the gap," how speed and capacity of phonological WM are ingredients of "memory for contingent speech," and how noticing the gap and memory for contingent speech form an aptitude complex (where one of the two ingredients can compensate to some extent for deficiencies in the other ingredient) that could be called "aptitude for focus on form," especially important for learning from recasts.

Third and finally, as the previous paragraphs already suggest, the importance of specific aptitudes depends very much on the context, which in the field of education typically means a treatment in the form of some kind of teaching method or technique. This interdependence of aptitude and context is what is called aptitude-treatment interaction (ATI) in educational psychology (Cronbach, 2002; Cronbach & Snow, 1977; Corno & Snow, 1986; Deary, 2001; Snow, 1988, 1998; Sternberg, Grigorenko, Ferrari & Clinkenbeard, 1999). While the practical impact of this line of research has been somewhat limited due to the difficulties of implementing any form of individualized instruction (even when "individualized" means adaptation to groups of students with certain aptitudes or aptitude profiles), individualization of instruction is one area where technology holds promise (because computers can give different amounts and kinds of instruction, practice and feedback to different individuals, depending on their aptitude profile, including previous performance). This research, therefore, may have a considerable pay-off in the near future.

Interesting recent examples of ATI research in the SLA domain include Erlam (2005) and Sheen (2007). Erlam showed an interaction between different aptitude profiles (inductive learning ability, phonetic sensitivity, WM) and inductive, deductive and structured-input teaching methodologies, in the sense that phonetic sensitivity (as measured by the PLAB) predicted success with deductive learning, the MLAT with both explicit-inductive learning and structured input, and WM with structured input. Sheen showed that aptitude (in the MLAT sense) was a more important predictor of achievement with metalinguistic than with direct error correction.

In conclusion, while the literature does provide a global picture of how aptitude predicts learning in SLA in general, and while some evidence exists at a more fine-grained level (different stages, different aspects of language, different learning contexts), the body of empirical research is rather limited. Only WM stands out as having received considerable attention in the literature of the last two decades. Therefore, the remainder of this chapter will be dedicated to a more in-depth account of the role of WM as (a component of) aptitude for SLA.

WM as SLA Aptitude

Described as a system responsible for both storing and manipulating temporary information, WM (Baddeley, 1986) has become a major focus in the study of SLA aptitude research. Individual differences in WM have been shown to impact L2 acquisition and use across age groups, proficiency levels and instructional settings. Theoretical accounts vary regarding the definition and structure of WM as well as the sources of variation between individuals (see Conway, Jarrold, Kane, Miyake & Towse, 2007). For example, Cowan (2008) provides three definitions of WM found in the current literature: short-term memory (STM) applied to cognitive tasks, a multi-component model used to hold and manipulate information in STM, and attentional control used to manage STM. Despite the ongoing debate on the exact nature and structure of WM, however, it is clear that WM is important for a wide range of cognitive functions, including those underpinning SLA. The cognitive psychology and SLA literatures clearly demonstrate a common trend: individuals with greater WM capacity consistently outperform individuals with lesser capacity on a wide range of complex cognitive tasks. This fact makes the study of WM and its role as aptitude for SLA an important endeavor. This is not only true for aptitude testing but also for better understanding of L2 learning and of underlying language processing, and potentially even for improving effectiveness of classroom language training through ATI. In this section, WM-focused SLA studies will be reviewed in an effort to highlight the critical role of WM across a wide range of SLA-related areas. First, however, a brief overview will be presented in order to define WM and highlight different conceptualizations that directly impact the study of WM as SLA aptitude.

In order to better understand the role of WM as SLA aptitude and the potential effects of individual differences in WM on L2 learning and use, it is important to clarify how WM is defined and operationalized. Currently, the most widely used model of WM in SLA research is Baddeley's (1986) multi-component model. Baddeley's WM framework consists of a capacity-limited attentional control system termed the central executive, aided by two subsidiary systems, the phonological loop and the visuo-spatial sketchpad (Baddeley & Hitch, 1974). The phonological loop is specialized for holding verbal and acoustic information using a temporary store and an articulatory rehearsal system. Remembering a string of digits such as a new phone number exemplifies the role of the phonological loop. The digits can be maintained for a very brief period of time within the temporary store with little effort. However, remembering the digits for a longer period of time often requires repeating the numbers, either out loud or sub-vocally. The articulatory rehearsal system similarly allows for the rehearsal of information within the phonological loop, thereby keeping the information available for further processing or later recall. The phonological loop is claimed to have evolved as a system for supporting language learning (Baddeley, Gathercole & Papagno, 1998) and is the focus of a great deal of WM-related research in SLA (e.g., Papagno & Vallar, 1995; Service & Kohonen, 1995; Masoura & Gathercole, 1999; Speciale, Ellis & Bywater, 2004; O'Brien, Segalowitz, Freed & Collentine, 2007). The sketchpad, which is posited to temporarily hold visuo-spatial information (as opposed to verbal or acoustic information), has been given far less attention in the SLA literature. In addition to the three original components of Baddeley's model, a final element termed the episodic buffer was later added. The episodic buffer allows for the combination of information from the subsidiary systems (the phonological loop and visuo-spatial sketchpad) and long-term memory into a single episodic representation (Baddeley, 2000). These four components of Baddeley's (2000, 2007) model form a framework popular in SLA-related WM research.

More recent conceptualizations of WM (e.g., Conway & Engle, 1994; Kane, Bleckley, Conway & Engle, 2001; Cowan, Elliott, Saults, Morey, Mattox, Hismjatullina & Conway, 2005) have produced models lacking the modality-specific systems found in Baddeley's (1986, 2000) framework (i.e., the models do not include a specified phonological loop or visuo-spatial sketchpad). Emphasizing "function and process over structure," Kane, Conway, Hambrick and Engle (2007, p. 21) offer an alternative WM model that explains domain specificity of temporary storage (apparent differences in storing verbal information compared to visuo-spatial information) as a reflection of the stimuli being processed. Different types of stimuli recruit distinct perceptual processes that, in turn, allow for different rehearsal activities. For example, a tourist following verbal directions to a famous land-mark in Beijing would likely utilize and benefit from sub-vocal rehearsal of the directions along the route. The nature of the to-be-remembered information makes this type of rehearsal possible. However, if successful navigation were based on remembering and recognizing street signs marked with Chinese characters, sub-vocal rehearsal would be useless for non-Chinese speakers as no pho-nological information is provided by the characters. In this case, the tourist might try to focus on repeatedly recalling the overall shape of the characters or focusing attention on certain components within a character. While this type of rehearsal is similar in function to sub-vocal rehearsal, the lack of acoustic information limits how the characters can be processed and held in WM. By focusing on characteristics of the stimuli (and subsequent processes available for certain types of stimuli), Kane et al.'s (2007) model accounts for domain specificity of temporal storage without the need for a dedi-cated phonological loop or visuo-spatial sketchpad.

A key characteristic of several recent WM models is the critical importance of attentional control (or executive attention). According to Cowan (1995, 2005), WM represents graded activation of portions of long-term memory held in a short-term store. Within this activated short-term store, a certain amount of information can be further activated by focused attention and then enters con-scious awareness. It is the size and capacity of this attentional focus that, Cowan claims, is responsible for variation in WM capacity. This is similar to the framework proposed by Kane and colleagues (Kane et al., 2001, 2007) with the exception that, instead of a true capacity limit (i.e., number of con-crete items that can be maintained within an attentional spotlight), variation in WM derives from the ability to actively maintain task-relevant information outside of consciousness and efficiently recover information despite various forms of interference inherent in complex processing opera-tions. Despite somewhat subtle differences, both models emphasize the role of attentional control in retrieving, holding and processing temporary information, often in the midst of interference and competition. This ability to control attention and ignore or inhibit interference is critical in several areas of SLA and use and is, therefore, a focal interest in SLA aptitude research.

Research in cognitive psychology increasingly supports the critical role of WM in reasoning, prob-lem solving and a myriad other complex processes. Latent variable analyses (e.g., Conway, Cowan, Bunting, Therriault & Minkoff, 2002) suggest that WM is a good predictor of general fluid intel-ligence (Gf)[2] in young adults. A reanalysis of 10 published studies, representing more than 3,100 young-adult participants, revealed a high correlation between WM and Gf (median $r = 0.72$), indi-cating that WM and Gf constructs share approximately 50% of their variance (Kane, Hambrick & Conway, 2005). It is not surprising, then, that individual differences in WM impact rate of learning and, quite possibly, ultimate attainment in SLA. Miyake and Friedman (1998) presented evidence suggesting that greater WM resources predict both a faster rate of learning and a higher attained level of proficiency. The predictive validity of WM remained even after controlling for individual differ-ences in general intelligence. While benefits of high language learning aptitude are particularly strong for adults (e.g., Abrahamsson & Hyltenstam, 2008; DeKeyser, 2000; DeKeyser et al., 2010; Harley & Hart, 1997), there is evidence to suggest that learning by children is also susceptible to the effects of differences in WM ability (e.g, Daneman & Carpenter, 1980; Gathercole & Baddeley, 1989, 1990; Hitch, Towse & Hutton, 2001), especially when considering rate of learning. Despite a prevalent belief that aptitude as traditionally thought of in the SLA field plays little role in child SLA, there is little reason to assume young learners are immune to the effects of individual differences in WM in instructed SLA settings. It is clear that WM is a critical component of aptitude for SLA. For whom, and under what conditions, are questions that can be informed by the ever-growing literature on the role of WM in SLA and use.

Robinson (2005) includes phonological WM capacity and phonological WM speed as basic abili-ties that contribute to a broad SLA aptitude complex. Phonological WM has been a key target of investigation for SLA researchers trying to explain WM's impact on L2 learning. Several studies from the early and mid-1990s demonstrated a positive effect of high phonological memory on language learning success. Service (1992) found that phonological short-term memory, as measured by the ability to repeat English-sounding pseudowords, predicted success in learning English as a foreign language over the course of three years. The link between phonological WM and language learning success also received support from Papagno and Vallar (1995), who tested polyglot and monolingual Italian participants on several measures, including phonological, visuo-spatial and long-term memory, general intelligence and vocabulary knowledge in their native language. The two groups differed significantly on several measures with the polyglots outperforming the monolinguals on the verbal STM tasks as well as a paired-associate learning test, which measured their ability to learn words in a new language (Russian). Performance on the measures of general intelligence, visuo-spatial short-term memory and Italian paired-associate learning did not differ significantly between the groups. The polyglots advantage in phonological memory and novel word pair learning led the authors to conclude that the ability to acquire a foreign language is closely tied to phonological memory. Further support for phonological memory's role in foreign language learning was provided by Service and Kohonen (1995) and Masoura and Gathercole (1999). Service and Kohonen utilized regression analyses on repetition data and learning measures to further strengthen the link between phonological memory and language learning, while Masoura and Gathercole verified and extended these findings by demonstrating an additional influence of L1 vocabulary knowledge.

More recent studies on the role of phonological memory have provided additional details regarding how individual differences in this area affect the acquisition of a second language. Speciale et al. (2004) conducted two experiments investigating the relative contributions of (university) students' short-term store and ability to learn phonological sequences on nonword repetition performance. In the first study, phonological sequence learning and phonological store made additive independent contributions to successful vocabulary learning. Experiment two included a longitudinal study of beginning Spanish learners during a 10-week university-level course and provided further support for the positive link between skill in phonological sequence learning and final levels of receptive Spanish ability and ability to repeat Spanish-word-like nonwords. This study extended the understanding of role of phonological memory by demonstrating that the phonological store and sequence learning are initially separable and both contribute to the acquisition of long-term phonological knowledge, which is necessary for foreign language vocabulary learning. Gathercole (2006) offers evidence from studies on both normal children and adults and people with language learning disorders that further establish the link between the nonword repetition ability and the learning of the phonological forms of novel words. One of Gathercole's (2006) major contributions to the subject is that nonword repetition and word learning both rely on phonological storage and are multiply determined, meaning that deficits in storage alone might not, by itself, lead to a substantial language learning deficit. The studies reviewed so far have shown a consistent relationship between phonological memory and foreign language vocabulary learning in both children and adults. This link has been supported in similarly-focused studies investigating language learning at home and abroad (e.g., O'Brien et al., 2007), in traditional (e.g., Speciale et al., 2004) and intensive (e.g., Kormos & Safar, 2008) learning environments, and with learners of different proficiency levels (Kormos & Safar, 2008).

WM has been shown to affect a broad range of language skills. Ellis and Sinclair (1996) demonstrated a positive relationship between WM and metalinguistic knowledge of grammatical regularities as well as some aspects of productive grammatical fluency and accuracy. This relationship was claimed to be WM-related as WM enables short-term maintenance and rehearsal of sequence information, which, in turn promotes long-term memory consolidation and learning. Williams and Lovatt (2003) provided further support for a relationship between phonological memory and grammar learning, finding that phonological memory contributed to the successful learning of determiner-noun agreement rules in a semi-artificial language. Investigating the link between phonological memory and grammar development in French-speaking children in a five-month English immersion course, French and O'Brien (2008) report two noteworthy findings. First, after controlling for initial grammar knowledge, phonological memory significantly predicted grammar development (approximately 28% of variance explained) at the end of the five-month time period. Second, the administration of two nonword span repetition tasks, one using actual Arabic words and the other using English nonwords, revealed a proficiency-related increase in ability to repeat English nonwords but not Arabic words. This finding is important as it demonstrates a positive effect of increased proficiency on English nonword span performance while, at the same time, suggesting that the underlying general phonological memory remains unchanged.

WM has also been credited with playing a vital role in noticing and benefiting from interactional feedback. Based on past research suggesting that learning cannot occur without noticing (Schmidt, 1990; Robinson, 1995), Mackey, Philp, Egi, Fujii and Tatsumi (2002) examined the effect of individual differences in WM on learning from interactional feedback. Trends emerged in which learners who indicated less noticing tended to have low WM capacities and students with higher capacities reported more noticing. This trend differed by proficiency level though as high WM capacity learners at lower developmental levels indicated more noticing than learners at higher developmental levels. Interestingly, Mackey et al. (2002) found no significant difference in immediate learning between high and low WM groups. However, this is in line with previous research (Ando, Fukunaga, Kurachachi, Suto, Nakano & Kage, 1992), which demonstrated no significant differences between high and low WM participants immediately after the instructional period but significant correlations with performance on a delayed posttest two months later. Mackey et al. (2002) suggest that the WM capacity of the high group individuals may have enabled them to pick up and hold more information than the low WM group. As a result, the larger amount of data might require a longer time period to process and consolidate, thereby explaining why no differences were found until the delayed posttest.

In conclusion, the literature on WM in SLA convincingly shows the critical position WM occupies in aptitude for SLA, over a wide range of learner ages, proficiency, language skills and learning environments.

Conclusions and Future Directions

The road ahead is still long. While the profession has known for decades how to measure aptitude with sufficient predictive validity for the situations where the measures were most needed, it is doubtful that these measures can be used equally successfully for all languages, learning contexts and proficiency levels, not to mention for all aspects of language, from pronunciation to grammar, vocabulary, pragmatics and writing systems.

One of the reasons why designing better tests is difficult is that the discipline does not have a good theoretical understanding yet of how the various components of aptitude interact with each other and with the learning context to predict success in different areas. Designing a better test means in the first place deciding what components need to be involved, and in the second place what the best way is to measure them if the goal is to use these measures as predictors of L2 learning. The only component that has received considerable attention so far, both in SLA research and in cognitive psychology more broadly, is WM. The results of research in this area are promising, but even there much work remains to be done to come to a fuller understanding of the exact role WM plays in the learning process for various aspects of languages and at different stages in the learning process.

A deeper understanding of the role that these various components play is unlikely to come from large amounts of simple correlational research in the sense of measuring the relationship between aptitude and broad outcome measures at the end of a given curriculum. Various research approaches, however, can all contribute to a better understanding:

- Longitudinal research is needed to assess the importance of the various aptitudes at different stages (the only way this can be done well is by tracking performance of the same individuals over time and see how their various aptitudes predict their performance at that stage, especially at the fine-grained level of stages of learning for specific structures).
- ATI research is needed, not only to investigate how learning context modulates the importance of different aptitudes in predicting achievement, but also to gain a better understanding of why these aptitudes tend to have predictive value in the first place (how they interact with the learning context suggests what role they play instead of just how much of a role they play).
- Even more narrowly focused research in a laboratory context is needed in order to take a more fine-grained process approach to the interaction between aptitudes and task characteristics for very specific learning tasks at very specific stages of the learning process (such as noticing verb suffixes that are typically not salient to the learner because of their inconspicuous forms and their limited communicative importance or taking knowledge of complex word order rules from the declarative to the procedural stage).

This chapter has shown that while definitive answers for most questions about aptitude are not available, many interesting hypotheses are ready to be tested in research that can at the same time make professionals understand the learning process better and produce better aptitude tests both for selection purposes and for more principled individualization of instruction.

Notes

1. Cognitive psychologists, in particular those interested in the acquisition of skills, often make a distinction between declarative and procedural knowledge (e.g. Anderson, 1993; Anderson, Bothell, Byrne, Douglass, Lebiere & Qin, 2004; Anderson & Lebiere, 1998; cf. also DeKeyser, 2001, 2007). Declarative knowledge is sometimes called "knowledge that" and procedural knowledge is then "knowledge how"; it is easy to see the difference between the two in the field of L2 learning, i.e., the difference between knowing a rule that one was taught and can verbalize more or less, e.g. "a verb in English takes an -s in the third person singular of the simple present tense," (declarative knowledge) and the kind of knowledge that lets the learner actually supply this -s each time it is required (procedural knowledge). Once a learner can use this procedural knowledge with a high degree of accuracy and fluency, one can speak of "automatized knowledge."
2. Fluid intelligence (Gf) and crystallized intelligence (Gc) (Cattell, 1971; Horn, 1989; cf. also Horn & Noll, 1997) are often seen as the two main components of intelligence in its most general sense (G). Gf shows far less influence from experience and education than Gc, and is sometimes argued to be equivalent to G. Research in the last decade or so has shown, however, that even a test such as Raven's Progressive Matrices, often considered the best measure of Gf, has shown large changes in averages scores in the last two generations, which strongly suggest that even this test of Gf is not free of environmental, presumably cultural, influences (see especially Flynn, 2007; Neisser, 1998).

References

Abrahamsson, N., & Hyltenstam, K. (2008). The robustness of aptitude effects in near-native second language acquisition. *Studies in Second Language Acquisition, 30*(4), 481–509.

Ackerman, P. L. (2003). Aptitude complexes and trait complexes. *Educational Psychologist, 38*(2), 85–93.

Anderson, J. R. (1993). *Rules of the mind.* Hillsdale, NJ: Lawrence Erlbaum.

Anderson, J. R., & Lebiere, C. (1998). *The atomic components of thought.* Mahwah, NJ: Lawrence Erlbaum.

Anderson, J. R., Bothell, D., Byrne, M. D., Douglass, S., Lebiere, C. & Qin, Y. (2004). An integrated theory of the mind. *Psychological Review, 111*(4), 1036–1060.

Ando, J., Fukunaga, N., Kurachachi, J., Suto, T., Nakano, T. & Kage, M. (1992). A comparative study on the two EFL teaching methods: The communicative and grammatical approach. *Japanese Journal of Educational Psychology, 40*, 247–256.

Baddeley, A. D. (1986). *Working memory.* Oxford: Oxford University Press.

Baddeley, A. D. (2000). The episodic buffer: A new component of working memory? *Trends in Cognitive Sciences*, 4, 417–423.

Baddeley, A. D. (2007). *Working memory, thought, and action.* Oxford: Oxford University Press.

Baddeley, A. D., Gathercole, S. E. & Papagno, C. (1998). The phonological loop as a language learning device. *Psychological Review*, *105*, 158–173.

Baddeley, A. D., & Hitch, G. J. (1974). Working memory. In G. A. Bower (Ed.), *The psychology of learning and motivation* (pp. 47–89). New York: Academic Press.

Carroll, J. B. (1981). Twenty-five years of research on foreign language aptitude. In K. C. Diller (Ed.), *Individual differences and universals in language learning aptitude* (pp. 83–118). Rowley, MA: Newbury House.

Carroll, J. B., & Sapon, S. (1959). *Modern Language Aptitude Test. Form A.* New York: The Psychological Corporation.

Cattell, R. B. (1971). *Abilities: Their structure, growth, and action.* Boston: Houghton Mifflin.

Conway, A. R. A., & Engle, R. W. (1994). Working memory and retrieval: A resource-dependent inhibition model. *Journal of Experimental Psychology: General*, *123*, 354–373.

Conway, A. R. A., Cowan, N., Bunting, M. F., Therriault, D. J. & Minkoff, S. R. B. (2002). A latent variable analysis of working memory capacity, short-term memory capacity, processing speed, and general fluid intelligence. *Intelligence*, *30*, 163–183.

Conway, A. R. A., Jarrold, C., Kane, M. J., Miyake, A. & Towse, J. N. (Eds.) (2007). *Variation in working memory.* New York: Oxford University Press.

Corno, L., & Snow, R. E. (1986). Adapting teaching to individual differences among learners. In M. C. Wittrock (Ed.), *Handbook of research on teaching* (3rd ed.) (pp. 605–629). New York: Macmillan.

Cowan, N. (1995). *Attention and memory: An integrated framework.* Oxford Psychology Series, No. 26. New York: Oxford University Press.

Cowan, N. (2005). *Working memory capacity.* New York: Psychology Press.

Cowan, N. (2008). What are the differences between long-term, short-term, and working memory? *Progress in Brain Research*, *169*, 323–338.

Cowan, N., Elliott, E. M., Saults, J. S., Morey, C. C., Mattox, S., Hismjatullina, A. & Conway A. R. A. (2005). On the capacity of attention: Its estimation and its role in working memory and cognitive aptitudes. *Cognitive Psychology*, *51*, 42–100.

Cronbach, L. J. (Ed.) (2002). *Remaking the concept of aptitude. Extending the legacy of Richard E. Snow.* Mahwah, NJ: Erlbaum.

Cronbach, L. J., & Snow, R. E. (1977). *Aptitudes and instructional methods: A handbook for research on interactions.* New York: Irvington.

Daneman, M., & Carpenter, P. A. (1980). Individual differences in working memory and reading. *Journal of Verbal Learning and Verbal Behavior*, *19*(4), 450–466.

Deary, I. J. (2001). Human intelligence differences: Towards a combined experimental-differential approach. *Trends in Cognitive Sciences*, *5*(4), 164–170.

DeKeyser, R. M. (2000). The robustness of critical period effects in second language acquisition. *Studies in Second Language Acquisition*, *22*(4), 499–533.

DeKeyser, R. M. (2001). Automaticity and automatization. In P. Robinson (Ed.), *Cognition and second language instruction* (pp. 125–151). New York: Cambridge University Press.

DeKeyser, R. M. (2007). Skill acquisition theory. In B. VanPatten & J. Williams (Eds.), *Theories in Second Language Acquisition: An introduction* (pp. 97–112). Mahwah, NJ: Erlbaum.

DeKeyser, R. M., Alfi-Shabtay, I. & Ravid, D. (2010). Cross-linguistic evidence for the nature of age effects in second language acquisition. *Applied Psycholinguistics*, *31*(3), 413–438.

Dewaele, J.-M. (2009). Individual differences in second language acquisition. In T. Bhatia & W. Ritchie (Eds.), *The new handbook of second language acquisition* (pp. 623–646). Bingley: Emerald Group.

Dörnyei, Z. (2009). *The psychology of second language acquisition.* Oxford: Oxford University Press.

Dörnyei, Z., & Ushioda, E. (Eds.) (2009). *Motivation, language identity, and the L2 self.* Bristol: Multilingual Matters.

Doughty, C., Campbell, S., Mislevy, M., Bunting, M., Bowles, A. & Koeth, J. (forthcoming). Predicting near-native ability: The factor structure and reliability of Hi-LAB. *Proceedings of the 2008 Second Language Research Forum.* Somerville, MA: Cascadilla Press.

Ehrman, M. E. (1996). *Understanding second language learning difficulties.* Thousand Oaks, CA: Sage.

Ehrman, M. E., & Oxford, R. L. (1995). Cognition Plus: Correlates of language learning success. *The Modern Language Journal*, *79*(1), 67–89.

Ellis, N. C., & Sinclair, S. G. (1996). Working memory in the acquisition of vocabulary and syntax: Putting language in good order. *The Quarterly Journal of Experimental Psychology A*, *49*(1), 234–250.

Erlam, R. (2005). Language aptitude and its relationship to instructional effectiveness in second language acquisition. *Language Teaching Research*, *9*(2), 147–171.

Flynn, J. R. (2007). *What is intelligence?* New York: Cambridge University Press.

French, L., & O'Brien, I. (2008). Phonological memory and children's second language grammar learning. *Applied Psycholinguistics*, *29*(3), 463–487.

Gathercole, S. E. (2006). Nonword repetition and word learning: The nature of the relationship. *Applied Psycholinguistics*, *27*, 513–543.

Gathercole, S. E., & Baddeley, A. D. (1989). Evaluation of the role of phonological STM in the development of vocabulary in children: A longitudinal study. *Journal of Memory and Language*, *28*, 200–214.

Gathercole, S. E., & Baddeley, A. D. (1990). The role of phonological memory in vocabulary acquisition: A study of young children. *British Journal of Psychology*, *81*(4), 439–454.

Goleman, D. (1996). *Emotional intelligence: Why it can matter more than IQ*. New York: Random House.

Goleman, D. (2006). *Social intelligence. The new science of human relationships*. New York: Random House.

Grigorenko, E., Sternberg, R. J. & Ehrman, M. E. (2000). A theory-based approach to the measurement of second-language learning ability: The CANAL-F theory and test. *The Modern Language Journal*, *84*(3), 390–405.

Harley, B., & Hart, D. (1997). Language aptitude and second language proficiency in classroom learners of different starting ages. *Studies in Second Language Acquisition*, *19*, 379–400.

Hitch, G. J., Towse, J. N. & Hutton, U. (2001). What limits children's working memory span? Theoretical account and applications for scholastic development. *Journal of Experimental Psychology: General*, *130*(2), 184–198.

Hokanson, S. (2000). Foreign language immersion homestays. Maximizing the accommodation of cognitive styles. *Applied Language Learning*, *11*(2), 239–264.

Horn, J. (1989). Models of intelligence. In R. L. Linn (Ed.), *Intelligence: Measurement, theory, and public policy* (pp. 29–73). Urbana, IL: University of Illinois Press.

Horn, J. L., & Noll, J. (1997). Human cognitive capabilities: Gf-Gc theory. In D. P. Flanagan, J. L. Genshaft & P. L. Harrison (Eds.), *Contemporary intellectual assessment. Theories, tests, and issues* (pp. 53–91). New York: Guilford.

Johnson, J., Prior, S. & Artuso, M. (2000). Field dependence as a factor in second language communicative production. *Language Learning*, *50*(3), 529–567.

Kane, M. J., Bleckley, M. K., Conway, A. R. A. & Engle, R. W. (2001). A controlled-attention view of working-memory capacity. *Journal of Experimental Psychology: General*, *130*, 169–183.

Kane, M. J., Conway, A. R. A., Hambrick, D. Z. & Engle, R. W. (2007). Variation in working memory as variation in executive attention and control. In A. R. A. Conway, C. Jarrold, M. J. Kane, A. Miyake & J. N. Towse (Eds.), *Variation in working memory* (pp. 21–48). Oxford: Oxford University Press.

Kane, M. J., Hambrick, D. Z. & Conway, A. R. A. (2005). Working memory capacity and fluid intelligence are strongly related constructs: Comment on Ackerman, Beier, and Boyle. *Psychological Bulletin*, *131*, 66–71.

Kormos, J., & Safar, A. (2008). Phonological short-term memory, working memory, and foreign language performance in intensive language learning. *Bilingualism: Language and Cognition*, *11*(2), 261–271.

Kozhevnikov, M. (2007). Cognitive styles in the context of modern psychology: Toward an integrated framework of cognitive style. *Psychological Bulletin*, *133*(3), 464–481.

Littlemore, J. (2001). An empirical study of the relationship between cognitive style and the use of communication strategy. *Applied Linguistics*, *22*(2), 241–265.

Mackey, A., Philp, J., Egi, T., Fujii, A. & Tatsumi, T. (2002). Individual differences in working memory, noticing of interactional feedback, and L2 development. In P. Robinson (Ed.), *Individual differences and instructed second language acquisition* (pp. 181–209). Amsterdam: Benjamins.

Masoura, E., & Gathercole, S. E. (1999). Phonological short-term memory and foreign language learning. *International Journal of Psychology*, *34*, 383–388.

Meara, P. (2005). LLAMA language aptitude tests. The manual. Unpublished manuscript.

Miyake, A., & Friedman, N. F. (1998). Individual differences in second language proficiency: Working memory as language aptitude. In A. E. Healy & L. E. Bourne (Eds.), *Foreign language learning: Psycholinguistic studies on training and retention* (pp. 339–364). Mahwah, NJ: Erlbaum.

Neisser, U. (Ed.) (1998). *The rising curve. Long-term gains in IQ and related measures*. Washington, DC: American Psychological Association.

O'Brien, I., Segalowitz, N., Freed, B. & Collentine, J. (2007). Phonological memory predicts second language oral fluency gains in adults. *Studies in Second Language Acquisition*, *29*, 557–582.

Papagno, C., & Vallar, G. (1995). Verbal short-term memory and vocabulary learning in polyglots. *Quarterly Journal of Experimental Psychology*, *48A*, 98–107.

Peterson, C. R., & Al-Haik, A. R. (1976). The development of the Defense Language Aptitude Battery (DLAB). *Educational and Psychological Measurement*, *36*, 369–380.

Pimsleur, P. (1966). *Pimsleur Language Aptitude Battery (PLAB)*. New York: The Psychological Corporation.

Price, L. (2004). Individual differences in learning: Cognitive control, cognitive style, and learning style. *Journal of Educational Psychology*, *24*, 681–698.

Ranta, L. (2002). The role of learners' language-analytic ability in the communicative classroom. In P. Robinson (Ed.), *Individual differences and instructed language learning* (pp. 159–179). Amsterdam: Benjamins.

Robinson, P. (1995). Attention, memory, and the "noticing" hypothesis. *Language Learning, 45*, 283–331.

Robinson, P. (2001). Individual differences, cognitive abilities, aptitude complexes, and learning conditions in SLA. *Second Language Research, 17*(4), 368–392.

Robinson, P. (2002). Learning conditions, aptitude complexes, and SLA. In P. Robinson (Ed.), *Individual differences and instructed language learning* (pp. 113–133). Amsterdam: Benjamins.

Robinson, P. (2005). Aptitude and second language acquisition. *Annual Review of Applied Linguistics, 25*, 46–73.

Schmidt, R. (1990). The role of consciousness in second language learning. *Applied Linguistics, 11*, 17–46.

Service, E. (1992). Phonology, working memory, and foreign-language learning. *Quarterly Journal of Experimental Psychology, 45A*, 21–50.

Service, E., & Kohonen, V. (1995). Is the relation between phonological memory and foreign language learning accounted for by vocabulary acquisition? *Applied Psycholinguistics, 16*, 155–172.

Sheen, Y. (2007). The effect of focused written corrective feedback and language aptitude on ESL learners' acquisition of articles. *TESOL Quarterly, 41*(2), 255–283.

Skehan, P. (1989). *Individual differences in second language learning.* London: Edward Arnold.

Skehan, P. (1998). *A cognitive approach to language learning.* Oxford: Oxford University Press.

Skehan, P. (2002). Theorising and updating aptitude. In P. Robinson (Ed.), *Individual differences and instructed language learning* (pp. 69–93). Amsterdam: Benjamins.

Slevc, L. R., & Miyake, A. (2006). Individual differences in second-language proficiency: Does musical ability matter? *Psychological Science, 17*(8), 675–681.

Snow, R. E. (1987). Aptitude complexes. In R. E. Snow & M. J. Farr (Eds.), *Aptitude, learning, and instruction* (pp. 13–59). Hillsdale, NJ: LEA.

Snow, R. E. (1988). *Aptitude-treatment interaction as a framework for research on individual differences* (No. 88-CERAS-16). Stanford, CA: Stanford University Press.

Snow, R. E. (1998). Abilities as aptitudes and achievements in learning situations. In J. J. McArdle & R. W. Woodcock (Eds.), *Human cognitive abilities in theory and practice* (pp. 93–112). Mahwah, NJ: Erlbaum.

Speciale, G., Ellis, N. & Bywater, T. (2004). Phonological sequence learning and short-term store capacity determine second language vocabulary acquisition. *Applied Psycholinguistics, 25*, 293–321.

Sternberg, R. J., Grigorenko, E. L., Ferrari, M. & Clinkenbeard, P. (1999). A triarchic analysis of an aptitude-treatment interaction. *European Journal of Psychological Assessment, 15*(1), 3–13.

Williams, J. N., & Lovatt, P. (2003). Phonological memory and rule learning. *Language Learning, 53*, 67–121.

Woltz, D. J. (2003). Implicit cognitive processes as aptitudes for learning. *Educational Psychologist, 38*(2), 95–104.

25

Around and Beyond the Critical Period Hypothesis

David Singleton and Carmen Muñoz

Introduction

The study of age effects in second or additional language (L2) learning has attracted the interest of researchers over many decades. The present survey presents and appraises research relating to the Critical Period Hypothesis (henceforth CPH) as well as a range of recent significant research conducted within a scenario that relies less and less on a single explanatory factor for age-related phenomena in L2 acquisition. The survey highlights a broad array of factors that may underlie the widely attested finding that L2 learners who begin to be exposed to their target language in their early years tend to reach higher levels of L2 proficiency than those who begin as adolescents or adults.

An illustration of what can be seen as an over-reliance on maturational explanations for findings related to later language acquisition in general is the manner in which the oft-cited case of Genie was dealt with by researchers. Until she was rescued at age 13, Genie spent most of her life sitting in a potty-chair and secluded from social contact. The fact that her subsequent language development showed some peculiarities (Curtiss, 1977) was interpreted by some as a demonstration of the closing at puberty of the window of opportunity for language acquisition. However, a complexity of factors must have played a role in such a situation. More than 50 years ago neurocognitive research reported an interaction between maturation and socialization in both monkeys (Harlow, 1958) and human children (Spitz, 1946). According to the classic studies of Spitz (1946), children who lacked proper maternal/parental care in the first year of their life were withdrawn and their intellectual performance was below standard. More recent research has shown that global neglect during the first five years of life leads to a permanently smaller head circumference, smaller brain size, and impaired ability to learn language and to develop normal social behaviour (e.g., Chugani, Behen, Muzik, Juhasz, Nagy & Chugani, 2001; see Uylings, 2006). In the case of Genie, global neglect, which includes minimal exposure to language, touch and social interaction, may seem to provide a more satisfactory explanation for her abnormal language development than an interpretation exclusively grounded in one single factor, such as that provided by the CPH.

Birdsong (2006) advises us that research in this area requires "clear-eyed and open-minded attempts to integrate biological, cognitive, experiential, linguistic, and affective dimensions of L2 learning and processing" (p. 37). In this chapter we argue that studies of age-related effects in L2 acquisition can greatly benefit from adopting a multi-factorial approach. In the service of this perspective, we begin by exploring and evaluating evidence and arguments relative to the CPH and then go on to discuss recent trends in the investigation of age-related effects in second language acquisition. Our conclusion is that such effects cannot be surgically separated from effects deriving from learners' learning environment and orientations, and that finer-grained research is needed in order fully to understand the attested variability in L2 outcomes, which has too often been attributed exclusively to the starting age of learning.

The Critical Period Hypothesis

The term *critical period* is used in biology to refer to a phase in the development of an organism during which a particular capacity or behaviour must be acquired if it is to be acquired at all. An example typically cited is that of imprinting in certain species. Thus, for instance, immediately after hatching, ducklings follow and become irreversibly attached to the first moving object they perceive—usually their mother. This following behaviour occurs only within a certain time period, after which the hatchlings develop a fear of strange objects and retreat instead of following. Within these time limits is what is seen as the critical period for the following behaviour (Clark & Clark, 1977, p. 520; De Villiers & De Villiers, 1978, p. 210; Lorenz, 1961). Another example is provided by the acquisition of birdsong: for instance, if a young chaffinch does not hear an adult bird singing within a certain period, the bird in question will apparently never sing a full song (Thorpe, 1954). Yet a further example relates to the development of binocularity:

> A critical period for the development of binocularity may begin when central nervous system cells driven by each eye grow and compete for cortical synapses … The critical period for development of binocularity may take place between weeks 4 and 12 in the cat; 1 and 9 in certain monkeys; and years 1 and 3 in man.
>
> (Almli & Finger, 1987, p. 126)

If language acquisition in human beings is constrained by the limits of a critical period on this kind of definition, the implication is that unless language acquisition gets under way before the period ends it simply will not happen. There may also be an implication that, even if language acquisition begins within the critical period, it does not continue beyond the end of that period and that additional languages acquired beyond the critical period will not ever be completely or "perfectly" acquired.

First Language Evidence of a Critical Period for Language Acquisition

The critical period idea was first applied to first language (L1) acquisition (see, e.g., Singleton & Ryan, 2004, chapters 2–3). Evidence sometimes cited in this connection is that furnished by cases of children who came into significant contact with language only around the age of puberty, the point at which the critical period for language acquisition supposedly ends according to many accounts. Two oft-cited cases of this kind are those of Victor, found running wild in the woods of Aveyron in late eighteenth-century France (see, e.g., Lane, 1976; Lebrun, 1980; Newton, 2002), and the aforementioned case of Genie, rescued from the cruel isolation imposed on her by her parents in late twentieth-century California (see, e.g., Curtiss, 1977; Jones, 1995; Rymer, 1993). Typically in such instances some post-rescue language development is observed—but of a limited and abnormal kind. Some researchers see this as "first language acquisition after the critical age" (De Villiers & De Villiers, 1978, p. 219); others see it as evidence of "specific constraints and limitations on … language acquisition outside of … the critical maturational period" (Curtiss, 1977, p. 234). Interestingly, Lenneberg, the "father" of the CPH, comments that all one can conclude from such cases is that "life in dark closets, wolves' dens, forests or sadistic parents' backyards is not conducive to good health and normal development" (Lenneberg, 1967, p. 142).

Another source of L1 evidence perceived as favouring the CPH is the mixed success exhibited by late acquirers of sign language—profoundly deaf subjects deprived of processable language input in their early years and who then acquire sign language as their L1 at a later stage (see, e.g., Curtiss, 1988; Emmorey, 2002; Mayberry & Fisher, 1989; Mayberry, Fischer & Hatfield, 1983; Morford & Mayberry, 2000; Newport, 1988; Singleton & Newport, 2004; Woodward, 1973). Such studies do not find that language completely fails to develop after a given maturational point but that some elements are observable in the language of the later signers that differentiate them from early signers. It can be argued that deprivation of language input during the phase in a child's life when cognitive development is at its most intense may have general cognitive effects, and that it may be these general effects that are reflected in later language development. It is noteworthy that some research (e.g. Peterson & Siegal, 1995; Schick & Gale, 1997; Woolfe, Want & Siegal, 2002) indicates that deaf children whose access to sign language is delayed have problems in the area of "theory of mind", i.e. in the understanding that individuals other than themselves have mental states—beliefs, desires, intentions, etc. The implications of such problems could be very far-reaching in terms of language development (cf. Lundy, 1999), and, moreover, other general cognitive problems associated with late L1 acquisition may well be revealed by further research.

As noted earlier, a very strong version of the CPH might posit that even if language development starts within the critical period, it does not continue beyond the end of the period. In a study of Down syndrome subjects Lenneberg, Nichols and Rosenberger (1964) were able to record progress in language development only in children younger than 14. This is interpreted by Lenneberg (1967, p. 155) to indicate that "progress in language learning comes to a standstill after maturity". Alternative interpretations are (1) that what Lenneberg et al. were observing was a general developmental phenomenon rather than specifically language-related; (2) that what was involved was not in fact a complete arrestation in development but a temporary plateau; and/or (3) that the halt in progress was due to an absence of the right kind of stimulation. One can in any case question the relevance of evidence from these abnormal situations for normal language development—especially in the light of the fact that there are ample indications that normal L1 development continues well beyond the childhood years (for further discussion see Nippold, 1998; Singleton & Ryan, 2004, pp. 55–60).

The CPH and L2 Acquisition: Naturalistic Evidence

The CPH swiftly became a theme also in the investigation of the acquisition of additional languages. L2-related interpretations of the CPH can be briefly summarized as follows: after a certain maturational point the L2 learner

- is no longer capable of attaining to native-like levels of proficiency;
- needs to expend more conscious effort than in earlier L2 acquisition; and/or
- makes use of different mechanisms from those deployed in L2 acquisition during childhood.

In any case, there is a sharp decline in L2 learning potential beyond a particular maturational stage. None of the above notions, let it be said, is unproblematic. At a general level it is worth bearing in mind that, as Aram, Bates, Eisele, Fenson, Nass, Thal & Trauner (1997) note, "the end of the critical period for language in humans has proven … difficult to find, with estimates ranging from 1 year of age to adolescence" (p. 85), and that, in addition, there is much dispute about what kinds of capacities are supposed to be affected by the critical period (see Singleton, 2005).

With regard to attaining native-like levels of proficiency, Scovel (1988) claims that those who begin to be exposed to an L2 after age 12 cannot ever "pass themselves off as native speakers phonologically" (p. 185) (a position since qualified—Scovel, 2000, 2006). Long (1990, p. 274) concurs with

Scovel's interpretation of the phonological evidence, and further suggests that for L2 morphology and syntax to reach native levels exposure to the L2 must begin before age 15 (see also Long, 2007). Such claims have been questioned by research and discussion focused on later beginners attaining to very high levels of L2 proficiency, e.g., Birdsong, 1992; Bongaerts, 1999, 2003; Bongaerts, Mennen & Van der Slik, 2000; Bongaerts, Planken & Schils 1995; Bongaerts, Van Summeren, Planken & Schils, 1997; Ioup, 1995; Ioup, Boustagui, Tigi & Moselle, 1994; Kinsella, 2009; Kinsella & Singleton, 2008; Moyer, 1999; Muñoz & Singleton, 2007; Palmen, Bongaerts & Schils, 1997; Singleton & Leśniewska, 2009). Hyltenstam and Abrahamsson (2000, p. 155) point out that there is no recorded case of a post-pubertal L2 beginner behaving in every single detail like a native speaker (cf. also Hyltenstam & Abrahamsson, 2003a, 2003b), but they also acknowledge that very early L2 beginners tend to differ too at the level of fine linguistic detail from monoglot native speakers. The maturational issue may be a good deal less important in this connection than the fact of possessing knowledge of another language (cf., e.g., Cook, 1995; Flege, 1999; Grosjean, 1992; Ioup, 2005, pp. 248ff.; Leather, 2002, p. 10f.).

Concerning the effortfulness of later language learning, Lenneberg (1967, p. 176) suggests that post-pubertal L2 learning requires "conscious and labored effort", a claim which some researchers (e.g. Hyltenstam & Abrahamsson, 2000, p. 152) have seen as a crucial aspect of the CPH. Many professionals involved in one way or another with language have simply assumed that later L2 learning requires more effort. Thus, in an Irish medical journal, of all places, we find an article (Breathnach, 1993) claiming that "the infant learns to pronounce and use the language he hears around him with ease and perfection", while adult L2 learning "demands a systematic and determined effort" (p. 44). Bongaerts, despite general scepticism towards the CPH, also remarks that the native-like L2 accents exhibited by the post-pubertal L2 learners he investigated may be partly explicable in terms of the very intensive training they had undergone (e.g. Bongaerts, 1999, pp. 154–155). However, such "input enhancement" may not be indispensable for successful late L2 learning. For example, one of Ioup's highly successful adult learners of Arabic was untutored, and her performance was native-like even in areas of which she had no awareness—e.g. subtle aspects of syntax and morphophonology (Ioup, 1995, p. 118). Even if later L2 learning *is* more effortful, this may bear absolutely no relation to the ending of a putative critical period for language. After all, the conscious, deliberate dimension of learning increases in *all* domains generally as cognitive development advances (cf. Feldman, 2009).

In relation to the idea that children and adults may have fundamentally different language-learning mechanisms at their disposal, some Chomskyans (e.g. Bley-Vroman, 1989; Schachter, 1988) have claimed that post-pubertal L2 language learning has no access to Universal Grammar (UG) (for discussion, see, e.g., Cook & Newson, 2007, pp. 237f.); the empirical basis for this perspective was always under question (cf., e.g., Flynn, 1987; Martohardjono & Flynn, 1995; see also Hawkins, 2001, pp. 353–359), and different schools of thought within the Chomskyan paradigm diverge on this issue (see, e.g., Mitchell & Myles, 2004, pp. 78f.). As Braidi (1999, p. 67) points out, "L2 learners do not seem to exhibit grammars that are not sanctioned by UG". Much research indicates that post-pubertal L2 learners deal in the same way as L1 acquirers with linguistic features purportedly having a UG basis (see, e.g., Birdsong, 2004, pp. 90ff.; Bruhn de Garavito, 1999; Dekydtspotter, Sprouse & Thyre, 1998).

Some non-UG-oriented research has also been interpreted as suggesting that different mechanisms subserve language learning in later years. Liu, Bates and Li's (1992) investigation of Chinese learners of English suggests that, whereas those whose exposure to English began after age 20 applied Chinese sentence-processing strategies to English, those whose learning of English began before age 13 deployed the same processing strategies as monolingual English speakers. In fact, this finding does not require a "different mechanisms" explanation, being explicable in terms of the increasing extent to which the L1 influences L2 processing as a function of years of experience of the L1 and the degree to which it is entrenched. Harley and Hart (1997) found that the early beginners' L2 outcomes "were much more likely to be associated with a memory measure than with a measure of language ability" (p. 395), whereas the reverse was true of the later beginners. DeKeyser's (2000) findings were not dissimilar: the adult beginners in his study who scored within the range of the child beginners manifested high levels of verbal analytical ability, an ability that seemed to play no role in the performance of the child beginners. The latter presented very little variation in their linguistic performance, however, and hence, as Ortega (2009, p. 158) notes, correlations were unlikely. DeKeyser interprets his results as signifying that maturational constraints apply only to implicit language learning mechanisms (cf. DeKeyser, 2003a, 2003b, 2006). Harley and Hart for their part point to the possible influence of primary- versus secondary-level instructional styles. A further possibility is that such findings reflect general cognitive changes affecting language learning but impacting on other areas of development also.

Turning to the question of the nature of the age-related decline in the language-acquiring capacity, the accumulated evidence from studies of "naturalistic" L2 acquisition has certainly favoured the notion that, while adolescent and adult subjects may have an initial advantage, eventually younger beginners are more likely to attain to native-like levels of proficiency (cf. Hyltenstam, 1992; Johnson & Newport, 1989; Krashen, Long & Scarcella, 1979; Oyama, 1976, 1978; Patkowski, 1980; Snow & Hoefnagel-Höhle, 1978). However, there is a question-mark over the notion that any such age-related decline is an abrupt one of the kind that a critical period, as classically understood, would entail—a so-called "elbow" or "7" shape (Bialystok & Hakuta, 1999; Birdsong, 2004, 2006; Flege, 1999). Bialystok and Hakuta's re-analysis of Johnson and Newport's data (Bialystok, 1997; Bialystok & Hakuta, 1994) suggests "that the tendency for proficiency to decline with age projects well into adulthood and does not mark some defined change in learning potential at around puberty" (Bialystok, 1997, p. 122); Bialystok and her colleagues (Bialystok & Hakuta, 1999; Hakuta, Bialystok, & Wiley, 2003; Wiley, Hakuta & Bialystok, 2005) also analysed census data on age of arrival in an English (L2) speaking environment and reported English proficiency; what emerges from this analysis is a steady linear decline of reported proficiency as age of arrival increases but no indication of a dramatically sharper rate of decline at any point between infancy and senescence; data on the relationship between L2 accent and age of arrival show a similarly continuous decline (cf. also Flege, 1999). Birdsong (2006) comments that "a recurrent finding is that a linear function captures the relationship between AoA [age of acquisition] and outcome over the span of AoA" (p. 12). His close analysis of the patterns of outcomes associated with different AoAs finds no evidence for the kind of shape of decline that would be indicative of a sharp maturational cut-off point—at least not at the end of maturation. In some of his own research (Birdsong & Molis, 2001) such a shape was identified, but at a much later chronological stage:

> [T]he best-fitting function placed the end of the ceiling period, and thus the beginning of the decline, at 27.5 years. In other words, the period of peak performance extends 10 or more years beyond the end of maturation. Thus, although the Birdsong and Molis results reveal a stretched "7" shape and its circumscribed period of full attainment, the temporal parameters do not mesh with a maturational-effects account of L2 ultimate attainment.
>
> (Birdsong, 2006, p. 18)

In any case: (1) the available evidence does not support the simplistic "younger = better in all circumstances over any timescale" optique that underlies some early treatments of this question (e.g., Lenneberg, 1967; Penfield & Roberts,1959; Stengel, 1939; Tomb, 1925); (2) even the "younger = better in the long run" position is sustainable only as a general tendency; an early start in an L2 is neither strictly necessary nor necessarily sufficient for the attainment of very high proficiency; age of first encounter is only one of the determinants of the ultimate level of proficiency attained. As mentioned earlier, even very young L2 beginners diverge at the level of fine linguistic detail from native speakers (see, e.g., Hyltenstam & Abrahamsson, 2000, p. 161; Flege, 1999).

Broadening Horizons

The CPH seeks to provide an explanation for age-related differences observed in L2 acquisition on the basis solely of neurobiological factors. In consonance with more general changes in the field of applied linguistics that recognize the systemic complexity of language learning, there has emerged a move towards explanations of age-related effects that involve the dynamic interaction of multiple variables. That is to say, long-term L2 attainment is increasingly seen as associated with social, environmental and affective variables, as well as with the AoA factor. For example, on this view a deeper understanding of L2 acquisition in the context of migration is sought by research that examines long-term L1 attainment (Jia, Aaronson & Wu, 2002; Jia & Aaronson, 2003) in relation to individual choices that are influenced by, among other factors, the modalities of the language environment and age-related opportunities and pressures.

In this section we present an overview of recent research that draws attention to the need to conduct more in-depth studies that integrate both quantitative and qualitative data and that question the traditional foci of age-related studies. This overview does not exhaust the multiple avenues along which age-related work is currently moving beyond the well-worn CPH pathways, but the research directions dealt with are representative of innovative developments: the role of input, the influence of learner orientations on ultimate attainment, the differences in age-effects in naturalistic and instructed L2 learning, and the influence of proficiency on L2 representation and processing, as gleaned from brain-based studies. To begin with, CPH research has typically examined L2 learners' mean performance across large-sized age groups, with the result that information about the participants' context of learning has been very broad and information about biographical variables has been scarce. Specifically, learners have not been matched in terms of experience with the L2, and so input across participants has not been comparable. Neither have their personal goals and expectations regarding long-term achievement in the L2 been explored, which may have led researchers to wrongly consider non-nativelikeness as failure on the learners' part. The current world-wide trend for an early start in foreign language acquisition has motivated a series of studies that have looked at the outcomes of early foreign language instruction against the background of expectations derived from L2 acquisition in a naturalistic learning environment. Finally, the advancement of brain-based studies has also allowed a more detailed exploration of the differences in brain location and timing derived from the interplay of learning age and language contact and L2 proficiency.

The Learning Environment: L2 Input

Maturational perspectives in L2 acquisition have tended to play down the role of the learning context, that is, the role that the nature of target language input and interaction with native/highly proficient target language-users play in L2 acquisition (Muñoz, 2009). In fact, it has often been noticed that adult learners (and also children) do not attain target levels in spite of prolonged access to input (Long, 1990), which constitutes a defining characteristic of the phenomenon labelled *fossilization* (Han & Odlin, 2006; Selinker, 1972). In accordance with CPH expectations, research has focused to an inordinate degree on the effects of age of onset (AoO) on L2 outcomes. Recent research has questioned the typical approach to the role of L2 exposure, however, both in its identification of what counts as age of onset or starting age and in the measurement of input.

AoO of L2 learning has traditionally been operationalized as age of arrival in the target language community, most often the age of immigration of L2 speakers. On the other hand, quantity of input received has been operationalized as length of residence (LoR), that is, the period of time learners have spent in the L2 community. A paradox has been observed when contrasting the effects of AoO and the effects of LoR: children learn L2s more slowly than adults; yet the earlier one starts to learn an L2 the better one will typically speak it in the long run. Snow (1983) observes that the paradox is methodological, since studies showing that older learners are better than younger ones have tested for L2 ability within the first years of learning, while studies showing child beginner superiority have tested after a longer period of exposure to the L2. In their review of age-related research, Krashen et al. (1979) concluded that LoR does not have a significant effect after an initial period of 5–10 years, while more recently DeKeyser (2000) extended this period to a minimum of 10 years. Along similar lines, Johnson and Newport (1989) found no LoR effect, and DeKeyser and Larson-Hall (2005) argue that input plays a very limited role once variation in age of arrival is controlled for statistically.

Recent evidence suggests that if the operationalization of AoO is the "age of onset of *significant* exposure" (full immersion in the L2 and interaction with native speakers) instead of simply the age of arrival, the number of later L2 learners who reach native-like levels of command of at least some aspects of the L2 may be higher. Hellman (2008) investigated ultimate attainment in the L2 lexical domain by looking at the size and depth of the lexicon of 33 Hungarian-L1 adult-onset learners who had had more than 20 years of significant exposure to English. AoO in this study was the time when significant daily interaction with native speakers of English began for each participant, and it did not always coincide with age at arrival. For example, although instruction in English as a foreign language in a classroom setting was not considered to give participants significant exposure, taking an English language MBA programme taught mainly by native speakers in the home country before arrival was. On the other hand, arrival in the US did not always mean the beginning of daily interaction with native speakers of English; sometimes it took participants many months to begin communicating regularly with native speakers of English, as in the case of a stay-at-home mother who did not begin to learn English until her children had started school. The results of the study showed that 76 per cent of the adult-onset L2 learner participants were native-like on all L2 vocabulary measures and that the accomplishments of five of them on those measures were above the comparably educated native-speaker mean.

Taking a similar tack, Flege and Liu (2001) found that years of residence in the target language country were predictive of success in L2 speech learning only when learners had received substantial amounts of native-speaker input, in contrast not only to L1 input provided by other immigrants from the same linguistic background but also to L2-accented input provided by non-native speakers. When Flege and Liu separated subjects by occupation, LoR was observed to have an effect on speech outcomes only in the case of students, who were likely to receive very substantial native-speaker input, in contrast to non-students, whose exposure to native-speaker input was less intense. Flege (2009) draws a similar conclusion from Winitz, Gillespie and Starcev's (1995) study of a Polish boy who arrived in the US at the age of seven and whose language development was followed over a seven-year period. This learner showed a strong LoR effect in contrast to other learners of similar age, and eventually became indistinguishable from native speakers. What was different in this case was that the young boy settled with his family in a small, rural town, attending a school that had very few non-English speaking children and did not offer English as a second language (ESL) classes. As a consequence, the boy received much more native-speaker input than most other children who immigrate in apparently similar circumstances but are enrolled in ESL classes in schools located in large cities and have much more contact with other immigrants. In a longitudinal study of 10 Chinese learners of English aged between 5 and 16, Jia and Aaronson (2003) observe how the same amount of LoR may involve L2 use in varying amounts and intensities. Specifically, these authors document how the children enjoyed more L2 contexts of use than the adolescents; for example, the former had a higher number of L2-speaking friends, while the latter chose more L1-speaking peers as their friends.

The new emphasis on input extends to its quantitative measurement. The main assumption in the proposal by Flege (2009, p. 184) is that the effects of input on ultimate attainment—generally around 10 per cent of the variance observed—may be stronger than so far perceived. Flege argues that age of arrival is a proxy for several variables including state of neurological development, state of cognitive development, state of L1 phonetic category development, levels of L1 proficiency, language dominance, frequency of L2/L1 use and kind of L2 input (native speaker versus foreign-accented). If age of arrival is seen as a "macrovariable" its effects cannot, says Flege, be compared to those of one "simple" variable such as percentage of L1 use. In a similar vein, Jia and Aaronson (2003) argue that arrival age is a confounded indicator of neurobiological maturation because it covaries with environmental factors.

Moyer (2004, p. 144) notes that the impact of AoO and LoR can be understood only in the context of specific information on quality of access to the L2, and that we can understand their contributions to attainment only through investigation of how they impact on the development of experience over time. Recent research in this area uses two more complex measures of input: language contact and language use (see Moyer, 2009). Language contact for naturalistic learners includes LoR, and also sometimes length of instruction (LoI) in the L2, as well as use of L2 relative to use of L1. Language contact for instructed learners in a foreign language setting includes number of hours, semesters or years of instruction—that is, LoI as well as numbers of hours spent using the L2 outside the classroom. In the case of foreign language learners who experience stays abroad, a measure of use of L2 relative to use of L1 is also relevant (eg. Freed, Dewey & Segalowitz, 2004). Moyer (2009, p. 168) notes that the measuring of language use is not just about time on task: beyond quantitative measurement, it is essential to find out "why learners use the target language as they do, that is, for what functions and to what social and psychological effects". In that respect, Moyer contends, there exists evidence that engagement in informal, personal domains—as opposed to the use of L2 in formal settings (e.g. school and work)—is clearly significant for long-term syntactic (Moyer, 2005), phonological (Flege, Munro & MacKay, 1995, Moyer, 2004, Purcell & Suter, 1980) and listening comprehension abilities (Moyer, 2006). A case in point is Marinova-Todd's (2003) finding that in her study of 30 post-pubertal learners of English the most proficient participants co-habited with native L2 speakers; the participants performed a series of tests focusing on several domains and the most successful participants attained native levels on all tasks, included accent in spontaneous speech. There exists evidence that where there is contact with the L2 in both formal and informal domains, this combination may lead to high attainment as well. In her study of late-beginning near-native L2 users, Kinsella (2009) found that her three participants who scored within native speaker ranges on all tasks had a number of factors in common: they were married to native speakers of the target language, they were immersed both at home and at work in the target language and they had the intention of residing permanently in the L2 country. Muñoz and Singleton (2007) also found that the most successful late L2 learner in their group of participants was married to a native speaker of English (L2), was immersed both at home and at work in the target language, and intended to stay permanently in the L2 country. Language use in meaningful interaction is also more conducive to higher long-term attainment than passive forms of language use. In her review, Moyer (2009) also underscores the combination of multiple contact domains (formal and informal, interactive and receptive) because this indicates that various communicative and social functions are being served.

Working in a different but related area of interest, that of the issue of incomplete acquisition in early bilingual acquisition and in post-pubertal L2 learning, Montrul (2006) also highlights the crucial importance of input. Specifically, Montrul suggests that amount and type of input as well as frequency of use may work together to promote incomplete grammatical states in bilinguals, when compared with L1-acquiring children, even when the language has been acquired before the posited end of the critical or sensitive period. To conclude, this section has discussed the need to measure

L2 input in relation to language contact and language use, which may be attainable only in research that pays more attention to the biographical and contextual circumstances of participants than has usually been the case in CPH research.

Learners' Orientations

As mentioned above, CPH research has tended to examine L2 learners' performance on average across age groups, disregarding the great variation existing among the older learners' achievements in the L2 (see Marinova-Todd, Marshall & Snow, 2000). Likewise, few studies so far have integrated both qualitative and quantitative perspectives. Recent research has thrown more light on some of the factors that together contribute to explaining the great variability observed in ultimate attainment. For example, in her study of 25 successful late L2 learners who were immigrants to Germany, Moyer (2004) concluded from her analysis of both quantitative and qualitative data that psychological factors such as satisfaction with attainment and personal motivation to acquire fluency in German accounted for 76 per cent of the variance in attainment. The extent to which an individual is actively engaged in seeking opportunities for interaction with native speakers, for instance, is closely connected with socio-psychological factors such as affiliation to the L2, both linguistically and culturally, and with identity issues. The significance of these issues has recently been researched mainly in relation to L2 phonology development (Major, 1993; Moyer, 2004; Piller, 2002). Also in this domain, an innovative proposal has included L2 acquisition motivation in the explanation of the link between ethnolinguistic affiliation (language identity) on the one hand and measures of L2 proficiency on the other (Segalowitz, Gatbonton & Trofimovich, 2009). This inclusion complements an explanation of the relationship between ethnolinguistic affiliation and the development of L2 proficiency that is seen as mediated by language contact. Specifically, on the basis of a series of recent studies (Gatbonton & Trofimovich, 2008; Trofimovich, Gatbonton & Segalowitz, 2007; Gatbonton, Trofimovich & Segalowitz, 2007) on the acquisition of the English voiced interdental fricative /ð/, often rendered as the voiced alveolar /d/ by French Canadian speakers of English, Segalowitz et al. (2009) suggest that aspects of ethnolinguistic affiliation are psychologically realized in terms of a multi-component, socially based L2 Motivation Self System (Dörnyei, 2005). These motivation system components are seen as affecting the amount of L2 use a person will engage in, and in turn some of these different uses of the L2 impact on the psycholinguistic processing mechanisms that ultimately affect the development of L2 proficiency and result in individual differences. Among these mechanisms, the authors highlight the fine-tuning of the speaker's perceptual and cognitive systems with respect to the processing of target language elements, reflecting, for example, awareness of the patterning that exists in the language. According to Segalowitz et al. (2009, p. 188):

> This patterning can be described as the frequency with which particular elements exist (e.g. how frequently a particular phonological target occurs), as regularities of co-occurrence of elements (e.g. the occurrence of particular targets in specific phonetic environments), and as the similarities and differences between L1 and L2 elements (e.g. aspects of phonetic similarity that will lead to perceptual assimilation).

Another important issue relates to the shift in language dominance towards the L2. Specifically, learners with very early AoO stand a very high chance of reaching near-nativelikeness while at the same time losing their mother tongue (Thompson, 1991). But then, as has also been observed, what is in question is no longer an L2 (Bialystok, 1997; Singleton, 2001). In this connection Moyer (2004, 2009) observes that once the transition in language affiliation is made, the relationship between accent and LoR becomes predictable. In a longitudinal study of a group of children and adolescents, Jia and Aaronson (2003) precisely tracked a language-dominance switch from L1 to L2 among the younger arrivals (9 years or younger) that did not occur among the older arrivals (older than 12) and related it to the superior gains in the morphosyntax domain shown by the former group. The study shows that language preference can be shaped by sociopsychological factors while at the same time it can also influence language use and proficiency. Specifically, Jia and Aaronson (2003, p. 153) suggest that the stronger willingness to use L2 and the subsequent greater L2 use by younger as compared with older L2 learners may partially explain the proficiency transition from the initial advantage of older learners (Snow & Hoefnagel-Höhle, 1978) to no age-related differences (Slavoff & Johnson, 1995) and then to the long-term advantage of younger arrivals (Flege, Yeni-Komshian & Liu, 1999). That is to say, over time, L1 and L2 environmental differences may accumulate and lead to language proficiency differences.

Learners' orientations can also impinge on their desire or willingness to become native-like speakers of the target language. Studies reporting on adults that have shown native-like performance in the L2 have highlighted their strong motivation to pass for native speakers (for a first-person account of identity phenomena in the appropriation of L2 accent see Marx, 2002; and also Kaplan, 1994). For instance, Bongaerts (1999) reported on Dutch learners with outstanding English pronunciation who were highly motivated to sound like native speakers for professional reasons. Similarly, the exceptional learner in Moyer's (1999) study was highly motivated to sound like a German native speaker. In both cases, learners had also received high-quality instruction on pronunciation. But not all learners have a desire to pass for a native speaker (and hence probably to take on an L2 identity). Birdsong and Paik (2008, p. 431) note that people vary in their experiences of society and culture and that "[w]hen the level of attainment and the way L2 knowledge is implemented in L2 use are determined by the learner, it would be pointless to speak of deficiencies in learning ability". In regard to accent in particular, not only must one be willing to sound like someone from the target culture, but one must also be willing to give up the protection that being foreign confers to non-native speakers, a risk not all L2 users are prepared to take (Obler 1989, p. 152; Schneiderman & Desmarais, 1988). Piller (2002) notes that many L2 users seem to weigh, consciously or not, the benefits and disadvantages of passing for a native speaker, and that this has consequences on their L2 speech, with resulting variations in perceived native-likeness. Relatedly, Pavlenko and Lantolf (2002) point out that more than anything else late or adult bilingualism requires agency and intentionality. Most frequently—these authors contend—people decide to learn their L2 "to a certain extent", which allows them to be proficient, even fluent, but without the consequences of losing the old and adopting the new ways of being in the world (2002, p. 162). Furthermore, the desire to pass for a native speaker may be temporary and lose its significance when speakers achieve what they consider to be a satisfactory level of fluency. The French-L2 speakers in Kinsella's study (2009) eventually learned to appreciate that their "foreignness" confered them an advantage they would not have otherwise had. It needs to be remarked, however, that in this study the social prestige of the learners' L1, English, may partly explain this finding. Learners with a less prestigious L1 or with a different position in society may not find their condition advantageous in the same way. Generally, it is reasonable to expect that learners will be satisfied with a level of L2 proficiency that allows them to use language effectively for their needs and purposes. In this vein, Marinova-Todd (2003, p. 68) suggests that from a practical point of view it may not be advantageous for many L2 learners to aim at higher levels of performance when resources can be applied towards alternative goals in their career. In sum, a qualitative examination of individuals' goals and actions, inasmuch as these have an impact on eventual attainment, together with a quantitative examination of their L2 attainment may allow us to better understand the variability found in late L2 learners.

The Case of Instructed Foreign Language Learning

Coming back to the importance of taking into account differences in amount and quality of input, the case of foreign language learning (see, e.g., Singleton, 1992; Singleton & Ryan, 2004, chapters 4 and 6; Stern, 1976; for a recent discussion see Nikolov, 2009), that is, where input and learning are mainly confined to the classroom, has warranted related attention. Until recently, differences in input between naturalistic learning settings and instructed foreign language settings have been considered influential principally in terms of the length of time needed for the younger starters to outperform older starters—an expectation derived from robust findings that, as seen above, point to an initial rate advantage on the part of older starters together with, as a general rule, an eventual long-term advantage on the part of younger starters in naturalistic settings (cf. Hyltenstam, 1992; Johnson & Newport, 1989; Krashen et al., 1979; Oyama, 1976, 1978; Patkowski, 1980; Snow & Hoefnagel-Höhle, 1978). For instance, on the basis of the study by Snow and Hoefnagel-Höhle (1978) that showed that younger starters were outperforming older starters after approximately one year in a naturalistic situation, estimations were made of the time needed for younger starters to outperform older starters in an instructed foreign language setting (e.g. Singleton, 1995).

Such estimations were essentially intended to point to the unlikelihood of younger instructed beginners ever manifesting an advantage within the span of normal formal education. More recently, Muñoz (2006a, 2008a, 2008c) has gone further, arguing that the generalization across learning contexts, namely, the expectation that younger starters—after an initial slower rate of learning—will in the long term outperform older starters after the same amount of hours or courses of instruction is not warranted in a typical limited-input instructed setting. Specifically, research in foreign language learning settings has confirmed the finding related to the faster rate of older starters (e.g. Álvarez, 2006; Cenoz, 2002, 2003; García Lecumberri & Gallardo, 2003; García Mayo, 2003; Kalberer, 2007; Lasagabaster & Doiz, 2003; Miralpeix, 2006; Mora, 2006; Muñoz, 2003, 2006a, 2006b; Navés, Torras & Celaya, 2003) but has not confirmed the long-term benefits of an early start when younger and older starters have had the same number of hours of instruction (Muñoz, 2006a; 2008b; Navés, 2009). On the basis of the findings from a large research project on the age factor (the BAF project), Muñoz (2006a) highlights the need to consider the influence of input on L2 outcomes. According to her explanation, young children may be superior to older learners at implicit learning but implicit learning requires massive amounts of input (DeKeyser & Larson-Hall, 2005) that a typical foreign language setting does not provide. In contrast, older learners are superior to young children at explicit learning owing to their superior cognitive development, and a typical foreign language setting, though deprived of rich and abundant input, provides many opportunities for explicit learning, which benefits older starters. In consequence, Muñoz (2006a) claims that in the long term older child starters will not outperform younger child starters any longer because the cognitive advantage of the former will have disappeared when the two groups reach late adolescence or adulthood. The absence of significant differences between early and late starters among learners in the same situation after a longer term (12 years) has recently been attested in research (see Navés, 2009).

The significance of the notion of "long term" in research in instructed L2 learning settings has also warranted a new focus of attention. As seen above, research in naturalistic settings has suggested that LoR has an effect in the first 10 years (Krashen et al., 1979; DeKeyser, 2000) or even 13 years (Moyer, 2009), which also constitutes the period of time during which the rate advantage of older learners may be manifest. After this initial period, LoR has failed to show a statistical significant effect (Long, 2005), which has been interpreted as signalling that learners have reached their ultimate attainment, and younger starters should then exhibit their long-term advantage. From a methodological point of view, research within a maturational approach should wait to compare learners' attainment until they have reached their ultimate uttainment, that is, when there is cessation of learning. Muñoz

(2008c) has argued that, logically, in order to evaluate long-term effects of starting age in a foreign language learning setting, learners' LoR or, more precisely, LoI should be equivalent to at least 10 years of immersion; this, however, is a period of time that extends beyond a lifetime. The obvious implication is that in the context of foreign language learning amount of exposure *never* ceases to be a determinant factor.

It was observed earlier that the age of significant exposure in naturalistic language acquisition does not always coincide with the age of arrival in the L2-speaking community. In this connection, it is to be noted that CPH-oriented researchers have often dismissed previous foreign instruction in the home country when they have identified AoO as the age of arrival in the target language community (e.g., Johnson & Newport, 1989), or as the age of actual significant exposure or immersion, socially or in an L2 educational programme (Hellman, 2008; White & Genesee, 1996). In other words, on this view, initial age of learning in a foreign language environment with limited input is not, by definition, the beginning of significant exposure and, in consequence, applying to instructed learning settings the same parameters as are used in naturalistic settings appears in principle to be misconceived.

Finally, the requisite that learners receive substantial amounts of native-speaker input, that is, an adequate provision of input for the attainment of native-likeness phonologically (Flege & Liu, 2001) or otherwise (Niżegorodcew, 2007), is not guaranteed in a foreign language setting either (see Muñoz, 2008a). In sum, in the light of Muñoz's arguments, there seems to be no reason to suppose that younger starters in a foreign language setting will *ever* outperform older starters in the long term, given that the necessary long term is not actually reachable, and given that the necessary quantity and quality of input is not guaranteed. Accordingly, any advantages of an early start in the instructional context need to be seen in terms of educational and attitudinal benefits that may accrue—benefits that do not automatically flow from early learners' biological circumstances but require, in addition to larger amounts of language input, high-quality teaching, including intensive high-grade input (see Muñoz, 2008a).

The Impact of Proficiency on L2 Representation and Processing

A further approach to the exploration of age constraints has been to claim that late language acquisition makes use of different areas of the brain as compared with early acquisition. For example, Weber-Fox and Neville (1996) collected data from measures of self-rated proficiency and from standardized tests of English grammar of L2 learners of different ages and conducted observations of the ERP (Event-Related Brain Potential) patterns in these learners. Their results indicated that learners who had been exposed to the L2 after the age of 11 showed a different pattern of responses to both detection of semantic anomalies and of grammatical anomalies. They concluded that their findings showed that different parts of the brain were specialized for processing different aspects of language and hence that the findings were consistent with the idea of sensitive periods for L2 acquisition. At around the same time, a study of the spatial representation of L1 and L2 in the cerebral cortex of early and late bilinguals during a sentence-generation task carried out by Kim, Relkin, Lee and Hirsch (1997) revealed little or no age-related separation of activity in Wernicke's area, but did reveal differences in respect of activity in Broca's area: among the late bilinguals two distinct but adjacent centres of activation showed up for L1 and L2, whereas in the early bilinguals there appeared to be a single area of activation for both languages. Marinova-Todd et al. (2000) point out that in Kim et al.'s study there was no control of the proficiency level of the later beginners and evoke the possibility "that the adult learners assessed … were poorly selected and do not represent highly proficient adult bilinguals" (Marinova-Todd et al., 2000, pp. 17–18). If this were the case, the neurological divergences observed might simply reflect differences in proficiency level, which some studies have found to be more important than AoO in determining brain organization in respect of additional languages (cf. Perani, Paulesu, Galles, Dupoux, Dehaene, Bettinardi, Cappa, Fazio & Mehler, 1998; Abutalebi, Cappa & Perani, 2001).

In general, recent findings point to a general congruence of brain areas activated in the L1 and the L2 by proficient later learners, although stronger activation tends to be found during L2 processing (Abutalebi et al., 2001, 2005; Stowe & Sabourin, 2005). Speaker characteristics that seem to play a role on the hemodynamic activation patterns observed during L1 and L2 processing are late L2 onset, low L2 proficiency and low L2 exposure. The relative influence of these three factors (onset, proficiency and exposure) appear to differ in accordance with the language processing components involved. For word-level production the three factors are reported to have a role, while for word-level semantic processing in comprehension only L2 proficiency seems to play a major role. By contrast, for activation differences related to syntactic processing in sentence comprehension, L2 onset seems to have the greatest influence, although stronger L2 syntactic processing activation seems to become visible only when subjects are required to make explicit metalinguistic judgments, even in late L2 learners (Indefrey, 2006, p. 299).

As regards the timing components of high-proficient L2 use, these are reported to be similar to those of L1 even if L2 learning began after age 12 (Hahne, 2001; Hahne & Friederici, 2001; Stowe & Sabourin, 2005, among others). These findings concur with Green's (2005) "convergence hypothesis", according to which, as L2 proficiency increases, the representation of L2 and its processing profile converge with those of native speakers of the language in question. This implies that any qualitative differences between native speakers of a language and L2 speakers of that language disappear as proficiency increases. However, as Green (2005, p. 520) notes, the convergence hypothesis is a claim about neural representation and processing profiles and not a claim about whether an L2 speaker of a language can simulate or pass for a native speaker of that language.

Conclusions

Postulating a critical period for language acquisition is fraught with problems, whether one is addressing the L1 or the L2 domain. As we have seen, there is no consensus regarding the duration and scope of such a critical period, and the evidence presented in support of the notion of a critical period is very far from conclusive. In the L1 area, findings regarding the language attainment of late-acquiring feral children and late signers can readily and plausibly be related to cognitive problems rather than being attributed (exclusively) to language acquisition issues. Concerning L2 acquisition, the propositions that have been put in respect of the absoluteness of late L2 learners' incapacity to attain native-like levels of proficiency, the absolute necessity of greater conscious effort on the part of late L2 learners and the absolute difference between mechanisms underlying early and late L2 learning have not been irrefutably demonstrated and have been beset by counter-evidence. This is not to deny the reality of maturational factors in language acquisition, but the critical period account of such factors is not the only possible one. The fact that children who start to play the violin early tend to reach higher levels of attainment that adult beginners does not lead us to conclude that there is a critical period for violin-playing. We simply recognize that the human learning capacity declines gradually over the lifespan in every sphere—from golf to higher mathematics. The operative word here is *gradually*. It is interesting to note in this connection that there has been no conclusive demonstration of an abrupt decline in language-acquiring capacity at a particular age—such as would be associated with the offset of a critical period. Instead, what seems to emerge is continuous linear decline of precisely the sort that we see in all other areas of learning.

L2 acquisition is clearly shaped by the dynamic interactions of multiple factors: cognitive, social and cultural variables interact with each other and shape the learners' language environments and in the end their language proficiency (Jia & Aaronson, 2003). As for the role of age, this in itself is no explanation of different attaiment levels if we cannot explain which precise aspects of maturation underlie the differences. In this chapter we have presented recent research that has emphasized the existence of a diversity of factors that mutually contribute to explaining the observed finding that younger starters achieve a higher level of L2 attainment than older starters in a naturalistic learning environment. In particular, the inclusion of a rigorous study of learners' input in research on the effects of age gives this line of research a new and richer angle. The consideration of the role of input in both naturalistic and instructed language learning settings reveals the need for including new perspectives, both quantitative, in the measurement of input, and qualitative, in the study of learn- ers' orientations. As regards the CPH proper, the implications are that this hypothesis may not be sufficient to explain L2 outcomes in a naturalistic setting and the enormous variability in attainment found by research, and that the hypothesis does not appear to have the explanatory power to deal with foreign language outcomes in an instructed setting.

References

Abutalebi, J., Cappa, S. F. & Perani, D. (2001). The bilingual brain as revealed by functional neuroimaging. *Bilingualism: Language and Cognition, 4*(2), 179–190.

Abutalebi, J., Cappa, S. F. & Perani, D. (2005). What can functional neuroimaging tell us about the bilingual brain? In J. F. Kroll and A. M. B. de Groot (Eds.), *Handbook of bilingualism: Psycholinguistic approaches* (pp. 497–515). New York: Oxford University Press.

Almli, C. R., & Finger S. (1987). Neural insult and critical period concepts. In M. H. Bornstein (Ed.), *Sensitive periods in devel- opment: Interdisciplinary perspectives* (pp. 123–143). Hillsdale, NJ: Lawrence Erlbaum.

Álvarez, E. (2006). Rate and route of acquisition in EFL narrative development at different ages. In C. Muñoz (Ed.), *Age and the rate of foreign language learning* (pp. 127–155). Clevedon: Multilingual Matters.

Aram, D., Bates, E., Eisele, J., Fenson, J., Nass, R., Thal, D. & Trauner, D. (1997). From first words to grammar in children with focal brain injury. *Developmental Neuropsychology, 13*(3), 275–343.

Bialystok, E. (1997). The structure of age: In search of barriers to second language acquisition. *Second Language Research, 13*(2), 116–137.

Bialystok, E., & Hakuta, K. (1994). *In other words: The science and psychology of second language acquisition.* New York: Basic Books.

Bialystok, E., & Hakuta, K. (1999). Confounded age: Linguistic and cognitive factors in age differences for second language acquisition. In D. Birdsong (Ed.), *Second language acquisition and the Critical Period Hypothesis* (pp. 161–181). Mahwah, NJ: Lawrence Erlbaum.

Birdsong, D. (1992). Ultimate attainment in second language acquisition. *Language, 68*(4), 706–755.

Birdsong, D. (2004). Second language acquisition and ultimate attainment. In A. Davies & C. Elder (Eds.), *The handbook of applied linguistics* (pp. 82–105). Oxford: Wiley-Blackwell.

Birdsong, D. (2006). Age and second language acquisition and processing: A selective overview. In M. Gullberg & P. Indefrey (Eds.), *The cognitive neuroscience of second language acquisition* (pp. 9–49). Malden, MA: Blackwell Publishing. Also published as *Language Learning, 56*, Supplement 1.

Birdsong, D., & Molis, M. (2001). On the evidence for maturational effects in second language acquisition. *Journal of Memory and Language, 44*(2), 235–249.

Birdsong, D., & Paik, J. (2008). Second language acquisition and ultimate attainment. In B. Spolsky & F. Hult, F. (Eds.), *Handbook of educational linguistics* (pp. 424–436). Oxford: Blackwell.

Bley-Vroman, R. (1989). What is the logical problem of foreign language learning? In S. M. Gass & J. Schachter (Eds.), *Linguistic perspectives on second language acquisition* (pp. 41–68). Cambridge: Cambridge University Press.

Bongaerts, T. (1999). Ultimate attainment in L2 pronunciation: The case of very advanced late L2 learners. In D. Birdsong (Ed.), *Second language acquisition and the Critical Period Hypothesis* (pp. 133–159). Mahwah, NJ: Lawrence Erlbaum,

Bongaerts, T. (2003). Effets de l'âge sur l'acquisition de la prononciation d'une seconde langue. *Acquisition et Interaction en Langue Étrangère, 18,* 79–98.

Bongaerts, T., Mennen, S. & Van der Slik, F. (2000). Authenticity of pronunciation in naturalistic second language acquisi- tion: The case of very advanced late learners of Dutch as a second language. *Studia Linguistica, 54*(2), 298–308.

Bongaerts, T., Planken, B. & Schils, E. (1995). Can late starters attain a native accent in a foreign language? A test of the criti- cal period hypothesis. In D. Singleton & Z. Lengyel (Eds.), *The age factor in second language acquisition* (pp. 30–50). Clevedon: Multilingual Matters Ltd.

Bongaerts, T., Van Summeren, C., Planken, B. & Schils, E. (1997). Age and ultimate attainment in the pronunciation of a foreign language. *Studies in Second Language Acquisition, 19*(4), 447–465.

Braidi, S. M. (1999). *The acquisition of second language syntax.* London: Edward Arnold.

Breathnach, C. (1993). Temporal determinants of language acquisition and bilingualism. *Irish Journal of Psychological Medicine, 10*(1), 41–47.

Bruhn de Garavito, J. L. S. (1999). Adult SLA of *se* constructions in Spanish: Evidence against pattern learning. *Proceedings of the Boston University Conference on Language Development, 23,* 112–119.

Cenoz, J. (2002). Age differences in foreign language learning. *I.T.L. Review of Applied Linguistics, 135–136,* 125–142.

Cenoz, J. (2003). The influence of age on the acquisition of English. In M. P. García Mayo & M. L.García Lecumberri (Eds.), *Age and the acquisition of English as a foreign language* (pp. 77–93). Clevedon: Multilingual Matters Ltd.

Chugani, H. T., Behen, M. E., Muzik, O., Juhasz, C., Nagy, F. & Chugani, D. C. (2001). Local brain functional activity following early deprivation: A study of post-institutionalized Romanian orphans. *NeuroImage, 14,* 1290–1301.

Clark, H. H., & Clark, E. V. (1977). *Psychology and language: An introduction to psycholinguistics.* New York: Harcourt Brace Jovanovich.

Cook, V. (1995). Multicompetence and effects of age. In D. Singleton & Z. Lengyel (Eds.), *The age factor in second language acquisition* (pp. 51–66). Clevedon: Multilingual Matters Ltd.,

Cook, V., & Newson, M. (2007). *Chomsky's Universal Grammar: An introduction* (3rd ed.). Oxford: Blackwell.

Curtiss, S. (1977). *Genie: A psycholinguistic study of a modern-day "wild child".* New York: Academic Press.

Curtiss, S. (1988). Abnormal language acquisition and the modularity of language. In F. J. Newmeyer (Ed.), *Linguistics: the Cambridge survey: Vol. 2. Linguistic theory: Extensions and implications* (pp. 96–116). Cambridge: Cambridge University Press.

DeKeyser, R. (2000). The robustness of critical period effects in second language acquisition. *Studies in Second Language Acquisition, 22*(4), 499–534.

DeKeyser, R. (2003a). Implicit and explicit learning. In C. Doughty & M. H. Long (Eds.), *The handbook of second language acquisition* (pp. 313–348). Malden, MA: Blackwell.

DeKeyser, R. (2003b). Confusion about confounding: The critical period and other age-related aspects of second language learning. Paper presented at ELIA VIII (Encuentros de Linguistica Inglesa Aplicada), "El factor edad en la adquisición y enseñanza de L2", Seville.

DeKeyser, R. (2006). A critique of recent arguments against the critical period hypothesis. In C. Abello-Contesse, R. Chacón-Beltrán, M. D. López-Jiménez & M. M. Torreblanca- López (Eds.), *Age in L2 acquisition and teaching* (pp. 49–58). Bern: Peter Lang.

DeKeyser, R., & Larson-Hall, J. (2005). What does the critical period really mean? In J. F. Kroll & A. M. D. De Groot (Eds.), *Handbook of bilingualism: Psycholinguistic approaches* (pp. 88–108). Oxford: Oxford University Press.

Dekydtspotter, L., Sprouse, R.A. & Thyre, R. (1998). Evidence of full UG access in L2 acquisition from the interpretive interface: quantification at a distance in English-French interlanguage. *Proceedings of the Boston University Conference on Language Development, 22,* 141–152.

De Villiers, J., & De Villiers. P. (1978). *Language acquisition.* Cambridge, MA: Harvard University Press.

Dörnyei, Z. (2005). *The psychology of the second language learner: Individual differences in second language acquisition.* Mahwah, NJ: Lawrence Erlbaum.

Emmorey, K. (2002). *Language, cognition, and the brain: Insights from sign language research.* Mahwah, NJ: Lawrence Erlbaum.

Feldman, R. S. (2009). *Development across the lifespan* (5th ed.). Upper Saddle River, NJ: Prentice Hall.

Flege, J. (1999). Age of learning and second language speech. In D. Birdsong (Ed.), *Second language acquisition and the Critical Period Hypothesis* (pp. 101–131). Mahwah, NJ: Lawrence Erlbaum.

Flege, J. (2009). Give input a chance! In T. Piske & M. Young Scholten (Eds.), *Input matters in SLA* (pp. 175–190). Clevedon: Multilingual Matters.

Flege, J., & Liu, S. (2001). The effect of experience on adults' acquisition of a second language. *Studies in Second Language Acquisition, 23*(4), 527–552.

Flege, J. E., Munro, M. & MacKay, I. (1995). Factors affecting strength of perceived foreign accent in a second language. *Journal of the Acoustical Society of America, 97*(5), 3125–3134.

Flege, J. E., Yeni-Komshian, G. H. & Liu, S. (1999). Age constraints on second-language acquisition. *Journal of Memory and Language, 41*(1), 78–104.

Flynn, S. (1987). *A parameter-setting model of L2 acquisition: Experimental studies in anaphora.* Dordrecht: Reidel.

Freed, B., Dewey, D. & Segalowitz, N. (2004). The language contact profile. *Studies in Second Language Acquisition, 26*(2), 349–356.

García Lecumberri, M. L., & Gallardo, F. (2003). English FL sounds in school learners of different ages. In M. P. García Mayo & M. L. García Lecumberri (Eds.), *Age and the acquisition of English as a foreign language* (pp. 115–135). Clevedon: Multilingual Matters Ltd.

García Mayo, M. P. (2003). Age, length of exposure and grammaticality judgements in the acquisition of English as a foreign language. In M. P. García Mayo & M. L. García Lecumberri (Eds.), *Age and the acquisition of English as a foreign language* (pp. 94–114). Clevedon: Multilingual Matters Ltd.

Gatbonton, E., & Trofimovich, P. (2008). The ethnic group affiliation and L2 proficiency link: Empirical evidence. *Language Awareness, 17*(13), 229–248.

Gatbonton, E., Trofimovich, P. & Segalowitz, N. (2007). Language and identity: Does ethnic group affiliation affect L2 performance? Paper presented at the International Symposium on Bilingualism (ISB6), June 2007. Hamburg, Germany.

Green, D. W. (2005). The neurocognition of recovery patterns in bilingual aphasics. In J. F. Kroll and A. M. B. de Groot (Eds.), *Handbook of bilingualism: Psycholinguistic approaches* (pp. 516–530). New York: Oxford University Press.

Grosjean, F. (1992). Another view of bilingualism. In R. Harris (Ed.), *Cognitive processing in bilinguals* (pp. 51–62). Amsterdam: North-Holland.

Hahne, A. (2001). What's different in second-language processing? Evidence from event-related brain potentials. *Journal of Psycholinguistic Research, 30*(3), 251–256.

Hahne, A., & Friederici, A. (2001). Processing a second language: Late learners' comprehension mechanisms as revealed by event-related brain potentials. *Bilingualism: Language and Cognition, 4*(2), 123–141.

Hakuta, K., Bialystok, E. & Wiley, E. (2003). Critical evidence: A test of the critical-period hypothesis for second-language acquisition. *Psychological Science, 14*(1), 31–38.

Han, Z.-H., & Odlin, T. (2006). Introduction. In Z.-H. Han & T. Odlin (Eds.), *Studies of fossilization in second language acquisition* (pp. 1–20). Clevedon: Multilingual Matters Ltd.

Harley, B., & Hart, D. (1997). Language aptitude and second language proficiency in classroom learners of different starting ages. *Studies in Second Language Acquisition, 19*(3), 379–400.

Harlow, H. F. (1958). The nature of love. *American Psychologist, 13*, 673–685.

Hawkins, R. (2001). *Second language syntax: A generative introduction.* Oxford: Blackwell.

Hellman, A. B. (2008). The limits of eventual attainment in adult-onset second language acquisition. Ed. D. dissertation, Boston University.

Hyltenstam, K. (1992). Non-native features of non-native speakers: On the ultimate attainment of childhood L2 learners. In R. Harris (Ed.), *Cognitive processing in bilinguals* (pp. 351–368). New York: Elsevier.

Hyltenstam, K., & Abrahamsson, N. (2000). Who can become native-like in a second language? All, some or none? On the maturational constraints controversy in second language acquisition. *Studia Lingüística, 54*(2), 150–166.

Hyltenstam, K., & Abrahamsson, N. (2003a). Maturational constraints in SLA. In C. Doughty & M. H. Long (Eds.), *The handbook of second language acquisition* (pp. 539–588). Malden, MA: Blackwell.

Hyltenstam, K., & Abrahamsson, N. (2003b). Âge de l'exposition initiale et niveau terminal chez les locuteurs du suédois L2. *Acquisition et Interaction en Langue Étrangère, 18*, 99–127.

Indefrey, P. (2006). A meta-analysis of hemodynamic studies on first and second language processing: Which suggested differences can we trust and what do they mean? In M. Gullberg & P. Indefrey (Eds.), *The cognitive neuroscience of second language acquisition* (pp. 279–304). Malden, MA: Blackwell Publishing. Also published as *Language Learning, 56*, Supplement 1.

Ioup, G. (1995). Evaluating the need for input enhancement in post-critical period language acquisition. In D. Singleton & Z. Lengyel (Eds.), *The age factor in second language acquisition* (pp. 95–123). Clevedon: Multilingual Matters Ltd.

Ioup, G. (2005). Age in second language development. In E. Hinkel (Ed.), *Handbook of research in second language teaching and learning* (pp. 419–435). London: Routledge.

Ioup, G., Boustagui E., Tigi, M. & Moselle, M. (1994). Reexamining the critical period hypothesis: A case study of successful adult SLA in a naturalistic environment. *Studies in Second Language Acquisition, 16*(1), 73–98.

Jia, G., & Aaronson, D. (2003). A longitudinal study of Chinese children and adolescents learning English in the United States. *Applied Psycholinguistics, 24*(1), 131–161.

Jia, G., Aaronson, D. & Wu, Y. (2002). Long-term language attainment of bilingual immigrants: Predictive variables and language group differences. *Applied Psycholinguistics, 23*(4), 599–621.

Johnson, J. S., & Newport, E. L. (1989). Critical period effects in second language learning: The influence of maturational state on the acquisition of ESL. *Cognitive Psychology, 21*(1), 60–99.

Jones, P. E. (1995). Contradictions and unanswered questions in the Genie case: A fresh look at the linguistic evidence. *Language and Communication, 15*(3), 261–280.

Kalberer, Urs. (2007). Rate of L2 acquisition and the influence of instruction time on achievement. Unpublished Master of Education dissertation, University of Manchester.

Kaplan, A. (1994). On language memoir. In A. Bammer (Ed.), *Displacements. Cultural identities in question* (pp. 59–70). Bloomington, IN: Indiana University Press.

Kim, K. H. S., Relkin, N. R., Lee, K.-M. & Hirsch, J. (1997). Distinct cortical areas associated with native and second languages. *Nature, 388*(6638), 171–174.

Kinsella, C. (2009). An investigation into the proficiency of successful late learners of French. Unpublished doctoral thesis, Trinity College Dublin.

Kinsella, C., & Singleton, D. (2008). Phonological attainment in late acquirers of French as an L2. Paper presented at the 20th International Conference on Foreign/Second Language Acquisition. Szczyrk, May.

Krashen, S. D., Long, M. H. & Scarcella, R. C. (1979). Age, rate, and eventual attainment in second language acquisition. *TESOL Quarterly, 13*(4), 573–582.

Lane, H. (1976). *The wild boy of Aveyron.* Cambridge, MA: Harvard University Press.

Lasagabaster, D., & Doiz, A. (2003). Maturational constraints on foreign-language written production. In M. P. García Mayo and M. L. García Lecumberri (Eds.), *Age and the acquisition of English as a foreign language* (pp. 136–160). Clevedon: Multilingual Matters Ltd.

Leather, J. (2002). Second language speech research: An introduction. *Language Learning, 49*(1), 1–56

Lebrun, Y. (1980). Victor of Aveyron: A reappraisal in light of more recent cases of feral speech. *Language Sciences, 2*(1), 32–43.

Lenneberg, E. H. (1967). *Biological foundations of language.* New York: Wiley.

Lenneberg, E. H., Nichols, I. A. & Rosenberger, E. F. (1964). Primitive stages of language development in mongolism. Research publication. *Association for Research in Nervous and Mental Disease, 42,* 119–137.

Liu, H., Bates, E. & Li, P. (1992). Grammaticality judgment in Chinese–English bilinguals: A gating experiment. In *Proceedings of the Fourteenth Annual Conference of the Cognitive Science Society* (pp. 95–99). Hillsdale, NJ: Lawrence Erlbaum.

Long, M. H. (1990). Maturational constraints on language development. *Studies in Second Language Acquisition, 12*(3), 251–285.

Long, M. H. (2005). Problems with supposed counter-evidence to the Critical Period Hypothesis. *International Review of Applied Linguistics, 43*(4), 287–317.

Long, M. H. (2007) *Problems in SLA.* Mahwah, NJ: Lawrence Erlbaum.

Lorenz, K. (1961). *King Solomon's ring.* Translated by Marjorie Kerr Wilson. London: Methuen.

Lundy, J. E. B. (1999). Theory of mind development in deaf children. *Perspectives in Education and* Deafness, *18*(1), 1–5.

Major, R. (1993). Sociolinguistic factors in loss and acquisition of phonology. In K. Hyltenstam & Å. Viberg (Eds.), *Progression and regression in language: Sociocultural, neuropsychological and linguistic perspectives* (pp. 463–478). Cambridge: Cambridge University Press.

Marinova-Todd, S. H. (2003). Know your grammar: What the knowledge of syntax and morphology in an L2 reveals about the critical period for second/foreign language acquisition. In M. P. Garcia-Mayo & M. L. Garcia-Lecumberri (Eds.), *Age and the acquisition of English as a foreign language: Theoretical issues and field work* (pp. 59–73). Clevedon: Multilingual Matters Ltd.

Marinova-Todd, S. H., Marshall, D. B. & Snow, C. E. (2000). Three misconceptions about age and L2 learning. *TESOL Quarterly, 34*(1), 9–34.

Martohardjono, G., & Flynn, S. (1995). Is there an age factor for Universal Grammar? In D. Singleton & Z. Lengyel (Eds.), *The age factor in second language acquisition* (pp. 135–153). Clevedon: Multilingual Matters Ltd.

Marx, N. (2002). Never quite a "native speaker": Accent and identity in the L2 and the L1. *The Canadian Modern Language Review/La Revue canadienne des langues vivantes, 59*(2), 264–281.

Mayberry R. I., & Fischer, S. D. (1989). Looking through phonological shape to lexical meaning: The bottleneck of non-native sign language processing. *Memory & Cognition, 17*(6), 740–754.

Mayberry, R. I., Fischer, S. D. & Hatfield, N. (1983). Sentence repetition in American Sign Language. In J. Kyle & B. Woll (Eds.), *Language in sign: International perspectives on sign language* (pp. 206–215). London: Croom Helm.

Miralpeix, I. (2006). Age and vocabulary acquisition in English as a foreign language. In C. Muñoz (Ed.), *Age and the rate of foreign language learning* (pp. 89–106). Clevedon: Multilingual Matters Ltd.

Mitchell, R., & Myles, F. (2004). *Second language learning theories* (2nd ed.). London: Arnold**.**

Montrul, S. (2006). Incomplete acquisition as a feature of bilingual and L2 grammars. In R. Slabakova, S. A. Montrul & P. Prevost (Eds.), *Inquiries in linguistic development. In honor of Lydia White* (pp. 335–359). Amsterdam and Philadelphia: John Benjamins.

Mora, J. C. (2006). Age effects on oral fluency development. In C. Muñoz (Ed.), *Age and the rate of foreign language learning* (pp. 65–88). Clevedon: Multilingual Matters Ltd.

Morford, J. P., & Mayberry, R. I. (2000). A reexamination of "early exposure" and its implications for language acquisition by eye. In C. Chamberlain, J. Morford & R. Mayberry (Eds.), *Language acquisition by eye* (pp. 111–128). Mahwah, NJ: Lawrence Erlbaum.

Moyer, A. (1999). Ultimate attainment in L2 phonology. The critical factors of age, motivation, and instruction. *Studies in Second Language Acquisition, 21,* 81–108.

Moyer, A. (2004). *Age, accent and experience in second language acquisition. An integrated approach to critical period inquiry.* Clevedon: Multilingual Matters Ltd.

Moyer, A. (2005). Formal and informal experiential realms in German as a foreign language: A preliminary investigation. *Foreign Language Annals, 38*(3), 377–387.

Moyer, A. (2006). Language contact and confidence in L2 listening comprehension: A pilot study of advanced learners of German. *Foreign Language Annals, 39*(2), 255–275.

Moyer, A. (2009). Input as a critical means to an end: Quantity and quality of experience in L2 phonological attainment. In T. Piske & M. Young-Scholten (Eds.), *Input matters in SLA* (pp. 159–174). Clevedon: Multilingual Matters Ltd.

Muñoz, C. (2003). Variation in oral skills development and age of onset. In M. P. García Mayo & M. L.García Lecumberri (Eds.), *Age and the acquisition of English as a foreign language* (pp. 161–181). Clevedon: Multilingual Matters Ltd.

Muñoz, C. (2006a). The effects of age on foreign language learning. In C. Muñoz (Ed.), *Age and the rate of foreign language learning* (pp. 1–40). Clevedon: Multilingual Matters Ltd.

Muñoz, C. (2006b). The BAF Project: Research on the effects of age on foreign language acquisition. In C. Abelló, R. Chacón, M.D. López & M. Torreblanca (Eds.), *Age in second language acquisition and teaching* (pp. 81–92). Bern: Peter Lang.

Muñoz, C. (2008a). Symmetries and Asymmetries of age effects in naturalistic and instructed L2 learning. *Applied Linguistics, 24*(4), 578–596.

Muñoz, C. (2008b). Age-related differences in foreign language learning. Revisiting the empirical evidence. *International Review of Applied Linguistics in Language Teaching, 46*(3), 197–220.

Muñoz, C. (2008c). When context matters: Age effects on FL learning. Plenary talk at the Second Language Research Forum, University of Hawai'i at Honolulu, October.

Muñoz, C. (2009). Input and long-term effects of early learning in a formal setting. In M. Nikolov (Ed.), *Contextualizing the age factor: Issues in early foreign language learning* (pp. 141–160). Berlin: Mouton de Gruyter.

Muñoz, C., & Singleton, D. (2007). Foreign accent in advanced learners: Two successful profiles. *The EUROSLA Yearbook, 7,* 171–190.

Navés, T. (2009). The "long-long" term effects of an early start on the learning of English as a Foreign Language. Paper presented at AAAL 2009, Denver, Colorado.

Navés, T., Torras, M. R. & Celaya, M. L. (2003). Long-term effects of an earlier start. An analysis of EFL written production. *The EUROSLA Yearbook, 3,* 103–130.

Newport, E. L. (1988). Constraints on learning and their role in language acquisition: Studies of the acquisition of American Sign Language. *Language Sciences, 10*(1), 147–172.

Newton, M. (2002). *Savage girls and wild boys: A history of feral children.* London: Faber & Faber.

Nikolov, M. (Ed.) (2009). *Early learning of modern foreign languages.* Bristol: Multilingual Matters Ltd.

Nippold, M. A. (1998). *Later language development: The school-age and adolescent years* (2nd ed.). Austin, TX: Pro-Ed.

Niżegorodcew, A. (2007). *Input for instructed L2 learners. The relevance of relevance.* Clevedon: Multilingual Matters Ltd.

Obler, L. (1989). Exceptional second language learners. In S. Gass, C. Madden, D. Preston & L. Selinker (Eds.), *Variation in second language acquisition: Psycholinguistic issues* (pp. 141–159). Clevedon: Multilingual Matters.

Ortega, L. (2009). *Understanding second language acquisition.* London: Hodder Education.

Oyama, S. (1976). A sensitive period for the acquisition of a nonnative phonological system. *Journal of Psycholinguistic Research, 5*(3), 261–285.

Oyama, S. (1978). The sensitive period and comprehension of speech. *Working Papers on Bilingualism, 16,* 1–17.

Palmen, M.-J., Bongaerts, T. & Schils, E. (1997). L'authenticité de la prononciation dans l'acquisition d'une langue étrangère au-delà de la période critique: Des apprenants parvenus à un niveau très avancé en français. *Acquisition et Interaction en Langue Etrangère, 9,* 173–191.

Patkowski, M. S. (1980). The sensitive period for the acquisition of syntax in a second language. *Language Learning, 30*(2), 449–472.

Pavlenko, A., & Lantolf, J. P. (2000). Second language learning as participation and the (re)construcion of selves. In J. P. Lantolf (Ed.), *Sociocultural theory and second language learning* (pp. 155–178). Oxford: Oxford University Press.

Penfield, W., & Roberts. L. (1959). *Speech and brain mechanisms.* Princeton, NJ: Princeton University Press.

Perani, D., Paulesu, E., Galles, N. S., Dupoux, E., Dehaene, S., Bettinardi, V., Cappa, S. F., Fazio, F. & Mehler, J. (1998). The bilingual brain: Proficiency and age of acquisition of the second language. *Brain, 121*(10), 1841–1852.

Peterson, C. C., & Siegal, M. (1995). Deafness, conversation, and theory of mind. *Journal of Child Psychology and Psychiatry, 36*(3), 459–474.

Piller, I. (2002). Passing for a native speaker: Identity and success in second language learning. *Journal of Sociolinguistics, 6*(2), 179–206.

Purcell, E., & Suter, R. (1980). Predictors of pronunciation accuracy: A re-examination. *Language* Learning, 30(2), 271–287.

Rymer, R. (1993). *Genie: An abused child's flight from silence.* New York: HarperCollins.

Schachter, J. (1988). Second language acquisition and its relationship to Universal Grammar. *Applied Linguistics, 9*(3), 219–235.

Schick, B., & Gale, E. (1995). Preschool deaf students interactions during ASL and English storytelling. *American Annals of the Deaf, 140*(4), 363–370.

Schneiderman, E. I., & Desmarais, C. (1988). A neuropsychological substrate for talent in second-language acquisition. In L. K. Obler & D. Fein (Eds.), *The exceptional brain. neuropsychology of talent and special abilities* (pp. 103–126). New York: The Guilford Press.

Scovel, T. (1988). *A time to speak: A psycholinguistic inquiry into the critical period for human language.* Rowley, MA: Newbury House.

Scovel, T. (2000). A critical review of the Critical Period Hypothesis. *Annual Review of Applied Linguistics, 20,* 213–223.

Scovel, T. (2006). Age, acquisition, and accent. In C. Abello-Contesse, R. Chacón-Beltrán, M. D. López-Jiménez & M. M. Torreblanca- López (Eds.), *Age in L2 acquisition and teaching* (pp. 31–48). Bern: Peter Lang.

Segalowitz, N., Gatbonton, E. & Trofimovich, P. (2009). Links between ethnolinguistic affiliation, self-related motivation and second language fluency: Are they mediated by psycholinguistic variables? In Z. Dörnyei & E. Ushioda (Eds.), *Motivation, language identity and the L2 self* (pp. 172–192). Bristol: Multilingual Matters.

Selinker, L. (1972). Interlanguage. *International Review of Applied Linguistics, 10*(2), 209–231.

Singleton, D. (1992). Second language instruction: The when and the how. *AILA Review, 9,* 46–54.

Singleton, D. (1995). Second languages in the primary school: The age factor dimension, *Teanga: The Irish Yearbook of Applied Linguistics, 15,* 155–166

Singleton, D. (2001). Age and second language acquisition. *Annual Review of Applied Linguistics, 21,* 77–89.

Singleton, D. (2005). The Critical Period Hypothesis: A coat of many colours. *International Review of Applied Linguistics in Language Teaching, 43*(4), 269–285.

Singleton, D., & Leśniewska, J. (2009). Age and SLA: Research highways and byeways. In M. Pawlak (Ed.), *New Perspectives on Individual Differences in Language Learning and Teaching* (pp. 109–124). Poznań-Kalisz: Adam Mickiewicz University Press.

Singleton, D., & Ryan, L. (2004). *Language acquisition: The age factor* (2nd ed.). Clevedon: Multilingual Matters Ltd.

Singleton, J. L., & Newport, E. L. (2004). When learners surpass their models: The acquisition of American Sign Language from inconsistent input. *Cognitive Psychology, 49*(4), 370–407.

Slavoff, G. R., & Johnson, J. S. (1995). The effects of age on the rate of learning a second language. *Studies in Second Language Acquisition, 17*(1), 1–16.

Snow, C. (1983). Age differences in second language acquisition: Research findings and folk psychology. In K. Bailey, M. Long & S. Peck (Eds.), *Second language acquisition studies.* (pp. 141–150) Rowley, MA: Newbury House Publishers.

Snow, C., & Hoefnagel-Höhle, M. (1978). The critical period for language acquisition: Evidence from second language learning. *Child Development, 49*(4), 1114–1128.

Spitz, R. A. (1946). Hospitalism: A follow-up report on investigation described in volume 1, 1945. *Psychoanalytical Study of Children, 2,* 113–117.

Stengel, E. (1939). On learning a new language. *International Journal of Psychoanalysis, 20,* 471–479.

Stern, H. H. (1976). Optimal age: Myth or reality? *Canadian Modern Language Review, 32*(3), 283–294.

Stowe, L. A., & Sabourin, L. (2005). Imaging the processing of a second language: Effects of maturation and proficiency on the neural processes involved. *International Review of Applied Linguistics in Language Teaching, 43*(4), 329–353.

Thompson, I. (1991). Foreign accents revisited: The English pronunciation of Russian immigrants. *Language Learning, 41*(2), 177–204.

Thorpe, W. H. (1954). The process of song-learning in the chaffinch as studied by means of the sound spectrograph. *Nature, 173,* 465–469.

Tomb, J. (1925). On the intuitive capacity of children to understand spoken languages. *British Journal of Psychology, 16*(1), 53–54.

Trofimovich, P., Gatbonton, E. & Segalowitz, N. (2007). A dynamic look at L2 phonological learning: Investigating effects of cross-language similarity and input frequency. *Studies in Second Language Acquisition, 29*(3), 407–448.

Uylings, H. B. M. (2006). Development of the human cortex and the concept of "critical" or "sensitive" periods. In M. Gullberg & P. Indefrey (Eds.), *The cognitive neuroscience of second language acquisition* (pp. 59–90). Malden, MA: Blackwell Publishing. Also published as *Language Learning, 56,* Supplement 1.

Weber-Fox, C. M., & Neville, H. J. (1996). Maturational constraints on functional specializations for language processing: ERP and behavioural evidence in bilingual speakers. *Journal of Cognitive Neuroscience, 8*(3), 231–256.

White, L., & Genesee, F. (1996). How native is near-native? The issue of ultimate attainment in adult second language acquisition. *Second Language Research, 12*(3), 233–265.

Wiley, E., Hakuta, K. & Bialystok, E. (2005). New approaches to using census data to test the critical period hypothesis for second language acquisition. *Psychological Science, 16*(4), 341–343.

Winitz, H., Gillespie, B. & Starcev, J. (1995). The development of English speech patterns of a 7-year-old Polish-speaking child. *Journal of Psycholinguistic Research, 24*(2), 117–143.

Woodward, J. C. (1973). Some characteristics of pidgin sign English. *Sign Language Studies, 2*(3), 39–46.

Woolfe T., Want, S. C. & Siegal, M. (2002). Signposts to development: Theory of mind in deaf children. *Child development, 73*(3), 768–778.

26

Interactional Competence in Language Learning, Teaching, and Testing

Richard F. Young

What is interactional competence? The term has been used by different scholars with different shades of meaning in several different areas of second language learning, teaching, and testing. In the pages that follow, I review some uses of the terms, but let's begin with an example of cross-cultural communication that brings into relief the fact that command of language forms is not enough to ensure successful communication. In her book on the ethnography of communication, Saville-Troike (1989, pp. 131–132) reported the following exchange in a kindergarten classroom on the Navajo Reservation:

> A Navajo man opened the door to the classroom and stood silently, looking at the floor. The Anglo-American teacher said "Good morning" and waited expectantly, but the man did not respond. The teacher then said "My name is Mrs. Jones," and again waited for a response. There was none.
>
> In the meantime, a child in the room put away his crayons and got his coat from the rack. The teacher, noting this, said to the man, "Oh, are you taking Billy now?" He said, "Yes."
>
> The teacher continued to talk to the man while Billy got ready to leave, saying "Billy is such a good boy," "I'm so happy to have him in class," etc.
>
> Billy walked towards the man (his father), stopping to turn around and wave at the teacher on his way out and saying, "Bye-bye." The teacher responded, "Bye-bye." The man remained silent as he left.

Saville-Troike explained the interaction as one in which two of the three parties were interpreting the conversational exchange in different ways. From a Navajo perspective, the Navajo man's silence is appropriate and respectful; his silence after the Anglo-American teacher's greeting is also a polite response to her greeting and, if he had identified himself by name, the man would have broken a traditional taboo that prohibits Navajos from saying their own name. The Anglo-American teacher follows her own expectations that her greeting would be returned and that the unknown man would identify himself. Billy, who is more used to Anglo ways than his father, displayed interactional competence by taking his leave of the teacher in the way she expected while his father remained silent.

What, then, is interactional competence (henceforth IC)? An examination of what these individuals did in this interaction reveals at least four aspects. The first is the fact that IC may be observed (or its absence noted) in spoken interaction. Almost all of the research on IC has focused exclusively on spoken interaction; if written language has been considered at all, it has played a very minor role in multimodal interaction. Although writing has not been considered as contributing substantially to IC, nonverbal semiotic resources such as gesture, gaze, posture, kinesics, and proxemics are frequently considered, as indeed are verbal prosody, rhythm, and intonation.

IC can be observed (or its absence noted) in a discursive practice. Discursive practices are recurring episodes of social interaction in context, episodes that are of social and cultural significance to a community of speakers. Such episodes have been called interactive practices (Hall, 1995), communicative practices (Hanks, 1996), while Tracy (2002) and Young (2007, 2008, 2009) use the term *discursive practice*. In Saville-Troike's example, greeting, leave-taking, and picking up a child from school are all discursive practices because they are episodes of spoken interaction that occur regularly and have significance in a community of speakers. Because discursive practices recur, participants have expectations about what happens in a practice and what linguistic and nonverbal resources people employ in constructing the practice. Thus, a second aspect of IC involves participants recognizing and responding to expectations of what to say and how to say it. These expectations lead participants to interpret forms of talk in a given practice with conventional meanings and may lead to misinterpretations when forms of talk do not meet their expectations. Such cross-cultural difficulties were described by Saville-Troike in her comments on the encounter between the Navajo man and the Anglo teacher. She wrote that, "[t]he encounter undoubtedly reinforced the teacher's stereotype that Navajo's are 'impolite' and 'unresponsive,' and the man's stereotype that Anglo-Americans are 'impolite' and 'talk too much'" (p. 132).

Viewing IC as simply a pragmatic match between cultural expectations and observed forms of talk in a discursive practice may lead us to believe that IC is simply a question of pragmatics, but this would be a mistake. Pragmatic meaning, as defined by Kasper and Rose (2002), arises "from choices between linguistic forms." Such choices are, however, "not unconstrained but are governed by social conventions, which can be flexed to different, contextually varying degrees but only entirely set aside at the peril of losing claims to face, insider status, or sanity" (pp. 2–3). The view of IC as essentially pragmatic competence is one underlying Hall's (1999, p. 137) oft-cited definition of the term as knowledge of:

(1) the goals of the interactive practice, the roles of the participants, and the topics and themes considered pertinent; (2) the optional linguistic action patterns along which the practice may unfold, their conventional meanings, and the expected participation structures; (3) the amount of flexibility one has in rearranging or changing the expected uses of the practice's linguistic resources when exercising these options and the likely consequences engendered by the various uses; and (4) the skill to mindfully and efficiently recognize situations where the patterns apply and to use them when participating in new experiences to make sense of the unknown.

However, pragmatic meaning in a discursive practice takes us only part of the way to understanding IC for, as Mehan (1982) wrote, "'Competence' becomes interactional in two senses of the term. One, it is the competence necessary for effective interaction. Two, it is the competence that is available in the interaction between people" (p. 65). Mehan's stress on interaction in IC was taken up later by Kramsch (1986, p. 367), who wrote:

Whether it is a face-to-face interaction between two or several speakers, or the interaction between a reader and a written text, successful interaction presupposes not only a shared knowledge of the world, the reference to a common external context of communication, but also the construction of a shared internal context or "sphere of inter-subjectivity" that is built through the collaborative efforts of the interactional partners.

Kramsch called the basis of successful interaction *interactional competence*, and it is Kramsch's view that forms the basis for contemporary understandings of the competence that is created by all participants in social interaction. The definition of IC that I will use here includes the pragmatic relationship between participants' employment of linguistic and interactional resources and the contexts in which they are employed. However, the third aspect of IC is not the ability of a single individual to employ those resources in any and every social interaction; rather, IC is how those resources are employed mutually and reciprocally by all participants in a particular discursive practice. This means that IC is not the knowledge or the possession of an individual person, but is co-constructed by all participants in a discursive practice, and IC varies with the practice and with the participants.

A fourth and final aspect of IC is the realization that discursive practices are not circumscribed by the time and place of occurrence, but must be viewed in a wider social and historical context. In research in anthropology by Bourdieu (1977, 1990), Ortner (1984), and Sahlins (1981, 1985) that led to the development of Practice Theory, of which discursive practice is an outcome, context is an essential part of practice. Context is larger than the place and time of interaction, and includes the network of physical, spatial, temporal, social, interactional, institutional, political, and historical circumstances in which participants do a practice. The relationship between context and practice is a complex one but it is not arbitrary. In the interaction described by Saville-Troike, for example, IC can be seen in the identities that Billy, his father, and the teacher attempt to establish through their interaction. For instance, in describing the Navajo man's reluctance to state his name, it is not enough to say that this is simply a Navajo custom, but we must understand the wider context of the role of personal names in Navajo life, the contexts in which personal names are spoken, and the occasions on which practices of naming are transgressed. The same goes for understanding the Anglo-American teacher's naming action: "My name is Mrs. Jones." How does the teacher's naming herself in this way construct her identity? What are the values associated with overtly naming oneself in Anglo-American culture? What are the meanings that the teacher creates by naming herself as "Mrs. Jones" rather than "Ms. Jones", or "Sally Jones", or simply "Sally"? And is naming oneself what Agar (1980) called a "rich point"—a departure from our expectations that signals a difference between Anglo-American and Navajo culture and gives direction to subsequent learning?

To summarize, then, the notion of IC has been used by different scholars in different ways, of which four aspects are foundational. First, discussions of IC have focused largely on spoken interaction, although nonverbal aspects of spoken interaction have often been seen as important. Second, in many discussions, the pragmatics of interaction—the relationships between the forms of talk chosen by participants and the social contexts in which they are used—has been considered as fundamental to IC. Third, IC is not to be described in the knowledge and actions of an individual participant in an interaction; instead, IC is the construction of a shared mental context through the collaboration of all interactional partners. Finally, the context of an interaction is not limited to the sequence of talk that occurs at a specific time and place; understanding IC thus requires an investigation of social, institutional, political, and historical circumstances that extend beyond the horizon of a single interaction.

Applied linguists' interest in IC has emerged in (applied) linguistic theory and in language assessment. In theoretical developments in linguistics and applied linguistics, changing views of the concept of competence have had significant effects on the aims and practice of second language teaching and testing. These theoretical developments are discussed in the following section.

Explaining Competence

Competence and Performance

In linguistic theory, the term *competence* has been taken to mean an individual's knowledge underlying the production and interpretation of well-formed sentences in a language. The term was first used in this sense by Chomsky (1965), who used it to distinguish between a speaker's knowledge of language in the abstract (competence) and the way in which that knowledge is realized in the production and interpretation of actual utterances (performance). Chomsky's idea of competence as knowledge of language apart from its use was criticized by Hymes (1972), who countered that not only does competence refer to the individual's knowledge of the forms and structures of language, but competence also extends to how the individual uses language in actual social situations. In effect, Hymes rejected Chomsky's dichotomy between competence and performance and argued that using language in social situations required as much knowledge and skill as knowledge of language as an idealized system—in Hymes's words, "[t]here are rules of use without which the rules of grammar are useless" (p. 278). Hymes then went on to specify the knowledge that speakers must have of at least four ways in which language is used in social situations: what is possible to do with language, what is feasible, what is appropriate, and what is actually done. This combination of ability and knowledge Hymes called *communicative competence*, which many people contrasted with Chomsky's theory, and the latter came to be known as *linguistic competence*.

Hymes's ideas were the basis for an applied linguistic theory of communicative competence put forward by Canale and Swain (1980) and for tests of *communicative language ability* theorized by Bachman (1990). These scholars tried to relate linguistic acts in social situations to an individual's underlying knowledge, and their views became very influential in second language teaching and testing. In both applied linguistic theory and language assessment, competence was recognized as a characteristic of a single individual. An individual's communicative competence was a complex construct composed of several component parts and it was something that differentiated one individual from others.

IC builds on the theories of competence that preceded it, but it is a very different notion from communicative competence and communicative language ability. He and Young (1998) wrote of two differences between IC and communicative competence. In one sense, IC simply adds further components to the four components of communicative competence. These were sketched by He and Young as linguistic and pragmatic resources that include, among others,

a knowledge of rhetorical scripts, a knowledge of certain lexis and syntactic patterns specific to the practice, a knowledge of how turns are managed, a knowledge of topical organization, and a knowledge of the means for signaling boundaries between practices and transitions within the practice itself.

(He & Young, 1998, p. 6)

Young (2008, p. 71) extended the list and wrote that IC includes the following seven resources that participants bring to interaction:

- Identity resources

  - *Participation framework*: the identities of all participants in an interaction, present or not, official or unofficial, ratified or unratified, and their footing or identities in the interaction

- Linguistic resources

  - *Register*: the features of pronunciation, vocabulary, and grammar that typify a practice
  - *Modes of meaning*: the ways in which participants construct interpersonal, experiential, and textual meanings in a practice

- Interactional resources

  - *Speech acts*: the selection of acts in a practice and their sequential organization
  - *Turn-taking*: how participants select the next speaker and how participants know when to end one turn and when to begin the next

- ◦ *Repair*: the ways in which participants respond to interactional trouble in a given practice
- ◦ *Boundaries*: the opening and closing acts of a practice that serve to distinguish a given practice from adjacent talk

IC involves knowledge and employment of these resources in social contexts. However, the fundamental difference between communicative competence and IC is that an individual's knowledge and employment of these resources is contingent on what other participants do; that is, IC is distributed across participants and varies in different interactional practices. And the most fundamental difference between interactional and communicative competence is that IC is not what a person *knows*, it is what a person *does* together with others.

Intersubjectivity

As mentioned earlier, Kramsch (1986) recognized that IC presupposes "a shared internal context or 'sphere of inter-subjectivity'" and this view is what most clearly distinguishes IC from previous theories of competence. What, then, is intersubjectivity? Developed originally as a philosophical theory in the phenomenology of Husserl (Beyer, 2007), intersubjectivity is the conscious attribution of intentional acts to others and involves putting oneself in the shoes of an interlocutor. Intersubjectivity was first inferred empirically from studies of infant development by Trevarthen (1977, 1979). In studies of interaction between preverbal infants and their mothers, Trevarthen noticed that at around two months of age, infants produced actions of body, hands, and face that were associated with the vocalizations of the mother. It seemed that, although each mother–infant pair was developing a different style of mutual activity, a general pattern of development in social behavior was common to all. Trevarthen (1977, p. 241) concluded:

I believe a correct description of this behaviour, to capture its full complexity, must be in terms of mutual intentionality and sharing of mental state. Either partner may initiate a "display" or "act of expression" and both act to sustain a sharing and exchange of initiatives. Both partners express complex purposive impulses in a form that is infectious for the other.

One example of the coordination of actions that led Trevarthen to infer intersubjectivity is when the child's eyes follow the direction of the mother's gaze or her act of pointing. Another example is when, in ritualized games of routine, the mother pauses before an expected action and the infant performs that action, a projection of the mother's action that underlies the development of turn-taking in conversation.

Trevarthen's research on intersubjectivity formed the basis for Wells's (1979, 1981) studies of children's language development through interaction. Wells's central argument was that collaborative activity provides the natural context for first language development and that children learn through exploring their surroundings with others. Intersubjectivity is explained by Wells (1981) as follows:

Linguistic interaction is a collaborative activity, and this applies just as much to the production and interpretation of individual utterances as it does to longer stretches of discourse. Any act of linguistic communication involves the establishment of a triangular relationship between the sender, the receiver, and the context of situation. The sender intends that, as a result of his communication, the receiver should come to attend to the same situation as himself and construe it in the same way. For the communication to be successful, therefore, it is necessary (a) that the receiver should come to attend to the situation as intended by the sender; (b) that the sender should know that the receiver is so doing; and (c) that the receiver should know that the sender knows that this is the case. That is to say they need to establish *intersubjectivity* about the situation to which the communication refers.

(Wells, 1981, pp. 46–47, emphasis in the original)

Wells's theory has inspired much work on the development of IC, and he has argued forcefully that teacher–student conversation in classrooms should be a genuine dialogic co-construction of meaning. Some studies of how learners develop IC have taken intersubjectivity as evidence of IC. Other studies have focused, instead, on the learners' developing employment of identity, linguistic, and interactional resources. These studies are reviewed in the following section.

The Development of Interactional Competence

In 1999, as notions of IC were still being developed, Young (1999, pp. 119–120) wrote:

At this point … no empirical studies have been carried out to test the claims [of IC]. We have, as yet, very few detailed descriptions of the configuration of interactional resources that constitute the interactional architecture of a given practice. […] And we await descriptive and pedagogical studies of how novices become expert participants and the degree to which interactional competence in a given practice can be generalized to other practices.

A decade later the situation has improved, with a number of published studies describing the development of IC in instructional, study-abroad, and professional contexts. In all these studies, IC has been described in spoken interaction and their longitudinal focus has been on the developing pragmatic relationship between learners' employment of interactional and linguistic resources and social context. Several studies have focused on the way that IC is co-constructed by all participants in dyadic or multi-party interaction, but only one researcher has investigated the social, institutional, political, and historical circumstances that extend beyond the horizon of particular interactions. These studies are summarized below.

Two studies by Young and Miller (2004) and Yagi (2007) have explored how IC develops in recurrent dyadic interactions in which one participant is a second language learner and the other participant a native speaker. The discursive practice that Young and Miller reported they called *revision talk*, which formed part of writing conferences between a Vietnamese student of English as a second language (ESL) and his American tutor. The conferences took place once a week over a period of four weeks. Before each writing conference, the student had written a draft of an essay on a topic assigned by the tutor, and during revision talk the tutor and student identified problem areas in the student's writing, talked about ways to improve the writing, and revised the essay. Young and Miller identified a sequence of eight actions constituting revision talk, which were performed several times during each writing conference: (1) display of attention to the student's paper; (2) identification of a problem in the student's paper; (3) explanation and/or justification of the need for a revision; (4) direction to the student to produce a candidate revision; (5) production of the candidate revision; (6) direction to the student to write the revision; (7) writing the revision; and (8) evaluation of the written revision.

In the first writing conference, the student's participation in revision talk was peripheral, consisting of minimal utterances, almost all limited to *yeah*. Most of the tutor's turns were completed with falling and often final-falling intonation, which helped establish potential turn transition relevance places, but a change of speaker did not occur and the tutor extended her turn, producing almost all of the eight actions of revision talk. The student's minimal responses of *yeah* showed him to be complicit in producing the tutor's extended turn. Thus, student and tutor co-constructed the asymmetric production of turns in this first occasion of revision talk. The student's peripheral participation was legitimated through the tutor's production of extended turns.

After four weeks, the participation framework of revision talk changed significantly. The student now performed many of the actions that were initially performed by the tutor. He identified the problem, he explained the need for a revision, he suggested a candidate revision, and he wrote the revision to his essay without being directed to do so by the tutor. Although the tutor's directive role in requiring that the student suggest a candidate revision and directing him to write it was never assumed by the student, it was hardly necessary for her to utter these directives because the student was ready to perform the required acts without direction. Not only did the quantity of the student's talk increase through the series of four conferences, but he also showed he had mastered the sequential structure of the practice by performing all acts except those that uniquely construct the role of tutor. It is in this sense that Young and Miller claimed that the student acquired IC in the practice of revision talk, which they noted was co-constructed by the tutor:

> It appears that the student is the one whose participation is most dramatically transformed, but the instructor is a co-learner, and her participation develops in a way that complements the student's learning. In fact, the effectiveness of the instructor is precisely in how she manages a division of participation that allows for growth on the part of the student.
>
> (Young & Miller, 2004, p. 533)

A second study of dyadic conversation between learners and native speakers in a single discursive practice is Yagi (2007). Yagi reported telephone calls by Japanese students of ESL in Hawai'i to various bookstores in the US inquiring whether the store had a particular title and asking about the store's opening hours. Students called bookstores ten times within approximately one hour. Although they received no feedback from Yagi or from their instructor, Yagi reports that by the end of the process, students came to communicate with bookstore staff more smoothly and effectively. The students experienced difficulty with certain unexpected phases of the interaction, including being put on hold while the store clerk searched for the requested title in the store's online database. One student employed a strategy to overcome interactional trouble by saying that he was Japanese and could not speak English very well. The sequence of opening actions in the telephone call also caused some difficulty. One previous study of telephone calls to a workplace (Bowles & Pallotti, 2004) had found that pre-request and initial inquiry actions often occur in place of the greeting found in openings of other kinds of calls, and Yagi found that some students consistently separated the greeting from the pre-request and initial inquiry. One student, however, performed both greeting and pre-request (e.g., "hello I'm looking for a book") or request (e.g., "hello I'm looking for a James Patterson's book") in the same turn, and Yagi reported that generally this student's interactions went smoothly. Yagi concluded that students are able to learn some aspects of IC through participation in a recurrent practice even without explicit feedback on their performance. He cautioned, however, that students' conscious attention to transcriptions of their interaction and guided reflection on their performance would be necessary to improve IC.

Second language learners' development of IC without overt study has also been observed in two reports of study abroad. The first, by Dings (2007), is the most extensive study to date of the development of IC. Dings reported on six 30-minute conversations in Spanish between Sophie, an American study-abroad student living in Granada, Spain and José, a native speaker of Spanish. The conversations were recorded at the beginning, middle, and end of two semesters of Sophie's sojourn in Granada. Dings reported on changes in Sophie's speaker selection, topic management, and alignment activity in her conversations with José over the year. In observing Sophie's developing employment of interactional resources, Dings focused attention on how Sophie selected either herself or

José as next speaker and how she initiated new conversational topics and managed transitions from one topic to another. Dings also developed a way to describe how Sophie and her interlocutor co-constructed the conversation by noticing alignment activity, defined as Sophie's assessment of her own and José's contributions and how Sophie collaborated with José in completing turns and extending topics. Dings summarized Sophie's development of IC as follows:

> Over the course of the year abroad Sophie showed some degree of development in all of the resources analyzed with the exception of topic initial elicitors. By the end of her stay abroad, she showed stronger skills in both speaker selection and alignment activity, and some skill in topic management in terms of topic transition markers.
>
> (Dings, 2007, p. 207)

In addition, Dings noticed development in ways in which Sophie collaboratively constructed the conversation with José:

> The most noticeable changes seen in co-construction while Sophie was holding the floor were the changing patterns in repair. [...] In general terms, José's role when holding the floor was relatively stable over the course of the year, while Sophie showed a growing involvement in elaborately co-constructing the interaction with José through her skillful deployment of alignment moves.
>
> (Dings, 2007, p. 215)

Another study that focused on learners' development of alignment in interactions with native speakers during study abroad is Ishida's (2009) report of an American student's conversations while studying abroad in Japan. The student, Fred, recorded eight 30-minute conversations once a month with Japanese people with whom he frequently interacted. The focus of Ishida's study was Fred's use of the Japanese particle *ne* [ね]. Ishida cited a number of studies of utterance-final *ne* that describe its wide range of interactional functions in Japanese including: an index of the speaker's epistemic and/or affective stance, the speaker's attempt to index a topic that the speaker believes to be known to the hearer, and an index of mutual alignment between speaker and hearer. Ishida reported, however, that Fred's development of IC was indexed by his use of *ne* in conversations with interlocutors. Initially, Ishida reported that Fred used *ne* only in turns that did not require "fine-tuning toward the previous speaker's turn" but in later conversations he "came to use [*ne*] as an immediate response to the previous speaker's turn and became more active in pursuing aligning responses through its use" (p. 382). In his later conversations, Fred used *ne* to index opinions that did not align with his interlocutor and his use of *ne* in assessments helped achieve mutual alignment with his interlocutors. By focusing on a learner's expanding interactional functions of a single linguistic form, Ishida's study showed how the learner developed overt attribution of intentional acts to others—intersubjectivity—and did so by means of expressions of alignment with what he perceived as the knowledge or stance of his interlocutor.

The studies reviewed thus far report the longitudinal development of IC of a single learner in dyadic interaction with a single native speaker.[1] Clearly, dyadic conversations like these allow comparisons between a learner's utterances in a recurrent discursive practice, but since learners do not generally interact with the same person over a long period of time, these nonetheless represent controlled experimental situations. A less controlled scenario is when learners interact with their teacher and classmates at school, and this is the context reported by Cekaite (2007) in her longitudinal study of one seven-year-old immigrant child's developing IC with her teacher and peers in a Swedish immersion language classroom. The child, Fusi, was a Kurdish girl from Iraq who spoke Kurdish and Arabic but whose Swedish was minimal at the beginning of the study.

Following Hall (1999) and Young and Miller (2004), Cekaite defined IC as participants' knowledge of the interactional architecture of a specific discursive practice, including knowledge of how to employ linguistic, pragmatic, and interactional resources in the construction of a discursive practice. Cekaite defined learning within Lave and Wenger's (1991) framework as evidenced by "novices' changing participation status and their move from peripheral to increasingly active participation in a given activity" (p. 46). The activities that Cekaite focused on were Fusi's topic initiation, her self-selection in multi-party turn-taking, and her construction of identity in the classroom.

Cekaite distinguished three phases in Fusi's development of IC over the school year. In the early phase, Fusi was mostly silent and participated only marginally in classroom activities. Her attempts to initiate a topic and to select herself as a conversational participant were nonverbal. Cekaite (2007, p. 49) reported that Fusi

> recurrently tried to get the teacher's and the children's attention by pretending to run away from the schoolyard or by pretending to cry in the classroom [...]. However, her peer group and her teachers rather quickly became bored with her staged escapes.

During the middle phase, Fusi's contributions were verbal but interactionally inappropriate. Cekaite reported that Fusi "frequently talked loudly, almost screaming, and her contributions were recurrently marked as unmitigated disagreements, which often resulted in conflict with the teachers or with the other children" (p. 50). In response, her teacher either ignored or explicitly disciplined her while her peers continued to self-select in conversations with the teacher. Cekaite commented that such responses to Fusi's attempts to participate provided her with explicit or implicit socialization to the norms of classroom conversation. In the final stage of observation, Fusi began to participate as a competent member of the classroom community. Cekaite reported that Fusi "mastered a more elaborate Swedish repertoire and developed interactional skills allowing her to participate in spontaneously evolving whole-group conversational activities, which in turn shaped interactional learning affordances" (p. 58). Her teachers paid attention to her initiatives and engaged in conversational exchanged with her. Thus, through participation in recurrent classroom discursive practices but with little explicit instruction in the norms of interaction, Fusi learned how classroom interaction was designed and how to participate effectively in it.

Cekaite's study is a valuable report of one child's development in the use of linguistic and interactional resources in the pragmatics of spoken interaction. Fusi's IC is also co-constructed by the reactions of her teachers and peers to her contributions, a development that eventually positioned her as a competent member of the classroom community. However, one feature of IC has only been hinted at by Cekaite and by authors of the other studies reviewed so far. A full understanding of IC requires an investigation of social, institutional, political, and historical circumstances that extend beyond the horizon of particular interactions. This wider context of interaction has been the focus of two studies by Nguyen (2006, 2008) of the development of IC in the counseling performed by two inexperienced pharmacists with patients during the course of the pharmacists' internships.

Nguyen's studies did not specifically address second language learning because her two subjects were both highly fluent English speakers. Nonetheless, their development of IC is relevant because of the clear relationship between the practice in which pharmacists and patients participated and the wider social order. US federal law and many states mandate that pharmacists provide instructions to patients about the medication they receive, and instruction in patient consultation is part of the curricula of many Schools of Pharmacy. Apart from these legislative mandates, the practice of patient consultation in a pharmacy is a site where a social hierarchy is constructed, in which the prescribing doctor occupies the highest rank, the patient the lowest, and the pharmacist an intermediary role between them. The two examples of interactions that I have excerpted from Nguyen's studies show clearly how the novice pharmacists negotiated their position in the hierarchy.

Nguyen (2006) compared two patient consultations performed by Jim, an advanced student of pharmacy employed as an intern at a community pharmacy. Over a period of three weeks, Jim demonstrated development of his participation status in patient consultations from *novice expert* to *experienced expert*. Nguyen (2006) explained the different statuses by citing Benner's (1984) work on the construction of expertise in health care practice:

> Unlike the novice expert, the experienced expert is someone who not only has access to professional knowledge, but also "no longer relies on analytic principles (rules, guidelines, maxims)", and "has an intuitive grasp of each situation and zeroes in on the accurate region of the problem without wasteful consideration of a large range of alternative diagnoses and solutions."
>
> (Nguyen, 2006, p. 148)

In an early patient consultation, Jim displayed his expert knowledge about administration and side effects of a medication using technical vocabulary despite the patient's apparent lack of interest; in doing so, Jim constructed an identity for himself that Nguyen called novice expert. In contrast, after working in the community pharmacy for three weeks and having participated in many patient consultations, Jim displayed an alignment with the patient's stance that was absent three weeks earlier. Nguyen (2006) went on to show how during his internship Jim developed other skills in patient consultations, including his responses to patients' challenges, the development of a shared perspective with his patients toward medication and toward the technical language provided in the patient information slips that are provided with every prescription. As his participation status as novice expert developed, Jim was able to utilize interactional and verbal resources more skillfully, both in displaying his expertise and in maintaining a stance of alignment with his patients—both of which are, according to Nguyen, important attributes of an experienced expert.

In her second study, Nguyen's (2008) focused on the development of IC in patient consultations involving another pharmacy intern, Mai, who negotiated her own role in the doctor–pharmacist–patient hierarchy. A template of interaction in patient consultation includes two pharmacist's actions that form part of a sequence of advice giving. The pharmacist refers to the doctor's prescription, including how frequently the medication should be taken and for how long, and the method by which it should be administered. The pharmacist also provides his/her own advice to the patient without referring to the doctor's prescription. These two actions are performed by experienced pharmacists in a fixed sequence: the doctor's instructions are given first, followed if necessary by an elaboration by the pharmacist. By referring to the doctor's instructions (in many cases indexing printed instructions by gesture and by referring to the doctor by name or simply as "they") the pharmacist creates a participation status for the doctor as author of the words that the pharmacist utters. The doctor's participation status is also principal, whose position is established by the words uttered and creates a context for the instructions that the pharmacist gives.

This sequence of actions in patient consultations appears to be crucial in establishing the pharmacist's role as intermediary between the prescribing doctor and the patient and, when the sequence is violated, interactional trouble results. In patient consultations performed early in her internship, Mai did not precede her own advice by reference to the doctor's prescription. In this case, Nguyen (2008) reported, "there were several instances of interactional trouble which were evident in the patient's lack of immediate receipt of the pharmacist's advice" (p. 536). Perhaps as a result of her experience of interactional trouble, over time Mai changed toward a less problematic sequence, specifically invoking the doctor as principal and author before giving her own advice.

The seven studies of the development of IC reported here show how the theoretical construct of IC can provide a new perspective on the second language learning process. Some but not all of the four aspects of IC can be seen in all these studies. First, all have been studies of spoken interaction and many have adopted the close analyses of spoken discourse that originate in conversation analysis. The studies by Young and Miller (2004) and by Nguyen (2006, 2008) have also included analyses of nonverbal communication including gesture, gaze, and body positioning. Second, the pragmatic relationships between forms of talk employed by learners and the cultural expectations of their interlocutors have been reported by Yagi (2007), Cekaite (2007), and Nguyen (2008), and these authors have remarked on how changes in learners' pragmatic competence has resulted in less problematic interactions. Third, the studies by Dings (2007), Ishida (2009), and Nguyen (2006) have shown how learners develop alignment with the knowledge or stance of their interlocutors, thus creating intersubjectivity—a shared mental context with their interactional partners. Dings (2007) reported that Sophie showed intersubjectivity by means of expressions of assessment of José's utterances, by collaboratively managing topics, and my managing smooth transitions from one topic to another; Ishida (2009) reported that Fred achieved alignment with his interlocutors through grammatical means; and Nguyen (2006) reported that Jim did so with his patients by means of changing stance from novice expert to experienced expert. Finally, the construction of an identity that persists beyond the spatial and temporal boundaries of a single interaction was reported by Cekaite (2007) and Nguyen (2008). Cekaite reported that after a considerable trajectory of interactional struggle, Fusi learned to perform as a socially competent student in the classroom who had learned to self-select and to participate in whole-group activities in accordance with the cultural norms of the classroom. Nguyen's comparison of Mai's identity construction in patient consultations also showed how the novice pharmacist changed the selection and sequence of activities in the patient consultations from a context in which the participation of the prescribing physician was not invoked to one in which she constructed the physician as principal and author of the instructions that she gave to the patient.

The authors of these studies have provided detailed descriptions of learners' development of IC, but they have provided little evidence of how the changes in IC occurred. One exception is Cekaite's description of how Fusi's teachers and classmates reacted to Fusi's violation of the norms of classroom participation. Ishida also speculated that the learners in her study may have been influenced by the booksellers' reactions to learners' actions in their first few telephone calls. In other words, no study so far has been designed to address the question of how to *teach* IC. Some scholars have, however, theorized how IC may be taught, and their work is briefly reviewed in the next section.

The Role of Instruction

Wong (2000) was among the first applied linguists to argue that second language learners can benefit from study of transcriptions of recorded naturally occurring conversations in order to learn how participants construct, reconstruct, and orient to social actions. Wong's call for attention to transcriptions of live interaction was echoed by Crandall and Basturkmen (2004) and Yagi (2007). Hall (1999) also maintained that second language learners can attain IC in part by the systematic study of discursive practices outside the classroom, a study that she termed "the prosaics of interaction." Hall explained what she meant as follows:

> By standing outside of interactive practices that are of significance to the group(s) whose language is being learned, and analyzing the conventional ways that verbal resources get used, the movement that occurs between their conventional meanings and their individual uses, and the consequences that are engendered by the various uses, we can develop a far greater understanding both of ourselves and of those in whose practices we aspire to become participants.
>
> (Hall, 1999, p. 144)

The process of teaching would then involve two moments. In the first, learners are guided through conscious, systematic study of the practice, in which they mindfully abstract, reflect upon, and speculate about the sociocultural context of the practice and the verbal, interactional, and nonverbal resources that participants employ in the practice. In the second moment, learners are guided through participation in the practice by more experienced participants. These two pedagogical moments, Hall argues, facilitate the development of IC in the second language.

In study abroad contexts, however, Dings (2007) and Ishida (2009) have both reported that learners sojourning in the community where the second language is used in everyday interactions have in fact developed aspects of IC, specifically the ability to take a point of view or stance of an interlocutor. If this is so, is it not enough to learn IC simply by extended interaction in the second language community? Relevant research on the effect of study abroad on the development of pragmatic competence was reviewed by Kasper and Rose (2002), who concluded that "[f]or developing pragmatic ability, spending time in the target community is no panacea, length of residence is not a reliable predictor, and L2 classrooms can be a productive social context" (p. 230). In other words, exposure alone to discursive practice in a second language community is not an efficient instructional strategy, no matter how long or how intense the exposure.

Young (2009) extended Kasper and Rose's conclusion about the development of pragmatic competence to IC and argued that there is considerable support for a pedagogy of conscious and systematic study of interaction in the work of the Soviet psychologist Gal'perin and his theory of systemic–theoretical instruction also known as concept-based instruction (Arievitch & Stetsenko, 2000; Gal'perin, 1989a, 1989b, 1989c; Haenen, 2001). Instruction, in Gal'perin's view, is the provision of efficient cultural psychological tools to learners so that they may solve problems in a specific domain. Comparing the kinds of cultural mediation available to learners in different types of instruction, Gal'perin concluded that the most efficient tool for learners is the provision of a general procedure that learners can use to solve any specific problem in a given instructional domain. For Gal'perin, the initial step in the procedure is construction of a "schema for a complete orienting basis for an action" (Gal'perin, 1989b, p. 70), which is in effect a theory of the domain of instruction. The new practice to be learned is first brought to the learner's attention, not in the small stages that characterize behaviorist instruction, but as a meaningful whole from the very beginning of instruction. Arievitch and Stetsenko (2000, p. 77) provided a general description of the procedure as follows: In concept-based instruction,

> students acquire a general method to construct a concrete orientation basis to solve any specific problem in a given subject domain. Such a general method involves a theoretical analysis of objects, phenomena, or events in various subject domains. The main feature of the analysis is that it reveals the "genesis" and the general structure of objects or phenomena (the general make-up of things). In such analysis, students learn to distinguish essential characteristics of different objects and phenomena, to form theoretical concepts on this basis, and use them as cognitive tools in further problem solving.

At the time of writing, there are very few applications of concept-based instruction to second language learning and those reported so far have focused on the acquisition of second language grammar (Negueruela, 2003; Negueruela & Lantolf, 2006). Despite what many have argued is an important pedagogy, no applications of concept-based instruction to the development of IC have been reported. In contrast, the field of language testing has seen an extensive discussion of how to assess IC, arising largely from work on performance testing and the realization that an individual score on a language test results from an interaction between the individual's ability and the context in which ability is measured. Recent research on interactional constructs in language testing is the topic of the next section.

Interactional Constructs in Language Testing

How has the concept of IC influenced the design of language tests and the interpretation tests results? The co-construction of IC by all participants in an interaction creates a challenge for assessment because, as Chalhoub-Deville and Deville (2005, p. 826) explain:

> Evaluating test-takers' performance according to this model offers a conundrum. Generally speaking, we administer tests to, assign scores to, and make decisions about individuals for purposes such as selection, placement, assignment of grades/marks, and the like. If we view language as co-constructed, how can we disentangle an individual's contribution to a communicative exchange in order to provide a score or assess a candidate's merit for a potential position?

In other words, if IC is the construct underlying test design, how can candidates' test performance be interpreted?

The general shape of the relationship between test performance and the construct underlying a test was laid out by Messick (1989, 1996) and Chapelle (1998). Chapelle distinguished among three perspectives on construct definition: a construct may be defined as a *trait*, as a *behavior*, or as *some combination of trait and behavior*. In a trait definition of a construct, consistent performance of a person on a test is related in a principled way to the person's knowledge and speech production processes. That is to say, a person's consistent performance on a test is taken to index a fairly stable configuration of knowledge and skills that the person carries around with them—and which that person can apply in all contexts. In contrast, in a definition of a construct as a behavior, the consistent performance of a person on a test is related in a principled way to the context in which the behavior is observed. That is to say, test performance is assumed to say something about a person's performance on a specific task or in a specific context, but *not* on other tasks or in other contexts—unless these can be shown to be related to the task or context that was tested.

Clearly, neither definition of a construct as trait or behavior is satisfactory for tests of IC because it includes *both* knowledge *and* the employment of that knowledge in different contexts of use. For this reason, it is desirable to consider the third of Messick's and Chapelle's definitions of a construct, which they refer to as the interactionalist definition. In an interactionalist validation of a test, a person's performance on a test is taken to indicate an underlying trait characteristic of that person and, at the same time, the performance is also taken to indicate the influence of the context in which the performance occurs. The interactionalist definition is, in other words, a way to infer from test performance something about *both* a practice-specific behavior *and* a practice-independent, person-specific trait. Moreover, the interactionalist definition of a construct refers not only to the trait and the context but also to some theory of how the two interact.

However, if interactionalist and behaviorist approaches to construct definition are to allow test users to generalize from performance in one context to another—that is, from the context of the performance elicited in the test to other non-test contexts—then what is needed is a theory that relates one context to another in a principled way. The question of generalizability of test results is a question of whether and how knowledge and ability employed by a person in one context of use can be redeployed in another.

If a person's knowledge is displayed in a participation framework in a certain context, then, because that framework has an architecture, elements of that architecture can be found, albeit in different configurations, in different contexts. What is needed is, as McNamara (1997) realized, a "close analysis of naturally occurring discourse and social interaction [to] reveal the standards that apply in reality in particular settings" (p. 457). Such an analysis of discourse and social interaction was the aim of Young's (2009) analysis of discursive practice. The architecture of any particular discursive practice is characterized by four features. First, analysis of language in social interaction is concerned with language used in specific discursive practices rather than with language ability independent of context. Second, it is characterized by attention to the co-construction of discursive practices by *all* participants involved rather than a narrow focus on a single individual. Third, as Young (2008) specified, analysis of social interaction identifies the set of seven identity, linguistic, and interactional resources that participants employ in specific ways in order to co-construct a discursive practice. And fourth, the problem of generalizability is resolved by identifying the particular configuration of resources that participants employ in a particular practice and, then, comparing the configuration of resources in that practice with others in order to discover what resources are local to that practice and to what extent the practice shares resources and a configuration with other practices.

This framework for understanding the construct of IC underlying a person's performance on a test is the interactionalist definition in Messick's (1989, 1996) and Chapelle's (1998) terms. The construct is local in the sense that it indicates the influence of the context in which the test performance was elicited. In addition, because the context involves other participants in addition to the candidate (interlocutors in an oral test, the designer of the test, the item writers, an oral examiner, members of an examination board, and others), the performance of a candidate must be understood as co-constructed and the contributions of others must be considered—those others "whose behavior and interpretation shape the perceived significance of the candidate's efforts but are themselves removed from focus" (McNamara, 1997, p. 459).

However, the redeployment of resources from one discursive practice to another—in other words the generalizability of an individual candidate's test performance—is within the scope of an analysis of context inspired by Practice Theory. The trait that an interactionalist theory of the construct considers is the configuration of identity, linguistic, and interactional resources employed in a test. But that does not mean that every discursive practice is *sui generis*. That configuration must then be compared with the configuration of resources employed in other contexts.

One clear example of portability of resources is provided by Young's (2003) analysis of the resources employed by international teaching assistants (ITAs) in office-hour conversations with students. Young compared an office-hour conversation conducted by an ITA in the Math Department at an American university with an office hour conducted by an ITA in the Italian Department. By comparing the resources employed in the two office-hour conversations, Young concluded that there were enough similarities to describe a genre of office-hour conversation. This genre is characterized by: a problem-statement/resolution script; an opening sequence that moves quickly to a statement of the problem; lexicogrammatical choices by both participants that mutually construct the ITA as an expert and the student as a novice; and a turn-taking system in which the ITA may take a turn at any time and may allocate the next turn to the student and may deny the floor to the student by means of overlapping speech. However, interactional differences in office-hour interactions in the two disciplines were apparent in the topics that were chosen and in the way that topics were sequenced. Discipline-specific modes of reasoning were instantiated in these office hours by the way that topics arose, persisted, and changed in conversation and by the semantic relations between adjacent topics. Young concluded that assessment of ITAs' IC in office hours was similar enough across disciplines to justify discipline-independent assessment.

Other well-known comparisons of the interactional resources in different practices are the studies of oral second-language proficiency interviews collected by Young and He (1998) and reviewed by Johnson (2001), Lazaraton (2002), and Young (2002). These studies compared the interactional resources employed by participants in mundane conversations with those required for participation in oral proficiency assessments. The differences in the interactional architectures of the two practices are so apparent that Johnson titled her analysis of oral proficiency interviews: *The art of non-conversation.* He and Young (1998) concluded that the resources employed by an examiner and a candidate in the assessment practice of an oral proficiency interview are very different from those employed by participants in conversations between native and nonnative speakers. Prior to the analyses that Young and He published, the similarity between interviews and conversations was something that was taken for granted because few researchers had made any systematic comparisons between the two practices. However, the results of the comparisons carried out on practices in several different languages revealed that the interactional architecture of interviews is very different from the interactional architecture of ordinary conversation. Interviews, that is, are not authentic tests of conversation, and generalization from a person's performance in a testing context to their performance in a non-testing context is problematic.

In conclusion, it can be seen that testing IC in a second language requires much greater analysis of the discursive architecture of language testing practices and systematic comparison with practices outside the testing room. This does not mean that generalization from test performance to non-test contexts is invalid. It does mean, however, that testers and applied linguists need to do much more work on the context of testing to elucidate the architecture of practices which language learners perform. As Anastasi (1986) stressed: "When selecting or developing tests and when interpreting scores, consider context. I shall stop right there, because those are the words, more than any others, that I want to leave with you: *consider context*" (p. 484, emphasis in original).

Future Directions for the Study of Interactional Competence

The following four aspects of IC have been cited in this review:

1. IC has been studied in spoken interaction, although nonverbal aspects of spoken interaction are seen as important.
2. The pragmatics of interaction—the relationships between the forms of talk chosen by participants and the social contexts in which they are used—are fundamental to IC.
3. IC is the construction of a shared mental context through the collaboration of all interactional partners.
4. The context of an interaction includes the social, institutional, political, and historical circumstances that extend beyond the horizon of a single interaction.

Learners' development in several of these four aspects has been reported in longitudinal studies in which learners' contributions to discursive practices have been compared over time. There is evidence from study abroad that IC does develop over time as a result of extended interaction by learners in a second language culture, but development may be slow and there is further evidence that simple exposure is not an effective learning strategy. Several authors have proposed that conscious systematic study by learners of the details of interaction in specific discursive practices may benefit development of IC, but we await empirical studies to test that claim.

In the assessment of IC, several authors have claimed that a close analysis needs to be made of the identity, linguistic, and interactional resources employed by participants in an assessment practice. This interactional architecture of the test may then be compared with discursive practices outside the testing room in which the learner wishes to participate. If the configuration of resources in the two practices is similar, then an argument can be made to support the generalization of an individual's test result because the testee can redeploy resources used in one practice to another. Is this truly a test of IC, however? Lee (2006) has argued that there is a tension between two interpretations of IC, one that admits stable and recognizable constructs of interaction, which can be transformed into language assessment and language learning objectives, and another that recognizes the contingency and variation of interactional organization. Lee (2006, p. 354) writes that this is precarious because it points to the discursive practice of interaction that is locally contingent and situationally specific while at the same time it attempts to create stable and unifying categories with which to compare language practices across contexts and even to document change.

Future work in the learning, teaching, and assessment of IC may resolve this tension.

Note

1. The sole exception is Ishida's (2009) study of Fred, in which several of Fred's eight conversations were with two people, and in one conversation one interlocutor was another American student.

References

Agar, M. (1980). *The professional stranger: An informal introduction to ethnography.* New York: Academic Press.

Anastasi, A. (1986). Evolving concepts of test validation. *Annual Review of Psychology, 37*(1), 1–16.

Arievitch, I. M., & Stetsenko, A. (2000). The quality of cultural tools and cognitive development: Gal'perin's perspective and its implications. *Human Development, 43*(2), 69–92.

Bachman, L. F. (1990). *Fundamental considerations in language testing.* New York: Oxford University Press.

Benner, P. E. (1984). *From novice to expert: Excellence and power in clinical nursing practice.* Menlo Park, CA: Addison-Wesley.

Beyer, C. (2007). Edmund Husserl [electronic version]. In *Stanford encyclopedia of philosophy.* Retrieved June 24, 2009 from http://plato.stanford.edu/entries/husserl/.

Bourdieu, P. (1977). *Outline of a theory of practice.* Translated by R. Nice. New York: Cambridge University Press.

Bourdieu, P. (1990). *The logic of practice.* Translated by R. Nice. Stanford, CA: Stanford University Press.

Bowles, H., & Pallotti, G. (2004). Conversation analysis of opening sequences of telephone calls to bookstores in English and Italian. *Textus, 17*(1), 63–88.

Canale, M., & Swain, M. (1980). Theoretical bases of communicative approaches to second language teaching and testing. *Applied Linguistics, 1*(1), 1–47.

Cekaite, A. (2007). A child's development of interactional competence in a Swedish L2 classroom. *The Modern Language Journal, 91*(1), 45–62.

Chalhoub-Deville, M., & Deville, C. (2005). A look back at and forward to what language testers measure. In E. Hinkel (Ed.), *Handbook of research in second language teaching and learning* (pp. 815–832). Mahwah, NJ: Erlbaum.

Chapelle, C. A. (1998). Construct definition and validity inquiry in SLA research. In L. F. Bachman & A. D. Cohen (Eds.), *Interfaces between second language acquisition and language testing research* (pp. 32–70). New York: Cambridge University Press.

Chomsky, N. (1965). *Aspects of the theory of syntax.* Cambridge, MA: MIT Press.

Crandall, E., & Basturkmen, H. (2004). Evaluating pragmatics-focused materials. *ELT Journal, 58*(1), 38–49.

Dings, A. (2007). Developing interactional competence in a second language: A case study of a Spanish language learner. Unpublished doctoral dissertation, University of Texas, Austin.

Gal'perin, P. Y. (1989a). Study of the intellectual development of the child. *Soviet Psychology, 27*(3), 26–44.

Gal'perin, P. Y. (1989b). Organization of mental activity and the effectiveness of learning. *Soviet Psychology, 27*(3), 65–82.

Gal'perin, P. Y. (1989c). The problem of attention. *Soviet Psychology, 27*(3), 83–92.

Haenen, J. (2001). Outlining the teaching-learning process: Piotr Gal'perin's contribution. *Learning and Instruction, 11*(2), 157–170.

Hall, J. K. (1995). (Re)creating our worlds with words: A sociohistorical perspective of face-to-face interaction. *Applied Linguistics, 16*(2), 206–232.

Hall, J. K. (1999). A prosaics of interaction: The development of interactional competence in another language. In E. Hinkel (Ed.), *Culture in second language teaching and learning* (pp. 137–151). New York: Cambridge University Press.

Hanks, W. F. (1996). *Language and communicative practices.* Boulder, CO: Westview.

He, A. W., & Young, R. (1998). Language proficiency interviews: A discourse approach. In R. Young & A. W. He (Eds.), *Talking and testing: Discourse approaches to the assessment of oral proficiency* (pp. 1–24). Amsterdam and Philadelphia: John Benjamins.

Hymes, D. (1972). On communicative competence. In J. B. Pride & J. Holmes (Eds.), *Sociolinguistics: Selected readings* (pp. 269–293). Harmondsworth: Penguin.

Ishida, M. (2009). Development of interactional competence: Changes in the use of *ne* in L2 Japanese during study abroad. In

H. t. Nguyen & G. Kasper (Eds.), *Talk-in-interaction: Multilingual perspectives* (pp. 351–385). Honolulu: University of Hawai'i National Foreign Language Resource Center.

Johnson, M. (2001). *The art of non-conversation: A re-examination of the validity of the oral proficiency interview.* New Haven, CT: Yale University Press.

Kasper, G., & Rose, K. R. (2002). *Pragmatic development in a second language.* Malden, MA and Oxford: Blackwell.

Kramsch, C. (1986). From language proficiency to interactional competence. *The Modern Language Journal, 70*(4), 366–372.

Lave, J., & Wenger, E. (1991). *Situated learning: Legitimate peripheral participation.* Cambridge and New York: Cambridge University Press.

Lazaraton, A. (2002). *A qualitative approach to the validation of oral language tests.* Cambridge: Cambridge University Press.

Lee, Y.-A. (2006). Towards respecification of communicative competence: Condition of L2 instruction or its objective? *Applied Linguistics, 27*(3), 349–376.

Markee, N. (2000). *Conversation analysis.* Mahwah, NJ: Lawrence Erlbaum.

McNamara, T. F. (1997). "Interaction" in second language performance assessment: Whose performance? *Applied Linguistics, 18*(4), 446–466.

Mehan, H. (1982). The structure of classroom events and their consequences for student performance. In P. Gilmore & A. A. Glatthorn (Eds.), *Children in and out of school: Ethnography and education* (pp. 59–87). Washington, DC: Center for Applied Linguistics.

Messick, S. (1989). Validity. In R. L. Linn (Ed.), *Educational measurement* (3rd ed.) (pp. 13–103). New York: American Council on Education and Macmillan Publishing Company.

Messick, S. (1996). Validity of performance assessments. In G. W. Phillips (Ed.), *Technical issues in large-scale performance assessment* (pp. 1–18). Washington, DC: US Department of Education, Office of Educational Research and Improvement.

Negueruela, E. (2003). Systemic-theoretical instruction and second language development. Unpublished doctoral dissertation, The Pennsylvania State University, State College, PA.

Negueruela, E., & Lantolf, J. P. (2006). Concept-based instruction and the acquisition of L2 Spanish. In R. A. Salaberry & B. A. Lafford (Eds.), *The art of teaching Spanish: Second language acquisition from research to praxis* (pp. 79–102). Washington, DC: Georgetown University Press.

Nguyen, H. t. (2006). Constructing "expertness": A novice pharmacist's development of interactional competence in patient consultations. *Communication and Medication, 3*(2), 147–160.

Nguyen, H. t. (2008). Sequence organization as local and longitudinal achievement. *Text and Talk, 28*(4), 523–550.

Ortner, S. B. (1984). Theory in anthropology since the sixties. *Comparative Studies in Society and History, 126*(1), 126–166.

Sahlins, M. D. (1981). *Historical metaphors and mythical realities: Structure in the early history of the Sandwich Islands kingdom.* Ann Arbor: University of Michigan Press.

Sahlins, M. D. (1985). *Islands of history.* Chicago: University of Chicago Press.

Saville-Troike, M. (1989). *The ethnography of communication: An introduction* (2nd ed.). Malden, MA: Blackwell.

Tracy, K. (2002). *Everyday talk: Building and reflecting identities.* New York: Guilford.

Trevarthen, C. (1977). Descriptive analyses of infant communicative behaviour. In H. R. Schaffer (Ed.), *Studies in mother-infant interaction: Proceedings of the Loch Lomond symposium, Ross Priory, University of Strathclyde, September, 1975* (pp. 227–270). London and New York: Academic Press.

Trevarthen, C. (1979). Communication and cooperation in early infancy: A description of primary intersubjectivity. In M. Bullowa (Ed.), *Before speech* (pp. 321–347). Cambridge: Cambridge University Press.

Wells, G. (1979). Describing children's linguistic development at home and at school. *British Educational Research Journal, 5*(1), 75–95.

Wells, G. (1981). *Learning through interaction: The study of language development.* Cambridge and New York: Cambridge University Press.

Wong, J. (2000). "Applying" conversation analysis in applied linguistics: Evaluating English as a second language textbook dialogue [electronic version]. *Paper presented at TESOL Convention, Vancouver, BC.* Retrieved June 2, 2009 from http://search.ebscohost.com/login.aspx?direct=true&db=eric&AN=ED444376&loginpage=Login.asp&site=ehost-live.

Yagi, K. (2007). The development of interactional competence in a situated practice by Japanese learners of English as a second language [electronic version]. *Hawaii Pacific University TESL Working Paper Series, 5(1).* Retrieved May 1, 2009 from http://www.hpu.edu/index.cfm?contentID=8064&siteID=1.

Young, R. (1999). Sociolinguistic approaches to SLA. *Annual Review of Applied Linguistics, 19,* 105–132.

Young, R. (2002). Discourse approaches to oral language assessment. *Annual Review of Applied Linguistics, 22,* 243–262.

Young, R. (2003). Learning to talk the talk and walk the walk: Interactional competence in academic spoken English. *North Eastern Illinois University Working Papers in Linguistics, 2,* 26–44.

Young, R. F. (2007). Language learning and teaching as discursive practice. In Z. Hua, P. Seedhouse, L. Wei & V. Cook (Eds.), *Language learning and teaching as social inter-action* (pp. 251–271). Basingstoke and New York: Palgrave Macmillan.

Young, R. F. (2008). *Language and interaction: An advanced resource book.* London and New York: Routledge.

Young, R. F. (2009). *Discursive practice in language learning and teaching.* Malden, MA and Oxford: Wiley-Blackwell.

Young, R., & He, A. W. (Eds.) (1998). *Talking and testing: Discourse approaches to the assessment of oral proficiency.* Amsterdam and Philadelphia: John Benjamins.

Young, R. F., & Miller, E. R. (2004). Learning as changing participation: Negotiating discourse roles in the ESL writing conference. *The Modern Language Journal, 88*(4), 519–535.

27
Second Language Speaking

I. S. P. Nation

This chapter focuses on research on speaking as it is relevant to gaining control of the speaking skill and to the use of speaking as a way of expanding language knowledge, such as vocabulary knowledge. It includes the learning of a clear pronunciation of the language, as well as control of grammatical and discourse features.

Speaking is typically seen as one of the four skills of language use, namely listening, speaking, reading and writing. In reality it is not always easy to distinguish these skills, particularly those of listening and speaking when they are involved in interaction. In this chapter a distinction is made between speaking in interaction and speaking monologue, which typically occurs in formal speaking.

The Role of Speaking in Language Learning

Although speaking has been seen as a central skill in the use of a language (we typically ask "Can you *speak* French? Can you *speak* Japanese?"), at various times in the history of foreign language teaching methodology, speaking has been relegated to being a minor skill, at least for certain stages of the language learning process.

Michael West (1955) who was involved in the teaching of English as a foreign language in Bengal in the 1930s suggested that "[t]he initial stage of learning a foreign language should, we believe, be to learn to read it—even in the case of the student who aims at complete mastery (of reading, writing, and speech)" (p. 5). The main justifications for this were the lack of substantial opportunity for spoken input in a foreign language situation, and the predominant need for the reading skill to access internationally available knowledge through English.

In the late 1970s and early 1980s, several writers advocated delaying speaking until learners had built up substantial knowledge of the language through mainly listening input (Nord, 1980). This was called "the comprehension approach" to language learning (Winitz, 1981). The title of Gary and Gary's (1981) article "Caution: talking may be dangerous for your linguistic health" indicates one of the justifications for such an approach, namely that if production is required too early, errors will be made and these errors could persist. By building up substantial receptive knowledge of the language system before learners have to produce, such errors could be avoided.

Krashen's (1985) input theory took a somewhat similar stance. That is, what is needed particularly in initial language learning is large quantities of comprehensible input that allows learners to gradually develop their knowledge of the language system.

While it makes good sense for learners to have large quantities of input at the right level for them, and there is evidence to show the beneficial effects of input for language learning (Elley & Mangub-hai, 1981), input alone is not sufficient. Swain (2005) has argued for the importance of output in language learning and her ideas will be looked at later in this chapter.

The position taken in this chapter is that there needs to be a balance of opportunities for learning across the four strands of meaning-focused input, meaning-focused output, language-focused learning, and fluency development (Nation, 2007). Thus a well-planned speaking course will build on learning through meaning-focused input, will provide substantial opportunities for meaning-focused output through speaking, will give deliberate attention to pronunciation, the learning of vocabulary and multiword units, handling discourse, and feedback on errors, and will develop fluency in speaking. We will look at each of these four strands in this chapter. Let us look first at the contribution of learning through input to developing the speaking skill.

Learning through Listening

The research on vocabulary learning through listening is still rather limited. A study by Elley (1989), which used stories repeated three times, showed that vocabulary learning was considerably increased by the teacher briefly noting words on the blackboard or by providing quick definitions or illustrations for the words. This suggests that in the context of a meaning-focused task, deliberately focused attention can yield useful results. Webb and Rodgers (2009a, 2009b) have carried out corpus-based studies of movies and television programmes to look at the opportunities for vocabulary learning, considering the vocabulary knowledge needed to cope with movies and television programmes, and the repetition of new vocabulary. They conclude that a vocabulary of around 6,000 words is needed to gain close to 98% coverage and that there are opportunities for learning through repeated meetings, particularly if several movies or television programmes are viewed.

Often foreign language learners have a very large reading vocabulary but they are less skilful at listening. This would mean that an extensive listening programme that allows them to listen to material containing familiar items may be useful in making the bridge between reading proficiency and listening proficiency.

If listening is intended to improve discourse skills in speaking, then focused listening with a very short list of things to observe could be a very useful way of training learners to listen like a speaker. Swain (2005) argues that pushing learners to speak can change the way in which they listen. Having to speak helps them to notice the gaps in their knowledge and these gaps may be filled through focused listening.

Learning through Pushed Speaking Output

Pushed output occurs when learners have to produce spoken language in tasks that they are not completely familiar with. That is, "pushed" means having to perform beyond their normal comfort level. There are several features of tasks that can result in pushed output.

First, learners may need to speak on topics that are not completely familiar to them. In speaking courses it is well worth planning a range of topics that learners will need to speak about, in order to make sure that they cover what needs to be covered, and that they have the opportunity to be pushed. The difficulty of topics is related to learners' previous experience and knowledge of the content matter of the topics. Previous content work can help support speaking tasks, and linked skills activities, where, for example, learners read about a topic, write notes about it, and then speak about it. This can provide useful support for speaking as learners deal with new topics.

Second, learners may need to use different text types in their speaking. Biber's (1989) research shows that there is a range of different text types that are distinguished from each other on the basis of the grammatical features and kinds of vocabulary that occur in the texts. Covering a range of text types results in learners meeting a range of different grammatical features and vocabulary. The biggest distinction in text types for speaking will be between formal prepared talks and informal interaction. Formal prepared talks typically involve the use of long turns, non-narrative subject matter and transactional speech which conveys important information (Brown, 1981).

Third, learners output can be pushed by the performance conditions under which they have to talk. Having time for preparation can affect the performance of a task (Ortega, 1999). Research on the effect of preparation typically shows that it can result in improvements in fluency and grammatical complexity, but seems to have unpredictable effects on accuracy. Repetition of a task is a kind of preparation. That is, by having to perform the task several times, learners can improve their performance. The early presentations can be seen as a form of preparation for the final presentation. We will look at this phenomenon more closely when we look at developing speaking fluency. Yuan and Ellis (2003) distinguish between on-line planning and pre-talk planning. On-line planning occurs when the learner is able to make planning decisions during the talk. This is helped, of course, by not having to deliver the talk under time pressure. On-line planning can have positive effects on grammatical accuracy. Another factor that can be included under performance conditions is the presence of support during the talk. This support can be in the form of written notes, pictures and guiding questions. Research by Joe (1998) showed that the presence of the written text during a retelling task resulted in richer vocabulary use but less creative use of that vocabulary. Retelling without the written text resulted in less use of the target vocabulary but more creative use of the vocabulary that was used.

So far we have looked at features that mainly apply to formal speaking, particularly monologues. Being able to sustain a long turn is an important speaking skill and one that deserves classroom practice. Planning for a formal talk can involve a group planning activity where learners in the group suggest ideas and help the speaker to organise them. It may also involve using a standard rhetorical framework for a talk such as setting up a range of points that will be attacked one by one, or by having several main points that each have their own examples. A useful way to practice such talks is to use the pyramid procedure (Jordan, 1990). In this procedure, the learner prepares the talk individually and then delivers the talk to a partner. Then the talk is given to a small group of perhaps four people. After that it is delivered to the whole class. The pyramid procedure involves the movement from individual to pair to group to the whole class.

Pushed output is not confined to formal speaking, but formal speaking provides very useful conditions to make pushed output manageable. Let us now look at how learners can be pushed to speak in interactive activities.

Interactive Speaking

Most often speaking is an interactive activity. That is, we speak with others and take account of them in our speaking by suiting our output to them, and by acknowledging their input and seeking clarification of what they say. This has two major effects—it strengthens relationships between the people involved in speaking so that they can more readily communicate with each other, and it provides opportunities for language development to occur, both for the listener and the speaker.

Here is part of a transcript of learners doing a task that involves exploring the meaning of the word *registration* (Nation & Hamilton-Jenkins, 2000, p. 17).

S12   bus driver? I don't think so
S10   bus driver because it is ...

S9   if you don't have a licence how can you drive a bus, the police will catch me
(The others agree)

S11   I see so we need **registoration**

S12   … so bus driver also need **reg … registration** because of competence so at first I think teacher, doctor, and lawyer is a very specific occupation so um it um at first they have to go to the university and polytech so they need require **registration** so ah in my opinion er I bus driver … if we want to be bus driver only we have ah licence and then we can ah get as a driver so I don't forget **registration** so I mistaked ah Japanese guess

S10   maybe it is not **registration**, maybe it is not **registration**, I think maybe it is only bus driver licence …

     … maybe **registration** is just like a list where you can find some name like doctor.

Notice in the conversation how learners are taking account of each other by asking questions, and by agreeing with others, and by taking up points that others have raised. Sometimes the agreement is marked by phrases like "I see". In the following transcript, we can see learners directly negotiating the meaning of a word:

S1   What means enclosure? Do you know?

S3   Close ah-   should be filled

S2   No I don't know enclos- enclosed

S1   Filled what means fill? Oh oh all enclosed, I think that all enclosed that means enclosed

S2   Fill

S3   Filled, filled

S2   Ohh

S1   Every every area yes should be filled

This negotiation may eventually result in the learners gaining some knowledge about the new word, *enclosure*. Since such negotiation is very effective in expanding learners' vocabulary knowledge, it has been a considerable focus of research for the development of knowledge of the grammar of language. Long (1996, p. 454) suggests

> tasks that stimulate negotiation for meaning may turn out to be one among several useful language-learning situations, in or out of classrooms, for they may be one of the easiest ways to facilitate a learner's focus on form without losing sight of a lesson's (or conversation's) predominant focus on meaning.

The way the tasks are designed can have a major effect on the type and amount of negotiation that occurs. Typically, split information tasks (two-way tasks where each learner has unique information) result in a great deal of negotiation. However, negotiation can occur for a variety of reasons and only some of these result in language learning. Newton (1995) found that using cooperative tasks, where learners have the same access to the same source of information, was more likely to result in the negotiation of the meanings of words.

Negotiation however does not just help language learning through the clarification of grammatical features and vocabulary items. It also has the major effect of making input comprehensible. This allows learners not only to understand the content of what they hear but also to learn language features incidentally that may not be explicitly negotiated in the input. Because negotiation can only focus on a very small proportion of the features in input, it is likely that most language learning from spoken input occurs through the incidental meeting of items in comprehensible contexts.

There are several ways in which spoken input can be made comprehensible. First, negotiation can be increased by having learners work in pairs rather than in small groups (Fotos & Ellis, 1991). Second, learners can receive training and practice in negotiation. This training can involve learning the phrases and signals that are needed when negotiating (this can be done with a rather small group of items such as *What?*, *Pardon?*, *They what?*), and can involve the deliberate study of interactions (Clennell, 1999). Third, learners can take part in speaking activities where understanding is particularly important in achieving the goal of the activity. Such activities include listen and do activities where one learner is given instructions about constructing an object from blocks or Lego parts, or has to draw a picture. Interactive dictation activities are also very effective in encouraging learners to seek clarification. Folse (1991) describes an activity where learners dictate to someone writing on the blackboard, but they cannot see what the person is writing because they are facing the other way. Fourth, learners can do activities where they bring substantial amounts of background knowledge to the activity. One way of arranging this is to set up activities involving expert groups and family groups. This works particularly well where learners are working on split information tasks. If the learners are working in pairs to find the differences in two pictures, then all the learners who have picture A form groups to practice improving their description of that picture. Similarly, learners who have picture B form groups to improve their description of their picture. After this expert group practice, they then form family groups (made up of one learner from the A group and one learner from the B group) to do the comparison task. The practice in the expert groups makes the performance in the family groups much more effective. Nation and Newton (2009) describe a range of tasks to encourage learning from input.

Deliberate Language-Focused Learning

Pronunciation

Although speaking is a meaning-focused activity, there is value in giving deliberate attention to a range of language features to improve the quality of spoken output. Most obvious of these is pronunciation. At times the deliberate teaching of pronunciation has fallen out of favour, but this has been largely the result of a reaction against far too much time being spent on deliberate learning to the detriment of meaning-focused activities. This unfavourable attitude has also been the result of pronunciation teachers taking too narrow a view of what is included in pronunciation. Deliberate attention to pronunciation can have positive effects (Trofimovich & Gatbonton, 2006), but it is important to see that giving deliberate attention to pronunciation is only one of a wide range of factors affecting pronunciation improvement.

There has been continuing debate on the goals and models for second language learners' pronunciation. Should the goal be a native speaker model or a non-native speaker model (Levis, 2005)? Should the model be British, American or a regional pronunciation of English? What should the criteria be for defining an acceptable pronunciation (Jenkins, 2002)? In many situations the answers to these questions are decided by factors that are beyond the control of the classroom teacher. If English is used outside the school, as in second language learning situations, then that model of English is likely to become the one determining learners' pronunciation. In a foreign language learning situation, political and economic alignments are likely to have a strong effect on the model chosen as the goal.

Research has shown that pronunciation is likely to be affected by the age at which the learner begins learning the language, the learner's first language, the attitude of the learner towards pronunciation, and the conditions in the classroom under which the learner learns the language. Let us look briefly at each of these factors in turn.

If a learner begins study of a language after the age of around 11, it is highly likely that they will speak that language with a foreign accent (Tahta, Wood & Lowenthal, 1981). There have been several attempts to explain why younger learners seem to achieve a better pronunciation than older learners. One explanation is that there are physical changes in the brain of the learner at a certain age that then make it difficult for the learner to acquire a good pronunciation. Teachers are reluctant to accept this explanation, and the evidence to support this physical explanation is not strong. A second kind of explanation is more cognitive. The cognitive explanation argues that as knowledge of the first language becomes more strongly established, it becomes a filter that affects observation and production of the second language (Flege, 1981). Thus, the older the learner is, the more strongly established the first language is likely to be, and thus the more difficult it will be to acquire a good pronunciation of the second language. A strong factor supporting this explanation is that the accent of a foreign speaker of the language is clearly affected by their first language. A third kind of explanation is psychological. This explanation argues that as we get older we become more protective of our personalities. Our pronunciation is a particularly sensitive part of our personality because it is a particularly noticeable part of the way with which we display our knowledge of a language. Research by Guiora, Beit-Hallami, Brannon, Dull and Scovel (1972) has shown that if we are made more relaxed, for example by the drinking of alcohol or through the use of a relaxing drug, then the quality of our pronunciation improves. Presumably, these relaxants lower the psychological barrier that we have erected to protect our personalities.

There is a very long history of contrastive analysis comparing the sound systems of the learner's first language and the target language. The basic premise behind early contrastive analysis was that the similarities will make learning easier and the differences will be sources of difficulty. Subsequent research showed that the picture was more complicated than this (Hammerly, 1982). It seems that small differences at the allophonic level are likely to be a source of greater difficulty than the presence of a sound in the second language that does not exist in the first.

A learner's attitude to pronunciation can affect the likelihood of gaining a good pronunciation (Purcell & Suter, 1980). Particularly important among the factors affecting attitude are learners' feelings toward speakers of the target language, the number of years that they had lived in an English-speaking country and lived with native speakers, and the strength of the learner's desire to have a good pronunciation. Several of these factors are clearly motivational and thus could be affected by a classroom teacher.

The way in which pronunciation is taught and practised in the classroom can also have a major effect on learning. It seems to be easier to learn a new sound in a word that has no previous associations for a learner, than to learn it as part of a known word. This effect is even stronger when doing remedial work on pronunciation errors. It is better to initially practise a difficult sound in nonsense words than to work on it in words that have previously been mispronounced. The written form of a word can also affect its pronunciation. If the spelling system of the language does not provide a regular match with the spoken form, then this can be a distraction for the learners. Where it does provide a match however, it can have a positive effect (Dickerson, 1990). Similarly, being able to observe mouth and tongue position may have positive effects on correcting pronunciation.

It is important to remember that the deliberate teaching of pronunciation is just one part of the language-focused learning strand of a course. The language-focused learning strand of a speaking course also needs to focus on the learning of vocabulary and multiword units, on control of the grammatical features of the language and on discourse strategies. This means that deliberate attention to pronunciation should not occupy a large amount of time in the classroom, but it does deserve some time.

Vocabulary

The minimum productive vocabulary size needed for largely unpredictable speaking activities is likely to be around 1,200 words (West, 1960, pp. 95–134). West checked that his minimum adequate speech vocabulary was "reasonably self-contained" by writing four plays using it, and by checking it against his defining vocabulary and seeing if the words not in the minimum adequate speech vocabulary could be replaced by items within the speaking vocabulary. It seems that almost all the words in the minimum adequate speech vocabulary were in his 2,000 word general service list.

This is a relatively small vocabulary and the words that it contains could be learnt fairly quickly. However, although vocabulary is, of course, an essential element of any language use, the words have to be put together in the right ways. A good step towards doing this involves gaining familiarity with the high-frequency multiword groups of the language. Shin (2007) and Shin and Nation (2008) provide lists of the most frequent multiword units in spoken language that are grammatically well structured, that is, that can exist as a whole sentence or as a complete part of a sentence.

Another source of immediately usable words and multiword units is Nation and Crabbe's (1991) survival vocabulary for foreign travel. This is a list of 120 words and phrases that are very useful when visiting another country as a tourist. The list has been tested in several different countries and is available in several different languages. It can be learned in about four hours of spaced study.

Grammar

Biber and Conrad (in press) have shown that the grammatical constructions used in the speech are typically very different from those that are used in written language. Complexity in speech is largely clausal, that is, speech contains a relatively large number of coordinated, noun and adverbial clauses. Complexity in written language on the other hand is largely phrasal, that is, written language contains a relatively large number of complex noun groups. The nature of complexity in spoken language is a direct result of the conditions under which spoken language is produced. The most important of these conditions is, of course, the time constraint on spoken language production. The nature of complexity in written English has changed over the past few centuries, and is likely to change in the future. Because the conditions under which spoken language is produced are very unlikely to change, it is very unlikely that the grammatical nature of spoken language will change very much.

This has several implications for language teaching and learning. First, it means that written language, especially formal written language, does not provide good grammatical models for spoken language. Second, it means that any direct teaching and instruction in grammar for spoken use should focus on clausal rather than phrasal constructions. Here are some typical clausal constructions that occur frequently in spoken English:

- What I mean to say is …
- I think that's a load of rubbish.
- She said that it wasn't going to happen.
- Do whatever you like!

Sociolinguistic Competence

Part of learning to speak another language involves learning how to say things and do things in appropriate ways. What do people say when they meet each other for the first time? How do you keep a conversation going? How do you signal to someone that you don't want to continue a conversation with them? How do you end a phone call? What do you say when someone asks you if you want a cup of tea?

The ways of dealing with these situations differ from language to language, and learning how to deal with them is an important part of learning a language. A particular useful strategy for learners to gain control of in the early stages of speaking is learning how to keep a conversation going.

Holmes and Brown (1976) describe a range of simple ways in which learners can be helped to manage conversation. For example, a useful way of keeping a conversation going is to answer questions with a short answer plus some extra related information. The extra information indicates a willingness to keep speaking, as well as providing something to keep talking about. When this simple strategy of giving a short answer with extra information has been well practised, a speaker can become very adept at using the extra information to steer the conversation towards topics that they are familiar with and want to talk about.

A great deal of sociolinguistic competence can be picked up through the careful observation of conversations if learners are aware of gaps in their own competence. For some very important language uses however, there is value in directly learning what to do.

Developing Fluency in Speaking

Speaking occurs under time constraints and thus it is very important that learners quickly become fluent in using the language items that they already know. For example, knowing the numbers in another language is of little value in spoken use unless these numbers can be accessed fluently. Thus, not only do the numbers need to be learnt, they also need to be practised until they can be quickly recognised when they are heard and quickly produced when they are needed. This is why the fourth strand of a well-balanced language course is fluency development.

Research on spoken fluency development has shown that the traditional separation between fluency and accuracy activities may not be well justified. The 4/3/2 activity involves learners working in pairs where one learner presents a talk to his/her partner with a four-minute time limit. They then change partners and the same speaker presents the same talk to a new partner with a three-minute time limit. They change partners again and the same speaker presents the talk for a third time to a new partner with a two-minute time limit. Arevart and Nation (1991) when doing research on this activity found that when comparing the four-minute talk with the two-minute talk, there was an increase in speaking speed as measured in words per minute, a decrease in the number of hesitations per hundred words, a reduction in the number of grammatical errors in repeated parts of the talk and an increase in the number of complex sentences in the two-minute talk. What is striking about this is that increases in fluency (as measured by speed and hesitations) were accompanied by positive changes in accuracy and grammatical complexity.

These changes fit with theories of fluency development (Schmidt, 1992), many of which see increases in speed triggering and resulting from changes in the organisation of the material being worked with. Palmer (1925) considered that the one of the fastest ways to develop fluency in the speaking skill was to memorise useful sentences and phrases. His fundamental guiding principle for a beginner learning to speak another language was—*Memorize perfectly the largest number of common and useful word groups!* Palmer (1933) produced a substantial list of these word groups and suggested the following: "Each [collocation] ... must or should be learnt, or is best or most conveniently learnt as an integral whole or independent entity, rather than by the process of piecing together their component parts" (Palmer, 1933, p. 4). He used the term *collocation* to describe these word groups and the term was later picked up by others.

Recent research on the nature of figuratives and collocations, however, shows that there is value in understanding how the parts of collocations fit together (Boers, Eyckmans & Stengers, 2007). Understanding the parts does help the learning of the whole, largely because collocations are not arbitrary occurrences of words, but are made up of words that occur together because their meanings relate to each other, and their use within the collocation is consistent with their normal use within the language. The use of collocations in speech has a positive effect on how others view the speaker's proficiency (Boers, Eyckmans, Kappel, Stengers & Demecheleer, 2006).

It is likely that fluency practice needs to be skill specific. That is, that speaking fluency requires speaking fluency practice, and reading fluency requires reading fluency practice. There is undoubtedly some transfer of fluency between the skills of listening, speaking, reading and writing, and it is likely that there will be the greatest transfer from productive to receptive use within the same mode, such as between the productive skill of speaking and the receptive skill of listening.

Fluency development requires the following conditions. First, the material worked with must be very familiar to the learners. That is, there should be no unfamiliar vocabulary or grammatical constructions or discourse features within the task. Second, the focus of the activity should be on conveying messages. The tasks should be communicative tasks. Third, there should be some pressure or encouragement to perform at a faster than usual speed. In the 4/3/2 activity briefly described above, the decreasing time available for each delivery of the talk provides an encouragement to speak faster. Fourth, there should be quantity of practice. Fluency development needs to make up a substantial proportion of the course. Fluency development requires practice and repetition, and the greater the amount of these, the greater the amount of fluency development.

The simplest spoken fluency development activities involve repetition. For example, developing fluency in the use of greetings or numbers can be done by firstly developing listening fluency where the teacher says a number and the learners quickly point to it. Once they become skilful at this, the roles can switch with the learners saying the numbers and the teacher pointing to them. This work can also be done very effectively in pairs in large classes. Repeated talks (such as 4/3/2), prepared talks, the say it activity, the best recording, and ask and answer are all very effective activities for developing spoken fluency (Nation & Newton, 2009).

Testing Speaking

The most researched way of testing speaking is through interviews and the use of scoring scales. Typically the interviews followed a set series of questions but allow for some flexibility. The scoring scales usually measure language use features such as fluency, intelligibility, grammatical accuracy and richness of vocabulary, with a scale for overall impression. It is not easy to get consistent agreement between raters (van Moere, 2006).

A more efficient way of testing speaking is to use a group oral exam. This involves a group of four or five people discussing a topic and observers grade each learner using a set of scales (Hilsdon, 1991). Instead of discussions there is a variety of tasks that can be used. The learners can do split information tasks where each learner has information that the other does not have but needs to complete the task, or the task could be a problem-solving task or a role-play. The difficulty with such tasks is that each learner's performance is to some degree dependent on the performance of others in the group (Norton, 2005).

There are methods of measuring speaking proficiency that do not involve the learners speaking. Obviously these lack face validity, but in some cases they have been shown to correlate well with performance measures of speaking. One example is conversational cloze (Brown, 1983). In this measure a conversation between native speakers is recorded and transcribed. It is turned into a cloze test by omitting every seventh word and leaving a space. The learners have to write in the missing words as in a normal cloze test. While such tests might be very practical in terms of saving time in administration and scoring, there are unlikely to be widely accepted in the place of performance tests.

Future Directions

A great deal of research on speaking has looked at the development of grammatical features through negotiation and interaction. With a few notable exceptions (Ellis, Tanaka & Yamazaki, 1994; Ellis &

He, 1999; Ellis & Heimbach, 1997; Newton, 1995), there has been a lack of research on vocabulary growth through speaking. This is surprising in that it would seem to be easier to measure growth in vocabulary knowledge with some degree of certainty than growth in the control of grammatical features. In addition, recent research (Elgort, 2007) has shown that, for vocabulary, explicit knowledge is likely to be accompanied by implicit knowledge, which does not seem to be true of grammatical knowledge. It would be good to see more research on how speaking activities can result in vocabulary growth.

Research on task-based learning has looked at a variety of variables affecting learning from speaking. These include the source of information (one-way versus two-way tasks), group size, topic and the proficiency levels of the participants. Recent developments in technique analysis (Laufer & Hulstijn, 2001) have suggested other factors, although these have largely been the focus of research on deliberate learning. Exploring these factors and others in spoken interaction will enrich our understanding of second language acquisition and provide guidelines for task design.

There is still a lack of substantial research on spoken fluency development. The research on the 4/3/2 activity (Nation, 1989) indicates how some of this might be done. As well as looking at the range of changes that occur as fluency develops, there is a need to look at how spoken fluency activities result in changes to speaking outside of the speaking course (Lennon, 1990).

There are commercially available spoken tests that are scored by a computer and that typically involve answering questions that the computer presents. There is a strong possibility that such tests will be very useful practical screening tests as a first step towards more time-consuming tests in a testing programme.

The movement towards more communicative language teaching has had very positive effects on the teaching and testing of speaking. In addition, research in sociolinguistics has helped broaden teachers' and researchers' views of the speaking skill. It is highly likely that future research will continue to enrich these views, and this can only be good news for language learners.

References

Arevart, S., & Nation, I. S. P. (1991). Fluency improvement in a second language. *RELC Journal, 22*(1), 84–94.

Biber, D. (1989). A typology of English texts. *Linguistics, 27*, 3–43.

Biber, D., & Conrad, S. (in press). *Register and genre variation*. Cambridge: Cambridge University Press.

Boers, F., Eyckmans, J. & Stengers, H. (2007). Presenting figurative idioms with a touch of etymology: More than mere mnemonics? *Language Teaching Research, 11*(1), 43–62.

Boers, F., Eyckmans, J., Kappel, J., Stengers, H. & Demecheleer, M. (2006). Formulaic sequences and perceived oral proficiency: Putting the lexical approach to the test. *Language Teaching Research, 10*(3), 245–261.

Brown, D. (1983). Conversational cloze tests and conversational ability. *ELT Journal, 37*(2), 158–161.

Brown, G. (1981). Teaching the spoken language. *Studia Linguistica, 35*(1–2), 166–182.

Clennell, C. (1999). Promoting pragmatic awareness and spoken discourse skills with EAP classes. *ELT Journal, 53*(2), 83–91.

Dickerson, W. B. (1990). Morphology via orthography: A visual approach to oral decisions. *Applied Linguistics, 11*(3), 238–252.

Elgort, I. (2007). The role of intentional decontextualised learning in second language vocabulary acquisition: Evidence from primed lexical decision tasks with advanced bilinguals. PhD thesis, Victoria University of Wellington, Wellington.

Elley, W. B. (1989). Vocabulary acquisition from listening to stories. *Reading Research Quarterly, 24*(2), 174–187.

Elley, W. B., & Mangubhai, F. (1981). *The Impact of a Book Flood in Fiji Primary Schools*. Wellington: NZCER.

Ellis, R., & He, X. (1999). The roles of modified input and output in the incidental acquisition of word meanings. *Studies in Second Language Acquisition, 21*, 285–301.

Ellis, R., & Heimbach, R. (1997). Bugs and birds: Children's acquisition of second language vocabulary through interaction. *System, 25*(2), 247–259.

Ellis, R., Tanaka, Y. & Yamazaki, A. (1994). Classroom interaction, comprehension and the acquisition of L2 word meanings. *Language Learning, 44*(3), 449–491.

Flege, J. E. (1981). The phonological basis of foreign accent: A hypothesis. *TESOL Quarterly, 15*(4), 443–455.

Folse, K. (1991). Could you repeat that? An innovative way of getting students to speak up. *TESL Reporter, 24*(2), 23–25.

Fotos, S., & Ellis, R. (1991). Communicating about grammar: a task-based approach. *TESOL Quarterly, 25*(4), 605–628.

Gary, J. D., & Gary, N. G. (1981). Caution: talking may be dangerous for your linguistic health. *IRAL, 19*(1), 1–13.

Guiora, A. Z., Beit-Hallami, B., Brannon, R. C. L., Dull, C. Y. & Scovel, T. (1972). The effects of experimentally induced changes in ego states on pronunciation ability in a second language: An exploratory study. *Comprehensive Psychiatry, 13*, 421–428.

Hammerly, H. (1982). Contrastive phonology and error analysis. *IRAL, 20*(1), 17–32.

Hilsdon, J. (1991). The group oral exam: Advantages and limitations. In J. C. Alderson & B. North (Eds.), *Language testing in the 1990s: The communicative legacy* (pp. 189–197). London: Macmillan.

Holmes, J., & Brown, D. F. (1976). Developing sociolinguistic competence in a second language. *TESOL Quarterly, 10*(4), 423–431.

Jenkins, J. (2002). A sociolinguistically based, empirically researched pronunciation syllabus for English as an international language. *Applied Linguistics, 23*(1), 83–103.

Joe, A. (1998). What effects do text-based tasks promoting generation have on incidental vocabulary acquisition? *Applied Linguistics, 19*, 357–377.

Jordan, R. R. (1990). Pyramid discussions. *ELT Journal, 44*(1), 46–54.

Krashen, S. D. (1985). *The input hypothesis: Issues and implications.* London: Longman.

Laufer, B., & Hulstijn, J. (2001). Incidental vocabulary acquisition in a second language: The construct of task-induced involvement. *Applied Linguistics, 22*(1), 1–26.

Lennon, P. (1990). Investigating fluency in EFL: A quantitative approach. *Language Learning, 40*(3), 387–417.

Levis, J. (2005). Changing contexts and shifting paradigms in pronunciation teaching. *TESOL Quarterly, 39*(3), 369–377.

Long, M. H. (1996). The role of the linguistics environment in second language acquisition. In W. C. Ritchie & T. K. Bhatia (Eds.), *Handbook of language acquisition* (Vol. 2: Second language acquisition) (pp. 413–468). New York: Academic Press.

Nation, I. S. P. (1989). Improving speaking fluency. *System, 17*(3), 377–384.

Nation, I. S. P. (2007). The four strands. *Innovation in Language Learning and Teaching, 1*(1), 1–12.

Nation, P., & Crabbe, D. (1991). A survival language learning syllabus for foreign travel. *System, 19*(3), 191–201.

Nation, I. S. P., & Hamilton-Jenkins, A. (2000). Using communicative tasks to teach vocabulary. *Guidelines, 22*(2), 15–19.

Nation, I. S. P. and Newton, J. (2009). *Teaching ESL/EFL listening and speaking.* New York: Routledge.

Newton, J. (1995). Task-based interaction and incidental vocabulary learning: A case study. *Second Language Research, 11*(2), 159–177.

Nord, J. R. (1980). Developing listening fluency before speaking: An alternative paradigm. *System, 8*(1), 1–22.

Norton, J. (2005). The paired format in the Cambridge Speaking Tests. *ELT Journal, 59*(4), 287–297.

Ortega, L. (1999). Planning and focus on form in L2 oral performance. *SSLA, 21*(1), 109–148.

Palmer, H. (1925). Conversation. In R. C. Smith (Ed.) (1999). *The writings of Harold E. Palmer: An overview* (pp. 185–191). Tokyo: Hon-no-Tomosha.

Palmer, H. E. (1933). *Second interim report on English collocations.* Tokyo: Kaitakusha.

Purcell, E. T., & Suter, R. W. (1980). Predictors of pronunciation accuracy: A re-examination. *Language Learning, 30*(2), 271–287.

Schmidt, R. W. (1992). Psychological mechanisms underlying second language fluency. *SSLA, 14*, 357–385.

Shin, D. (2007). The high frequency collocations of spoken and written English. *English Teaching, 62*(1), 199–218.

Shin, D., & Nation, P. (2008). Beyond single words: The most frequent collocations in spoken English. *ELT Journal, 62*(4), 339–357.

Swain, M. (2005). The output hypothesis: Theory and research. In E. Hinkel (Ed.), *Handbook of research in second language teaching and learning* (pp. 471–483). Mahwah, NJ: Lawrence Erlbaum Associates.

Tahta, S., Wood, M. & Lowenthal, K. (1981). Age changes in the ability to replicate foreign pronunciation and intonation. *Language and Speech, 24*(4), 363–372.

Trofimovich, P., & Gatbonton, E. (2006). Repetition and focus on form in processing L2 Spanish words: Implications for pronunciation instruction. *The Modern Language Journal, 90*(4), 519–535.

van Moere, A. (2006). Validity evidence in a university group oral test. *Language Testing, 23*(4), 411–440.

Webb, S., & Rodgers, M. P. H. (2009a). The vocabulary demands of television programs. *Language Learning, 59*(2), 335–366.

Webb, S., & Rodgers, M. P. H. (2009b). The lexical coverage of movies. *Applied Linguistics, 30*(3), 407–427. Advance Access published on March 26, 2009.

West, M. (1955). *Learning to read a foreign language* (2nd ed.). London: Longman.

West, M. (1960). *Teaching English in difficult circumstances.* London: Longman.

Winitz, H. (Ed.) (1981). *The comprehension approach to foreign language instruction.* Rowley, MA: Newbury House.

Yuan, F., & Ellis, R. (2003). The effects of pre-task planning and on-line planning on fluency, complexity and accuracy in L2 monologic oral production. *Applied Linguistics, 24*(1), 1–27.

28
Second Language Listening
Presage, Process, Product, and Pedagogy

Larry Vandergrift

Listening is perhaps the most essential skill for second/foreign (L2) language learning; it internalizes the rules of language and facilitates the emergence of other language skills (e.g., Dunkel, 1991; Rost, 2002; Vandergrift, 2007). Listening is also a critical part of everyday life; we spend about 45% of our waking hours listening (Lee & Hatesohl, 1993).

Listening is a particularly complex cognitive skill. It is perceived as the most difficult skill to learn because of its temporal and implicit nature (Graham, 2006). Listeners must process speech while simultaneously attending to new input at a speed controlled by the speaker; process input that can be characterized by phonological vagaries (enunciation, pronunciation and accent); parse the input into meaningful units where, unlike in reading, word boundaries are often hard to determine; and, inhibit the natural compulsion to apply native language (L1) segmentation procedures to a rhythmically different language (Cutler, 2001). This is no small feat. Helping learners to become aware of and regulate these processes can improve their listening comprehension and enhance overall L2 learning success.

This chapter will examine L2 listening using a model recently exploited by Imhof and Janusik (2006) to frame the process of oral information processing and listening. This model, based on a systems model of study processes (Biggs, 1999), identifies three interdependent factors: presage (individual and context variables), process and product. This is a useful heuristic for exploring the listening construct since it is an integrated system where presage variables (listener, task and context) affect the quality of the listening process and resulting product (comprehension or lack of it). Vice versa, the product (e.g., miscomprehension) can affect presage variables (e.g., motivation) and the listener's efforts at processing subsequent input. This model will frame this chapter's examination of the basic principles and recent research in L2 listening and their implications for pedagogy. A discussion of the processes underlying L2 listening comprehension will be followed by an examination of the research related to the presage variables that affect the quality of the comprehension process and the product of listening, i.e., the variables that characterize skilled listeners. After a brief discussion related to the product of listening, the chapter will conclude with pedagogical implications. It is argued that helping language learners develop a greater awareness of the process of listening can help them better regulate the listening process and become more successful listeners.

Process

Listening comprehension is an active process of meaning construction in which listeners, based on their purpose for listening, attend to and process aural and relevant visual input, automatically in real time, in order to understand what is unequivocally stated and to make all necessary inferences implied in the input (Buck, 2001).

Top-Down and Bottom-Up Processing

Fundamental to an understanding of comprehension processes is the distinction between bottom-up and top-down processing, the types of knowledge each process applies to the input and the interaction between these processes (Vandergrift, 2004). Bottom-up processing involves decoding, i.e., segmenting the sound stream into meaningful units. Listeners who decode in a bottom-up manner construct meaning by accretion, gradually combining increasingly larger units of meaning from the phoneme-level up to discourse-level features. On the other hand, top-down processing involves the application of context and prior knowledge to build a conceptual framework for interpretation purposes. Listeners use initial cues (linguistic or other) in the input or the context of the listening act to activate a conceptual framework for interpreting the input, much of which may be unintelligible to them. The different types of knowledge listeners can apply to this interpretation process include experiential, cultural, textual, linguistic and pragmatic knowledge. Top-down and bottom-up processes rarely operate independently. Linguistic knowledge gleaned from the decoding process and prior knowledge applied from the interpretation process interact in parallel fashion as listeners create a mental representation of what they have heard (Hulstijn, 2003). Research in L1 speech perception provides evidence for these processes and their interactive nature, particularly how information from top-down processing drives and constrains interpretation (Davis & Johnsrude, 2007).

While successful listening comprehension involves a judicious interplay between the two processes, the degree to which listeners use one process more than the other will depend on the purpose for listening, learner characteristics (e.g., language proficiency) and the context of the listening event. A listener who needs to verify a specific detail, the date before an event for example, will engage in more bottom-up processing than a listener who is interested in obtaining an overview of what happened at that particular event.

Perception, Parsing, and Utilization

Another representation of listening, useful for gaining greater insight into how listeners construct meaning while bottom-up and top-down processing occurs, is Anderson's (1995) differentiation of listening comprehension into three interconnected phases: perceptual processing (perception), parsing and utilization. Although this representation may suggest a sequence, the phases have a two-way relationship with each other. The interactive and integrated nature of the processes is reflected in the arrows between the component processes illustrated in Figure 28.1.

During the perception phase, listeners recognize sound categories of the language, pauses and acoustic emphases in the speech they hear and hold these briefly in working memory (WM). Perception involves primarily the bottom-up dimension of listening. Listeners encode incoming speech by (1) attending to the text over against to the exclusion other sounds in the environment; (2) noting similarities, pauses and acoustic emphases in the sound stream relevant to a particular language; and then (3) grouping these according to the categories of the identified language. This is the initial stage in the word segmentation process. Difficulties reported by L2 listeners during this stage include: (1) not recognizing words; (2) neglecting what follows; (3) not chunking the stream of speech; (4) missing the beginning;

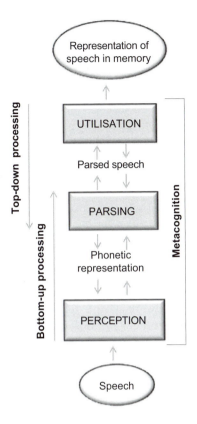

Figure 28.1 Cognitive processing in L2 listening comprehension

Source: Based on Anderson (1995).

and (5) concentration problems (Goh, 2000). A phonetic representation of what listeners are able to retain is passed on to the parser for further processing.

Development of word segmentation skills is a major challenge faced by L2 listeners (Cutler, 2001). Unlike readers, listeners do not have the luxury of spaces to help them determine word boundaries. Listeners must parse the sound stream into meaningful units and, due to stress patterns, elisions and reduced forms, word boundaries are often difficult to determine. Moreover, even if they can recognize individual words, listeners may not always recognize those same words in connected speech (Broersma & Cutler, 2008). Furthermore, word segmentation skills are language-specific, acquired early in life, and so solidly engrained in the listener's processing system that they are involuntarily applied when listening to a non-native language.

During the parsing phase (bottom-up processing that can be influenced by top-down processes), listeners segment what was retained in WM and also begin to activate potential word candidates (Rost, 2005). Listeners retrieve word candidates from long-term memory (LTM)-based cues such as word onset, likely due to the prosodic information accompanying the word (Field, 2004; Harley, 2000), or phonotactic conventions (rules that apply to the sequencing of phonemes) (Al-jasser, 2008) and create propositions in order to hold a meaning-based representation of these words in WM as new input is processed. Meaning is often the principal clue in segmentation (Sanders, Neville & Woldorff, 2002) and, as language proficiency develops, listeners can more quickly activate successful word candidates (for the context) and hold meaning in increasingly larger chunks of propositional content (Broersma & Cutler, 2008; Field, 2008a). With regard to the processing and identification of function and content words, L2 listeners appear to be more successful in identifying content words (Field, 2008b). This is not surprising, since content words carry meaning and, because of limitations of WM, L2 listeners need to selectively attend to the input. Difficulties reported by listeners during this phase include: (1) quickly forgetting what is heard; (2) an inability to form a mental representation from words heard; and (3) not understanding subsequent parts because of what was missed earlier (Goh, 2000). The parsed speech (identified words) is then sent for interpretation; however, there is likely a great deal of back and forth processing as new information is interpreted against world knowledge and integrated with what has been understood so far (co-text).

Finally, in the utilization phase, listeners relate the resulting meaningful units to information sources in LTM to interpret the intended or implied meanings and create a representation in memory of what they understood. An important characteristic of this phase, which involves top-down processing, is that listeners use information from outside the linguistic input to interpret what they have retained. Using world knowledge (different types of knowledge stored as schemata in LTM) listeners elaborate on the new information and monitor it for congruency with their previous knowledge and their developing interpretation of the text (co-text) as often as necessary within the time available. Listeners generate a conceptual framework against which to match the emerging meaning of the text or utterance and to go beyond the literal meaning of the input. This is the process underlying the cognitive strategy of elaboration (Vandergrift, 2003b). Listening comprehension then becomes a problem-solving activity where listeners reconcile linguistic input with their store of knowledge in order to solve the problem of what is meant by the speaker. Difficulties reported by listeners during this phase include (1) understanding the words but not the message; and (2) confusion because of seeming incongruences in the message (Goh, 2000).

These processes, which take place within milliseconds, involve cognitive fluency (Segalowitz, 2007), i.e., access fluidity (connecting the knowledge of the language system to meaning) and attention control (focusing and refocusing on the unfolding message in real time). Successful listening depends, obviously, on the degree to which listeners can coordinate these processes efficiently. L1 listeners do this automatically, with little conscious attention to individual words. L2 listeners, on the other hand, usually have limited language knowledge; therefore, not everything they hear may be automatically processed. Depending on their level of L2 proficiency, listeners may need to consciously focus on some of the input, using controlled processing, or learn to selectively attend to basic elements of meaning, such as content words (as noted above). Whatever listeners cannot immediately process and map onto LTM is subject to controlled processing, time permitting. Controlled (as opposed to automatic) processing requires more time and, given the limitations of WM and the speed of new incoming input, comprehension will suffer. Comprehension either breaks down or listeners may use compensatory strategies, contextual factors and any other relevant information available to them, to guess at what they did not understand.

Metacognition

The success with which listeners are able to regulate these processes to achieve comprehension depends on their awareness of these cognitive processes; that is, their metacognitive knowledge about listening (Goh, 2008). Metacognitive knowledge consists primarily of knowledge and beliefs about the task-, person- and strategy-related factors that interact during any cognitive activity (Flavell, 1979). Application of metacognitive knowledge (regulation of the cognitive processes) is a mental characteristic shared by successful learners; in fact, metacognition accounts for a relatively high percentage of variance in learner performance (Veenman, Van Hout-Walters & Afflerbach, 2006).

There is extensive evidence that learners' metacognition can directly affect the process and the outcome of their learning (Wenden, 1998; Zimmerman & Schunk, 2001), that it is positively linked to motivation and self-efficacy (Paris & Winograd, 1990; Vandergrift, 2005) and that it can help learners regulate their comprehension (Pressley, 2002). In fact, with regard to listening, Vandergrift, Goh, Mareschal and Tafaghodtari (2006) observed that about 13% of variance in listening achievement could be explained by metacognition. In sum, listeners who are aware of the cognitive processes underlying successful comprehension are better able to regulate these processes.

The interrelationships between the various components in comprehension processing are summarized and illustrated in Figure 28.1. The chapter will now move to a discussion of the presage variables that influence the quality and efficiency of L2 comprehension processes: individual listener factors and contextual factors.

Presage

Individual Listener Variables

Pragmatic Knowledge

Listeners use pragmatic knowledge when they apply information regarding a speaker's intention that goes beyond the literal meaning of an utterance (Rose & Kasper, 2001). Listeners apply pragmatic knowledge during the utilization phase of the comprehension process to make contextually informed elaborations in order to determine the speaker's implied meaning. Most research on the use of pragmatic knowledge has been conducted with reference to speech acts; however, research on the application of pragmatic knowledge to L2 comprehension is growing. The ability to activate pragmatic knowledge appears to depend on language proficiency: lower-proficiency listeners have greater difficulty processing both contextual and linguistic information for comprehending request strategies (Cook & Liddicoat, 2002). Garcia (2004) arrived at similar conclusions concerning conversational implicatures (understanding the attitude and intentions of a speaker). These differences can be explained by the limitations of WM for lower-proficiency listeners whose comprehension processes are not sufficiently automatic for them to attend to both contextual and linguistic information. Taguchi (2005) investigated pragmatic comprehension in greater depth by exploring the role of speed and accuracy in the comprehension of implied meaning. More conventional implicatures (indirect requests and refusals) appear to be more difficult and take longer to interpret than less conventional ones (indirect opinions). She also found a strong proficiency effect for accuracy of both types of implicatures but not for speed of interpretation.

Metacognitive Knowledge

Research on differences in listening strategy use (using a think-aloud methodology) has highlighted some important differences between skilled and less-skilled listeners (Goh, 2002a; O'Malley & Chamot, 1990; Vandergrift, 2003b). Skilled listeners report using about twice as many metacognitive strategies as their less-skilled counterparts, as well as greater use of comprehension monitoring and questioning elaboration (flexibility in using a combination of questions and world knowledge in interpretation during the utilization phase of the comprehension process). A qualitative analysis of the think-aloud protocols (Vandergrift, 2003b) further revealed that the skilled listeners used effective combinations of metacognitive and cognitive strategies, a finding also noted by Goh (2002a) and O'Malley, Chamot and Küpper (1989). Successful L2 listening appears to involve a skillful orchestration of metacognitive and cognitive strategies to regulate listening processes and achieve comprehension.

Less-skilled listeners, on the other hand, report greater use of on-line translation (Vandergrift, 2003b). Such an approach to listening, often fostered by an overemphasis on word-for-word understanding in listening instruction (Osada, 2001), neither allows listeners to keep up with the input nor leaves them with adequate WM resources to apply prior knowledge and construct meaning. Comprehension breaks down unless listeners also activate top-down processes through the use of compensatory strategies and other relevant available information to inference what they did not understand. L2 listeners must resist the compulsion to mentally translate if they are to become skilled listeners.

Prior Knowledge

The role of prior knowledge (e.g., Long, 1990; Macaro, Vanderplank & Graham, 2005) in successful L2 listening comprehension has long been established. Research into pre-listening activities has documented positive effects on listening performance for visuals (e.g., Ginther, 2002), advance organizers (e.g., Chung, 2002) and questions (e.g., Flowerdew & Miller, 2005). Contextualized listeners have the resources to activate prior knowledge and to develop a conceptual framework for inferencing (top-down processing). This allows them to process the linguistic input more efficiently, freeing up WM resources. Tyler (2002) found that when listeners had access to the topic through an advance organizer, there were no differences in WM consumption between L1 and L2 listeners. However, when the topic was not available, WM consumption was much higher in L2 listeners.

Although prior knowledge is important for facilitating comprehension, it can also be misleading when used inflexibly. Listener use of prior knowledge can lead to inaccurate comprehension if it is not supported by corroborating evidence as the text unfolds (Macaro et al., 2005). This underscores the importance of flexibility in the comprehension process and of continually elaborating, through a combination of questions and prior knowledge, to consider possibilities and to monitor for congruency in the interpretation process (Vandergrift, 2003b).

Other Knowledge Sources

Identifying any additional variables related to L2 listening can better elucidate the listening construct and provide empirical data to inform a model of L2 listening comprehension. Research exploring the variables that might contribute to L2 listening achievement is just emerging. Phonological memory skill contributes to growth in listening ability and vocabulary learning, particularly with children at a beginning level of language proficiency (French, 2003). Mecartty (2000) also found that vocabulary knowledge emerged as a significant predictor, explaining about 14% of L2 listening ability. Grammatical knowledge, however, failed to emerge as a predictor, explained, perhaps, by Field's (2008b) finding that L2 listeners attend to content words, not function words. In a study examining the potential contribution of L1 listening ability, Vandergrift (2006) found that L1 listening ability could account for about 14% of L2 listening ability. Current research by Vandergrift and Tafaghodtari (2009) seeks to obtain empirical evidence for additional factors and their relative contribution to listening success of students in the first year of French immersion, an academic context where listening comprehension is the foundation for L2 acquisition. Initial findings suggest that French vocabulary, English vocabulary, sound discrimination ability, WM span, and metacognition all correlate significantly with L2 listening ability.

Affect: Anxiety, Self-Efficacy, and Motivation

L2 learners' perception that listening is the most difficult skill (Graham, 2006), coupled with a classroom practice that often associates listening with evaluation (Mendelsohn, 1994), lead learners to associate listening with a high degree of anxiety (e.g., Elkhafaifi, 2005; Mills, Pajares & Herron, 2006). High levels of anxiety often lead to low levels of confidence and self-efficacy because L2 listeners attribute L2 listening success to factors outside their control (Graham, 2006). Self-efficacy theory maintains that when learners attribute success to factors within their control, they will be more motivated to attempt future tasks (Bandura, 1993). This would suggest that if L2 learners could be taught to regulate their comprehension processes, self-efficacy beliefs regarding listening should improve. Graham and Macaro (2008) did indeed demonstrate that listening strategy instruction improved comprehension and had salutary effects on listener self-efficacy. Mills et al. (2006) also showed that L2 learner judgments of their self-efficacy can influence their approach to listening tasks and performance. Students who participate in study-abroad experiences (Cubillos, Chieffo & Fan, 2008) or maintain contact with native speakers (Moyer, 2006) also demonstrate greater confidence and a greater sense of self-efficacy with regard to listening.

There is some initial evidence for a positive relationship between motivation and L2 listening achievement (Vandergrift, 2005). Students who scored low on motivation, perhaps because of a lack of self-confidence and self-efficacy, demonstrated a passive attitude toward L2 learning, and also reported using ineffective listening strategies. On the other hand, students who indicated high levels of motivation appeared to engage in listening behaviors that were more metacognitive in nature. Motivation, self-efficacy and (reduced) anxiety appear to form a cluster of interrelated affective variables that contribute to L2 listening success. In fact, research by Tafaghodtari, inspired by work on variance in L2 reading by Bernhardt (2005), provides empirical evidence for the contribution of both cognitive and affective variables (metacognition and motivation) to variance in L2 listening ability, suggesting that these variables contribute to variance in an interactive manner (Tafaghodtari & Vandergrift, 2008; Tafaghodtari, 2009).

Contextual Variables

Listening in Interaction

When engaged in interactive listening, listeners must process linguistic input in real time, clarify understanding when comprehension is uncertain, and respond appropriately. At the same time, they need to attend to prosodic (e.g., sarcasm), non-verbal (e.g., furrowed eyebrows) and other culturally-bound cues (e.g., pointing and the finger used for pointing) which can add to, or change, the literal meaning of an utterance. In this listening context, listeners can generally exert greater control, using reception strategies such as requests for clarification (to signal a comprehension problem), repetition (of what was just said) or a request that the interlocutor speak more slowly. Interactive listening may be easier than one-way listening, particularly if the context is familiar and the interlocutors are comfortable with each other. On the other hand, status relationships can negatively affect comprehension and the freedom to negotiate meaning, particularly when one interlocutor is in a power relationship over the other (Carrier, 1999); for example, the interviewee in a job interview.

Interactive listening involves more than comprehension clarification, however. Good listeners use culturally acceptable receipt tokens (uptakes or backchannels) to signal understanding and move the conversation forward. This type of reception strategy may transfer from the L1, if both languages share similar conversational norms. Farrell and Mallard (2006) found that L2 listeners engaged in an information gap task, without any strategy training, used primarily three strategies: backchannels to signal understanding, hypothesis testing to check understanding, and reprises to confirm understanding. Backchannels can be culturally bound and used incorrectly, thus affecting the quality of the interaction and leading to negative perceptions of the other. For example, Japanese learners of English, to be polite and to avoid confrontation, used backchannels (nod, "mmm") that frustrated their English L1 interlocutors who were not certain to what degree their partners understood them or not (Cutrone, 2005). The potential to learn the use of backchannels in interactive listening, using a multimedia environment, has been successfully demonstrated (Ward, Escalante, Al Bayyari & Solorio, 2007) with L2 learners of Arabic who listened to examples of the cue, observed correct visual representations of voice pitch for the cue, received auditory and visual feedback on their attempts to produce the cue and, finally, received feedback on their performance on simulated dialogues where they took on the role of listener.

Listening in Multimedia Environments

New technologies and increased accessibility to these tools make multimedia environments an especially important context for listening development (Goodwin-Jones, 2007; Robin, 2007). Increasingly widespread use of personal iPods makes podcasting a rich source of linguistic input and listening instruction in classrooms, particularly in independent learning contexts (O'Bryan & Hegelheimer, 2007).

Multimedia environments allow listeners to work with audio, video and text, in addition to other types of support (e.g., annotations, dictionaries). Pictorial support and written annotations can help L2 listeners acquire more vocabulary and recall the aural text better than pictorial annotations alone or written annotations alone (Jones, 2004; Jones & Plass, 2002). Video with multilingual soundtracks and captions offer L2 listeners the choice of captions in L1 or L2 to facilitate comprehension. The consensus of research conducted on the usefulness of captions for listening comprehension is that L2 captions facilitate comprehension (e.g., Guichon & McLornan, 2008); however, long-term effects of learning, in terms of listening improvement and vocabulary learning, still need to be determined (Jones, 2006; Robin, 2007). Although captions may facilitate immediate comprehension, their usefulness for learning to listen, however, is still a matter of debate; students will not *learn* how to listen if they read to understand L2 aural texts (Stewart & Pertusa, 2004; Vandergrift, 2004).

Technology can also be harnessed to develop perception skills. Repeated audio delivery, slowed audio text delivery and transcripts of digitized audio texts can be particularly helpful for segmenting or analyzing the individual components of concatenated speech. Multimedia software such as 123LISTEN (Hulstijn, 2003) for segmenting digitized video or audio texts, or on-line tutorials focusing on decoding skills (Klein & Robert, 2004) can also provide practice in perception and parsing of extended discourse in oral texts. It is important, however, that listeners use these tools only after an initial attempt to interpret what they hear, using real-life listening strategies such as prediction and monitoring. These tools can then be used to verify comprehension or problem-solve.

Computer technology can also provide greater insight into listener decision-making as listeners attempt to comprehend texts. For example, using Realplayer and Camstudio, Roussel (2008) compared the performance of listeners under three different conditions: (1) listened once; (2) listened twice; and (3) regulated their own listening. Overall, each group recalled more idea units under the self-regulated condition, although there was a wide range of differences in performance. In the self-regulated condition, the advanced proficiency group used the pause and replay functions more actively than the two other groups, suggesting that they knew exactly what needed verification or closer attention. Tracking the use of self-help functions, Hegelheimer and Tower (2004) found that lower proficiency students used the "repeat previous sentence and transcription" function, which was negatively related to performance. This may be reflective of a translation strategy, characteristic of beginner-level listeners who have not learned how to use contextual information and compensatory strategies to predict and monitor (Eastman, 1991; Osada, 2001). In a study on the use of subtitles or transcripts while listening to a web-based academic lecture, Grgurović and Hegelheimer (2007) observed that, when comprehension broke down, listeners interacted with subtitles more frequently and longer than with transcripts. In another study using web-delivered English as a second language

(ESL) lectures, Smidt and Hegelheimer (2004) were able to ascertain, through an analysis of the answers to comprehension questions, that students consulted the slides rather than the oral text, leading the researchers to conclude that any incidental acquisition of vocabulary was likely due to reading, not listening.

Studies that track listener behavior on the use of help functions in multimedia settings are helpful for determining what listeners deem to be useful for comprehension purposes. These data become more useful, however, when complemented by stimulated recall protocols, where listeners attempt to recall and explain what may have motivated their behavior (Gruba, 2004; Vandergrift, 2010).

Listening in Academic Environments

Students who choose to study in another language face the double challenge of comprehending complex information, in addition to unfamiliar language terms (Miller, 2009). Research on academic listening highlights a number of factors that facilitate lecture comprehension. In addition to valuing generic pedagogical strategies such as variety in presentation, relaxed learning environment and passion for the subject matter, L2 students point to the importance of examples, visual support, lecture handouts and lectures faithful to the handout (Miller, 2009). Gestures and facial cues can also facilitate comprehension; however, the degree to which these cues are used by listeners varies by level of language proficiency (Sueyoshi & Hardison, 2005).

Discourse markers also affect lecture comprehension, i.e., markers that help contextualize listeners by signaling the relative importance of ideas (e.g., let me repeat it) or cohesive links (e.g., first, second). For example, students who listened to unscripted lectures recalled more main ideas and supporting ideas than students who listened to the same lectures with discourse markers removed (Jung, 2006). Camiciottoli (2004) noted similar salutary effects on lecture comprehension for the use of metadiscursive comments such as "what I will do now is," particularly for L2 listeners.

Vocabulary is often a major challenge in academic listening. The use of metaphorical language, in particular, can lead to misunderstandings by L2 listeners (Littlemore, 2001). To alleviate this problem, lecturers can increase redundancy, stating the same information in a different way. On the other hand, lectures can also be a source of rich language input, due to their focus on a defined topic and their inherent redundancy. Vidal (2003) observed significant vocabulary gains after students listened to three short lectures on the same topic. Most of the vocabulary gains were retained four weeks later, particularly for the lower proficiency group.

The nature of academic listening is changing with the increased use of PowerPoint and other visuals (e.g., on-line internet access). Because visual input is often an integral part of a lecture, this information must be processed simultaneously with auditory input (Gruba, 2004), competing for the limited WM resources of L2 listeners. Consequently, research on academic listening in multimedia environments is inconclusive about the value of written visual support (Gruba, 2007; Smidt & Hegelheimer, 2005). McKnight (2004), for example, found that students focused their attention on copying the visually presented material instead of listening to the lecture, thereby missing out on the elaborations of the lecturer.

Product

It goes without saying that the desired product of listening is comprehension, as determined by the purpose for listening. However, as stated earlier in this chapter, listening can also contribute to the language acquisition.

Given that the resourceful nature of the comprehension process allows L2 listeners to understand yet-to-be acquired structures (Izumi, 2003), can L2 listeners be taught to focus on these structures and acquire them? There is some research evidence that a focus on phonological form allowed students to acquire the rule of gender agreement for French adjectives (Arteaga, Herschensohn & Gess, 2003), and that receptive training in adjective agreement in Spanish increased aural processing speed of meaningful sentences (DeJong, 2005). Leeser (2004), on the other hand, found that listeners did not demonstrate comprehension of a perceptually salient targeted form in Spanish. Leeser attributes the difference in results to the nature of the stimulus materials. Because the targeted form was embedded in a short narrative (instead of isolated sentences), listeners focused on comprehension, leaving inadequate WM resources for attention to the targeted form. To overcome WM constraints and still make listening a vehicle for language acquisition, Richards (2005) proposes attention to form as a second phase of listening practice, following a focus on comprehension.

Vocabulary acquisition can also be a by-product of the listening process, as evidenced in the Vidal (2003) study on academic listening. Furthermore, Mason and Krashen (2004) present evidence for more efficient acquisition of incidental vocabulary by a group listening to stories only, compared to a group that engaged in vocabulary activities, in addition to listening.

Pedagogy

Since comprehension is the overriding desired outcome, L2 teaching typically focuses on the product of listening: the correct answer. Consequently, research on improving L2 listening achievement has focused primarily on manipulating the presage variables through experimental studies in order to increase scores on a measure of listening comprehension (Goh, 2002b; Vandergrift, 2010). This body of research has demonstrated that it is helpful to contextualize L2 listeners and that they can be taught to use a number of cues to improve comprehension of oral texts (Hinkel, 2006). Generally, there is no interest, however, in determining *how* listeners use these cues to improve comprehension.

While an exclusive focus on the product of listening allows teachers to verify comprehension, the answer (correct or incorrect) does not help listeners gain an insight into the metacognitive processes underlying successful comprehension so that they can better regulate these processes and become more successful listeners. Furthermore, an exclusive interest in the right answer often creates a high level of anxiety, especially since an interest in the correct answer is often associated with evaluation. Therefore, this section of the chapter will focus on the growing body of research that examines a process approach to the teaching of L2 listening. It will be argued that an emphasis on the process of listening through regular classroom practice, unencumbered by the threat of evaluation, can better enable L2 listeners to control comprehension processes on their own. This section provides an overview of the research demonstrating that L2 learners can gain greater control of the bottom-up and top-down processes underlying the comprehension process and argues for an integrated model that leads L2 listeners to strategically orchestrate these processes and attain comprehension goals.

Bottom-Up Approaches

The bottom-up dimension of listening involves decoding the linguistic input. Research shows that when listeners attempt to parse linguistic input in a new language, they are confronted with three basic challenges: processing problems (an inability to rapidly locate word boundaries), text problems (inadequate L2 vocabulary knowledge) and intrusion problems (involuntarily applying L1 segmentation procedures) (Cross, 2009a). Although L2 listeners can learn to inhibit the compulsion to apply L1 segmentation procedures to a new language (Cutler, 2001), the difficulty presented by word segmentation is particularly acute for lower-proficiency L2 listeners (Goh, 2000; Graham, 2006). Consequently, an important skill to develop in L2 listening instruction is rapid word recognition.

L2 decoding skills, crucial to successful word recognition, have been extensively investigated by Field (2008a). For example, using a "gating" technique, he demonstrated differences in the speed at which L1 listeners are able to abandon a potential word candidate as incorrect compared to L2 listeners who are more reluctant to abandon appropriate word candidates (Field, 2008c). In another series of experiments with word sets and isolated "garden path" sentences, he explored how L2 listeners rely too heavily on top-down interpretative processes, even when confronted by conflicting evidence (Field, 2004). This body of research, however, generally uses psycholinguistic laboratory methods. While helpful for the insights they provide into listener decoding problems and consequent remedial work, these studies lack ecological validity in that they rob listeners of the contextual support that usually supports real-life listening. A more realistic account of listener decoding difficulties is proposed by Cross (2009a) through the use of authentic materials (news videotexts) in a classroom setting. An analysis of notes written by the listeners after each of two listenings revealed specific decoding problems (e.g., clitisization, resyllabification, poor word choices) that could be addressed with specific remedial activities.

Although the decoding problems of L2 listeners have been researched extensively, there is very little research on the types of activities that help learners "make themselves familiar with the phonetic and phonological properties of the L2, learn large amounts of words and automatize their ability to recognize words in speech" (Hulstijn, 2003, p. 419). Al-jasser (2008) provides empirical evidence for teaching English phonotactic constraints (illegal consonant clusters) to Arabic English as a foreign language (EFL) learners, using a Word Spotting Task, resulting in better word segmentation skills. Exact repetition and altering the speech rate were examined by Jensen and Vinther (2003). Although they determined that repetition can facilitate the acquisition of phonological decoding strategies, reduced speed did not account for better performance.

Training in perception can take many forms. Teachers can engage students in an analysis of parts of the text transcript, in dictation or analogy exercises, all within the context of a listening task, so that these exercises are part of meaningful language use (Goh, 2002b). Field (2003) provides a framework of remedial activities to rectify listening problems. To develop automaticity in word recognition, Hulstijn (2001) recommends listening to "i-1 level" texts so that listeners can attend to slight discrepancies between the aural and written forms of the text. Dictogloss can help L2 listeners notice differences between their reconstructed text and a written transcription of the original (Wilson, 2003) and gain greater insight into their comprehension errors. Although these exercises show promise for the development of perception skills, they do not yet have empirical support.

Top-Down Approaches

The top-down dimension of listening involves the application of listener knowledge sources to the decoding process. Listeners apply prior knowledge (world, linguistic, textual, pragmatic and cultural) as well as metacognitive knowledge about listening processes to the comprehension process. Since the role of prior knowledge was examined earlier, this section will focus on metacognition: namely development of metacognitive knowledge and strategy instruction.

Research on the systematic development of metacognition, i.e., listeners' awareness of the L2 listening process and their ability to regulate the underlying processes (prediction, monitoring, evaluating and problem-solving) is a relatively recent development (Vandergrift, 2007). Questionnaires (Goh, 2000) and process-based discussions (Goh & Taib, 2006; Vandergrift, 2002, 2003a) can provide learners and instructors with important information concerning L2 listeners' degree of awareness of listening problems and how to rectify them. The Metacognitive Awareness Listening Questionnaire (MALQ), a 21-item self-report instrument grounded in listening theory, is helpful to learners for raising their awareness of the processes underlying L2 listening and to language instructors for diagnostic purposes (Vandergrift et al., 2006). Listening diaries, with or without prompts, can also stimulate awareness of listening and growth in metacognitive awareness and listening success (Goh, 1997, 2002b). L2 listeners of different ages and backgrounds engaged in process-based listening tasks that raise awareness of metacognitive processes underlying listening have reported increased motivation, confidence and strategy knowledge (Goh & Taib, 2006; Vandergrift, 2002, 2003a).

Research in explicit strategy instruction suggests that L2 listeners can be successfully taught to use strategies (Chamot, 2005). However, these studies tend to report positive results for the use of only one or two strategies, and only immediately following the instruction period (Graham, 2003). Research evidence for the long-term benefits of this kind of strategy instruction remains inconclusive (Field, 2001; Graham & Macaro, 2008). Furthermore, given that skilled listeners appear to use strategies in an interconnected fashion (e.g., Vandergrift, 2003b), instruction in individual strategies may not necessarily lead to overall listening improvement (Field, 2001, 2008c). A recent study by Cross (2009b) found no differences for the group receiving explicit strategy instruction. Cross suggests that the significant improvement of both groups might be attributed to the use of a task-based pedagogical cycle reflecting real-life listening similar to the pedagogical cycle advocated by Vandergrift (2007). Finally, a recent study by Graham and Macaro (2008) demonstrated considerable success in the explicit "awareness raising" of multiple strategies over a period of six months. Both a high- and a low-scaffolded group outperformed a control group at the end of the study and six months later. Interestingly, the researchers attribute improved listening performance to the "clustering of strategies" and the task-specific and learner-centered characteristics of the intervention, which echo key elements of the pedagogical cycle advocated by Vandergrift (see below).

Integrating Bottom-Up and Top-Down Approaches

Little attention has been given to systematic practice in L2 listening (see DeKeyser, 2007), i.e., on the integrated instruction of a sequential repertoire of strategies to help L2 learners develop comprehension skills for real-life listening (Berne, 2004; Mendelsohn, 1994; Vandergrift, 2004). Integrated instruction of a sequential repertoire of strategies, or metacognition about strategies (Sternberg, 1998), has already been documented in reading research, where there is general consensus that this kind of instruction is more effective than individual strategy instruction for teaching comprehension skills (Grabe, 2004). A task-based, pedagogical cycle that leads listeners through the processes underlying real-life listening can develop both the top-down and bottom-up dimensions of listening as well as metacognitive awareness of the cognitive processes underlying successful L2 listening (see Field, 2001; Vandergrift, 2004, 2007). Through an orchestrated use of hypothesis formation (planning) and verification (monitoring), with the judicious application of prior knowledge to compensate for gaps in understanding (problem-solving), along with opportunities for reflection (evaluation) listeners can acquire implicit knowledge about listening processes and achieve greater listening success.

This pedagogical cycle has strong theoretical support, in that it closely parallels research findings demonstrating implicit learning through task performance (Johnston & Doughty, 2006). It also finds empirical support in a number of recent studies. Over the period of one semester, intermediate-level learners of French who were guided through this process approach to listening significantly outperformed learners in the control group (Vandergrift & Tafaghodtari, 2010). To control for the teacher variable, both groups were taught by the same instructor using the same texts. The less-skilled listeners in the experimental group made greater gains than their more-skilled peers, demonstrating that less-skilled listeners, in particular, can benefit from this kind of guided listening practice.

Cross (2009c) investigated the development of metacognition, through the lens of socio-cultural theory, by examining the collaborative dialogue emerging from the use of the same pedagogical cycle with more advanced Japanese learners of English. Through collaborative dialogue, diaries and interviews, listeners demonstrated the usefulness of collaborative dialogue in mediating metacognitive development, in particular, strategy awareness, comprehension awareness and text awareness. Finally, using this same cycle with low-proficiency and high-proficiency civil servants in intensive language training, Mareschal (2007) was able to document, from triangulated data (MALQ responses, stimulated-recall protocols, diaries, think-aloud protocols and a final summative open-ended questionnaire), how these learners of French were better able to regulate their listening processes as a result of the pedagogical intervention, particularly the low-proficiency group. It appears that systematically leading language learners through the process of listening as part of regular listening activities encourages these learners to practice the metacognitive processes involved in listening. This approach, which reflects real-life listening, can enable language learners to participate in communicative activities outside of class at an early stage of language learning (Field, 2008a).

Fundamental to this pedagogical cycle is repeated and systematic exposure to the same sequence of metacognitive processes used by skilled listeners. Although the teacher will initially play a greater role, scaffolding should be gradually removed so that students do the work themselves and the process becomes automatic. Furthermore, matching all or parts of the aural text with the written text helps listeners develop awareness of form-meaning relationships and word recognition skills. It is important, however, that the latter step takes place only after listeners have engaged in the cognitive processes underlying comprehension, using only cues that underlie real-life listening.

Conclusion

This chapter has provided an overview of L2 listening as an integrated system where presage variables (listener, task and context) interact with the quality of the listening process to determine the product. It is argued that a greater awareness of the process can help L2 listeners better regulate the process, leading to a pedagogy for overall listening improvement. Some the areas for future research that have emerged from this overview include investigating:

- the interaction between various sources of information in academic listening (lecturer, Power-Point, visuals, preparatory reading), student note-taking and comprehension success;
- how multimedia can be exploited for teaching L2 learners how to listen; in particular, how to incorporate the pedagogical cycle for use in independent learning environments;
- the pedagogical cycle with different languages learners of different ages;
- additional factors that can explain more of the variance in L2 listening and models of how these factors interact;
- the success of different perception activities for developing word segmentation skills; and
- sociocultural influences on learning to listen.

Interested readers are also encouraged to consult Vandergrift (2007) for more details on these suggestions, in addition to other potential directions for future research.

Acknowledgments

The author wishes to thank Catherine Mareschal, Jerry Cross, and Eli Hinkel for their comments and suggestions for revision.

References

Al-jasser, F. (2008). The effect of teaching English phonotactics on the lexical segmentation of English as a foreign language. *System, 36,* 94–106.

Anderson, J. R. (1995). *Cognitive psychology and its implications* (4th ed.). New York: Freeman.

Arteaga, D., Herschensohn, J. & Gess, R. (2003). Focusing on phonology to teach morphological form in French. *The Modern Language Journal, 87,* 58–70.

Bandura, A. (1993). Perceived self-efficacy in cognitive development and functioning. *Educational Psychologist, 28,* 117–148.

Berne, J. E. (2004). Listening comprehension strategies: A review of the literature. *Foreign Language Annals, 37,* 521–531.

Bernhardt, E. (2005). Progress and procrastination in second language reading. *Annual Review of Applied Linguistics, 25,* 133–150.

Biggs, J. (1999). *Teaching for quality learning at university.* Buckingham: SRHE.

Broersma, M., & Cutler, A. (2008). Phantom word activation in L2. *System, 36,* 22–34.

Buck, G. (2001). *Assessing listening.* Cambridge: Cambridge University Press.

Camiciottoli, B. C. (2004). Interactive discourse structuring in L2 guest lectures: Some insights from a comparative corpus-based study. *Journal of English for Academic Purposes, 3,* 39–54.

Carrier, K. (1999). The social environment of second language listening: Does status play a role in comprehension? *The Modern Language Journal, 83,* 65–79.

Chamot, A. U. (2005). Language learning strategy instruction: Current issues and research. *Annual Review of Applied Linguistics, 25,* 98–111.

Chung, J. M. (2002). The effects of using two advance organizers with video texts for the teaching of listening in English. *Foreign Language Annals, 35,* 231–241.

Cook, M., & Liddicoat, A. J. (2002). The development of comprehension in interlanguage pragmatics: The case of request strategies in English. *Australian Review of Applied Linguistics, 25,* 19–39.

Cross, J. D. (2009a). Diagnosing the process, text and intrusion problems responsible for L2 listeners' decoding errors. *Asian EFL Journal, 11,* 31–53.

Cross, J. D. (2009b). Effects of listening strategy instruction on news videotext comprehension. *Language Teaching Research, 13,* 151–176.

Cross, J. D. (2009c). The development of metacognition of L2 listening in joint activity. Unpublished PhD dissertation, University of Melbourne, Australia.

Cubillos, J. H., Chieffo, L. & Fan, C. (2008). The impact of short-term study abroad programs on L2 listening comprehension skills. *Foreign Language Annals, 41,* 157–185.

Cutler, A. (2001). Listening to a second language through the ears of a first. *Interpreting, 5,* 1–23.

Cutrone, P. (2005). A case study examining backchannels in conversations between Japanese-British dyads. *Multilingua, 24,* 237–274.

Davis, M. H., & Johnsrude, I. S. (2007). Hearing speech sounds: Top-down influences on the interface between audition and speech perception. *Hearing Research, 229,* 132–147.

De Jong, N. (2005). Can second language grammar be learned through listening? An experimental study. *Studies in Second Language Acquisition, 27,* 205–234.

DeKeyser, R. (2007). *Practice in a second language: Perspectives from applied linguistics and cognitive psychology.* Cambridge: Cambridge University Press.

Dunkel, P. (1991). Listening in the native and second/foreign language: Toward an integration of research and practice. *TESOL Quarterly, 25,* 431–457.

Eastman, J. K. (1991). Learning to listen and comprehend: The beginning stages. *System, 19,* 179–187.

Elkhafaifi, H. (2005). Listening comprehension and anxiety in the Arabic language classroom. *The Modern Language Journal, 89,* 206–220.

Farrell, T. C., & Mallard, C. (2006). The use of reception strategies by learners of French as a foreign language. *The Modern Language Journal, 90,* 338–352.

Field, J. (2001). Finding one's way in the fog: Listening strategies and second-language learners. *Modern English Teacher, 9,* 29–34.

Field, J. (2003). Promoting perception: Lexical segmentation in second language listening. *ELT Journal, 57,* 325–334.

Field, J. (2004). An insight into listeners' problems: Too much bottom-up or too much top-down? *System, 32,* 363–377.

Field, J. (2008a). *Listening in the language classroom.* Cambridge: Cambridge University Press.

Field, J. (2008b). Bricks or mortar: Which parts of the input does a second language listener rely on? *TESOL Quarterly, 42,* 411–432.

Field, J. (2008c). Revising segmentation hypotheses in first and second language listening. *System, 36,* 35–51.

Flavell, J. H. (1979). Metacognition and cognitive monitoring: A new area of cognitive-developmental inquiry. *American Psychologist, 34*, 906–911.

Flowerdew, J., & Miller, L. (2005). *Second language listening: Theory and practice*. New York: Cambridge University Press.

French, L. (2003). Phonological working memory and L2 acquisition: A developmental study of Quebec francophone children learning English. Unpublished PhD dissertation, Université Laval, Canada.

Garcia, P. (2004). Pragmatic comprehension of high and low level language learners. *TESL-EJ 8*. Retrieved May 26, 2009 from http://tesl-ej.org/ej30/a1.html.

Ginther, A. (2002). Context and content visuals and performance on listening comprehension stimuli. *Language Testing, 19*, 133–167.

Goodwin-Jones, R. (2007). Digital video update: YouTube, Flash, High-Definition. *Language Learning & Technology, 11*, 16–21.

Goh, C. (1997). Metacognitive awareness and second language listeners. *ELT Journal, 51*, 361–369.

Goh, C. (2000). A cognitive perspective on language learners' listening comprehension problems. *System, 28*, 55–75.

Goh, C. (2002a). Exploring listening comprehension tactics and their interaction patterns. *System, 30*, 185–206.

Goh, C. (2002b). *Teaching listening in the language classroom*. Singapore: SEAMEO Regional Language Centre.

Goh, C. (2008). Metacognitive instruction for second language listening development: Theory, practice and research implications. *RELC Journal, 39*, 188–213.

Goh, C., & Taib, Y. (2006). Metacognitive instruction in listening for young learners. *ELT Journal, 60*, 222–232.

Grabe, W. (2004). Research on teaching reading. *Annual Review of Applied Linguistics, 24*, 44–69.

Graham, S. (2003). Learner strategies and advanced level listening comprehension. *Language Learning Journal, 28*, 64–69.

Graham, S. (2006). Listening comprehension: The learners' perspective. *System, 34*, 165–182.

Graham, S., & Macaro, E. (2008). Strategy instruction in listening for lower-intermediate learners of French. *Language Learning, 58*, 747–783.

Grgurović, M., & Hegelheimer, V. (2007). Help options and multimedia listening: Students' use of subtitles and the transcript. *Language Learning & Technology, 11*, 45–66.

Gruba, P. (2004). Understanding digitized second language videotext. *Computer Assisted Language Learning, 17*, 51–82.

Gruba, P. (2007). Decoding visual elements in digitized foreign newscasts. *Proceedings ascilite Singapore 2007*. Retrieved May 26, 2009 from http://www.ascilite.org.au/conferences/singapore07/procs/gruba.pdf.

Guichon, N., & McLornan, S. (2008). The effects of multimodality on L2 learners: Implications for CALL resource design. *System, 36*, 85–93.

Harley, B. (2000). Listening strategies in ESL: Do age and L1 make a difference? *TESOL Quarterly, 34*, 769–776.

Hegelheimer, V., & Tower, D. (2004). Using CALL in the classroom: Analyzing student interaction in an authentic classroom. *System, 32*, 185–205.

Hinkel, E. (2006). Current perspectives on teaching the four skills. *TESOL Quarterly, 40*, 109–131.

Hulstijn, J. H. (2001). Intentional and incidental second language vocabulary learning: A reappraisal of elaboration, rehearsal and automaticity. In P. Robinson (Ed.), *Cognition and second language instruction* (pp. 258–286). Cambridge: Cambridge University Press.

Hulstijn, J. H. (2003). Connectionist models of language processing and the training of listening skills with the aid of multimedia software. *Computer Assisted Language Learning, 16*, 413–425.

Imhof, M., & Janusik, L. (2006). Development and validation of the Imhof–Janusik listening concepts inventory to measure listening conceptualization differences between cultures. *Journal of International Communication Research, 35*, 79–98.

Izumi, S. (2003). Comprehension and production processes in second language learning: In search of the psycholinguistic rationale of the output hypothesis. *Applied Linguistics, 24*, 168–196.

Jensen, E. D., & Vinther, T. (2003). Exact repetition as input enhancement in second language acquisition. *Language Learning, 53*, 373–428.

Johnston, J., & Doughty, C. (2006). *L2 listening sub-skills*. Center for Advanced Study of Language Technical Report, University of Maryland, College Park.

Jones, L. (2004). Testing L2 vocabulary recognition and recall using pictorial and written test items. *Language Learning & Technology, 8*, 122–143.

Jones, L. (2006). Listening comprehension in multimedia environments. In L. Ducate & N. Arnold (Eds.), *Calling on CALL: From theory and research to new directions in foreign language teaching* (pp. 99–125). San Marcos, TX: CALICO.

Jones, L., & Plass, J. (2002). Supporting listening comprehension and vocabulary acquisition in French with multimedia annotations. *The Modern Language Journal, 86*, 546–561.

Jung, E. H. (2006). Misunderstanding of academic monologues by non-native speakers of English. *Journal of Pragmatics, 38*, 1928–1942.

Klein, H. & Robert, J. M. (2004). L'eurocompréhension (EUROCOM), une méthode de compréhension des langues voisines. *Études de linguistique appliquée, 136*, 403–418.

Lee, D., & Hatesohl, D. (1993). *Listening: Our most used communication skill.* Retrieved May 21, 2009 from http://extension.missouri.edu/publications/DisplayPub.aspx?P=CM150.

Leeser, M. J. (2004). The effects of topic familiarity, mode and pausing on second language learners' comprehension and focus on form. *Studies in Second Language Acquisition, 26,* 587–615.

Littlemore, J. (2001). The use of metaphor in university lectures and the problems that it causes for overseas students. *Teaching in Higher Education, 6,* 333–349.

Long, D. R. (1990). What you don't know can't help you. *Studies in Second Language Acquisition, 12,* 65–80.

Macaro, E., Vanderplank, R. & Graham, S. (2005). A systematic review of the role of prior knowledge in unidirectional listening comprehension. In *Research Evidence in Education Library.* London: EPPI-Centre, Social Science Research Unit, Institute of Education, University of London. Retrieved August 17, 2010 from http://eppi.ioe.ac.uk/cms/Default.aspx?tabid=299.

McKnight, A. (2004). Learning by listening and note-taking? International students and academic lectures. Unpublished PhD dissertation, La Trobe University, Australia.

Mareschal, C. (2007). Student perceptions of a self-regulatory approach to second language listening comprehension development. Unpublished PhD dissertation, University of Ottawa, Canada.

Mason, B., & Krashen, S. (2004). Is form-focused vocabulary instruction worthwhile? *RELC Journal, 35,* 179–185.

Mecartty, F. (2000). Lexical and grammatical knowledge in reading and listening comprehension by foreign language learners of Spanish. *Applied Language Learning, 11,* 323–348.

Mendelsohn, D. (1994). *Learning to listen: A strategy-based approach for the second-language learner.* San Diego, CA: Dominie.

Miller, L. (2009). Engineering lectures in a second language: What factors facilitate students' listening comprehension? *Asian EFL Journal, 11,* 8–30.

Mills, N., Pajares, C. & Herron, C. (2006). A re-evaluation of the role of anxiety: Self-efficacy, anxiety and their relation to reading and listening proficiency. *Foreign Language Annals, 39,* 276–295.

Moyer, A. (2006). Language contact and confidence in second language listening comprehension: A pilot study of advanced listeners of German. *Foreign Language Annals, 39,* 255–275.

O'Bryan, A., & Hegelheimer, V. (2007). Integrating CALL into the classroom: The role of podcasting in an ESL listening strategies course. *ReCALL, 19,* 162–180.

O'Malley, J. M., & Chamot, A. U. (1990). *Learning strategies in second language acquisition.* Cambridge: Cambridge University Press.

O'Malley, J. M., Chamot, A. U. & Küpper, L. (1989). Listening comprehension strategies in second language acquisition. *Applied Linguistics, 10,* 418–437.

Osada, N. (2001). What strategy do less proficient learners employ in listening comprehension? A reappraisal of bottom-up and top-down processing. *Journal of the Pan-Pacific Association of Applied Linguistics, 5,* 73–90.

Paris, S. G., & Winograd, P. (1990). How metacognition can promote academic learning and instruction. In B. F. Jones & L. Idol (Eds.), *Dimensions of thinking and cognitive instruction* (pp. 15–51). Hillsdale, NJ: Lawrence Erlbaum.

Pressley, M. (2002). Metacognition and self-regulated comprehension. In A. Farstrup & S. Samuels (Eds.), *What research has to say about reading instruction* (pp. 291–309). Newark, DE: International Reading Association.

Richards, J. C. (2005). Second thoughts on teaching listening. *RELC Journal, 36,* 85–92.

Robin, R. (2007). Learner-based listening and technological authenticity. *Language Learning & Technology, 11,* 109–115.

Rose, K. R., & Kasper, G. (Eds.) (2001). *Pragmatics in language teaching.* Cambridge: Cambridge University Press.

Rost, M. (2002). *Teaching and researching listening.* London: Longman.

Rost, M. (2005). L2 Listening. In E. Hinkel (Ed.), *Handbook of research in second language teaching and learning* (pp. 503–527). Mahwah, NJ: Erlbaum.

Roussel, S. (2008). Les stratégies d'autorégulation de l'écoute et leur influence sur la compréhension de l'orale chez des apprenants de l'allemand langue seconde. Unpublished PhD dissertation, Université de Toulouse 2, France.

Sanders, L. D., Neville, N. J. & Woldorff, M. G. (2002). Speech segmentation by native and non-native speakers: The use of lexical, syntactic, and stress-pattern cues. *Journal of Speech, Language and Hearing Research, 45,* 519–530.

Segalowitz, N. (2007). Access fluidity, attention control and the acquisition of fluency in a second language. *TESOL Quarterly, 41,* 181–186.

Smidt, E. & Hegelheimer, V. (2004). Effects of online academic lectures on ESL listening comprehension, incidental vocabulary acquisition and strategy use. *Computer Assisted Language Learning, 17,* 517–556.

Sternberg, R. J. (1998). Metacognition, abilities and developing expertise: What makes an expert student? *Instructional Science, 26,* 127–140.

Stewart, M. A., & Pertusa, I. (2004). Gains to language learners from viewing target language close-captioned films. *Foreign Language Annals, 37,* 438–447.

Sueyoshi, A., & Hardison, D. M. (2005). The role of gestures and facial cues in second-language listening comprehension. *Language Learning, 55,* 661–699.

Tafaghodtari, M. H. (2009). L2 listening development as a component of multiple literacies: A mixed methods study. Unpublished PhD dissertation, University of Ottawa, Canada.

Tafaghodtari, M. H., & Vandergrift, L. (2008). Second/foreign language listening: Unraveling the construct. *Perceptual and Motor Skills, 107,* 99–113.

Taguchi, N. (2005). Comprehending implied meaning in English as a foreign language. *The Modern Language Journal, 89,* 543–562.

Tyler, M. (2001). Resource consumption as a function of topic knowledge in nonnative and native comprehension. *Language Learning, 51,* 257–280.

Vandergrift, L. (2002). It was nice to see that our predictions were right: Developing metacognition in L2 listening comprehension. *The Canadian Modern Language Review, 58,* 555–575.

Vandergrift, L. (2003a). From prediction through reflection: Guiding students through the process of L2 listening. *The Canadian Modern Language Review, 59,* 425–440.

Vandergrift, L. (2003b). Orchestrating strategy use: Toward a model of the skilled second language listener. *Language Learning, 53,* 463–496.

Vandergrift, L. (2004). Learning to listen or listening to learn? *Annual Review of Applied Linguistics, 24,* 3–25.

Vandergrift, L. (2005). Relationships among motivation orientations, metacognitive awareness and proficiency in L2 listening. *Applied Linguistics, 26,* 70–89.

Vandergrift, L. (2006). Second language listening: Listening ability or language proficiency? *The Modern Language Journal, 90,* 6–18.

Vandergrift, L. (2007). Recent developments in second and foreign language listening comprehension research. *Language Teaching, 40,* 191–210.

Vandergrift, L. (2010). Researching listening in applied linguistics. In B. Paltridge & A. Phakiti (Eds.), *Companion to research methods in applied linguistics* (pp. 160–173). London: Continuum.

Vandergrift, L., & Tafaghodtari, M. (2009). Explaining variance in second language listening. Paper presented at the annual meeting of the American Association of Applied Linguistics, Denver, CO.

Vandergrift, L., & Tafaghodtari, M. H. (2010). Teaching students how to listen does make a difference: An empirical study. *Language Learning, 65.*

Vandergrift, L., Goh, C., Mareschal, C. & Tafaghodatari, M. H. (2006). The Metacognitive Awareness Listening Questionnaire (MALQ): Development and validation. *Language Learning, 56,* 431–462.

Veenman, M., Van Hout-Wolters, B. & Afflerbach, P. (2006). Metacognition and learning: conceptual and methodological considerations. *Metacognition and Learning, 1,* 3–14.

Vidal, K. (2003). Academic listening: A source of vocabulary acquisition? *Applied Linguistics, 24,* 56–89.

Ward, N. G., Escalante, R., Al Bayyari, Y. & Solorio, T. (2007). Learning to show you're listening. *Computer Assisted Language Learning, 20,* 35–51.

Wenden, A. (1998). Metacognitive knowledge and language learning. *Applied Linguistics, 19,* 515–537.

Wilson, M. (2003). Discovery listening—improving perceptual processing. *ELT Journal, 57,* 335–343.

Zimmerman, B. J., & Schunk, D. H. (2001). *Self-regulated learning and academic achievement.* Mahwah, NJ: Erlbaum.

29
Second Language Literacy

Lee Gunderson, Dennis Murphy Odo, and Reginald D'Silva

Introduction

Learning to read and write is viewed as a key to success in many local, national, and international societies (Gunderson, 2007, 2009) and success is often related to learning second language literacy (L2L) skills. The terms literacy, multiliteracies, second language (L2), and L2L are defined. A review of the number of first and second languages in the world is presented. A brief overview of L2L in China, India, Africa, North and South America, and Europe is given. Non-standard views of L2L are presented such as digital and programing code as L2L. It is concluded that L2L is a vast and complex issue that has not been fully addressed in the literature.

Defining Literacy

The origin of the word literacy is Latin meaning "one who knows the letters." Literate was often used to connote an educated or learned man. Read, to "understand the meaning of written symbols," is unique to Old English, while write meant to scratch or draw (Diringer, 1968). Willinsky (1990) notes, "'literate,' dates back to the fifteenth century, and was used to describe one who can read and write" (p. 14).

The word "read" represents a large number of concepts. Gaining meaning from print is a standard interpretation, however, reading is more complex. Leu (1981) proposed that it involves "production" and/or "comprehension." We propose that production without comprehension is a feature of L2L.

PISA (2009) notes: "Reading literacy is understanding, using, reflecting on and engaging with written texts, in order to achieve one's goals, to develop one's knowledge and potential, and to participate in society" (p. 23). This definition appears to include reading but not writing:

> Reading literacy includes a wide range of cognitive competencies, from basic decoding, to knowledge of words, grammar and larger linguistic and textual structures and features, to knowledge about the world. It also includes metacognitive competencies: the awareness of and ability to use a variety of appropriate strategies when processing texts.
>
> (PISA, 2009, p. 23)

In 2003 UNESCO adopted the following definition:

> Literacy is the ability to identify, understand, interpret, create, communicate and compute using printed and written materials associated with varying contexts. Literacy involves a continuum of learning in enabling individuals to achieve his or her goals, develop his or her knowledge and potentials, and participate fully in the community and wider society.
>
> (UNESCO, 2003, p. 25)

A serious difficulty with measuring literacy levels around the world is that it normally involves researchers interviewing individuals and basically asking, "are you literate" and the responses are normally coded as either yes or no. Who would want to say "no I am not literate?" UNESCO has developed a somewhat more expanded view (see http://www.uis.unesco.org/ev.php?ID=6411_201&ID2=DO_TOPIC).

Wiley (2005) describes *minimal literacy*, *conventional literacy*, *basic literacy*, and *functional literacy*. He argues that " *[f]unctional* literacy refers to the ability to use print in order to achieve individual goals as well as the print-related obligations of employment, citizenship, daily problem solving *and* participation in the community" (p. 532; emphasis in original). He notes that the concept has been criticized for its middle-class western bias.

Some suggest that a more useful concept is "multiple literacies." In this respect literacy is viewed as ways of "reading the world" in different contexts in different ways (see Cope & Kalantzis, 2000; Lankshear & Knobel, 2003; Street, 2003). The area of New Literacy Studies (NLS) focuses on the local, everyday experience of literacy in particular communities of practice (Barton, 1994; Barton & Hamilton, 1998). In this sense literacy only has meaning within its particular context of social practice and does not transfer easily across contexts. There are different literacy practices in different areas such as education, religion, workplace, public services, and family and community activities. Practices change over time and are supported and shaped by different institutions and social relationships.

The term "multiliteracies" was advocated by the "New London Group" who argued that the term represents "the multiplicity of communications channels and media" and the "increasing salience of cultural and linguistic diversity" (Cope & Kalantsis, 2000, p. 5). They also note that, "[w]hat we might term 'mere literacy' remains centred on language only, and usually on a singular national form of language at that, being conceived as a stable system based on rules such as mastering sound-letter correspondence" (p. 5).

There is a deep-seated relationship between technology and literacy. Cuneiform writing, one of the very earliest systems, involved the use of wooden implements designed to make marks in clay in order to record inventories (Diringer, 1968). The early Romans used chisels in marble and later in their history brushes on scrolls. Their choice of technology changed their writing and the invention of the printing press tended to fix it for some time (Diringer, 1968). Lead pencils, pens of various kinds, the typewriter, radio, television, the word processor, the computer, cellular technology, the internet, and social networking have all been associated with different, sometimes subtle, changes in the concept of literacy. Watching the 2010 Winter Olympics live on television while tweeting with others about what is happening as it happens argues for an expanded view of literacy.

We applaud Lo Bianco's (2000, pp. 93–94) notion that

> [l]anguages caught up in the multimodal environment of contemporary communication, which combine verbal linguistics meaning-making with the gestural, visual, spatial, and the radically altered writing and reading regimes of computer literacy, such as the oral-like writing and writing-like oralism in voice instruction, complicate literacy practices with multicultural contexts as the modes, codes and cultural meaning interact with each other.

We explore L2L with the goal of indentifying some of the complex interactions occurring in multiple multimodal environments. We have chosen to organize the discussion situated in L2L events differing across nations, languages, practices, contexts, and modes. The task is complex because it is difficult to disambiguate the terms reading and literacy since some authors use them interchangeably (see, for instance, Koda, 2008) and L2L turns out to be complex.

Second Language Defined

The term "second language" is used to designate the language of those who speak one language at home (perhaps, a mother tongue) and an additional language (or more) outside of the home. The term is misrepresentative in many cases. There are human beings who speak multiple languages. So when we refer to L2 in this chapter it may actually be the third or fourth language. L2 is used here as a term to represent "not the first language or mother tongue."

First Languages

Lewis (2009, p. 7), editor of *Ethnologue: Languages of the World*, notes:

> Because languages are dynamic and variable and undergo constant change, the total number of living languages in the world cannot be known precisely. In this edition, we tally 6,909 languages which are known to have living speakers who learned them by transmission from parent to child as the primary language of day-to-day communication. These languages are commonly referred to as a person's "first language" or "mother tongue".

The history of languages is fascinating, but incredibly complex and well beyond the scope of this chapter. Many languages are represented by writing of some kind (Daniels, 1996). Joshi and Aaron (2006) broadly classify writing systems as "morphemic writing (Chinese), syllabic writing (Japanese Kana), alphabetic-syllabic system (Kanada and Tamil), and alphabetic writing (Italian and Spanish)" (p. xiii). They also note that there are different scripts: "The graphic format in which writing is presented" (p. viii). The Roman, Arabic, and Indic scripts are used in many countries to represent many different languages. In many cases a script is borrowed or adopted to represent a language for various complex reasons. Urdu, for instance, is written in a modified Arabic script in Pakistan and in some cases in Devanagari script in India (D'Silva, personal communication, April 2010). Many L2s are written in a script different from the script used to write L1s.

Second Languages

Lewis (2009) reports that 389 (about 6%) languages have at least one million speakers and account for 94% of the languages spoken. He notes that various dialects of Chinese make up the world's largest language group by number of speakers (1,213,000,000); followed by Spanish (329,000,000), English (328,000,000), Arabic (221,000,000), Hindi (182,000,000), Bengali (181,000,000), Portuguese (178,000,000), Russian (144,000,000), Japanese (122,000,000), and German (90,000,000). Ostler (2005) estimates the number of L2 users to be: Mandarin (1,052,000,000), English (508,000,000), Hindi (487,000,000), Spanish (417,000,000), Russian (277,000,000), Bengali (211,000,000), Portuguese (191,000,000), German (128,000,000), French (128,000,000), and Japanese (126,000,000). Mandarin, Spanish, English, French, and Hindi are major L2s.

There are millions of human beings learning L2L skills around the world. Immigrants and others learn Norwegian, Danish, Swedish, French, German, Italian, Spanish, Portuguese, Arabic,

Kurdish, Malay, Indonesian, Turkish, Russian, Hebrew, Swahili (Kiswahili), English, Mandarin, and hundreds of other languages as L2s as a result of migration, economics, technology, and governmental educational policies. Some are doing so because the language of instruction is different from their L1 as a result of colonialism, some are doing so because of immigration, and some are doing so because the L2 is thought to be the key to technology or to access to the local, national, or world economy.

Second Language Literacy

It seems counterintuitive, however, it is true that there are more human beings involved in L2L then in first language literacy (L1L). An early study of "reading literacy" in 32 countries by the International Association for the Evaluation of Educational Achievement (IAEEA) included the issue of home language versus school language (Elley, 1992). The author found "a consistency in patterns of achievement across countries favoring girls, students who speak the language of the school, and students from urban areas" (p. 64). Students involved in reading literacy in an L2 at school generally scored lower than those who spoke the language of instruction at home.

Re-Production

There are a number of influential L2s that are employed around the globe. The following discussion will include several of the major ones. In some cases, L2L involves the re-production of, but not necessarily the comprehension of, the L2. Examples in popular culture are numerous. Singers can learn to produce songs in an L2 without comprehending their meanings. Human beings can learn to reproduce a language from printed text without understanding the text. We have encountered individuals who can decode Greek, Arabic, Korean, and Hindi, but do not understand the discourse. They have learned the sound–symbol relationships and can "read," that is decode, L2 texts without understanding them. DMO, a bilingual English–Korean speaker, argues that one can learn to decode Korean orthography in an hour or two because it is very shallow. In many respects decoding without comprehension appears to be a fairly robust feature of L2 learning (Gunderson, 2009). Often students can decode L2 because of their knowledge of the phoneme-graphemc of their L1. They are helped to read an L2 by their knowledge of their L1 (see discussion of the CUP model below). There are instances in which learning to decode an L2 is an integral part of a culture.

Kalaodi is a village on the island of Tidore in eastern Indonesia. "In the late fifteenth century the first Tidorean ruler converted to Islam" (Baker, 1992, p. 99). Baker adds: "Today, being a Muslim is integral to the ethnic identity of being Tidorese" (p. 99). The Tidorese learn to read the Koran in the sense that they can decode the orthography into Arabic. "The skill of recognizing Arabic characters and producing the sounds encoded by them is taught to children as a basic part of their formal education" (p. 102). Baker notes: "For the Kalaodi, the activity of reading remains formal and ritualistic and an enlightened comprehension of what they are reading and affirming remains blocked by the foreignness of the language" (p. 107). In this case, the readers can reproduce with great accuracy the Arabic they read, but they do not understand the text, although Baker notes they do recognize and understand the significance of some names that have meaning for them. L2 learners can learn to decode an L2 without necessarily being able to comprehend it. It is not clear, however, that they can write an L2 without being able to comprehend it. Except, perhaps, in the case in which the "writing" involves the production of iconic visual symbols that may transcend languages. An X across an icon of some sort, for instance, means "forbidden" and can be "written" by a Chinese speaker and understood by a Farsi speaker.

Chinese: Second Language Literacy

Lewis (2009) reports that there are 293 languages in China; one having no known speakers. There is one national language (Mandarin) and seven regional languages. "More and more Chinese nowadays are able to communicate with Chinese Mandarin, says a survey that indicates that 53 per cent of the population can communicate with the language known as putonghua" (http://www.chinadaily. com.cn/english/doc/2004-12/26/content_403419.htm). Putonghua is the language taught to students in school in China. It has also been adopted in Singapore as one of the four official languages even though very few individuals in Singapore speak it as an L1. In essence, for the large majority of Chinese in China and in Singapore, Putonghua is a second language. Cheung, McBride-Chang and Chow (2006) argue that "[o]ne obvious advantage of adopting the logographic principle (i.e., graphemes directly representing meaning) in written Chinese is that it greatly facilitates communication among people speaking different Chinese languages … most of them mutually unintelligible" (p. 422). Chinese instruction is interesting:

> Students in China are taught literacy skills initially through the use of the international phonetic alphabet (i.p.a.), called Pinyin, as a method to introduce sound-symbol relationships to students. Pinyin was adopted in 1958 (http://en.wikipedia.org/wiki/Zhuyin) to replace the previous system that had been in place called guóyǔzìmǔ (or bopomofo in Taiwan). In addition, in 1949 the People's Republic of China adopted a simplified orthography (see http://www.omniglot.com/writing/chinese_simplified.htm#simp) so that the first characters students learn are simplified from the classic form. Simplified characters are introduced with Pinyin added so that students are able to "decode" the characters. This system is used until about the third grade, with new characters being introduced with Pinyin, but not thereafter (Hudson-Ross & Dong, 1990).
>
> In Taiwan, students are introduced to a phonetic transcription system that involves non-Roman syllables called zhùyīnfúhào or bopomofo. Developed in 1913 by the Ministry of Education in the Republic of China, the system was originally called guóyǔzìmǔ or the National Phonetic Alphabet. In 1986, the Republic of China (Taiwan) adapted the system to assist learners in learning to read and write Mandarin, re-naming it zhùyīnfúhào (bopomofo). The characters/symbols are based on calligraphic forms and some are derived from Chinese characters (see http://en.wikipedia.org/wiki/Bopomofo). Students in Taiwan learn to read standard, classic Chinese characters that have not been simplified. Finally, in Hong Kong, until recently, learning to read Cantonese was by a system that involved drill and rote memorization of classic Chinese characters using a "flash card" approach that begins at about age three for many students.
>
> (Gunderson, 2007, pp. 195–197)

The research related to the teaching and learning of Chinese as an L2 is sparse. The commonly held view, however, is that spoken Chinese is not difficult to learn because it has simple phonological (except tones) and grammatical structures. The most difficult aspect, however, is to learn to recognize and write the calligraphy. Erard (2004) reported there were 30 million people around the world learning Chinese as an L2 and that the goal was to increase it to 100 million in four years. It is unclear that this goal has been met world wide, but the number of learners continues to increase internationally as China becomes a significant member of the world economic society.

Putonghua appears to have been adopted to unify China in terms of language. "One obvious advantage of the logographic and morphosyllabic nature of Chinese is that the same script can be used in a large population in which people speak different dialects" (Ho, Chan, Tsang, Chan, & Lee, 2002, p. 544). There are cases where the L2 has not been adopted but has been imposed.

Spanish: Second Language Literacy

Spanish is spoken in 44 countries (Lewis, 2009). It is an L2 in many of these countries. In Mexico, for instance, there are 298 languages, but seven have no known speakers (Lewis, 2009). The national language is Spanish. López-Gopar (2007, p. 159) notes:

> Mexican indigenous people not only face discrimination but also struggle in the current education system. Silvia Schmelkes (2004), General Coordinator of Intercultural and Bilingual Education in Mexico, reported that indigenous children's education in Mexico is in a critical state. The lowest level of literacy and the highest level of dropout rates are found among the indigenous population.

López-Gopar adds: "For 500 years, Indigenous people have been discriminated against and manipulated to believe that they need to abandon their language and culture if they want to succeed in Mexican society" (2007, p. 161). In essence, L2L skills are promoted as a key to success in Mexico at the expense of the L1.

López-Gopar (2007, p. 166) states that "[t]he writing systems developed by Aztecs, Mayans, Zapotecs, and Mixtecs are represented in what are generically called codices." Codices involve images, logograms, and phonetic representations. L2L instruction has had a negative effect on many students from different L1 backgrounds in Mexico (López & Gunderson, 2006).

Spanish as an L2 has had similar effects on L1s in South and Central America. Spanish is the official language in Argentina (25 living languages), Bolivia (37), Columbia (80), Costa Rica (10), Ecuador (23), El Salvador (5), Guatemala (53), Honduras (10), Nicaragua (7), Panama (14), Paraguay (20), and Peru (92) (Lewis, 2009). Most students in these countries are involved in L2L instruction, often to the exclusion of their L1s. For instance, Peréz (2009) in reference to Peru notes: "Formal education has played a central role in the promotion of a Spanish-only policy" (p. 202). She states that "90% of indigenous pupils still receive education that does not involve their language or culture" (p. 206). She notes that Spanish as an L2 has been promoted and is rapidly expanding in Brazil where the national language is Portuguese.

English: Second Language Literacy

English is spoken in 112 countries as an official or major language (Lewis, 2009). Australia, Canada, New Zealand, the United Kingdom, and the United States are the countries most often identified with English. They are also the countries with millions of immigrants who are involved in English as an L2L.

The British Council reports that:

> English has official or special status in at least seventy five countries with a total population of over two billion; English is spoken as a first language by around 375 million and as a second language by around 375 million speakers in the world; speakers of English as a second language probably outnumber those who speak it as a first language; around 750 million people are believed to speak English as a foreign language, and one out of four of the world's population speak English to some level of competence; demand from the other three-quarters is increasing.
>
> (http://www.britishcouncil.org/learning-faq-the-english-language.htm)

It is also argued that

English is the main language of books, newspapers, airports and air-traffic control, international business and academic conferences, science, technology, diplomacy, sport, international competitions, pop music and advertising, over two-thirds of the world's scientists read in English, three quarters of the world's mail is written in English, eighty per cent of the world's electronically stored information is in English and, of the estimated 200 million users of the Internet, some thirty-six per cent communicate in English.

(http://www.britishcouncil.org/learning-faq-the-english-language.htm)

Literacy learning in English and in English as a second language (ESL), especially reading, appears to have received the most research attention over the years (Gunderson, D'Silva, & Chen, 2010). Joshi and Aaron (2006) note: "Until about two decades ago, the study of writing systems and its relationships to literacy acquisition has been generally modeled after studies of the English language" (p. xiii). Mohanty argues:

As the voiceless minorities suffer the sinister exclusion of mother tongues, the silent elites enjoy the pre-eminence of dominant languages such as English. In the post-colonial world, '*the killer languages*' thrive at the cost of other languages, and in many countries the myth of English-medium superiority is propagated to the detriment of the poor and the marginalised.

(Mohanty, 2009, p. 5; emphasis in original)

English is strongly associated with the United States, arguably one of the most powerful countries in the world and, perhaps, as a result it has received more research attention (Gunderson et al., 2010); both as a first and as a second or foreign language. A major ESL authority and researcher, Jim Cummins of the University of Toronto in Canada, has developed a number of influential L2 notions related primarily to English.

The "Common Underlying Proficiency" (CUP) model is based on the view that literacy-related features of a bilingual's proficiency in L1 and L2 are seen as common or interdependent across languages (Cummins, 1983, 1984, Cummins & Swain, 1986). There is evidence to support CUP (Baker & deKanter, 1981; Cummins, 1983, 2000). Hakuta, Butler, and Witt (2000) have shown more recent evidence that transfer does occur. CUP is also been referred to as the interdependence principle.

In addition, Cummins (1979, 1980, 1981a, 1981b) proposed that there are two types of language to be learned, "basic interpersonal communicative skill" (BICS), the language of ordinary conversation or "the manifestation of language proficiency in everyday communicative contexts" (Cummins, 1984, p. 137), and "cognitive academic language proficiency" (CALP), the language of instruction and academic texts.

Threshold is another concept discussed by Cummins (2000). Threshold is related to a hypothesis by Alderson (1985) that one has to acquire a certain level of L2 proficiency to learn to read in the L2 (Cummins, 1979). Cummins (1979) notes that "a cognitively and academically beneficial form of bilingualism can be achieved only on the basis of adequately developed first language (L1) skills" (p. 222). He adds that "[t]he threshold hypothesis assumes that those aspects of bilingualism which might positively influence cognitive growth are unlikely to come into effect until the child has attained a certain minimum or threshold level of competence in a second language" (p. 229). Cummins also spoke of a lower and an upper threshold. In essence, the lower threshold allows the learner to develop interpersonal competence, while the upper threshold allows students to be involved in learning that involves complex cognitively difficult language. Despite criticism, the terms continue to be used.

Millions of all ages are learning to read and write English around the globe. Many immigrants to the major English-speaking nations appear to be at-risk in various ways. They appear to be failing to learn English literacy skills, are failing to read and learn from their textbooks, are failing to learn from lectures in their academic classes, and are failing to acquire the literacy skills they need to get work in anything but low-level labor-intensive work (Gunderson, 2007). Joshi and Aaron (2006) state: "It was also tacitly believed, if not overtly stated, that what is true of English is also true for other writing systems" (p. xiii). The problem is that the learning of English literacy skills is likely one of the most difficult L2L tasks (Gunderson et al., 2010).

L2 problems appear often to be related to the learning of ESL. Ziegler, Perry, Ma-Wyatt, Ladner, and Schulte-Körne (2003) note that "[t]he slower rate of learning to read in English does not seem to occur because of variations in teaching methods across different countries, rather it seems due to the relatively low orthographic consistency of English" (p. 13). English is the most difficult language to learn to read and there appear to be more individuals who have trouble learning to read it. "The empirical evidence that is presented … clearly suggests that reading acquisition in the English writing system proceeds more slowly than any other orthography that has been looked at so far" (Landerl, 2006, p. 514). Hispanic students who are born in the United States and immigrants who have Spanish as their L1 are over-represented in remedial reading and special education classes (Klingner, Artilles, & Barletta, 2006; Rueda & Windmueller, 2006). Languages such as Spanish have fairly shallow orthographies since there is a high degree of regularity in grapheme-phoneme correspondence. In general, it appears that students who first learn to read in a shallow orthography, depending on their age, may experience initial difficulty learning an L2 with a deep orthography such as English. There are also associated difficulties in learning to spell in English.

In Australia, Canada, New Zealand, and the United States, English has had a deleterious effect on the languages of indigenous peoples. McCarty (2009), for instance, notes that while there are 62 classes of Native American languages, "[e]very one of these languages is in a perilous state of decline" (p. 125), while Nicolas (2009) states that before colonization there were "63 languages in Canada belonging to 11 different language families" (p. 221), while only three "are considered healthy enough to survive the present century" (p. 221). English has had a profound effect on the L1s of the indigenous people of North America. Ostler (2005) concludes that "[i]n the present situation, the prospect for long-term survival of any of North America's own languages, even in coexistence with English, seems very bleak" (p. 490).

Some speak of the hegemony of English. In the 1800s and early 1900s bilingual programs were fairly common in the United States and a large-scale Spanish–English bilingual program was established in the 1960s in Miami, Florida (Gunderson, 2008). Since then the use of languages other than English has become a politically-charged contentious issue. English-only laws were passed and a group called US English organized to lobby for an amendment to the United States constitution that would establish English as the official language (Crawford, 1989). In 1998, 63% of the voters in California supported an anti-bilingual proposition called Proposition 227 (Crawford, 1997). In 2006 a majority of voters in Arizona voted 849,772 (66%) to 295,632 (26%) in favor of Proposition 103 to make English the official language and businesses to enforce the measure (accessed on April 15, 2010 at http://www.azsos. gov/election/2006/info/pubpamphlet/sun_sounds/english/prop103.htm). English-only instruction has not improved the ESL population's English achievement. In essence, learners are losing their L1s and in addition are not becoming proficient enough in L2L to succeed at school or in society (Gunderson, 2007, 2008, 2009).

India: Second Language Literacy

There are 438 living languages in India. English and Hindi are the national "official" languages. In addition there are 22 official scheduled languages associated with different geographic regions. Lewis (2009) reports that there are 179,000 native English speakers in India, but there are also 11,021,610

English L2 speakers. Hindi speakers include 180,000,000 L1 and 120,000,000 L2 individuals (Lewis, 2009). The L2 issues in India are so complex it is impossible to adequately address them here.

Hundreds of millions are involved in L2 literacy in India. The overall picture is incredibly complex. One of the authors of this chapter (Reginald D'Silva), for instance, speaks six languages. He is L1 literate in English. He subsequently learned Hindi, Kannada, Konkani, Tulu, and German literacy skills. Kannada, Konkani, and Tulu in his region are represented by the same orthography, but not in other regions. That he is able to read and write these three languages with a single orthography is evidence that CUP mentioned above is a feature in multi-lingual literacy.

Jhringran notes:

> In some areas, children have to learn four or five languages by the time they complete primary school. For example, a child in a Mundari-speaking household in Raigarh district in Chattisgarh would speak Mundari with his parents, Chattisgarhi with his/her friends and neighbours and learn *Hindi* at school as the language used for instruction and try to pick up English from grade 3 onwards.
>
> (Jhingran, 2009, p. 265; emphasis in original)

He also notes that "[a] rough assessment indicates that almost 25% of primary school children face moderate to severe problems in the initial months and years of primary school because their home language differs from the school language" (p. 267) and that 103,732 primary schools have populations of 90% who have a home language different from the language of instruction.

Mohanty, Mishra, Reddy, and Ramesh (2009) argue that "[f]orced submersion of minority children in dominant or majority language classrooms with subtractive effects on their mother tongues continues to be the most pressing educational issue in multilingual settings" (p. 283). Although the L2L situation is complex in India, it is safe to say that language minority students are often in peril of failure to learn literacy skills and dropping out. Authorities such as Jhringran (2009) suggest that multilingual programs would support the use of home languages and home cultures in early grades and provide a stronger language base to the learning of a dominant language such as Hindi or English. India has dramatic regional differences in literacy achievement. The consequences are significant. According to the National Network of Educaton (2010) there are about 106 million people in the age group of 15–24 years in north India alone, but only about 33.4 million are likely to enroll for higher and vocational education. This is a rate that is significantly lower than other regions such as Kerala. Indian Human Resource Development (HRD) Minister Kapil Sibal concluded that "north Indian states cannot emulate the model of education in southern states as they have an inherently indigenous culture of learning" (http://www.indiaedunews.net/Today/Northern_India_fares_low_in_literacy_rate,_says_study_11184/).

Same language subtitling (SLS) has proven to be a simple yet effective way of providing literacy, including L2L, to people of all ages through high-interest television programing. Successfully used in rural India to promote mass literacy usually in Hindi or an official scheduled language, this feature also called "literacy karaoke" uses subtitles in the same language as the visual content to promote reading. This highly cost-effective literacy tool is also a winner of the 2002 World Bank's Global Innovation Competition (planetread.org). The SLS technology has now extended to educational resources such as digital books in over 20 languages (bookbox.com). It appears to help students improve their L2L skills.

India has a complex L2L environment. It seems that the majority of students in India are involved in learning literacy skills in an L2 and that the L2 varies both between and within regions. Success in learning L2L skills is difficult for many students, particularly those who speak a language at home other than the language of instruction.

Africa: Second Language Literacy

Africa has about one-third of the languages in the world (Bendor-Samuel, 1996). Colonists brought both their religions and their alphabets to Africa. The Church Missionary Society in 1848 established an approach for writing different African languages using a Roman alphabet (Bendor-Samuel, 1996). In 1928 the International African Institute published "The Practical Orthography of African Languages" which established the "Africa" alphabet (Bendor-Samuel, 1996). Most African languages, mostly sub-Saharan, are written using either a modified Roman alphabet or the International Phonetic Alphabet. Africa is unique and complex in terms of orthographies (Heine & Nurse, 2000; Prah, 1998).

Heugh (2009) notes: "European languages have generally come to be used for high-level purposes in each African country south of the Sahara" (p. 105). She notes that English has come to be used even in countries that were never British colonies i.e., Namibia and Ethiopia. Heugh's (2009) review is an excellent overview. The following is a sampling of the complexities of L2Ls in Africa.

The following data are from Lewis (2009). Angola has 41 living languages and the official language is Portuguese. Benin has 54 living languages with French as a national or official language. Botswana's official language is English with 29 living languages. Burundi has three national or official languages: French, Rundi, and Swahili. Chad's official languages are Standard Arabic and French with 131 living languages. Equatorial Guinea has two official languages; Spanish and French. Ethiopia has Amharic, English, and Tigrinia as official languages, with 85 living languages. Hassaniyya is the official language of Mauritania. South Africa has Afrikaans, Ndebele, Northern Sotho, Southern Sotho, Swati, Tsonga, Tswana, Venda, Xhosa, Zulu, and English as national or official languages. L2L and bilingual instruction are features of many countries in Africa.

Okedara and Okedara (1992) claimed that mother-tongue literacy was important, especially for a country such as Nigeria. They concluded that "[a] local language or mother tongue facilitates the acquisition of literacy" (p. 92). An interesting point of view was that "[a]n individual illiterate may thus end up being bilingual or multilingual before he or she can truly be regarded as functionally literate since he or she has to be able to communicate with neighbours but also the wider community" (p. 102).

"Swahili is now the official language in the states of Tanzania and Kenya, and widely used in the neighbouring countries of Uganda, Mozambique, Burundi, the Congos, Madagascar and the Comoros" (Ostler, 2005, pp. 104–105). It is mostly an L2. "Despite the vast number who use it (estimated at 40 million), Swahili is learnt as a native language only on the islands and coast close to Zanzibar" (p. 105).

Heugh (2009) argues that "literacy instruction and language learning programmes and materials that originate from or that may be currently fashionable in English-dominant contexts beyond Africa cannot be trans/imported successfully to Africa" (p. 122). She speaks of Mother Tongue (MT) and Mother Tongue Medium (MTM). She also notes that "explicit teaching of literacy in the MT and the L2; and that MTM education is required for at least eight years of schooling, along with L2 teaching and learning" (pp. 104–105). In general it appears that L2 literacy across Africa often results in lower achievement than bilingual programs. UNESCO (2008) states that "the detailed analysis of these regional patterns shows that: whilst there have been substantial gains in East Asia and especially China, the Arab States, Bangladesh and Sub-Saharan Africa are lagging behind" (p. 48).

Europe: Second Language Literacy

It is not unusual for Europeans to be literate in several languages. The history of language is complex and involves the influence of Greek, Latin, German, French, English, and other languages

(Ostler, 2005). It is impossible to describe the complexities in this chapter (see Ostler, 2005). L2L is a feature of Finland (12 living languages), Norway (10), and Sweden (12) (Lewis, 2009). Each has an immigrant population so many individuals are involved in Finnish, Norwegian, and Swedish L2L programs. The Sámi in Finland, Norway, and Sweden have "their own language(s) and distinct culture(s)" (Aikio-Puoskari, 2006, p. 238). "From the mid-19th to the mid-20th century, the Sámi were subjected to a conscious and, at times, very harsh assimilation policy" (Aikio-Puoskari, 2006, p. 238). However, "the Sámi language can be the language of instruction, or a subject called 'the mother tongue/first language,' or 'a foreign/second language' in the schools of Norway Sweden and Finland" (p. 245). Overall, there are hundreds of L1s in Europe (Lewis, 2009) and they are often not represented in schools (Ostler, 2005). Phillipson (2006) concludes that, "roughly 300 languages are in use in EU member states ...." (p. 90). It is clear that many learners are involved in L2L in their home countries.

Russian is the official language of both the Russian Federation (60 living languages) and the Russian Federation Europe (100) (Lewis, 2009). Russian is widely spoken in the former Soviet Republics and in the former Warsaw Pact countries of Eastern and Central Europe, where many learn it as a second language in schools (Ostler, 2005). There are millions who learn Russian as an L2.

Many immigrants who speak languages other than that spoken in their new countries are involved in L2 programs. Arabic-speaking immigrants, for example, are involved in English, French, Dutch, Spanish, German, Portuguese, Italian, and other L2L instruction across Europe. L2L learning is a significant feature of teaching and learning in Europe. Some are concerned about the hegemony of English in Europe. Phillipson (2006) concludes that "English linguistic hegemony has been progressively asserted in the EU system" (p. 91).

Programing Code: Second Language Literacy

There are a number of languages that are not typically identified as L2s. Musical notation literacy skills are used around the world. The L2 transcends the L1. An Urdu speaker can read and write music that a Zambuangan speaker can read and understand, although they cannot communicate in L1 with each other. Math is also an international L2. There are others. However, the most significant is likely to be programing language.

Programing has been around for quite a while. The perforated paper roll used in player pianos to control the playing of the piano is a kind of program. Programing code for computers has been around since the 1940s. There are about 2,500 programing languages and hundreds of "dialects," which are variants of programs. Computers are inflexible machines that only accept specific forms of input. Program languages have syntactic and semantic features. Syntax refers to the grammar and "spelling" of a program language. In essence, the syntax of a language determines the expected form and different programs have defined their own syntactical rules that determine which words, what order the words should be in, and what punctuation that the computer can "understand." Semantics refers to meaning and in many cases is written in natural language, often English, or mathematical terms. The following is a program provided by Reginald D'Silva in Java (Figure 29.1). This is a typical program written by students to practice writing different languages such as BASIC, Fortran IV, and COBAL. The program tells a computer to print out on the screen the phrase "Hello World."

Syntax statements include English, mathematical, and punctuation components that follow particular language-specific syntactic patterns. A compiler is a language specific program that is used to make the program computer readable. A program may run successfully because of its syntax, but results in an incorrect outcome because of semantic problems in the program. A programer can both read and write code. The underlying syntax and semantics of programing code are related to English in significant ways.

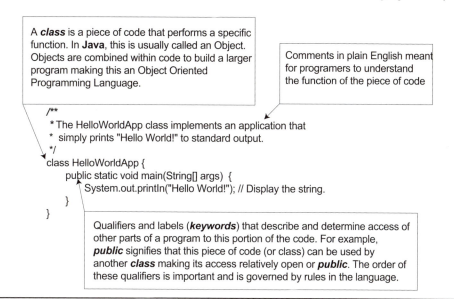

Figure 29.1 An example of a Java program

Source: Reginald D'Silva.

There are those who write and read programing code, but cannot communicate orally or in writing with each other because their L1s are different. The proliferation of computer viruses, worms, and trojans argues for the position that programing code is a major L2L. Programing code also makes possible a great variety of digital applications, including, of course, the internet.

Multiliteracies: Second Language Literacy

Online Literacy

Mode, medium, context, and *purpose* are elements that usually define literacy. The *importance* and *relevance* of literacies are also essential elements that are established by the communities that create, shape, and *legitimize* them. One or more of these elements in essence defines any kind of literacy.

Kress (2003) identifies two distinct modes—*writing* and *image*—and their associated media, namely the *book* and *screen* respectively. The shift in dominance from the book to the screen appears to be the driving force behind how literacy is envisioned in this millennium. Some identify *web literacies* as making meaning in the *context* of the web (Eagleton & Dobler, 2007). Indeed every literary act has a *purpose*, which may be one of making meaning or that of communicating with another human being. However, the *importance, relevance,* and *legitimacy* of these literacy skills are determined by the communities where these literacies are situated.

With the rapid advancement of information and communication technology (ICT) the importance, relevance, and legitimacy of online literacy is growing at an unprecedented rate. "The former constellation of *medium of book* and *mode of writing* is giving way, and in many domains has already given way, to the new constellation of *medium of screen* and *mode of image*" (Kress, 2003, p. 9). In the last decade internet use has grown dramatically by around 400% (Internetworldstats.com, 2010) making online literacy, the skills needed to read, write, publish, and interact online, one of the most important and relevant concepts in academic and non-academic domains in the developed world. Some believe in the notion of a *digital language* that mediates online literacy and suggest that those born into the age of ICTs are native speakers of this language or *digital natives*. On the other hand, those who have acquired the skills to use these technologies and have been socialized into these environments are *digital immigrants* (Prensky, 2001). With only 26.6 % of the world currently online (Internetworldstats.com, 2010), this view of online literacy implies that an overwhelming majority of the world's population either have or will have digital as a second language (DSL) (Haynes, 2007). Experts have suggested that changes in ICT will influence how we define literacies in the twenty-first century (Leu, 2000). Online literacy is a "deictic" term, which means that "what it means to be literate has become a moving target, one we can never completely define because information and communication technologies continually change" (Leu, 1999). Our knowledge and understanding of online literacy will probably continue to remain in a constant state of flux as internet use widens. The net, in part, is associated with multiliteracies.

Multiliteracies and L2 Students

Cummins (2006) noted that "literacy as it is taught and tested in our schools is still conceived as linear, text-based reading and writing skills. These are the skills tested in high school graduation examinations or literacy tests" (p. 5) "To view literacies as multiple, multilingual, multicultural, situated and fluid is, in itself, to contest and subvert the singularity of dominant cultural approaches to national print literacy" (Pegrum, 2008, p. 140). "Teachers typically assume that 'literacy' refers only to literacy in the dominant language and that students' first language proficiency is irrelevant to their educational progress" (Cummins, 2006, p. 6). These flawed assumptions lead to perceptions that "digital, multimodal forms of literacies are not the core of a literacy curriculum" (Mills, 2007, p. 230). As a result, some teachers have been found to limit certain non-mainstream learners' access to multiliteracies instruction and the opportunities that knowledge of these literacies can bring (Mills, 2007). This is similar to the notion that comic books are inappropriate for both L1 and L2 learners, while there is evidence that L2 learners benefit in various ways from them (Norton & Vanderheyden, 2004).

Multiliteracies pedagogical approaches encourage learners to draw on their own cultural and multilingual knowledge to produce multimodal texts using digital media (Lotherington, 2007), photography (Stein, 2000), film (Pegrum, 2008), and have been shown to improve L2 learners' skills with more traditional forms of literacy such as academic essays (Stein, 2000). Multiliteracy pedagogy emphasizes the growing diversity in our globalized world. Our multicultural and pluralistic society requires citizens who can proficiently negotiate "the code switching often to be found within a text among different languages, dialects, or registers; different visual and iconic meanings and variations in the gestural relationships among people, language and, material objects" (New London Group, 1996, p. 69). When learners are able to "juxtapose different languages, discourse, styles, and approaches, they gain substantially in meta-cognitive and meta-linguistic abilities and in their ability to reflect critically on complex systems and their interactions" (New London Group, 1996, p. 69). It seems that use of the internet may be a significant L2 multiliteracy influence.

English (495.8 million), Chinese (407.7), Spanish (139.8), Japanese (96.0), and Portuguese (77.6) are the top five internet languages (http://www.internetworldstats.com/stats7.htm). It is possible to search and access non-English websites by conducting searches in English (Gunderson, 2009). The World Wide Web represents a vast resource that involves L2L in many different modes. Multiliteracies also include drama, painting, poetry, and a wide variety of other genres and modes. One large-scale coordinated project developed in Canada can be seen at http://multiliteracies.ca. Both L1 and L2 literacies are found on this page, including multiple L1s, print, "claymation" productions, and other L2Ls.

Conclusion

More people around the world learn literacy skills in an L2 than they do in their own L1. It appears to us that many view English as *the* primary L2. This is, of course, an English-centric notion that does not reflect the realities of the world. Chinese appears to be the major L2. Spanish, Russian, English, Hindi, Swahili, and others are also significant L2s. It appears that learners involved in L2L instruction generally do not do as well in learning the L2 as those involved in L1 literacy instruction. L2 is the language of instruction as a result of colonialism, political choice, immigration, or overt assimilationist policies.

The term "second language literacy" is inadequate to describe the complex interactions occurring in multiple multimodal environments. A single human being has the potential to learn literacy skills in a number of second or additional languages that are not necessarily traditional in nature. A monolingual Farsi speaker, for instance, may have programing code literacy skills, digital as an L2, and music or math as an L2. Rather than the term "second", it may be more appropriate to categorize these languages as "additional." English, for the moment, does appear to be a significant component of the World Wide Web. However, this seems to be changing as use of the Web increases around the globe. The underlying program codes continue to employ English-like languages.

Multiliteracies broaden the view of what literacy activities L2 students should and can be involved in. There is a significant need to explore L2L issues as the scope of multiliteracies expands and the world itself grows smaller. As our understanding of what constitutes multiliteracies expands, defining the term will become more complex and difficult.

References

Aikio-Puoskari, U. (2009). The ethnic revival, language and education of the Sámi. In T. Skutnabb-Kangas, R. Phillipson, A. K. Mohanty, & M. Panda (Eds.), *Social justice through multilingual education* (pp. 238–262). Bristol: Multilingual Matters.

Alderson, J. C. (1985). Reading in a foreign language: A reading problem or a language problem? *RELC Journal, 16*(2), 1–24.

Baker, J. N. (1992). The presence of the name: Reading scripture in an Indonesian village. In J. Boyarin (Ed.), *The ethnography of reading* (pp. 98–138). Berkeley, CA: University of California Press.

Baker, K. A., & deKanter, A. A. (1981). *Effectiveness of bilingual education: A review of the literature.* Washington, DC: Office of Planning and Budget, US Department of Education.

Barton, D. (1994). *Literacy: An introduction to the ecology of written language.* Malden, MA: Blackwell.

Barton, D., & Hamilton, M. (1998). *Local literacies: Reading and writing in one community.* London: Routledge.

Bendor-Samuel, J. (1996). African languages. In P. T. Daniels & W. Bright (Eds.), *The world's writing systems* (pp. 689–691). New York: Oxford University Press.

Cheung, H., McBride-Chang, C., & Chow, B. (2006). Reading Chinese. In R. M. Joshi & P. G. Aaron (Eds.), *Handbook of orthography and literacy* (pp. 421–438). Mahwah, NJ: Lawrence Erlbaum Associates.

Cope, B., & Kalantzis, M. (Eds.) (2000). *Multiliteracies: Literacy learning and the design of social features.* New York: Routledge.

Crawford, J. (1989). *Bilingual education: History politics, theory, and practice.* Trenton, NJ: Crane Publishers.

Crawford, J. (1997). *Best evidence: Research foundation of the bilingual education act.* National Clearing House for Bilingual Education. Retrieved September 8, 2010, from http://www.ncela.gwu.edu/files/rcd/BE020829/Best_Evidence_Research.pdf.

Cummins, J. (1979). Cognitive/academic language proficiency, linguistic interdependence, the optimum age question and some other matters. *Working papers on bilingualism, 19,* 197–205.

Cummins, J. (1980). The entry and exit fallacy in bilingual education. *NABE Journal, 4,* 25–59.

Cummins, J. (1981a). Age on arrival and immigrant second language learning in Canada: A reassessment. *Applied Linguistics, 2,* 132–149.

Cummins, J. (1981b). The role of primary language development in promoting educational success for language minority students. *Schooling and language minority students.* Los Angeles: California State University.

Cummins, J. (1983). Language proficiency and academic achievement. In J. W. Oller, Jr (Ed.), *Issues in language testing research* (pp. 108–129). Rowley, MA: Newbury House.

Cummins, J. (1984). *Bilingualism and special education: Issues in assessment and pedagogy.* Clevedon: Multilingual Matters.

Cummins, J. (2000). *Language, power and pedagogy.* Toronto: Multilingual Matters Limited.

Cummins, J. (2006). Multiliteracies and equity: How do Canadian schools measure up? *Education Canada, 46*(2), 4–7.

Cummins, J., & Swain, M. (1986). Linguistic interdependence: A central principle of bilingual education. In *Bilingualism in education* (pp. 80–95). New York: Longman Group UK Limited.

Daniels, P. T. (1996). The study of writing systems. In P. T. Daniels & W. Brigfht (Eds.), *The world's writing systems* (pp. 1–20). New York: Oxford University Press.

Diringer, D. (1968). *The alphabet* (Vols 1 & 2). New York: Funk & Wagnalls.

Eagleton, M. B., & Dobler, E. (2007). *Reading the web: Strategies for internet inquiry.* New York: The Guilford Press.

Elley, W. B. (1992). *How in the world do students read?* Hamburg: The International Association for the Evaluation of Educational Achievement.

Erard, M. (2004). The Mandarin offensive: Inside Beijing's global campaign to make Chinese the number one language in the world. *Wired, 4*, 1–2.

Gunderson, L. (2007). *English-only instruction and immigrant students in secondary school: A critical examination.* Mahwah, NJ: Lawrence Erlbaum and Associates.

Gunderson, L. (2008). The state of the art of secondary ESL teaching and learning. *Journal of Adolescent and Adult Literacy, 52*(3), November, 184–188.

Gunderson, L. (2009). *ESL (ELL) literacy instruction: A guidebook to theory and practice.* New York: Routledge.

Gunderson, L., D'Silva, R., & Chen, L. (2010). Second language reading disabilities: International themes. In R. Allington & A. McGill-Franzen (Eds.), *Handbook of research in reading disabilities* (pp. 13–24). New York: Routledge.

Hakuta, K., Butler, Y. G., & Witt, D. (2000). *How long does it take English learners to attain proficiency?* Santa Barbara, CA: University of California Linguistic Minority Research Institute.

Haynes, J. (2007). *DSL—Digital as a Second Language.* Retrieved 15 March, 2010, from http://www.everythingesl.net/inservices/dsl__digital_second_language_11955.php.

Heine, B., & Nurse, D. (Eds.) (2000). *African languages: An introduction.* Cambridge: Cambridge University Press.

Heugh, K. (2009). Literacy and bi/multilingual education in Africa. In T. Skutnabb-Kangas, R. Phillipson, A. K. Mohanty, & M. Panda (Eds.), *Social justice through multilingual education* (pp. 103–124). Bristol: Multilingual Matters.

Ho, C. S.-H., Chan, D. W.-O., Tsang, S.-M., Chan, S.-H., & Lee, S.-H. (2002). The cognitive profile and multiple-deficit hypothesis in Chinese developmental dyslexia. *Developmental Psychology, 38*, 543–553.

Hudson-Ross, S., & Dong, Y. R. (1990). Literacy Learning as a reflection of language and culture: Chinese elementary school education. *The Reading Teacher, 44*, 110–123.

Internetworldstats.com. (2010). *World internet usage statistics.* Retrieved March, 15, 2010, from http://www.internetworldstats.com/stats.htm.

Jhingran, D. (2009). Hundreds of home languages in the country and many in most classrooms: Coping with diversity in primary education in India. In T. Skutnabb-Kangas, R. Phillipson, A. K. Mohanty, & M. Panda (Eds.), *Social justice through multilingual education* (pp. 263–282). Bristol: Multilingual Matters.

Joshi, R. M., & Aaron, P. G. (2006). Introduction to the volume. In R. M. Joshi & P. G. Aaron (Eds.), *Handbook of orthography and literacy* (pp. xiii–xiv),. Mahwah, NJ: Lawrence Erlbaum Associates.

Klingner, J. K., Artilles, A. J., & Barletta, L. M. (2006). English language learners who struggle with reading? Language acquisition or LD? *Journal of Learning Disabilities, 39*, 108–128.

Koda, K. (2008). Looking back and thinking forward. In K. Koda & A. M. Zehler (Eds.), *Learning to read across languages* (pp. 222–234). New York: Routledge.

Kress, G. (2003). *Literacy in the new media age.* London and New York: Routledge.

Landerl, K. (2006). Reading acquisition in different orthographies: Evidence from direct comparisons. In R. M. Joshi & P. G. Aaron (Eds.), *Handbook of orthography and literacy* (pp. 513–530). Mahwah, NJ: Erlbaum.

Lankshear, C., & Knobel, M. (2003). *New literacies: Changing Knowledge and classroom practice.* Buckingham: Open University Press.

Leu, D. (1981). Questions from a metatheoretical perspective: The interdependence of solutions to issues involved in the development of reading comprehension models. In M. Kamil (Ed.), *Directions in reading: Research and instruction* (pp. 96–107). Washington, DC: The National Reading Conference.

Leu, D. (1999). *Caity's question: Literacy as deixis on the internet.* Retrieved March 15, 2010, from http://www.readingonline.org/electronic/elec_index.asp?HREF=/electronic/RT/caity.html.

Leu, D. (2000). How will literacy be defined in the new millennium? *Reading Research Quarterly, 35*(1), 64–71.

Lewis, M. P. (Ed.) (2009). *Ethnologue: Languages of the world* (16th ed.). Dallas, TX: SIL International. Online version: http://www.ethnologue.com/.

Lo Bianco, J. (2000). Multiliteracies and multilingualism. In B. Cope & M. Kalantzis (Eds.), *Multiliteracies: Literacy learning and the design of social features* (pp. 92–105). New York: Routledge.

López, M., & Gunderson, L. (2006). Oaxacan parents' perception of literacy. In V. Pang & R. Jimenez (Eds.), *Race, ethnicity and education: Language, literacy and schooling* (pp. 95–113). Wesport, CT: Praeger.

López-Gopar, M. (2007). Beyond the alienating alphabetic literacy: Multiliteracies in indigenous education in Mexico. *Diaspora, Indigenous and Minority Education, 1*(3), 159–174.

Lotherington, H. (2007). Rewriting traditional tales as multilingual narratives at elementary school: Problems and progress. *Canadian Journal of Applied Linguistics, 10*, 241–256.

McCarty, T. L. (2009). Empoering indigenous languages—What can be learned from Native American Experiences? In T. Skutnabb-Kangas, R. Phillipson, A. K. Mohanty, & M. Panda (Eds.), *Social justice through multilingual education* (pp. 125–139). Bristol: Multilingual Matters.

Mills, K. A. (2007). "Have You Seen *Lord of the Rings*?" Power, pedagogy, and discourses in a multiliteracies classroom. *Journal of Language, Identity and Education, 6*, 221–241.

Mohanty, A. K. (2009). Multilingual education: A bridge too far? In T. Skutnabb-Kangas, R. Phillipson, A. K. Mohanty, & M. Panda (Eds.), *Social justice through multilingual education* (pp. 3–15). Bristol: Multilingual Matters.

Mohanty, A. K., Mishra, M. K., Reddy, N. U., & Ramesh, G. (2009). Overcoming the language barrier for tribal children: Multilingual education in Andhra Pradesh. In T. Skutnabb-Kangas, R. Phillipson, A. K. Mohanty, & M. Panda (Eds.), *Social justice through multilingual education* (pp. 283–297). Bristol: Multilingual Matters.

National Network of Education. (2010) February 5. Retrieved March 15, 2010, from http://www.indiaedunews. net/Today/Northern_India_fares_low_in_literacy_rate,_says_study_11184/.

New London Group. (1996). A pedagogy of multiliteracies: Designing social futures. *Harvard Educational Review, 66*, 60–92.

Nicolas, A. B. (2009). Reversing language shift through a native language immersion teaching programme in Canada. In T. Skutnabb-Kangas, R.Phillipson, A. K. Mohanty, & M. Panda, M. (Eds.), *Social justice through multilingual education* (pp. 220–237). Bristol: Multilingual Matters.

Norton, B., & Vanderheyden, K. (2004). Comic book culture and second language learners. In B. Norton & K. Toohet (Eds.), *Critical pedagogies and language learning* (pp. 201–221). Cambridge: Cambridge University Press.

Okedara, J. T., & Okedara, C. A. (1992). Mother-tongue literacy in Africa. *Annals of the American Academy of Political and Scoial Science, 520*, 91–102.

Ostler, N. (2005). *Empires of the word: A language history of the world.* New York: HarperCollins.

Pegrum, M. (2008). Film, culture and identity: Critical intercultural literacies for the language classroom. *Language and Intercultural Communication, 8*, 135–154.

Peréz, S. J. (2009). The contribution of post-colonial theory in intercultural bilingual education in Peru: An indigenous teacher education programme. In T. Skutnabb-Kangas, R.Phillipson, A. K. Mohanty, & M. Panda, M. (Eds.), *Social justice through multilingual education* (pp. 201–219). Bristol: Multilingual Matters.

Phillipson, R. (2006). The tension between linguistic diversity and dominant English. In T. Skutnabb-Kangas, R. Phillipson, A. K. Mohanty, & M. Panda, M. (Eds.), *Social justice through multilingual education* (pp. 85–102). Bristol: Multilingual Matters.

PISA (Programme for International Student Assessment). (2009). *Assessment framework—Key competencies in reading, mathematics, and science.* Paris: Organisation for Economic Co-operation and Development.

Prah, K. K. (Ed.) (1998). *Between distinction and extinction: The harmonisation and standardization of African Languages.* Johannesburg: Witwaterstrand University Press.

Prensky, M. (2001). Digital natives, digital immigrants. *On the Horizon, 9*(5), 1–6.

Rueda, R., & Windmueller, M. P. (2006). English language learners, LD, and overrepresentation: A multiple-level analysis. *Journal of Learning Disabilities, 39*, 99–107.

Schmelkes, S. (2004). La educación intercultural: Un campo en proceso de consolidación [Intercultural education: A field in consolidation process]. *Revista Mexicana de Investigación Educativa, 9*(20), 9–13.

Stein, P. (2000). Rethinking resources: Multimodal pedagogies in the ESL classroom. *TESOL Quarterly, 34*, 333–336.

Street, B. (2003). What's "new" in New Literacy Studies? Critical approaches to literacy in theory and practice. *Current Issues in Comparative Education, 5*(2), 72–91.

UNESCO (2003). *Literacy: A UNESCO perspective.* Paris: UNESCO.

UNESCO (2008). *International Literacy Statistics: A review of concepts, Methodology, and current data.* Montreal: UNESCO Institute for Statistics.

Wiley, T. (2005). Second language literacy and biliteracy. In E. Hinkel (Ed.), *Handbook of research in second language teaching and learning* (pp. 529–544). Mahwah, NJ: Lawrence Erlbaum Associates.

Willinsky, J. (1990). *The new literacy: Redefining reading and writing in the schools.* New York: Routledge.

Ziegler, J. C., Perry, C., Ma-Wyatt, A., Ladner, D., & Schulte-Körne, G. (2003). Developmental dyslexia in different languages: Language specific or universal? *Journal of Experimental Child Psychology, 86*, 169–193.

30

Out of My Orthographic Depth
Second Language Reading

Barbara Birch

Vagary: an unpredictable turn of events, dating in English from the 1500s, by semantic drift from "a wandering journey" apparently borrowed from Latin vagārī "to wander."

Because of a vagary of my recent years, I have been able to study both Macedonian and Mongolian in their home countries. The former, a Southern Slavic language, has a shallow Cyrillic orthography dating from the 1940s; its letters correspond one-to-one with its phonemes. The latter, a Mongolic language, has a mid twentieth century Cyrillic orthography as well, but it is deep; the correspondence between the visual appearance of the word and its pronunciation is not always predictable. Macedonian was easy for me to decode very quickly, but learning to decode Mongolian literally made my head hurt. As a reading researcher, I wrote this chapter in an attempt to understand my experiences as acquisition phenomena (and not merely the effects of aging) and their implications for second language (L2) reading instruction.

It is impossible to convey the diverse breadth and depth of reading research and applications available for the interested teacher, but everyone agrees that the purposes for reading are generally similar among readers, to get information, to study and learn, to access sacred, classical, and popular literature, and to escape everyday realities by entering a fictional world. Given these purposes, an early goal for reading instruction is for learners to achieve efficient automatic decoding abilities, so they have enough mental attention left over for comprehension, internalization of ideas, appreciation, and relaxation. The purposes for L2 reading are much the same as they are for first language (L1) reading, but research is uncovering a paradox in early L2 reading acquisition.

The paradox is that the very same efficiency and automaticity that lead to fluent L1 reading may in fact hinder acquisition of fluent L2 reading. This effect might be greater when the L1 and L2 orthographies are very different and when the L2 has a difficult (deep or opaque) writing system or orthography. As it turns out, I experienced these effects as a beginning reader of Macedonian and Mongolian. In learning to read Mongolian, I found myself out of my orthographic depth.

Nomenclature

To start with, Perfetti and his colleagues are careful to distinguish writing system, orthography, and script (Perfetti & Dunlap, 2008, pp. 14–22).

- A *writing system* is a technology that encodes speech by representing units of language with graphemes. Simplifying the situation, speech units can be phonemic as in alphabetic European languages, syllabic as in Japanese kana, or logographic as in Chinese characters, which encode meanings and morphemes. Making an analogy between millet, rice, and maize, researchers refer to graphemes as having different *grain-sizes*. Logographic graphemes have a larger grain-size than syllabic graphemes, which are larger than phoneme-based graphemes. Macedonian and Mongolian both use an alphabetic writing system.
- An *orthography* is the implementation of a writing system technology in a specific language. Macedonian orthography and Mongolian orthography are quite different from each other, although they use more or less the same Cyrillic graphemes. Cyrillic is quite different from the Roman alphabet; there is only a little overlap in the graphemes.
- A *script* is a font used to represent an orthography. Different scripts are made up of different graphic styles. For instance, I never learned to decode Cyrillic handwriting script; I could read some conventionalized cursive on signs, but people's handwriting was a code I could not crack. (I have much more sympathy for my students now.)

A distinction between various writing systems and orthographies comes from a comparison of how close or direct the correlation is between the graphemes used and the unit of language represented in the writing.

- *Transparency* means that graphemes encode language in shallow and predictable one-to-one correlations. Macedonian orthography is shallow and transparent.
- *Opacity* means that the graphemes encode language units in deep and unpredictable many-to-many correlations. English is opaque especially in its vowel bi-directional mappings from letter to sound. Mongolian orthography is also somewhat opaque to the beginning reader.

People acquire their L1 in infancy and childhood, and their L1 knowledge affects their acquisition of L2s. The potential relationship that L1 has on L2 acquisition is called *transfer*. In reading, L1 to L2 transfer effects occur at the level of system, orthography, or script, but most research focuses on the first two. L1 systemic and orthographic knowledge and processing strategies become hard-wired into our brains as we become fluent readers. The hard-wiring that allows for fluency and automaticity in reading has an effect on reading acquisition of later-learned languages.

- *Facilitation* refers a positive relationship between L1 knowledge and processing strategies and L2 acquisition. In reading, facilitation means that L1 knowledge and processing strategies are useful and helpful in learning to read an L2 writing system or orthography with fluency.
- *Interference* refers to a negative relationship between L1 knowledge and processing strategies and L2 acquisition. For reading, interference means that L1 knowledge and processing strategies delay, obstruct, or prevent learning to read an L2 writing system or orthography.

To continue our discussion of transfer and its effects on L2 reading, we must turn to certain aspects of L1 reading.

L1 Reading Acquisition

Researchers posit some important commonalities, or universal principles, in first reading experiences regardless of writing system or orthography. Nevertheless, despite the universal commonalities, there are also important learner variables and linguistic variation to be found in people's first experiences with print and text.

Universals of L1 Reading

Lengthy and extensive research into L1 reading can be summarized into four principles.

- The *Processing* Principle: Successful reading rests both on general knowledge storage in long-term memory and on-line processing components, procedures, and strategies that use short-term memory (Birch, 2006, pp. 2–7).
- The *Interactive* Principle: Successful reading simultaneously involves well-developed cognition, language knowledge, general comprehension, and language-specific in-take strategies (Birch, 2006, p. 3).
- The *Mapping* Principle: Successful reading involves a mapping (or correlation) between speech and graphemes at different grain-sizes (writing systems). In addition, each orthography has different language-specific *mapping details* (Koda, 2008, p. 73).
- The *Phonology* Principle: Despite different mapping grain-sizes and details, reading always recruits phonology, so it involves language-related phonemic awareness and listening skills. However, phonology may be involved in different ways in reading different writing systems and orthographies (Perfetti & Dunlap, 2008, p. 14).

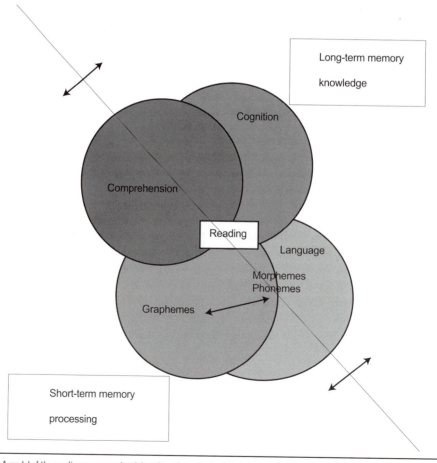

Figure 30.1 A model of the reading processor involving the universal principles of processing, interaction, mapping, and phonology

These principles are illustrated in models of reading, like that described in Perfetti, Liu, and Tan (2002), or as I illustrate here in Figure 30.1. Interaction is illustrated by the intersecting circles of language, cognition, comprehension, and processing strategies with reading at the center. Processing refers to the connections between long-term memory components and short-term processing components. The mapping is the arrow between graphemes and phonemes or morphemes (phonology).

Cognition contains declarative knowledge about the world, culture, experiences, and so on. This area interacts with general comprehension processes such as meaning-construction, interpretation, inference, and so on. Language is systemic knowledge about semantics, syntax, phonology, morphology, and word meaning that increases as children learn their L1. Once children learn to read, they connect their knowledge about orthography and the writing system to phonology and morphology. The processing component also develops as children learn to understand speech; phonemic, morphological, lexical, syntactic, and discourse strategies increase and become automatic. At the point where children begin learning to read and write, the language-specific mapping details between graphemes and speech phonemes, syllables, and morphemes form.

L1 Learner Variables

This model predicts a lot of variation in how people learn to read. Most L1 reading research revolves around the variables correlated with good comprehension abilities as opposed to those correlated with poor comprehension abilities. Again, diverse variables have been studied: *sociocultural attitudes* toward literacy; *personal variables* such as gender, age, or parental behaviors, motivation, amount of leisure, or peer group influences; *cognitive factors* such as memory limitations, attention span, or intelligence; *physical factors* such as vision, hearing, or speech; and *linguistic factors* such as degree of phonological, morphological, and syntactic awareness, amount and depth of vocabulary knowledge, and so on. In this section, I focus on one L1 learner variable associated with the *Phonology* Principle (Rayner, Foorman, Perfetti, Pesetsky, & Seidenberg, 2001, p. 44).

The *Phonological Deficit* Hypothesis

Because knowledge of phonology and phonemic processing strategies are both necessary for reading, children who have a deficit in phonological knowledge or processing will have impairments or delays in learning to read, especially in learning to read opaque writing systems.

Dyslexia is a complex impairment of reading that seems to involve problems with phonological processing. The *Phonological Deficient* Hypothesis predicts that people with impairments in phonological processing will have difficulty learning to read. Goswami (2002) presents a cross-linguistic overview of dyslexia, with the assumption that the primary cause for developmental dyslexia in all languages comes from readers' difficulties with representing speech sounds in their mind and that these problems are exacerbated by opaque orthographies. Since the problem of dyslexia is also language-dependent, that evidence will be reviewed below.

Linguistic Variation

In Birch (2006) I review cross-linguistic research into the effect of different writing systems on readers' psycholinguistic processing and brain activation. Quite a few brain activation studies as well as other robust psycholinguistic evidence show that learning different writing systems forces the brain to develop different low-level knowledge and processing strategies. It's true that all writing systems involve some kind of phonological processing. However, Chinese, with its characters, is based on retrieving phonology when the word or morpheme is recognized. Alphabetic languages are based on assembling phonology so as to retrieve the word from memory (Perfetti, Liu, Fiez, Nelson, Bolger, & Tan, 2007).

Two hypotheses have emerged from L1 reading acquisition research regarding variation in reading ability due to writing system and orthography. First, the *Orthographic Depth* Hypothesis predicts that some writing systems are easier to learn and some are harder to learn. Second, the *Syllable Complexity* Hypothesis predicts that languages with complex syllables will be harder to read (Seymour, Aro, & Erskine, 2003, p. 145).

The *Orthographic Depth* Hypothesis

Shallow (or transparent) orthographies are easier to read using phonological processes, so children learning a shallow L1 orthography learn to read faster than children learning a deep (or opaque) L1 orthography.

The *Syllable Complexity* Hypothesis

Complex syllable structures (many different syllable structures with different consonant clusters as onsets and codas) increase the difficulty of acquiring literacy.

There is ample evidence that these linguistic variables make some writing systems and orthographies harder to acquire than others, which should come as no surprise to perceptive teachers and learners around the world. Therefore, it is worthwhile reviewing some of the literature on cross-linguistic comparisons of difficulty.

Cross-Linguistic Comparisons of Difficulty

As we have seen, studies show that some writing systems and some orthographies are more transparent than others and some have easier syllable structures. These are easier to learn. Some writing systems and orthographies are more opaque and/or have complex syllable structures; these should be more complicated to learn. There is also evidence for different degrees of difficulty for writing systems and orthographies when we look at the common instructional methodologies used to instruct children and non-native speakers to read. Finally, studies of dyslexia also indicate that some systems and orthographies facilitate recovery and others don't.

Transparency

Within alphabetic systems, transparency means that one grapheme spells one phoneme and one phoneme only. Opaque means that each grapheme spells more than one phoneme and each phoneme may have a number of spellings. Perfetti and Dunlap (2008) provide an orthographic depth chart for alphabetic languages with Finnish, Welsh, Italian, Serbo-Croatian, Spanish, Portuguese, Korean, and German as transparent or shallow orthographies. Danish and Dutch are intermediate. Lao, Khmer, French, English, Arabic, and Hebrew are opaque or deep alphabetic orthographies. Syllabic systems such as Japanese kana are shallow and transparent, and so is the mixed syllabo-alphabetic system in Korean.

Tseng (2002, p. 3), using the slightly different notion of "ease of predicting the pronunciation of a word from the surface structure of its written form," calls Chinese "one of the world's most phonologically 'deep' orthographies." Chinese writing is a complicated system that encodes both semantic units and phonological units, but they are both highly irregular. Chinese readers must memorize thousands of sinograms in order to read. Thus, there is a scale of difficulty from the most shallow or transparent of writing systems (Finnish, Japanese kana) and orthographies (Finnish, Italian) to the deeper and more opaque (English, Chinese) just in terms of how predictable the pronunciation is from the visual word.

The more transparent the mapping from grapheme to phoneme, the more the reader can simply rely on print-to-sound conversion to get to phonology. The more opaque the orthography, the more the reader must come to rely on other strategies for reading such as probabilistic reasoning, reasoning by analogy to known spelling patterns, morphological processing, accessing whole words from memory, interpreting context, and the like.

Syllable Complexity

Seymour et al. (2003) studied literacy acquisition in five European orthographies. They classified European languages by two dimensions, orthographic depth and syllabic complexity. Syllable complexity contrasts Romance languages with a predominantly CV structure and few complex consonant clusters versus Germanic languages with CVC syllables and complex consonant clusters in initial or final position. The study confirmed that syllable complexity affected decoding ability; complex syllables were a disadvantage for beginning readers. It also confirmed the effect of orthographic depth.

Finnish is a language with the simplest syllabic structures and orthographic transparency. Greek, Italian, and Spanish also have simple syllables and are relatively shallow. Portuguese and French have simple syllables and more opaque orthography. German, Norwegian, and Icelandic have complex syllabic structures but shallow orthography. Dutch, Swedish, and Danish are a bit more complex in syllable structure and also more opaque in orthography. Of the European languages, English has the most complex syllabic structures and the greatest opacity of the languages studied.

Seymour et al. (2003) measured children's general decoding skills by testing their ability to read nonwords, concluding:

> The results demonstrate that the capacity to develop simple nonword decoding skills varies substantially between orthographies. There was evidence that these skills might be more difficult to establish in the context of complex syllable languages than in the context of simple syllable languages. Nonwords were read more accurately and more rapidly by simple syllable than by complex syllable samples. There was also evidence of orthographic depth effects …. Reductions in accuracy and fluency were apparent in French and Portuguese among the simple syllable languages, and in Danish, and, to a lesser extent, Swedish and Dutch, among the complex syllable languages.
>
> (Seymour et al., 2003, pp. 159–160)

English has the most complex syllabic structures and the greatest opacity. Seymour et al. (2003, p. 160) discovered that

> [t]he most striking outcome was the evidence of profound delays in the development of simple decoding skills in English. The performance of the Scottish P1 sample fell far below the range for all other groups. Quantification of this effect … suggested that a reading age of 7.5 years or above was necessary before accuracy and fluency matched the European levels.

In fact, Seymour et al. (2003, p. 167) found that the "normal" reading accuracy and fluency rates for English readers fell within the "disability" rates for readers of many shallow European languages. The researchers felt that the delayed reading in English was caused by the combined factors of syllable complexity and orthographic depth. Overall, they found that readers of English require two and a half or more years of learning to achieve mastery of familiar word recognition and simple decoding, which is approached by readers of other European orthographies within their first year. The rate of foundation literacy acquisition in English is slower by a ratio of 2.5 to 1 compared to languages with simple syllables and shallow orthographies.

Instructional Methodologies

Seymour (1990, 1997, 1999) proposed that, for alphabetic writing systems, "foundation literacy" is acquired in phases. *Phase 1* includes acquisition of the basic components, generally grapheme-to-phoneme correspondences and, for English, familiar sight words. *Phase 2* includes acquisition of more complex orthographic and morphographic processing of larger units such as syllables, onsets and rimes, and morphemes. Transparent alphabets are generally taught using a method combining synthetic phonics (letters are isolated from words and taught along with their pronunciations) and blending (mmmm aaaaaa = ma). Reading acquisition can generally be achieved in phase one of foundation literacy. Extensive practice with reading leads to fluency and automaticity.

On the contrary, English reading instruction begins with synthetic phonics and some blending, but sight words are also taught as wholes. Since the grapheme-to-phoneme correspondences are irregular, children need ample experience and practice to acquire unconscious knowledge of the probabilities that a grapheme will be pronounced a certain way (Birch, 2006). In addition, children are often given instruction in onsets and rimes (e.g., a larger grain-size) and an analogical strategy based on known spelling patterns: If you know "tank," then you can read "pr-ank." Children are sometimes taught about common morphemes as well. It is this secondary phase of strategic acquisition that may account for some of the lag in reading development among English-speaking children. We will return to a discussion of this lag in English reading acquisition later.

Fender (2008) summarized research on children learning to read Arabic. Children learn to read Modern Standard Arabic (MSA) or Classical Arabic (CA), not their own native colloquial dialect. According to Fender (2008), MSA differs from local dialects in vocabulary and some aspects of phonology and grammar. Fender (2008, p. 112) argues that learning MSA is learning to read an L2 for many children. Smythe, Everatt, Al-Menaye, He, Capellini, Gyarmathy, and Siegel (2008) studied word-level literacy among Grade 3 children in Arabic and other languages. MSA has an alphabetic writing system that relies heavily on consonants to represent morphemic roots. Some texts are fully marked with vowel diacritics (highly transparent) and some texts omit vowel diacritics and are highly opaque. Children are expected to have learned the vowelized text by Grade 3, when they are exposed to non-vowelized text. Thus, it appears that they develop phonemic awareness, synthetic phonics, and blending strategies to decode.

To read the non-vowelized text, Fender (2008, p. 113) says "children need to learn to use their morphological knowledge, knowledge of sentence syntax, and the context to identify words that are ambiguous due to the incomplete vowel spellings." Indeed, the claim is made that literacy in Arabic requires fluent word recognition skills incorporating both spelling and contextual information (Abu-Rabia, 1997a, 1997b, 1998). Shimron (1999) makes similar claims for Hebrew. However, given the larger number of countries that teach MSA as the standard language, it is nearly impossible to generalize about how teachers teach reading at present.

There is some literature about children learning to read Chinese. According to Wang and Yang (2008), within the vast area that Chinese reading is taught as an L1, many children first learn a phonetic alphabet called Pinyin (People's Republic of China—PRC), or Zhu-Yin-Fu-Hao in Taiwan, within the first ten weeks of first grade, at six to seven years of age. Teachers use a synthetic/blending method. The phonetic alphabet with diacritics for the Mandarin tones is then used to teach the characters. The alphabet is not used for conventional reading; instead, the sound of the word the character represents is spelled in the phonetic alphabet above the characters in the text. However, in Hong Kong, children are taught using a whole character approach and rote-learning. After hearing the teacher say the characters aloud and explaining their meanings, children copy and memorize them. Children who are taught with a phonetic bootstrap acquire better phonological awareness than those who are taught using the whole character method. In this fashion, children memorize 2,600 to 2,800 characters during their elementary grades (Ho, 2003, p. 282).

Tan, Spinks, Eden, Perfetti, and Siok (2005, p. 8781), in their study of reading acquisition in Chinese, found that, unlike for alphabetic languages, Chinese character reading seems more associated with writing skills than with listening. They report that there is significant spatial analysis necessary to learn each Chinese character, and visual-orthographic processing is an important part of reading characters. The strokes that make up the character are usually done in a particular order, so children need to practice creating the character with the correct order of strokes. They suggest that these demands necessitate a particular instructional methodology, namely

> asking children to repeatedly copy, by writing down, samples of single characters. Through writing, children learn to deconstruct characters into a unique pattern of strokes and components and then regroup these subcharacters into a square linguistic unit. This type of decoding occurs at the visual-orthographic level and is assumed to facilitate children's awareness of the character's internal structure (orthographic awareness). This awareness supports the formation of connections among orthographic, semantic, and phonological units of the Chinese writing system and may be associated with the quality of lexical entries in long-term memory.

To summarize, evidence from instructional methodology shows that transparent alphabetic writing systems can be taught with a simple synthetic strategy with blending in Phase 1. Opaque alphabetic writing systems such as Arabic or English require beginning readers to develop further strategies to cope with text in subsequent phases. They either induce these strategies or they are directly instructed by their teachers. Chinese requires many more years to memorize all of the characters and each individual character is practiced over and over again to the point of automatic recognition.

Brain researchers attribute different brain activation patterns in reading to the characteristics of the script, but also to the instructional methodology. Since Chinese children learners spend a lot of time copying single characters to learn how to make them, Tan et al. (2005) found that children's reading ability in Chinese is more strongly related to handwriting skills than to phonological awareness or listening. Learning Chinese is based on acquiring specific character forms and not general decoding procedures, such as in alphabetic languages, and this becomes hard-wired into the brain. English readers learn to decode the graphemes into phonemes, onsets, rimes, common syllables, and morphemes, and use various processing strategies such as analogy to known spelling patterns in order to read new words. There are different patterns of brain activation associated with different writing systems and orthographies.

Dyslexia

If the *Phonological Deficit* Hypothesis holds, we should find that reading disorders such as dyslexia are more frequent among learners of an opaque writing system or orthography. In fact, this finding is supported by developmental psychology, genetics, and brain imaging. Children with dyslexia have difficulty with tasks involving phonological awareness, short-term memory, and naming. Goswami (2002, p. 149) found that "literacy problems are greater for dyslexic children learning to read inconsistent orthographies (e.g. English) than consistent orthographies (e.g. Italian, German, Greek)."

Goswami cites evidence supporting the hypothesis that, based on syllable complexity and orthographic depth, there should be increasingly greater difficulty on the complex and deep end than on the shallow and transparent end of the writing spectrum. The idea is that children with phonological representation deficits simply recover better, because in learning to read a transparent orthography, they can more easily form grapheme-to-phoneme matchings. If the matching details are easier, they can learn to read more accurately, although they rarely learn to read as well as their non-disabled peers.

Paulesu, Demonet, Fazio, McCrory, Chanoine et al. (2001) compared brain activity of Italian, French, and English speakers with dyslexia while they were reading. All of them showed deficits when compared with the control non-impaired readers. Positron emission tomography (PET) scans showed reduced activity in the same area of the left hemisphere for all of the dyslexic readers, regardless of L1. Nevertheless, when the actual reading performances were compared, the Italian readers were more accurate on word and nonword reading than the French or the English readers, as would be expected given the different transparencies of the languages. They suggested that the same neurocognitive bases cause dyslexia but that different orthographies influence the seriousness of the reading deficits and the ability to recover. In Birch (2006, pp. 168–169) I report some evidence that dyslexic readers can recover in English with targeted interventions designed to improve their bottom-up reading knowledge and strategies.

Ho (2003) finds that, contrary to what some people believed a generation ago, dyslexia does occur among Japanese and Chinese readers as well. She suggests that "phonological processing skills such as phonological awareness, phonological memory, and phonological retrieval are important contributors to early reading success in Chinese" (p. 283) and that "Chinese dyslexic children also have phonological deficits in line with those of their alphabetic counterparts" (p. 290). Little is known about recoverability, however. The overall picture seems to be that phonological deficits and impairments such as those found in dyslexia are at least partially "hidden" by proficiency in and ease with transparent languages because dyslexic readers can recover more easily than similarly impaired readers of opaque languages. The complex and unpredictable matching details of opaque systems and orthographies cause reading problems, and it is more difficult for impaired readers to recover.

L2 Reading Acquisition

L2 reading researchers have become more and more concerned about possible transfer of L1 language knowledge and processing strategies to L2. They have also looked at learner variables in L2 reading acquisition and the different reading strategies that L2 learners employ to read in their L2.

Transfer

Although there has long been anecdotal evidence about transfer, Koda (2008, pp. 70–71) traces a *theory* of transfer back to Krashen (1983), who believed that learners simply fall back on L1 knowledge when L2 knowledge is missing. In a more sophisticated formulation, Gass and Selinker (1983) thought that transfer of L1 knowledge to L2 results in interlanguage characteristics that, when compared to the target L2, can be "positive," "negative," and "neutral." Both of these views rest on the idea that knowledge of language is composed of a set of rules and forms, and that people rely on L1 knowledge because L2 knowledge is insufficient. Theoretically, transfer should disappear once sufficient L2 proficiency is reached and at that point, L1 knowledge and processing strategies will no longer affect the L2.

Koda points out that modern theories of transfer are based on functional notions of language and language learning. In the functionalist view, language is a conventional and culturally-embedded set of correlations between forms/structures and the functions they perform. L1 acquisition means that over time a learner internalizes the form-to-function correlations through daily use of language to communicate; thus, as long as there is use, acquisition doesn't ever stop. When people learn L2s, they internalize new form-to-function mappings; however, it seems clear that earlier knowledge of forms, functions, and the mappings between them creates a complex background for new acquisition.

In this view, the earlier language background is a resource that can help later-language learners if the forms, functions, and the mappings are similar. At the same time, if they are substantially different, they may hinder (or at least not help) the internalization of new forms, functions, and mappings. That is where the possibility of facilitation or interference emerges. In L2 reading, acquisition involves acquiring new knowledge of writing system and orthography and internalizing new correlations between printed text and the units of language represented. L1 to L2 transfer between writing systems and orthographies takes on more complicated aspects at different levels. We can discuss these complexities as learner variables and as processing variables.

Learner Variables

L2 reading is fundamentally different from L1 reading. This seems so obvious now that it is easy to forget that for many years, it was thought that there was universal proficiency that was common to L1 and L2 reading. In the 1980s, reading researchers focused primarily on syntactic, semantic, and discourse strategies, and, of course, vocabulary, and assumed that there was a common cognitive academic language proficiency (CALP), a kind of metalinguistic awareness, underlying L1 and L2 reading ability (Cummins, 1979).

The assumption was that if people were fluent readers in their L1, it was because they had strong syntactic, semantic, and discourse awareness, and then they should be fluent readers in their L2 too. If learners were poor readers in their L2 it was because they lacked CALP and would be expected to be poor L1 readers too. This led to the idea that learners should always become proficient readers in their L1 and develop their CALP before attempting to learn a L2. Once proficient in L1, a L2 could simply be added on. Nevertheless, there was little empirical evidence to substantiate this theory.

Asking whether poor foreign language reading was a "reading problem" or a "language problem," Alderson (1984, p. 4) reviewed the available research and carefully posed two hypotheses about learner variables, which he hoped would stimulate more empirical research and better pedagogic implications. In formulating the two hypotheses, Alderson used the word "strategies" to mean syntactic, semantic, and discourse comprehension strategies, not intake processing strategies related to writing system or orthography.

The *Developmental Interdependence* Hypothesis I

Poor reading in a foreign language is due to poor reading ability in the first language. Poor first language readers will read poorly in the foreign language and good first language readers will read well in the foreign language … [or] poor foreign language reading is due to incorrect strategies for reading that foreign language, strategies which differ from the strategies for reading the native language.

The *Linguistic Threshold* Hypothesis I

Poor reading in a foreign language is due to inadequate knowledge of the target language … [or] poor foreign language reading is due to reading strategies in the first language not being employed in the foreign language, due to inadequate knowledge of the foreign language. Good first-language readers will read well in the foreign language once they have passed a threshold of foreign language ability.

The *Developmental Interdependence* Hypothesis represents the common underlying proficiency or the CALP hypothesis. It suggests that problems in L2 reading acquisition are attributable to the readers' use of incorrect syntactic, semantic, and discourse comprehension strategies because they are simply poor readers in general (e.g., the reading problem). The *Linguistic Threshold* Hypothesis assumes that the syntactic, semantic, and discourse strategies would be the similar for successful reading in both languages, and that learners are poor readers simply because of their lack of proficiency in the L2 (e.g., the language problem).

In those days, there was as yet little research on or even awareness of the lower level phonemic, syllabic, morphemic, and orthographic intake strategies that we now consider important in reading. As Alderson put it:

> If transfer of reading ability takes place across the native/non-native language divide … readers who are poor in foreign language reading but not in their first language are either logical impossibilities or *merely in need of familiarization with the foreign language code*.
>
> (Alderson, 1984, p. 6; emphasis mine)

To understand how much is included in the word "merely," and to update these hypotheses about learner variables, we go now to an examination of lower level strategies in reading.

Reading Strategies

Ehri (1998) provides a good starting point for strategic comparisons among languages. For English reading development, Ehri proposed that there are four stages. In the first stage, reading is *pre-alphabetic*. It is top-down and meaning-based, and relies on long-term memory of the visual appearance of whole words as symbols. As readers acquire the matching details for English, they begin to connect graphemes to phonemes using *partial alphabetic* knowledge and processing strategies (stage 2). With sufficient practice, the connections between graphemes and phonemes become complete and firm until, at the *fully alphabetic* stage (3), readers have a good knowledge of probabilities and contingencies that allow them to read graphemes as accurately and automatically as possible for English. In the *consolidated alphabetic* stage (4), readers use their extensive knowledge of graphemic/phonemic mappings, as well as larger grain-sized onsets, rimes, morphemes, and syllables to apply a strategy based on reasoning by analogy to known spelling patterns.

For English, because of its opaque vowel representations and its syllable complexity, the transition from stage 3 probabilistic reasoning to stage 4 analogical reasoning is crucial. In other words, as English L1 readers experience more and more exposure to print, the grapheme-to-phoneme patterns that reoccur time and time again begin to merge and consolidate. Isolated bits of information restructure themselves into larger chunks of information: morphemes (-tion, -ness, pre-), syllables (at, in, ten), or smaller parts of syllables called onsets and rimes. The onset is the first consonant or consonant sequence in a one syllable word if there is one (p-, pl-, spl-); the rime is the vowel and final consonant or consonants (-it, -op, -ash) .

English L1 readers undergo *cognitive restructuring* because of the processing demands of an opaque script for a language with a complex syllable structure. Up to a certain point, readers get by on their knowledge of how individual graphemes are to be read, along with some contextual information. After a while, readers realize unconsciously that there is a more efficient way to read vowels if the common spelling patterns of English are stored in memory too. English readers then begin amassing a store of chunked information with which to assign vowel pronunciations by analogy. This stage 4 strategy allows the reader to resolve important intake decisions quickly and accurately. Ehri thinks that it is in second grade that English readers begin the consolidated alphabetic phase. This coincides with Seymour et al.'s research findings discussed earlier, when English readers begin catching up to their European counterparts in reading abilities.

In Birch (2006), I describe how the strategies proposed in Ehri's first three stages of reading development are reminiscent of the strategies that are described in the brain activation and psycholinguistic studies for learners of different L1 writing systems. There is evidence that L1 readers of sinograms and kanji use, for English, a meaning-based strategy in which the symbol is visually associated with a meaning and then with a set of phonemes.

Tan, Spinks, Feng, Siok, and Perfetti et al. (2003) studied moderately fluent Chinese/English graduate students who began learning English after the age of 12. A comparison group was a set of English monolinguals. They found that phonological processing of Chinese characters recruits portions of the brain that contribute to spatial information representation, spatial working memory, and coordination of cognitive resources as a central executive system. They thought that the high activation of this system was related to the square configuration of the sinogram, which then maps onto a monosyllabic unit of speech. When their Chinese subjects performed a phonological task on English words, the same neural system was active. These areas were unlike the brain areas activated by the English monolinguals when they performed phonemic analyses. Tan et al. felt that their Chinese subjects applied their L1 system to the task of reading in English. Since they lacked grapheme-to-phoneme knowledge and processing strategies, they were less capable of processing English similar to how the English readers did.

Tan et al. also report that their moderately fluent English L2 graduate students did not automatically use the letter-to-sound conversion rules like the English monolinguals did. Tan et al. don't mention the onset-rime strategy or probabilistic reasoning, but presumably the Chinese readers were not using those strategies either. In other words, it seems that the Chinese graduate students were using their habitual visual and semantic processing to read English, not taking advantage of the alphabetic writing system and not using those processing strategies that are most effective for English.

Likewise, some evidence indicates that Arabic or Hebrew readers might transfer a strategy such as Ehri's partial alphabetic reading strategy to read English, in which readers use their knowledge of consonant grapheme-to-phoneme correspondences, syntactic knowledge, and context to guess what English words are. Similarly, Italian or Spanish L1 readers may initially be using a fully alphabetic strategy to process graphemes in English since this strategy yields good results for transparent orthographies. In fact, there would be no need to develop the consolidated alphabetic strategy if the L1 writing system is transparent.

Indeed, Goswami (1998) reported that the correlation between rime awareness and reading ability has not been consistently found for early readers of alphabetic languages other than English. Goswami theorized that the importance of rime units in reading different languages could be studied by looking at whether familiarity with rimes aided reading for early readers. English, French, and Greek were studied. Greek has a nearly one-to-one correspondence between graphemes and phonemes and French has a closer connection between them than English. Goswami found that rime familiarity aided English readers quite a bit, French readers somewhat, and Greek readers not at all. It seemed that the Greek children were not using rimes in reading their orthography.

If we look back at Ehri's (1998) phases, it is possible that, since Greek writing has great consistency in grapheme-to-phoneme correspondences, Greek readers can read efficiently at the fully alphabetic stage. There is no need for them to develop further strategies, like English readers do. In fact, Goswami (1998) argued that it is dealing with English writing that causes strategies based on using rimes to emerge. Cognitive restructuring only happens if it is necessary. There is further evidence that students from transparent alphabetic writing systems acquire a syllabic processing strategy, dividing words into predictable syllables based on the vowels, for the purposes of reading (Aidinis & Nunes, 1998).

To summarize this section, L1 reading development can be described as a somewhat sequential set of stages of knowledge acquisition and strategic development that readers go through to cope with the properties of their L1 language and writing system. Figure 30.2 is one possible model; it could be amended easily for kana systems for Japanese and hangul orthography for Korean as well.

Thus, when researchers now talk about low-level transfer, they are referring to the transfer of these low level strategies acquired to handle L1 reading to L2 reading acquisition, as Koda (2005, p. 72) does.

1. L2 readers from diverse L1s use qualitatively different procedures when reading the same target language.
2. The procedural diversity can be identified with structural variations in the L1s.
3. Transferred L1 competencies interact with L2 print input in complex but predictable ways.
4. Therefore, L1 reading experience has lasting impacts on L2 reading development and alters processing procedures for L2 print.

If transferred L1 competencies and experiences interact with L2 print input in complex but predictable ways, have lasting impacts on L2 reading development, and alter the processing procedures for L2 print, then we must be able to explain when and why facilitation sometimes occurs instead of interference.

Facilitation or Interference

Perfetti et al. (2007) discuss two hypotheses about what happens to the L1 reading system so as to handle L2 reading.

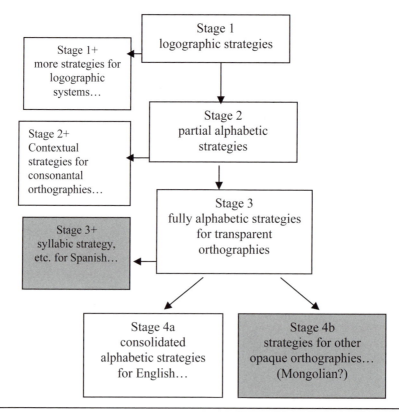

Figure 30.2 Stages of development of reading strategies in various languages

System Assimilation or System Accommodation

Perfetti et al. (2007) hypothesize that the L1 reading system can react in one of two ways to L2 reading acquisition. First, the L1 system can attempt to *assimilate* to the L2 writing system and orthography without changing itself. If assimilation occurs, then brain activation patterns continue to show the same pattern as the L1. Alternatively, the L1 reading system can adapt or *accommodate* to the features of the L2 writing system. If accommodation occurs, then brain activation patterns should show a change to handle the L2 print input.

The *System Assimilation* Hypothesis

The brain uses its L1 processing network *as is* to read a later orthography or writing system, with no adjustment.

The *System Accommodation* Hypothesis

The brain figures out a way to apply different appropriate processing strategies to handle the new writing system or orthography.

The psycholinguistic and the brain activation evidence from Chinese learners of English support *System Assimilation*. That is, Chinese readers of English, even apparently successful graduate students, appear to read English as if it were Chinese, applying a visual and meaning-based strategy rather than a decoding strategy. In contrast, there is at least a little evidence for *System Accommodation* as well. In a recent study, Liu, Perfetti, and Wang (2006) studied first and second semester English-speaking learners of Chinese and found that their brain activation revealed that their processing strategies became more like native Chinese readers over time, as the sinograms they were exposed to became more familiar to them.

Perfetti et al. suggest that

> [t]he accommodation process may be asymmetrical, applying to an alphabetic learner of Chinese more than to a Chinese learner of English. We found the Chinese-English bilinguals tend to show the same bilateral activation of visual areas, including the fusiform, when they read English as well as when they read Chinese. We also found some evidence that Chinese-English bilinguals may use frontal Chinese L1 areas for English. The interesting implication of this asymmetry is that *it is actually Chinese that provides the more universal system for reading. Chinese reading procedures can be applied to English and other alphabetic writing in a way the alphabetic reading procedures cannot be applied to Chinese.*
>
> (Perfetti et al., 2007, p. 143; emphasis mine)

Their intriguing results and their observation that logographic writing may be universal demand further elucidation. We can phrase Perfetti et al.'s conclusion more specifically by returning to the proposed stages of reading acquisition in Figure 30.2.

Strategic Availability

Let us suppose that all readers go through a stage of visual meaning-based reading to start with, as in Ehri's (1998) pre-alphabetic stage. This stage can be used to read numbers and other logographic symbols like @, !, or %. Chinese readers continue to rely on this reading strategy because that is the basis for their writing system. In addition, they acquire other processing strategies to deal with other components of the characters (stage 1+). In learning English, their visual meaning-based strategies are extended to English print because they have no alphabetic strategies to transfer. Hebrew and Arabic alphabetic readers continue through the partial alphabetic stage (stage 2) and possibly on to the fully alphabetic stage to deal with the vowelized texts that they read initially. Then they must develop additional contextual strategies to handle nonvowelized texts and to cope with the lack of vowel diacritics (stage 2+). When learning English, they transfer these strategies to reading English.

Readers of transparent and syllabically simple languages stop developing strategies when they can read their orthography with automaticity (stages 3 and 3+). Readers of opaque and syllabically difficult orthographies continue to develop additional strategies to cope with the complexities of their mapping details. For instance, English readers undergo cognitive restructuring to use reasoning by analogy to known spelling patterns for rimes and morphemes (stage 4a). Readers of other opaque and difficult orthographies develop other strategies as yet unknown to cope with the complexities of their orthography (stage 4b).

Let us further propose that reading stages and strategies acquired earlier continue to be available to readers. That means that it should be relatively easy for English readers to accommodate to a transparent alphabetic system. It should be possible for English readers to go back to a visual meaning-based strategy based on long-term memory and/or rely on strategies used for numbers and other logograms for accommodating to Chinese. Their reading system, having passed through these earlier stages, can accommodate to the demands of these diverse writing systems. However, the complex visual processing and memory load still make Chinese difficult to for English readers to learn.

Chinese readers, on the other hand, do not seem to have developed any useful strategies for coping with alphabets. That is, either they are from Hong Kong and have never learned a phonetic alphabet, or they are from PRC or Taiwan and have never used a phonetic alphabet for conventional reading although they have some phonemic awareness. They do not have an alphabetic system available as a resource. This would predict that Chinese adult readers will find it very difficult (or impossible?) to accommodate their reading strategies to reading an alphabetic L2. If these suppositions are true, then we can posit two tentative hypotheses that reformulate system accommodation or assimilation.

The *Strategic Availability* Hypothesis

System accommodation will occur if earlier stages and/or other processing strategies are available to the L2 reader. Assimilation will happen when other (earlier) stages and strategies of reading are not available to the L2 reader.

The *Universal Logographic* Hypothesis

Logographic reading strategies are universal (possibly because they are innate symbolic processing procedures) so accommodation to a logographic system is always possible for L1 readers of alphabetic (or syllabic) languages. (However, this does not make learning a logographic system easy.)

The *Universal Logographic* Hypothesis states that humans have a possibly innate ability to use graphic symbols to represent concepts. Some of the experimental work with other primates shows that they can use symbols to stand for things, and in humans we see early indications of symbolic representations in cave paintings and artifacts. The earliest writing systems used pictographs and tallies to refer to things, and over time they became stylized and a few developed into the alphabets we know today.

Tang, Zhang, Chen, Feng, Ji, Shen, and Reiman (2006, p. 10776) studied the brain activation of Chinese readers and English readers looking at numbers. They found that Chinese readers and

English readers have some differences in how they process numbers, but they also have a large area of overlap in the occipital-parietal pathway, the sensorimotor areas, and the frontal cortex. This area of overlap was congruent with a common number processing model that has verbal, analogue, and visual components.

Liu, Dunlap, Fiez, and Perfetti (2007) discuss the left middle frontal gyrus (LMFG) as a crucial part of the Chinese reading network because it supports a brief sustainable memory image of the character so that its associated phonological and semantic constituents can be recovered. In studying English learners of Chinese, they found that English learners of Chinese, after instruction in some 60 characters, showed two new activation patterns distinctive to reading by native Chinese readers. The first was a bilateral activation pattern for occipital and fusiform regions and the second was a left middle frontal activation (with right middle front gyrus also showing increased activation). They argued that the learners of Chinese were developing the characteristic LMFG necessary to read sinograms. It is unclear at this point how the LMFG might be related to the area of overlap found in the processing of numbers by English and Chinese readers by Tang et al. (2006). In any case, these two hypotheses account for the transfer data found for Chinese and other learners of English, as well as for English learners of Chinese and other languages. It seems that L2 readers do sometimes face a potential "reading" problem.

Language Proficiency

However, there may also be proficiency effects, especially with opaque languages and/or languages with complex syllable structures. Perfetti et al. (2007, p. 143) suggest that although Chinese readers can read English as if it were Chinese, that success may be limited:

> Higher levels of second language skill show brain-related as well as behavioral differences from lower levels of skill (Abutalebi, Cappa, & Perani, 2001). We should not be surprised to discover a similar result in cross-writing-system reading skill. High levels of L2 alphabetic reading skill for an L1 Chinese reader may arise with experience at alphabetic decoding that requires accommodation to brain structures that serve alphabetic procedures.

We don't know, as yet, whether Chinese readers of English can learn to read English by decoding graphemes to phonemes and by using probabilistic reasoning and reasoning by analogy to known spelling patterns if they become more proficient or if they have more experience with reading. We don't even know, at this point, whether they need to learn to read English the way native readers do or if their logographic reading of English is "okay." However, for some learners, L2 reading success may be a matter of language proficiency as well as strategic availability.

The *Developmental Interdependence* Hypothesis II

Poor L2 reading is due to the unavailability of processing strategies from experience reading earlier languages. This causes the brain to attempt to assimilate the existing processing strategies, which may or may not lead to success.

The *Linguistic Threshold* Hypothesis II

Poor L2 reading is because readers have not reached a threshold of L2 knowledge and processing strategies that allow them to access available strategies or acquire new ones. If and when the threshold is reached, the accumulation of L2 knowledge and experience causes cognitive restructuring, with accommodation to the new writing system.

Orthographic Distance

There is a third factor related to the reading and/or proficiency problem that I have discussed only peripherally: *orthographic distance*. Since decoding skills acquired in the L1 affect L2 reading acquisition in the ways discussed above, the closer (or more similar) the two writing systems are in their properties, the more facilitative transfer there will be. The more similar two languages are in terms of syllable structure or orthography, the easier reading acquisition should be. It should be rather easy for a Spaniard to learn to read Portuguese or Italian.

Conversely, the more distant (or different) the systems and orthographies are, the more difficulty there will be. This can happen in two ways. First, the more distant two writing systems are in their mapping grain sizes, the less the likelihood that there will be available processing strategies in common, as in Chinese readers of English. Nevertheless, the "distance" from Chinese to English is greater than the "distance" from English to Chinese because English readers potentially have available strategies for Chinese. Another aspect of distance has to do with the *secondary* strategies that develop in response to the mapping details of orthographies.

The *Orthographic Distance* Hypothesis

L2 reading will be affected by the degree to which the L2 orthography employs the same grain-size and mapping details as earlier languages. In particular, at the same grain-size, the more mapping details orthographies have in common, the more strategic availability for learners; the fewer mapping details there are in common, the less strategic availability for learners.

My Reading Vagaries

I learned to read Spanish very fluently as a teenager and young adult. Since I had a fully alphabetic processing strategy available to me (stage 3 in Figure 30.2), it was not hard to read Spanish after learning its mapping details. I was already adept at probabilistic reasoning for English; it was not difficult to read using a fully alphabetic strategy since the probabilities that a grapheme will represent a phoneme are near 100% in Spanish. Over time, as I became more proficient, I acquired the syllabic strategy as well (stage 3+). After eight years in Spain and two years in Ecuador, I had expert-level fluency in reading Spanish. Those strategies were still available to me at the time I started learning Macedonian, so I had many resources from my earlier reading experiences to bootstrap decoding.

Macedonian, a fusional language, has a transparent alphabetic orthography and simple syllables much like Spanish. In Macedonian, most syllables are CV, CVC, CVCC, V, or VC (Koneska, E., personal communication, 5/1/09). Macedonian orthography was very carefully updated in the 1940s by local linguists using the alphabetic principle, one symbol for one sound because they wanted to differentiate Macedonian from Bulgarian and Serbian. The fully alphabetic strategy and the syllabic strategy facilitated my reading Macedonian because of its regularity. After a short period of adjustment to Cyrillic (facilitated by two semesters of Russian 20 years earlier in college), I was ready to decode Macedonian words. My reading performance was affected, however, by the length of the words in Macedonian and by the complex morphology of the case and gender systems because I didn't, in my time there, develop enough language proficiency to acquire adequate processing strategies for them. Thus, up to the level of morphology, Macedonian was fairly easy for me because I had several available strategies to facilitate my reading acquisition.

In contrast, Mongolian is an agglutinative language with an opaque orthography and a complex syllable structure. Syllables can be as complex as CVVCCC. There are many sight words: words that simply have to be memorized as units. Mongolia has a complex history of writing systems. In 1204, a scribe of Chingiis Khan's adapted an existing alphabet to write Mongolian; this orthography is still used in Inner Mongolia in China and for calligraphy in Mongolia. I do not know how transparent or opaque this orthography is in present days. The Mongolian Cyrillic writing system was created in 1941 under the direct order of Stalin in the guise of increasing literacy rates. Apparently, designers of the writing system at the time didn't consider the specific features of the spoken language, so the spelling doesn't correlate with the sounds. (Jamyan, D., personal communication, 5/1/09). It may be possible that the classic Mongolian orthography was simply transliterated to Cyrillic without much consideration for some of the phonological changes that had occurred in the spoken language in the intervening centuries. Little seems to be known about the 1941 transliteration process at this time.

Bolor, my Mongolian teacher, tried to teach me to decode the words, to little avail. I was already familiar with the Cyrillic alphabet from Russian and Macedonian, but I had only one transferable processing strategy: memorization of sight words, the least efficient strategy for alphabetic reading (and similar to logographic reading?). Without available resources, I attempted to read by assimilating; that is, I tried to read Mongolian as if it were English (or Spanish or Macedonian). Nothing worked. Although English and Mongolian use alphabetic writing, their mapping details were too distant from each other for much strategic availability. In terms of Figure 30.2, I could not easily get from the 3, 3+, or 4a box to the 4b box. In my time in Mongolia, I never passed through the language threshold where efficient and automatic reading kicked in. If there was a common underlying proficiency, I was not able to access it. And that's how I found myself out of my orthographic depth.

Implications

It is easy to make some naive recommendations for language planning, for instance, that Finnish should be adopted as the international language, not English or Chinese. A little more thoughtfully, we might consider revisions to writing systems to make them easier to learn. But the immediate implications fall in the areas of research and pedagogy. In research, we simply need more information about the universals and the hypotheses of L1 and L2 reading. We need more information about the primary and secondary strategies for reading various languages. We need to know more about transfer. We need to know if it is better in some way to read English alphabetically or if it doesn't really matter in the long run if Chinese readers read it logographically. This information will surely affect instructional methodologies. At the very least, we need to recognize that it takes longer to become a proficient reader of some languages and that learners need to acquire specific knowledge and intake strategies directly to facilitate their learning.

References

Abu-Rabia, S. (1997a). Reading in Arabic orthography: The effect of vowels and context on reading accuracy of poor and skilled native Arabic readers. *Reading and Writing, 9*(1), 65–78.

Abu-Rabia, S. (1997b). Reading in Arabic orthography: The effect of vowels and context on reading accuracy of poor and skilled native Arabic readers in reading paragraphs, sentences, and isolated words. *Journal of Psycholinguistic Research, 26*(4) 465–482.

Abu-Rabia, S. (1998). Reading Arabic texts: Effects of text type, reader type and vowelization. *Reading and Writing, 10*(2), 105–119.

Abutalebi, J., Cappa, S. F., & Perani, D. (2001). The bilingual brain as revealed by functional neuroimaging. *Bilingualism: Language & Cognition, 4*, 179–190.

Aidinis, A., & Nunes, T. (1998). The role of different levels of phonological awareness in the development of reading and spelling in Greek. *Reading and Writing, 14*(1–2) (March 2001), 145–177.

Alderson, J. (1984). Reading in a foreign language: A reading problem or a language problem? In J. C. Alderson and A. H. Urquhart (Eds.), *Reading in a foreign language* (pp. 1–24). London: Longman.

Birch, B. (2006). *English L2 Reading: Getting to the bottom* (2nd ed.). Mahwah, NJ: Lawrence Erlbaum Associates.

Cummins, J. (1979). Linguistic interdependence and educational development of bilingual children. *Review of Educational Research, 49*, 222–251.

Ehri, L. (1998). Grapheme-phoneme knowledge is essential for learning to read words in English. In J. Metsala & L. Ehri (Eds.), *Word recognition in beginning literacy* (pp. 3–40). Mahwah, NJ: Lawrence Erlbaum Associates.

Fender, M. (2008). Arabic literacy development and cross-linguistic effects in subsequent L2 literacy development. In K. Koda and A. Zehler (Eds.), *Learning to read across languages: Cross-linguistic relationships in first- and second-language literacy development* (pp. 101–124). London: Routledge.

Gass, S., & Selinker, L. (Eds.) (1983). *Language transfer in language learning*. Rowley, MA: Newbury House.

Goswami, U. (1998). The role of analogies in the development of word recognition. In J. Metsala & L. Uhri (Eds.), *Word recognition in beginning literacy* (pp. 41–63). Mahwah, NJ: Lawerence Erlbaum Associates.

Goswami, U. (2002). Phonology, reading development, and dyslexia: A cross-linguistic perspective. *Annals of Dyslexia, 52,* 141–163.

Ho, C. (2003). Reading acquisition and developmental dyslexia in Chinese: A cognitive perspective. In N. Goulandris (Ed.), *Dyslexia in different languages: Cross-linguistic comparisons* (pp. 277–296). London: Whurr Publishers.

Koda, K. (2005). *Insights into second language reading: A cross-linguistic approach.* Cambridge: Cambridge University Press.

Koda, K. (2008). Impacts of prior literacy experience on second language learning to read. In K. Koda & A. Zehler (2008). *Learning to read across languages: Cross-linguistic relationships in first- and second-language literacy development* (pp. 68–96). London: Routledge.

Krashen, S. (1983). Newmark's "Ignorance Hypothesis" and current second language acquisition theory. In S. Gass & L. Selinker (Eds.), *Language transfer in language learning* (pp. 135–153). Rowley, MA: Newbury House.

Liu, Y., Dunlap, S., Fiez, J., & Perfetti, C. (2007). Evidence for neural accommodation to a writing system following learning. *Human Brain Mapping, 28,* 1223–1234.

Liu, Y., Perfetti, C., & Wang, M. (2006). Visual analysis and lexical access of Chinese characters by Chinese as second language readers. *Linguistics and Language, 7*(3), 637–657.

Paulesu, E., Demonet, J.-F., Fazio, F., McCrory, E., Chanoine, V., Brunswick, N., Cappa, S. F., Cossu, G., Habib, M., Frith, C. D., & Frith, U. (2001). Dyslexia: Cultural diversity and biological unity. *Science, 291,* 2165–2167.

Perfetti, C., & Dunlap, S. (2008). Learning to read: General principles and writing system variations. In K. Koda & A. Zehler (Eds.), *Learning to read across languages: Cross-linguistic relationships in first- and second-language literacy development* (pp. 13–38). London: Routledge.

Perfetti, C., Liu, Y., Fiez, J., Nelson, J., Bolger, D., & Tan, L. (2007). Reading in two writing systems: Accommodation and assimilation in the brain's reading network. *Bilingualism: Language and Cognition, 10*(2), 131–146. Special issue on Neurocognitive approaches to bilingualism: Asian languages, edited by P. Li.

Perfetti, C., Liu, Y., & Tan, L. (2002). How the mind can meet the brain in reading: A comparative writing systems approach. In H. S. R. Kao, C. K. Leong, & D.-G. Gao (Eds.), *Cognitive neuroscience studies of the Chinese language* (pp. 36–60). Hong Kong: Hong Kong University of Press.

Rayner, K., Foorman, B., Perfetti, C., Pesetsky, D., & Seidenberg, M. (2001). How psychological science informs the teaching of reading. *Psychology Science in the Public Interest, 2*(2), 31–74. A supplement to *Psychological Science*.

Seymour, P. (1990). Developmental dyslexia. In M. Eysenchk (Ed.), *Cognitive psychology: An international review* (pp. 135–196). Chichester: Wiley.

Seymour, P. (1997) Foundations of orthographic development. In C. Perfetti, L. Rieben, & M. Fayol (Eds.), *Learning to spell* (pp. 319–337). Hillsdale, NJ: Erlbaum.

Seymour, P. (1999) Cognitive architecture of early reading. In I. Lundberg, F. Tonnessen, & I. Austad (Eds.), *Dyslexia: Advances in theory and practice* (pp. 59–73). Dordrecht: Kluwer.

Seymour, P., Aro, M., & Erskine, J. (2003). Foundation literacy acquisition in European orthographies. *British Journal of Psychology, 94,* 143–174.

Shimron, J. (1999). The role of vowel signs in Hebrew: beyond word recognition. *Reading and Writing, 11*(4), 301–319.

Smythe, I., Everatt, J., Al-Menaye, N., He, X., Capellini, S., Gyarmathy, E., & Siegel, L.(2008). Predictors of word-level literacy amongst grade 3 children in five diverse languages. *DYSLEXIA, 14,* 170–187.

Tan, L., Spinks, J., Eden, G., Perfetti, C., & Siok, W. (2005). Reading depends on writing, in Chinese. *Proceedings of the National Academy of Science USA, 102*(24), June 14, 8781–8785.

Tan, L, Spinks, J., Feng, C., Siok, W., Perfetti, C., Xiong, J., Fox, P., & Gao, J. (2003). Neural systems on second language reading are shaped by native language. *Human Brain Mapping, 3,* 158–166.

Tang, Y., Zhang, W., Chen, K., Feng, S., Ji, Y., Shen, J., & Reiman, M. (2006). Arithmetic processing in the brain shaped by cultures. *Proceedings of the National Academy of Sciences, 103*(28), 10775–10780.

Tseng, O. (2002). Current issues in learning to read in Chinese. In W. Li, J. Gaffney, & J. Packard (Eds.), *Chinese children's reading acquisition: theoretical and pedagogical issues* (pp. 3–16). Dordrecht: Kluwer.

Wang, M., & Yang, C. (2008). Learning to read Chinese: Cognitive consequences of cross-language and writing system differences. In K. Koda & A. Zehler (Eds.), *Learning to read across languages: Cross-linguistic relationships in first- and second-language literacy development* (pp. 125–153). London: Routledge.

31
Grammar Teaching
Research, Theory, and Practice

Penny Ur

Introduction

The teaching of grammar holds a central position in the literature on language teaching, largely—but not only—for historical reasons. The teaching of living languages was in mediaeval times and later modeled on the teaching of Latin and Greek, which stressed the learning of the rules of grammar and their application in translation exercises. More recently, influential linguists in the mid-twentieth century continued to see grammar as the fundamental component of language, whether based on structuralism (Bloomfield, 1933) or, later, transformational-generative theory (Chomsky, 1957). The influential audio-lingual language-teaching methodology was developed (Rivers, 1968) as a result of structuralist theories combined with behaviorism (Skinner, 1957). Transformational-generative grammar moved language teaching toward more cognitive and analytical methods. But the main goal was consistently a mastery of the grammatical system of the target language, with its phonology, lexis, and general communicative function seen as secondary.

In such approaches grammar has been seen primarily as a set of structures, and conventionally defined as relating to forms: to this day dictionary definitions of the word typically relate to rules and formal correctness rather than to meanings. But recent years have seen increasing focus on the function of grammar in creating and adapting meanings (Widdowson, 1990; Larsen-Freeman, 2002). Corpus-based research has furnished the basis for some influential modern grammars, which devote most of their space to aspects of meaning and use (Biber, Johansson, Leech, Conrad, & Finegan, 1999; Carter & McCarthy, 2006), with relatively little attention to rules of form. Parallel to this trend has been the rise in the perceived importance of vocabulary as the main component in language proficiency and, by implication, in teaching (D. Willis, 1990).

The communicative approach, which began to gain popularity in the 1970s (Hymes, 1972; Widdowson, 1978) and prevails in language-teaching methodological theory to this day, implies a lowering of the importance of grammatical accuracy as compared to communicative effectiveness. However, perhaps surprisingly, grammar teaching has maintained a central position both in the research literature on second-language teaching and learning and in classroom materials and practice. The enormous amount of published research and theory on grammar and its teaching in a second language over the last two or three decades, only a small selection of which can be summarized in this chapter, and the regular appearance of "state-of-the-art" articles in major periodicals (for example, Spada, 1997; Nassaji & Fotos, 2004; R. Ellis, 2006), indicate the importance that is attached to it by both descriptive and applied linguists. And in spite of the current promotion of communicative and task-based methodologies by ministries of education worldwide, grammatical explanations and exercises continue to be prominent both in coursebooks and in the classroom practice of teachers in school-based foreign-language courses.

Correctness and Acceptability

One issue which has been widely discussed, particularly in connection with the use of English as a lingua franca, has been the standards of correctness or acceptability that should be aimed for by teachers and students. The term *correct* has usually been used to refer to accurate grammatical usage as prescribed by academic grammars of the language (*prescriptive* grammar), whereas the term *acceptable* is usually taken to refer to the way the grammar is used by the majority of the language users (*descriptive* grammar): in the case of English this is revealed by an analysis of language corpora.

In practice, however, the two are very similar. There are some minor differences, such as the increasingly acceptable use of *who* in English rather than the formally correct *whom* when this is the object of a verb, but these are few and fairly trivial. Even where teachers explicitly take descriptive grammar as their model, these standards in fact become prescriptive within the context of classroom practice, so that in most cases acceptable usages are treated as correct, and unacceptable ones as wrong and needing to be corrected.

English as a Lingua Franca

An interesting partial exception to this generalization can be seen in the discussion of research based on the Vienna-Oxford International Corpus of English (VOICE, 2009), which is a corpus of speakers of English as a lingua franca. VOICE provides a record of a million words of oral interaction between people from different (mainly European) first-language backgrounds using English in a variety of conversational contexts. The evidence that is beginning to emerge from this corpus suggests that certain forms that would be defined as incorrect by pedagogical or academic grammars are in fact widely used by such speakers and cause no problems in spoken communication. Examples of these are the omission of the third-person -*s* suffix, or the use of relative *which* to refer to a person instead of *who*, and vice versa. In contexts where the purpose is to learn English for international/intercultural spoken communication, teachers and materials writers could use these insights as guidance for the selection of grammatical forms to teach and test. It is not suggested that teachers actually teach forms such as *she go* as acceptable: rather, that the teaching of the corresponding correct form should simply have a lower priority than those forms that appear to be more crucial to the communication of meanings (Seidlhofer, 2004, 2006). A more extreme approach would see the insistence on "correct" forms such as *she goes* as an example of an unjustified imposition of native-speaker norms on the non-native majority of English speakers. Supporters of this position would therefore legitimize *she go* as acceptable usage for a variety of English as a lingua franca as used by non-native speakers and suggest that assessment of such speakers' performance in English should take this into account (Jenkins, 2006). However, there is, at the time of writing, no evidence that those users of English as a lingua franca who do in fact regularly omit the third-person -*s* and so on in their speech constitute a majority. Until and unless such evidence is forthcoming, this approach seems unlikely to be adopted by practitioners or learners, particularly as the claims do not extend to written discourse. The more moderate position expressed by Seidlhofer and her colleagues is, however, gaining support and may be expected to have some influence on the treatment of grammar in curriculum and materials design, at least as far as the teaching of the spoken language is concerned. The latter, indeed, has grammatical norms of its own even in the discourse of its native speakers, which merit separate discussion.

Spoken Language

Spoken language displays a range of grammatical features that, in the case of English, has been extensively documented in recent years using corpus resources (Biber et al., 1999; Timmis, 2005). These include aspects such as the use of coordination of sentences rather than subordination, grammatical reduction, or ellipsis ("Don't know," "Trouble is ..."), "heads" and "tails" ("My sister, she lives in ..." or "He's nice, that guy"); unconventional, non-clausal, inconsistent, or fragmentary grammar ("There's a lot of people out there," "He wasn't hurt wasn't it?"); and an enormous number of colloquial prefabricated lexico-grammatical chunks, many of them fillers or expressions of vagueness, ("you know," "or something") (Liu, 2003; Dongkwang & Nation, 2007). Some have argued for the inclusion of a selection of these features in second-language courses (Timmis, 2005). However, it appears that few coursebooks do in fact include them (Cullen & Cho, 2007), and even if they do, coverage appears usually to be limited to lexico-grammatical chunks.

One problem with teaching spoken grammar is, of course, that the features listed above, though perfectly acceptable in informal speech, are largely unacceptable in more formal discourse, whether written (letters, reports, academic papers) or spoken (formal speeches, news broadcasts). Most teachers would have reservations about teaching forms that have only limited applicability and that might impact negatively on students' ability to express themselves in appropriate forms outside informal conversation. Another consideration is that there is no evidence that these features, with the exception of the chunks, are language-specific. On the contrary, it seems very likely that features such as "heads" and "tails" and inconsistent or fragmentary grammatical constructions are the result of natural strategies rooted in the circumstances of the composition of "online" spoken discourse, which cannot be planned or edited in advance and is very often constructed in collaboration with an interlocutor. Such features are very likely, therefore, to appear in informal registers of any natural language, and will tend to appear in learners' speech even if we do not deliberately teach them.

It might be useful and interesting, therefore, for teachers to raise learners' awareness of some of the features of spoken grammar by drawing their attention to them when they occur in discourse (audio/video recordings, the teacher's own speech). But pro-active deliberate teaching should probably be limited to the most useful lexico-grammatical chunks that are specific to the target language.

E-Grammar

The grammar used in most written electronic texts and the vast majority of websites accords with the conventional prescriptions of grammar books; however, this is not true of informal interactive written communication such as instant messaging and many emails. Here we can talk about the evolving of a distinct discourse variety (Crystal, 2001a) that has some grammatical peculiarities of its own. Some of these—lack of subordination, ellipsis, some inconsistency of construction—are similar to those of spoken discourse, owing to similar if less extreme constraints: rapid composition and little opportunity for preparation or editing. However, other elements such as the insertion of prefabricated chunks to serve as "fillers" do not occur, since the fundamental principle of such compositions is what Crystal calls the "save-a-keystroke" rule: do not hit an extra key if you can possibly avoid it. One interesting result of this may be the use of shorter grammatical options: for example, the substitution in English of the simple aspect in verb forms for progressive or perfect.

However, there is little or no evidence that the grammatical features of such types of communication are influencing mainstream written discourse of other types, whether on paper or on the Internet, and it seems unlikely that such influence will make itself felt in the future (Crystal, 2001b; Baron, 2005). It does not seem to be particularly important, therefore, for teachers to provide instruction in such features, though as with spoken grammar there may be a place for awareness-raising through tasks contrasting computer-mediated informal written interaction with more formal types of written text. It is important for learners to distinguish between the different types of grammatical usages that they may encounter, and to learn which are more, or less, appropriate for the various contexts within which they may be called upon to function.

Implicit and Explicit Teaching

Implicit knowledge of grammar is that which is demonstrated through students' actual production of speech or writing in communication and does not imply the ability to explain underlying rules. Explicit knowledge is the ability to verbalize a rule or description of usage, often using grammatical metalanguage. Implicit teaching means exposing students to or getting them to use grammatical forms and meanings but without actually discussing the rules, whereas explicit teaching involves verbal explanations of form and use.

The goal of grammar teaching is that learners should be able to produce grammatical features in their output accurately and appropriately: that is, implicit knowledge. The question is whether explicit teaching does or does not contribute to achieving this goal.

Implicit Teaching

Models of implicit grammar teaching are based mostly on the way the grammar of a first language is acquired: through extensive exposure and the mediation of parents, teachers, and other interlocutors, without any conscious instruction. Stephen Krashen, arguably the most influential proponent of implicit teaching, claims in his *input hypothesis* (1981, 1999 and elsewhere) that grammar—indeed, language in general—is best taught through exposing learners to a large amount of comprehensible input, without any deliberate explanation, practice, or correction of language features. He makes a distinction between *acquisition* and *learning*: acquisition being the natural internalization of language forms and meanings through exposure, and learning, in contrast, being the conscious understanding and application of rules provided by the teacher or textbook. Learning, thus defined, can provide a means of consciously monitoring output, but acquisition is the only means by which real mastery may be achieved. An additional claim is that there is no transfer from "learning" to "acquisition": learned rules cannot lead to implicit knowledge.

Another theoretical research-based model of implicit grammar learning is the *interaction hypothesis* (Long & Porter, 1985; Long, 1996), which states that the main means of acquisition of new language features is through the negotiation of meaning that takes place during interaction between the learner and another interlocutor, who is ideally a more advanced, or native, speaker of the target language, but may also be another learner. Long, therefore, in contrast with Krashen, sees an important role for output and learner interaction as well as input. An alternative model is proposed by Swain (1995), based on longitudinal studies of Canadian immersion programs in French, where Anglophone school students are taught at least 50% of their content lessons in French. These studies found that the speech of graduates of these immersion programs was characterized by basic grammatical errors that would not have occurred in the speech of native speakers. It is certainly not feasible that these learners did not receive plenty of comprehensible input, but was noticeable that the Anglophone learners volunteered little output in comparison with Francophone classmates. Swain therefore suggests in her *output hypothesis* that "pushed output" is also necessary for mastery of the grammatical forms of the language. She posits that learner output within communicative interaction provides opportunities for the learner to become aware of what he or she does not know how to express and to check hypotheses.

Exemplar-based models of language learning also entail implicit learning of grammar. N. Ellis (2002) claims that repeated encounter with formulaic or semi-formulaic morpho-syntactic constructions results in the learner accumulating a vast number of exemplars that furnish the basis for implicit knowledge of grammatical forms and meanings. This model is essentially connectionist and probabilistic: learners acquire the ability to guess how morphemes, words, and expressions are likely to combine with one another to make meanings, based on their previous encounters with similar combinations. Critics have found substantial flaws in this theory (Gass & Mackey, 2002): for example, that there are some features that seem to be absorbed after relatively few encounters, whereas others are not; and that many second-language learning contexts do not allow for the immense amount of exposure that would be needed to supply an adequate "pool" of language experience. Nevertheless, the idea of language acquisition based largely on the learning of exemplars retains a place in the research literature. Some have suggested, for example, that the learning of formulaic utterances or collocations may play an important role in the acquisition of grammar (Wray, 2000; Fitzpatrick & Wray, 2006; Taguchi, 2007), and that such learning may be a result of deliberate teaching or learning by heart rather than of accumulation of incidental encounters. The learning of formulaic language that exemplifies grammatical features enables the learner to recognize and even produce similar language later by analogy and implicit acquisition processes. More elaborate learning by heart of texts by Chinese learners, with excellent results for both accuracy and fluency, is reported by Ding (2007).

Explicit Teaching

Altogether, although there is some research to support the idea that implicit teaching brings about good learning of grammar, there is also substantial evidence in favor of explicit teaching.

Some writers commenting on the Canadian immersion programs referred to above would suggest that the addition of "pushed output" is not enough, but that some explicit teaching procedures such as error correction and explanations could also contribute to higher levels of mastery of the grammar (Swain, 2000).

A survey article by Spada (1997) looking at various studies of the teaching of grammatical features of French and English came to the conclusion that, though results are mixed, on the whole explicit procedures tended to produce better results. Later Norris and Ortega (2001) conducted a meta-analytic review of a large number of empirical studies, and again demonstrated a clear advantage for explicit teaching over implicit. Their conclusions have been supported by more recent research (Leow, 2007).

A reasonable conclusion is that in second-language teaching and learning in formal contexts it is very likely that an explicit component within a basically communicative or task-based methodology will make a substantial contribution to the achievement of grammatical accuracy.

The Relationship between Implicit and Explicit Teaching

The possible relationships between implicit and explicit knowledge of grammar have been described as *interface*, *non-interface*, and *weak interface* (R. Ellis, 2005).

The non-interface position expressed by Krashen in his various books and articles, states that there is no connection between implicit and explicit knowledge, and that the mastery of explicit knowledge will not feed into the (implicit) acquisition system. In other words, if you consciously learn a rule, this will not enable you to produce the target item accurately in your own output in real-time communication, but can contribute only as a conscious "monitor." This approach would furnish the basis for methodologies based on the provision of comprehensible input or communicative tasks.

The weak interface position suggests that there can be indirect transfer from explicit to implicit knowledge. This transfer, however, cannot be predicted or directly caused by teaching: it will depend primarily on the learner's readiness to integrate the new feature into his or her own language system. Such integration can be facilitated or accelerated by the existence of explicit knowledge. This view is compatible with the *consciousness-raising* model of grammar teaching (R. Ellis, 2001b) discussed later in this chapter.

According to the strong interface position supported by Dekeyser (1998, 2007) there certainly can be, and often is, a direct transfer from explicit to implicit knowledge. Such a transfer is effected by (normally teacher- or textbook-initiated) practice. This position is the basis of practice-based methodologies such as those suggested by Johnson (1996) and Ur (2009) (see later in this chapter).

Before discussing how such positions are implemented in grammar-teaching methodologies it is worth looking at two further research-based hypotheses that have had a fundamental influence on thinking in this field.

Influential Second-Language Acquisition Theories

Noticing

The concept of "noticing" in second-language acquisition has been proposed by Schmidt (2001 and elsewhere) based on a study of his own experiences learning a second language (Schmidt & Frota, 1986). Schmidt spent some time in Brazil studying Portuguese: initially he took a course in the language, but later continued learning through conversational interaction with Brazilian interlocutors. His progress was documented both through a personal journal and through recordings of his conversations. Schmidt and Frota found that in almost all cases features (mainly grammatical) that appeared in his own speech were those he had earlier consciously noted and written down in his journal. Based on this finding, he concluded that language learning, as in this case, results from some degree of conscious noticing. He rejects the possibility of "subliminal" or unconscious acquisition of language features, and suggests that input, even comprehensible, will only become intake that can be used as a basis for development of the learner's own second language if it is noticed. This does not mean that incidental learning cannot take place, but that it will do so only if features encountered incidentally are to some degree brought to the conscious attention of the learner.

There are, of course, various levels of noticing, ranging from the briefest fleeting perception to verbalized metalinguistic analysis. But very fleeting perception is unlikely to lead to learning. Higher levels of attention lead to higher levels of learning.

The influence of this hypothesis on later writers has been immense. In principle, noticing can, and does, occur within an implicit language-learning process: thus a simple flood of comprehensible input will not in itself promote acquisition until and unless the learner notices and pays attention to language features within it. Hence, methodological models were developed that promoted such noticing within communicative tasks (see, for example, the section on "Focus on Form and Consciousness-Raising", p. 516). But perhaps even more, Schmidt's ideas, taken together with the research mentioned above, accelerated the movement toward more use of explicit grammar-teaching procedures in second-language teaching.

The Teachability Hypothesis

The teachability hypothesis was proposed by Pienemann (1984), based on his studies of the acquisition of German. He found that there was a natural developmental sequence of acquisition of morpho-syntactic structures, which is apparently unaffected by the order in which such structures are taught. So a learner will only acquire a new structure if he or she is developmentally ready for it, i.e. has already mastered those structures that precede it in the developmental sequence. Teaching a structure for which the learner is not ready will not only fail to result in learning, but may also have a detrimental effect. He further predicted that learners cannot skip stages in a developmental sequence. Pienemann therefore suggests that teaching of grammatical structures will be effective only if and when it coincides with the stage at which the learner is ready to acquire them.

Pienemann's findings have been explored in later studies (for example R. Ellis, 1989; Spada & Lightbown, 1999) and have, to some extent, been confirmed. R. Ellis's study found that certain structures in German were acquired in the order predicted in the natural developmental sequence even when this was different from the order in which they were taught. Spada and Lightbown's study looked at the acquisition of interrogative forms in English and found that learners did indeed progress in the order predicted, but that teaching of a structure a stage or two ahead of the apparent readiness of the learner did not have a detrimental effect: on the contrary, it apparently contributed to progress to the next stage.

There are various problems with implementing the recommendation that the teaching of new structures should take place as and when the learners are ready for them, in a syllabus based on a developmental sequence:

- The lack of any fully comprehensive list of the developmental sequence of acquisition of morpho-syntactic structures in any language, further complicated by the fact that this is apparently likely to vary according to the learners' L1.
- The impractibility within the time constraints of ongoing coursework of the teacher working out exactly where each individual student is in terms of his/her developmental sequence at any given time.
- The impossibility of timing teaching of grammatical structures so that it is appropriate for every learner in the class, since they are unlikely ever to be all at the same stage at the same time.
- As shown in the Spada and Lightbown study, some stages in the developmental sequence are actually ungrammatical; no teacher is going to teach an ungrammatical structure even if it features as a documented stage in development and is apparently the next form to be acquired for a particular learner.

Nevertheless, the overriding hypothesis that a developmental sequence exists and that it constrains the ability of the learner to acquire new grammatical structures, regardless of the order in which these are taught, has been generally accepted, and has led applied linguists to try to design methodological options that take it into account (see later sections). There are also two major implications for the practicing teacher. First, the hypothesis provides a reassuring explanation of the well-documented fact that teaching and extensive practice often do not result in (immediate) acquisition; this may not be fault of the teaching, nor because the learner is unintelligent or lazy: it may simply be that he or she was not "ready" to acquire the structure. Second, it implies the necessity of re-teaching crucial grammatical structures at intervals in order to cater for students' different rates of progress along the developmental sequence: teaching a structure once only may neglect the learning needs of a substantial proportion of any specific class.

Methodological Models of Grammar Teaching

Traditional (or PPP)

Traditionally, grammar has been taught by a presentation-practice-production (PPP) process: a new grammatical structure is presented and explained, it is then practiced and finally students are expected to produce it in their own spoken and written discourse. PPP is strongly associated with the existence of a synthetic grammatical syllabus, which dictates in what order grammatical structures are to be taught in the course.

The PPP model has been roundly condemned in the literature as representing an ineffective methodology that does not accord with current representations of language acquisition processes (for example, R. Ellis, 1993; Skehan, 1997). At the same time, it does, however, persist in most English language teaching (ELT) textbooks (Nitta & Gardner, 2005), and probably classrooms as well.

Various arguments have been adduced to support the predominant opposition to traditional PPP-based grammar-teaching methods.

On the practical side, it has been found—and this is a common experience of many teachers—that even after getting explanations, and after performing well on grammar exercises and tests, learners continue to make errors in their own language production: practice does not make perfect. The more modest claim that while practice does not make perfect, it does improve performance is more difficult to refute. R. Ellis brings some research evidence that practice does not lead to improvement (for example, Ellis & Rathbone, 1987); other studies show that it does (for example, Salaberry, 1997). As with many areas in second-language acquisition research, it is difficult to draw clear-cut conclusions, but see further discussion in the "Skill-theory-based instruction" section, p. 516.

Other arguments against PPP are based on underlying language-acquisition theory. It is held by many that second languages are best learnt the same way that first languages are, through communicative activity, whether input- or output-based, and that, therefore, a presentation-practice model is in principle doomed to failure. It has, however, been acknowledged (as described above) that some explicit teaching of grammar (the first "P"), though not a part of natural first-language acquisition, can probably enhance the second-language learning process. This has led to a number of methodological models that have attempted to combine a basically communicative task-based methodology with some explicit grammar-teaching procedures.

Then there is the teachability hypothesis: if learners acquire morpho-syntactical features in a set order that is impervious to order of instruction, then it would appear useless to provide practice. The argument runs as follows: if the learner is ready to acquire the feature, then he or she will do so through noticing it in input when he or she is ready; if he or she is not ready, then practice will not help.

All this has led applied linguists to search for alternatives to the traditional methods that make sense in terms of second-language acquisition research and are likely to work better.

Input- or Task-Based Instruction

Those who assume that grammar is best acquired primarily through implicit learning processes base their methodologies on analytic syllabuses. Such syllabuses do not consist of a list of language features (grammatical structures, lexis, or functions/notions) but rather of opportunities—whether task- or text-based—for the learners to encounter the language naturally in the context of communicative interaction. The language may be simplified in order to make it comprehensible to the learner, but it will not be deliberately designed or manipulated in order to teach particular grammatical items.

The Natural Approach

This approach derived from Krashen's input hypothesis, is based on the provision of a large amount of comprehensible input, whether spoken or written, at a level of "i + 1" (just above the learner's present level of acquisition), on the assumption that accurate and appropriate grammar will best be acquired through the resulting intake (Krashen & Terrell, 1983).

This approach has been extensively criticized (for example, Brumfit, 1984; Long & Robinson, 1998), and has not on the whole been adopted by teachers. Research, such as the Canadian immersion studies (Swain, 2000), provides strong evidence that comprehensible input is not enough to produce learners with a full command of the target-language grammar. And most people today would accept that even if explicit teaching may not be necessary, some degree of conscious noticing (Schmidt, 2001) is essential in the learning of a second language in formal courses of study. Such considerations led to practical models that were more output- and interaction-based, though still essentially based on implicit acquisition.

Task-Based Instruction

The procedural syllabus proposed in the 1980s by Prabhu (1987) was the precursor of a number of books and articles in favor of task-based instruction as a more effective model for the learning of a second language, including its grammar: for example, Long and Crookes (1992), Skehan (1997, 2003), R. Ellis (2003), and Nunan (2004). Proponents of task-based instruction as a basis for learning grammar accept the learnability hypothesis and therefore reject as unrealistic the idea that grammar can be learnt piece by piece in a linear syllabus: it is preferable to provide learners with plenty of encounters with varied natural language in input and their own interactions. In this way they are likely to have more opportunities to encounter the different grammatical items as they are ready for them. These writers would agree with Krashen that language is best learnt through naturalistic processes, but include active output as well as input as a means of acquisition (the output hypothesis), and in particular, the negotiation that takes place between interlocutors while attempting to understand each other in the course of a conversation in the target language (the interaction hypothesis). They would also differ from Krashen in accepting that there is a place for noticing and occasional explicit focus on form, but stress that the main source of learning is the communicative task, as described by Skehan (1997, p. 95): "Instruction in which learners are given tasks to complete in the classroom makes the assumption that transacting tasks in this way will engage naturalistic acquisitional mechanisms, cause the underlying interlanguage system to be stretched, and drive development forward."

However, research such as the documentation and analysis of interactive tasks in process, as carried out by Seedhouse (1999), casts doubt on the effectiveness of tasks as a vehicle for grammar learning: in Seedhouse's transcripts of such tasks there was little evidence of interlanguage systems being "stretched"; on the contrary, participants seemed to go for the simplest and most basic utterances possible in order to achieve the task goal, often simple lexical items with no grammar at all, so that little grammar-learning results. Task-based instruction as a means for learners to acquire the grammar of a target language has been criticized on these and other grounds by Richards (2002) and Swan (2005).

There has, therefore, in recent years, been a tendency for writers to move away from the purely communicative task as a basis for language learning, and towards more deliberate teaching of grammatical forms and meanings during, or as an accompaniment to, task-based procedures (J. Willis, 1996).

Focus on Form and Consciousness-Raising

Focus on form has been proposed (Long, 1991; Long & Robinson, 1998) as a way to provide for "noticing" of grammatical features during a communicative task. It is, rather confusingly, contrasted with *focus on forms*, the systematic teaching of grammatical structures according to a predetermined grammatical syllabus. In practice, focus on form may involve "time out" to talk about a particular grammatical form in the course of an otherwise communicative procedure, or involve paying attention, while focusing on the meaning of a text, to some feature that is salient in its grammar. In any case, it is in principle brief and unobtrusive, and the attention of the learner is primarily and consistently directed to communicative meaning.

Originally such procedures were intended to include only spontaneous reactions to perceived problems of form. Later interpreters of the term have, however, interpreted the concept more flexibly. R. Ellis (2001a), for example, draws a distinction between planned and incidental focus on form. Planned focus on form means that it has been predetermined which feature is to be attended to, usually through text or task design: so a text may contain a large number of exemplars of past progressive forms, or a task may be designed to be based on interrogatives. Incidental focus on form, in contrast, is unplanned, and takes place mainly during oral interaction: spontaneous error correction, for example. In practice what often happens is that the intervention is based on "planned spontaneity": the text or task may or may not in itself focus on a particular feature, but the teacher plans in advance to exploit some aspect of it for the teaching or review of a grammatical form or meaning at the point where it is encountered in the course of the lesson.

Focus on form has been extensively discussed in the literature, and its interpretation in practice has been even more flexible than implied by the above definitions and examples. In Shak and Gardner (2008) for example, grammar activities are suggested under the heading "focus on form" that involve completing sentences with a correct grammatical form, or matching active or passive sentences to a picture. These involve more than a brief and unobtrusive focus on form and are arguably functionally indistinguishable from meaningful grammar practice exercises.

Another model, compatible both with focus on form and task-based learning, but rejecting practice as a useful contributor to learning, is *consciousness-raising* (R. Ellis, 2001b). Consciousness-raising is the deliberate teaching and learning of explicit knowledge of a grammatical feature, often (though not always) involving the articulation of a rule. Its usefulness is based on the premise that the integration of a grammatical feature within the learner's implicit language knowledge system will take place only when the learner is developmentally ready to acquire it (see "The Teachability Hypothesis" section, p. 512) and "notices" it in communicative output (see "Noticing" section, p. 512). This noticing may, however, be substantially facilitated by previous conscious knowledge of the feature: hence the usefulness of occasional consciousness-raising lessons, aimed at the acquisition of explicit knowledge.

But in general, as evidenced by the Shak and Gardner (2008) article mentioned above, there has been a perceptible trend in recent years back to a legitimization of practice as a useful component of grammar teaching, whether based on a systematic grammatical syllabus or on response to learner errors or perceived gaps in knowledge.

Skill-Theory-Based Instruction

In contrast to the essentially communication-based models of task-based learning and focus on form, Johnson (1996), Dekeyser (1998, 2007), and others have suggested that a second language, including its grammar, is largely learnt the same way as skills such as playing an instrument or flying an aircraft: through declarative knowledge transformed into procedural knowledge by practice. The term *practice* is understood to mean deliberate rehearsal of the target skill, whose objective is to bring about automatization.

This is to some extent a reversion to an essentially PPP model, but with some crucial changes in emphasis. One of these is the stress on the use of meaningful, or communicative practice—what Larsen-Freeman (2003) calls "grammaring"—rather than the traditional focus on mechanical, accuracy-focused drills (gapfills, multiple choice, matching exercises, and so on), making it more likely that there will be some transfer of knowledge to communicative situations. Although the traditional drills are still found in many workbooks, there is increasing use of communicative grammar activities in both coursebooks and teacher materials (for example, Ur, 1996, 2009). The last two Ps of PPP are thus combined into one, and the component of traditional mechanical drills is reduced or eliminated (Dekeyser, 1998).

For those who believe that grammar is acquired through experience of examplars, the use of practice may, incidentally, have another function: it simply provides for frequency of encounter in situations where the language is used very little outside the limited hours of classroom lessons, and where, therefore, the learner may have fewer opportunities to come across the rarer features within natural communicative situations.

Some researchers have accepted a place for (meaningful) practice, but have limited this to input processing. There is evidence (VanPatten & Cadierno, 1993; VanPatten, 2003) that grammatical features are best learnt when learners are given opportunities to process the input (by identifying meanings associated with between different features, for example), rather than to produce correct sentences themselves. Such processes resulted in better comprehension and at least equal levels of production as those shown by learners who had experienced conventional output-based practice. Later studies have partially confirmed this hypothesis (Qin, 2008), but others have shown an equal, sometimes superior, result for output (Dekeyser & Sokalski, 1996; Morgan-Short & Bowden, 2006).

Classroom Implementation

The research on grammar teaching and learning and its interpretation in the provision of possible practical teaching models, as outlined above, provide some interesting and thought-provoking insights. It is, however, impossible, I believe, for research to furnish a firm basis for the choice of a practical classroom grammar-teaching methodology, for two main reasons.

The first has been mentioned earlier in this chapter. It is difficult, if not impossible, to reach definite, generalizable conclusions from the results of any one empirical study of a group of learners in a specific context. No one group of learners is exactly like any other, no teacher is like any other, nor is any context of learning and teaching. It is impossible to neutralize all surrounding factors that enhance, or interfere with, learning in order to identify the effect of the particular factor that the researcher is interested in. This is perhaps the main reason underlying the differing and often contradictory results produced by research: for example, the research on the efficacy, or not, of focused grammar practice, as noted previously. Even meta-analytic studies, which in principle should be able to reach more reliable conclusions, cannot completely free themselves from such reservations. All this does not mean, of course, that the research is useless for the practitioner. On the contrary, it is very useful, but only insofar as we realize that its function is to raise our awareness of the different scenarios that have been explored and to propose rational interpretations of such scenarios. It is not a question of "right" or "wrong"; it is a question of understanding and awareness of the various factors influencing learning (R. Ellis, 2006).

The second reason is that empirical research on grammar teaching/learning, being largely based on second-language acquisition research, has disregarded some crucial aspects of "teaching" in order to focus on the "learning." The implication is that teaching is a mere mirror-image of learning: if we can establish how languages are learnt, we can define and determine how to teach them. But this is simply not true. The practice of a second-language teaching involves not only second-language acquisition processes but also things such as students' socio-cultural backgrounds, relationships, and personalities; motivation; their expectations, learning styles and preferences; the influence of stake-holders such as parents, ministries of education, and school principals; aspects of lesson design and planning; time available for preparation and correction of notebooks; classroom management and discipline; upcoming exams … to mention but a few. Such features often actually have more influence on how grammar is taught, and whether it is successfully learnt, than any of those dealt with in research described in preceding sections of this chapter. For example: even if a teacher is convinced of the validity of a task-centered approach with incidental focus on form, he or she might decide not to implement such an approach because his or her students—or their parents—believe they learn better from systematic, traditional "focus on forms." Conversely, one who is convinced in principle of the importance of traditional forms-focused grammar practice may abandon it not because he or she feels it is useless, but because he or she finds that it does not make for learner interest and motivation. Or certain types of procedure are used because these are the ones that are going to come up in a high-stake exam at the end of the course. And so on.

Any recommended model of grammar teaching must therefore take into account not only insights from research but also pedagogical judgment based on professional experience and aspects of the particular context of teaching/learning.

A Possible Solution: Mix and Match?

Individual research-based studies such as those summarized in this chapter typically convey a clear message as to how their results might be implemented in practice: a procedure or set of procedures. But in attempting to draw some kind of general conclusion for the practitioner, it is impossible, owing to the reservations stated in the discussion above, to claim with any confidence that one model or approach has proved its case and is likely to produce good results in a variety of contexts.

This does not mean that "anything goes." It means that the teacher needs to assess the relevance of research results to his or her teaching context, and apply insights selectively. In any case a single specific methodology, which adopts only one model to the exclusion of others, is unlikely to be universally effective. It is a question of mixing and matching the different options according to the individual teacher's needs, situation, and professional judgment.

In this section I will attempt to describe five such options in practical teaching terms, and suggest how these may be combined in different situations. Each is defined in terms of a lesson, or part of a lesson.

> *Option 1: Task plus focus on form.* The lesson is based on a communicative task that may involve a written or spoken text. Occasionally time is devoted to clarification of grammatical forms, and possibly even practice activities. Such "time out" may be initiated by either teacher or students, may be either spontaneous or pre-planned by the teacher. But in any case, most of the lesson time and effort is devoted to the task and its meaning-focused outcomes.
>
> *Option 2: Grammar explanation plus practice.* The lesson is based on a grammatical structure, whose rule is explained (inductively or deductively), and which is then practiced. The practice activities may include a brief stage of mechanical drills, but are mainly meaningful and communicative, using the grammatical feature to understand and produce purposeful messages. They may include also communicative tasks designed to provide a natural context for the target grammatical feature.

Option 3: Communication. The lesson consists only of a communicative task that does not focus overtly on any grammatical feature. It may be based on components such as extensive reading, story-telling, problem-solving, interactive group work, or role-play. The aim (as far as grammar learning is concerned) is to provide opportunities for students to consolidate implicit knowledge of grammatical features.

Option 4: Consciousness-raising. The lesson, or part of a lesson, consists of a discussion of a grammar point, with no attempt to provide practice or implement in communication. The teacher may, for example, display sentences and invite students to try to identify the grammatical rule underlying them, or compare a particular grammatical feature of the target language with the equivalent in the students' L1. The aim is to raise awareness of a grammatical feature, as a basis for later noticing and acquisition.

Option 5: Exemplar-learning. The teacher invites students to familiarize themselves with or learn by heart texts that exemplify grammatical features: formulaic phrases, dialogues, chants, songs, poems and rhymes, tongue-twisters, proverbs, plays etc. This may take only a few minutes, or an entire lesson or series of lessons. The aim is for learners to acquire a repertoire of ready-made correct and meaningful grammatical forms that will furnish a basis for later acquisition through "noticing" and analogy. Some of these include an aspect of "play" (Cook, 2000) that is also likely to contribute to interest and motivation.

All the above have been justified in different situations as providing for useful learning. An optimum program of grammar teaching—indeed, of language teaching in general—should not confine itself to one of them, but rather include most or all, in varying proportions. Which are likely to predominate and which to be used very little if at all will, obviously, depend mainly on the teaching context and pedagogical considerations. More advanced adult learners (in academic programs in a target-language-medium university courses for example), are likely to improve their grammatical accuracy best if most lessons are based on task plus incidental focus on form, with occasional consciousness-raising and purely communicative activities. They are probably already familiar with much of the grammar of the target language and mainly need to "mop up" errors or gaps in their knowledge; they are highly motivated and of a high enough intellectual level to function well in group activities and tasks involving grammatical analysis. In contrast, teachers of schoolchildren in a state school in a country where the target language is not spoken outside the classroom are likely to get best results in grammar learning through systematic explanation plus practice, supplemented by smaller proportions of the other options. This is for various reasons: the relatively low starting level of proficiency and limited time available; learner and parent expectations; widespread lack of learner motivation, and discipline problems that make it difficult to run communicative tasks in groups. Such classes will also need a lot of communicative input—stories, for example—since the lessons are often their only opportunity to encounter the language, and varied lessons with plenty of games and short "fun" activities (as suggested in Ur & Wright, 1991). Exemplar-based learning is particularly useful for young learners but also sometimes for older ones, as the Chinese experience referred to previously (Ding, 2007) indicates.

These examples obviously cover only a small proportion of possible teaching contexts, but they give a taste of the context-dependent factors influencing teacher decisions how best to teach the target grammar.

Future Directions

The general impression one gets from reading the current literature is that it is assumed that some kind of task-based communicative approach is in principle "best," and it is only a question of how to persuade the teachers to adopt it (e.g., Carless, 2007; Gatbonton & Segalovitz, 2005; Littlewood, 2007). If, as suggested here, it is not a question of what is in principle "best" but rather what is the most appropriate combination of methods for a particular situation, then what is needed is longitudinal qualitative studies of grammar teaching situated within specific contexts. Such studies would provide a richly-textured description of situated processes and outcomes, enabling researchers to draw conclusions that may provide useful and reliable insights for other teachers working in similar circumstances.

References

Baron, N. S. (2005). Instant messaging and the future of language. *Communications of the ACM, 48*(7), 29–31.

Biber, D., Johansson, S., Leech, G., Conrad, S., & Finegan, E. (1999). *Longman grammar of spoken and written English.* Harlow: Pearson Education Limited.

Bloomfield, L. (1933). *Language.* New York: Holt.

Brumfit C. J. (1984). *Communicative methodology in language teaching.* Cambridge: Cambridge University Press.

Carless, D. (2007). The suitability of task-based approaches for secondary schools: Perspectives from Hong Kong. *System, 35*(4), 595–608.

Carter, R., & McCarthy, M. (2006). *Cambridge grammar of English.* Cambridge: Cambridge University Press.

Chomsky, N. (1957). *Syntactic structures.* The Hague: Mouton.

Cook, G. (2000). *Language play, language learning.* Oxford: Oxford University Press.

Crystal, D. (2001a). *Language and the internet.* Cambridge: Cambridge University Press.

Crystal, D. (2001b). Twenty-first century English. In A. Pulverness (Ed.), *IATEFL 2001: Brighton conference selections* (pp. 137–154). Cambridge: Cambridge University Press.

Cullen, R., & Cho, I-Chun. (2007). Spoken grammar and ELT course materials: A missing link? *TESOL Quarterly, 41*(2), 361–386.

Dekeyser, R. M. (1998). Beyond focus on form: Cognitive perspectives on learning and practising second language grammar. In C. Doughty & J. Williams (Eds.), *Focus on form in classroom second language acquisition* (pp. 42–63). Cambridge: Cambridge University Press.

Dekeyser, R. M. (2007). Introduction: Situating the concept of practice. In R. M. Dekeyser (Ed.), *Practice in a second language: Perspectives from applied linguistics and cognitive psychology* (pp. 1–18). Cambridge: Cambridge University Press.

Dekeyser, R. M., & Sokalski, K. J. (1996). The differential role of comprehension and production practice. *Language Learning, 46*(4), 613–642.

Ding, Y. (2007). Text memorization and imitation: The practices of successful Chinese learners of English. *System, 35*(2), 271–280.

Dongkwang, S., & Nation, P. (2007). Beyond single words: The most frequent collocations in spoken English. *ELT Journal, 62*(4), 339–348.

Ellis, N. (2002). Frequency effects in language processing. *Studies in Second Language Acquisition, 24*(2), 143–188.

Ellis, R. (1989). Are classroom and naturalistic acquisition the same? A study of the classroom acquisition of German word order rules. *Studies in Second Language Acquisition, 11*(3), 305–328.

Ellis, R. (1993). Talking shop: Second language acquisition research: How does it help teachers? *ELT Journal, 47*(1), 3–11.

Ellis, R. (2001a). Introduction: Investigating form-focused instruction. *Language Learning, 51*, 1–46.

Ellis, R. (2001b). Grammar teaching—Practice or consciousness-raising?. In J. C. Richards & W. A. Renandya (Eds.), *Methodology in language teaching* (pp. 167–174). Cambridge: Cambridge University Press.

Ellis, R. (2003). *Task-based language learning and teaching.* Oxford: Oxford University Press.

Ellis, R. (2005). Principles of instructed language learning. *System, 33*(2), 209–224.

Ellis, R. (2006). Current issues in the teaching of grammar: An SLA perspective. *TESOL Quarterly, 40*(1), 83–107

Ellis, R., & Rathbone, M. (1987). *The acquisition of German in a classroom context.* London: Ealing College of Higher Education.

Fitzpatrick, T., & Wray, A. (2006). Breaking up is not so hard to do: Individual differences in L2 memorization. *Canadian Modern Language Review, 63*(1), 35–57.

Gass, S., & Mackey, A. (2002). Frequency effects and second language acquisition: A complex picture? *Studies in Second Language Acquisition, 24*(2), 249–260.

Gatbonton, E., & Segalovitz, N. (2005). Rethinking communicative language teaching: a focus on access to fluency. *Canadian Modern Language Review, 61*(3), 325–353.

Hymes, D. (1972). On communicative competence. In J. B. Pride & J. Holmes (Eds.), *Sociolinguistics: Selected readings* (pp. 269–293). Harmondsworth: Penguin Books.

Jenkins, J. (2006). The spread of EIL: A testing time for testers. *ELT Journal*, *60*(1), 42–50.

Johnson, K. (1996). *Language teaching and skill learning.* Oxford: Blackwell.

Krashen, S. D. (1981). *Second language acquisition and second language learning.* Oxford: Pergamon.

Krashen, S. D. (1999). Seeking a role for grammar: A review of some recent studies. *Foreign Language Annals*, *32*(2), 245–257.

Krashen, S. D., & Terrell, T. (1983). *The natural approach.* Oxford: Pergamon.

Larsen-Freeman, D. (2002). The grammar of choice. In E. Hinkel & S. Fotos (Eds.), *New perspectives on grammar teaching in second language classrooms* (pp. 103–118). New York: Lawrence Erlbaum Associates.

Larsen-Freeman, D. (2003). *Teaching language: From grammar to grammaring.* Boston: Heinle.

Leow, R. P. (2007). Input in the L2 classroom: An attentional perspective on receptive practice. In R. M. Dekeyser (Ed.), *Practice in a second language: Perspectives from applied linguistics and cognitive psychology* (pp. 21–50). Cambridge: Cambridge University Press.

Littlewood, W. (2007). Communicative and task-based language teaching in East Asian classrooms. *Language Teaching*, *40*(3), 243–249.

Liu, D. (2003). The most frequently used spoken American English idioms: A corpus analysis and its implications. *TESOL Quarterly*, *37*(4), 671–700.

Long, M. (1991). Focus on form: A design feature in language teaching methodology. In K. De Bot, D. Coste, R. Ginsberg, & C. Kramsch (Eds.), *Foreign language research in cross-cultural perspective* (pp. 39–52). Amsterdam: John Benjamins.

Long, M. (1996). The role of the linguistic environment in second language acquisition. In W. Ritchie & T. Bhatia (Eds.), *Handbook of language acquisition, volume II: Second language acquisition* (pp. 413–468). New York: Academic Press.

Long, M. H., & Crookes, G. (1992). Three approaches to task-based syllabus design. *TESOL Quarterly*, *26*(1), 27–56.

Long, M. H., & Porter, P. A. (1985). Group work, interlanguage, talk and second language acquisition. *TESOL Quarterly*, *19*(2), 207–228.

Long, M. H., & Robinson, P. (1998). Focus on form: Theory, research and practice. In C. Doughty & J. Williams (Eds.), *Focus on form in classroom second language acquisition* (pp. 15–41). Cambridge: Cambridge University Press.

Morgan-Short, K., & Bowden, H. W. (2006). Processing instruction and meaningful output-based instruction: Effects on second language development. *Studies in Second Language Acquisition*, *28*(1), 31–65.

Nassaji, H., & Fotos, S. (2004). Current developments in research in the teaching of grammar. *Annual Review of Applied Linguistics*, *24*, 126–145.

Nitta, R., & Gardner, S. (2005). Consciousness-raising and practice in ELT course books. *ELT Journal*, *59*(1), 3–13.

Norris, J. M., & Ortega, L. (2001). Does type of instruction make a difference? Substantive findings from a meta-analytic review. *Language Learning*, *51*, Supplement 1, 157–213.

Nunan, D. (2004). *Task-based language teaching.* Cambridge: Cambridge University Press.

Pienemann, M. (1984). Psychological constraints on the teachability of language. *Studies in Second Language Acquisition*, *6*, 186–214.

Prabhu, N. S. (1987). *Second language pedagogy.* Oxford: Oxford University Press.

Qin, J. (2008). The effect of processing instruction and dictogloss tasks on acquisition of the English passive voice. *Language Teaching Research*, *12*(1), 61–82.

Richards, J. C. (2002). Accuracy and fluency revisited. In E. Hinkel & S. Fotos (Eds.), *New perspectives on grammar teaching in second language classrooms* (pp. 35–50). New York: Lawrence Erlbaum Associates.

Rivers, W. (1968). *Teaching foreign language skills.* Chicago: University of Chicago Press.

Salaberry, M. R. (1997). The role of input and output practice in second language acquisition. *Canadian Modern Language Review*, *53*(2), 422–451.

Schmidt, R. (2001). Attention. In P. Robinson (Ed.), *Cognition and second language instruction* (pp. 3–32). Cambridge: Cambridge University Press.

Schmidt, R., & Frota, S. (1986). Developing basic conversational ability in a second language: a case study of an adult learner of Portuguese. In R. Day (Ed.), *Talking to learn: Conversation in second language acquisition* (pp. 237–322). Rowley, MA: Newbury House.

Seedhouse, P. (1999). Task-based interaction. *English Language Teaching Journal*, *53*(3), 149–156.

Seidlhofer, B. (2004). Research perspectives on teaching English as a lingua franca. *Annual Review of Applied Linguistics*, *24*, 209–239.

Seidlhofer, B. (2006). English as a lingua franca in the expanding circle: What it isn't. In R. Rubdy & M. Saraceni (Eds.), *English in the world: Global rules, global roles* (pp. 40–50). London: Continuum.

Shak, J., & Gardner, S. (2008). Young learner perspectives on four focus-on-form tasks. *Language Teaching Research*, *12*(3), 387–408.

Skehan, P. (1997). A rationale for task-based instruction. In *A cognitive approach to language learning* (pp. 93–120). Oxford: Oxford University Press.

Skehan, P. (2003). Task-based instruction. *Language Teaching, 36*, 1–14.

Skinner, B. F. (1957). *Verbal behavior.* New York: Appleton-Century-Crofts.

Spada, N. (1997). Form-focussed instruction and second language acquisition: A review of classroom and laboratory research. *Language Teaching, 30*, 73–85.

Spada, N., & Lightbown, P. M. (1999). Instruction, first language influence, and developmental readiness in second language acquisition. *Modern Language Journal, 83*(1), 1–22.

Swain, M. (1995) The output hypothesis: Theory and research. In E. Hinkel (Ed.), *Handbook of research in second language teaching and learning* (pp. 471–484). Oxford: Oxford University Press.

Swain, M. (2000). French immersion research in Canada: Recent contributions to SLA and applied linguistics. *Annual Review of Applied Linguistics, 20*, 199–211.

Swan, M. (2005). Legislation by hypothesis: The case of task-based instruction. *Applied Linguistics, 26*(3), 376–401.

Taguchi, N. (2007). Chunk learning and the development of spoken discourse in a Japanese as a foreign language classroom. *Language Teaching Research, 11*(4), 433–457.

Timmis, I. (2005). Towards a framework for teaching spoken grammar. *English Language Teaching Journal, 59*(2), 117–125.

Ur, P. (1996). *A course in language teaching.* Cambridge: Cambridge University Press.

Ur, P. (2009). *Grammar practice activities* (2nd ed.). Cambridge: Cambridge University Press.

Ur, P., & Wright, A. (1991). *Five minute activities.* Cambridge: Cambridge University Press.

VanPatten, B. (2003). Processing instruction: An update. *Modern Language Journal, 52*(4), 755–803.

Van Patten, B., & Cadierno, T. (1993). Explicit instruction and input processing. *Studies in Second Language Acquisition, 15*, 225–243.

VOICE (2009). Accessed January 11 from http://www.univie.ac.at/voice/index.php.

Widdowson, H. G. (1978). *Teaching language as communication.* Oxford: Oxford University Press.

Widdowson, H. G. (1990). Grammar, and nonsense, and learning. In *Aspects of language teaching* (pp. 79–98). Oxford: Oxford University Press.

Willis, D. (1990). *The lexical syllabus.* London: Collins.

Willis, J. (1996). A flexible framework for task-based learning. In D. Willis & J. Willis (Eds.), *Challenge and change in language teaching* (pp. 52–62). Oxford: Heinemann.

Wray, A. (2000). Formulaic sequences in second language teaching: Principle and practice. *Applied Linguistics, 21*(4), 463–489.

32
What Research on Second Language Writing Tells Us and What it Doesn't

Eli Hinkel

Introduction

Over the past half century, the overarching goal of research on second language (L2) writing has been to create pedagogical models for teaching L2 writing. Many of these models have sought to identify instructional areas and techniques for constructing discourse and text in order to shed light on the tasks of teachers and their students who need to learn to write in an L2.

Formal investigations in L2 writing began to emerge as a research venue in the 1950s and 1960s when international students first began to enroll in colleges and universities in substantial numbers in English-speaking countries. In keeping with the classical western literary tradition, early studies focused primarily on discourse and ideational structuring, and they brought to the foreground the fact that discourse and ideational paradigms differ greatly in and across languages and cultures.

In a large measure, the theoretical frameworks and research methods for analyses of L2 writing are derived from those developed and formulated in various domains of applied linguistics such as text linguistics, discourse analysis, ethnography, and cross-cultural communication. Although much research on first language (L1) English-language writing has been carried out in such disciplines as rhetoric and composition, on the whole, the study of rhetoric has had a minimal influence on the investigations of L2 text.

Speaking generally, discourse analysis undertakes to study global (macro) features of text, such as the sequencing of ideas, and the organization of information in writing. The original and primary goal of such analyses was to examine the structure of discourse in the writing of L2 students in US universities in the early days of applied linguistics. Many studies undertaken in the 1960s and 1970s had the objective of developing new knowledge, based on empirical studies, that could provide a theoretical and practical foundation for the teaching of L2 writing and teacher education. However, L2 studies and publications achieved prominence and began to proliferate only in the 1980s and 1990s, largely as an outcome of a dramatic growth in the enrollments of students who were nonnative speakers (NNSs) of English.

In the past three decades, an ever expanding body of work has come to elucidate a broad range of properties of L2 discourse and text, as well as regularities in the structure of L2 written prose. For instance, since the 1990s, much has been learned about the structuring of ideas in written prose and the smaller, essential components of discourse, also called discourse moves (e.g., Hinds, 1987;

Swales, 1990). Along these lines, cross-cultural investigations in the uses of L2 linguistic properties of learner writing also began to take a closer look at the local (micro) features of L2 text.

A large number of investigations in the language and discourse features of L2 prose have identified important and significant differences among the properties of L1 and L2 text in similar or proximate written genres. To a great extent, research on discourse construction and language usage patterns in L2 writing has led to a greater understanding of many issues that confound English as a second language/English as a foreign language (ESL/EFL) writing and its teaching and learning. These studies have provided important insights into a broad range of connections between L2 discourse and text, such as advance discourse organizers and divisions, topic introductions and shifts, persuasion devices, and lexical and syntactic means of establishing cohesion, e.g., lexical ties, repetitions, and the uses of tenses, pronouns, and sentence adverbials (Aziz, 1988; Choi, 1988; Field & Oi, 1992; Hinkel, 2001a, 2002a, 2002b, 2003a; Mauranen, 1996; Montano-Harmon, 1991; Poole, 1991).

To make sense of the enormous number of studies, this chapter provides a brief overview of L2 writing research and its findings to highlight what is known and what still requires further investigation.

Cross-Cultural and Cross-Linguistic Research in L2 Writing

Analyzing written discourse frameworks and text properties became the objective of many studies that worked with L1 writing of native speakers (NSs) of English in, for example, Australia, Canada, the US, the UK, and New Zealand, and those in the English L2 writing of speakers of many other languages. To date, research has thus far compared discourse and textual features employed in L2 writing of speakers of such languages as (in alphabetical order, not a complete list by any measure):

- Amharic
- Arabic
- Bengali
- Bulgarian
- Burmese
- Cambodian
- Catalan
- Chinese (Cantonese Mandarin, Han)
- Czech
- Dutch
- Farsi
- Finish
- French
- Haitian Creole
- Hawaiian Creole
- Hebrew
- Hindi
- Hmong

- Hungarian
- German
- Gola
- Greek
- Gurjartic
- Ibo
- Indonesian
- Italian
- Japanese
- Kanjoval
- Korean
- Lambya
- Lao
- Malay
- Marathi
- Navajo
- Norwegian
- Polish
- Portuguese

- Romanian
- Russian
- Serbo-Croatian
- Sinhala
- Somali
- Spanish
- Swedish
- Tahitian
- Tagalog
- Tamil
- Telugu
- Thai
- Tigringa
- Turkish
- Ukrainian
- Urdu
- Vietnamese
- Western Apache, and
- several varieties of English.

By and large, the studies of L2 discourse and text have sought to address immediate and long-term research, curriculum, and instructional development goals, as well as pedagogical needs of specific groups of L2 learners in various locations, available sources of text data, and/or attempts to apply the findings of predominantly English language-based text linguistics to L2 text (e.g. Al-Khatib, 2001; Carlson, 1988; Hinkel, 1999, 2005; Laufer, 2003; see also Grabe & Kaplan, 1996) for a discussion).

Despite a great deal of research into L2 writing, a coherent picture of syntactic, lexical, rhetorical, or discoursal features of L2 text has yet to emerge. However, in sum total, much has been learned about features of text produced by L2 writers in different contexts and for divergent academic, social, and communication purposes, as discussed throughout this chapter.

The Range of Research in L2 Writing

An enormous number of works on writing in general and L2 writing specifically are published every year. In fact, the quantity of publications and research reports has become so overwhelming that a new genre of work has begun to appear in growing numbers: research syntheses. The emergence of this type of work has been driven predominantly by the need to make sense of the vast body of research on L2 writing. A few examples below include the recent research synthesis publications to demonstrate how vast the body of work on L2 writing actually is (Table 32.1).

A vast body of published studies has investigated discoursal, rhetorical, cohesive, lexical, and syntactic properties of L1 and L2 writing. To date, research into L2 discourse and text has identified the important and systematic differences in how L1 and L2 writing are constructed. These will be reviewed in broad strokes later in this chapter.

Educational and Social Contexts of L2 Writing

To date, the majority of investigations into L2 writing have focused on the organizational and ideational structure of L2 discourse and the morphosyntactic and lexical characteristics of L2 text. Comparative studies have sought to account for differences and similarities between the properties of L2 discourse and text and those identified in the L1 writing of English NSs who can be, for example, university students, authors of published research articles, or employees of multinational companies.

In such examinations, comparisons can be made in regard to L1 and L2 global (macro) discourse construction, arrangements of ideas, cohesion, and coherence. Additionally, researchers can

Table 32.1 Examples of Recent Synthesis Publications and Writing Research Overviews (in Reverse Chronological Order)

Author	Years covered	Number of works examined	Research areas covered
Leki, Cumming, and Silva (2008)	1984–2004	1,144	Contexts for L2 writing; Curriculum, instruction, and assessment; Basic research on L2 writing
Troia (2007)	1983–2005	150	Writing instruction only primarily in L1 English and some L2
Juzwik, Curcic, Wolbers, Moxley, Dimling, and Shankland (2006)	1999–2004*	1,502 total; 387 analyzed	Contexts for writing only (L1 and L2)
Hedgcock (2005)	1985–2005	135	L2 writing research and pedagogy
Paltridge (2004)	—	255	Academic writing (mostly L2)
Silva and Brice (2004)	2000–2003	360	Around 20 research areas related to teaching L2 writing, e.g. written texts, assessment, plagiarism, grammar and vocabulary, reading and writing, computers and technology
Weigle (2002)	—	255	Assessment and testing

Note: * Books excluded, journal articles only.

scrutinize textual (micro) features that have the function of marking discourse organization and aiding in the development of cohesive and coherent prose (e.g. Cutting, 2000; Hinkel, 2001b, 2002b; Markkanen & Schroeder, 1997). As with the research on L2 discourse, the primary objectives of practically all L2 text analyses and comparative studies have stemmed from instructional or curriculum development needs for teaching or learning to write in L2.

Learners of L2 writing can be, for example, school-age youngsters or adults, new immigrants who seek employment on their arrival in a new country or region of residence, professionals, employees of a broad range of organizations as well as their family members, university students, or academically-bound language learners who seek to obtain L2 writing skills prior to the beginning of their careers. Furthermore, research has examined the properties of L2 text produced by adult L2 writers in colleges and universities with an English medium of instruction (e.g. in Hong Kong, the Philippines, India, or Singapore), as well as the writing of young language learners in the course of their schooling. In short, those who undertake to learn to write in a L2 can be of all ages and as young as five years of age, and they can come from all walks of life and pursue their learning objectives in practically any location around the globe.

Predictably enough, L2 writing takes place at all levels of educational, vocational, community, and professional enterprise, as well as literacy training. Some specific contexts for L2 writing and writing development include:

- elementary school
- secondary school
- school-based newcomer programs for young learners
- undergraduate and graduate studies in colleges and universities
- community programs
- resettlement, refugee, and adult education centers
- professional contexts
- academic and scholarly pursuits
- the workplace.

With the possible exception of resettlement and refugee programs, which are rarely established for L1 writers who are, by definition not resettled in a new location, L2 writing probably takes place in the same contexts as L1 writing does.

Research Findings on Discourse (Macro) Properties of L2 Writing

Studies of L2 writing have delved into such global features of writing as discourse organization and information structuring, topic appropriateness, development, and continuity, types and arrangement of evidence, as well as text cohesion, coherence, clarity, and style. These constructs appear to be greatly influenced by the rhetorical and text construction norms that can differ substantially across languages and cultures. As has been mentioned, it is crucially important that comparative analyses of discourse and language features employed in L1 and L2 prose be carried out on the basis of similar or proximate written genres. For example, a comparison of linguistic properties of romantic fiction with its flourish of adjectives and adverbs to published scholarly articles in, say, biology or business memos may render results of any study less than valid. For this reason, discussion below is concerned only with the findings of many studies of L2 discourse (macro) properties, as well as the linguistic (micro) features, based on similar and comparable genres of writing.

By and large, the analyses of discourse properties in L2 writing pivot on scores and rankings assigned by raters, whose judgments are required to be consistent (see, for example, Connor-Linton, 1995;

Crowhurst, 1980; or Hamp-Lyons, 1995 for detailed discussions of the rating processes involved in evaluating L2 writing). Speaking broadly, virtually all studies to date have identified fundamental and pronounced differences between all facets of writing in L1 and L2 discourse and text. For example, the process of constructing L2 discourse is consistently and significantly different from that involved in producing L1 written prose, and L2 writers undertake less discourse planning, reviewing, and revising than L1 basic writers.

According to some researchers, however, the divergences between L1 and L2 discourse structuring, paragraph organization, and ideational cohesion can also be attributed to L2 writers' developmental constraints and inexperience rather than the transfer of L1 rhetorical paradigms (Mohan & Lo, 1985). Along these lines, examinations of published reports written by Chinese and English speakers (Taylor & Chen, 1991), and essays written by Korean students in a US university (Choi, 1988) demonstrated that discourse structuring in L1 and L2 writing can show both differences and similarities. In both cases, the authors note that due to the internationalization of scientific discourse and the impact of English writing instruction in many countries, the paradigmatic disparities between the Anglo-American discourse structuring patterns and those in other rhetorical traditions have been noticeably declining over time and are likely to become even less pronounced in the future.

Based on the findings of hundreds of studies, compared to the discourse structuring and ideational development in L1 writing, the following characteristics of L2 writing seem to be prominent.

Discourse Structuring and Ideational Development in L2 Writing

Compared to L1 writers of similar social and educational backgrounds, and based on research in similar genres, L2 writers

- organize and structure discourse moves differently
- utilize discourse moves and their contents differently and inconsistently, primarily due to the negative transfer of discourse structuring conventions across various cultures
- construct or place thesis statements differently, as well as omitting them altogether
- take a logically and conceptually different approach to rhetorical development, argumentation, persuasion, and exposition/narration
- often neglect to account for counterarguments and to anticipate audience reactions
- support their arguments and claims by means of statements of personal opinions and beliefs in lieu of more substantive information
- significantly more often leave their argumentation unsupported
- sequence ideas and explanatory information differently: the norms of rhetorical structuring of discourse often do not conform to those expected in comparable written genres in English
- construct less fluent and less detailed/explanatory prose
- produce shorter and less elaborated texts
- rely more on personal opinions and include less fact-based evidence in argumentation and exposition
- over- or under-estimate the amount of readers' background knowledge and the need for textual clarity, explicitness, and specificity
- differently orient the reader to the content, as well as differently introduce and develop topics;
- delay or omit thesis/main point statements, and also omit or dramatically shorten conclusions/ closings (e.g. one-sentence closings, as in: *Hopefully, scientists will find a solution to this problem soon.*)
- employ different strategies for extracting/citing information from sources, as well as paraphrasing, quoting, and including source material in their writing

- develop text cohesion differently, with weak lexical/semantic ties and theme connections, and a preponderance of overt discourse-level conjunctions
- rely on different given–new (theme–rheme) idea development
- use different sequencing, parsing, ordering, and connecting paragraph divisions, e.g., in some cases, such as those found in academic essays, L2 paragraphs need to be re-organized or divided into shorter ones, or short paragraphs need to be combined into longer ones
- differently—and often inconsistently—establish text cohesion: less frequent and less dense usage of cohesion devices, such as lexical, discoursal, and referential cohesive ties
- rely on repetition in order to paraphrase or establish cohesion at rates twice as high as those found in L1 writing
- develop prose that is oblique (e.g., hints) and vague (e.g., questions and allusions in lieu of direct statements)
- often take moralistic and emotionally appealing approaches to argumentation and persuasion (e.g. Field & Oi, 1992; Indrasuta, 1988; Johnson, 1992; Hinkel, 1997, 2001b; Leki, 2007; Leki, Cumming, & Silva, 2008; Mauranen, 1996; Paltridge, 2001, 2004; Silva, 1993; Spack, 1997; Swales, 1990; Markkanen & Schroeder, 1997).

Many researchers have concluded that L2 written discourse paradigms are principally, strategically, and globally different from those found in L1 writing. In light of these crucial and profound differences, it stands to reason that instruction in constructing L2 written discourse cannot be derived from that developed for L1 writing pedagogy; that is, learning to write in an L2 is a process foundationally and substantively distinct from learning to write in an L1.

The effects of L1 discourse structuring and rhetorical organization of information represents a prolific area taken up in numerous studies of L2 writing. Many investigations of written discourse paradigms in a range of rhetorical traditions and cultures have shed a great deal of light on various issues that continue to confound the teaching and learning of writing.

To this end, research into how L2 discourse and text are constructed, as well as comparative analyses of discourse in similar genres, have proven to be highly fruitful in the teaching of L2 writing and creating more appropriate curricula in L2 writing instruction (e.g., Leki, 1992; Reid, 1993; Weigle, 2002). In particular, an important outcome of research into L2 written discourse is the increased knowledge about discourse and text in writing traditions other than Anglo-American, including such written genres as news reports, academic publications, student writing, email messages, business letters, recommendation letters, email messages, article abstracts, conference proposals, sales letters, grant proposals, formal essays, university term papers, and diploma projects produced by L2 writers (e.g., Al-Khatib, 2001; Bouton, 1995; Choi, 1988; Hinkel, 2001a, 2001b; Jenkins & Hinds, 1987).

Morphosyntactic and Lexical Attributes of L2 Text

Unlike the ratings of the discourse attributes of L2 prose, studies of morphosyntactic and lexical features of L2 text, as well as error analyses, are typically quantitative. Such investigations allow for identifying statistically significant differences between the textual properties of L1 and L2 prose. To date, much research has investigated a broad range of lexical and syntactic features of L2 prose, such as the uses of personal and other types of pronouns, modal verbs, sentence structure (e.g., subordination and coordination), phrase and sentence conjunctions (e.g., sentence transitions), prepositional phrases, concrete and abstract nouns, verb tenses and aspects, cohesive devices (e.g., lexical repetition), lexical synonyms and ties, active and passive voice constructions, and lexical and grammatical errors. Much research, for example, investigated the uses of discourse markers (e.g., *well, you know,* or *I mean*), cohesion and coherence devices (e.g., *so, the cause of, a result*), modal verbs, hedges, and modifiers in L1 and L2 prose (Field & Oi, 1992; Flowerdew, 2000; Hinkel, 1995, 2001b, 2002a, 2004; Johns, 1984, 1990; Johnson, 1992; Khalil, 1989; Mauranen, 1996; Swales, 1990).

For this purpose, researchers may compare the frequencies and contexts of sentence conjunctions (e.g., *furthermore*, *however*, and *thus*), coordinating conjunctions (e.g., *and*, *but*, *yet*, and *so*), and/or summary markers (e.g., *in short* and *in sum*) (e.g. Field & Oi, 1992; Hinkel, 1999, 2001a, 2003a, 2003b; Schleppegrell, 2002). Similarly, to analyze the uses of modal verbs, usage measurements can be computed separately or together for possibility and ability modals (e.g., *can*, *may*) or obligation and necessity modals (e.g., *must*, *should*).

Overall, based on a vast body of research, limited vocabulary and grammar are the most frequently cited/noted properties of L2 text.

Micro Features (Grammar and Vocabulary) of L2 Writing

Compared to L1 prose, L2 texts

- exhibit less lexical variety and sophistication
- contain significantly fewer idiomatic and collocational expressions
- have smaller lexical density and lexical specificity, and more frequent vocabulary misuses
- rely on shorter sentences and clauses (aka T-units) with fewer words per clause and fewer words (e.g., nouns and modifiers) per verb
- involve high rates of incomplete or inaccurate sentences (e.g., missing sentence subjects or verbs, incomplete verb phrases, sentence fragments)
- repeat content words more often (i.e., nouns, verbs, adjectives, and adverbs)
- provide twice as many simple paraphrases or avoid paraphrasing altogether with a preponderance of referential pronouns (e.g., *this*, *that*, *it*)
- use shorter words (fewer words with two or more syllables), more conversational and high frequency words (e.g., *good*, *bad*, *ask*, *talk*)
- incorporate fewer modifying and descriptive prepositional phrases, as well as a higher rate of misused prepositions
- employ less subordination and two to three times more coordination.

L2 texts also employ

- fewer passive constructions
- fewer lexical (e.g., adjectives and adverbs) and syntactic modifiers (e.g., subordinate clauses) of sentences, nouns, and verbs
- inconsistent uses of verb tenses
- more emotive and private verbs (e.g., *believe*, *feel*, *think*)
- significantly higher rates of personal pronouns (e.g., *I*, *we*, *he*) and lower rates of impersonal/referential pronouns (e.g., *it*, *this*, *one*)
- markedly fewer of abstract and interpretive nouns, and nominalizations (e.g., *rotation*, *cognition*, *analysis*)
- fewer adverbial modifiers and adverbial clauses
- fewer epistemic and possibility hedges (e.g., *apparently*, *perhaps*) and more conversational hedges (e.g., *sort of*, *in a way*)
- more conversational intensifiers, emphatics, exaggeratives, and overstatements (e.g., *totally*, *always*, *huge*, *for sure*)
- fewer downtoners (e.g., *almost*, *hardly*)
- more lexical softening devices (e.g., *maybe*).

At present, research has clearly and unambiguously demonstrated that L2 writers' skill level in vocabulary and grammar disadvantages the quality of their formal prose. A number of studies report that, even after several years of language learning, the micro properties of L2 writers' text continue to differ significantly from that of novice NS writers in regard to a broad range of features. The results of dozens of analyses indicate that even advanced and highly educated L2 writers, such as doctoral students enrolled in universities in English-speaking countries and professionals, have a severely limited lexical and syntactic repertoire, compared to their NS peers. In many cases of undergraduate L2 writers, for example, a restricted access to advanced language features results in simple texts that rely on the most common language features that occur predominantly in conversational discourse. In fact, today, in light of a large body of research findings obtained after about a half a century of comparative L1 and L2 text analyses, this conclusion seems rather obvious and trite (Carson, 2001; Hamp-Lyons, 1991, 1995; Hedgcock, 2005; Hinkel, 2009; Jenkins & Hinds, 1987; North, 1986).

Analyses of Errors in L2 Prose

It is important to note at the outset that L2 writers' ability to identify and correct grammar and vocabulary errors is a developmental process at least to some extent. That is, as their experience with constructing L2 text grows, the frequency of errors in many instances of L2 writing can decline. However, researchers have also found that, for a majority of L2 learners, eliminating all morpho-syntactic and lexical errors is virtually impossible. Furthermore, while some types of sentence- and phrase-level errors can be reduced with experience, other classes of errors are a great deal more difficult to eliminate. Although studies of L2 writing have shown that errors can occur in the L2 uses of a broad range of language constructions, the following error types have been recognized as highly common and pervasive (e.g., Ferris, 1995, 1997, 2002; Ferris & Roberts, 2001; Cutting, 2000; McCretton & Rider, 1993; Schleppegrell, 2002).

Examples of Frequent Error Types in L2 Writing

The following error types have been found to be frequent in L2 writing:

- Sentence divisions, fragmented and clipped sentences, and run-ons, e.g., *So, I ask. *Sometime, one can be lack.
- Subject and verb agreement, e.g., *Teachers of math and reading is serious about teaching.
- Verb tenses and aspects, and verb phrases, e.g., *I remember the time when I receive a phone call from my boss that they were not satisfy with the work we've done.
- Word-level morphology (i.e., absent or incorrect affixes) and incorrect word forms, e.g., *nation pride, *America class is more interested than in my country.
- Incomplete or incorrect subordinate clause structure (e.g., missing subjects, verbs and clause subordinators), e.g., *when try to be success, *although economic is not a factor.
- Misuses (or under-uses and over-uses) of coherence and cohesion markers, such as coordinating conjunctions and demonstrative pronouns, e.g., *At last, I completely agree with this. *The next reason is not willing to try again.
- Singular or plural nouns and pronouns. *People want to go to school, so he work very hard on his subjects. *The elder are given many equipments to help them in the old age.
- Incorrect or omitted prepositions, e.g., *from my opinion, *At some time there is this young businessman who just about takes a taxi of the airport.
- Incorrect or omitted articles, e.g., *Finally, some people can not take good exam and telling very sad. *Some students sleep in classroom, play cellphone, play game.

- Incorrect modal verbs, e.g., *It is also important to have adults by their side whom could advice them when they may make a mistake.*
- Spelling errors.

Since the 1980s, analyses of L2 language errors have become a familiar venue in investigations of written computer corpora of learner writing (Granger, 1998; Granger & Tribble, 1998; Green, Christopher, & Lam, 2000; Nesselhauf, 2005). In general terms, the analysis of grammatical and lexical errors in L2 prose is rooted in the contrastive (error) analysis that predominated in L2 learning research between the 1950s and 1970s.

One of the most popular comments on the studies of errors in L2 writing is that L1 writers who are NSs of English also make mistakes. This observation is unquestionably true. A recent empirical study of L1 undergraduate writing in 24 US universities (Lunsford & Lunsford, 2008) identified the most frequent types of errors (in declining order):

- wrong word
- spelling (including homonyms)
- incomplete or missing documentation
- mechanical error with a quotation
- missing comma after an introductory element
- missing word
- unnecessary or missing capitalization
- vague pronoun reference
- unnecessary comma
- unnecessary shift in verb tense
- missing comma in a compound sentence.

It seems clear from this list that the L1 errors in formal prose are fundamentally distinct from those in L2 university writing because the former are unlikely to impede comprehension (see also studies of error gravity in L2 writing, e.g., Vann, Lorenz, & Meyer, 1991; Vann, Meyer, & Lorenz, 1984; and Santos, 1988).

Research in L2 Writing Instruction and Curricula

To date, research in effective writing instruction lags far behind studies into the features of L2 written discourse and text. As Leki, Cumming, and Silva (2008, pp. 72–73) point out,

> indeed, one would be hard pressed to identify foundational concepts that have aspired to provide a single, guiding basis on which to organize writing curricula comprehensively. … [L]ittle research and few models of L2 writing have tried to relate curriculum content directly with L2 students' writing achievements.

These authors further note that abundant research is available about cross-cultural variations in discourse paradigms and "L2 composing processes" and that it may inform certain curricular decisions about teaching or organizing of teaching activities for specific groups of learners. However, research on principles for effective curriculum design or instructional methods for L2 writing is conspicuously missing.

In this light, the trends in L2 writing instruction and curricula have gravitated toward various sets of incremental teaching techniques and theoretical approaches that have gathered enough momentum to form particular schools of thought (e.g., Ferris & Hedgcock, 2005; Grabe & Kaplan, 1996; Paltridge, 2004). It is important to note, though, that few, if any, combinations of techniques or theoretical models have been empirically validated in terms of their pedagogical effectiveness or even usefulness. Rather, many of the currently prevalent approaches to teaching L2 writing have become established instructional practices that typically fall under the umbrella term of "what works" (also known as "best practice") in pedagogy and curriculum design. However, this term can refer to any number of issues in teaching or learning L2 writing. In some educational contexts, it can point practicing teachers to a productive activity that can help learners to improve the quality of their discourse organization, or enrich their vocabulary in writing, or provide for an enjoyable classroom task. Although in the teaching of L1 writing to school-age learners and college students a number of studies have undertaken to determine whether specific teaching techniques do in fact lead to a noticeable improvement in writers' skills, few such investigations have been carried out in the contexts of L2 writing (see Troia, 2007 for a thorough discussion).

Techniques in Teaching L2 Writing

In the 1970s and 1980s, much in the methods and techniques for teaching L2 writing was derived from pedagogy in L1 composition. In later years, L2 writing instruction has striven to move away from composition studies at least to some extent (Frodesen, 2001; Hinkel, 2006). For past two or three decades, techniques prevalent in the teaching of L2 writing have sought to address an extensive array of issues that have traditionally represented major and minor foci of instruction modified to meet the needs of L2 learners specifically. These techniques encompass generating ideas and producing L2 text, organizing ideas in keeping with L2 discourse conventions, planning and outlining, paragraph and text development, drafting, revising at the discourse and sentence levels, considerations of audience, lexical choice, precision, and vocabulary changes, dictionary uses, spelling, punctuation, editing, and error correction, as well as using computers for writing, grammar practice, and vocabulary development.

In many prototypical activities, students are expected to read one or more selections on particular topics that vary in the degree of their content complexity and language sophistication depending on learners' proficiency levels. While at the beginning or intermediate levels, the selected readings can be on such simple topics as "preparing for a trip" or "holidays in my country," at advanced or pre-academic levels, the model texts can deal with more elaborate material on consumer behavior, psychology, or climate change. Following the reading portion of the activity, learners can be asked to perform a variety of tasks that include responding to the excerpt, recounting their own experiences associated with the topic, or providing their views on the subject matter.

By and large, these activities have the goal of teaching L2 writers how to construct meaningful and reasonably fluent and accurate texts, and organize ideas to meet particular communicative goals in context (e.g., see Ferris & Hedgcock, 2005, for a detailed overview). As a follow-up, learners usually receive instruction in paragraphing, discourse structuring and organization, sentence construction, vocabulary, narrative or argumentation conventions, cohesion development, revising, and editing, as well as linguistic aspects of text (Silva & Brice, 2004). More recently, additional and innovative teaching techniques have also gained popularity, e.g., dialog journals, writing from sources, analyses of language uses in print and online media, examinations of language elements in model texts, such as those in academic disciplines or business writing, producing critiques or letters to express a point of view, or collaborative writing (e.g., Basturkmen & Lewis, 2002; Coffin, Curry, Goodman, Hewings, Lillis, & Swann, 2003; Cotterall & Cohen, 2003; Myers, 2001).

Methodological and Theoretical Directions in L2 Writing Curricula and Instruction

As Leki, Cumming, and Silva (2008) comment, "there have been surprisingly few research-based descriptions of L2 writing classroom instruction" (p. 80). A handful of publications that have appeared since the early 1990s take the form of professional reflections or testimonials to recount teachers' experiences in L2 writing classes or working with individual L2 writers enrolled in writing courses (e.g., Ferris, 2001; Lillis, 2001). In part, due to the fact that various techniques and theoretical approaches to teaching L2 writing have not been substantiated by empirical research, several prevalent methods and schools of thought have evolved in tandem, and in addition to these, other pedagogical schemes continue to thrive.

Generally speaking, a number of methodological approaches to developing curricula and teaching L2 writing, as well as academic L2 writing, have emerged in the past half century. These have diverged to varying extents depending on the prevailing fashions and contemporary views on the effectiveness of a particular writing instruction, political trends in academic writing and composition teaching, language learning, L2 learning, human development, and cognitive maturation (e.g., Paltridge, 2004). Although novel perspectives on the teaching of L2 writing continue to emerge regularly, few (if any) of the once-predominant methods or sets of particular teaching techniques have disappeared completely. Each of the once-popular approaches to teaching L2 writing has its core of devoted supporters among researchers and instructors who remain steadfast when another methodological innovation appears on the disciplinary scene (see, for example, an extensive discussion of historically dominant and now less prevalent methods in Ferris & Hedgcock, 2005).

In this light, the brief discussion below touches only on the prevailing trends among the many methodological and theoretical directions that currently predominate in the curriculum design and teaching approaches in L2 writing pedagogy.

At present, different schools of thought on L2 writing curricular and pedagogy predominate in different world regions. These are distinct in regard to how L2 writing should be taught, what L2 types of writing L2 learners should be able to produce, and what type of curricula and instruction best serves the needs of these learners. For instance, content-based language and writing instruction is commonly found in the US-based curricula, while genre-based teaching of L2 writing is prevalent in the UK, Australia, and New Zealand.

Content-based instruction and L2 curricula occupy a prominent place in the teaching of L2 writing to school-age learners and academically-bound students in Enlgish for academic purposes (EAP) and English for specific purposes (ESP) programs (Mohan, 1986). According to the principles of content-based teaching, L2 reading, writing, and language instruction are integrated together with that in content, while grammar and vocabulary play the role of attendant foci (e.g., Snow, 2005; Snow & Brinton, 1997). In content-based instruction, L2 reading and writing play a central role, and the instruction in these skills is typically combined to improve the quality of L2 prose in terms of both discourse (macro) and morphosyntactic and lexical (micro) properties. For example, combined with instruction in content and language uses in thematically-selected readings, the teaching of L2 writing can address matters of discourse structuring and information flow, as well as the uses of grammar structures and contextualized vocabulary. Additionally, features of formal written register and academic language can be emphasized in context (Celce-Murcia & Olshtain, 2000, 2005). Content-based teaching can also have supplementary foci on teaching incremental academic skills, such as text and information analysis, text and discourse construction, critical thinking, library research, or information gathering (Paltridge, 2004).

A wide adoption of content-based instruction in L2 reading and writing has given rise to numerous variations of the prototypical content-based instructional models that include such representative exemplars as immersion learning, partial immersion learning, sheltered instruction, or academic language learning. Other instructional variants have more closely followed approaches popular in the teaching of writing to L1 school-age learners and college students, such as academic literacy learning, cooperative learning, whole language instruction, or language-content-task instruction (e.g., Mohan, Leung, & Davison, 2001; Snow, 2005).

In practical terms, however, several important issues have been noted in connection with content-based instruction and the teaching of L2 writing. One of these, for instance, regards the level of expertise in matters of content and writing in the disciplines required of language teachers who work with content-based teaching and curricula. Many published reports have pointed out that practicing L2 teachers are well-equipped to deal with language instruction, but far less so in the areas of content and discipline-specific academic writing and discourse frameworks (e.g., Met, 1998; Snow, 2005). Along these lines, in the context of L2 writing curricula, it is not always clear what content should be included for the purposes of language and L2 writing instruction in content-based courses. In addition, given the great amount of work entailed in teaching content to L2 learners, in many cases, the teaching of grammar and the features of formal academic prose often receive short shrift. At present, practically all pedagogical materials on content-based instruction explicitly direct teachers to focus intensively on L2 writers' needs for grammar and language instruction (e.g., Celce-Murcia & Olshtain, 2005; Hinkel, 2004; Paltridge, 2004; Snow, 2005).

In the UK and Australia in particular, *genre-based approaches* have predominated among methodological and theoretical directions in L2 writing instruction and curricular designs. Like content-based instruction, genre-based pedagogy also represents an integrated approach to teaching L2 writing together with reading and supplementary foci on attributes of written registers. The genre-based approach and teaching techniques draw on the foundations of the systemic functional linguistics and genre theory. These analytical approaches have informed the teaching of L2 writing mostly for academic and special purposes (EAP and ESP), as well as research in the uses of language in written discourse and texts in diverse genres, such as, say, university essays, assignments, or technical communications, ranging from email messages to news reports and to doctoral dissertations. Genre-based instruction seeks to enable L2 learners to analyze academic discourse while reading and to produce academic writing that adheres to the sociocultural norms of a particular academic (or professional) genre (e.g., Christie, 1999; Christie & Derewianka, 2008; Cope & Kalantzis, 1993, 2000; Martin, 1992). More recently, genre approaches to teaching L2 writing have made important inroads in North American research of school discourse, writing pedagogy, and, to some extent, instructional practices and teacher education (e.g., see Schleppegrell, 2004; Schleppegrell & Columbi, 2002).

In genre-based instruction, the language focus addresses features of discourse and text in the social, cultural, and practical contexts in which the written prose is constructed and the purposes that it is expected meet. Thus, pedagogical activities may undertake to analyze written prose in an array of genres, such as narrative, exposition, or argumentation, with the goal of increasing learners' awareness of how particular grammar and vocabulary are employed in authentic written text and discourse. Such practice in text analysis can become a useful springboard for an instructional focus on the specific uses of grammar structures and contextualized lexis. Similarly, the features of school writing or formal written discourse and register are emphasized in conjunction with the social and situational variables of language in the context of its use (e.g., Christie, 1999; Schleppegrell, 2002, 2004).

However, usage of a genre-based methodology and teaching activities in education, and more specifically in L2 curricula and instruction, have not been without controversy. Many experts in writing pedagogy and, more generally, in L2 teaching and learning believe that genres and their linguistic features may be subjective, culture-bound, vaguely defined, or even irrelevant to diverse types of ESL/EFL learners (e.g., see Silva & Brice, 2004 or Leki, 2007 for a discussion). For example, Widdowson (2003, p. 69) states that "the conception of genres as stable entities is only a convenient fiction: they are in reality sociocultural processes, continually in flux." He goes on to say that genres "are not controlled by native speakers of English, so neither is the language which is used to realize them" (p. 69). According to Widdowson, the findings of genre analyses represent impressionistic judgments about their distinctiveness, and, therefore, such findings simply have limited validity. Thus, given that genres are far from well-defined, the pedagogic viability of the genre-based approach and the attendant teaching of genre-driven discourse conventions and language features is in fact "limited" (p. 70).

As has been mentioned, in addition to these dominant methodological and theoretical directions in L2 writing instruction, other models of curricular and pedagogical orientation have made their mark on the vast expanse of L2 writing research and practice. These include, for instance, innovative work on L2 literacy and biliteracy, a broad-based construct of multiliteracy, as well as literacy instruction with multimedia and technology (e.g., Hornberger, 2003; Kress, 2003; Luke, 2004). Research on the meanings and implications of literacy, multiliteracy, and literate discourse in the contemporary age of technology and international communication is that, for L2 learners and writers, it is essential to attain capacities for multimodal communication in order to achieve social and educational equality and opportunity. Of this, there is no doubt.

Conclusions and Future Research Directions

In the past half century, a large body of work has been developed to identify the uses of discoursal, textual, syntactic, and lexical properties of L2 prose. Many studies of L2 text have identified the important and significant differences that exist between L1 and L2 writing in similar genres and among similar populations of writers. To date, research findings have established that L2 writers need intensive and extensive instruction in practically all aspects of constructing discourse and reasonably fluent and accurate text. Research has also demonstrated that, in many cases, crucial factors that confound L2 writing and text have to do with shortfalls of writers' language proficiencies and restricted linguistic repertoire that significantly undermine L2 writers' ability to produce high-quality texts. Based on the results of their studies, many researchers of L2 learning and development have emphasized that even school-age children or highly educated adult L2 learners require years of language training to attain the levels of proficiency necessary to produce effective written prose.

However, it also seems clear that research on what L2 writers need to learn, what they should be able to do, and how L2 writing can be efficaciously taught is conspicuously lacking. As Leki, Cumming, and Silva (2008, p. 81) note, "the curriculum and instructional practice has been a perplexingly overlooked and underrepresented aspect of research on L2 writing." While there are a number of theoretical and methodological approaches to curriculum and pedagogy in L2 writing, such as content-based and genre-based instruction, none has been empirically and practically validated. Admittedly, the range of settings and contexts where L2 writing is taught and learned is enormous, as are the types of learners who set out to attain language proficiency and skills requisite to produce quality L2 writing. Nonetheless, the need for research in comprehensive curriculum design and effective instruction in L2 writing is indisputably great.

The well-established research venue on the properties of L2 written prose has also been accompanied by a vast literature on English language corpora, the features of formal academic writing in published works or that written by professional writers. Similarly, much has been learned about how L1 writers, who are NSs of English or other languages construct formal prose in school- or university-level writing. At present, however, it is not known what L2 writers are to be taught to enable them to meet their academic, occupational, professional, and vocational goals. New research, the development of principled classroom practice, and well-rounded teacher education are urgently needed. In the end, the overarching objective of novel and empirically-grounded and principled pedagogical models is to provide L2 writers with access to social, educational, and economic opportunities and to enable L2 writers to communicate effectively in a broad range of contexts.

References

Al-Khatib, M. (2001). The pragmatics of letter-writing. *World Englishes, 20*, 170–200.

Aziz, Y. (1988). Theme-theme organization and paragraph structure in standard Arabic. *Word, 39*(3), 117–128.

Basturkmen, H., & Lewis, M. (2002). Learner perspectives of success in an EAP writing course. *Assessing Writing, 8*, 31–46.

Bouton, L. (1995). A cross-cultural analysis of the structure and content of letters of reference. *Studies in Second Language Acquisition, 17*, 211–244.

Carlson, S. (1988). Cultural differences in writing and reasoning skills. In A. Purves (Ed.), *Writing across languages and cultures: Issues in contrastive rhetoric* (pp. 109–137). Newbury Park, CA: Sage.

Carson, J. (2001). Second language writing and second language acquisition. In T. Silva & P. Matsuda (Eds.), *On second language writing* (pp. 191–199). Mahwah, NJ: Lawrence Erlbaum Associates.

Celce-Murcia, M., & Olshtain, E. (2000). *Discourse and context in language teaching.* New York: Cambridge University Press.

Celce-Murcia, M., & Olshtain, E. (2005). Discourse-based approaches: A new framework for second language teaching and learning. In E. Hinkel (Ed.), *Handbook of research in second language teaching and learning* (pp. 729–742). Mahwah, NJ: Laurence Erlbaum.

Choi, Y. (1988). Text structure of Korean speakers' argumentative essays in English. *World Englishes, 7*, 129–142.

Christie, F. (1999). Genre theory and ESL teaching: A systemic functional perspective. *TESOL Quarterly, 33*(4), 759–763.

Christie, F., & Derewianka, B. (2008). *School discourse: Learning to write across the years of schooling.* London: Continuum.

Coffin, C., Curry, M., Goodman, S., Hewings, A., Lillis, T., & Swann, J. (2003). *Teaching academic writing: A toolkit for higher education.* London: Routledge.

Connor-Linton, J. (1995). Looking behind the curtain: What do L2 composition ratings really mean? *TESOL Quarterly, 29*, 762–765.

Cope, B., & Kalantzis, M. (Eds.) (1993). *The powers of literacy: A genre approach to teaching writing.* Pittsburgh: University of Pittsburgh Press.

Cope, B., & Kalantzis, M. (Eds.) (2000). *Multiliteracies: Literacy learning and the design of social futures.* New York: Routledge.

Cotterall, S., & Cohen, R. (2003). Scaffolding for second language writers: Producing an academic essay. *ELT Journal, 57*, 158–166.

Crowhurst, M. (1980). Syntactic complexity and teachers' quality ratings of narrations and arguments. *Research in the Teaching of English, 14*, 223–231.

Cutting, J. (2000). Written errors of students in higher education and English native speaker students. In G. M. Blue, J. Milton, & J. Saville (Eds.), *Assessing English for academic purposes* (pp. 97–113). Oxford: Peter Lang.

Ferris, D. (1995). Can advanced ESL students be taught to correct their most serious and frequent errors? *CATESOL Journal, 8*(1), 41–62.

Ferris, D. (1997). The influence of teacher commentary on student revision. *TESOL Quarterly, 31*, 315–339.

Ferris, D. (2001). Teaching "writing for proficiency" in summer school: Lessons from a foxhole. In J. Murphy & P. Byrd (Eds.), *Understanding the courses we teach: Local perspectives on English language teaching* (pp. 328–345). Ann Arbor: University of Michigan Press.

Ferris, D. (2002). *Treatment of error in second language student writing.* Ann Arbor: University of Michigan Press.

Ferris, D., & Hedgcock, J. (2005). *Teaching ESL composition* (2nd ed.). Mahwah, NJ: Lawrence Erlbaum Associates.

Ferris, D., & Roberts, B. (2001). Error feedback in L2 writing classes: How explicit does it need to be? *Journal of Second Language Writing, 10*, 161–184.

Field, Y., & Oi, Y.L.M. (1992). A comparison of internal conjunctive cohesion in the English essay writing of Cantonese speakers and Native speakers. *RELC Journal, 23*, 15–28.

Flowerdew, L. (2000). Using a genre-based framework to teach organizational structure in academic writing. *ELT Journal, 54*, 369–378.

Frodesen, J. (2001). Grammar in writing. In M. Celce-Murcia (Ed.), *Teaching English as a second or foreign language* (3rd ed.) (pp. 233–248). Boston: Heinle & Heinle.

Grabe, W., & Kaplan, R. B. (1996). *Theory and practice of writing.* London: Longman.

Granger, S. (1998). The computer learner corpus: A versatile new source of data for SLA research. In S. Granger (Ed.), *Learner English on computer* (pp. 3–18). London: Longman.

Granger, S., & Tribble, C. (1998). Learner corpus data in the foreign language classroom: Form-focused instruction and data-driven learning. In S. Granger (Ed.), *Learner English on computer* (pp. 199–209). London: Longman.

Green, C., Christopher, E., & Lam, J. (2000). The incidence and defects on coherence of marked themes in interlanguage texts: A corpus-based enquiry. *English for Specific Purposes, 19*, 99–113.

Hamp-Lyons, L. (1991). Reconstructing "academic writing proficiency." In L. Hamp-Lyons (Ed.), *Assessing second language writing in academic contexts* (pp. 127–153). Norwood, NJ: Ablex.

Hamp-Lyons, L. (1995). Rating nonnative writing: The trouble with holistic scoring. *TESOL Quarterly, 29*, 759–762.

Hedgcock, J. (2005). Taking stock of research and pedagogy in L2 writing. In E. Hinkel (Ed.), *Handbook of research in second language teaching and learning* (pp. 597–614). Mahwah, NJ: Lawrence Erlbaum.

Hinds, J. (1987). Reader versus writer responsibility: A new typology. In U. Connor & R. B. Kaplan (Eds.), *Writing across languages: Analysis of L2 text* (pp. 141–152). Reading, MA: Addison-Wesley.

Hinkel, E. (1995). The use of modal verbs as a reflection of cultural values. *TESOL Quarterly, 29*, 325–343.

Hinkel, E. (1997). Indirectness in L1 and L2 academic writing. *Journal of Pragmatics, 27*, 360–386.

Hinkel, E. (1999). Objectivity and credibility in L1 and L2 academic writing. In E. Hinkel (Ed.), *Culture in second language teaching and learning* (pp. 90–108). Cambridge: Cambridge University Press.

Hinkel, E. (2001a). Giving examples and telling stories in academic essays. *Issues in Applied Linguistics, 12*, 149–170.

Hinkel, E. (2001b). Matters of cohesion in L1 and L2 academic texts. *Applied Language Learning, 12*, 111–132.

Hinkel, E. (2002a). *Second language writers' text.* Mahwah, NJ: Lawrence Erlbaum Associates.

Hinkel, E. (2002b). Teaching grammar in writing classes: Tenses and cohesion. In E. Hinkel & S. Fotos (Eds.), *New perspectives on grammar teaching in second language classrooms* (pp. 181–198). Mahwah, NJ: Lawrence Erlbaum Associates.

Hinkel, E. (2003a). Simplicity without elegance: Features of sentences in L2 and L1 academic texts. *TESOL Quarterly, 37*, 275–301.

Hinkel, E. (2003b). Adverbial markers and tone in L1 and L2 students' writing. *Journal of Pragmatics, 35*, 1049–1068.

Hinkel, E. (2004). *Teaching academic ESL writing: Practical techniques in vocabulary and grammar.* Mahwah, NJ: Lawrence Erlbaum Associates.

Hinkel, E. (2005). Analyses of L2 text and what can be learned from them. In E. Hinkel (Ed.), *Handbook of research in second language teaching and learning* (pp. 615–628). Mahwah, NJ: Lawrence Erlbaum.

Hinkel, E. (2006). Current perspectives on teaching the four skills. *TESOL Quarterly, 40*(1), 109–131.

Hinkel, E. (2009). The effect of essay prompts and topics on the uses of modal verbs in L1 and L2 academic writing. *Journal of Pragmatics, 41*(4), 667–683.

Hornberger, N. H. (Ed.) (2003). *Continua of biliteracy: An ecological framework for educational policy, research and practice in multilingual settings.* Clevedon: Multilingual Matters.

Indrasuta, C. (1988). Narrative styles in the writing of Thai and American students. In A. Purves (Ed.), *Writing across languages and cultures: Issues in contrastive rhetoric* (pp. 206–227). Newbury Park, CA: Sage.

Jenkins, S., & Hinds, J. (1987). Business letter writing: English, French, and Japanese. *TESOL Quarterly, 21*, 327–349.

Johns, A. (1984). Textual cohesion and the Chinese speaker of English. *Language Learning and Communication, 3*, 69–74.

Johns, A. (1990). Coherence as a cultural phenomenon: Employing ethnographic principles in the academic milieu. In U. Connor & A. Johns (Eds.), *Coherence in writing* (pp. 211–225). Alexandria, VA: TESOL.

Johnson, P. (1992). Cohesion and coherence in compositions in Malay and English. *RELC Journal, 23*, 1–17.

Juzwik, M., Curcic, S., Wolbers, K., Moxley, K., Dimling, L., & Shankland, R. (2006). Writing into the twenty- first century: An overview of research on writing, 1999–2004. *Written Communication, 23*(4), 451–476.

Khalil, A. (1989). A study of cohesion and coherence in Arab EFL college students' writing. *System, 17*, 359–371.

Kress, G. (2003). *Literacy in the new media age.* London: Routledge.

Laufer, B. (2003). The influence of L2 on L1 collocational knowledge and L1 lexical diversity in written expression. In V. Cook (Ed.), *Effects of second language learning on the first* (pp. 19–31). Clevedon: Multilingual Matters.

Leki, I. (1992). *Understanding ESL writers.* Portsmouth, NH: Boynton/Cook Heinemann.

Leki, I. (2007). *Undergraduates in a second language: Challenges and complexities of academic literacy development.* New York: Lawrence Erlbaum.

Leki, I., Cumming, A., & Silva, T. (2008). *A synthesis of research on second language writing in English.* New York: Routledge.

Lillis, T. (2001). *Student writing: Access, regulation, desire.* London: Routledge.

Luke, A. (2004). On the material consequences of literacy. *Language and Education, 18*(4), 331–335.

Lunsford, A., & Lunsford, K. (2008). Mistakes are a fact of life: A national comparative study. *College Composition and Communication, 59*(4), 781–806.

McCretton, E., & Rider, N. (1993). Error gravity and error hierarchies. *International Review of Applied Linguistics, 31*(3), 177–188.

Markkanen, R., & Schroeder, H. (1997). Hedging: A challenge for pragmatics and discourse analysis. In R. Markkanen & H. Schroder (Eds.), *Hedging and discourse: Approaches to the analysis of a pragmatic phenomenon in academic texts* (pp. 3–20). Berlin: Walter de Gruyter.

Martin, J. (1992). *English text: System and structure.* Philadelphia: John Benjamins.

Mauranen, A. (1996). Discourse competence: Evidence from thematic development in native and non-native texts. In E. Ventola & A. Mauranen (Eds.), *Academic writing: Intercultural and textual issues* (pp. 195–230). Amsterdam/Philadelphia: John Benjamins.

Met, M. (1998). Curriculum decision-making in content-based teaching. In F. Genesee & J. Cenoz (Eds.), *Beyond bilingualism: Multilingualism and multilingual education* (pp. 35–63). Clevedon: Multilingual Matters.

Mohan, B. (1986). *Language and content.* Reading, MA: Addison-Wesley.

Mohan, B., Leung, C., & Davison, C. (2001). *English as a second language in the mainstream: Teaching, learning and identity.* Harlow: Longman.

Mohan, B., & Lo, W. (1985). Academic writing and Chinese students: Transfer and developmental factors. *TESOL Quarterly, 19*, 515–534.

Montano-Harmon, M. (1991). Discourse features of written Mexican Spanish: Current research in contrastive rhetoric and its implications. *Hispania, 74*, 417–425.

Myers, J. (2001). Self-evaluations of the "stream of thought" in journal writing. *System, 29*, 481–488.

Nesselhauf, N. (2005). *Collocations in a learner corpus.* Amsterdam: John Benjamins.

North, S. (1986). Writing in philosophy class: Three case studies. *Research in the Teaching of English, 20*(3), 225–262.

Paltridge, B. (2001). *Genre and the language learning classroom.* Ann Arbor: The University of Michigan Press.

Paltridge, B. (2004). State of the art review: Academic writing. *Language Teaching, 37*(2), 87–105.

Poole, D. (1991). Discourse analysis in enthnographic research. *Annual Review of Applied Linguistics, 11*, 42–56.

Reid, J. (1993). *Teaching ESL writing.* Englewood Cliffs, NJ: Prentice Hall.

Santos, T. (1988). Professors' reactions to the academic writing of nonnative-speaking students. *TESOL Quarterly, 22*, 69–90.

Schleppegrell, M. (2002). Challenges of the science register for ESL students: Errors and meaning-making. In M. Schleppegrell & M. Colombi (Eds.), *Developing advanced literacy in first and second languages* (pp. 119–142). Mahwah, NJ: Lawrence Erlbaum Associates.

Schleppegrell, M. (2004). *The language of schooling.* Mahwah, NJ: Lawrence Erlbaum.

Schleppegrell, M., & Columbi, M. (2002). *Developing advanced literacy in first and second languages: Meaning with power.* Mahwah, NJ: Lawrence Erlbaum.

Silva, T., & Brice, C. (2004). Research in teaching writing. *ARAL*, 70–106.

Silva, T. (1993). Toward an understanding of the distinct nature of L2 writing: The ESL research and its implications. *TESOL Quarterly, 27*, 657–677.

Snow, M. (2005). A model of academic literacy for integrated language and content instruction. In E. Hinkel (Ed.), *Handbook of research in second language teaching and learning* (pp. 693–712). Mahwah, NJ: Lawrence Erlbaum.

Snow, M., & Brinton, D. (1997). *The content-based classroom: Perspectives on integrating language and content.* White Plains, NY: Addison-Wesley Longman.

Spack, R. (1997). The rhetorical construction of multilingual students. *TESOL Quarterly, 31*, 765–774.

Swales, J. (1990). *Genre analysis.* Cambridge: Cambridge University Press.

Taylor, G., & Chen, T. (1991). Linguistic, cultural, and subcultural issues in contrastive discourse analysis: Anglo-American and Chinese scientific texts. *Applied Linguistics, 12*, 319–336.

Troia, G. (2007). Research in writing instruction: What we know and what we need to know. In M. Pressley, A. Billman, K. Perry, K. Reffitt, & J. Reynolds (Eds.), *Shaping literacy achievement: Research we have, research we need* (pp. 129–156). New York: Guilford.

Vann, R., Lorenz, F., & Meyer, D. (1991). Error gravity: Response to errors in the written discourse of nonnative speakers of English. In L. Hamp-Lyons (Ed.), *Assessing second language writing* (pp. 181–196). Norwood, NJ: Ablex.

Vann, R., Meyer, D., & Lorenz, F. (1984). Error gravity: A study of faculty opinion of ESL errors. *TESOL Quarterly, 18*, 427–440.

Weigle, S. (2002). *Assessing writing.* Cambridge: Cambridge University Press.

Widdowson, H. (2003). *Defining issues in English language teaching.* Oxford: Oxford University Press.

V
Methods and Instruction in Second Language Teaching

33
Communicative Language Teaching
An Expanding Concept for a Changing World

William Littlewood

Introduction

A Problem of Identity

A recurrent comment about communicative language teaching is that nobody knows what it is. For example, in questioning Bax's (2003) provocative announcement of "the end of CLT", Harmer (2003, p. 289) suggests that "the problem with communicative language teaching (CLT) is that the term has always meant a multitude of different things to different people". Spada (2007, p. 272) expresses a similar view at the start of her review of CLT: "What is communicative language teaching? The answer to this question seems to depend on whom you ask." With the development of task-based language teaching (TBLT), the situation has become even more complex than before: TBLT has developed an identity of its own (as witnessed by the many publications that bear its name (such as Ellis, 2003; Estaire & Zanon, 1994; Nunan, 2004; Willis, 1996), but is also viewed by many as one specific realization within the CLT framework (e.g. by Hu, 2005; Littlewood, 2004a; Nunan, 2004; Richards, 2005).

Of course no approach or method can be defined completely unambiguously, since there are too many variables that intervene between theoretical conception, explicit formulation and practical implementation. The audiolingual method may serve as an example. By the 1960s it seemed that its principles and practices had been neatly defined in works such as Brooks (1964), so that on this basis, a research team directed by Philip D. Smith could embark on the large-scale experimental Pennsylvania Project in schools to demonstrate the superiority of this method over "traditional" cognitive methods. The results (which the director described as "personally traumatic" to the project staff) proved to be inconclusive and in the controversy that resulted, a common conclusion was precisely this problem of definition that bedevils CLT: although the audiolingual method had been extensively described in both principle and practice, and the teacher-participants had been given clear guidelines on how to use it, it was found that when they came to actually implement it, they did so in significantly different ways (see Lynch, 1996, pp. 26–30, for description and analysis).

With CLT the situation is further complicated by a number of factors. For example:

- From the outset, people have discussed two "versions" of CLT, often called (after Howatt, 1984) a "weak" and a "strong" version. These differ significantly in their underlying assumptions, notably about the relative contributions of "experiential" and "analytic" strategies of learning and teaching (which will be discussed later).

- Related to this, it is often unclear whether people are discussing "communicative language teaching" in the sense of an overarching curriculum framework for achieving communicative goals (often through a combination of "non-communicative" as well as "communicative" learning activities) or in the sense of a methodology in which students are *always* engaged in communication.

- CLT emerged partly as a specific response to dissatisfaction with preceding methods but its further development has coincided with the so-called "postmethod" attitude that questions the very concept of definable methods (see, e.g. Allwright & Hanks, 2009, pp. 37–57; Kumaravadivelu, 2003 and 2006a). So one could say, paradoxically, that indefinability has become one of the defining characteristics of all approaches to language teaching, whether or not they carry the label CLT.

- It is therefore not surprising that (1) different people focus on different elements in characterizing CLT, but also (2) these same elements are found in other approaches that are *not* explicitly described as CLT. For example, Byrne (1986) does not use the label "communicative" to describe his approach (in his Preface, his aim is "successful language teaching"), but a large proportion of the activities he describes (such as information-gap activities, role-plays, problem-solving, using visual stimuli and authentic materials) form part of the basic repertoire of teachers who *would* hope to be identified as "communicative".

Richards and Rodgers (2001, p. 173) reflect this problem of identity when they say that many of the characteristics usually cited for CLT "address very general aspects of language learning and teaching that are now largely accepted as self-evident and axiomatic throughout the profession". A similar view is expressed by Harmer (2007, p. 70), for whom CLT is simply "a generalized 'umbrella' term to describe learning sequences which aim to improve the students' ability to communicate" in contrast to "teaching which is aimed more at learning bits of language just because they exist—without focusing on their use in communication".

So Does the Term "CLT" Serve a Useful Function?

In spite of the uncertainties outlined above, it is not time (*pace* Bax above) to abandon the term, at least not until a better one is found. The value of CLT as an "umbrella term" should not be underestimated. In almost every country that has been documented, there is a tradition of language teaching that aims to transmit "bits of language just because they exist" without relating them to their meaning or how they are used for communication. The strength of this tradition still comes through in many lessons as teachers embark on mini-lectures about language as an object with little or no relevance to communication or students' interest. Although its precise content is variable, the term CLT still serves as a valuable reminder that the aim of teaching is not to learn bits of language but to "improve the students' ability to communicate".

Although it is important to avoid assuming that approaches developed in Western contexts are also suited to other contexts (an issue we will return to later), it is also clear that in today's globalized world, every country needs people who can communicate internationally. A small selection of the countries from different parts of the world whose members have expressed this need in recent publications includes China (Wang, 2007; Wang & Lam, 2009), Japan (Butler & Iino, 2005; Nishino & Watanabe, 2008), Korea (Shin, 2007), Libya (Orafi & Borg, 2009), Thailand (Prapaisit de Segovia & Hardison, 2009), Uzbekistan (Hasanova & Shadieva, 2008), Vietnam (Pham, 2007), fifteen countries across East Asia (Ho & Wong, 2004) and seven countries across the Asia-Pacific Rim (Nunan, 2003).

As Pham (2007, p. 196) puts it, "while teachers in many parts of the world may reject the CLT techniques transferred from the West, it is doubtful that they reject the spirit of CLT". Pham formulates this "spirit of CLT" in terms compatible with Harmer's "umbrella" definition above: that "learning is likely to happen when classroom practices are made real and meaningful to learners" and that the goal is to teach learners "to be able to use the language effectively for their communicative needs" (p. 196).

This appears then to be the consensus on the meaning of CLT that is now establishing itself. The meaning of CLT is disengaging itself from any *necessary* association with "techniques transferred from the West" or indeed any other *specific* set of techniques for designing "real and meaningful learning experiences" for improving students' ability to communicate. This is a wide definition suited to developing a postmethod pedagogical framework in a globalized world, within which teachers can design methods appropriate to their own contexts but based on principled reflection. It focuses broadly on a framework of means and ends that few would call into doubt, but also, in the words of Kumaravadivelu (2006b, p. 20), encourages teachers to seek "a context-sensitive postmethod pedagogy that encompasses location-specific teaching strategies and instructional materials".

This Chapter

The concepts and terms in the preceding paragraph underlie the main organizational framework for this article:

- What insights does CLT offer into the *goals* of language learning and teaching, that is, into the ability to communicate that learners need to acquire? (The minority of learners who have other goals will not fall within the scope of this article.)
- What insights does CLT offer into the *learning experiences* that might take learners towards their goals in "real and meaningful ways"?
- What insights does CLT offer into the *pedagogy* that might facilitate these experiences, that is, about possible teaching strategies?
- Moving from the "possible" to the "actual", what have been the *experiences with CLT* in specific contexts around the world?
- How might these experiences, and teachers' responses to them, affect *how CLT is characterized* in a globalized, postmethod era?
- What aspects of CLT should have priority in *future research*?

Before embarking on this plan, however, the article gives a brief outline of the emergence of CLT. This outline is linked with my own formative experiences with CLT because, as we have seen, CLT is both interpreted in various ways and in constant evolution. This means that the experience of the individual is a key influence on what aspects of it are highlighted and how they are interpreted. My own experience with CLT has been mainly in the UK and other parts of Europe until 1991 and in Asia since then. The American dimension has for me been mainly secondhand. However, that dimension is strongly represented in the first edition of this handbook (Savignon, 2005) as well as in the accounts by Wesche and Skehan (2002) and Spada (2007).

Formative Influences on CLT: A Personalized Perspective

My own experience with CLT dates back almost to its inception. When I entered the field of applied linguistics in 1972, two linguists were publishing work that was seminal in laying the conceptual basis of CLT: Michael Halliday was exploring the "functions of language" and how these are expressed though the grammar (e.g. Halliday, 1973) and Dell Hymes was establishing the notion of "communicative competence" in contrast to the narrow linguistic competence studied by Chomsky and his followers. (Extracts from the work of Halliday and Hymes are in Brumfit & Johnson, 1979.) In the field of philosophy, J.L. Austin's (1962) theory of speech acts was already an established part of discourse about language. In the European context, this work was a major source of inspiration for a Council of Europe team that developed a new framework for syllabus design based on communicative categories such as "functions" (e.g. "asking somebody's name", "saying what somebody's job is") and "notions" (e.g. "future time", "quantity and degree") (Van Ek, 1975; Wilkins, 1976). At the same time, Henry Widdowson and others were exploring the implications for methodology of "teaching language as communication" (Widdowson, 1972 and especially 1978). (The key impacts of Wilkins, 1976, and Widdowson, 1978, are evaluated respectively by Johnson, 2006, and Littlewood, 2008). In the English-teaching field, a multitude of course books began to appear bearing the description "functional", "notional" and/or "communicative", and including a large proportion of meaning-oriented activities such as pair work, role-play, discussion and the use of authentic materials (e.g. the course books of Abbs, Ayton & Freebairn, 1975 and Jones, 1979; activities discussed in Johnson & Morrow, 1981). As Morrow and Johnson (1983, p. 4) indicate in connection with a seminar that they organized at the University of Reading in 1978, in the early days, "functional syllabuses seemed to offer an automatic solution to all the problems of language teaching".

In the teaching of modern languages (mainly French and German) in the UK, functional syllabuses also entered the scene in the 1970s, but under a different label and with a more pragmatic motivation. The move to a "comprehensive school" system in which modern languages were taught to all secondary school children (rather than only the select few in "grammar schools") had resulted in large cohorts of students who could not cope with the dominant structure-based approaches (mainly grammar-translation or audio-visual). A grass-roots movement of teachers in different localities set out to change this and saw a function-based approach as a way to focus on what students could *achieve* with language (e.g. simple communicative objectives such as "asking the way") rather than what they found too difficult (e.g. grammar and accuracy). This so-called "graded objectives" movement (Page, 1983; Page & Hewett, 1987) led directly to the reform of the 16+ examination, which introduced innovations such as role-play as an assessment task and criterion-referenced grading based on what students could do with the language. The success rate with the new examination was much higher than with the old one, thus justifying the new approach in pedagogical terms but also attracting criticism that the examination was too easy and failed to differentiate between students of different proficiency levels.

From the other side of the Atlantic, the most prominent messages were related not so much to the nature of communicative ability as to the processes by which it is acquired. In 1968, Leonard Newmark and David Reibel had shocked the world with the idea that teaching is not only unhelpful but actually "interferes" with learning. This idea was later reflected in Stephen Krashen's "input hypothesis": that learning depends primarily on comprehensible input and teachers should therefore concentrate on creating conditions for "natural acquisition" (as in the "Natural Approach" of Krashen & Terrell, 1983). It was also expressed in the "Communicational Language Teaching" project of N. S. Prabhu in Bangalore, in which explicit teaching and error correction were avoided (Prabhu, 1987). The input hypothesis later led to the "interaction hypothesis", which sees not only input but also output and interaction as important for learning (see, e.g. Allwright & Bailey, 1991; Gass & Selinker, 2008). The importance of learning through communication was supported empirically by Sandra Savignon's study (1972, reported also in, e.g. Savignon, 2005), which found that students who had engaged in communication tasks outperformed (in accuracy as well as fluency) those who had spent the same amount of time carrying out pattern practice. From another perspective, the role of communication was affirmed by advocates of "humanistic" teaching such as Moskowitz (1978) and

Stevick (1980, 1990); their emphasis was on the need to engage the "whole person" in meaningful communication. In the UK this strand has been represented by work emanating from the Pilgrims School of English in Canterbury (e.g. Deller, 1990; Spaventa, 1980). To the criticism that the communication stimulated by humanistic techniques is too intrusive on learners' feelings and inner life, Arnold (1998) gives an informative and well-balanced response.

Referring to a distinction made earlier, a broad generalization (subject to the usual caveats about such generalizations) is that in the first two decades of CLT, work rooted in the American context tended to contribute to the "strong" version of CLT, in which students learn through the experience of communication, whilst the European work tended more to support the "weak" version, in which analytic strategies (based on functions as well as grammar) have a prominent role *in addition to* experiential strategies. It was in this second tradition that my own book on CLT (Littlewood, 1981) was written. If now, some thirty years later, the book is still in print in English and translated versions, this is due not only to the book itself but also to the developing world around it: over these thirty years, as national boundaries have weakened under the influence of globalization, more and more countries have felt an intensified need for English as a medium of international communication and developed CLT-based policies in order to meet this need.

What Insights Does CLT Offer into the Goals of Language Learning and Teaching?

At the core of CLT is a more thoroughgoing analysis than previously of the nature of communication and the role that language plays in it. It is not that communication was ignored by previous approaches—it figures prominently in all "active" methods such as the situational-structural approach and the audiolingual method (for an overview of these, see Littlewood, 1999; Richards & Rodgers, 2001). But before CLT, it was usually assumed (implicitly or explicitly) that the route to this goal lies simply through mastering the structures and vocabulary of the language, that is, through *linguistic* competence. The emergence of the key concept of *communicative* competence, which includes linguistic competence but goes beyond it, revolutionized language teaching by redefining its goals and the methods to achieve them. It also helped to explain why so many learners achieve poor levels of communicative ability through structure-based methods.

In a short but influential article, Widdowson (1972) drew attention to why students who have been taught English for several years frequently remain deficient in the ability to actually use the language. He pointed out that the approach currently recommended in UK-based English language teaching (ELT), combining situational presentation with structural practice, neglects an essential fact about the nature of communication: that it depends on the ability not only to "compose sentences" but also, crucially, to use these sentences to perform a variety of "acts of communication". For example, when a teacher demonstrates meaning by walking to the door and saying *I am walking to the door*, then asks students to describe someone else with *He is walking to the door* (etc.), "[these sentences] are being used to perform the act of commentary in situations in which in normal circumstances no commentary would be called for" (p. 17). We are teaching the *signification* of the sentences but not their communicative *value*. Widdowson (1978) explores further the nature and pedagogical implications of this distinction between "signification" and "value" (as well as related ones such as that between "usage" and "use"), which have become fundamental ideas within CLT. With CLT, the teaching of the "communicative value" (i.e. functional aspects) as well as structural and semantic aspects of language is accepted as one of its essential principles, both in courses for general learners and in teaching language for specific purposes (see, e.g. Hutchinson & Waters, 1987).

The relation between form and function does not consist of direct equivalents that can simply be learnt. For example, an apparently straightforward declarative sentence such as *The door's open* could function as an explanation ("that's why it's so cold"), a reassurance ("don't worry, you'll be able to get out"), a request ("close it, please"), and in many other ways, depending on the situation. Conversely, the request could be expressed not only through the above sentence but also more directly through, for example, *Would you mind closing the door?* or simply *Close the door, please.* The selection of one form rather than the other is governed not only by linguistic factors but also by situational factors and conventions of social appropriacy (e.g. one is more likely to be direct with a friend than a stranger). In order to communicate both effectively and appropriately, learners must therefore be aware of the links between language forms and all aspects of meaning (conceptual, functional and social) and also be able to express and interpret specific links in specific situations. Moreover, it is not enough to learn to do this for individual utterances. Communication is an interactive process in which meanings are developed and negotiated over longer stretches of discourse. This involves developing effective ways of structuring information, creating cohesive links over longer stretches of discourse, opening and closing conversations appropriately, initiating as well as responding, expressing disagreement without producing confrontation and so on. These issues are explored further in, for example, Richards and Schmidt (1983).

This process of interpretation and negotiation is sometimes unsuccessful. Recently, in an introductory seminar on second language learning with students I had never met before, I had spent about ten minutes introducing "interlanguage theory" when a student asked: "Why are we doing this?" "Why" questions often function as protests (*Why haven't you washed your cup?*) as well as requests for information and I assumed that the students had already studied this topic in depth and wanted to move quickly to more recent developments. It was only later that I realized: the student was not protesting but literally asking why the topic was relevant. She had not done the background reading and felt completely confused ("not waving, but drowning") and my own communicative competence had not led me to see this until too late. Littlewood (2001) and Thomas (1983) give similar examples; implications for teaching are discussed in Eslami-Rasekh (2005) and Rose and Kasper (2001).

An important orientational framework in discussions of the nature of communicative competence in a second language is still that of Canale and Swain (1980), expanded in Canale (1983). The terminology is adapted slightly here and I have added a fifth dimension to the four proposed in Canale (1983):

- *Linguistic competence* includes the knowledge of vocabulary, grammar, semantics and phonology that have been the traditional focus of second language learning.
- *Discourse competence* enables speakers to engage in continuous discourse, e.g. by linking ideas in longer written texts, maintaining longer spoken turns, participating in interaction, opening conversations and closing them.
- *Pragmatic competence* enables second language speakers to use their linguistic resources to convey and interpret meanings in real situations, including those where they encounter problems due to gaps in their knowledge.
- *Sociolinguistic competence* consists primarily of knowledge of how to use language appropriately in social situations, e.g. conveying suitable degrees of formality, directness and so on.
- *Sociocultural competence* includes awareness of the cultural knowledge and assumptions that affect the exchange of meanings and may lead to misunderstandings in intercultural communication.

A development of this framework by Bachman (1990) groups a similar (not identical) set of basic elements into three main components: *language competence*, which includes grammatical, textual and sociolinguistic competence; *strategic competence*, which includes pragmatic competence as described above; and *psychophysiological mechanisms*, which enable productive and receptive use. This last component introduces psycholinguistic aspects of second language proficiency that are not included in the Canale and Swain framework but are of course fundamental to communicative language use. For further exploration, see for example Harley, Allen, Cummins and Swain (1990) and Benati (2009).

What Insights Does CLT Offer into the Learning Experiences that Can Lead to This Goal?

As well as this extended notion of the goals of language teaching, CLT also works within a broader framework for designing the learning experiences that can help learners move towards these goals. This framework can be usefully described in terms of the distinction referred to earlier between "analytic" and "experiential" dimensions. These dimensions are analysed in, for example, Stern (1990, 1992), as well as in Allen (1983), where the analytic dimension is further divided into "structural-analytic" and "functional-analytic" in his "three-level curriculum framework".

The Analytic Dimension in CLT

The analytic dimension of language teaching dominated most widely-used approaches before CLT and indeed, so far as one is able to generalize (see the later section on experiences with CLT), still does. Sometimes the learners themselves are involved in analysing the language (e.g. in the grammar-translation approaches). In the more active, practice-oriented approaches that superseded grammar-translation in many contexts, learners practise language items that have been isolated as discrete "part-skills" by the teacher and sequenced into a teaching syllabus. Learners practise the items until they can produce them as automatically as possible and later engage in "whole-task" practice, where they integrate the separate items in order to communicate (on this skill-learning perspective on language learning, see for example Johnson, 1996). These stages underlie the familiar "PPP" (Presentation—Practice—Production) sequence described in many teachers' handbooks. One of the main contributions of the early work in CLT was to expand this analytic dimension by adding a functional-communicative element, so that learners are more aware of the functional and social aspects of the language they are practising. For example, they may carry out a controlled pair-work activity in which they "make suggestions" in various situations and later engage in a less controlled role-play based on a similar situation.

In the analytic dimension of learning, CLT has strengthened awareness of the need to relate forms to meanings in the learning process, both for motivational reasons and to establish the form-meaning connections that are a necessary basis for communication (see, for example, Batstone & Ellis, 2009 and Ur, 1988, on ways to achieve this in grammar teaching).

The Experiential Dimension in CLT

Another important feature of CLT is that it attaches special importance to the experiential dimension of learning. There are three main reasons for this:

- The goal of learning—communicative competence—is itself experiential. That is, it does not involve knowing separate items but being able to integrate these items in the context of real communicative experience. The way towards this goal has to include "situated learning" (Lave & Wenger, 1991) in which learners actually perform this integration, first with appropriate scaffolding, leading to gradually increasing autonomy (this is a focus of the sociocultural perspective on learning as discussed in, for example, Lantolf, 2007).
- If we adopt the skill-learning perspective outlined in the previous section, real communicative experience (or "practice") facilitates the transition from "controlled" to "automatic" processing

(clear explanations of these terms can be found in Johnson, 1996; McLaughlin, 1987; Mitchell & Myles, 2004). In fluent communication, lower-level operations such as formulation and articulation can occur automatically, allowing controlled processing to be allocated to higher-level operations such as conceptualization.

- The experience of natural, untutored second language acquisition shows that through participating in interaction, learners not only consolidate their capacity to communicate with their existing knowledge of the language but actually extend this knowledge. Studies of learners' "interlanguage" (surveyed in, for example, Lightbown & Spada, 2006; Littlewood, 2004b) highlight some of the internal processes by which this takes place. The "interaction hypothesis" referred to earlier focuses on how output and interaction push learners to refine their language knowledge.

The complementary roles of the two dimensions in contributing to communicative competence may be represented as in Figure 33.1. It should be noted that the two dimensions are at two ends of a continuum and that most specific learning activities will have features of each, to varying degrees. For example, in what will be called "communicative language practice" in the following section, learners engage in communication but with pre-taught forms. On the other hand, during "authentic communication", they may sometimes focus analytically on specific forms which cause difficulties (on the issue of proactive "focus on form*s*" and reactive "focus on form", see, for example, Doughty & Williams, 1998; Ellis, 2005). Also, at any particular moment during an activity, different learners will focus on form or meaning to different degrees.

What Insights Does CLT Offer into the Pedagogy that Can Facilitate these Learning Experiences?

There have been several lists in the literature of the core principles that characterize CLT. For example, Richards and Rodgers (2001, p. 172) state that its main principles include:

- Learners learn a language through using it to communicate.
- Authentic and meaningful communication should be the goal of classroom activities.
- Fluency is an important dimension of communication.
- Communication involves the integration of different language skills.
- Learning is a process of creative construction and involves trial and error.

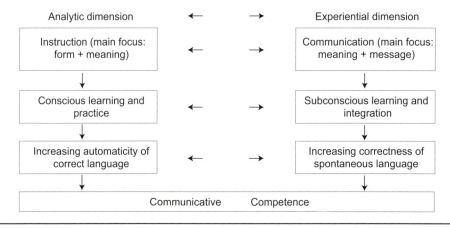

Figure 33.1 Two dimensions of learning in CLT

The main qualities of "communicative classrooms" mentioned by Wesche and Skehan (2002, p. 208) have a similar focus on communication and learner-centredness:

- Activities that require frequent interaction among learners or with other interlocutors to exchange information and solve problems.
- Use of authentic (nonpedagogic) texts and communication activities linked to "real-world" contexts, often emphasizing links across written and spoken modes and channels.
- Approaches that are learner centred in that they take into account learners' backgrounds, language needs and goals, and generally allow learners some creativity and role in instructional decisions.

The specific features of classroom methodology that these authors mention as supporting a communicative approach (here consolidated from both sources) are: message focus, e.g. information sharing and information transfer; cooperative learning, such as group and pair work; free practice; risk taking; communicative tasks as a basic organizing unit; the use of substantive content such as school subject matter to develop language; psycholinguistic processing; attention to appropriateness of language use; and opportunities for learners to focus on the learning process. Richards' (2005) "ten core assumptions of current CLT" recognize that activities involving "language analysis and reflection" may also have a role but these have no place in Jacobs and Farrell's (2003) suggestions for "changes in the way second language teaching is conducted and conceived" as a result of the "CLT paradigm shift": learner autonomy; social nature of learning; curricular integration; focus on meaning; diversity; thinking skills; alternative assessment; teachers as co-learners. As these references suggest, much CLT discourse has emphasized experiential aspects of learning (i.e. the "strong" version of CLT), with only a fleeting indication that more analytic, form-focused activities may also perform a productive role. It is not surprising that Thompson (1996, p. 10) found, from his experience in workshops across the world, that the most widespread misconceptions about CLT amongst teachers were that it means "not teaching grammar" and "teaching only speaking".

A more inclusive account of CLT is important not only for representing more adequately its claims and purposes but also for facilitating its acceptance at the practical level. Figure 33.2 (elaborated in Littlewood, 2000, 2004a) presents a framework for CLT methodology that seeks to accommodate both experiential and analytical aspects of teaching and learning along a continuum from non-communicative activities to authentic communication. It gives oral activities as examples but the same principles may be applied to written activities.

Brandl (2008), Littlewood (2000) and Ma (2008) give examples of activities from different parts of the continuum, which has proved an accessible basis for teacher education as well as for analysing the classroom practice of teachers seeking to establish a more communicative classroom (e.g. Chen, 2008; Deng & Carless, 2009). For teachers accustomed to a tradition dominated by controlled, form-oriented activities, the framework provides dimensions for innovation and expansion. They can maintain their base in activities represented in the first and second categories, but gradually expand their repertoire into the other three. In this way they can grow but retain a sense of security and value in what they have done before, two important conditions for the postmethod pedagogy that CLT has now become.

Operating within an overall analytic-to-experiential framework such as that in Figure 33.2, a teacher may also seek his or her ways of implementing "macrostrategies" such as the ones below, which are explored in depth by Kumaravadivelu (2003, 2006a). (The glosses in brackets are my own.)

- maximize learning opportunities;
- facilitate negotiated interaction (i.e. classroom interaction with a communicative purpose);

- minimize perceptual mismatches (i.e. conflict between what is intended and what is understood);
- activate intuitive heuristics (i.e. capacity for independent discovery);
- foster language awareness (i.e. conscious awareness of aspects of language);
- contextualize linguistic input;
- integrate language skills;
- promote learner autonomy;
- raise cultural consciousness;
- ensure social relevance.

Like the continuum in Figure 33.2, these strategies can provide links between familiar activities and new ones that serve context-specific needs, and serve as a framework to inspire teachers to explore their current practice and generate further possibilities.

What Have Been the Experiences with CLT in Specific Contexts around the World?

This section will focus primarily on Asian (particularly East Asian) countries, which have been major "recipients" of CLT ideas and practices since their emergence in the 1970s. The word "recipients" is used advisedly, because for many years the attitude was often transmission-oriented—the ideas and practices were held to be "top-quality" and fit for export over the world. Gupta (2004) gives a graphic account of how, when CLT was first introduced at a leading Indian university in 1989, the implicit message accompanying it corresponded to the "CLT attitude" attacked by Bax (2003):

1. Assume and insist that CLT is the whole and complete solution to language learning.
2. Assume that no other method could be any good.
3. Ignore people's own views of who they are and what they want.
4. Neglect and ignore all aspects of the local context as being irrelevant.

Countering this CLT attitude, there has been a steady output of publications questioning the assumption that an approach originating in one context (specifically here: the West) can simply be exported elsewhere. Holliday (1994) and Ellis (1996) deal with the overall issue of developing "appropriate methodology" for different contexts. The (lack of?) compatibility between CLT and

Analytic Strategies		← →		Experiential Strategies
Non-communicative learning	**Pre-communicative language practice**	**Communicative language practice**	**Structured communication**	**Authentic communication**
Focusing on the structures of language, how they are formed and what they mean, e.g. substitution exercises, inductive 'discovery' and awareness-raising activities	Practising language with some attention to meaning but not communicating new messages to others, e.g. describing visuals or situational language practice ('questions and answers')	Practising pre-taught language but in a context where it communicates new information, e.g. information gap activities or 'personalised' questions	Using language to communicate in situations which elicit pre-learnt language but with some unpredictability, e.g. structured role-play and simple problem-solving	Using language to communicate in situations where the meanings are unpredictable, e.g. creative role-play, more complex problem-solving and discussion
Focus on forms and meanings		← →		**Focus on meanings and messages**

Figure 33.2 The "communicative continuum" as a basis for CLT

the beliefs and traditions of specific contexts have been the main focus of many articles (e.g. for Cambodia: Jones, 1995; for China: Hu, 2002, 2005; for Hong Kong: Carless, 2004, 2007; for Korea: Li, 1998; for Vietnam: Kramsch & Sullivan, 1996) and highlighted as a major factor in many others, for example, in the reports about the experiences with CLT in East Asian countries found in Ho and Wong (2004) and Littlewood (2007).

These reports support the general finding that CLT means "different things to different teachers" (Ho & Wong, 2004, p. xxxiv). It has consequently been implemented in many different ways but most often means "providing the teachers with communicative activities in their repertoire of teaching skills and giving learners the opportunity in class to practise the language skills taught" (Ho, 2004, p. 26) (i.e. the "weak" version of CLT referred to earlier). The main challenges that this has raised for teachers have been in the domains of classroom management; students' avoidance of English, especially in group work; teachers' own lack of confidence in using English; the feeling that many communicative tasks do not require students to use more than a minimal level of English; incompatibility between CLT and the demands of examinations and expectations of parents; and conflict with current practices, values and beliefs about teacher–student roles.

Chow and Mok-Cheung (2004, p. 158) refer to the shift from a teacher-centred to a student-centred CLT pedagogy as a "quantum leap" in the transmission-oriented context of Hong Kong schools. This quantum leap is reflected in Wang's (2007, p. 101) summary of the changes expected from teachers in Mainland China, as they make the transition to a new communication-oriented English curriculum. Teachers are expected to:

- change their views about language teaching from a knowledge-based one to a competence-based one;
- change their traditional role as a knowledge transmitter to a multi-role educator;
- develop new teaching skills;
- change their ways of evaluating students;
- develop the ability to adapt the textbooks;
- use modern technology; and
- improve their own language proficiency.

In many cases these expectations have resulted in teachers' rejection of official CLT policies. For example, Hu (2004, p. 43) found in his survey that "the intensive top-down promotion of CLT notwithstanding, pedagogical practices in many Chinese classrooms have not changed fundamentally". In South Korea, Shim and Baik (2004, p. 246) state that many teachers "write up reports that comply with government recommendations while continuing to practise examination-oriented classroom instruction". Pandian (2004, p. 280) writes that in Malaysia, after the "initial euphoria" of implementing CLT concepts, "classroom teaching seems to have returned to the chalk-and-talk drill method".

Of special interest from a "postmethod" perspective are the ways in which teachers have accepted the "spirit of CLT" (as described earlier) but developed a methodology to suit their own contexts. We can identify three ways (forming a continuum) in which this takes place:

- Li (1998, p. 696) writes of *adapting* (rather than adopting) the practices of CLT. This approach recognizes the authority of CLT as the base-framework from which the adaptations depart.
- Rao (1996, p. 467) writes of ways of *reconciling* the traditional approach and CLT. This approach still accepts CLT as a definable reference framework but places a traditional (here: Chinese) approach next to it in an equal relationship.
- Wong and Ho (2004, p. 464) write of the *cross-breeding of elements* from different ELT techniques, methods and approaches *to form a localized methodology*. In this approach, CLT is one amongst many sources of ideas for an appropriate local pedagogy.

Some reports tell how these processes can take place. In Hong Kong, for example, Carless (2004) observed that many teachers reinterpret the use of communicative tasks as "contextualised practice" rather than activities in which learners negotiate meaning independently of the teacher. Mitchell and Lee (2003) found that both an English teacher of French and a Korean teacher of English interpreted CLT in a similar way to the Hong Kong teachers: "Teacher-led interaction, and the mastery of correct language models, took priority over the creative language use and student centring which have been associated with more fluency-oriented or 'progressivist' interpretations of the communicative approach" (p. 56). Zheng and Adamson (2003) analyse how a secondary school teacher of English "reconciles his pedagogy with the innovative methodology in a context constrained by examination requirements and the pressure of time" (p. 323) by "expanding his repertoire rather than rejecting previous approaches" (p. 335). He maintains many traditional elements, such as his own role as a knowledge transmitter, the provision of grammatical explanations, and the use of memorization techniques and pattern drills. However, he integrates new ideas into his pedagogy by including more interaction and more creative responses from the students in his classes, "usually in the context provided by the textbook, but sometimes in contexts derived from the students' personal experience" (p. 331). Zheng and Davison (2008) give more extended discussion of this teacher and others.

CLT: A Transnational Ideoscape?

The "CLT attitude" in the form criticized by Bax (2003) conceptualizes CLT as a package of ideas and practices to be exported around the world. This corresponds to early conceptions of globalization and modernization as unidirectional processes in which ideas and forms are transmitted from centre to periphery and, in the words of the social anthropologist Ulf Hannerz (1992, p. 219), "when the centre speaks, the periphery listens, and mostly does not talk back". Gradually, supported by "the world-wide development of a new cultural self-confidence", this unidirectional conception has been overtaken by one in which "inflowing cultural forms and meanings [meet] existing local forms and meanings" and the resulting "creative mixture of 'global' elements with local meanings and cultural forms" leads to innovation and diversity (Schuerkens, 2004, p. 19, p. 23). Schuerkens characterizes this as a "cosmopolitan conversation of humankind" (p. 15) in which all participants have a voice. This is reflected in the processes of adaptation, reconciliation and above all cross-breeding mentioned in the preceding section.

As we continue to move further into an era of globalization and postmethodism, perhaps the most valuable contribution of CLT is to act not as a specific set of practices and ideas but as a transnational "ideoscape" (Apparudai, 1996; discussed also in Holton, 2005), that is, as an *ideational landscape* that provides a location for deepening and extending the "cosmopolitan conversation" about second language pedagogy.

CLT and the Future: What Are the Research Priorities?

To conclude, this section will outline six areas that need special attention as we take CLT into the future:

1. *Supporting wider participation in the "cosmopolitan conversation" about language pedagogy.* A frequently mentioned obstacle to innovation is that teachers are not adequately supported in their attempts to process new ideas and develop their pedagogy in contextually appropriate ways. Akbari (2008) emphasizes the need to bridge the gap between the "academic discourse community" and the "community of practice" of language teachers. Wedell (2003) discusses factors that planners need to consider when asking teachers to innovate. Research is needed into effective ways of giving this support at the pre- and in-service stages.
2. *Developing the base of postmethod principles.* The ten "macrostrategies" explored by

Kumaravadivelu (2003, 2006a) as well as the "communicative continuum" proposed by Littlewood (2000, 2004a) are two attempts to find principles that are (a) sufficiently universal to serve as a context-free basis for pedagogy but also (b) sufficiently goal-related to guide practice in specific situations. They are only a first step, however, and further enquiry is needed into whether these principles (and others still to be developed) are indeed well-founded and suited to support the development of "microstrategies" and techniques in the classroom.

3. *Deepening the content of communication in the classroom.* Pennycook (1994, p. 311) writes of the "empty babble of the communicative language class". This is an obvious overgeneralization but it alerts us to the superficial nature of much communication in CLT classrooms. Students are sometimes given a steady diet of activities such as "planning a party" that will never take place or "giving directions to the station" on the map of a non-existent town. It is important to explore ways of making the communication more engaging and substantial. These may include linking language development to other subject content (as proposed by Wesche & Skehan, 2002), developing project work (Legutke & Thomas, 1991), exploring the "three generations of tasks" described in Ribé and Vidal (1993), using drama techniques (e.g. Maley & Duff, 1978) or focusing systematically on other techniques for "personalization" (e.g. Griffiths & Keohane, 2000), whilst remembering that not all students in all contexts are happy to engage in self-disclosure (Pegrum, 2004). A reconsideration of the role of the mother tongue in second language learning (see below) should also generate further options.

4. *Exploring the complementary functions of analytic and experiential strategies.* Perhaps the most significant strategic decisions that classroom teachers have to make relate to the complementary functions of analytic and experiential strategies in furthering learning. There is now strong evidence that experiential learning alone is not enough and that direct intervention that focuses on forms is also important. Ellis (2005, p. 717) classifies these forms of intervention into explicit instruction, implicit instruction, structured input, production practice and negative feedback. Further research is needed into the most effective ways of conducting these and into their relation to other learning experiences.

5. *Structuring classroom interaction more effectively.* A major hindrance to many teachers in their implementation of communication activities (or "tasks") in the classroom, especially with monolingual classes at primary or secondary level, is that when students are not closely monitored, many of them revert to the mother tongue and do not challenge themselves linguistically. More effective ways need to be found of scaffolding group work, for example, through task design features that give better direction and support to independent interaction, even in the absence of direct teacher intervention. Techniques in cooperative learning (e.g. Littlewood, 2009) are a promising avenue for exploration.

6. *Creating a rich target language environment.* There is now lively debate about the role of the mother tongue in the second language classroom (see, e.g. Littlewood & Yu, 2010 for an overview of issues and approaches). In many contexts where it has been officially banned, teachers have nonetheless used it extensively (see, e.g. Mitchell, 1988 on teachers in the UK). In other contexts, the use of the mother tongue has long been normal practice, but official policy now urges teachers to use the target language (e.g. in South Korea; see Liu, Ahn, Baek & Han, 2004). Since the classroom is the only context of interaction and source of input for many students, most teachers agree that they should aim for *maximal* use of the target language, but feel constrained by factors such as the students' language proficiency and sometimes their own. Further exploration is needed into the respective roles of the mother tongue and the target language as well as into more effective strategies for increasing the use of the latter. Also significant here are recent discussions that affirm the validity of teachers' own local models of English as a medium of communication (e.g. Kirkpatrick, 2007).

This is only a small sample of areas where research is needed. Indeed within the broad definition of CLT that has now emerged, one may say that there is no distinction between research into CLT and all other research that sets out to further an engaging, communication-oriented approach to language teaching.

References

Abbs, Brian, Ayton, Angela & Freebairn, Ingrid (1975). *Strategies.* London: Longman.

Akbari, Ramin (2008). Postmethod discourse and practice. *TESOL Quarterly, 42*(4), 641–652.

Allen, J. Patrick B. (1983). A three-level curriculum model for second language education. *Canadian Modern Language Review, 40*(1), 23–43.

Allwright, Dick, & Bailey, Kathleen M. (1991). *Focus on the language classroom: An introduction to classroom research for language teachers.* Cambridge: Cambridge University Press.

Allwright, Dick, & Hanks, Judith (2009). *The developing learner: An introduction to exploratory practice.* Basingstoke: Palgrave Macmillan.

Appadurai, Arjun (1996). *Modernity at large: Cultural dimensions of globalization.* Minneapolis: University of Minnesota Press.

Arnold, Jane (1998). Towards more humanistic English teaching. *ELT Journal, 53*(2), 235–242.

Austin, John L. (1962). *How to do things with words.* Oxford: Oxford University Press.

Bachman, Lyle (1990). *Fundamental considerations in language testing.* Oxford: Oxford University Press.

Batstone, Rob, & Ellis, Rod (2009). Principled grammar teaching. *System, 37*(2), 194–204.

Bax, Stephen (2003). The end of CLT: A context approach to language teaching. *ELT Journal, 57*(3), 278–287.

Benati, Alessandro, G. (Ed.) (2009). *Issues in second language proficiency.* London: Continuum.

Brandl, Klaus (2008). *Communicative language teaching in action: Putting principles to work.* Upper Saddle River, NJ: Pearson Prentice Hall.

Brooks, Nelson H. (1964). *Language and language learning: Theory and practice.* New York: Harcourt, Brace & World.

Brumfit, Christopher J., & Johnson, Keith (Eds.) (1979). *The communicative approach to language teaching.* Oxford: Oxford University Press.

Butler, Yuko Goto, & Iino, Masakazu (2005). Current Japanese reforms in English language education: The 2003 "Action Plan". *Language Policy, 4*(1), 25–45.

Byrne, Donn (1986). *Teaching oral English* (2nd ed.). London: Longman.

Canale, Michael (1983). From communicative competence to communicative language pedagogy. In Jack C. Richards & Richard W. Schmidt (Eds.), *Language and communication* (pp. 2–27). London: Longman.

Canale, Michael, & Swain, Merrill (1980). Theoretical bases of communicative approaches to second language teaching and testing. *Applied Linguistics, 1*(1), 1–47.

Carless, David (2004). Issues in teachers' reinterpretation of a task-based innovation in primary schools. *TESOL Quarterly, 38*(4), 639–662.

Carless, David (2007). The suitability of task-based approaches for secondary schools: Perspectives from Hong Kong. *System, 35*(4), 595–608.

Chen, Pei (2008). Implementation of task-based instruction in language learning classrooms in China. Unpublished doctoral dissertation, University of Macau.

Chow, Alice W. K., & Mok-Cheung, Angela H. M. (2004). English language teaching in Hong Kong SAR: Tradition, transition and transformation. In W. K. Ho & R. Y. L. Wong (Eds.), *English language teaching in East Asia today* (pp. 150–177). Singapore: Eastern Universities Press.

Deller, Sheelagh (1990). *Lessons from the learner.* London: Longman.

Deng, Chun-Rao, & Carless, David (2009). The communicativeness of activities in a task-based innovation in Guangdong, China. *Asian Journal of English Language Teaching, 19,* 113–134.

Doughty, Catherine, & Williams, Jessica (Eds.) (1998). *Focus on form in classroom second language acquisition.* New York: Cambridge University Press.

Ellis, Greg (1996). How culturally appropriate is the communicative approach? *ELT Journal, 50*(3), 213–218.

Ellis, Rod (2003). *Task-based learning and teaching.* Oxford: Oxford University Press.

Ellis, Rod (2005). Instructed language learning and task-based teaching. In Eli Hinkel (Ed.), *Handbook of research in second language learning and teaching* (pp. 713–728). Mahwah, NJ: Lawrence Erlbaum.

Eslami-Rasekh, Zohreh (2005). Raising the pragmatic awareness of language learners. *ELT Journal, 59*(3), 199–208.

Estaire, Sheila, & Zanon, Javier (1994). *Planning classwork: A task-based approach.* Oxford: Macmillan Heinemann.

Gass, Susan M., & Selinker, Larry (2008). *Second language acquisition: An introductory course* (3rd ed.). New York: Routledge.

Griffiths, Griff, & Keohane, Kathy (2000). *Personalizing language learning*. Cambridge: Cambridge University Press.

Gupta, Deepti (2004). CLT in India: Context and methodology come together. *ELT Journal*, *58*(3), 266–269.

Halliday, Michael (1973). *Explorations in the functions of language*. London: Edward Arnold.

Hannerz, Ulf (1992). *Cultural complexity: Studies in the social organization of meaning*. New York: Columbia University Press.

Harley, Birgit, Allen, Patrick, Cummins, Jim & Swain, Merrill (Eds.) (1990). *The development of second language proficiency*. Cambridge: Cambridge University Press.

Harmer, Jeremy (2003). Popular culture, methods and context. *ELT Journal*, *57*(3), 288–294.

Harmer, Jeremy (2007). *The practice of English language teaching* (4th ed.). London: Longman.

Hasanova, Dilbarhon, & Shadieva, Tatyana (2008). Implementing communicative language teaching in Uzbekistan. *TESOL Quarterly*, *42*(1), 138–143.

Ho, Wah Kam (2004). English language teaching in East Asia today: An overview. In W. K. Ho & R. Y. L. Wong (Eds.), *English language teaching in East Asia today* (pp. 1–32). Singapore: Eastern Universities Press.

Ho, Wah Kam, & Wong, Ruth Y. L. (Eds.) (2004). *English language teaching in East Asia today*. Singapore: Eastern Universities Press.

Holliday, Adrian (1994). *Appropriate methodology and social context*. Cambridge: Cambridge University Press.

Holton, Robert J. (2005). *Making globalization*. Basingstoke: Palgrave Macmillan.

Howatt, Anthony P. R. (1984). *A history of English language teaching*. Oxford: Oxford University Press.

Hu, Guangwei (2002). Potential cultural resistance to pedagogical imports: The case of communicative language teaching in China. *Language, Culture and Curriculum*, *15*(2), 93–105.

Hu, Guangwei (2004). Pedagogical practices in Chinese EFL classrooms. *Asian Englishes*, *7*(1), 42–59.

Hu, Guangwei (2005). English language education in China: Policies, progress, and problems. *Language Policy*, *4*(1), 5–24.

Hutchinson, Tom, & Waters, Alan (1987). *English for specific purposes: A learning-centred approach*. Cambridge: Cambridge University Press.

Jacobs, George M., & Farrell, Thomas C. M. (2003). Understanding and implementing the CLT (Communicative Language Teaching) paradigm. *RELC Journal*, *34*(1), 4–30.

Johnson, Keith, & Morrow, Keith (Eds.) (1981). *Communication in the classroom: Applications and methods for a communicative approach*. London: Longman.

Johnson, Keith (1996). *Language teaching and skill learning*. Oxford: Blackwell.

Johnson, Keith (2006). Revisiting Wilkins' *Notional Syllabuses*. *International Journal of Applied Linguistics*, *16*(3), 414–418.

Jones, Jeremy F. (1995). Self-access and culture: Retreating from autonomy. *ELT Journal*, *49*(3), 228–234.

Jones, Leo (1979). *Notions in English*. Cambridge: Cambridge University Press.

Kirkpatrick, Andy (2007). *World Englishes: Implications for international communication and English language teaching*. Cambridge: Cambridge University Press.

Kramsch, Claire, & Sullivan, Patricia (1996). Appropriate pedagogy. *ELT Journal*, *50*(3), 199–212.

Krashen, Stephen D., & Terrell, Tracy D. (1983). *The natural approach: Language acquisition in the classroom*. Oxford: Pergamon.

Kumaravadivelu, B. (2003). *Beyond methods: Macrostrategies for language teaching*. New Haven: Yale University Press.

Kumaravadivelu, B. (2006a). *Understanding language teaching: From method to postmethod*. Mahwah, NJ: Lawrence Erlbaum.

Kumaravadivelu, B. (2006b). Dangerous liaison: Globalization, empire and TESOL. In Julian Edge (Ed.), *(Re-)Locating TESOL in an age of empire* (pp. 1–26). Basingstoke: Palgrave Macmillan.

Lantolf, James P. (2007). Sociocultural theory: A unified approach to L2 learning and teaching. In J. Cummins & C. Davison (Eds.), *International handbook of English language teaching* (pp. 693–700). Boston: Springer Science & Business Media. Online access via SpringerLink.

Lave, Jean, & Wenger, Etienne (1991). *Situated learning: Legitimate peripheral participation*. Cambridge: Cambridge University Press

Legutke, Michael, & Thomas, Howard (1991). *Process and experience in the language classroom*. London: Longman.

Li, Defeng (1998). "It's always more difficult than you plan and imagine": Teachers' perceived difficulties in introducing the communicative approach in South Korea. *TESOL Quarterly*, *32*(4), 677–703.

Lightbown, Patsy, & Spada, Nina (2006). *How languages are learned* (3rd ed.). Oxford: Oxford University Press.

Littlewood, William T. (1981). *Communicative language teaching: An introduction*. Cambridge: Cambridge University Press.

Littlewood, William T. (1999). Second language teaching methods. In Bernard Spolsky (Ed.), *The concise encyclopedia of educational linguistics* (pp. 658–668). Oxford: Pergamon.

Littlewood, William T. (2000). Task-based learning of grammar. *Teaching Update*, *1*, 40–57. Retrieved 12 August 2010 from http://www.edb.gov.hk/FileManager/EN/Content_3997/task_based.doc.

Littlewood, William T (2001). Cultural awareness and the negotiation of meaning in intercultural communication. *Language Awareness, 10*(2&3), 189–199.

Littlewood, William T. (2004a). The task-based approach: Some questions and suggestions. *ELT Journal, 58*(4), 319–326.

Littlewood, William T. (2004b). Second language learning. In Alan Davies & Catherine Elder (Eds.), *The handbook of applied linguistics* (pp. 500–524). Oxford: Blackwell.

Littlewood, William T. (2007). Communicative and task-based language teaching in East Asian classrooms. *Language Teaching, 40*(3), 243–249.

Littlewood, William T. (2008). Thirty years later: Henry Widdowson's *Teaching Language as Communication. International Journal of Applied Linguistics, 18*(2), 212–217.

Littlewood, William T. (2009). Chinese learners and interactive learning. In Tricia Coverdale-Jones & Paul Rastall (Eds.), *Internationalising the University: The Chinese context* (pp. 206–222). Basingstoke: Palgrave Macmillan.

Littlewood, William T., & Yu, Baohua (2011). First language and target language in the foreign language classroom. *Language Teaching 44*(1).

Liu, Dilin, Ahn, Gil-Soon, Baek, Kyung-Suk & Han, Nan-Ok (2004). South Korean high school English teachers' code switching: Questions and challenges in the drive for maximal use of English in teaching. *TESOL Quarterly, 38*(4), 605–638.

Lynch, Brian K. (1996). *Language progamme evaluation: Theory and practice.* Cambridge: Cambridge University Press.

Ma, Anne (Ed.) (2008). *A practical guide to a task-based curriculum: Planning, grammar teaching and assessment.* Hong Kong: City University of Hong Kong Press.

Maley, Alan, & Duff, Alan (1978). *Drama techniques in language learning.* Cambridge: Cambridge University Press.

McLaughlin, Barry (1987). *Theories of second-language learning.* London: Edward Arnold.

Mitchell, Rosamond (1988). *Communicative language teaching in practice.* London: Centre for Information on Language Teaching and Research.

Mitchell, Rosamond, & Lee, Jenny Hye-Won (2003). Sameness and difference in classroom learning cultures: Interpretations of communicative pedagogy in the UK and Korea. *Language Teaching Research 7*(1), 35–63.

Mitchell, Rosamond, & Myles, Florence (2004). *Second language learning theories.* London: Arnold.

Morrow, Keith, & Johnson, Keith (1983). Introduction. In Keith Johnson & Keith Morrow (Eds.), *Functional materials and the classroom teacher: Some background issues* (pp. 4–5). Oxford: Modern English Publications.

Moskowitz, Gertrude (1978). *Caring and sharing in the foreign language class.* Rowley, MA: Newbury House.

Newmark, Leonard, & Reibel, David (1968). Necessity and sufficiency in language learning. *International Review of Applied Linguistics, 6*(2), 145–164.

Nishino, Takako, & Watanabe, Michinobu (2008). Classroom-oriented policies versus classroom realities in Japan. *TESOL Quarterly, 42*(1), 133–138.

Nunan, David (2003). The impact of English as a global language on educational policies and practices in the Asia-Pacific region. *TESOL Quarterly, 37*(4), 589–613.

Nunan, David (2004). *Task-based language teaching.* Cambridge: Cambridge University Press.

Orafi, Senussi M. S., & Borg, Simon (2009). Intentions and realities in implementing communicative curriculum reform. *System, 37*(2), 243–253.

Page, Brian (1983). Graded objectives in modern language learning. *Language Teaching, 16*(4), 292–308.

Page, Brian, & Hewett, Derrick (1987). *Languages step by step: Graded objectives in the UK.* London: Centre for Information on Language Teaching and Research.

Pandian, Ambigapathy (2004). English language teaching in Malaysia today. In W. K. Ho & R. Y. L. Wong (Eds.), *English language teaching in East Asia today* (pp. 272–293). Singapore: Eastern Universities Press.

Pegrum, Mark (2004). Selling English: Advertising and the discourses of ELT. *English Today, 20*(1), 3–10.

Pennycook, Alastair (1994). *The cultural politics of English as an international language.* London: Longman.

Pham, Hoa Hiep (2007). Communicative language teaching: Unity within diversity. *ELT Journal, 61*(3), 193–201.

Prabhu, N. S. (1987). *Second language pedagogy.* Oxford: Oxford University Press.

Prapaisat de Segovia, Lakhana, & Hardison, Debra M. (2009). Implementing education reform: ELF teachers' perspectives. *ELT Journal, 63*(2), 154–162.

Rao, Zhenhui (1996). Reconciling communicative approaches to the teaching of English with traditional Chinese methods. *Research in the Teaching of English, 30*(4), 458–471.

Ribé, Ramon, & Vidal, Nuria (1993) *Project work: Step by step.* Oxford, Heinemann.

Richards, Jack. C. (2005). *Communicative language teaching today.* Singapore: RELC.

Richards, Jack C., & Rodgers, Theodore S. (2001). *Approaches and methods in language teaching* (2nd ed.). Cambridge: Cambridge University Press.

Richards, Jack C., & Schmidt, Richard W. (Eds.) (1983). *Language and communication.* London: Longman.

Rose, Kenneth R., & Kasper, Gabriele (Eds.) (2001). *Pragmatics in language teaching.* Cambridge: Cambridge University Press.

Savignon, Sandra (1972). *Communicative competence: An experiment in Language teaching*. Philadelphia: Center for Curriculum Development.

Savignon, Sandra J. (2005). Communicative language teaching: Strategies and goals. In Eli Hinkel (Ed.), *Handbook of research in second language learning and teaching* (pp. 635–651). Mahwah, NJ: Lawrence Erlbaum.

Schuerkens, Ulrike (2004). The sociological and anthropological study of globalization and localization. In Ulrike Schuerkens (Ed.), *Global forces and local life-worlds: Social transformations* (pp. 14–26). London: Sage.

Shim, Rosa Jinyoung & Baik, Martin Jonghak (2004). English education in South Korea. In W. K. Ho & R. Y. L. Wong (Eds.), *English language teaching in East Asia today* (pp. 241–261). Singapore: Eastern Universities Press.

Shin, Hyunjung (2007). English language teaching in Korea: Towards globalization or *glocalization*? In Jim Cummins & Chris Davison (Eds.), *International handbook of English language teaching* (pp. 75–86). Boston: Springer Science & Business Media. Online access via SpringerLink.

Spada, Nina (2007). Communicative language teaching: Current status and future prospects. In Jim Cummins & Chris Davison (Eds.), *International handbook of English language teaching* (pp. 271–288). Boston: Springer Science & Business Media. Online access via SpringerLink.

Spaventa, Lou (1980). *Towards the creative teaching of English*. London: Heinemann.

Stern, H. H. (David) (1990). Analysis and experience as variables in second language pedagogy. In Birgit Harley, Patrick Allen, Jim Cummins & Merrill Swain (Eds.), *The development of second language proficiency* (pp. 93–109). Cambridge: Cambridge University Press.

Stern, H. H. (David) (1992). *Issues and options in language teaching*. Oxford: Oxford University Press.

Stevick, Earl W. (1980). *Teaching languages: A way and ways*. Rowley, MA: Newbury House.

Stevick, Earl W. (1990). *Humanism in language teaching*. Oxford: Oxford University Press.

Thomas, Jenny (1983). Cross-cultural pragmatic failure. *Applied Linguistics*, 4(1), 91–112.

Thompson, Geoff (1996). Some misconceptions about communicative language teaching. *ELT Journal*, 50(1), 9–15.

Ur, Penny (1988). *Grammar practice activities*. Cambridge: Cambridge University Press.

Van Ek, Jan (1975). *Systems development in adult language learning: The threshold level in a European unit credit system for modern language learning by adults*. Strasbourg: Council of Europe.

Wang, Qiang (2007). The National Curriculum changes and their effects on English language teaching in the People's Republic of China. In Jim Cummins & Chris Davison (Eds.), *International handbook of English language teaching* (pp. 87–105). Boston: Springer Science & Business Media. Online access via SpringerLink.

Wang, Wenfang, & Lam, Agnes S. L. (2009). The English language curriculum for senior secondary school in China: Its evolution from 1949. *RELC Journal*, 40(1), 65–82.

Wedell, Martin (2003). Giving TESOL change a chance: Supporting key players in the curriculum change process. *System*, 31(4), 439–456.

Wesche, Marjorie Bingham, & Skehan, Peter (2002). Communicative, task-based, and content-based instruction. In Robert B. Kaplan (Ed.), *The Oxford handbook of applied linguistics* (pp. 207–228). New York: Oxford University Press.

Widdowson, Henry G. (1972) The teaching of English as communication. *ELT Journal*, 27(1), 15–19. (Reprinted in Brumfit & Johnson, 1979.)

Widdowson, Henry G. (1978) *Teaching language as communication*. Oxford: Oxford University Press.

Wilkins, David (1976) *Notional syllabuses*. Oxford: Oxford University Press.

Willis, Jane (1996). *A framework for task-based learning*. London: Longman.

Wong, Ruth Y. L., & Ho, Wah Kam (2004). The future of English language teaching in East Asia. In W. K. Ho & R. Y. L. Wong (Eds.), *English language teaching in East Asia today* (pp. 455–465). Singapore: Eastern Universities Press.

Zheng, Xin-min, & Adamson, Bob (2003). The pedagogy of a secondary school teacher of English in the People's Republic of China: Challenging the stereotypes. *RELC Journal*, 34(3), 323–337.

Zheng, Xin-min, & Davison, Chris (2008). *Changing pedagogy: Analyzing ELT teachers in China*. London: Continuum.

34

Re-Evaluating Traditional Approaches to Second Language Teaching and Learning

Lixian Jin and Martin Cortazzi

The Paradox of Traditional Approaches and Contexts of Criticism

Traditional approaches (TAs) to teach and learn second or foreign languages have been around for many years. They are often thought of as "grammar-translation": a cluster of practices including explicit grammatical explanations, detailed examples illustrating grammatical rules, bilingual vocabulary lists and translation exercises, and perhaps a focus on reading literary texts. For years they have been widely criticized on the grounds that they do not develop learners' communication skills. However, paradoxically traditional approaches have continued in some ways and in some contexts. In many second language (L2, which also covers foreign language learning) classrooms in different countries some elements of these traditions persist, especially those that are more teacher-led or focus on explicit explanations of the L2 grammar and the classroom uses of learners' first language (L1), translation between L1 and L2, or bilingual vocabulary lists and memorization.

In this paradox, there is a tradition of dismissing traditions. This is most evident in the English-speaking regions in relation to TESOL (teaching English to speakers of other languages) or when English teachers encounter TAs outside the English-speaking centres of the globe. In a whole-world vision that includes the teaching and learning of many languages besides English, this might alert researchers to a need to re-evaluate TAs and to question the contexts of criticisms and the relations between the critic, the critique, the criticized and the audience for criticism.

TAs have a historical role and it is valid to study them as background contexts to trace influences and developments, to understand precedents or to locate sites of change. But there is more than this. Practices of TAs (and critiques of them) often relate to points of dissemination over time, to particular languages and to geography and economics. Broadly, since the 1970s the global role of English has attracted considerable financial and political support for TESOL; hence there has been more research, more pedagogic development, greater innovations in curricula, teacher development and publications—and far more learners and teachers—in an ever-expanding cycle into the 2000s. This has clearly outstripped L2 education developments for other languages in this period, and it has influenced them at different rates: the teaching and learning of central or "major" languages has adopted developments much more quickly than that of peripheral or "minor" languages. At the same time, TAs have persisted for longer in most developing areas of the world than in more economically developed ones, due to the slower development of educational systems and language teacher training, cultural perceptions and different ways of change, limited learning resources and finance. This means that there may be different perceptions of "traditional" for different languages—and from learners from such language backgrounds—and in TESOL in less developed areas in a time lag: developmental cycles are smaller and slower.

This paradox and the apparent hierarchical differences of language teaching approaches between languages and places over time are worth investigating because there may be a concern that criticisms of TAs come most strongly from English speakers and may be targeted mainly at the teaching of other L2s or at those who have been learning English from the linguistic and cultural backgrounds of those languages. Given that English is the most widely taught and the most influential L2 and that some other languages are taught with strong elements of TAs, the criticisms may look uncomfortably hierarchical, stemming from the dominant linguistic centres and targeting the less developed language teaching contexts. In any case, studying TAs where they continue may inform us about sociocultural practices around pedagogic ideas and such reflections can be turned to current situations elsewhere. Extant traditional practices can be studied in order to reflect on one's own pedagogic position and practices in the light of common and different features.

TAs are often described as a baseline at some point in time before modern practices were introduced, yet dividing lines of historical change between one approach and another may not be clear in real contexts and some current approaches have traditional elements that are packaged within much broader orientations. To label a method of language teaching as "traditional" has generally come to mean that the user of the term is dismissing what is referred to as outdated and probably dysfunctional. TAs, it is said, may give learners knowledge of the target language (L2) and the ability to compare it with their L1 but they leave learners unable to engage in social interaction to use the language for practical communication. In the 1970s or 1980s critics often quoted polarities: "form" or "meaning" (Wilkins, 1972); "usage" or "use" (Widdowson, 1978); "academic" or "practical" (Strevens, 1980); "formalist" or "activist" (Rivers, 1981). TAs and some others fell into the first category of each pair as advocates of a subsequent approach aligned themselves with the second category. A more careful reading of these sources would show that both poles are necessary but that they might receive different emphasis in different contexts or for different proficiency levels.

This critique revolves around the purposes of language learning. There is a current presupposition that the dominant purpose for language learning is social, professional or economic: that learners wish to communicate in L2 for social interaction with target language speakers, employment opportunities and professional activity, and social life goals. However, although the nineteenth-century TAs did not ignore oral skills (as is sometimes stated), they often emphasized academic or cultural presuppositions: learners should develop their thinking through learning analytical skills in working with grammar; their knowledge of other peoples and cultures and their sensitivity towards humanity through reading L2 literature and learning about the L2 civilization. While communication skills are currently highlighted world-wide, these other broad traditional educational goals of L2 learning (academic, cultural and the humane) haven't gone away—they remain of crucial importance in educational institutions, although they may be handled much more interactively and with global awareness (e.g. in cultural awareness and intercultural communication).

In this chapter we elaborate the themes introduced above. We distinguish five versions of "traditional" and discuss TAs in terms of historical perspectives; we examine textbooks as evidence of persisting traditions, and then as a significant case study we look at TAs in current practices in China. The chapter has some emphasis on grammar-translation approaches, which are often negatively stereotyped. A consequence of the reactions to grammar-translation has been a common rejection of translation in favour of sole or main use of the L2 in classrooms, yet translation is a common activity around the world in school and college language teaching contexts where learners share the same L1.

In this chapter we are not supporting TAs. We suggest that they may need re-evaluating from a broader sociocultural and world-wide perspective in order to identify what can be learned from them and why some teachers and learners still use some features. We consider elements of teaching grammar, the place of translation, memorizing, and literature that might be appropriately used within contemporary orientations.

Defining, Debating, and Evaluating Approaches or Methods

Defining an "approach" or "method" usefully starts from Anthony's (1963) distinction: an "approach" is a set of assumptions dealing with the nature of language, learning and teaching; a "method" is the overall plan for systematic presentation of language based on an approach; a "technique" is a specific classroom activity that is consistent with a method. While a particular approach may be associated with a method or technique, there is no fixed correspondence between them: a given technique may be associated with more than one method and teachers could flexibly adapt a technique or method from one approach within another approach—the key issue is how and why they are used (Larsen-Freeman, 2000).

Richards and Rogers (2001) reformulated the above terms by using "method" as the overarching term to specify and relate theory and practice, within which an "approach" defines assumptions, beliefs and theories about the nature of language and language learning; a "design" specifies six necessary features of objectives, syllabus, activities, learner roles, teacher roles, and the role of materials; and "procedure" refers to techniques and classroom practices derived from an approach and design. Brown (1994) argues that usage in the field seems more in line with Anthony's and that "methodology" (as the study of pedagogical practices in general, with considerations of "how to teach") is a better overarching term, while "methods" refers to a generalized set of classroom specifications for accomplishing linguistic objectives, mainly teacher and student roles, but also lesson objectives, sequencing and materials. Here we focus on approach, which includes methods and techniques (Anthony's terms); this is in line with Celce-Murcia (2001) but could be translated as "method" by others (e.g. Larsen-Freeman, 2000).

Much criticism of TAs and other approaches has been directed by a search for the "right" one that would "work with all learners in all contexts" (Nunan, 1991, p. 228) but it is recognized that this search rests on two false assumptions: first, "that language learning is sufficiently homogenous for a single method to fit all circumstances" and, second, "that the achievement of relative success or failure in language learning is to be ascribed, above all to method, and not significantly to other factors" and because classrooms vary so much in participants and circumstances it is "inconceivable that any single method could achieve optimum success in all circumstances" (Strevens, 1977, pp. 4–5). So as Stern (1992, p. 14) concludes,

> each new approach has presented a plausible case for its particular emphasis, but ultimately no single method has been sufficient in itself to deal with the great variety of circumstances, types of learners, and levels of instruction that constitute second language pedagogy.

Stern calls this "the predicament of the 'method' solution: an excessive emphasis on a single concept" and argues that a wider and more differentiated interpretation of teaching is needed "to overcome the narrowness, rigidities, and imbalances which have resulted from conceptualizing language teaching purely or mainly through the concept of method" (1983, p. 477). The persistent use of the definite article in chapter headings in descriptions of methods ("*The* grammar-translation method", "*the* audio-lingual method" etc. in, say, Rivers, 1981; Howatt, 1984; Larsen-Freeman, 2000; Richards & Rogers, 2001) may implicitly reinforce this identification of an approach or method with a single concept and might encourage polarized debates of an approach as a homogeneous package rather than as a looser cluster of methods and techniques. However, there is now a general recognition in teachers' handbooks that

> there never was and probably ever will be a method for all, and the focus in recent years has been on the development of classroom tasks and activities which are consonant with what we know about the processes of second language acquisition and which are also in keeping with the dynamics of the classroom itself.
>
> (Nunan, 1991, p. 228)

So rather than a one-size-fits-all solution of using a single approach everywhere, a more contextualized approach is to be informed of different approaches and methods (including TAs), to understand their principles and practices, and then to examine one's own beliefs and context to base pedagogic decisions on informed reflection (Larsen-Freeman, 2000, pp. 1, 141). This may mean going "beyond method" and to have "an approach for enlightened eclectics" (Brown, 1994). This approach would be flexible, based on an analysis of local circumstances and needs, with a theoretical rationale and coherent principles and a philosophy of exploration with reflection.

Interestingly, there is some tradition of being eclectic in this way among prestigious language teachers. It was advocated by Rivers (1981, pp. 54–55), who cites Henry Sweet (1889, p. 3): "A good method must, before all be comprehensive and eclectic. It must be based on a thorough knowledge of the science of language" and general principles rather than the "one absolutely invariable method" and Harold Palmer's (1921, p. 141) "multiple line of approach", which "embodies the eclectic principle": "we use each and every method, process, exercise, drill, or device … to select judiciously and without prejudice all that is likely to help us in our work". Conversely, inflexibility is likely to become dysfunctional: "Any method ceases to be efficient when it is applied inflexibly, according to set procedures, in every situation" (Rivers, 1981, p. 27).

So the question of "What is the best one?" becomes "How do we look at different approaches and methods?" and subsequently, "What do named approaches (such as 'traditional') offer in relation to particular teachers, learners and contexts?" This last question is a matter of relevance, so researchers can examine TAs for knowledge, insights or applications (Wilkins, 1972). Approaches, methods or techniques can be combined for knowledge or insights, and in practice aspects can be used selectively.

Larsen-Freeman (2000, pp. 2–3) offers an accessible list of evaluative questions. These are important for researchers: a crucial point is what questions one is asking, and why they are worth asking. She asks about the goals of teachers and roles of teachers and students, the characteristics of the teaching/learning process and the nature of student–teacher or student–student interaction. She also asks about the feelings of the students dealt with, how language and culture are viewed, about which areas or skills of language (listening, speaking, reading and writing) are emphasized. Further questions relate to the role of the students' L1 and how the teacher responds to student errors. In similar lists, others may add different questions. Richards and Rogers (2001, p. 28) add questions about how an approach views the nature of language and the nature of language learning, and about selection and organization of language/content in the design of a syllabus; Nunan (1989 cited in Brown, 1994, pp. 70–71) adds questions about activity types and the role of materials; McDonough (2002, pp. 108–110) adds questions about whose culture is represented in materials, and about whether or how a lesson plan sequences a presentation, practice and production of target language items; Stern (1983, pp. 477–482) in evaluating teaching guides includes broader questions about historical, sociopolitical and educational contexts and about specific content (areas of language, culture, and literature).

Stern (1983, pp. 505–507, 1992, pp. 279–348) gives considerable attention to three sets of these questions as dimensions of instructional options: an "*intralingual-crosslingual*" dimension, which concerns the use (or not) of L1 in L2 learning; an "*analytic-experiential*" dimension where the focus may be on form, skill-getting and language practice compared with a focus on communication, skill-using and language use; and an "*explicit-implicit*" dimension, where the learner is encouraged to consciously analyse language, learn rules and be reflective or to take a more intuitive approach and work for subconscious acquisition and more automatic or intuitive responses. TAs relate strongly to the cross-lingual, analytic and explicit options, but Stern would argue that both dimensions are needed in an integrated model.

Historical Perspectives on Traditional Approaches

The term "traditional" in language teaching is a moving target. Each generation of teachers and researchers may include newly added elements from previous generations in their perceptions of a TA: thus after 2010 one might count 1960s structural drills and pattern practice from audiolingual methods as traditional.

We suggest that "traditional" can be seen as a series of five possible definitions (see Figure 34.1), which move on from a classical definition to progressively more flexible and more diverse ones.

1. A *classical definition* of "grammar-translation" with: a deductive focus on grammatical paradigms, with analyses, examples and explanations in L1, perhaps with Latin grammatical terms (e.g. nominative, accusative, genitive, dative); lengthy bilingual vocabulary lists; use of L1 for classroom communication; extensive use of translation exercises for application of rules and practice; and maybe extended reading texts.
2. A *wider definition* of "grammar-translation" with lesson organization centred around grammatical explanations, examples and the extensive use of translation but also including other exercises and activities and both reading texts and dialogues and therefore with a much stronger oral element (which may also be seen in the use of phonetics and detailed pronunciation guidance).
3. An *audiolingual approach* that was well-established over the 1940s–1960s but that was then thought to be largely or entirely superseded by communicative approaches; this includes a

Table 34.1 Defining "Traditional" Approaches as Five Different Versions

Conceptions of "traditional"	Approximate timescale	Some key features
Classical grammar-translation	Up to 1900s	Uses of grammatical paradigms, explanations, bilingual vocabulary lists, translation exercises, use of L1 in classroom
Wider grammar-translation	1900s–2000s	Grammatical explanations, bilingual vocabulary lists, translation exercises, also oral elements and other practice exercises
Audiolingual	1940s–1960s	Emphasis on structures, oral skills, mimicry, memorization, substitution and pattern drills
Mainstream EFL	1930s–2000s	Mixed approach, includes presentation, practice, production, communicative activities,
"Humanistic" or alternative	1970s–2000s	Total Physical Response, The Silent Way, Community Language Learning, Suggestopedia, and The Natural Approach

stress on oral skills with lessons organized through dialogues; emphasis on grammatical structures and patterns (rather than rules), inductive teaching of grammar; the use of substitution tables and pattern drills with techniques of mimicry and memorization to develop language habits.

4. A general term for the established *mainstream* approach, especially for teaching English as a foreign language (EFL), which began around the 1930s and continues with a practical or eclectic mix from other approaches; this includes a strong communicative orientation and classroom practices but also grammatical explanation, some structural practice, use of situations, role plays and dialogues, often in a sequence of presentation, practice and production but with variety.

5. Some diverse approaches generally known collectively as "*humanistic*" or "*alternative*", which although not practised on a global scale are widely known about (Total Physical Response, The Silent Way, Community Language Learning, Suggestopedia and perhaps The Natural Approach); since the 1970s, these are generally considered in teacher training programmes through studying readings or handbooks, in brief classroom exercises or viewing videos of lessons. These traditions seem influential in informing teachers' thinking in theory but are peripheral to the majority in practice.

These versions of TAs will now be considered in more detail.

The Classical Tradition of Grammar-Translation

The classical tradition of grammar-translation developed from around the second century BC with the Roman tradition of learning Greek grammar through Greek–Latin translation with literary, moral and Roman nationalist themes (Kelly, 1969; Howatt, 1984). Translation and grammar re-emerged in education during the Renaissance and Reformation in Europe (fifteenth–seventeenth centuries), developing the Roman tradition of normative, conservative and often elitist attitudes, with a focus on literature and social and religious agendas (Benson, 2000). In the nineteenth century elite schools grammatical paradigms, rules, lists of vocabulary and translation exercises were central to learning the classical languages of Latin and ancient Greek. It was natural to emphasize reading and writing of classics as oral skills were no longer necessary with the rise of vernacular languages in literacy, education, religion and government (and, obviously, there were no native speakers of ancient languages). The grammatical terminology of the classics and the teaching approach became the "modern" model used to teach English and European languages in schools for the general population.

Grammar-translation spread rapidly. It was aimed academically at mental training through the analysis and memorizing of rules, paradigms, sentence examples and vocabulary lists but it maintained cultural aims through the study of literature and civilization. It neglected speaking, relied on translation of discrete sentences for practical application of skills at lower levels but moved to reading of literary texts later. These grammar-translation approaches are deductive: starting typically with the presentation and explanation of a rule with examples, students practise through translation of further sentence examples (translating both ways, from and into L2). The curriculum was graded and sequenced: vocabulary and grammar needed for translation were confined to words and structures students had already encountered. This TA continued in school systems and universities: written tests on grammar through translation fitted into the newly emerging exam systems from around 1850; in more elitist and conservative contexts it showed a respect for regularity, literature and the past; it provided mental training (as would many other disciplines); and teachers who had learned through the approach as students tended to continue to use it in their teaching.

Criticisms of this classical approach (e.g. Rivers, 1981; Larsen-Freeman, 2000; Richards & Rogers, 2001) are based on communicative models of language learning: communication is not a goal, oral skills are not developed, and there is little use of L2 as the medium of instruction in the classroom since the learners' L1 is used for instructions and explanations. At its worst, this is paralysis by analysis. Less gifted students find the approach "tedious", "laborious" and "monotonous" (Rivers, 1981, pp. 30–31). Other criticisms relate to the deductive approach and the memorization of paradigms and vocabulary lists. The grammar-translation approach is criticized for a lack of theory: it is "still widely practised", but it "has no advocates"; it is "a method for which there is no theory"; "there is no literature that offers a rationale or justification for it or that attempts to relate it to issues in linguistics, psychology, or educational theory" (Richards & Rogers, 2001, p. 5).

However, just as approaches change, criticisms also change over time. Cook (2001, p. 204) notes that this "academic style" of language teaching may suit academically gifted students in some contexts: "If the society and the students treat individual goals as primary, language use as secondary, and the students are academically gifted, then the academic style is appropriate." It may match somewhat with current ideas about the raising of conscious grammatical knowledge (though the model of grammar is weak); it should be supplemented with language use; teachers would need to remember to develop learners' goals beyond the knowledge of grammar. Additionally, we can note how the approach seems useful with large classes and that many people, including language teachers, learned languages successfully with this method. It is true that generally additional exposure (beyond school) to the L2 was needed to develop more advanced skills in communication, but this is generally true of most school subjects.

A basic problem is that this approach seems invariant and inflexible and, as Rivers comments: "Any method ceases to be efficient when it is applied inflexibly, according to set procedures in every situation" (1981, p. 27). Some of the criticism of version 1 of "traditional" does not apply to version 2, which is the more flexible version that is most likely to be used today where grammar-translation is used.

Wider Grammar-Translation

Reactions against grammar-translation approaches in the nineteenth and twentieth centuries were generally based on the role of communication and the development of oral skills. In the 1880s and 1890s a group of linguists, some of whom had been schoolteachers, co-operated in founding the International Phonetics Association (IPA) and developing shared aims of L2 teaching (Howatt, 1984). This influenced many teachers in what was called the Reform Movement that led to the later name of the Direct Method, which is a major influence on mainstream EFL (Rivers, 1981; Larsen-Freeman, 2000; Richards & Rogers, 2001). Priority was given to oral skills (supported by the science of phonetics); the order of skills for development and lesson organization became listening, speaking, reading and writing, so that when learners read something they had already discussed it orally and early writing was a summary of what had been read. There was an inductive approach to the teaching of grammar; first, examples were met in meaningful contexts and situations directly associating words and phrases with objects and actions (without using L1) and grammar rules were taught after they have been practised. The L2 became the normal language for classroom communication in "the monolingual principle". For some, this meant banning translation but for others it meant using learners' L1 only for briefly explaining new vocabulary or grammar points; the L2 was supposed to be learnt without mediation through L1. In classes where learners have a large variety of L1s, this monolingual principle is almost inevitable. This approach, Rivers (1981, pp. 33–34) concludes, "provides an exciting and interesting way of learning a language through activity". It was later elaborated into the Oral Situational Approach in the 1940s–1960s (Richards & Rogers, 2001).

This Direct Approach seems the direct opposite of grammar-translation, but surprisingly, the wider grammar-translation approach has survived, although it was modified. This can best be shown through examining textbooks. These give an idea of what is intended to happen in classrooms, and they represent a key aspect of an approach, but they cannot tell the whole story: good teachers would always adapt, edit and supplement what is in the textbook and the book does not represent classroom interaction.

Table 34.2 summarizes some relevant features of a range of textbooks for learning languages other than English (but written for English speakers) first published between 1853 and 1997. The languages are European (German, Italian, Portuguese, Greek, Dutch), Middle Eastern (Persian, Arabic, Turkish) or Southeast Asian (Gujerati, Urdu, Malay, Hindi) but apart from Fijian we have not included Asian-Pacific languages or other groups. The books are intended for students at university, colleges or other adult classes or for independent learners but not for schools. A number of points can be made. First, a similar table for TESOL textbooks would look quite different, especially those used internationally; since the 1960s there would be shorter and fewer grammatical explanations; translation would most likely not be included at all; exercises and activities would be varied and there would be little literary or historical content. A table for TESOL would thus reflect the standard historical developments of periods in language teaching and learning. These books for many other languages do not reflect that conventional periodization.

Second, within these textbooks for these languages, grammar translation elements seem to be remarkably uniform features throughout. Detailed grammatical explanations are widespread; they are usually illustrated with examples in L2 which are translated into English. Bilingual vocabulary lists and frequent translations of texts and dialogues (side by side versions or translations given below) confirm this major role of translation; so does the obvious common use of translation exercises, often with translation keys provided for students to check their answers.

Third, the grammar is deductively presented in earlier books but either deductively or inductively in later books, thus the precise role and sequencing of grammar can vary. Some books specify that parts of the grammar and lists of vocabulary are given for reference; they do not expect students to memorize these parts; most books say nothing about memorization, even for vocabulary. There may well have been classroom practices of memorization but this is not evident in the books and criticisms of reference materials on grounds that they are intended to be learned by heart misses the authors' guidance.

Fourth, reading passages are generally included, although some books have only sentence-based exercises; other books have additional reading texts in a special section with additional vocabulary; thus reading skills are developed and often reading passages are also translated.

Fifth, oral elements are also strong, even early books in this period have dialogues and conversations; the use of IPA or similar phonetics is quite frequent (note that this does not include "imitated" pronunciation, which is basically coding L2 in L1 pronunciation systems). The more recent books are accompanied by audio-recordings. None of these oral elements seems to have affected the strong presence of features of grammar-translation, thus criticisms of wider grammar-translation approaches about the lack of oral skills development is not supported at all by these books.

Sixth, activities that are not translation exercises do appear, most obviously in recent books but occasionally in others; in some recent books translation is present but is only one of a wide range of activities. A count of translation activities in these books would show diminishing percentages but a continuing use.

Finally, the traditional focus on literature is more evident in earlier books; for Persian this is often linked with texts about history. Social and cultural content (which might be expected in most books) is actually variable: it is clearest for the Fijian example but inclusion of sociocultural elements is not related to specific languages.

Table 34.2 Textbooks for Speakers of English to Learn Foreign Languages

Textbook examples: Target languages and authors	Detailed grammar and examples	Translation of grammar examples	Translation of vocabulary lists	Texts and dialogues	Translation of texts and dialogues	Translation exercises, both ways	Answer key to translations	Other exercises, not translation	Additional reading and vocabulary	Use of IPA or similar phonetics	Audio-recordings	Social and cultural content	Literary and historical content
Persian: Bleeck (1853)	√	√	√	√	√				√			√	√
German: Müller-Strübing and Quick (1874)	√	√				√							√
Gujerati: Tisdall (1892)	√	√	√						√	√		√	√
Greek: Vincent and Dickson (1879)	√	√	√	√	√				√				√
Italian: Grandgent and Wilkins (1887)	√	√	√			√			√				√
Persian: Rosen (1898)	√	√		√	√					√		√	√
Persian: Tisdall (1902)	√	√	√	√	√	√	√		√	√		√	√
Portuguese: Hills, Ford and Coutinho (1925)	√	√	√			√		√		√		√	
Arabic: Kapilawatsky (1940)	√	√	√	√		√	√		√			√	√
Dutch: Koolhoven (1941)	√	√	√			√	√			√		√	
Urdu: Bailey, Firth and Harley (1942)	√	√	√	√	√					√			
Arabic: Tritton (1943)	√	√	√			√	√			√			
Portuguese: Barker (1945)	√	√	√	√		√	√	√	√	√		√	
Malay: Lewis (1947)	√	√	√	√	√	√	√					√	
Greek: Pring (1950)	√	√	√					√		√			
Turkish: Lewis (1953)	√	√	√	√		√	√					√	√
Malay: Hamilton (1953)	√	√	√	√	√								
Fijian: Milner (1956)	√	√					√				√	√	
Arabic: Ziadeh and Winder (1957)	√		√	√	√	√							
Dutch: Shetter (1958)	√	√	√	√		√	√				√	√	√
Italian: Jones (1960)	√	√	√	√		√		√					
Malay: King (1960)	√	√	√	√	√	√	√	√					
Persian: Mace (1962)	√	√	√	√		√	√						√
Persian: Lambton (1963)	√	√	√			√	√			√			√
Persian: Elwell-Sutton (1963)	√	√	√			√	√			√			√
Portuguese: Naar (1963)	√	√	√			√	√						
Portuguese: Willis (1965)	√	√	√			√	√		√				
Gujerati: Lambert (1971)	√	√	√	√	√				√	√	√	√	
Hindi: McGregor (1972)	√	√	√	√		√	√	√	√			√	
Turkish: Underhill (1976)	√	√	√	√	√	√		√					
Greek: Tofallis (1977)	√	√	√	√		√		√	√			√	√
Dutch: Fenoulhet (1983)	√	√	√	√	√	√	√		√		√		
Malay: Othman and Atmosumarto (1995)	√	√	√	√	√	√	√	√				√	√
Turkish: Pollard and Pollard (1996)	√	√	√	√		√	√	√				√	√
Portuguese: Osborne, Sampaio and McIntyre (1997)	√	√	√	√		√	√	√				√	√

Overall, these textbooks illustrate a version 2 TA in action over a considerable period of time. The persistent nature of this wider version (and presumably the market demand for the books) is confirmed by the publication of many later editions and reprints, e.g. Vincent (1879/1919), Gradgent and Wilkins (1887/1904), Tisdall (1902/1943/1959), Hills, Ford and Coutinho (1925/1944), Shetter (1958/1994), King (1960/1988/2004). Generally, some criticisms of grammar-translation that apply to the classical version do not apply to these books illustrating the wider version.

Audiolingual Approaches

Audiolingual approaches (1940s–1960s) carried forward basic ideas of Direct, Oral and Situational Approaches but additionally applied structural linguistics (as a theory of language) and behaviourism (as a theory of learning) to language teaching: these were both well-supported theories at the time (Larsen-Freeman, 2000; Richards & Rogers, 2001). With an emphasis on speech, audiolingual lessons generally started with a dialogue which exemplified structures (grammatical patterns, graded and sequenced, then taught one at a time) and pronunciation, including stress and intonation (Fries, 1945; Brooks, 1964). Classroom techniques centred around combinations of mimicry (imitating pronunciation and model sentences, often heard on audiotapes), memorization (of dialogues)—hence the catchphrase "mim-mem"—and drills on structures using substitution tables or through pattern practice. There were many types of drills (Lado & Fries, 1958; Krohn, 1971) but they mostly involved the class in chorus or small groups in repetition, short responses or grammatical manipulations (e.g. of present tenses to past tenses), and they were conducted by the teacher in an effort for students to form correct habits of speech and avoid making errors (reading and writing came later recycling the oral material). Grammatical explanations were minimal; translation and use of learners' L1 was strongly discouraged. Vocabulary teaching was minimal initially and was well-controlled.

Contrastive analysis (comparing L1 and L2 phonology, grammar, semantics and, interestingly, culture) was used to predict learners' difficulties based on interference from their L1 (Lado, 1957). This is still useful cross-linguistic knowledge for teachers (Odlin, 1989; Swan & Smith, 2001), but it has been largely overtaken by more learner-centred ideas of error analysis, learners' interlanguage and acquisition processes (James, 1980; Selinker, 1992) and has evolved into broader areas such as contrastive rhetoric (Connor, 1996).

Criticisms of audiolingual approaches came from the theoretical undermining of structural linguistics and behaviourism (both of which had been somewhat distorted in audiolingualism), but in any case teachers and learners had found that predicted results fell far short of expectations for real communication (Richards & Rogers, 2001). Finocchiaro and Brumfit (1983, p. 7) concluded:

> Learners parroted incomprehensible material, reading was deferred, the study of grammar ("talking about language") was banned in many school systems, and pattern practice drills were the main activities of the lesson. And since students were being taught to parrot patterns they often became very good at it—without communication and without interaction. In fact learners were often prevented from saying what they wanted to say because that was against the "rules" of the theory.

The teacher-centred nature of the approach was a problem, too, not only because of post-1970s beliefs that classrooms should be more learner-centred, but also because so much of the move from intensive practice to personal communication depended on the teacher: the techniques could be "tedious and boring" and teachers needed "energy", "imagination and enterprise" to make material "acquire reality and relevance" (Rivers, 1981, pp. 47–48). Diller (1971, p. 78) concluded that the direct method is inherently interesting, while mim-mem and pattern drill have to be made interesting by the teacher. It is fun to establish communication in the foreign language as the direct method has us do. But with mim-mem and pattern drill, communication in the foreign language is postponed until after a reliable set of habits has been drilled into the student. Drill is not very much fun; meaningful practice is.

However, in an eclectic application of audiolingual techniques, Paulston and Bruder (1976, pp. 3–47) suggest a sequence of presenting a pattern in context, comprehension questions, identification of a pattern with a formal explanation, then mechanical drills followed by meaningful and communicative ones. Similarly, Rivers (1981, pp. 96–111, 228–231), shows appreciation for drills for specific language points at lower levels, but concludes that they cannot be an end in themselves and that there is a need to move from structured practice to spontaneous expression: "Language teachers must learn how to promote language-using activities in which there is as much student involvement and as little teacher direction as possible" (1981, p. 230). Audiolingual approaches did not do this. Nevertheless, Cook (2001, p. 210) concludes that audiolingual approaches still have a pervasive influence on mainstream EFL:

> Though few teachers nowadays employ a "pure" audiolingual style, many of the ingredients are present in today's classrooms. The use of short dialogues, the emphasis on spoken language, the value attached to practice, the emphasis on the students speaking, the division into four skills, the importance of vocabulary control, the step-by-step progression, all go back to audiolingualism.

Mainstream EFL Traditions

As described above, these tend to be eclectic. They have absorbed some aspects of traditional approaches but not translation (see below). However, eclecticism does not mean just any combination of approaches, methods or techniques: there needs to be an analysis and rationale for sequences of whatever elements are chosen for effective learning (Marton, 1988). These mainstream approaches can be readily investigated starting with handbooks for teachers (e.g. Nunan, 1991; Brown, 1994; Carter & Nunan, 2001; Celce-Murcia, 2001) and by examining current international textbooks or observing classes. Since the 1970s they have been increasingly influenced by communicative approaches. Language is held to be learnt though realistic use. Teachers work with more complex ideas of language from applied linguistics: phonetics, phonology, discourse and culture. The four skills are taught both separately and in integrated ways. Mainstream approaches have been steadily influenced by teacher development programmes and especially by postgraduate courses in applied linguistics and language teaching: these have made many teachers far more aware of theoretical and research dimensions and many EFL teachers have become more reflective and innovative (e.g. in using technology). This means that it is a much more radical position to use "traditional" as a negative label for this approach compared to other versions of traditional.

Humanistic or Alternative Approaches

There has been a lack of consideration of the role of affective factors in L2 pedagogy (Arnold, 1999). Humanistic approaches pay great attention to feelings and self-actualization (as part of "the whole person"); to communication that has personal meaning for learners; to class atmosphere, peer support and quality of interaction by encouraging friendship, cooperation and mutual responsibility between learners (Stevick, 1976, 1980, 1990; Larsen-Freeman, 2000; Richards & Rogers, 2001). There are huge differences between the outward techniques in the approaches grouped under the humanistic heading, but between them they show interesting features of their inner life that might constitute a basis to evaluate other approaches from alternative perspectives. These features include the role of real, personal or imagined experience (in the Silent Way, Community Language Learning and Suggestopedia); the roles of confidence (in the Silent Way and Suggestopedia); concentration (in the Silent Way and Total Physical Response); the use of students' inner resources (in the Silent Way and Community Language Learning); and—reflecting themes of other TAs—the roles of memory (in the Silent Way and Total Physical Response), translation (in Community Language Learning and the Silent Way) and the importance given to vocabulary (in the Silent Way and Suggestopedia).

The Status of Grammar, Translation, Memorization and Literature

Various strands of grammar-translation traditions live on, though somewhat transformed and developed in practice. The nature of this continuation should be considered in re-evaluating TAs.

Grammar after being in a bypass in audiolingual and early communicative periods is widely reinstated to a more central position in TESOL theories. This is evident in streams of corpus-based reference and pedagogic grammars (e.g. Collins Cobuild, 2005; Swan, 2005; Greenbaum & Nelson, 2010). It is clear from the steady flow of research-based rationales and considerations for applying grammar in L2 classrooms (e.g. Rutherford, 1987; Rutherford & Sharwood Smith, 1988; Batstone, 1994; Bygate, Tonkyn & Williams, 1994; Odlin, 1994; Hinkel & Fotos, 2002). Questions remain about attention to form (when and how, at which language levels); about whether and how to integrate grammar with other skills or have some separate treatment, about deductive or inductive treatment, or both; and about the use of descriptive terms in grammar teaching. In mainstream textbooks grammar is usually a focus in specific sections of explanations followed by limited practice after considerable work with language in texts and classroom interaction so that grammatical patterns under consideration will have already been exemplified in meaningful contexts.

Memory is clearly a crucial factor in L2 learning, but memorization of vocabulary (as distinct from simply learning vocabulary) seemed to have suffered negative connotations of rote-learning from criticisms of grammar-translation. This is revised in the extensive research on learner strategies related to vocabulary where memory strategies are recognized as being used, often spontaneously, by learners and are potentially part of the repertoire of vocabulary learning strategies that are trainable in broad approaches to teaching vocabulary (Schmitt, 1997, 2000; Nation, 2001; Nyikos & Fan, 2007).

Translation is often wrongly bracketed with grammar-translation, so translation activities have been hugely diminished in language teaching pedagogy by criticisms of grammar-translation approaches. Widdowson (1979, p. 101) expresses a popular mistrust: "The use of translation as a teaching technique has long been viewed with suspicion by language teachers and many, of course, proscribe it altogether as a matter of principle." Finocchiaro and Brumfit (1983, p. 5) indicate that this reaction to an excessive use of a TA is itself excessive: "But translation, both oral and written, may still have a role to play, even though the reaction to the excessive use of grammar-translation led some teachers to reject both parts of the method on principle." Since the impact of Direct Approaches and later, it is widely felt that only a minimum of oral translation should be used for teachers' explanations, and many teachers feel this is a last resort. In mainstream English language teaching (ELT), translation by students is out of fashion; it is rarely mentioned in teacher training handbooks.

Yet the discipline of translation studies is a field in its own right, and a sub-field of applied linguistics; there are translation theories, methods, practices, approaches to teaching, and research issues (Bell, 1991; Baker, 1992; Gentzler, 1993; Hatim, 2001; Venuti, 2000). This means that translation aspects of TAs can be theoretically justified and that this aspect of critiques of grammar-translation approaches seems unjustified. Classroom translation is arguably useful on utilitarian grounds (many exams contain translation elements) and through a social recognition of L2 uses in the real world (for professional and informal translation and interpreting, and L2 learners often use L1 in their heads) (Cook, 2001). Translation activities can raise language awareness through explorations of equivalence. Older models of translation tend to be based on formal equivalence (literal translations or the best language), whereas more recent models include pragmatic and functional equivalence, notions of discourse, genre and style, plus the purpose of the L1 text and its audience, the purpose of the L2 translation, the nature of the L2 audiences. These models require not only linguistic competence but sociocultural and intercultural competence, which are high on the agenda in twenty-first-century language teaching. Translation need not be translation of isolated sentences, of memorizing words and using dictionaries to understand and translate; there are creative ways of using translation in classrooms and a great variety of translation tasks (Rivers & Temperley, 1978; Duff, 1989). Widdowson (1978, 1979) advocates translating using non-verbal devices (e.g. translating diagrams to text) and semantic and pragmatic translation across types of texts, which can be a communicative activity. All of this is an argument that translation can be included in language teaching as a fifth skill.

Explicit links between L2 learning and literature, challenged by utilitarian aspects of communicative approaches and languages for specific purposes, experienced a revival in the 1980s and 1990s and partly continues this strand of TAs. Exploring literature in language classrooms has been linked to developing specific L2 skills, understanding cultural issues, and personal growth through engagement with literature; it can be language-based or linked to a literature curriculum (Brumfit & Carter, 1986; Carter & Long, 1987, 1991); it can be a context for imaginative, creative and communicative activities (Maley & Duff, 1989). Literature-based activities can be linked to specific linguistic domains such as pragmatics (Sell, 1995) and are seen in TESOL programmes around the world, particularly at university level (Brumfit & Benton, 1993).

Some Traditional Strands in TESOL in Modern China

TESOL in China represents a significant case where some traditional strands continue in a rapidly modernizing context. China has the world's largest education system and there are an estimated 300 million learners of English in Chinese schools, colleges, universities and English language institutes (British Council, 2009). Approaches to TESOL at colleges in China are considerably reoriented by recent curriculum guidelines (Ministry of Education, 2007), which include a new emphasis on oral English skills and practical abilities for real life applications, developing critical thinking, creativity and intercultural awareness through English, besides strong encouragement to incorporate e-learning and develop whole-person approaches and students' learning capacities. There are parallel requirements for junior and senior middle schools and English is now established in primary schools. There is mass involvement and widespread enthusiasm for English in modern China but putting these new requirements into practice is challenging, partly because of the strength of TAs (Cortazzi & Jin, 1996a; Jin & Cortazzi, 2006). Teachers are required to shift from a teacher-centred, knowledge-based approach to a much more learner-centred interactive style of skills development, which at the same time develops independent learning.

Traditionally between the early twentieth century and the late 1990s or early 2000s, students were taught to pay great attention to English grammar, vocabulary and reading. This was required for exams, notably to enter university—and to pass required levels of English to graduate. So many students would learn some texts as models, practise grammar through multi-choice exercises, read and learn long vocabulary lists (often whole books of bilingual lists). Outside class, students could be seen reading and heard reciting texts and vocabulary aloud for their class preparation. In class, the common procedure for the premier course in intensive reading was a teacher-led, text-centred lesson: reading a text, going through bilingual vocabulary lists and grammar points, answering comprehension questions before completing traditional vocabulary and grammar exercises, and finally doing translations and a guided writing task.

Here are strands of a wider version of a grammar-translation approach and some elements remain official in the recent developments, which overall are not traditional. Translation is commonly quoted as a fifth skill and is listed as number five in the new college requirements for basic, intermediate and advanced levels (Ministry of Education, 2007, pp. 19–23); thus intermediate requirements for non-English majors ask for correct and fluent translations on familiar topics published in English with the help of a dictionary, translations of idiomatic English writing within their speciality into Chinese and of general topics from Chinese into English. Recommended vocabulary is listed as number six, almost as a sixth skill, confirming a central role of vocabulary: at all levels, students should acquire specified numbers of words and the words themselves are listed. Knowing that they will be tested on these, students will learn them through their teachers and textbooks, through note-taking, memorization and practice, but not just rote-learning (Cortazzi & Jin, 1996c).

Research on broader features of Chinese cultures of learning suggests that they apparently persist, often with a positive effect, to influence L2 learning (Cortazzi & Jin, 1996b; Jin & Cortazzi, 1998). "Cultures of learning" describes taken-for-granted frameworks of expectations, attitudes, values and beliefs about successful learning and teaching, about learning and using different language skills in classrooms, and about how interaction should be accomplished. For students, this includes ways of preparing for English exams, self-study practices and class work. It includes giving great importance to the teacher, to the book, to models and explanations, to mimicking and memorizing, to practising and performing (which matches TAs rather well). It also includes deeper values of the importance of learning and study; their respect for teachers for their knowledge, cultivation of learning and morality; their awareness of teachers' guidance, care, concern, devotion and sacrifice (cognitive, social and affective dimensions). It includes a deep belief that making a continuous effort leads to success (not just having talent), that success is possible and that difficulties and hardships can be endured and surmounted (Cortazzi, Jin & Wang, 2009). This list gives insights for successful language learning in this context—and some features are traditional in the Confucian heritage.

Such a culture of learning (which likely has a different nature or emphasis elsewhere) is consonant with TAs but might lead to tacit resistance to aspects of some approaches imported from outside. In China in the 1980s and 1990s the national take-up of communicative approaches was slow; teachers often spoke of "the Chinese context" and of "the need for an eclectic approach", which took account of some communicative techniques but also maintained TAs. After all, some students only needed to read English and they were achieving this through TAs. These observations indicate a need to understand TAs in their educational and cultural contexts; perhaps we should ask whether students have a right to learn as they wish (using TAs or not). But this is a complex question. L2 learning, practically by definition, involves the challenge for learners to go beyond a comfort zone not only into new languages and cultures with new levels of proficiency but also into new ways of learning. Approaches to L2 learning and teaching—as Ting-Toomey (1999) points out for communicating across cultures—need to be not only appropriate and effective, but also satisfying for participants. A significant part of satisfaction for students and teachers resides in how a new approach to learning and teaching fits in with their cultures of learning and relates to their beliefs about change and long-term traditions. Education in languages always balances the known with the unknown, a given element of transmission and a new element of innovation; in reaching an appropriate, effective and satisfying balance traditional approaches to L2 teaching and learning may need re-evaluation.

Researching Traditional Approaches

This last section outlines a number of ways to research TAs, which can be used singly or in combination. Most obviously, a researcher can examine historical sources. Study could start with accessible critical summaries (Mackey, 1965; Rivers, 1981; Stern, 1983; Larsen-Freeman, 2000; Richards & Rogers, 2001) and move on to detailed histories of language teaching: Howatt's (1984) chronological study has detailed chapters on language teaching in the nineteenth and early twentieth century, and features studies and biographical notes of outstanding individuals who contributed to developments of EFL; Kelly's (1969) work is thematically organized around teaching meaning, grammar, pronunciation, language skills, selection and organization of content, and the reception of ideas. For the classical tradition of medieval grammar and changes in the teaching of Latin as L2, see Law (1997) and for a focus on grammar and learning to read, with comments from teachers' marginal notes on Latin texts, see Reynolds (1996). Histories of linguistics provide useful understanding of changing concepts and contexts of language study (Robins, 1997; Seuren, 1998; Law, 2003). As case studies, methods books by influential figures who promoted what was later called grammar translation include Ahn (1849) on learning German and parallel books for English, Dutch, French, and Ollendorf (1838) on learning German and other books for learning English. Other key figures wrote books to emphasize oral methods, often with ideas which were ahead of their time (Sweet, 1899; Jesperson, 1904; Palmer, 1921; Fries, 1945; Lado, 1957). Research would need to be contextualized within the historical milieu, sociocultural contexts, institutional and curriculum developments in general education, and changes within particular periods, so histories of education are relevant and sometimes have surprising quotations about grammar and language teaching and learning from leading scholars—such as John Milton, John Locke, Jean Jacques Rousseau (Rusk, 1965; Cole, 1950; Bowen, 1975; Wagoner, 2008).

Second, researchers can examine original educational documents in a particular country to locate statements about language teaching and examples of practice (e.g. policy documents, inspectors' reports, exam papers, school records and reports). The most available document is the older L2 textbook; however, one should remember that printed materials are often not the same as actual practice and may not relate closely to classroom interaction. A third approach is to observe, record and analyse classroom practices in which TAs have a role and interview the participants later for their comments on a lesson transcript or video recording. This suggests, fourth, interviewing teachers and older adults singly or in focus groups to ask about experiences of remembered TAs. Researchers should be aware that recall of personal experiences can be shaped or distorted so cross-checking information is useful. A survey questionnaire could prove fruitful for a wider study of present attitudes to TAs, perhaps with a comparison across age groups, in different countries or languages. Similarly, it would be interesting to examine accounts of traditional language learning in autobiography and fiction. Bearing in mind the points made earlier about the contexts of criticism and about cultures of learning, it would be appropriate for those who critique TAs to consider their own experiences and stance regarding cultures of learning.

References

Ahn, F. (1849). *A new practical and easy method of learning the German language.* Frankfurt: Brockhaus & Avenarius.
Anthony, E. (1963). Approach, method, technique. *English Language Teaching, 17,* pp. 63–66. (Also in Allen, H. B., & Campbell, R. N. (1971). *Teaching English as a second language.* London: McGraw-Hill.)
Arnold, F. (1999). *Affect in language learning.* Cambridge: Cambridge University Press.
Baker, M. (1992). *In other words, a course book on translation.* London: Routledge.
Batstone, R. (1994). *Grammar.* Oxford: Oxford University Press.
Bell, R. T. (1991). *Translation and translating: Theory and practice.* London: Longman.

Benson, M. J. (2000). The secret life of grammar-translation. In H. Trappes-Lomax (Ed.), *Change and Continuity in Applied Linguistics* (pp. 35–50). Clevedon: Multilingual Matters.

Bowen, J. (1975). *A history of western education, vol. 2, civilization of Europe, sixth to sixteenth century.* London: Methuen.

British Council (2009). *India and China ELT today* (seminar, 21 May). London: The British Council.

Brooks, N. (1964). *Language and language learning.* New York: Harcourt.

Brown, H. D. (1994). *Teaching by principles: An interactive approach to language pedagogy.* New York: Prentice Hall Regents.

Brumfit, C., & Benton, M. (Eds.) (1993). Teaching literature: A world perspective. *Review of ELT, 2*(3). London: Modern English Publications/The British Council.

Brumfit, C., & Carter, R. (Eds.) (1986). *Language and literature teaching.* Oxford: Oxford University Press.

Bygate, M., Tonkyn, A. & Williams, E. (Eds.) (1994). *Grammar and the language teacher.* Hemel Hempstead: Prentice Hall.

Carter, R., & Long, M. (1987). *The web of words, exploring literature through language.* Cambridge: Cambridge University Press.

Carter, R., & Long, M. (1991). *Teaching literature.* London: Longman.

Carter, R., & Nunan, D. (Eds.) (2001). *The Cambridge guide to teaching English to speakers of other languages.* Cambridge: Cambridge University Press.

Celce-Murcia, M. (Ed.) (2001). *Teaching English as a second or foreign language* (3rd ed.). Boston: Heinle & Heinle.

Cole, L. (1950). *A history of education, Socrates to Montessori.* New York: Holt, Rinehart & Winston.

Collins Cobuild (2005). *English grammar* (2nd ed.). London: Collins.

Connor, U. (1996). *Contrastive Rhetoric, cross-cultural aspects of second-language writing.* Cambridge: Cambridge University Press.

Cook, V. (2001). *Second language learning and language teaching.* London: Arnold.

Cortazzi, M., & Jin, L. (1996a). ELT in China: State of the art article. *Language Teaching, 29*(2), 61–80.

Cortazzi, M., & Jin, L. (1996b). Cultures of learning: Language classrooms in China. In H. Coleman (Ed.), *Society and the language classroom* (pp. 169–206). Cambridge: Cambridge University Press.

Cortazzi, M., & Jin (1996c). Changes in learning English vocabulary in China. In H. Coleman & L. Cameron (Eds.), *Change and language* (pp. 153–165). Clevedon: Multilingual Matters.

Cortazzi, M., Jin, L. & Wang, Z. (2009). Cultivators, cows and computers: Chinese learners' metaphors of teachers. In T. Coverdale-Jones & P. Rastall (Eds.), *Internationalizing the university, the Chinese context* (pp.107–129). London: Palgrave Macmillan.

Diller, K. C. (1971). *Generative grammar, structural linguistics, and language teaching.* Rowley, MA: Newbury House.

Duff, A. (1989). *Translation.* Oxford: Oxford University Press.

Finocchiaro, M., & Brumfit, C. (1983). *The functional-notional approach, from theory to practice.* New York: Oxford University Press.

Fries, C. (1945). *Teaching and learning English as a foreign language.* Ann Arbor: University of Michigan Press.

Genzler, E. (1993). *Contemporary translation theories.* London: Routledge.

Greenbaum, S., & Nelson, G. (2010). *An introduction to English grammar* (3rd ed.). London: Longman.

Hatim, B. (2001). *Teaching and researching translation.* London: Longman.

Hinkel, E., & Fotos, S. (Eds.) (2002). *New perspectives in grammar teaching in second language classrooms.* Mahwah, NJ: Lawrence Erlbaum Associates.

Howatt, A. P. R. (1984). *A history of English language teaching.* Oxford: Oxford University Press.

James, C. (1980). *Contrastive analysis.* Harlow: Longman.

Jesperson, O. (1904). *How to teach a foreign language.* London: Allen & Unwin.

Jin, L., & Cortazzi, M. (1998). The culture the learner brings: A bridge or a barrier? In M. Byram & M. Fleming (Eds.), *Language learning in intercultural perspective* (pp. 98–118). Cambridge: Cambridge University Press.

Jin, L., & Cortazzi, M. (2006). Changing practices in Chinese cultures of learning. *Language, Culture and Curriculum, 19*(1), 5–20.

Kelly, L. G. (1969). *25 centuries of language teaching.* Rowley, MA: Newbury House.

Krohn, R. (1971). *English sentence structure.* Ann Arbor: University of Michigan Press.

Lado, R. (1957). *Linguistics across cultures.* Ann Arbor: University of Michigan Press.

Lado, R., & Fries, C. F. (1958). *English pattern practice* (3rd ed.). Ann Arbor: University of Michigan Press.

Larsen-Freeman, D. (2000). *Techniques and principles in language teaching* (2nd ed.). New York: Oxford University Press.

Law, V. A. (1997). *Grammarians in the middle ages.* London: Longman.

Law, V. (2003). *The history of linguistics in Europe from Plato to 1600.* Cambridge: Cambridge University Press.

McDonough, S. (2002). *Applied linguistics in language education.* London: Arnold.

Mackey, W. (1965). *Language teaching analysis.* London: Longman.

Maley, A., & Duff, A. (1989). *The inward ear, poetry in the language classroom.* Cambridge: Cambridge University Press.

Marton, W. (1988). *Methods in English language teaching, frameworks and options.* New York: Prentice Hall.

Ministry of Education (2007). *College English curriculum requirements*. Beijing: Foreign Language Teaching and Research Press.

Nation, I. S. P. (2001). *Learning vocabulary in another language*. Cambridge: Cambridge Press.

Nunan, D. (1991). *Language teaching methodology, a handbook for teachers*. New York: Prentice Hall.

Nyikos, M., & Fan, M. (2007). A review of vocabulary learning strategies: Focus on language proficiency and learner voice. In A. D. Cohen & E. Macaro (Eds.), *Language learner strategies: Thirty years of research and practice* (pp. 251–275). Oxford: Oxford University Press.

Odlin, T. (1989). *Language transfer, cross-linguistic influence in language learning*. Cambridge: Cambridge University Press.

Odlin, T. (Ed.) (1994). *Perspectives on pedagogical grammar*. Cambridge: Cambridge University Press.

Ollendorf, H. G. (1838). *A new method of learning to read, write and speak a language in six months, adapted to the German*. London: Whittaker.

Palmer, H. E. (1921). *The oral method of teaching foreign languages*. Cambridge: Heffer.

Paulston, C. B., & Bruder, M.N. (1976). *Teaching English as a second language: Techniques and procedures*. Cambridge, MA: Winthrop.

Reynolds, S. (1996). *Medieval reading: Grammar, rhetoric and the classical text*. Cambridge: Cambridge University Press.

Richards, J. C., & Rodgers, T. S. (2001). *Approaches and methods in language teaching*. Cambridge: Cambridge University Press.

Rivers, W. M. (1981). *Teaching foreign language skills*. Chicago: University of Chicago Press.

Rivers, W. M., & Temperley, M. S. (1978). *A practical guide to the teaching of English as a second or foreign language*. New York: Oxford University Press.

Robins, R. H. (1997). *A short history of linguistics*. London: Longman.

Rusk, R. R. (1965). *The doctrines of the great educators* (3rd ed.). London: Macmillan.

Rutherford, W. E. (1987). *Second language grammar: Learning and teaching*. London: Longman.

Rutherford, W. E., & Sharwood-Smith, M. (1988). *Grammar and second language teaching*. Boston: Heinle and Heinle.

Schmitt, N. (1997). Vocabulary learning strategies. In N. Schmitt & M. McCarthy (Eds.), *Vocabulary, description, acquisition and pedagogy* (pp. 199–227). Cambridge: Cambridge University Press.

Schmitt, N. (2000). *Vocabulary in language teaching*. Cambridge: Cambridge University Press.

Sell, R. D. (Ed.) (1995). Literature throughout foreign language education: The implications of pragmatics. *Review of ELT*, *5*(1). London: Modern English Publications/The British Council.

Selinker, L. (1992). *Rediscovering interlanguage*. London: Longman.

Seuren, P. A. M. (1998). *Western linguistics, an historical introduction*. Oxford: Blackwell.

Stern, H. H. (1983). *Fundamental concepts in language teaching*. Oxford: Oxford University Press.

Stern, H. H. (1992). *Issues and options in language teaching*. Oxford: Oxford University Press.

Stevick, E. W. (1976). *Memory, meaning and method, some psychological perspectives on language learning*. Rowley, MA: Newbury House.

Stevick, E. W. (1980). *Teaching languages, as way and ways*. Rowley, MA: Newbury House.

Stevick, E. W. (1990). *Humanism in language teaching, a critical perspective*. Oxford: Oxford University Press.

Strevens, P. (1977). *New orientations in the teaching of English*. Oxford: Oxford University Press.

Strevens, P. (1980). *Teaching English as an international language*. Oxford: Pergamon.

Swan, M. (2005). *Practical English usage* (3rd ed.). Oxford: Oxford University Press.

Swan, M., & Smith, B. (2001). *Learner English* (2nd ed.). Cambridge: Cambridge University Press.

Sweet, H. (1899/1964). *The practical study of languages: A guide for teachers and learners*. London: Dent/Oxford: Oxford University Press.

Ting-Toomey, S. (1999). *Communicating across cultures*. New York: The Guilford Press.

Venuti, L. (Ed.) (2000). *The translation studies reader*. London: Routledge.

Wagoner, J. L. (2008). *American education, a history*, (4th ed.). New York: Routledge.

Widdowson, H. G. (1978). *Teaching language as communication*. Oxford: Oxford University Press.

Widdowson, H. G. (1979). *Explorations in applied linguistics*. Oxford: Oxford University Press

Wilkins, D. A. (1972). *Linguistics and language teaching*. London: Edward Arnold.

Additional references (language textbooks referred to in Table 34.2)

Bailey, T. G, Firth, J. R. & Harley, A. H. (1942/1950/1972). *Urdu*. London: Teach Yourself Books.

Barker. J. W. (1945). *Portuguese*. London: Hodder & Stoughton.

Bleeck, A. H. (1853). *A concise grammar of the Persian language, containing dialogues, reading lessons and a vocabulary*. London: Bernard Quaritch.

Elwell-Sutton, L. P. (1963). *Elementary Persian grammar.* Cambridge: Cambridge University Press.

Fenoulhet, J. (1983/1994). *Dutch in three months.* London: Hugo's Language Books.

Grandgent, C. H., & Wilkins, E. H. (1887/1904). *Italian grammar.* Boston: Heath.

Hamilton, A. W. (1953/1985/1995). *Malay made easy.* Singapore: Eastern Universities Press.

Hills, E. C., Ford, J. D. M. & Coutinho, J. de S. (1925, revised by L. G. Moffatt 1944). *Portuguese grammar.* Boston: Heath.

Jones, F. J. (1960). *A modern Italian grammar.* London: University of London Press.

Kapliwatzky, J. (1940/1960). *Arabic language and grammar* (Vol. 1). Jerusalem: Rubin Mass.

King, E. S. (1960/1988/2004). *Speak Malay.* London: University of London Press.

Koolhoven, H. (1941/1977). *Dutch.* London: Hodder & Stoughton.

Lambert, H. M. (1971/1985). *Gujarati language course.* Cambridge: Cambridge University Press.

Lambton, A. K. S. (1963). *Persian grammar.* Cambridge: Cambridge University Press.

Lewis, M. B. (1947). *Teach yourself Malay.* London: English Universities Press.

Lewis, G. L. (1953/1989). *Teach yourself Turkish.* London: Hodder & Stoughton.

Mace, J. (1962). *Teach yourself modern Persian.* London: Teach Yourself Books.

McGregor, R. S. (1972). *Outline of Hindi grammar.* Oxford: Clarendon Press.

Milner, G. B. (1956/1972). *Fijian grammar.* Suva, Fiji: Government Press.

Müller-Strübing, H., & Quick, R. H. (1874). *Companion to Schiller's Wilhelm Tell, being a complete vocabulary.* London: David Nutt.

Naar, M. E. de A. (1963/1974). *Colloquial Portuguese.* London: Routledge.

Osborne, E. S., Sampaio, J. & McIntyre, B. (1997/2002). *Colloquial Portuguese of Brazil.* London: Routledge.

Othman, Z., & Atmosumarto, S. (1995). *Colloquial Malay, a complete language course.* London: Routledge.

Pollard, A. C., & Pollard, D. (1996). *Turkish.* London: Hodder & Stoughton.

Pring, J. T. (1950/1961). *A grammar of modern Greek on a phonetic basis.* London: University of London Press.

Rosen, F. (1898). *Modern Persian colloquial grammar.* London: Luzac & Co.

Shetter, W. Z. (1958/1994). *Dutch: An essential grammar.* London: Routledge.

Tisdall, W. S.-C.(1892/1961). *A simplified grammar of the Gujarati language.* London: Kegan Paul/Trench & Trübner.

Tisdall, W. S.-C. (1902/1943/1959). *Modern Persian conversation-grammar with reading lessons.* London: Nutt.

Tofallis, K. (1977/1984). *A textbook of modern Greek.* Nicosia: Cosmos Press.

Tritton, A. S. (1943/1983). *Arabic.* London: Hodder & Stoughton.

Underhill, R. (1976/1997). *Turkish grammar.* Cambridge, MA: MIT Press.

Vincent, E., & Dickson, T. G. (1879/1919). *A handbook of modern Greek.* London: Macmillan.

Willis, R. C. (1965/1984). An essential course in modern Portugese. Walton-on-Thames: Nelson.

Ziadeh, F. J., & Winder, R. B. (1957). *An introduction to modern Arabic.* Princeton, NJ: Princeton University Press.

35
Focus on Form

Shawn Loewen

This chapter examines research that has looked at form-focused instruction (FFI) generally, and at focus on form (FonF) more specifically. An initial challenge in this endeavor is to arrive at definitions of FFI and FonF and to establish the boundaries of these constructs, as the terms have been used in multiple, overlapping, and sometimes contradictory ways (Ellis, 2008; Doughty & Williams, 1998a; Williams, 2005). Subsequently, it is important to consider the theoretical and pedagogic implications of FonF and to explore the controversies surrounding it.

Definitions

FFI is a component of instructed second language acquisition (SLA), which, in turn, is a subcategory of general SLA that is concerned with all aspects of the learning of languages other than one's first (L1). Instructed SLA focuses on "any systematic attempt to enable or facilitate language learning by manipulating the mechanisms of learning and/or the conditions under which these occur" (Housen & Pierrard, 2005, p. 3). Generally, instructed SLA is seen as occurring inside the second language (L2) classroom, and as such it contrasts with naturalistic SLA, which occurs in the course of learners' contact and interaction with the L2 in everyday life.

Instructed SLA can be further divided according to the emphasis that is placed on either meaning or linguistic form. Thus meaning-focused instruction (MFI) (also known as communication-focused instruction) is based on the premise that the L2 should be treated as a tool for communication and not as an object of study in itself and that there should be an overall emphasis on the communication of meaning in L2 classes. Proponents of MFI argue that learning discrete linguistic items and grammar rules does not help learners develop their interlanguage systems. Examples of MFI include communicative language teaching (Savignon, 2005), content-based instruction (Lyster, 2007), and task-based language teaching (Ellis, 2003). It should be noted, however, that while the primary focus of various types of MFI is on communication, many of them also encourage, or at least allow, some attention to linguistic form as well.

While the parameters of MFI are relatively straightforward, the definition and operationalization of FFI are somewhat less clear. It is perhaps best to begin by considering Long's (1991, 1996; Long & Robinson, 1998) categorization of language teaching options into focus on meaning, focus on form and focus on forms (FonFS). Focus on meaning clearly corresponds to MFI. FonF was defined as "overtly draw[ing] students' attention to linguistic elements as they arise incidentally in lessons whose overriding focus is on meaning or communication" (Long, 1991, pp. 45–46). A common example illustrating this definition of FonF is the provision of corrective feedback in response to learners' erroneous utterances during communicative activities. Long contrasted FonF with FonFS, which he described as the presentation and practice of isolated linguistic structures apart from any communicative need (Long, 1991; Long & Robinson, 1998). An example of FonFS is traditional grammar instruction in which explicit rules about language are taught. In an effort to use an adjectival descriptor for one or both of these constructs, the term "form-focused instruction" has been used. However, Doughty and Williams (1998b) discuss the terminological conundrum brought about by such usage because FFI could potentially refer to either FonF or FonFS instruction. As a result, Doughty and Williams recommended avoidance of the term; however, SLA researchers have ignored this sage advice, with the result that FFI has become a commonly, though inconsistently used term. Therefore it is important to delineate FFI and to specify its relationship to FonF and FonFS.

One early and frequently cited definition of FFI comes from Spada (1997), who defines FFI as "any pedagogical effort which is used to draw the learners' attention to language form either implicitly or explicitly" (p. 73). Spada goes on to state that her use of FFI is similar to Long's (1991) FonF, with both terms encompassing "pedagogical events which occur within meaning-based approaches to L2 instruction" (p. 73); however, Spada emphasizes that Long's definition of FonF is restricted to spontaneous attention to form, while her definition of FFI includes focusing on language in either spontaneous or predetermined ways. Therefore, Spada's definition of FFI represents an expansion of FonF to include proactive attention to language items; however, it contrasts with FonFS by stipulating that the proactive focus must still occur within a meaning-focused context. Examples of predetermined FonF could include the systematic provision of corrective feedback on the incorrect production of specific, recently taught linguistic items or the seeding of a communicative activity with multiple exemplars of a targeted linguistic form.

A subsequent definition by Ellis (2001) states that FFI refers to "any planned or incidental instructional activity that is intended to induce language learners to pay attention to linguistic form" (pp. 1–2). Ellis proceeds to divided FFI into three categories:

- FonFs, which encompasses traditional structural approaches to instruction and corresponds with Long's (1991, 1996) use of the term.
- Incidental FonF, which involves brief and spontaneous attention to language items during communicative activities and corresponds with Long's definition of FonF.
- Planned FonF, which consists of attention to preselected language items during communicative activities and takes into account Spada's concern for FonF that occurs in predetermined ways.

Thus, Ellis's (2001) definition of FFI can be viewed as a superordinate category that contrasts with MFI and subsumes FonF and FonFS. This definition has been used in numerous subsequent investigations into FFI, including Housen and Pierrard's (2005) edited volume on instructed SLA and Nassaji and Fotos's (2007) volume on FFI and teacher education. Ellis's (2008) recent encyclopedic volume on SLA also provides a similar definition. Given this common usage, FFI in this chapter will refer to any instructional activity attempting to draw learners' attention to specific linguistic items.

In order to illustrate graphically the various components of instructed SLA, Figure 35.1 builds on previous taxonomies (Long & Robinson, 1998; Williams, 2005) and presents the taxonomic relationships among the constructs under consideration. MFI and FFI are superordinate categories that refer to instruction emphasizing either communication or linguistic items respectively. FFI is further divided into FonF and FonFS. The definition of FonFS follows Long's and Ellis's definitions in that it maintains an overall emphasis on discrete components of language and treats language as an object to be studied. While this chapter will not explore FonFS instruction in detail, it will consider its

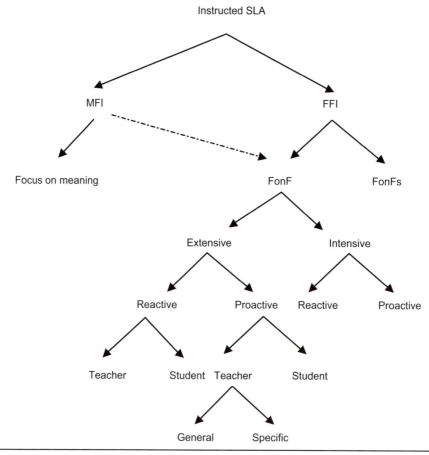

Figure 35.1 A taxonomy of instructed SLA

relationship to FonF, particularly in comparing the effectiveness of the two constructs for L2 learning.

In comparison to FonFS, the definition of FonF is slightly more complicated. In an attempt to bring some order to the multiple views of FonF, Williams (2005) provides a helpful overview of the definitions of FonF and FFI presented in Long and Robinson (1998), Doughty and Williams (1998a), Spada (1997), and Ellis (2001). She uses the criteria below in order to compare the components of FonF that are either required, possible or prohibited in the various definitions.

- an overall emphasis on the communication of meaning.
- a brief diversion from that emphasis on communication to focus on language as object.
- a problem-based trigger for the diversion.

(Williams, 2005, p. 672)

According to Williams, the one characteristic shared by these definitions is a focus on language as object and, apart from Ellis's (2001) category of FFI, that focus must occur in a context that is primarily meaning-focused. Implicit in Williams's three features is Doughty and Varela's (1998) statement that "a quintessential element of the theoretical construct of focus on form is its dual requirement that the focus must occur in conjunction with—but must not interrupt- communicative interaction" (p. 114). Based on these features, FonF in this chapter will refer to brief attention, either planned or incidental, to problematic language items within a larger communicative context. Consequently, Figure 35.1 shows FonF as a subcategory of FFI, but a dashed line from MFI to FonF indicates the communicative context in which FonF occurs. The various subcategories of FonF will be explored in more detail below as the essential components of FonF, and their operationalization, are considered.

Before delving more deeply into the various options in FonF, it is important to consider its relationship to theoretical and pedagogical issues. The impetus for FonF comes from Long's view that language teaching should focus on "psycholinguistically relevant design features" (Long, 1991, p. 41). He argues that teaching isolated linguistic structures using FonFS is psycholinguistically untenable, given what is known about learners' interlanguage and developmental sequences (Long, 2007). Additionally, interactionist approaches to SLA (Gass, 1997; Gass & Mackey, 2007) propose that FonF can be an important part of interaction, particularly as it can help facilitate the noticing of linguistic items, which is considered essential for L2 learning (Schmidt, 1995, 2001).

In addition to theoretical concerns for SLA, FonF is clearly linked to L2 pedagogy, with obvious implications for the organization of L2 classroom instruction. On the one hand, the implementation of FonF in the classroom reduces or eliminates instructional activities that isolate linguistic items and separates them from meaningful interaction. On the other hand, FonF draws attention to the accurate use of language items in MFI contexts that might otherwise exclude such a focus. These pedagogical options in FonF will be considered subsequently in the chapter.

Trends and Controversies

Having established some of the differences between FonF and FonFS, this chapter will now consider various issues related specifically to FonF. The list below provides definitions of the taxonomic categories proposed in Figure 35.1:

1. FonF—brief attention to (problematic) language as object during communicative activities.
    1.1. Extensive FonF—no single linguistic item is targeted, rather limited attention may be given to a variety of structures.
        1.1.1. Reactive—attention to form can occur sporadically in response to any errors produced by the student. Example: corrective feedback.
            1.1.1.1. Teacher-initiated—error correction done by the teacher.
            1.1.1.2. Learner-initiated—error correction done by other students.
        1.1.2. Proactive—attention is given to linguistic items identified as problematic, although no immediate error has been produced.
            1.1.2.1. Teacher-initiated—attention drawn to a linguistic item by the teacher.
                1.1.2.1.1. General—an overall emphasis on accuracy, Example: the provision of guided planning time prior to a communicative activity, a general admonishing to pay attention to accuracy.
                1.1.2.1.2. Specific—the teacher draws attention to specific linguistic items that he/she perceives may be problematic for learners.
            1.1.2.2. Learner-initiated—student asks about a specific linguistic item that they perceive as problematic.
    2.1. Intensive focus on form—one or two linguistic items are targeted continually during an activity.
        2.1.1. Reactive—attention to form occurs consistently in response to a specific error.
        2.1.2. Proactive—specific forms are embedded in the input.

FonF is first divided according to the intensity of the focus on a particular linguistic item, with both intensive and extensive FonF having the possibility of occurring reactively or proactively. Furthermore, extensive FonF can be carried out by either the teacher or the student. Finally, teachers' proactive FonF can target specific linguistic items or can draw learners' attention to linguistic accuracy more generally. These features represent possible options in the manifestation of FonF in the classroom, and the issues surrounding them will now be discussed.

Should FonF Occur at all in the L2 Classroom?

Before examining potential design features of FonF, it is necessary to justify its presence in the classroom at all. Some proponents of MFI argue that overt attention to linguistic items in the classroom does not lead learners to develop proceduralized and implicit L2 knowledge; therefore, it is best to provide learners with an input-rich, communicative classroom environment without specifically teaching about language (Krashen, 1982, 1985, 1994; Krashen & Terrell, 1983; Schwartz, 1993). According to this view, attention to form may provide learners with explicit knowledge about language; nevertheless, FonF will have little impact on learners' ability to use the L2 for communication.

In contrast to strong MFI approaches that reject FonF because it provides too much attention to linguistic items, others argue that FonF does not provide enough attention to language. For example, Sheen (2003, 2005) argues that FonF has not lived up to its claimed effectiveness and that FonFS instruction is necessary for L2 learning.

In spite of these criticisms, there is a growing consensus that FonF can be beneficial for L2 learning and that it does have a place in the classroom (Ellis, 2002, 2006; Doughty, 2003). For example, Norris and Ortega's (2000) meta-analysis of instructed SLA found that both FonF and FonFS were effective for L2 learning. They also found that explicit types of instruction in both categories were more effective than implicit types. In addition to Norris and Ortega, several other meta-analyses have found an effect for at least one type of FonF, namely corrective feedback (Li, 2010; Russell & Spada, 2006). As a result of such studies, Spada and Lightbown (2008) claim that "the most engaging questions and debates in L2 pedagogy are no longer about whether CLT [communicative language teaching] should include FFI but rather how and when it is most effective" (p. 184).

It should be noted, though, that while FonF is generally considered to be potentially beneficial for learners, most researchers do not propose that FonF is essential for L2 learning or that learning cannot occur in FonFS and/or MFI contexts (Doughty & Williams, 1998c; Long, 2007). Indeed, different types of instruction may be better for different structures and different types of learning. For example, Laufer (2005) maintains that vocabulary can be taught through both FonF and FonFS instruction. Meanwhile, Ellis (2006) contends that as of yet, no firm conclusion can be reached about the relative effectiveness of FonF and FonFS. Therefore, FonF can be considered a legitimate option in the L2 classroom.

What Constitutes a Communicative Context for FonF?

Given that one of the central components of FonF is an "overall and primary focus on meaning" (Williams, 2005, p. 672), a fundamental consideration is how that primary focus is operationalized. Ellis (2006) stresses that "it is crucially important to distinguish the context in which attention to form takes place" (p. 23). Of course, form and meaning are inextricably linked, so that it is difficult, if not impossible, for one to occur without the other; nevertheless, it is possible to prioritize either form or meaning in at least three types of instructional contexts, namely curricular, course, and classroom activity. At the curricular level, the goal of a meaning-focused instructional program is to provide opportunities for learners to interact with, and in, the L2 or for learners to study academic subjects through the medium of the L2. An example of a curricular emphasis on meaning can be found in content-based instruction in Canadian French immersion classes (Lyster, 2007). Indeed, several descriptive studies have examined how FonF occurred in content classes such as science, social studies, and math (Lyster, 1998a, 1988b; Lyster & Ranta, 1997). Another example is the use of a syllabus comprised of communicative tasks, such as can be found in task-based language teaching (Ellis, 2003; Skehan, 2003; Van den Branden, 2006). Such curricula exemplify an overall emphasis on meaning within which FonF can occur.

Another recent approach to FonF and FFI that defines "overall emphasis" at the curricular level is Spada and Lightbown's (2008) introduction of the terms integrated FFI and isolated FFI. Within a communicative language teaching or content-based instruction context, integrated FFI is incorporated into communicative activities, while isolated FFI occurs in lessons that are separate from communicative activities. Spada and Lightbown point out that isolated FFI differs from FonFS at the level of syllabus, with language-focused activities occurring within a broader MFI program. Integrated FFI, on the other hand, corresponds closely to the general definition of FonF used in this chapter, with attention to language items occurring within communicative activities themselves.

However, not all L2 instructional contexts follow an entirely meaning-focused curriculum. Many institutions provide a modular approach to L2 instruction in which semester- or term-long courses have differing emphases (Pica, 2002; Zyzik & Polio, 2008). For example, a language school might offer some courses that focus on grammar and others that focus on communication skills. An advanced, university-level foreign language program may require students to take courses that focus on linguistic aspects of the L2 in addition to courses that teach academic content, such as literature, in the L2. In these contexts, then, the primary emphasis is determined at the course level, and students may be enrolled simultaneously in courses that have a primary emphasis on meaning and those that focus on language form.

Finally, within a single class, there may be alternation between activities that focus primarily on meaning and on language forms. Ellis (2006) suggests that what determines the emphasis of the context is the teachers' instructions in setting up the classroom activities. Thus, a class may begin with a communicative activity in which learners discuss their opinions about a specific topic, and that activity may be followed by an explicit grammatical lesson, or vice versa. Several FonF studies have been conducted in such contexts where the overall emphasis is determined at the level of classroom activity (Ellis, Basturkmen, & Loewen, 2001a, 2001b; Loewen, 2003, 2004).

Ellis (2006) argues that communicative and learning contexts, as he calls them, constitute a dichotomy, rather than poles on a continuum. By that definition, most language classes, apart from content-based or immersion ones, presumably have an overall context of L2 learning rather than a primary emphasis on communication. That is, the main purpose of a school or course is to teach language and students come to learn language. However, within the school or course context, the types of classes and activities that learners engage in may have different foci. Thus the contextual emphasis of specific activities might clearly be on meaning or form, but other activities may blur that line. Additionally, Batstone (2006) argues that patterns of classroom discourse in which the teacher is seen to value linguistic accuracy can create a predisposition among students to pay attention to form, even in more meaning-focused contexts.

Because of the high priority that FonF places on an overall emphasis on meaning, it is important to consider how the operationalization of context might influence the effectiveness of FonF. In considering the merits of each context, it seems that each overlooks specific issues. For example, Ellis's proposition of context at the level of classroom activity ignores the larger course and curricular contexts. If a communicative activity is preceded by several FonFS activities, will learners view the communicative activity as truly communicative? In addition, learners who are at a language school to learn the L2 (which is often conceptualized as learning grammar) may view communicative activities as simply another opportunity to learn more about the language. In contrast, it is unclear how an overarching communicative syllabus influences learners' perceptions of grammar activities, such as those suggested in Spada and Lightbown's isolated FFI. The line between isolated FFI and FonFS seems a very fine one. The question to investigate, then, is how does a primary emphasis on meaning at the curricular, course, or classroom activity level influence the effects of FonF?

How Explicit Should FonF Be?

Another important consideration for FonF is its degree of obtrusiveness or explicitness. FonF is supposed to draw learners' attention to form as they are experiencing a communicative need, thereby optimizing the learning potential by combining attention to input, learner internal processes, and output in productive ways (Long, 1991, 1996). While proponents of FonF agree that noticing is essential, there is controversy regarding the explicitness of FonF necessary to induce learners' noticing. On the one hand, it is important not to disrupt the communicative flow of the activity, which would call for implicit types of FonF (Doughty & Varela, 1998; Long, 2007). On the other hand, implicit types of FonF may not be salient to learners, and therefore more explicit interventions may be necessary for FonF to be effective (Lyster, 1998a; Ellis, Loewen, & Erlam, 2006).

Several researchers have proposed that explicitness should be viewed as a continuum rather than a dichotomy, with various FonF options being placed on that continuum. For example, more implicit types of FonF would include input flood, input enhancement, and recasts, while more explicit FonF could include metalinguistic feedback, consciousness-raising tasks, structured input, and the combination of several types of FonF (Doughty, 2003; Doughty & Williams, 1998c; Nassaji & Fotos, 2007; Norris & Ortega, 2000). These methodological options will be considered in more detail below; however, some of the latter are so explicit that there are arguments about whether or not they constitute FonF or FonFS.

Considerable research has gone into comparing FonF activities with differing degrees of explicitness. Much of this research has been conducted with corrective feedback, and several recent studies have found that while implicit feedback such as recasts can be effective for L2 learning, more explicit types of feedback have an even greater effect (Ellis et al., 2006; Sauro, 2009; Sheen, 2007). Norris and Ortega's (2000) meta-analysis results also favored explicit treatment; however, the possible bias due to the types of testing instruments used in the studies is acknowledged, and Doughty (2003) argues that the case of explicit instruction is overstated.

One attempt to combine the issues related to context and explicitness is the counterbalance hypothesis (Lyster, 2007; Lyster & Mori, 2006), which states that

> instructional activities and interactional feedback that act as a counterbalance to the predominant communicative orientation of a given classroom setting will be more facilitative of interlanguage restructuring than instructional activities and interactional feedback that are congruent with the predominant communicative orientation.
>
> (Lyster & Mori, 2006, p. 294)

Thus, the contrast between a communicative activity and a brief attention to a language item can help learners notice and potentially benefit from such a focus.

How Intensive Should FonF Be?

Related to explicitness is the issue of the intensity of the FonF. Intensity can be operationalized as how frequently a specific linguistic form is focused on, with repeated focuses being more intensive and possibly more salient to learners. In Long's (1991) original definition of FonF, attention to language was brief and in reaction to learner errors, with the idea being that many forms might be targeted on only one, or maybe two, occasions. This type of spontaneously-provided FonF corresponds with what Ellis (2001) calls incidental FonF, and its occurrence, both reactive and proactive, has been documented in several different L2 classroom contexts (Ellis et al., 2001a, 2001b; Loewen, 2004; Lyster, 1998a, 1998b; Lyster & Ranta, 1997; Sheen, 2004; Yoshida, 2008). However, it is difficult to experimentally investigate the effectiveness of something that occurs spontaneously, particularly since it is not possible to test learners' prior knowledge of such forms. Consequently, quasi-experimental studies of FonF have tended to investigate linguistic structures that the researchers had chosen ahead of time (e.g., Doughty & Varela, 1998; Long, Inagaki, & Ortega, 1998; Mackey & Philp, 1998). However, the effects of such planned FonF may differ from those of incidental FonF because the former is intensive and targets only one or two structures but on multiple occasions, whereas the latter is extensive, targeting many linguistic structures with each structure receiving attention on only one or two occasions (Ellis, 2001).

In considering the nature of planned FonF, it is possible that the issue of planning distracts from the more important distinction of intensity of focus. Although planning is important from a pedagogical perspective, it is not a theoretically interesting construct for FonF since it is not the teachers' prior decision to target specific forms that affects learners' interlanguage systems. Rather it is the amount of focus that learners receive on a specific linguistic item as a result of that prior decision that potentially influences the impact of different types of FonF. For this reason, FonF in Figure 35.1 is divided into intensive and extensive categories, rather than planned and incidental as Williams (2005) proposed.

The intensity of FonF may be measured in several ways. Traditionally, studies of FonF have reported the amount of time spent on the treatment, with studies typically ranging from between 30 minutes to over 120 minutes. In these cases, length of treatment has stood as a proxy for intensity, and indeed length of treatment has been found to be a significant variable in the effectiveness of FonF (Norris & Ortega, 2000). Most recently, Li's (2010) meta-analysis of corrective feedback found that treatments of 50 minutes or less had a significantly higher effect size than did longer treatments.

Nevertheless, the length of treatment may not necessarily correspond with the actual amount of time spent focusing on a specific linguistic item. Researchers are beginning to acknowledge this issue by, for example, documenting how many instances of feedback are provided to learners during treatment sessions (e.g., Loewen & Nabei, 2007). In addition, some studies have investigated the intensity of FonF as an independent variable. For example, Havranek (2002) examined linguistic items that received just one correction, versus those that received two, three, or more corrections. Her individualized testing did not find different effects for single and multiple corrections. Additionally, Ellis, Sheen, Murakami, and Takashima (2008) investigated what they called focused and unfocused recasts in which two groups of learners received differing amounts of feedback on the same error. They found no differences between the two groups, although the difference in the average number of corrections on the target structure was not large (5.4 corrections for the focused group and 3.7 for the unfocused feedback group). Finally, Grim (2008) examined the effects of planned FonF, incidental FonF, and focus on meaning in helping second- and third-semester French students learn specific grammar, vocabulary, and culture content. He concluded that while the planned FonF group performed slightly better than the other two groups on the immediate posttest, there were no significant differences on the delayed tests.

Although these few studies suggest limited differences between intensive and extensive FonF, Ellis (2008) suggests that a key factor in the effectiveness of FFI and FonF is the length of treatment, and he asserts that treatments of less than one or two hours may not be effective, particularly if the treatment is directed at complex structures. Nevertheless, the logical conclusion of Long's (1991, 1996) definition of FonF is that even a single focus on a language item may influence the learning process. Therefore, empirical evidence from additional studies investigating both intensive and extensive FonF is needed.

When Should a FonF Occur?

The issue of problematicity is central to the definition of FonF (Long, 1991, 2007; Williams, 2005), and it provides a guide for when to focus on form. FonF is supposed to occur because of a learner problem. This design feature helps contrast it with FonFS where specific linguistic structures are taught regardless of learners' needs. Long (2007) argues that evidence of learner difficulty with a structure, coupled with teachers' intuitions about the learnability of that structure, combine to provide attention to language at a time when learners are developmentally ready. Furthermore, the reactive nature of FonF anticipates that meaning will already be evident to the learner, thereby freeing up attentional resources for the learner to notice form–meaning connections. The need to communicate effectively is also argued to draw learners' attention to the necessary forms (Long, 2007).

In spite of Long's (1991, 2007) insistence that FonF is by definition reactive, subsequent studies have argued that FonF can occur in predetermined ways (Ellis, 2001; Ellis et al., 2001b; Spada, 1997). As has already been discussed, it is possible for teachers to preselect specific linguistic items that are considered to be problematic for learners and then to intensively correct learners' errors in the use of those items. Numerous studies of corrective feedback have employed this option (Doughty & Varela, 1998; Long et al., 1998; Mackey & Philp, 1998, among others). An additional possibility is for teachers to make note of problematic linguistic items and then design a subsequent FonF activity to target the items.

Another type of proactive FonF that occurs in anticipation of an error is what Ellis et al. (2001b) called teacher-initiated FonF. In this option, the teacher chooses to focus on a language item, even though no error in production has occurred. Thus, teachers are anticipating that learners will have problems. Williams (2005) rejects this as a type of FonF stating that it does not meet the requirement of problematicity. It is true that teachers may not be entirely accurate in predicting which forms learners will have difficulty with and that teachers may be relying on their intuitions in trying to predict problematic items for the learners. However, it is presumably those same intuitions, based on previous interaction with numerous L2 learners that help teachers in creating other proactive FonF activities. Furthermore, even if teachers design FonF activities targeting a linguistic item identified as problematic for a specific learner, it does not mean that the item will be problematic for all learners. Thus, further investigation into the issue of problematicity may help determine in which manner linguistic "problems" should be addressed.

While problematicity has often been considered in terms of grammatical structures, other aspects of language can also be targeted in FonF. Descriptive studies (Ellis et al., 2001a; Loewen, 2005; Lyster & Ranta, 1997) have found that grammar, vocabulary, and pronunciation all receive FonF in the classroom. In addition, experimental studies have investigated the effects of FonF on vocabulary (de la Fuente, 2006; Laufer, 2005, 2006; Laufer & Girsai, 2008), as well as pronunciation (Trofimovitch & Gatbonton, 2008; Arteaga, Herschensohn, & Gess, 2003) and pragmatics (Lyster, 1994).

Several issues arise when considering the problematicity of grammatical items. For instance, Ellis (2006) suggests that FFI on simple morphological structures will be more effective than treatment directed at complex structures. Additionally, Spada and Lightbown (2008) discuss factors that might influence a choice between whether a grammatical feature should receive isolated or integrated FFI, suggesting that more problematic structures may need more explicit attention. For example, isolated FFI may be necessary for grammatical structures that are difficult due to L1 influence. Examples of such structures would include English adverb placement (White, 1991) and possessive pronoun gender (Ammar, 2008; Ammar & Spada, 2006; Spada, Lightbown, & White, 2005) for French L1 speakers. Other grammatical structures that may necessitate more obtrusive FonF are those with low salience, low communicative value or low frequency in the input. Additionally, isolated FFI may be more appropriate for lower proficiency learners, older learners, lower aptitude students, and those students and teachers who prefer such an approach.

Another way of dealing with problematic features is to provide attention that contrasts an L2 feature with an L1 feature, drawing attention to the similarities and differences. Several studies have found such contrastive emphasis to be helpful for learning (Laufer & Girsai, 2008; Spada et al., 2005).

Who Should Initiate a FonF?

A further variable in FonF is who initiates it (Nassiji & Fotos, 2007; Williams, 2005). Generally it has been considered to be the job of the teacher (or researcher) to initiate FonF, particularly if there is to be an intensive focus on a specific linguistic form. Indeed, the preceding questions in this chapter have assumed that it is the teacher who initiates the FonF. Nevertheless, it is possible for students to focus on form as well, and several such possiblities will now be considered.

Reactive FonF usually consists of the teacher providing corrective feedback to learners' errors; however, it is also possible for students to correct each other. Studies investigating peer corrective feedback have found that while students do correct each other, they do so considerably less frequently than do teachers (Oliver, 2000; Zhao & Bitchener, 2007), and although there is some concern that students may provide incorrect feedback, there is evidence to suggest that their feedback is generally accurate (Adams, 2007).

In addition to reactive FonF, students may also initiate proactive FonF. Student-initiated FonF occurs when learners query a linguistic item during a communicative activity, even though no error in production has occurred (Ellis et al., 2001b). One proposed benefit of student-initiated FonF is that students themselves focus on linguistic items that they identify as problematic. Studies of student-initiated FonF have found that it does occur in communicative L2 interaction (Alcón, 2007; Ellis et al., 2001b; Williams, 1999), although younger learners may ask about linguistic items less frequently than do older ones (van den Branden, 2008). When students do initiate questions about form, they generally focus on vocabulary and they ask questions primarily of their teachers (Alcón & Garcia Mayo, 2008; Ellis et al., 2001b; Williams, 1999; Zhao & Bitchener, 2007). In addition, higher proficiency learners tend to ask more questions and appear to benefit more from the attention to form (Williams, 2001). Finally, Alcón and Garcia Mayo (2008) found strong, positive correlations among noticing, uptake, and individualized test scores for student-initiated FonF; however, Loewen (2006) found no significant differences in posttest scores following reactive and student-initiated FonF.

Given these studies, it is clear that students can and do take initiative in raising attention to language forms. Indeed, student topicalization, in which students, rather than teachers, nominate a specific topic of attention, is argued to be beneficial for learning (Slimani, 1989); this argument is borne out by several of the previously mentioned studies that reported accurate production on subsequent posttests of the language items queried by students.

What FonF Options Are Available in the L2 Classroom?

Having considered some of the more theoretically-based issues regarding FonF, we can turn to pedagogical concerns. Various FonF instructional options will be considered in turn, going from more implicit to more explicit types of FonF. In addition, these options will be considered in relation to their position on the taxonomy of instructed SLA in Figure 35.1. It should be noted that several instructional options have been referred to by various researchers as constituting either FonF or FonFS. In this chapter, a fairly strict interpretation of FonF will be used to classify instructional activities; however, instructional types that have been classified as both FonF and FonFS will also be briefly discussed.

Input Flood

One of the most implicit types of FonF is input flood (also known as enriched input). In this option communicative tasks are seeded with specific grammatical structures or vocabulary in the hope that the increased frequency of the forms will be salient to learners or that learners will produce errors in the targeted forms that can then receive corrective feedback. As such, it is an example of an intensive, proactive type of FonF because there are usually multiple tokens of the same form in the input and the decision of which forms to focus on is made ahead of time.

There have not been many studies of input flood by itself, and those that compare it to input enhancement will be considered in the next section. However, one study, Trahey and White (1993), found that input flood was enough for French learners of English to learn the correct placement of adverbs, but it was not enough to help them avoid making an incorrect, L1 transfer-related error. In a more recent study of input flood, Loewen, Erlam, and Ellis (2009) considered learners' ability to benefit from substantial exposure to English third person -s during FFI activities targeting English articles. Results did not indicate any increase in learners' accuracy scores.

Input Enhancement

A slightly more explicit option than input flood is input enhancement, which involves increasing the visual (or auditory) effect of specific linguistic items in the input (Sharwood Smith, 1993). Input enhancement can take the form of bolding, underlining, capitalization, italics, color, etc. Research on input enhancement has investigated the effects of different types of enhancement as well as its effectiveness in comparison to other types of FonF. For example, Simard (2009) compared seven different types of input enhancement with a comparison group, and found that the use of capital letters and a combination of three cues resulted in the best test scores. Jourdenais, Ota, Stauffer, Boyson, and Doughty (1995) found that learners in an input enhancement condition reported higher levels of noticing than did an input flood group, while Leeman, Arteagoitia, Fridman, and Doughty (1995) found that their input enhancement group outperformed an input flood group in the accurate use of Spanish preterit and imperfect tenses.

In a recent meta-analysis of 20 visual input enhancement studies, Lee and Huang (2008) found a very small effect size difference between input enhancement and input flood. There was also a small, but negative effect for comprehension, suggesting that input enhancement can distract from the meaning of the text. Lee and Huang also concluded that most input enhancement studies have not included a true control group, but rather made comparisons with groups that received input flood. Finally, in a review of input enhancement research, Han, Park and Combs (2008) note the need for studies that investigate the effects of input enhancement in relation to noticing, comprehension, and learning.

Corrective Feedback

As previously stated, corrective feedback has received considerable attention as a type of FonF. Corrective feedback occurs in response to learners' production errors during communicative activities, and the correction can take the form of a recast, elicitation, or metalinguistic feedback. Recasts tend to be more implicit, but they provide the correct form for the learners (Ellis & Sheen, 2006; Loewen & Philp, 2006; Long, 2007; Sheen, 2006). Elicitations provide an opportunity for learners to self-correct, and thus are argued to be better for L2 learning (Lyster, 2004). Metalinguistic feedback is more explicit, which may interrupt the communicative flow, but this type of feedback makes the error more noticeable (Ellis et al., 2006). Russell and Spada's (2006) recent meta-analysis of corrective feedback found it to be more effective than no feedback; however, they did not have a sufficient number of studies to compare the various types of feedback. Studies that have compared different types of feedback have produced varying results. In general, corrective feedback appears to be beneficial and it would seem that more explicit feedback options may be somewhat more effective.

Corrective feedback may occur in several positions in the taxonomy of FonF. It is always reactive; however, it may be either extensive or intensive, depending on whether it is targeting multiple, different errors or concentrating on only one or two errors. In addition, extensive feedback can be given by either the teacher or students.

Planning Time

Planning time is generally associated with studies of accuracy, fluency, and complexity in learner L2 production during communicative tasks (Ellis, 2003), and as such it has not been generally associated with FonF. However, Mochizuki and Ortega (2008) argue that the provision of guided planning time may help draw learners' attention to language items during subsequent communicative activities. As such, the provision of planning time would be a type of extensive, proactive, teacher-initated, general type of FonF.

FFI

There are a number of instructional activities, such as dictogloss, structured input, and consciousness-raising tasks, that have been, at one time or another, labeled as FonF; however, by strict definition, they arguably should not be considered FonF activities because they do not maintain an overall emphasis on meaning with only brief attention to language form. On the other hand, these instructional activities do not fit the strict definition of FonFS either because they do not generally present linguistic structures in a discrete, isolated fashion apart from a reference to meaning. Rather, they appear to have an equal focus on both meaning and form at the same time. If FonF and FonFS were seen as two ends of a continuum rather than as a dichotomy, then these activities would fall somewhere in the middle of that continuum. In Doughty and Williams's (1998c) continuum of obtrusiveness, the change from FonF to non-FonF activities, as defined above, seems to coincide with a change in two features: learning condition and the inclusion of metalinguistic information. Thus, FonF activities could be classified as inductive and without metalinguistic information, while non-FonF activities would be deductive and include metalinguistic information. These types of activities will be considered briefly.

One such activity is dictogloss in which students hear a passage and then work in pairs or groups to reconstruct it (Wajnryb, 1990; Swain & Lapkin, 2001). As students work to reconstruct the meaning of the text, they may encounter difficulties in producing accurately the forms that realize their intended meanings, and thus a focus on form ensues. While dictogloss has been classified by some as a FonF activity, its primary goal is the reconstruction of a linguistic text. However, within the activity, learners may notice gaps between their own interlanguage resources and the language necessary to reconstruct the text.

Another type of instruction that has been classified as a type of FonF is consciousness-raising tasks (Doughty & Williams, 1998c); however, Ellis (2003) states that "the desired outcome of a [consciousness-raising] task is awareness of how some linguistic feature works" (p. 163). In addition, the "content" in consciousness-raising tasks is language itself, with learners talking about the targeted language feature, similar to how linguists talk about language. In consciousness-raising tasks, learners are given exemplars of targeted linguistic items and are expected to induce rules about the forms. Therefore, consciousness-raising tasks do not appear to conform to a strict definition of FonF by having a primary emphasis on meaning.

Another instructional activity that has been categorized as both FonF and FonFS is structured input, which is a type of enriched input that requires learners to demonstrate that they have comprehended the target structure (Ellis, 2008). Ellis (2001) explicitly classifies structured input as a type of FonFS "because it is designed to enable learners to give primary attention to form rather than meaning" (p. 19); however, in Ellis (2006) he classifies structured input as a type of FonF. One specific type of structured input is processing instruction (VanPatten, 2002), which identifies a faulty processing strategy, draws learners' attention to this inaccurate strategy, and provides input for the learners that will help them process the input appropriately. Again, if we follow the strict definition of FonF, then structured input is excluded; however, there is a strong dual focus on both meaning and form, thus placing it in the middle of a FonF/FonFS continuum.

Combined FonF Options

While it is possible to identify individual treatment options in FFI, often studies incorporate several of them (Ellis, 2006). One of the more common designs is to combine some type of more explicit focus on grammar, either before or after an interactive, communicative task, with communicative activities that include corrective feedback on the targeted structure. For example, Lyster (2004) investigated the effects of FFI with and without different types of corrective feedback. The FFI consisted of enhanced input, awareness raising activities, and practice activities; the corrective feedback consisted of either recasts or prompts. Lyster found that FFI was better than no FFI, and that it was even better when combined with corrective feedback in the form of prompts. In a similar study, Lyster and Izquierdo (2009) found that consciousness-raising exercises coupled with either prompts or recasts were equally effective in improving learners' ability to mark grammatical gender in French. In another study, Muranoi (2000) compared implicit corrective feedback with and without subsequent explicit grammar explanation; he found that feedback followed by FFI showed the greatest effect for learning. In sum, these studies have generally found that combinations of FonF and FFI can also be effective for L2 learning.

Future Directions

In considering the prospects of FFI and FonF research, it appears that this rich vein of investigation will continue in the foreseeable future. An indication of the interest in this area of research is evident in the emerging number of meta-analyses of various FonF topics. However, these meta-analyses have been hampered by the small number of appropriately rigorous studies that could be included, and, as a result, such studies have not been able to directly compare different types of FonF. It is necessary, therefore, for continued high-quality research into the effectiveness of FonF.

Although it is naive to expect that a consistent set of terminology will be used in ongoing research, it is important for researchers to be aware of the varying theoretical and methodological concerns that underlie the FonF options they investigate in order to ensure valid comparisons. For example, there are different possibilities regarding the overall emphasis on meaning that constitutes the context in which FonF is conducted. It is important to investigate and compare the nature and effectiveness of FonF in curricular, course, and classroom activity contexts. In this respect, the counterbalance hypothesis (Lyster, 2007; Lyster & Mori, 2006) is beginning to address this issue. In addition, Spada and colleagues are conducting studies which compare integrated and isolated FFI (Spada, Barkaoui, Peters, So, & Valeo, 2009). It is also possible to examine students' and teachers' perceptions of the primary focus of the contexts and activities in which they are involved. Several studies have begun to use stimulated recall (Gass & Mackey, 2000) or post-activity interviews to comparing students' and teachers' perceptions of corrective feedback (Kim & Han, 2007).

Another unresolved issue related to FonF, and indeed to instructed SLA more generally, concerns the level of explicitness that is optimal for L2 learning. Additional studies are necessary to further tease out the effects of explicit and implicit types of FonF. For example, how does the intensity of the focus influence the salience of various forms and what level of frequency is most effective for which linguistic items?

In conclusion, I would echo Williams's (2005, p. 687) statement that "sometimes FonF works; sometimes it does not". The role of research is to continue to investigate which variables contribute to the effectiveness of FonF in order to better inform both SLA theory and pedagogy.

References

Adams, R. (2007). Do second language learners benefit from interacting with each other? In A. Mackey (Ed.), *Conversational interaction in second language acquisition* (pp. 29–52). Oxford: Oxford University Press.

Alcón, E. (2007). Incidental focus on form, noticing and vocabulary learning in the EFL classroom. *International Journal of English Studies, 7*(2), 41–60.

Alcón, E., & Garcia Mayo, M. (2008). Incidental focus on form and learning outcomes with young foreign language classroom learners. In J. Philp, R. Oliver, & A. Mackey (Eds.), *Second language acquisition and the younger learner: Child's play?* (pp. 173–192). Amsterdam: John Benjamins.

Ammar, A. (2008). Prompts and recasts: Differential effects on second language morphosyntax. *Language Teaching Research, 12*(2), 183–210

Ammar, A., & Spada, N. (2006). One size fits all? Recasts, prompts and L2 learning. *Studies in Second Language Acquisition, 28*(4), 543–574.

Arteaga, D., Herschensohn, J., & Gess, R. (2003). Focusing on phonology to teach morphological form in French. *The Modern Language Journal, 87*(1), 58–70.

Batstone, R. (2006). A role for discourse frames and learner interpretation in focus on form. *New Zealand Studies in Applied Linguistics, 12,* 50–63.

de la Fuente, M. (2006). Classroom L2 vocabulary acquisition: Investigating the role of pedagogical tasks and form-focused instruction. *Language Teaching Research, 10*(3), 263–295.

Doughty, C. (2003). Instructed SLA: Constraints, compensation, and enhancement. In C. Doughty & M. Long (Eds.), *The handbook of second language acquisition* (pp. 256–310). Malden, MA: Blackwell.

Doughty, C., & Varela, E. (1998). Communicative focus on form. In C. Doughty & J. Williams (Eds.), *Focus on form in classroom second language acquisition* (pp. 114–138). Cambridge: Cambridge University Press.

Doughty, C., & Williams, J. (1998a). *Focus on form in classroom second language acquisition.* Cambridge: Cambridge University Press.

Doughty, C., & Williams, J. (1998b). Issues and terminology. In C. Doughty & J. Williams (Eds.), *Focus on form in classroom second language acquisition* (pp. 1–12). Cambridge: Cambridge University Press.

Doughty, C., & Williams, J. (1998c). Pedagogical choices in focus on form. In C. Doughty & J. Williams (Eds.), *Focus on form in classroom second language acquisition* (pp. 197–262). Cambridge: Cambridge University Press.

Ellis, R. (2001). Introduction: Investigating form-focused instruction. *Language Learning, 51*(Supplement 1), 1–46.

Ellis, R. (2002). Does form-focused instruction affect the acquisition of implicit knowledge?: A review of the research. *Studies in Second Language Acquisition, 24,* 223–236.

Ellis, R. (2003). *Task-based language learning and teaching.* Oxford: Oxford University Press.

Ellis, R. (2006). Researching the effects of form-focussed instruction on L2 acquisition. *AILA Review, 19,* 18–41.

Ellis, R. (2008). *The study of second language acquisition, 2nd edition.* Oxford: Oxford University Press.

Ellis, R., Basturkmen, H., & Loewen, S. (2001a). Learner uptake in communicative ESL lessons. *Language Learning, 51*(2), 281–318.

Ellis, R., Basturkmen, H., & Loewen, S. (2001b). Pre-emptive focus on form in the ESL classroom. *TESOL Quarterly, 35*, 407–432.

Ellis, R., Loewen, S., & Erlam, R. (2006). Implicit and explicit corrective feedback and the acquisition of L2 grammar. *Studies in Second Language Acquisition, 28*, 339–368.

Ellis, R., & Sheen, Y. (2006). Reexamining the role of recasts in second language acquisition. *Studies in Second Language Acquisition, 28*(4), 575–600.

Ellis, R., Sheen, Y., Murakami, M., & Takashima, H. (2008). The effects of focused and unfocused written corrective feedback in an English as a foreign language context. *System, 36*(3), 353–371.

Gass, S. (1997). *Input, interaction, and the second language learner.* Mahwah, NJ: Lawrence Erlbaum Associates.

Gass, S., & Mackey, A. (2000). *Stimulated recall methodology in second language research.* Mahwah, NJ: Lawrence Erlbaum Associates.

Gass, S., & Mackey, A. (2007). Input, interaction and output in second language acquisition. In B. VanPatten & J. Williams (Eds.), *Theories in second language acquisition: An introduction* (pp. 175–200). Mahwah, NJ: Lawrence Erlbaum Associates.

Grim, F. (2008). Integrating focus on form in L2 content-enriched instruction lessons. *Foreign Language Annals, 41*(2), 321–346.

Han, Z., Park, E., & Combs, C. (2008). Textual enhancement of input: Issues and possibilities. *Applied Linguistics, 29*(4), 597–618.

Havranek, G. (2002). When is corrective feedback most likely to succeed? *International Journal of Educational Research, 37*, 255–270.

Housen, A., & Pierrard, M. (2005). *Investigations in instructed second language acquisition.* New York: Mouton de Gruyter.

Jourdenais, R., Ota, M., Stauffer, S., Boyson, B., & Doughty, C. (1995). Does textual enhancement promote noticing?: A think-aloud protocol analysis. In R. Schmidt (Ed.), *Attention and awareness in foreign language learning* (pp. 183–216). Honolulu: University of Hawai'i Press.

Kim, J., & Han, Z. (2007). Recasts in communicative EFL classes: Do teacher intent and learner interpretation overlap? In A. Mackey (Ed.), *Conversational interaction in second language acquisition* (pp. 269–297). Oxford: Oxford University Press.

Krashen, S. (1982). *Principles and practice in second language acquisition.* Oxford: Pergamon.

Krashen, S. (1985). *The input hypothesis: Issues and implications.* London: Longman.

Krashen, S. (1994). The input hypothesis and its rivals. In N. Ellis (Ed.), *Implicit and explicit learning of languages* (pp. 45–77). London: Academic Press.

Krashen, S., & Terrell, T. (1983). *The natural approach: Language acquisition in the classroom.* Oxford: Pergamon.

Laufer, B. (2005). Focus on form in second language vocabulary learning. *EUROSLA Yearbook, 5*, 223–250

Laufer, B. (2006). Comparing focus on form and focus on formS in second-language vocabulary learning. *The Canadian Modern Language Review/La Revue canadienne des langues vivantes, 63*(1), 149–166.

Laufer, B., & Girsai, N. (2008). Form-focused instruction in second language vocabulary learning: A case for contrastive analysis and translation. *Applied Linguistics, 29*, 694–716.

Lee, S., & Huang, H. (2008). Visual input enhancement and grammar learning: A meta-analytic review. *Studies in Second Language Acquisition, 30*, 307–331.

Leeman, J., Arteagoitia, I., Fridman, B., & Doughty, C. (1995). Integrating attention to form with meaning: Focus on form in content-based Spanish instruction. In R. Schmidt (Ed.), *Attention and awareness in foreign language learning* (pp. 217–259). Honolulu: University of Hawai'i Press.

Li, S. (2010). The effectiveness of corrective feedback in SLA: A meta-analysis. *Language Learning, 60*(2), 309–365.

Loewen, S. (2003). Variation in frequency and characteristics of incidental focus on form. *Language Teaching Research, 7*, 315–345.

Loewen, S. (2004). Uptake in incidental focus on form in meaning-focused ESL lessons. *Language Learning, 54*(1), 153–187.

Loewen, S. (2005). Incidental focus of form and second language learning. *Studies in Second Language Acquisition, 27*, 361–386.

Loewen, S. (2006). Autonomy and language learning behaviour: The role of student initiation in meaning-focused L2 lessons. In T. Lamb & H. Reinders (Eds.), *Supporting Independent Language Learning: Issues and Options* (pp. 37–53). Peter Lang.

Loewen, S., Erlam, R., & Ellis, R. (2009). The incidental acquisition of third person -s as implicit and explicit knowledge. In R. Ellis, S. Loewen, C. Elder, R. Erlam, J. Philp, & R. Reinders (Eds.), *Implicit and explicit knowledge in second language learning, testing and teaching* (pp. 262–280). Bristol: Multilingual Matters.

Loewen, S., & Nabei, T. (2007). Measuring the effects of oral corrective feedback on L2 knowledge. In A. Mackey (Ed.), *Conversational interaction in second language acquisition* (pp. 361–378). Oxford: Oxford University Press.

Loewen, S., & Philp, J. (2006). Recasts in the adult English L2 classroom: Characteristics, explicitness, and effectiveness. *The Modern Language Journal, 90*, 536–556.

Long, M. (1991). Focus on form: A design feature in language teaching methodology. In K. de Bot, R. Ginsberg, & C. Kramsch (Eds.), *Foreign language research in cross-cultural perspective* (pp. 39–52) Amsterdam: John Benjamins.

Long, M. (1996). The role of the linguistic environment in second language acquisition. In W. Ritchie & T. Bhatia (Eds.), *Handbook of second language acquisition* (pp 413–468). San Diego: Academic Press.

Long, M. (2007). Recasts in SLA: The story so far. In M. Long (Ed.), *Problems in SLA* (pp. 75–118). Mahwah, NJ: Lawrence Erlbaum Associates.

Long, M., Inagaki, S., & Ortega, L. (1998). The role of implicit negative feedback in SLA: Models and recasts in Japanese and Spanish. *The Modern Language Journal, 82*, 357–371.

Long, M., & Robinson, P. (1998). Focus on form: Theory, research and practice. In C. Doughty & J. Williams (Eds.), *Focus on form in classroom second language acquisition* (pp. 15–41). Cambridge: Cambridge University Press.

Lyster, R. (1994). The effect of functional-analytic teaching on aspects of French immersion students' sociolinguistic competence. *Applied Linguistics, 15*, 263–287.

Lyster, R. (1998a). Recasts, repetition and ambiguity in L2 classroom discourse. *Studies in Second Language Acquisition, 20*(1), 51–81.

Lyster, R. (1998b). Negotiation of form, recasts, and explicit correction in relation to error types and learner repair in immersion classrooms. *Language Learning, 48*(2), 183–218.

Lyster, R. (2004). Differential effects of prompts and recasts in form-focused instruction. *Studies in Second Language Acquisition, 26*, 399–432.

Lyster, R. (2007). *Learning and teaching languages through content: A counterbalanced approach*. Amsterdam: John Benjamins.

Lyster, R., & Izquierdo, J. (2009). Prompts versus recasts in dyadic interaction. *Language Learning, 59*(2), 453–498.

Lyster, R., & Mori, H. (2006). Interactional feedback and instructional counterbalance. *Studies in Second Language Acquisition, 28*, 269–300.

Lyster, R., & Ranta, L. (1997). Corrective feedback and learner uptake: Negotiation of form in communicative classrooms. *Studies in Second Language Acquisition, 19*(1), 37–66.

Mackey, A., & Philp, J. (1998). Conversational interaction and second language development: Recasts, responses and red herrings? *The Modern Language Journal, 82*(3), 338–356.

Mochizuki, N., & Ortega, L. (2008). Balancing communication and grammar in beginning-level foreign language classrooms: A study of guided planning and relativization. *Language Teaching Research, 12*, 11–37.

Muranoi, H. (2000). Focus on form through interaction enhancement: Integrating formal instruction into a communicative task in EFL classrooms. *Language Learning, 50*, 617–673.

Nassaji, H., & Fotos, S. (2007). *Form-focused instruction and teacher education: Studies in honor of Rod Ellis*. Oxford: Oxford University Press.

Norris, J. M., & Ortega, L. (2000). Effectiveness of L2 instruction: A research synthesis and quantitative meta-analysis. *Language Learning, 50*, 417–528.

Oliver, R. (2000). Age differences in negotiation and feedback in classroom and pairwork. *Language Learning, 50*, 119–151.

Pica, T. (2002). Subject-matter content: How does it assist the interactional and linguistic needs of classroom language learners? *The Modern Language Journal, 86*, 1–19.

Russell, J., & Spada, N. (2006). The effectiveness of corrective feedback for the acquisition of L2 grammar: A meta-analysis of the research. In J. Norris & L. Ortega (Eds.), *Synthesizing research on language learning and teaching* (pp. 133–164). Amsterdam: John Benjamins.

Sauro, S. (2009). Computer-mediated corrective feedback and the development of L2 grammar. *Language Learning and Technology, 13*(1), 96–120.

Savignon, S. (2005). Communicative language teaching: Strategies and goals. In E. Hinkel (Ed.), *Handbook of research in second language teaching and learning* (pp. 635–652). Mahwah, NJ: Lawrence Erlbaum Associates.

Schmidt, R. (1995). *Attention and awareness in foreign language learning*. Honolulu: University of Hawai'i Press.

Schmidt, R. (2001). Attention. In P. Robinson (Ed.), *Cognition and second language instruction* (pp. 3–32). Cambridge, Cambridge University Press.

Schwartz, B. (1993). On explicit and negative data effecting and affecting competence and linguistic behavior. *Studies in Second Language Acquisition, 15*, 147–163.

Sharwood Smith, M. (1993). Input enhancement in instructed SLA: Theoretical bases. *Studies in Second Language Acquisition, 15*, 165–179.

Sheen, R. (2003). Focus-on-form—a myth in the making. *ELT Journal, 57*, 225–233.

Sheen, R. (2005). Focus on formS as a means of improving accurate oral production. In A. Housen & M. Pierrard (Eds.), *Investigations in instructed second language acquisition* (pp. 271–310). New York: Mouton de Gruyter.

Sheen, Y. (2004). Corrective feedback and learner uptake in communicative classrooms across instructional settings. *Language Teaching Research*, 8(3), 263–300.

Sheen, Y. (2006). Exploring the relationship between characteristics of recasts and learner uptake. *Language Teaching Research*, 10(4), 361–392.

Sheen, Y. (2007). The effects of corrective feedback, language aptitude and learner attitudes on the acquisition of English articles. In A. Mackey (Ed.), *Conversational interaction in second language acquisition* (pp. 301–322). Oxford: Oxford University Press.

Simard, D. (2009). Differential effects of textual enhancement formats on intake. *System*, 37(1), 124–135.

Skehan, P. (2003). Focus on form, tasks and technology. *Computer Assisted Language Learning*, 16, 391–411.

Slimani, A. (1989). The role of topicalization in classroom language learning. *System*, 17, 223–234.

Spada, N. (1997). Form-focussed instruction and second language acquisition: A review of classroom and laboratory research. *Language Teaching*, 30, 73–87.

Spada, N., Barkaoui, K., Peters, C., So, M., & Valeo, A. (2009). Developing a questionnaire to investigate second language learners' preferences for two types of form-focused instruction. *System*, 37, 70–81.

Spada, N., & Lightbown, P. (2008). Form-focused instruction: Isolated or integrated? *TESOL Quarterly*, 42(2), 181–207.

Spada, N., Lightbown, P., & White, J. (2005). The importance of form/meaning mappings in explicit form-focused instruction. In A. Housen & M. Pierrard (Eds.), *Investigations in instructed second language acquisition* (pp. 199–234). New York: Mouton de Gruyter.

Swain, M., & Lapkin, S. (2001). Focus on form through collaborative dialogue: Exploring task effects. In M. Bygate, P. Skehan, & M. Swain (Eds.), *Researching Pedagogic tasks, second language learning, teaching and testing* (pp. 99–118). Harlow: Longman.

Trahey, M., & White. L. (1993). Positive evidence and preemption in the second language classroom. *Studies in Second Language Acquisition*, 15, 181–204.

Trofimovitch, P., & Gatbonton, E. (2008). Repetition and focus on form in processing Spanish L2 words: Implications for pronunciation instruction. *The Modern Language Journal*, 90, 519–535.

Van den Branden, K. (2006). *Task-based language education*. Cambridge: Cambridge University Press.

Van den Branden, K. (2008). Negotiation of meaning in the classroom: Does it enhance reading comprehension? In J. Philp, R. Oliver, & A. Mackey (Eds.), *Second language acquisition and the younger learner: Child's play?* (pp. 149–169). Amsterdam: John Benjamins.

VanPatten, B. (2002). Processing instruction: An update. *Language Learning*, 52, 755–803.

Wajnryb, R. (1990). *Grammar dictation*. Oxford: Oxford University Press.

White, L. (1991). Adverb placement in second language acquisition: Some effects of positive and negative evidence in the classroom. *Second Language Research*, 7, 133–161.

Williams, J. (1999). Learner-generated attention to form. *Language Learning*, 49, 583–625.

Williams, J. (2005). Form-focused instruction. In E. Hinkel (Ed.), *Handbook of research in second language teaching and learning* (pp. 671–691). Mahwah, NJ: Lawrence Erlbaum Associates.

Yoshida, R. (2008). Teachers' choice and learners' preference of corrective feedback types. *Language Awareness*, 17(1), 78–93.

Zhao, Y., & Bitchener, J. (2007). Incidental focus on form in teacher–learner and learner–learner interactions. *System*, 35, 431–447.

Zyzik, E., & Polio, C. (2008). Incidental focus on form in university Spanish literature courses. *The Modern Language Journal*, 92, 53–70.

36
Corrective Feedback in Language Teaching

Younghee Sheen and Rod Ellis

Corrective feedback (CF) refers to the feedback that learners receive on the linguistic errors they make in their oral or written production in a second language (L2). Both oral and written CF have attracted considerable attention in recent years because of their significance for the development of theories of L2 acquisition and because they have held an important place in L2 pedagogy. We begin with a brief description of what oral and written CF entail and then move on to consider a number of theories of L2 learning where CF holds a central place. We will then consider the key issues that surround the provision of CF in language pedagogy. Finally, we review the empirical research that has investigated oral and written CF.

Types of Corrective Feedback

Oral CF can involve both on-line attempts to make learners aware that they have produced an utterance that contains an error (i.e., the feedback is provided more or less immediately following the utterance that contained an error) and off-line attempts (i.e., the feedback is withheld until the communicative event the learner is participating in has finished). Oral CF can be input-providing (i.e., the learner is supplied with the correct form) or output-prompting (i.e., it can attempt to elicit a correction from the learner). Oral CF can also be implicit as when the teacher simply requests clarification in response to the learner's erroneous utterance or explicit as when the teacher directly corrects the learner and/or provides some kind of metalinguistic explanation of the error.[1] A common form of CF is a recast. Recasts can be conversational and implicit when they take the form of a confirmation check as a response to a failure to understand the learner's utterance or didactic and more explicit when the learner's erroneous utterance is reformulated even though it has not caused a communication problem (see Ellis & Sheen, 2006; Sheen, 2006). Definitions of these different types of oral CF are provided in Table 36.1.

Written CF almost always involves off-line (i.e., delayed) corrections of the errors that students have committed in a written text. As with oral CF, this can involve both input-providing feedback (usually referred to as "direct correction") and output-prompting feedback (referred to as "indirect correction"). Direct correction involves supplying learners with the correct form or reformulating the entire text; indirect correction involves indicating that an error has been committed either in the margin of the text or within the text where the error occurs. Both direct and indirect written CF may or may not be accompanied with metalinguistic information. However, the distinction between

Table 36.1 A Taxonomy of Oral CF Strategies

	Implicit	Explicit
Input-providing	• Conversational recasts (i.e., the correction consists of a reformulation of a student utterance in the attempt to resolve a communication problem; such recasts often take the form confirmation checks where the reformulation is followed by a question tag as in "Oh, so you were sick, were you?").	• Didactic recasts (i.e., the correction takes the form of a reformulation of a student utterance even though no communication problem has arisen). • Explicit correction only (i.e., the correction takes the form of a direct signal that an error has been committed and the correct form is supplied). • Explicit correction with metalinguistic explanation (i.e., in addition to signaling an error has been committed and providing the correct form, there is also a metalinguistic comment).
Output-prompting	• Repetition (i.e., the learner's erroneous utterance is repeated without any intonational highlighting of the error). • Clarification requests (i.e., attention is drawn to a problem utterance by the speaker indicating he/she has not understood it).	• Metalinguistic clue (i.e., a brief metalinguistic statement aimed at eliciting a correction from the learner). • Elicitation (i.e., an attempt is made to verbally elicit the correct form from the learner by, for example, a prompting question). • Paralinguistic signal (i.e., an attempt is made to non-verbally elicit the correct form from the learner).

implicit and explicit CF does not apply in the case of writing; all written CF is necessarily explicit (i.e., the student knows he/she has been corrected—see Sheen, 2010). A description of these written CF strategies is provided in Table 36.2.

Table 36.2 A Taxonomy of Written CF Strategies

	Direct	Indirect
Metalinguistic information	• Provision of the correct form with brief grammatical explanation.	• Use of error code (e.g., symbols such as VT to signal a verb tense error or WO a word order error are inserted into the text). • Use of brief grammatical explanation (e.g., error types are numbered in the text and then a brief explanation of each type of error is provided at the end of the text).
No metalinguistic information	• Provision of the correct form only. • Reformation of the entire sentence or paragraph.	• Errors are indicated but not located and the correct form is not supplied (e.g., a cross is placed in the margin next to the line where an error has occurred). • Errors are indicated and located but the correct form is not supplied (e.g., an error is underlined in the place in the text in which it occurs).

Theoretical Positions

Corrective feedback is addressed in just about every theory of L2 acquisition. However, in this section we will consider only those theories that view CF as making a major contribution to L2 acquisition (i.e., we will not consider theories that claim that CF has no or only a very limited role). We feel this is justified given the very substantial empirical evidence now available that shows that CF can affect acquisition (see later sections in this chapter).

Cognitive Theories of Corrective Feedback

The main cognitive theoretical perspectives are the Interaction Hypothesis (Long, 1983, 1996), the Output Hypothesis (Swain, 1985, 1995) and the Noticing Hypothesis (Schmidt, 1994, 2001). Table 36.3 below provides a brief account of these hypotheses. They come together in what Long (1991) termed "focus on form," of which CF is one manifestation. They also figure in skill-acquisition theory (Johnson, 1996), which emphasizes the importance of learners receiving feedback in the context of the real-life behaviors they are trying to learn. However, rather than examining these different theories in detail, we will offer a composite account of how cognitive theories see CF as facilitating L2 acquisition.

Cognitive theories emphasize the fact that CF assists acquisition when the participants are focused primarily on meaning, commit errors and receive feedback that they recognize as corrective. In this way, learners receive information not just about linguistic form but also about form-meaning mappings (i.e., they are able to see how a particular linguistic form realizes a particular meaning in context). An example will make this clear:

S1: What do you spend with your wife?
T: What?
S1: What do you spend your extra time with your wife?
T: Ah, how do you spend?
S2: How do you spend.

(Ellis & Sheen, 2006, p. 581)

Here Student 1 (S1) asks the teacher a question about how he spends time with his wife but erroneously uses "what" instead of "how." This elicits a request for clarification from the teacher (T), to which S1 responds by extending his original utterance but with the same error. T then recasts S1's utterance and this is uptaken by Student 2 (S2). In this way the learners are able to see that the meaning they wish to convey in this context requires the use of the linguistic form "how," not "what."

Table 36.3 Three Hypotheses That Inform Cognitive Accounts of Corrective Feedback

Hypothesis	Description
Interaction Hypothesis	This claims that the negotiation of meaning that occurs when a communication problem arises results in interactional modifications that provide learners with the input needed for L2 learning.
Output Hypothesis	This claims that learners also learn from their own output when this requires them to "stretch their interlanguage in order to meet communicative goals" (Swain, 1995, p. 127).
Noticing Hypothesis	This claims that L2 learning is enhanced when learners pay conscious attention to specific linguistic forms in the input to which they are exposed.

In this example, corrective feedback occurred as a result of a communicative breakdown. That is, it involved "negotiation of meaning." However, it can also occur when the teacher (or another learner) chooses to focus attention on form even though no communication breakdown has taken place, as in this example also taken from Ellis and Sheen (2006, p. 292):

S: Korean is more faster.
T: Is faster.
S: Is faster than English.

Here the learner makes the common error of double marking a comparative adjective ("more faster"). The teacher clearly understands the learner but goes ahead and provides the explicit correction ("is faster"). This results in the learner's modified uptake ("is faster than English"). In this case, the CF is "didactic" rather than "conversational" and involves "negotiation of form."

In both cases, CF works by causing learners to notice the errors they have committed. In particular, it affords an opportunity for them to "notice-the-gap," i.e., to compare their own production with that provided for them in the CF move. CF may also assist acquisition when learners have the opportunity to repair/correct their initial error following the CF move. This is known as "uptake"; it constitutes one type of "modified output" (as illustrated in the examples above). It may help learners to rehearse the correct form in their short-term memory and consolidate a form-function mapping and thus enable them to incorporate the corrected feature more fully into their interlanguage. However, the role of uptake/modified ouput remains controversial, with some researchers (e.g., Lyster, 1998a) suggesting it is beneficial and others (e.g., Long, 2007) arguing that CF promotes acquisition through the input it provides rather than through opportunities for modifying output.

Cognitive theories also make claims about the type of CF strategy most likely to enhance acquisition but, again, the claims are conflicting. Long (1996, 2007) argues that recasts are especially beneficial in that they provide learners with positive evidence of what is correct as well as negative evidence showing an error has been committed and minimally disturb the focus on communication. Lyster (2004) makes a theoretical case to suggest that what he calls "prompts" (i.e., CF strategies that elicit a self-repair/correction from the learner) are more effective than recasts. Other theorists have argued that explicit feedback (e.g., involving metalinguistic information) is especially effective as it not only induces noticing of an error and its correction but also fosters understanding of the nature of the error.

Cognitive theories seek to account for how CF assists acquisition in interaction. Thus, a key feature of such theories is that the feedback is provided on-line in what Doughty (2001) has called "a window of opportunity" (i.e., at a time that the learner is cognitively primed to attend to the correction). Doughty argues that feedback needs to be attended to more or less immediately if it is to activate the cognitive mechanisms responsible for acquisition.

Cognitive theories have generally sought to account for how oral CF assists acquisition. Constructs such as "negotiation of meaning," "negotiation of form" and "window of opportunity" apply primarily to oral CF. However, cognitive theories can also be applied to written CF. For example, as illustrated in Sheen (2010), the distinction between "input-providing" and "output-prompting" CF is equally applicable to both oral and written CF. So too are the key notions of "noticing" and "noticing-the-gap." Even "uptake/modified output" can be applied to written CF if learners are given the opportunity to incorporate corrections into a second draft (revision) of their written text. As already noted, written CF is invariably explicit and thus is perhaps more likely to invite metalinguistic understanding of an error.

Cognitive theories, therefore, can account for how CF works in both oral and written communication. The differences between the two media also afford a means of testing some of the claims made about CF (e.g., whether CF can only produce change in the learner's L2 system if it is provided on-line in "a window of opportunity").

Corrective Feedback in Sociocultural Theory

In sociocultural theory (SCT), learning is "participation" rather than "acquisition"; that is, it is mediated by and is evident in social interaction rather than in the mind of the learner. Thus, to explicate how SCT views CF it is necessary to understand how participation in interaction creates affordances for learning. According to SCT, there is no single set of characteristics of social interaction that constitute affordances for all learners. Rather, affordances arise out of the successful tailoring of the interaction to the developmental level of individual learners. They occur when the interaction enables the participants to construct a "zone of proximal development" for the learner—that is, the learners come to be able to perform a language feature through the scaffolding provided by an interlocutor when they are not able to do so independently. The aim of interaction (including corrective feedback) is to assist the learner to move from other-regulation in the zone of proximal development to self-regulation, where the learner is finally able to use a linguistic feature correctly without assistance. According to this view of CF, what constitutes a facilitative form of correction for one learner might not be so for another, either because it is pitched at a level too far in advance of the learner or because it fails to "stretch" the learner by posing a sufficient challenge.

This approach to the mediating role of CF is well represented in Aljaafreh and Lantolf's (1994) study. They developed a "regulatory scale" to reflect the extent to which a tutor's oral feedback on the errors students had made in their writing was implicit or explicit. For example, asking learners to find and correct their own errors was considered an implicit strategy, while providing examples of the correct pattern was highly explicit. An intermediate level occurred when the tutor indicated the nature of an error without identifying it for the learner. Aljaafreh and Lantolf showed how the degree of scaffolding provided by the tutor for a particular learner in oral conferences diminished (i.e., the help provided became more implicit over time). This was possible because the learners assumed increased control over the L2 and therefore needed less assistance. Aljaafreh and Lantolf identified a number of general principles governing the effectiveness of CF: (1) it must be graduated—no more help than is necessary should be provided at any single time; (2) it must be contingent—it must reflect actual need and be removed when the learner demonstrates an ability to function independently; and (3) it is dialogic—it involves dynamic assessment of a learner's Zone of Proximal Development.

An SCT view of corrective feedback is also reflected in Poehner and Lantolf's (2005) account of "dynamic assessment." Some examples from Poehner's (2008) research with advanced learners of L2 French will illustrate this. Poehner asked the learners to construct a past-tense oral narrative in French after watching a short video-clip. They were given no feedback or mediation in this first task. Then they repeated the task after watching a second clip. This time "they interacted with a mediator who offered suggestions, posed questions, made corrections, and helped them think through decisions concerning selection of lexical items, verb tense, and other language difficulties" (Poehner & Lantolf, 2005, p. 246). This interactive assistance, which was provided in English, was "highly flexible, emerging from the interaction between the student and the mediator" (Poehner & Lantolf, 2005, p. 246). For example, in the case of one learner, the teacher initially used quite direct clues (for example, "in the past") and subsequently, when addressing the same linguistic problem, more indirect means (for example, "there's something there with the verb").

In SCT corrective feedback is seen as a key element in how teachers (or other learners) can assist a learner to achieve self-regulation through self-correction and thereby ultimately learn how to use a feature correctly without assistance. Two points need to be emphasized. First, a SCT perspective on corrective feedback rejects the view adopted in cognitive accounts, namely that it is possible to identify specific corrective strategies that are the most effective in promoting learning. Rather, SCT emphasizes the importance of varying the strategies employed to suit the developmental level of the learner. Second, as Aljaafreh and Lantolf's (1994) and Poehner and Lantolf's (2005) studies make clear, CF in this theoretical framework is necessarily oral in nature. It is not clear how written CF can be tailored to the learner's developmental level given that there is typically no opportunity to engage in social interaction when teachers correct and simply return their students' written work.

Pedagogical Positions

The key issues facing teachers and teacher educators were identified by Hendrickson in 1978 while Chaudron (1988) reviewed research that has addressed these issues. These issues are still current today. Here we will focus on what teacher educators and teachers have had to say about these issues, noting that there is considerable disagreement evident in their opinions.

Should Learner Errors Be Corrected?

Hendrickson's (1978) review article focused on oral CF. He argued that teachers should definitely correct learners' oral errors. This conclusion was based on both theoretical grounds (i.e., CF helps learners to engage in the process of hypothesis testing) and on empirical grounds (i.e., studies had shown that students wished to be corrected). However, not all language teaching methods view CF so positively. Ur (1996) summarized the position adopted by different methods. She noted that errors in audiolingualism need to be prevented so that bad habits do not develop and, for this reason, "negative assessment" plays little part in learning and ideally should be avoided. In humanistic methods, "assessment should be positive or non-judgmental" in order to "promote a positive self-image of the learner as a person and language learner," while in skill theory "the learner needs feedback on how well he or she is doing" (Ur, 1996, p. 243). In the post-method era, methodologists are more likely to affirm the need for oral CF, recognizing the cognitive contribution it can make while also issuing warnings about the potential affective damage it can cause. Ur concluded that "there is certainly a place for correction" but "we should not over-estimate this contribution" (1996, p. 255) because it often fails to eliminate errors and concluded that she would rather invest time in avoiding errors than in correcting them.

Similar differences in opinion exist where written CF is concerned as is evident in the debate between Truscott and Ferris (Truscott, 1996, 1999, 2007; Ferris 1999, 2004). Truscott, reflecting the views of teachers who adhere to process theories of writing, advanced the strong claim that correcting learners' errors in a written composition may enable them to eliminate the errors in a subsequent draft but has no effect on grammatical accuracy in a new piece of writing (i.e., it does not result in acquisition). Ferris (1999) disputed this claim, arguing that it was not possible to dismiss correction in general as it depended on the quality of the correction—in other words, if the correction was clear and consistent it could work for acquisition. Truscott (1999) replied by claiming that Ferris (1999) failed to cite any evidence in support of her contention. Writers of handbooks for teachers almost invariably adopt Ferris' (2004) position in arguing that there is a need for teachers to correct their students' written work. However, they also point out the danger of over-correcting and the importance of providing feedback on other aspects of writing (e.g., content and organization) as well as linguistic problems. How to balance content-correction and corrective feedback is a major issue where writing is concerned. Indeed, as Ferris (2003a) noted a common refrain is that teachers focus too much on correcting linguistic errors at the expense of content and organization.

When Should Learner Errors Be Corrected?

In the case of oral CF, teachers are faced with the choice of either correcting immediately following the learner's erroneous utterance or delaying the correction until later. Teacher educators often distinguish between "accuracy" and "fluency" work, arguing that CF has a place in the former but not in the latter. Harmer (1983), for example, argued that when students are engaged in communicative activity, the teacher should not intervene by "telling students that they are making mistakes, insisting on accuracy and asking for repetition etc." (p. 44). Bartram and Walt (1991) similarly argued that students should not be interrupted while speaking. Hedge (2000) listed a number of techniques that can be used in delayed CF (e.g., recording an activity and then asking students to identify and correct their own errors or simply noting down errors as students perform an activity and going through these afterwards). Teachers also appear to favor delayed correction in fluency work. Basturkmen, Loewen and Ellis (2004) found language teachers believed that it was best not to correct students during a communicative activity. However, they also found that the teachers did not always conform to this belief in their actual practice of CF. Rolin-Ianzati (2010) identified two different approaches that teachers of L2 French used when providing delayed feedback following a role-play activity—they either initiated repair by the student or simply reviewed the errors students had made. She argued that initiating repair was a more effective strategy as it led to more self-repair by the students.

When to correct is less of an issue in written CF as correction is nearly always delayed to some extent—unless, as in Aljaafreh and Lantolf's (1994) study, teachers ask students to read out their written text and correct errors orally. However, the issue of timing arises in process writing instruction where students produce multiple drafts. Teachers need to decide whether to stage their feedback, focusing initially on content and organization and only in later drafts on linguistic errors. McGarrell and Verbeen (2007) argue that corrective feedback should be delayed as it constitutes a form of assessment that may deter students from revising their ideas and organization of the text.

Which Learner Errors Should Be Corrected?

A key issue is whether teachers should aim to correct all the linguistic errors in a text or only some. Selective correction is widely promoted by language teaching methodologists (e.g., Byrne, 1988; Edge, 1989; Raimes, 1983; Ferris, 1999). Various proposals—relevant to both oral and written CF—have been advanced regarding which errors to correct. Some methodologists have suggested that teachers should focus only on "errors" and ignore "mistakes" as these are merely performance phenomena (see Corder (1967) for a discussion of this distinction). Another favored approach is to recommend correcting "global" rather than "local" errors (Burt, 1975) on the grounds that the former are more likely to interfere with communication. Global errors are errors that affect overall sentence organization while local errors are errors that affect single elements in a sentence (for example, errors in morphology). Krashen's (1982) proposal that CF should be limited to features that are simple and portable (i.e., "rules of thumb") and therefore "learnable" has also attracted attention from methodologists.

In fact, none of these proposals is easy to implement in practice. The distinctions between an "error" and a "mistake" and a "local" and "global" error are not as clear-cut as Corder (1967) and Burt (1975) made out. There is no widely accepted theory of grammatical complexity to help teachers decide which rules are simple and portable. Hard-pressed teachers may not have the time to ascertain which features are problematic. As Truscott (1996) noted, there is good reason to doubt teachers' ability to engage systematically with selective correction.

A different approach to selective correction, however, does hold out more promise. Teachers can elect to focus on one specific category of error (i.e., adopt what Sheen (2007a) called "focused corrective feedback"). For example, they could correct just past-tense errors at one time and article errors at another. As the review of the research below shows, focused correction has been the approach adopted in experimental studies of both oral and written CF.

How Should Learner Errors Be Corrected?

A feature of teachers' actual practice of CF is its inconsistency and lack of precision. Inconsistency arises when teachers respond variably to the same error made by different students in the same class, correcting some students and ignoring others. Such inconsistency is not necessarily detrimental, however, for, as Allwright (1975) pointed out, it may reflect teachers' attempts to cater for individual differences among the students.

Reflecting this, teacher educators have been understandably reluctant to prescribe or proscribe the strategies that teachers should use. In part this is because they are uncertain as to which strategies are the effective ones. But it also almost certainly reflects their recognition that the process of correcting errors is a complex one, involving a number of competing factors. The approach adopted by Ur (1996) is to raise a number of questions for teachers to consider and then to offer answers based on her own practical teaching experience.

Who Should Correct Learner Errors?

Teachers are often advised to give students the opportunity to self-correct and, if that fails, to invite other students to perform the correction (e.g., Hedge, 2000). Such advice can be seen as part and parcel of the western educational ideology of learner-centeredness.

Some CF strategies automatically place the burden of correction on the learner—for example, signaling an error by means of a clarification request or by simply repeating the erroneous utterance. In the case of written CF, "indirect correction" (e.g., indicating the presence of an error without supplying the correct form or using an error-coding system to signal the general category of an error) constitutes a half-way house—the teacher takes on some responsibility for correcting but leaves it up to the individual student to make the actual correction.

There are, however, a number of problems with learner self-correction. First, learners typically prefer the teacher do the correction for them. Second, and more importantly, learners can only self-correct if they possess the necessary linguistic knowledge. Other (typically teacher) correction will be necessary to enable learners to identify forms that have not yet been acquired. Third, although output-prompting CF strategies signal that there is some kind of problem with the learner's utterance they do not make it clear that the problem is a linguistic one (as opposed to just a communicative one). Thus, there are clear grounds (theoretical and practical) for encouraging self-correction but this will not always be possible, as methodologists such as Hedge acknowledge. This poses teachers with a conundrum—should they push the learner to self-correct or provide the correction directly themselves? One solution sometimes advocated to this problem is to conduct CF as a two-stage process: first encourage self-correction and, if that fails, provide the correction. Such an approach is, of course compatible with a SCT view of CF.

Another alternative is peer-correction. Methodologists generally endorse the importance of allowing learners opportunities to correct their fellow learners' oral errors. However, peer correction has been more extensively practiced in the case of writing. Ferris (2003b) reports that first language (L1) writing scholars (many of whom are skeptical of the value of teacher correction) give "nearly unqualified endorsement" (p. 15) to peer-correction. She also notes that many L2 process writing methodologists (e.g., Zamel, 1985) are similarly in favor of peer-correction. However, Hyland and Hyland (2006) advise against "idealizing L2 peer group interactions as sites of constructive interaction, since the reality can be quite different" (p. 6) while Ferris (2003b) herself argues that students need careful training in how to conduct a peer review.

Two points emerge from this brief review of pedagogical positions regarding CF. The first is that CF is a very complex issue with no simple rules-of-thumb available to guide teachers. The second, a corollary of the first point, is that considerable disagreement exists over how best to conduct CF. Hyland and Hyland (2006) rightly point out that CF is "a form of social action designed to accomplish educational and social goals" (p. 10) and for this reason needs to be viewed contextually. Thus there can be no single set of guidelines for conducting either oral or written CF that is appropriate for all instructional contexts. Nor, we would argue, is it likely that research will provide definitive answers to the pedagogical questions that Hendrickson (1978) raised. It can, however, illuminate the issues involved, and suggest possible strategies that teachers can explore in their own contexts.

Research into Corrective Feedback

Studies of oral and written CF have been conducted separately with almost no reference to each other. For this reason we will consider them separately here.

Oral Corrective Feedback

We will focus exclusively on the classroom-based CF research. The research has been both interpretative (i.e., descriptive and ethnographic) and confirmatory (i.e., correlational and experimental) in design.

Much of the earlier research was descriptive. A number of studies (e.g., Allwright, 1975; Chaudron, 1977; Long, 1977) set out to develop typologies of CF strategies with a view to identifying which strategies teachers typically used and how consistent they were in their use of them. This work has carried on into recent times. In an often cited study, Lyster and Ranta (1997), for example, identified the strategies used by teachers in French immersion classrooms in Canada. A feature of this more recent research has been to examine the frequency with which the different strategies are used. Lyster and Ranta reported that recasts were by far the preferred means of correcting students. Seedhouse (1997), who examined classroom repair sequences, also found that teachers generally showed a preference for mitigated, indirect forms of correction (e.g., recasts) rather than more direct forms (e.g., explicit correction). However, other studies have shown considerable variation in teachers' handling of errors both within and across classrooms. Van Lier (1988), for example, showed that the type of repair work reflects the nature of the context which the teacher and learners jointly create. Seedhouse (2004) emphasized that there is "no single, monolithic organization of repair in the L2 classroom" (p. 179), with the type of organization varying depending on whether the pedagogic focus is on accuracy or fluency. Sheen (2004) reported significant differences in the types of CF in four macro teaching contexts (Canada immersion, Canada English as a second language (ESL), New Zealand ESL and Korea English as a foreign language (EFL)). The frequency of recasts, for example, varied significantly from one context to the next. Explicit correction was rare in Canada ESL classes but quite common in New Zealand ESL ones. This descriptive/ethnographic research has provided a useful set of categories for investigating CF and also demonstrated the complexity of CF as an interactional phenomenon.

Recasts have received special attention from researchers. In a descriptive study, Sheen (2006) distinguished a number of different characteristics of recasts. They can occur in a single-move or multiple-move. Single-move recasts can vary in terms of mode, scope, whether they are reduced or not reduced, the number of changes made to the learner's utterances, the type of change and the linguistic focus. For example, the recast in the following sequence can be coded in terms of mode

(= declarative), scope (= isolated), reduction (= non-reduced), length (= clause), number of changes (= one change), type of change (= addition), and linguistic focus (= grammar).

S: I think she'll travel together her boyfriend after the course.
T: I think she'll travel together with her boyfriend.

(Sheen, 2006, p. 372)

Such a description is useful because it enables researchers to examine the relationship between different types/characteristics of recasts and learner repair (i.e., whether the learner's response successfully incorporates the correction) and acquisition (i.e., whether as a result of exposure to a recast the learner is subsequently able to use the corrected form more accurately). Studies that have attempted this will be considered below.

Reflecting the complexity of CF, research has shown that teachers are often inconsistent and imprecise in how they correct learner errors. Long (1977) noted that teachers often give more than one type of feedback simultaneously and that often their feedback moves go unnoticed by the students. Yoshida's (2008) study helps to explain why teachers vary in the practice of CF. This study used a stimulus recall interview to examine teachers' choice of and learners' preferences for different CF types. The findings shed light on when and why teachers use recasts, elicitation and metalinguistic feedback. For example, the teachers claimed they used recasts because of the time limitation of classes and in response to learners' differing cognitive styles. On the other hand, the teachers stated they used prompts (e.g., elicitation or metalinguistic clue) when they felt sure that the learner was able to self-correct the error. Also most of the student participants Yoshida interviewed preferred to receive output-prompting CF before recasts so that they had the chance to work out and correct their errors themselves.

Correlational studies have examined the relationship between different types of CF and learner uptake/repair (e.g., Sheen, 2004; Lyster & Mori, 2006) and between uptake and acquisition (e.g., Williams, 2001; Loewen, 2005). This research has been motivated by Schmidt's (1994) Noticing Hypothesis, Swain's (1995) Output Hypothesis and Long's (1991, 1996) claims regarding the importance of focus on form. Thus, corrective feedback is hypothesized to facilitate acquisition if learners first notice the correction and second repair their own erroneous utterance, especially when this occurs in a context where they are primarily focused on meaning rather than form.

Lyster (1998b) found that learner repair of lexical and grammatical errors was more likely after elicitations, requests for clarification, and metalinguistic clues (all examples of output-prompting CF—see Table 36.1) than other types. Sheen (2004), in the study referred to above reported that New Zealand ESL and Korea EFL produced significantly higher uptake and repair following recasts than Canada Immersion and Canada ESL, suggesting that recasts do not necessarily lead to less uptake in instructional contexts where teachers and students are oriented towards language as form. Lyster and Mori (2006) also reported differences in uptake and repair according to instructional context, in this case two different immersion contexts—French immersion in Canada and Japanese immersion in Japan. They advanced the "counterbalance hypothesis," which predicts that the extent to which different CF strategies lead to uptake/repair is influenced by whether the overall instruction orients learners to attend to form as it did in Japan but not in Canada. Oliver and Mackey (2003) found differences according to the specific contexts found within child ESL classrooms with uptake more frequent in explicit language contexts and least frequent in management-related exchanges. Thus, as with corrective feedback itself, uptake and repair have been shown to be highly variable.

Studies that have investigated the relationship between uptake and acquisition have reported mixed results. Loewen (2005) found that learners' successful uptake in classroom-based communicative lessons was a strong predictor of their ability to subsequently correct their errors in tailor-made tests administered to individual students. Loewen and Philp (2006) investigated the effect of different characteristics of recasts (e.g., linguistic focus, length, number of changes, segmentation) on individual learners' uptake and acquisition, as measured by tailor-made tests. They found that those recasts with explicit linguistic characteristics were more likely to result in both uptake and learning. McDonough and Mackey (2006), however, found no evidence that the learners' repetitions of recasts assisted acquisition although they did find that what they called "primed production" (i.e., the learner correctly produced the corrected form within six turns of the recast that provided it) predicted acquisition.

Classroom-based experimental studies have focused on investigating the effects of two broad types of oral CF—implicit vs. explicit and input-providing vs. output-prompting (see Table 36.1 for the specific corrective strategies involved). Ellis, Loewen and Erlam (2006) compared the effects of implicit CF in the form of recasts and explicit CF in the form of metalinguistic comments on adult ESL learners' acquisition of regular past tense. In the implicit CF, the teacher simply recast the verb in the past tense as in this example:

S: Yesterday two boys, Joe and Bill visit their rich uncle
T: Visited
S: Visited their rich uncle.

(Ellis et al., 2006, p. 362)

In the explicit CF, the teacher repeated the learner's error and then provided a metalinguistic clue:

S: Yesterday Joe and Bill ah went to ah Bill's grandmother and visit their grandmother
T: and visit—you need past tense
S: Visited, yes.

(Ellis et al., 2006, p. 362)

This study found no effect for either treatment on the immediate post-tests but the students receiving the explicit CF outperformed both the control group and the group receiving implicit feedback on the delayed post-tests. The tests were designed to provide measures of both implicit and explicit L2 knowledge. Sheen (2007b) compared the effects of implicit CF in the form of recasts and explicit CF in the form of explicit correction together with metalinguistic comments on adult ESL learners' acquisition of definite and indefinite articles. Whereas the explicit correction resulted in significant gains in learning in both immediate and post-tests, the implicit did not. Thus, in a classroom context, it would appear that explicit CF is more effective.

Other experimental studies have investigated the relative effects of input-providing and output-prompting CF. Lyster (2004) investigated grade 5 French immersion learners, comparing the effects of recasts (as an input-providing strategy) and a mixture of output-prompting CF strategies (including explicit CF) on the acquisition of gender marking on articles and nouns. Both groups also received initial form-focused instruction (FFI). There was also a group that just received the FFI (i.e., no CF) and a control/comparison group. The FFI-prompt group was the only group to outperform the control group on all eight measures of acquisition. The FFI-recast group outperformed the control group on five out of eight measures while the FFI-only group outperformed control group on four out eight measures. Statistically significant differences were found between the FFI-prompt and FFI-only groups but not between FFI-recast and FFI-prompt groups. Ammar and Spada (2006) investigated learners in grade 6 intensive ESL classes, comparing the effects of recasts and prompts on their acquisition of possessive pronouns. They found that the high proficiency learners benefitted equally from both types of CF but that the prompts were more effective than the recasts with the low proficiency learners. These studies suggest that output-prompting feedback is more effective than input-providing feedback although, clearly, this can only be true for learners who have at least begun to acquire the target feature.

Researchers have also explored the role of computer-mediated corrective feedback involving recasts (e.g., Loewen & Erlam, 2006; Sachs & Suh, 2007; Sauro, 2009; Smith, 2005). Smith (2005) found no relationship between degree of uptake (with or without repair) and the acquisition of L2 vocabulary items by intermediate-level ESL learners, who participated in computer-mediated communication based on jigsaw tasks. Loewen and Erlam (2006) compared recasts and metalinguistic prompts during group text-chat interaction and found that neither type of CF resulted in significantly greater gains in linguistic accuracy than no CF. Sachs and Suh compared enhanced and non-enhanced recasts, reporting no difference in learning gains for these two types of recasts. However, Sauro's (2009) study produced results more favorable to computer-mediated CF. She reported that two different types of CF (recasts and metalinguistic prompts) did not differ in the learning gains they produced but did have a positive effect on learners' short-term development of L2 grammar. There is a need for studies that compare traditional face-to-face oral CF and synchronous computer-mediated CF.

It is not easy to reach clear conclusions about such issues as the importance of uptake/repair or the type of CF most likely to promote acquisition. One reason is that many other variables that interact with the feedback are involved. Sheen (2008), for example, reported that recasts do result in acquisition but only in learners with low foreign language speaking anxiety. Individual difference factors and contextual factors will clearly influence whether, how and when oral CF is effective. For this reason, the idea of an overall "best" CF strategy may prove to be a chimera (Ellis, 2010). Overall, however, there is now clear evidence that oral CF—in one form or another—can benefit acquisition.

Written Corrective Feedback

Teacher feedback received a bad press in the 1980s and early 1990s. Ferris and Hedgcock (2005) list the following adjectives that L1 researchers used to describe the nature of teachers' feedback: "exercise in futility" (Knoblauch & Brannon, 1981, p. 1), "arbitrary, idiosyncratic" (Sommers, 1982, p. 149), "overly directive, removing students' rights to their own texts" (Ferris & Hedgcock, 2005, p. 186), and "short, careless, exhausted, or insensitive comments" (Connors & Lunsford, 1993, p. 215). However, Ferris and Hedgcock (2005) pointed out that this negative view of teacher feedback arose from critiques of feedback directed at justifying a grade or at providing very general comments to assist students when revising their drafts and ignored the fact that written CF can serve other functions.

Descriptive studies that have examined the relationship between teacher feedback and students' revisions have employed analytic models (Hyland & Hyland, 2001). For example, Ferris (1997), in a study that employed such a model, found that students were able to revise 73% of the grammatical errors teachers corrected. She further reported that her students (1) revised consistently and successfully following feedback involving form, (2) revised less successfully following comments about content or questions seeking further information, and (3) revised or did not revise irrespective of whether the teacher attempted to hedge on critical comments.[2]

A number of studies of students' perceptions have been conducted using survey and self-report data (e.g., Cohen & Cavalcanti, 1990; Ferris, 1995; Hedgcock & Lefkowitz, 1994, 1996; Leki, 1991). These studies have consistently shown that learners value teacher feedback highly and believe that it helps improve their writing. More specifically, students prefer comments that explain specific problems in their texts and make concrete suggestions about how to revise them. Conversely, they report that teachers' short, general comments are not very helpful, especially when these take the form of content-related questions.

Leki (1991) found that most students desired to be corrected by their teachers. Hedgcock and Lefkowitz (1994) also reported that both ESL and foreign language (FL) learners have a positive attitude toward written CF. In comparing ESL and FL students, however, they noted that whereas FL students tend to prefer CF directed at grammar, the lexicon and mechanics of their written texts to feedback directed at content and style, ESL students expressed a preference toward feedback on the content and organization of their writing. In other words, the learning context may determine how learners respond to the CF they receive. Furthermore, as Conrad and Goldstein (1999) rightly pointed out, students may differ individually in their reaction to feedback depending on such factors as language aptitude, learning style, personality and motivation. Hyland's (2000) case study showed how a learner's own values and preferences influenced the use made of the CF received from the teacher.

These different assumptions about written CF and learners' differing preferences may explain why teachers practice CF the way they do. However, according to a recent study by Lee (2009), a considerable gap exists between teachers' beliefs and their practice of CF. She reported that while teachers reported they were selective in correcting errors, they often adopted a comprehensive approach to correcting errors. They also indicated a preference for indirect CF but in practice frequently used direct correction.

Discussions of written CF have centered on whether or not it is effective in helping improve learners' linguistic accuracy. In a controversial paper, Truscott (1996) concluded that written grammar correction has no effect on L2 acquisition and, in some cases, may even be harmful and thus should be abandoned. Truscott emphasized the fact that teachers' feedback is unsystematic and arbitrary and concluded that teachers could serve L2 writers better by helping them with the content of their writing and by providing reading activities that will enhance writing abilities. He argued for the complete abandonment of written CF. As noted earlier in this chapter, this conclusion has been challenged by a number of L2 writing researchers and practitioners (e.g., Chandler, 2003; Ferris, 1999, 2004).

This debate has spawned a number of empirical studies of written CF using quasi-experimental designs to investigate if CF is effective and which types of CF are more effective. These studies fall into three major categories: (1) studies that have examined the effect of CF on learners' revised texts; (2) studies that have compared different types of CF—e.g., feedback on form vs. feedback on content, direct CF vs. indirect CF, error codes vs. underlining; and (3) studies that have investigated the effect of CF on new pieces of writing over time. While studies in category (1) are of obvious relevance to L2 writing teachers, they do not shed any light on whether written CF facilitates L2 acquisition. As Sheen (2007a) and Truscott (2007) pointed out, the fact that students are able to edit their papers when revising does not constitute evidence that they will be able to transfer this skill to a new piece of writing. Nor do studies in category (2) demonstrate that written CF affects acquisition unless they included a control group.

Much of the earlier research that responded to the Truscott/Ferris debate sought to compare the effects of different types of error feedback. In particular, they examined different ways in which direct feedback (where errors are indicated and corrected) and indirect feedback (where errors are just indicated) are provided to L2 writers (e.g., Chandler, 2003; Ferris & Roberts, 2001; Robb, Ross & Shortreed, 1986; Semke, 1984). These studies produced mixed and inconclusive findings. They were dismissed by Truscott (2004) because they did not include a control group, making it impossible to say whether any gains in accuracy were the result of the feedback or simply of practice in writing and general exposure to the L2. The studies all had another feature in common—they all examined unfocused written CF (i.e., CF that was directed broadly at many types of linguistic errors) and in this respect differed from oral CF research, which as we have seen typically examined focused CF.

A number of recent studies (e.g., Bitchener, 2008; Sheen, 2007a) have set out to investigate focused CF and to address the methodological problems evident in the earlier written CF research by including a control group in a pre-test/post-test design. These studies have shown that focused CF does lead to gains in linguistic accuracy and also that the more explicit the feedback is, the bigger the benefit for the students. Sheen (2007a), for example, measured students' progress over time (in post-tests and delayed post-tests) and also included a control group (which received no feedback at all) and reported that both direct CF and direct + metalinguistic CF led to significant gains in accuracy, with the latter having a stronger effect than the former. However, these studies of focused CF have all investigated the same grammatical feature—English articles—so it is not clear whether focused CF will prove generally effective in improving learners' linguistic accuracy. What they do suggest is that written CF, when focused on a single feature, can be effective and thus this constitutes evidence to refute Truscott's (1996, 2004) claims.

From a pedagogic standpoint, given that the practice of written CF is generally unfocused in nature, it is important to examine the *relative* efficacy of unfocused and focused CF. Only two studies to date have addressed this, both using English definite and indefinite articles as the target feature. Ellis, Sheen, Murakami and Takashima (2008) failed to find any difference between unfocused and focused CF, both proving to be equally effective. However, as they admitted, this may have been because the distinction between the two types of CF in this study was not made sufficiently clear. Sheen, Wright and Moldawa (2009) overcame this problem by carefully distinguishing unfocused and focused CF. They also, importantly, investigated the effects of CF not just on a single grammatical feature (articles) but also on a broader range of features. Their results led to the conclusion that unfocused CF is of limited pedagogical value and that much can be gained by focused CF where grammatical accuracy in L2 writing is concerned.

It is likely that the debate concerning the value of written CF will continue. One or two studies showing that focused written CF can lead to acquisition are unlikely to convince the skeptics. So, clearly, more research is needed. Also, it will be necessary to show that written CF does not have some of the negative effects that Truscott (1996, 2007) has considered likely—for example, on students' fluency in writing.

Conclusion

Recently a number of meta-analyses of empirical CF studies have been published (Lyster & Saito, 2010; Mackey & Goo, 2007; Norris & Ortega, 2000; Russell & Spada, 2006; Li, 2010). By and large, these meta-analyses point to the importance of taking into account various moderating factors, such as feedback type, error type, interaction type, mode (oral/written/computer-mediated), L2 instructional contexts, age, gender, proficiency, L1 transfer, schema, anxiety and cognitive abilities, which in turn influence the extent to which CF can be beneficial to L2 learners. In other words, they support the position we have adopted in our review—namely that CF constitutes a highly complex *social* activity.

We conclude with some general statements about what is currently known about CF that can inform pedagogic practice:

1. Learners almost invariably express a wish to be corrected.
2. CF—both oral and written—is effective in assisting learners to improve their linguistic accuracy over time; in other words, CF promotes acquisition.
3. The positive effect of CF is evident not just in careful, planned language use where learners are able to make use of their explicit knowledge of L2 features, but also in meaning-centered, unplanned language use, which calls for implicit knowledge.
4. There is no clear evidence that CF needs to be provided on-line—in a "window of opportunity"—in order to impact on interlanguage development. The clearest evidence for this comes

from the fact that written CF (which is invariably delayed) has shown to be effective. Both on-line/immediate and off-line/delayed CF can promote linguistic development.

5. In general, the types of CF that have the greatest impact on L2 development in a classroom context are those that are explicit and output-prompting rather than implicit and input-providing. For example, explicit feedback in conjunction with metalinguistic clues is more likely to result in learning than recasts.

6. For CF to work for acquisition, learners must be conscious that they are being corrected. CF that is conducted in the guise of some other speech act (for example, a confirmation check or a discourse-supporting move) may not be seen as corrective and, as a result, be ineffective.

7. One function of CF is to assist the learner to self-correct (i.e., to uptake the correction by repairing the error). While the role of self-correction in oral language use and of revision in writing remains to be clearly established, there is increasing evidence to suggest that when learners do self-correct, learning is more likely to occur.

8. If learner self-correction is the goal of CF, then this might be best achieved by means of CF that is fine-tuned to individual learners' level of L2 development and their capacity to benefit from CF. One way in which this might be achieved is by teachers systematically probing for the most implicit form of CF that will enable the learner to self-correct.

Corrective feedback constitutes an area where the discourses of theory and practice can comfortably rub shoulders. It affords an ideal area for researchers and teachers to engage in collaborative enquiry.

Notes

1. The distinction between implicit and explicit oral CF strategies is less clear when the CF is off-line (delayed). Arguably, delayed oral CF is invariably explicit as it will be clear to the students that the focus is on correcting errors.
2. Hedging strategies teachers use include: (1) lexical hedges (e.g., *maybe, please*); (2) syntactic hedges (e.g., "Can you add an example here?"); and (3) positive softeners (e.g., "You've raised some good points, but …").

References

Aljaafreh, A., & Lantolf, J. (1994). Negative feedback as regulation and second language learning in the zone of proximal development. *Modern Language Journal, 78*, 465–483.

Allwright, R. (1975). Problems in the study of the language teacher's treatment of learner error. In M. Burt & H. Dulay (Eds.), *On TESOL '75: New directions in language learning, teaching, and bilingual education* (pp. 96–109). Washington, DC: TESOL.

Ammar, A., & Spada, N. (2006). One size fits all? Recasts, prompts, and L2 learning. *Studies in Second Language Acquisition, 28*, 543–574.

Bartram, M., & Walt, R. (1991). *Correction: Mistake management: A positive approach for language teachers.* Hove: Language Teaching Publications.

Basturkmen, H., Loewen, S. & Ellis, R. (2004). Teachers' stated beliefs about incidental focus on form and their classroom practices. *Applied Linguistics, 25*, 243–272.

Bitchener, J. (2008). Evidence in support of written corrective feedback. *Journal of Second Language Writing, 17*, 102–118.

Burt, M. (1975). Error analysis in the adult EFL classroom. *TESOL Quarterly, 9*, 53–63.

Byrne, D. (1988). *Teaching writing skills.* London: Longman.

Chandler, J. (2003). The efficacy of various kinds of error feedback for improvement in the accuracy and fluency of L2 student writing. *Journal of Second Language Writing, 12*, 267–296.

Chaudron, C. (1977). A descriptive model of discourse in the corrective treatment of learners' errors. *Language Learning, 27*, 29–46.

Chaudron, C. (1988). *Second language classrooms: Research on teaching and learning.* Cambridge: Cambridge University Press.

Cohen, A., & Cavalcanti, M. (1990). Feedback on written compositions: Teacher and student verbal reports. In B. Kroll (Ed.), *Second language writing: Research insights for the classroom* (pp. 155–177). Cambridge: Cambridge University Press.

Connors, R., & Lunsford, A. (1993). Teachers' rhetorical comments on student papers. *College Composition and Communication, 44*, 200–223.

Conrad, S., & Goldstein, L. (1999). ESL student revision after teacher-written comments: Text, contexts, and individuals. *Journal of Second Language Writing, 8*, 147–179.

Corder, P. (1967). The significance of learners' errors. *International Review of Applied Linguistics, 5*, 161–170.

Doughty, C. (2001). Cognitive underpinnings of focus on form. In P. Robinson (Ed.), *Cognition and second language instruction* (pp. 206–257). Cambridge: Cambridge University Press.

Edge, J. (1989). *Mistakes and correction.* New York: Longman.

Ellis, R. (2010). Cognitive, social, and psychological dimensions of corrective feedback. In R. Batstone (Ed.), *Sociocognitive perspectives on language use and language learning* (pp. 151–165). Oxford: Oxford University Press.

Ellis, R., Loewen, S. & Erlam, R. (2006). Implicit and explicit corrective feedback and the acquisition of L2 grammar. *Studies in Second Language Acquisition, 28*, 339–368.

Ellis, R., & Sheen, Y. (2006). Re-examining the role of recasts in L2 acquisition. *Studies in Second Language Acquisition, 28*, 575–600.

Ellis, R., Sheen, Y., Murakami, M. & Takashima, H. (2008). The effects of focused and unfocused written corrective feedback in an English as a foreign language context. *System, 36*, 353–371.

Ferris, D. (1995). Teaching ESL composition students to become independent self-editors. *TESOL Journal, 4*(4), 18–22.

Ferris, D. (1997). The influence of teacher commentary on student revision. *TESOL Quarterly, 31*, 315–339.

Ferris, D. (1999). The case for grammar correction in L2 writing classes: A response to Truscott (1996). *Journal of Second language Writing, 8*, 1–10.

Ferris, D. (2003a). Responding to writing. In B. Kroll (Ed.), *Exploring the dynamics of second language writing* (pp. 119–140). Cambridge: Cambridge University Press.

Ferris, D. (2003b). *Response to student writing: Implications for second language students.* Mahwah, NJ: Lawrence Erlbaum.

Ferris, D. (2004). The "grammar correction" debate in L2 writing: Where are we and where do we go from here. *Journal of Second Language Writing, 13*, 49–62.

Ferris, D., & Hedgcock, J. (2005). *Teaching ESL composition: Purpose, process, and practice.* Mahwah, NJ: Erlbaum.

Ferris, D., & Roberts, B. (2001). Error feedback in L2 writing classes: How explicit does it need to be? *Journal of Second Language Writing, 10*, 161–184.

Harmer, J. (1983). *The practice of English language teaching.* London: Longman.

Hedgcock, J., & Lefkowitz, N. (1994). Feedback on feedback: Assessing learner receptivity to teacher response in L2 composing. *Journal of Second Language Writing, 3*, 141–163.

Hedgcock, J., & Lefkowitz, N. (1996). Some input on input: Two analyses of student response to expert feedback on L2 writing. *Modern Language Journal, 80*, 287–308.

Hedge, T. (2000). *Teaching and learning in the language classroom.* Oxford: Oxford University Press.

Hendrickson, J. (1978). Error correction in foreign language teaching: Recent theory, research and practice. *Modern Language Journal, 62*, 387–398.

Hyland, F. (2000). ESL writers and feedback: Giving more autonomy to students. *Language Teaching Research, 4*, 33–54.

Hyland, F., & Hyland, K. (2001). Sugaring the pill: Praise and criticism in written feedback, *Journal of Second Language Writing, 10*(3), 185–212.

Hyland, K., & Hyland, F. (2006). Contexts and issues in feedback on L2 writing: An introduction. In K. Hyland & F. Hyland (Eds.), *Feedback in second language writing: Contexts and issues* (pp. 1–19). Cambridge: Cambridge University Press.

Johnson, K. (1996). *Language teaching and skill learning.* Oxford: Blackwell.

Knoblauch, C., & Brannon, L. (1981). Teacher commentary on student writing: The state of the art. *Freshman English News, 10*, 1–4.

Krashen, S. (1982). *Principles and practice in second language acquisition.* Oxford: Pergamon.

Lee, I. (2009). Ten mismatches between teachers' beliefs and written feedback practice. *ELT Journal, 63*(1), 13–22.

Leki, I. (1991). The preferences of ESL students for error correction in college-level writing classes. *Foreign Language Annals, 24*, 203–218.

Li, S. (2010). The effectiveness of corrective feedback in SLA: A meta-analysis. *Language Learning, 60*, 309–365.

Loewen, S. (2005). Incidental focus on form and second language learning. *Studies in Second Language Acquisition, 27*, 361–386.

Loewen, S., & Erlam, R. (2006). Corrective feedback in the chatroom: An experimental study. *Computer Assisted Language Learning, 19*(1), 1–14.

Loewen, S., & Philp, J. (2006). Recasts in the adult English L2 classroom: Characteristics, explicitness, and effectiveness. *Modern Language Journal, 90*, 536–556.

Long, M. (1977). Teacher feedback on learner error: Mapping cognitions. In H. D. Brown, C. A. Yorio & R. H. Crymes (Eds.), *On TESOL '77* (pp. 278–293). Washington, DC: TESOL.

Long, M. (1983). Native speaker/non-native speaker conversation in the second language classroom. In M. Clarke & J. Handscombe (Eds.), *On TESOL '82* (pp. 207–225). Washington, DC: TESOL.

Long, M. (1991). Focus on form: A design feature in language teaching methodology. In K. de Bot, R. Ginsberg & C. Kramsch (Eds.), *Foreign language research in cross-cultural perspective* (pp. 39–52). Amsterdam: John Benjamins.

Long, M. (1996). The role of the linguistic environment in second language acquisition. In W. Ritchie & T. Bhatia (Eds.), *Handbook of second language acquisition* (pp. 413–468). San Diego, CA: Academic Press.

Long, M. (2007). Recasts in SLA: The story so far. In M. H. Long (Ed.), *Problems in SLA* (pp. 75–116). Mahwah, NJ: Laurence Erlbaum.

Lyster, R. (1998a). Recasts, repetition, and ambiguity in L2 classroom discourse. *Studies in Second Language Acquisition, 20*, 51–81.

Lyster, R. (1998b). Negotiation of form, recasts, and explicit correction in relation to error types and learner repair in immersion classrooms. *Language Learning, 48*, 183–218.

Lyster, R. (2004). Differential effects of prompts and recasts in form-focused instruction. S*tudies in Second Language Acquisition, 19*, 37–66.

Lyster, R., & Mori, H. (2006). Interactional feedback and instructional counterbalance. *Studies in Second Language Acquisition, 28*, 269–300.

Lyster, R., & Ranta, L. (1997). Corrective feedback and learner uptake. *Studies in Second Language Acquisition, 19*, 37–66.

Lyster, R., & Saito, K. (2010). Effects of oral feedback in SLA classroom research: A meta-analysis. *Studies in Second Language Acquisition, 32*, 265–302.

McDonough, K., & Mackey, A. (2006). Responses to recasts: Repetitions, primed production, and linguistic development. *Language Learning, 56*, 693–720.

McGarrell, H., & Verbeen, J. (2007). Motivating revision of drafts through formative feedback. *ELT Journal, 61*, 228–236.

Mackey, A., & Goo, J. (2007). Interaction research in SLA: A meta-analysis and research synthesis. In A. Mackey (Ed.), *Conversational interaction in second language acquisition: A collection of empirical studies* (pp. 407–452). Oxford: Oxford University Press.

Norris, J., & Ortega, L. (2000). Effectiveness of L2 instruction: A research synthesis and qualitative meta-anaylsis. *Language Learning, 50*, 417–528.

Oliver, R., & Mackey, A. (2003). Interactional context and feedback in child ESL classrooms. *Modern Language Journal, 87*, 519–533.

Poehner, M. E. (2008). *Dynamic assessment: A Vygotskian approach to understanding and promoting second language development.* Berlin: Springer Publishing.

Poehner, M., & Lantolf, J. (2005). Dynamic assessment in the language classroom. *Language Teaching Research, 9*, 233–265.

Raimes, A. (1983). *Techniques in teaching writing.* New York: Oxford University Press.

Robb, T., Ross, S. & Shortreed, I. (1986). Salience of feedback on error and its effect on EFL writing quality. *TESOL Quarterly, 20*, 83–93.

Rolin-Ianziti, J. (2010). The organization of delayed second language correction. *Language Teaching Research, 14*, 183–206.

Russell, J., & Spada, N. (2006). The effectiveness of corrective feedback for the acquisition of L2 grammar: A meta-analysis of the research. In J. Norris and L. Ortega (Eds.), *Synthesizing research on language learning teaching* (pp. 133–164). Amsterdam: John Benjamins.

Sachs, R., & Suh, B. (2007). Textually enhanced recasts, learner awareness, and L2 outcomes in synchronous computer-mediated interaction. In A. Mackey (Ed.), *Conversational interaction in second language acquisition: A collection of empirical studies* (pp. 197–227). Oxford: Oxford University Press.

Sauro, S. (2009). Computer-mediated corrective feedback and the development of L2 grammar. *Language Learning & Technology, 13*(1), 96–120.

Schmidt, R. (1994). Deconstructing consciousness in search of useful definitions for applied linguistics. *AILA Review, 11*, 11–26.

Schmidt, R. (2001). Attention. In P. Robinson (Ed.), *Cognition and second language instruction* (pp. 3–32). Cambridge: Cambridge University Press.

Seedhouse, P. (1997). The case of the missing "no": The relationship between pedagogy and interaction. *Language Learning, 47*, 547–583.

Seedhouse, P. (2004). *The interactional architecture of the language classroom: A conversation analysis perspective.* Malden, MA: Blackwell.

Semke, H. (1984). The effects of the red pen. *Foreign Language Annals, 17*, 195–202.

Sheen, Y. (2004). Corrective feedback and learner uptake in communicative classrooms across instructional settings. *Language Teaching Research, 8*, 263–300.

Sheen, Y. (2006). Exploring the relationship between characteristics of recasts and learner uptake. *Language Teaching Research, 11*(4), 361–392.

Sheen, Y. (2007a). The effect of focused written corrective feedback and language aptitude on ESL learners' acquisition of articles. *TESOL Quarterly*, 41(2), 255–283.

Sheen, Y. (2007b). The effect of corrective feedback, language aptitude and learner attitudes on the acquisition of English articles. In A. Mackey (Ed.), *Conversational interaction in second language acquisition* (pp. 301–322). Oxford: Oxford University Press.

Sheen, Y. (2008). Recasts, language anxiety, modified output and L2 learning. *Language Learning*, 58(4), 835–874.

Sheen, Y. (2010). Differential effects of oral and written corrective feedback in the ESL classroom. *Studies in Second Language Acquisition*, 32, 203–234.

Sheen, Y., Wright, D. & Moldawa, A. (2009). Differential effects of focused and unfocused written correction on the accurate use of grammatical forms by adult ESL learners. *System*, 37(4), 556–569.

Smith, B. (2005). The relationship between negotiated interaction, learner uptake and lexical acquisition in task-based computer-mediated communication. *TESOL Quarterly*, 39, 33–58.

Sommers, N. (1982). Responding to student writing. *College Composition and Communication*, 33, 148–156.

Swain, M. (1985). Communicative competence: Some roles of comprehensible input and comprehensible output in its development. In S. M. Gass & C. Madden (Eds.), *Input and second language acquisition* (pp. 91–103). Rowley, MA: Newbury House.

Swain, M. (1995). Three functions of output in second language learning. In G. Cook & B. Seidlhofer (Eds.), *Principle and practice in applied linguistics: Studies in honor of H. G. Widdowson* (pp. 125–144). Oxford: Oxford University Press.

Truscott, J. (1996). The case against grammar correction in L2 writing classes. *Language Learning*, 46, 327–369.

Truscott, J. (1999). The case for "the case for grammar correction in L2 writing classes": A response to Ferris. *Journal of Second Language Writing*, 8, 111–122.

Truscott, J. (2004). Evidence and conjecture on the effects of correction: A response to Chandler. *Journal of Second Language Writing*, 13, 337–343

Truscott, J. (2007). The effect of error correction on learners' ability to write accurately. *Journal of Second Language Writing*, 16, 255–272.

Ur, P. (1996). *A course in language teaching.* Cambridge: Cambridge University Press.

Van Lier, L. (1988). *The classroom and the language learner.* London: Longman.

Williams, J. (2001). The effectiveness of spontaneous attention to form. *System*, 29, 325–340.

Yoshida, R. (2008). Teachers' choice and learners' preference of corrective feedback types. *Language Awareness*, 17(1), 78–93.

Zamel, V. (1985). Responding to student writing. *TESOL Quarterly*, 19, 79–102.

37
Content-Based Second Language Teaching

Roy Lyster

Introduction

Content-based second language teaching is an instructional approach in which non-linguistic content, including subject matter such as social studies or mathematics, is taught to students through the medium of a language that is not their first, so that while they are learning curricular content they are also learning an additional language. Good reasons abound in support of teaching additional languages through content-based instruction rather than through traditional methods. As Snow, Met, and Genesee (1989) argued, language development and cognitive development go hand-in-hand, yet more traditional methods tend to separate language development from general cognitive development, isolating the target language from any substantive content except for the mechanical workings of the language itself. Content-based instruction, in contrast, is designed to integrate language and cognitive development.

Content-based instruction is known to come in many different shapes and sizes. Met (1998) described a range of content-based instructional settings along a continuum varying from more content-driven programs, such as total and partial immersion, to more language-driven programs, which include language classes either based on thematic units or with frequent use of content for language practice. Towards the middle of the continuum are program models in which students study one or two subjects in the target language along with a more traditional language class; an example would be the "adjunct" format adopted at the post-secondary level in which students are integrated into a content course offered for native speakers "but sheltered as a group in a separate credit language course related to the content course" (Burger & Chrétien, 2001, p. 85).

Immersion education refers to additive bilingual programs designed for majority-language speakers in which at least half of their subject-matter instruction is in a language that they are learning as a second or foreign language; they also receive some instruction through a shared first language, which normally has majority status in the community. Two-way immersion programs normally integrate a similar number of children from two different mother-tongue backgrounds (e.g., Spanish and English in the US) and provide curricular instruction in both languages (Lindholm-Leary, 2001). In many European contexts, content-based instruction is known as "content and language integrated learning" or "CLIL" (Dalton-Puffer, 2007; Mehisto, Marsh, & Frigols, 2008).

Cloud, Genesee, and Hamayan (2000) used the term "enriched education" to refer to school programs that integrate bilingual proficiency as a full-fledged objective along with other curricular objectives. Enriched education includes second and foreign language immersion programs as well as two-way immersion programs. Also included under the rubric of enriched education are developmental bilingual education programs, designed for minority-language students in the US who receive at least half of their instruction through their primary language throughout elementary school.

Content-based instruction also encompasses content-based ESL and "sheltered instruction." In content-based English as a second language (ESL), "teachers seek to develop the students' English language proficiency by incorporating information from the subject areas that students are likely to study," and sheltered instruction entails content courses for ESL learners taught normally by content (rather than ESL) specialists with grade-level objectives and modified instruction to facilitate comprehension of the material (Echevarría, Vogt, & Short, 2008, p. 13).

Content-based instruction thus crosses a wide range of international contexts, including elementary, secondary, and post-secondary institutions, and, by encompassing both majority-language learners (as in immersion and CLIL programs) and minority-language learners (as in ESL learners in sheltered or mainstream content courses in the US), ensures first language support in some contexts but not in others. In spite of the tremendous differences across these contexts, there are some common pedagogical issues that arise at the interface of language and content teaching and that will be highlighted throughout this chapter. As Wesche (2001, p. 1) argued, "the contexts have much in common, each involving learners struggling to master academic concepts and skills through a language in which they have limited proficiency, while at the same time striving to improve that proficiency." She suggested that learners' efforts in this endeavor "can be facilitated by considerably good teaching." Drawing on classroom research, this chapter aims to identify various types of "good teaching" that that are apt to facilitate the learning of a new language while learning curricular content through that language.

Two for One?

Content-based second language teaching has often been referred to as the "two for one" approach (e.g., Lightbown & Spada, 2006), because learners in these programs learn subject matter and the target language at the same time. It has been widely documented that majority-language speakers learning an additional language through immersion indeed succeed in mastering the content as well as if they were learning it through their first language, at no expense to their first language (e.g., Genesee, 1987; Turnbull, Lapkin, & Hart, 2001). However, contrary to the "two for one" nomenclature, nothing comes for free. That is, by learning content through a second language, the second language does not come "for free." Instead, as will be illustrated throughout this chapter, a great deal of attention still needs to be drawn to the second language, which needs to be manipulated and enhanced during content teaching.

Amid the flourishing movement of naturalistic and communicative language teaching methods, which assumed that implicit acquisition determines second language performance and obviates the need for explicit instructional intervention (e.g., Krashen, 1981), studies of second language learners in programs such as French immersion in Canada revealed that, even after many years of exposure to the target language, students demonstrated a lack of second language accuracy (e.g., Swain, 1985). Since then, researchers have concurred that, for content-based instruction to be effective, it must be language-rich and discourse-rich (e.g., Duff, 2001; Genesee, 1987; Harley, Cummins, Swain, & Allen, 1990; Hoare & Kong, 2008; Musumeci, 1996; Netten, 1991; Lyster, 2007; Swain, 1988, 1996). Instructional practices that emphasize discourse and the use of language as an instrument for learning, Day and Shapson (1996) noted, have much to contribute to improving the second language learning environment in immersion classes. They observed marked differences in instructional strategies employed by immersion teachers during science lessons. In one science classroom, students were seen "as a community of learners engaged in discourse about science" (p. 80), while in another the limitations of traditional pedagogy were more evident as the teacher "repeated or rephrased what [students] said, wrote the answers on the board, and had students take notes" (p. 56). Genesee (1987) as well argued that more discourse-rich approaches are needed for immersion programs to fulfill their potential, but acknowledged that "many immersion programs, and indeed many regular school programs, do not do this" (p. 77). Such an approach requires a great deal of systematic planning and does not necessarily come naturally to content-based teachers. At the interface of content and language teaching are challenging obstacles that prevent content teaching from being ipso facto good language teaching (Swain, 1985, 1988).

Language and Content: Separation or Integration?

In their immersion classroom observation study, Swain and Carroll (1987) noted an important paradox: "Although one goal of immersion is to learn language through learning content, a general observation about the classes is that form and function are kept surprisingly distinct" (p. 191). They found that it was relatively rare for teachers (1) to refer during content-based lessons to what had been presented in a grammar lesson and (2) to set up content-based activities specifically to focus on form related to meaning. Netten (1991) reported that the instructional strategies used by elementary-level immersion teachers appeared incommensurate with the fact that they were teaching both content and a second language: "Teachers expected that the pupils would learn the target language as they were learning the content of the prescribed curriculum" (p. 288). A kindergarten Swedish immersion teacher in Finland observed by Södergård (2008) avoided mentioning to the children that they were learning a new language in order for their language learning "to happen unnoticed" (p. 170). Two of the teachers described by Lyster (1998c), also in elementary immersion classrooms, were unaware of how they focused on language as they interacted with students because, they both acknowledged, "their real concern was content" (p. 74). Fortune, Tedick, and Walker (2008) found that, although Spanish immersion teachers readily described their instruction as focusing on language, the targets of their language instruction could be summed up in two words: "vocabulary and verbs" (p. 76).

It is often reported that immersion and content-based approaches entail language learning through content alone, without any accompanying second language instruction. If ever there is attention drawn to language, this is reportedly done so incidentally. However, this is not an accurate representation. A great deal of language instruction has in fact been observed in immersion classrooms, although with indeterminate effectiveness. Incidental references to language (or none at all) have been observed in subject-matter lessons, whereas language arts lessons tend toward a much more intentional and also explicit focus on language. Swain and Carroll (1987), for example, observed many lessons set aside to focus on grammar, during which time formal rules, paradigms, and grammatical categories were presented. These decontextualized grammar lessons emphasized the learning and categorizing of forms rather than relating these forms to their communicative functions, and appeared to have minimal effect on students whose exposure to the target language was primarily message-oriented and content-based (Swain, 1996).

Teacher Collaboration

Whether working in content-based foreign language instruction (e.g., Pessoa, Hendry, Donato, Tucker, & Lee, 2007) or content-based ESL (e.g., Duff, 2001), researchers concur that the success of content-based instruction is contingent upon ongoing collaboration among teachers. Yet, even in the case of mainstream classrooms with two teachers—a subject-matter specialist working in partnership with an ESL specialist—institutional constraints appear to militate against equitable integration of content and language. In her study of ESL students in mainstream classrooms in the UK, for example, Creese (2002, p. 611) observed that "knowledge about language was positioned as less important in the subject classroom. Knowledge and pedagogies associated with language learning and languages for learning were pushed to the periphery of the schools' agendas" (see also Arkoudis, 2006; Creese, 2006). Short's (2002) observational study of four teachers in sheltered ESL middle school classrooms in the US included two teachers trained as ESL instructors and two with certification as social studies instructors. Her analysis of 14 hours of classroom interaction revealed that 44% of the teacher utterances addressed content, 35% addressed tasks, and only 20% addressed language. Even the trained ESL teachers devoted only one-fifth or less of their interactions to language. When teachers did address language, 95% of their comments focused on vocabulary comprehension or pronunciation. Short attributed these findings to the pressure that teachers in sheltered classrooms feel as they prepare students for state and local testing, and also to the content specialists' lack of background in language. In fact, one of the social studies teachers said about language teaching: "I thought that was someone else's job" (p. 21). Having observed many teachable moments for language teaching slip away, Short concluded that both ESL and content teachers alike need to expand their conception of language beyond vocabulary comprehension to include explicit instruction in language learning strategies, language functions, vocabulary, grammar, mechanics, and the four language skills. Observations in other content-based instructional contexts also reveal that content-trained teachers tend to focus mainly on content at the expense of language while language-trained teachers tend to focus more on language but often at the expense of greater in-depth exploration of content (e.g., Dalton-Puffer, 2007; Hoare & Kong, 2008; Kong, 2009; Pessoa et al., 2007).

In immersion contexts, where students receive instruction in two languages, collaboration between teachers of each language is likely to strengthen the academic literacy development of children in both languages. In this vein, Lyster, Collins, and Ballinger (2009) conducted a study in Quebec of three French immersion classrooms composed heterogeneously of French-dominant, English-dominant, and French/English bilingual students. Their study aimed to facilitate collaboration between the French and English teachers of the same group of students as a means of reinforcing students' biliteracy skills and creating opportunities for cross-linguistic connections. The two teachers of each class read aloud to their students from the same storybooks over four months, alternating the reading of one chapter in French and another in English. Prior to each read-aloud session (all of which were video taped and transcribed for analysis), teachers asked their students to summarize the content of the previous reading, which had taken place in the other language of instruction, and after each reading they asked their students to make predictions about the next chapter. The read-aloud sessions generated a great deal of interaction, some of which involved cross-linguistic connections made incidentally, especially in the case of new concepts being reinforced by both teachers in both languages. Actual collaboration, however, between the French and English teachers, on either content- or language-based objectives, was minimal.

Obstacles to Integration

Obstacles preventing a more systematic integration of language and content instruction, as well as more explicit connections between first and second language literacy development, may derive from at least two unresolved issues about the nature of language instruction in content-based approaches.

First, is language learning in content-based second language teaching a primary or secondary goal? Genesee (1994) argued that "language learning in immersion is secondary to academic achievement" (p. 2). However, Met (1998, p. 40) suggested that, in content-driven immersion programs, "student mastery of content may share equal importance with the development of language proficiency." Allen, Swain, Harley, and Cummins (1990, p. 75) stated that, in immersion, "language and content learning are equally important goals," and Echevarría et al. (2008) advocated clear identification of both content and language objectives in their model of sheltered content-based ESL instruction. The perspective expressed throughout this chapter is that second language learning and academic achievement are inextricably linked and thus share equal status in terms of educational objectives.

Second, 'incidental' is a word that was initially attributed to the process of both teaching and learning language through content (e.g., Genesee, 1987; Snow, 1987; Swain & Lapkin, 1982; more recently, see Long, 2007), usually with a disclaimer, however, that "incidental" is neither tantamount to "haphazard" (Snow, 1987) nor at odds with systematicity (Genesee, 1987). Yet it remains unclear how an incidental approach to language instruction can, at the same time, be systematic. Lyster (2007) illustrated how incidental attention to language is often too brief and perfunctory to convey sufficient information about certain grammatical subsystems and thus, in those cases, can be considered neither systematic nor apt to make the most of content-based instruction as a means for teaching language.

Because it otherwise lacks such an intentional and systematic focus on language, an incidental approach to teaching language through content, to borrow the encapsulating title of Swain's (1988) seminal paper, falls inadequately short of "manipulating and complementing content teaching to maximize second language learning." Content-based instruction that draws students' attention only incidentally to language provides substantial exposure to contextualized language use and promotes primarily lexically oriented learning, but does not ensure the learning of less salient yet crucial morphosyntactic features of the target language (Harley, 1994; Swain, 1988). The next section proposes a tentative framework for addressing more systematically the integration of language and content in content-based second language instruction.

Counterbalanced Instruction

Observation studies of immersion classrooms revealed that a typical way to approach content-based instruction is to focus exclusively on content and to refer to language only incidentally as the need arises by chance. Then, if more attention to language is called for, a traditional approach is adopted in language arts classes to engage in structural analyses of the target language out of context. A case will be made here for eschewing this non-integrated approach and instead for integrating content-based and form-focused instruction through *counterbalanced instruction*. According to the *Oxford English Dictionary* (Brown, 1993), the term "counterbalance" refers to "a power or influence that balances the effect of a contrary one" and is used here in this sense to bring a new perspective to the seemingly paradoxical endeavor of learning and teaching language through non-linguistic curricular content. This issue parallels Stern's (1990, 1992) concern for integrating "analytic" and "experiential" instructional strategies to maximize second and foreign language. He recommended more systematic integration of analytic strategies in contexts of immersion and content-based instruction, and at the same time, more emphasis on experiential strategies in traditional programs where the target language is taught as a subject. When instruction is counterbalanced in this way, learners in content-based classrooms are expected to benefit from a greater focus on language that pushes them forward in their language development, and learners in language-focused classrooms are expected to benefit from a greater emphasis on substantive content that enriches classroom discourse. In content-based second language teaching, to incite students to vary their attentional focus between the content to which they usually attend in classroom discourse and target language features that are not otherwise attended to, teachers can draw on form-focused instruction.

Form-focused instruction includes pedagogical techniques that draw learners' attention to form/function relationships in the target language that would otherwise not be noticed in content-based input. Form-focused instruction is usually embedded in meaning-based tasks and thus differs in important ways from traditional grammar lessons that emphasize memorization of forms out of context (see Chapter 35 by Loewen in this volume). With its goal of integrating both form-focused and content-based instruction in conjunction with language across the curriculum and other pivotal literacy-based approaches at the heart of school-based learning (see Lyster, 2007), counterbalanced instruction promotes continued second language growth by developing students' awareness of learning both language and content together. In short, counterbalanced instruction gives language and content objectives equal and complementary status.

Figure 37.1 (from Lyster, 2007, p. 135) illustrates the content-based and form-focused instructional options that are essential components of content-based second language teaching. Content-based instructional options include: (1) techniques that teachers employ to make subject matter comprehensible to second language learners; (2) opportunities for students to use the second language to mediate content learning during academic tasks; (3) negotiation replete with questions and feedback employed by teachers to scaffold verbal exchanges with students in ways that ensure their participation and appropriation of the targeted content. Form-focused instructional options include: (1) noticing and awareness activities designed to make input features salient and to facilitate their intake; (2) production practice activities designed to facilitate the proceduralization of target language knowledge; (3) negotiation involving teacher prompts and other engaging feedback that push students to draw optimally on their developing knowledge of the target language and increasingly to take responsibility for their learning.

Although content-based and form-focused instructional options appear as discrete options in Figure 37.1, they are best seen as complementary pairs that interact dialectally to foster a dynamic interplay between communication and reflection on that communication. By the same token, the vertical orientation of Figure 37.1 is not intended to depict any hierarchical or linear relationships

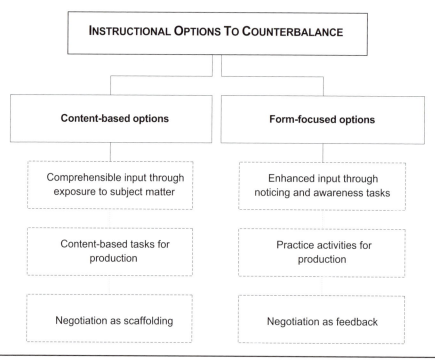

Figure 37.1 Instructional options to counterbalance

among instructional options that differentially emphasize input, production, and negotiation. The following sections further develop the rationale for counterbalancing content-based and form-focused instruction across these three key components of content-based second language teaching: (1) instructional input; (2) student production; and (3) classroom interaction. To conclude, a set of teacher vignettes will be presented as snapshots of practitioners in the field integrating language and content in this way.

Instructional Input

Content-based second language teachers need to counterbalance instructional strategies that are designed to make content-based input more comprehensible and strategies designed to make input features more salient. Students in content-based classrooms benefit from a broad spectrum of repeated opportunities to process language for comprehension as well as for developing their metalinguistic awareness.

Content-Based Input

The goal of teachers throughout any type of content-based program is to enable students to comprehend the curriculum presented through the second language. Making subject-matter input comprehensible through a learner's second language is no small undertaking because it is imperative that curricular content itself not be simplified to the point of shortchanging students (Echevarría et al., 2008; Met, 1994, 1998).

Content-based second language teachers are known to modify their speech by speaking more slowly in the beginning grades, emphasizing key words or phrases and using cognates, restricted vocabulary, and shorter phrases. They build redundancy into their speech by using discourse modifications such as self-repetition, modeling, and paraphrase (Tardif, 1994), as well as multiple examples, definitions, and synonyms to give students many chances to understand the target language. Ideally, teachers provide natural pauses between phrases to give students time to process language and also to give students appropriate "wait time" to interpret questions and formulate responses (Cloud et al., 2000). In tandem with their verbal input, teachers use props, graphs, and other graphic organizers (see Early, 2001; Mohan, 1986), as well as various visual and multimedia resources (see Echevarría et al., 2008). To further facilitate comprehension, teachers rely on extensive body language, including gestures and facial expressions, and a range of paralinguistic elements. Content-based teachers ensure predictability and repetition in instructional routines by using clear boundary markers between activities to orchestrate daily routines in a way that maximizes classroom discipline and opportunities for learning (Mendez, 1992; Salomone, 1992a). Content-based teachers draw extensively on their students' background knowledge to aid comprehension, and they also draw on students to help one another understand content lessons.

Instructional techniques that ensure the comprehension of subject matter taught through the medium of the students' second language are at the core of content-based approaches and are requisite for students' academic success. The notion that learners can and should be exposed to language just ahead of their current level of ability (e.g., Krashen, 1982, 1985, 1994), rather than being exposed only to language they already know, is essential to content-based second language teaching. However, the limits of an exclusively comprehension-based approach to language instruction are now well known, especially in the long run and for learners aspiring to reach beyond beginner levels of proficiency and to develop literacy skills in the target language (e.g., Lightbown, Halter, White, & Horst, 2002). That is, the continued use of strategies that rely too much on gestures and other visual and non-linguistic support may, over time, have negative effects on the development of students' communicative ability in the second language. Such strategies are unlikely to make the kinds of increasing demands on the learners' language system that Genesee (1987) suggested are necessary for continuous second language learning. Swain (1985) argued that exposure to extensive input via subject-matter instruction engages comprehension strategies that enable students to process language semantically but not necessarily syntactically, allowing them to bypass structural information and to rely instead on pragmatic and situational cues.

There is now considerable theoretical support as well as empirical evidence—much of it from immersion settings—that exposure to comprehensible input alone is insufficient for continued language growth. Swain (1988, 1996) argued accordingly that content teaching needs to be manipulated and complemented in ways that maximize second language learning, and suggested that, to do so, teachers need to draw students' attention to specific form/meaning mappings by creating contrived contexts that allow students to notice second language features in their full functional range (see also Harley & Swain, 1984).

Form-Focused Input

The need for learners to notice target features in the input, in order to process them as intake, is a crucial first step in second language learning (Schmidt, 1990). In order for input to become intake, some degree of noticing must occur, and what gets noticed in the input depends on mediating factors such as prior knowledge and skill, task demands, frequency, and perceptual salience (Gass, 1988; Schmidt, 1990, 1994). In classroom settings, noticing can also be triggered by input features that have been contrived for instructional purposes through "input enhancement" designed to make certain forms more salient in the input, through color coding or boldfacing in the case of written input, and through intonational stress and gestures in the case of oral input (Sharwood Smith, 1993).

At least two phases are required for learners to notice target features in a manner robust enough to make the forms available as intake: a noticing phase and an awareness phase. In the noticing phase, learners engage primarily in receptive processing during activities designed to move the learner toward more target-like representations of the second language. Noticing activities serve as catalysts for drawing learners' attention to problematic target features that have been contrived to appear more salient and/or frequent in oral and written input. In the awareness phase, learners engage either receptively or productively, or both, in activities designed to consolidate the cognitive restructuring of rule-based declarative representations. Awareness activities require learners to do more than merely notice enhanced forms in the input and instead to engage in some degree of elaboration (Sharwood Smith, 1981, 1993). Such elaboration may include inductive rule-discovery tasks and opportunities to compare and contrast language patterns, followed by different types of metalinguistic information.

Noticing and awareness activities (see examples from classroom studies summarized in Lyster, 2007) aim to strengthen students' metalinguistic awareness, which then serves as a tool for extracting linguistic information from content-based input and thus for learning language through subject-matter instruction. Even young learners in content-based classrooms benefit from the inclusion of age-appropriate noticing and awareness activities that enable them to draw on their linguistic sensitivity in a way that primes them for the kind of implicit analysis of naturalistic input they need to engage in to drive their interlanguage development forward (see Ranta, 2002; Skehan, 1998). Moreover, because young learners rely heavily on the use of formulaic chunks in their early production (e.g., Weber & Tardif, 1991), teachers can exploit their students' emerging metalinguistic awareness to engage increasingly over time in analyses of formulaic items as a means of developing a more generative rule-based system.

Student Production

To complement input-driven instructional techniques, content-based second language teachers need also to ensure that their students' opportunities to use the second language continue to expand both in quantity and quality. An argument is made in this section for counterbalancing student production opportunities to ensure target language use in contexts ranging from content-based tasks to more form-focused practice activities.

Content-Based Tasks

Content-based instruction is thought to provide ideal contexts for second language learning to occur naturally, because of the countless opportunities for authentic and purposeful use of the target language generated by the study of subject matter (Snow et al., 1989). Genesee (1987, p. 176) argued that the academic curriculum stimulates language development by placing increasingly high levels of cognitive and linguistic demands on students. He proposed academic (i.e., content-based) tasks themselves, rather than a language-based syllabus, as a basis for stimulating second language development, but added that "maximum language learning in immersion will probably result only to the extent that the curriculum exploits opportunities for discourse in the service of academic achievement." He proposed a process approach to content-based second language teaching whereby "certain interactional processes of a discoursal nature," hypothesized to contribute to language development, are instantiated in academic tasks, which in turn govern the actual units of language to be learned: "It follows that second language learning will then proceed in response to the communication demands of academic work, given certain motivational conditions" (see also Brinton, Snow, & Wesche, 2004).

The argument that second language development will be driven primarily by the discourse in which students need to engage to complete academic tasks is premised on the theoretical assumption that communicative language ability is acquired through purposeful communication. Not accounted for, however, are research findings that have documented the ineffectiveness of immersion for promoting levels of accuracy that match its success in developing fluency.

Effective content teaching is generally considered to include hands-on tasks that engage learners in opportunities for in-depth understanding and for "learning by doing" (Bruner, 1971). Content-based tasks undertaken with the strategic support of concrete materials and graphic aids fit well with what are considered best practices in content instruction (see Lyster, 2007) but, as Ellis (2000) argued: "It cannot be assumed that achieving communicative effectiveness in the performance of a task will set up the interactive conditions that promote second language acquisition" (p. 213). Even in the tasks used in the intervention studies by Harley (1989) and Day and Shapson (1991), which were specifically designed to encourage the productive use of specific target forms during oral interaction, target forms were avoided and superseded by spontaneous expression and the concomitant use of simplified forms. In achieving oral fluency by ignoring accuracy or by concentrating on a narrow repertoire of language, learners are not necessarily pushed to extend and refine their interlanguage system. Therefore, content-based tasks need also to include a writing phase that requires learners to use the target language for academic purposes without the contextual support that normally scaffolds oral interaction.

Form-Focused Practice

Practice can be broadly defined as "engaging in an activity with the goal of becoming better at it" (DeKeyser, 1998, p. 50) and more specifically in reference to second language learning as "specific activities in the second language, engaged in systematically, deliberately, with the goal of developing knowledge of and skills in the second language" (DeKeyser, 2007, p. 1). Researchers in immersion settings have been advocating the importance of both receptive and production practice activities for years (e.g., Harley & Swain, 1984). In their observation study of immersion classrooms, Allen et al. (1990) reported that the "speech acts which occur naturally in the classroom context may provide little opportunity for students to produce the full range of target language forms" (p. 74) and recommended that teachers implement "carefully planned and guided communicative practice that will push students towards the production of comprehensible output" (p. 76).

At one end of the practice spectrum, controlled practice activities engage learners' awareness of rule-based representations and are thus useful for circumventing their over-reliance on communication strategies and effecting change in the interlanguage (Ranta & Lyster, 2007). At the other end of the practice spectrum, communicative practice activities engage learners in more open-ended and meaning-focused tasks with fewer constraints to ensure accuracy, thus proving effective for promoting confidence and motivation to use the second language, and for providing a safe playing field for students to try out communication strategies. Lyster (2004b) found that, in cases where the areas of linguistic difficulty were sources of persistent errors for immersion students, controlled practice was more effective than communicative practice. However, Segalowitz (2000) argued that second language fluency develops as a result of practice that has not only been extensive and repetitive, thus building automaticity, but that has also been genuinely communicative in nature and therefore transfer-appropriate. To promote second language development, therefore, practice activities, whether considered controlled or communicative, need to involve the processing of the target language for communicative purposes.

A good example of both controlled and communicative practice is evident in the content-driven activities used in Doughty and Varela's (1998) classroom study, which took place in a content-based ESL science class, targeting the simple past and the conditional past in the context of science experiments. A group of 11–14-year-old students conducted a set of experiments in accordance with their regular science curriculum. To report their results accurately, they needed to use the simple past and the conditional past. For example, in one of the experiments, students were asked first to make the following prediction: "Which ball do you think will bounce the highest: a basketball, a rubber ball, or a soccer ball?" After completing the experiments, students produced written lab reports and were also questioned orally about their experiments. They were asked to recount the procedure they had followed to complete the experiment and also to report the results relative to their initial prediction, thus creating an obligatory context for use of the past tense (e.g., "I thought the rubber ball would bounce the highest"). Similarly, Fortune et al. (2008) reported on a 5th-grade Spanish immersion teacher who implemented a content-based activity requiring students to use both their content knowledge and specific language forms. To demonstrate their understanding of human rights in social studies class, students participated in small groups to complete a creative writing task called the Bill of Rights activity, which required the use of the subjunctive mood, an aspect of Spanish verb morphosyntax rarely used by immersion students. Students had to generate 13 rights using a complex sentence structure to first express the right and then a limiting factor, introduced by a connective such as *aunque* ("although"), which created an obligatory context for the subjunctive.

Designing practice activities that are "task-essential" in this way (i.e., they cannot be completed unless the elicited structure is used—Loschky & Bley-Vroman, 1993) is no small undertaking. Yet content-based second language teachers have another, arguably more feasible, option at their disposal. That is, given the generally rich context for language use in content-based classrooms, drawing on opportunities to push learners in their output during the course of interaction about curricular content may prove more efficient than designing relatively contrived practice activities. As Lightbown (1998, p. 194) argued:

Work on improving output is better done in the context of more interactive activities, in which the main focus is on communication, but in which the accuracy or sophistication can be improved via focus on form via feedback and learners' self-corrections.

Classroom Interaction

This section considers the central role played by teachers as they interact with students during whole-class activities with the dual aim of enhancing their students' content knowledge and second language development. Content-based second language teachers need to counterbalance diverse opportunities to negotiate language through content by means of instructional options that include a wide range of questioning and scaffolding techniques as well as a variety of corrective feedback moves.

In the context of science lessons in a mainstream classroom with ESL learners, Gibbons (2003) observed many teacher-fronted lessons used effectively in combination with group and pair work in complementary ways. Some lessons consisted entirely of students carrying out experiments in small groups, while in other lessons the teacher played a major role in initiating talk. Gibbons concluded that the quality of the interaction and the extent to which it contributes to educational objectives are more important than whether the lesson is a whole-class or small-group activity.

Language teachers' extensive use of display questions has been well documented and is often criticized for limiting possibilities for students to try out their own ideas. Yet teachers have been observed using both display and referential questions with equal effectiveness. Specifically in immersion classrooms, Salomone (1992b) remarked that display questions "are an important part of content learning" (p. 104), because they help teachers to verify content mastery and, thus, are not limited to inciting students only to display linguistic knowledge. Similarly, in Italian content-based classes, Musumeci (1996) found that display questions served effectively to verify comprehension of subject matter delivered in the second language and were just as effective as referential questions for eliciting extensive responses from students (see also Dalton-Puffer, 2006). In content-based classrooms, notwithstanding a constructivist rationale for co-constructing knowledge and negotiating content, it appears both improbable and undesirable for subject-matter specialists to ask a preponderance of questions to which they do not know the answers. As they work dialogically with students, teachers need to exercise their responsibility as mentors interacting with novices by providing scaffolding that necessitates a variety of questioning techniques ranging from display to referential questions.

Arguably more important than the teacher's initiating question in the well-known tripartite exchange of initiating, responding, and follow-up moves (Sinclair & Coulthard, 1975) is the teacher's choice of follow-up move and the extent to which it allows the teacher to work with the student's response in a variety of ways (Nassaji & Wells, 2000). Specifically in the context of sheltered ESL instruction, Echarvarría and Graves (1998) identified questioning techniques designed to enrich "instructional conversations" (see Tharpe & Gallimore, 1988) and to facilitate students' understanding of ideas and concepts that they would otherwise be unable to express on their own. They recommended the use of fewer known-answer questions and more questions eliciting complex language, as well as requests for students to justify their positions. Similarly, to create more opportunities for extended student responses specifically in CLIL classrooms, Dalton-Puffer (2006) recommended that teachers use fewer questions eliciting facts, which tend to result in minimal responses, and more questions about students' beliefs and opinions that require them to explain, define, or give reasons.

In addition to various questioning techniques, teacher follow-up moves include feedback. Early research studies conducted in immersion classrooms suggested that the use of feedback was not high on teachers' list of priorities. The observation study of immersion classrooms described by Allen et al. (1990) revealed that error treatment was dealt with in "a confusing and unsystematic way" (p. 67) and that "teachers spent only minimal amounts of observed time asking students what they intended in producing a specific utterance or written text" (p. 77; see also Day & Shapson, 1996). Netten (1991) found that immersion teachers encouraged communication by correcting oral errors "as unobtrusively as possible, usually by echoing the pupil's response" (p. 299). It seems highly probable that a correlation exists between immersion teachers' tendency to use random implicit feedback and immersion students' tendency to reach a developmental plateau in their communicative ability. As Allen et al. (1990) cautioned, "unsystematic, possibly random feedback to learners about their language errors" (p. 76) could have a "detrimental effect on learning" (p. 67).

Still other studies revealed rather more consistent use of feedback by immersion teachers after learner errors: 67% of learner errors were followed by teacher feedback in French immersion classrooms (Lyster & Ranta, 1997), 61% in Japanese immersion classrooms (Lyster & Mori, 2006), and 64% in English immersion classrooms (Lee, 2007). The French immersion teachers observed by Chaudron (1977, 1986) provided feedback, but did so more during language arts classes than subject-matter lessons and earlier in the school year than later. In all cases, the majority of the feedback used by immersion teachers involves recasting: that is, a reformulation of the learner's utterance, minus the error.

Content-Based Negotiation

In second language acquisition research, conversational moves used in dyadic interaction to facilitate comprehension and hypothesized to benefit second language development are generally subsumed under the rubric of "negotiation for meaning," which comprises clarification requests, confirmation checks (including recasts and repetition), and comprehension checks (Long, 1996). Although negotiation for meaning has been advocated as a central feature of content-based instruction (e.g., Genesee, 1987; Met, 1994; Rebuffot, 1993; Tardif, 1991), its component moves, while useful for moving conversations forward, have not proven as effective in classroom settings as in laboratory settings for focusing learners' attention on form (Aston, 1986; Foster, 1998; Foster & Ohta, 2005; Lyster; 2002, 2007). For example, in post-secondary content-based classes of Italian as a foreign language, Musumeci (1996) reported that the teachers viewed negotiation for meaning less as a language teaching strategy and more as a social strategy "to help the student get through the exchange as painlessly as possible" (p. 316). Musumeci (1996) also found that teachers "appear to understand absolutely everything the students say" (p. 314). They strove to derive meaning from students' speech and, to do so, "supplied key lexical items and provided rich interpretations of student responses, rather than engage in the kind of negotiation which would have required learners to modify their own output" (p. 314). Musumeci further argued:

> While this kind of "filling in the spaces" by the teacher may have helped to create coherent conversational texts, it also made the teachers responsible for carrying the linguistic burden of the exchange, and it reduced the students' role to one of supplying linguistic "hints" to the teacher, rather than functioning as full partners in the exchange.
>
> (Musumeci, 1996, p. 315)

Her observation is thus reminiscent of Harley's (1993, p. 248) finding that, in immersion classrooms with younger learners,

> a substantial portion of the effort in the communicative enterprise may be off-loaded onto the teacher [which] is doubtlessly appropriate and necessary in the early stages but in the long run may not encourage an independent approach to SLA [second language acquisition] that is seen as a prerequisite for expertise in any domain.

Similarly, in the context of content-based ESL classrooms, Pica (2002) found very little negotiation for meaning that might be expected to move second language development forward. Instead, as students and teacher negotiated for meaning to guarantee comprehensibility during discussion of film reviews, the majority of students' non-target utterances went unaddressed in any direct way. In her analysis of negotiation for meaning in high school CLIL classrooms in Italy, Mariotti (2006) found that negotiation moves produced by students consisted primarily of repetition of lexical items extracted from classroom input and that those produced by teachers did not entail the use of corrective feedback that would otherwise push learners to produce more target-like utterances.

Central to negotiation for meaning are recasts, which are reformulations of learner utterances, minus the error but with the original meaning intact. Recasts have been hypothesized to create ideal opportunities for learners to notice the difference between their interlanguage forms and target-like reformulations (e.g., Doughty, 2001; Long, 1996, 2007). Because recasts preserve the learners' intended meaning, Long (1996) claimed, they free up cognitive resources that would otherwise be used for semantic processing. Specifically with respect to content-based and immersion classrooms, Long (2007) suggested that recasts provide teachers with "the option of dealing with many of their students' language problems *incidentally* while working on their subject matter of choice" (pp. 76–77). However, empirical research conducted in the context of content-based and immersion classrooms indicates instead that the strength of recasts may lie more in their propensity for facilitating the delivery of complex subject matter and for providing helpful scaffolding to learners when target forms are beyond their current abilities (Gibbons, 1998, 2003; Lyster, 1998a, 2002; Mohan & Becket, 2001). That recasts occur so frequently during content-based instruction can be seen as well tuned to the objectives of content-based second language instruction. That is, recasts serve to maintain the flow of communication, to keep students' attention focused on content, and to provide scaffolds that enable learners to participate in interaction about subject matter that requires linguistic abilities exceeding their current developmental level.

Form-Focused Negotiation

Swain (1985) argued that teachers, in order to benefit their students' interlanguage development, need to incorporate ways of "pushing" students to produce language that is not only comprehensible, but also accurate. Lyster and Ranta (1997) observed different feedback types that immersion teachers have at their disposal and then identified which feedback types tended more than others to "push" learners to modify their non-target output. They observed six different types of feedback: recasts, explicit correction, clarification requests, repetition of error, elicitation, and metalinguistic clues. Recasts and explicit correction both supply learners with target reformulations of their non-target output. Whereas a recast is considered implicit insofar as it contains no metalinguistic information, an explicit correction contains the correct form as well as a clear indication that what the student said was inaccurate. In contrast, clarification requests, repetition of error, elicitation, and metalinguistic clues were grouped together as "prompts," because they withhold correct forms and instead offer learners an opportunity to self-repair by generating their own modified response (Lyster, 2004a; Lyster & Mori, 2006; Ranta & Lyster, 2007). When a teacher's prompt is followed by a learner repair move, the teacher–student exchange is said to involve the "negotiation of form" (Lyster & Ranta, 1997; Lochtman, 2005), because it serves to hand the floor over to students while drawing attention to accuracy. Prompts thus fit well with instructional discourse and are especially compatible with content teaching, as they resemble the "clueing" procedure or "withholding phenomenon" identified by McHoul (1990) in his study of feedback in subject-matter classrooms.

Prompts have generally proven more effective than recasts across a range of instructional settings, including French immersion (Lyster, 2004a), intensive ESL (Ammar & Spada, 2006), and English as a foreign language (EFL) in China (Yang & Lyster, 2010). Their effectiveness has been explained in part through skill acquisition theory, which entails a gradual transition from effortful use to more automatic use of target language forms, brought about through practice and feedback in meaningful contexts (DeKeyser, 2003, 2007). Proponents of skill acquisition theory advocate instructional techniques that help second language learners develop automaticity in target language use, including a judicious use of various prompts that push second language learners to notice their interlanguage forms and to practice emergent target forms in contexts of interaction (e.g., Lyster, 2007; Ranta & Lyster, 2007).

Teacher Vignettes

Despite the many obstacles arising at the interface of language and content teaching, examples abound in the research literature of teachers counterbalancing instructional strategies to engage students with language during subject-matter instruction. What follows is a selection of teacher vignettes, drawn from classroom studies of content-based second language teaching in both ESL and immersion settings, to illustrate teachers drawing attention to both curricular content and the target language as they interact with their students.

Vignette 1 (Gibbons, 1998, 2003). In a mainstream science classroom in Australia, a teacher of 9–10-year-old learners of English implemented an instructional sequence about magnetism with a view to helping students develop an academic register appropriate to the language of science. The sequence consisted of small-group work, teacher-guided reporting, and journal writing. To push students to use a more scientific register during the teacher-guided reporting stage, the teacher used explicit comments such as: "We're trying to talk like scientists," "Your language has got to be really precise," and "The language you choose is very important." The teacher interacted with individual students in ways that scaffolded their contributions, allowing for communication to proceed while providing access to new linguistic data. The teacher's elicitation of more appropriate language ("let's start using our scientific language") resulted in longer and more complete learner discourse than did simply recasting.

Vignette 2 (Laplante, 1993). Mme Legault, a 1st-grade French immersion teacher, counterbalanced language and content instruction as she interacted with students during science lessons. She provided rich and varied input and then helped students to improve the form and content of their own utterances by providing feedback that included questions, paraphrases, comments, translation, elaboration, and requests for translation or elaboration. Her interaction with students had a pedagogical function that encouraged language production on the part of the students and allowed them to negotiate the unfolding of certain activities.

Vignette 3 (Lyster, 1998b). Rachelle, a 4th-grade French immersion teacher, drew attention to relevant language features as she interacted with students during a science lesson about mammals and their natural defenses against predators. During these lively discussions, she maintained a central focus on meaning yet succeeded in eliciting synonyms, antonyms, homophones, more precise terms, words with similar structural properties, as well as correct grammatical gender, spelling, and pronunciation. She frequently used prompts that led students to experiment with language in creative ways, and also led students along a continuum from hearing and using general all-purpose verbs to more specific ones.

Vignette 4 (Day & Shapson, 1996). Claudette, a 7th-grade French immersion teacher created a language-rich science classroom that became a veritable arena of communication. Her students engaged in both "doing" science and collaboratively talking about it. Students were encouraged to speculate, justify, and be comfortable with the view that there might be "no right answer" to some questions, even though the teacher had clear learning objectives and structured her classes accordingly. Many opportunities for students to produce the second language and to communicate with one another arose inherently out of what was being learned, fusing language and science "into a unified whole" (p. 55) and enabling students to use a wide variety of language functions and structures.

Vignette 5 (Lapkin & Swain, 1996). Leonard, an 8th-grade French immersion teacher, presented a combined science and language arts lesson on the greenhouse effect, which was carefully planned yet presented in the guise of a spontaneous class discussion. He adopted a multifaceted approach to lexical instruction, drawing attention to phonological, grammatical, syntactic, sociolinguistic, and discourse-related aspects of vocabulary, in addition to meaning. His strategies included repetition, use of multiple synonyms in their characteristic syntactic frames, and revisiting words in a variety of contexts and in different parts of the lesson.

Vignette 6 (Kong, 2009). This comparative study of teachers in Hong Kong late immersion classrooms and in content-based foreign language classrooms in China revealed various instructional practices propitious for integrating language and content. For example, effective teachers implemented cyclical lessons (i.e., exploration with students from multiple perspectives) rather than linear lessons (i.e., coverage of a list of facts) as a way of providing students with multiple opportunities to explore and revisit content and content-related language. Effective teachers also organized complex content according to knowledge relationships (e.g., cause–effect, hypothesis, comparison), which were actualized in targeted language forms used explicitly and consistently (e.g., "lead to" and "result in" for cause-effect relationships; *if*-conditional clauses for hypothesis).

Summary and Conclusion

For years now, there have been calls for greater emphasis on language development in content-based instructional settings. Yet teaching with a dual focus on language and content continues to be challenging, for many reasons. This chapter addressed some of the pedagogical challenges at the interface of language and content, and proposed a counterbalanced approach that integrates both content-based and form-focused instruction as complementary ways of promoting continued second language growth.

Content-based and form-focused instructional options can be counterbalanced through activities that interweave balanced opportunities for input, production, and negotiation. In terms of classroom input, teachers need to cover a range of instructional options, from instruction designed to make content-based input comprehensible by means of various techniques that facilitate comprehension, to instruction designed to make language features more salient. Learners in immersion and content-based classrooms benefit from a broad spectrum of continual opportunities to process input for comprehending subject matter as well as for restructuring their representations of the target language through noticing and awareness activities. In terms of target language production, teachers need again to create a range of opportunities, which vary from content-based tasks designed to promote the use of the target language for academic purposes, to practice activities designed to promote the proceduralization of target language forms that tend otherwise to be avoided, misused, or unnoticed. In terms of classroom interaction, teachers and students need to negotiate language across the curriculum, as teachers exploit a range of interactional techniques that vary from the use of implicit feedback in the form of recasts that scaffold interaction in ways that facilitate students' participation, to feedback in the form of prompts and other signals that push learners beyond their use of recalcitrant interlanguage forms.

More research is needed to explore how learners can effectively and systematically engage with language in classrooms that emphasize content-driven input, purposeful tasks, and meaning-focused interaction. Counterbalanced instruction brings language to the forefront of content-based instruction, providing a tentative framework for systematically addressing the integration of language and content so that educators in content-based classrooms will be better positioned to integrate more focus on language, and that those in traditional language-focused classrooms will be inspired to integrate more content-based instruction as a means of enriching classroom discourse. That is, while there is a need to continue exploring effective ways of integrating more focus on language in content-based classrooms, there are also benefits to exploring ways of integrating more content-based instruction as a means of enriching classroom discourse in traditional language classrooms. Given their predominant focus on meaning, content-based classrooms provide a rich context for reflecting on and experimenting with innovative ways of second language teaching and learning.

Although content-based programs have far-reaching potential to innovate, they have not yet necessarily reached their full potential. As for any educational initiative, content-based programs need to continue to evolve in ways that (1) respond to the needs of changing student populations and their communities; (2) incorporate relevant research findings about effective instructional practices in specific contexts; and (3) adopt instructional practices that situate teachers in a more interactive relationship with students and knowledge than do transmission models of teaching. Agreeing with Swain (1988) that not all content teaching is necessarily good language teaching, Handscombe (1990) argued further that "the best content teaching is also the best language teaching" (p. 185). To attain such exemplary levels of instructional practice where the best content teaching and the best language teaching coalesce, content-based approaches to second language teaching have much to gain from social-constructivist views of education (e.g., Day & Shapson, 1996; Laplante, 1997), which seek to minimize transmission models of instruction and attribute considerable importance to language as both a cognitive and social tool in all learning.

References

Allen, P., Swain, M., Harley, B., & Cummins J. (1990). Aspects of classroom treatment: Toward a more comprehensive view of second language education. In B. Harley, P. Allen, J. Cummins, & M. Swain (Eds.), *The development of second language proficiency* (pp. 57–81). Cambridge: Cambridge University Press.

Ammar, A., & Spada, N. (2006). One size fits all? Recasts, prompts and L2 learning. *Studies in Second Language Acquisition, 28*, 543–574.

Arkoudis, S. (2006). Negotiating the rough ground between ESL and mainstream teachers. *International Journal of Bilingual Education and Bilingualism, 9*, 415–433.

Aston, G. (1986). Trouble-shooting in interaction with learners: The more the merrier? *Applied Linguistics, 7*, 128–143.

Brinton, D., Snow, M., & Wesche, M. (2004). *Content-based second language instruction.* Ann Arbor: University of Michigan Press.

Brown, L. (Ed.) (1993). *The new shorter Oxford English dictionary.* Oxford: Clevedon Press.

Bruner, J. (1971). *The relevance of education.* New York: Norton.

Burger, S., & Chrétien, S. (2001). The development of oral production in content-based second language courses at the University of Ottawa. *The Canadian Modern Language Review, 58*, 84–102.

Chaudron, C. (1977). A descriptive model of discourse in the corrective treatment of learners' errors. *Language Learning, 27*, 29–46.

Chaudron, C. (1986). Teachers' priorities in correcting learners' errors in French immersion classes. In R. Day (Ed.), *Talking to learn* (pp. 64–84). Rowley, MA: Newbury House.

Cloud, N., Genesee, F., & Hamayan, E. (2000). *Dual language instruction: A handbook for enriched education.* Boston: Heinle & Heinle.

Creese, A. (2002). The discursive construction of power in teacher partnerships: Language and subject specialists in mainstream schools. *TESOL Quarterly, 36*, 597–616.

Creese, A. (2006). Supporting talk? Partnership teachers in classroom interaction. *International Journal of Bilingual Education and Bilingualism, 9*, 434–453.

Dalton-Puffer, C. (2006). Questions in CLIL classrooms: Strategic questioning to encourage speaking. In A. Martinez-Flor & E. Usó (Eds.), *Current trends in the development of the four skills within a communicative framework* (pp. 187–213). Berlin: Mouton de Gruyter.

Dalton-Puffer, C. (2007). *Discourse in content and language integrated learning (CLIL) classrooms.* Amsterdam/Philadelphia: John Benjamins.

Day, E., & Shapson, S. (1991). Integrating formal and functional approaches to language teaching in French immersion: An experimental study. *Language Learning, 41*, 25–58.

Day, E., & Shapson, S. (1996). *Studies in immersion education.* Clevedon: Multilingual Matters.

DeKeyser, R. (1998). Beyond focus on form: Cognitive perspectives on learning and practicing second language grammar. In C. Doughty & J. Williams (Eds.), *Focus on form in classroom second language acquisition* (pp. 42–63). Cambridge: Cambridge University Press.

DeKeyser, R. (2003). Implicit and explicit learning. In M. Long & C. Doughty (Eds.), *Handbook of second language acquisition* (pp. 313–348). Malden, MA: Blackwell.

DeKeyser, R. (Ed.) (2007). *Practice in a second language: Perspectives from applied linguistics and cognitive psychology.* Cambridge: Cambridge University Press.

Doughty, C. (2001). Cognitive underpinnings of focus on form. In P. Robinson (Ed.), *Cognition and second language instruction* (pp. 206–257). New York: Cambridge University Press.

Doughty, C., & Varela, E. (1998). Communicative focus on form. In C. Doughty & J. Williams (Eds.), *Focus on form in classroom second language acquisition* (pp. 114–138). Cambridge, UK: Cambridge University Press.

Duff, P. (2001). Language, literacy, content, and (pop) culture: Challenges for ESL students in mainstream courses. *The Canadian Modern Language Review, 58*, 103–132.

Early, M. (2001). Language and content in social practice: A case study. *The Canadian Modern Language Review, 58*, 156–179.

Echevarría, J., & Graves, A. (1998). *Sheltered content instruction.* Boston: Allyn & Bacon.

Echevarría, J., Vogt, M., & Short, D. (2008). *Making content comprehensible for English learners: The SIOP model.* Boston: Pearson Education.

Ellis, R. (2000). Task-based research and language pedagogy. *Language Teaching Research, 4*, 193–220.

Fortune, T., Tedick, D., & Walker, C. (2008). Integrated language and content teaching: Insights from the immersion classroom. In T. Fortune & D. Tedick (Eds.), *Pathways to bilingualism and multilingualism: Evolving perspectives on immersion education* (pp. 71–96). Clevedon: Multilingual Matters.

Foster, P. (1998). A classroom perspective on the negotiation of meaning. *Applied Linguistics, 19*, 1–23.

Foster, P., & Ohta, A. (2005). Negotiation for meaning and peer assistance in second language classrooms. *Applied Linguistics, 26*, 402–430.

Gass, S. (1988). Integrating research areas: A framework for second language studies. *Applied Linguistics, 9*, 198–217.

Genesee, F. (1987). *Learning through two languages: Studies of immersion and bilingual children.* Cambridge, MA: Newbury House.

Genesee, F. (1994). *Integrating language and content: Lessons from immersion.* Educational Practice Report No. 11. Santa Cruz, CA: National Center for Research on Cultural Diversity and Second Language Learning.

Gibbons, P. (1998). Classroom talk and the learning of new registers in a second language. *Language and Education, 12*, 99–118.

Gibbons, P. (2003). Mediating language learning: Teacher interactions with ESL students in a content-based classroom. *TESOL Quarterly, 37*, 247–273.

Handscombe, J. (1990). The complementary roles of researchers and practitioners in second language education. In B. Harley, P. Allen, J. Cummins, & M. Swain (Eds.), *The development of second language proficiency* (pp. 181–186). Cambridge: Cambridge University Press.

Harley, B. (1989). Functional grammar in French immersion: A classroom experiment. *Applied Linguistics, 10*, 331–359.

Harley, B. (1993). Instructional strategies and SLA in early French immersion. *Studies in Second Language Acquisition, 15*, 245–259.

Harley, B. (1994). Appealing to consciousness in the L2 classroom. *AILA Review, 11*, 57–68.

Harley, B., Cummins, J., Swain, M., & Allen, P. (1990). The nature of language proficiency. In B. Harley, P. Allen, J. Cummins, & M. Swain (Eds.), *The development of second language proficiency* (pp. 7–25). Cambridge: Cambridge University Press.

Harley, B., & Swain, M. (1984). The interlanguage of immersion students and its implications for second language teaching. In A. Davies, C. Criper, & A. Howatt (Eds.), *Interlanguage* (pp. 291–311). Edinburgh: Edinburgh University Press.

Hoare, P., & Kong, S. (2008). Late immersion in Hong Kong: Still stressed or making progress? In T. Fortune & D. Tedick (Eds.), *Pathways to bilingualism and multilingualism: Evolving perspectives on immersion education* (pp. 242–263). Clevedon: Multilingual Matters.

Kong, S. (2009). Content-based instruction: What can we learn from content-trained teachers' and language-trained teachers' pedagogies? *The Canadian Modern Language Review, 66*, 233–267.

Krashen, S. (1981). *Second language acquisition and second language learning.* Oxford: Pergamon.

Krashen, S. (1982). *Principles and practice in second language acquisition.* New York: Pergamon.

Krashen, S. (1985). *The input hypothesis: Issues and implications.* London: Longman.

Krashen, S. (1994). The input hypothesis and its rivals. In N. Ellis (Ed.), *Implicit and explicit learning of languages* (pp. 45–77). London: Academic Press.

Lapkin, S., & Swain, M. (1996). Vocabulary teaching in a grade 8 French immersion classroom: A descriptive study. *The Canadian Modern Language Review, 53,* 242–256.

Laplante, B. (1993). Stratégies pédagogiques et enseignement des sciences en immersion française : le cas d'une enseignante. *The Canadian Modern Language Review, 49,* 567–588.

Laplante, B. (1997). Teachers' beliefs and instructional strategies in science: Pushing analysis further. *Science Education, 81,* 277–294.

Lee, J. (2007). Corrective feedback and learner uptake in English immersion classrooms at the primary level in Korea. *English Teaching, 62*(4), 311–334.

Lightbown, P. M. (1998). The importance of timing in focus on form. In C. Doughty & J. Williams (Eds.), *Focus on form in classroom second language acquisition* (p. 177–196). Cambridge: Cambridge University Press.

Lightbown, P. M., Halter, R., White, J., & Horst, M. (2002). Comprehension-based learning: The limits of "Do it yourself." *The Canadian Modern Language Review, 58,* 427–464.

Lightbown, P. M., & Spada, N. (2006). *How languages are learned* (3rd ed.). Oxford: Oxford University Press.

Lindholm-Leary, K. (2001). *Dual language education.* Clevedon: Multilingual Matters.

Lochtman, K. (2005). Negative feedback and learner uptake in analytic foreign language teaching. In A. Housen & M. Pierrard (Eds.), *Investigations in instructed second language acquisition* (pp. 333–352). Berlin and New York: Mouton de Gruyter.

Long, M. (1996). The role of the linguistic environment in second language acquisition. In W. C. Ritchie & T. K. Bhatia (Eds.), *Handbook of second language acquisition* (pp. 413–468). San Diego, CA: Academic Press.

Long, M. (2007). *Problems in SLA.* Mahwah, NJ: Lawrence Erlbaum.

Loschky, L., & Bley-Vroman, R. (1993). Grammar and task-based methodology. In G. Crookes & S. Gass (Eds.), *Tasks and language learning: Integrating theory and practice* (pp. 123–167). Clevedon: Multilingual Matters.

Lyster, R. (1998a). Recasts, repetition, and ambiguity in L2 classroom discourse. *Studies in Second Language Acquisition, 20,* 51–81.

Lyster, R. (1998b). Immersion pedagogy and implications for language teaching. In J. Cenoz & F. Genesee (Eds.), *Beyond bilingualism: Multilingualism and multilingual education* (pp. 64–95). Clevedon: Multilingual Matters.

Lyster, R. (1998c). Form in immersion classroom discourse: In or out of focus? *Canadian Journal of Applied Linguistics, 1,* 53–82.

Lyster, R. (2002). Negotiation in immersion teacher–student interaction. *International Journal of Educational Research, 37,* 237–253.

Lyster, R. (2004a). Differential effects of prompts and recasts in form-focused instruction. *Studies in Second Language Acquisition, 26,* 399–432.

Lyster, R. (2004b). Research on form-focused instruction in immersion classrooms: Implications for theory and practice. *Journal of French Language Studies, 14,* 321–341.

Lyster, R. (2007). *Learning and teaching languages through content: A counterbalanced approach.* Amsterdam: John Benjamins.

Lyster, R., Collins, L., & Ballinger, S. (2009). Linking languages: A bilingual read-aloud project. *Language Awareness, 18*(3/4), 366–383.

Lyster, R., & Mori, H. (2006). Interactional feedback and instructional counterbalance. *Studies in Second Language Acquisition, 28,* 269–300.

Lyster, R., & Ranta, L. (1997). Corrective feedback and learner uptake: Negotiation of form in communicative classrooms. *Studies in Second Language Acquisition, 19,* 37–66.

McHoul, A. (1990). The organization of repair in classroom talk. *Language in Society, 19,* 349–377.

Mariotti, C. (2006). Negotiated interactions and repair patterns in CLIL settings. *Vienna English Working Papers, 15* (3), 33–39.

Mehisto, P., Marsh, D., & Frigols, M. (2008). *Uncovering CLIL: Content and language integrated learning in bilingual and multilingual education.* Oxford: Macmillan.

Mendez, C. (1992). How many Wednesdays? A portrait of immersion teaching through reflection. In E. Bernhardt (Ed.), *Life in language immersion classrooms* (pp. 45–63). Clevedon: Multilingual Matters.

Met, M. (1994). Teaching content through a second language. In F. Genesee (Ed.), *Educating second language children* (pp. 159–182). New York: Cambridge University Press.

Met, M. (1998). Curriculum decision-making in content-based language teaching. In J. Cenoz & F. Genesee (Eds.), *Beyond bilingualism: Multilingualism and multilingual education* (pp. 35–63). Clevedon: Multilingual Matters.

Mohan, B. (1986). *Language and content.* Reading, MA: Addison-Wesley.

Mohan, B., & Beckett, G. H. (2001). A functional approach to research on content-based language learning: Recasts in causal explanations. *The Canadian Modern Language Review, 58,* 133–155.

Musumeci, D. (1996). Teacher–learner negotiation in content-based instruction: Communication at cross-purposes? *Applied Linguistics, 17*, 286–325.

Nassaji, H., & Wells, G. (2000). What's the use of "triadic dialogue"?: An investigation of teacher–student interaction. *Applied Linguistics, 21*, 376–406.

Netten, J. (1991). Towards a more language oriented second language classroom. In L. Malavé & G. Duquette (Eds.), *Language, culture and cognition* (pp. 284–304). Clevedon: Multilingual Matters.

Pessoa, S., Hendry, H., Donato, R., Tucker, G. R., & Lee, H. (2007). Content-based instruction in the foreign language classroom: A discourse perspective. *Foreign Language Annals, 40*, 102–121.

Pica, T. (2002). Subject-matter content: How does it assist the interactional and linguistic needs of classroom language learners? *The Modern Language Journal, 86*, 1–19.

Ranta, L. (2002). The role of learners' language analytic ability in the communicative classroom. In P. Robinson (Ed.), *Individual differences and instructed language learning* (pp. 159–180). Amsterdam andPhiladelphia: John Benjamins.

Ranta, L., & Lyster, R. (2007). A cognitive approach to improving immersion students' oral language abilities: The Awareness-Practice-Feedback sequence. In R. DeKeyser (Ed.), *Practicing for second language use: Perspectives from applied linguistics and cognitive psychology* (pp. 141–160). Cambridge: Cambridge University Press.

Rebuffot, J. (1993). *Le point sur l'immersion au Canada*. Montreal: Éditions CEC.

Salomone, A. (1992a). Immersion teachers' pedagogical beliefs and practices: Results of a descriptive analysis. In E. Bernhardt (Ed.), *Life in language immersion classrooms* (pp. 9–44). Clevedon: Multilingual Matters.

Salomone, A. (1992b). Student–teacher interactions in selected French immersion classrooms. In E. Bernhardt (Ed.), *Life in language immersion classrooms* (pp. 97–109). Clevedon: Multilingual Matters.

Schmidt, R. (1990). The role of consciousness in second language learning. *Applied Linguistics, 11*, 129–158.

Schmidt, R. (1994). Deconstructing consciousness in search of useful definitions for applied linguistics. *AILA Review, 11*, 11–26.

Segalowitz, N. (2000). Automaticity and attentional skill in fluent performance. In H. Riggenbach (Ed.), *Perspectives on fluency* (pp. 200–219). Ann Arbor: University of Michigan Press.

Sharwood Smith, M. (1981). Consciousness-raising and the second language learner. *Applied Linguistics, 2*, 159–168.

Sharwood Smith, M. (1993). Input enhancement in instructed SLA. *Studies in Second Language Acquisition, 15*, 165–179.

Short, D. (2002). Language learning in sheltered social studies classes. *TESOL Journal, 11*, 18–24.

Sinclair, J., & Coulthard, R. M. (1975). *Towards an analysis of discourse: The English used by teachers and pupils*. Oxford: Oxford University Press.

Skehan, P. (1998). *A cognitive approach to language learning*. Oxford: Oxford University Press.

Snow, M. (1987). *Immersion teacher handbook*. Los Angeles: UCLA.

Snow, M., Met, M., & Genesee, F. (1989). A conceptual framework for the integration of language and content in second/foreign language instruction. *TESOL Quarterly, 23*, 201–217.

Södergård, M. (2008). Teacher strategies for second language production in immersion kindergarten in Finland. In T. Fortune & D. Tedick (Eds.), *Pathways to bilingualism and multilingualism: Evolving perspectives on immersion education* (pp. 152–173). Clevedon: Multilingual Matters.

Stern, H. H. (1990). Analysis and experience as variables in second language pedagogy. In B. Harley, P. Allen, J. Cummins, & M. Swain (Eds.), *The development of second language proficiency* (pp. 93–109). Cambridge: Cambridge University Press.

Stern, H. H. (1992). *Issues and options in language teaching*. Oxford: Oxford University Press.

Swain, M. (1985). Communicative competence: Some roles of comprehensible input and comprehensible output in its development In S. Gass & C. Madden (Eds.), *Input in second language acquisition* (pp. 235–253). Rowley, MA: Newbury House.

Swain, M. (1988). Manipulating and complementing content teaching to maximize second language learning. *TESL Canada Journal, 6*, 68–83.

Swain, M. (1996). Integrating language and content in immersion classrooms: Research perspectives. *The Canadian Modern Language Review, 52*, 529–548.

Swain, M., & Carroll, S. (1987). The immersion observation study. In B. Harley, P. Allen, J. Cummins, & M. Swain (Eds.), *Development of bilingual proficiency. Final report. Volume II: Classroom treatment* (pp. 190–316). Toronto: Modern Language Centre, OISE/UT.

Swain, M., & Lapkin, S. (1982). *Evaluating bilingual education in Ontario: A Canadian case study*. Clevedon: Multilingual Matters.

Tardif, C. (1991). Quelques traits distinctifs de la pédagogie d'immersion. *Études de linguistique appliquée, 82*, 39–51.

Tardif, C. (1994). Classroom teacher talk in early immersion. *The Canadian Modern Language Review, 50*, 466–481.

Tharpe, R., & Gallimore, R. (1988). *Rousing minds to life: Teaching, learning, and schooling in social context*. New York: Cambridge University Press.

Turnbull, M., Lapkin, S., & Hart, D. (2001). Grade 3 immersion students' performance in literacy and mathematics: Province-wide results from Ontario (1989–99). *The Canadian Modern Language Review, 58,* 9–26.

Weber, S., & Tardif, C. (1991). Assessing L2 competency in early immersion classrooms. *The Canadian Modern Language Review, 47,* 916–932.

Wesche, M. (Ed.) (2001). French immersion and content-based language teaching in Canada. Special issue. *The Canadian Modern Language Review, 58*(1).

Yang, Y., & Lyster, R. (2010). Effects of oral production practice and feedback on EFL learners' acquisition of regular and irregular past-tense forms. *Studies in Second Language Acquisition, 32*(2), 235–263.

38
Content-Based Instruction and Vocabulary Learning

I. S. P. Nation and Stuart Webb

Content-based instruction involves the learning of language while studying content matter subjects such as mathematics, science, English literature, and technology. It is also known as teaching language through the curriculum and sustained-content language teaching (SCLT). Typically, the subject matter of English teaching courses consists of a variety of topics or themes selected to be interesting or generally useful for the language learners (Cook, 1983). In content-based instruction however, the learners are studying the content as a part of their normal education, and as well as learning the content matter they need to increase their English proficiency. In Malaysia, for example, mathematics and science are taught in English in the secondary schools with the two goals of the learners learning mathematics and science, and becoming proficient in both the receptive and productive use of English in an academic setting. In other subject areas in Malaysia, study is done in the first language.

The Value of Content-Based Instruction

There is plenty of evidence that content-based instruction can be effective for both of these goals. In a very useful and wide-ranging review Stoller and Grabe (1997) show that there is strong theoretical and experimental support for the principles and practice of content-based instruction. Their evidence is drawn from a variety of areas of research on educational and cognitive psychology, and from research on content-based instruction itself. There are also plenty of reasons why content-based instruction could help vocabulary learning:

1. By limiting the content matter of the lessons to a particular subject area, the vocabulary load becomes much less. Research by Sutarsyah, Nation, and Kennedy (1994) compared the vocabulary of an economics textbook with the vocabulary of a similarly-sized collection of texts on a variety of different topics. There were well over twice as many word families in the collection of texts than in the single textbook, even though they were the same length. Most of these extra words were words not in the high frequency words of the language and not in the Academic Word List (Coxhead, 2000). Having a wide variety of topics in a course results in a heavy vocabulary load. Sticking to one subject area makes the amount of new vocabulary much more manageable.
2. Keeping within the same subject area increases the repetitions of the vocabulary, both high frequency and academic vocabulary as well as technical vocabulary (Hwang & Nation, 1989;

Schmitt & Carter, 2000; Sutarsyah et al., 1994). This increases the amount of the vocabulary being learned.

3.   Limiting the content matter to a particular subject area allows learners to build up knowledge of the subject area. This means that later study in that area will become easier because the content is increasingly familiar. This makes it easier to guess from context, and to develop and establish new concepts.

     If the content matter knowledge is already well established in the first language, then dealing with second language texts is much easier.

4.   Subject matter study involves learning new ideas and applying them. This application results in the vocabulary being used in new ways and this is an ideal situation for vocabulary learning (Joe, 1998). This is probably the most striking in mathematics where the learning of mathematics largely consists of a variety of different kinds of applications of the basic mathematical rules and principles. The various kinds of applications range from those involving just figures and symbols, such as,

$$3x + 4x =$$

to those which are very contextualized:

A rotary sprinkler waters a lawn in a circular pattern. The water can reach up to 8 m from the sprinkler. What area of the lawn can be watered from one position?

(Barton, 1999, p. 195)

In good science texts, there are also many opportunities for applying new ideas. These applications require learners to understand the vocabulary involved, to process the vocabulary thoughtfully, to use this vocabulary both receptively and productively in new ways (generative use). Generative use is increased when learners interact with each other about the task and interact with the teacher about the task. Generative use and the development of the concepts involved and their application are closely linked (Nation & Gu, 2007, pp. 50–51).

The aim of this chapter is to consider what vocabulary should be focused on, how much vocabulary could be set as a goal, and what opportunities for learning vocabulary there can be in content-based instruction.

What Vocabulary Should Be Focused on?

Content-based instruction typically involves using texts that are written for native speakers of English. That is, they are unsimplified texts, and although they may be written to suit the age of the learners, they will typically have the same vocabulary characteristics as unsimplified texts. These characteristics include the use of vocabulary from a range of frequency levels likely to be familiar to native speakers, the occurrence of a large number of words that occur only once in the text, and the occurrence of a topic-based technical vocabulary.

High-Frequency Words

Most of the vocabulary in the text will be accounted for by the first 2,000 words of English. It is likely that most learners involved in content-based instruction will already know these words, but if they don't then their task will be very hard indeed. It is thus worth checking for some learners that these words are known by using the Vocabulary Levels Test (Schmitt, Schmitt, & Clapham, 2001) or the bilingual versions of the first 2,000 words of English (see the Vocabulary Resource Booklet at http://www.victoria.ac.nz/lals/staff/paul-nation/nation.aspx). The Vocabulary Levels Test tests vocabulary knowledge at the 2,000 word level, the 3,000 word level, the 5,000 word level, the Academic Word List, and the 10,000 word level. The test can be sat quite quickly and not all levels need be administered. The test is also easy to mark and interpret. It is clearly essential that learners need to know at least the first 2,000 words of English to cope with content-based instruction. The first 2,000 words of English cover around 80% or more of the running words in academic texts.

The Academic Word List

The words from the Academic Word List (Coxhead, 2000) will cover around 10% of the running words in a school or university text. It is thus very important that learners know these words. Although these words occur often in non-fiction texts, they are not easily learnt during the reading of such texts (Cohen, Glasman, Rosenbaum-Cohen, Ferrara, & Fine, 1988; Donley & Reppen, 2001). This is probably because they are not as salient in such texts as the topic-related technical vocabulary of the text, and because these words are not usually defined in the text. Academic words are very important in content-based instruction, because they help the writer perform the academic functions of such texts. That is, they are called on when reviewing previous research, when explaining the methodology used in a study, when presenting the results of the study, and when discussing these results. A teacher involved in content-based instruction needs to know whether the learners know the words in the Academic Word List or not. This can be checked by using the Academic Word List section of the Vocabulary Levels Test. If the teacher discovers that the learners are not familiar with most of these words, then it is important that they are given deliberate attention, and that learners are made aware of the importance of knowing them. Some words from the Academic Word List may actually be technical words within a subject area (Chung & Nation, 2003).

Technical Vocabulary

The most striking words in content-based instruction will be the technical vocabulary of the subject area. Learners seem to have little difficulty in picking up this vocabulary. Technical vocabulary typically occurs quite frequently in its subject area, is often formally defined within the text, and will need to be used in most activities involving the application of ideas in the course. Around 20% to 30% of the running words in a subject matter text are likely to be technical words that are strongly related to that subject area.

The technical vocabulary of a subject area can range from a few hundred words to several thousand words depending on the particular subject area (Chung & Nation, 2003). This vocabulary will certainly attract the attention of both the teacher and the learners, and the content-based teachers will be the best qualified to deal with such vocabulary because of their knowledge of the subject area. Technical vocabulary is best learned while studying the subject matter.

Low-Frequency Words

So far, we have looked at high-frequency vocabulary, academic vocabulary, and technical vocabulary. In any text the remaining words are likely to be proper nouns and low-frequency words. To be able to read an academic text without the assistance of dictionaries or other supports, a learner needs a vocabulary of around 8,000 word families. Even with this number of words there will still be many unknown words within the text, probably around five or six per page on every page of the book (Nation, 2006).

Ideally, if content-based texts were specially prepared for learners of English, there would be almost no low-frequency words in the texts, and there should certainly be no low-frequency words that occur only once or twice within the texts. It is likely that in most technical texts, at least two or three words per page are low-frequency words that only occur once within the text. When preparing content-based texts for learners of English, an ideal first step would be to make sure that there were no low-frequency one timers in the texts. An ideal second step would be to remove all of the low-frequency words that are not technical words beyond the fourth or fifth 1,000 words of English. Surprisingly, not a lot of changes need to be made to a text in order to get rid of many of its low-frequency words.

Let us now look briefly at an example of part of a secondary school text in order to see the different kinds of vocabulary in the text:

Among our nations, *Aotearoa* is the only one with *pounamu*, greenstone. *Pounamu* is highly prized for its *versatility*, beauty, and *rarity*. In *Aotearoa*, it is found only in the South Island, known to the *Maori* as *Te Wai Pounamu*—water of greenstone.

Pounamu is *carved* into *jewellery*, weapons, and tools, and these would be used, exchanged or handed on as family *taonga*, precious belongings or *heirlooms*. On occasions of importance people may wear *Pounamu*. Many of the pieces may go back **generations** within a family.

The unmarked words (among, our, nations) are from the first 2,000 high-frequency words of English. The word in bold (**generations**) is from the Academic Word List. The words in italics (*Aotearoa*, *pounamu*, *versatility*) are from the low-frequency words of English or are proper nouns or foreign words. Note that most of the text consists of high-frequency words. Note also that many of the low-frequency words are very important for the message of the text.

In order of priority, the vocabulary goals of content-based vocabulary instruction should be (1) to firmly establish knowledge of the most frequent 2,000 words of English, (2) to help learners develop both receptive and productive control of academic vocabulary, (3) to develop a good working knowledge of the technical vocabulary of the subject area, and (4) to expand learners' knowledge of the low-frequency words of English in frequency-based stages.

How Much Vocabulary Can Learners Be Expected to Learn?

As we have seen, content-based instruction should not only increase learners' knowledge of the technical vocabulary of the subject they are studying, but should also contribute significantly to their knowledge of other vocabulary, namely high-frequency vocabulary, academic vocabulary, and low-frequency vocabulary. How much vocabulary can learners be expected to gain control of over a year? Native speakers of English seem to learn vocabulary at a rate of around 1,000 words a year through their wide variety of experiences with language. This is largely receptive knowledge, and a 13-year-old native speaker would not be expected to be able to produce all of the thousands of words that they know.

Second language learners should at least try to match the native speaker rate of learning. This means that in one year of study they should learn about a thousand words, or in a 40-week school year around 25 words a week. This averages out to around five words a day. This is still quite a lot of learning, because the second language learner will not have the same amount of meaning-focused input that a first language learner will have. Deliberate learning however is a way of speeding up the learning process, at least in the initial stages.

Teachers cannot be responsible for all of this learning, although they should be guiding learners in their choice of the words to learn. Teachers should also provide training in learning words from word cards, because this is a very effective learning technique that provides the kind of knowledge that is needed for normal language use (Elgort, 2007). There are efficient ways of learning from word cards (Nation, 2008, pp. 104–114), and there are inefficient ways. Learners can benefit from training in how to do this kind of learning.

The older the learners, the more valuable it is that they are explicitly aware of their learning goals. This can have very good effects on motivation, and can be an encouragement for them to take responsibility for their own learning.

How Can a Teacher Provide Opportunities for Vocabulary Learning?

In language courses, learning can occur through four major kinds of tasks—experience tasks, shared tasks, guided tasks, and independent tasks. In this section we will look at how experience tasks, shared tasks, and guided tasks can be used in content-based instruction to help vocabulary learning. In many of these tasks, vocabulary learning will not be the main goal of the task. The main goal will usually be the learning of the subject matter of the lesson. However as we shall see it is possible to design tasks that have a content learning focus, but that also provide good opportunities for vocabulary learning. Being able to do independent tasks is the eventual goal of working with experience, shared, and guided tasks. Independent tasks involve the learners working largely without support.

Conditions for Vocabulary Learning

Each of the four major kinds of tasks draw on the same conditions for vocabulary learning. If these conditions are present, then vocabulary learning has a good chance of occurring. Let us now look briefly at the five conditions, and then see how they can be helped to occur in each of the tasks.

1. *Motivation*: The learners are interested and attentive. Motivation is a pre-requisite for attention. Tseng and Schmitt (2008) see motivation of various kinds as being central to vocabulary learning.
2. *Repetition*: The learners have repeated opportunities to meet the word. Although there have been many attempts to find the number of repetitions that are needed for a word to become established, this research has not given consistent results. It does confirm the commonsense notion however that the more often a word is met, the more likely it is to be known (Webb, 2007).
3. *Four strands*: There is a balance of opportunities for learning (Nation, 2007a). That is, there are opportunities for learning through meaning-focused input, meaning-focused output, language-focused learning, and fluency development. One effect of this will be that the learners have opportunities to produce the word. Productive use requires greater and more specific knowledge than receptive use. Having to produce a word encourages the learner to give it different kinds of attention when it is again met in input (Swain, 2005).
4. *Thoughtful processing*: The learners have opportunities to notice, retrieve, or to make generative use of the vocabulary. The levels of processing hypothesis (Craik & Lockhart, 1972) says the critical factor in memory is the depth or thoughtfulness of the mental processing at the moment of learning. Laufer and Hulstijn (2001) have operationalized this in the involvement load hypothesis, which makes use of the conditions of need, search, and evaluation. In this discussion however we will draw on the conditions of noticing, retrieval, and generative use. Noticing involves giving some degree of conscious attention to an item (Schmidt, 1990). Conscious, deliberate attention helps learning. Retrieval involves recalling aspects of a word (its form, meaning, or use). For example, retrieval is involved when a word is met in reading

and its meaning is recalled. Retrieval is also involved when a speaker recalls the word form needed to express a wanted meaning. Baddeley (1990) considers retrieval to be one of the most robust mechanisms available to improve memory of items. Generative use (Joe, 1998) involves meeting or using a word in a way that is different from previous meetings or uses. The more generatively a word is used, the stronger the memory of it.

5. *Meaningful relationships*: The learning is set within a knowledge framework that helps storage and recall. Opposites, near synonyms, and members of a lexical set such as furniture, days of the week, fruit are more difficult to learn if they occur within the same lesson. These different meaning relationships bring items together in ways that resemble a list. However, meaning relationships that bring items together in ways that resemble the kinds of relationship within a sentence have a positive effect on learning (Nation, 2000). For example, learning words such as *conditions*, *apply*, *frequently* together has a positive effect on learning because they can relate to each other in the way that a subject relates to a verb, or a verb to an adverb.

These five conditions apply to experience, shared, guided, and independent tasks. Let us look at each type of task and how each type of task can bring these conditions into play.

Experience Tasks

In an experience task, a learner performs a normal language use activity in much the same way that a native speaker would do it, but because the learner brings a lot of relevant previous experience to the task, the task is easy to do. The best known use of experience tasks occurs in teaching first language reading (Ashton-Warner, 1963). In an experience approach to reading, a young learner draws a picture of something that recently happened to them. The teacher then asks the learner what the picture is about, and writes the learner's description at the bottom of the picture using exactly the same words that the learner used. This then becomes the learner's reading text for the day. The learner brings a great deal of experience to the reading of this text. First, the learner is very familiar with the language in the text, because the learner produced the text. Second, the learner is very familiar with the ideas in the text, because it is based on the picture that the learner drew. Third, the learner is very familiar with the discourse features of the text, because it is the text that the learner produced. The only unfamiliar part of the task is making the connection between the written text and the meaning it conveys. This is the goal of the reading lesson. Clearly, the learner brings a lot of experience to this task and thus can perform it with a high degree of success.

Experience tasks are very well suited to content-based instruction. If the work in the course is usefully sequenced so that each task that the learners do is well supported by the learning that has gone before, then each task is in effect an experience task. Each task that the learner does makes the next task easier to do.

There are many ways of sequencing tasks so that each one builds on the previous ones (Nation, 2007b). A very useful way of doing this is to use linked skills. In a linked skills activity, a series of tasks focuses on the same topic. For example, first the learners may read about the topic, then they can talk about it in groups, and finally they write about it. This particular sequence begins with the skill of reading, then moves to speaking, and finally to writing. The word *skills* in the term *linked skills* refers to the skills of listening, speaking, reading, and writing. Many possible sequences can be made from the four skills, and a sequence need not involve all different skills. For example, the learners can read about a subject, then talk about it, and then read something more difficult about it. In a course where English is taught through the curriculum, there are useful sequences of activities that build on each other. This means that the later activities rely a lot on what has been learned before. Often the effect of this is to help learners develop fluency with the ideas and vocabulary.

If a task is too difficult for the learners to do, the teacher can (1) change the task so it only draws on what the learners already know, (2) talk about the ideas needed to do the task, reminding the learners of things they have already studied but may have forgotten, or (3) pre-teach the ideas and language needed to do the task (Nation & Gu, 2007, p. 73).

How do experience tasks help vocabulary learning? In experience tasks, the prototypical means of vocabulary learning is through guessing from context. If the learners bring a lot of background knowledge and experience to a task, then this will provide a very supportive language and knowledge context for any unknown language items. Let us look at an example of an experience task to show how this might happen.

For the example we will take a unit of work on electrolysis in a junior high school science textbook (Noor, Mak, Quek, & Chong, 2005). The unit begins with examples of electrolysis in daily life, as in plating medals and spoons. This introduction deliberately stimulates previous knowledge and relates it to the topic. The main goal is to help learners gain control of the ideas that the unit will deal with. The next section of the unit defines electrolysis and explains how it occurs. This is a kind of pre-teaching and makes the following activity easier. The following activity deals with three examples of electrolysiselectroplating involving copper, silver, and chromium; the extraction of metals involving aluminum; and the purification of metals involving copper. So far the unit has given some familiar examples of electrolysis, has defined what it is and how it occurs, and has examined three extended examples, each using electrolysis for a different purpose. The next part of the unit is a self-assessment test. The unit then continues with a related topic on the production of electrical energy from chemical reactions.

The sequence of activities provides good conditions for vocabulary learning. (The italic mini-headings below refer back to the list of conditions described at the beginning of this section.)

Motivation: The content matter of the unit is interesting and challenging and it is likely to gain the learners' attention. The unit involves discovery learning where the learners are active in doing experiments and solving problems that should challenge them.

Repetition: The different parts of the unit provide an opportunity for the technical vocabulary to be repeated. The design of the unit as a series of experience tasks, each one building on the other, helps learners understand the meaning of the new words, and in a few cases the technical vocabulary is specifically defined. Because the topic of each part of the unit is increasingly familiar as learners move through it, it becomes much easier to guess new words from context when they occur.

Four strands: There are opportunities for both receptive and productive use of the target vocabulary, as well as some deliberate learning. As students become more familiar with the vocabulary the focus may move toward fluency.

Thoughtful processing: Because experience tasks involve the application of previously met ideas to new situations, there are plenty of opportunities for retrieval and generative use.

Meaningful relationships: All of this vocabulary learning is taking place within a well structured unit of work. It would be quite easy to draw a diagram showing how the ideas in each of the parts of the unit (definitions, analysis, examples, applications) fit together to make up the topic of electrolysis. The vocabulary learning is thus taking place within a set of meaningful relationships. These relationships are likely to have a very positive effect on learning because they involve syntagmatic rather than paradigmatic relationships between the words (Nation, 2000). That is, the learners are not studying lists of related words, but are studying words that are being used to do things.

From the perspective of experience tasks, a well-designed unit will have parts that build on each other typically involving linked skills activities, will make obvious and meaningful connections to what the learners already know about the topic, will provide opportunities for application and analysis of the ideas involved both receptively and productively, and will stay largely within the topic area so that there are plenty of opportunities for repetition.

Shared Tasks

Shared tasks, or group work, provide the opportunity for learners to learn from each other. In experience tasks, the support comes from the design of the tasks and their relationship with previous knowledge. In shared tasks, learners support each other, and by working as a group individuals are able to do things that they could not easily do by themselves. Shared tasks can set up the same conditions for vocabulary learning as experience tasks, but they do this in different ways.

Here is an example of a task from a science text on radioactive substances (Noor et al., 2005, p. 36):

Aim: to study radioactive substances

1. Your teacher will show videos or charts about radioactive substances, radioactive radiation and radioisotopes.
2. Discuss the following in groups:

    (a) radioactive substances and examples
    (b) the process of radioactive decay and the types of radiation emitted
    (c) what are radioisotopes?

Let us compare this with the following task from a unit on combustion (Yeoh, Sim, Tan, & Jamaludin, 2002, pp. 56–57) (see Figure 38.1).

There are some very important differences between these two tasks, which make the second task more suitable for vocabulary learning. The task on combustion contains much more written input than the task on radiation. Having plenty of written input for a shared task provides plenty of opportunity for vocabulary in the input to be noticed, retrieved, and used during related speaking activities. The task on combustion also has a much more focused outcome to the task. In the task on radioactive substances, only the question "What are radioisotopes?" has a clear outcome. If the learners are told to discuss a topic, it may not be clear to them what they should do and when they have done enough. In the task on combustion however there are very clear questions for the learners to answer. They know what they have to do and they will know when they have done that. Having a focused outcome to a speaking task tends to get learners more involved in the task. The task on combustion involves two parts—setting up and doing the experiment, and answering the questions and drawing a conclusion. Because the same vocabulary and ideas are involved in each of the two parts, the learners will explore these ideas thoroughly and will need to use the right vocabulary to express these ideas.

Let us now look at how the activities in the shared tasks can provide the conditions for vocabulary learning using the same set of headings we used for experience tasks.

Motivation: Learners tend to like working together and this can increase their motivation and involvement in the activity. Shak and Gardner (2008) found that younger learners were motivated by group work. The task on combustion also involves discovery learning. Group work is well-suited for discovery learning because of the support that learners give each other during the activity.

Repetition and the four strands: In shared tasks, learners hear each other use the target vocabulary and may also have a chance to produce it themselves. Discussion typically involves a lot of repetition. In shared tasks learners can negotiate the meanings of words with each other. Negotiation of the meanings of words has been shown to have a high likelihood of resulting in the learners remembering those words (Newton, 1995). Discussion also provides input which is additional to the written text. This additional input provides additional examples for guessing from context.

Thoughtful processing: Negotiation typically involves the generative use of a word, and it also involves some degree of deliberate attention to the word.

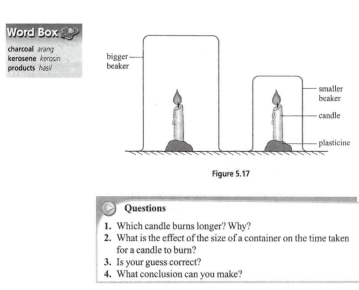

Figure 5.17

Questions

1. Which candle burns longer? Why?
2. What is the effect of the size of a container on the time taken for a candle to burn?
3. Is your guess correct?
4. What conclusion can you make?

A bigger container contains more air than a smaller container. A candle will burn for a longer time in a bigger container. There is more oxygen to support combustion.

Activity 5.4 Finding out the products of combustion of charcoal

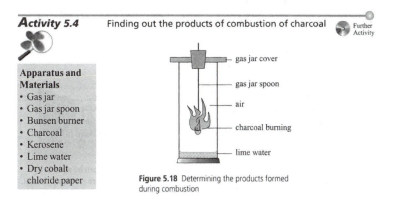

Figure 5.18 Determining the products formed during combustion

Figure 38.1 Candle exercise

Source: Yeoh, Sim, Tan, and Jamaludin (2002, pp. 56–57).

Meaningful relationships: As with most content-based tasks, the vocabulary involved in the activities is related to each other in meaningful ways.

From the perspective of shared tasks, a well-designed unit will provide the learners with opportunities to work together, will have well focused group work tasks to solve problems and discuss ideas, will provide plenty of written input to use as the basis for this discussion, and will encourage the learners to use the language and ideas from the written input in new ways (Joe, Nation, & Newton, 1996).

Guided Tasks

There are two main kinds of guided tasks, those where the learners gain outside assistance from dictionaries, glossaries, or concordances, and those where the support comes in the activity itself in the form of guiding questions or a set of points to address, models for the learners to follow, or activities where the learners make choices, classify items, or complete items. Here are examples of each of these types of guidance. The examples are from Yeoh et al. (2002).

Guiding questions are a very useful way of making a speaking or writing task easier. The greatest guidance is provided when the words used in the questions can also be used in the answers. Here are some questions that get learners to reflect on an experiment they have just completed:

1. Why can sand be separated from the salt solution?
2. What is the white solid formed in the evaporating dish?
3. Suggest one method to obtain salt from seawater?

This kind of activity does not require all the vocabulary to be retrieved from memory, but it does slightly change the context in which the vocabulary appears, that is, a question becomes a statement. This provides a small degree of generative use that helps learning. Item 3 above, on making salt from seawater, provides good opportunities for retrieval and generative use. The answer requires making some changes to the experiment that the learners have just completed on separating salt from a mixture of sand and salt. This is in effect having a model to follow.

Having items to classify or re-organize requires three major kinds of speaking—mentioning the names of the items, seeking information about the items, and deciding where they should be put. Mentioning the names develops familiarity with the forms of the words. Seeking or providing information about the nature of the items develops understanding of the concepts. Deciding where they should be put can develop knowledge of both the form and concepts of the items and the classification categories. Such activities are thus very useful for developing vocabulary knowledge.

Here is an example of a classification activity:

The following are examples of common substances.

Carbon dioxide	Sodium
Calcium carbonate	Water
Glucose	Iodine
Sulphuric acid	Bronze
Mercury	Orange juice
Ice-cream	Silver

Classify these substances into elements, compounds and mixtures. Write your answers in the form of a table.

(Yeoh et al., 2002, p. 34)

Completion activities provide excellent opportunities for retrieval. In some content-based tasks, completion activities are used to revise and summarize what the learners have just studied (see Figure 38.2).

When learners do the activity, they should be encouraged to try to recall the missing items rather than going back and looking for them. The more different the chart is in its format from what the learners have studied before, the greater the likelihood of deeper processing, which helps learning. The same comments apply to sentence completion activities such as the one below. If the sentence to be completed is not an exact copy of a previously met sentence, then the greater the amount of generative use, which helps learning, will be greater than if it was an exact copy.

An .... is the simplest form of matter. It cannot be broken down into two or more simpler substances by any chemical method.

(Yeoh et al., 2002, p. 33)

BUILDING A SUMMARY CHART

Copy and complete the summary chart below.

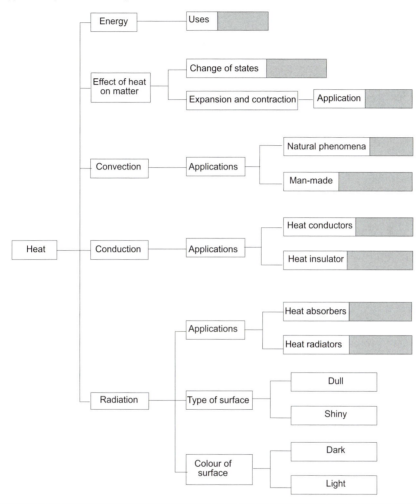

Figure 38.2 An example of how to build a summary chart

Source: Yeoh et al. (2002, p. 127).

Multiple-choice items provide a chance for strengthening receptive learning—seeing a word and retrieving its meaning. As the example below shows, they can make learners think carefully about word meanings.

Test yourself

1   What method of heat flow causes sea breezes?

A Conduction in air
B Convection in air
C Absorption of heat in air
D Radiation of heat in air

(Yeoh et al., 2002, p. 129)

Guided tasks provide useful support while the activity is being done. They are particularly useful when there is a standard way of expressing something. Their main disadvantage (which can also be seen as an advantage) is that part of the work is already done for the learner. Guided tasks may be modified according to the level of the learners. Greater guidance can be provided for those who need it, while less guidance can be provided for more capable learners. To get the greatest benefit from guided tasks, this guidance should be gradually removed as the learners get more proficient (Nation & Gu, 2007, pp. 66–68).

Let us now look at how guided tasks can help vocabulary learning.

Motivation: Learners are likely to have a high degree of success when working on guided tasks, because most of the work has already been done for them. This is one reason why guided tasks in the form of multiple-choice questions, summary charts, or completion activities based on what learners have just studied are particularly useful for revision.

Repetition: Guided activities typically reuse what the learners have met before and so this can provide meaningful repetition of vocabulary.

Four strands: Guided activities such as multiple-choice questions are particularly good for receptive use. Completion activities, questions, following models, and classification activities can encourage productive use.

Thoughtful processing: Because most of the context is provided in the activity in a guided task, there is little difficulty in understanding the target words. Definitions or glosses may be provided as a part of the activity. Guided activities typically involve learners in providing answers to items that are somewhat like tests. If more than verbatim knowledge is being sought, this then provides opportunities for retrieval and generative use.

Meaningful relationships: Guided activities are usually set within the framework of the whole meaningful unit of work. There is a slight danger in guided activities that they will move into list making, as, for example, in classification activities.

From the perspective of guided tasks, a well-designed unit will require the learners to understand and produce the target vocabulary, will involve recycling of previously met vocabulary, will provide language contexts that differ in useful ways from the previous input, and will provide learners with a good chance of being successful when doing them.

Independent Tasks

Experience, shared, and guided tasks all involve some kind of support for the learner while doing the task. Independent tasks on the other hand do not have any accompanying support or previous preparation. For learners of limited language proficiency, independent tasks will be very difficult, but they are the goal of any language proficiency program. Learners can apply strategies to make independent tasks easier and the strategies may be related to experience, shared, or guided tasks. For example, if the learner has to read a difficult text, this could be made easier by reading a simpler text on the same topic, thus turning reading the later text into an experience task. Similarly when doing an independent task learners could go and seek help from someone else thus turning it into a shared task. Using a dictionary during an independent task gives it a guided element. If content-based instruction is properly sequenced and graded, then there are probably no truly independent tasks involved in it.

Vocabulary learning is only one of many goals that are involved in content-based instruction. However, vocabulary knowledge plays a very important role in content lessons. The learners' vocabulary size may indicate which types of vocabulary need to be learned together with the subject. The technical vocabulary of a subject area is inextricably related to knowledge of that area. However, determining the extent to which learners know the high-frequency, low-frequency, academic, and technical vocabulary may show which words need the most attention.

Content-based instruction may provide many opportunities for vocabulary learning, but with an awareness of how learning can be enhanced in experience, shared, and guided tasks, teachers can increase and strengthen these opportunities. The means of increasing and strengthening learning include providing motivating activities, ensuring target words are encountered repeatedly, providing opportunities for balanced learning which include receptive and productive use, language-focused learning, and fluency, and arranging for retrieval and generative use. The nature of content-based instruction typically ensures that meaningful relationships exist between the content vocabulary involved in content-based lessons and units of work. Creating or modifying tasks that draw on these conditions will increase the potential for vocabulary learning.

The principles that should guide vocabulary teaching and learning are the same for both English language courses and content-based instruction. However, content-based instruction provides particularly helpful circumstances for putting these principles into practice. This chapter has tried to show this.

References

Ashton-Warner, S. (1963). *Teacher*. New York: Simon and Schuster.

Baddeley, A. (1990). *Human memory*. London: Lawrence Erlbaum Associates.

Barton, D. (1999). *Alpha mathematics*. Auckland: Longman Pearson Education Ltd.

Chung, T. M., & Nation, P., (2003). Technical vocabulary in specialised texts. *Reading in a Foreign Language*, *15*(2), 103–116.

Cohen, A. D., Glasman, H., Rosenbaum-Cohen, P. R., Ferrara, J., & Fine, J. (1988). Reading English for specialised purposes: Discourse analysis and the use of student informants. In P. Carrell, J. Devine, & D. E. Eskey (Eds.), *Interactive approaches to second language reading* (pp. 152–167). Cambridge: Cambridge University Press.

Cook, V. J. (1983). What should language teaching be about? *ELT Journal*, *37*, 229–234.

Coxhead, A. (2000). A new academic word list. *TESOL Quarterly*, *34*, 213–238.

Craik, F. I. M., & Lockhart, R. S. (1972). Levels of processing: A framework for memory research. *Journal of Verbal Learning and Verbal Behavior*, *11*, 671–684.

Donley, K., & Reppen, R. (2001). Using corpus tools to highlight academic vocabulary in SCLT. *TESOL Journal*, *10*(2–3), 7–12.

Elgort, I. (2007). The role of intentional decontextualised learning in second language vocabulary acquisition: Evidence from primed lexical decision tasks with advanced bilinguals. PhD thesis, Wellington: Victoria University of Wellington.

Hwang, K., & Nation, P. (1989). Reducing the vocabulary load and encouraging vocabulary learning through reading newspapers. *Reading in a Foreign Language*, *6*(1), 323–335.

Joe, A. (1998). What effects do text-based tasks promoting generation have on incidental vocabulary acquisition? *Applied Linguistics*, *19*(3), 357–377.

Joe, A., Nation, P., & Newton, J. (1996). Vocabulary learning and speaking activities. *English Teaching Forum*, *34*(1), 2–7.

Laufer, B., & Hulstijn, J. (2001). Incidental vocabulary acquisition in a second language: The construct of task-induced involvement. *Applied Linguistics*, *22*(1), 1–26.

Nation, I. S. P. (2000). Learning vocabulary in lexical sets: Dangers and guidelines. *TESOL Journal*, *9*(2), 6–10.

Nation, I. S. P. (2006). How large a vocabulary is needed for reading and listening? *Canadian Modern Language Review*, *63*(1), 59–82.

Nation, I. S. P. (2007a). The four strands. *Innovation in Language Learning and Teaching*, *1*, 1–12.

Nation, I. S. P. (2007b). Vocabulary learning through experience tasks. *Language Forum*, *33*(2), 33–43.

Nation, I. S. P. (2008). *Teaching vocabulary: Strategies and techniques*. Boston: Heinle Cengage Learning.

Nation, I. S. P. & Gu, P. Y. (2007). *Focus on vocabulary*. Sydney: NCELTR/Macquarie.

Newton, J. (1995). Task-based interaction and incidental vocabulary learning: A case study. *Second Language Research*, *11*(2), 159–177.

Noor, H., Mak, S. Y., Quek, Y. H., & Chong, K. Y. (2005). *Science, form 4*. Selangor: Pustaka Alhas Sdn Bhd.

Schmidt, R. W. (1990). The role of consciousness in second language learning. *Applied Linguistics*, *11*(2), 129–158.

Schmitt, N., & Carter, R. (2000). The lexical advantages of narrow reading for second language learners. *TESOL Journal*, *9*(1), 4–9.

Schmitt, N., Schmitt, D., & Clapham, C. (2001). Developing and exploring the behaviour of two new versions of the Vocabulary Levels Test. *Language Testing*, *18*(1), 55–88.

Shak, J., & Gardner, S. (2008). Young learner perspectives on four focus-on-form tasks. *Language Teaching Research, 12,* 387–408.

Stoller, F., & Grabe, W. (1997). Content-based instruction: Research foundations. In M. A. Snow and D. M. Brinton (Eds.), *The content-based classroom: Perspectives on integrating language and content* (pp. 78–94). White Plains, NY: Addison Wesley Longman.

Sutarsyah, C., Nation, P., & Kennedy, G. (1994). How useful is EAP vocabulary for ESP? A corpus based study. *RELC Journal, 25*(2), 34–50.

Swain, M. (2005). The output hypothesis: Theory and research. In E. Hinkel (Ed.), *Handbook of Research in Second Language Teaching and Learning* (pp. 471–483). Mahwah, NJ: Lawrence Erlbaum Associates.

Tseng, W., & Schmitt, N. (2008). Toward a model of motivated vocabulary learning: A structural equation modelling approach. *Language Learning, 58,* 357–400.

Webb, S. (2007). The effects of repetition on vocabulary knowledge. *Applied Linguistics, 28,* 46–65.

Yeoh, S. L., Sim, B. L., Tan, Y. H., & Jamaludin, S. (2002). *Science form 1, vol. 2.* Kuala Lumpur: Bakaprep Sdn Bhd.

39
Written Discourse Analysis and Second Language Teaching

Dana Ferris

Introduction

The analysis of written discourse as a research approach in applied linguistics is a relatively recent phenomenon. Nonetheless, its insights and applications have been influential in a variety of second language (L2) teaching contexts (Connor & Kaplan, 1987; Polio, 1997, 2001, 2003). However, it is also fair to say that some controversy—both philosophical and methodological—surrounds the theory and especially the pedagogical applications of written discourse analysis in L2 classrooms.

In Kaplan and Grabe's (2002) "modern history of written discourse analysis," they observed that text/written discourse analysis is a research approach that crosses an extraordinarily wide range of disciplinary and subdisciplinary boundaries, from many different applications within linguistics, to literary studies, rhetoric, and even cognitive psychology. In this chapter, it is not my intention to duplicate that overview but rather to look at written discourse analysis specifically through the lens of how it has been applied to L2 pedagogy. I will argue that while the contributions of written discourse analysis to L2 teaching are many, varied, and helpful, a number of practical issues constrain its impact on L2 classrooms. In short, while a great deal has been accomplished in a short period of time, there is still a way to go; as Enkvist put it back in 1987, "we need a special race of applied linguists to carry messages across the buffer zone between pure linguistics and language teaching … But there seem to be few such people" (pp. 23–24).

To further focus this discussion, I will divide the chapter into several sections. First, I will look briefly at definitions and specific ways that "written discourse" or "text" analysis have been approached in applied linguistics, noting specifically the distinctions between the analysis of first language (L1) or native speaker texts and those written by L2 or non-native speakers. From there, I will move into discussion of three specific subfields of written discourse analysis: contrastive (or intercultural) rhetoric research, corpus linguistics research, and genre research. I emphasize these areas of research rather than the many others possible because these are the ones with the most direct applications to L2 pedagogy, the main focus of this particular chapter. For each area, I will briefly review the research trends, discuss how they have been applied to L2 teaching, and evaluate (to the degree it is possible) their influence on classroom teaching to date. The chapter will conclude with suggestions of ways in which (1) the three subfields could better utilize areas of possible overlap in research and application;

and (2) the broader concerns regarding the pedagogical application of written discourse analysis could be productively addressed.

Written Discourse Analysis: Definitions and Descriptions

Definitions

Kaplan and Grabe (2002) intentionally delimited their own wide-ranging "modern history" by defining written discourse analysis as the *"systematic analyses of the linguistic features and patterns occurring in written texts,"* further noting that "a number of new and emerging disciplines and fields have contributed to" its development (p. 192, emphasis added). An earlier definition provided by Connor and Kaplan (1987) described the analysis of written discourse as the examination of "various levels of language … which interact within a text [including] … the *intrasential* structure, the *intersentential* structure, and the *discourse* structure (p. 2). *Written* discourse analysis is further distinguished from the broader realm of *discourse analysis*, which includes *spoken discourse or conversational analysis*, though Kaplan and Grabe (2002) acknowledge that such distinctions can at times be problematic. For Kaplan and Grabe, the key element of the definition is that such analyses "explore the *actual structuring of the text via some consistent framework*" (2002, p. 192, emphasis added).

Descriptions

General Concerns of Text Analysis Research

Having thus defined written discourse analysis, we can illustrate some of the ways in which written discourse analysis has historically been approached. For example, as to "intrasentential" structure, researchers have looked at issues such as how information is ordered within a sentence (e.g., old vs. new information, subject-predicate or topic-comment structures), the use of coordinating or subordinating connectors, the presence or absence of hedges, the use of various types of modals, and so forth (see Kaplan & Grabe, 2002; Schleppegrell, 2009). Examinations of "intersentential" structure have focused on features such as reference, adverbial connectors such as "however," or lexical cohesion (repetition, synonymy, etc.) (Halliday & Hasan, 1976). At the discourse level, researchers have examined macro- and micro-structures of texts, propositional structures, and topical structures (e.g., de Beaugrande, 1980; de Beaugrande & Dressler, 1981; Connor, 1987; Dressler, 1978; Kinneavy, 1971; Lautamatti, 1987; Meyer, 1975; van Dijk, 1972, 1977, 1980, 1985).

Text Analytic Research on L2 Writing/Writers

Considering the focus of this chapter on applications of written discourse analysis to L2 teaching, one important body of research concerns studies of L2 writers and their texts (Hinkel, 2002, 2005). Text analytic studies of L2 writing have covered a range of issues. Text analytic research methods have been used to describe and characterize the nature of L2 writing (e.g., Hinkel, 2002; Hyland, 2002; Silva, 1993), including in some instances direct comparisons with texts produced by L1 writers (Ferris, 1994b; Hinkel, 2002; Silva, 1993). Text analyses have also been used to identify text features of stronger vs. weaker L2 writers (e.g., Ferris, 1994a; Jarvis, Grant, Bikowski, & Ferris, 2003) and/or of texts rated higher or lower by teacher/raters in assessment contexts (Jarvis et al., 2003).

In addition to such descriptive efforts, written discourse analysis has been utilized, sometimes in combination with other research methods, to assess the effectiveness of various types of instructional interventions with student writers (mostly in L2 settings, but occasionally in L1 classes as well).

Examples include studies of the effects of teacher–student writing conferences on students' revisions and/or subsequent texts (e.g., Goldstein & Conrad, 1990; Patthey-Chavez & Ferris, 1997); descriptions and/or assessments of the influence of written teacher commentary on student writing (Conrad & Goldstein, 1999; Ferris, 1997; Ferris, Pezone, Tade, & Tinti, 1997; F. Hyland, 1998; Hyland & Hyland, 2001; Straub & Lunsford, 1995; Zamel, 1985); studies of the effects of written error correction on student revision or later writing (for reviews, see Ferris, 2002, 2003; Ferris & Hedgcock, 2005; Truscott, 1996, 2007); and studies of the nature and effects of peer feedback on student writing (e.g., Connor & Asenavage, 1994; Liu & Hansen, 2002; Mendonça & Johnson, 1994).

While this latter group of written discourse analyses focused on classroom practices has certainly been influential, this work has also not been without controversy. In particular, there remains considerable debate to this day about what the research base really shows about written corrective feedback, or error correction (see Ferris, 2004; Truscott, 2007; Truscott & Hsu, 2008). Similarly, some researchers and classroom practitioners remain unconvinced of the merits of peer feedback for L2 student writers, who may not have the linguistic knowledge base or intuitions to give accurate or helpful information to their classmates (for discussion and reviews, see Jacobs, Curtis, Braine, & Huang, 1998; Ferris, 2003; Leki, 1990; Liu & Hansen, 2002; Zhang, 1995, 1999). Finally, much of the classroom-oriented text analysis research on L2 writers has been criticized for being too decontextualized (Goldstein, 2001; Silva, 2005) or simply too small and too centered on a specific context to be generalizable (see Hinkel, 2005; for an early discussion of this methodological issue, see Kaplan, 1987). Also, as noted by Polio (1997, 2001, 2003), many text analysis studies have been flawed or limited as to their methodology, for example by failing to calculate or report statistics on reliability or validity of the measures used to examine the texts and make claims about them.

To summarize, written discourse analysis, in its brief but active history, has focused on "text" at a number of different levels, in a broad range of contexts, and for a variety of fairly distinct purposes. The remaining sections of this chapter highlight several specific applications of the analysis of written discourse that have had (or been claimed to have) important implications for L2 classroom teaching: contrastive rhetoric, corpus linguistics, and genre studies.

Specific Emphases in Written Discourse Analyses and L2 Instruction

Contrastive or Intercultural Rhetoric

The Beginnings of Constrastive Rhetoric

The term *contrastive rhetoric* (hereafter CR) was not invented by Robert Kaplan, but it was certainly popularized by his seminal, frequently cited, and multiply reprinted 1966 *Language Learning* article. In Kaplan's own words, his 1966 "doodles article" was intended "to call attention to … a pedagogical problem" (Kaplan, 1987, p. 9) and "to educate the teachers of L2 writing" (Kaplan, 2005, p. 387). The "problem" he was highlighting was stated as follows:

> Foreign students who have mastered syntactic structures have still demonstrated inability to compose adequate themes, term papers, theses, and dissertations. Instructors have written, on foreign-student papers, such comments as: "The material is all here, but it seems somehow out of focus," or "Lacks organization," or "Lacks cohesion." And these comments are essentially accurate. *The foreign-student paper is out of focus because the foreign student is employing a rhetoric and a sequence of thought which violate the expectations of the native reader.*
>
> (Kaplan, 1966, pp. 3–4, emphasis added)

648 · Dana Ferris

To provide empirical support for his claim that L2 writers produce texts that "violate the expectations of the native reader," Kaplan analyzed over 600 compositions ("themes") written by university international ("foreign") students, finding divergent paragraph structures across writers who were L1 speakers from different language families that he characterized in a series of diagrams (or "doodles," as they were later called).

In an era when "the teaching of English largely focused on grammar and phonology" (Kaplan, 2005, p. 388), Kaplan's attempt to broaden the discussion of contrastive analyses across languages beyond the sentence/utterance level was intriguing. CR work quickly inspired pedagogical applications such as explicitly teaching L2 writers to produce the "linear" English paragraph depicted in Kaplan's diagram. In addition, Kaplan's work was followed by many research attempts to confirm or disconfirm what became known as the "Contrastive Rhetoric Hypothesis": that different languages and cultures do, in fact, employ a "rhetoric and sequence of thought" that vary in observable ways from other languages and that may, by extension, create difficulties for L2 writers and for their L1 readers.

Research on CR

CR research over the subsequent decades has taken a variety of forms (Connor, 1996, 2003; Connor & Kaplan, 1987; Grabe & Kaplan, 1996; Kaplan & Grabe, 2002; Leki, 1991; Purves, 1988). These include identifying specific discourse features (e.g., personal vs. impersonal, abstract vs. concrete, coherence patterns, presence or absence of narration) and comparing those across L1s (e.g., Purves, 1986). They also have included descriptions of how different text-types vary cross-culturally (e.g., Hinds's well-known 1987 typology of "writer-responsible" and "reader-responsible" rhetorics); and even attempts to induce the "personality" of a culture or the worldview of its inhabitants based on examinations of its texts (or texts written in English by students from that L1 group) (e.g., Indrasuta, 1988).

Kaplan's claims also raised various criticisms. Some researchers (e.g., Mohan & Lo, 1985) claimed that what Kaplan was characterizing as "contrastive" rhetorical patterns in L2 student writing were in fact due to developmental issues (i.e., the students were not writing effectively in the L2 because they were not yet competent enough to do so, not because their L1 rhetorics were "interfering"). Others worried about the implied ethnocentrism of the claims and/or about the deterministic pedagogy that it suggested or at least appeared to privilege: "When the findings of contrastive rhetoric have been applied to L2 writing, they have, almost by definition, been prescriptive: In English we write like this; those who would write well in English must look at this and imitate it" (Leki, 1991, p. 123).

Earlier work on CR was also criticized for ignoring issues of genre and audience. For example, Grabe (1987) reminded researchers that "[i]f contrastive rhetoric is to examine text materials in a number of languages, at some point in the future, the research will first need to establish which texts in different languages are, in fact, similar" (p. 136). Thus, for instance, comparing narratives in Chinese with newspaper editorials in English—or student argumentative essays with opinion pieces written by professional journalists—would likely lead to some specious findings and conclusions. Complicating the discussion even further is the understanding that writers write for specific audiences, and the production of even similar text-types across languages will be constrained by the knowledge base and expectations of the targeted readership. However, by the late 1980s, there appeared to be more awareness among CR researchers of these interacting variables; as Kaplan wrote in 1987: "If one of the objectives … is to teach people to write, then it is logical to ask 'to write what, for whom, and to what end'?" (p. 20). By his self-described "final word" on CR in 2005, Kaplan had developed these ideas even further, listing three pairs of related questions addressed by CR research (pp. 378–379):

1a. Who has the authority to write?
1b. Who may be addressed?
2a. What may be discussed?
2b. What form may the writing take?
3a. What constitutes evidence?
3b. How can the evidence be convincingly arranged?

Leki (1991) also acknowledged this move toward a broader, more complex model of CR: "they now also include investigations of the broad political and historical contexts for writing and recognize that not simply rhetorical style but also purpose, task, topic, and audience are culturally informed" (p. 133).

After more than 40 years of research on CR, there appears to be at least some agreement on what these studies have shown us: "scholars looking at other *languages have perceived significant differences between languages in their rhetorical structure*, even if … they *have not agreed on the nature of the differences*" (Kaplan, 1987, p. 10, emphases added) and

> in the past half a century, a number of studies have been published to show that *rhetorical organization of text does indeed differ across various languages*. However, *the specifics of those differences diverge*, depending on who conducted the studies and where they conducted them.
>
> (Kaplan, 2005, p. 388, emphases added)

Even Leki (1991) who as a reviewer of "twenty-five years of contrastive rhetoric" can fairly be characterized as wary of the entire enterprise and especially of its pedagogical applications, acknowledged that contrastive rhetoric as an area of inquiry has value: "Contrastive rhetoric studies can, thus, *add to our understanding of the structure of texts* and perhaps eventually to *a deeper understanding of cultures*" (p. 133, emphases added).

L2 Classroom Applications of CR

As already noted, one of the most immediate objections to CR was that Kaplan's 1966 diagrams were reproduced in English as a second language (ESL) composition texts and used as justification for prescriptive, formulaic teaching of the "correct" way to write in English. Such applications, which Leki (1991) noted were consistent with the "current-traditional" methodology in vogue in L1 composition at the time (Ferris & Hedgcock, 2005; Silva, 1990), became immediate targets for L1/L2 composition scholars promoting a process-oriented approach to writing instruction which focused on students' evolving texts and ideas rather than prescribing "Ideal Texts" (Brannon & Knoblauch, 1982) that students must emulate. Despite the objections of Kaplan (and others) that CR as a hypothesis/construct was never designed to promote rigidity or ethnocentrism, Leki (1991) nonetheless claimed that "the findings of early contrastive rhetoric studies were whole-heartedly embraced in many ESL writing classes, which actually taught that English speakers think in a straight line while Asians think in circles and others think in zigzags" (pp. 123–124).

While the scholarly objections to current-traditional/CR-based pedagogy have been well established for some decades, it is interesting to note that it is alive and well in many L2 writing classrooms and textbooks. Students themselves will sometimes voice the opinion that learning "structure" (of the American academic essay or paragraph) helped them to navigate the challenge of reading and writing in a L2. Pre-service and in-service teachers often will defend teaching even "the five-paragraph essay," arguing, like the students, that it provides a "foundation" from which students can expand their rhetorical repertoires. This is to say that not all L2 professionals or students necessarily think the more "structural" applications of CR are always a bad thing. However, an overly narrowly drawn approach to teaching L2 composition will sometimes cause a mismatch between ESL writing programs below the college level (i.e., intensive English programs, community college classes, or developmental university writing courses) and those administered by a composition or English department (see Atkinson & Ramanathan, 1995).

Beyond the specific application of teaching paragraph/essay structure, Leki argued that the appropriately more complex lenses through which CR research is now conducted make its findings "much less immediately importable than they once seemed" (1991, p. 134). However, Leki also claimed that broader implications of CR research for the L2 classroom include the "instant enlightenment" and "metacognitive awareness" that CR insights can provide to L2 writing students (Leki, 1991, p. 138). Further, Kaplan (2005) noted the benefits of CR research for writing teachers: it helps them think beyond the sentence level; it helps them to be more aware of discourse differences across languages; and it helps them to understand some of the background knowledge, assumptions, and practices that their L2 students may bring into the writing classroom (pp. 386–387). Increased awareness of the experience and knowledge base a specific group of students may possess—on the part of both students and teachers—can only facilitate more effective teaching and learning (Ferris & Hedgcock, 2005).

All that said, I must end this section with a caveat, or at least a note of caution. Recent work over the past 10–15 years has highlighted differences across groups of L2 writers and necessitated re-examinations of who or what an "L2 writer" really is. In particular, the increased focus on resident L2 students, especially "Generation 1.5" or "early arriving resident" students (Ferris, 2009; Harklau, Losey, & Siegal, 1999; Hedgcock & Ferris, 2009; Reid, 2006; Roberge, Siegal, & Harklau, 2009), has further complicated discussions and especially applications of CR. Specifically, to what extent do CR findings apply to students who *speak* a particular language with their parents but who have never been educated in it? Are CR insights completely irrelevant for them, or are they somehow still impacted by exposure to the language and culture of their parents when they approach L2 writing tasks? What about later-arriving resident students, those who have received part of their education in another language and culture? These distinctions are important because many programs or courses preparing future teachers of L2 writers routinely talk about CR (and often the pre-service teachers read Kaplan's 1966 article). Along with such discussions, teachers need to be reminded that L2 writers are not all alike and that the impact and relevance of CR insights may vary according to the student audience being addressed.

Corpus Linguistics

Scope and Characteristics

In his 1987 paper, "Cultural thought patterns revisited," Kaplan noted that the future of written discourse analysis in general and CR research in particular would be limited by the practical concern of how much time it takes:

> [I]n order to make significant claims about the nature of written text, it will be necessary to examine *rather long segments* … progress in this area will be slow simply by virtue of the *time required* to perform analyses of long texts.
>
> (Kaplan, 1987, pp. 18–19, emphases added)

At its most basic level, *corpus linguistics* addresses this practical problem by providing methodology and technology to rapidly analyze not only large *quantities* of texts but also *multiple dimensions* (or interacting features) of texts (Biber, 1988). Because of the power and sophistication of the tools developed for corpus linguistics research, its findings now undergird nearly all types of written discourse analysis and many classroom teaching endeavors, from vocabulary and grammar instruction to dictionary use to oral skills for comprehending and participating in classroom language.

However, corpus researchers would object to the notion that corpus linguistics can be narrowly defined as a type of research technology (Tardy & Swales, 2008), arguing that it is also "unified by certain philosophical tenets which make it an identifiable approach" (Conrad, 2005, p. 393). Conrad (2005, pp. 394–396) summarizes the characteristics of corpus linguistics research as follows:

1. It uses a *corpus*: "a large, principled collection of naturally occurring texts that is stored in electronic form" (p. 394).
2. It uses *computer-assisted automatic analysis* techniques to tag, code, and count occurrences or co-occurrences of specific linguistic features under consideration.
3. It is *empirical* in that its intent is to describe language patterns rather than relying on intuitions or observations.
4. It is essentially *quantitative* in approach, although, as noted by Conrad (2005), the interpretation of quantitative findings entails some qualitative aspects; further, some recent corpus studies have included qualitative elements (such as interviews and case studies) within their design (e.g., Hyland, 2000; see also discussion in Kaplan & Grabe, 2002, p. 214).

Corpora can be very large (hundreds of millions of words) or relatively small (samples of student writing within a particular program), and there is some discussion in the literature about how large a corpus needs to be for the analysis to be reliable and valid (Biber, 1993). Corpora can include written or transcribed spoken text, and, in recent work, can also include video that is linked to transcriptions of accompanying speech (Reder, Harris, & Setzler, 2003). The focus of corpus design can be very general (British English) or quite specific (academic research articles in a particular discipline). The important common element is that corpora are selected or collected not haphazardly but intentionally to examine some "naturally occurring" sample of language that is the subject of the researchers' interest.

History and Major Research Trends

Though corpora were collected and corpus research conducted prior to late twentieth-century technological developments, the development of automatic analysis procedures (i.e., computer programs to tag and count linguistic features specified by algorithms) together with advanced statistical techniques (in particular, the multi-feature/multi-dimensional analysis pioneered by Biber in the 1980s, e.g., 1985, 1988) have allowed corpus research to develop rapidly and dramatically in a short period of time. In addition to the advantages provided by sophisticated programming and statistical analyses, it is now much easier, given advancements in scanning and production of electronic texts, to assemble a substantial corpus than it used to be. In short, events over the past 25 years have created a "perfect storm" of factors that have enabled corpus linguistics as a subfield not only to make progress toward fulfilling its own research agenda but also to influence research and pedagogy across different areas of applied linguistics and L2 teaching.

Concerns of Corpus Research

Early corpus linguistics work focused on issues such as differences between speech and writing (Biber, 1988), across text-types (Grabe, 1987), and in specific academic disciplines over time (e.g.,

Atkinson, 1992, 1999). Along with conducting his own corpus research, Biber and his students/ colleagues also articulated methodological guidelines for conducting corpus research (Biber, 1990, 1993; Biber, Conrad, & Reppen, 1998) and finished the 1990s with the publication of an ambitious and influential corpus-based reference grammar (Biber, Johannsson, Leech, Conrad, & Finegan, 1999). Biber and colleagues have focused much of their work in the past decade on both spoken and written university language (Biber, 2006; Biber, Conrad, Reppen, Byrd, & Helt, 2002). Besides Biber and his colleagues, another prolific corpus researcher has been Ken Hyland, who during the 1990s published a series of studies on specific issues and genres in academic writing (e.g., Hyland, 1998, 1999, 2001; see also Biber's 2006 summary). As noted by Tardy and Swales (2008), a great deal of the corpus linguistics work takes place outside of the US. Finally, recent researchers, such as Reppen (2001) and Reynolds (2005), have examined corpora of learner English.

L2 Classroom Applications of Corpus Linguistics

As noted by Conrad (2005), there has been some disagreement about the degree to which corpus linguistics findings are "useful" in the language classroom. Can empirical descriptions of how language features (co)occur in natural language and in learner language be transformed into teaching materials, and should corpus researchers even attempt to do so? Objections to the application of corpus linguistics findings to L2 teaching are both philosophical and practical.

Philosophically, some theorists and practitioners wonder whether teaching suggestions derived from corpus research are not simply "dressed up" modern versions of older pedagogy that fell from favor decades ago with the advent of communicative language teaching methods and the "natural approach" (Krashen & Terrell, 1983). For instance, in a recently published article providing suggestions of how to apply corpus findings to L2 teaching, van Zante and Persiani (2008) began thus: "ESL instructors, curriculum designers, and materials writers must make decisions about *which linguistic features to teach and the sequence in which to present them*" (p. 95, emphasis added). However, this assertion begins with the assumption that ESL instructors follow a structural syllabus that is organized around "linguistic features" that will be explicitly "presented" in some "sequence." While some ESL teachers in some contexts may well do so, many others prefer and utilize a holistic, content-based approach that focuses primarily or even exclusively on learners' top-down processing and access of background knowledge. Whether such instructors should, in fact, be more intentional about the principled selection and presentation of specific language features is an argument that is beyond the scope of this particular chapter (see Byrd & Bunting, 2008; Coxhead & Byrd, 2007; Folse, 2004, 2008), but it is important to observe that some instructors may resist/ignore/avoid the findings of corpus research because their specific applications strike them as too narrowly focused and not consistent with their views of how language is learned or acquired.

While the philosophical issues surrounding corpus linguistics and L2 teaching are significant, they pale in scope and substance against the practical ones. In order to design, conduct, and apply corpus linguistics research, teachers must

1. know how to select and assemble a corpus;
2. be able to select or design and then use the appropriate computer software for analysis;
3. be able to select and utilize the best statistical procedures;
4. be able to understand the statistical results; and
5. be able to take the findings and transform them into useful classroom materials.

Even if teachers are not attempting to carry out their own corpus studies, just interpreting the ones that have been published usually requires substantial training in both formal linguistics and advanced statistics. L2 teachers come from a wide range of academic backgrounds and teacher preparation programs, and they may not always have had extensive formal training in these issues.

Despite these objections, corpus linguistics research nonetheless has much to offer to classroom L2 teachers. First, corpus linguistics research has informed the development of a variety of useful materials, including learner dictionaries, word lists, grammar and vocabulary student texts, and reference grammars for teachers (especially Biber et al., 1999). While all of these resource types existed prior to the recent advances in corpus linguistics, the current versions are based on empirical data rather than textbook developers' intuitions or best guesses about the most important structures or features to teach. Of particular note is the corpus-research-based Academic Word List (or AWL; Coxhead, 2000), which has led to the development of various online and print teaching resources (see Coxhead, 2006; Coxhead & Byrd, 2007). Tools based on the AWL have been used for teacher preparation (Coxhead, 2006; Hedgcock & Ferris, 2009) and for student analyses of academic texts they are reading for classes (Conrad, 2005).[1]

Second, corpus-based analyses of L2 student writing have added valuable information to existing research about L2 writers and their texts. While Hinkel (2005) correctly noted that corpus linguistics studies have largely focused on similar features to those "carried out prior to the technological and methodological innovations in text linguistics" (p. 623), corpus studies have the advantage of being larger, faster, and probably more accurate overall (a computer cannot get bored or tired in the way that a researcher counting features manually can). Hinkel also (p. 623) notes several specific research questions regarding the nature of L2 text that have been productively examined due to the availability of corpus research techniques.

Finally, Conrad (2005, 2008) and others (e.g., Byrd & Bunting, 2008; Coxhead & Byrd, 2007) have argued not only for *applying* corpus research findings to classroom instruction and materials but for *utilizing* corpus techniques in the language classroom as a means to "observe language and make generalizations," to promote "hypothesis formation and testing" and "noticing and grammatical consciousness-raising" (Conrad, 2005, p. 402). While these all appear to be legitimate and valuable goals for bringing corpus linguistics into the L2 classroom, it is unlikely that these suggestions will be widely adopted unless appealing user-friendly materials are created and disseminated to classroom teachers, as the practical issues noted above make it difficult for many instructors to do their own analyses and design their own instructional materials.[2]

Genre Studies

Overview

The final area of written discourse analysis I will discuss is *genre studies*. As outlined by Hyon (1996), Johns (1997, 2003) and Johns, Bawarshi, Coe, Hyland, Paltridge, Reiff, and Tardy (2006), genre research (outside of literary studies) is conducted by at least three distinct groups of scholars: (1) The Sydney School, based on the Systemic Functional Linguistics approach; (2) English for specific purposes (ESP) researchers, of whom the most famous is John Swales (1990); and the (3) New Rhetoric group, composed mainly of North American rhetoricians and compositionists (e.g., Freedman & Medway, 1994; Herrington & Moran, 2005; Russell, 1997). Though the scholarship and concerns of all three groups definitely inform and influence one another, I will focus in this section on the first two, as they are most concerned with analysis of written discourse as we have defined it in this chapter, and their findings are the most directly applicable to L2 instruction.[3]

Definitions of Genre

In reality, genre studies are "defined" by their very complexity (see Tardy in Johns et al., 2006), but at their core, they focus on the real-world contexts in which texts are produced and received, on recognizable features of texts produced for specific audiences or discourse communities, and on ways to help novices trying to enter those communities analyze the characteristics of those text-types so that they can successfully produce texts that will be understandable and—more importantly—acceptable to their target audiences. Genre has been broadly defined as "actions we want to accomplish" (Miller, 1984, p. 151); as "ways in which people get things done through their use of language in particular contexts" (Paltridge in Johns et al. 2006, p 236); and as "purposeful, social, and situated" (Johns, 2009, p. 2005). Johns made these rather abstract constructs more concrete by explaining that genres simultaneously include "repeated or conventional features" and also "situational" features (2009, p. 206), providing the example of résumés: writers learn their general, conventional characteristics but also that these documents often need to be adapted in response to a specific job advertisement. As a result, Johns claimed that "genre knowledge provides a shortcut … to the processing and production of familiar texts" (1997, p. 21).

Research Emphases

For the past several decades, the Sydney School has focused on identifying the features of "elemental genres" found in schools and workplaces and designing curriculum to help students (both younger students and adult L2 learners) analyze and respond to the requirements of specific communicative contexts. These various genres are described according to their purposes, the contexts in which they are typically used/found, their macro-structures, and the typical internal progression of ideas (or "stages") (see Johns, 2003, pp. 201–202). For example, the "procedure" genre provides a sequence of steps and explains how to do something, can be found in reports of science experiments, and has a macro-structure of "Goal–Steps–(desired) Results", with the "stages" being the more detailed explanations of the parts of the macro-structure. In addition to these rhetorical descriptions, the Sydney School follows the principles of Systemic Functional Linguistics (SFL) in identifying particular features of language needed for the specific genres under consideration. Findings from the Sydney School have been used to effect dramatic changes in school curricula and teacher preparation in Australia (Cope, Kalantzis, Kress, & Martin, 1993; Feez, 2002; Hyon, 1996; Johns, 1997, 2003; Mackin-Horarik, 2002). In recent years, there have also been increased attempts to apply SFL principles to English language/literacy/writing instruction in North America (see, e.g., Schleppegrell, 1998, 2001, 2008, 2009; Schleppegrell & Colombi, 2002).

ESP researchers have also focused on both the structure and language of specific genres. As explained by Johns (2003), the differences between the two "schools" lie primarily in the focus of their investigations (academic disciplines and professional settings) and in the more precise ways in which genre is targeted to specific discourse communities. For example, rather than describing the "procedure" or "narrative" genres in broad terms, ESP researchers look at narrower areas such as the "court order" or the "academic research article." Finally, most ESP research and pedagogy has been focused on and designed for adult learners, who bring different knowledge bases and motivations to the task of genre-learning than do, say, secondary school students in English language arts courses in the US or Australia. The most famous genre researcher from the ESP school is John Swales, whose analysis of "moves" (or sections or subsections) in academic research articles (1990) has been widely applied and replicated by ESP researchers and practitioners all over the world. Similar to the Sydney School, ESP researchers also focus on the common language characteristics in the genres (and within the moves) being studied.

L2 Classroom Applications of Genre Studies

As noted above, genre studies are essentially pedagogical in their orientation. Indeed, the Sydney School purposefully developed genre pedagogy as a means to help disadvantaged secondary and adult school students (including L2 students) to enter the mainstream of academic and workplace communication by deconstructing and demystifying the "rules" of the particular genres. Similarly, ESP was developed as a way to move from "general" English language pedagogy to helping learners (particularly in English as a foreign language (EFL) contexts) target their English language study and acquisition to their particular instrumental purposes. Thus, for example, doctors and nurses could study medical English; businesspeople could study business English; scientists could study scientific English; and so forth. ESP has also influenced the development of English for academic purposes (EAP), curricula and materials designed to help L2 undergraduate and graduate students successfully negotiate the academic demands of English-medium institutions. Though much of this work has focused on literacy development (e.g., the popular ESP-based graduate writing textbook by Swales & Feak, 2004), there have also been applications to academic aural/oral skills (e.g., Flowerdew, 1994; Murphy, 2006).

As with all of our subtopics, however, the applications of genre studies to pedagogy have aroused some controversy. Critics of the Sydney School/SFL approach raise concerns about the possibility of reductionist pedagogy that teaches school-based genres as static, rather than as forms constantly evolving and changing and in need of contextualized analysis. Further, some English/writing instructors might question the intensive bottom-up language analysis suggested by SFL wondering if/how it fits into a writing course syllabus that also includes engaging content and process elements.

ESP approaches in the US have generated disagreement when there are attempts to apply their findings to undergraduate, especially lower-division, composition instruction. While many might acknowledge the value of a genre-based, discipline-specific approach for graduate students or even upper-division undergraduates who have chosen a major field of study, there is disagreement on its benefits for first-year composition, for several practical reasons. First, students at that level often have not even selected a major (at least in the US); even if they have, they may be completing breadth requirements rather than specific disciplinary coursework. Second, composition instructors may not be adequately prepared to teach specialized content related to specific disciplines (see Spack, 1988). These critics suggest that it is more appropriate at this level to teach students the conventions of "general academic English" (Johns, 2003, p. 207). To the degree there is any agreement as to whether there *is* such a thing as "general academic English," most would say it consists of understanding how argument works and the ways in which arguments can be structured; conventions of using/citing/integrating work from a variety of sources; and control of various language and usage options from which writers may choose. To these general areas (argument, sources, language), Johns (2003, p. 208) added a helpful list of characteristics of academic expository writing that appear to cross disciplines and genres.

Nearly all of Johns's work, dating back some 20 years, has emphasized training students to be "researchers" of various genres, a theme that has been expressed by other genre scholars as well (see Johns et al., 2006, for various treatments of this principle; see also Tardy & Courtney, 2008). While it is not desirable to teach genres as set, static forms, nor is it likely possible to prepare students, whether in entry-level writing courses or even in advanced writing in the disciplines courses, to master all of the genres they are likely to encounter, what *is* possible is to help students know what to look for and what questions to ask as they encounter various tasks, texts, and evaluators (e.g., professors, reviewers, etc.). Johns (2009, pp. 209–214) provided a very practical and useful outline for a lower-division academic writing course that could help all students (but especially those who arrive in college with language/literacy challenges and struggle with the complexity of academic reading/writing tasks) to develop "rhetorical flexibility"—the ability and the tools to research and analyze the various contexts they will encounter beyond the beginning writing class.

There is no doubt that genre studies have been very influential in the application of written discourse analysis to L2 teaching. In particular, the effects of ESP research and pedagogy, together with work in composition/rhetoric in writing across the curriculum/writing in the disciplines, have changed the face of both secondary and postsecondary writing and language instruction. Though there are legitimate pitfalls to be avoided and questions to be resolved, there is no question that genre research and its pedagogical application have been useful, especially as they help students who are simultaneously grappling with content, language, and rhetoric to gain some control and understanding of the contextual factors working for or against their success—and to learn not only specific genre conventions but general metacognitive awareness of the reality of genre in every communicative situation they will encounter.

Conclusion

Productive Possibilities for Overlap in Written Discourse Analysis

A careful reader of this chapter thus far will note an interesting fact: while there is clearly and inevitably overlap between the three subtopics—contrastive rhetoric, corpus linguistics, and genre studies—subsumed under the broad topic of analysis of written discourse and its applications to L2 teaching, they nonetheless all have their own separate research traditions, seminal works, and well-known scholars strongly associated with them. This is a somewhat counterintuitive observation and an unfortunate one, as well. There are several obvious ways in which researchers in these subcategories of written discourse analysis could productively build upon each other's work to a greater degree than they now do.

Overlaps Between Corpus Linguistics and CR/Genre

As already noted, the computational tools developed by corpus linguists have great potential to assist researchers concerned with contrastive rhetoric, particularly for studies that focus on groups of L2 writers from different L1 backgrounds. Tardy and Swales (2008) further note with some puzzlement that the tools and approaches of corpus linguistics have been underutilized or even ignored in genre studies. Given that at least part of genre-based research focuses on the language of texts (beyond the context and the rhetorical moves or stages), it would seem that the large, rapid, and sophisticated analyses of corpora could yield insights useful for genre studies and especially for SFL.

Overlaps Between CR and Genre Studies

It is also worth mentioning that the principles articulated in genre pedagogy could also be quite useful in applying contrastive rhetoric work. As most thoughtful observers of CR would agree, its primary "practical" application is not (or should not be) prescriptive: "Maybe your home language/culture presented ideas that way, but here we do things differently, so you'd better learn to do it our way." However, in the same way that students can be asked to investigate genre differences, they could also be asked to research the ways in which ideas and evidence are presented in their home language/culture (and then to compare them to the target language/culture). Such investigations might help students to understand more explicitly and consciously what are some of the tacit assumptions (of both the home/target language) that might be impeding their success in the new setting.

Genre studies and CR can inform each other in another way. If genres are inherently socially situated, then the rhetorical patterns or traditions of different cultures may well affect the shape of even the "same" genre in different contexts. For example, opinion columns or editorials in newspapers (a ubiquitous genre that is easy to access and to study) will most likely vary in important and observable ways depending upon the author, the target audience, and even the type of publication in which those opinion pieces appear. There could be a great deal more productive work that blends the principles and discoveries of CR with the specific findings and research paradigms of genre studies.

Problems With Application

As I have noted in the previous sections, attempts to apply research findings from written discourse analyses to the L2 classroom have met with criticism, philosophical disagreements, and practical obstacles. Broadly speaking, there are three major criticisms of written discourse analysis as it is applied to the L2 classroom. The first is that its findings can be oversimplified and turned into rigid formulae that learners must follow (e.g., write in a "straight line" like English speakers do; model your writing after these genre specifications). This concern can be addressed by encouraging teachers to engage students in text research so that they can learn more about the target discourses they are trying to produce successfully (Johns, 2009; Johns et al., 2006; Tardy & Courtney, 2008), rather than by teaching prescriptively and/or having students simply emulate "correct" models.

The second criticism (aimed primarily at corpus linguistics and SFL) is that the emphasis is on specific linguistic features (grammatical and lexical) and not enough on overall comprehension and communication. Even if teachers were capable of performing the sophisticated analyses required and developing classroom activities based on the findings, they still might not want to take the amount of time and energy it would require (both for themselves and in the classroom) to explicitly highlight features that may or may not help the students become more effective users of the L2. There is definitely a need for much more classroom-based empirical research to demonstrate that such intensive word- and sentence-based interventions is effective as a pedagogical strategy, compared with other approaches to developing student competence (see Tardy, 2006).

This concern can be addressed by careful and thoughtful prioritizing on the part of curriculum/course designers, materials developers, and teachers. For instance, if teaching units that successfully blend interactive reading strategies, writing processes, and bottom-up language concerns are presented to teachers, they may well respond favorably to them.[4] Most L2 instructors know that they should be integrating presentation of linguistic features along with more "top-down" reading strategies and writing processes, but they are not sure how to do so in a balanced and effective (and engaging) way (see Schleppegrell & Oliveira, 2005, for one such model).

The third and final concern about the written discourse analysis is its complexity: it is time-consuming (and often tedious); it often requires advanced linguistic training; and in some instances it also involves sophisticated computer and statistics knowledge. As a result, advances in written discourse analysis are often slow, the published findings are sometimes beyond the expertise of the classroom teachers who might read them, and suggestions that teachers conduct such research themselves to design materials for their own students seem frankly unrealistic. These practical problems are substantial but not insurmountable, and solutions will require (most likely) some productive partnerships between researchers and classroom practitioners. Researchers need the "reality check" that teachers can provide: the "What does it mean?" and "Why should anyone care?" questions that so often divide research and practice. They further need the teacher's assessment of whether their ideas for application of their findings will actually work in a classroom. Teachers, on the other hand, need researchers' time and technical expertise. It is unlikely that busy classroom teachers are going to conduct their own corpus studies or genre analyses; in fact, it is unusual for many teachers to develop their own classroom materials outside of their chosen/assigned textbook. The researcher has the time, focus, resources, and training to design the studies and present findings that can be applied productively, helping to identify new, data-driven solutions to vexing classroom problems. Ideally, the researchers would be in constant consultation with the practitioners as they identify research questions and ways to investigate them—more typically, researchers pursue questions that are of theoretical interest to them and then later try to convince practitioners of the findings' relevance and usefulness.

Notwithstanding these legitimate and substantial concerns, written discourse analysis is an indispensable part of applied linguistics research, and it has tremendous potential for L2 classroom teaching—but only if the researchers and teachers listen to each other and collaborate.

Notes

1. Useful tools include the Vocabulary Profiler (lextutor.ca/vp) and the AWL Highlighter (http://www.nottingham.ac.uk/~alzsh3/acvocab/awlhighlighter.htm). These free and easy-to-use online tools allow teachers or students to upload or paste texts that can help them to identify and analyze vocabulary in the specific text(s) they are considering or using. Though these URLs were current at the time this chapter was written, readers are reminded that they tend to change.
2. Conrad (2005, p. 405) noted a "critical need for more computer programmers in corpus linguistics," further highlighting some of the methodological and practical gaps potentially constraining future investigations and classroom applications.
3. Johns (2009) notes that much of her approach to teaching students to become researchers of genres is inspired by the New Rhetoric school.
4. The 2005 textbook series *College writing* (Houghton Mifflin) is a good example of this approach. Students are introduced in each unit to "Power Grammar," carefully selected linguistic items (based on corpus/SFL insights) that are integrated with unit readings and writing tasks. Thus, the structures are never presented or taught in isolation.

References

Atkinson, D. (1992). The evolution of medical research writing from 1735–1985: The case of the *Edinburgh Medical Journal*. *Applied Linguistics*, *13*, 337–374.

Atkinson, D. (1999). *Scientific discourse in sociohistorical context: The philosophical transactions of the Royal Society of London, 1675–1975*. Mahwah, NJ: Erlbaum.

Atkinson, D., & Ramanathan, V. (1995). Cultures of writing: An ethnographic comparison of L1 and L2 university writing/language programs. *TESOL Quarterly*, *29*(3), 539–568.

Beaugrande, R., de (1980). *Text, discourse, and process: Toward a multi-disciplinary science of texts*. Norwood, NJ: Ablex.

Beaugrande, R., de, & Dressler, W. (1981). *Introduction to text linguistics*. London: Longman.

Biber, D. (1985). Investigating macroscopic textual variation through multi-feature/multi-dimensional analysis. *Linguistics*, *23*, 337–360.

Biber, D. (1988). *Variation across speech and writing*. Cambridge: Cambridge University Press.

Biber, D. (1990). Methodological issues regarding corpus-based analyses of linguistic variation. *Literary and Linguistic Computing*, *5*, 257–269.

Biber, D. (1993). Representativeness in corpus design. *Literary and linguistic computing*, *8*, 243–257.

Biber, D. (2006). *University English: A corpus-based study of written and spoken registers*. Amsterdam: John Benjamins.

Biber, D., Conrad, S., & Reppen, R. (1998). *Corpus linguistics: Investigating language structure and use*. Cambridge: Cambridge University Press.

Biber, D., Conrad, S., Reppen, R., Byrd, P., & Helt, M. (2002). Speaking and writing in the university: A multi-dimensional comparison. *TESOL Quarterly*, *36*, 9–48.

Biber, D., Johansson, C., Leech, S., Conrad, S., & Finegan, E. (1999). *The Longman grammar of spoken and written English*. London: Longman.

Brannon, L., & Knoblauch, C.H. (1982). On students' rights to their own texts: A model of teacher response. *College Composition and Communication*, *33*, 157–166.

Byrd, P., & Bunting, J. (2008). Myth 3: Where grammar is concerned, one size fits all. In J. Reid (Ed.), *Writing myths: Applying second language research to classroom teaching* (pp. 42–69). Ann Arbor: Michigan.

Connor, U. (1987). Argumentative patterns in student essays: Cross-cultural differences. In U. Connor & R. B. Kaplan (Eds.), *Writing across languages: Analysis of L2 text* (pp. 57–71). Reading, MA: Addison-Wesley.

Connor, U. (1996). *Contrastive rhetoric: Cross-cultural aspects of second-language writing.* Cambridge: Cambridge University Press.

Connor, U. (2003). Changing currents in contrastive rhetoric: Implications for teaching and research. In B. Kroll (Ed.), *Exploring the dynamics of second language writing* (pp. 218–241). Cambridge: Cambridge University Press.

Connor, U. & Asenavage, K. (1994). Peer response groups in ESL writing classes: How much impact on revision? *Journal of Second Language Writing, 3,* 257–276.

Connor, U., & Kaplan, R. B. (1987). Introduction. In U. Connor & R. B. Kaplan (Eds.), *Writing across languages: Analysis of L2 text* (pp. 1–5). Reading, MA: Addison-Wesley.

Conrad, S. M. (2005). Corpus linguistics and L2 teaching. In E. Hinkel (Ed.), *Handbook of research in second language teaching and learning* (pp. 393–409). Mahwah, NJ: Erlbaum.

Conrad, S. M. (2008). Myth 6: Corpus-based research is too complicated to be useful for writing teachers. In J. Reid (Ed.), *Writing myths: Applying second language research to classroom teaching* (pp. 115–139). Ann Arbor: University of Michigan Press.

Conrad, S. M., & Goldstein, L. M. (1999). ESL student revision after teacher-written comments: Text, contexts, and individuals. *Journal of Second Language Writing, 8,* 147–180.

Cope, B., Kalantzis, M., Kress, G., & Martin, J. (1993). Bibliographical essay: Developing the theory and practice of genre-based literacy. In B. Cope & M. Kalantzis (Eds.), *The power of literacy: A genre-based approach to the teaching of writing* (pp. 231–247). London: Falmer Press.

Coxhead, A. (2000). A new academic word list. *TESOL Quarterly, 34*(2), 213–238.

Coxhead, A. (2006). *Essentials of teaching academic vocabulary.* Boston: Houghton Mifflin.

Coxhead, A., & Byrd, P. (2007). Preparing writing teachers to teach the vocabulary and grammar of academic prose. *Journal of Second Language Writing, 16*(3), 129–147.

Dressler, W. (Ed.) (1978). *Current trends in text linguistics.* Berlin: de Gruyter.

Enkvist, N. E. (1987). Text linguistics for the applier: An orientation. In U. Connor & R. B. Kaplan (Eds.), *Writing across languages: Analysis of L2 text* (pp. 23–43). Reading, MA: Addison-Wesley.

Feez, S. (2002). Heritage and innovation in second language education. In A. Johns (Ed.), *Genre in the classroom: Multiple perspectives* (pp. 47–68). Mahwah, NJ: Erlbaum.

Ferris, D. R. (1994a). Lexical and syntactic features of ESL writing by students at different levels of L2 proficiency, *TESOL Quarterly, 28,* 414–420.

Ferris, D. R. (1994b). Rhetorical strategies in student persuasive writing: Differences between native and non-native speakers. *Research in the Teaching of English, 28,* 45–65.

Ferris, D. R. (1997). The influence of teacher commentary on student revision. *TESOL Quarterly, 31,* 315–339.

Ferris, D. R. (2002). *Treatment of error in second language student writing.* Ann Arbor: University of Michigan Press.

Ferris, D. R. (2003). *Response to student writing.* Mahwah, NJ: Erlbaum.

Ferris, D. R. (2004). The "grammar correction" debate in L2 Writing: Where are we, and where do we go from here? (and what do we do in the meantime …?). *Journal of Second Language Writing, 13,* 49–62.

Ferris, D. R. (2009). *Teaching college writing to diverse student populations.* Ann Arbor: University of Michigan Press.

Ferris, D. R., & Hedgcock, J. S. (2005). *Teaching ESL composition: Purpose, process, and practice* (2nd Ed.). Mahwah, NJ: Erlbaum.

Ferris, D. R., Pezone, S., Tade, C. R., & Tinti, S. (1997). Teacher commentary on student writing: Descriptions and implications. *Journal of Second Language Writing, 6,* 155–182.

Flowerdew, J. (Ed.) (1994). *Academic listening: Research perspectives.* Cambridge: Cambridge University Press.

Folse, K. S. (2004). *Vocabulary myths.* Ann Arbor: University of Michigan Press.

Folse, K. S. (2008). Myth 1: Teaching vocabulary is not the writing teacher's job. In J. Reid (Ed.), *Writing myths* (pp. 1–17). Ann Arbor: University of Michigan Press.

Freedman, A., & Medway, P. (Eds.) (1994). *Genre and the new rhetoric.* London: Taylor & Francis.

Goldstein, L. (2001). For Kyla: What does the research say about responding to ESL writers? In T. Silva & P. K. Matsuda (Eds.), *On second language writing* (pp. 73–90). Mahwah, NJ: Lawrence Erlbaum Associates.

Goldstein, L., & Conrad, S. (1990). Student input and the negotiation of meaning in ESL writing conferences. *TESOL Quarterly, 24,* 443–460.

Grabe, W. (1987). Contrastive rhetoric and text-type research. In U. Connor & R. B. Kaplan (Eds.), *Writing across languages: Analysis of L2 text* (pp. 115–137). Reading, MA: Addison-Wesley.

Grabe, W., & Kaplan, R. B. (1996). *Theory and practice of writing: An applied linguistics perspective.* London: Longman.

Halliday, M. A. K., & Hasan, R. (1976). *Cohesion in English.* London: Longman.

Harklau, L., Losey, K., & Siegal, M. (Eds.) (1999). *Generation 1.5 in college composition.* Mahwah, NJ: Erlbaum.

Hedgcock, J. S., & Ferris, D. R. (2009). *Teaching readers of English: Students, texts, and contexts.* New York: Routledge/Taylor & Francis.

Herrington, A., & Moran, C. (Eds.) (2005). *Genre across the curriculum.* Logan, UT: Utah State University Press.

Hinds, J. (1987). Reader versus writer responsibility: A new typology. In U. Connor & R. B. Kaplan (Eds.), *Writing across languages: Analysis of L2 text* (pp. 141–152). Reading, MA: Addison-Wesley.

Hinkel, E. (2002). *Second language writers' text.* Mahwah, NJ: Erlbaum.

Hinkel, E. (2005). Analyses of second language text and what can be learned from them. In E. Hinkel (Ed.), *Handbook of research in second language learning and teaching* (pp. 615–628). Mahwah, NJ: Erlbaum.

Hyland, F. (1998). The impact of teacher-written feedback on individual writers. *Journal of Second Language Writing, 7*(3), 255–286.

Hyland, F., & Hyland, K. (2001). Sugaring the pill: Praise and criticism in written feedback. *Journal of Second Language Writing, 10*(3), 185–212.

Hyland, K. (1998). *Hedging in scientific research articles.* Philadelphia: John Benjamins.

Hyland, K. (1999). Talking to students: Metadiscourse in disciplinary textbooks. *English for Specific Purposes, 18*, 3–26.

Hyland, K. (2000). *Disciplinary discourse.* London: Longman.

Hyland, K. (2001). Bringing in the reader: Addressee features in academic articles. *Written Communication, 18*, 549–574.

Hyland, K. (2002). *Teaching and researching writing.* London: Longman.

Hyon, S. (1996). Genres in three traditions: Implications for second language teaching. *TESOL Quarterly, 30*, 693–722.

Indrasuta, C. (1988). Narrative styles in the writing of Thai and American students. In A.C. Purves (Ed.), *Writing across languages and cultures: Issues in contrastive rhetoric* (pp. 206–226). Newbury Park, CA: Sage.

Jacobs, G. M., Curtis, A., Braine, G., & Huang, S. (1998). Feedback on student writing: Taking the middle path. *Journal of Second Language Writing, 7*, 307–318.

Jarvis, S., Grant, L., Bikowski, D., & Ferris, D. R. (2003). Exploring multiple profiles of learners' writing proficiency. *Journal of Second Language Writing, 12*, 377–403.

Johns, A. M. (1997). *Text, role, and context: Developing academic literacies.* Cambridge: Cambridge University Press.

Johns, A. M. (2003). Genre and ESL/EFL composition instruction. In B. Kroll (Ed.), *Exploring the dynamics of second language writing* (pp. 195–217). Cambridge: Cambridge University Press.

Johns, A. M. (2009). Situated invention and genres: Assisting Generation 1.5 students in developing rhetorical flexibility. In M. Roberge, M. Siegal, & L. Harklau (Eds.), *Generation 1.5 in college composition* (pp. 203–220). New York: Routledge.

Johns, A. M., Bawarshi, A., Coe, R. M., Hyland, K., Paltridge, B., Reiff, M. J., & Tardy, C. (2006). Crossing the boundaries of genre studies: Commentaries by experts. *Journal of Second Language Writing, 15*, 234–249.

Kaplan, R. B. (1966). Cultural thought patterns in intercultural education. *Language Learning, 16*, 1–20.

Kaplan, R. B. (1987). Cultural thought patterns revisited. In U. Connor & R. B. Kaplan (Eds.), *Writing across languages: Analysis of L2 text* (pp. 9–21). Reading, MA: Addison-Wesley.

Kaplan, R. B. (2005). Contrastive rhetoric. In E. Hinkel (Ed.), *Handbook of research in second language learning and teaching* (pp. 375–391). Mahwah, NJ: Erlbaum.

Kaplan, R. B., & Grabe, W. (2002). A modern history of written discourse analysis. *Journal of Second Language Writing, 11*, 191–223.

Kinneavy, J. L. (1971). *A theory of discourse.* Englewood Cliffs, NJ: Prentice-Hall.

Krashen, S. D., & Terrell, T. (1983). *The natural approach: Language acquisition in the classroom.* San Francisco: The Alemany Press.

Lautamatti, L. (1987). Observations on the development of the topic in simplified discourse. In U. Connor & R. B. Kaplan (Eds.), *Writing across languages: Analysis of L2 text* (pp. 87–114). Reading, MA: Addison-Wesley.

Leki, I. (1990). Potential problems with peer responding in ESL writing classes. *CATESOL Journal, 3*, 5–19.

Leki, I. (1991). Twenty-five years of contrastive rhetoric: Text analysis and writing pedagogies. *TESOL Quarterly, 25*, 123–143.

Liu, J., & Hansen, J. (2002). *Peer response in second language writing classrooms.* Ann Arbor: University of Michigan Press.

Mackin-Horarik, M. (2002). "Something to shoot for": A systemic functional approach to teaching genre in secondary school science. In A. Johns (Ed.), *Genre in the classroom: Multiple perspectives* (pp. 17–46). Mahwah, NJ: Erlbaum.

Mendonça, C. O., & Johnson, K.E. (1994). Peer review negotiations: Revision activities in ESL writing instruction. *TESOL Quarterly, 28*, 745–769.

Meyer, B. J. F. (1975). *The organization of prose and its effects on memory.* Amsterdam: North Holland Publishing Company.

Miller, C. (1984). Genre as social action. *Quarterly Journal of Speech, 70*, 151–167.

Mohan, B. A., & Lo, W. A-Y. (1985). Academic writing and Chinese students' transfer and developmental factors. *TESOL Quarterly, 19*(3), 515–534.

Murphy, J. (2006). *Essentials of teaching academic oral communication.* Boston: Houghton Mifflin.

Patthey-Chavez, G. G., & Ferris, D. R. (1997). Writing conferences and the weaving of multi-voiced texts in college composition. *Research in the Teaching of English, 31*, 51–90.

Polio, C. (1997). Measures of linguistic accuracy in second language writing research. *Language Learning, 47*, 101–143.

Polio, C. (2001). Research methodology in second language writing research: The case of text-based studies. In T. Silva & P. Matsuda (Eds.), *On second language writing* (pp. 91–116). Mahwah, NJ: Erlbaum.

Polio, C. (2003). Research on second language writing: An overview of what we investigate and how. In B. Kroll (Ed.), *Exploring the dynamics of second language writing* (pp. 35–65). Cambridge: Cambridge University Press.

Purves, A. (1986). Rhetorical communities, the international student, and basic writing. *Journal of Basic Writing, 5,* 38–51.

Purves, A. (Ed.) (1988). *Writing across languages and cultures.* Newbury Park, CA: Sage.

Reder, S., Harris, K., & Setzler, K. (2003). A multimedia adult learner corpus. *TESOL Quarterly, 37,* 546–556.

Reid, J. M. (2006). *Essentials of teaching academic writing.* Boston: Houghton Mifflin.

Reppen, R. (2001). Register variation in student and adult speech and writing. In S. Conrad & D. Biber (Eds.), *Variation in English: Multi-dimensional studies* (pp. 187–199). London: Longman.

Reynolds, D. (2005). Linguistic correlates of second language literacy development: Evidence from middle-grade learner essays. *Journal of Second Language Writing, 14*(1), 19–45.

Roberge, M., Siegal, M., & Harklau, L. (Eds.) (2009). *Generation 1.5 in college composition.* New York: Routledge/Taylor & Francis.

Russell, D. (1997). Rethinking genre in school and society: An activity theory analysis. *Written Communication, 14,* 504–554.

Schleppegrell, M. (1998). Grammar as resource: Writing a description. *Research in the Teaching of English, 32,* 182–211.

Schleppegrell, M. (2001). Linguistic features of the language of schooling. *Linguistics and Education, 12,* 431–459.

Schleppegrell, M. (2008). Grammar, the sentence, and linguistic analysis. In C. Bazerman (Ed.), *Handbook of research on writing* (pp. 549–564). Mahwah, NJ: Erlbaum.

Schleppegrell, M. (2009). Grammar for Generation 1.5: A focus on meaning. In M. Roberge, M. Siegal, & L. Harklau (Eds.), *Generation 1.5 in college composition* (pp. 221–234). New York: Routledge.

Schleppegrell, M., & Colombi, C. (Eds.) (2002). *Developing advanced literacy in first and second languages: Meaning with power.* Mahwah, NJ: Erlbaum.

Schleppegrell, M., & Oliveira, L. (2005). An integrated language and content approach for history teachers. *Journal of English for Academic Purposes, 5,* 254–269.

Silva, T. (1990). ESL composition instruction: Developments, issues and directions. In B. Kroll (Ed.), *Second language writing: Research insights for the classroom* (pp. 11–23). Cambridge: Cambridge University Press.

Silva, T. (1993). Toward an understanding of the distinct nature of L2 writing: The ESL research and its implications. *TESOL Quarterly, 27,* 657–677.

Silva, T. (2005). On the philosophical bases of inquiry in second language writing: Metaphysics, inquiry paradigms, and the intellectual zeitgeist. In P.K. Matsuda & T. Silva (Eds.), *Second language writing research: Perspectives on the process of knowledge construction* (pp. 3–15). Mahwah, NJ: Erlbaum.

Spack, R. (1988). Initiating students into the academic discourse community: How far should we go? *TESOL Quarterly, 22,* 29–52.

Straub, R., & Lunsford, R. F. (1995). *Twelve readers reading: Responding to college student writing.* Creskill, NJ: Hampton Press.

Swales, J. (1990). *Genre analysis: English in academic and research settings.* Cambridge: Cambridge University Press.

Swales, J., & Feak, C. (2004). *Academic writing for graduate students* (2nd ed.). Ann Arbor: University of Michigan Press.

Tardy, C. (2006). Researching first and second language genre learning: A comparative review and a look ahead. *Journal of Second Language Writing, 15,* 79–101.

Tardy, C., & Courtney, J. (2008). Assignments and activities in teaching academic writing. In P. Friedrich (Ed.), *Teaching academic writing* (pp. 73–92). London: Continuum.

Tardy, C., & Swales, J. (2008). Form, text organization, genre, coherence, and cohesion. In C. Bazerman (Ed.), *Handbook of research on writing* (pp. 565–581). Mahwah, NJ: Erlbaum.

Truscott, J. (1996). The case against grammar correction in L2 writing classes. *Language Learning, 46,* 327–369.

Truscott, J. (2007). The effect of error correction on learners' ability to write accurately. *Journal of Second Language Writing, 16*(4), 255–272.

Truscott, J., & Hsu, A. Y.-p. (2008). Error correction, revision, and learning. *Journal of Second Language Writing, 17*(4), 292–305.

van Dijk, T. A. (1972). *Some aspects of text grammars.* The Hague: Mouton.

van Dijk, T. A. (1977). *Text and context.* London: Longman.

van Dijk, T. A. (1980). *Macrostructures: An interdisciplinary study of global structures in discourse, interaction, and cognition.* Hillsdale, NJ: Erlbaum.

van Dijk, T.A. (1985). *Handbook of discourse analysis* (Vols. I and II). London: Academic Press.

van Zante, J., & Persiani, R. (2008). Using corpus-linguistics findings in the classroom: A rationale with practical applications. *CATESOL Journal, 20,* 95–109.

Zamel, V. (1985). Responding to student writing. *TESOL Quarterly, 19*, 79–102.

Zhang, S. (1995). Reexamining the affective advantage of peer feedback in the ESL writing class. *Journal of Second Language Writing, 4*, 209–222.

Zhang, S. (1999). Thoughts on some recent evidence concerning the affective advantage of peer feedback. *Journal of Second Language Writing, 8*, 321–326.

40

Computer-Assisted Language Learning

Dorothy M. Chun

Introduction

The purpose of this chapter is to provide an overview of the research in computer-assisted language learning (CALL). The field of CALL is multidisciplinary, drawing upon a number of disciplines, including linguistics, psychology, sociology, education, computer science, and natural language processing, to name several of the most important. This particular sub-discipline fits within the larger domains of research on second language acquisition (SLA) and foreign language teaching (FLT). Therefore, the same issues that are treated by SLA and FLT will be addressed, but in this case from the perspective of how technology and computers can aid in these processes.

Since it is not possible to discuss all of the subareas of SLA and FLT, the sections in this chapter will focus on the most important developments and trends in CALL, and in particular, the areas in which technology may be particularly well suited to enhancing teaching and learning. CALL is not a methodology; it is an emerging field that studies how technology is used as one (of many) tool(s) for language learning.

The position taken in this chapter is that technology should be used primarily in service of language learning and teaching and secondarily because it is integral to academic life in the twenty-first century. Just as there is no one universally accepted theory of SLA or one universally proven methodology of language teaching, so too are there no CALL tools that are effective universally for all learners. A key theme throughout this chapter is that CALL research shows how certain CALL tools are effective for certain learners (e.g., particular levels of learners, learners with particular learning styles) and for certain aspects of language and cultural competence (e.g., vocabulary, grammar, speaking, reading, communicative and pragmatic competence, intercultural understanding). Simply stated, what will be examined is the research on how people learn with computers, multimedia, and social networks, and how particular features can be effective for particular learners for particular aspects of language and culture learning within a particular teaching methodology.

There are many ways in which a chapter on CALL could be organized. A *historical* approach could be taken and the development of the field of CALL could be traced historically, as Bax (2003) and Warschauer (2004) have done (see Table 40.1). The chapter could be structured based on the *technologies* used in CALL, e.g., earlier uses of the computer as a tutor or a drill-and-test machine, use of videodiscs for teaching culture, first generation Web-based tools for computer-mediated communication (CMC 1.0), and more recent Web 2.0 tools for social networking and virtual worlds (CMC 2.0), "edutainment" and gaming, to name but a few (Hubbard, 2009, Vol. III; Levy & Stockwell,

Table 40.1 The Three Stages of CALL

Stage	1970s–1980s: structural CALL	1980s–1990s: communicative CALL	Twenty-first century: integrative CALL
Technology	Mainframe	PCs	Multimedia and Internet
English teaching paradigm	Grammar translation and audiolingual	Communicative language teaching	Content-based, English for specific purposes (ESP)/ English for academic purposes (EAP)
View of language	Structural (a formal structural system)	Cognitive (a mentally constructed system)	Sociocognitive (developed in social interaction)
Principal use of computers	Drill and practice	Communicative exercises	Authentic discourse
Principal objective	Accuracy	Fluency	Agency

Source: Warschauer (2004, p. 22).

2006, Warschauer & Grimes, 2007). Another approach could be to organize the chapter by *language component* or *skill*, with sections devoted to pronunciation, grammar, vocabulary, speaking, listening, reading, writing, culture, and intercultural competence, as Ducate and Arnold (2006) and Hubbard (2009, Vol. II) have done effectively (see Table 40.2). Since technologies change and evolve so rapidly, yet another approach would be to discuss the most recent trends in using technology for language/culture learning (Blake, 2008).

Table 40.2 CALL for Individual Language Skills

Skill	CALL tools	Research results
Pronunciation: vowels and consonants	Visualizations of articulation, automatic speech recognition (ASR)	Levis, 2008, O'Brien, 2006
Prosody, intonation	Visualizations of pitch curves, ASR	Chun, 2002; Hardison, 2004, 2005
Vocabulary	Tutorials, multimedia glosses, CMC	Chun, 2006; Horst, Cobb, and Nicolae, 2005; Taylor, 2006
Grammar and syntax	Tutorials, iCALL, CMC	Heift and Schulze, 2007; Kern, 1995; Nagata, 1999
Pragmatics	CMC 1.0 & 2.0	Belz and Kinginger, 2003; Sykes, 2005
Speaking	CMC 1.0 & 2.0, audio and videoconferencing	C. Blake, 2009; R. Blake, 2005; Payne and Ross, 2005
Listening	Multimedia glosses, audio and videoconferencing	Jones, 2006; Jones and Plass, 2002
Reading	Multimedia annotations; electronic dictionaries	Abraham, 2008; Chun, 2006
Writing	CMC 1.0 and 2.0	Ducate and Lomicka, 2008; Murray and Hourigan, 2006
Culture	Videos, films, CMC 1.0 & 2.0	Abrams, 2006; Dubreil, 2006
Intercultural communicative competence	CMC 1.0 & 2.0	Lomicka, 2006; O'Dowd and Ritter, 2006
Multiliteracies	Viewing and creating Web pages	Gonglewski and DuBravac, 2006; Kern, 2000
Assessment	Web-based tools	Carr, 2006; Douglas and Hegelheimer, 2008

Table 40.3 CALL for SLA Based on SLA Theories

Theory	Focus	Technology
Psycholinguistic SLA— *individual*	Vocabulary, grammar, reading, collocations	Multimedia, iCALL, CMC Corpus linguistics
Interactionist SLA— *individual + interlocutor*	Communication: negotiation of meaning	CMC 1.0 (email, forums, chat); CMC 2.0 (blogs, wikis)
Sociocultural SLA— *individual + society/culture*	Mediation of understanding and action through cultural tools Intercultural competence	CMC 1.0 (audio- and video-conferencing), 2.0 (podcasts, vodcasts, social networking sites, virtual worlds) Corpus linguistics
Ecological SLA— *individual + environment*	Audience, author agency, identity	CMC 1.0, 2.0 Hybrid/blended models

Based on the premise that CALL should be discussed in relation to how it can enhance SLA, I have chosen to organize this chapter based on the most prevalent theories of SLA and discuss research on how technology can be used in service of second language (L2) learning and teaching (similar to Chapelle, 2007). An excellent panel at the CALICO Conference (Computer Assisted Language Instruction Consortium) represented the state of the art in "Second Language Acquisition Theories, Technologies, and Language Learning." The four main theoretical bases discussed, moving from narrower to broader spheres, from individuals to groups and communities, were (1) psycholinguistic approaches (Payne), (2) interactionist approaches (Smith), (3) sociocultural or cultural-historical approaches (Thorne), and (4) ecological approaches (van Lier) (see Table 40.3). This chapter will therefore present research on the use of CALL in relation to each of these underlying theories of SLA. Incorporated into these sections will be discussions of effectiveness research, noting the trend away from comparing technology vs. no technology toward investigating the features of technology that are helpful for language learning (Felix, 2005).

Digital Literacy and Multiple Literacies

Before discussing the four main SLA theories as applied to CALL research, it has been suggested that new online media are helping to transform language and literacy in general. Warschauer (2001, p. 49) states that online communications and other forms of transnational media provide L2 learners with greater communicative opportunities, and

> digital media are changing reading and writing practices, giving rise to a new set of literacies incorporating onscreen reading, online navigation and research, hypermedia interpretation and authoring, and many-to-many synchronous and asynchronous communication. The computer thus becomes more than an optional tool for language tutoring, but rather an essential medium of literacy and language use.

Even for the current generation of students, the so-called "digital natives," simply growing up surrounded by technology does not ensure that they will be effective communicators in online realms, just as growing up in a print world did not automatically make one a good reader and writer (Warschauer, 2001, p. 56).

Students still need help in developing multiple literacies, both in first (L1) and second languages. Kern (2000) proposes a working definition of literacy in the specific context of academic second and foreign language education that weaves together linguistic, cognitive, and sociocultural strands:

"Literacy is the use of socially-, historically- and culturally-situated practices of creating and inter-preting meaning through texts" (p. 16). He describes how computer environments can foster the development of sociocognitive literacy in a number of ways, starting with how worldwide networks initially allowed cross-national and cross-cultural interpersonal exchange of text but have evolved to multi-modal means of expression and representation of information, so that multiple literacies, such as visual literacy, cultural literacy, etc. must be acquired (p. 259).

Gonglewski and DuBravac (2006) discuss some general categories to incorporate into teaching multiliteracy, which include the use of authentic materials, the fostering of authentic communica-tion, the study of alternative modes of expressing meaning (specifically via hypermedia—viewing or creating Web pages—or via CMC, which "flouts the stark delineation between written and oral communication," p. 49), a focus on cultural conventions, critical thinking, and process-oriented approaches.

Research Perspectives

In the inaugural issue of *Language Learning & Technology*, Chapelle (1997) recommended that instructed SLA provide guidance for framing CALL research questions. It is this recommenda-tion that guides the organization of this chapter. In the following four sub-sections, the research on psycholinguistic approaches, interactionist approaches, sociocultural approaches, and ecological approaches to SLA and CALL will be discussed.

Each sub-section will summarize the most important results from the research to date on CALL tools that have been found to be effective for particular aspects of L2 learning. At the end of each sub-section, directions for future research and development will be outlined based on the current CALL tools that are available and on the particular theoretical premise of that sub-section. Kern, Ware, and Warschauer (2004) noted: "In each area [of networked language learning], research has indicated that there is no single *effect* of using online communication, but rather that process and results vary widely depending on a range of logistical, pedagogical, and social factors" (p. 243).

Psycholinguistic Approaches to SLA and CALL

As the name indicates, psycholinguistic theories of L2 learning focus on the cognitive processes in *individuals* involved with language learning—how the brain processes language—including both learning processes that involve memory, attention, and noticing, as well as individual differences in how multi-modal information is processed. Psycholinguistic CALL research is able to go beyond observations of behavior (language output) and has examined mental representations of linguistic information, e.g., the mental lexicon, lexical access in sentence processing, the effects of the fre-quency of hearing words or phrases on how well they are learned, and individual differences in cognitive capacity (e.g., differences in verbal and spatial abilities or differences in working memory (WM) capacity) that could constrain processing of multimedia in the L2.

Many of the psycholinguistic CALL studies are based in part on the cognitive theory of multime-dia learning (Mayer, 2005), which posits that when presenting multi-modal information, the use, for example, of pictures vs. text, or of audio vs. text, must be based on the cognitive processes aided by this information and on how these processes can be supported by the characteristics of the par-ticular mode. Specifically for L2 learning, while a picture may be effective for depicting a word that represents an object, for an advance organizer, a video with an audio narration may be preferable to aid the integration of information into an existing mental model of the subject matter. In addition, research on cognitive load (Sweller, 2005) has shown that due to limitations in WM, problems arise when information is presented in multiple modes and cannot be processed simultaneously in WM.

For example, if L2 learners must process textual, visual, and audio information at the same time, depending on their WM capacity, they may or may not be successful in integrating these multiple sources of information and comprehending all of it.

Vocabulary Acquisition and Reading Comprehension

Since L2 vocabulary knowledge is widely held to be one of the primary factors in L2 reading comprehension, many CALL studies have investigated the effect of multi-modal vocabulary glosses (text definitions, visuals/graphics, videos, audio) on vocabulary learning and reading comprehension. The research is summarized in Chun (2006) and in a meta-analysis (Abraham, 2008). Although different studies report differing results on which types of multimedia glosses or annotations are best for L2 vocabulary acquisition, many studies suggest that image-based annotations are helpful, particularly in combination with text-based annotations (Chun & Plass, 1996; Kost, Foss, & Lenzini, 1999; Yoshii & Flaitz, 2002). In his meta-analysis of 11 studies of computer-mediated glosses, Abraham (2008) found an overall large effect of computer-mediated glosses on L2 vocabulary learning, both on immediate and delayed post-tests, and that glosses were most effective for intermediate-level learners.

Interestingly, a number of studies have found that, when multimedia glosses are available and learners are free to look up annotations of their choice, they actually prefer to look up definitions or translations of L2 words into L1 rather than graphic, visual, or audio glosses (Ercetin, 2003; Laufer & Hill, 2000). In contrast, Sakar and Ercetin (2005) reported that participants in their study preferred visual annotations significantly more than textual or audio annotations.

The important issue here is that while learners may prefer one type of gloss to another, research shows that looking up a text-based annotation in combination with an image-based annotation results in better vocabulary learning. Therefore, it may be necessary to train learners to use CALL materials rather than to assume that learners will know how to use them or to let them rely on their natural preferences (Hubbard, 2004).

Since it cannot be assumed that learners will use CALL materials in the most effective ways, one essential aspect of CALL research is thus tracking user behavior. A CALL psycholinguistic study that tracked lookup behavior and multimedia glosses by Chun and Payne (2004) found that learners used different types of support differently. Learners with lower individual WM capacity made greater use of multimedia resources and bootstrapped their way to greater vocabulary acquisition; they compensated for their limited WM capacity by looking up more multimedia glosses than those learners with greater WM capacity.

Another psycholinguistic aspect of CALL studies involves individual differences among learners, namely, the question of for whom multimedia can be effective. Research by Plass, Chun, Mayer, and Leutner (1998, 2003) showed that visual learners are aided by graphic information, but learners will low spatial ability are *not* helped by visual glosses of unknown L2 words. Similarly, low verbal-ability learners do not learn vocabulary words better if they have to process *both* verbal and visual information. In each case, the high cognitive load resulting for the low ability learners actually hindered learning. Thus, the paradox is that although in general a combination of verbal and visual glosses is more effective for most learners, it can be detrimental for low ability learners (or less effective for lower-level learners, as Abraham, 2008 found in his meta-analysis).

The theoretical framework of attention (Schmidt, 1995) and noticing has also been widely studied in psycholinguistic SLA research. In a CALL study, Yanguas (2009) found that learners who frequently requested or accessed multimedia glosses noticed this input and performed significantly better on vocabulary tests than those who used the glosses infrequently or did not have access to any glosses.

In terms of reading comprehension, the effect of different types and modes of glosses is less clear and generally weaker than for vocabulary learning. However, there do seem to be some definitive results in the literature: in a meta-analysis of the effects of CALL vs. traditional textual glosses on reading comprehension, Taylor (2006) found that learners who were provided with computer-assisted L1 glosses comprehended significantly more text than learners who used traditional, paper-based L1 glosses. In Abraham's (2008) meta-analysis, he found a medium overall effect of computer-mediated glosses on reading comprehension (as compared with a large overall effect on vocabulary learning).

Some studies have found that multimedia glosses are helpful for L2 reading comprehension (Chun & Plass, 1996; Lomicka, 1998). Yanguas (2009), in a replication study of Bowles (2004), specifically investigated whether multimedia glosses promoted noticing and led to better text comprehension and found that learners who received both textual and pictorial glosses of vocabulary words while reading significantly outperformed the groups of learners who received only textual or pictorial glosses or no glosses at all on the comprehension test.

In contrast to these positive results, others have found that multimedia glosses do *not* aid comprehension significantly (Ariew & Ercetin, 2004). Sakar and Ercetin (2005) found that although their learners preferred visual annotations significantly more than textual and audio annotations, there was a *negative* relationship between reading comprehension and the use of pronunciation, audio, and video annotations. Similarly, studies on individual differences in reading comprehension have shown mixed results. For example, a negative effect of visual glosses for text comprehension was found by Plass et al. (2003) and attributed to high cognitive load imposed by the visual annotations for all learners, independent of their abilities.

Oral Proficiency

At the sentence level, psycholinguistic research by Payne and Whitney (2002) and Payne and Ross (2005) investigated whether CMC could indirectly improve L2 oral proficiency by developing the same cognitive mechanisms underlying spontaneous conversational speech. The 2002 study found that the oral proficiency of learners who spent two of four contact hours in a chatroom was significantly higher than participants whose four contact hours were in traditional classrooms. The 2005 study lent support to the notion that chatrooms might provide a unique form of support to certain types of learners, specifically those with lower phonological working memory capacity, in developing L2 oral proficiency. These types of learners might be able to take advantage of the reduced cognitive burden introduced by the chatroom to produce more extensive and elaborate constructions, something they may have found difficult in a face-to-face (FTF) setting (p. 49).

Corpus Linguistics and SLA/CALL

The final point of discussion in this section is an example of how current research in the field of linguistics is influencing applied linguistics, and in particular, SLA/CALL research. Corpus linguistics is one of the fastest-growing methodologies in contemporary linguistics, and many SLA researchers have also begun to employ this methodology, which is facilitated by computers, in a number of different ways (Gries, 2008). Very briefly, and at the expense of overgeneralization, it is important for CALL in the following ways. First, the *frequency* of patterns in the input learners receive (Ellis, 2006) is a critical aspect of psycholinguistic CALL research as it could determine the amount of input that is ideal for SLA. Second, research in cognitive and corpus linguistics on *collocations*, or the co-occurrences of lexical elements or phrases in corpora, can also inform SLA, both in terms of what students should learn and in terms of the kinds of input teachers should provide. Third, *concordances* have been used for many years by linguistics and applied linguists to show how words and phrases are used in larger contexts (clauses and sentences), and this has direct implications for L2 learning and teaching. In addition, SLA/CALL researchers can examine L2 learners' output in search of patterns and errors in their interlanguage (Gries & Wulff, 2005).

Summary

In summary, research on psycholinguistic approaches to CALL focus on how cognitive processes involved in SLA can be enhanced (or in some cases, hindered) by computer-based tools such as electronic dictionaries, multimedia glosses, and synchronous chat programs. Research during the last decade of the twentieth century and the first decade of the twenty-first century has found that computer-based dictionaries and multimedia glosses have a direct, positive impact on L2 vocabulary acquisition and a lesser or mixed overall effect on reading and listening comprehension. In addition, text chatting appears to serve as a preparatory tool for oral production.

Future Directions

Research in neuroscience (e.g., brain imaging) and cognitive science (e.g., eye-tracking, WM capacity studies) appears to be a fruitful avenue for informing SLA research. Specifically, eye-tracking technology could provide eye gaze fixation data, which could be used to study "noticing" or attention to words while reading. The focus on cognitive capacity limitations will add to the understanding of how the ability to maintain information (words, ideas) in WM can have a direct impact on L2 performance.

Interactionist Approaches to CALL-Based SLA

Despite advances in psycholinguistic research, acquisition of an L2 is not restricted to cognitive processes alone, and this section discusses interactionist approaches to CALL-based SLA, approaches that move beyond the individual and consider the *interlocutors* with whom the individual *interacts.*

It should be noted at the start that although the interactionist approach is one of the most widely researched theoretical perspectives in the field of SLA, it too does not account for all of the issues in the complex process of learning an L2. It does not provide a complete causal theory of SLA but is compatible with many other theories and approaches, e.g., it also incorporates the cognitive constructs of attention and noticing, which were mentioned above in the psycholinguistic approach section, and acknowledges the importance of social factors, which will be discussed in the following section.

When considering how the interactionist approach can be applied to CALL, the question is: how do computer-mediated and Internet environments provide opportunities for *input, interaction, attention, feedback,* and *output,* and in turn to the benefits that have been seen to accrue through the *negotiation of meaning* in "traditional" FTF classroom interaction?

In the last decade, there has been an explosion of research on interaction using CMC tools for SLA and FLT. The two primary modes of first generation CMC 1.0 that have been studied are asynchronous computer-mediated communication (ACMC) and synchronous computer-mediated communication (SCMC). Until recently, these tools were primarily text-based, but in the last few years they have increasingly expanded to other media, namely audio and video, and to so-called Web 2.0 types of tools involving extensive social networks (see Figures 40.1 and 40.2). The Internet provides the medium both for extended discourse and for direct contact with local classmates and global partners. In addition, and importantly for both pedagogical and for research purposes, records of these interactions are easily (sometimes automatically) compiled for use by both learners and researchers.

One of the common early themes in this body of research was comparing CMC to FTF interaction. When analyzing the similarities and differences between CMC and FTF, a key question is whether and how the differences affect learning processes. Specifically, how do the differences between a text chat interface and a FTF conversation affect the linguistic, sociolinguistic, and pragmatic aspects of the language produced? Is online discourse different from discourse found in FTF discourse in

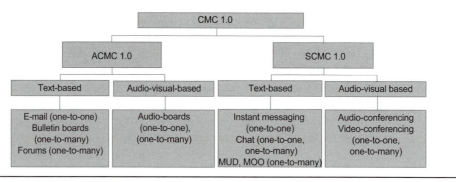

Figure 40.1 Types of CMC 1.0

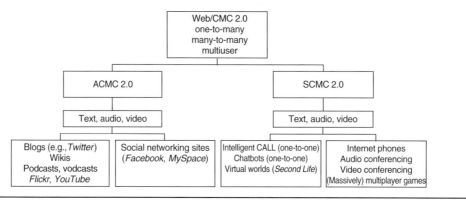

Figure 40.2 Types of CMC 2.0

foreign language classrooms? What type of language is used in pedagogical activities? Do exchanges with other cultures require a change in discourse practices? These questions will be addressed in the sub-sections below.

Recent research tends to focus less on comparisons of FTF and CMC discourse and more on how CMC can achieve the goals of interactionist approaches. The research on CMC in instructed environments is summarized in Chun (2008) and Thorne and Payne (2005). The following sub-sections discuss research on interactionist approaches to learning vocabulary and grammar via CMC and studies of CMC for learning discourse-level aspects of language.

Lexical Development Through Negotiation of Meaning, Attention to Form, and Feedback

Many studies of negotiation of meaning in CMC activities have shown that it is the lexis that is negotiated first and foremost. Blake (2000) found that pairs of L2 Spanish learners negotiated synchronously online with each other often about lexical confusions but not as frequently about grammatical or syntactic issues. In a study of synchronous communication between native speaking teachers and L2 learners of Spanish, Lee (2006) looked in particular at the relationship among error type, feedback types, and responses; she found that lexical, rather than syntactic errors were the main triggers for negotiation moves.

Grammatical Development Through Negotiation of Meaning, Attention to Form, and Feedback

Early studies of computer-assisted classroom discussion, i.e., networked discussion *within* a class found that SCMC improved grammatical competence (Beauvois, 1998; Kern, 1995). Salaberry

(2000) found more accurate usage of past-tense morphological markers in written chat interactions than in oral FTF conversations. A number of recent studies have suggested that text-based *intra*-group chatting provides learners with more time and opportunities than FTF conversations to notice and correct their linguistic errors (Lai & Zhao, 2006; Pellettieri, 2000).

In a study of linguistic accuracy in *inter*-class interactions between L2 learners and native speakers (NSs) of the target language, Sotillo (2005) found that in problem-solving activities via an instant-messaging system, NSs provided only indirect corrective feedback focusing primarily on grammatical and lexical errors to L2 learners (non-native speakers, NNSs), and that there was evidence of successful learner uptake of this feedback. On the other hand, Lee's (2001, 2002) research provided tempering evidence about the value of CMC for promoting linguistic accuracy: learners tended to ignore each other's mistakes, focusing on the meaning of the communication rather than the form itself.

In terms of complexity of language produced, Warschauer (1996) showed that students tended to produce more complex language when chatting online than in FTF discussions. In a study comparing SCMC and ACMC, Sotillo (2000) found that the delayed nature of *asynchronous* discussions gave learners more opportunities to produce syntactically complex language than in *synchronous* discussions.

Discourse and Pragmatic Development Through Negotiation of Meaning

In addition to investigating lexical and grammatical development, early studies comparing SCMC and FTF discussions within classes focused on discourse-level issues. For example, Kern (1995) found that the amount of language produced by L2 French learners was two to four times greater in SCMC discussions than in oral FTF discussions. Abrams (2003) compared three groups of L2 German learners (a control group, an SCMC group, and an ACMC group) and confirmed an increase in quantity of language produced by students in the SCMC group, as compared to the other two groups. However, in contrast to earlier studies, her analyses of the quality of language indicated no significant differences among the three groups, either lexically or syntactically.

Other work has also shown that real-time, online conversations via text may indirectly help to develop L2 speaking ability (Abrams, 2003; Blake, 2009). Dussias (2006) compared a group of L2 Spanish learners who engaged in inter-class interactions with NSs in Spain with a group of learners who participated in ACMC and SCMC intra-class discussions. ACTFL Oral Proficiency Interviews with both groups suggested that the group that engaged in NS–NNS partnerships benefited from the CMC tools more than the intra-class group *and* that language learning mediated by these tools appeared to transfer readily to spontaneous oral production.

In terms of the use of CMC for developing pragmatic competence, the focus is on how learners acquire knowledge that allows them to use appropriate utterances or speech acts in particular discourse contexts and to manage conversations. An early study of L2 German learners by Chun (1994) found that *intra*-class SCMC allowed students to generate and initiate more types of speech acts than they typically would in FTF oral conversations in the classroom. Sotillo's (2000) study of advanced ESL writing classes showed that the quantity and types of discourse functions present in SCMC were similar to the types of interactional modifications found in FTF conversations that are deemed necessary for SLA. Interestingly, discourse functions in ACMC discussions were more constrained than those found in the SCMC discussions and similar to the question–response–evaluation sequence typical of the traditional classroom (p. 82).

Research on communication strategies (i.e., discourse strategies that are used to keep a conversation going and avoid communication breakdowns) within CMC environments has indicated that learners use a wide variety of such strategies to negotiate and create meaning, particularly in task-based activities. Lee's (2001, 2002) L2 Spanish learners used requests for help, clarification requests, and comprehension checks. Smith (2003b) studied ESL learners' strategy use and differentiated between the use of communication strategies employed during problem-free discourse and compensatory strategies used to compensate for a lack of competence in the target language when problems in communication arise. He found that students used a wide variety of communication strategies, such as substitution, politeness, framing, and fillers, and that compensatory strategies were a popular and efficient means for preemptively addressing unknown lexical items.

Sykes (2005) systematically compared the effects of three types of synchronous group discussion (written chat, oral chat, FTF discussion) on the acquisition of the speech act of refusing an invitation among intermediate Spanish learners and found in her role-play data that the students in all three discussion groups improved their pragmatic competence in some way. However, the written CMC group outperformed the others in terms of both complexity and variety of strategies used.

Due to space constraints, it is not possible to discuss all of the uses of CMC within interactionist approaches to language learning (e.g., tandem learning, Kötter, 2003, O'Rourke 2005; bimodal communication using both oral and written CMC in distance education, Blake, 2005).

Summary

Despite the obvious and seemingly simple advantages of extended interactions online and direct contact with speakers of the L2, research has shown that while CMC may provide opportunities for learners to negotiate about lexical and grammatical questions and to notice and correct errors, they do not always take advantage of these opportunities, or, in the case of NSs, correct the NNSs errors. Positive results of CMC environments include greater lexical range, improved grammatical accuracy, production of more complex language, use of more speech acts and communication strategies in CMC environments than in FTF discussions, and the apparent transfer to oral proficiency. Researchers have also noted the need for teachers to invest time and effort in designing appropriate tasks for learners, in monitoring the online discourse, and in following up in the classroom.

Future Directions

Although there is a substantial body of research on CMC in interactionist approaches to SLA, many avenues for future research may be pursued. For example, Smith (2003a) proposed a model of computer-mediated negotiated interaction that adapts and expands Varonis and Gass's (1985) model to account for the fact CMC interactions can be different from FTF conversations. Furthermore, it may not be sufficient to simply examine the final transcripts or output logs of a CMC chat session, as these end products do not take into account the false starts, self-repairs, or interruptions in the chat (O'Rourke, 2008; Smith, 2008).

In the future, researchers could use new and varied technologies, such as eye-tracking or a combination of video screen capture and keystroke logging to capture the richness of language production. In addition, audio-conferencing would capture intonation, and video-conferencing would capture gestures and facial expressions, which are all part of communication. Other experimental methodologies might be used, such as think alouds, retrospective reports, or stimulated recall protocols in order to study the effects of feedback, immediate vs. delayed uptake, and discourse-level issues such as communication strategy use.

In addition to using CMC for negotiation of meaning among L2 learners or between NSs and NNSs to enhance lexical, grammatical, and pragmatic development, research has shown that in the case of telecollaborative environments or exchanges between groups in different countries, *intercultural competence* can be developed as well. Thus, moving along the continuum from individuals to larger communities, the research on sociocultural or cultural historical approaches to SLA and CALL will be examined in the next section.

Cultural-Historical Approaches

Cultural historical approaches to SLA and CALL are based in large measure on the sociocultural theory of Vygotsky as applied to L2 learning (Lantolf & Thorne, 2006). This theory of mediated action proposes that we mediate our understanding and our actions through the use of cultural tools, a subset of which consists of technological tools such as CMC. If culture is defined by concrete, objective, social-material conditions, and if individuals carry out social actions and create social relationships, then these actions using language have consequences in the broader social context. Starting at turn of the millennium, there has been a distinct trend in SLA research and teaching to embrace the teaching of culture and integrate it with language teaching. This section presents research on how learners carry out social actions with an L2, how they maintain social relationships and enter into virtual online relationships via telecollaboration, and how they create or expand their identities with various CMC tools, both the "traditional" CMC 1.0 and, increasingly, Web 2.0 or CMC 2.0 tools. In addition, recent SLA/CALL research is being conducted with tools from the emerging field of corpus linguistics.

Negotiation for Meaningfulness

In showing the overlap between interactionist and sociocultural approaches, Reinhardt's (2008) study of advanced proficiency learners of L2 German and L2 English found that there is not as much negotiation for meaning for the purpose of rectifying or repairing breakdowns in communication as with beginning or intermediate learners. He suggested rather that negotiation for *meaningfulness* is

> prolific, as the participants attempt to create meaningful relationships with the other participants, the other language, and the other culture. Self-noticing and task-appropriate responses … are integrated into the discourse and can be seen from a socio-cognitive perspective to be motivated by the participants' moves to establish and negotiate face and solidarity.
>
> (Reinhardt, 2008, p. 236)

The creation and maintenance of interpersonal relationships is a cornerstone of sociocultural and cultural historical approaches to SLA.

Developing Intercultural Competence

Numerous intercultural exchanges that employed first-generation CMC tools (e.g., ACMC tools such as email and forums, SCMC tools such as instant messaging, chatting, MUD (multi-user domain) object oriented systems (MOOs), audio- and video-conferencing) have been reported in journals, in Belz and Thorne (2006), in O'Dowd (2007), and summarized by Chun (2008) and Lomicka (2006). Many projects and studies were based on the excellent *Cultura* model of Furstenberg, Levet, English, and Maillet (2001). At first blush, it would seem that online exchanges and collaborations between learners of different cultures would be ideal for enhancing Byram's (1997) construct of intercultural communicative competence (ICC), and many studies have documented this (Müller-Hartmann, 2000; O'Dowd, 2006).

But even within a partly successful exchange, obstacles such as cultural presumptions sometimes hindered communication. For example, Kramsch and Thorne (2002) reported on certain problematic scenarios during an email exchange between a French class in the US and a high school class in France that were "characterized by different discourse styles" (p. 96) due to the fact that "neither the French nor the American students were aware that the global medium [email] only exacerbated the discrepancies in social and cultural genres of communication" (p. 100).

Studies by Itakura (2004) and Chun and Wade (2004) explored how cultural stereotypes are formed, modified, or reinforced during intercultural exchanges. Itakura's email project between

Hong Kong university learners of Japanese and Japanese university students revealed that learners were able to modify existing stereotypes by negotiating with their partners, but they also were influenced by remarks made by the native Japanese speakers, which sometimes caused the formation of new stereotypes. Chun and Wade found in their email exchanges and online forum discussions that both the German and the American students were able to construct new intercultural knowledge, but that the generally positive results were tempered by the fact that learners made erroneous generalizations as well. An interesting finding was that in the email exchanges, learners were more inclined to ask questions, express curiosity, negotiate the meaning of concepts and practices, and make observations and hypotheses (including reflection on their own culture) than in the forum discussions. Due to the nature of the one-on-one email exchanges, they engaged in more direct forms of address and dialogue as well as rapport management than in the general, class-based forums (which contradicted findings by Furstenberg et al., 2001).

Empowering Learners to Express Their Identities

In addition to creating and maintaining social relationships, other studies have found that online chatting can empower L2 learners to express themselves and reflect on their identities, as Kramsch, A'Ness, and Lam (2000) reported, "multimedia and the Internet enable learners to find a voice for themselves at the intersection of multiple time scales, to represent their own version of reality through multimodal texts, and to confront a broad public audience with that reality" (p. 98).

Two recent studies examined how CMC activities are used beyond the classroom. Using CMC 1.0 tools, Van Deusen-Scholl, Frei, and Dixon (2005) examined the relationship between in-class, online, and out-of-class learning, proposing the concept of spiraled interaction: "the dynamic interplay of in-class activities that in part focus on meaning and focus on form and online collaborations that have as their primary goal student-constructed representations of knowledge" (p. 657). They found that learners became part of a community of practice outside the classroom and took on social and communicative roles that are quite different from those inside the classroom (p. 672).

Thorne (2009) reported on the use of CMC 2.0 tools in a high school L2 Spanish Advanced Placement class, in which students used Spanish as a resource, not as "foreign language," to create their personas in their personal online lives. He suggested that learners were de-emphasizing language and emphasizing personal goals, e.g., wanting to be clever, becoming socially engaging while using L2 online. Students wrote Spanish blogs for their Spanish class, then posted these same blogs to their personal blog or their *Facebook* page; some even translated postings on their personal site into Spanish and posted the translations on their Spanish class site. This is in line with sociocultural theory, in which learning is defined not as the acquisition of information but as developing as a person, becoming a person with particular capacities to engage and participate. This engagement and participation is accomplished now in ways that were not possible or available before, i.e., in online CMC 2.0 environments.

Summary

For sociocultural and cultural historical approaches to SLA, both first- and second-generation CMC tools provide the most appropriate CALL tools. Research thus far primarily on CMC 1.0 has shown that intermediate and advanced L2 learners are able to negotiate for meaningfulness, reflect on and develop their identities, and increase their intercultural understanding. But sometimes learners were not aware of different discourse styles and new stereotypes were formed or misunderstandings occurred. Instructors must be aware of their role in helping learners take an intercultural stance (Ware, 2005; Ware & Kramsch, 2005). A number of different factors that appear to be responsible for "failed communication" in telecollaborative exchanges are discussed by O'Dowd and Ritter (2006).

At the present time, research investigating SLA through the use of Web/CMC 2.0 tools has only begun to emerge.

Future Directions

The use of first-generation CMC 1.0 tools will continue to be employed, and the broader socially-oriented Web 2.0/CMC 2.0 networking tools will no doubt increase in prevalence in L2 classrooms and research, creating new communities for L2 learners. As a preview of emerging research, Lomicka and Lord's (2009) *The Next Generation: Social Networking and Online Collaboration in Foreign Language Learning* contains chapters on podcasting, social networking sites in foreign language classes, microblogging on Twitter, really simple syndication (RSS) and social personalized start pages, collaborative writing in wikis, chatbots as either a peer or a tool for language learners, the virtual world *Second Life*, and multiuser virtual environments for L2 pragmatics acquisition.

Ecological Approaches to SLA

In moving to the fourth and final approach to language learning, the broadest of the four, it is important to note that there is considerable overlap among all of these approaches. The title of one of the most influential books on ecological approaches to SLA by van Lier (2004), *The Ecology and Semiotics of Language Learning: A Sociocultural Perspective*, indicates that it encompasses both a sociocultural and an ecological perspective. Van Lier takes an ecological world view and applies it to language education, hoping that such an approach can galvanize many different perspectives, in particular, sociocultural theory, semiotics, ecological psychology, and the recent focus on self and identity. Ecology broadly studies organisms in their relations with their environment. Key constructs in this approach to language learning are *affordances* and *scaffolding*, with an affordance defined as the relationship between an organism and something in the environment that can potentially be useful for that organism. Technology is a source of affordances and learning opportunities for language learners; in addition, appropriate scaffolding, i.e., help from peers, teachers, or technology itself, might also be necessary.

In this vein, Wildner-Bassett (2005, p. 651) proposed a model for a critical social-constructivist (CS-C) approach to the use of CMC in language and culture education, with the goal of leading participants

> toward making connections between their own personal and individual histories, experiences, and the meanings and values they have found in their life stories so far and those of their classmates, those of others in our society, and those of members, past and present, of ... [other] societies.

By encouraging a CS-C learning ecology in which learner voices are all-important and where CMC contexts help understand the "other" in relation to the self, "all participants' multiple identities and cultural positionings can be expressed with the temporal and spatial independence offered by CMC" (p. 654).

Another example of how technology can be used for cross-cultural comparison, intercultural reflection, and the development of intercultural identity is seen in autobiography–biography–cross-cultural analysis (ABC) projects (Schmidt & Finkbeiner, 2006). Exchanges involving tandem learning have been conducted for many years, based on principles of reciprocity and learner autonomy (Kötter, 2003; Schwienhorst, 2003).

Increasingly, ecological approaches to SLA recognize that a significant amount of language (and other) learning can and does take place outside of the classroom. Examples of informal settings for L2 use and development are online gaming and open Internet environments, as examined by Thorne

(2008). Cilesiz (2009) provided an example of Turkish adolescents who built their identities as learners of English and as future professionals in Internet cafés.

Summary and Future Directions

Ecological approaches to SLA focus on issues of agency, identity, and voice, in other words, on how learners interact with and influence their environment. Web/CMC 2.0 tools in particular can serve as affordances for learners to express multiple voices and identities. In addition, one trend is to look beyond the language classroom in studying how learners develop L2s and themselves as multilingual individuals.

Summary and Conclusions

As technology continues to be an integral part of academic life in the twenty-first century, it is being used in many ways in second and foreign language teaching. Research has shown that certain multimedia and CMC tools can be effective for facilitating the learning of particular aspects of language and culture for particular types or levels of learners, but that no one medium or tool is effective for all learners.

An extensive body of literature exists on multimedia annotations for vocabulary acquisition and reading comprehension and on CMC tools for improving linguistic (grammatical and lexical) ability and communicative (sociolinguistic and pragmatic) ability. But the variety of CMC activities and the many factors that must be considered do not allow for a simple "yes" or "no" answer as to whether CMC is effective. For example, CMC tools can be asynchronous or synchronous, text-based or audio-visual-based, used intra-class or inter-class (between NSs and NNSs). Although many CMC projects have experienced successful outcomes in terms of language and/or cultural learning, a number of studies have shown that intercultural exchanges do not always result in the desired goals, due to such factors as the learners' prior knowledge and experience, the tasks chosen, the incompatibility of the groups, and misunderstandings due to cultural differences in communicative style.

The newer CMC 2.0 tools facilitate one-to-many and many-to-many interactions (blogs, wikis, podcasts, vodcasts, and much wider social networking (e.g., *Facebook, Twitter*). Virtual worlds (such as *Second Life*) and multiuser online games are popular because they are life-like 3-D environments and are being touted as potentially effective affordances for language and culture learning. But the jury is still out, particularly for the CMC 2.0 tools. Great strides have been made in corpus linguistics, and this methodology holds promise for SLA and CALL research as well.

For the future, CALL scholars look toward developing appropriate theoretical frameworks for using technology in service of L2 learning. Teachers and researchers who use technology are well aware that significant time and effort must be invested in the implementation and study of CALL, which are informed by contemporary approaches to teaching (e.g., communicative language teaching, task-based language teaching). The greatest promise is in hybrid or blended learning environments, in which technology is seamlessly integrated into everyday teaching, learning, and communicating. Thorne and Black (2007) even hypothesize that "for many individuals, performing competent identities in second and additional language(s) now involves Internet mediation as or more often than face-to-face and nondigital forms of communication" (p. 149). In developing multiliteracies, learning takes place in and beyond the L2 classroom.

References

Abraham, L. (2008). Computer-mediated glosses in second language reading comprehension and vocabulary learning: A meta-analysis. *Computer Assisted Language Learning, 21*(3), 199–226.

Abrams, Z. I. (2003). The effect of synchronous and asynchronous CMC on oral performance in German. *Modern Language Journal, 87*, 157–167.

Abrams, Z. I. (2006). From theory to practice: Intracultural CMC in the L2 classroom. In L. Ducate & N. Arnold (Eds.), *Calling on CALL: From theory and research to new directions in foreign language teaching* (pp. 181–209). San Marcos, TX: CALICO.

Ariew, R., & Ercetin, G. (2004). Exploring the potential of hypermedia annotations for second language reading. *Computer Assisted Language Learning, 17*(2), 237–259.

Bax, S. (2003). CALL: Past, present and future. *System, 31*(1), 13–28.

Beauvois, M. H. (1998). Conversations in slow motion: Computer-mediated communication in the foreign language classroom. *Canadian Modern Language Review, 54*(2), 198–217.

Belz, J. A., & Kinginger, C. (2003). Discourse options and the development of pragmatic competence by classroom learners of German: The case of address forms. *Language Learning, 53*(4), 591–647.

Belz, J. A., & Thorne, S. L. (2006). *Computer-mediated intercultural foreign language education.* Boston: Heinle & Heinle.

Blake, C. (2009). Potential of text-based Internet chats for improving oral fluency in a second language. *Modern Language Journal, 93*(2), 227–240.

Blake, R. J. (2000). Computer mediated communication: A window on L2 Spanish interlanguage. *Language Learning & Technology, 4*(1), 120–136.

Blake, R. J. (2005). Bimodal CMC: The glue of language learning at a distance. *CALICO Journal, 22*(3), 497–511.

Blake, R. J. (2008). New trends in using technology in the foreign-language curriculum. *Annual Review of Applied Linguistics, 27*, 76–97.

Bowles, M. A. (2004). L2 glossing: To CALL or not to CALL. *Hispania, 87*(3), 541–552.

Byram, M. (1997). *Teaching and assessing intercultural communicative competence.* Clevedon: Multilingual Matters.

Carr, N. T. (2006). Computer-based testing: Prospects for innovative assessment. In L. Ducate & N. Arnold (Eds.), *Calling on CALL: From theory and research to new directions in foreign language teaching* (pp. 289–312). San Marcos, TX: CALICO.

Chapelle, C. (1997). CALL in the year 2000: Still in search of research paradigms? *Language Learning & Technology, 1*(1), 19–43.

Chapelle, C. A. (2007). Technology and second language acquisition. *Annual Review of Applied Linguistics, 27*, 98–114.

Chun, D. M. (1994). Using computer networking to facilitate the acquisition of interactive competence. *System, 22*(1), 17–31.

Chun, D. M. (2002). *Discourse intonation in L2: From theory and research to practice.* Amsterdam: Benjamins.

Chun, D. M. (2006). CALL technologies for L2 reading. In L. Ducate & N. Arnold (Eds.), *Calling on CALL: From theory and research to new directions in foreign language teaching* (pp. 69–98). San Marcos, TX: CALICO.

Chun, D. M. (2008). Computer-mediated discourse in instructed environments. In S. Magnan (Ed.), *Mediating discourse online* (pp. 15–45). Amsterdam: Benjamins.

Chun, D. M., & Payne, J. S. (2004). What makes students click: Working memory and look-up behavior. *System, 32*(4), 481–503.

Chun, D. M., & Plass, J. L. (1996). Effects of multimedia annotations on vocabulary acquisition. *Modern Language Journal, 80*(2), 183–198.

Chun, D. M., & Wade, E. R. (2004). Collaborative cultural exchanges with CMC. In L. Lomicka & J. Cooke-Plagwitz (Eds.), *Teaching with technology* (pp. 220–247). Boston: Heinle.

Cilesiz, S. (2009). Educational computer use in leisure contexts: A phenomenological study of adolescents' experiences at Internet cafés. *American Educational Research Journal, 46*(1), 232–274.

Douglas, D., & Hegelheimer, V. (2008). Assessing language using computer technology. *Annual Review of Applied Linguistics, 27*, 115–132.

Dubreil, S. (2006). Gaining perspective on culture through CALL. In L. Ducate & N. Arnold (Eds.), *Calling on CALL: From theory and research to new directions in foreign language teaching* (pp. 237–268). San Marcos, TX: CALICO.

Ducate, L., & Arnold, N. (Eds.) (2006). *Calling on CALL: From theory and research to new directions in foreign language teaching.* San Marcos, TX: CALICO.

Ducate, L. C., & Lomicka, L. L. (2008). Adventures in the blogosphere: From blog readers to blog writers. *Computer Assisted Language Learning, 21*(1), 9–28.

Dussias, P. E. (2006). Morphological development in Spanish-American telecollaboration. In J. A. Belz & S. L. Thorne (Eds.), *Internet-mediated intercultural foreign language education* (pp. 121–146). Boston: Thomson Heinle.

Ellis, N. C. (2006). Cognitive perspectives on SLA: The Associative-Cognitive CREED. *AILA Review, 19*(1), 100–121.

Ercetin, G. (2003). Exploring ESL learners' use of hypermedia reading glosses. *CALICO, 20*, 261–283.

Felix, U. (2005). Analysing recent CALL effectiveness research—Towards a common agenda. *Computer Assisted Language Learning, 18*(1/2), 1–32.

Furstenberg, G., Levet, S., English, K., & Maillet, K. (2001). Giving a virtual voice to the silent language of culture: The *Cultura* project. *Language Learning & Technology, 5*(1), 55–102.

Gonglewski, M., & DuBravac, S. (2006). Multiliteracy: Second language literacy in the multimedia environment. In L. Ducate & N. Arnold (Eds.), *Calling on CALL: From theory and research to new directions in foreign language teaching* (pp. 43–68). San Marcos, TX: CALICO.

Gries, S. T. (2008). Corpus-based methods in analyses of SLA data. In P. Robinson & N. C. Ellis (Eds.), *Handbook of cognitive linguistics and second language acquisition* (pp. 406–431). New York: Routledge.

Gries, S. T., & Wulff, S. (2005). Do foreign language learners also have constructions? Evidence from priming, sorting, and corpora. *Annual Review of Cognitive Linguistics, 3,* 182–200.

Hardison, D. M. (2004). Generalization of computer-assisted prosody training: Quantitative and qualitative findings. *Language Learning & Technology, 8,* 34–52.

Hardison, D. M. (2005). Contextualized computer-based L2 prosody training: Evaluating the effects of discourse context and video input. *CALICO Journal, 22*(2), 175–190.

Heift, T., & Schulze, M. (2007). *Errors and intelligence in computer-assisted language learning: Parsers and pedagogues.* New York: Routledge.

Horst, M., Cobb, T., & Nicolae, I. (2005). Expanding academic vocabulary with an interactive on-line database. *Language Learning & Technology, 9*(2), 90–110.

Hubbard, P. (2004). Learner training for effective use of CALL. In S. Fotos & C. Browne (Eds.), *New perspectives on CALL for second language classrooms* (pp. 45–67). Mahwah, NJ: Lawrence Erlbaum.

Hubbard, P. (Ed.) (2009). *Computer assisted language learning* (Vols I–IV). Critical Concepts in Linguistics series. New York: Routledge.

Itakura, H. (2004). Changing cultural stereotypes through e-mail assisted foreign language learning. *System, 32*(1), 37–51.

Jones, L. (2006). Listening comprehension in multimedia environments. In L. Ducate & N. Arnold (Eds.), *Calling on CALL: From theory and research to new directions in foreign language teaching* (pp. 99–125). San Marcos, TX: CALICO.

Jones, L., & Plass, J. (2002). Supporting listening comprehension and vocabulary acquisition in French with multimedia annotations. *Modern Language Journal, 86*(4), 546–561.

Kern, R. G. (1995). Restructuring classroom interaction with networked computers: Effects on quantity and characteristics of language production. *Modern Language Journal, 79,* 457–476.

Kern, R. G. (2000). *Literacy and language teaching.* Oxford: Oxford University Press.

Kern, R. G., Ware, P., & Warschauer, M. (2004). Crossing frontiers: New directions in online pedagogy and research. *Annual Review of Applied Linguistics, 24,* 243–260.

Kost, C., Foss, P., & Lenzini, J. (1999). Textual and pictorial gloss: Effectiveness on incidental vocabulary growth when reading in a foreign language. *Foreign Language Annals, 32*(1), 89–113.

Kötter, M. (2003). Negotiation of meaning and codeswitching in online tandems. *Language Learning & Technology, 7*(2), 145–172.

Kramsch, C., & Thorne, S. (2002). Foreign language learning as global communicative practice. In D. Block & D. Cameron (Eds.), *Globalization and language teaching* (pp. 83–100). London: Routledge.

Kramsch, C., A'Ness, A., & Lam, E. (2000). Authenticity and authorship in the computer-mediated acquisition of L2 literacy. *Language Learning & Technology, 4*(2), 78–104.

Lai, C., & Zhao, Y. (2006). Noticing and text-based online chat. *Language Learning & Technology, 10*(3), 102–120.

Lantolf, J., & Thorne, S. L. (2006). *Sociocultural theory and the genesis of second language development.* Oxford: Oxford University Press.

Laufer, B., & Hill, M. (2000). What lexical information do L2 learners select in a CALL dictionary and how does it affect word retention? *Language Learning & Technology, 3*(2), 58–76.

Lee, L. (2001). Online interaction: Negotiation of meaning and strategies used among learners of Spanish. *ReCALL, 13*(2), 232–244.

Lee, L. (2002). Synchronous online exchanges: A study of modification devices on non-native discourse. *System, 30* (3), 275–288.

Lee, L. (2006). A study of native and nonnative speakers' feedback and responses in Spanish-American networked collaborative interaction. In J. A. Belz & S. L. Thorne (Eds.), *Internet-mediated intercultural foreign language education* (pp. 147–176). Boston: Thomson Heinle.

Levis, J. (2008). Computer technology in teaching and researching pronunciation. *Annual Review of Applied Linguistics, 27,* 184–202.

Levy, M., & Stockwell, G. (2006). *CALL dimensions: Options and issues in computer-assisted language learning.* Mahwah, NJ: Erlbaum.

Lomicka, L. L. (1998). "To gloss or not to gloss": An investigation of reading comprehension online. *Language Learning & Technology, 1*(2), 41–50.

Lomicka, L. (2006). Understanding the other: Intercultural exchange and CMC. In L. Ducate & N. Arnold (Eds.), *Calling on CALL: From theory and research to new directions in foreign language teaching* (pp. 211–236). San Marcos, TX: CALICO.

Lomicka, L., & Lord, G. (Eds.) (2009). *The next generation: Social networking and online collaboration in foreign language learning*. San Marcos, TX: CALICO

Mayer, R. E. (2005). *The Cambridge handbook of multimedia learning*. Cambridge: Cambridge University Press.

Müller-Hartmann, A. (2000). The role of tasks in promoting intercultural learning in electronic learning networks. *Language Learning & Technology, 4*(2), 129–147.

Murray, L., & Hourigan, T. (2006). Using micropublishing to facilitate writing in the foreign language. In L. Ducate & N. Arnold (Eds.), *Calling on CALL: From theory and research to new directions in foreign language teaching* (pp. 149–179). San Marcos, TX: CALICO.

Nagata, N. (1999). The effectiveness of computer-assisted interactive glosses. *Foreign Language Annals, 32*(4), 469–479.

O'Brien, M. G. (2006). Teaching pronunciation and intonation with computer technology. In L. Ducate & N. Arnold (Eds.), *Calling on CALL: From theory and research to new directions in foreign language teaching* (pp. 127–148). San Marcos, TX: CALICO.

O'Dowd, R. (2006). The use of videoconferencing and e-mail as mediators of intercultural student ethnography. In J. A. Belz & S. L. Thorne (Eds.), *Internet-mediated intercultural foreign language education* (pp. 86–120). Boston: Thomson Heinle.

O'Dowd, R. (Ed.) (2007). *Online intercultural exchange: An introduction for foreign language teachers*. Clevedon: Multilingual Matters.

O'Dowd, R., & Ritter, M. (2006). Understanding and working with "failed communication" in telecollaborative exchanges. *CALICO Journal, 23*(3), 623–642.

O'Rourke, B. (2005). Form-focused interaction in online tandem learning. *CALICO Journal, 22*(3), 433–466.

O'Rourke, B. (2008). The other C in CMC: What alternative data sources can tell us about text-based synchronous computer mediated communication and language learning. *Computer Assisted Language Learning, 21*(3), 227–251.

Payne, J. S., & Ross, B. M. (2005). Synchronous CMC, working memory, and L2 oral proficiency development. *Language Learning & Technology, 9*(3), 35–54.

Payne, J. S., & Whitney P. J. (2002). Developing L2 oral proficiency through synchronous CMC: Output, working memory, and interlanguage development. *CALICO Journal, 20*(1), 7–32.

Pellettieri, J. (2000). Negotiation in cyberspace: The role of chatting in the development of grammatical competence. In M. Warschauer & R. Kern (Eds.), *Network-based language teaching: Concepts and practice* (pp. 59–86). Cambridge: Cambridge University Press.

Plass, J. L., Chun, D. M., Mayer, R. E., & Leutner, D. (1998). Supporting visual and verbal learning preferences in a second language multimedia learning environment. *Journal of Educational Psychology, 90*(1), 25–36.

Plass, J. L., Chun, D. M., Mayer, R. E., & Leutner, D. (2003). Cognitive load in reading a foreign language text with multimedia aids and the influence of verbal and spatial abilities. *Computers in Human Behavior, 19*, 221–243.

Reinhardt, J. (2008). Negotiating meaningfulness: An enhanced perspective on interaction in computer-mediated foreign language learning environments. In S. Magnan (Ed.), *Mediating discourse online* (pp. 219–244). Amsterdam: Benjamins.

Sakar, A., & Ercetin, G. (2005). Effectiveness of hypermedia annotations for foreign language reading. *Journal of Computer Assisted Learning, 21*(1), 28–38.

Salaberry, R. (2000). L2 morphosyntactic development in text-based computer communication. *Computer Assisted Language Learning, 13*(1), 5–27.

Schmidt, R. (1995). Consciousness and foreign language learning. In R. Schmidt, (Ed.), *Attention and awareness in foreign language learning* (pp. 1–63). University of Hawai'i at Manoa: Second Language Teaching and Curriculum Center.

Schmidt, P. R., & Finkbeiner, C. (Eds.) (2006). *The ABC's of cultural understanding and communication: National and international adaptations*. Greenwich, CT: Information Age Publishing.

Schwienhorst, K. (2003). Learner autonomy and tandem learning: Putting principles into practice in synchronous and asynchronous telecommunications environments. *Computer-Assisted Language Learning, 16*(5), 427–443.

Smith, B. (2003a). Computer-mediated negotiated interaction: An expanded model. *Modern Language Journal, 87*(1), 38–57.

Smith, B. (2003b). The use of communication strategies in computer-mediated communication. *System, 31*, 29–53.

Smith, B. (2008). Methodological hurdles in capturing CMC data: The case of the missing self-repair. *Language Learning & Technology, 12*(1), 85–103.

Sotillo, S. (2000). Discourse functions and syntactic complexity in synchronous and asynchronous communication. *Language Learning & Technology, 4*(1), 82–119.

Sotillo, S. (2005). Corrective feedback via instant messenger learning activities in NS–NNS and NNS–NNS dyads. *CALICO Journal, 22*(3), 467–496.

Sweller, J. (2005). Implications of cognitive load theory for multimedia learning. In R. E. Mayer (Ed.), *The Cambridge handbook of multimedia learning* (pp. 19–30). Cambridge: Cambridge University Press.

Sykes, J. (2005). Synchronous CMC and pragmatic development: Effects of oral and written chat. *CALICO Journal, 22*(3), 399–431.

Taylor, A. (2006). The effects of CALL versus traditional L1 glosses on L2 reading comprehension. *CALICO Journal, 23*(2), 309–318.

Thorne, S. L. (2008). Transcultural communication in open Internet environments. In S. Magnan (Ed.), *Mediating discourse online* (pp. 303–327). Amsterdam: Benjamins.

Thorne, S. L. (2009). Sociocultural approaches to SLA. Paper presented at CALICO, Tempe, AZ, March.

Thorne, S. L., & Black, R. (2007). Language and literacy development in computer-mediated contexts and communities. *Annual Review of Applied Linguistics, 27*, 133–160.

Thorne, S. L., & Payne, J. S. (Eds.) (2005). Special issue on computer-mediated communication and foreign language learning: Context, research, and practice. *CALICO Journal, 22*(3).

Van Deusen-Scholl, N., Frei, C., & Dixon, E. (2005). Coconstructing learning: The dynamic nature of foreign language pedagogy in a CMC environment. *CALICO Journal, 22*(3), 657–678.

van Lier, L. (2004). *The ecology and semiotics of language learning: A sociocultural perspective.* Boston and Dordrecht: Kluwer.

Varonis, E. M., & Gass, S. M. (1985). Non-native/non-native conversations: A model for negotiation and meaning. *Applied Linguistics, 6*, 71–90.

Ware, P. (2005). "Missed" communication in online communication: Tensions in a German-American telecollaboration. *Language Learning & Technology, 9*(2), 64–89.

Ware, P. D., & Kramsch, C. (2005). Toward an intercultural stance: Teaching German and English through telecollaboration. *Modern Language Journal, 89*(2), 190–205.

Warschauer, M. (1996). Comparing face-to-face and electronic discussion in the second language classroom. *CALICO Journal, 13*(2), 7–26.

Warschauer, M. (2001). Millennialism and media: Language, literacy, and technology in the 21st century. *AILA Review, 14*, 49–59.

Warschauer, M. (2004). Technological change and the future of CALL. In S. Fotos & C. Browne (Eds.), *New perspectives on CALL for second and foreign language classrooms* (pp. 15–25). Mahwah, NJ: Erlbaum.

Warschauer, M., & Grimes, D. (2007). Audience, authorship, and artifact: The emergent semiotics of Web 2.0. *Annual Review of Applied Linguistics, 27*, 1–23.

Wildner-Bassett, M. (2005). CMC as written conversation: A critical social-constructivist view of multiple identities and cultural positioning in the L2/C2 classroom. *CALICO Journal, 22*(3), 635–656.

Yanguas, I. (2009). Multimedia glosses and their effect on L2 text comprehension and vocabulary learning. *Language Learning & Technology, 13*(2), 48–67.

Yoshii, M., & Flaitz, J. (2002). Second language incidental vocabulary retention: The effect of picture and annotation types. *CALICO Journal, 20*(1), 33–58.

41
Second Language Learner Strategies

Andrew D. Cohen

The Focus

The first consideration will be definitional issues regarding *second- or foreign-language (L2)*[1] *learner strategies.* Then the roles played by language learner strategies in research will be the focus of attention: the good language learner studies, strategies for learning a skill (listening, reading, speaking, writing, vocabulary, and grammar), strategies for learners in distance learning courses, test-taking strategies, and research on validating measures of learner strategies. Next, controversy and developments in the field will be discussed, and the chapter ends with the author's stance on L2 learner strategies.

Definitional Issues Regarding Language Learner Strategies

Surveying the Experts

Twenty-three international scholars met at Oxford University to advance the work on language learning and language use: (1) defining language learner strategies; (2) relating strategies to learners' short- and long-term goals; (3) relating strategies to individual and situational difference; and (4) demonstrating and communicating the importance of strategies to the end-user (i.e., bridging the gap between strategy theory and classroom practice) (Macaro & Cohen, 2007, pp. 2–3).

An outgrowth of the meeting was a survey of the views of respected strategy experts concerning terms and issues in the language learner strategy field. Altogether, 18 at the meeting and one other responded to the questionnaire. The results from this survey revealed a lack of consensus as to a unified theory, with agreement by learner strategy experts on some concepts and definitions and not on others (Cohen, 2007).

The survey found, for example, that experts lacked consensus as to how conscious of and attentive to their language behaviors learners need to be in order for those behaviors to be considered strategies. While there was consensus that learners deploy strategies in sequences or clusters, there was some disagreement as to the extent to which a behavior needs to have a mental component, a goal, an action, a metacognitive component (involving planning, monitoring, and evaluation of the strategy), and a potential that its use will lead to learning in order for it to be considered a strategy.

So, in essence, two contrasting views emerged—that strategies need to be specific, small, and most likely combined with other strategies for completing a given task, and that strategies need to be kept at a more global, flexible, and general level. There was consensus that strategies enhance performance in language learning and use, both in general and on specific tasks, and that strategies are used to help make language learning easier, faster, and more enjoyable. The experts were found to be somewhat unlikely to see strategies as compensating for a deficit.

A Working Definition of Language Learner Strategies

Language learner strategies can be defined as thoughts and actions, consciously selected by learners, to assist them in learning and using language in general, and in the completion of specific language tasks. Such strategies have been classified in different ways—for example, strategies for learning and use, strategies according to skill area, and strategies according to function (i.e., metacognitive, cognitive, affective, or social).

The first distinction, then, is between language learning strategies (i.e., strategies for the learning of language material for the first time) and language use strategies (i.e., strategies for using the material that has already been learned to some degree) (see Cohen & Weaver, 2006). It could be argued that *communication strategies* are a type of language use strategy. When learners experience problems or breakdowns in communication, they may use communication strategies to avoid the problematic areas and express their meaning in some other way. For example, learners may paraphrase words or concepts (e.g., "I'd like something to dry my hands with" when they don't know the word for "towel"), coin words ("air maker" when they don't know "bicycle pump"), or use facial expressions or gestures in an effort to communicate and to create more time to think (e.g., hoping that a frown will signal that they do not approve of the other person's behavior). At times, learners also compensate for gaps by using literal translation from their native language or switching to their native language altogether. Finally, communication strategies include conversational interaction strategies such as asking for help, seeking clarification or confirmation, and using fillers (such as *uh* and *uhm*) for pauses (see Erard, 2007, for more on this), along with other hesitation devices such as repeating key words.

A second way to classify strategies is by skill area. In this approach, then, strategies are viewed in terms of their role in listening, reading, speaking, and writing. There are also strategies that apply to all four of these basic skill areas, namely, vocabulary, grammar, and translation strategies.

A third way to classify strategies is in terms of their function, namely, metacognitive, cognitive, affective, or social (Chamot, 1987; Oxford, 1990). *Metacognitive strategies* are considered valuable in that they allow learners to control their language learning by planning what they will do, checking on progress, and then evaluating their performance on a given task. *Cognitive strategies* deal with the crucial nuts and bolts of language use since they involve the processes that learners go through in both learning the target language (e.g., identification, grouping, retention, and storage of language material) and in using it (e.g., retrieval of language material, rehearsal, and comprehension or production of words, phrases, and other elements of the target language). *Social strategies* encompass the means employed by learners for interacting with other learners and native speakers, such as through asking questions to clarify social roles and relationships, asking for an explanation or verification, and cooperating with others in order to complete tasks. Finally, *affective strategies* help students regulate their emotions, motivation, and attitudes. In addition, they are used to reduce anxiety and provide self-encouragement.

One area of concern that emerged from the above-mentioned survey of experts was that strategies often occur in sequences or clusters (see Cohen, 2007). Consequently, it may be difficult for researchers to isolate the impact of a single strategy because its actual impact is cumulative, and is based on the effect of other strategies as well. So, while it may be more elegant to list out the strategy types (metacognitive, cognitive, social, and affective) for definitional purposes, the reality is that strategies are actually deployed in complex, interacting ways such that at a given moment it may be a challenge to determine the type of strategy that is being utilized.

The Roles Played by L2 Learner Strategies in Research

Various topics that language learner strategy research has encompassed will now be considered: the good language learner; strategies for the various skill areas; strategies for students in distance learning courses; test-taking strategies; and research on validating the measures of learner strategies.

The Good Language Learner

The field of language learner strategies got its start with an article by Rubin (1975) on what the good language learner can teach us. This article was an outgrowth of Rubin's experiences sitting in on French, German, and Spanish classes, and her efforts to follow what learners were doing in those class sessions. She would watch them as they attended to class activities, listened attentively when students spoke up in class, and observed what they wrote in their notebooks—even taking notes on what they took notes on. During the breaks, she would go up to students that she had observed and would ask them to explain their class interventions and the notes that they had taken. She wanted to better understand their rationale for doing what she observed them to be doing. At that time (1970), there was no focus on what learners were doing in language classrooms. It was assumed that good teaching automatically meant good learning.

A recent volume edited by Griffiths (2008) celebrated more than three decades of research since the appearance of that Rubin article. The book included chapters that dealt with strategies used by good language learners for the receptive and productive skills, and for grammar and vocabulary. While it is true that there is no one model of a good language learner, one of the findings to emerge from the good language learner literature was that, as just noted above, good learners use a variety of strategies to accomplish what they accomplish, especially metacognitive ones.

Strategies for the Various Skill Areas: Listening, Reading, Speaking, Writing, Vocabulary, and Grammar

The following section provides a sampling of the literature on language learner strategies in the skill areas (listening, reading, speaking, writing, vocabulary learning, and grammar), categorized in four ways: (1) a review of strategy studies in the skill area; (2) group studies of strategy performance in that skill; (3) case studies of strategy use for that skill; and (4) studies involving strategy instruction for that skill area. With regard to strategy instruction in general, interest in enhancing the learning and use of an L2 through strategy instruction has been on the rise at the elementary- and secondary-school and university levels, at adult centers, as well as in self-access centers (Rubin, Chamot, Harris, & Anderson, 2007; Chamot, 2008). While strategy instruction may vary in form, it is likely to have the following features:

1. raising awareness of the strategies that learners are already using;
2. presenting and modeling strategies so that learners become increasingly aware of their own thinking and learning processes;
3. providing multiple practice opportunities to help learners move toward autonomous use of the strategies through gradual withdrawal of teacher scaffolding; and
4. getting learners to evaluate the effectiveness of the strategies used and any efforts that they have made to transfer these strategies to new tasks.

The effectiveness of strategy instruction with given learners depends on the specific learning context, the tasks at hand, and the characteristics of the learners (i.e., the learners' background knowledge, their goals for learning the particular language, their style preferences, and their language strategy repertoire). While a given teacher's knowledge about how to conduct strategy instruction plays a role, the impact of any given effort at strategy instruction is differential at best, due to the host of learner variables involved. There are also teachers' guides that provide numerous examples of activities to be used by an instructor for the purposes of strategy instruction. The Cohen and Weaver volume (2006), which is intended for delivery of strategy instruction at all levels, and that by Chamot (2009), which is intended for levels K-12, are examples of these kinds of publications, which provide teachers guidelines for how to administer and supervise such activities.

As it constitutes a major concern of research on language learner strategies, a sampling of studies by skill area will now be described, organized according to whether it is a review of the strategy literature for a particular skill, a group study of strategy use by skill, a case study of strategy use by skill, or a report on strategy instruction by skill.

Listening Strategies

REVIEW ARTICLE ON LISTENING STRATEGIES

A review of listening strategy research looked at studies on approaches to strategy elicitation, on the relationship between strategy use and listening success, on prior knowledge as a processing strategy, and on efforts to improve strategy use (Macaro, Graham, & Vanderplank, 2007). The conclusions were that the relationship between successful listening and strategy use needs to be explored more rigorously, that prior knowledge can easily be misused, and that, although there is a considerable body of literature exploring listening strategy use, the literature related to strategy instruction is more sparse.

GROUP STUDY OF LISTENING STRATEGIES

A qualitative, classroom-based investigation serves as an illustrative study of listening strategies (Farrell & Mallard, 2006). The study described the types and frequency of receptive strategies used by 14 learners at three different proficiency levels in French while engaged in a two-way information-gap task. The findings were that the learners at all proficiency levels were able to use three types of strategies: (1) obtaining new information from interlocutors (forward inference, uptaking—indicating they were listening and presumably understanding, and faking—indicating comprehension when they had not understood); (2) confirming old information (hypothesis testing and text-level reprise—repeating the speaker's words with a rising or falling intonation); and (3) clarifying old information (sentence-level reprise—repeating a word or words without understanding them at the sentence level, and global reprise—signaling a comprehension problem but without indicating what). Despite the findings that learners across proficiency levels used these strategies when needed, the researchers still recommended strategy instruction, especially for beginning L2 learners.

CASE STUDY ON LISTENING STRATEGIES

An illustrative case study of listening strategies is that of an advanced English-as-a-foreign-language (EFL) listener in Taiwan (Chen, 2007). The subject was a 30-year-old Taiwanese woman who had majored in English. Verbal report revealed that she used 18 strategies in order to comprehend four audio texts: (1) prediction; (2) using background knowledge; (3) listening for key words; (4) grammar analysis;

(5) note taking; (6) inferring the context of the text; (7) message integration; (8) translation; (9) visualization; (10) reinterpretation; (11) selecting strategies; (12) increasing concentration; (13) prediction confirmation; (14) problem identification; (15) selective attention; (16) evaluation; (17) recalling the main idea; and (18) deleting impossible answers. Through the use of verbal report, the researcher was able to demonstrate how listening comprehension strategies varied by task. The reported strategies were categorized into three main groups: strategies for monitoring comprehension; strategies for assisting comprehension; and strategies for enhancing comprehension. These strategies were used in three listening phases: pre-listening; while-listening; and post-listening.

STRATEGY INSTRUCTION IN LISTENING

A recent study looked at the impact of strategy instruction in listening (and reading) relative to other powerful factors such as socio-economic background (Harris & Grenfell, 2008). The researchers conducted a quasi-experimental study, involving 120 from intact experimental and control classes of 12-to-13-year-olds learning French. Whereas the experimental class was exposed to explicit strategy instruction in listening and reading during their French lessons, the control class was not. Over a nine-month period, the experimental classes were taught 25 lessons or parts of lessons incorporating strategy instruction. The results were that listening strategy instruction benefited all students regardless of their prior attainment or prior attitude, their gender, or bilingual status.

Another study involving strategy instruction investigated the effects of a metacognitive, process-based approach to teaching L2 listening over a semester (Vandergrift & Tafaghodatari, 2010). The 106 participants came from six intact sections of a French L2 course at the University of Ottawa, Canada. The 60 students in the experimental group listened to texts using a methodology that led them through the metacognitive processes (prediction/planning, monitoring, evaluating and problem-solving) that underlie successful L2 listening. The 46 control-group students, taught by the same teacher, listened to the same texts the same number of times, but without any guided attention to process. As hypothesized, the experimental group significantly outperformed the control group on the final comprehension measure, after statistical adjustment for initial differences. Transcript data from stimulated-recall sessions provided further evidence of a growing learner awareness of the metacognitive processes underlying successful L2 listening, as student responses on the *Metacognitive Awareness Listening Questionnaire* changed over the duration of the study.

Reading Strategies

REVIEW ARTICLE ON READING STRATEGIES

A review of reading strategy research presents an overview of empirical research published since the 1970s on strategies for L2 reading comprehension, beginning with a conceptualization of the processes involved in reading, and noting that research findings are still not conclusive as to whether these processes are, on the whole, universal or language specific (Erler & Finkbeiner, 2007). They look at various aspects of how first language (L1) reading impacts L2 reading, and consider the non-linguistic factors as well, such as cultural knowledge, motivation, and interest.

GROUP STUDIES OF READING STRATEGIES

An illustrative example of a group study of reading strategies is that by Ho and Teng (2007). The participants of the study were 152 11th-grade EFL students at a vocational high school in northern Taiwan. The study administered two instruments to these low-intermediate-level English students:

(1) a 32-item questionnaire asking participants to report the frequency with which they used certain EFL reading strategies; and (2) an interview guide used to probe participants' reading strategies. The results showed that compensatory strategies were reportedly used the most frequently, with translation being the most frequently-reported strategy in this category. Metacognitive strategies were reportedly the strategies least used by these vocational high-school students. In addition, female students had higher mean scores on most of the reading strategy items, and proficient students used more strategies than less proficient ones. The explanation offered was that the proficient students chose to use various EFL reading strategies in order to comprehend the text, while less proficient students tended to skip the unknown parts.

CASE STUDY OF READING STRATEGIES

A case study illustrative of work on reading strategies examined the sociocultural variables that influenced the strategy choices of two international students studying in the US, one at law school and the other doing a masters in business administration (Uhrig, 2006). The study documented how the two students used language strategies differently to succeed in their respective programs. The researcher used verbal report protocols, strategy logs, and interviews to arrive at a picture of how these students handled assigned readings and other course demands. Uhrig found that learning style preferences had a notable influence on language strategy choices. This finding confirmed and expanded the hypothesis that strategy use can be predicted by an analysis of task and learning style (Cohen, 2003). For example, the business student's response to the teamwork requirement of the MBA program was to worry about communication in English. Because of his concrete-sequential and introverted learning style, he adapted to this challenge by creating and relying on summaries, and by working individually and comparing results with team members after establishing his own understanding. The law student, on the other hand, responded to the workload in his program with a general strategy of extending the minimum effort sufficient for getting by. His abstract-intuitive and extroverted learning styles led him to rely on his background knowledge and on other students as resources to minimize his efforts.

STRATEGY INSTRUCTION IN READING

Two studies are illustrative of strategy instruction in reading, one involving elementary-level students and the other involving college-bound students. The first study was of strategy instruction at the upper elementary level in Singapore, where learning to read in English is regarded as essential because it is the medium of instruction in the education system, although the majority still learn it as an L2 (Zhang, Gu, & Hu, 2008). The participants were 18 pupils in grades 4, 5, and 6 from three neighborhood primary schools. The results suggested that the use of reading strategies varied according to language proficiency and grade level. High-proficiency learners seemed to be more concerned about meaning and knew that they needed to predict, summarize, infer meaning, and monitor their comprehension processes. For the low-proficiency learners, the attempt to read in English possibly terminated at the perceptual processing stage, and in other cases wild speculation and guessing permeated the process.

The second study examined the willingness of English-as-a-second-language (ESL) students to be engaged in strategic reading instruction in Singapore (Zhang, 2008). The study involved classroom activities over two months, following a social constructivist approach where meaning was constructed through dialog between an "expert" (i.e., a more competent learner/peer) and a "novice," during which the latter internalized the new concepts under the teacher's guidance as facilitator, participant, and interactant throughout each lesson. This quasi-experimental study involved an experimental and a control group of 99 college-bound ESL students from the People's Republic of China (average age of 18). The strategy instruction program started with awareness-raising activities, followed by explaining, modeling, monitoring, and evaluating strategy use. The results showed that the teacher's strategy-based instructional intervention evolving around participatory activities affected changes in the ESL students' use of reading strategies and improvement in comprehension. The experimental group benefited more than the control group from group sharing and discussion of many of the instances or contexts where particular strategies were used. The two most prominent strategies distinguishing the two groups were previewing or survey texts and identifying organizational patterns of text.

Speaking Strategies

REVIEW ARTICLE OF SPEAKING STRATEGIES

A review article by Nakatani and Goh (2007) examined trends in L2 communication strategy research from both an interactional approach (i.e., a focus on the way learners use strategies during interaction that could help to improve negotiation of meaning and the overall effectiveness of their message) and a psycholinguistic view (i.e., a focus on mental processes that underlie learners' language behavior when dealing with lexical and discourse problems). They highlighted how different researchers have described communication strategies and how the use of such strategies is examined in relation to learner and task variables in different contexts. They also examined intervention studies involving strategy instruction and their pedagogical implications.

GROUP STUDIES OF SPEAKING STRATEGIES

A recent study of speaking strategies at the group level involved 94 Taiwanese junior-college English majors (Wu & Gitsaki, 2007). The study found that in general the higher-level English speakers reported themselves as using more oral communication strategies than the lower-level speakers. The only two strategies with an opposite result were "message reduction and alteration strategies" and "nonverbal strategies while speaking." The results showed that the high-proficiency subjects reported making significantly more use of fluency-maintaining, accuracy-oriented, and social affective strategies than the low-proficiency subjects.

CASE STUDY OF SPEAKING STRATEGIES

An illustrative example of a case study of speaking strategies is Carson's study of her strategies for learning Spanish in Argentina (Carson & Longhini, 2002). Carson kept a diary of her Spanish learning for eight weeks of her Fulbright in Rio Cuarto, where she lived with a monolingual Spanish speaker and spent considerable time with the family of her colleague. Her data included 32 diary entries, which took into account her learning style preferences and language strategy choices. Metacognitive strategies prevailed, and she was able to link her strategy choices to her style preferences. For example, she found she was visual, introverted, intuitive-random, closure-oriented, and global. Consistently, she reported writing down material to use in oral language work (e.g., verb forms).

STRATEGY INSTRUCTION IN SPEAKING

One study involved 30 participants receiving one week of strategy instruction and 30 receiving two weeks, with 15 in a control group (Iwai, 2006). The principal finding was that teaching communication strategies has a potential for L2 learners' declarative knowledge to become proce-dural knowledge, thus enhancing oral performance. A second study looked at strategies for oral com-munication, the degree to which these strategies could be explicitly taught, and the impact of strategy use on communicative ability (Nakatani, 2005). In a 12-week EFL course based on a communicative approach, 28 female learners received metacognitive strategy instruction, focusing on strategy use for oral communication, whereas the 343 females in the control group received only the normal communicative course, with no explicit focus on communication strategies. The findings revealed that participants in the strategy instruction group significantly improved their oral proficiency test scores, whereas improvements in the control group were not significant. The results of transcription and retrospective protocol data analyses confirmed that the participants' success was partly due to an increased general awareness of oral communication strategies and the use of specific strategies, such as maintenance of fluency and negotiation of meaning to solve interactional difficulties.

A third study focused on the effect of a cooperative strategy instruction program on the patterns of interaction that arose as small groups of students participated in an oral discussion task (Naugh-ton, 2006). Intact classes of Spanish EFL students from the University of Granada were randomly assigned to three experimental groups ($n = 24$) and two control groups ($n = 21$), and triads from within each group were videotaped at the beginning and end of the experimental intervention. The pretest showed that prior to strategy instruction, interaction patterns frequently did not reflect those interactions deemed important for language acquisition as identified within both traditional L2 acquisition and sociocultural research. The posttest revealed, however, that the program of strategy instruction was largely successful in encouraging students to engage in these types of interactional sequences (i.e., use of follow-up questions, requesting and giving clarification, repair, and requesting and giving help).

Writing Strategies

REVIEW ARTICLE ON WRITING STRATEGIES

Manchón, Roca de Larios, and Murphy (2007) conducted a systematic review of the empirical research on composing strategies published in English since 1980. They analyze how the strategy construct has been conceptualized in the empirical research on composing and identify the frame-works informing these conceptualizations. They summarize the main research insights regarding descriptive studies of the strategies used by L2 writers, and the impact of strategy instruction on writ-ing strategy use. They also discuss the use of the L1 in planning, writing, revising, and monitoring L2 writing; strategies internal to the writer and socio-cognitive variables that are external to the writer; and studies dealing with the transfer of strategies across languages.

STRATEGY INSTRUCTION IN WRITING

A study of strategy instruction for business writing was conducted at a technical college in Tai-wan (Huang, 2007). The instructor-researcher drew heavily on a metacognitive framework in her approach to teaching 34 3rd-year students the basics of business writing—including explicit instruc-tion, scaffolded instruction, expert modeling, think-aloud training, and self-questioning. While the study intended to explore how a metacognitive approach could enhance students' ability to deal with business English writing tasks, low proficiency level and lack of motivation shifted the focus to describing reasons why learners did not make use of metacognitive strategies in dealing with prob-lems in their business correspondence. Qualitative data were collected through: (1) information about work experience from a pre-course questionnaire; (2) students' reactions to the instruction from a mid-term course feedback; (3) students' comments in class, including oral feedback, group discussions and presentations, and individual students' verbal report protocols; (4) students' written assignments, feedback, and responses on test; and (5) the instructor's reflective notes.

Vocabulary Strategies

REVIEW ARTICLE ON VOCABULARY STRATEGIES

Nyikos and Fan (2007) consider the lexical dimension of language learning in a report on studies that describe strategies through which L2 learners discover the meaning of unknown words, and integrate and consolidate newly acquired vocabulary. This chapter examines vocabulary learning strategies (VLS) with particular focus on *learner voice* (i.e., how learners report their own perceptions regarding their actual use of VLS). They look both at decontextualized VLS (memorization strategies, repetition, association, and keyword mnemonics) and at contextualized vocabulary inferencing strategies, as well as at dictionary and electronic look-up strategies. They also consider factors that affect VLS use, including proficiency, individual variation, and learning environment.

GROUP STUDY OF VOCABULARY STRATEGIES

A study looked at word-decision strategies while reading among 40 US college learners of Chinese at the beginning and advanced levels (Shen, 2008). The study compared the strategies used by these two groups and then identified the most effective out of 100 strategies. It was found that both the beginning and the advanced learners accessed their mental lexicon in the decision process. Other strategies both groups used included making guesses based on intuition, combining the semantic information of each constituent character, deriving word meaning based on the semantic information about the constituent characters, applying knowledge of parts of speech to the target item or adjacent characters, and using contextual information. The advanced learners were more likely to use contextual knowledge. Word-decision accuracy rating for beginners was 50%, and perhaps surprisingly, only somewhat higher (54%) for advanced learners.

STRATEGY INSTRUCTION IN VOCABULARY

Out of 106 college English majors in Hong Kong who responded to a questionnaire about their dictionary use, 25 agreed to participate in a strategy-instruction workshop (Chan, 2005). The participants were given a list of 25 erroneous sentences and were asked to use the dictionary that they would regularly consult. Areas of incorrect usage included the transitivity of verbs, countability of nouns, choice of verb forms, and choice of prepositions. Verbal report was used for recording the process of locating a target word, searching for the appropriate usage, and determining which was correct. Although students regularly consulted one or more dictionaries in their ESL learning, their dictionary skills were found to be inadequate and the recommendation was that they get instruction in it.

Grammar Strategies

REVIEW ARTICLE ON GRAMMAR STRATEGIES

Although it was the intention of Oxford and Lee (2007) to review the literature on grammar strategy studies, they found that there was such a paucity of studies that instead they wrote a position paper instead on how grammar strategies had largely been ignored in the research literature. Their chapter starts by offering an overview of the instructional modes that teachers employ for dealing with grammar in L2 classrooms. The first two entail either implicit instructional treatment of grammar with a focus on meaning or with a focus on form. The third and fourth entail either an explicit instructional treatment of grammar with an inductive focus on forms or a deductive focus on forms. Next, the authors explore diverse types of grammar strategies in connection with different kinds of grammar learning. As a link to the real world, they quote from a teacher's diary about grammar instruction and grammar strategies.

GROUP STUDIES OF GRAMMAR STRATEGIES

One recent study conducted during a 20-week course entitled "English for Living and Working in New Zealand," investigated the students' attitudes about ways that grammar could be dealt with in the course (Bade, 2008). The 14 students taking the course were all immigrants to New Zealand with less than two years in the country. The students responded to a 20-item questionnaire in the first week of the course, with 15 of the items focused, and another five open-ended (e.g., what they were doing with their knowledge and why they were doing it). The questionnaire related grammar to course content, inquiring about the kinds of resources that students used to assist in language learning, and the students' preferred teaching methodology, kinds of feedback, and types of error correction. Reported strategies included using time outside of class to practice each grammar point for 10 minutes, trying out grammar forms in their own sentences based on a model sentence, and basing their learning of a grammar point on explicit rules and a text that exemplified these rules so that they could learn the points accurately.

In another study, 20 highly-motivated students of Spanish were asked to describe their strategies primarily for dealing with grammar (Morales & Smith, 2008b). These were students who had attained high levels of proficiency on the ACTFL proficiency scale as compared to average students of Spanish. Nine were studying Spanish in university classes and 11 were home-schooled. The authors give examples of how the students used strategies involving mental images in order to remember the correct use of grammatical forms (verb inflections, *por-para*, *ser-estar*, direct vs. indirect pronouns, gender of nouns, and article use).

STRATEGY INSTRUCTION IN GRAMMAR

While much attention is focused on the teaching of grammar, not much attention has been paid to how learners are to go about learning and performing it. And the somewhat unfortunate reality is that grammar forms are not just magically acquired. Even though in this era of communicative language teaching, there is a tendency to play down the issue of grammar and even relegate grammar learning to homework assignments, the hard fact is that learners encounter grammar forms that are problematic and may well cause them repeated difficulties, regardless of how well they are presented in textbooks, drilled in class, or exercised in homework assignments. As Oxford and Lee note in their review of grammar strategy issues, "grammar learning might or might not occur for a particular student. At heart, learning depends on the student" (Oxford & Lee, 2007, p. 119).

One strategy instruction study focusing on grammar entailed exposing American university students of Spanish to mental image associations in order to assist them in differentiating the uses of the verbs *ser* and *estar* (Morales & Smith, 2008a). The reason for the strategy instruction was that the uses of these verbs were seen to present special challenges to the learners, for whom the verb "to be" was generally used for both *ser* and *estar*. The study demonstrates that the 113 students with brief exposure to visual images associated with the uses of *ser* and *estar* showed a greater improvement in their ability to distinguish the correct use of each verb than did the 90 students in the control group who did not get exposure to visual images to help in learning the distinction. The article provides useful samples of the instructional materials used to teach the distinction.

Another effort at grammar strategy instruction involved the construction of a website featuring over 70 strategies deployed successfully by learners of Spanish grammar, including strategies from nonnative teachers of Spanish—who need to learn Spanish grammar in order to teach it (Cohen & Pinilla-Herrera, 2010).[2] The website has audio- and video-clip descriptions from learners and nonnative teachers of Spanish about strategies that they have used for successfully learning problematic grammar forms. The website also includes diagrams, mental maps, charts, visual schemes, and drawings used to convey strategy information. The website can be used for obtaining strategies to enhance the learning of specific grammar forms, or to get ideas for strategies that could be applied to the learning of various grammar forms.

In the summer of 2008, 12 learners of Spanish participated in a usability testing of the website, and changes were made to the site based on the feedback. In the spring of 2009, two University of Minnesota undergraduates similar in age and status to the website potential users conducted evaluational research with 15 undergraduate students of Spanish to determine the strategies that they chose to incorporate into their grammar strategy repertoire and what they thought of the experience. The study consisted of a website orientation session and two follow-up interviews. Findings suggested that students appreciated the practical nature of the website and the usefulness of the strategies. They tended to find that the strategies that the students incorporated into their repertoire helped to improve their oral and written work, and had a positive effect on their achievement in class (Cohen, Pinilla-Herrera, Thompson, & Witzig, in press).

Strategies for Students in Distance Learning Courses

One study focused on the use of course management software (CMS) to improve the English language proficiency of international students (Weasonforth, Meloni, & Biesenbach-Lucas, 2005). Emphasizing that their aim was to demonstrate that the technologies available to distance teachers can be effective in fostering language autonomy, they showed how CMS enabled their students to work without supervision, to become teachers and researchers, to exercise choice, and to benefit from feedback other than the "right answer." They also touched on issues that may mitigate against success in the use of CMS, such as resistance on the part of students to becoming autonomous due to often interrelated factors such as age, lack of experience with computers and online environments, and a preference for more dependent learning styles.

Another study looked at ways in which learners conceptualize the process of distance language learning in terms of the interface that develops between the learner and the learning context in the course of learning experiences (White, 2005). The author explored the different dimensions of the theory, together with the purposes that the interface serves for distance language learners. Commentaries given by learners provided a link between the theory and realities of distance language learning.

Test-Taking Strategies

An area with robust research on language learner strategies over the last 25 years or more is that of test-taking strategies. Technically, such test-taking strategies are not language learning or language use strategies, but rather consist of either test-management or test-wiseness strategies (see Cohen, 2006). Yet, responding to a language measure invariably involves drawing on strategies for the various language skill areas as well. One issue that arises in language assessment tasks is the extent to which learners as respondents make use of their L1 and/or other language while performing in the target language. The review notes the valuable role that verbal report methods have played in the process of understanding what tests actually measure. A challenge for test-taking strategy research is that of finding ways to make the research effort as unobtrusive as possible, while at the same time tapping the test-taking processes.

Research on Validating Measures of Learner Strategies

Measures for Assessing Language Strategy Use Among Young Children

One type of study is that which has investigated the effectiveness of means for collecting empirical data on lower-primary-school pupils' use of language learner strategies (Gu, Hu, & Zhang, 2005). Verbal reports were elicited from the children as they performed listening, reading, and writing tasks. Since most had difficulty in verbalizing their mental processes while performing a language task, the researchers had to ask probing questions in order to reveal their mental processes and strategies. The researchers encountered problems in four areas: (1) communication between interviewer and respondent; (2) strategy elicitation process; (3) silence, voice level, body language, and covert strategies; and (4) recording and transcribing data. The researchers felt that using specific questions to elicit verbal reporting could put strategies in the child's mouth, and thus result in misrepresentation and overestimation of children's strategies. The primary 3 students produced longer verbal reports and identified more strategies than the primary 1 students. Also, the higher-achieving students produced more strategies and better quality ones than the lower-achieving students (see Gu, Hu, & Zhang, 2005).

Measures for Assessing Language Strategy Use Among Adults

As an example of a study to validate measures with adults, Oxford's 50-item *Strategy Inventory for Language Learning* (SILL) was administered to 137 first-year Taiwanese EFL college students (Hsiao, 2005). Respondents were asked to indicate not only their frequency of use of the strategies, but also their knowledge of them, how effective they perceived the strategy to be, how anxious they were about using it, and how difficult it was for them to use. Knowledge of the strategy was found to be the most important condition for using it, followed by the perceived difficulty associated with using it.

Another study reported on the validation of an EFL listening questionnaire designed to assess learners' listening practice strategies in outside-class learning situations, and the frequency of practicing strategy use (Lee, 2007). A total of 206 freshmen non-English majors at a university in southern Taiwan participated in this study. The main instrument in the study was a *Listening Practice Strategy Questionnaire* (LPSQ) developed by the researcher. The reliability of the LPSQ was found to be high (Cronbach alpha reliability coefficient = .88). A factor analysis yielded five distinctive factors: problem-solving (i.e., through use of metacognitive, cognitive, and compensatory strategies), deliberate practice (i.e., regularity, effort, seriousness, and rehearsal); aural immersion (i.e., creating environments for aural immersion, such as through song); English-comprehension strategies (i.e., through listening to the English directly rather than reading the Chinese subtitles); and problem-avoiding (skipping incomprehensible portions). The findings showed that the students used problem-solving most and English-comprehension strategies the least.

A study by Nakatani (2006) dealt with how valid information about learners' perception of strategy use during communicative tasks can be gathered systematically from EFL learners. The study had as its goal to develop a questionnaire, the *Oral Communication Strategy Inventory* (OCSI). The research first called for the development of an open-ended questionnaire to identify learners' general perception regarding strategies for language interaction (*n* = 80 first-semester EFL students). Then a factor analysis was run with 400 respondents to obtain a stable self-report measure. The resulting OCSI included eight categories of strategies for coping with speaking problems and seven categories for coping with listening problems during communication. The applicability of the survey instrument was subsequently examined in a simulated communicative test for EFL students ($n = 62$) that involved a travel agency vignette to role-play. Directly after the task, the students filled out the OCSI, indicating the strategies that they had used on the task. It was found that high-oral-proficiency students tended to use social and affective strategies, fluency-oriented strategies, and negotiation of meaning more than the low-proficiency students.

Another study drew on work done in educational psychology to propose a new approach to generating a psychometrically-based measure of L2 learners' strategic learning of vocabulary, operationalized as their *self-regulatory capacity*, as an alternative to the scales traditionally used to quantify language learning strategy use (Tseng, Dörnyei, & Schmitt, 2006). The findings showed that the proposed instrument had satisfactory psychometric characteristics and that the hypothesized theoretical model had a good fit with the data, providing evidence for the validity of transferring the theoretical construct of self-regulation from educational psychology to the area of L2 acquisition.

The final study to be described in this section focused on verbal report, providing a detailed analysis of issues in think-aloud studies and recent methodological refinements (White, Schramm, & Chamot, 2007). The authors argue for the value of a contextual approach to developing an understanding of learner strategy use, so as to better understand how it relates to students' experiences and the actions that they take as learners. They then consider methodological applications in two relatively new research contexts—online language learning and the learning of heritage languages. The final section of the chapter points to the value of widening research methods to include action research approaches. A case is made for collaborative action research as having much to offer in extending and illuminating our understanding of learner strategies, in strengthening the often tenuous links between theory, research and practice, and in demonstrating the ongoing relevance of language learner strategy research.

Controversy and Developments Regarding L2 Learner Strategies

The field of language learner strategies has always had its detractors over the years. A prominent critic of late is Dörnyei (2005, 2006), who—although endorsing strategy instruction for the sake of language pedagogy—has expressed skepticism about the construct *strategy* at the theoretical level. He has questioned whether language learner strategies actually exist as a psychological construct given what he sees as persistent ambiguity, and hence recommends referring simply to learner *self-regulation* rather than to *strategies*. In his view the process of self-regulation generates strategies as a product. He asks if what distinguishes an ordinary learning activity (e.g., using a bilingual vocabulary list) from a strategic one (e.g., adding color coding to a vocabulary list) is really enough to consider the latter strategic. Dörnyei also directs his criticism at the well-known strategy taxonomies (e.g., O'Malley & Chamot, 1990; Oxford, 1990) in that there are categories in which individual items overlap (e.g., cognitive strategies and memory strategies). Finally, he considers the most used strategy inventory, the SILL (Oxford, 1990), seriously flawed in that it employs a frequency-of-use scale, which implies a linear relationship between item scores and total scale scores. He would argue that given the diversity of the items, the scales in the SILL are not cumulative and computing mean scores "is psychometrically not justifiable" (Dörnyei, 2005, p. 182).

In response to the claim that the language learner strategy theory is weak, there have appeared a series of reviews highlighting theoretical underpinnings of the strategy field, with some of these review chapters described above (Cohen & Macaro, 2007). The opening chapter of the book provides the most direct reply to the criticism at both a theoretical and a practical level (Grenfell & Macaro,

2007). *Styles and Strategies-Based Instruction: A Teachers' Guide* (Cohen & Weaver, 2006) and the *Cognitive Academic Language Learning Approach (CALLA) Handbook* (Chamot, 2009) would attest to the fact that language learner strategies are alive and well both theoretically and practically, as does the work on embedding strategies into L2 pragmatics instruction through websites for Japanese and Spanish L2 pragmatics websites under the auspices of the Center for Advanced Research on Language Acquisition (CARLA) at the University of Minnesota. Perhaps one of the best exemplars of the language strategy field in action would be that of the above-mentioned Spanish grammar strategies website since it operationalizes the notion of strategy so explicitly in example after example.

As to the issue of strategy inventory design, Lee and Oxford (2008) cite confirmatory factor analyses of the SILL but also note the addition of new items to enhance its value in recent work in Korea. There are also other inventories, such as the *Language Strategy Use Survey* (Cohen, Oxford, & Chi, 2002), which have undergone confirmatory factor analysis with good results (Paige, Cohen, & Shively, 2004, pp. 264–265).

Another development is the work being done to provide taxonomies for strategies in the non-traditional skill areas, such as in L2 pragmatics, where strategies are needed for dealing with intended meaning in the given speech community. In an effort to make strategy instruction for pragmatics more concrete, a taxonomy was generated of strategies for learning L2 pragmatics, strategies for performing pragmatics (i.e., use strategies), and metapragmatic strategies (i.e., strategies for evaluating how effectively the learning and use strategies are being applied; Cohen, 2005). The complex nature of speech acts (such as requests, complaints, apologies, and the like) and the challenge that learning how to perform them presents seemed ample justification for the creation of such a strategy taxonomy.

In order to empirically validate this taxonomy, the taxonomy was embedded into a website for learning Spanish pragmatics and an online virtual environment for practicing the performance of this knowledge. The validation effort consisted of a comparison of two environments for Spanish pragmatics, the above-mentioned Spanish pragmatics website, *Dancing with Words: Strategies for Learning Pragmatics in Spanish* http://www.carla.umn.edu/speechacts/sp_pragmatics/home and *Croquelandia*, virtually authentic space for pragmatic interactions (Cohen, 2008; Sykes & Cohen, 2008, 2009). In the synthetic immersive environment, learners were able to move their avatar (i.e., personalized graphic representation) throughout the environment and do voice and written chat with a native speaker via a controlled avatar. These results suggest that the reported learning and use strategies, albeit modest, could be attributed to the strategy overlay that each group of learners received through the website and the immersive environment respectively. Since explicit identification and exploration of each of the strategies was included as part of the instructional activities, it was thus concluded that strategy instruction played an important role in pragmatics instruction on the web. It was also found that language students appreciated strategy instruction that was salient and explicit.

Another development is the context-based approach to learners' strategy use: seeing it as dynamic and varying across contexts, and hence a temporarily and contextually-situated phenomenon, as illustrated by the following two studies. The first is an autobiographical case study of how the college professor subject reported embracing different sets of strategies for dealing with English in six distinct phases in her life (He, 2003). Another study of 14 Chinese learners of English found that while popular language learning discourses, assessment methods, and influential agents (including teachers, experts, friends, and family members) had an influence on the learners' frequency and choices of strategy use in China, strategy patterns changed when the learners moved to England (Gao, 2005). Some learners stopped their uses of memorizing, note taking, and regular reviewing strategies to retain new words. Instead, they relied on using more social strategies to guess, acquire, and apply meanings of new words in actual conversations. The interpretation was that the Chinese influences on language strategy use were perhaps undermined when the students started studying in British institutions.

The Author's Stance on L2 Learner Strategies

In an ideal language learner situation learners become savvy consumers of L2s at an early age, maximize their experiences in and out of class, and become life-long users of a host of languages, thus facilitating their interactions with others in a variety of speech communities throughout the world, and enhancing their employment prospects and performance globally (see Cohen & White, 2008, for more on this approach). Learners start their language learning trajectory by taking a learning style preference measure and a language strategy inventory to see how style preferences and language strategy choices relate to each other. If the fit is not good, then the learners vary their repertoire or style-stretch to match their preferred strategy choices. Learners also check the fit between survey responses and what transpires when they engage in actual tasks.

Beyond creating more savvy language learners is the need to further the work in specific domains of strategy use, such as strategies for grammar and for pragmatics, and to further develop websites where this information can be posted to the international community. In addition, strategy instruction should be embedded into language instruction so that learners are provided an opportunity to enhance their language learning experiences. While language learners around the world are becoming increasingly multilingual, there are still numerous cases of monolinguals and even among the multilinguals skills are not developed at a level that would be considered "professional." A real concern is that the attained proficiency may not be adequate to guard against attrition, so as the years progress, the learners forget whatever it was that they had learned.

Finally, given the accumulation of studies looking just at frequency of strategy use, there is a commensurate need to look at knowledge about the strategies that language learners use, the perceived ease at using them, and the perceived effectiveness of the strategies over time.

As can be seen from the research studies reviewed in this chapter, language learner strategies have played a highly varied role in research, with the bulk of the studies looking at the use of strategies in a given skill area, such as speaking or reading. While the language learner strategy field has most certainly come into its own in recent years, there is still much to do. It is an especially propitious moment to do the kinds of fine-tuning recommended in this chapter in order to enhance language strategy use.

Notes

1. For the purposes of this chapter, L2 will serve as a generic label, including both the context where the language is spoken widely and the context where it is not. In principle, L2 development will be faster in the former context than in the latter, but it depends largely on how the learner makes use of the available resources.
2. As of July 2009, the website is accessible at http://www.carla.umn.edu/strategies/sp_grammar.

References

Bade, M. (2008). Grammar and good language learners. In C. Griffiths (Ed.), *Lessons from good language learners* (pp. 174–184). Cambridge: Cambridge University Press.

Carson, J. G., & Longhini, A. (2002). Focusing on learning styles and strategies: A diary study in an immersion setting. *Language Learning, 52*(2), 401–438.

Chamot, A. U. (1987). The learning strategies of ESL students. In A. Wenden & J. Rubin (Eds.), *Learner strategies in language learning* (pp. 71–84). Englewood Cliffs, NJ: Prentice-Hall.

Chamot, A. U. (2008). Strategy instruction and good language learners. In C. Griffiths (Ed.), *Lessons from good language learners* (pp. 266–281). Cambridge: Cambridge University Press.

Chamot, A. U. (2009). *The CALLA handbook: Implementing the cognitive academic language learning approach* (2nd ed.). White Plains, NY: Longman.

Chan, A. Y. W. (2005). Tactics employed and problems encountered by university English majors in Hong Kong in using a dictionary. *Applied Language Learning, 15*(1 & 2), 1–27.

Chen, I.-J. (2007). Listening strategies used by the advanced listener: A case study. In Y.-N. Leung et al. (Eds.), *Selected papers from the 16th International Symposium and Book Fair on English Teaching* (pp. 34–41). Taipei: English Teachers' Association, Republic of China.

Cohen, A. D. (2003). The learner's side of foreign language learning: Where do styles, strategies, and tasks meet? *IRAL, 41*(4), 279–291.

Cohen, A. D. (2005). Strategies for learning and performing L2 speech acts. *Intercultural Pragmatics, 2*(3), 275–301.

Cohen, A. D. (2006). The coming of age of research on test-taking strategies. *Language Assessment Quarterly, 3*(4), 307–331.

Cohen, A. D. (2007). Coming to terms with language learner strategies: Surveying the experts. In A. D. Cohen & E. Macaro (Eds.), *Language learner strategies: 30 years of research and practice* (pp. 29–45). Oxford: Oxford University Press.

Cohen, A. D. (2008). Teaching and assessing L2 pragmatics: What can we expect from learners? *Language Teaching, 41*(2), 215–237.

Cohen, A. D., & Macaro, E. (Eds.) (2007). *Language learner strategies: 30 years of research and practice*. Oxford: Oxford University Press.

Cohen, A. D., Oxford, R. L., & Chi, J. C. (2002). *Language strategy use survey*. Minneapolis, MN: Center for Advanced Research on Language Acquisition, University of Minnesota. http://www. carla.umn.edu/maxsa/documents/ LanguageStrategy-Survey_MAXSA_IG.pdf (accessed May 19, 2009).

Cohen, A. D., & Pinilla-Herrera, A. (2010). Communicating grammatically: Constructing a learner strategies website for Spanish. In T. Kao and Y. Lin (Eds.) *A new look at language teaching and testing: English as a subject and vehicle* (pp. 63–83). Taipei: Language Teaching and Testing Center.

Cohen, A. D., Pinilla-Herrera, A., Thompson, J. R., & Witzig, L. E. (in press). Communicating grammatically: Evaluating a learner strategies website for Spanish grammar. *CALICO Journal, 29*(1).

Cohen, A. D., & Weaver, S. J. (2006). *Styles and strategies-based instruction: A teachers' guide*. Minneapolis, MN: Center for Advanced Research on Language Acquisition, University of Minnesota.

Cohen, A. D., & White, C. (2008). Language learners as informed consumers of language instruction. In A. Stavans & I. Kupferberg (Eds.), *Studies in language and language education: Essays in honor of Elite Olshtain* (pp. 185–205). Jerusalem: The Hebrew University Magnes Press.

Dörnyei, Z. (2005). *The psychology of the language learner*. Mahwah, NJ: Lawrence Erlbaum.

Dörnyei, Z. (2006). Researching the effects of form-focused instruction on L2 acquisition. *AILA Review, 19*, 42–68.

Erard, M. (2007). *Um: Slips, stumbles, and verbal blunders, and what they mean*. New York: Pantheon.

Erler, L., & Finkbeiner, C. (2007). A review of reading strategies: Focus on the impact of first language. In A. D. Cohen & E. Macaro (Eds.), *Language learner strategies: 30 years of research and practice* (pp. 187–206). Oxford: Oxford University Press.

Farrell, T. C., & Mallard, C. (2006). The use of reception strategies by learners of French as a foreign language. *Modern Language Journal, 90*(3), 338–352.

Gao, X. (2005). Understanding changes in Chinese students' uses of learning strategies in China and Britain: A socio-cultural re-interpretation. *System, 34*(1), 55–67.

Grenfell, M., & Macaro, E. (2007). Claims and critiques. In A. D. Cohen & E. Macaro (Eds.), *Language learner strategies: 30 years of research and practice* (pp. 9–28). Oxford: Oxford University Press.

Griffiths, C. (Ed.) (2008). *Lessons from good language learners*. Cambridge: Cambridge University Press.

Gu, P. Y., Hu, G., & Zhang, L. J. (2005). Investigating language learner strategies among lower primary school pupils in Singapore. *Language and Education, 19*(4), 281–303.

Harris, V., & Grenfell, M. (2008). Learning to learn languages: The differential response of learners to strategy instruction. Unpublished manuscript, London: Department of Educational Studies, University of London.

He, A. E. (2003). Learning English in different linguistic and socio-cultural contexts. *Hong Kong Journal of Applied Linguistics, 7*(2), 107–121.

Ho, P.-Y., & Teng, H.-C. (2007). A study of EFL reading strategies used by vocational high school students in Taiwan. In Y. Leung et al. (Eds.), *Selected papers from the 16th International Symposium and Book Fair on English Teaching* (pp. 95–103). Taipei: English Teachers' Association, Republic of China.

Hsiao, T.-Y. (2005). Testing a social psychological model of strategy use with students of English as a foreign language. *Psychological Reports, 95*, 1059–1071.

Huang, P.-C. (2007). A metacognitive approach to the task demands encountered in business English writing. In Y. Leung, H. Chang, K. Cheung, & W. Dai (Eds.), *Selected papers from the 16th International Symposium and Book Fair on English Teaching* (pp. 255–265). Taipei: English Teachers' Association—Republic of China.

Iwai, C. (2006). *Linguistic and pedagogical values of teaching communication strategies: Integrating the notion of communication strategies with studies of second language acquisition.* Hiroshima: Hiroshima City University.

Lee, H.-M. (2007). A study of listening practice strategies of non-English major freshmen. In Y. Leung et al. (Eds.), *Selected papers from the 16th International Symposium and Book Fair on English Teaching* (pp. 448–458). Taipei: English Teachers' Association, Republic of China.

Lee, K. R., & Oxford, R. (2008). Understanding EFL learners' strategy use and strategy awareness. *Asian EFL Journal, 10*(1), 7–32.

Macaro, E., & Cohen, A. D. (2007). Introduction. In A. D. Cohen & E. Macaro (Eds.), *Language learner strategies: 30 years of research and practice* (pp. 1–5). Oxford: Oxford University Press.

Macaro, E., Graham, S., & Vanderplank, R. (2007). A review of listening strategies: Focus on sources of knowledge and on success. In A. D. Cohen & E. Macaro (Eds.), *Language learner strategies: 30 years of research and practice* (pp. 165–185). Oxford: Oxford University Press.

Manchón, R. M., Roca de Larios, J., & Murphy, L. (2007). A review of writing strategies: Focus on conceptualizations and impact of first language. In A. D. Cohen & E. Macaro (Eds.), *Language learner strategies: 30 years of research and practice* (pp. 229–250). Oxford: Oxford University Press.

Morales, M., & Smith, D. J. (2008a). Las imágenes mentales en la adquisición de la gramática de la segunda lengua: El caso de "ser" y "estar" en español (Mental images in the acquisition of L2 grammar: The case of *ser* and *estar* in Spanish). *Revista Nebrija de Lingüística Aplicada a la Enseñanza de Lenguas, 2*(3), 1–24.

Morales, M., & Smith, D. J. (2008b). Spanish learning strategies of some good language learners. *Porta Linguarum, 9,* 167–177.

Nakatani, Y. (2005). The effects of awareness-raising training on oral communication strategy use. *Modern Language Journal, 89*(1), 76–91.

Nakatani, Y. (2006). Developing an oral communication strategy inventory. *Modern Language Journal, 90*(2), 151–168.

Nakatani, Y., & Goh, C. (2007). A review of oral communication strategies: Focus on interactionist and psycholinguistic perspectives. In A. D. Cohen & E. Macaro (Eds.), *Language learner strategies: 30 years of research and practice* (pp. 207–227). Oxford: Oxford University Press.

Naughton, D. (2006). Cooperative strategy training and oral interaction: Enhancing small group communication in the language classroom. *The Modern Language Journal, 90*(2), 169–184.

Nyikos, M., & Fan, M. (2007). A review of vocabulary learning strategies: A focus on language proficiency and learner voice. In A. D. Cohen & E. Macaro (Eds.), *Language learner strategies: 30 years of research and practice* (pp. 251–273). Oxford: Oxford University Press.

O'Malley, J. M., & Chamot, A. U. (1990). *Learning strategies in second language acquisition.* Cambridge: Cambridge University Press.

Oxford, R. L. (1990). *Language learning strategies: What every teacher should know.* New York: Newbury House/Harper Collins.

Oxford, R. L., & Lee, K. R. with Park, G. (2007). L2 grammar strategies: The second Cinderella and beyond. In A. D. Cohen & E. Macaro (Eds.), *Language leaner strategies: 30 years of research and practice* (pp. 117–139). Oxford: Oxford University Press.

Paige, R. M., Cohen, A. D., & Shively, R. L. (2004). Assessing the impact of a strategies-based curriculum on language and culture learning abroad. *Frontiers: The Interdisciplinary Journal of Study Abroad, 10,* 253–276.

Rubin, J. (1975). What the "good language learner" can teach us. *TESOL Quarterly, 9*(1), 41–51.

Rubin, J., Chamot, A. U., Harris, V., & Anderson, N. J. (2007). Intervening in the use of strategies. In A. D. Cohen & E. Macaro (Eds.), *Language learner strategies: 30 years of research and practice* (pp. 141–160). Oxford: Oxford University Press.

Shen, H. A. (2008). An analysis of word decision strategies among learners of Chinese. *Foreign Language Annals, 41*(3), 501–524.

Sykes, J. M., & Cohen, A. D. (2008). Observed learner behavior, reported use, and evaluation of a website for learning Spanish pragmatics. In M. Bowles, R. Foote, & S. Perpiñán (Eds.), *Second language acquisition and research: Focus on form and function. Selected Proceedings of the 2007 Second Language Research Forum* (pp. 144–157). Somerville, MA: Cascadilla Press.

Sykes, J. M., & Cohen, A. D. (2009). Learner perception and strategies for pragmatic acquisition: A glimpse into online learning materials. In C. R. Dreyer (Ed.), *Language and linguistics: Emerging trends* (pp. 99–135). Hauppauge, NY: Nova Science Publishers.

Tseng, W.-T., Dörnyei, Z., & Schmitt, N. (2006). A new approach to assessing strategic learning: The case of self-regulation in vocabulary acquisition. *Applied Linguistics, 27*(1), 78–102.

Uhrig, K. (2006). Sociocognitive influences on strategies for using language in English for academic purposes: Two case studies. Unpublished doctoral dissertation, Indiana University.

Vandergrift, L., & Tafaghodatari, M. H. (2010). Teaching L2 learners how to listen does make a difference: An empirical study. *Language Learning, 60*(2), 470–497.

Weasonforth, D., Meloni, C. F., & Biesenbach-Lucas, S. (2005). Learner autonomy and course management software. In B. Holmberg, M. Shelley, & C. White (Eds.), *Distance education and languages: Evolution and change* (pp. 195–211). Clevedon: Multilingual Matters.

White, C. (2005). Towards a learner-based theory of distance language learning: The concept of the leaner-context interface. In B. Holmberg, M. Shelley & C. White (Eds.), *Distance education and languages: Evolution and change* (pp. 55–71). Clevedon: Multilingual Matters.

White, C., Schramm, K., & Chamot, A. U. (2007). Research methods in strategy research: Re-examining the toolbox. In A. D. Cohen & E. Macaro (Eds.), *Language learner strategies: 30 years of research and practice* (pp. 93–116). Oxford: Oxford University Press.

Wu, H.-F., & Gitsaki, C. (2007). Taiwanese EFL junior college learners' use of oral communication strategies. In Y. Leung et al. (Eds.), *Selected papers from the 16th International Symposium and Book Fair on English Teaching* (pp. 259–268). Taipei: English Teachers' Association–Republic of China.

Zhang, L. J. (2008). Constructivist pedagogy in strategic reading instruction: Exploring pathways to learner development in the English as a second language (ESL) classroom. *Instructional Science, 36*(2), 89–116.

Zhang, L. J., Gu, P. Y., & Hu, G. (2008). A cognitive perspective on Singaporean primary school pupils' use of reading strategies in learning to read English. *British Journal of Educational Psychology, 78*(2), 245–271.

VI

Second Language Assessment

Guest editor: Carol Chapelle

42
How Language Ability Is Assessed[1]

Rob Schoonen

The title of this chapter suggests a description of a *common* practice of assessing language ability in second language acquisition (SLA) and applied linguistic research. However, the reader might be disappointed to learn that there is no common practice. The assessment of language ability is too complex to be captured in one common practice. Language ability per se is a complicated, multi-faceted construct, consisting of many interdependent or independent subskills, and each subskill can be operationalised in many different ways. Moreover, language ability is assessed for many different purposes, and these purposes affect decisions about how language tests are designed.

It would be impossible to discuss all options for defining language ability and designing language assessments in one chapter. However, for the validity of research in SLA and applied linguistics that draws upon test scores, researchers need to provide justification for the options they choose. Doing so requires an understanding of choices we as researchers have in designing language assessments, and of the consequences of choosing one of the options over another. In this chapter, "researchers" is the term used to denote those concerned with choosing, developing and investigating assessments because they are responsible for justifying test score use. The focus will be tests used in a second and foreign language context, for which the generic term "second language acquisition" will be used. In such contexts, language learners are the test-takers, and therefore these terms will be used interchangeably, as are the terms "assessment" and "test."

Central to language test design is the construct the researcher intends to measure; therefore, we begin with a discussion of issues involved in defining the construct of language ability. Operationalisation of a construct in any particular test is related to the function the language test needs to perform. The second part of the chapter will discuss why researchers need to be aware of the context of assessment, that is, why are they assessing language ability and what information needs to be obtained from the assessment. The construct definition as well as the reasons for and context of language assessment feed back to the decisions to be made about the features of the assessment. Next, we will look in closer detail into features of operationalisations of language assessments exemplified by language assessment practices appearing in recent SLA research studies.

Defining Language Ability

A working definition of language ability can be expressed as the *ability to perform language tasks in real life and real time, that is, the ability to convey or understand a content message through the medium of spoken or written language.*[2] As such language performance entails the successful execution of cognitive processes from a pool of relevant processes. Different language tasks will draw upon a slightly or substantially different set of processes from the pool. For example, monologues call more heavily upon such processes as establishing coherence and structure than short contributions to a dialogue; compositions should be comprehensible, independent of the presence of the writer and the context of the writing, which requires knowledge or awareness of the "naive" reader and thus, among other things, a skilled use of anaphoric pronouns and avoidance of deictic references, such that the text is comprehensible without physical contextual support.

The interesting and most challenging part of language assessment, or the assessment of any other construct, is that it always leads one back to theoretical questions about what is being measured, such as the following: What is language ability? What do we mean by proficient reading? Or, what is speaking proficiency? These kinds of hard questions always underlie, or should underlie, test use in an SLA study. Such questions are sometimes answered implicitly when researchers make decisions in test design. However, whether the answers are implicit or explicit, they always pertain to the construct validity of the measurement, be it in large-scale assessments or in small-scale, in-depth linguistic studies. Although validity is considered a "psychometric" feature of a measurement, any researcher who thinks that a methodologist or psychometrician can solve this kind of measurement problems or can answer these validity questions might be disappointed. Or as Borsboom and colleagues put it: "Validity is the one problem in testing that psychology [or SLA] cannot contract out to methodology" (Borsboom, Mellenbergh & Van Heerden, 2004, p. 1062). Instead, developing a defensible, appropriate construct definition of language ability is the responsibility of the content specialist. Unfortunately, there is no single, generally accepted and universally useful theory of language ability that can answer questions about how to define the construct of language ability (Bachman, 2007). Many scholars have made important contributions to the development of theoretical models of language proficiency (Bachman, 1990; Bachman & Palmer, 1996; see also McNamara, 1996 for an overview) and different approaches have been debated (Bachman, 2007; Chalhoub-Deville, 2003; Chapelle, 1998; McNamara, 1996). Some of the main questions that can be derived from these discussions and that we will briefly address here are *which capacities should be included in a construct of language ability, and which should not* and *should language ability be considered as one monolithic ability or not?* And if not, *how should we value the contributions of constituent component abilities?*

The Linguistic Aspects of Language Ability

In delineating language ability, the researcher has to decide how *linguistic* the language ability definition should be. On the one hand, when language ability is assessed, the researcher wants to assess language ability and nothing else. Score users do not expect, for example, differences in language learners' guessing strategies in multiple-choice tasks to be reflected in their scores for reading proficiency. If a score also reflects such test-taking strategies, it includes undesirable "construct-irrelevant variance" (Messick, 1989, p. 34). On the other hand, researchers want to be sure that all relevant components of language ability are reflected in the scores. For example, scores on a multiple-choice writing test are unlikely to capture the rich and complex process of composing a text. They would therefore be considered to reflect an "underrepresentation" of the construct (Messick, 1989, p. 34). The problem of delineating language ability is thorniest in contexts where tests of language production are needed. A definition of writing ability, for instance, needs to take into account the initial stages of writing—content generation. However, to what extent should the poor content of an impromptu essay about, let us say, the "history of cricket" be considered a language problem or just lack of content knowledge? A researcher needs to decide whether content is considered part of the construct and thus should be part of the assessment procedure. This issue is especially relevant assessing language for specific purposes (cf. Douglas, 2000).

At the final stages of producing the same written composition, one might question whether handwriting is part of the writing ability that should be measured. Illegible handwriting can be fatal to the communication of ideas but at the same time an intensive language course will most likely not solve the problem. Most people probably would agree that handwriting is not a language ability. This agreement may disappear when we have to decide whether spelling and punctuation are part of the construct language ability or not. There is no absolute and independent criterion to make such decisions: researchers operationalising language ability must determine and make explicit whether a certain aspect of a language performance is part of the language ability construct they wish to measure for a particular purpose.

For defining language ability as a construct in language assessment, researchers often conceptualise language use as a single act of an individual language user. In reality however, most language use is in communication with other language users. In other words, actual language use is different and perhaps more difficult than language use as it is conceived by many researchers. Language users need to switch roles of listener and speaker swiftly in dynamic contexts that are more complex than the models devised by researchers. The interlocutor brings additional conditions and constraints to any given language use task: what is his or her status and background, what kind of knowledge can be expected to be shared knowledge with the interlocutor and what are possible cultural differences that might affect production and comprehension of each contribution to the conversation? These broader communicative and strategic skills (cf. Bachman, 1990) complicate a possible definition of language ability even further. Cultural and sociolinguistic factors interact with linguistic choices a language user makes. An important research issue is how these factors influence each other. Is one communicative task just harder to fulfil than another when skills and knowledge remain constant, or do different tasks appeal to a different subset of skills and knowledge resources? It is easy to see that trying to define language ability is getting more and more complex. Bachman states that

> the issues and questions in language testing research are far too complex, and the perspectives that are involved far too diverse to admit to any doctrinaire positions, with respect to either what the *true* construct is or what the *correct* methodological approach is.
>
> (Bachman, 2007, p. 68; italics in original)

Nevertheless, for any specific context of testing, it is necessary for researchers in designing tests to state explicitly what the test is intended to measure, i.e., "what's the construct?"

Dimensionality of Language Ability

The first question about how linguistic language ability should be delineated is related to the second about the dimensionality of the language ability construct. Several proposals have been put forth concerning the dimensionality of language proficiency, ranging from one general ability (unidimensionality, Oller, 1979 cited in Bachman, 2007 and McNamara, 1996) to 14 "components of language competence" (Bachman, 1990) up to 30 language-related ("semantic") abilities in Guilford's (1971) model of the structure of intellect. It is no easy task to decide about the dimensionality of the construct. One approach is to administer language learners a large battery of language (sub)tests and subsequently to analyse the intercorrelations of the scores by means of factor-analytic techniques (see Purpura, Chapter 44, this volume). Can the intercorrelations be described in terms of one single underlying factor (i.e. general language ability), or are they better described by two or more underlying factors, for example lexical, syntactic and socio-pragmatic abilities? From this point of view of measurement, dimensionality can be defined as the number of factors required to describe the intercorrelations between possible language (sub)tests. To a large extent this is an empirical question to be addressed in empirical factor-analytic studies. However, the interpretations of correlations can misguide us (cf. Borsboom et al., 2004; Henning, 1992). In a language learning context, certainly in a usage-based paradigm (Tomasello, 2003) where exposure to language input is the dominant factor for language learning, language exposures will be exposure to *both* syntactic structures and lexical items. Thus, in real life, syntactic and lexical ability may develop hand-in-hand, which will lead to high intercorrelations between these subskills. Consequently, it might be difficult to distinguish them *empirically* as separate abilities whereas in other contexts, such as intervention studies, the training of lexical abilities might not affect syntactic abilities, and the two abilities might no longer correlate.

Another, more psychological approach might be to define dimensionality as subskills that can—potentially—vary independently and as such contribute to the overall score (variance) (see also Henning, 1992; Snow & Lohman, 1989). We could theorize about the number of subskills based on how learners acquire a second language. Can we imagine a language learner who has a very rich vocabulary (lexical ability), but produces poor simple sentences (syntactic ability), or vice versa, a language learner who produces long complex sentences but knows few words. Although these language learners may be hard to find, we probably can imagine such cases, which may suggest that lexical and syntactic ability are *theoretically* speaking independent abilities. The question remains of what are candidates for constituent abilities. Cognitive studies of language use have led to models of reading, writing, listening and speaking that unravel these macro processes into numerous micro processes (cf. Cutler & Clifton, 1999; Levelt, 1999; Perfetti, 1999; Hayes, 1996).[3] Thus, from this cognitive perspective (Snow & Lohman, 1989), every subprocess can be a source of variance in the execution of the macro process, i.e., reading, listening, writing or speaking. A language user has to go through all these processes and must be able to execute those processes adequately and successfully. For example, a speaker in interaction must access the previous discourse, value the position of his interlocutor, generate the content of a response, decide on given and new in his response, access the lemmata that represent the concepts in the message and so forth, and finally has to execute a phonetic plan by activating the articulatory muscles. This leads to tens of subprocesses, which potentially all (imaginably independently) contribute to the quality of the speaking performance. However, some of these subprocesses we do not want to consider language use because they are at (or across) the border of what we consider language or linguistic (see previous section). Other subprocesses might not be relevant because they do not vary that much or do not or hardly contribute to the quality of the overall performance. For instance, the speed of launch of the articulatory apparatus probably does not differ much among speakers and the differences that do exist do not affect the speaking performance noticeably (De Jong, Steinel, Florijn, Hulstijn & Schoonen, 2011). In a similar vein, Gough (1972) describes what happens in just one second of reading. Are all these small subprocesses executed by relevant abilities? Or, to put it differently, is improving speed or accuracy of these micro processes noticeably beneficial to the overall language performance, and thus worth to be considered separate subskills? See Snow and Lohman (1989) for an extensive general introduction to this cognitive approach.

Up till now we do not exactly know which subprocesses, and under which conditions, do and which do not contribute to the eventual language performance quality. Addressing this issue is part of fundamental construct validity research. The cliché "nothing as practical as a good theory" applies here more than anywhere else. It is not just a matter of test scores correlating (moderately) with other test scores; we need to know what psycholinguistic processes are involved. In the late 1950s Cronbach made a plea for an integrated experimental and correlational approach to the study of cognitive processes and abilities: "A true federation of the disciplines is required. Kept independent, they can give only wrong answers or no answers at all regarding certain important problems" (Cronbach, 1957, p. 673). This plea is still valid, and is implicitly echoed in Borsboom et al.'s (2004) call for study of response behaviour in testing research (see also Snow & Lohman, 1989). Models such as the afore-mentioned ideally form point of departure in defining the language abilities we intend to assess.

Integration of Knowledge and Processes

Language performance is not the simple addition of the outcomes of several cognitive subprocesses. To get every subprocess in gear in a well-organized and timely order in real time might cause some difficulties in itself. In their writing process model, Flower and Hayes called this "juggling with constraints" (Flower & Hayes, 1980). Carroll (1968) in his chapter on the psychology of language testing recognised the importance of *performance testing* in which a complex language task as such has to be performed, next to so-called discrete point testing intended to call on isolated subskills or language features:

> But since the use of language in ordinary situations calls upon all these aspects [of linguistic competence], we must further recognize that linguistic performance also involves the individual's capability of mobilizing his linguistic competence and performance abilities in an integrated way, i.e. in the understanding, speaking, reading or writing of connected discourse.
>
> (Carroll, 1968, p. 56)

It is an empirical question to what extent the sum of the subskills adds up to the total language performance in a given context and whether language learners use their resources in the same way (cf. Snow & Lohman, 1989). One study investigating this issue found that four discrete knowledge tests and two productive speed tests explained 80% of the variance in writing scores for English as a foreign language (EFL) young students (Schoonen, Van Gelderen, De Glopper, Hulstijn, Simis, Snellings & Stevenson, 2003). Three of these knowledge tests and two other receptive speed tests explained 83% of the variance in EFL reading of the same group of students (Van Gelderen, Schoonen, De Glopper, Hulstijn, Simis, Snellings & Stevenson, 2004).[4]

Integration of subskills may be facilitated if some of the cognitive subprocesses are automatised, that is, run fast without much cognitive attention or central resources (cf. Segalowitz & Hulstijn, 2005). Automatic subprocesses leave cognitive resources available to the more complex, non-automatic processes (Snow & Lohman, 1989) and thus a fluent integration of subskills is more likely to occur. In recent years, there have been developments and debates about the operationalisation of automaticity (Segalowitz & Segalowitz, 1993; Hulstijn, Van Gelderen & Schoonen, 2009). In assessing the level of second language proficiency or evaluating the efficacy of language education, it might be relevant to learn that participants not only enlarged their repertoire of words and structures, but also reached a certain level of automaticity in using these language resources (Fukkink, Hulstijn & Simis, 2005; Gatbonton & Segalowitz, 2005; Harrington, 2006; Snellings, Van Gelderen & De Glopper, 2004). Thus, speed and automaticity are essential aspects of the development of language ability, in addition to the increase in the available linguistic knowledge resources (Snow & Lohman, 1989).

In sum, there are different approaches to the construct of language ability, each of which foregrounds a different aspect of the construct in accordance with the function of the assessment in the studies concerned. Some researchers focus on the overall language performance including the integration of knowledge and processes and the interaction with communicative context. In these cases it is essential that the language test task elicits target language use (TLU; cf. Bachman & Palmer, 1996; see Bachman, 1990 for a discussion about authenticity). Other researchers will be orientated towards the building blocks of the language performance, that is the knowledge resources used, the cognitive processes involved and the resulting linguistic features of the performance. The former approach we encounter in large-scale assessments for selection and placement, the latter is more common in theory building and diagnostics in SLA research. Our initial working definition (pp. 701–702) that language proficiency is the *ability to perform language tasks in real life and real time, that is, the ability to convey or understand a content message through the medium of (spoken or written) language* could be refined with respect to the linguistic abilities and knowledge resources that may underlie language performance as well as the ability to integrated these in a dynamic way in communicative interactions.

Reasons for the Assessment

Language tests are used for different reasons and can be classified accordingly. In all cases, test users make inferences about some aspects of the test-takers' language ability. However, the inferences are used for different purposes. Davies (1990, p. 20) distinguishes four purposes for testing, that is: selection, feedback, evaluation and experimentation; Bachman (1990, pp. 54ff.; Bachman & Palmer, 1996, pp. 95ff.) refers to the different kinds of decisions we make on the basis of the inferences about language proficiency, that is—at the level of the individual test-taker—selection, placement, diagnosis and progress and grading. Apart from the use at the individual level, test scores are also used to evaluate treatments and teaching programs and to "verify scientific hypotheses" (Cronbach, 1961; Bachman, 1990). For *selection*, test-takers usually have to meet a certain criterion or to reach a certain ranking to be admitted to a college, a university or even a country. A single overall score might suffice, as long as the overall score represents the target proficiency well enough. For example, are students applying for university admission able to understand a lecture (cf. Buck, 2001; Sawaki & Nissan, 2009)? Or, do immigrants have the linguistic skills to survive in society as part of citizenship or immigration testing (cf. Shohamy & McNamara, 2009)?

Placement or classification is much like selection, except that decisions concern multiple levels, for example, in placement for academic EFL writing courses. Generally the levels are related to the overall performance on language tasks, but it is also conceivable that the different "levels" are related to different profiles of performance. In our example, some students might be referred to a course for those who perform weakly in structuring their texts, or to a course for those who need extra training in English punctuation, spelling and mechanics. Depending on the situation and information needed different operationalisations of writing proficiency are required. In the latter case we are basically dealing with a *diagnostic* purpose of language testing, that is, deciding on the strengths and weaknesses of the language learner. Such educational settings as much as clinical settings, where language problems have to be treated, require a detailed model of language use and the cognitive processes underlying it (cf. Snow & Lohman, 1989). Alderson (2005, 2007) calls for the development of good diagnostic language tests, but at the same time he acknowledges that "[w]hat we appear to lack … is any theory of what abilities or components of abilities are thought to contribute to language development, or whose absence or underdevelopment might *cause* weaknesses" (Alderson, 2007, pp. 28–29; italics in the original). According to Alderson, we should pay more attention to what language learners "cannot (yet) do" (2007, p. 29).

Progress and grading are needed when test users want to evaluate the language development of language learners, for instance, in a school or in a national assessment. A "simple" criterion as in selection will not suffice. The assessment must be fine-grained in order to be able to detect progress. The operationalisation of the construct will usually focus on overall performance, but, of course, depending of the kind of development one wants to detect or the kind of programme one is evaluating, the operationalisation can zoom in on component skills as well. In particular in programme evaluation, the construct measured in the language tests should be determined by the syllabus of the programme.

Most schemes for describing test purposes (Bachman, 1990; Bachman & Palmer, 1996; Cronbach, 1961; Davies, 1990) include a special niche for scientific research, experimentation or "verification of scientific hypotheses" (Cronbach, 1961, p. 20). Such uses are not so much concerned with decisions about test-takers, but more so with the tenability of hypotheses about, for example, the relation between subskills, the effects of interventions or experimental task manipulations, subgroups of language learners to explore the effects of background variables such as first-language or second-language level, or about the way language is processed (Bachman, 1990). Operationalisations will often be at the level of subskills and/or underlying cognitive processes. However, if the researcher wants to relate subskills to the overall language performance, overall language ability will need to be tested as well.

Detailed information about test-takers' language ability can be obtained either by using selected response tasks that have a narrow focus on subskills or subprocesses, such as multiple-choice tests or fill-in-the-gap tasks, or by applying specific scoring criteria (or analytic rating scales) to language performance on a constructed-response test, such as a measure of lexical diversity in a test of speaking performance (e.g. Tavakoli & Foster, 2008). If these two approaches to gain detailed information about test-takers' language proficiency are used in combination, their results should ideally converge. However, there is an essential difference between the two approaches that many researchers fail to recognize, and that may cause incomparability. The former type of test is what Cronbach (1961) calls a "test of ability", the latter type is more a "test of typical behaviour" (p. 29). Language learners' typical behaviour may not reflect their highest possible level of performance, but had they known they may have performed differently. We may refer to this phenomenon as the *had-I-known* effect.

For the researcher, the question is whether the research goal requires assessment of performance on every (sub)process or every detailed piece of knowledge (e.g. domain of vocabulary knowledge or morphological feature) or whether it suffices to collect more general information about the level of performance on certain language tasks (i.e. the result of the full orchestration of all component skills)? The decision about the definition of language ability rests on the purpose of the assessment, and therefore the purpose also affects the way that the language test tasks are designed.

Facets of Language Assessment Tasks

A number of schemes exist for describing language assessment tasks (Carroll, 1968; Bachman, 1990, ch. 5; Bachman & Palmer, 1996, ch. 3; Mackey & Gass, 2005, ch. 3; Gass & Mackey, 2007) because facets of a language task will affect the knowledge resources and subskills being tested. Bachman and Palmer's (1996) framework includes five aspects for the description of task features: setting, test rubric, input, expected response and relationship between input and response (p. 47), which have been used extensively in language assessment (e.g. see Alderson, 2000 and Fulcher, 2003 for applications in reading and speaking assessment, respectively). This framework includes three basic questions that test developers and researchers need to address: *What is available?*, i.e. the prompt including stimulus materials, *What has to be done?*, i.e. the instructions and the constraints that come with the instruction, and finally *How is it evaluated?*, that is, what scoring or interpretative procedures are used to go from the (language) performance to a score or any other kind of evaluative statement. In the following subsections we illustrate how researchers have addressed these questions in constructing assessments for studying SLA. In particular, examples come from the 2008 volumes of two leading journals in SLA, *Language Learning* and *Studies in Second Language Acquisition*.

What Is Available?

The materials in a language test usually consist of two parts, one being the instructions and the other optional part being the stimulus materials. The instructions should be easily accessible to the test-takers, because we have to be sure that the test-takers know what they are expected to do. In SLA studies this requirement might not be as straightforward as it seems. With young children the instruction should not be too abstract or too complex, with beginning second language learners the language of the instructions should be simple. A researcher does not want the challenge of deciphering the instructions in a composition or a grammar test to be so great that the test becomes a reading test. Instructions in the first language might be a solution if the number of first languages in the study is limited, as might be instructions in a shared third language when that solution is feasible. The instructions can be given orally by test assistants with the opportunity to verify comprehension, or in writing with the opportunity for the test-taker to refer back to them. In most cases it is safest to do both.

Apart from the accessibility of the instructions the stimulus materials may contain information that is part of the language task, for example a reading text that has to be processed or content information for letter writing. Obviously, the characteristics of these materials will affect the cognitive processes that are triggered in the test task performance. In the case of writing assessment, the information that is provided to test-takers (propositional, but also wordings) may marginalise the role of some component processes. For instance, providing all test-takers with the required content information most likely decreases the role of content *generation* as a possible critical subprocess in the writing performance. Writing tasks that differ only slightly will—to a large extent—draw upon the same subprocesses, but they may have their own specific requirements as well. Writing a letter to your pen pal versus writing a letter to an admission officer at a university will call for some different processes to be executed, and some different language knowledge resources to be called upon. The writer will "interact" with the intended reader. However, in both cases there will be an appeal to the writer's syntactic repertoire, mental lexicon and discourse organizational proficiency. In the research practice, the stimulus materials range from nothing (write a personal narrative or recount a fairy-tale; Ayoun & Salaberry, 2008) to an audio presentation that has to be reproduced (e.g. Graham & Macaro, 2008) to animated cartoons that have to be retold (e.g. Choi & Lantolf, 2008; Brown & Gullberg, 2008; Tavakoli & Foster, 2008). In some cases written production is guided, i.e. the test-takers are given prompt nouns, verbs and/or certain sentence frames (e.g. Kempe & Brooks, 2008; Sheen, 2008; Toth, 2008) to elicit target forms.

For reading, characteristics of the stimulus text will elicit certain reading behaviours and marginalise others (Deane, Sheehan, Sabatini, Futagi & Kostin, 2006). A well-structured text with intermediate summaries will require less higher-order summarising and interpretive skills from the test-taker than a text that is less well organised. A reading test with simply structured texts with many infrequent words may become more of a vocabulary test when the infrequent words are essential to understanding the texts and answering the test items (cf. Drum, Calfee & Cook, 1981). Focusing on the decoding part of the reading process, some studies use irregular pseudo-word lists (e.g. Hamada & Koda, 2008). Also, specially designed sentence structures are presented to test-takers to assess their ability for resolution of ambiguity or pronominal reference (e.g. Jackson, 2008; Roberts, Gullberg & Indefrey, 2008) and comprehension of subjunctive structures (e.g. Fernández, 2008).

In order to be able to make the right choices and decisions concerning the materials in developing a language test, the test developer needs an explicit construct definition and needs to consider the expected response behaviour that will be triggered by the materials. It is obvious that this might not be the same for each and every test-taker (cf. Snow & Lohman, 1989). Piloting of materials is essential, preferably with some form of think-aloud protocols or stimulated recall in order to gain insights in the cognitive processes involved in performing the test tasks.

What Has to Be Done?

In tests assessing productive language abilities, the test-taker is often asked to perform in some kind of role-play. Therefore, it is of the utmost importance that the test-takers know what is expected of them. Clear instructions are crucial to a valid assessment; they define the language-testing task to the test-taker. The test-taker must know what the context of the TLU is: "why do I have to write a letter?", "who is the addressee?", "what does the addressee already know?" and so forth. Apart from these essential aspects of the task that are included to reflect the TLU situation, where language users know their purpose and audience, there will also be requirements and constraints, which are evoked by the testing situation and which are enforced by the researcher, such as the time allotted to the task, the minimum (or maximum) length of the contribution, the use of dictionaries and so on. Again, in all cases researchers have to ask themselves how changes in the test task are to affect the processes and abilities involved in the test-task performance and then whether the measured processes and abilities still match the intended construct. To allow the test-takers to use a dictionary might increase the authenticity of a writing assessment (assuming that writers use dictionaries to solve word searches, cf. Weigle, 2002), but at the same time a lexical diversity measure for the written letter might become a less valid index of the test-taker's productive vocabulary and more of an index for fast dictionary use (see Hurman & Tall, 2002 and East, 2007 for the effects of dictionary use on writing performance).

In assessing receptive language skills, *mutatis mutandis* the same kind of requirements apply. Although language learners can read or listen to a text and just try to comprehend it, their reason for reading or listening makes a difference. Reading for pleasure or aesthetic reasons is different from searching for a certain piece of information or remembering the content for later reproduction. The instructions should be clear about the purpose for reading or listening, and about the testing conditions. For instance, the test-taker must know from the start whether or not the text will remain available when answering questions, that is, will there be a need to memorise (the propositional content or surface form of) the text? Reading strategies will differ and cognitive processes involved will differ consequently. In the same vein, on a listening test, it must be clear whether the spoken text will be repeated or not, as is sometimes the case in listening tests (cf. Buck, 2001 and Sherman, 1997 for the effect of different listening conditions).

The core question a researcher needs to consider in developing assessment tasks is what cognitive processes and skills the test-taker needs to engage in to reach a correct answer or to produce an acceptable communicative contribution. This means that it is not necessary per se that the tests be authentic. Rather what is essential is that they appeal to the processes and skills (and no others) that the research aims to assess (cf. Bachman, 1990, and see Alderson, 2007 for a similar position regarding diagnostic testing). Extensive validity studies are required to evaluate the aptness of a test.

The range of tasks administered in SLA research is enormous. Language learners have to read words aloud (e.g. Hamada & Koda, 2008), read from a computer screen at their own pace (e.g. Jackson, 2008; Lazarte & Barry, 2008), choose answers to multiple choice and yes/no questions (e.g. Tseng & Schmitt, 2008; Taguchi, 2008a, 2008b), translate or fill in gaps (e.g. Tseng & Schmitt, 2008; Bowles, 2008; Ayoun & Salaberry, 2008). They are also invited to self-report word knowledge (e.g. Kim, 2008; Min, 2008), to judge utterances for their acceptability or grammaticality (e.g. Abrahamsson & Hyltenstam, 2008; Anderson, 2008; Lee, 2008; Roberts et al., 2008; Toth, 2008). All these formats can be considered tests of ability and they will be recognized by the test-takers as such. However, test-takers are also asked to join in conversations in which the instructions are to get to know each other, to produce questions forms or Vietnamese tones (e.g. Dimroth, 2008; Jansen, 2008; McDonough & Mackey, 2008; Nguyen & Macken, 2008). These tests are usually unobtrusive regarding the linguistic features and/or errors counted and one could say that in these cases test-takers will show "typical behaviour" more so than their best performance (cf. Cronbach, 1961).

How Is Performance Evaluated?

The language performance of the test-takers has to be converted to estimated levels of language proficiency. For the receptive skills, i.e., reading and listening, the language performance, that is the comprehension of the discourse, is less visible and often has to be derived from the selected responses in a test. The criteria for correct answers are usually predetermined and the score is the weighted sum of the correct answers (e.g. Berent, Kelly, Porter & Fonzi, 2008; Leow, Hsieh & Moreno, 2008; Taguchi, 2008a, 2008b; Tseng & Schmitt, 2008; Webb, 2008). This way of evaluating the test-taker's language ability is often called "objective scoring" or "objective tests", but this qualification pertains to the final checking of the scores only. Determining which of the alternatives is the correct one is not always self-evident and maybe not objectively determined. Distracters in multiple-choice items can anticipate certain false interpretations of a text or the use of inappropriate strategies and as such the "wrong" choices can provide diagnostic information as well (cf. Snow & Lohman, 1989). This multiple-choice and yes/no format is well-known from reading and listening tests, but is basically also underlying grammaticality judgments (e.g. Abrahamsson & Hyltenstam, 2008; Anderson, 2008; Lee, 2008; Roberts et al., 2008; Toth, 2008).

In some cases receptive-language tests require (limited or extended) constructed responses, as in gap-filling tests (e.g. Ayoun & Salaberry, 2008; Bowles, 2008; Tseng & Schmitt, 2008) and story-retellings, respectively (e.g. Lazarte & Barry, 2008; see Alderson, 2000 and Buck, 2001 for the assessment of reading and listening respectively). In these cases, the scoring of the answers will usually be more difficult. For example, if the word that has to fill the gap is misspelled, the researcher has to make scoring guidelines for acceptable misspellings. Penalising misspellings means that correct spelling becomes a prominent aspect of the reading test, which might cause "construct-irrelevant variance" (Messick, 1989).

In receptive tests the range of expected constructed responses will be limited due to the input text. This range of possible responses will be much larger in productive tests. There are innumerable ways "to write an essay for a school magazine" (Schoonen et al., 2003; see Weigle, 2002, Jarvis, Grant, Bikowski & Ferris, 2003) or to orally "describe an accident to a judge" (De Jong et al., 2011), and actually, there are numerous ways to judge the writing and speaking performances. Assessing language learners' ability, the rating criteria should reflect the instructions in order to avoid the aforementioned *had-I-known* effect. This implies that a response to a general writing task, for instance to persuade a reader, should be rated according to its persuasiveness, which almost inevitably leads to some form of general impression or holistic scoring, or context-bound primary-trait scoring (i.e. "Does the text fulfil its purpose?"; cf. Lloyd-Jones, 1977; Weigle 2002; Fulcher, 2003). From a diagnostic perspective, we would like to have more detailed information about the language performances. What are the strong and weak aspects of the performance? Analytic rating is intended to provide such detailed information. The dimensions of an analytic scoring grid implicitly refer to subskills, such as the ability to generate and organise content, the ability to use a wide vocabulary range, or to be grammatically accurate and such. The raters rate according to scale descriptions and descriptions of (some of) the scale points (see, for some examples, Bachman & Palmer, 1996; Luoma, 2004; Fulcher, 2003; Weigle, 2002; Council of Europe, 2001; see also Brindley, 1998). The *Common European framework of reference for languages* (Council of Europe, 2001) provides an extensive set of scales for various aspects of language use, each with descriptors at six levels of the corresponding scales, and as such this framework is a very rich document. At the same time, a critical review of these descriptors (and the framework as a whole) shows that language performance and successive levels of language development can not easily be captured in "simple" descriptions of linguistic features (see also the debate in *Modern Language Journal*'s 2007 winter issue).

Rating language performances requires some level of skill and training of the rater (see Shohamy, Gordon & Kraemer, 1992), but this required level probably depends on the dimension or feature that has to be rated. Schoonen, Vergeer and Eiting (1997) found that lay readers rated "content and organization" of texts equally well as so-called expert readers, but when it came to rating "language usage", the experts turned out to be more reliable (Schoonen et al., 1997). Thus, the intended addressees of a writing or speaking task are not necessarily the best judges of the successfulness of the performances, although in a sense, it might seem very authentic to employ them as raters (see Munro & Derwing, 2008 for the rating of vowel quality by untrained raters). Holistic and analytic ratings of performances consist of an implicitly weighted sum of several features, taking into account the goal and function of the language performance. In the studies examined from *Language Learning* and *Studies in Second Language Acquisition,* direct evaluations of (second language) language performance, that is, holistic or analytic ratings of samples of spoken or written performances, were rare, and as a dependent variable non-existent. Just a few studies refer to general unspecified language tests and/or self-ratings that concern general language proficiency (e.g. Jackson, 2008; Min, 2008). In any case, the use of semi-"authentic" tasks is rather limited and if they are used, they are predominantly used to collect written or spoken language samples for subsequent linguistic analysis.

In general, in SLA research the focus is narrower and often researchers count all kinds of linguistic features to accomplish a linguistically detailed description of the language performance (see Wolfe-Quintero, Inagaki & Kim, 1998 for an overview of linguistic measures for fluency, accuracy and complexity in writing performances). Researchers focus on, among other things, word order (e.g. Jansen, 2008), question formation (e.g. McDonough & Mackey, 2008), syntactic functions in clause initial position (e.g. Bohnacker & Rosén, 2008), utterance length (e.g. Tavakoli & Foster, 2008) or features as negation and finiteness in verbs (e.g. Dimroth, 2008), use of English articles (e.g. Sheen, 2008) and gender agreement (e.g. Montrul, Foote & Perpiñán, 2008). If we assume that typical behavior reflects ability, the descriptive models of language performance and error analyses can give the researcher insights in the stage of interlanguage development of the language learner (e.g. Pienemann's (1998) model of developmental stages). Linguistic features emerge in the language of the learner (see Pallotti, 2007 criteria thereof), occur increasingly frequently, and stabilise or sometimes disappear again in favour of a more advanced structure.

However, the relation between task instructions and scoring criteria is not always transparent; that is, language learners are usually unaware of the features that are scored in their language sample (cf. Cronbach's tests of typical behaviour). Furthermore, it is not always evident what the relationship is between the scored features and the underlying cognitive processes and language skills, which makes the assessment *as an assessment of language ability* problematic.

In sum, every facet of a test task potentially contributes to or affects the processes involved in the task execution and thus the processes that contribute to the variance in responses. Researchers should therefore make with great care decisions about the wording of a prompt, the features of the context the test taker is to imagine, information provided, the timing and the response mode. When we design a reading test asking test-takers to respond orally, we might have a *reading* assessment that is different from an assessment with a test asking test-takers to respond in writing. In Messick's terminology, the assessments probably share the same reading processes "construct representation", but they will differ in construct-irrelevant processes, which may lead to different research outcomes. To counter these response mode effects we need to choose a response mode that is easily do-able for all participants, i.e. reducing the construct-irrelevant variance, or we might want to use multiple tasks with different response modes, in which way the different effects of the construct-irrelevant processes may level out, and thus the generalisability of the overall assessment outcome is enhanced (e.g. Dekydtspotter, Donaldson, Edmonds, Liljestrand Fultz & Petrush, 2008 using a listening and a reading test to assess the resolution of ambiguous relative pronouns, implicitly claiming that this subprocess of language use is part of both the written and oral mode of language use).[5]

Conclusions

In view of the working definition proposed at the beginning of this chapter (i.e. the ability to perform language tasks in real time …), the examples of languages assessment discussed in this chapter are notable in that they are not focused on a general communicative language ability or even on performance of tasks requiring conveying meaning through writing, and speaking or understanding meaning through reading and listening. Also noteworthy is that hardly any study is concerned with language above the sentence level. This sentence and below level focus goes back to the predominance of generative paradigm in linguistics, but other reasons may be involved as well. Practically speaking, the sentence level can be relatively easily controlled in research; for example, in language production a limited set of constructed responses is easier to evaluate. In language understanding, the processing of language input can be controlled better when test-takers need to comprehend short language units. However, without correlations between enabling skills, detailed processes and features and major language skills in (second language) language use (cf. Snow & Lohman's, 1989, pp. 312ff. "cognitive correlates"), it is not clear to what extent these analyses of short segments of language relate to everyday language use in larger discourse units. Validation studies that investigate the causal relations between test performance and overall language performance are needed to address such questions.

Another important area pertaining to validation is the underlying ability continuum that is assumed to span a range of ability from less to more proficient. In the course of the second language development, language proficiency is expected to improve. In developmental research, achievement assessment and programme evaluation, we want test scores to reflect these improvements. However, measurement of development through the use of frequency counts for certain structures or lexical features of a written text or spoken discourse does not always reflect such a continuum. For example, embedded clauses or longer utterances do not always improve the text or discourse quality. Instead, the relevant dimension for capturing development needs to be in the improvements in the language choices that improve the meaning making (see Mohan, Chapter 45, this volume). Thus, there is no underlying ability continuum that maps to the quantity of linguistic features used or understood. This should make us cautious in using these kind of measures as part of the assessment of language proficiency. They can be interesting tools to describe language use (as "typical behaviour"), but inferences about language ability might be one step too far.

More practically, when we develop or choose tests or measurement procedures, we should ask these questions: what do we offer as stimuli and instruction materials, what do we expect test-takers to do and are the instructions coercive enough to make those expectations realistic? Are our evaluation criteria in line with the task instructions and the claims we intend to make about the knowledge and skills of the test-taker? All are seemingly self-evident questions, but when we seriously consider those questions and think about the possible answers, we will be led to more fundamental validity questions like: what is the construct we are measuring? What kind of underlying language use model do we presume? And what does it take for a test-taker to reach an adequate response? Addressing these questions should lead to a theory of response behaviour (cf. Borsboom et al., 2004; Snow & Lohman, 1989); a response behaviour in which the abilities we want to measure are essential and causally related to the outcomes, that is the quality of the language performance, so that we learn how language ability is best assessed for a given purpose.

Notes

1. The author wishes to thank Carol Chapelle and Jan Hulstijn for their helpful comments on an earlier draft of this chapter, and Sophie ter Schure for her help classifying studies.
2. This chapter focuses on spoken and written language, but the definition can easily be extended to include sign language as well.
3. It should be recognised that these models usually are very summary regarding the impact of social and interactional parameters. In more recent years, researchers have tried to integrate affect and motivation in cognitive models (e.g. Hayes, 1996; Guthrie & Wigfield, 1999; Laufer & Hulstijn, 2001; Dörnyei, 2005).

4. The analyses concerned so-called latent variables and as a consequence correlations and regressions are generally higher than in analyses with manifest variables because there is no attenuation due to unreliable measures.

5. One way to test such claims would be to report correlations between measures for the "same trait" measured with "multiple methods". See Bachman and Palmer (1982) and Llosa (2007) for examples of "multi-trait, multi-method" (MTMM) (validity) research. See Chapelle (1999) and Bachman (2004) for more general information about MTMM designs in language testing.

References

Abrahamsson, N., & Hyltenstam, K. (2008). The robustness of aptitude effects in near-native second language acquisition. *Studies in Second Language Acquisition, 30*(4), 481–509.

Alderson, J. C. (2000). *Assessing reading.* Cambridge: Cambridge University Press.

Alderson, J. C. (2005). *Diagnosing foreign language proficiency. The interface between learning and assessment.* London/New York, Continuum.

Alderson, J. C. (2007). The challenge of (diagnostic) testing: Do we know what we are measuring? In J. Fox, M. Wesche, D. Bayliss, L. Cheng, C. E. Turner & C. Doe (Eds.), *Language testing reconsidered* (pp. 21–39). Ottawa: University of Ottawa Press.

Anderson, B. (2008). Forms of evidence and grammatical development in the acquisition of adjective position in L2 French. *Studies in Second Language Acquisition, 30*(1), 1–29.

Ayoun, D., & Salaberry, M. R. (2008). Acquisition of English tense-aspect morphology by advanced French instructed learners. *Language Learning, 58*(3), 555–595.

Bachman, L. F. (1990). *Fundamental considerations in language testing.* Oxford: Oxford University Press.

Bachman, L. F. (2004). *Statistical analyses for language assessment.* Cambridge: Cambridge University Press.

Bachman, L. F. (2007). What is the construct? The dialectic of abilities and contexts in defining constructs in language assessment. In J. Fox, M. Wesche, D. Bayliss, L. Cheng, C. E. Turner & C. Doe (Eds.), *Language testing reconsidered* (pp. 41–71). Ottawa: University of Ottawa Press.

Bachman, L. F., & Palmer, A. S. (1982). The construct validation of some components of communicative proficiency. *TESOL Quarterly, 16*(4), 449–465.

Bachman, L. F., & Palmer, A. S. (1996). *Language testing in practice. Designing and developing useful language tests.* Oxford: Oxford University Press.

Berent, G. P., Kelly, R. R., Porter, J. E. & Fonzi, J. (2008). Deaf learners' knowledge of English universal quantifiers. *Language Learning, 58*(2), 401–437.

Bohnacker, U., & Rosén, C. (2008). The clause-initial position in L2 German declaratives: Transfer of information structure. *Studies in Second Language Acquisition, 30*(4), 511–538.

Borsboom, D., Mellenbergh, G. J. & Van Heerden, J. (2004). The concept of validity. *Psychological Review, 111*(4), 1061–1071.

Bowles, M. A. (2008). Task type and reactivity of verbal reports in SLA: A first look at a L2 task other than reading. *Studies in Second Language Acquisition, 30*(3), 359–387.

Brindley, G. (1998). Describing language development? Rating scales and SLA. In L. F. Bachman & A. D. Cohen (Eds.), *Interfaces between second language acquisition and language testing research* (pp. 112–140). Cambridge: Cambridge University Press.

Brown, A., & Gullberg, M. (2008). Bidirectional crosslinguistic influence in L1–L2 encoding of manner in speech and gesture: A study of Japanese speakers of English. *Studies in Second Language Acquisition, 30*(2), 225–251.

Buck, G. (2001). *Assessing listening.* Cambridge: Cambridge University Press.

Carroll, J. B. (1968). The psychology of language testing. In A. Davies (Ed.), *Language testing symposium: A psycholinguistic approach* (pp. 46–69). London: Oxford University Press.

Chalhoub-Deville, M. (2003). Second language interaction: Current perspectives and future trends. *Language Testing, 20*(4), 369–383.

Chapelle, C. A. (1998). Construct definition and validity inquiry in SLA research. In L. F. Bachman & A. Cohen (Eds.), *Interfaces between second language acquisition and language testing research* (pp. 32–70). Cambridge: Cambridge University Press.

Chapelle, C. A. (1999). Validity in language assessment. *Annual Review of Applied Linguistics, 19*, 254–272.

Choi, S., & Lantolf, J. P. (2008). Representation and embodiment of meaning in L2 communication: motion events in the speech and gesture of advanced L2 Korean and L2 English speakers. *Studies in Second Language Acquisition, 30*(2), 191–224.

Council of Europe. (2001). *Common European framework of reference for languages: Learning, teaching, assessment.* Cambridge: Cambridge University Press.

Cronbach, L. J. (1957). The two disciplines of scientific psychology. *American Psychologist, 12*(11), 671–684.

Cronbach, L. J. (1961). *Essentials of psychological testing* (2nd ed.). New York and London: Harper & Row and John Weatherhill, Inc.

Cutler, A., & Clifton Jr, C. (1999). Comprehending spoken language: A blueprint of the listener. In C. M. Brown & P. Hagoort (Eds.), *The Neurocognition of Language* (pp. 123–166). Oxford: Oxford University Press.

Davies, A. (1990). *Principles of language testing.* Cambridge, MA: Basil Blackwell.

Deane, P., Sheehan, K. M., Sabatini, J., Futagi, Y. & Kostin, I. (2006). Differences in text structure and its implications for assessment of struggling readers. *Scientific Study of Reading, 10*(3), 257–273.

De Jong, N., Steinel, M., Florijn, A., Hulstijn, J. & Schoonen, R. (2011). Facets of speaking proficiency. *Studies in Second Language Acquisition* (accepted for publication).

Dekydtspotter, L., Donaldson, B., Edmonds, A. C., Liljestrand Fultz, A. & Petrush, R. A. (2008). Syntactic and prosodic computations in the resolution of relative clause attachment ambiguity by English–French learners. *Studies in Second Language Acquisition, 30*(4), 453–480.

Dimroth, C. (2008). Age effects on the process of L2 acquisition? Evidence from the acquisition of negation and finiteness in L2 German. *Language Learning, 58*(1), 117–150.

Dörnyei, Z. (2005). *The psychology of the language learner: Individual differences in second language acquisition.* Mahwah, NJ: Lawrence Erlbaum Associates.

Douglas, D. (2000). *Assessing languages for specific purposes.* Cambridge: Cambridge University Press.

Drum, P. A., Calfee, R. C. & Cook, L. K. (1981). The effects of surface structure variables on performance in reading comprehension tests. *Reading Research Quarterly, 16*(4), 486–514.

East, M. (2007). Bilingual dictionaries in tests of L2 writing proficiency: Do they make a difference? *Language Testing, 24*(3), 331–353.

Fernández, C. (2008). Reexamining the role of explicit information in processing instruction. *Studies in Second Language Acquisition, 30*(3), 277–305.

Flower, L. S., & Hayes, J. R. (1980). The dynamics of composing: Making plans and juggling constraints. In L. W. Gregg & E. R. Steinberg (Eds.), *Cognitive processes in writing* (pp. 31–50). Hillsdale, NJ: Lawrence Erlbaum Associates.

Fukkink, R. G., Hulstijn, J. & Simis, A. (2005). Does training in second-language word recognition skills affect reading comprehension? An experimental study. *The Modern Language Journal, 89*(1), 54–75.

Fulcher, G. (2003). *Testing second language speaking.* London: Pearson Longman.

Gass, S. M., & Mackey, A. (2007). *Data elicitation for second and foreign language research.* Mahwah, NJ: Lawrence Erlbaum Associates.

Gatbonton, E., & Segalowitz, N. (2005). Rethinking communicative language teaching: A focus on access to fluency. *Canadian Modern Language Review/La Revue canadienne des langues vivantes, 61*(3), 325–353.

Gough, P. B. (1972). One second of reading. In H. Singer & R. B. Ruddell (Eds.), *Theoretical models and processes of reading* (pp. 661–686). Newark, DE: International Reading Association. (Reprint, 1985.)

Graham, S., & Macaro, E. (2008). Strategy instruction in listening for lower-intermediate learners of French. *Language Learning, 58*(4), 747–783.

Guilford, J. P. (1971). *The nature of human intelligence.* London: McGraw-Hill.

Guthrie, J. T., & Wigfield, A. (1999). How motivation fits into a science of reading. *Scientific Studies of Reading, 3*(3), 195–208.

Hamada, M., & Koda, K. (2008). Influence of first language orthographic experience on second language decoding and word learning. *Language Learning, 58*(1), 1–31.

Harrington, M. (2006). The lexical decision task as a measure of L2 proficiency. *EUROSLA Yearbook, 6*(1), 147–168.

Hayes, J. R. (1996). A new framework for understanding cognition and affect in writing. In C. M. Levy & S. Ransdell (Eds.), *The science of writing: Theories, methods, individual differences and applications* (pp. 1–27). Mahwah, NJ: Lawrence Erlbaum Associates.

Henning, G. (1992). Dimensionality and construct validity of language tests. *Language Testing, 9*(1), 1–11.

Hulstijn, J., Van Gelderen, A., & Schoonen, R. (2009). Automatization in second-language acquisition: What does the coefficient of variation tell us? *Applied Psycholinguistics, 30*(4), 555–582.

Hurman, J., & Tall, G. (2002). Quantitative and qualitative effects of dictionary use on written examination scores. *Language Learning Journal, 25*(1), 21–26.

Jackson, C. (2008). Proficiency level and the interaction of lexical and morphosyntactic information during L2 sentence processing. *Language Learning, 58*(4), 875–909.

Jansen, L. (2008). Acquisition of German word order in tutored learners: A cross-sectional study in a wider theoretical context. *Language Learning, 58*(1), 185–231.

Jarvis, S., Grant, L., Bikowski, D. & Ferris, D. (2003). Exploring multiple profiles of highly rated learner compositions. *Journal of Second Language Writing, 12*(4), 377–403.

Kempe, V., & Brooks, P. J. (2008). Second language learning of complex inflectional systems. *Language Learning*, 58(4), 703–746.

Kim, Y. (2008). The role of task-induced involvement and learner proficiency in L2 vocabulary acquisition. *Language Learning*, 58(2), 285–325.

Laufer, B., & Hulstijn, J. (2001). Incidental vocabulary acquisition in a second language: The construct of task-induced involvement. *Applied Linguistics*, 22(1), 1–26.

Lazarte, A. A., & Barry, S. (2008). Syntactic complexity and L2 academic immersion effects on readers' recall and pausing strategies for English and Spanish texts. *Language Learning*, 58(4), 785–834.

Lee, S.-Y. (2008). Argument–adjunct asymmetry in the acquisition of inversion in Wh-questions by Korean learners of English. *Language Learning*, 58(3), 625–663.

Leow, R. P., Hsieh, H.-C. & Moreno, N. (2008). Attention to form and meaning revisited. *Language Learning*, 58(3), 665–695.

Levelt, W. J. M. (1999). Producing spoken language: A blueprint of the speaker. In C. M. Brown & P. Hagoort (Eds.), *The Neurocognition of Language* (pp. 83–122). Oxford: Oxford University Press.

Llosa, L. (2007). Validating a standards-based classroom assessment of English proficiency: A multitrait-multimethod approach. *Language Testing*, 24(4), 489–515.

Lloyd-Jones, R. (1977). Primary trait scoring. In C. R. Cooper & L. Odell (Eds.), *Evaluating writing: Describing, measuring, judging* (pp. 33–66). Urbana, IL: NCTE.

Luoma, S. (2004). *Assessing speaking*. Cambridge: Cambridge University Press.

McDonough, K., & Mackey, A. (2008). Syntactic priming and ESL question development. *Studies in Second Language Acquisition*, 30(1), 31–47.

Mackey, A., & Gass, S. M. (2005). *Second language research. Methodology and design*. Mahwah, NJ: Lawrence Erlbaum Associates.

McNamara, T. F. (1996). *Measuring second language performance*. London: Longman.

Messick, S. (1989). Validity. In R. L. Linn (Ed.), *Educational measurement* (3rd ed.) (pp. 13-103). New York/London: American Council on Education/Macmillan.

Min, H.-T. (2008). EFL vocabulary acquisition and retention: Reading plus vocabulary enhancement activities and narrow reading. *Language Learning*, 58(1), 73–115.

Montrul, S., Foote, R. & Perpiñán, S. (2008). Gender agreement in adult second language learners and Spanish heritage speakers: The effects of age and context of acquisition. *Language Learning*, 58(3), 503–553.

Munro, M. J., & Derwing, T. M. (2008). Segmental acquisition in adult ESL learners: A longitudinal study of vowel production. *Language Learning*, 58(3), 479–502.

Nguyen, H. t., & Macken, M. A. (2008). Factors affecting the production of Vietnamese tones: A study of American learners. *Studies in Second Language Acquisition*, 30(1), 49–77.

Pallotti, G. (2007). An operational definition of the emergence criterion. *Applied Linguistics*, 28(3), 361–382.

Perfetti, C. A. (1999). Comprehending written language: A blueprint of the reader. In C. M. Brown & P. Hagoort (Eds.), *The neurocognition of language* (pp. 167–208). Oxford: Oxford University Press.

Pienemann, M. (1998). *Language processing and second language development*. Amsterdam: John Benjamins.

Roberts, L., Gullberg, M., & Indefrey, P. (2008). Online pronoun resolution in L2 discourse: L1 influence and general learner effects. *Studies in Second Language Acquisition*, 30(3), 333–357.

Sawaki, Y., & Nissan, S. (2009). *Criterion-related validity of the TOEFL iBT Listening section* (No. RR-09-02). Princeton, NJ: ETS.

Schoonen, R., Van Gelderen, A., De Glopper, K., Hulstijn, J., Simis, A., Snellings, P. & Stevenson, M. (2003). First language and second language writing: The role of linguistic fluency, linguistic knowledge and metacognitive knowledge. *Language Learning*, 53(1), 165–202.

Schoonen, R., Vergeer, M., & Eiting, M. (1997). The assessment of writing ability: Expert readers versus lay readers. *Language Testing*, 14(2), 157–184.

Segalowitz, N., & Hulstijn, J. (2005). Automaticity in second language learning. In J. F. Kroll & A. M. B. De Groot (Eds.), *Handbook of bilingualism: Psycholinguistic approaches*. (pp. 371–388). New York: Oxford University Press.

Segalowitz, N. S., & Segalowitz, S. J. (1993). Skilled performance, practice, and the differentiation of speed-up from automatization effects: Evidence from second language word recognition. *Applied Psycholinguistics*, 14(3), 369–385.

Sheen, Y. (2008). Recasts, language anxiety, modified output, and L2 learning. *Language Learning*, 58(4), 835–874.

Sherman, J. (1997). The effect of question preview in listening comprehension tests. *Language Testing*, 14(2), 185–213.

Shohamy, E., Gordon, C. M. & Kraemer, R. (1992). The effect of raters' background and training on the reliability of direct writing tests. *The Modern Language Journal*, 76(1), 27–33.

Shohamy, E., & McNamara, T. F. (Eds.) (2009). Language assessment for immigration, citizenship, and asylum. Special issue of *Language Assessment Quarterly. An International Journal*, 6(1).

Snellings, P., Van Gelderen, A. & De Glopper, K. (2004). The effect of enhanced lexical retrieval on L2 writing. A classroom experiment. *Applied Psycholinguistics, 25*(2), 175–200.

Snow, R. E., & Lohman, D. F. (1989). Implications of cognitive psychology for educational measurement. In R. L. Linn (Ed.), *Educational measurement* (3rd ed.) (pp. 263–331). New York/London: American Council on Education/Macmillan.

Taguchi, N. (2008a). Cognition, language contact, and the development of pragmatic comprehension in a study-abroad context. *Language Learning, 58*(1), 33–71

Taguchi, N. (2008b). The role of learning environment in the development of pragmatic comprehension: A comparison of gains between EFL and ESL learners. *Studies in Second Language Acquisition, 30*(4), 423–452.

Tavakoli, P., & Foster, P. (2008). Task design and second language performance: The effect of narrative type on learner output. *Language Learning, 58*(2), 439–473.

Tomasello, M. (2003). *Constructing a language. A usage-based theory of language acquisition.* Cambridge, MA: Harvard University Press.

Toth, P. D. (2008). Teacher- and learner-led discourse in task-based grammar instruction: Providing procedural assistance for L2 morphosyntactic development. *Language Learning, 58*(2), 237–283.

Tseng, W.-T., & Schmitt, N. (2008). Toward a model of motivated vocabulary learning: A structural equation modeling approach. *Language Learning, 58*(2), 357–400.

Van Gelderen, A., Schoonen, R., De Glopper, K., Hulstijn, J., Simis, A., Snellings, P. & Stevenson, M. (2004). Linguistic knowledge, processing speed and metacognitive knowledge in first and second language reading comprehension. A componential analysis. *Journal of Educational Psychology, 96*(1), 19–30.

Webb, S. (2008). Receptive and productive vocabulary sizes of L2 learners. *Studies in Second Language Acquisition, 30*(1), 79–95.

Weigle, S. C. (2002). *Assessing writing.* Cambridge: Cambridge University Press.

Wolfe-Quintero, K., Inagaki, S. & Kim, H.-Y. (1998). *Second language development in writing: Measures of fluency, accuracy & complexity.* Honolulu: University of Hawaii Press.

43
Validation in Language Assessment

Carol Chapelle

Validation is the process researchers engage in to produce evidence pertaining to the *meaning of test scores* and *their appropriateness for making decisions.* Test score meaning, as Schoonen (Chapter 42, this volume) illustrated, can refer to a variety of constructs such as knowledge of wh-question formation, reading comprehension, or language ability (see also Bachman, 2007; Chapelle, 1998; McNamara, 1996). Decisions may include students' decisions to drop a course or to study harder; teachers' decisions to teach something a different way or to assign a particular grade to a student; institutional decisions to admit, hire, or advance a candidate; or the government's decision to increase funding for a school (see Ross, Chapter 47, this volume). Because of the decisions that stem from language test scores, the professional practices entailed in validation are of fundamental importance to language test developers, testing researchers, test score users, and test takers. Everyone involved with language testing relies on the quality of the procedures used for investigating and establishing validity, and they count on professionals in language assessment to know the procedures and be able to apply them appropriately.

Many test users assume that the application of such methods is a mechanical process yielding results indicating test validity. They would be surprised and alarmed to read in the first volume of the *Handbook of Research in Second Language Teaching and Learning* that many unresolved issues surround language test validation practices. Reflecting a social turn in language assessment, Davies and Elder (2005) introduced the topic of validation in language assessment with recognition of the ongoing debates in the field. They explicitly brought into the discussion the social context of language assessment, which amplified the situated human judgment involved in validation. They introduced validity not as a conclusion about *a test* to be proven scientifically but rather as a judgment about *test interpretation and use* to be arrived at from a rhetorically-framed argument supported by data. Their characterization of the knowledge in this area provides a good starting point for understanding how the field has progressed to its current state.

The current state, I will suggest, moves beyond the social turn by taking what I call "a praxis step." The praxis step has focused on the need to make practical and useable the concepts, theory, and philosophy associated with validity and validation over the past years. The chapter begins with a brief background of how theory and practice in validation have evolved over recent history, and then explains the key concepts that are important in the current praxis step. The chapter illustrates a modern validity argument for a high stakes language test, the Test of English as a Foreign Language (TOEFL) because even though few language testing programs command the will and resources to undertake such a program of validation, the thinking behind it and the approach taken in developing this validity argument is instructive for any type of language assessment. In other words, the example illustrates how the praxis step in validation has resulted in concrete, useful guidance for developing validity arguments. The chapter ends with a statement about the limitations of the guidance offered by the praxis step.

Historical Background

> Does the test measure what it claims to measure? If it does, it is valid.
>
> (Lado, 1961, p. 321)

Most language professionals today would agree with this characterization of a valid test from the first book on language assessment in the modern era. Moreover, it would be difficult to find dispute as to whether or not validity is a good thing. Who would want a language test that failed to measure what it claims to measure? Whether it be an assessment of material taught over the course of a unit in class (see Jamieson, Chapter 46, this volume) or a test of an ability necessary for job performance, anyone would agree that the test needs to measure what it claims to measure. Despite agreement on this issue, it is less clear what kind of evidence a test developer should provide in order to demonstrate that a test measures what it claims to measure. The question about selection of appropriate evidence, which has been central for many years (Cronbach & Meehl, 1955; Oller, 1979; Shepard, 1993), remains at the core of an evolving discussion about validity in language assessment.

Evidence for Validity

Researchers in language testing would point out three complexities that arise in attempting to gather appropriate evidence for validity. First, evidence can be gathered in the process of designing a test and conducting research on it, but precisely what evidence should be gathered, how much is needed, and how it should be combined to demonstrate validity have proven to be complex issues. For example, many researchers would consider as evidence for validity high correlations between their new reading test and an existing reading test. A correlation would indicate that the students who did well on the new reading test had also done well on the existing reading test. This correlation, then, would serve as evidence of the new test as a measure of reading ability. The case of the hypothetical new reading test, however, fails to reflect the relevant facts of real test development. Most importantly, developers typically do not attempt to construct a new test that measures exactly what another test measures. The point of developing a new test is to fulfill the need for a new and better test for the same purpose as an existing test or to develop a new test for a new testing purpose. In both cases, it is easy to see why a correlation with the existing test would be somewhat limited in its utility. As a consequence, methods are needed that do not rely on an existing test as a model and criterion.

Second, the practice of gathering evidence for the types of tests that are actually developed and used in language teaching and research require testing researchers to question what the evidence is for. "Does the test measure what it claims to measure?" provides a starting point, but hardly an adequate frame for designing research. What the test claims to measure is an aspect of language knowledge, ability, or performance capacity. As Shoonen pointed out in Chapter 42, even defining what a test is intended to measure is a complex issue as many perspectives on language constructs have been developed to provide a means of stating what a test is intended to measure. In examining what types of evidence should be gathered, researchers have revised the initial frame for the inquiry to focus not on the test but upon the *interpretation* to be made on the basis of test scores.

Third, test score interpretation is important in the validation process, but it is rather abstract as a sole basis for guiding validation research. Moreover, some would argue that it is the *test score use*, or *the actions resulting from test scores*, that should motivate the validation. For example, if a language test score is used to determine whether a candidate is eligible for a job, the validation process should provide evidence that the candidate who obtains a passing test score can actually do the job better than one who fails to obtain a passing score. The interpretation made on the basis of the test score in this case would be language ability whereas the use would be the employment decision.

Because of their struggles to conduct research that gathers the appropriate evidence, most language testing researchers conceive of validity as a quality that can pertain to the interpretations made on the basis of test scores and to their use. In other words, evidence is sought not to support the validity of the test, but rather to support the validity of test score interpretation and use. In language testing, the idea that validity pertains to test score interpretation and use is made explicit in Bachman's (1990) book, *Fundamental Considerations in Language Testing*, where he draws upon the thinking in educational measurement, and particularly on the work of Messick (1989).

Messick and the Social Turn

In his seminal paper entitled "Validity" in the third edition of *Educational measurement*, Messick defined validity as "an overall evaluative judgment of the degree to which evidence and theoretical rationales support the adequacy and appropriateness of interpretations and actions based on test scores" (Messick, 1989, p. 13). This statement ties together the *evidence*, the *interpretations*, and the *actions* based on test scores. At the same time, it frames validity as an evidence-based judgment rather than as a quality a test can possess. This framing of validity as a judgment implies a community for whom an argument is made. The argument is to include evidence about the actions or consequences of test use on test users, institutions, and society more broadly. For example, the argument would not be limited to the test measuring the intended construct, but might include facts about the effects of placement decisions on the quality of instruction, and in turn, the quality of performance of graduates in their future jobs. These two factors—the argument with an audience, and the social consequences of testing—in the validation process are the primary impetus for Davies and Elder's (2005) reference to the social turn in language testing.

The influence of Messick's conception of validity has been pervasive through work in language assessment, in part because it provides such a far-reaching frame for conceptualizing validation research. The ideas from Messick's 1989 paper are also reflected in the *Standards for Educational and Psychological Testing* (AERA/APA/NCME, 1999) that are intended to provide a lingua franca for measurement across academic fields. An examination of the primary journal for our field, *Language Testing*, reveals the influence of Messick, sometimes through the *Standards* (AERA/APA/NCME, 1999) or Bachman (1990) on the way in which authors describe their validation research, discuss what their tests are intended to measure, and raise questions about the effects that their tests have on teachers and students.

In Volume I of the *Handbook*, Davies and Elder identified four challenges the social turn brings. First, they point out that validity and the process of validation requires that those attempting to argue the validity of test interpretation and use must do so by appealing to logic, in other words constructing an argument whose conclusion can be justified on the basis of premises that are shown to be connected to conclusions in a defensible way.

The second challenge is the question about the role of reliability within a validity argument. Is reliability best seen as a quality, alongside validity, that is another, perhaps complementary, way of conceptualizing test quality? Is it a prerequisite for validity? Or is it one of many factors that can be drawn upon in developing a validity argument? Long debated in professional testing circles, these questions require a consensus in the professional community if a test developer is to construct a defensible validity argument.

The third challenge pertains to identifying the audience for a validity argument. An argument is typically made in a particular context with an audience or range of audiences in mind. Test developers are therefore faced with the question of determining the scope of the audience they intend to affect with a validity argument for test use. Moreover, test developers have to decide whether or not a unique argument is needed for each test score use from a particular test in view of the fact that a validity argument is needed to justify test score interpretation and use.

The fourth challenge, which Davies and Elder refer to as "unitary and divisible," pertains to the challenge of gathering evidence and presenting theoretical rationales from a number of sources, and then integrating them into a single or unitary validity argument. Part of the challenge, in view of the social turn in language testing, is that the theory and evidence that can be brought to bear on test interpretation and use can come from a broad range of sources pertaining to use(s) of the test. Such a potentially diverse set of evidence needs to be integrated in view of the conception that validity is to be seen as unitary, referring to an overall judgment, rather than divisible types of validities (e.g., content validity, construct validity, etc.).

These challenges in arguing validity are amplified within the social turn in language assessment in a way that renders the study of validity an interesting academic topic from multiple angles. However, for test developers and researchers who wish to develop sound validity arguments, accepted procedures are needed. As Davies and Elder pointed out the following:

> If the notion of test validity and the process of test validation discussed in this chapter are to be regarded as credible rather than dismissed as the arcane practices of a self-serving élite, they need to be simplified or at least rendered more transparent to test users.
>
> (Davies & Elder, 2005, p. 810)

In response to this need, language testing researchers such as Bachman and Palmer (1996) and Weir (2005) have outlined categories or components pertaining to language assessment that can be used to organize validation research. In language assessment, these efforts represent part of what I call the praxis step for validation in language assessment. Whereas the social turn raises many relevant issues and reveals complexity, the praxis step aims to create a usable set of concepts and procedures for developing validity arguments.

Kane and the Praxis Step

In his chapter, "Validation," in the fourth edition of *Educational Measurement*, Kane's (2006) presentation of a validity argument attempts a praxis step by providing guidance as to how to decide what kind of evidence a validity argument requires. The editor, Brennan (2006), contrasted the presentation on validity given by Kane (2006) with that of Messick: "the chapter in the 2006 edition aims at making validation a more accessible enterprise for educational measurement practitioners" (p. 3). It does so by focusing of the validation efforts in four ways as outlined in Table 43.1, which contrasts Kane's perspective with that presented in the 1999 AERA/APA/NCME *Standards for Educational and Psychological Testing* (Chapelle, Enright, & Jamieson, 2010).

Kane's presentation of validity shifts the framing of score interpretation from a construct such as reading comprehension or grammatical ability alone to an interpretive argument, which refers to an explicit statement of what score meaning entails. An interpretive argument can include a construct, but in Kane's approach, does not rely completely upon a construct. Instead, the test developer articulates an interpretive argument by defining the inferences that are important for test interpretation and use.

Table 43.1 Key Aspects in the Process of Validation in the *Standards* (AERA/APA/NCME, 1999) and in *Educational Measurement* (Kane, 2006)

Three aspects characterizing approaches to validity	Standards (AERA/APA/ NCME, 1999)	Kane (2006)
Framing the intended score interpretation	A construct	An interpretive argument
Outlining the essential research	Propositions consistent with the intended interpretation	Inferences and their assumptions
Structuring research results into a validity argument	Listing types of evidence	Series of inferences linking grounds with conclusions

Adapted from Chapelle et al. (2010).

Since an interpretive argument is constructed with inferences, *inference* a key concept in understanding the praxis step. Kane (1992, 2001) and Mislevy, Steinberg, and Almond (2003) defined and used inference in a way that is consistent with Toulmin's (2003) description of informal or practical arguments, such as those used in nonmathematical fields such as law. In this sense an inference is a logical movement from one fact or proposition to another, as illustrated in the diagram in Figure 43.1.

In this example, the inferences connecting an examinee's score, the interpretation and the decision are explicitly drawn as inferences. When test users are given a test score for an individual, they decide whether or not the individual is capable of performing in a particular context and therefore make a decision about admission, employment, or a pay raise, for example. Two inferences are involved in this process. The score represents one fact, i.e., that the student obtained a particular score on a test. The first inference moves from the fact of that score to another proposition, i.e., that the examinee who obtained the score has the ability to perform successfully in a particular context. This inferred

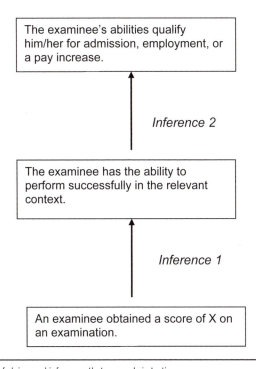

Figure 43.1 Example of the types of claims and inferences that are made in testing

proposition then is used as a basis for the next inference which moves to a decision to admit, employ, or increase the salary of the individual.

The interpretive argument defined by the test developer provides the basis for setting the agenda for validation research. Such an interpretive argument as a guide to research contrasts with the approach outlined in the *Standards*, which suggests that the test developer generate some propositions that are consistent with the intended test score interpretation. The *Standards* provide some examples of propositions, but this process is too open-ended to offer sufficient guidance. The interpretive argument is developed from inferences as described above, and Kane provides a finite number of these that set some parameters for test developers. The test developer defines the inferences underlying score interpretation and use as well as the assumptions that need to be made in order for the inferences to be made legitimately. The specific research that must be carried out in validation, then, is research that supports these assumptions.

The result of validation research is evidence supporting score interpretation and use. The *Standards* do not provide any particular structure for the validity argument other than listing types of evidence. Kane's approach, in contrast, structures the validity evidence according to the interpretive argument, which provides a stepwise progress in which certain inferences can be made only if others have been. Finally, Kane provides a mechanism for challenging the validity argument.

In language assessment, the influence of Kane's framing of validation has been present for several years, particularly in the papers of Bachman (2002, 2005) and Mislevy (e.g., Mislevy & Chengbin, 2009), who draw upon a similar structure for defining an "assessment use argument." Kane's work containing some of the fundamental components of the argument-based approach to validity began to appear in the 1990s (e.g., 1992; Kane, Cohen, & Crooks, 1999). However, the specifics of Kane's approach to developing a validity argument include some precise methodological concepts and procedures that had not appeared in the papers in *Language Testing* by mid-2009. An example of this approach can be found, however, in a book-length presentation of the validity argument for the TOEFL.

Validity Argument

The concepts of inference, interpretive argument, and validity argument are best understood through an example of how these terms have been used in language assessment. In view of the complexity of developing a validity argument, however, it is difficult to find complete examples in which validation practice displays the principles outlined by Kane. Instead, one finds research pertaining to test score meaning and use reported in journal articles with the assumption that such research results would form part of a validity argument. Such individual studies are intended to contribute to a validity argument, but in view of space limitations as well as the fact that all of the necessary research may not have been done at the time of publication of an individual study; it is unusual to find a validity argument laid out and supported in a single publication. The validity argument that I will use as an illustration appears in an edited volume, in which individual chapters report different studies that aimed at supporting particular claims in the interpretive argument that is outlined in the first chapter. Beyond this chapter, then, readers can therefore seek additional explanation and detail in a published account of the validity argument, as well as in the research that the book refers to. At the same time, however, it is important to recognize that this is an example of how Kane's concepts can be used rather than a formula for how all validity arguments for language tests are to be constructed.

The TOEFL Interpretive Argument

To understand the validity argument, one must start with the interpretive argument. The interpretive argument for the TOEFL is complex, so as a first step to understanding it, Figure 43.2 illustrates the beginning and ending claims in the interpretive argument. The arrow between the starting and ending points of the argument is used to provide a simple representation of the inferences in this simplified diagram. A successful argument about the validity of TOEFL score use needs to point one to the conclusion that the scores are useful for making decisions about university admissions, as illustrated in Figure 43.2. The starting point for such a conclusion would be the claim that the sample of performance elicited by the test tasks was appropriate for drawing such a conclusion. Therefore, the interpretive argument begins with the claim that the examinee provided a sufficient sample of performance on a set of relevant tasks.

A number of inferences and intermediary claims make up the intermediary steps that connect the beginning and ending claims. Figure 43.2 is a very simple version of the interpretive argument without all of the intermediary inferences articulated, but those inferences need to be specified in order to identify the validation research to be completed. The validation research is aimed at providing support for the claims that are associated with the inferences.

Figure 43.3 shows the additional detail of the inferences and intermediary claims that connect the claim about appropriate performance (the second claim in the argument) with the conclusion about test use (at the top). Each of the inferences in Figure 43.3 is labeled with a name that is consistent with Kane's presentation of possible inferences in an interpretive argument (e.g., generalization and explanation). The intermediary conclusion that (2) observations of performance on the TOEFL reveal relevant knowledge, skills, and abilities in situations representative of those in the target domain of language use in the English-medium universities is based on an analysis of language use in an academic domain. But this conclusion is only warranted, i.e., that inference can only be made, if test developers have done an accurate and credible job of describing the domain of academic language use in a relevant way.

Observations of performance remain some distance from the score use claim (7). To move the argument closer to the desired conclusion, the evaluation inference is the next link in the chain. The evaluation inference can be made if good evidence exists that evaluators are focusing on and evaluating the relevant features of examinees' responses such that the following conclusion (3) is warranted: observations on the TOEFL tasks are evaluated to provide observed scores reflective of

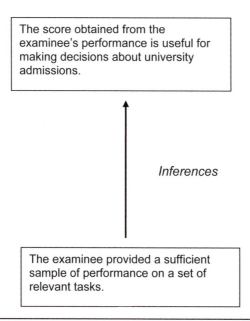

Figure 43.2 Claims and inferences underlying the use of TOEFL scores for university admissions decisions

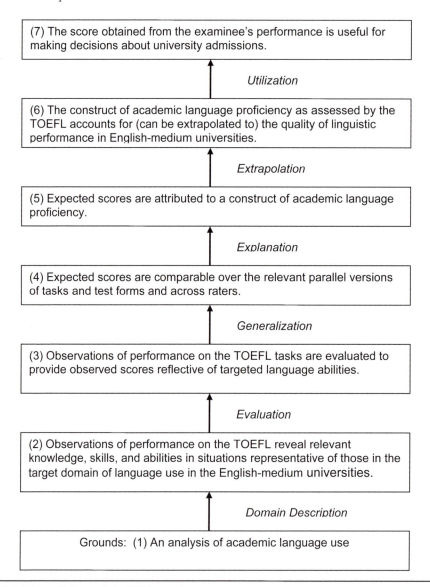

Figure 43.3 Claims and inferences in the TOEFL interpretive argument

targeted language abilities. This conclusion serves as the basis for the generalization inference which, if supported, warrants the conclusion (4) that expected scores are comparable over the relevant parallel versions of tasks and test forms and across raters.

The theorized expected score, or perfectly reliable score, is the starting point for the explanation inference, which, if supported, warrants the conclusion (5) that the expected scores are attributed to the construct of academic English language proficiency. This is the construct that the test is intended to measure, but in the interpretive argument, it appears as just one of several links in an explicit chain of inferences. This conclusion about the construct provides the basis for the extrapolation inference, whose support would warrant the conclusion (6) that the construct as measured by the test can be extrapolated to the quality of the test taker's linguistic performance in English-medium universities. This conclusion, in turn, provides the basis for the final conclusion that the score obtained from the examinee's performance is useful for making decisions about university admissions, provided that evidence is found to warrant the utilization inference.

The TOEFL Validity Argument

What appears in Figure 43.3 depicts the interpretive argument, which outlines the structure that the validity argument takes. The validity argument, however, needs to include the evidence that supports each of the inferences. In other words, a validity argument needs to demonstrate how each of the inferences is warranted. Kane's approach to outlining the validity argument actually uses the term "warrant" to refer to the statements that need to be supported if inferences are to be legitimately made. The second column of Table 43.2 summarizes the warrants associated with each of the inferences in the TOEFL validity argument.

The third column shows the assumptions that underlie each of the inferences. For example, the warrant that needs to be supported if the generalization inference to be made is that expected scores are comparable over parallel versions of tasks and test forms and across raters. The assumptions are an important part of the thinking leading up to the construction of a validity argument because they point to the areas where research is needed to support the validity argument. For the generalization inference, assumptions about appropriate quantities and configurations of tasks were supported through quantitative research, and in particular research on generalizability, reliability, scaling, and equating.

As Purpura (Chapter 44, this volume) points out, a variety of quantitative studies can be used to provide backing for many of the assumptions in a validity argument. In the minds of many applied linguists, such quantitative studies form the cornerstone of language testing research, but it should be apparent that from the variety of assumptions that appear in Table 43.2 that both quantitative and qualitative research is needed to provide backing in a validity argument. Qualitative research is used, for example, to provide backing for the assumption that the linguistic knowledge, processes, and strategies required to successfully complete tasks vary across tasks in keeping with theoretical expectations. Moreover, as Mohan (Chapter 45, this volume) demonstrates, fundamental assumptions about the nature of assessment tasks, the appropriateness of response evaluation, the pertinence of the construct definition, and the justifiability of the extrapolation all rest on qualitative issues of how language is defined and analyzed.

Table 43.2 outlines the types of research that were used in the validity argument for the TOEFL. This research is explained in greater detail in the edited volume outlining the TOEFL validity argument (Chapelle, Enright, & Jamieson, 2008), but it should be noted here that these are not the only types of research that can be used to support the TOEFL validity argument in particular, or validity arguments in general. Moreover, as Mohan points out, support for such a validity argument in terms of qualitative discourse analysis is an area that remains problematic for all tests of academic language ability, including TOEFL.

It should be evident from this example that the praxis step in language assessment builds upon the changes brought about by the social turn, and provides a stronger basis for those who are responsible for planning and carrying out validation research than what was provided by the social turn. The example should also illustrate that validation of language assessments is a process of conducting multiple types of research pertaining to inferences that test developers intend to be made on the basis of particular test scores. The path for such research typically begins with the test developers' need to support an interpretive argument, but research can and should extend beyond what the test developer presents. As inferences entail different types of assumptions, research can and should encompass appropriate quantitative and qualitative methods. The resulting composite of validation research provides a good example of mixed methods research in applied linguistics.

Table 43.2 Inferences, Warrants, Assumptions in the TOEFL Validity Argument and Examples of the Research That Provides Backing for Each

Inference in the TOEFL interpretive argument	Warrant supporting the inference	Assumptions underlying warrant	Example of backing sought to support assumption
Domain description	Observations of performance on the TOEFL reveal relevant knowledge, skills, and abilities in situations representative of those in the target domain of language use in the English-medium institutions of higher education.	Assessment tasks that are representative of the academic domain can be identified.	Domain analysis
		Critical English language skills, knowledge, and processes needed for study in English-medium colleges and universities can be identified.	Domain analysis
		Assessment tasks that require important skills and are representative of the academic domain can be simulated.	Task modeling
Evaluation	Observations of performance on TOEFL tasks are evaluated to provide observed scores reflective of targeted language abilities.	Rubrics for scoring responses are appropriate for providing evidence of targeted language abilities.	Rubric development
		Task administration conditions are appropriate for providing evidence of targeted language abilities.	Prototyping studies
		The statistical characteristics of items, measures, and test forms are appropriate for norm-referenced decisions.	Item and test analysis
Generalization	Expected scores are comparable over the relevant parallel versions of tasks and test forms and across raters.	A sufficient number of tasks are included on the test to provide stable estimates of test takers' performances	Generalizability and reliability studies
		Configuration of tasks on measures is appropriate for intended interpretation.	Generalizability and reliability studies
		Appropriate scaling and equating procedures for test scores are used.	Scaling and equating studies
		Task and test specifications are well defined so that parallel tasks and test forms are created.	Generalizability and reliability studies
Explanation	Expected scores are attributed to a construct of academic language proficiency.	The linguistic knowledge, processes, and strategies required to successfully complete tasks vary across tasks in keeping with theoretical expectations.	Discourse analyses and cognitive processing studies
		Task difficulty is systematically influenced by task characteristics.	Task characteristic-item difficulty studies
		Performance on new test measures relate to performance on other test-based measures of language proficiency as expected theoretically.	Concurrent correlational studies
		The internal structure of the test scores is consistent with a theoretical	Studies of reliability and factor

		view of language proficiency as a number of highly interrelated components.	analysis
		Test performance varies according to amount and quality of experience in learning English.	Comparison studies of group differences
Extrapolation	The construct of academic language proficiency as assessed by TOEFL accounts for the quality of linguistic performance in English-medium institutions of higher education.	Performance on the test is related to other criteria of language proficiency in the academic context.	Criterion-related validity studies
Utilization	Estimates of the quality of performance in the English-medium institutions of higher education obtained from the TOEFL are useful for making decisions about admissions and appropriate curriculum for test takers.	The meaning of test scores is clearly interpretable by admissions officers, test takers, and teachers.	Standard setting studies Score interpretation materials
		The test will have a positive influence on how English is taught.	Availability of instructional materials Washback studies

From Chapelle, Enright, & Jamieson (2008, pp. 19–21).

Evaluating the Validity Argument

If test developers and testing researchers who are working for the institutions that produce tests are the ones developing interpretive and validity arguments, how do such arguments get evaluated? If test developers set out to create new tests in order to conduct post hoc research on whether assumptions in the interpretive argument can be supported, the test development cycle would be long and inefficient. Instead, the development process entails research whose outcomes are used to make design decisions that will result in a test whose interpretation and use can be supported. In this sense, the validity argument that is put forth by the test developers can be said to have a confirmatory bias (Cronbach, 1988). Such an argument needs to be seen for what it is, as Briggs (2004) put it, a design validity argument, which is presented by the test designers' team as a statement that provides evidence in support of intended score interpretations and uses.

Such an argument needs to be evaluated by the community of test users in view of the soundness of the argument, the strength of the support, and the lack of support for any possible rebuttals. Like development of a validity argument, such evaluations require expertise. One approach to evaluating a validity argument is to evaluate its clarity and scope. In order to do so, one needs to understand the approach taken to the validity argument as well as some alternatives. Questions posed by an evaluator at this stage would include whether or not (1) the logical progression of the inferences makes sense, (2) all of the assumptions that underlie each warrant have been identified, and (3) all of the relevant consequences of the test have been identified. Such consequences can extend into society as tests are used for many purposes such as those described by Ross (Chapter 47, this volume).

A second approach to evaluating a validity argument is to evaluate the quality of the support for each assumption that has been identified. In order to do so, an evaluator needs to be able to understand the logic of the research and to evaluate the quality of the execution of the research methods that are used to supply the backing for each assumption. As the TOEFL validity argument demonstrates, both qualitative and quantitative methods are used to provide backing for assumptions. For example, one assumption underlying the explanation inference is supported through the use of qualitative analysis of learners' strategies during test task completion. Other assumptions are supported though the use of correlations between the test scores and other measures of language ability, structural equation modeling investigating the underlying structure of the abilities tested, and ANOVA to test for significant differences across groups of different ability levels (see Purpura, Chapter 44, this volume). Therefore, an evaluation of a validity argument requires an understanding of a variety of research methods that are used in applied linguistics.

A third approach to evaluating a validity argument is to identify "unless-statements," facts or conditions that would weaken the argument in all or some cases. For example, in the case of the TOEFL validity argument that concludes test scores reflect academic English ability, a possible rebuttal one might make is "unless test takers are unfamiliar with completion of test tasks on a computer." Such a statement alone would not weaken the argument, but if research were conducted that provided support for the statement that such construct irrelevant factors consistently affected test performance, the rebuttal would be supported. This approach to evaluating a validity argument, therefore, requires a good understanding of the specific validity argument, an ability to identify potential rebuttals to the argument, and the capability to undertake credible qualitative or quantitative research that supports a rebuttal.

Conclusion

Many applied linguists wish the rules for validation would remain stationary and provide clear formulas for practice so they could simply use tests in research, classrooms, businesses, and government. For these people, the praxis step may come as welcome news. In my view the news is indeed good; however, it needs to be welcomed with at least three caveats.

The praxis step does indeed provide what is needed to step beyond the complexity of the social turn prompted by Messick's far-reaching perspective in 1989. However, those wishing to step beyond a complex conception of validity and validation probably need to first take the social turn though which they understand the multifaceted notion of validity. In other words, applied linguists who conceive of validity as meaning that the test measures what it is supposed to measure are probably not in the position to take the praxis step. The validity argument outlined by Kane is built from concepts that were presented, reviewed, and richly explored by Messick and others over the past 20 years. In this case, then, "praxis" should not be interpreted to mean "quick and easy," or "immediately accessible." What it does mean is that for professionals in language testing, concepts about validity so richly crystallized by Messick have been rendered usable in Kane's practice-oriented approach to interpretive and validity arguments.

Second, although Kane's argument-based approach to validation provides a means of working around some thorny issues in language testing, it does not preclude the need for applied linguists to be able to define the language constructs they measure. Technically speaking, one can write a validity argument without including an "explanation" inference and therefore without a language construct. However, typically test scores users do want to interpret test scores with reference to test takers' language ability; moreover, other inferences such as domain definition and extrapolation and evaluation are also based on assumptions about the nature of language. In short, regardless of how one presents an interpretive argument for a language tests, one still needs to have an means of defining and analyzing language today as in the past (e.g., Stansfield, 1986). Therefore, even a praxis step in validation does not mean that validity arguments preclude the need for useful and appropriate linguistic analysis.

Third, what I have presented here necessarily simplified what is actually a dynamic area of inquiry in which disagreement exists. The process of wrestling with the complexity of Messick's perspective on validity has sent some researchers back to the safer clarity of the idea that validity should be seen simply as whether or not a test measures what it is intended to measure (e.g., Borsboom, 2006). Some continue to work with Messick's perspective and operationalizing it in a variety of productive ways. Some offer different conceptualizations of validity altogether. The range of perspectives currently in play in educational measurement was brilliantly captured at a conference held at the University of Maryland in 2008, and the resulting papers provide support and detail for the assertion that this as an area that is very much under discussion and revision (Lissitz, 2009).

In the meantime, professionals concerned with language teaching and research are faced with many test uses and validation needs. So praxis oriented are applied linguists' concerns that within the many voices and perspectives currently in play, a praxis-oriented step has attained a status of salience to my eye. I have therefore presented here what appears to be a step that will be taken by many in language testing.

References

AERA/APA/NCME. (1999). *Standards for educational and psychological testing.* Washington, DC: AERA.

Bachman, L. F. (2007). What is the construct? The dialectic of abilities and contexts in defining constructs in language assessment. In J. Fox, M. Wesche & D. Bayliss (Eds.), *What are we measuring? Language testing reconsidered* (pp. 41–71). Ottawa: University of Ottawa Press.

Bachman, L. F. (1990). *Fundamental considerations in language testing.* Oxford: Oxford University Press.

Bachman, L. F. (2002) Alternative interpretations of alternative assessments: Some validity issues in educational performance assessments. *Educational Measurement: Issues and Practice, 21*(3), 5–18.

Bachman, L. F. (2005). Building and supporting a case for test use. *Language Assessment Quarterly, 2*(1), 1–34.

Bachman, L. F., & Palmer, A. S. (1996). *Language testing in practice.* Oxford: Oxford University Press.

Borsboom, D. (2006). The attack of the psychometricians. *Psychometrika, 71*(3), 425–440.

Brennan, R. L. (Ed.) (2006). Perspectives on the evolution and future of educational measurement. In R. Brennen, (Ed.), *Educational measurement* (4th ed.) (pp. 1–16). Westport, CT: Greenwood Publishing.

Briggs, D. C. (2004). Comment: Making an argument for design validity before interpretive validity. *Measurement: Interdisciplinary Research and Perspectives, 2*(3), 171–174.

Chapelle, C. A. (1998). Construct definition and validity inquiry in SLA research. In L. F. Bachman and A. D. Cohen (Eds.), *Interfaces between second language acquisition and language testing research* (pp. 32–70). Cambridge: Cambridge University Press.

Chapelle, C. A., Enright, M. E., & Jamieson, J. (2010). Does an argument-based approach to validity make a difference? *Educational Measurement: Issues and Practice, 29*(1), 3–13.

Chapelle, C. A., Enright, M. K., & Jamieson, J. (Eds.) (2008). *Building a validity argument for the Test of English as a Foreign Language.* London: Routledge.

Cronbach, L. (1988). Five perspectives on validity argument. In H. Wainer & H. Braun (Eds.), *Test validity* (pp. 3–17). Hillsdale, NJ: Lawrence Erlbaum.

Cronbach, L. J., & Meehl, P. E. (1955). Construct validity in psychological tests. *Psychological Bulletin, 52,* 281–302.

Davies, A., & Elder, C. (2005). Validity and validation in language testing. In E. Hinkel (Ed.), *Handbook of research in second language teaching and learning* (pp. 795–813). Mahwah, NJ: Lawrence Erlbaum Associates.

Kane, M. T. (1992). An argument-based approach to validity. *Psychological Bulletin, 112,* 527–535.

Kane, M. T. (2001). Current concerns in validity theory. *Journal of Educational Measurement, 38,* 319–342.

Kane, M. (2006). Validation. In R. Brennen, (Ed.), *Educational measurement* (4th ed.) (pp. 17–64). Westport, CT: Greenwood Publishing.

Kane, M., Crooks, T., & Cohen, A. (1999). Validating measures of performance. *Educational Measurement: Issues and Practice, 18*(2), 5–17.

Lado, R. (1961). *Language testing: The construction and use of foreign language tests.* New York: McGraw Hill.

Lissitz, R. W. (Ed.) (2009). *The concept of validity: Revisions new directions and applications.* Charlotte, NC: Information Age Publishing, Inc.

McNamara, T. (1996). *Measuring second language performance.* London: Longman.

Mislevy, R. J., & Chengbin, Y. (2009). If language is a complex adaptive system, what is language assessment? *Language Learning, 59*(Supplement 1), 249–267.

Mislevy, R. J., Steinberg, L. S., & Almond, R. G. (2003). On the structure of educational assessments. *Measurement: Interdisciplinary Research and Perspectives, 1,* 3–62.

Messick, S. (1989). Validity. In R. L. Linn (Ed.) *Educational measurement* (3rd ed.) (pp. 13–103). New York: Macmillan Publishing Co.

Oller, J. (1979). *Language tests at school.* London: Longman.

Shepard, L. A. (1993). Evaluating test validity. *Review of Research in Education, 19,* 405–450.

Stansfield, C. W. (Ed.) (1986). *Toward communicative competence testing: Proceedings of the second TOEFL invitational conference. TOEFL Research Reports,* 21, Princeton: Educational Testing Service.

Toulmin, S. E. (2003). *The uses of argument* (updated edition). Cambridge: Cambridge University Press.

Weir, C. J. (2005). *Language testing and validation: An evidence-based approach.* Basingstoke: Palgrave Macmillan.

44
Quantitative Research Methods in Assessment and Testing

James E. Purpura

Introduction

Over the years language assessment researchers have provided reflective reviews of the current thinking and practices in the use of quantitative methods in language test validation research (e.g., Palmer, Groot, & Trosper, 1981; Anivan, 1991; Douglas & Chapelle, 1993; Alderson, 1991, 1994; Cumming, 1996; Bachman & Eignor, 1997; Hamp-Lyons & Lynch, 1998; Kunnan, 1998, 1999; Chapelle, 1999; Bachman, 2000; Alderson & Banerjee, 2001, 2002; Lumley & Brown, 2005; Chalhoub-Deville & Deville, 2005, 2008). These reviews have summarized the state of the field and initiated deliberation on where the field might be headed or, in some cases, should be headed. They have also described quantitative research methods used in published research, explained refinements to the current methods along with examples of their applications, and revealed advances in educational measurement with reflections of how new research methods might be applied to questions in language assessment and practice. Finally, some of these reviews (e.g., Palmer et al., 1981; Cumming, 1996; Bachman & Eignor, 1997; Kunnan, 1998; Xi, 2008) have related the use of quantitative methods to the types of validity evidence needed to support or refute claims of particular meanings or uses of language assessments. In this regard, as theories of validation and understandings of language constructs have evolved, so have the methods and associated technologies used to provide evidence of validity claims.

While considerable confusion exists in the literature regarding definitions of quantitative methods, I will use "quantitative methods" to refer collectively to the manner in which data are collected—that is, by means of experimental, quasi-experimental, or non-experimental quantitative designs (e.g., *ex post facto* correlational or survey research designs). Quantitative methods in this chapter also involve the collection of quantitative data regardless of the process used in quantification or the measurement scale used to characterize attributes or abilities. Finally, I use quantitative methods to refer to procedures involving both parametric and nonparametric statistical analysis (Grotjahn, 1987).

The purpose of this chapter is to present concepts, explain practices, and examine trends in the use of quantitative methods for language test validation. As I am neither the first nor will I be last to offer an admittedly biased view of quantitative research methods in language validation research over the years, I will begin by discussing the summaries provided in previous reviews. Then, building on Chapelle's chapter in this volume (Chapter 43), I will discuss validation theories since the 1980s and show how quantitative methods have served to provide validity evidence in language assessment research and practice. In this section, I will examine an argument-based approach to validity in an attempt to relate quantitative research methods in language assessment to the provision of empirical evidence in support of claims or counterclaims in a validity argument.

Prior Reviews of Quantitative Methods in Language Assessment

One set of reviews of quantitative methods (e.g., Douglas & Chapelle, 1993; Alderson, 1991, 1994; Hamp-Lyons & Lynch, 1998; Kunnan, 1998, 1999; Chalhoub-Deville & Deville, 2005, 2008) examined research in the field in order to characterize current trends, point out gaps, and suggest future research directions. For example, Hamp-Lyons and Lynch (1998) surveyed abstracts from the Language Testing Research Colloquium from 1979 to 1994 to examine how validity in language assessment had been conceptualized and investigated. They concluded that while some in-roads had been made for the inclusion of papers drawing on "alternative paradigms" of validity research (i.e., qualitative, ethnographic, discursive, narrative paradigms), language testing research reflected predominately positivist thinking at the time with a strong dependence on psychometric methods to support claims of validity. In a more recent study, Chalhoub-Deville and Deville (2008) surveyed articles in the two major language assessment journals from their beginnings to 2005. They also concluded that while qualitative research methods had indeed begun to appear more frequently in the journals, quantitative data and psychometric methods dominated the language testing research agenda. This set of reviews confirmed the emphasis on quantitative methods in language test validation research and the need to review these methods. At the same time, it highlighted the lack of evidence obtained through qualitative methods that might provide alternative interpretations of language assessment phenomena (Moss, 2003).

A second set of reviews (e.g., Palmer et al., 1981; Bachman & Eignor, 1997; Kunnan, 1999; Bachman, 2000; Lumley & Brown, 2005) described quantitative research methods currently used in the testing literature along with the latest enhancements and their application to language assessment research. For example, Bachman and Eignor (1997) described advances in the 1990s with respect to item response theory (IRT). IRT is a family of statistical models used to estimate the psychometric characteristics of items (e.g., their difficulty level) in concert with characteristics of examinees (e.g., their ability level) in a way that the estimates for the items and examinees are not dependent on any one sample of items or examinees (Hambleton, Swaminathan, & Rogers, 1991). IRT is also used to describe how items, examinees, or other facets of the measurement interact (Yen & Fitzpatrick, 2006). For example, IRT assumes that the chances of an examinee getting an item right on a test is a function of both the difficulty level of the item and the examinee's ability level. It could also be impacted by the severity of the judges scoring performance. Bachman and Eignor were especially interested in how, in the late 1990s, IRT was being used in computer-adaptive testing (CAT), specifically with respect to how test items were selected based not only on statistical constraints, but also on complex test specifications. They explained that these new item-selection procedures were already being used to generate test forms in some large-scale testing programs. Bachman and Eignor further described advances in the use of partial-credit IRT models and their generalized extensions to examine polytomously-scored (i.e., partial credit) data in some language performance tests (Masters, 1982; Muraki, 1992; Linacre, 1989). They reported studies that used simultaneous estimation procedures to examine both dichotomously-scored and polytomously-scored data together (e.g., Tang & Eignor, 1996). Finally, Bachman and Eignor reported on advances in the generation of examinee ability descriptors based on combinations of multiple-choice and constructed-response scores by means of IRT-based scale anchoring (Beaton & Allen, 1992) and a number of other procedures. Many of the topics in their review still have resonance with language testers today.

Kunnan (1999) also reviewed some of the quantitative advances in language testing in the late 1990s, focusing on the use of structural equation modeling (SEM). SEM uses a set of data analysis tools to conceptualize, specify, estimate, and test theoretically-derived hypotheses about substantively meaningful interrelationships among observed and unobserved variables (Bentler, 1992). While SEM had been used in language test validation research as early as 1982 (e.g., Bachman & Palmer, 1982), this method had recently gained in popularity due to the availability of user-friendly computer software. Kunnan described five ways in which structural equation modeling could be used in language assessment research and cited a number of studies at the time that had successfully used SEM to examine the hypothesized factor structure of assessment instruments as well as hypothesized relationships among a range of latent and observed variables in models of second language ability (e.g., Sasaki, 1993; Kunnan, 1995; Purpura, 1996, 1997, 1998; Ginther & Stevens, 1998; Bae & Bachman, 1998).

In a more ambitious accounting of the field of language testing at the turn of the century, Bachman (2000) described how increasingly more powerful quantitative methodologies were used to investigate a range of research questions. He first discussed advances in criterion-reference measurement (see Jamieson, Chapter 46, this volume). Bachman described some of the applications of criterion-referenced (CR) measurement to language test development and analysis (e.g., Hudson & Lynch, 1984; Hudson, 1991, 1993; Lynch & Davidson, 1997; Brown, 1988). He then described generalizability theory (G-theory) along with recent applications of G-theory to language validation research. Drawing on the framework of factorial design and ANOVA (Cronbach, Gleser, Nanda, & Rajaratnam, 1972; Brennan, 1983; Shavelson & Webb, 1991), G-theory is a measurement model used to identify and estimate the variances associated with multiple sources of error (e.g., the severity of the raters) in test scores by examining group-level effects (Wolfe & Dobria, 2008). G-theory has been used to examine rater consistency in oral and written performance assessments (e.g., Bachman, Lynch, & Mason, 1995; Lynch & McNamara, 1998). After that, he discussed IRT applications to language test analysis, noting the growing popularity of many-facet Rasch measurement to examine the simultaneous effects of several facets of measurement in language performance assessments. Finally, Bachman discussed a number of studies that used SEM to investigate the factorial structure of measurement instruments as well as the interrelationships among constructs.

Lumley and Brown (2005) provided brief summaries of four types of quantitative research methods in language assessment research. They first described studies that used simple correlations and some advanced correlational procedures (e.g., multiple linear regression, exploratory factor analysis or structural equation modeling) to examine linear associations among variables or to investigate the effect of observed or latent variables on other such variables. They then reported on studies that had used statistical procedures such as *t*-tests, ANOVA, and MANOVA to compare hypotheses related to differences in scores from two or more groups of test takers. For example, they discussed studies examining differences in essay scores from raters with or without an English as a second language (ESL) background (e.g., Brown, 1991) and differences in scores from examinees responding to different test tasks (e.g., Stansfield & Kenyon, 1992). They also described the use of the Mantel-Haenszel or Mann Whitney procedures for examining the differential functioning of items (DIF) by diverse test-taker groups. Finally, Lumley and Brown reported briefly on studies that used many-facet Rasch measurement—an extension and refinement of Rasch measurement, and G-theory to investigate different sources of variability (i.e., facets) entailed in performance-based assessments. This second set of reviews described some of the latest quantitative methods that had gained currency at the time and provided brief summaries of the studies and the types of questions they were addressing.

A third set of reviews sought to describe language assessment research within a concrete framework of language test validation (e.g., Palmer et al., 1981; Cumming, 1996; Bachman & Eignor, 1997; Kunnan, 1998; Xi, 2008). These studies viewed quantitative methods in language assessment research as a means of providing different types of empirical evidence in the support of claims or counterclaims about test score interpretation or use. Relating language assessment research to a framework of test validation has had a long history in language assessment, and as theories of test validation have evolved, so have the types of research being addressed. Similarly, deeper understandings of language test constructs and the availability of increasingly more sophisticated, user-friendly technologies for test construction, administration, scoring, and analysis, have also impacted the types of validation studies conducted to provide empirical support of validity. In the next section, I will discuss three theories of validation that have impacted language assessment research. With each theory, I will discuss the role that quantitative methods have played in justifying—or refuting—claims of test validity.

Relating Quantitative Methods to Theories of Test Validation

Quantitative Methods and the Trinitarian Model of Test Validity

In the early 1980s, validation was defined in terms of the trinitarian notion of validity (Cronbach, 1971; Guion, 1980), where score-based interpretations were justified by providing evidence of content, concurrent/predictive, and construct validity. In language assessment, Palmer et al. (1981) used the trinitarian framework of validity in their edited volume to organize studies designed to investigate tests of communicative competence. Several studies used quantitative methods to provide evidence of reliability and validity. In an inquiry of the concurrent validity of a cloze test and an oral interview, Shohamy (1981) used Cronbach's alpha to provide evidence of high inter-rater reliability. She then used correlations to provide evidence of high intra-rater reliability to show a strong relationship between the oral interview and the cloze tasks. Hinofotis, Bailey, and Stern (1981), in developing an instrument to measure the oral proficiency of international teaching assistants, used correlations and ANOVA to examine the consistency of rater judgments. They then used multiple linear regression to examine which components of speaking ability best predicted the ratings in several aspects of the rating scales. These analyses led to several refinements in the scales used to assess speaking ability.

Finally, two studies in the volume, Clifford (1981) and Bachman and Palmer (1981) were conducted in response to Oller's (1976, 1979) influential studies, which had led to the hypothesis that language proficiency was a unitary trait. Oller's research used exploratory factor analysis (EFA) to provide evidence in support the hypothesis. EFA involves "a variety of statistical techniques whose common objective is to represent a set of variables in terms of a smaller number of hypothetical [i.e., latent] variables" (Kim & Mueller, 1978, p. 9). In EFA terms, confirmation of the unitary trait hypothesis would result in a one-factor solution of multiple observed variables. In these studies Oller factor analyzed scores obtained from a wide range of task types in order to understand the factor structure of tests designed to measure listening, speaking, reading, writing, and grammatical ability. In each analysis, Oller found that the pattern of loadings in the factor structure favored a unitary competence hypothesis. While technical concerns with Oller's implementation of EFA presented serious concerns for a unitary trait hypothesis (Farhardy, 1983; Volmer & Sang, 1983), EFA became a valuable quantitative method in language test validation.

Clifford (1981) and Bachman and Palmer (1981) analyzed a multi-trait-multimethod matrix of correlations, based on the work of Campbell and Fiske (1967), to examine hypotheses regarding the convergent and divergent validity of tests. Clifford (1981) examined convergent and divergent validity of four components of language proficiency and two test methods, whereas Bachman and Palmer (1981) investigated the convergent and divergent validity of six tests of speaking and writing ability and three test methods. Both studies concluded that test performance is influenced by both the traits being measured and the methods used to measure them. Both studies, along with later studies (Bachman & Palmer, 1982; Harley, Allen, Cummins, & Swain, 1990), showed support for the componentiality of language proficiency. Thus, the validation evidence in these studies was offered to support the "accuracy of a specific prediction or inference made from a test score" (Cronbach, 1971, p. 443) based on a theory of language proficiency.

Quantitative Methods and Test Validity as a Unified Notion

The notion of "validity" was refined in the fourth edition of the *Standards for Educational and Psychological Testing* (AERA, APA, & NCME, 1985), where it is defined as the "appropriateness, meaningfulness and usefulness of the specific inferences made from test scores" (p. 9) and "validation" involved "the process of accumulating evidence to support such inferences" (p. 9). Messick (1989) proposed a progressive matrix (see Table 44.1) for examining a "unified notion of validity" in which construct validity plays a central role. In his framework, the process of validation entails collection of evidence that can justify the interpretation of test scores as an indicator of some ability being tested (i.e., construct-related evidence of validity). Evidence is also gathered to support the value implications associated with this interpretation—for example, the implications of classifying a person in terms of high or low speaking ability based on a score from an oral proficiency interview. The assessment is then examined for relevance or utility. In other words, if the scores from a speaking test are generated by scoring a prospective international teaching assistants' (ITAs) ability to use grammatical and phonological resources to deliver content intelligibly in class, logical rationales, or empirical evidence are needed to show that these resources are relevant to being an effective ITA. Finally, the social consequences of test use need examining. For example, what are the social consequences of basing decisions on our score-based interpretations or what are the potentially beneficial and harmful consequences of using our scores to certify that an examinee has the required level of speaking ability to teach at a university? In sum, Messick viewed validity as "an inductive summary of both the existing evidence for and the potential consequences of score interpretation and use" (p. 13).

Messick's (1989) unified notion of validity has served as a valuable framework for language test validation. Researchers have attempted to use theory and supporting empirical evidence to justify interpretations of test scores for a specific purpose and the use of these score-based inferences to make decisions. Much of the supporting evidence has been obtained through a wide range of quantitative methods. To illustrate, Douglas and Chapelle (1993) published an edited volume of papers from the 1990 Language Testing Research Colloquium in which they classified studies according to Messick's notion of validity. Eleven of the 13 studies used quantitative analysis as supporting evidence. Clapham (1993) used repeated measures analysis of variance (ANOVA) and repeated measures multivariate analysis of variance (MANOVA) to examine whether students in three groups reading texts within their subject area (along with texts from two other subject areas) scored significantly higher than those outside it. She concluded that, in fact, subject area (not background knowledge) seemed to have no deleterious effect on reading scores. Hudson (1993) used two-parameter IRT to examine the internal structure of items and skills on a reading test, concluding that different levels of gram-

Table 44.1 Progressive Matrix of Validity

	Test interpretation	**Test use**
Evidential basis	Construct validity	Construct validity + relevance/utility
Consequential basis	Construct validity + value implications	Construct validity + relevance/utility + value implications + social consequences

Messick (1989).

matical knowledge are essential to process text at different reading ability levels. Bachman, Davidson, and Foulkes (1993) used several quantitative methods to examine the comparability of abilities measured by University of Cambridge *First Certificate of English (FCE)* (University of Cambridge ESOL) and Educational Testing Service's *Test of English as a Foreign Language, the Test of Written English and the Test of Spoken English*. They used descriptive statistics to examine central tendencies, variabilities, and differences between the measures, KR20 to examine internal consistency reliability, and EFA to investigate the second-order factor structure of each exam battery. They concluded that the two test batteries appeared to measure similar constructs, thereby making it justifiable to make meaningful score comparisons. However, they noted that such comparisons must be made cautiously given the levels of reliability across the two tests and the lack of parallel form equivalence in the *FCE*. Finally, in an impressive study designed to create a CR language testing program, Brown (1994) used a variety of quantitative methods to analyze two forms of a CR test administered in a counterbalanced design at the beginning and end of the semester. Exams were created for two levels in the reading and listening classes, and three in the writing classes. Descriptive statistics were used to examine central tendencies and variablilities across the different level tests within each class. Item statistics were investigated by means of three quantitative methods: norm-reference (NR) testing procedures (e.g., item facility and item discrimination), CR procedures (e.g., estimates for the difference index, item phi, *B*-index, and item agreement index), and two-parameter IRT procedures (e.g., item difficulty and discrimination estimates). Consistency was examined by two method: NR test procedures (Cronbach's alpha, split-half adjusted, and Guttman estimates) and CR test procedures (ϕ domain score dependability index and ϕ [λ] squared-error loss agreement coefficient). Brown concluded that the quantitative analyses provided complementary information, noting that the CR test indices appear to be more useful for pass–fail decisions than the analogous NR test reliability estimates.

Cumming and Berwick (1996) also prepared an edited volume on validation in language testing in which studies were organized around Messick's unified concept of validity. Several studies used quantitative methods to provide evidence of all four cells in Messick's matrix. For example, to provide evidence of construct validity, Milanovich, Saville, Pollitt, and Cook (1996) and Tyndall and Kenyon (1996) used many-facet Rasch measurement to examine the functionality of newly-developed rating scales. Weigle and Lynch (1996) used MANOVA to examine hypotheses regarding differences between graduate students' and immigrant undergraduates' performance on a formal grammar test and subtests of a newly designed ESL placement test. As for evidence of test relevance and utility, Stansfield and Kenyon's (1996) paper used many-facet Rasch analysis to investigate French, Spanish, and bilingual education teachers' perceptions regarding the level of difficulty needed to perform tasks of differing levels of complexity, as hypothesized in the ACTFL proficiency scales. Results showed that while teachers were able to distinguish among the 38 speaking tasks, considerable variability in the scaling by the French and Spanish teachers on the one hand and the bilingual teachers on the other was observed.

Kunnan (1998) also used Messick's validity framework to categorize validation research from approximately 1980 to 1997, identifying a number of themes within each quadrant. In providing an evidential basis for test interpretation, he identified the themes of investigating proficiency components of language ability, test dimensionality, studies related to test development, and validation of specific exams or methods used to present validity evidence. Then, in providing an evidential basis for test use, he described studies examining test relevance and utility. The themes in this section included test-taking processes, test-taking strategies, and a wide range of test taker characteristics. In supplying a consequential basis for test interpretation, Kunnan identified studies that examined value systems differences, mostly where test takers were asked to report on some aspect of the testing process. Finally, with regard to a consequential basis for test use, he highlighted studies involving social consequences of tests and washback, ethics, standards and equality, and alternative assessment approaches. The predominant means of providing support for validity claims in these studies was through quantitative methods. While most studies obviously used descriptive statistics, classical test analyses, and simple correlation, a few used ANOVA, MANOVA, and multiple linear regression. The majority, however, used sophisticated statistical procedures such as factor analysis, multi-trait multi-method analysis, Rasch measurement, G-theory, or structural equation modeling.

While Messick's (1989) validity framework has been useful for generating and organizing logical and empirical evidence for the purpose of a unified evaluative judgment of language test validation, testing researchers (e.g., Bachman, 2005; Chapelle, Enright, & Jamieson, 2008), drawing on Cronbach (1988), Kane (1992, 2001, 2006) and Kane, Crooks, and Cohen (1999) currently conceptualize validity as an argument involving multiple inferences in a chain of inferences and implications.

Quantitative Methods and the Argument-Based View of Test Validity

In order for researchers to justify the proposed interpretation and use of test scores for decision-making purposes, Kane (2006) proposed the formulation of two kinds of arguments: an interpretative argument and a validity argument (see Chapelle, Chapter 43, this volume). "An *interpretative argument* specifies the proposed interpretations and uses of test results by laying out the network of inferences and assumptions leading from the observed performances to the conclusions and decisions based on the performance" (Kane, 2006, p. 23). In other words, the interpretative argument makes explicit the inferences that need to be made (and ultimately supported) prior to using score-based interpretations for decision-making. According to Bachman (2005), Kane (2006), and Chapelle et al. (2008), the chain of inferences in the interpretative argument can include: domain description, scoring (or evaluation), generalization, explanation, extrapolation, and utilization. In the interpretative argument, each of these inferences is associated with certain assumptions, or warrants, that must also be explicitly identified, and each assumption is supported with logical or empirical backing (in the validity argument).

In language assessment, the interpretative argument makes explicit several types of inferences and assumptions that link language test performance to the use of score-based interpretations for assessment purposes. As seen in Figure 44.1, the *domain description* inference links performance in the target domain to the sample of observations on the test (Chapelle et al., 2008). This inference assumes that the performance sample entailed in the completion of the task reflects the relevant knowledge, abilities, and skills one would expect to find in the target domain. It also assumes that the language and processes invoked by these tasks can be specified so that similar tasks can be generated. Another inference in the network connects a sample of performance on a language assessment to an observed score. This is referred to as *scoring* and is based on the assumption that construct-relevant observations of language performance have been elicited from examinees and that the procedures used to convert these samples to scores are appropriate, consistent, accurate, and bias free. Another inference in the network is *generalization*, which links the examinees' observed score to their expected score (i.e., their "universe" or "true" score) across equivalent tasks, occasions, administration conditions, and scoring procedures. This inference assumes that if examinees receive tasks drawn from a pool of possible tasks within a specified domain of generalization, then their observed score would generalize to their expected score on equivalent tasks from that domain.

Another inference in the network links this expected score to the underlying theoretical test construct.[1] This inference is referred to as *explanation* and assumes that consistencies in the performance can be attributed to an underlying construct (Chapelle et al., 2008). This inference also relates to how the construct is affected by a web of other observed and latent variables (e.g., grammatical knowledge, strategic competence, exposure to the second language culture), how the construct (e.g., second language pragmatic ability) may change over time or across different groups, or how the construct's underlying structure accounts for test score variability. Next, the construct is linked to the "target" score—that is, the score that an examinee might receive for real-life language use. This inferential link is called *extrapolation*, and refers to the extent to which performance on a test (reflected in the construct) is comparable to performance on real-life tasks in terms of both the underlying processes and the underlying knowledge, abilities, and skills engaged in task completion. This inference assumes that performance on test tasks (e.g., a report writing task) compares favorably to performance on appropriate criterion measures drawn from the target language use domain (e.g., writing a real lab report). The final inference, *utilization*, connects the target score to test use[2] (Bachman, 2005). This inference extends the interpretation of score meaning to the use of test scores for "beneficial, fair, and equitable" decision-making in a wide range of educational, social, cultural, political, ethical, economic, technological, and legal contexts (Kunnan, 2008; Shohamy & McNamara, 2009). In other words, the utilization inference assumes that test score use for decision-making can be justifiably used when the introduction and use of assessments incur intended, beneficial, and fair consequences for stakeholders (Kunnan, 2000; Taylor & Weir, 2009), operating in contexts ranging from an examinee's individual language learning (Purpura, 2009) to contexts that involve international migration (Saville, 2009).

Based on Kane (2006) with refinements made by Chapelle et al. (2008) and Bachman (2005), Figure 44.1 represents the measurement procedure and interpretative argument for trait interpretation.

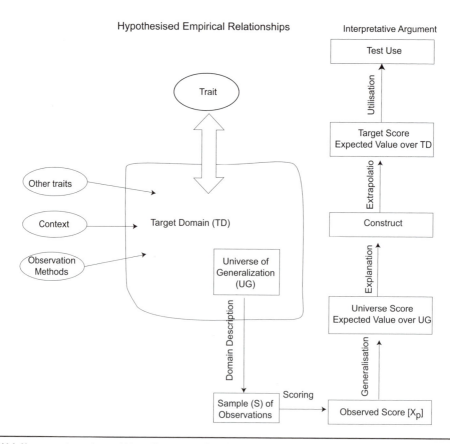

Figure 44.1 Measurement procedure and interpretive argument for trait interpretation

Based on Bachman (2005); Chapelle et al. (2008, p. 15); and Kane (2006, p. 33).

Once the chain of inferences leading from performance to claims of trait interpretation and use has been laid out along with its supporting assumptions, the argument is evaluated by means of a *validity argument*. A validity argument provides a coherent means by which to assess the plausibility of the theoretical and empirical evidence used to support or refute the inferences and assumptions associated with a proposed test interpretation or use (Kane, 2006). For example, if the interpretative argument includes claims about the interchangeability of raters in a performance assessment, then the validity argument should evaluate the dependability of this generalization across raters. Or if the interpretative argument includes a claim that the underlying test construct accounts for regularities in performance, then the validity argument should evaluate the appropriateness of the trait indicators in terms of the factor loadings and model-data fit. Finally, if the interpretative argument includes claims about the stability of examinee attributes across different demographic groups, then evidence for the invariance of scores across these groups would contribute to the plausibility of that claim. In providing theoretical and empirical evidence to support or refute inferences and assumptions leading from performance to trait interpretation and use, the validity argument offers multiple opportunities for the use of quantitative methods.

Quantitative Research Methods as Evidence in a Validity Argument

Xi (2008) provided an excellent overview of both qualitative and quantitative methods used to provide empirical evidence in support of validity inferences and assumptions in an argument-based approach to language test validation. While her study did not draw on the exact same validity framework depicted in Figure 44.1, this chapter builds on Xi's work focusing specifically on quantitative methods and the types of empirical supports they provide in the validity argument.

Domain Description Inference: From the Target Domain to the Performance Sample

The domain description inference links performance in the target domain to performance that can be elicited and measured in assessment tasks. In other words, domain description involves the identification and description of tasks in the TLU domain, which reflect the types of language and processes one would like to measure in the assessment context. A wide variety of quantitative methods have been used to provide backing for inferences about the domain description inference, including descriptive statistics, frequency analyses, ANOVA and other group comparison statistical procedures, chi-square, correlations, factor analysis, and many more.

Such studies involve the collection and examination of language corpora or surveys of features in the TLU domain. To describe features of language use in the academic English domain for use in the TOEFL, Biber et al. (2004) examined the linguistic patterns of register variation in academic speaking and writing at universities in the United States. They generated a spoken corpus of 1,665,500 words and a written corpus of 2,737,200 words. They then tagged the words for specific lexico-grammatical features. Several methods were used to analyze the data quantitatively. Token counts of words and lexical bundles (i.e., four-word sequences) were tabulated, frequencies calculated, and register differences and distributional factors examined. Then, EFA was used to investigate the underlying dimensions of variation in the data, followed by a comparison of the registers, disciplines, and levels of the corpus data. Finally, ANOVA was used to test differences among the university registers with respect to the mean dimension scores.

In another corpus study aimed at describing the TLU domain, Neff-VanAertselaer (2008) examined the use of metadiscourse strategies in the construction of persuasive texts by Spanish and English expert writers. In order to understand group differences in pragmatic-rhetorical metadiscourse strategies, she tagged three interpersonal markers (i.e., hedges, certainty markers, and attitude markers) in the English–Spanish contrastive corpus of argumentative texts and tested their differences by means of chi-square. Chi-square is a nonparametric, statistical procedure used with count data (frequencies, proportions, probabilities, or percentages) to test whether the observed frequencies in these categories differ from the expected ones (Shavelson, 1981). Neff-VanAertselaer's study provided an interesting description of the cross-linguistic differences and genre characterizations of Spanish and Anglo writers' attempts to persuade—descriptions that testers might expect to observe in performance samples of persuasive texts.

Scoring Inference: From the Observed Performance to the Observed Score

The scoring inference links a sample of performance on a language assessment to an observed score. This inference is based on the assumption that performance on tasks provides observed scores that are viable samples of the test construct. Empirical backing to support assumptions about the scoring inference might come from studies of the effect of test task characteristics (e.g., variations in task input or expected response characteristics) on scores, the impact of test administration conditions (e.g., variations in test medium such as computer vs. pencil-and-paper) on performance, the influence of the scoring method (e.g., variations in rater background) on performance, and the lack of test bias—more commonly referred to as "differential item functioning" (DIF). Further backing might involve scaling studies and studies examining the fit of data to model expectations.

Language testing researchers have performed countless studies since the 1990s designed to provide backing for scoring assumptions. Several researchers have used ANOVA and other group-comparison methods, multidimensional scaling, and a range of statistical procedures used to investigate DIF. Ferne and Rupp (2007), in an excellent synthesis of DIF research in language testing, defined DIF as "the statistical detection of potentially biased items" (p. 114). Some procedures to detect DIF are rooted to classical test theory, such as Mantel-Haenzel and Generalized Mantel-Haenzel (Su & Wang, 2005) and logistic regression (Swaminathan & Rogers, 1990) while others are grounded in IRT. The vast majority of language testing studies investigating the scoring inference have used many-facet Rasch measurement.

Test Method and Performance

Several studies have investigated the effects of test method characteristics on performance (see Bachman, 1990). Kobayashi (2002) investigated the effect of differences in text organization (i.e., association, causation, description, problem-solving) and response format (cloze, open-ended versus summary writing) on reading proficiency levels (high, medium, low). The mean differences were tested by means of one- and two-way ANOVA. The results showed that these methods had a clear effect on scores.

In a study examining the effect of channel differences on listening test performance, Wagner (2006) administered three dialogue and three lecturette listening tasks to two groups of students. One group saw the video and the other had audio only. He used multivariate analysis of variance (MANOVA) and multivariate analysis of covariance (MANCOVA) to test differences in students' listening test scores, finding that the video group outperformed the audio-only group. MANOVA is an extension of univariate analysis of variance (ANOVA), and is used to simultaneously test differences among groups on more than one dependent variable (Pedhazur, 1982). MANCOVA is used when the initial difference among groups are found to be statistically different. This procedure permits the measurement of the dependent variable to be adjusted for these initial differences (Hatch & Lazaraton, 1991).

In'nami and Koizumi (2009), in an effort to examine assumptions related to the scoring inference, investigated the effect of task format (multiple-choice and open-ended tasks) on first language reading, second language reading, and second language listening test performance by conducting a meta-analysis. A meta-analysis is a set of quantitative methods designed to synthesize empirical research evidence across a sample of studies that focus on a specific topic or hypothesis (Hedges & Olkin, 1985). In these studies estimates of effect size (e.g., standardized mean difference, a correlation coefficient or an odds ratio) are first calculated as indicators of magnitude of association for the variable of interest (Konstantopoulos, 2008). Then, the effect size estimates are combined and tested for significance, producing a summary indicator of the relationship across the studies. In In'nami and Koizumi's study, the mean effect size estimates for the effects of format differences in first language reading, second language reading, and second language listening from five data sources were computed. The aggregate effect size was then computed by means of the mixed effects model, which assumes variability across studies due to specific characteristics of the studies or to other unaccounted sources of variability. Their results showed that multiple-choice formats were easier than open-ended formats in first language reading and second language listening, but with second language reading multiple-choice formats were easier in only some conditions.

Finally, Weigle (1998) examined the scoring inference by investigating the effects of raters with varying degree of experience (novice and expert) on writing performance using analytic rating scale. The analyses were performed by means of many-facet Rasch measurement (MFRM) (Linacre, 2006). MFRM is a probabilistic mathematic model within IRT that estimates an examinee's performance as a function of both the ability of the test taker and the difficulty of the item. MFRM is also capable of simultaneously estimating other sources of variability (e.g., rater severity) (i.e., *facets*) in the assessment context that might impact scores. MFRM, unlike two- or three-parameter IRT, is able to analyze items scored partial credit or tasks scored by means of a rating scale.

Test Administration Conditions and Performance

Test administration conditions may also have a direct impact on performance associated with the test construct described in the target domain, and fluctuations in test administration conditions may introduce extraneous sources of variability into the scores. Coniam (2005) investigated claims that wearing a face mask during a speaking test as a result of the SARS epidemic in Hong Kong would have a negative impact on speaking scores. To examine this, he asked examinees to perform a role-play and have group discussion with and without a mask. Their performance was then judged by two raters on six scales. The data were analyzed by means of a five-facet design using MFRM. The facets were: rater severity, the test takers' speaking ability, difficulty of the input prompts, scale difficulty, and the differential performance of groups with or without the mask. The results suggested that wearing a face mask did not have a negative effect on speaking scores.

Other studies using MFRM include Davis' (2009) examination of the effect of interlocutor proficiency (high/low with high/low) on examinee speaking performance when engaged in a paired oral test. Bonk and Ockey (2003) investigated the performance of Japanese students of English engaged in a group discussion task across two consecutive administrations of the test. An examination of the facets across these administrations showed that group oral testing might provide a viable and efficient means of measuring speaking ability. Wigglesworth (1997) investigated the use of use of planning time on speaking scores for high- and low-proficiency level test takers in the context of semi-direct oral assessment. MFRM was used to provide difficulty estimates for each task on each criterion so that a hierarchy of task difficulty could be established prior to subsequent analyses of the grammar.

Test administration conditions and performance have also been investigated by means of MANCOVA. Ockey (2009) used MANCOVA to investigate the extent to which assertive and non-assertive test takers' scores were affected by the levels of assertiveness of their group members. The study failed to find an effect for grouping based on assertiveness for non-assertive test takers' scores.

Scoring Method and Performance

Many of studies of scoring have focused on the consistency and accuracy of scoring, the absence of bias, the development and evaluation of scoring rubrics, the appropriateness of scoring procedures for the performance elicited, and the training and monitoring of rater performance. For example, looking at rater consistency and the extent to which rater judgments might constitute a source of measurement error, Kondo-Brown (2002) used MFRM to examine the consistency with which trained teachers judged certain types of candidates and several components of Japanese writing performance. She detected significant bias patterns in many of the raters. She also looked at the viability of using a rating scale for measuring Japanese writing ability. Schaefer (2008) used Rasch-based bias analysis to explore rater interaction patterns of native English-speaker raters when rating English as a foreign language (EFL) essays with a six-category analytic rating scale. Bias was identified by means of rater-rubric interactions and rater–writer interactions. Lumley and O'Sullivan (2001) and O'Loughlin (2002) used MFRM to examine the impact of gender in oral proficiency scores, and Brown (1995) compared the effect of rating behavior of raters from different professional and linguistics backgrounds on test performance. Finally, Di Gennaro (2009) used MFRM to look at differences in writing performance of international (IL2) and generation 1.5 (G1.5) students. The results showed the differences were only detected in their score for rhetorical control.

In an attempt to discern the relationship between different rater types, their background, and their scoring patterns on a standardized test, Eckes (2008) asked experienced raters to judge the importance of certain categories (e.g., correctness, fluency, train of thought) in the rating scale. MFRM analyses revealed very different views on these categories. Then, a two-mode cluster analysis was performed to test three rater type hypotheses. According to Eckes (2008) "the general goal of cluster analysis is to construct a common categorical representation of two different sets of elements such as a set of raters and a set of scoring criteria" (p. 165). The results showed that with respect to the importance of the criteria, six rater types (from a pool of 64 raters) were identified and their scoring profiles appeared to be related to their background variables (e.g., age, years abroad).

Other studies examining the scoring inference have focused on the development and examination of rating scales. Upshur and Turner (1999) used two empirically-derived rating scales to assess grammatical accuracy and communicative effectiveness of a story-retell and an audiotaped letter task. Empirically-derived rating scales were constructed by means of binary questions relating to boundaries between categories on a rating scale. They used MFRM in a three-facet (examinee, rater, task), partial credit design to examine the step structure of the scales. When rater-task bias analyses were performed, they found, in fact, interactions among the raters, tasks, and scales.

Chalhoube-Deville (1995) also examined the scoring inference by investigating the criteria/dimensions of a holistic rating scale, designed to measure Arabic as a foreign language (AFL) speaking ability, across three tasks and three rater groups. The ratings were analyzed by means of speech sample analysis, regression and INDSCAL multidimensional scaling models. Multidimensional scaling, similar to EFA, is an exploratory, data reduction/clustering procedure used to determine the number of underlying dimensions that exist in interval or ordinal data. This procedure provides graphic representations of variable coordinates that cluster together in a given space, allowing the researcher to label the dimensions (Hatch & Lazaraton, 1991). With a nonmetric, three-dimensional solution as the best fit to the data, Chalhoube-Deville found that the rater groups were perceiving the speaking performance samples differentially.

More recently, assumptions relating to the scoring inference have been examined by investigating the use of automated engines for scoring constructed-response data. To do this, two studies (Xi, Higgins, Zechner, & Williamson, 2008; De Jong, Lenning, Kerkhoff, & Poelmans, 2009) examined scoring algorithms to ensure that automated scores accurately represent the performance and correspond to human assigned scores. This was examined by means of reliability analysis, correlation analysis, and multiple linear regression.

Generalization: From the Observed Score to the Universe Score

The generalization inference links the examinees' observed score to their "expected" score. This is based on the assumption that if examinees are given tasks similar to other test tasks in the domain, then their observed scores on these tasks should be considered an estimate of their expected scores if certain conditions of the assessment varied. According to Kane (2006), the degree to which scores can be assumed to generalize over replications of the measurement procedure is a function of the facets in the procedure allowed to vary. Thus, scores should be comparable regardless of which test form or equivalent task examinees are given, or which rater judges the performance. Empirical backing for these assumptions might come from studies on the consistency or dependability of scores across a sample of observations, from the stability of the performance estimates based on the optimal number of tasks or raters, and from the precision of the scores in light of estimates of the standard error of measurement. Further backing might come from scaling and norming or linking and equating studies. Some quantitative methods used to provide backing for the generalization inference include reliability analyses, IRT, and, more recently, generalizability theory and SEM.

Brown (1999) examined the generalizability inference by investigating relative contributions of person ability, item difficulty, subtest difficulty, first language differences and their interactions to TOEFL score dependability (analogous to classical theory reliability). The analyses included descriptive statistics, classical theory reliability estimates, and a series of generalizability studies conducted to examine estimates of the variance components attributed to persons, items, subtests and languages, and their relative effects on test dependability. The results showed that language differences alone accounted for a small proportion of the variance when estimates of other sources of variance were modeled simultaneously.

More recently, several studies in language testing (Sawaki, 2003; Lee & Cantor, 2005; Lee, 2006; Park, 2007; Liao, 2009) have examined the generalizability inference by means of multivariate generalizability (MG) theory. MG theory is used in situations where more than one trait is evaluated simultaneously as it provides information on multiple universe scores, derived from analytic scoring situations, and allows for the inspection of the universe score correlations (Brennan, 2001).

In a study on the generalizability of speaking test scores, Grabowski (2009) examined the extent to which scores at different proficiency levels were affected by grammatical ability (i.e., accuracy, meaningfulness) and pragmatic ability (i.e., sociolinguistic, sociocultural, and psychological appropriateness) as opposed to method factors (i.e., task types). The examinees took four reciprocal, role-play tasks designed to elicit sociolinguistic, sociocultural, and psychological meanings. Grabowski used MG theory to examine the relative effects of examinees, raters, and tasks on total score variability (and dependability) and to investigate simultaneously the rating scales across the four tasks. She also used MFRM to examine claims about the equivalence of the facets (raters, tasks, scales) prior to making generalizations about the test takers' ability or their proficiency levels. Her results, drawing also on an interactional sociolinguistics analysis, showed differential contributions of each subscale to the composite universe score variance, suggesting that each subscale was important for measurement purposes. She also found that the grammatical knowledge subscale was the most stable across the proficiency levels, but grammar was increasingly more important at the lower levels, while pragmatics was increasingly more important at the upper ones.

Kim (2009) also examined the generalizability inference by investigating claims relating to the effects of variations in context and task type on speaking tasks. Students took eight semi-direct, speaking tasks (independent and integrated skills), which represented the academic and general TLU domains. Speaking ability was judged on six scales (grammatical, discourse, sociolinguistic competence, intelligibility, meaningfulness, and task completion). MG theory was used to examine the effects of rating and tasks on the dependability of speaking scores. Kim also investigated the dependability of scores for the academic and general domains and for the independent and integrated tasks. Finally, the relationships between the different contexts and task types were examined. Following these analyses, Kim modeled these relationships in a multi-trait, multi-method structural equation model, where the analytic components of the rubric were the traits and context and task type variables were the method. The results showed considerable variation in scores according to domain and task type. More specifically, she found that grammatical competence and intelligibility seemed stable across different domains and task types, while sociolinguistic competence and task completion showed greater variation. She also found that grammatical competence was relatively constant across tasks, suggesting that it could be a more accurate predictor of second language ability than the other components.

Explanation: From the Expected Score to the Construct

The explanation inference links the expected score to the underlying test construct, and is based on the assumption that regularities in the observed scores on target-like tasks reflect the trait(s) or constructs being measured (Chapelle et al., 2008). Explanation also assumes the internal structure of the test is consistent with the theory of the construct and that the nature of the construct might be affected by change over time (due to an intervention, for example) or across group differences. Several researchers (Kunnan, 1995; Bae & Bachman, 1998; Sawaki, 2007; Phakiti, 2003, 2008) have examined this inference over the years by using SEM. Other methods (e.g., correlation, multiple regression, EFA, path analysis, MG theory, IRT, and hierarchical linear modeling) have also been used as support for the explanation inference.

To examine the explanation inference with respect to the University of Cambridge *FCE*, Purpura (1997) investigated the relationships between strategy use and second language test performance. Examinees took the *FCE* anchor test and a Cognitive and Metacognitive Strategy Questionnaire. Analyses were performed by means of reliability analyses, EFL, and SEM. The results produced a model of the *FCE* that showed lexico-grammatical knowledge to be an extremely strong predictor of reading ability. The strategy use model showed that metacognitive strategy use had a strong direct effect on cognitive strategy use. The results also showed that metacognitive strategy use had a strong, positive effect on cognitive strategy use, but no direct effect on performance. Cognitive strategy use, however, had a mixed effect on lexico-grammatical ability, and no direct effect on reading ability, suggesting that the more examinees invoked memory strategies in the context of a test-taking, the worse they performed, and the less they used the memory strategies, the better they performed.

Purpura (1998) then used multi-group SEM to examine the differential effects of strategy use and second language test performance with high- and low-ability test takers. Separate baseline models of strategy use and second language performance were first established for each group. These models were then estimated simultaneously with cross-group equality constraints imposed. The similarities and differences in this multi-group model provided the means for evaluating the viability of the parameter estimates across ability levels. The results showed that the metacognitive strategy use and second language performance models produced almost identical factorial structures for each group, while the cognitive strategy use models were somewhat different. In fact, the two underlying models of strategy use were similar with the low-ability model being much less parsimonious than the high-ability model. The data provided evidence of cross-group invariance when it came to the effect of lexico-grammatical ability on reading ability, but as expected, the hypotheses of cross-group invariance with regard to the effects of metacognitive strategy use on cognitive strategy use for high and low-ability examinees did not hold.

Sawaki, Stricker, and Oranje (2009) investigated the factor structure of the Test of English as a Foreign Language™ Internet-based test (TOEFL® iBT) by means of an item-level confirmatory factor analysis. The data were modeled as a higher-order factor model with one higher-order general factor (ESL/EFL ability) and four first-order factors representing reading, listening, speaking, and writing ability. Integrated speaking and writing tasks defined the modalities. The results supported the current practice of reporting a total score and four modality scores. They also supported the claim that the integrated tasks contributed only to the scores of the target modalities.

In a more recent study, Ameriks (2009) provided support for the generalizability and explanation inferences in her study examining the comparability of the underlying trait structure of the two forms of one section of the University of Michigan *Examination for the Certificate of Proficiency in English (ECPE)*. Separate baseline models of the hypothesized relationships between lexico-grammatical knowledge and reading ability were modeled in both forms using confirmatory factor analysis. The results produced identical factorial models, suggesting that the forms were comparable when modeled separately. The two models were then estimated simultaneously to test the invariance of the parameters across both forms by means of multi-group SEM. The results surprisingly showed that invariance across forms could not be supported, raising questions about the equivalence of the underlying structure across test forms.

Finally, Llosa (2007) examined the extent to which standards-based assessments of English language development used in language classrooms measure the same constructs as the statewide standardized English proficiency test. These relationships were modeled in a multi-trait, multi-method design and examined longitudinally over three years. The findings showed that the classroom-based assessments were consistent with those provided by the standardized exam.

Extrapolation: From the Construct to Target (Real-Life) Score

The extrapolation inference relates the examinee's universe score to the score s/he might receive for performance on real life tasks. This inference is based on the assumption that performance on test tasks compares favorably to performance on representative criterion measures drawn from the TLU domain. Backing for this assumption might be provided by evidence that a high score on a test corresponds to effective performance on corresponding real-like tasks that engage the same knowledge, ability, and skills.

Sawaki and Nissan (2009) investigated the extrapolation assumption in a study investigating the relationship between scores from the listening section of the TOEFL® iBT and three videotaped lectures created by content experts at the university. These criterion measures and the TOEFL® iBT were given to examinees, and high correlations were observed between the measures. Also, the mean scores of the criterion measures for different ability groups showed that those who scored high on the TOEFL scored well on the criterion measures.

Xi (2007) also examined the extrapolation inference by investigating the use of TOEFL®iBT scores as a screening measure for ITAs. The TOEFL®iBT scores were correlated with scores from the local ITA screening tests or with teacher recommendations. High observed correlations suggested that the TOEFL could be used as a screening device for ITAs.

Utilization: From the Target (Real-Life) Score to Test Use

The utilization inference links the target score to the use of that score for decision-making purposes (Bachman, 2005). It assumes that scores can be justifiably used to make appropriate decisions about examinees, and that the score-based decisions are meaningful and appropriate (Messick, 1989). This inference also assumes that information provided to stakeholders is relevant, useful, and sufficient for stakeholders to make appropriate decisions (Bachman, 2005). Finally, it assumes that the consequences of using these scores for decision-making are beneficial, fair, and equitable in relevant contexts (Kunnan, 2008; Shohamy & McNamara, 2009).

Several studies have provided evidence of the utilization inference by investigating assumptions related to decision-making based on score-based interpretations (e.g., Cheng, Klinger, & Zheng, 2007; Liao, 2009). Liao (2009) sought to understand classification decisions related to performance on the *General English Proficiency Test (GEPT)* (LTTC, 2004) in Taiwan by means of discriminant analysis. Discriminant analysis is a statistical procedure used for describing group differences and for classifying cases into groups based on multiple predictors (Stevens, 2002, cited in Liao, 2009). Since the *GEPT* distinguished masters (those who pass the exam) from non-masters (those who fail it), Liao examined the extent to which predictor variables (grammatical form and semantic meaning) served as predictors of mastery/non-mastery on the listening and reading sections of the *GEPT*. She found that based on these predictors, 79 percent of the masters and 64 percent of the non-masters were classified correctly.

Sawaki (2009) examined ways in which examinees could be classified as masters or non-masters by means of cognitive diagnosis. Cognitive diagnosis is a method for extracting fine-grained linguistic and skill-based information from items so that this information can be presented to learners for further development (Lee & Sawaki, 2009). Sawaki compared the functioning of three psychometric models for cognitive diagnosis in the context of second language listening and reading comprehension tests (i.e., the general diagnostics model, the fusion model, and the latent class model). She found that all three models adequately classified examinees into masters and non-masters on most items, while a moderate level of across-form consistency of skill mastery classification was observed for the majority of reading and listening skills. Several examinees showed "flat" profiles.

Many studies over the years have provided evidence of the utilization inference by examining the impact of test scores on different stakeholders (Taylor & Weir, 2009). Green (2007) examined the impact of Academic Writing Module of the *International English Language Testing System (IELTS)* (University of Cambridge ESOL) on *IELTS* test preparation and on English for academic purposes courses. Test takers took *IELTS* tests, questionnaires, grammar and vocabulary tests, and questionnaires. The data were analyzed by means of descriptive statistics, reliability analysis, frequency analysis, MFRM, *t*-tests, ANCOVA, and multiple regression analysis, and several implications were presented.

Finally, studies have provided evidence of the utilization inference by investigating how information on the strengths and weaknesses of learner performance can be extracted from the data and provided to examinees for the purpose of closing learning gaps by means of cognitive diagnosis. For example, Jang (2009) used cognitive diagnosis modeling in order to make diagnostic inferences about second language reading ability. She constructed a Q-matrix by identifying reading attributes that emerged from a verbal report protocols. She then used the fusion model to examine test taker abilities on the skills required to respond to test items correctly. She detected nine reading skills relating to a wide range of reading processes and cognitive reading abilities.

Conclusion

As validation frameworks have become more sophisticated, the number of quantitative methods used to argue for or against validity claims has increased. Nonetheless, additional relevant quantitative methods exist. For example, I know of no published studies in language assessment to date that have used latent curve analysis for examining latent growth at three or more points in time or that have used multidimensional IRT. Nor have I seen studies that have used hierarchial linear modeling or mixed effects regression for use with hierarchial or nested data structures, or studies using Bayesian modeling, where large amounts of information can be incorporated in the analysis. I hope that in the next volume of this volume, this will not be the case.

Notes

1. While Kane (2006) links the expected or universe score directly to the target score as in task-based language assessment (see Norris, Brown, Hudson, & Yoshioka, 1998), Chapelle et al. (2008) explain that most language testers would prefer to make explicit the preliminary link between the universe score and the underlying theoretical test construct.
2. Kane (2006) refers to the link between the target score and trait interpretation as *implications*.

References

AERA, APA, & NCME. (1985). *Standards for educational and psychological testing*. Washington, DC: American Psychological Association.

Alderson, J. D. (1991). Language testing in the 1990s: How far have we come? How much further have we to go? In S. Anivan (Ed.), *Current development in language testing* (pp. 1–26). Singapore: SEAMEO Regional Language Centre.

Alderson, J. D. (1994). The state of language testing in the 1990s. In A. Huhta, K. Sajavaara, & S. Takala (Eds.), *Language testing: New openings* (pp. 1–19). Jyväskyla: University of Jyväskyla.

Alderson, J. D., & Banerjee, J. (2001). Language testing and assessment (Part 1). *Langauge Teaching, 34*, 213–236.

Alderson, J. D., & Banerjee, J. (2002). Language testing and assessment (Part 2). *Language Teaching, 35*, 70–113.

Ameriks, Y. (2009). Investigating validity across two test forms of the Examination for the Certificate of Proficiency in English (ECPE): A multi-group structural equation modeling approach. Unpublished doctoral dissertation, Teachers College, Columbia University, New York.

Anivan, S. (Ed.) (1991). *Current development in language testing*. Singapore: SEAMEO Regional Language Centre.

Bachman, L. F. (1990). *Fundamental considerations in language testing*. Oxford: Oxford University Press.

Bachman, L. F. (2000). Modern testing at the turn of the century: Assuring that we count counts. *Language Testing, 17*(1), 1–42.

Bachman, L. F. (2005). Building and supporting a case for test use. *Language Assessment Quarterly, 2*(1), 1–34.

Bachman, L. F., Davidson, F., & Foulkes, J. (1993). A comparison of the abilities measured by the Cambridge and Educational Testing Service EFL test batteries. In D. Douglas & C. Chapelle (Eds.), *A new decade of language testing research: Selected papers from the 1990 Language Testing Research Colloquium* (pp. 25–45). Alexandria, VA: TESOL.

Bachman, L. F., & Eignor, D. R. (1997). Recent advances in quantitative test analysis. In C. Clapham & D. Corson (Eds.), *Encyclopedia of language and education. Volume 7: Language testing and assessment* (pp. 227–242). Dordrecht: Kluwer Academic Publishers.

Bachman, L. F., Lynch, B. K., & Mason, M. (1995). Investigating variability in tasks and rater judgments in a performance test of foreign language speaking. *Language Testing, 12*(2), 238–257.

Bachman, L. F., & Palmer, A. S. (1981). A multitrait-multimethod investigation into the construct validity of six tests of speaking and reading. In A. S. Palmer, P. J. M. Groot, & G. A Trosper (Eds.), *The construct validation of tests of communicative competence* (pp. 149–165). Washington, DC: TESOL.

Bachman, L. F., & Palmer, A. S. (1982). The construct validation of some components of communicative proficiency. *TESOL Quarterly, 16*(4), 449–465.

Bae, J.-O., & Bachman, L. F. (1998). A latent variable approach to listening and reading: Testing factorial invariance across two groups of children in the Korean/English Two-Way Immersion Program. *Language Testing, 15*(3), 380–414.

Beaton, A. E., & Allen, N. L. (1992). Scaling through scale anchoring. *Journal of Educational Statistics, 17*(2), 191–204.

Bentler, P. M. (1992). *EQS Structural Equation Modeling Program Manual*. Los Angeles, CA: BMDP Statistical Software.

Biber, D., Conrad, S. M., Reppen, R., Byrd, H. P., Helt, M., Clark, V., Cortes, V., Cosmay, E., & Urzua, A. (2004). *Representing language use in the university: Analysis of the TOEFL 2000 spoken and written academic language corpus*. Princeton, NJ: Educational Testing Service.

Bonk, W. J., & Ockey, G. J. (2003). A many-facet Rasch analysis of the second language group oral discussion task. *Language Testing, 20*(1), 89–110.

Brennan, R. L. (1983). *Elements of generalizability theory*. Iowa City: The American College Testing Program.

Brennan, R. L. (2001). *Generalizability theory*. New York: Springer-Verlag.

Brown, J. D. (1988). Tailored cloze: Improved with classical item analysis techniques. *Language Testing, 5*(1), 19–31.

Brown, J. D. (1991). Do English and ESL faculties rate writing samples differently? *TESOL Quarterly, 25*(4), 587–603.

Brown, J. D. (1994). A comprehensive criterion-referenced language testing project. In D. Douglas & C. Chapelle (Eds.), *A new decade of language testing research: Selected papers from the 1990 Language Testing Research Colloquium* (pp. 163–184). Alexandria, VA: TESOL.

Brown, A. (1995). The effect of rater variables in the development of an occupation-specific language performance test. *Language Testing, 12*(1), 1–15.

Brown, J. D. (1999). Relative importance of persons, items, subtests and languages to TOEFL test variance. *Language Testing, 16*(2), 216–237.

Campbell, D. T., & Fiske, D. W. (1967). Convergent and discriminant validation by the multitrait-multimethod matrix. In W. A. Mehrens & R. L. Ebel (Eds.), *Principles of educational and psychological measurement* (pp. 273–302). Chicago: Rand McNally.

Chalhoube-Deville, M. (1995). A contextualized approach to describing oral language proficiency. *Language Learning, 45*(2), 251–281.

Chalhoub-Deville, M., & Deville, C. (2005). A look back and forward to what language testers measure. In E. Hinkel (Ed.), *Handbook of research in second language teaching and learning* (pp. 815–831). Mahwah, NJ: Lawrence Erlbaum Associates.

Chalhoub-Deville, M., & Deville, C. (2008). Utilizing psychometric methods in assessment. In E. Shohamy & N. H. Hornberger (Eds.), *Encyclopedia of language and education, 2nd edition, Volume 7: Language testing and assessment* (pp. 211–224). New York: Springer Science + Business Media LLC.

Chapelle, C. A. (1999). Validity in language assessment. *Annual Review of Applied Linguistics, 19*(1), 254–272.

Chapelle, C. A., Enright, M. K., & Jamieson, J. M. (2008). *Building a validity argument for the test of English as a foreign language.* New York: Routledge, Taylor & Francis Group.

Cheng, L., Klinger, D. A., & Zheng, Y. (2007). The challenges of the Ontario Secondary School Literacy Test for second language students. *Language Testing, 24*(2), 185–208.

Clapham, C. (1993). Is ESP testing justified? In D. Douglas & C. Chapelle (Eds.), *A new decade of language testing research: Selected papers from the 1990 Language Testing Research Colloquium* (pp. 257–271). Alexandria, VA: TESOL.

Clifford, R. (1981). Convergent and divergent validation of integrated and unitary language skills: The need for a research model. In A. S. Palmer, P. J. M. Groot, & G. A Trosper (Eds.), *The construct validation of tests of communicative competence* (pp. 62–70). Washington, DC: TESOL.

Coniam, D. (2005). The impact of wearing a face mask in a high-stakes oral examination: An exploratory post-SARS study in Hong Kong. *Language Assessment Quarterly, 2*(4), 235–261.

Cronbach, L. J. (1971). Test validation. In R. L. Thorndike (Ed.), *Educational measurement* (2nd ed.). Washington, DC: American Council on Education.

Cronbach, L. J. (1988). Five perspectives on validity argument. In H. Wainer & H. Braun (Eds.), *Test validity* (pp. 3–17). Hillsdale, NJ: Lawrence Erlbaum.

Cronbach, L. J., Gleser, G. C., Nanda, H., & Rajaratnam, N. (1972). *The dependability of behavioral measurement: Theory of generalizability for scores and profiles.* New York: John Wiley.

Cumming, A. (1996). Introduction: The concept of validation in language testing. In. A. Cumming & R. Berwick (Eds.), *Validation in language testing* (pp. 1–14). Clevedon: Multilingual Matters.

Cumming, A., & Berwick, R. (Eds.) (1996). *Validation in language testing.* Clevedon: Multilingual Matters.

Davis, L. (2009). The influence of interlocutor proficiency in a paired oral assessment. *Language Testing, 26*(3), 367–296.

De Jong, J. H. A. L., Lenning, M., Kerkhoff, A., & Poelmans, P. (2009). Development of the test of spoken Dutch for prospective immigrants. *Language Assessment Quarterly, 6*(1), 41–60.

Di Gennaro, K. (2009). Investigating differences in the writing performance of international and Generation 1.5 students. *Language Testing, 26*(4), 533–559.

Douglas, D., & Chapelle, C. (Eds.) (1993). *A new decade of language testing research: Selected papers from the 1990 Language Testing Research Colloquium.* Washington, DC: TESOL.

Eckes, T. (2008). Rater types in writing performance assessments: A classification approach to rater variability. *Language Testing, 25*(2), 155–185.

Farhardy, H. (1983). On the plausibility of the unitary language proficiency factor. In J. W. Oller (Ed.), *Issues in language testing research* (pp. 11–28). Rowley, MA: Newbury House Publishers.

Ferne, T., & Rupp, A. A. (2007). A synthesis of 15 years of research on DIF in language testing: Methodological advances, challenges, and recommendations. *Language Assessment Quarterly, 4*(2), 113–148.

Ginther, A., & J. Stevens. (1998). Investigating the differential test performance of native language groups on an Advanced Placement Examination in Spanish. In A. J. Kunnan (Ed.), *Validation in language assessment* (pp. 169–194). Mahwah, NJ: Lawrence Erlbaum.

Grabowski, K. (2009). Investigating the construct validity of a test designed to measure grammatical and pragmatic knowledge in the context of speaking. Unpublished doctoral dissertation, Teachers College, Columbia University, New York.

Green, T. (2007). *IELTS washback in context: Preparation for academic writing in higher education.* Cambridge: Cambridge University Press.

Grotjahn, R. (1987). On the methodological basis of introspective methods. In C. Faerch & G. Kasper (Eds.), *Introspection in second language research* (pp. 54–81). Clevedon: Multilingual Matters.

Guion, R. M. (1980). On trinitarian conceptions of validity. *Professional Psychology, 11,* 385–398.

Hambleton, R. K., Swaminathan, H., & Rogers, H. J. (1991). *Fundamentals of item response theory.* Newbury Park: Sage Publications.

Hamp-Lyons, L., & Lynch, B. K. (1998). Perspectives on validity: A historical analysis of language testing conference abstracts. In A. J. Kunnan (Ed.), *Validation in language assessment* (pp. 253–276). Mahwah, NJ: Lawrence Erlbaum Associates.

Harley, B., Allen, P., Cummins, J., & Swain, M. (1990). *The development of second language proficiency.* Cambridge: Cambridge University Press.

Hatch, E., & Lazaraton, A. (1991). *The research manual: Design and statistics for applied linguistics.* New York: Newbury House Publishers.

Hedges, L. V., & Olkin, I. (1985). *Statistical methods for meta-analysis.* New York: Academic Press.

Hinofotis, F. B., Bailey, K. M., & Stern, S. L. (1981). Assessing the oral proficiency of prospective foreign teaching assistants: Instrument development. In A. S. Palmer, P. J. M. Groot, & G. A. Trosper (Eds.), *The construct validation of tests of communicative competence* (pp. 106–126). Washington, DC: TESOL.

Hudson, T. D. (1991). Relationships among IRT item discrimination and item fit indices in criterion-referenced language testing. *Language Testing, 8*(2), 160–181.

Hudson, T. D. (1993). Testing the specificity of ESP reading skills. In D. Douglas & C. Chapelle (Eds.), *A new decade of language testing research: Selected papers from the 1990 Language Testing Research Colloquium* (pp. 58–82). Alexandria, VA: TESOL.

Hudson, T. D., & Lynch, B. (1984). A criterion-referenced measurement approach to ESL achievement testing. *Language Testing, 1,* 171–201.

In'nami, Y., & Koizumi, R. (2009). A meta-analysis of test format effects on reading and listening test performance: Focus on multiple-choice and open-ended formats. *Language Testing, 26*(2), 219–244.

Jang, E. E. (2009). Demystifying a Q-matrix for making diagnostic inferences about L2 reading ability. *Language Assessment Quarterly, 6*(3), 210–238.

Kane, M. T. (1992). An argument-based approach to validity. *Psychological Review, 112,* 527–535.

Kane, M. T. (2001). Current concerns in validity theory. *Journal of Educational Measurement, 38,* 319–342.

Kane, M. T. (2006). Validation. In R. L. Brennan (Ed.), *Educational measurement* (4th Ed.) (pp. 18–64). Westport, CT: American Council on Education/Praeger.

Kane, M. T., Crooks, T., & Cohen, A. (1999). Validating measures of performance. *Educational Measurement: Issues and Practice, 18*(2), 5–17.

Kim, H. (2009). Investigating the effects of context and task type on second language speaking ability. Unpublished dissertation, Teachers College, Columbia University, New York.

Kim, J. O. & Mueller, C. W. (1978). *Introduction to factor analysis: What it is and how to do it.* Newbury Park: Sage Publications

Kobayashi, M. (2002). Method effects on reading comprehension test performance: Text organization and response format. *Language Testing, 19*(2), 193–220.

Kondo-Brown, K. (2002). FACETS analysis of rater bias in measuring Japanese second language writing performance. *Language Testing, 19*(1), 3–31.

Konstantopoulos, S. (2008). An introduction to meta-analysis. In J. W. Osborne (Ed.), *Best practices in quantitative methods* (pp. 177–194). Los Angeles: Sage Publications.

Kunnan, A. J. (1995). *Test taker characteristics and test performance: A structural modeling approach.* Cambridge: Cambridge University Press.

Kunnan, A. J. (1998). *Validation in language assessment: Selected papers from the 17th Language Testing Research Colloquium, Long Beach.* Mahwah, NJ: Lawrence Erlbaum Associates.

Kunnan, A. J. (1999). Recent developments in language testing. *Annual Review of Applied Linguistics, 19*(1), 235–253.

Kunnan, A. J. (Ed.) (2000). *Fairness and validation in language assessment.* Cambridge: Cambridge University Press.

Kunnan, A. J. (2008). Towards a model of test evaluation: Using the test fairness and wider context frameworks. In L. Taylor & C. Weir (Eds.), *Multilingualism and assessment: Achieving transparency, assuring quality, sustaining diversity* (pp. 229–251). Cambridge: Cambridge University Press.

Lee, Y.-W. (2006). Dependability of scores for a new ESL speaking assessment consisting of integrated and independent tasks. *Language Testing, 23,* 131–166.

Lee, Y.-W., & Cantor, R. (2005). *Dependability of new ESL writing test scores: Evaluation prototype tasks and alternative rating schemes (TOEFL Monograph No. MS-30).* Princeton, NJ: ETS.

Lee, Y.-W., & Sawaki, Y. (2009). Cognitive diagnosis and Q-matrices in language assessment. *Language Assessment Quarterly*, 6(3), 169–171.

Liao, Y.-F. (2009). A construct validation study of the GEPT reading and listening sections: Re-examining the models of L2 reading and listening abilities and their relations to lexico-grammatical knowledge. Unpublished doctoral dissertation, Teachers College, Columbia University.

Linacre, J. M. (1989). *Many-faceted Rasch measurement*. Chicago: MESA.

Linacre, J. M. (2006). *Facets Rasch measurement computer program*. Chicago: Winsteps.com.

Llosa, L. (2007). Validating a standards-based classroom assessment of English proficiency: A multitrait-multimethod approach. *Language Testing, 24*(4), 489–515.

LTTC (Language Training and Testing Center). (2004). *General English Proficiency Test*. Taiwan: Ministry of Education.

Lumley, T., & Brown, A. (2005). Research methods in language testing. In E. Hinkel (Ed.), *Handbook of research in second language teaching and learning* (pp. 833–855). Mahwah, NJ: Lawrence Erlbaum Associates.

Lumley, T., & O'Sullivan, B. (2001). The effect of test-taker sex, audience, and topic on task performance in tape-mediated assessment of speaking. *Melbourne Papers in Language Testing, 10*(2), 59–74.

Lynch, B. K., & Davidson, F. (1997). Criterion Referenced Testing. In C. Clapham & D. Corson (Eds.), *Encyclopedia of language and education. Volume 7: Language testing and assessment* (pp. 263–274). Dordrecht: Kluwer Academic Publishers.

Lynch, B. K., & McNamara, T. F. (1998). Using g-theory and many-facet Rasch measurement in the development of performance assessments. *Modern Language Journal, 15*(2), 158–180.

Masters, G. (1982). A Rasch model for partial credit scoring. *Psychometrika, 47*, 149–174.

Messick, S. (1989). Validity. In R. Linn (Ed.), *Educational measurement* (pp. 13–103). New York: Macmillan.

Milanovich, M., Saville, N., Pollitt, A., & Cook, A. (1996). Developing rating scales for CASE: Theoretical concerns and analyses. In A. Cumming & R. Berwick (Eds.), *Validation in language testing* (pp. 15–38). Clevedon: Multilingual Matters.

Moss, P. A. (2003). Reconceptualizing validity for classroom assessment. *Educational Researcher, 25*(1), 20–28.

Muraki, E. (1992). A generalized partial credit model: Application of an EM algorithm. *Applied Psychological Measurement, 16*, 159–176.

Neff-VanAertselaer, J. (2008). Arguing in English and Spanish: A corpus study of stance. *University of Cambridge ESOL Examinations Research Notes, 33*, 28–33.

Norris, J. M., Brown, J. D., Hudson, T., & Yoshioka, J. (1998). Designing second language performance assessments (Vol. SLTCC Technical Report #18). Honolulu: Second Language Teaching & Curriculum Center, University of Hawai'i at Manoa.

Ockey, G. (2009). The effects of group members' personalities on test taker's L2 group oral discussion test scores. *Language Testing, 26*(2), 161–186.

Oller, J. W. (1976). Evidence of a general language proficiency factor: An expectancy grammar. *Die Neuren Sprachen, 76*, 165–174.

Oller, J. W. (1979). *Language tests at school*. London: Longman.

O'Loughlin, K. (2002). The impact of gender in oral proficiency testing. *Language Testing, 19*(2), 169–192.

Palmer, A. S., Groot, P. J. M., & Trosper, G. A. (1981). *The construct validation of tests of communicative competence*. Washington, DC: TESOL.

Park, T. (2007). Investigating the construct validity of the Community Language Program English writing test. Unpublished doctoral dissertation, Teachers College, Columbia University, New York.

Pedhazur, E. J. (1982). *Multiple regression in behavioral research: Explanation and prediction* (2nd ed.). Chicago: Holt, Rinehart and Winston, Inc.

Phakiti, A. (2003). A closer look at the relationship of cognitive, and metacognitive strategy use to EFL reading achievement test performance. *Language Testing, 20*(1), 26–56.

Phakiti, A. (2008). Strategic competence as a fourth-order factor model: A structural equation modeling approach. *Language Assessment Quarterly, 5*(1), 20–42.

Purpura, J. E. (1996). Modeling the relationships between test takers' reported cognitive and metacognitive strategy use and performance on language tests. Ph.D. dissertation, University of California, Los Angeles.

Purpura, J. E. (1997). An analysis of the relationships between test takers' cognitive and metacognitive strategy use and second language test performance. *Language Learning, 47*(2), 289–325.

Purpura, J. E. (1998). Investigating the effects of strategy use and second language test performance with high and low ability test takers: A structural equation modeling approach. *Language Testing, 15*(3), 333–379.

Purpura, J. E. (2009). The impact of large-scale and classroom-based language assessments on the individual. In L. Taylor & C. J. Weir (Eds.), *Language testing matters: Investigating the wider social and educational impact of assessment—Proceedings of the ALTE Cambridge Conference, April 2008* (pp. 301–325). Cambridge: Cambridge University Press.

Sasaki, M. (1993). Relationships among second language proficiency, foreign language aptitude and intelligence: A structural equation modeling approach. *Language Learning, 43*, 313–344.

Saville, N. (2009). Language assessment in the management of international migration: A framework for considering the issues. *Language Assessment Quarterly, 6*(1), 17–29.

Sawaki, Y. (2003). A comparison of summarization and free recall as reading comprehension tasks in a Web-based assessment of Japanese as a foreign language. Unpublished doctoral dissertation, University of California, Los Angeles.

Sawaki, Y. (2007). Construct validation of analytic rating scales in a speaking assessment: Reporting a score profile and a composite. *Language Testing, 24*(3), 355–390.

Sawaki, Y. (2009). Application of three cognitive diagnosis models to ESL reading and listening assessments. *Language Assessment Quarterly, 6*(3), 239–263.

Sawaki, Y., & Nissan, S. (2009). *Criterion-related validity of the TOEFL iBT Listening Section* (Research Report, No. 09-02). Princeton, NJ: ETS.

Sawaki, Y., Stricker, L. J., & Oranje, A. H. (2009). Factor structure of the TOEF Internet-based test. *Language Testing, 26*(1), 5–30.

Schaefer, E. (2008). Rater bias patterns in an EFL writing assessment. *Language Testing, 25*(4), 465–493.

Shavelson, R. J. (1981). *Statistical reasoning for behavioral sciences* (2nd ed.). Boston: Allyn and Bacon, Inc.

Shavelson, R. J., & Webb, N. M. (1991). *Generalizability theory: A primer.* Los Angeles: Sage Publications.

Shohamy, E. (1981). Inter-rater and intra-rater reliability of the oral interview and concurrent validity with cloze procedure. In A. S. Palmer, P. J. M. Groot, & G. A. Trosper (Eds.), *The construct validation of tests of communicative competence* (pp. 94–105). Washington, DC: TESOL.

Shohamy, E., & McNamara, T. (2009). Editorial: Language tests for citizenship and asylum. *Language Assessment Quarterly, 6*(1), 1–5.

Stansfield, C. W., & Kenyon, D. M. (1992). Research on the comparability of the oral proficiency interview and the simulated oral proficiency interview. *System, 20*(3), 347–364.

Su, Y.-H., & Wang, W.-C. (2005). Efficiency of the Mantel, generalized Mantel-Haenzel and logistic discriminant function analysis methods in detecting differential item functioning for polytomous items. *Applied Measurement in Education, 18,* 313–350.

Swaminathan, H., & Rogers, J. (1990). Detecting differential item functioning using logistical regression procedures. *Journal of Educational Measurement, 27,* 361–370.

Tang, K. L., & Eignor, D. R. (1996). *Concurrent calibration of dichtomously and polytomously scored TOEFL items using IRT models.* Princeton, NJ: Educational Testing Service.

Taylor, L., & Weir, C. J. (2009). *Language testing matters: Investigating the wider social and educational impact of assessment— Proceedings of the ALTE Cambridge Conference, April 2008.* Cambridge: Cambridge University Press.

Tyndall, B., & Kenyon, D. M. (1996). Validation of a new holistic rating scale using Rasch multi-faceted analysis. In A. Cumming & R. Berwick (Eds.), *Validation in language testing* (pp. 39–57). Clevedon: Multilingual Matters.

Upshur, J., & Turner, C. E. (1999). Systematic effects in the rating of second-language speaking ability: Test method and learner discourse. *Language Testing, 16*(1), 82–111.

Volmer, H. J., & Sang, F. (1983). Competing hypotheses for second language ability: A plea for caution. In J. W. Oller (Ed.), *Issues in language testing research* (pp. 29–79). Rowley, MA: Newbury House Publishers.

Wagner, E. (2006). Utilizing the visual channel: An investigation of the use of video texts on tests of second language listening ability. Unpublished dissertation, Teachers College, Columbia University, New York.

Weigle, S. (1998). Using FACETS to model rater training effects. *Language Testing, 15*(2), 263–287.

Weigle, S. C., & Lynch, B. K. (1996). Hypothesis testing in construct validation. In A. Cumming (Ed.), *Selected papers from the 1992 Language Testing Research Colloquium* (pp. 58–71). Clevedon: Multilingual Matters.

Wigglesworth, G. (1997). An investigation of planning time and proficiency level on oral test discourse. *Language Testing, 14*(1), 85–106.

Wolfe, E. W., & Dobria, L. (2008). Applications of the multifaceted Rasch model. In J. W. Osborne (Ed.), *Best practices in quantitative methods* (pp. 71–85), Los Angeles: Sage Publications.

Xi, X. (2007). Validating TOEFL iBT Speaking and setting score requirements for ITA screening. *Language Assessment Quarterly, 4*(4), 318–351.

Xi, X. (2008). Methods of test validation. In E. Shohamy & N. H. Hornberger (Eds.), *Encyclopedia of language and education, 2nd edition, Volume 7: Language testing and assessment* (pp. 177–196). New York: Springer Science + Business Media LLC.

Xi, X., Higgins, D., Zechner, K., & Williamson, D. M. (2008). Automated scoring of spontaneous speech using SpeechRater v. 10. (ETS Research Report No. 08-62). Princeton, NJ: Educational Testing Service.

Yen, W. M., & Fitzpatrick, A. R. (2006). Item response theory. In B. Brennan (Ed.), *Educational Measurement* (4th ed.) (pp. 111–153). Westport, CT: ACE/Praeger Series on Higher Education.

45
Qualitative Research Methods in Second Language Assessment

Bernard A. Mohan

In the previous volume of the *Handbook of Research in Second Language Teaching and Learning*, Lumley and Brown (2005, p. 840) observe that qualitative methods have become increasingly used to examine issues of language testing, and that a number of commentators relate this to the conception of validity in assessment widening from a solely quantitative view to a integrated holistic view based on a range of quantitative and qualitative evidence. They then review studies of the qualitative research methods more popular in language assessment (discourse analysis, introspection and ethnographic methods) and note how they raise problems about language assessment. Discourse analysis, for example, has raised concerns about the nature of oral interview discourse by contrast with conversational interaction outside the testing situation, the way in which candidate performance may be influenced by variation in interviewer behaviours, task type and so on. In other words, Lumley and Brown start from qualitative research methods and discuss the problems that they raise with assessment practices.

In this review we will reverse this procedure. We will examine the problems of assessment practices and enquire about what qualitative methods might throw light on them. Because the problems are complex, we will take two related and important examples—the assessment of academic language ability in high-stakes testing and assessment of language and content knowledge. In both cases, the validation of assessment practices requires researchers to demonstrate that assessment outcomes accurately reflect the learners' capacity for using language to construe academic meanings. We will argue that research with such a goal needs to be conducted within an analytic framework capable to analysing the quality of learners' language use for construing academic meaning. In the validation of tests of academic language ability, models of discourse and language competence have been used, but due to a simplistic view of language, they fail to provide the needed basis for discourse analysis. We therefore begin by demonstrating the current problem with testing of academic language ability and illustrate how a functionally-based framework for discourse analysis could be used to address the qualitative need. To further exemplify the types of discourse analytic results obtained from the approach, we discuss additional examples that come from classroom assessment of content and language. These examples illustrate just a few of the findings that can come from qualitative methodology of language assessment if the theoretical basis is a linguistic model that relates wording and meaning.

Qualitative Issues in Tests of Academic Language Ability

Tests of academic English ability such as the Test of English as a Foreign Language (TOEFL) and the International English Language Testing System (IELTS) are used to make high-stakes decisions about whether or not examinees should be considered for admission to universities in English speaking countries. As a consequence, such tests are subjected to research aimed to investigate the extent to which their use can be justified (e.g., Chapelle, Enright & Jamieson, 2008). In that volume about the foundations for and validation research on TOEFL, Taylor and Angelis (2008) summarise almost a half century of thought and investigation about the design of the TOEFL. The first TOEFL in the 1960s was essentially based on a language code and skills model. Following the structuralist linguistic theory of the time, which has had an enormous influence on second language testing (see Lado, 1961), the language system was viewed and tested as discrete components such as a sound system, grammar and vocabulary. The communicative "skills" of reading, writing, speaking and listening were tested separately. There was little attempt to relate the language system to the communicative "skills".

Test developers for the new TOEFL have moved to a very different set of presuppositions about language and communication (see Taylor & Angelis, 2008, p. 50). First, they evolved in keeping with validation practices from a purely quantitative view of validity to a multi-faceted view which includes qualitative evidence. This evolution creates an important opening for the contribution of qualitative research methods. Second, with regard to test content, they favour a task-centred approach that aims to take into account the context of language use in academic tasks. This creates the need for qualitative research methods that can investigate academic discourse and academic contexts. Third, with regard to the test construct they ask: "How can an appropriate theoretical perspective based on communicative competence be articulated to underlie score interpretation?" In effect, this calls for theory that can address how examinees draw on their linguistic knowledge of the language system and their knowledge of context to construct and comprehend meaning in discourse or text. In other words, instead of a *structural* theory, this calls for a *functional* theory that combines a theory of the language system and a theory of text in context, and that relates wording (the language system) to meaning in text and context.

Qualitative validation research methods are needed that can relate wording to academic meanings in text and context, and are backed by a functional linguistic theory. Of the three main qualitative methods selected by Lumley and Brown (2005) (introspection, ethnographic methods and discourse analysis), only a few forms of discourse analysis have any intrinsic connection with functional linguistic analysis. We need to ask: what model of language and text does a qualitative method assume, if any? This is an important question for qualitative researchers since it is often claimed that qualitative research uses language as data while quantitative research uses numbers as data. But the question is seldom asked, perhaps because of Descartes' historically influential, but highly questionable, epistemological view that research method provides reliable knowledge only by following the correct research procedure and *by rejecting any prior framework of interpretation* (see Abbey, 2000, pp. 172–176). In our case we need qualitative methods that provide an appropriate framework of interpretation. Otherwise they are not relevant to the problem situation we face.

The structural assumptions on which tests such as the first TOEFL were based made it impossible to relate wording to meaning in text in context. Structural linguistics aims to describe structures of linguistic form in language e.g. patterns of grammar in sentences. Like earlier "traditional grammars", structural linguistics is concerned with language as a set of rules, though structural linguists take a behaviourist view and describe rules as "behaviour patterns". North American structural linguists for whom Bloomfield was the central figure did not consider meaning to be part of the structure of language: "meaning had no status as a real entity within language nor as a category within the Bloomfieldian theory of language description" (Fought, 1999, p. 147). Meaning was thus assumed to be separate from linguistic form rather than related to it. In this assumption they were very different from European linguists such as de Saussure who saw the linguistic sign as an expression united with a meaning.

On these assumptions of language as rule and language as form but not meaning, second language (L2) assessment is the assessment of correctness or error in language form, and L2 development is conceived of as a movement towards correct language form. A written or spoken text is merely a display of language form, not a structure of meaning larger than the clause or sentence, and accordingly discourse processes of reading, writing, speaking and listening are reduced to matters of decoding and encoding sequences of language form. In this "language code and language skills model", there is an unbridgeable gap between code and skills, between grammar and meaning in discourse as they would need to be conceived in a task-centred testing approach that aims to take into account language use in academic contexts.

Grabe (2009, pp. 21–58) reviews recent psycholinguistic reading research that bridges this gap and shows the fundamental importance of grammatical information for constructing the meaning of discourse in reading comprehension. Comprehension contains lower-level processes, which include word recognition, syntactic parsing and semantic-proposition encoding. With regard to the latter he states:

> At the same time that the first words are being activated during reading and the first structural grouping of the words is parsed for its syntactic information, information being extracted from the words and structures is used to build semantic units that are approximately equivalent to phrase and clause units.
>
> (Grabe, 2009, pp. 30–31)

Comprehension also contains higher-level processes "including text-model formation (what the text is about), situation-model building (how we decide to interpret the text), inferencing, executive-control processing (how we direct our attention), and strategic processing" (2009, p. 21). Grammar also plays a role in these higher-level processes e.g. in tracking participants and events. Text-model formation is centrally important, since it requires us to relate different semantic elements in the text and arrive at a coherent idea of what the text is about. However, an account of comprehension that includes both text models and situation models helps us explain how we read different texts in different ways and allows us to take into account genre and register differences in reading comprehension (2009, p. 46).

Accordingly, validation research for a test of academic reading ability would need to investigate how the linguistic choices authors had made while writing in various registers affected reading interpretations and reading comprehension scores. Grabe (2009, pp. 203ff.) shows how a basis for an *explanation* of the way grammar processing contributes to the meaning of discourse in reading comprehension is provided by the sustained work of Gernsbacher and Givon (Gernsbacher & Givon, 1995; Givon, 2005). Gernsbacher's Structure Building model of discourse comprehension is supported by Givon's linguistic analysis of how grammar systems functionally provide information for building discourse coherence. Thus a discourse analysis that aims to describe test takers' reading processes and comprehension from a linguistic point of view needs to draw on a theory that describes how lexicogrammar constructs the meaning of discourse and that combines the language system and text in context; in brief, a theory that relates wording to meaning of text in context. With proposition encoding at the phrase and clause level, it relates grammatical and lexical information to the semantic units of phrase and clause; with text-model formation at the text-level, it connects the lexicogrammar of clause relations to the semantic elements of the text as a whole; and at the situation-model level it connects the text to its context.

The need of a systematic approach to discourse analysis in language assessment is even more evident in research on the assessment of productive L2 skills. In a review of studies that analysed demands for writing that second language students encounter, Cumming asserts that

> systematic modes of analysing students' written texts are needed because rating scales typically used to evaluate students writing in a second language are simply too imprecise, or lack theoretical rigour or validation, to be able to provide useful indicators of students' achievement.
>
> (Cumming, 1998, p. 65)

The result of this lack of theoretical rigour and precision is demonstrated by Low (in press), who conducted a qualitative discourse analysis of teacher decision-making in writing assessment. She studied teachers of L2 students, sitting next to them as they marked student essays about the topics of the content curriculum and articulated the decisions they made as they reflected on student work. She worked in two very different sites, a college in Western Canada and an upper elementary school in Samoa, but found very similar themes. A recurrent dilemma was that teachers wanted to respond to the way students make meaning with language yet they had no way of doing so, apparently because their thinking was dominated by a structuralist notion of grammar as form without meaning. As one teacher deliberated:

> Although this student still has problems with grammar, the ideas are there. He is working through the choices the community has about their need for a better water supply system. Hmm, this is difficult. I just wish his grammar errors weren't so bad then I could give him an "A".

Thus teachers struggled with and were disturbed by the gap between a grammar of form and their recognition of their students' abilities to make meaning with language in discourse. They were unable to find a satisfactory resolution because they could not readily draw upon a framework that explained how grammar constructed meaning in discourse.

Possible Approaches to the Problem

The qualitative issues in language assessment exemplified above provide the necessary background for examining qualitative discourse analysis methods. However, the methods of discourse analysis typically favoured in L2 studies do not provide a systematic account of how lexicogrammar builds meaning in discourse.

Consider two frameworks motivating discourse analysis highlighted by McNamara, Hill and May (2002) as most significant for disturbing and challenging the assumptions underlying current assessment practices, Conversation Analysis and Vygotskyan sociocultural theory (McNamara et al., 2002, p. 222). Conversation Analysis (Schegloff, Koshik, Jacoby & Olsher, 2002), as a field of sociology, is concerned with describing the interactional practices used to accomplish social action through conversation, including such matters as turn-taking and repair. It provides methodological tools for transcription of conversation data that allow the researcher to examine details of interaction as it is accomplished. But as a sociological approach to grounded analysis of interactional meaning, it does not deal with the linguistic question of a systematic account of how lexicogrammar builds meaning in discourse. Therefore it does not provide a basis for analysing the ways in which texts provided in reading tests, or text produced in writing tests, construe academic meanings. Discourse analysis conducted within the framework of Vygotskyan sociocultural theory of mind points analysts to aspects of dialogue theorised to be relevant to L2 learning such as scaffolding used in collaborative dialogue and miscommunication in cross-cultural communication (e.g., Swain, Brooks & Tocalli-Beller,

2002). But as a sociocultural theory, it does not attempt to deal systematically with the linguistic question of how lexicogrammar builds meaning in discourse.

The framework that has been influential in language assessment originated in the well-known model of communicative competence developed by Canale and Swain. This model consists of four linguistic and language-related components. Grammatical competence is "knowledge of lexical items and of rules of morphology, syntax, sentence-grammar semantics, and phonology" (Canale & Swain, 1980, p. 29). Discourse competence is mastery of rules that determine ways in which forms and meanings are combined to achieve a meaningful unity of spoken or written texts. Sociolinguistic competence was made up of "sociocultural rules of use and rules of discourse" (Canale & Swain, 1980, p. 29). Strategic competence covers the strategies used to compensate for communication breakdowns. Bachman (1990) and Bachman and Palmer (1996) elaborated and adapted this model further to increase its utility for specifying what language assessments measure.

There has been wide agreement with the aim of this model, which is to specify a framework for assessing L2 learners' ability to communicate linguistic meaning within particular contexts, not just to produce correct language code. However, critics have noted that this model of communicative competence has fatal weaknesses. Widdowson (2001) objects to the Canale and Swain/Bachman and Palmer communicative competence approaches to describing communicative language ability on the grounds that offering a mere list of competences is not sufficient, and that they have not specified how the components of communicative language ability are dynamically *related* in actual communication. In other words, it is not sufficient simply to have grammar and discourse as separate components, it is necessary to say how they are related in communication. This indeed is the central point of Grabe's discussion outlined above of research in reading comprehension: to explain reading comprehension it is necessary to explain how grammar constructs meaning in discourse. The model of communicative competence does not do this. A further objection that must be raised is that the communicative competence model describes competences in terms of a "language as rule" view of language, as the first three competences show. This is consistent with explaining correctness and error in the language code, but it does not explain the communication of meaning, which calls for a "language as choice of meanings" view. There is a parallel between the weaknesses of the model as a framework for discourse analysis in validation research and the weaknesses of the structural view of language. The model mirrors the structuralist separation of form and meaning in its separation of grammatical, discourse and sociolinguistic competences, and its reliance on language as rule. In sum, if we are to account for how forms and meanings are combined in actual communication we need to look for a view of language and discourse which is more adequate to the task.

In seeking an alternative, Widdowson (2001) dismisses Chomsky's view of linguistic competence as "a knowledge of the formal properties of sentences in isolation" (p. 18). Instead, aiming to find a way of conceiving linguistic capacity as part of a more general ability to communicate, he argues in favour of Halliday's concept of a speaker's "meaning potential", the language options or choices that are available to the language user to construct meanings in particular contexts. Halliday holds a theory of language as choice and views language as a resource for making meaning by choosing language options.

The speaker's "meaning potential" is central to systemic functional linguistics (SFL), which is oriented to "the description of language as a *resource for meaning* rather than as a system of rules" i.e. to speakers' meaning potential (what they can mean) rather than constraints on what they can say (see Halliday & Martin, 1993, pp. 22–23). SFL is "concerned with *texts*, rather than sentences, as the basic unit through which meaning is negotiated". SFL focuses on mutually predictive *relations between texts and social contexts* rather than on texts as decontextualised structural entities. SFL is "concerned with language as a system for construing meaning, rather than as a conduit through which thoughts and feelings are poured. In other words, it views language as a meaning-making system rather than a meaning-expressing one." This is a constructivist view of language: "language is not passively reflecting some pre-existing conceptual structure; on the contrary, it is actively engaged in bring such structures into being … The grammar of every natural language … is already a theory of experience … It transforms our experience into meaning" (Halliday & Martin, 1993, p. 10).

Functional Assessment of Text

Discourse analysis in language assessment should provide the framework for examining the way the language is used to make meaning through the oral and written texts that learners are provided and those they help construct during assessment events. The framework should contain categories and concepts for identifying aspects of discourse that are relevant to the understanding the quality of academic meaning making. An assessor should be able to explain or justify her/his judgement of the meaning of a text on the basis of the wording of the text, and such judgements should draw upon a linguistically principled basis such as SFL to take account of the text as a whole in its context (see Macken & Slade, 1993, Mohan, Leung & Slater, in press).

An SFL Register Analysis of Text

In what follows we will illustrate how assessment in an SFL register approach would judge text as making meaning with language resources in context. We will show how it is possible to assess meaning and wording in discourse on a linguistically principled basis. That is, we will show how a functional approach to language can provide the theory and analysis needed to relate meaning and wording systematically in a manner that is relevant to understanding the quality of academic language. We will limit text description to that purpose.

The following two explanations, from Mohan and Slater (2004), were elicited using a diagram of the water cycle. Each builds a line of meaning (Longacre, 1996). Explanation A is essentially a time line of events. Explanation B is essentially a causal line of events and actions. Explanation B would usually be judged a better scientific explanation of the water cycle because it explains some of the causal relations of the water cycle. One would reasonably expect a competent assessor or system of language assessment to be able to judge that the two explanations were different in meaning in this way:

Explanation A (writer: a secondary school teacher whose first language (L1) is English):

The water cycle.
What are the processes that "water" goes through?
1) Initially, the water cycle begins as snow melts from the glaciers.
2) The water then meanders through various water sheds until it reaches rivers and lakes. Water eventually reaches the oceans.
3) Water then becomes water vapour (it evaporates into the air) and accumulates in what we call clouds.
4) The "clouds" then distribute water in the form of rain, snow, or sleet back to the mountains where the cycle begins again.

Explanation B (writer: a university student who speaks English as an L2):

The water cycle: The sun is the source of our water. The water, or hydrological, cycle begins when the sun heats up the ocean to produce water vapour through evaporation. This water vapour mixes with dust in the atmosphere and forms clouds. Cool air causes condensation of water droplets in the clouds, bringing about precipitation, or rain. This rain then falls into rivers, streams and lakes and eventually returns to the ocean, where the cycle begins again.

In SFL the immediate context of a text is called the context of situation. A context of situation is described through three main variables that affect language use: field covers the topic or content of the text and the social activity it is part of; tenor deals with the social roles and relations between the people involved in the text; mode relates to the role and medium of language in the situation (spoken or written, accompanying the activity or constitutive of it). Each variable is related to a component of the language system. Field is related to ideational meaning, which represents experience; tenor is related to interpersonal meaning, which enables interaction; mode is related to textual meaning, which manages coherence and connectedness in text. Explanations A and B are similar in mode, since they are both written, they are similar in tenor, as "objective" scientific accounts written for language research purposes, but they are somewhat different in field, since they provide rather different accounts of the water cycle. We will therefore focus on ideational meaning.

Ideational meaning covers three main realms of experience: the identification and classification of things, qualities or processes; the representation of events and activity sequences; and human consciousness, including mental and verbal processes. Explanations A and B both treat the water cycle as an activity sequence of events, so we will focus on the representation of events and activity sequences. The representation of events is typically realised by material transitivity (verbs of happening and doing): X happens, A did B. The representation of activity sequences is typically realised by logical relations such as time and cause: X happens, then Y happens, X happens because Z happens (Painter, 1999, p. 74).

Explanation A represents events mainly with verbs of happening (e.g. *melts, meanders, becomes*) and one verb of doing (*distribute*). It represents its activity sequence with the logical relation of time, using time conjunctions (*initially, then, eventually*). It also uses dependent clauses of time (*as* snow melts, *until* it reaches) and lexical verbs of time (*begin*).

Explanation B represents events with verbs of happening (*falls, returns*) and of doing (*heats up*). It represents its activity sequence with the logical relation of cause, using causal dependent clauses (*to produce water vapour*), cause/means as circumstance (*through* evaporation), lexical verbs of cause (*produces, causes, brings about*), nominalisation of causal processes (*evaporation, condensation, precipitation*), and a causal metaphor (the sun is *the source* of our water).

An assessor who judged Explanation A as a temporal explanation and Explanation B as a causal explanation would be able to justify this judgement of meaning by pointing to how these two different ideational meanings were constructed by the different wording of each text. The assessor would be working with the meaning–wording relations in the two texts. In this way the assessor would judge the two texts as making different meanings with different language resources. Notice that the judgement is not based on whether or not an explanation breaks grammar rules or discourse conventions, as the communicative competence model would guide the analysis to do.

The following objection to the discourse analysis above was stated by a language assessment specialist accustomed to rating based on a communicative competence model: "Both Explanations A and B are competent. I don't see why you have to bother to say anything further than that." In other words, if the two texts did not display errors, there was no need for the SFL discourse analysis of wording and meaning. Mohan and Slater (2004) explored whether L2 assessors using a version of the communicative competence model could recognise the discourse differences between Explanation A and Explanation B. The assessors were using a locally developed test for assessing the communicative competence of potential L2 teachers based on Canale and Swain (1980). In the assessment of a candidate's text, the raters classified errors in standard categories of competence: linguistic, sociolinguistic, discursive and strategic. The raters could give one point to a category if there were no problems exhibited and zero if there were one or more examples of errors. Instead of noticing a difference in the two texts and crediting Explanation B as being the better of the two, these raters judged them as equal. The writer of Explanation A was faulted in the area of mechanics because she spelled *watersheds* as two words. A supposed mechanics problem was the reason for an imperfect score for Explanation B: the raters felt that it was wrong to use an upper case letter after a colon. Unfortunately, there was nothing in the assessment instrument that allowed the raters to add points for what they considered exceptional because it was assessing the errors made rather than the linguistic resources each writer was exhibiting. Intuitively, however, these raters judged Explanation B as definitely "more advanced", "scientific" and at a "higher caliber than" the Explanation A, yet they admitted that the assessment instrument would not account for this discrepancy: they stated that the only way they could distinguish levels with this assessment instrument was when there were errors. Mohan and Slater (2004) found a similar pattern of results with a group of assessors using the Test of Written English protocol.

The assessors recognised the quality of Explanation B as more sophisticated academic discourse, but, following their understanding of the assessment procedure, they assigned scores on the basis of mechanical "errors", for construct irrelevant reasons. It must be clearly recognised that a theoretical framework supporting such assessment practices that attend to errors only and ignore the functional quality of L2 writers' texts does not provide a basis for discourse analysis that can investigate construct validity.

Academic Discourse and Grammatical Metaphor

One feature contributing to the sophistication of academic discourse is the linguistic concept of grammatical metaphor (GM). GM was important in Explanation B, which used nominalisations such as *evaporation* and *precipitation*. Control over grammatical metaphor is vital for success in secondary schooling and beyond, for it is involved in building disciplinary knowledge and in enabling argumentation. With native speakers of English, the more complex forms of grammatical metaphor do not appear until adolescence; and while able writers achieve considerable control of it in the mid-secondary years, many others struggle with it (see Christie & Derewianka, 2008, pp. 24–25).

GM refers to "a substitution of one grammatical class, or one grammatical structure by another; for example, *his departure* instead of *he departed*. Here the words (lexical items) are the same; what has changed is their place in the grammar" (Halliday, 1993, p. 79). In conversation, processes tend to be realised "congruently" as verbal groups, participants as nominal groups and circumstances as prepositional phrases or adverbs (e.g. he removed the plaster slowly). In adult written language the action may be realised "metaphorically" as a noun, the participant as a determiner or postmodifying phrase, and the "how" as an adjective (e.g. his slow removal of the plaster).

GM is an aspect of the historical development of scientific English in general and of causal discourse in particular. Halliday and Martin (1993) show that in the historical development of scientific English, causal discourse has taken the following developmental path:

from A happens; so X happens

    because A happens, X happens

        that A happens causes X to happen

           happening A causes happening X

to   happening A is the cause of happening X

(Halliday & Martin, 1993, p. 66)

As one might expect, the development of causal discourse is a significant component of learners' development of capacity to use academic discourse. The SFL analysis of cause includes reason, purpose and condition and recognises an "external" sense of cause (A causes B to happen) and an "internal" sense (A is proof, evidence or a reason for believing that B is the case). Asking for evidence is a familiar classroom questioning strategy (see Painter, 1999, p. 245).

The development of GM in L2 learners has been studied by Byrnes (2009), who traced longitudinal changes in GM and textual meaning-making capacities of L2 German learners as they moved from an intermediate to an advanced level of performance in written German. GM was seen as a key feature of movement from oral to written academic language. Subjects were 14 students who had completed at least three consecutive curricular levels in a university German program in a curriculum based on genres. Each student wrote a writing task based on a genre at the end of curricular levels 2, 3 and 4. Each written text was analysed for type and frequency of GM. Results showed that students used GM increasingly throughout the levels, with the greatest increase between levels 3 and 4. A detailed case study of one student showed that GM was used initially to express emotions and personal experiences that were being objectified (e.g. I chose the university → My choice of university). Then at level 4, GM was used prospectively to outline topics to be discussed, and GM was used retrospectively to structure an extended argument by reiterating and concluding. In sum, the results suggested GM was a valuable marker of L2 development in written academic German, and that it was used developmentally to accomplish an increasing range of textual meaning-making functions.

In a study of oral discourse, Slater and Mohan (in press) described how students who are native speakers of English and English as a second language (ESL) students develop their resources to express causal explanations using grammatical metaphor. They outlined a model for the development of causal meaning and wording with two dimensions, one being increasing grammatical metaphor and the other being a semantic shift from time to cause to proof. They applied this model to ten hours of oral data of interviews that elicited causal explanations from English language learners (ELLs) and native speakers of English from two classes at Grade 1/Grade 2 level and two classes at Grade 9 level. They found developmental differences in the construction of causal explanations between the younger and older groups that were consistent with the model. When they compared ELLs and native speakers at the Grade 1/2 level, they discovered surprisingly that the ELLs performed better. This was possibly because the teacher of the ELLs had taught the language of science very systematically. When they compared ELLs and native speakers at the Grade 9 level they found that the native speakers performed better, that is, they found that the Grade 9 English L1 speakers in oral conversation could draw on causal language resources when needed much more readily than the Grade 9 ELLs.

These examples demonstrate the utility of a functional discourse analysis as a means of examining the aspects of texts that are relevant to assessment of academic language ability. Whereas a structural approach and the related communicative competence model prompts assessors to see text as a display of grammatical forms, SFL sees text as making meaning through the use of language resources in context. Whereas a structural approach would value language rules (competence) rather than text (performance), SFL relates language system to text and values both. Whereas a structural approach would view language learning as acquiring correct forms, SFL would view language learning as extending resources for making meaning in context. SFL provides a productive framework for analysis of discourse in language assessment enables the assessment of wording–meaning relations to be systematically based on a linguistically principled approach, supported by a functional grammar of English (see Halliday & Matthiessen, 2004). Such a framework that provides the concepts and categories relevant to analysis of how people make academic meaning is needed if discourse analysis is to be used to investigate the validity of assessments of academic language.

Further examples of studies that examine the assessment of academic writing from an SFL perspective include Coffin and Hewings (2004) and Mickan and Slater (2003) who critique the assessment of academic writing in the IELTS test and Brisk and Zisselsberger (2007), Gebhard, Harman and Seger (2007) and Schleppegrell and Go (2007) who explore how an SFL approach using register and genre impacts the teaching of writing and student writing development in mainstream elementary classrooms with bilingual learners.

Qualitative Issues in Language and Content Assessment

The need for a relevant framework for discourse analysis is equally apparent in language and content assessment practices. In recent years, assessing language and content has also become a high-stakes issue (see review by Byrnes, 2008). For example, learners in the US, including ELLs, must be assessed for learning outcomes, due to the demands of the federal No Child Left Behind (NCLB) legislation. US testers have responded in terms of "accommodation", maintaining the test task and content-relevant terminology but modifying the noncontent vocabulary and linguistic structures and thereby enabling Limited English Proficiency students to achieve higher performances (e.g. Abedi, 2004). More generally, similar language and content assessment issues arise when L2 learners are assessed for content standards at all parts of the education system and in the professions. This is a large area because the underlying issue is that language is the major means of assessment for *all* learners. Language assessors cannot ignore this issue.

Summarising her review, Byrnes (2008, pp. 46–47) reports that the field of assessing content and language struggles with the major difficulty that the L2 profession has a history of describing learners' L2 knowledge in terms of formal features, separate from knowing a content area, and cannot readily draw on "a theory of language that places meaning and content at the center of its interests" like SFL. As a result, "to date only sporadic work exists that explicitly targets the implications of that [theory] for assessment".

The key to a productive understanding of the assessment of language and content is given by Halliday and Mattthiessen (1999, pp. 1–3) who see knowledge as meaning, a resource for understanding and acting on the world, and language as a means of learning. In their view, all knowledge is constituted in semiotic systems with language as the most central. Knowledge or content, then, is meaning. When a teacher assesses a science essay, s/he understands the meaning or content of the essay using the evidence of the wording of the essay. Similarly, when a teacher assesses an English essay, s/he understands the meaning or content of the essay using the evidence of the wording of the essay. The different evaluations they make are both based on, and presuppose, an understanding of how the wording constructs meaning in the text and context. This common ground should be a focus of discourse analysis of language and content assessment.

As noted above, an SFL approach provides the tools to analyse wording and meaning in text, including ideational meaning, which is closest to "meaning in the sense of content" in everyday terms (Halliday, 1985, p. 101) and which constructs our knowledge of the world from our experience. It enables us to address a learner's knowledge of a content area by examining a learner's construction of the wordings and meanings of its register. This is what was done in part for the assessment of Explanations A and B, and it is explored in greater depth in the next section.

Classroom Formative Assessment of L2 Learners

In this section we want to demonstrate how formative classroom assessment provides cases where teachers of L2 learners assess language and content intuitively (but not necessarily consciously) as part of the flow of classroom interaction. This is not surprising in view of the fact that language is the main means of learning content and it is also likely to be the main means of assessing content. However, to recognise these cases we need qualitative methods that incorporate a linguistic model of language that relates wording and meaning. Research on functional formative classroom assessment is vitally important in its own right, but the cases it analyses can point the way to greater use of language and content assessment in future in other areas of language assessment. As with our earlier register analysis, we will concentrate on examples of the wording and meaning of causal explanations. We will first deal with assessment in recasts and then with assessment in a unit of classroom work.

Wiliam (2007/2008) reports that syntheses of more than 4,000 research studies have shown that formative assessment for learning practices can double the rate of student learning, so this area is likely to be very important for student learning of academic language and content. The Assessment Reform Group (2002, p. 2) helpfully describes classroom formative assessment as follows:

> [T]asks and questions prompt learners to demonstrate their knowledge, understanding and skills. What learners say and do is then observed and interpreted, and judgements are made about how learning can be improved. These assessment processes are an essential part of everyday classroom practice.

One type of formative assessment is provided by formal recasts of learner errors of grammatical form:

(1) ELL: Uh yes ... a woman **drinking** (and bottle) wine, uh bottle ...
(2) NS: [RECAST] Yes and she**'s drinking** a glass or a bottle of wine?
(3) ELL: No, uh, she? ... She**'s drinking** in (no) glass.

(Long, 1996, p. 429)

The ELL's grammatical error of omitting the auxiliary in (1) is correctively recast by NS, the native speaker, in (2), who thereby assesses (1) as grammatically incorrect and provides detailed feedback to the ELL, who corrects the error in (3), showing evidence of learning. Thus the participants have interacted to construct a brief formative cycle of utterance, feedback and uptake.

A different type of formative assessment is provided by *functional* recasts, which assess learners' functional integration of wording and meaning:

(4) ELL: To extend his power in Babylon, Hammurabi made his code. He ... um ... enforce the code and limit the power of the king.
(5) T: [RECAST] So, Hammurabi extended his power throughout Babylon **by enforcing** his code and **limiting** the power of kings ... right ... good.

(Early, 2001, p. 168)

In (4) the ELL offers a social studies causal explanation of the purpose of Hammurabi's code in two sentences, but the actions of the second sentence are not explicitly related to those in the first. In (5) T, the teacher, recasts it to make the relation explicit by subordinating the second sentence to the first and making it a causal circumstance of the first (*by enforcing*). T's recast makes the meaning of causal relations more explicit through the use of the grammar, which makes the grammatical form of the original more complex. As a causal explanation, as social studies discourse and as academic discourse generally, (5) is more elaborate and "developed" than (4). Thus T's recast provides guidance for the ELL's development in academic language and content.

A more elaborate example of a functional recast by a teacher of ELLs' causal explanations occurred during a project on the human brain in a content-based language learning classroom at the university level (see Mohan & Beckett, 2003):

(6) S: We can relax our brain **by wave.**
(7) T: We can relax our brain **by wave**? How does that work? [RECAST] How does **a wave** help us relax our brains?

(8) S: Because ... **the cerebral wave** of the stable type appears when the mind relaxes, and **it improve the centering power.**

(Mohan & Beckett, 2003, p. 430)

This example shows T using a recast as part of a larger strategy for scaffolding causal explanation by formatively probing for an explanation. S, the student, offers a causal explanation in (6). In (7), T assesses (6) as needing causal elaboration, and uses the recast to pose a guiding question, making "wave" the agent of the explanation, not the means, as it is in "by wave", and offering "help" as a causal process. S's uptake in (8) offers a much more elaborated causal explanation, making "wave" the agent, using "improve" as a causal process, and adding a causal nominalization "the centering power". As a causal explanation, as scientific discourse, and as academic discourse generally, (8) is more elaborate and "developed" than (6).

As with the formal recast above, the participants in the functional recast construct a brief formative cycle of utterance, feedback and uptake. The difference here concerns the focus of the assessment, whether on wording independent of meaning as in the formal recast, or on adjusting the wording to elaborate on the meaning and thus help expand the student's language resources in context.

But functional recasting also covers cases where an utterance is made less elaborate and *accommodated* to a learner. Wording and meaning can be negotiated "down" rather than "up" (see Mohan & Beckett, 2003):

(9) S: **Mentally and physically active**? What's that?
(10) T: **It's using our brain and doing things with our hands and legs ...**

(Mohan & Beckett, 2003, p. 428)

Further evidence of functional recasting of causal explanations includes Gibbons (2006), a book-length study of teachers and learners in an ESL content-based classroom and their patterns of discourse that support both L2 development and curriculum learning, and Mohan and Luo (2005), who studied online computer-mediated communication in a graduate language education course, where ESL students skillfully functionally recast their peers' discourse as part of the normal practice of online academic discussion. Functional recasts are, of course, not limited to causal explanations but include all types of recasting that can help expand the student's language resources in context.

The qualitative functional discourse analysis of such cases shows how it is possible to study classroom assessment of language and content by assessing wording and meaning. These cases have the potential to expand conceptions of academic discourse and advanced L2 learning. When teachers are involved in examining their classroom language from this perspective, such an analysis can help them to reflect upon their intuitive functional assessment practices and build on them consciously and systematically.

Assessment of Register in a Unit of Teaching

We now illustrate a broader level, functional discourse analysis of the teaching and assessment phases of a unit of classroom teaching We will discuss a study of a Western Canadian Grade 9 mainstream science class on the theory of matter (ToM), which contained a mix of native speakers of English and ELLs (see Mohan & Slater, 2006). The field of knowledge in our example is ToM at the Grade 9 level. The teacher is one who knows the field and therefore, in functional terms, we would say that he has already constructed for himself the meaning potential of ToM. The learners, however, have to build up this meaning potential, or frame of meaning, through the process of learning the discourse of ToM. If we wish to assess their success in doing so, we need to ask the following questions: what register meanings are the learners expected to develop? How can one gather inductive evidence to assess that they understand these meanings, and have not simply memorized register wordings or are guessing?

In the teaching and learning phase of the unit, the teacher (his pseudonym: "Mr Peterson") conducted "theory" lessons on the physical properties of matter, helping students develop a register framework of ideational meanings: the taxonomy of physical properties of matter and the effects of these properties. Three physical properties of matter central to the later problem-solving task were density, magnetism and solubility. In the case of density, for instance, he engaged students in discussion of how density is defined in terms of mass and volume, and of the density of various substances (e.g. "Gold's one of the most dense [metals]"). Later he illustrated the effects of density, putting a cork and a rubber stopper in water, and explained: "why things sink or float in water is dependent on density".

In order to provide a meaningful discourse analysis of the classroom conversation about these topics, we need to draw upon three main realms of ideational meaning defined in SFL: (1) taxonomy involves the classification of things; (2) causal relations involves the representation of events; and (3) human consciousness involves perception of events. From this perspective, the problem-solving assessment task can be analysed as the third realm, human consciousness, being applied to the other two realms.

In a formative assessment phase of the lesson, the teacher aimed to assess the students' understanding of ToM by having them use their "frame of ideational meanings" to solve a separation task, where they had to separate a mixture of iron, salt, sand and gold. From a linguistic perspective they being asked to draw semantic inferences from their "frame of ideational meanings" in order to direct their actions. Introducing the task, he guided student decision-making. He emphasised that students should use their understanding of physical properties and their causal relations to draw inferences about what to do in the task. He distinguished between the "thinking science nine students way" where the students "think physical properties" (i.e. solve the problem by inferences from physical properties) and the "extremely tedious way", of sorting particles by their physical appearance (i.e. work only from what is physically obvious). He then made it clear that the property should differentiate between substances: "What's the physical property this stuff has that the others don't?" Later he returned to this point and modelled considering possible properties ("Like you can go crystal shape? No, not going to help"). In the starred examples below, Mr Peterson recast a student answer so that it clearly stated the physical property "this stuff has that the others don't" that will separate the substances. In other words, he highlighted how the student choice should be justified with an adequate reason that makes a clear inference from a distinctive physical property. Note that in the third answer the student Mike showed uptake and independently and adequately justified his choice with a reason that stated gold's distinctive property and drew the correct semantic inference that it would sink ("The gold is more dense, so it will sink to the bottom").

Processes of human consciousness are underlined. Lexis related to the problem-solving process is in upper case. Teacher recasts of student answers are double-starred (**).

Mr Peterson:	Now your JOB is to SEPARATE them into four piles. How would you do that? There's the THINKING SCIENCE NINE STUDENT'S WAY ... and then there's the EXTREMELY TEDIOUS "well, you could get a microscope or a magnifying glass and a pair of tweezers and you pick out all the things"—it'd take you forever! ... THINK PHYSICAL PROPERTIES. What's the PHYSICAL PROPERTY this stuff has that the others don't? Stan?
Stan:	Use a magnet to separate the iron? ...
Mr Peterson:	Right. There's one. ** IRON'S ATTRACTED. NONE of the OTHERS are. What's next? What would you do next? Yeah?
Student:	Dissolve the salt in water.
Mr Peterson:	Add water. ** the SALT will DISSOLVE. The SAND and GOLD won't. Good ... Okay what's next? You've got sand and gold ...
Keith:	Pan for gold.

Mr Peterson:	THINK of a PHYSICAL PROPERTY that SEPARATES the two. Like you can go crystal shape? No not going to help. Solubility? No neither of them dissolve. No viscosity? No that's for liquid. Magnetism? Neither are magnetic. Color? Well that's good if you want to do the tweezers METHOD okay? … How does panning work? …
Mike:	Add water to it. And shake it around and the GOLD is MORE DENSE, so it'll SINK to the bottom and the SAND will –
Mr Peterson:	But the SAND would SINK too wouldn't it?
Mike:	No. It would SINK but if you keep SPINNING it wouldn't.

To illustrate how answers as semantic inferences relate back to the theory, the answer "Add water to it. And shake it around" is warranted by the reason "the gold is more dense [than sand], so it [the gold]'ll sink to the bottom", which is based on the general causal statement that "why things sink or float in water is dependent on density" and on the general taxonomic statement that "Gold's one of the most dense [metals]."

The teacher's register assessment strategy was: (1) to pose a problem case that needed the theory/register that was taught for its solution; (2) to identify a set of possible alternatives to choose among (the physical properties); (3) to ask for an answer that required semantic inferences about the case from the theory; and (4) to scaffold the students to provide reasons based on the theory for these semantic inferences. Note how the teacher explicitly guided the students' decision-making process, from (1) through (4).

In our example of register analysis of ideational meaning, content is meaning in text, encoded in wording. Teaching and learning involved building meaning, building taxonomies and causal relations, and engaging learners in talking and thinking about them. Assessing content was assessing meaning, constructing decision-situations to assess the learners' ability to interpret a case by drawing inferences, and justifying them, from the theory, the register frame of meanings. In sum, our example showed both how language can be the major means of learning content and how language can be the major means of assessing content.

Since semantic inference is central to this teacher's assessment strategies, it is worthwhile drawing a parallel with research on inference in reading assessment. Grabe (2009, pp. 68–70) points out how inferencing is a highly important and ubiquitous cognitive process and how reading research demonstrates that making inferences to interpret academic texts is critical for reading comprehension, can be a very demanding skill, and is one that begins by explicitly learning academic inferencing as a strategy. However, in a discussion of test design in reading, Alderson (2000, p. 164) states that the distinction between a language user understanding information explicitly stated in the text and making inferences about information is a distinction that has been very difficult to categorise reliably in reading research. By contrast, it seems that the distinction between theory and inferences from it in a problem task is very well-marked in our example. It would appear therefore that discourse analysis that would reveal strategies of semantic inferencing and inference justification in teacher functional formative assessment could pay considerable dividends in understanding both language and content in the classroom and academic reading.

Conclusion

The brief examples from academic language assessment and the language of content in the classroom reveal the critical qualitative issue in L2 assessment. Language assessments need to provide learners with the opportunities to demonstrate their capacity for using their linguistic resources for constructing and interpreting academic meanings. Assessments that fail to provide such opportunities cannot be argued to provide scores indicating learners' ability to do so, nor can they be argued as useable for academic gatekeeping and formative classroom assessment. Qualitative research in language assessment needs to be appropriately framed to investigate how meaning is made in assessment contexts because it is ability for meaning making that is central to the construct that is assessed.

If the ability of interest is learners' use of language for making meaning, it is hard to see how language assessment can ignore wording–meaning relations. We have therefore exemplified the academic meanings (e.g. causal relationships, taxonomy) and linguistic resources (e.g. grammatical metaphor) that are included with an SFL framework to guide a relevant approach to discourse analysis. We focused on the language of education because this is an area where the meanings learners need to construe are particularly complex. However, in all forms of communicative language testing, task-based language testing or performance testing the basic issue is the same: if the construct of interest is examinees' ability to use language to make meaning, the qualitative discourse analysis used in validation research needs to be capable of revealing the types of linguistic meanings that are made.

References

Abbey, R. (2000). *Charles Taylor.* Princeton, NJ: Princeton University Press.

Abedi, J. (2004). The No Child Left Behind Act and English language learners: Assessment and accountability issues. *Educational Researcher, 33,* 4–14.

Alderson, J. C. (2000). *Assessing reading.* Cambridge and New York: Cambridge University Press.

Assessment Reform Group. (2002). Assessment for learning: 10 principles. Cambridge: Faculty of Education, University of Cambridge.

Bachman, L. (1990). *Fundamental considerations in language testing.* Oxford: Oxford University Press.

Bachman, L. F., & Palmer, A. S. (1996). *Language testing in practice.* Oxford: Oxford University Press.

Brisk, M., & Zisselsberger, M. (2007). We've let them in on the secret: using SFL theory to improve teaching of writing to bilingual learners. In T. Lucas (Ed.), (forthcoming) *Envisioning possibilities: Preparing all teachers to teach English language learners.* Mahwah, NJ: Lawrence Erlbaum.

Byrnes, H. (2008). Assessing content and language. In E. Shohamy & N. H. Hornberger (Eds.), *Encyclopedia of language education. 2nd edition. Volume 7: Language testing and assessment* (pp. 37–52). Dordrecht: Springer/Kluwer Academic Publishers.

Byrnes, H. (2009). Emergent L2 German writing ability in a curricular context: A longitudinal study of grammatical metaphor. *Linguistics & Education, 20*(1), 50–66.

Canale, M., & Swain, M. (1980). Theoretical bases of communicative approaches to second language teaching and testing. *Applied Linguistics, 1*(1), 1–47.

Chapelle, C. A., Enright, M. K. & Jamieson, J. M. (Eds.) (2008). *Building a validity argument for the Test of English as a Foreign Language.* New York and London: Routledge.

Christie, F., & Derewianka, B. (2008). *School discourse.* London and New York: Continuum.

Coffin, C., & Hewings, A. (2004). IELTS as preparation for tertiary writing: Distinctive interpersonal and textual strategies. In L. Ravelli & R. Ellis (Eds.), *Analysing academic writing* (pp. 153–171). London: Continuum.

Cumming, A. (1998). Theoretical perspectives on writing. *Annual Review of Applied Linguistics, 18,* 61–78.

Early, M. (2001). Language and content in social practice: A case study. *Canadian Modern Language Review, 59*(1), 157–179.

Fought, J.G. (1999). *Leonard Bloomfield.* London and New York: Routledge.

Gebhard, M., Harman, R. & Seger, W. (2007). Reclaiming recess in urban schools: The potential of systemic functional linguistics for ELLs and their teachers. *Language Arts, 84*(5), 419–430.

Gernsbacher, M. A., & Givon, T. (Eds.) (1995). *Coherence in spontaneous text.* Philadelphia: Benjamins.

Gibbons, P. (2006). *Bridging discourses in the ESL classroom.* London and New York: Continuum.

Givon, T. (2005). *Context as other minds.* Amsterdam: Benjamins.

Grabe, W. (2009). *Reading in a second language.* Cambridge and New York: Cambridge University Press.

Halliday, M. A. K. (1985). *An introduction to functional grammar.* London: Edward Arnold.

Halliday, M. A. K. (1993). The act of meaning. Applied Linguistics Association of Australia occasional paper 13, 42–61.

Halliday, M. A. K., & Martin, J. (1993). *Writing science: Literacy and discursive power.* Pittsburgh: University of Pittsburgh Press.

Halliday, M. A. K., & Matthiessen, C. M. I. M. (1999). *Construing experience through meaning: A language-based approach to cognition*. London and New York: Cassell.

Halliday, M. A. K., & Matthiessen, C. M. I. M. (2004). *An introduction to functional grammar* (3rd ed.). London: Arnold.

Lado, R. (1961). *Language testing*. New York: McGraw-Hill.

Long, M. H. (1996). The role of the linguistic environment in second language acquisition. In W. Ritchie & T. Bhatia (Eds.), *Handbook of second language acquisition* (pp. 413–468). New York: Academic Press.

Longacre, R. E. (1996). *The grammar of discourse*. New York and London: Plenum Press.

Low, M. (in press). Teachers and texts: Judging what ELLs know from what they say. In A. Paran & L. Sercu (Eds.), *Testing the untestable in language education*. Clevedon: Multilingual Matters.

Lumley, T., & Brown, A. (2005). Research methods for language testing. In E. Hinkel (Ed.), *Handbook of research in second language teaching and learning* (pp. 833–856). London: Lawrence Erlbaum.

Macken, M., & Slade, D. (1993). Assessment: A Foundation for effective learning in the school context. In B. Cope & M. Kalantzis (Eds.), *The powers of literacy: A genre approach to teaching writing* (pp. 203–220). Pittsburgh: University of Pittsburgh Press.

McNamara, T., Hill, K. & May, L. (2002). Discourse and assessment. In M. McGroarty (Ed.), *Annual Review of Applied Linguistics, 22*, 221–242. New York: Cambridge University Press.

Mickan, P., & Slater, S. (2003). Text analysis and the assessment of academic writing. In R. Tulloh (Ed.), *IELTS research reports* (Vol. 4). Canberra: IELTS Australia.

Mohan, B., & Beckett, G. H. (2003). A functional approach to research on content-based language learning: Recasts in causal explanations. *Modern Language Journal, 87*(iii), 421–432.

Mohan, B., Leung, C. & Slater, T. (in press). Assessing language and content: A functional perspective. In A. Paran & L. Sercu (Eds.), *Testing the untestable in language education*. Clevedon: Multilingual Matters.

Mohan, B., & Luo, L. (2005). A systemic functional linguistics perspective on CALL. In J. Egbert and G. Petrie (Eds.), *Research perspectives in CALL* (pp. 87–96). Mahwah, NJ: Lawrence Erlbaum Associates, Inc.

Mohan, B., & Slater, T. (2004). The evaluation of causal discourse and language as a resource for meaning. In J. A. Foley (Ed.), *Language, education, and discourse: Functional approaches* (pp. 255–269). New York: Continuum.

Mohan B., & Slater T. (2006). Examining the theory/practice relation in a high school science register: A functional perspective. *Journal of English for Academic Purposes, 5*, 302–316.

Painter, C. (1999). *Learning through language in early childhood*. London: Continuum.

Schegloff, E., Koshik, I., Jacoby, S. & Olsher, D. (2002). Conversation Analysis and applied linguistics. In M. McGroarty (Ed.), *Annual Review of Applied Linguistics, 22*, 3–31. New York: Cambridge University Press.

Schleppegrell, M., & Go, A. (2007). Analyzing the writing of English learners: A functional approach. *Language Arts, 84*(6), 529–538.

Slater, T., & Mohan, B. (in press). Towards systematic and sustained formative assessment of causal explanations in oral interactions. In A. Paran & L. Sercu (Eds.), *Testing the untestable in language education*. Clevedon: Multilingual Matters.

Swain, M., Brooks, L. & Tocalli-Beller, A. (2002). Peer-peer dialogue as a means of second language learning. In M. McGroarty (Ed.), *Annual Review of Applied Linguistics, 22*, 171–185. New York: Cambridge University Press.

Taylor, C. A., & Angelis, P. (2008). The evolution of the TOEFL. In C. A. Chapelle, M. K. Enright & J. M. Jamieson (Eds.), *Building a validity argument for the Test of English as a Foreign Language* (pp. 27–54). New York and London: Routledge.

Widdowson, H. G. (2001). Communicative language testing: The art of the possible. In C. Elder, A. Brown, N. Iwashita, E. Grove, K. Hill, T. Lumley, T. McNamara & K. O'Loughlin (Eds.), *Experimenting with uncertainty: Essays in honour of Alan Davies* (pp. 12–21). Cambridge: Cambridge University Press.

Wiliam, D. (2007/2008). Changing classroom practice. *Educational Leadership, 65*(4), 36–42.

46
Assessment of Classroom Language Learning

Joan Jamieson

In the 2005 *Handbook*, Constance Leung discussed one central aspect of classroom language assessment—research and practice in teacher assessment. He defined teacher assessment as "the noticing and gathering of information about student language use in ordinary (non-contrived) classroom activities, and the use of that information to make decisions about language teaching without necessarily quantifying it or using it for reporting purposes" (Leung, 2005, p. 871). Leung showed how such assessment events, which are woven into fabric of language classroom teaching, rely on teachers' understanding of the constructs and proficiency frameworks with which they are working. Leung argued that such assessment knowledge and practice is central to language learning in the classroom.

In this volume of the *Handbook*, the focus is on a complementary type of classroom assessment that can reflect and support learning—criterion-referenced assessment. Criterion-referenced assessment is used both during and at the end of instruction. It is often seen as more traditional than alternative, more contrived than authentic, and more formal than informal. Criterion-referenced assessment has a well-established history in language assessment as well as in other areas of education as a means of focusing the attention of both teachers and learners on important areas of instruction. Because of the formal and explicit character of much criterion-referenced assessment, in teacher education it provides a useful starting point for helping teachers to gain an understanding of assessment practices, which they can draw upon in developing other classroom assessments, as well as in understanding principles of assessments that are external to their classrooms.

Criterion-Referenced Assessment

What is criterion-referenced assessment? According to Robert Linn (1994, p. 12) criterion-referenced assessment is a concept that "ranks high among a small list of seminal ideas that have had a lasting impact on the thinking and practice of educational measurement." The idea was put forth in a brief article by Robert Glaser (1963, pp. 519–520):

> Achievement measurement can be defined as the assessment of terminal or criterion behavior; this involves the determination of the characteristics of student performance with respect to specified standards ... The scores obtained from an achievement test provide primarily two kinds of information. One is the degree to which the student has attained criterion performance, for example, whether he can satisfactorily prepare an experimental report ... The second type

of information … is the relative ordering of individuals with respect to their test performance … The principal difference between these two types of information lies in the standard used as a reference. What I shall call criterion-referenced measures depend upon an absolute standard of quality, while what I term norm-referenced measures depend upon a relative standard … Underlying the concept of achievement measurement is the notion of a continuum of knowledge acquisition ranging from no proficiency at all to perfect performance … The term "criterion," when used is this way, does not necessarily refer to final end-of-course behavior. Criterion levels can be established at any point in instruction where it is necessary to obtain information as to the adequacy of an individual's performance.

Note that criterion-referenced assessment is explained in contrast to norm-referenced assessment, which up to that time had been the prevailing approach to the interpretation of test scores (Brown & Hudson, 2002; Popham, 1978). Similarities and differences between norm-referenced and criterion-referenced tests representing two ends of a continuum are summarized in Table 46.1.

Uses of Criterion-Referenced Assessment

Two important instructional decisions involve deciding what learners can do at a certain point in time in relation to the achievement of particular instructional goals (a summative purpose) and monitoring learner progress during instruction (a formative purpose). Criterion-referenced assessment is used for both purposes and it provides a means of targeting feedback. Feedback serves to reinforce successful learning and to identify learning errors and misconceptions. Feedback can also

Table 46.1 Comparison of Norm-Referenced and Criterion-Reference Test Characteristics

Comparison of norm-referenced tests (NRT) and criterion-referenced tests (CRT)		
Similarities	**Differences in emphasis**	
	NRT	**CRT**
1. Both require specification of the achievement domain to be measured.	1. Typically cover a large domain of learning tasks, with just a few items measuring each specific task.	1. Typically focuses on a delimited domain of learning tasks, with a relatively large number of items measuring each specific task.
2. Both require a relevant and representative sample of test items.	2. Emphasizes discrimination among individuals in terms of relative level of learning.	2. Emphasizes description of what learning tasks individuals can and cannot perform.
3. Both use the same types of test items.	3. Favors items of average difficulty and typically omits very easy and very hard items.	3. Matches item difficulty to learning tasks, without altering item difficulty or omitting easy or hard items.
4. Both use the same rules for item writing (except for item difficulty).	4. Interpretation requires a clearly defined group.	4. Interpretation requires a clearly defined and delimited achievement domain.
5. Both are judged by the same qualities of goodness (validity and reliability).		
6. Both are useful in educational assessment.		

Adopted with formatting changes from Miller, Linn, and Gronlund (2009, p. 42).

lead to further action—giving teachers the opportunity to modify instruction and giving learners the opportunity for individualized practice (Miller et al., 2009; Rea-Dickins, 2006). Frequent use of different types of assessment in the classroom, whether formative, summative, or both, underscores the need to examine its intended and unintended effects. Such examination clarifies the extent to which assessment promotes learning (Linn, Baker, & Dunbar, 1991; Rea-Dickins, 2001).

Educational research has long found assessment to be effective for student learning. Reasons proposed for positive effects include that assessments can show students what is important, provide relevant feedback on performance, provide practice and active processing of content, consolidate learning, develop students' study skills, and increase their positive attitudes and motivation (e.g., Baker, Herman, & Linn, 2005; Bangert-Drowns, Kulik, & Kulik, 1991; Black & Wiliam; 1998; Crooks, 1988; Jones, 1923; Maloney & Ruch, 1929; Stiggins, 2004).

The effect of directing attention to what is tested is well documented. Assessment influences the kinds of preparations students make, it shows students what is important or valued, and by doing so it influences teaching and learning (e.g., Bloom, 1986). Having such influence can have unintended consequences: "We start out with the intention of making the important measureable, and end up making the measurable important" (Wiliam, 2000, p. 165). By focusing too closely on the assessment, teachers and students may have a tendency to de-emphasize material that is not included in assessment (Frederiksen, 1984; Linn et al., 1991). Apart from narrowing the curriculum, tests may have adverse consequences on those students whose talents are not tapped by traditional achievement tests (Black & William, 1998; the Assessment Reform Group (ARG), 1999). To counter negative effects, ARG developed *Assessment for learning*, "the process of seeking and interpreting evidence for use by learners and their teachers to decide where the learners are in their learning, where they need to go, and how best to get there" (Assessment Reform Group, 2002).

While the function of summative assessment is mainly reporting on students' achievement, the function of formative assessment is to affect students' learning. Black and Wiliam (1998) defined formative assessment as a sequence of two events. First, the learner has to perceive a gap between her/his present state and her/his desired goal, and second, the learner has to do something to close that gap so that s/he can reach that goal. The first event, the perception of a gap, is often a result of feedback. Response to feedback may lead the learner to close the gap. Feedback has been defined as any of numerous procedures, such as a comment or information from a teacher, other learners, or from oneself, that is used to tell a learner if an instructional response is right or wrong (Bangert-Drowns, Kulik, Kulik, & Morgan, 1991; Colby-Kelly & Turner, 2007; Kulhavy, 1977; Rea-Dickins, 2001). In some studies, feedback was most effective when the learner made an error while having high confidence that s/he was correct (Kulhavy & Stock, 1989). In our own field, similar ideas are found in the work of Schmidt (1993), Gass (1997), and Swain (1993), for example. Feedback is thought to play a facilitative role in focus-on-form instruction in which teachers provide corrective feedback, often in the form of recasts, metalinguistic explanations for oral language, and the location of the error for written language (e.g., Lyster, 2007; Russell & Spada, 2006; Williams, 2005). Recent findings regarding the benefit of responding to feedback have been mixed (e.g., Mackey & Goo, 2007; McDonough & Mackey, 2006).

Challenges in Constructing Criterion-Referenced Assessment

Criterion-referenced assessment requires that the criterion must be clearly defined, because, as Brindley (1989) noted, learners' success cannot be determined if there are no criteria on which the learner is to be judged. This belief is in contrast to that put forward by Wiliam (2000; cf. Davison, 2004), who advocates no attempt to define a criterion, but instead to rely on the consensus of teachers making the assessments. How, then, is the "criterion" defined? Consider a horizontally-oriented continuum. At one end, we place Wiliam's view. At the other end, we place the view of Cartier (1968) who thought it necessary to include a complete inventory of all of the behaviors of adequate performance of second language tasks. Middle ground was suggested by Linn (1994), who urged test developers not to be too literal in trying to define a criterion and suggested we consider Glaser's example of preparing an experimental report. He would not define all elements that go into report writing, but instead keep in mind that the criterion is a construct—a construct that is defined according to a reasonable set of characteristics that reflect valued performance. The definition of these valued characteristics may vary along abstract and concrete ends of an explanation continuum. Envisioning this continuum vertically instead of horizontally, these "planes of explanation" move from abstract theories of language proficiency, to psycholinguistic processes and strategies, to concrete features of language tasks, ideally all systematically related to each other (Chapelle, 2008).

Two approaches for defining our instructional values are based on content objectives and classroom objectives. The content approach samples information included in a text. Tyler (1934) and Bloom (1986) found this approach disappointing as it often resulted in assessments that required simple recall of information; instead, they advocated objective-based assessments requiring students' reasoning and skill in interpreting relevant data, reflecting their interests and attitudes. Hughes (1989) described the situation for second language assessment. The view that test content should be based directly on a textbook has appeal as the test only contains what students have been exposed to. A disadvantage is that successful performance on a test that requires students to read aloud sentences containing phonemic contrasts may not indicate successful achievement of a classroom objective of the development of conversational ability.

Today, many published instructional materials including books and websites utilize the content approach in their accompanying criterion-referenced assessments. Examples include *NorthStar* for English (Boyd & Numrich, 2009), *Rendez-vous* for French (Muyskens & Omaggio Hadley, 2002), *Kontakte* for German (Terrell, Tschirner, & Nikolai, 2005), *Nakama* for Japanese (Hatasa, Hatasa, & Makino, 2010), and *Puntos en breve* for Spanish (Knorre, Dorwick, Perez Girones, Glass, & Villarreal, 2007). Such text/assessment combinations are important because of their widespread use. To illustrate, a representative of Pearson publishing company estimated that between 300 and 400 million people are currently using published materials to study English as a second or foreign language (based on a broad definition of published materials as new, used, handed down, etc., and estimates that of the one billion people currently studying English worldwide, 30–40% are using published materials; P. Alongi, personal communication, October 16, 2009). For students, these assessments provide feedback about what was learned, help them to recognize the important material in a unit, and motivate them to study. For teachers, they provide ready-made tests that are easy to administer and score. One important difference between textbook assessment and teacher-made assessments lies in the fact that these published tests are necessarily based on content objectives rather than classroom objectives. Due to their prevalence, both materials-based and classroom-based assessments reflect contemporary implementations of applied linguistics theory and research and as such need to be understood by practitioners.

One implication of criterion-referenced assessment is the requirement for test developers, whether textbook writers or classroom teachers, to reflect on their objectives and then to develop tasks and assess students in relation to those objectives. This notion is reflected in the expectations for teachers in *Assessment for learning* (Assessment Reform Group, 2002; Stiggins, 2005), which allow for a wide array of tools that teachers can use in classroom assessment. Black and Wiliam (1998, 2006) organize these tools into five components of a teacher's kit: choice of task, discourse, questions, tests, and feedback. It is important for each teacher to choose among the tools, selecting those which work best in a given context. However, teachers need support in implementing new assessment practices. Teachers' practices in formative assessment have been found to be weak (Black & Wiliam, 1998, 2006; Brindley,

2001; Crooks, 1988; Rea-Dickins & Gardner, 2000). Because much of formative assessment, as well as summative assessment, includes achievement tests as indicators of student learning, it seems wise that teachers' professional development should provide a grounding in criterion-referenced assessment, an important assessment concept.

Assessment Based on Language Learning Materials

Content Objectives of a Reading/Writing Textbook Unit

One popular textbook series, *NorthStar* (Boyd & Numrich, 2009) serves as an example. This integrated skills series for English as a second or foreign language to young adults includes two textbooks at five levels of ability. One textbook is for reading/writing and the other is for listening/speaking. Every unit is divided into three parts: focus on the topic, focus on reading (or listening), and focus on writing (or speaking).

As with many published language learning materials, each unit follows the same format in which topics, linguistic content, and exercise types vary. This structure, presented in the material's scope and sequence, provides an outline for test design, filled in with the help of a content analysis. A content analysis describes a unit's written and/or spoken texts, tasks and task types, requirements of the student to complete the task, objective of the task, and number of items for each task. The content analysis of Reading/Writing Unit 6 in the intermediate level textbook is partially reproduced below (Barton & Sardinas, 2009). In Table 46.2, we see the three parts of the unit that are further divided into sections including one or more tasks. Some tasks direct students to work in small groups and to integrate skills, whereas others direct students to work alone, answering multiple choice questions or writing sentences. The objectives for the tasks are keyed to the scope statements. The number of items along with the suggestions for customizing the units in the *Teacher's manual* helps the test developer to determine the appropriate weighting of test tasks. The test should reflect the content in the book, while conforming to constraints such as time. An end-of-unit test should be efficient, using only a minimum of class time. Considering both content and time, for this example the test design included three parts—vocabulary, reading, and writing—and would take no more than 45 minutes.

Specifications

One method for displaying overall test design is to create a matrix, called a "Table of Specifications" whose main purposes are to guard against the omission of key material or the overemphasis of relatively unimportant material, and to ensure that there is a representative sample of tasks (Miller et al., 2009; Millman & Green, 1989; Ruch, 1929). Table 46.3 displays the Table of Specifications for our example assessment (Jamieson & Chapelle, 2009).

The task of setting forth the objectives (i.e., what is valued) is necessary to indicate what the test is intended to measure. This step has been, and continues to be, explicit in design of criterion-referenced achievement tests (e.g., Davidson & Lynch, 2002; Miller et al., 2009; Popham, 1978; Tyler, 1934). The scope of each unit in the reading and writing textbooks of *NorthStar* includes language objectives in five areas: critical thinking skills, reading skills, writing skills, vocabulary, and grammar.

When creating this Table of Specifications, five steps were followed. First the objectives and the content were listed. Then, percentages were determined. Next, the total number of items was estimated. Then, the number of items per objective and content was distributed. Finally, the number of items per cell was computed.

Table 46.2 Excerpt of Content Analysis for *NorthStar* Unit 6, Book 3

Part	Section	Description of task	Requirement for student	Task type	Task objective(s)	Number of items
1. Focus on topic	A. Predicting	Look at answer three questions; discuss with classmates	Express and map; share opinions	Integrated: R, S, L	R: predict	3
	C. Background and vocabulary	Read definitions multiple choice questions in which key word is underlined	Study and use vocabulary	Multiple choice (4 options)	V: definitions	10
2. Focus on reading	A. Reading 1: Tourists in a Fragile Land; 555 words; first person scientist; formal	Read five paragraphs and order three main ideas as they appear in text	2. Read and order main ideas	Order events	R: identify chronology	3
		Fill in outline with details from reading	3. Read for details	Fill in the blank	R: details	6
3. Focus on writing	A. Vocabulary	Match key vocabulary with adjective/noun	1. Review vocabulary in 1C	Match	V: collocations	8
	B. Grammar for writing: because/even though	Read two sentences; rewrite into one sentence using target forms	2. Use because and even though	Short answer: sentence	W: grammar	7
	C. Focused writing task	Write essay and check it for errors against checklist	4. Write and edit	Write an essay	W: opinion CT: point of view	1

The Table of Specifications lists the textbook's objectives across the top row, and lists the content down the first column. The last row at the bottom of the chart displays the percentage allocation for each objective. Critical thinking skills cover 10% of the test, reading skills cover 15%, writing skills cover 42.5%, vocabulary covers 25%, and grammar covers 7.5%. These percentages comprise 100% of the test. In a similar manner, the last column on the right displays the percentage allocation for the parts of the test. The unit's vocabulary makes up 25% of the test; reading makes up an additional 25%, divided among two readings and an integrated task; and writing makes up 50% of the test, with 25% for grammar, style, editing, and revision tasks, and the other 25% for an essay. Once the percentages have been decided on, then the total number of items (or points) needs to be determined; keeping in mind that there should be about 10 items per objective and considering the

Table 46.3 Table of Specifications for *NorthStar Reading and Writing*

	Critical thinking skills	Reading skills	Writing skills	Vocabulary	Grammar	No. of tasks/ points	Percentage of total tasks
Part 1. Key words							
Unit vocabulary (5 min.)				10		**10**	25%
Part 2. Reading							
Reading #1 (5 min.)		3				**3**	7.5%
Reading #2 (5 min.)		3				**3**	7.5%
Integrate readings (5 min.)	4					**4**	10%
Part 3. Writing							
Grammar/Style/ Editing/Revising (5 min.)			7		3	**10**	25%
Paragraph/Essay (20 min.)			1 (10 points)			**10**	25%
No. of points on test	**4**	**6**	**17**	**10**	**3**	**40**	
Percentage of total tasks	10%	15%	42.5%	25%	7.5%		100%

amount of time available, a total of 40 points was decided upon. Then, to determine the number of items per content area and objective the total number of points was multiplied by the proportion of tasks on the test. For example, 10 vocabulary items were needed (40 × 0.25). Because only one extended writing sample could be expected in 20 minutes, it was worth 10 points to represent 25% of the total score.

Once these numbers were computed, it was then a matter of filling in the cells in the body of the table. Four items (10%) measured critical thinking skills; two readings were needed to have the test-taker relate information across reading passages. Six items (15%) were to measure reading skills; three items were allocated to each reading passage. In a similar way, the 10 writing items were to be divided among grammar, style, editing, and revising.

The Table of Specifications provides the design for the test. Once this is determined, it must be fleshed out. Five test specification components for criterion-referenced tests outlined by Popham (1978) are described in detail for second language teachers by Davidson and Lynch (2002; see also Bachman & Palmer, 1996). For this particular unit test, content elements to consider were the topic (i.e., tourism), key vocabulary (e.g., coastal, fragile, landscape), and task objectives such as main idea and detail, predicting, collocations, writing sentences with adverbial clauses, and stating opinions. Item types needed to be specified. Because these tests were to be delivered both on paper and on-line, many of the items needed to be machine scorable. All of these decisions require the test developer to return to the original design and make adjustments, but having an original design makes it easier to keep the lesson and test objectives in mind.

In this example, the writing task would be scored by the teacher. The writing rubric was modeled after the TOEFL iBT™'s integrated writing rubric (Pearlman, 2008) and illustrates a middle ground between norm-referenced and criterion-referenced assessments alluded to earlier. The scale ranges from a high score of 5 to a low score of 0. In order to account for the 10 points required in the Table of Specifications, the 0–5 score was multiplied by two. Whereas the TOEFL iBT™ scoring rubric is intended to distinguish levels of English proficiency, this *NorthStar 3* scoring rubric is intended to show progress in students' writing at the third level. An example of the scoring rubric for score levels 3 and 5 is shown in Table 46.4.

Because the *NorthStar 3* scoring bands were intended to show criterion-referenced achievement within the duration of a period of instruction rather than norm-referenced proficiency among a group of test-takers at one point in time, they make finer distinctions than TOEFL iBT™'s scoring bands. You can see that TOEFL iBT™'s band 3 is expanded to scores 3, 4, or 5 for *NorthStar 3* (Table 46.5). In this way, it is hoped that students will be able to both see improvement in their scores and receive high marks, while still writing at the level that would receive a score of 3 on TOEFL.

Table 46.4 *NorthStar 3* Achievement Test Scoring Rubric—Writing

Score	Description
5	A response at this level contains relevant information from the test reading passage; the information is generally coherent and connected and is marked by several of the following: • Adequate organization; effective use of transition words and phrases to display unity and progression of information. • A clearly identifiable introduction, body, and conclusion although the introduction or conclusion might need more development; there is a main idea and multiple supporting sentences per paragraph. • Consistent, generally correct use of word order, pronouns, relative clauses, modals, and auxiliary + main verbs; sentences often include multiple clauses or subordination. • Appropriate use of a variety of vocabulary items from the unit. • Several language errors throughout.
3	A response at this level contains relevant information from the test reading passage; the information is not coherent or connected and is marked by several of the following: • Somewhat adequate organization; there is a somewhat effective attempt to use transition words and phrases to sequence and organize information. • More than one paragraph; there is a main idea and multiple supporting sentences per paragraph. • Consistent, correct use of subject–verb agreement, pronouns, relative clauses, infinitives, modals, and simple verb tenses. • Appropriate use of a variety of vocabulary items from the unit. • Several language errors throughout.

Table 46.5 Correspondence between Scores on TOEFL iBT™ and *NorthStar* Writing

TOEFL iBT		NorthStar 3
3–4	⟵⟶	5
3	⟵⟶	4
3	⟵⟶	3
2	⟵⟶	2
1–2	⟵⟶	1
0–1	⟵⟶	0

Paper-Based vs. Computer-Based

Designing tests for textbooks for both paper-based and on-line administration involves consideration of layout, scoring of answers, and feedback to students. One difference involves the very nature of reading. Reading passages on paper and on computer screen may have some differential effects on test performance (e.g., Bridgeman, Lennon, & Jackenthal, 2003; Kim & Huynh, 2008), although recent research surveys indicate the difference in general is not significant (e.g., Wang, Jiao, Young, Brooks, & Olson, 2008). Also, the ease with which a reader can go back over a text on paper is different from the links within a text that can be active on-line (De Ridder, 2003). Paper-based tests will be scored by the teacher and so there is flexibility in the types of responses students provide. Computer-based scoring is often limited to machine matching between the input of the student and the pre-programmed answer; the longer the string of language, the more problematic the accuracy of machine scoring. A final consideration involves feedback to the test-taker. Both a teacher and a computer program have the flexibility to give students feedback and to assign additional materials, providing for the positive effects of formative assessment. However, the time it takes for a teacher to compute total scores and scores for each objective for each student is nontrivial. For the computerized version of the test, it was possible to immediately summarize performance on all machine scored items to the student (for all but the writing section of the test). Information was also provided as to which questions were answered correctly and incorrectly (showing the correct answer). Based on the number of incorrect answers for an objective, a student was provided a link to review the material and to practice with new tasks (Jamieson, Grgurovic, & Becker, 2008).

Assessment Based on a Language Classroom

Turning to classroom objectives, we continue with our example now with a teacher of an intermediate-level reading/writing class in an intensive English program[1,2] using the *NorthStar* textbook.

Classroom Objectives of a Reading/Writing Class

The teacher's course objectives are displayed in the first column of Table 46.6. Comparing this list with the objectives presented in the Scope and Sequence section of the textbook (see Table 46.3), the teacher has adopted many of the text's objectives, and has added a few of her own, namely increasing reading fluency and extensive reading, and writing summaries. The teacher is responsible for summative evaluation of the students. In the United States, this is often done using percentages which are translated into letter grades: 90% to 100% = A, 80% to 89% = B, 70 to 79% = C, 60 to 69% = D, and below 59% = F, or failure.

In this example, both criterion-referenced tests and other assessments are used to monitor student progress and determine end-of-course achievement, as indicated by the presence of crosses in the cells in Table 46.6. Tests account for 50% of the final grade, homework accounts for 30%, a speed chart and an outside reading chart each account for 10%.

Classroom Test Design

For this class, tests needed to cover seven different learning objectives. Except for summary writing, the tests designed for the textbook series seemed suitable. There were, however, changes that were needed to reflect classroom realities and the course objectives. First, the teacher wanted to give a test after every three units. Second, the teacher was interested in having students demonstrate that they understood the meaning and/or morphology of the key words, and also show that they understood

Table 46.6 Objectives and Weight for Summative Evaluation of a Reading/Writing Class

Objectives chart	Tests	Homework	Speed chart	Reading
Understanding and using key vocabulary	X	X		
Understanding main ideas, details, inferences	X	X		
Comparing and evaluating ideas across readings	X	X		
Summarizing reading in own words	X	X		
Increasing reading speed			X	
Reading books and longer, more complex texts				X
Organizing writing	X	X		
Conveying ideas in writing	X	X		
Writing grammatical sentences	X	X		
Weight	50%	30%	10%	10%

them in context, and could use them correctly in essays. The teacher wanted the students to show their understanding of a text by writing a summary. Also, the teacher did not want students to write discrete sentences, but rather to use sentences accurately in their writing. Here we see an example of the way classroom objectives would not have been assessed if only the publisher's content-based test had been used.

These changes are reflected in the Table of Specifications outlined in Table 46.7. The course objectives included in the test are in the top row. There are five main objectives. The bottom row shows that vocabulary counted for 15% of the total score; reading comprehension counted for 30%; essay writing, 30%; summary writing, 15%; and organization, 10%. The numbers in the cells refer to the part, section, and item numbers in the test. The vocabulary items are discrete items (those beginning with 1), reading in context items (those beginning with 2), and using vocabulary in essay "items" (those beginning with 4). The two vocabulary in context items were scored two times, once for the vocabulary score, and once for the reading score; this points to the fact that in classroom testing content concerns often outweigh psychometric concerns. (Two excellent resources for psychometric concerns in language testing are Bachman, 2004 and Brown & Hudson, 2002.)

Writing Rubrics

The rubrics developed for the textbook provided a good starting point for the classroom rubrics. The holistic score, though, did not provide the teacher with a formative assessment tool to show students their strengths and weaknesses. So, the components of the holistic rubric were teased out according to the three classroom objectives of writing about content, in an organized way, with grammatical sentences and appropriate word choice, shown in Table 46.8.

For summary writing, the analytic rubric was modified to include the teacher's objective to have students develop skills to paraphrase rather than to copy; an excerpt of this rubric is shown in Table 46.9. By using these analytic rubrics the teacher could show a student where s/he is, and where s/he needs to go.

Another change worth noting regards the scale and its implications for summative assessment. The textbook tests use a scale of 5, 4, 3, 2, 1, 0. In a US classroom setting, teachers often convert such a scale to letter grades where a 5 = A, 4 = B, 3 = C, etc. In the Table of Specifications and the rubric, we saw that a student's essay could receive a maximum of 15 points, as it was scored by two people its total weight was 30 points.

Table 46.7 Table of Specifications for Classroom-Based Test Using *NorthStar Reading and Writing 3*

| Objective | Vocabulary | Reading comprehension | | | | Essay writing | Summary writing | Organization | Total items | % |
Text type		Main idea and details	Inference	Connecting info	Vocabulary	Writing				
Unit 6 333 word passage 9.0 grade level	2 1.1.1 2.3.5	3 2.3.1 2.3.2 2.3.4	1 2.3.3	5 2.5.1 2.5.2 2.5.3 2.5.4 2.5.5	1 2.3.5		1 4.1	2 3.1.1 3.1.2	18	41.5
Unit 6 252 word passage 9.7 grade level		3 2.4.1 2.4.2 2.4.3								
Unit 7 69 word passage 10.8 grade level	3 1.2.1 1.2.2 1.2.3		1 2.1					3 3.2.1 3.2.2 3.2.3	7	12
Unit 8 189 word passage 9.3 grade level	5 1.1.2 2.2.6 4.2.1 4.2.2 4.2.3	3 2.2.1 2.2.2 2.2.5	2 2.2.3 2.2.4		1 2.2.6	1 4.2			12	46.5
Total items	10			20		1	1	5	37	
Points	10			20		15	15	5		
Weight	1.5			1.5		* 2 raters	* 2 raters / 2	2		
%	15			30		30	15	10		100

Table 46.8 Analytic Essay Rubric for Classroom Use Based on *NorthStar 3* Writing Rubric

| | High ←--→ Low | | | | |
	5	4.25	3.75	3.25	2.75
Organization	The essay consists of one or more paragraphs and contains a clearly identifiable introduction and body. Generally effective use of transition words and phrases to sequence and organize information.	The essay contains at least one paragraph and uses some transition words and phrases to sequence and organize information.	The essay consists of one paragraph. The writer is just beginning to use transition words to sequence information.	The essay consists of several complete sentences and beginning levels of organization.	The essay consists of several complete and incomplete sentences; the writer needs to organize the information.
Content	The essay very coherently addresses the topic of the assignment. The essay contains a clear main idea and multiple supporting sentences.	The essay addresses the topic of the assignment and is coherent. The essay contains a main idea and multiple supporting sentences.	The essay somewhat addresses the topic of the assignment. The essay includes a simple main idea and several supporting sentences.	The essay partially addresses the topic of the assignment. It includes a simple main idea and few supporting sentences.	The essay largely does not address the topic of the writing assignment. The writer needs to provide a main idea and supporting sentences.
Language use	Consistent, correct use of grammatical features studied to date. Appropriate use of three or more vocabulary items from the prompt. Some language errors throughout.	Consistent, generally correct use of grammatical features studied to date. Appropriate use of two to three vocabulary items from the prompt. Several language errors throughout.	Generally consistent, correct use of grammatical features studied to date. Appropriate use of one to two of the vocabulary items from the prompt. Several language errors in paragraph.	Some consistent, correct use of grammatical features studied to date. Appropriate use of one vocabulary item from the prompt. Numerous language errors per sentence.	Needs to practice consistent, correct use of grammatical features studied to date. No vocabulary from the prompt. Numerous language errors per phrase.

Table 46.10 illustrates that a linear conversion of score points is not justified. As shown in columns 1–4, if a student receives a perfect score of 5 in every category by both raters, all is well; the student's score is equivalent to 100% and the grade of A. If a student receives all scores of 4, he will get the expected grade of B, but in terms of points, he will receive the minimum number of points for a B. The problem becomes apparent for the student who gets all 3s. We expect that this student is in the

Table 46.9 Paraphrase Section of Analytic Summary Rubric

	5 points	4.25 points	3.75 points	3.25 points	2.75 points
Paraphrase	The writer restates the ideas of the text in own words using attributive language and paraphrasing correctly.	Mostly the writer restates the ideas of the text in own words using attributive language and paraphrasing correctly.	The writer restates the ideas of the text in a limited way, copying some phrases from the text.	The writer restates the ideas of the text in a very limited way, copying many phrases (i.e., 40–70% of the summary) from the text.	The writer fails to restate the ideas of the text in his/her own words, copying most of the phrases and even sentences (i.e., over 75% of the summary) from the text.

Table 46.10 Example of Two Scales and Their Resulting Grades for Essays

1. Scores in organization, content, language use	2. Total score by two raters	3. Percent of 30	4. US grade	5. New scores	6. Total score by two raters	7. Percent of 30	8. US grade
All 5	30	100%	A	All 5	30	100%	A
All 4	24	80%	B	All 4.25	25.5	85%	B
All 3	18	60%	D	All 3.75	22.5	75%	C
All 2	12	40%	F	All 3.25	19.5	65%	D
All 1	6	20%	F	All 2.75	16.5	55%	F

middle, or average, and should get the grade of C. Instead, this student receives the lowest percentage score possible for the unsatisfactory grade of D. The situation gets continually worse for students with lower scores. It can be remedied by changing the scale to reflect the skewed nature of the scoring distribution in US schools, as illustrated in columns 5–8.

Homework

The notion that homework leads to student learning is related to theory and research that more time on task, or engaged time, increases academic achievement (e.g., Edelenbos & Vinje, 2000; Frederiksen, 1984; Richards, 1987). An influential article on this topic was written by John Carroll (1963, p. 730) in which he proposed a model of five factors affecting success in school learning, including learning a foreign language. The five factors are the amount of time needed to learn (aptitude), the ability to understand directions (general intelligence), the quality of instruction, the time allowed for learning (opportunity), and perseverance (the amount of time a student is willing to spend). In school, the time allowed for learning any one task (opportunity) is often insufficient due to the number of tasks that must be covered. This lack of opportunity is made up for by perseverance. People in different circumstances, such as those of greater or lesser aptitude or with better or worse quality of instruction, will need different amounts of time outside of regular school hours to learn a given task. So, it is not the amount of time one spends doing homework that matters; what matters is doing the homework so that less than optimum conditions in any of the other categories can be compensated for by perseverance.

Homework and its subsequent use in the classroom provide numerous opportunities for learning and for formative assessment through classroom discussion and questions (Black & Wiliam, 1998). In a series of reviews, Cooper and his colleagues (Cooper, 2001; Cooper, Lindsay, Nye, &

Greathouse, 1998; Cooper, Robinson, & Patall, 2006) reported a positive link between homework and achievement in the US in grades 7–12. Focusing on students in grade 8 learning French as a second language in Switzerland, it was found that frequent homework assignments predicted achievement (Trautwein, Schnyder, Niggli, Neumann, & Ludtke, 2009). Both of these teams reached their conclusions somewhat tentatively, discussing the issues of the operationalizations of homework, the levels of analysis used, and flaws in many research designs. Factors such as effort, ability, time, attitude, motivation, feedback, and parental involvement all seem to influence the benefits of homework (e.g., Hong, Peng, & Rowell, 2008; Sagarra & Zapata, 2008). In our example, the teacher assigned individual as well as group homework, and kept records of each student's percentage of completed assignments.

Reading Speed

Another non-test measure of achievement in our example class concerned reading speed. One of the objectives of the course was to increase students' reading rate, based on the belief that reading fluency will not simply develop on its own (Anderson, 2008; Carver, 1992; Stoller & Grabe, 2009). One way to measure increases in reading fluency is to average the results of in-class paired fluency practice, and then to compare the results over time (e.g., Grabe, 2009; Opitz, 2007). This alternative assessment technique paired two students, and had one student reading aloud to the other for a set amount of time (e.g., 30 seconds). The student marked her place and then the students changed roles. Next, they repeated the practice. Each student kept a log of reading rates which were expected to increase over time. Achievement was measured by increases for an individual student, not in comparison to others.

Extensive Reading

The final non-test measure for the reading portion of the objectives addressed extensive reading. This objective is based on the belief that to become a better reader, it is essential to read—a lot (Bamford & Day, 2004; Grabe, 1991, 2009; Renandya, 2007). Anticipated advantages to linguistic ability as opposed to general reading skills have been somewhat controversial but findings do support an improvement in general reading skills (e.g., Green, 2005; Yamashita, 2008). For our reading-writing class example, students were required to read and report on three books from a set of graded readers that were at or beyond their level to receive the grade of C. Thirty minutes of in-class time per week were devoted to sustained silent reading in order to promote extensive reading.

Directions in Research and Practice

These examples illustrate how criterion-referenced assessments in classroom instruction are central to student learning. While theory and research have attempted to better understand their roles in strengthening second language learning, at least three areas are in need of further investigation—objectives, feedback, and training.

Research and training are needed to improve teachers' ability to understand and interpret objectives, and to ensure the inclusion of all objectives. First, objectives need to be both defined and illustrated better (e.g., Baker, 2001). For example, increasing reading speed is often an objective in second language reading classes. There is little guidance, however, for teachers to link development of such a process-oriented objective to a more abstract understanding of reading and a more concrete view of the text's discourse features (Chapelle, 2008). Second, different teachers need to share common interpretations of objectives. Conducting a study on standards-based English assessments in the US, Llosa's

(2008) results indicated that a number of factors apart from the standards influenced the teachers, resulting in inconsistencies in both the scores and the application of the standards. Similar findings were reported by Davison (2004) in a comparison of teacher practices in Australia and Hong Kong.

Although this article has mainly presented cognitive views, there can be no question of the importance and relevance of constructivist and socio-cultural perspectives in contemporary second language teaching, learning, and assessment. As foreseen by Shepard (2000, p. 6): "Though these camps are sometimes warring with each other, I predict that it will be something like this merged, middle-ground theory that will eventually be accepted as common wisdom and carried into practice." A third issue regarding objectives, then, is how they reflect not only cognitive but also constructivist and socio-cultural perspectives. Collaborative project work and interaction, developing metacognitive abilities, and fostering positive self-image, as well as increasing peer- and self-assessment are all valued but how can these be reflected for both formative and summative purposes? Some examples for incorporating them into both dynamic, formative and summative assessment are available for teachers (e.g., Clarke & Gipps, 2000; Kim, 2008; Lantolf & Poehner, 2004, 2007). More examples on how to integrate objectives from different perspectives are needed.

A second area that would benefit from further investigation concerns feedback. What difference in language learning is there between receiving feedback and responding to it? Findings in second language acquisition are inconclusive. In the broader field of instructional technology although the idea of individualized feedback and practice based on student performance has been described and modeled (e.g., Alderson, 2005; Levy & Mislevy, 2004; Jang, 2009), little work has been done in terms of actual implementation, with few reading studies focusing on the effects of additional practice (e.g., Landauer, Lochbaum, & Dooley, 2009; Murphy, 2007). Early researchers of feedback suggested that it would be most effective in situations where the learner made an error while having a high degree of certainty that the response was correct, that is, over-confidence (e.g., Kulhavy, 1977). Its inclusion in a few second language studies describe confidence as something to be improved, assuming that more is beneficial (de Saint Leger & Storch, 2009; Issitt, 2007). While there is empirical evidence that individuals can be classified as confident or over-confident, there is little research in second language learning that directly takes confidence into account in either providing feedback or encouraging individual students to respond to feedback, and then estimating its effects on learning.

Finally, are language teachers trained in the types of tools they will need in their kit, as suggested by Black and Wiliam (2006)? A recent study of language assessment courses in applied linguistics' graduate programs indicated little emphasis on hands-on experience in designing, developing, and administering language tests with most hands-on experiences in test analysis and test critiquing (Brown & Bailey, 2008). Design of language tests was barely mentioned in the article. Results also showed that the match between items and objectives and specifications was not covered in most courses. This is unfortunate as design and development of criterion-referenced tests could address the difficulty teachers have had in assessing higher order skills in both their classroom questions and the items they include in tests. Most classroom teachers use tests that come with texts or make their own tests to be able to report students' progress on their class objectives. This is why the simple tool of the Table of Specifications is so useful. It provides teachers with the space to determine the coverage of their objectives on a test. In so doing, the teacher can see what is and is not included, as was the case in our reading and writing class example.

Notes

1. Examples adapted from the Program in Intensive English, Northern Arizona University.
2. I would like to acknowledge the work of my Northern Arizona University colleagues that I made use of for this article, namely Tony Becker, Jackie Evans, and Jonathan Smart on the writing rubrics; Bill Grabe, Eun-Hee Jeon, and Fredricka Stoller on the reading measures; and Kum Young Chang, Bill Crawford, YouJin Kim, and Don Miller on the tests.

References

Alderson, J. C. (2005). *Diagnosing foreign language proficiency: The interface between learning and assessment.* London: Continuum.

Anderson, N .J. (2008). *Practical English language teaching: Reading.* New York: McGraw Hill.

Assessment Reform Group. (1999). *Beyond the black box.* Retrieved from the Internet October 10, 2009: http://www.assessment-reform-group.org/AssessInsides.pdf.

Assessment Reform Group. (2002). *Assessment for learning.* Retrieved from the Internet October 10, 2009: http://www.assessment-reform-group.org/CIE3.PDF.

Bachman, L. (2004). *Statistical analyses for language assessment.* New York: Cambridge University Press.

Bachman, L., & Palmer, A. (1996). *Language testing in practice.* Oxford: Oxford University Press.

Baker, E. (2001). Testing and assessment: A progress report. *Educational Assessment, 7*(1), 1–12.

Baker, E., Herman, J., & Linn, R. (2005). Evidence-based rationales for assessment systems. *CRESST Line, 2*(Winter), 6–7.

Bamford, J., & Day, R. (Eds.) (2004). *Extensive reading activities for teaching language.* New York: Cambridge University Press.

Bangert-Drowns, R., Kulik, J., & Kulik, C.-L. (1991). Effects of frequent classroom testing. *Journal of Educational Research, 85,* 89–99.

Bangert-Drowns, R., Kulik, C.-L., Kulik, J., & Morgan, M. (1991). The instructional effect of feedback in test-like events. *Review of Educational Research, 61,* 213–238.

Barton, L., & Sardinas, C. D. (2009). *NorthStar 3 reading and writing.* White Plains, NY: Pearson Longman.

Black, P., & Wiliam, D. (1998). Assessment and classroom learning. *Assessment in Education: Principles, Policy & Practice, 5*(1), 7–74.

Black, P., & Wiliam, D. (2006). Assessment for learning in the classroom. In J. Gardener (Ed.), *Assessment & learning* (pp. 9–25). London: Sage.

Bloom, B. (1986). Ralph Tyler's impact on evaluation theory and practice. *Journal of Thought, 21,* 36–46.

Boyd, F., & Numrich, C. (Series Eds.) (2009). *NorthStar.* White Plains, NY: Pearson Longman.

Bridgeman, B., Lennon, M. L., & Jackenthal, A. (2003). Effects of screen size, screen resolution, and display rate on computer-based test performance. *Applied Measurement in Education, 16,* 191–205.

Brindley, G. (1989). A*ssessing achievement in the learner-centred curriculum.* Sydney: National Centre for English Language Teaching and Research, Macquarie University.

Brindley, G. (2001). Outcomes-based assessment in practice: Some examples and emerging insights. *Language Testing, 18,* 393–407.

Brown, J. D., & Bailey, K. (2008). Language testing courses: What are they in 2007? *Language Testing, 25,* 349–383.

Brown, J. D., & Hudson, T. (2002). *Criterion-referenced language testing.* New York: Cambridge University Press.

Carroll, J. B. (1963). A model of school learning. *Teachers College Record, 64,* 723–733.

Cartier, F. (1968). Criterion-referenced language skills. *TESOL Quarterly, 2,* 27–32.

Carver, R. (1992). Reading rate: Theory, research, and practical implications. *Journal of Reading, 36,* 84–95.

Chapelle, C. (2008). The TOEFL validity argument. In C. Chapelle, M. Enright, & J. Jamieson (Eds.), *Building a validity argument for the Test of English as a Foreign Language* (pp. 319–352). New York: Routledge.

Clarke, S., & Gipps, C. (2000). The role of teachers in teacher education assessment in England 1996–1998. *Evaluation and Research in Education, 14*(1), 38–52.

Colby-Kelly, C., & Turner, C. (2007). AFL research in the L2 classroom and evidence of usefulness: Taking formative assessment to the next level. *Canadian Modern Language Review, 64,* 9–38.

Cooper, H. (2001). Homework for all—in moderation. *Educational Leadership, 58,* 34–38.

Cooper, H., Lindsay, J., Nye, B., & Greathouse, S. (1998). Relationships among attitudes about homework, amount of homework assigned and completed, and student achievement. *Journal of Educational Psychology, 90,* 70–83.

Cooper, H., Robinson, J., & Patall, E. (2006). Does homework improve academic achievement? A synthesis of Research, 1987–2003. *Review of Educational Research, 76,* 1–62.

Crooks, T. (1988). The impact of classroom evaluation practices on students. *Review of Educational Research, 58,* 438–480.

Davidson, F., & Lynch, B. (2002). *Testcraft. A teacher's guide to writing and using language test specifications.* New Haven, CT: Yale University Press.

Davison, C. (2004). The contradictory culture of teacher-based assessment: ESL teacher assessment practices in Australian and Hong Kong secondary schools. *Language Testing, 21,* 305–334.

De Ridder, I. (2003). *Reading from the screen in a second language: Empirical studies on the effect of marked hyperlinks, on incidental vocabulary learning, text comprehension, and the reading process.* Antwerp: Garant.

de Saint Leger, D., & Storch, N. (2009). Learners' perceptions and attitudes: Implications for willingness to communicate in an L2 classroom. *System, 37,* 269–285.

Edelenbos, P., & Vinje, M. (2000). The assessment of a foreign language at the end of primary (elementary) education. *Language Testing, 17,* 144–162.

Frederiksen, N. (1984). The real test bias. Influences of testing on teaching and learning. *American Psychologist, 39,* 193–202.

Gass, S. (1997). *Input, interaction, and the second language learner.* Mahwah, NJ: Lawrence Erlbaum Associates.

Glaser, R. (1963). Instructional technology and the measurement of learning outcomes: Some questions. *American Psychologist, 18,* 519–521.

Grabe, W. (1991). Current developments in second language reading research. *TESOL Quarterly, 25,* 375–406.

Grabe, W. (2009). *Reading in a second language: Moving from theory to practice.* New York: Cambridge University Press.

Green, C. (2005). Integrating extensive reading in the task-based curriculum. *ELT Journal, 59,* 306–311.

Hatasa, Y., Hatasa, K., & Makino, S. (2010). *Nakama 1* (2nd ed.). Florence, KY: Heinle Cengage.

Hong, E., Peng, Y., & Rowell, L. (2009). Homework self regulation: Grade, gender, and achievement-level differences. *Learning and Individual Differences, 19,* 269–276.

Hughes, A. (1989). *Testing for language teachers.* Cambridge: Cambridge University Press.

Issitt, S. (2007). Improving scores on the IELTS speaking test. *ELT Journal, 62,* 131–138.

Jamieson, J., & Chapelle, C. (2009). *NorthStar achievement tests.* White Plains, NY: Pearson Education.

Jamieson, J., Grgurovic, M., & Becker, T. (2008). Using diagnostic information to adapt traditional textbook-based instruction. In C. Chapelle, Y.-R. Chung, & J. Xu (Eds.), *Toward adaptive CALL: Natural language processing for diagnostic language assessment* (pp. 25–39). Ames, IA: Iowa State University.

Jang, E. E. (2009). Cognitive diagnostic assessment of L2 reading comprehension ability: Validity arguments for Fusion Model application to *LanguEdge* assessment. *Language Testing, 26,* 31–76.

Jones, H. E. (1923). Experimental studies of college teaching. *Archives of Psychology, 10,* 1–70.

Kim, D.-H., & Huynh, H. (2008). Computer-based and paper-and-pencil administration mode effects on a statewide end-of-course English test. *Educational and Psychological Measurement, 68,* 554–570.

Kim, Y. (2008). The contribution of collaborative and individual tasks to the acquisition of L2 vocabulary. *Modern Language Journal, 92,* 114–130.

Knorre, M., Dorwick, T., Perez Girones, A., Glass, W., & Villarreal, H. (2007). *Puntos en breve.* Columbus, OH: McGraw-Hill.

Kulhavy, R. (1977). Feedback in written instruction. *Review of Educational Research, 47*(1), 211–232.

Kulhavy, R., & Stock, W. (1989). Feedback in written instruction: The place of response certitude. *Educational Psychology Review, 1,* 279–308.

Landauer, T., Lochbaum, K., & Dooley, S. (2009). A new formative assessment technology for reading and writing. *Theory into Practice, 48,* 44–52.

Lantolf, J., & Poehner, M. (2004). Dynamic assessment of L2 development: Bringing the past into the future. *Journal of Applied Linguistics, 1,* 49–72.

Lantolf, J., & Poehner, M. (2007). *Dynamic assessment: A teacher's guide.* State College, PA: Pennsylvania State University.

Leung, C. (2005). Classroom teacher assessment of second language development: Construct as practice. In E. Hinkel (Series Ed.), T. McNamara, A. Brown, L. Grove, K. Hill, & N. Iwashita (Eds.), *Handbook of research in second language teaching and learning* (pp. 869–888). Mahwah, NJ: Lawrence Erlbaum Associates.

Levy, R., & Mislevy, R. (2004). Specifying and refining a measurement model for a computer-based interactive assessment. *International Journal of Testing, 4,* 333–369.

Linn, R. (1994). Criterion-referenced measurement: A valuable perspective clouded by surplus meaning. *Educational Measurement: Issues and Practice, 13*(4), 12–14.

Linn, R., Baker, E., & Dunbar, S. (1991). Complex, performance-based assessment: Expectations and validation criteria. *Educational Researcher, 20*(8), 15–21.

Llosa, L. (2008). Building and supporting a validity argument for a standards-based classroom assessment of English proficiency based on teacher judgments. *Educational Measurement: Issues and Practice, 27*(3), 32–42.

Lyster, R. (2007). *Learning and teaching languages through content.* Philadelphia: John Benjamins Publishing Co.

McDonough, K., & Mackey, A. (2006). Responses to recasts: Repetition, primed production, and linguistic development. *Language Learning, 56,* 693–720.

Mackey, A., & Goo, J. (2007). Interactional research in SLA: A meta-analysis and research synthesis. In A. Mackey (Ed.), *Conversational interaction in second language acquisition* (pp. 407–452). Oxford: Oxford University Press.

Maloney, E., & Ruch, G. (1929). The use of objective tests in teaching as illustrated by grammar. *The School Review, 37,* 62–66.

Miller, M. D., Linn, R., & Gronlund, N. (2009). *Measurement and evaluation in teaching.* (10th ed.). Upper Saddle River, NJ: Merrill, Prentice Hall.

Millman, J., & Greene, J. (1989). The specification and development of tests of achievement and ability. In R. Linn (Ed.),

Educational measurement (3rd ed.) (pp. 335–366). New York: American Council on Education and Macmillan Publishing Company.

Murphy, P. (2007). Reading comprehension exercises online: The effects of feedback, proficiency and interaction. *Language Learning & Technology, 11*(3), 107–129.

Muyskens, J., & Omaggio Hadley, A. (2002). *Rendez-vous.* Columbus, OH: McGraw-Hill.

Opitz, M. (2007). *Don't speed. Read! Twelve steps to smart and sensible fluency instruction.* New York: Scholastic.

Pearlman, M. (2008). Finalizing the test blueprint. In C. Chapelle, M. Enright, & J. Jamieson (Eds.), *Building a validity argument for the Test of English as a Foreign Language* (pp. 227–258). New York: Routledge.

Popham, W. J. (1978). *Criterion-referenced measurement.* Englewood Cliffs, NJ: Prentice-Hall, Inc.

Rea-Dickins, P. (2001). Mirror, mirror on the wall: Identifying processes of classroom assessment. *Language Testing, 18,* 429–462.

Rea-Dickins, P. (2006). Currents and eddies in the discourse of assessment: A learning-focused interpretation. *International Journal of Applied Linguistics, 16,* 163–188.

Rea-Dickins, P., & Gardner, S. (2000). Snares and silver bullets: Disentangling the construct of formative assessment. *Language Testing, 17,* 215–243.

Renandya, W. (2007). The power of extensive reading. *RELC Journal, 38*(2), 133–149.

Richards, J. (1987). The dilemma of teacher education in TESOL. *TESOL Quarterly, 21,* 209–226.

Ruch, G. M. (1929). *The objective or new-type examination.* Chicago: Scott, Foresman and Company.

Russell, J., & Spada, N. (2006). The effectiveness of corrective feedback. In J. Norris and L. Ortega (Eds.), *Synthesizing research on language learning and teaching* (pp. 133–164). Philadelphia: John Benjamins Publishing Co.

Sagarra, N., & Zapata, G. (2008). Blending classroom instruction with online homework: A study of student perceptions of computer-assisted L2 learning. *ReCALL, 20,* 208–224.

Schmidt, R. (1993). Awareness in second language learning. *Applied Linguistics, 13,* 206–226.

Shepard, L. (2000). The role of assessment in a learning culture. *Educational Researcher, 29*(7), 4–14.

Stiggins, R. (2004). New assessment beliefs for a new school mission. *Phi Delta Kappan, 86*(1), 22–27.

Stiggins, R. (2005). *Assessment for learning defined.* Retrieved from the Internet on October 9, 2009, http://www.assessmentinst.com/wp-content/uploads/2009/05/afldefined.pdf.

Stoller, F., & Grabe, W. (2009). Debunking myths about L2 reading instruction. Presentation at TESOL conference, Denver, Colorado, March.

Swain, M. (1993). The Output Hypothesis: Just speaking and writing aren't enough. *Canadian Modern Language Review, 50,* 158–165.

Terrell, T., Tschirner, E., & Nikolai, B. (2005). *Kontakte: A communicative approach.* Columbus, OH: McGraw-Hill.

Trautwein, U., Schnyder, I., Niggli, A., Neumann, M., & Ludtke, O. (2009). Chameleon effects in homework research: The homework-achievement association depends on the measures used and the level of analysis chosen. *Contemporary Educational Psychology, 34,* 77–88.

Tyler, R. (1934). *Constructing achievement tests.* Columbus, OH: The Bureau of Educational Research, Ohio State University.

Wang, S., Jiao, H., Young, M., Brooks, T., & Olson, J. (2008). Comparability of computer-based and paper-and-pencil testing in K-12 reading assessments. A Meta-analysis of testing mode effects. *Educational and Psychological Measurement, 68,* 5–24.

Wiliam, D. (2000). An overview of the relationship between assessment and the curriculum. In D. Scott (Ed.), *Curriculum & assessment* (pp. 165–181). Westport, CT: Greenwood Publishing Group.

Williams, J. (2005). Form-focused instruction. In E. Hinkel (Ed.), *Handbook of research in second language teaching and learning* (pp. 671–691). Mahwah, NJ: Lawrence Erlbaum Associates.

Yamashita, J. (2008). Extensive reading and development of different aspects of L2 proficiency. *System, 36,* 661–672.

47

The Social and Political Tensions of Language Assessment

Steven J. Ross

The Politics of Assessment

Different constituencies and stakeholders such as immigrants, government bureaucrats, politicians, citizens, teachers, parents, industrialists, publishers, and examination makers all play a role in influencing language education and language assessment policy. The complex interaction of these different interests and worldviews produces tensions among the varying and often conflicting goals and interests. The goal of this chapter will be to provide a sketch of the focal points of these tensions in a number of current language assessment contexts, and a summary of issues that have recently been the thematic focus of colloquia and symposia at international conferences related to applied linguistics and language assessment.

Language assessment is an endeavor that inevitably involves values, ideologies, and sometimes interests driven by nationalism, xenophobia, and also vested interests that may be motivated to acquire, retain, or expand economic or strategic power. Alderson (2009a) addresses different political facets affecting language education and assessment, and outlines the distinction between macropolitics and micropolitics, which differ primarily in terms of their scope and magnitude. At the macro level, the power and prestige of languages operate at the national and international level, and involve strategic and economic interests, both overt and covert. In contrast, micropolitics focuses on issues related to power struggle at the institutional level, though even at the micro level, the personal preferences and prejudices of individuals may be driven by ideology, values, or vested interests. The tensions language assessment specialists face can involve the macro and micro levels, depending on the particular combination of stakeholders involved in the political decision to deploy language assessments to achieve their ends.

Assessment policies are normally determined by governments or institutions for specific reasons such as to determine the veracity of language-related claims, qualification, merit, and relative and absolute ability. Because the consequences of assessments affect the life paths of test takers, testing practices and policies are subject to critical scrutiny at many levels. As Bachman and Purpura (2008) suggest, language assessment will be seen as a vehicle to provide opportunities for some, or a barrier to exclude others. Because testing is now considered a political act, the traditional approaches to the evaluation of assessment practices that have focused almost entirely on the technical issues of reliability and validity are no longer considered sufficient. A more recent focus has been on the evaluation of policies that guide decisions about who is to be assessed, by whose authority, and for what ends (Kunnan, 2005). In this way language testing is seen as a tool of the parties with the power to legislate their use. The recent critical focus on political aspects of language assessment has made it an increasingly complex affair, for the conventional criteria for test quality are no longer the only benchmarks for demonstrating best practice (Kunnan, 2009). The injection of the critical component, which examines the agendas of the governments, institutions, and schools requiring asylum seekers, immigrants, job applicants, and limited English proficiency school learners to take language tests, makes for challenging complexities because the traditional foundations for validation now are seen by many stakeholders as insufficient.

Assessment practices that hitherto would have been considered adequate in terms construct validity may now be seen through the critical lens as wanting in terms of economic and social justice criteria (Shohamy, 2001). The trend toward critical evaluation of language assessment practices has resulted in a paradigm shift away from relying on the technical aspects of testing to a new emphasis on social consequences (McNamara & Roever, 2007). The trend favoring decentralized and intentionally unstandardized language assessment practices that may appear to be democratic because of greater accommodation to local exigencies can, however, prove faulty in terms of reliability and construct validity. Assessment policy makers like never before face tensions when required to adjudicate on which practices are simultaneously fair, ethical, just, reliable, and valid.

The Assessment of Immigrants

The use of language tests for migration continues to be a hot button issue in a number of nations. Sweden, Australia, Canada, and New Zealand, for instance, are contexts where commercial language tests and specifically-designed assessments have been used to examine potential migrants. Issues of content validity, standards, score interpretation, the role of language assessment professionals, and ethical standards all make language testing of immigrants a particularly sensitive issue. Language testing deployed for the purpose of screening and excluding potential immigrants has a long and tarnished history (see Kunnan, 2005) for a summary.

With increased globalization of economies, immigration has spread to virtually all industrialized nations. Migration policy is nearly universally controversial, and enmeshed in the controversy is the role of language testing. Milani (2008) in the European context examines the ideologies that motivate the language assessment of immigrants to Sweden. Central to the assessment policy is an assimilation ideology that aims to avoid the non-integration of immigrants into Swedish society. Through the tool of language testing, it argued that potential long-term social integration of immigrants will be made possible when citizenship qualification is anchored onto successful language acquisition. The dual use of language assessments as a vehicle for gauging migrants' qualification for social integration is a further complication for construct validation. Policies that require citizenship testing for social integration primarily use the host nation language as the medium of testing (Blackledge, 2009), and thus potentially confound the proficiency construct with content knowledge.

A major rationale for immigration policy is the projected economic benefit the host country can accrue from migration, which in many circumstances presumes rapid linguistic assimilation on the part of newcomers. Immigration policy is often predicated on applicants' qualification and merit in terms of both occupational skills and linguistic readiness to assimilate. McNamara (1998) notes the tendency for governments to rely on language assessment to screen the linguistic qualifications of potential migrants. The actual ways language assessments are implemented, however, can sometimes deviate from the original rationale and idealized methods. Hawthorne (1997) provides a case in point, noting how language tests in Australia have been used for political purposes. The use of language tests to justify granting permanent residence to Chinese students stranded in Australia after the crackdown on student dissidents by the Chinese government was an ad hoc political expedient constructed independently of the meritocratic standards required of all other potential immigrants. Special English language tests were thus devised to avoid political problems and embarrassment to the government. Here the immigration tests were used as a humanitarian quick fix, but nevertheless provided grist for the critical mill.

The post-9/11 reaction has had an adverse influence on language assessment policies and procedures, particularly in the testing of border crossers. It also presents a potential ethical dilemma to language assessment professionals. Applied linguists may feel compelled to protest at what they perceive as unjust policies with regard to asylum seekers and migrants, and opt to decline participatory roles as advisors to the agencies charged with implementing such policies. The non-participation of applied linguists in the formation and articulation of immigration testing policies could thus paradoxically potentially produce even more injustice and faulty practices on the part of paraprofessional language testers. Eades, Fraser, Siegel, McNamara, and Baker (2003), for example, describe the procedures used by immigration authorities to identify asylum seekers' nationality through linguistic means. At issue here is the potential impact applied linguists could have to correct and thus possibly validate a practice that would be made more unjust and even more onerous by authorities employing will-o'-the-wisp procedures and criteria. Eades (2009) alludes to such practices as a number of countries have invoked language analysis for the determination of origin (LADO). Eades suggests that the role of the linguist should be that of the referee in the interpretation of LADO reports asserting that asylum or migration cases are not from a claimed country of origin.

Preexisting policies favoring language assessment of migrants prior to arrival is a system devised to assist in migrant settlement. In recent decades Australia and Canada, both with large numbers of immigrants, have proactively supported and assessed post-migration language learning. The rationale for continued language learning support is multifaceted. Cumming (1994) asserts that the benefits of language assessment are that it can facilitate and hasten the settlement of newcomers to Canada, and can assist migrants to get past the various barriers standing in their way to employment and education. In this regard, assessment is for "door opening."

Publically sponsored language learning usually requires an assessment component for accountability purposes. To this end, Norton and Stewart (1999) describe the Canadian Language Benchmarks Assessment (CLBA) for immigrants to Canada and outline the challenges of accountability when different stakeholders are involved. A key issue is the authenticity of tasks used in such assessments, which for different stakeholders may appear to be biased. Blackledge (2009) endorses language courses devised to introduce citizenship in lieu of language testing in the UK migration context. Such a strategy skirts the ethical difficulties associated with high stakes tests, but invites other kinds of complications when language teachers are then charged with devising assessments that guarantee core knowledge deemed necessary for citizenship and social integration. Responsibility for assessment in such a scenario would be pushed onto language teaching institutes that may be unprepared for conducting high stakes assessments.

In the Australian context, Burns (1996) provides an outline of the evolution of the Certificate in Spoken and Written English, used in the Australian Adult Migrant English Program. Burns describes the issues associated with a focus on competency assessment through tasks devised to simulate different way-stages of settlement into work and society. The Certificate in Spoken and Written English was devised not to be a standardized test, but a set of assessment specifications that could be interpreted by language teachers and converted into locally constructed assessment tasks. As Brindley (1998) discovered, the task specification approach to assessment invited considerable variation in actual task difficulty, compounded by substantial variation in task performance judgments. Research on identifying features of task difficulty for the purpose of precise task specifications has suggested there may be a point of diminishing returns for a system of local autonomy in assessment task construction. Brindley and Slatyer (2002) point out that task conditions and characteristics interact with texts, item formats, and response requirements enough to make task specifications multidimensional and difficult to articulate as a task construction recipe.

Task variation inevitably leads to performance differences, which, if not accounted for, would lead to faulty inferences about migrants' readiness for integration into society. More complex is the ambiguity that occurs when tallies of task successes are used as indicators of learner competency as well as for program accountability purposes. A policy of making locally constructed versions of assessment tasks the basis for determining competence can ironically inject fundamental questions of equity and fairness when learners are assessed with non-standardized tasks, which are then reported as tallies of competence for the migrants, and as indictors of efficacy on the part of instructional service providers. In such accountability systems, service providers competing for contracts have an increased incentive to assess learners with optimally "doable" tasks, or may seek to exempt clients with learning problems from the assessment data.

Brindley (2001) concludes that a happy medium may need to be reached between the local autonomy model of task development and some form of standardized assessment procedures. Through task bank development and professional development, outcomes-based assessment can be made more valid and potentially generalizable. Even with such efforts to articulate compromise, the policy choice between stipulating assessment standardization and granting local autonomy is a perennial source of tension.

Language Education, Identity Politics, and Assessment Policies in Asia

Language education policy in many industrial and post-industrial nationals is driven primarily by economic factors. Given the dominance of English as a lingua franca, this means that in most contexts language education policy translates to issues of instruction of English as a foreign or second language (EFL), as well as to the instruction of the national language. In some instances, the national language and English as a global language come into conflict, especially when assessment procedures weight foreign language proficiency over school-based indicators of foreign language achievement. Educational policy makers rationalize foreign language instruction (primarily English) as a component of national economic development strategy, which tends to value tangible results more than for the traditional survey of culture and literature. The goal then becomes the development of measurable outcomes made observable on standardized proficiency tests. A basic tension is the conflict between assessment practices that do not easily lend themselves to accountability, and those that allow for macro-level evaluation of language learning programs. Mackay and Brindley (2007) outline the issues related to this tension.

Language education policy in Asian nations is particularly driven by economic goals. In Korea, foreign language testing is seen as vital to national economic and strategic interests. Kwon (2000) traces the evolution of language policy in Korea, and outlines the factors that have influenced the current emphasis on the national effort to increase EFL proficiency. A core tension exists between the economic development strategy and the preservation of cultural identity. At the heart of this tension is the influence of English, and especially American popular culture, on the core values of Korean students exposed to it. Yim (2007) explores how textbook makers in Korea aim to countervail the perceived threat of identity erosion by including in their EFL textbooks personalities manifesting essential Korean identity and values. The impetus for counterbalancing EFL instruction with subtle social engineering of a Korean identity in the same texts is the fear that too much foreign language learning may rob Korean youth of their essential Korean spirit.

The potential conflict of interest between language education for economic development and preservation of core cultural values is one that extends to language testing. Here, what aspects of a foreign language, and how it is to be assessed, serve to define what is to be considered as meritorious. In an overview of the issues associated with the rapid expansion of language proficiency testing in Korea, Choi (2008) traces factors influencing how language testing has grown dramatically over the last few decades, and the ways standardized tests are used, sometimes with questionable ecological validity, across all levels of Korean education to gauge language proficiency.

The tension between the need for Japanese who can use English for business and cultural exchange, and the perceived threat of cultural identity erosion has led to political maneuvering not unlike that seen in Korea. Hashimoto (2007) describes how government ministries have redefined the goals of school-based English language learning as a rationale for young Japanese to use their foreign language abilities to convey the "glory of Japanese culture" to the rest of the world. A perusal of middle and high school EFL texts provides examples how Japanese cultural values are injected into materials as subthemes in the English language lessons.

When cultural identity reinforcement goals are merged into language education policy, the content and construct validity of language assessments used to fabricate the meritocratic order becomes suspect. The economic development strategy would reward practical proficiency, while the "cultural core" maintenance goal might not do so. Language assessment practices in Japan are thus split into two main spheres: one for school and university admissions, and a different one emphasizing proficiency qualifications for job seekers after they have found their place in the social hierarchy extrapolated from the relative prestige ranking of their Alma Mater (Cutts, 1997). The chief rationale for EFL in Japan has primarily been for economic purposes, though assessment practices in schools do not clearly align to this goal. Sasaki (2008) describes the evolution and growth of "examination English," which defines pathways to school admission in Japan. Merit for learning EFL in Japan has historically been given to those who have learned English the Japanese way—by memorization and translation. This pervasive teaching and testing method has ensured that test takers demonstrate basic knowledge of the written code of both Japanese and the foreign language. The testing of comprehension of spoken language has not until very recently, and then only on a limited scale, even been mandated. Credit is rarely given for unbridled English proficiency, which could be developed through exposure without extensive scholarly effort and costly preparation. "Achievement" of the socially sanctioned variety of EFL knowledge is thus integrated into a system impervious to modernization.

The growth of the Test of English for International Communication (TOEIC) has been an ironic consequence of the dual purpose of language assessment in Japan. Useful proficiency is rarely developed as a consequence of preparation for "examination English," so as a proficiency measure that extends beyond the type of foreign language knowledge useful for school admissions, the TOEIC has added a post-school admissions tier to the language knowledge meritocratic system in Japan. It is noteworthy that TOEIC was a Ministry of Economics, Trade, and Industry (METI) initiative, though the test was developed "off shore" by the Educational Testing Service. By establishing the test making process overseas, the standards for determining merit for proficiency are placed outside the immediate control of the test prep industry, though it may be argued that after 30 years of TOEIC testing in Japan, cramming for proficiency tests has become a new facet of the industry.

Kobayashi (2007) notes that in spite of "objective" qualifications that relative EFL proficiency test scores on tests such as TOEIC might indicate, many of the prestigious Japanese companies still select only male employees for overseas postings, and for the intensive language training programs that prepare them for such postings. It is said that human resource departments even add the prestige ranking of each candidate's Alma Mater to his proficiency score to link school careers to current proficiency. Practices like these run contrary to governmental pronouncements (Ministry of Education, Sports and Technology, 2003) about the national policy for foreign language learning, because they serve to distribute the meritocratic rewards of language learning to males from the "right" schools, perpetuating the elitism Cutts (1997) describes. Further, because extensive test preparation with private tutors, local after school test practice centers, and dedicated cram schools for high school students requires considerable investment, the use of language tests promotes a plutocracy more than the idealized system based on scholastic merit.

Language Assessment in Asian Ex-Colonies

The Hong Kong and Singapore contexts differs considerably from Japan and Korea in some respects, but converge in others. In both Hong Kong and Singapore, English evolved into a widely used second language, and after independence, English has been increasing rivaled by Mandarin as the language of education and commerce. In Hong Kong, Tsui (2004) describes policy initiatives to increase the teaching of Mandarin. The preference for English-medium schools has remained strong, however, and the danger that the medium of instruction divide in Hong Kong will lead to a two-tier system looms large.

There has also been a shift in focus from large scale norm-referenced tests to more locally-determined school-based assessment practices. Davison (2007) examines the validity argument supporting the use of school-based assessment, which is grounded on the premise that assessment at the school level ought to be conducive to formative purposes rather than for merely summarizing learning outcomes. In counterpoint, Qian (2008) examines some of the problems in initiating EFL test policy reform in Hong Kong. Qian provides an outline of the complexities associated with the introduction of large-scale school-based assessment practices into public schools, and suggests that while the desirability of the rationale for formative assessment is clear, practical logistics work against widespread implementation. Qian also summarizes potential problems about the fairness of school-based assessment. Specifically, without standardization of tasks and procedures, task incomparability across assessors and institutions can be seen as potential threats to the validity of localized assessment. In this respect, the tension between local and centralized control over testing standards and content is similar to that seen in migrant testing in Australia.

In contrast with Hong Kong, where the impetus to enhance the status of Mandarin as a medium of instruction is motivated by political ends, language policy initiatives in Singapore are more motivated by economic pragmatism (Chew, 2007). There, the governmental priority is not so much identity maintenance, as much as reaping the long-term economic benefits of English language bilingualism for the city-state. At issue in Singapore is the status of the local variety "Singlish." Initiatives to get Singaporeans to "speak good English" reveal policy-makers' perception that language is a tool of economic advantage, and that linguistic capital can be nurtured into a valuable currency in the global economy. In a parallel movement, government initiatives to encourage a shift from "low value" dialects to Mandarin suggest how ethno-linguistic heritage can be less valued than the lure of economic benefits of proficiency in Mandarin and English. Chew (2007) points out that the critics of these diversity-eliminating language policies tend be members of the academy, or those who are themselves users of "premium" languages.

Policies without coherent programs of implementation usually result in ideological positioning rather than tangible change. Pakir (2004) notes the tension between the segment of Singapore society aiming for globalization and another that aspires more to heritage language maintenance. For the former group, the allure of English and Mandarin bilingualism is strong, for it provides access onto the fast lanes of social and economic mobility. For the latter, the dilemma is to forfeit the heritage language, at least in terms of the development of literacy, and select a language of instruction such as English or Mandarin for linguistic capital development. The resultant policy thus prioritizes the languages that offer cross-national access but allow multilingualism to be elective, though increasingly less valued options for heritage language speakers.

Language Assessment Policies in Europe

The politics of language training and assessment in Europe are primarily driven by the expansion of the North Atlantic Treaty Organization (NATO), issues of worker qualifications within the European Union, and increasing numbers of migrants. These issues have made language assessment practices and policies the focus of considerable debate in recent years. The evolution of the Common European Framework for assessing proficiency has resulted in no small number of controversies. The adoption of a "language passport" portfolio system (Little, 2007), which includes a self-assessed profile, language biography, and dossier of work samples, invites questions of comparability across different groups of portfolio users. The Common European Framework for defining proficiency levels across languages has also met with challenges concerning the validity of the proficiency levels (Moonen, 2006).

Setting standards for language proficiency in the military has also met with some degree of controversy. Crossey (2009) describes how the decision making about which languages are to be tested, by what instruments, and to what standard, is not necessarily the prerogative of language assessment specialists. Rather, competing constituencies within NATO vie for control over assessment policy, and may not prioritize the conventional criteria for assessing assessment validity. Different views on what should be prioritized vary according to the interests at stake, the ideologies that motivate policy endorsement, and the degree of focus on technical quality as opposed to ideological criteria. Green and Wall (2005) outline possible adverse consequences that could be expected to arise if language tests are not designed to professional standards. The struggle for standards versus local autonomy in Europe suggests that less than optimal assessment methods and criteria win out because of the endorsement of powerful individuals rather than because of their validity. Language assessment policies can be influenced by political factions aiming to control access, or by champions of particular ideological views, and less frequently by assessment specialists who might prioritize measurement quality.

In the immigrant assessment domain, the work of De Jong, Lenning, Kerkhoff, and Poelmans (2009), is a case in point. They go to great lengths to demonstrate the technical quality of an assessment instrument devised to validate the Dutch language proficiency of immigrants to the Netherlands. The assumption they appear to make is that the technical quality of the test for migrants should be the primary basis for its endorsement. Shohamy and McNamara (2009) apparently take an oppositional view on what the most important criteria for any assessment policy should be when it is applied to immigration. The contrast here reflects an increasingly frequent tension among language assessment specialists—whether ideological justification for tests should be considered more important than substantive arguments that focus on psychometric criterion first and foremost.

Macro-political movements endorsing standards and comparability often face sizable problems of implementation at the local level, especially in contexts without extensive resources available for training language assessment specialists (Eckes, Ellis, Kalnberina, Pizorn, Springer et al., 2005), or strong precedents for considering language assessment as a specialized domain not subsumed under language pedagogy. When reform movements gain momentum, they often pit traditionalists, conservatives, and factions with a financial stake in preserving the status quo against potential reformers who often champion modern measurement concepts and procedures. The vested interests often can be traced to institutions providing "traditional" training, publishing concerns with "market share" preservation motives, and even individuals in positions of power who may stand to lose from reforms (Alderson, 2009b). These interests may function at the national level, and thus imply macro-economic interests, or they may be particular to the individual micro-economic interests of individuals involved with assessment reform. Summarizing case studies from the Eastern European context, Pizorn and Nagy (2009) outline how individuals, internal factions, and vested interests find ways to undermine reform efforts and thus waste considerable resources earmarked for providing training for modernizing assessments. Pizorn and Nagy note that the motives of factions of stakeholders for derailing language assessment reforms can also be cloaked in the guise of nationalism and preservation of what is seen as tradition.

The Politics of National Standards and Accountability

Accountability in education has been in recent decades a political touchstone in many industrialized nations and has been a polarizing factor among the differing factions holding opposing views about what is to be taught and assessed (Young, 2008). Accountability has been particularly controversial in the USA, where an increasingly large fraction of the school aged learners are not native speakers of English (Duran, 2008). The issue of national standards and accountability in the US context is not a new one. Jennings (1998) outlines the history of the political issue of standards and accountability in the USA, and notes that it has not always been clearly aligned with conservative or liberal political ideology. Proponents of equality in education monitored and enforced by centralized governmental supervision have always been at odds with "states rights" local autonomists. Jennings describes how efforts to formulate national educational standards started with President Johnson's Civil Rights initiatives, later expanded by President Nixon, then set aside by President Reagan, the champion of "small government" and laissez-faire, before again being taken up by Presidents Bush and Clinton. The momentum established by these two presidents in particular led to the eventual formulation of the No Child Left Behind Act under the G. W. Bush administration.

Under the No Child Left Behind Act each state still retains some degree of autonomy in how accommodations and transitional bilingual programs for English language learners (ELLs) are implemented or phased out. The variation in the way the policy is carried out across different states has led to no small degree of controversy (Linn, Baker, & Betebenner, 2002). An increasingly common trend has been for states to require ELLs to reach grade-level benchmarks without the benefit of bilingual education or the option of taking the standardized tests in their native language (Wright, 2005).

Although there is a paucity of large-scale empirical research on the effects of interventions comparing the impacts of bilingual transitional programs, the few that have been conducted, e.g., Slavin and Madden (1999), suggest positive benefits for particular types of curricula when they are delivered and tested in Spanish. An important complication in many contexts, however, is that ELLs are not exclusively Spanish speakers. Datnow, Bormean Stringfiled, Overman, and Castellano (2003), for instance, discovered in their comparison of different instructional interventions in a large urban school district in California that ELLs were too diverse for equivalent and efficient bilingual delivery of instruction and assessment. Nevertheless, they concluded that one of the programs assessed, "Success for All," yielded significant gains in reading and math for the ELLs even though the program was delivered and tested in English. In a similar vein, Robinson (2008) describes comparatively large reading ability growth among Spanish-speaking ELLs who were ability-streamed, relative to learners in mixed ability class configurations. This outcome underscores the problem of generalizability in assessing accountability policies (Laguardia & Goldman, 2007). Sometimes they work, sometimes they don't. Programs that apparently provide evidence of success in some multilingual contexts might not yield the best outcomes in other contexts where the linguistic homogeneity of the ELL community would make bilingual transitional programs more feasible. Cultural and sociological explanations (Ream, 2005; Tyler, Uqdah, Dilihunt, Beaty-Hazelbaker, & Conner et al., 2008) for differential school success are often not considered when the issue of language-of-assessment is in focus. These cultural interpretations about the reasons for the lack of academic success suggest that the educational problems experienced by ELLs are not exclusively linguistic, and that they predate the onset of the No Child Left Behind policy ostensibly designed to alleviate them.

Although the results of empirical investigations of the relative benefits of first language instruction are varied, and focus mainly on Spanish-speaking children, the overall trends suggest that the educational outcomes of bilingually educated children are comparable to reference groups (Lindholm-Leary & Borsato, 2006). This general summary of the available research would suggest that the most just and rational policy would be one that supports and augments bilingual transitional programs in the elementary years, wherever it is feasible to do so.

The crux of the policy evaluation problem is that many individual states have opted out of bilingual programs because of the diversity of ELLs and the added cost of delivery. It is also likely that post-9/11 reactive xenophobia has also fueled the spread of assimilation ideology leading to the repeal of bilingual education and associated accommodations to ELLs in a number of these states. The net result has been an increase in the phenomena the No Child Left Behind policy was designed to reduce: an increase in the drop-out rate and non-education of ELLs. Heilig and Darling-Hammond (2008) describe as a case in point how schools facing sanctions because they are below the mandated average benchmarks are increasingly motivated to transfer, nudge out, or otherwise find ways to exempt ELL students likely to fail mandated tests by tracking them into special education programs. Jennings and Beveridge (2009) found that exempting students likely to fail measures used for assessing school accountability resulted in inflated achievement outcomes for such schools. Holding schools accountable according to benchmarks thus promotes "gaming" the system such that school administrators have incentives to save themselves at the expense of the at-risk students. In such school districts, the No Child Left Behind policy paradoxically exacerbates the problems it was devised to solve.

A core issue is how curriculum content can be validly assessed to demonstrate that target-level benchmarks have been reached. It is well established that the language of the test affects the performance of ELLs (Wiley & Wright, 2004). At issue is the validity of assessments of ELLs when the language of the assessment is English. Butler and Stevens (2001) warn that test results will at best be ambiguous when learners do not reach benchmarked grade-level standards. Punitive sanctions leveled at schools or districts not meeting standards may in such cases be unjust. The issue for language assessment specialists concerns not just the ideology that drives language assessment, but extends to the threats to reliability and validity that loom large when curricular content is tested in a second language. The key issue here is that benchmarks in core subject areas cannot be validly assessed (Abedi, 2004; Rossell, 2005) when ELL language accommodations are no longer allowed (Wright, 2005; Wright & Li, 2008; Gandara & Baca, 2008). Even if accommodations are permitted, for instance, with the use of translated tests, the assumption that the subject matter tests rendered into different languages are parallel is usually not justified (Wainer, 1999; Huempfner, 2004; cf. Stansfield, 2003).

The role of language assessment in macro-level educational accountability schemes such as No Child Left Behind is essential and complex. The tension is between the practical feasibility of providing instruction and assessment in the native languages of ELLs in a manner that provides equal opportunity for successful social and economic integration, and the ideology of assimilation that has progressively sought to eliminate accommodations and transitional programs. Policies driven by ideology alone without the counterweight of rigorous empirical verification are notoriously risky and tend to produce more problems than they cumulatively solve. In the case of No Child Left Behind, there is currently insufficient empirical evidence to conclude that it has not succeeded in its main objectives. However, because the assessment of ELLs injects much more complexity than the main curricular reforms and standards set down in the policy can address, the current ledger suggests that ELLs are more likely to be disenfranchised and less socially integrated in communities where ELLs are in the majority.

Conclusions

The survey of socio-political issues related to language assessment suggests that language assessment cannot be understood exclusively as limited to the technical issues of reliability and validity. Language assessment is infused with issues of power, identity, national sovereignty, macro- and micropolitics, as well as macro- and microeconomics. Tensions exist between competing ideologies and practices that promote language assessment for managerial and accountability purposes, and those seeking alternatives predicated on the belief that locally-decided assessment practices are ultimately more democratic. In either case, policies driven exclusively by ideology alone are likely to lead to unacceptable results. While the tensions outlined in this chapter may suggest contrastive and mutually exclusive worldviews, it can be argued that such tensions are necessary (Kuhn, 1977) for substantive progress to be achieved. Ideology-driven policies result in practices that must be rigorously interrogated for validity. Technically efficient measurement systems likewise need to be justified in terms of ethical criteria. Language assessment policies that will be seen as successful will likewise be those that can eventually find the optimal utilitarian common ground satisfying all the important criteria for ethical, just, reliable, and valid tests.

References

Abedi, J. (2004). The No Child Left Behind Act and English language learners: Assessment and accountability issues. *Educational Researcher*, *33*(1), 4–14.

Alderson, J. C. (2009a). Setting the scene. In J. C. Alderson (Ed.), *The politics of language education: Individuals and institutions* (pp. 8–44). Bristol: Multilingual Matters.

Alderson, J. C. (2009b). The micropolitics of research and publication. In J. C. Alderson (Ed.), *The politics of language education: Individuals and institutions* (pp. 222–236). Bristol: Multilingual Matters.

Bachman, L., & Purpura, J. (2008). Language assessments: Gate-keepers or door closers? In B. M. Spolsky & F. M. Hult (Eds.), *Blackwell handbook of educational linguistics* (pp. 456–468). Oxford: Blackwell Publishing.

Blackledge, A. (2009). "As a country we do expect": The further extension of language testing regimes in the United Kingdom. *Language Assessment Quarterly*, *6*, 6–16.

Brindley, G. (1998). Assessment in the AMEP: Current trends and future directions. *Prospect*, *13*, 59–71.

Brindley, G. (2001). Outcomes-based assessment in practice: Some examples and emerging insights. *Language Testing*, *18*, 393–407.

Brindley, G., & Slatyer, H. (2002). Exploring task difficulty in ESL listening assessment. *Language Testing*, *19*(4), 369–394.

Burns, A. (1996). Collaborative research and curriculum change in the Australian Adult Migrant English Program. *TESOL Quarterly*, *30*(3), 591–598.

Butler, F., & Stevens, R. (2001). Standardized assessment of the content knowledge of English language learners K-12: Current trends and old dilemmas. *Language Testing*, *18*(4), 409–427.

Chew, P. G. L. (2007). Remaking Singapore: Language, culture, and identity in a globalized world. In A. Tsui & J. Tollefson (Eds.), *Language policy, culture, and identity in Asian contexts* (pp. 73–94). Mahwah, NJ: Lawrence Erlbaum and Associates.

Choi, I. C. (2008). The impact of EFL testing on EFL education in Korea. *Language Testing*, *25*(1), 39–62.

Crossey, M. (2009). The role of micropolitics in multinational, high stakes language assessment systems. In C. Alderson (Ed.), *The politics of language education: Individuals and institutions* (pp. 147–164). Bristol: Multilingual Matters.

Cumming, A. (1994). Does language assessment facilitate recent immigrants' participation in Canadian Society? *TESL Canada Journal/Revue TESL du Canada*, *11*(2), 117–133.

Cutts, R. L. (1997). *An empire of schools: Japan's universities and the molding of a national power elite*. Armonk, NY: M. E. Sharpe.

Datnow, A. Borman, G., Stringfield, S., Overman, L., & Castellano, M. (2003). Comprehensive school reform in culturally and linguistically diverse contexts: Interpretations and outcomes from a four-year study. *Educational Evaluation and Policy Analysis*, *25*(2), 143–171.

Davison, C. (2007). Views from the chalkface: English language school-based assessment in Hong Kong. *Language Assessment Quarterly*, *4*, 37–68.

De Jong, J., Lennig, M., Kerkhoff, A., & Poelmans, P. (2009). Development of a test of spoken Dutch for prospective immigrants. *Language Assessment Quarterly 6*, 41–60.

Duran, R. (2008). Assessing English language learners' achievement. In G. Kelly, A. Luke, & J. Green (Eds.), *Review of educational research. What counts as knowledge in educational settings: Disciplinary knowledge, assessment, and the curriculum* (pp. 292–327). Thousand Oaks, CA: Sage.

Eades, D. (2009). Testing the claims of asylum seeker: The role of language analysis. *Language Assessment Quarterly, 6,* 30–40.

Eades, D., Fraser, H., Siegel, J., McNamara, T., & Baker, B. (2003). Linguistic identification in the determination of nationality: A preliminary report. *Language Policy, 2,* 179–199.

Eckes, T., Ellis, M., Kalnberzina, V., Pizorn, K., Springer, C., Szollas, K., & Tsagari, C. (2005). Progress and problems in reforming public language examinations in Europe: Cameos from the Baltic States, Greece, Hungary, Poland, Slovenia, France, and Germany. *Language Testing, 22,* 355–377.

Gandara, P., & Baca, G. (2008). NCLB and California's English language learners: The perfect storm. *Language Policy, 7,* 201–216.

Green, R., & Wall, D. (2005). Language testing in the military: Problems, politics and progress. *Language Testing, 22,* 379–398.

Hashimoto, K. (2007). Japan's language policy and the "lost decade." In A. Tsui & J. Tollefson (Eds.), *Language policy, culture, and identity in Asian contexts* (pp. 25–36). Mahwah, NJ: Lawrence Erlbaum.

Hawthorne. L. (1997). The political dimension of English language testing in Australia. *Language Testing, 14*(3), 248–260.

Heilig, J., & Darling-Hammond, L. (2008). Accountability Texas-style: The progress of urban minority students in a high-stakes testing context. *Educational Evaluation and Policy Analysis, 30,* 75–110.

Huempfner, L. (2004). Can one size fit all? The imperfect assumptions of parallel achievement tests for bilingual students. *Bilingual Research Journal, 28*(3), 379–399.

Jennings, J. (1998). *Why national standards and tests? Politics and the quest for better schools.* Thousand Oaks, CA: Sage.

Jennings, J., & Beveridge, A. (2009). How does test exemption affect schools' and students' academic performance? *Educational Evaluation and Policy Analysis 31,* 153–175.

Kobayashi, Y. (2007). TEFL policy as part of a stratified Japan and beyond. *TESOL Quarterly, 41*(3), 566–571.

Kuhn, T. (1977). *The essential tension.* Chicago: University of Chicago Press.

Kunnan, A. (2005). Language assessment from a wider context. In E. Hinkel (Ed.), *Handbook of second language teaching* (pp. 779–794). Mahwah, NJ: Lawrence Erlbaum Associates.

Kunnan, A. (2009). Testing for citizenship: The U.S. Naturalization Test. *Language Assessment Quarterly, 6,* 89–97.

Kwon, O. (2000). Korea's English language education policy changes in the 1990's: Innovations to gear the nation for the 21st century. *English Teaching, 55*(1), 47–91.

Laguardia, A., & Goldman, P. (2007). School reform, standards testing and English language learners. *International Journal of Inclusive Education, 11*(2), 111–131.

Lindholm-Leary, K., & Borsato, G. (2006). Academic achievement. In F. Genessee, K. Lindholm-Leary, W. Saunders, & D. Christian (Eds.), *Educating English language learners: A synthesis of research evidence* (pp. 176–222). New York: Cambridge University Press.

Linn, R., Baker, E., & Betebenner, D. (2002). Accountability systems: Implications of requirements of the No Child Left Behind Act of 2001. *Educational Researcher, 31*(6), 3–16.

Little, D. (2007). The Common European Framework of Reference for Languages: Perspectives on the making of supranational language education policy. *Modern Language Journal, 91,* 645–685.

McKay, P., & Brindley, G. (2007). Educational reform and ESL assessment: New roles and new tensions. *Language Assessment Quarterly, 4,* 69–84.

McNamara, T. (1998). Policy and social considerations in language assessment. *Annual Review of Applied Linguistics, 18,* 304–319.

McNamara, T., & Roever, C. (2007). *Language testing: The social dimension.* Malden, MA: Blackwell Publishing.

Milani, T. (2008). Language testing and citizenship: A language ideological debate in Sweden. *Language in Society, 37,* 27–59.

Ministry of Education, Culture, Sports, Science and Technology. (2003). *Regarding the establishment of an action plan to cultivate "Japanese with English abilities."* Retrieved April 15, 2003, from http://www.mext.go.jp/english/topics/03072801.htm.

Moonen, E. (2006). Scales and Europidgin: On the theoretical assumptions of the Common European Framework of Reference for Languages. *Neusprachliche Mitteilungen aus Wissenschaft und Praxis, 59*(2), 6–16.

Norton, B., & Stewart, G. (1999). Accountability in language assessment of adult immigrants to Canada. *Canadian Modern Language Review/La revue Canadienne des langues vivantes, 56*(2), 223–244.

Pakir, A. (2004). Medium-of-instruction policy in Singapore. In J. Tollefson & A. Tsui (Eds.), *Medium of instruction policies: Which agenda? Whose agenda?* (pp. 117–133). Mahwah, NJ: Lawrence Erlbaum and Associates.

Pizorn, K., & Nagy, E. (2009). The politics of examination reform in central Europe. In C. Alderson (Ed.), *The politics of language education: Individuals and institutions* (pp. 185–202). Bristol: Multilingual Matters.

Qian, D. (2008). English language assessment in Hong Kong: A survey of practices, developments and issues. *Language Testing, 25*(1), 85–111.

Ream, R. (2003). Counterfeit social capital and Mexican-American underachievement. *Educational Evaluation and Policy Analysis, 25*, 237–262.

Robinson, J. (2008). Evidence of a differential effect of ability grouping on the reading achievement growth of language-minority Hispanics. *Educational Evaluation and Policy Analysis, 30*, 141–180.

Rossell, C. (2005). The flawed requirements of limited English proficiency children of the No Child Left Behind Act. *Journal of Education, 186*(3), 29–40.

Sasaki, M. (2008). The 150 year history of English language assessment in Japanese education. *Language Testing, 25*(1), 63–84.

Shohamy, E. (2001). *The power of tests: A critical perspective of the uses of language tests.* London: Longman.

Shohamy, E., & McNamara, T. (2009). Editorial: Language tests for citizenship, immigration, and asylum. *Language Assessment Quarterly, 6*, 1–5.

Slavin, R., & Madden, N. (1999). Effects of bilingual and second language adaptations for Success for All on reading achievement of students acquiring English. *Journal of Education for Students Placed at Risk, 4*, 393–416.

Stansfield, C. (2003). Test translation and adaptation in public education in the USA. *Language Testing, 20*, 189–207.

Tsui, A. (2004). Medium of instruction in Hong Kong: One country, two systems, whose language? In J. Tollefson & A. Tsui (Eds.), *Medium of instruction policies: Which agenda? Whose agenda?* (pp. 97–116). Mahwah, NJ: Lawrence Erlbaum and Associates.

Tyler, K., Uqdah, A., Dilihunt, M., Beaty-Hazelbaker, R., Conner, T., Gadson, N., Henchy, A., Hughes, T., Mulder, S., Owens, E., Roan-Belle, C., Smith, L., & Stevens, R. (2008). Cultural discontinuity: Toward a quantitative investigation of a major hypothesis in education. *Educational Researcher, 37*(5), 298–301.

Wainer, H. (1999). Comparing the incomparable: An essay on the importance of big assumptions and scant evidence. *Educational Measurement: Issues and Practice, 18*(4), 10–16.

Wiley, T., & Wright, W. (2004). Against the undertow: Language minority education policy and politics in the "Age of Accountability." *Educational Policy, 18*(1), 142–168.

Wright, W. (2005). English language learners left behind in Arizona: The nullification of accommodations in the intersection of federal and state policies. *Bilingual Research Journal, 29*(1), 1–29.

Wright, W., & Li, X. (2008). High-stakes math tests: How No Child Left Behind leaves newcomer English language learners behind. *Language Policy, 8*(7), 237–266.

Yim, S. (2007). Globalization and language policy in South Korea. In A. Tsui & J. Tollefson (Eds.), *Language policy, culture, and identity in Asian contexts* (pp. 37–54). Mahwah, NJ: Lawrence Erlbaum.

Young, M. (2008). From constructivism to realism in the sociology of the curriculum. In G. Kelly, A. Luke, & J. Green (Eds.), *Review of educational research. What counts as knowledge in educational settings: Disciplinary knowledge, assessment, and the curriculum* (pp. 1–28). Thousand Oaks, CA: Sage.

VII
Ideology, Identity, Culture, and Critical Pedagogy in Second Language Teaching and Learning

48
Ideology in Second Language Education

James W. Tollefson

Research on ideology has generated a remarkably extensive scholarly literature across the full range of the social sciences. Nowhere has it been more important than in communication and language studies, particularly in critical approaches such as critical discourse analysis (Fairclough, 1995; Hodge & Kress, 1993; van Dijk, 1993a, 1993b; Wodak, 1996). Despite the extensive body of published research, perhaps no concept in language studies is more characterized by confusion, contradiction, competing methodologies, and controversies about fundamental terminology. This chapter begins by summarizing the complex meanings of ideology, and then examines certain aspects of ideology in second language (L2) theories and research methods, teaching practice, and teacher education.

The Concept of Ideology

As a theoretical concept in the social sciences, ideology was originally drawn from Marxism. In its classic Marxist formulation, the concept of ideology begins with the fundamental idea that social knowledge represents as natural, necessary, and inevitable social relations that are in fact contingent, historical, and advantageous to the ruling class. Ideology consists of the processes by which prevailing ideas (e.g., individualism) that favor the ruling class come to be "naturalized," which means that their role in sustaining the interests of the ruling class becomes invisible.

The proliferation of research on ideology has been so extensive, however, that the Marxist understanding has become one approach among many. Given the wide range of approaches, it is impossible to survey the full diversity of meanings of the term. Broad categories of research, however, as well as trends in current meanings, can be identified.

First, understandings of the concept of ideology fall into two broad categories. (For a full analysis, see Blommaert, 2005.) In one, it refers to a specific set of "discourses, terms, arguments, images, stereotypes, serving a specific purpose and operated by specific groups" (Blommaert, 2005, p. 158). That is, ideologies are viewed as specific sets of ideas that individuals and groups advocate (e.g., liberalism, socialism, and communism). The limitations of this notion of ideology led to a major reconsideration and reformulation of the concept in the 1970s, which yielded the second broad category of meanings, in which ideology is the cultural perspective toward social and political systems. In this view, ideology penetrates all aspects of societies and leads to hidden systems of thought, assumptions, beliefs, and behaviors that come to be seen as natural, normal, and inevitable. Research on ideology within this category is aimed at "unpacking" these naturalized systems (Auerbach, 1995). Language is a central concern because it is viewed as always ideological, never a "transparent medium through which truth can be observed" (O'Sullivan, Hartley, Saunders, Montgomery, & Fiske, 1994, p. 142). This approach to ideology encompasses a very wide range of perspectives, including Althusser (1971), Gramsci (1988), Foucault (1972, 1980), Bourdieu (1991), van Dijk (1993a), and many others.

It is this second broad category of research on ideology that has played an important role in studies of L2 education. This research may be placed more or less along a continuum from primarily cognitive approaches to ideology on the one hand, to a focus on institutional practices on the other.

Cognitive Approaches to Ideology

Cognitive approaches to ideology (termed "cognitive-ideational" by Blommaert, 2005, p. 161) are best exemplified by van Dijk's socio-cognitive approach, in which a major concern is "social knowledge," particularly social representations of individuals or groups, for example "Black," "White," "Asian," or "Native Speaker." The reason for calling these representations "social" is that they entail *shared* beliefs, values, norms, and attitudes that one needs in order to function as a culturally competent member of a society.

Social representations are important in many ways. One particularly significant way is that they influence individuals' understanding of *specific,* personal experiences. For example, imagine a white, middle-class individual in a park in Los Angeles observing a mother and child walking together speaking Spanish. This particular, specific event becomes part of the observer's personal experience and memory, but that experience and memory are fundamentally shaped by the observer's "social knowledge" about Latinos, which in this case might be the belief that "Latinos hold on to Spanish and refuse to learn English."

As this example suggests, a particularly important type of social representation is stereotypes. In popular usage, stereotyping is often viewed as a form of cognition called "categorization"; the difference between stereotypes and other categories is usually considered to be a matter of accuracy or legitimacy. In this popular view, categorization is a necessary and natural part of human cognition, but sometimes it "goes too far," resulting in an exaggerated, distorted, or overly negative representation (i.e., a stereotype). From this perspective, stereotypical representations are overly broad categories that can be corrected through education and more accurate or complete information.

In contrast to this view is one that emphasizes the ideological nature of stereotypes, as a particular and distinctive form of social cognition. Usually categories are not fixed, but somewhat flexible, and they can be modified as needed, with new categories formed on the basis of new information. Stereotypes, on the other hand, are relatively rigid, and they severely limit the formation of new categories. The social representation of Latinos as "holding on to Spanish and refusing to learn English" may be considered a stereotype. Moreover, stereotypes have an important social function that mere categories do not. As Pickering (2001, p. 3) points out:

> Stereotyping may operate as a way of imposing a sense of order on the social world in the same way as categories, but with the crucial difference that stereotyping attempts to deny any flexible thinking with categories. It denies this in the interests of the structures of power which it upholds. It attempts to maintain these structures as they are, or to realign them in the face of a perceived threat. The comfort of inflexibility which stereotypes provide reinforces the conviction that existing relations of power are necessary and fixed.

In other words, the social function of stereotypes is that they help to maintain existing, unequal social relations that favor powerful, dominant groups. Socio-cognitive research on ideology attempts to discover and make explicit stereotypes and other social representations, the processes by which groups share this "knowledge," and the ways that it is used as a basis for interpreting the meaning of individual experience.

Within this socio-cognitive approach to ideology, how are social representations communicated and shared? It is here that discourse becomes crucial, because discourse is the interface between the social and the cognitive (van Dijk, 1990, 1993a). Social representations are acquired, communicated, and reproduced through various forms of discourse, including peer talk, parent-child communication, classroom interaction, and mass media. Yet not all forms of discourse are equally significant. Van Dijk calls for special attention to the discourses produced by social elites, which are

> groups in society that have special power resources [such as] property, income, decision control, knowledge, expertise, position, rank, as well as social and ideological resources such as status, prestige, fame, influence, respect, and similar resources ascribed to them by groups, institutions, or society at large.
>
> (Van Dijk, 1993b, p. 44)

Two examples of elite discourse are political and academic discourse. In political discourse, political leaders appear in the mass media, where they routinely define "problems" or "issues" for others to discuss; in this sense, they establish social agendas. In educational discourse, researchers, administrators, and other "expert-professionals" examine educational issues (such as L2 learning), offer technical analysis and advice, and develop programs, teaching methods, materials, tests, and other professional products that become the naturalized artifacts of educational systems.

One reason elite discourse is important is that it has the social function of gaining the consent of individuals and groups to systems in which they are exploited. The social function of discourse can be seen when it is compared to explicit forms of coercion, such as violence. For example, violent racist coercion (termed "old racism" [van Dijk, n.d.]) may be relatively rare in some settings, but racism persists (often not termed "racism" at all), and is passed on (or "reproduced") through forms of discourse such as racist (often termed "cultural") stereotypes that are believed to be based on reality (e.g., "Latinos hold on to Spanish and refuse to learn English"; "immigrant students are slow learners"). In L2 education, socio-cognitive approaches to ideology focus on ways that such discourse naturalizes representations of students, teachers, and others, and thereby gains their cooperation with educational practices that sustain their marginal position in systems of social inequality.

Institutional Approaches to Ideology

The main limitation with the socio-cognitive analysis of ideology is that it does not make explicit how social knowledge is created, nor how it is systematically manifest in everyday life. In order to understand these issues, a large body of research on ideology focuses on practices within institutions. The central claims within this research are that ideology is always experienced in institutional forms, and that dominant ideologies are always complex, contested, and in conflict with alternative ideologies. Institutional forms of ideology have been termed the "ideological state apparatuses" (Althusser, 1971), which includes education, communication systems, and the mass media. Their function is to reproduce ideologies that serve the interests of socially dominant groups (the ruling class, in Marxist terms). The ideological state apparatuses have the important disciplinary function of gaining the consent of the governed by transforming class interests into other terms, such as (in liberal states) "equal opportunity," "educational meritocracy," and other liberal discourses (Tollefson & Tsui, 2004).

Among the important institutions providing this disciplinary function is education. Bourdieu (1991) is one of the most influential scholars working within this institutional approach to ideology in education. His primary claim is that schools reproduce unequal social relations by requiring particular educational practices, which thereby legitimize particular forms of knowledge (those of the upper-middle class). Bourdieu's theory of social reproduction, which rests on his theoretical concepts of *habitus* and *capital*, has been influential in L2 research. An important claim of many scholars working within this tradition is that language in educational institutions is a key factor in reproducing systems of inequality (Tollefson, 1991).

The range of research on ideology—from van Dijk's socio-cognitive theory of discourse to Bourdieu's analysis of social reproduction in schools and to other institutional analyses of ideology—suggests that there are many disagreements, and indeed it is difficult to summarize research on ideology in a way that captures the contributions of the full continuum of approaches, from the cognitive to the material and institutional. Blommaert (2005) proposes a "safe position" that encompasses much of this range: a complete analysis of ideologies would have to include the cognitive (such as assumptions, beliefs, and forms of knowledge) and the material (including institutional practices). Such a perspective results in the definition of ideology as "materially mediated ideational phenomena" (p. 164).

Power, Discourse, and Ideology

Thus far I have not mentioned power, but any analysis of ideology inevitably entails an analysis of power. Here again there is significant disagreement and confusion about fundamental concepts and terms. The material base of ideology is central to this debate. One key issue, as Pennycook (2001) summarizes it, is that scholars differ on whether their core concern is ideology or discourse (also see Mills, 1997). The essential difference is whether to analyze "discourse *and* ideology as opposed to discourse *or* ideology" (Pennycook, 2001, p. 83). Many approaches to ideology are the former, which assume a close, even essential link with discourse. Within this view, ideologies (such as standard language ideology [see Lippi-Green, 1997]) are associated with specific discourses (such as a discourse of stable national unity supported by a single standard language).

Other scholars, however, reject the necessary link between ideology and discourse, and argue instead that discourse is the preferred concept. One difficulty with ideology-and-discourse, according to these scholars (e.g., Foucault, 1980) is that it assumes that "truth" is in opposition to ideologies, which are sometimes seen as "false or ungrounded constructions of society" (Wodak, 1996, p. 18). A second difficulty is that ideology is often viewed as dependent on its social and economic foundation, which is particularly evident in Marxist and neo-Marxist analysis. Critics argue that such material analysis leads to forms of determinism. A third difficulty with ideology-and-discourse is that power is a given (based on historical factors such as class), and it is maintained through language, whereas the alternative focus on discourse emphasizes instead that power is a crucial factor requiring explanation. Thus Foucault, Pennycook, and others (e.g., Canagarajah, 1999) argue that a focus on ideology over-emphasizes the role of the material, and it results in a material (usually economic) determinism that cannot explain the role of individuals as "agents," for example, in resisting powerful social groups. If discourse rather than ideology becomes the fundamental concept, then power becomes a central concern not as a result of class relations or state authority, but rather as ever-present and inevitable in all social relations.

The implications of the difference between these two positions on power, ideology, and discourse are crucial in L2 research. A focus on ideology emphasizes the positioning of individuals in social roles within educational institutions, the close relationship between power and socio-economic factors, the fundamental importance of coercion, and the ways in which language learners and their teachers are largely blocked from access to powerful institutional roles. In contrast, a focus on discourse emphasizes acts of resistance by learners and their teachers, the myriad of practices over which they have significant control, and the complex interplay of coercion and resistance. Although in both views power is a central concern, a focus on ideology views power as resulting primarily from historically determined social and economic structures, while a focus on discourse explores a wide range of ways that power is imminent in everyday life.

L2 Education

I have spent considerable time describing some of the complexities of theoretical and conceptual research on ideology, which suggests that ideology in L2 education is characterized by many of the same contradictions and confusions as theoretical work. In order to organize a complex and contradictory body of work on ideology in L2 education, I divide the discussion into five broad categories: cognitive and methodological research in SLA; experimentalism; pragmatism; critical approaches; and teacher education.

Cognitive and Methodological Research in SLA

For the past 40 years, the academic discipline of second language acquisition (SLA) has evolved considerably, so that teacher education programs and graduate programs in language learning routinely include a course surveying SLA research. The scope of the field is determined in part by the main aim of the discipline: to explain differences in outcomes among L2 learners (Gass & Selinker, 2001). Over the years, an impressive body of published research in SLA has focused attention on variables that might explain learner outcomes. Beginning with Schumann's (1978) early taxonomy of factors affecting L2 learning, these variables have been largely limited to the learner and to the immediate environment of learning (e.g., input, the curriculum and classroom activities). Among major SLA models (e.g., Dörnyei, 2006; Krashen, 1981; Naiman, Frölich, Stern, & Todesco, 1996; Schumann, 1978; Zuengler & Miller, 2006), there is general agreement that factors affecting L2 learning are primarily learner variables, including (but not limited to) personality, aptitude, affective factors (e.g., motivation and language shock), cognitive factors (e.g., level of cognitive development, unconscious and conscious processes), personal factors (e.g., age, anxiety, and learning strategies), and input. Most SLA models include "social factors" (e.g., Schumann, 1978), but these are narrowly limited to such matters as opportunities for input and L2 use, attitudes toward assimilation, and attitudes toward the target language group. Thus the core of research in SLA focuses on cognitive, affective, and other individual factors, which have been termed mainly "within-the-individual" variables (Lantolf, 2005, p. 340).

In response to this limitation in SLA research, social-psychological and sociocultural approaches have been developed. The most influential social-psychological theory is Gardner's (1985), which focuses on learners' attitudes and motivation, and therefore remains firmly grounded within the range of traditional SLA variables. Sociocultural research has ventured beyond the limits of the individual L2 learner, by seeking to understand the relationship between the cognitive and emotional development of the individual and the cultural and historical context. (For an overview, see Lantolf, 2006.) Yet, despite its attention to the broader context, sociocultural theory remains focused primarily on the processes of L2 development and L2 use, and thus economic, structural, and discursive analysis (the major focus of ideology) remains largely beyond its scope and attention.

A full analysis of the ideologies of SLA theories and the academic discipline of SLA remains to be undertaken. Nevertheless, we can begin to understand ideology in SLA by noting what most SLA research does *not* investigate. First, by focusing on individual cognitive and affective variables, SLA represents L2 learning as fundamentally an individual rather than a social phenomenon. As a result, crucial concerns such as power and socioeconomic class are ignored, even when they are clearly central to learner performance and related matters such as the medium of instruction in L2 learning (Canagarajah, 1999; Luk & Lin, 2007; Ramanathan, 2005). Second, by seeking explanations for learner performance within the individual, SLA research cannot explain major historical, socioeconomic, and institutional constraints on learners, including the different benefits that accrue to successful L2 learners (which are obviously not distributed equally to all learners), differential access to high-quality learning opportunities (also varying widely), the "deskilling" of teachers (Baumann, 1991), and the socially-constructed meanings of particular forms of language and patterns of language use. Because traditional research in SLA largely ignores such matters, a growing body of socio-historical (Hall, 1996) and historical-structural (Tollefson, 1991) research, published in a new generation of scholarly journals (such as the *Journal of Language, Identity and Education* and *Critical Inquiry in Language Studies*), seems to be diverging from SLA, perhaps eventually forming a distinct discipline with its own research questions, methodologies, and epistemology (e.g., Cooke, 2008). Such research includes both cognitive and institutional approaches to ideology in L2 education.

A second major ideological issue is SLA research methodology. A central aim of SLA research is to determine causation, specifically why some learners out-perform others ("why most learners do not achieve the same degree of proficiency in a second language as they do in their native language ... [and] why only some learners appear to achieve native-like proficiency in more than one language" [Gass & Selinker, 2001, p. 1]). The concern with causation is so deeply embedded in SLA research (and in educational research generally) that it is rarely questioned. Indeed, many researchers claim that the fundamental aim—perhaps the only aim—of research is to determine what variables lead to what learning outcomes (Eisenhart, 2005). For such research, the main criterion for evaluating the effectiveness of research methodologies is whether they can provide convincing accounts of causation. From this perspective, other goals, such as exploring important social issues, deepening our understanding of complex phenomena, or seeking changes in L2 education based on values such as social justice, may be viewed as secondary and peripheral compared to determining causation, and indeed may not be considered research at all (Davies, 1996).

The focus on causation leads to the privileging of research methods that specifically permit causal claims. The most prominent category of these methods is experimentalism, the goal of which is "to establish a cause-effect relationship between two phenomena" (Johnson, 1992, p. 165). Of course there is a rich tradition of opposition to experimentalism and a range of qualitative, process-oriented methods such as ethnography that insist on careful consideration of the power relationship between researchers and their subjects (Cameron, Frazer, Harvey, Rampton, & Richardson, 1992). Nevertheless, in L2 research "quantitative (especially experimental) approaches have been viewed as the most important and given top priority" (Johnson, 1992, p. 18). In addition, after a decade in which qualitative research has greatly expanded, experimentalism has recently reemerged as a preferred approach in educational research. Therefore I focus here on experimental approaches, and I make only brief comments on the ideologies of other research methods.

Experimentalism

Since the late 1990s, the long debate about quantitative and qualitative methods in L2 research has receded somewhat, perhaps because advocates have separated into different institutions and academic departments, they publish in different scholarly journals, and they have reduced interaction in academic meetings and conferences. In educational research, however, a new debate over methodology has emerged within public policy.

Many discussions about research methodology in L2 education are carried out within larger debates involving individuals and groups seeking to influence public policy, particularly education for immigrants and minorities. Politicians, lobbying groups, political parties, and the popular media have increasingly weighed in with their views about educational research. In the United States, the question of which research methodologies in education are most appropriate—and which should receive government funding—has been addressed by the important federal education law called the No Child Left Behind Act of 2001, the newly created Institute of Education Sciences, and the influential National Research Council. In these and other contexts, experimental research is touted as the "gold standard" in education. For example, in its report on education research, the National Research Council (2002) declared that "in estimating the effects of [educational] programs, we urge the expanded use of random assignment" (p. 125). Similarly, the influential Coalition for Evidence-Based Policy (2002) has argued that randomized, controlled trials should be the "gold standard" (pp. 7–8) in educational research, that the failure to adopt this approach is one of the major reasons that many educational interventions have not achieved their desired results, and that federal research funding should be channeled primarily to experimental research. (For extended discussion, see Howe, 2004.) This new discussion of research methods is particularly important in public policy debates about the achievement gap between "native English" and "limited English proficient" speakers. In this debate, there is a renewed call for experimental research.

The debate in education about research methodology raises many issues that are beyond the scope of this chapter. For our purposes, the question is: in what sense does experimentalism raise ideological issues? A key feature of randomized experiments is that they require tight restrictions on the population and the treatment; indeed, what defines experimentalism is the emphasis on careful attention to ensuring that control and experimental groups differ only in the treatment they receive. The difficulty in L2 education is that such control reduces the relevance of experiments to real-world educational settings, where groups are always highly complex, with multiple levels of overlapping similarities and differences.

In practice, experimentalism means that researchers' attention focuses primarily on factors that can be measured and controlled, such as age, first language (L1), motivation, and L2 proficiency. In contrast, social, economic, cultural, and historical factors, which are difficult to measure or control, are ignored or are absent from the list of investigated explanatory variables. Indeed, experimentalism encourages research that simply ignores social, economic, cultural, and historical factors, and thus it contributes to the dominance of cognitive research in SLA.

The ideologies of other, non-experimental approaches to research also may be examined. What kinds of variables are most likely to be examined in a qualitative focus on process (rather than on cause and effect)? How do correlational studies, which examine relationships among variables, often for the purpose of predicting the effects of teaching practice, affect the kinds of research questions that are raised? Why have case studies traditionally had low status in educational research, but found greater acceptance in recent years? What are the implications of the recent popularity of ethnographic research in L2 education? Such questions point us toward the ideological underpinnings of each of the major research methods in L2 education.

Pragmatism

Pragmatism is an important tradition in education generally, and particularly in L2 education. Pragmatism has influenced L2 education in two main areas: teaching practices and research methods. In L2 teaching, pragmatism refers to the belief that teachers and students are engaged in a practical, non-ideological project of language education using any approaches, methods, and techniques that work. Describing the teaching of English as a second language composition, for example, Santos (1992) writes that it is "unprejudiced by value judgments about the linguistic system, its speakers, and ... the sociopolitical circumstances attached to the system" (p. 8). Advocates of pragmatism claim that it has a common-sense view of L2 education: good teachers use whatever practices "work" to help students learn the language they want to know.

In her critique of pragmatism in English for academic purposes, Benesch (1993) argues that much of the practical advice to teachers throughout the recent history of L2 education expresses an implicit ideology of pragmatism (e.g., Reid, 1989). A key principle of this ideology is that learners should develop the language skills they need to be successful in educational institutions and the workplace. In this sense, teachers and students, in their focus on a pragmatic approach to learning and teaching, may uncritically accept common institutional practices; good teaching and successful learning are defined as developing the ability to meet institutional requirements (e.g., specific genres of writing such as academic term papers on assigned topics). A second principle of the ideology of pragmatism is that learners are expected to "adapt … to the existing curriculum" (Benesch, 1993, p. 712), even if the curriculum is irrelevant to their learning goals or needs. Success, in other words, is defined by the institution rather than the learners, and critical analysis of institutional requirements is avoided, such as in "survival English" and "English for academic purposes." Third, pragmatism assumes that there is a set of key ideas and associated teaching practices that constitute "methods that work" (e.g., Oller, 1993) or "best practice" (e.g., Daniels & Bizar, 2004). Such a belief leads to a social-educational hierarchy in which certain individuals (researchers, textbook writers, curriculum coordinators) possess the knowledge of good teaching practice, whereas teachers are required to accept and use that knowledge to teach students who are in no position to question the effectiveness of the "best practices" to which they are subjected. Thus the ideology of pragmatism encourages students and teachers to accommodate to institutional demands and to maintain institutional positions in which they have relatively little power and control. In Bourdieu's terms, pragmatism encourages teachers and students to cooperate in reproducing unequal social relations, by legitimizing particular educational practices and forms of knowledge.

A second major area in which pragmatism has influenced L2 education is research methods. In research methods, pragmatism advocates a "scientific orientation" (Santos, 1992, p. 11) that avoids commitment to particular epistemologies, philosophies, or research methods. Pragmatism underpins the rise of "mixed methods" research that is oriented toward solving practical educational problems in real-world educational institutions (Greene, 2007). Encouraging researchers to choose freely any research methods and techniques that meet their needs, Creswell (2009) notes that "pragmatism opens the door to multiple methods, different worldviews, and different assumptions, as well as different forms of data collection and analysis" (p. 11).

The prevalence of mixed methods research in education in recent years suggests that many researchers accept the ideology of pragmatism, particularly the "compatibility thesis," that there is no ontological or epistemological conflict between positivist-quantitative research and constructivist-qualitative research (see Teddlie & Tashakkori, 2003). Addressing a key issue in ideology (the role of structural determinism and human agency), pragmatism claims that some realities can be objectively observed and measured, while other realities are socially constructed through the decisions of human agents. Although such a claim has a common-sense appeal in its acceptance of all sides in ideological debates and in its positioning as "non-ideological," there is little likelihood that the ideology of pragmatism will end the important disagreements over research methods in L2 education. Nevertheless, mixed methods research and the ideology of pragmatism that supports its use are likely to continue to influence L2 research for many years to come.

Critical Approaches to L2 Education

Critical approaches to L2 education have become increasingly prominent in recent years. For our purposes, what distinguishes critical approaches is that they *explicitly* focus on ideology, and in that sense they are diametrically opposed to pragmatism. Although some critical scholars seem to suggest that their work is relatively free of ideology because it seeks to undermine existing, unequal social relations, a more inclusive understanding of ideology suggests that critical approaches are distinct not because they are non-ideological, but because their underlying ideologies can be distinguished from those of other approaches to L2 education. In this section, I examine critical L2 research, emphasizing its use of key concepts that are central to ideology, including power and inequality. In the next section on teacher education, I briefly discuss critical pedagogy.

Critical L2 research covers a vast range of topics, major issues, and research methods. Among the branches of critical language studies are discourse analysis (Fairclough, 1989, 1995; Pennycook, 2001), language policy (Tollefson & Tsui, 2004; Tsui & Tollefson, 2007), curriculum and instruction (Gegeo & Watson-Gegeo, 2002), English language teaching (Auerbach, 1995), educational innovation and change (Gourd, 1998), and teacher education (Luk & Lin, 2007).

In general, critical approaches to L2 education explicitly focus on ideology. That is, their major aim is to make explicit the systems of thought, the assumptions and beliefs, and the systems of behavior that are seen as natural and normal within educational institutions. For example, Phillipson (1992) outlines five principles of English language teaching that support English linguistic imperialism: that English is best taught monolingually; that the ideal teacher is a native speaker; that English should be introduced at the youngest age possible; that English should constitute as much of the curriculum as possible in order to maximize learning opportunities; and that the use of other languages threatens English language learning and proficiency standards. These principles are sufficiently naturalized that they are implicit in much of the teacher training, curriculum planning, educational policies, and classroom practices of English language education worldwide, despite the fact that there is little empirical evidence to support any of them. In Phillipson's view, these principles help to sustain the privileged position of monolingual teachers and other specialists in "core" English speaking countries (especially the UK and the US), and thus they may be termed "ideological."

Also working within a critical approach, Lippi-Green (1997) describes standard language ideology, which she defines as "a bias toward an abstract, idealized homogeneous language, which is imposed and maintained by dominant institutions and which has as its model the written language, but which is drawn primarily from the spoken language of the upper middle class" (p. 64). Lippi-Green's material-institutional analysis explores ways that standard language ideology impacts language practices in many institutions and social domains, including the use of standard language varieties in schools, restrictions on the use of stigmatized home varieties in public domains, depictions of accent in children's media, and judgments about individuals' veracity and trustworthiness.

As Phillipson's and Lippi-Green's research suggests, critical L2 research undertakes a project of discovery of implicit ideologies that are seen as natural and normal within institutions, including schools. A critical approach to this project of discovery can be characterized by three major tenets (cf. Norton, 1995) that align closely with the understanding of ideology outlined in the first section of this chapter.

The first tenet of critical L2 research is that research itself is always historically situated, always reflects in deep and implicit ways the social position of the researcher, and can never provide the kind of unbiased, objective truth-claims demanded by allegedly "objective" approaches such as experimentalism. In contrast to experimentalism, critical research requires that researchers make explicit their personal histories and social positions, and that they critically reflect on their institutional roles, their relationship of power with their subjects, and the aims and uses of their research (Cameron et al., 1992; Norton, 1995).

A second major tenet of critical L2 research is that it investigates how social inequalities, particularly involving unequal power relations, are central to L2 teaching and learning. This focus on power and inequality requires explicit attention to class, race, gender, and sexual orientation in L2 education, and to the ways that institutional structures and roles determine L2 learning. This work initially focused on constraints on L2 learning imposed by class, race, and other social factors, and by the institutions of the ideological state apparatuses (e.g., Tollefson, 1991). Since the 1990s, critical research has gradually shifted toward greater emphasis on human agency and has sought to avoid structural determinism. Accordingly, critical L2 research has increasingly focused on acts of resistance, opportunities for anti-hegemonic and counter-hegemonic action, and the complex ways that teachers and students in the everyday interactions of teaching and learning shape their social positions independently of the demands of the ideological state apparatuses. (For examples of such research, see Canagarajah, 1999, and Gegeo & Watson-Gegeo, 2002.) Thus while critical research explores the impact of power and inequality in L2 education, it also seeks ways to transform L2 education through the classroom practices of what has come to be called "critical pedagogy" (see Tollefson, 2002a).

Critical pedagogy suggests a third tenet of critical L2 research: that the goal of research is social change. Although related to action research (Nunan, 1990), critical research is distinguished by being grounded in analysis of ideology, power, and inequality, and in addition it seeks the transformation of schools and other institutions, in order to undermine social hierarchies that are sustained by these institutions. This task is a formidable one, requiring not only carefully considered research methods, but also an analysis of educational innovation and change, an understanding of the local politics of language policy in schools, and a practical involvement in the daily work of teaching and learning (Morgan & Ramanathan, 2005). In this undertaking, the hierarchical separation of research and teaching, and of researchers and language teachers, must also be critically examined and transformed. Thus I turn to what it means to be a teacher, and to ideologies of teacher education.

Teacher Education

In the past 20 years, a growing scholarly literature on ideology in teacher education has emerged. To some extent, this attention is due to two major and contradictory teacher-education reform movements. One of these movements is the effort to professionalize teaching and teacher education, often linked to discourses of professionalism and accountability (Cochran-Smith & Fries, 2001). In L2 education, this movement is evident in the push to adopt standards for English language teaching programs, led by the Standards Standing Committee of the international TESOL organization and the Commission on English Language Program Accreditation (TESOL, 2006). In K–12 education, the professionalization movement in the United States is led by the National Commission on Teaching and America's Future (1997), the National Council for the Accreditation of Teacher Education (2002), and other associated groups, with individual leadership provided by Linda Darling-Hammond (Darling-Hammond, 2000).

A second reform movement in teacher education—opposed to the professionalization movement—is the effort to deregulate teacher education by eliminating most authority currently exercised by state licensing agencies and dismantling teacher-education program in universities. This movement is led by several conservative foundations, including the Thomas B. Fordham Foundation (1999) and the Heritage Foundation. (For a survey of the tensions between these two movements, see Cochran-Smith & Fries, 2001.)

The debate between professionalization and deregulation is partly carried out with reference to research evidence, advocates of both movements arguing that *their* position is best supported by research findings. Indeed, certain areas of ideological agreement between the two movements are noteworthy. Most importantly, all discussants agree that empirical evidence should be the main determinant of any reforms and policy initiatives. For example, in supporting deregulation, the Fordham Foundation states: "We are struck by the paucity of evidence linking inputs with actual teacher effectiveness ... very little connection was found between the degrees teachers had earned or the experience they possessed and how much their students learned" (Thomas B. Fordham

Foundation, 1999, p. 18). In response, advocates of professionalization state that "reviews of more than two hundred studies contradict the long-standing myths that 'anyone can teach' and that 'teachers are born and not made'" (National Commission on Teaching and America's Future, 1997, p. 10). Such claims are based on a fundamental assumption in teacher education: that the quality of teaching can and must be assessed, and that one way to do so is to measure gains in students' learning. This common-sense approach is claimed by professionalization advocates and those who support deregulation.

In L2 teaching and learning, such debates take concrete form in several controversies in teacher education, including the importance of "native-speaker" language ability among teachers (Leung, Harris, & Rampton, 1997); the relationship between research and practice (Erben, 2004); the best practices movement (Samway & McKeon, 2007); and approaches to language assessment (McNamara, 2000). Perhaps nowhere, however, is there greater controversy in teacher education than over what some critics term "the ideological indoctrination" of teachers (Hare, 2007).

This controversy emerges in debates over a fundamental question: what is a good teacher? In the United States, the standards of the National Council for Accreditation of Teacher Education include certain dispositions that teachers are required to hold and to demonstrate in their practice. These dispositions include "beliefs and attitudes related to values such as caring, fairness, honesty, responsibility, and social justice" (National Council for Accreditation of Teacher Education, 2002, p. 53). In practice, one commonly required disposition is a commitment to critical thinking.

Critics argue, however, that such standards for teachers—and the attention given to these standards in teacher education programs—constitute indoctrination to a political agenda (Hare, 2003). Critics ask: what is meant by "critical thinking," by "responsibility," and by a commitment to "social justice"? How are teachers expected to demonstrate their understanding of these values and incorporate them into their practice? What happens when teachers impose their own perspectives on students? For example, examining social constructionist approaches to composition theory, Santos (1992) argued that they deny "individuality" and are "allied with a political ideology which is left-wing or Marxist in nature," whereas preferred approaches are "pragmatic" and "avoid ideology" (p. 4). Critics who insist on a non-ideological approach to teacher education implicitly argue that *their* approach has no ideology, and that *their* programs of teacher education do not indoctrinate (Hare, 2003).

Although most approaches to teacher education do not investigate their underlying ideologies (Cochran-Smith & Fries, 2001), educators have a responsibility to articulate (rather than ignore, disguise, or naturalize) their ideologies. A common feature of critical teacher education, for example, is a commitment to the "joint goals" of developing "English communication abilities and the ability to apply them to developing a critical awareness of the world and the ability to act on it to improve matters" (Crookes & Lehner, 1998). Thus the approach emphasizes "critical thinking" and focuses on the crucial importance of power and inequality in L2 teaching and learning and the need for social change.

By investigating and articulating ideologies of teacher education, teachers can become cautious about generalizations about L2 education. For example, in one setting, learning English may be a practical way to get a better job, but in another setting, learning English may entail important changes in individual or group identity, perhaps even a threat to ethnic group survival. Thus in some contexts, learning English may be a problem rather than a solution. In India, for instance, teaching English in early elementary school may undermine education in the local language that is more effective for subject-matter teaching (Dua, 1985).

The ideologies of all aspects of language education should be examined in teacher education programs, including theories of language learning, research practices, teaching methods, and textbooks and other materials—all of which may be viewed as historical and cultural artifacts. What factors in language learning are highlighted in current learning theories and what do those factors imply about the causes of successful and unsuccessful L2 learning? Why are particular teaching methods and materials popular at particular periods in history? Who benefits from the spread of particular methods and materials? These and similar questions focus attention on the historical context of theory and practice, and their ideological function. For example, Ager (1999) argues that literacy programs in France often have an implicit ideological aim: to define "illiteracy" as a form of social deprivation. In such programs, immigrants are represented as culturally and educationally deficient, and thus literacy education has the political function of placing blame for illiteracy on immigrants and their sending countries. The implicit "solution" therefore is cultural assimilation, language shift, and loss of ethnic identity. Ager's argument suggests that common literacy teaching practices in France support the recent upsurge of anti-immigrant sentiment. Such an analysis demonstrates that attention to ideology in teacher education can help to create an intense skepticism about claims made in support of theories, methods, and classroom practice.

Finally, a focus on ideology in teacher education means that self-reflection and self-critique are fundamental, not only for teachers in training, but for faculty who direct graduate courses, for supervising teachers, and for other mentors (Nunan, 1992). Ideologies of language and teaching are largely implicit and unconscious, and only intense critical reflection can help make them explicit and thus open to change. To be effective, however, self-reflection and critique must take place within an administrative framework that rewards these important processes.

Ideology and L2 Research: Two Examples

Although a focus on ideology calls into question research methods, the role of research, and the relationship between researchers and the people they investigate, empirical research remains central to understanding L2 education. That is, an ideological focus does not mean that research is irrelevant to important issues in language teaching and learning. Rather, attention to ideology can open new perspectives that can strengthen research findings, providing a level of confidence in research that is impossible when ideology is ignored. In this section, I offer two examples of key issues in L2 education in which attention to ideology is particularly useful.

Language Variation and Target Language in L2 Learning

The tradition of L2 teaching has long relied on the concept of "target language" (Tollefson, 2002b). Although there are exceptions, the target language for much of L2 education is a standard language variety, typically described by language texts that specify rules of grammar and pronunciation. Within this perspective, the learners' goal is to learn and use the standard model, and the teachers' expert position in schools is grounded on expertise in this model. This approach to language education (in which teachers, texts, and other sources of authority define a "target" for students to learn) is based on what Cameron (1995) calls an "ideology of variation," in which the target language is fixed, and variation in learners' language is assumed to be the result of learners' "carelessness … or incompetence" (p. 39). Students' output is expected to conform to the invariant target language, and thus assessment and error correction become important techniques for enforcing the ideology of variation. Although variation is fundamental to all language use, L2 education is often assumed to be exempt from variation (except as a marker of "failed" learning). As a result, the field has adopted concepts such as "interlanguage," "fossilization," and "error correction," which reflect the belief that learners are involved in (and should be involved in) learning the target (standard) language. An additional problem, as Lippi-Green (1997) points out, is that the concept of standard language is an idealized construct that has only indirect relationship to actual language use.

The failure to incorporate a theory of variation in L2 education has important consequences in the analysis of language and identity. Many learners are involved not in acquiring a prestige standard variety, but instead multiple stigmatized varieties and hybrid varieties that have social value in groups with multiple and hybrid identities (Rampton, 2006). When such common L2 learning is ignored, the result is an idealized (and ideological) version of the process of L2 learning: a one-to-one link between language and identity; an image of individuals attempting to learn and use standard languages according to native-speaker norms; teachers, texts, and tests that insist on learners' ability to comprehend and produce standard languages; and a conceptual framework that makes this process seem natural, normal, and desirable (Tollefson, 2007). In contrast, a focus on ideology reveals that language and identity have complex and varied relationships; many learners are not involved in the process of learning standard varieties defined by native-speaker norms; and few adult learners will ever produce (or need to produce) the target standard.

Bilingual and Monolingual Approaches to L2 Teaching

Despite a large body of research demonstrating that language learning is facilitated by using learners' L1s in classrooms (Auerbach, 1993; Tollefson & Tsui, 2004), target-language-only instruction remains a common practice, particularly English-only. Similarly, in English literacy in the United States and elsewhere, initial L1 literacy is often ignored, despite research suggesting that it can have a beneficial impact on L2 literacy (Auerbach, 2000). The insistence on English-only practices in English language teaching entails restrictions on use of "non-standard," stigmatized varieties, such as pidgins and creoles, regional varieties, and working class or "ethnic" varieties such as African American English. Although research over many years suggests that using such varieties can aid L2 learning (Siegel, 1999), a long tradition in education insists that stigmatized varieties are inappropriate in classrooms and disruptive to learning, and ultimately delay acquisition of the standard target variety. Monolingual practices in the face of empirical evidence to the contrary serve the ideological function of limiting the use of minority languages in education, restricting learning, and sustaining the social representation of marginal groups as lacking motivation and the ability to learn, and even racist stereotypes of minorities as slow learners with low expectations for future learning (Cooke, 2008). Thus a monolingual ideology, often rationalized on pedagogical grounds, helps to sustain systems of inequality in which language plays a crucial role.

As these examples suggest, empirical research that is linked to analysis of ideology offers provocative possibilities for understanding fundamental practices in L2 education. What exactly are learners learning? What uses of language can be observed in their lives? How are relationships among teachers and students shaped by common teaching practices? Who really benefits from those practices? Such questions direct our attention to social relations in L2 learning and to the complex and often invisible forces that structure those relations.

Conclusion: The Importance of Ideology in L2 Education

Ideological analysis in L2 education reveals that social and political agendas call ideologies into service in the process of allocating resources and benefits to different social groups. Standard language ideology, the ideology of monolingual (English) classrooms, the ideology of variation, and implicit ideologies in teacher education, SLA, research methods, and other aspects of L2 education have direct consequences for the social positions of learners, teachers, and others; and it is in such social positions that individuals gain (or are denied) access to economic resources and political power.

A focus on ideology is also crucial in the larger context of the role of language and L2 education in the enormous challenges facing humanity: national and ethnic conflicts, economic and social inequality, and crises of the environment, economy, and international security. Because these multiple challenges are intractable and overwhelming for individual nation-states, even those with the greatest wealth and resources, it is only through the participation of peoples worldwide in coordinated, international action that these problems can be confronted. Yet ethnic, linguistic, national, and cultural differences persist at the core of political and military conflict around the world, including the UK, France, Italy, Turkey, the United States, China, India, Russia, Iraq, Pakistan, Mexico, Guatemala, and many other countries.

In such circumstances, the central importance of cooperation and active participation in policymaking means that language, literacy, and L2 education are more important than ever. It is only through international cooperation—multilingual, multicultural, multiethnic, and multinational—that solutions to the great problems facing humanity can be developed. To find ways to create cooperation requires a deeper understanding of the processes by which social, economic, and political inequalities are created, masked, and sustained. It is for this reason that analysis of ideology deserves the highest priority in L2 research and education.

References

Ager, D. E. (1999). *Identity, insecurity and image: France and language.* Clevedon: Multilingual Matters.

Althusser, L. (1971). Ideology and ideological state apparatuses. In *Lenin and philosophy and other essay* (pp. 127–186). (Ben Brewster, trans.). New York: Monthly Review Press.

Auerbach, E. (1993). Reexamining English only in the ESOL classroom. *TESOL Quarterly, 27*(1), 9–32.

Auerbach, E. (1995). The politics of the ESL classroom: Issues of power in pedagogical choices. In J. W. Tollefson (Ed.), *Power and inequality in language education* (pp. 9–33). Cambridge: Cambridge University Press.

Auerbach, E. (2000). When pedagogy meets politics: Challenging English only in adult education. In R. D. Gonzales with I. Melis (Eds.), *Language ideologies: Critical perspectives on the official English movement* (Vol. I) (pp. 177–204). Urbana, IL and Mahwah, NJ: NCTE and Lawrence Erlbaum.

Baumann, J. F. (1991). Basel reading programs and the deskilling of teachers. Paper presented at the Annual Meeting of the American Education Research Association, Chicago. ED329906.

Benesch, S. (1993). ESL, ideology, and the politics of pragmatism. *TESOL Quarterly, 27*(4), 705–717.

Blommaert, J. (2005). *Discourse.* Cambridge: Cambridge University Press.

Bourdieu, P. (1991). *Language and symbolic power* (G. Raymond & M. Adamson, trans.). Oxford: Polity Press.

Cameron, D. (1995). *Verbal hygiene.* London: Routledge.

Cameron, D., Frazer, E., Harvey, P., Rampton, M. B. H., & Richardson, K. (1992). *Researching language: Issues of power and method.* London: Routledge.

Canagarajah, A. S. (1999). *Resisting linguistic imperialism in English teaching.* Oxford: Oxford University Press.

Coalition for Evidence-Based Policy. (2002). Bringing evidence-driven progress to education: A recommended strategy for the U.S. Department of Education (ERIC Document Reproduction Service No. 474378). Retrieved May 17, 2009, from http://www.eric.ed.gov/PDFS/ED474378.pdf.

Cochran-Smith, M., & Fries, M. K. (2001). Sticks, stones, and ideology: The discourse of reform in teacher education. *Educational Researcher, 30*(8), 3–15.

Cooke, M. (2008). "What we might become": The lives, aspirations, and education of young migrants in the London area. *Journal of Language, Identity, and Education, 7*(1), 22–40.

Creswell, J. W. (2009). *Research design: Qualitative, quantitative, and mixed methods approaches.* London: Sage.

Crookes, G., & Lehner, A. (1998). Aspects of process in an ESL critical pedagogy teacher education course. *TESOL Quarterly, 32*(2), 319–328.

Daniels, H., & Bizar, M. (2004). *Teaching the best practice way: Methods that matter, K-12.* Portland, ME: Stenhouse Press.

Darling-Hammond, L. (Ed.) (2000). *Studies of excellence in teachers.* Washington: National Commission on Teaching and America's Future.

Davies, A. (1996). Review article: Ironising the myth of linguistic imperialism. *Journal of Multilingual and Multicultural Development, 17*(6), 485–496.

Dörnyei, Z. (2006). Individual differences in second language acquisition. *AILA Review, 19,* 42–68.

Dua, H. (1985). *Language planning in India.* New Delhi: Harnam.

Eisenhart, M. (2005). Hammers and saws for the improvement of educational research. *Educational Theory, 55*(3), 245–261.

Erben, T. (2004). Emerging research and practices in immersion teacher education. *Annual Review of Applied Linguistics, 24,* 320–338.

Fairclough, N. (1989). *Language and power.* London: Longman.

Fairclough, N. (1995). *Critical discourse analysis.* London: Longman.

Foucault, M. (1972). *The archaeology of knowledge.* Harmondsworth: Penguin.

Foucault, M. (1980). *Power/knowledge: Selected interviews and other writings, 1972–1977.* New York: Pantheon.

Gardner, R. C. (1985). *Social psychology and second language learning: The role of attitudes and motivation.* London: Edward Arnold.

Gass, S., & Selinker, L. (2001). *Second language acquisition: An introductory course.* Mahwah, NJ: Lawrence Erlbaum Associates.

Gegeo, D. W., & Watson-Gegeo, K. A. (2002). The critical villager: Transforming language and education in Solomon Islands. In J. W. Tollefson (Ed.), *Language policies in education: Critical issues* (pp. 309–325). Mahwah, NJ: Lawrence Erlbaum.

Gourd, K. (1998). Freire's liberatory model of education: Transformation at the classroom level. Unpublished Ph.D. dissertation, University of Washington, Seattle.

Gramsci, A. (1988). *A Gramsci reader: Selected writings* (D. Forgacs, Ed.). London: Lawrence & Wishart.

Greene, J. C. (2007). *Mixed methods in social inquiry.* San Francisco: Jossey-Bass.

Hall, S. (1996). The question of cultural identity. In S. Hall, D. Held, D. Hubert, & K. Thompson (Eds.), *Modernity: An introduction to modern societies* (pp. 595–634). Cambridge, MA: Blackwell.

Hare, W. (2003). The ideal of open-mindedness and its place in education. *Journal of Thought, 38,* 3–10.

Hare, W. (2007). Ideological indoctrination and teacher education. *Journal of Educational Controversy, 2*(2). Retrieved May 6, 2009, from http://www.wce.wwu.edu/Resources/CEP/eJournal/v002n002/a006.shtml.

Hodge, R. & Kress, G. (1993). *Language as ideology (second edition).* London: Routledge.

Howe, K. R. (2004). A critique of experimentalism. *Qualitative Inquiry, 10*(4), 42–61.

Johnson, D. M. (1992). *Approaches to research in second language learning.* London: Longman.

Krashen, S. D. (1981). *Second language acquisition and second language learning.* London: Pergamon.

Lantolf, J. P. (2005). Sociocultural and second language learning research: An exegesis. In E. Hinkel (Ed.), *Handbook of research in second language teaching and learning* (pp. 335–353). Mahwah, NJ: Lawrence Erlbaum Associates.

Lantolf, J. P. (2006). Sociocultural theory and the L2: State of the art. *Studies in Second Language Acquisition, 28,* 67–109.

Leung, C., Harris, R., & Rampton, B. (1997). The idealized native speaker, reified ethnicities, and classroom realities. *TESOL Quarterly, 31*(3), 543–560.

Lippi-Green, R. (1997). *English with an accent.* London: Routledge.

Luk, J. C. M., & Lin, A. M. Y. (2007). *Classroom interactions as cross-cultural encounters: Native speakers in EFL lessons.* Mahwah, NJ: Lawrence Erlbaum.

McNamara, T. F. (2000). *Language testing.* Oxford: Oxford University Press.

Mills, A. (1997). *Discourse.* London: Routledge.

Morgan, B., & Ramanathan, V. (2005). Critical literacies and language education: Global and local perspectives. *Annual Review of Applied Linguistics, 25,* 151–169.

Naiman, N., Frölich, M., Stern, H. H., & Todesco, A. (1996). *The good language learner.* Clevedon: Multilingual Matters.

National Commission on Teaching and America's Future. (1997). *Doing what matters most: Investing in quality teaching.* New York: National Commission on Teaching and America's Future.

National Council for Accreditation of Teacher Education. (2002). *Professional standards for the accreditation of schools, colleges, and departments of education.* Washington: National Council for Accreditation of Teacher Education.

National Research Council. (2002). *Scientific research in education.* Washington: National Academy Press.

Norton, B. (1995). The theory of methodology in qualitative research. *TESOL Quarterly, 29*(3), 569–576.

Nunan, D. (1990). Action research in the language classroom. In J. Richards & D. Nunan (Eds.), *Second language teacher education* (pp. 62–81). Cambridge: Cambridge University Press.

Nunan, D. (1992). *Research methods in language learning.* Cambridge: Cambridge University Press.

Oller, J. (1993). *Methods that work: Ideas for literacy and language teachers.* New York: van Nostrand Reinhold.

O'Sullivan, T., Hartley, J., Saunders, D., Montgomery, M., & Fiske, J. (1994). *Key concepts in communication and cultural studies.* London: Routledge.

Pennycook, A. (2001). *Critical applied linguistics: A critical introduction.* Mahwah, NJ: Lawrence Erlbaum.

Phillipson, R. (1992). *Linguistic imperialism.* Oxford: Oxford University Press.

Pickering, M. (2001). *Stereotyping: The politics of representation.* London: Palgrave Macmillan.

Ramanathan, V. (2005). *The English-vernacular divide: Postcolonial language politics and practice.* Clevedon: Multilingual Matters.

Rampton, B. (2006). *Language in late modernity: Interaction in an urban school.* Cambridge: Cambridge University Press.

Reid, J. M. (1989). English as a second language composition in higher education: The expectations of the academic audience. In D. M. Johnson & D. H. Roen (Eds.), *Richness in writing: Empowering ESL students* (pp. 220–234). New York: Longman.

Samway, K. D., & McKeon, D. (2007). *Myths and realities: Best practices for English language learners* (2nd ed.). Portsmouth, NH: Heinemann.

Santos, T. (1992). Ideology and composition: L1 and ESL. *Journal of Second Language Writing, 1*, 1–15.

Schumann, J. (1978). *The pidginization process: A model for second language acquisition*. Rowley, MA: Newbury House.

Siegel, J. (1999). Stigmatized and standardized varieties in the classroom: Interference or separation? *TESOL Quarterly, 33*(4), 701–728.

TESOL. (2006). *TESOL ESL Standards for PreK-12 Students*. Retrieved May 17, 2009, from http://www.tesol.org/s_tesol/seccss.asp?CID=1186&DID=5348.

Teddlie, C., & Tashakkori, A. (2003). Major issues and controversies in the use of mixed methods in the social and behavioural sciences. In A. Tashakkori & C. Teddlie (Eds.), *Handbook of mixed methods in social and behavioural sciences* (pp. 3–50). Thousand Oaks, CA: Sage.

Thomas B. Fordham Foundation. (1999). *The quest for better teachers: Grading the states*. Washington: Thomas B. Fordham Foundation.

Tollefson, J. W. (1991). *Planning language, planning inequality: Language policy in the community*. London: Longman.

Tollefson, J. W. (2002a). Introduction: Critical issues in educational language policy. In J. W. Tollefson (Ed.), *Language policies in education: Critical issues* (pp. 3–15). Mahwah, NJ: Lawrence Erlbaum.

Tollefson, J. W. (2002b). Reconsidering "target language." *Language Research Bulletin, 17*, 143–152.

Tollefson, J. W. (2007). Ideology, language varieties, and ELT. In J. Cummins & C. Davison (Eds.), *International handbook of English language teaching, Part I* (pp. 25–36). New York: Springer.

Tollefson, J. W., & Tsui, A. B. M. (Eds.) (2004). *Medium of instruction policies: Which agenda? Whose agenda?* Mahwah, NJ: Lawrence Erlbaum Associates.

Tsui, A. B. M., & Tollefson, J. W. (Eds.) (2007). *Language policy, culture and identity in Asian contexts*. Mahwah, NJ: Lawrence Erlbaum Associates.

van Dijk, T. (1990). Social cognition and discourse. In G. Giles & R. P. Robinson (Eds.), *Handbook of social psychology and language* (pp. 163–183). Chichester: Wiley.

van Dijk, T. (1993a). Discourse and cognition in society. In D. Crowley & D. Mitchell (Eds.), *Communication theory today* (pp. 107–126). Oxford: Pergamon Press.

van Dijk, T. (1993b). *Elite discourse and racism*. London: Sage.

van Dijk, T. (n.d.). New(s) racism: A discourse analytical approach. Retrieved September 5, 2008, from http://www.discourses.org/OldArticles/New(s)%20racism%20-%20A%20discourse%20analytical%20approach.pdf.

Wodak, R. (1996). *Disorders of discourse*. London: Longman.

Zuengler, J., & Miller, E. R. (2006). Cognitive and sociocultural perspectives: Two parallel SLA worlds? *TESOL Quarterly, 40*(1), 35–58.

49

Identity in Second Language Teaching and Learning

Brian Morgan and Matthew Clarke

No, an identity is never given, received or attained; only the interminable and indefinitely phantasmatic process of identification endures.

(Derrida, 1998, p. 28)

Identity has become one of the most frequently employed concepts in the social sciences and humanities (Bendle, 2002) and the fields of education (Gee, 2000) and applied linguistics have proved no exception to this trend (Belcher & Lukkarila, forthcoming; Block, 2007; Cummins, 2006; Dörnyei & Ushioda, 2009; Fleming, 2003; Lin, 2008; Menard-Warwick, 2005; Morgan, 2007; Norton, 2000; Pavlenko & Blackledge, 2004). Part of the reason for this popularity can be traced to the term's capacity to provide a conceptual link between seemingly opposed tendencies; indeed, echoing Eagleton's (2000, p. 2) comments on culture, a similarly prolific term, it is possible to argue in relation to identity that "within this single term, questions of freedom and determinism, agency and endurance, change and identity, the given and the created, come dimly into focus". Eagleton's use of the term "identity" in the above quote, as something that is opposed to, or in tension with, "change", suggests that identity is about the psychic, social and semiotic work necessary to sustain a sense of unity and sameness across time and space. Yet, as we will discuss in more detail below, identity relies on difference and on *social* categories in order to achieve its coherence. The social origins and traces of the "other" within identity have led some to argue that identity is a "fiction" rather than an "existential fact" (Menard-Warwick, 2005). This distinction between identity as an existential fact and as a fiction echoes the divide highlighted by Mansfield (2000) between theories and approaches which see identity/subjectivity[1] as a "thing" to be discovered, liberated, examined and/or explained, as, for example, in most psychoanalytic theories, and theories that see identity as an effect, of discourse or power, as is the case with postmodern and poststructuralist approaches to identity (Mansfield, 2000).

Whichever of these views we adopt, identity relies on a repertoire of communicative resources (e.g. rituals, texts and signs) through/by which categories of difference/individuality are perceived, maintained or resisted and these communicative resources are fundamentally social in nature. Indeed, it is the importance attached to the representational means/tools involved that underpins Blommaert's (2005) conceptualization of identity as "semiotic potential", a perspective that aligns closely with the mediational foci of socio-cultural and activity theories (see e.g. Lantolf & Thorne, 2006; van Lier, 2004).

Indeed, the above tensions between identity as *sameness/uniqueness* and identity as *difference (from)* parallel debates around the continuity versus the malleability of identity, debates that form a significant fault line in research on identity in second language education (SLE) (Menard-Warwick, 2005). In turn, these identity debates echo debates centring on the ontological/existential status of languages and cultures. For example, minority/indigenous language rights debates typically rely on the objectification/demarcation of languages into discrete, enumerative entities, with populations ascribed to them, in order to make them the "legitimate" objects of expert intervention for revitalization purposes. Yet other work confounds the very possibility of talking about the existence of discrete languages per se (Makoni & Pennycook, 2007; Reagan, 2004) and it can be argued that such objectifying, reificatory approaches lend themselves to cultural stereotyping (Holliday, 2005; Kubota, 2004).

The rise of identity as a concept in the social sciences also requires attention to historical factors such as the long process of Western secularization from the seventeenth to the twentieth centuries—the shift from theocentric to anthropocentric visions of the universe, and from the "soul" to the "mind" as the locus of what we now refer to as identity (Porter, 2004). This shift brought with it a concomitant emphasis on worldly life, self-fulfilment and activity, a process reflected in and supported by the late twentieth-century burgeoning of media and consumer cultures and practices targeting the individual, for example, lifestyle shows and self-help manuals. However, despite the dominant Western narrative, which views these developments in terms of the growth of individual choice and freedom, they can also be seen as reflective of our increasing (self-)subjection to discourses of commoditization and consumption, an issue we address below in a section on neoliberalism and SLE.

The "Inner World" of the Subject: Language, Identity, and Psychoanalytic Theory

Perhaps the epitome of an anthropocentric world view is to be found in Descartes' (in)famous *cogito*, "I think, therefore I am", with its assertion of self-conscious reflection as the founding principle of knowledge and truth and its assumption of the self's separateness and individuality (Hall, 2004). However, the idea of a self-sufficient individual self took a potentially disturbing turn in the late nineteenth and early twentieth centuries, as the new science of psychology sought to unlock the hidden secrets of the human mind, while psychoanalysis uncovered the dark forces lurking beneath consciousness. Freud's notion of the unconscious was taken in a new—and for the purposes of this chapter vitally important, given the significance attached to language and identity in his theories (Roseboro, 2008)—direction by Lacan, whose subversion of the Cartesian cogito is reflected in his statement, "I think where I am not, therefore I am where I do not think" (Chiesa, 2007, p. 39). For Lacan, identity formation occurs through a double process of misrecognition, or alienating identification. This first occurs in the "mirror stage", which entails momentous changes for the child, including a distinction between itself and the (m)other/mirror-image (self as "other"), coupled with the (illusory) promise of potential for self-reliance and mastery.

The alienation of the mirror stage is redoubled with entry into the symbolic order (language), a social system of signification, which precedes and exceeds any given individual, yet which, at the same time, mediates the individual's relations with others and with the world. As Butler puts it, "when the 'I' seeks to give an account of itself, it can start with itself, but it will find that this self is already implicated in a social temporality that exceeds its own capacities for narration" (2005, p. 8). This alienation is compounded by the insufficiency of language to convey the individual's intentions and desires completely, whilst also, paradoxically, often conveying more than the individual intended (Chiesa, 2007). In Eagleton's words, "we are fated, then, to express ourselves in a tongue which is forever foreign" (2008, p. 86, cf. Derrida, 1998). Such insights confound received understandings that by acquiring additional languages we move ever closer to the promise of complete communication, or that second languages are necessarily alienating, given that all language is alienating (McNamara, 2009). As Granger's (2004) psychoanalytic study of silence in second language acquisition (SLA) suggests, the transition from first to second language compounds the unconscious loss and emotional displacement inherent in first language acquisition.

Indeed, it could be argued that Lacan provides a theoretical underpinning for the liberating effect that some commentators have described as an important element of second language learning (House, 2003), given that this learning bypasses the initial trauma of entering the symbolic realm that learning the "mother tongue" entails. However, it would be simplistic or essentializing to depict the translingual subject as residing in permanent states of either abjection or emancipation. As Pavlenko (2006) reports, many translingual writers find the latter learned language as a medium of emotional release, offering "new 'clean' words, devoid of anxieties and taboos, freeing them from self-censorship, from prohibitions and loyalties of their native culture" (p. 20). Yet, they also recognize that "the use of the 'stepmother tongue' comes with a price: the ever-present nostalgia for the primeval emotionality of the selves linked to the mother tongue, the language that retains the incomparable ability to wound, to heal, and to caress" (p. 20). Clearly, both emotional loss and liberation can arise from the psychic/semiotic mediation of translingual practices. At the same time, the fact that such perspectives and evocative descriptions have arisen at all in SLE sheds light on the degree to which psychoanalytic perspectives have invigorated research on the "inner world" of bilinguals and second language learners (cf. Granger, 2004; McNamara, 2009; Pavlenko, 2006), and in ways profoundly different from earlier considerations of affect and motivation in the SLA literature.

Identity, Agency, and Power

Misrecognition and alienation are not only concerns/conditions of the mind but also of the social world. Indeed, they are central to Althusser's notion of identity formation through ideological interpellation, or "hailing", as when, in a scene that is at once "exemplary and allegorical" (Butler, 1997, p. 106), the police office calls "hey you" and we guiltily turn around regardless of whether or not we are the one being hailed. We accept the legitimacy of the state and its institutions, despite knowing at some level that the state has no claim on us: "Law abiding behaviour results not from the threat of punishment, but from a complex complicity with power" (Kay, 2003, p. 105). Or to put it in more Foucauldian terms, we might say that identity positions are materializations of discursively structured power relations.

Indeed, Foucault is probably the theorist most linked to the view that sees the individual not as a pre-given entity but as an effect of discourse, of subjectivity as something that takes shape within the operations of the Foucauldian couplet, power/knowledge. Foucault rejects the notion of the individual as the self-originating source of her/his own meaning: "one has to dispense with the constituent subject, to get rid of the subject itself … [in order to] … account for the constitution of the subject within an historical framework" (Foucault, 1980, p. 115). Still, to understand identity as subjectivity, on these terms defined by Foucault, does not reduce us to the status of "puppets on a string", helpless in the face of power and blinded by "false consciousness". But it does frame our capacity to act or imagine otherwise—to have *agency*—since, following Foucault, discourses also create the conditions for their transgression.

Across identity work in the social sciences, and inherent in the seminal texts and theorists cited in this introduction, the issue of *agency* is crucial, especially in relation to its causal connections with language and its implications for SLE (Ahearn, 2001; Flowerdew & Miller, 2008). Echoing the rational, free-willed subject of the *cogito*, to what extent are our thoughts our own—their essence conveyed intact through a putatively transparent and neutral medium of language? Or, conversely, to what extent are we *determined*—"spoken" by the language we use, the discourses we inhabit, or by the primordial structures of culture and mind against which we are relatively powerless? Perhaps it is both and "in-between" whereby agency is not a universal, a priori condition but one socially embedded and enabled through specific discursive constraints, a conceptualization that seems to align with Bakhtin's dialogical notions of voice and answerability (e.g. Hall, Vitanova & Marchenkova, 2005; Thorne, 2005). These kinds of questions—and the theoretical answers to which we subscribe—define the *horizons of possibility* (cf. Simon, 1992) for identity work in SLE.

Identity Work in SLE: Selective Appropriations

In her survey of identity theory in SLA and literacy studies, Menard-Warwick (2005) astutely notes how these sub-fields have selectively appropriated (p. 253) conceptual elements from key figures such as Foucault (e.g. discourse) and Bourdieu (e.g. habitus, capital). The broader point is crucial: though the boundaries of fields have become increasingly blurred, common interests serve to maintain a sense of disciplinary cohesion. Periodically, however, persistent field-internal problems are recognized, prompting researchers to look outside their existing knowledge base for ideas that might serve to revitalize tired habits of thought. An underlying and persistent field-internal problem in applied linguistics and SLE has been an overwhelming reliance on psycholinguistic and social psychological explanation in SLA research, on the one hand, and a strong bias against openly ideological and ethnographic inquiry, on the other (e.g. Block, 2003). Through membership in discrete and stable communities, learners were assumed to possess particular traits and language habits, whose estimated proximity or distance from the target language and culture, served to "explain" failure or success in SLA. Indeed, as Firth and Wagner (1997) noted, the native speaker and non-native speaker seemed to be the only two identities entertained in SLA and applied linguistics. Based on this somewhat insular model, pedagogical interventions were directed entirely towards informing/changing learner attributes to align ever more closely with the target of native speaker competence—an inherently political approach that ironically disavowed politics and ignored mainstream prejudices and power hierarchies that marginalized learner opportunities.

This authoritative, disciplinary canon was challenged by Norton Peirce's 1995 *TESOL Quarterly* article (see also Norton, 2000). Drawing on poststructural notions of subjectivity and discourse (cf. Weedon, Foucault), Norton (2000) proposed a dynamic notion of identity as "multiple and contradictory" and "a site of struggle" (p. 127), in which neither students nor teachers could be seen as speaking or behaving in predictable ways that indexed stable ethnolinguistic categories or that offered straightforward evidence of the attitudinal and motivation types deemed essential for SLA. In addition, Norton's influential construct of *investment*—informed by Bourdieu (cf. cultural and symbolic capital)—similarly challenged the apolitical and psycholinguistic biases of much interlanguage research, offering "the right to speak" and "the power to impose reception" (2000, p. 8) as ideological/discursive criteria necessary for an adequate understanding of second language competence.

The SLE field has since witnessed an extraordinary growth in identity-based research, in parts refining and extending the complexities that Norton's investigation prompted. There have also been important critiques, particularly of the poststructural "subject-in-discourse"—a construct whose dynamic, multiple and contradictory qualities may be somewhat exaggerated and whose capacity for individual agency may be similarly over-stated (e.g. Luke, 2009, pp. 292–293). Despite these concerns, Norton's work opened up new conceptual spaces.

In terms of lasting appropriations, poststructural metaphors of mobility across time, place and category/structure have become preferred means of explaining and framing self and collective understanding and for identity work in general. Notions of the *transcultural* and *transnational*, for example, allude to a world of intensified migration across political states—and states of mind—of *global flows* (e.g. ethnoscapes, mediascapes, technoscapes, ideoscapes, financescapes; cf. Appadurai, 1996) and of shifting and multiple allegiances brought about by newcomers who ultimately diversify and hybridize the urban spaces, language practices and identity regimes into which they are ostensibly integrated/assimilated (Pavlenko & Blackledge, 2004). Equally fluid metaphors can be cited here—ones that foreground provisionality and indeterminacy (e.g. *performativity*,[2] cf. Pennycook, 2004; *ethnography of performance*, Ibrahim, 2003), or that seek to explain syncretic and emergent phenomena in identity negotiation (e.g. *crossing*, cf. Rampton, 1995; *hybridity*, *third spaces*, cf. Bhabha, 1994; *contact zones*, cf. Pratt, 1991; *cosmopolitanism*, e.g. Kumaravadivelu, 2008, Ch. 7). Indeed, such notions of "mobility" are increasingly viewed as desirable outcomes for SLE curricula, recent examples being research on *intercultural rhetoric* in second language writing (Connor, Nagelhout & Rozycki, 2008), or the notions of *interculturality*, *cosmopolitanism* and *global citizenship* as identity-based competencies to be nurtured through English as a lingua franca pedagogy, albeit with ideological concerns as to how and in whose interests—centre or periphery—these concepts are defined and realized (cf. "elite" and "deficit" cosmopolitanisms, Guilherme, 2007; Starkey, 2007).

One final metaphorical observation can be made: for a field aligned with the deep structures of mind (cf. Chomsky) and with synchronic description (cf. Saussure), and with an abiding fascination for closely-specified taxonomies of tasks and strategies, it is interesting to observe the extent to which the "linguistic turn" characteristic of postmodern thought has entered professional conversations beyond identity work. Witness, for example, the shifts in thinking encouraged by de-nominalized variants transformed though continuous aspect: e.g. *languaging* in SLA studies (Swain, 2006) and in nation-state formation (Ramanathan, 2009a), as well as the notions of *grammaring* (Larsen-Freeman, 2003), or of *discoursing* in activity theory (Wells, 2007). Such morphological/semantic shifts allude to a key poststructural insight—that discourse and language practices—even at word level—are "person-formative" (Morgan & Ramanathan, 2005), shaping our own *subjectivities*, and the ways in which we understand ourselves, our communities and our fields/places of work, and more importantly, the degree to which we see ourselves as active participants in their unfolding. These are central concerns for identity pedagogies in SLE.

Conceptual Vernacularization: Identity as Pedagogy and Text in SLE

Selective appropriation of theory is not just about solving field-internal problems; it is also a process of *conceptual vernacularization*; that is, of engaging with concepts and contextualizing them in ways that reflect field specializations with the subsequent potential of developing unique understandings of interdisciplinary significance. In relation to identity, two areas of SLE expertise are especially important: a concern with pedagogy and a concern with language/texts/signs. Once grounded in these specializations, many of the postmodern metaphors described above take on important pedagogical and textual functions.

The notion of *transnationalism*, for example, serves as a unifying theme for a special issue on transnational literacies related to language learning and identity, edited by Warriner (2007). *Transcultural flows* frame Pennycook's (2007) original analyses of global rap and hip hop and the performative identity work being done though the creative appropriation of English, in which the trans-semiotic texts of local and global hip hop provide strong evidence of new youth solidarities and modes of identity-based political activity; at the same time, they offer researchers a generous source of data with which to unsettle many prevailing assumptions regarding the appropriate sites and functions of SLA, particularly around the notion of English as an international or world language (e.g. Alim, Ibrahim & Pennycook, 2009; Ibrahim, 2003; Sarkar & Allan, 2007). Equally productive in application, Louise Pratt's notion of *contact zones* has become a robust concept for research on the internationalization of university EAP (English for academic purposes) programs (see e.g. Nelson, 2005;

Singh & Doherty, 2004). Meanwhile, Deleuzean notions of *de-territorialization and nomadology* serve as conceptual lens for a recent anthology explicating multiple literacies theory in bilingual education (Masny & Cole, 2009) and foreground the complications/compromises (and inherent "rootlessness" invoked through the Deleuzean metaphor of "rhizome") of postcolonial translation in Ramanathan's (2005, 2006) work on the English-vernacular divide in the Indian state of Gujarat.

Beyond singular concepts, general identity categories and theories have become pedagogically "vernacularized". A key example is the category/issue of race and racism as they align with SLE concerns and as comprehensively examined in a 2006 special issue of *TESOL Quarterly* and a 2009 collected volume, both edited by Ryuko Kubota and Angel Lin. Both publications detail key theoretical points, the socio-historical construction of racial categories (i.e. racialization), systemic and colour-blind discrimination (cf. whiteness studies), complex intersections with class, gender, ethnicity and nation (Amin & Dei, 2006), and how they articulate with professional roles and constructs in SLE (i.e. language ideologies regarding native-speakerness, accent intelligibility, standardized English; see e.g. Curtis & Romney, 2006; Shuck, 2006). Within this field of inquiry, the relevance of Critical Race Theory (CRT) is most often cited. Originating in legal studies, CRT challenges the discursive construction of impartiality and colour-blind neutrality in the law, revealing deeply ingrained and persistent racial inequalities tied to property rights and unacknowledged white privilege within the justice system (Ladson-Billings & Tate IV, 2006).

In Sara Michael-Luna's (2009) classroom-based study, CRT becomes vernacularized as reading methodology, providing a critical lens with which to problematize the exotic and subordinate representations of ethnic and racial minorities in English as a second language (ESL) texts used for early childhood bilingual education. As Michael-Luna's data shows, CRT also informs a pedagogy of *counter-storytelling* whereby students are encouraged to produce texts that celebrate the accomplishments of minority leaders less present or invisible in mainstream texts. Similarly inspiring, the pedagogical potential of CRT is elaborated in Lisa Taylor's (2006) qualitative study of an anti-discrimination leadership camp for ESL youth in Toronto. Utilizing an experiential, problem-posing approach (cf. Freire), the students and camp counsellors explored common sense prejudices and racial hierarchies that persist within Canada's liberal multicultural framework. Following CRT principles, the students developed ways of analysing/identifying racist practices as well as action plans to counter them in their schools and communities. In this respect, both these studies from Taylor and Michael-Luna exemplify the transformative potential of SLE pedagogies and textual practices, when grounded in local contexts and experiences.

Critical engagement and transformative pedagogies are also priorities in vernacularizing the notion of *sexuality*, arguably the most neglected aspect of identity studies in SLE until Cynthia Nelson (1999, 2005) introduced queer theory to the field, highlighting its priorities for second/foreign language research, pedagogy and teacher education. Queer theory, drawing inspiration from Butler (cf. performativity) and Foucault (cf. power/knowledge, discourse and subjectivity), is concerned not just with understanding the putatively "abnormal" (i.e. pathologized and stigmatized categories of gay and lesbian), but rather in how the discursive production and regulation of "normal" sexualities and gender roles in society requires the visible demarcation and abjection of "abnormal" practices. This focus on understanding and transgressing "heteronormativity", suggests pedagogies whose ambitions extend beyond promoting mainstream tolerance for difference. As Nelson (2005) states: "Thinking queerly about teaching, then, means not just 'including gay people' but prompting inquiry about the cultural and linguistic production of sexual identities in day-to-day practices and discourses" (p. 110). In SLE, the ubiquitous reinforcement of heterosexual norms through language learning tasks, course texts and teaching habits has presented itself as an especially important focus for queer pedagogies. One key intervention has been the inclusion of the voices of gay, lesbian, bisexual and transgendered ESL/EFL (English as a foreign language) students—again, thinking queerly, not to build sympathy or tolerance, but to reveal to teachers the discursive normalization of *all* identities arising through SLE curricula and the silencing of particular minorities that can arise through unintended and unexamined classroom practices (e.g. Dumas, 2008; Kapra & Vandrick, 2006; Liddicoat, 2009; Vandrick, 2009, Ch. 7).

Queer consciousness-raising and counter-discourse extend, as well, to students' beliefs and assumptions, as demonstrated in a special issue on *Queer Inquiry in Language Education* (*Journal of Language Identity and Education*, 2006, 5(1); edited by Nelson), in which several contributors detail innovative, vernacularized approaches to teaching queerly across a remarkable variety of SLE settings (e.g. Curran, 2006; Moita-Lopes, 2006; Ó'Móchain, 2006). Whereas conventional research on teacher–student interactions has been concerned with the provision of "comprehensible input" (cf. Initiation-Response-Feedback patterns; e.g. Block, 2003), Curran (2006) examines the potential for disrupting and deconstructing heteronormative stereotypes through his own answers/responses to student questions in an Australian adult-ESL classroom. Based on ethnographic data from a fifth-grade class in Brazil, Moita-Lopes (2006) combines queer theory with critical discourse analysis and provides a set of reading guidelines for understanding the normalization of dominant sexualities in texts. Of note, for what might appear to be an especially unreceptive setting for sexual discussions of any kind—a Christian women's college in Japan—Ó'Móchain (2006) describes how he integrated the narratives of Japanese gays and lesbians into a content-based EFL course (e.g. cultural studies) in ways non-threatening while supportive of academic language learning. Ó'Móchain's students showed a new-found empathy based on awareness of the painful familial and social ostracism faced by lesbian and gay youth in Japan.

Whether or not the primary focus is on race as conceptualized through CRT, or on sexuality conceptualized through queer theory, the common thread running through these vernacularized identity practices is the intent to "distance" students from "taken-for-granted" internalized beliefs/norms (see Morgan & Ramanathan, 2005), in a sense, productively harnessing the affective tensions of misrecognition and alienating identification (cf. Lacan) detailed in theory and described in our introduction. Luke (2004) aptly describes this process as "an analytic move to self-position oneself as Other … from dominant text and discourse [which] can be cognate, analytic, expository, and hypothetical, and it can, indeed, be already lived, narrated, embodied, and experienced" (p. 26). Towards this attainment, texts are strategically deployed and sequenced, but also diversified—"lived, narrated, embodied", as well as digitized, visualized, spatialized—in the recognition that varied and integrated modes of communication contain signifying capacities or affordances for meaning-making that engage identities and realize experiences in ways unmet through other modalities, a reiteration of Blommaert's (2005) depiction of identity as "semiotic potential" (see e.g. Unsworth, 2008). It is also a potential recognized and promoted through *multiliteracies* pedagogies (e.g. Cope & Kalantzis, 2000; Cummins, 2006), which seek to utilize the expansion of new networks and audiences, text-types and literacy practices in affirming and transforming ways.

In Jim Cummins' (2006) notion of "identity texts", the social and semiotic are effectively aligned with social justice concerns for minority language students in English-dominant schools. Based on a large multiliteracies project in Toronto and Vancouver schools, Cummins' data demonstrate that the authoring of compositions combining first and second languages—their production and circulation enhanced through digital and multimodal platforms—facilitates minority students' academic achievement by combining "maximum cognitive engagement and maximum identity investment" (p. 60). The enhanced capacity to "act on social realities" underscores Cummins' framework. As he persuasively argues, the positive reception generated for students' bilingual "identity texts" serves to redress a deficit orientation towards first language in mainstream schools and, in the long term, emboldens minority communities to challenge "common-sense" prejudices that devalue their traditions, knowledge forms and language practices.

The capacity for texts and pedagogies to (re)position identities vis-à-vis power relations and colonial histories similarly informs Bhattacharya, Gupta, Jewitt, Newfield, Reed and Stein's (2007) comparative analysis of the policy-practice nexus across three sites of English instruction (e.g. Delhi, Johannesburg, London). The unit of analysis for their classroom study is the *textual cycle*—the selection, sequencing and integration of texts, both conventional and multimodal—and its role in "the shaping of student identities in the English classroom" (p. 19). In examining teachers' methodological decisions and their effects on students, the authors argue that these micro-sites reveal the (re)production of particular stances in relation to the nation-state's appropriation and ownership of English. In the textual cycle in Delhi, for example, a lack of ownership is most pronounced through teaching decisions that emphasize the mastery of external standards and content disconnected from the life worlds of students. English thus becomes an imported commodity, acquired and reproduced for its socioeconomic utility. In the London classroom, the teacher's treatment of *Macbeth* indicates greater efforts at engaging with students' out-of-school identities, but primarily and instrumentally as preparation for state examinations. In Johannesburg, in contrast, the teaching of ninth-grade English through a popular teenage novel, *Who Killed Jimmy Valentine?*, demonstrates a textual cycle grounded in students' lived realities, involving them in a variety of meaning-making activities that position them as "potential transformers of their worlds" (p. 20).

These multimodal/multiliteracies case studies from Cummins and Bhattacharya et al., similar to the classroom realizations of CRT and queer theory described above, exemplify the notion of conceptual vernacularization that frames this section. Through close attention to texts and pedagogies, especially in second/foreign language learning contexts, researchers in SLE can be seen contributing unique field-internal insights that contribute to identity work across disciplinary fields. In the following sections we shall describe some of the more recent issues and innovative practices undertaken by SLE/applied linguistics researchers concerned with identity.

Identity Work in SLE: Recent Themes and Priorities

The relevance of postmodern and poststructural notions of identity continues to be explored and debated in a number of SLE publications (e.g. Block, 2007; Clarke, 2008; Lin, 2008; Menard-Warwick, 2005; Morgan, 2007). And as described in the previous section, theory often informs pedagogy in ways distinctively and indelibly SLE in focus. In second language pronunciation work, for example, the goal of intelligibility through syllabus design has been reconceptualized through poststructural identity in articles by Golombek and Jordan (2005) and Morgan (2003). In an second language reading context, Moffatt and Norton (2005) contrast a "traditional feminist" approach (i.e. the social/textual reproduction of patriarchy) with one informed by feminist-poststructuralism whereby a popular cultural text (e.g. an Archie comic) is depicted as having multiple meanings that both reproduce and critique dominant gender norms and whereby school-aged readers are affirmed as active meaning-makers and not passive recipients of the dominant gendered positions offered.

In addition, poststructural theory can be seen informing research on the identities/subjectivities and professional roles specific to SLE/applied linguistics and the kinds of deficit orientations and expert interventions that are operationalized on those brought into discourse. The label *ESL*, as a prominent example, fails to recognize multilingual competencies or dialect differences, as Waterstone (2008) observes. For adult learners, particularly in English-only classrooms, preoccupations with code proficiency often come at the expense of meaningful content, contributing to an infantilization of ESL curricula, and the inculcation of passive citizenship practices (e.g. Morgan & Fleming, 2009). Similarly, the construct of *Generation 1.5*, commonly evoked in the EAP literature to describe the second language phenomena/performance of adolescent migrants, is critiqued for its "discourses of partiality" by Benesch (2008), its underlying monolingual/monocultural assumptions and elision of race as factors in the academic inadequacies ascribed to these youth. In the same vein, recent work has critiqued the ways in which discursive notions of a "standard" language, with clearly defined "native-speakers", have contributed to the professional marginalization of those labelled non-native English-speaking teachers (see the collection in Braine, 1999).

Language teacher identity itself has become the focus of renewed investigation, and of pedagogical concerns beyond the native-speaker/non-native speaker divide. To reiterate an earlier point, once we re-conceptualize language and knowledge in post-positivistic terms that foreground their contingent and socially constructed development (e.g. Canagarajah, 2005; Makoni & Pennycook, 2007; Reagan, 2004) then we place the teacher (as well as, of course, the students) in a very different role from the traditional image of a transmitter (or receiver) of neutral knowledge. We start to recognize the co-implicated nature of knowledge, power, and identity, in which the teacher's own identity suddenly takes on a new significance in understanding the dynamics of the language classroom (e.g. "teacher identity as pedagogy", Morgan, 2004). Language teacher identity thus becomes a potential site of pedagogical intervention and an area of explicit focus in teacher preparation (Brogden & Page, 2008; Mantero, 2004; Varghese, Morgan, Johnston & Johnson, 2005).

Aligned with this new focus is a heightened attention to context and the ways in which socioeconomic and sociopolitical changes impact on the ways in which teachers' identities are constructed in professional settings (Johnson, 2006; cf. our discussion of neoliberalism). Reflecting such concerns, Phan (2008) examines how the identities of English teachers in Vietnam are shaped through negotiation between competing discourses and values, while Clarke (2008) explores the connections between individual and social identity formation and the often invisible influences of wider sociopolitical factors in what initially appears to be purely pedagogical dimensions of the identity formation of a cohort of new English teachers in the United Arab Emirates (UAE). Employing a more narrative approach, Tsui (2007) examines the complexities of identity formation through the lens of one teacher's struggles to negotiate multiple identities, meanings and practices, as he navigated his way through the complex process of becoming a teacher in contemporary China.

Perhaps the most significant development in language teacher identity research is the turn towards values, morals and ethics in the work of teachers (Crookes, 2009; Hafernik, Messerschmitt & Vandrick, 2002; Johnston, 2003) and how it relates to teacher decision-making around curricula and school-based language policies (Farrell & Tan, 2008; Ramanathan & Morgan, 2007; Stritikus & Varghese, 2005) and the conduct of interpersonal relations with students (Richards, 2006). Clarke (2009a, 2009b), in particular, recognizes the centrality of ethics to the work of teachers, but re-theorizes traditionally understood notions of morality and ethics in terms of Foucauldian notions of "ethical self-formation" and "care of the self" in order to explore the ways in which individual pre-service teachers exercised agency in the face of pressures to conform to, and be bounded by nationalistic discourses that predominate in the UAE context and by the powerful peer maintenance and monitoring of professional beliefs that reflected the social cohesion of the cohort. As we shall discuss below in a section on "the politics of identity", the monitoring of beliefs—informally with peers, or formally through journals, web logs, narratives, etc.—can be professionally rewarding but also personally intrusive, and in ways that promote conformity rather than teacher autonomy.

Gender, in many respects, was the first and most prominent demographic domain through which identity work was introduced to SLE (e.g. Norton Peirce, 1995). In spite of its categorical longevity, it continues to be an area of renewed conceptual interest, and for reasons not unrelated to the demographics of SLE classrooms and the over-representation of women in a profession characterized by limited job security and poor working conditions (see e.g. Haque & Cray, 2007). The year 2004 saw the publication of two special journal issues and an edited volume focused on research on gender in SLE (*TESOL Quarterly*, 2004, edited by Kathy Davis & Ellen Skilton-Sylvester; *Journal of Language, Identity & Education*, 2004, edited by Juliet Langman; Norton & Pavlenko, 2004). More recent publications (Carroll, Motha & Price, 2008; Menard-Warwick, 2009; Park, 2009), utilizing ethnographic and narrative perspectives, illuminate the contingent ways in which gendered discourses not only constrain female students and teachers but also offer potential sites of transformative agency. Park's (2009) article, for example, examines the ways in which, Han Nah, a Korean immigrant enrolled in a TESOL program in the US, strategically positions her cultural and linguistic resources—resources that are all too often dismissed, silenced or overlooked in educational settings—as assets by teaching Korean and promoting bilingual education in the Korean-American community. A similar duality of constraint and opportunity is foregrounded in the identity negotiation of two college ESL students and four, first-year ESOL instructors in a recent study by Carroll, Motha and Price (2008). Integrating both critical narrative inquiry and critical feminist ethnography, the researchers found evidence of "imagined communities" (cf. Kanno, 2003) whose membership accorded liberating, non-traditional gender roles, but also the co-existence of "regimes of truth" (cf. Foucault) restricting the kinds of identity options and professional roles that these women might imagine and subsequently act upon. Indeed, the realization that imagined communities and language learner narratives are most often populated by women's voices speaks volumes to the "real-world" constraints that continue to restrict their participation.

In assessing the future of *indigenous identity*, the accelerated shift from and loss of aboriginal or First Nation languages in the world is most often raised as existential threat by the various stakeholders involved, and it has accelerated efforts at documentation and revitalization through a broad range of educational policies and practices as well as formalized rights-based initiatives (e.g. special issues in *Canadian Modern Language Review*, 2009, 66(1); *Teaching Education*, 2009, *20*(1); Hornberger, 2006). Critical reflections on the efficacy of such interventions have also been raised, for example, by Patrick (2005) who questions the extent to which top-down, language rights policies can effectively motivate young Inuit in Arctic Quebec, and by Johnston (2002) whose case study of a failed Dakota immersion pre-school illustrates the crucial need to generate consensus amongst local stakeholders irrespective of the intrinsic merits of the curriculum being offered. Such an approach underpins Martin and Tagalik's (2004) commissioned research project to promote the Inuit language of Inuktitut as a full functioning official language alongside English in Nunavut schools, workplaces and public places. Central to their recommendations for a language of instruction framework are indigenous notions of *Aajiiqatigiingniq* ("consensual-decision-making") and principles of *Inuit Qaujimajatuqangit* (i.e. Inuit traditional knowledge) as well as training and support for local, Nunavumniut language and culture researchers as crucial to building long term community involvement and trust in the study's recommendations. As the authors note, "[h]istorically, research has been 'done to' Inuit communities as opposed to being 'done with' them" (p. 180), an experience common to all indigenous peoples and one that rightfully engenders scepticism of outsider intentions and capacities for genuine dialogue.

Menezes de Souza's (2005, 2007) work with the Kashinawa in Amazonian Brazil, demonstrates that scepticism of "expert" intervention, particularly the work of linguists and language policy makers, is indeed justified. Drawing on postcolonial theory, Menezes de Souza details a contact history of religious, colonial and anthropological paternalism, a relationship codified and perpetuated through the grammatical and orthographic (mis)representation of indigenous oral languages and in ways that invent the conceptual primitiveness required as justification for a "civilizing", domesticating agenda. As counter-discourse, the author portrays the Kashinawa in active and contemporary terms, as engaged in the performativity of a contact-based identity through syncretic, multimodal texts that integrate both alphabetic writing and Kashinawa visual patterns. This ongoing process of Kashinawa re-traditionalization and ethnogenesis is aptly described as "'entering a culture quietly' … but not to remain, or to stay put … but to appropriate and transform, *in order to preserve* one's own (indigenous) culture" (2007, p. 166, italics in original).

This last observation from Menezes de Souza raises a provocative question in respect to indigenous peoples; that is, to what extent is a language—especially as it is demarcated and formalized by Western-trained linguists—essential to the preservation (i.e. performativity) of indigenous self-understanding? Given the diversity of aboriginal peoples and of colonial histories in the world, it is a question requiring context-specific answers. At the same time, it reconfirms the need for ongoing critical reflection amongst language specialists in light of our professional predispositions towards lingua-centric solutions for social problems, which may not always correspond with indigenous perceptions and priorities.

New Domains and Neglected Areas of Research

While we have foregrounded the conceptual and pedagogical contributions of poststructural theory in many of the sections above, it would nonetheless be misleading and limiting to address identity exclusively through such a framework, as aptly demonstrated, for example, by recent research on language education informed by a neo-Vygotskian, communities of practice perspective (Tsui, 2007; see also Haneda, 2006), as well as publications in applied linguistics/SLE informed by sociolinguistics (Omoniyi & White, 2006), language socialization (Bayley & Schecter, 2003), eco-semiotics (van Lier, 2004), sociocultural and activity theories (e.g. Lantolf & Thorne, 2006) or by way of postcolonial theory (e.g. Lin & Luke, 2006). Indeed, it is possible to argue that poststructuralism has been (over)used to the point of saturation in studies of identities in SLE/ELT (English language teaching) (Block, 2007), contributing to a more general sense that after some twenty years or more of research in SLE, identity work has become conceptually exhausted, resulting in a kind of "identity fatigue". However, significant new areas of interest have emerged recently, some of which are outlined briefly below.

One such recent research focus addresses the subjectivization of the body through various discourses of disease and disability (e.g. breast cancer, Alzheimer's disease, diabetes, epilepsy, autism), the theme of Ramanathan's new book, *Bodies and Language* (2009b) as well as a forthcoming special issue on *Language Policies and Health* (2009, 8(4)) also edited by Ramanathan. Specific to schooling, a related research concern examines the complexities and consequences of (mis)diagnosing learning disabilities (LD) in English language learners as well as the types of pedagogical interventions that might preclude such remedial interventions (e.g. Bernhard, Cummins, Campoy, Ada, Winsler & Bleiker, 2006; Lesaux, 2006). Yet, as Mayer (2009) cautions, interventions on behalf of LD communities are not easily generalizable. Based on her work with deaf second language literacy learners, Mayer outlines several factors (e.g. absence of a standard first language print form in American Sign Language; inadequate phonological awareness supporting literate discourse, etc.) that complicate the potential for cross-linguistic transfer in the development of Cognitive Academic Language Proficiency (cf. Cummins, 2006).

Another area of increasing interest and debate in SLE is the domain of *spirituality* (Smith, 2007). For many language professionals, spirituality is coterminous with formal religion, and hence has no place in SLE. Such a view is reinforced by SLE's focus on *form*al aspects of language, its emphasis on purely cognitive dimensions of learning, and its privileging of scientific and secular worldviews, which engender a wariness of religious/spiritual domains of experience and a consequent disregard for the more visceral and intense registers of thinking and being associated with these domains (e.g. Connolly, 1999). Some critique this wariness of spirituality through postcolonial experience, arguing that the association of secularism with modernity and religion/spirituality with tradition has become an ideological tool to discriminate against non-Western/non-liberal societies in general and Islamic ones in particular (Kumaravadivelu, 2008; Scott, 2007). Others question the desirability or even the possibility of hiding this dimension of identity in SLE settings. Moreover, they find the voiced proscriptions against religious identity work in SLE as somewhat hypocritical given the field's current preoccupation with the kinds of engaged identity pedagogies described in this chapter (Baurain, 2007).

For those opposed to the integration of spiritual themes and content in SLE, the main object of concern has not been intrinsic matters of faith, but rather on their worldly articulation, more specifically, a concern based on the historical alignment of English with colonialism and Christian missionary work, and its current alignment with Evangelical Christian teachers and organizations in the SLE field, utilizing the global demand for English as an opportunity and vehicle for the spread of gospel and the conversion of impressionable students (e.g. Johnston & Varghese, 2006; Pennycook & Coutand-Marin, 2003). That this evangelical work is sometimes advanced via covert avenues and by "teachers" with little SLE training outside the parsing of biblical text is problematic not only for critical educators but also for SLE language professionals who self-identify as Christians. Such concerns, and the ways in which they address the secular/spiritual divide in SLE, are detailed and debated in a book edited by Mary Wong and Suresh Canagarajah (2009) titled, *Christian and Critical English Language Educators in Dialogue: Pedagogical and Ethical Dilemmas.* Though evidence of consensus across chapters in this remarkable book is limited, the fact that this conversation takes place at all is a significant accomplishment.

Given the worldly alignment of English with Christianity, and with forms of colonial, military and economic power from past to present, many SLE researchers have debated the extent to which English can and should be taught in Islamic societies, a theme developed in a special issue of *Journal of Language, Identity & Education* (2004, 4(2)) titled, *Islam and English in the Post-9/11 Era*, edited by Sohail Karmani. This was also the focus of a comprehensive website called TESOL Islamia (http://www.tesolislamia.org/), which addressed the challenges of teaching English in ways compatible with Islamic values and the lingua franca needs of Muslim nation-states and citizens. However, this website is no longer available. Towards this end, Mahboob's (2009) recent article, "English as an Islamic language", provides numerous examples of Islamic ideologies/values present in the discourse structures of Pakistani English language textbooks—proof that English can be appropriated and decolonized to serve local needs and interests. Still, the global reach of English and the dominant values and power relations that align with its expansion are likely to put increased pressure on less powerful faiths and structures of feeling, resulting in the kinds of hyperbolized practices of identity maintenance noted by Fader (2006) in her study of the language socialization of young Hasidic girls in New York. As we forecast the future of identity in SLE, the global expansion of neoliberalism—with English as its default language—poses a particular threat to all understandings of self and community outside the calculation of their utility and instrumentality. We now turn to that discussion.

Neoliberalism and Regimes of Accountability

Neoliberalism[3] has been a powerful force for homogenization and of creating/inventing systems of equivalency by which the relative value of all things and practices can be established—i.e. commoditized—for sale and exchange (cf. language as commodity, Tan & Rubdy, 2008). As Wendy Brown (2005) points out, the neoliberal state is not focused on the economy as an end in itself; rather it seeks to extend and disseminate market values to all institutions and social actions, thereby (re)constructing *identities* as entrepreneurial agents, solely and wholly responsible for their own success or failure. This assumption of individual responsibility is nonetheless carefully monitored by the state on the grounds that "in an age of universal welfare, the perceived possibilities of slothful indolence create necessities for new forms of vigilance, surveillance and 'performance appraisal' and forms of control generally" (Olssen, 2003, p. 200).

With the expansion of global media networks, neoliberal values have become hegemonic in respect to the lifestyles and aspirations people imagine for themselves and their families. Luke, Luke and Graham (2007) aptly describe this development as "a planetary 'newspeak' that lines the pages of newspapers, blogs, and screens with the language of the 'market', and with its images and discourses of competitive and possessive individualism" (Luke, Luke & Graham, 2007, p. 4)—which has led to the ascendancy of business and market ideologies in education generally (Luke, 2006; Marginson, 2006; Sleeter, 2007), as well as in teacher education and professional development (Cochran-Smith, 2005; Day, 2007), and, of particular concern for this chapter, language education (Chun, 2009; Corson, 2002; Harvey, 2006; Holborow, 2007; Jordao, 2009; Phillipson, 2008). However, neoliberalism is not only a matter of ideology and discourse, but also expands its reach through material practices such as global modes of production and divisions of labour. Here, English increasingly takes on a key instrumental and value-adding function, a most prominent example being the outsourcing of the call-centre industry (e.g. special issue on Language Policies and International Call Centers, in the journal *Language Policy*, 2009, *8*(1), edited by Kendal King). Newly globalized divisions of labour have also precipitated transformations of language policies and practices in major immigration-receiving nations such as Canada, where provisions for a "knowledge economy" have resulted in shifts from settlement ESL curricula to those more closely aligned with sector-specific language skills, a provision Gibb (2008) sees as consistent with "human capital theory".

In a similar vein, technocratic discourses of management and finance have come to justify the predominance of excolonial languages as compulsory subjects *and* as preferred media for learning and teaching other subjects (Rassool, 2007), most visibly the promotion of English. This has led to debates about the opportunities and perils of justifying language education programmes in the materialist, cost-benefit terms of the contemporary economics-dominated political climate, and the problems of "collusion" (McGroarty, 2006; Petrovic, 2005). The neoliberal hegemony has also prompted debates about what constitutes appropriate and effective critical language education, about how to ensure that this is more than just "an uncritical education in technocratic English as globalized and globalizing *lingua franca*, in 'financial literacy', 'entrepreneurial literacy', 'information literacy' and so forth" (Luke et al., 2007, p. 12). As one example of what such critical work might look like, Chun (2009) describes his pedagogical interventions in the EAP classroom, challenging neoliberalism's preferred subjectivities by encouraging students to interrogate and critique neoliberal assumptions about the self as a project whereby individuals are behooved to engage in a lifelong quest for "success". Jordao describes a dialogic pedagogy, underpinned, like Chun's, by poststructuralist notions about the power of discourse and the contested nature of truth claims, in which students and teachers engage in "conceptual questioning in open spaces", about, for example, "different views on the role of English in local and global contexts" or about "appreciating elements other than exclusive improvement of linguistic competence as signs of effective educational processes" (2009, p. 100, p. 103). Whether or not we view such pedagogies as insignificant or hopelessly out-of-touch, the fact is that a growing number of SLE professionals recognize an urgent need, in Phillipson's (2008) words, for language policies based on "ethical human rights principles" as a means to "counteract neoliberal imperialism" (pp. 38–39).

Conclusions: The Future Politics of Identity

My point is not that everything is bad, but that everything is dangerous, which is not exactly the same as bad. If everything is dangerous, then we always have something to do.

(Foucault, 1983, pp. 231–232)

As we have tried to demonstrate in this chapter, identity has become a major conceptual lens for understanding theory and pedagogy in SLE, where through processes we call *conceptual ver-nacularization*, SLE specialists have contributed unique interdisciplinary insights across the social sciences. But here too we need to be continually mindful of the politics of identity. In this vein, it is reassuring to note a number of insightful critiques regarding identity's ideological and discursive underpinnings. For Cameron and Kulich (2003), our current fascination with identity obscures the significance and power in language education of emotional factors such as desire. Such gaps, as we note above, are partially addressed though the emergence of more poststructural and psychoanalytic approaches to affective domains and emotional understanding in SLE (cf. Granger, 2004; McNamara, 2009; Pavlenko, 2006).

From Skeggs (2008), another future concern regards the ways that "identity reproduces the tradition of possessive individualism … [and] the Western obsession with visibility as the major way of knowing" (pp. 26–27), an inherently conservative politics available only to elites capable of creating and mobilizing their visibility in ways officially acknowledged by the nation-state (cf. a politics of recognition, Fraser, 1997). Still, for SLE, the visibility and agency of the individual language learner have been welcome correctives in a field whose structuralist and positivistic roots have resulted in "the consistent anonymising, if not the actual eclipsing, of the learner" (Candlin, 2000, p. xiii). In this respect, we would argue that identity continues to be a tremendously illuminating and productive notion for SLE; yet we would also want to highlight some of its risks, not so as to replace it with another, less dangerous concept, but as part of an ongoing critical vigilance in the spirit of Foucault's comment that introduces this section.

As we look forward, one area of potential concern may lie in the growing interest in compiling and assessing evidence of the inner thoughts and motivations of teachers and learners through various forms of journal writing, narrative inquiry, auto-ethnography, counter storytelling, etc., all of which are useful tools for learning yet always potentially "dangerous", we would argue. The preoccupation with identity tends to promote a "confessional" obligation, as students are exhorted to reveal and share their personal narratives and their innermost selves and desires that many may find obtrusive (e.g. Sharkey, 2004). In SLE settings, this obligation can also engender resentment when "inauthentic" stories are committed to text, as Harklau's (2003) discussion reveals. The compulsion for second language writers to produce an "Ellis Island" discourse of gratitude, as Harklau's study shows, reveals a discursive urgency for the newcomer's voice to affirm the voice and values of the teacher—and of all longstanding citizens—particularly when the legitimacy and central organizing myths of the imagined nation are in doubt (Honig, 2001).

One final "danger" to consider is the extent to which identity loses its "cutting-edge" lustre in the future, becoming an exhausted footnote in the history of SLE research. We suggest that identity will remain a prominent concern for years to come, in large part because of its salience as liberal democratic states re-organize themselves in ways described by Nancy Fraser (1997) as the "post-socialist condition", a pronounced shift from a *politics of redistribution* (e.g. increased unionization, higher wages and pensions, universal health care) to a *politics of recognition* (e.g. the provision of rights and resources in support of ethno-linguistic vitality). For SLE, this new political imperative works on the identity/subjectivity of language learners in ways similar to the performative experiences Ibrahim (2003) observed in his research participants' *becoming* Black upon entry into Canada's already racialized polity. For all newcomers, a politics of recognition demands that they negotiate/perform the hyphenated identities that already precede them and that embody unfamiliar historical grievances to which they must add their voices in demanding recognition and/or restitution from the nation-state. Such identity-based grievances are often first voiced or discovered in SLE settings and through curricular content, placing issues of self and collective understanding at the centre of what it means to learn or teach a second/additional language. Maintaining critical awareness of such challenges and resisting the dangers of conceptual complacency is essential if identity is to continue to be employed productively in the SLE field. As Foucault would say, "we will always have something to do".

Notes

1. Hall (2004) argues that the term subjectivity implies a self-conscious reflection on the self, whereas the term identity lacks this self-reflexivity. We see both terms as potentially, but not necessarily, entailing self-awareness and will use the two terms interchangeably.
2. The notion of performativity originated with Austin's "performative" speech acts, utterances that created that which they named in language (e.g. "Let the games begin"). Butler (1990) adopted the performative as a way of reconceptualizing gender. She argued that gender was something that must be continually re-established, or iteratively *performed*—in large part through language—rather than being something that is merely given or a priori, thus opening up spaces for slippage, dissonance, contradiction or subversion.
3. See Olssen (2003) for a discussion of key differences between liberalism and neoliberalism.

References

Ahearn, L. M. (2001). Language and agency. *Annual Review of Anthropology*, 30, 109–137.

Alim, H. S., Ibrahim, A. & Pennycook, A. (Eds.) (2009). *Global linguistic flows: Hip hop cultures, youth identities, and the politics of language*. New York: Routledge.

Amin, N., & Dei, G. S. (Eds.) (2006). *The poetics of anti-racism*. Halifax: Fernwood.

Appadurai, A. (1996). *Modernity at large: Cultural dimensions of globalization*. Minneapolis: University of Minnesota Press.

Bayley, R., & Schecter, S. R. (Eds.) (2003). *Language socialization in bilingual and multilingual societies*. Clevedon: Multilingual Matters.

Baurain, B. (2007). Christian witness and respect for persons. *Journal of Language, Identity, & Education*, 6, 201–219.

Belcher, D., & Lukkarila, L. (forthcoming). ESP and identity. In D. Belcher, A. Johns & B. Paltridge (Eds.), *New directions for ESP research*. Ann Arbor: University of Michigan Press.

Bendle, M. (2002). The crisis of "identity" in high modernity. *The British Journal of Sociology*, 53(1), 1–18.

Benesch, S. (2008). "Generation 1.5" and its discourses of partiality: A critical analysis. *Journal of Language, Identity, & Education*, 7, 294–311.

Bernhard, J. K., Cummins, J., Campoy, F. I., Ada, A. F., Winsler, A. & Bleiker, C. (2006). Identity texts and literacy development among preschool English language learners: Enhancing learning opportunities for children at risk for learning disabilities. *Teachers College Record*, 108(11), 2380–2405.

Bhabha, H. (1994). *The location of culture*. New York: Routledge.

Bhattacharya, R., Gupta, S., Jewitt, C., Newfield, D., Reed, Y. & Stein, P. (2007). The policy-practice nexus in English classrooms in Delhi, Johannesburg, and London: Teachers and the textual cycle. *TESOL Quarterly*, 41(3), 465–488.

Block, D. (2003). *The social turn in second language education*. Washington: Georgetown University Press.

Block, D. (2007). *Second language identities*. London: Continuum.

Blommaert, J. (2005). *Discourse: A critical introduction*. Cambridge: Cambridge University Press.

Braine, G. (Ed.) (1999). *Non-native educators in English language teaching*. Mahwah, NJ: Lawrence Erlbaum Associates.

Brogden, L. M., & Page, B. (2008). Ghosts on the cupboard: Discursive hauntings during the first year of French immersion teaching in Canada. In T. S. C. Farrell (Ed.), *Novice language teachers: Insights and perspectives for the first year* (pp. 118–131). London: Equinox Publishers.

Brown, W. (2005). *Edgework: Critical essays in knowledge and politics*. Princeton, NJ: Princeton University Press.

Butler, J. (1990). *Gender trouble: Feminism and the subversion of identity*. New York: Routledge.

Butler, J. (1997). *The psychic life of power: Theories in subjection*. Stanford, CA: Stanford University Press.

Butler, J. (2005). *Giving an account of oneself*. New York: Fordham University Press.

Cameron, D., & Kulick, D. (2003). *Language and sexuality*. Cambridge: Cambridge University Press.

Canagarajah, S. (Ed.) (2005). *Reclaiming the local in language policy and practice*. Mahwah, NJ: Lawrence Erlbaum Associates.

Candlin, C. (2000). General editor's preface. In B. Norton, *Identity and language learning* (pp. xiii–xxi). London: Longman.

Carroll, S., Motha, S. & Price, J. N. (2008). Accessing imagined communities and reinscribing regimes of truth. *Critical Inquiry in Language Studies*, 5, 165–191.

Chiesa, L. (2007). *Subjectivity and otherness: A philosophical reading of Lacan*. Cambridge, MA: The MIT Press.

Chun, C. W. (2009). Contesting neoliberal discourses in EAP: Critical praxis in an IEP classroom. *Journal of English for Academic Purposes*, 8(2), 111–120.

Clarke, M. (2008). *Language teacher identities: Co-constructing discourse and community*. Clevedon: Multilingual Matters.

Clarke, M. (2009a). The ethico-politics of teacher identity. *Educational Philosophy & Theory*, 41(2), 185–200.

Clarke, M. (2009b). Doing "identity work" in teacher education: The case of a UAE teacher. In R. Sultana & A. Mazawi (Eds.), *World yearbook of education 2010: Education and the Arab world: Local dynamics, global resonances* (pp. 145–162). New York: Routledge.

Cochran-Smith, M. (2005). The new teacher education: For better or for worse? *Educational Researcher*, *34*(7), 3–17.

Connolly, W. (1999). *Why I am not a secularist*. Minneapolis: University of Minnesota Press.

Connor, U., Nagelhout, E. & Rozycki, W. (Eds.) (2008). *Contrastive rhetoric: Reaching to intercultural rhetoric*. Amsterdam: John Benjamins.

Cope, B., & Kalantzis, M. (Eds.) (2000). *Multiliteracies: Literacy learning and the design of social futures*. London: Routledge.

Corson, D. (2002). Teaching and learning for market-place utility. *International Journal of Leadership in Education*, *1*, 1–13.

Crookes, G. (2009). *Values, philosophies, and beliefs in TESOL: Making a statement*. Cambridge: Cambridge University Press.

Cummins, J. (2006). Identity texts: The imaginative construction of self through multiliteracies pedagogy. In O. Garcia, T. Skuttnabb-Kangas & M. E. Torres-Guzman (Eds.), *Imagining multilingual schools: Languages in education and glocalization* (pp. 51–68). Clevedon: Multilingual Matters.

Curran, G. (2006). Responding to students' normative questions about gays: Putting queer theory into practice in an Australian ESL class. *Journal of Language, Identity, and Education*, *5*(1), 85–96.

Curtis, A., & Romney, M. (Eds.) (2006). Color, race, and English language teaching: Studies of meaning. Mahwah, NJ: Lawerence Erlbaum Associates.

Day, C. (2007). School reform and transitions in teacher professionalism and identity. In T. Townsend & R. Bates (Eds.), *Handbook of teacher education: Globalization, standards and professionalism in times of change* (pp. 597–612). Dordrecht: Springer.

Derrida, J. (1998). *Monolingualism of the other, or, The prosthesis of origin* (P. Mensah, trans.). Stanford, CA: Stanford University Press.

Dörnyei, Z., & Ushioda, E. (Eds.) (2009). *Motivation, language identity and the L2 self*. Clevedon: Multilingual Matters.

Dumas, J. (2008). The ESL classroom and the queerly shifting sands of learner identity. *TESL Canada Journal*, *26*(1), 1–10.

Eagleton, T. (2000). *The idea of culture*. Oxford: Blackwell.

Eagleton, T. (2008). *Trouble with strangers: A study of ethics*. Chichester and Malden, MA: Wiley-Blackwell.

Fader, A. (2006). Learning faith: Language socialization in a community of Hasidic Jews. *Language in Society*, *35*, 205–229.

Farrell, T.S.C., & Tan, S. (2008). Language policy, language teachers' beliefs and classroom practices. *Applied Linguistics*, *29*(3), 381–403.

Firth, A., & Wagner, J. (1997). On discourse, communication, and (some) fundamental concepts in SLA research. *The Modern Language Journal*, *81*(3), 285–300.

Fleming, D. (2003). Building personal and nation-state identities: Research and practice. *TESL Canada Journal*, *20*(2), 65–79.

Flowerdew, J., & Miller, L. (2008). Social structure and individual agency in second language learning: Evidence from three life histories. *Critical Inquiry in Language Studies*, *5*(4), 201–224.

Foucault, M. (1980). *Power/knowledge: Selected interviews and other writings 1972–1977*. Brighton: Harvester.

Foucault, M. (1983). On the genealogy of ethics: An overview of a work in progress. In H. Dreyfus & P. Rabinow (Eds.), *Michel Foucault: Beyond structuralism and hermeneutics* (2nd ed.) (pp. 229–252). Chicago: The University of Chicago Press.

Fraser, N. (1997). *Justice interruptus: Critical reflections on the "postsocialist" condition*. New York: Routledge.

Gee, J. P. (2000). Identity as an analytic lens for research in education. *Review of Research in Education*, *25*, 99–125.

Gibb, T. L. (2008). Bridging Canadian Adult second language education and essential skills policies: Approach with caution. *Adult Education Quarterly*, *58*, 318–334.

Golombek, P., & Jordan, R. S. (2005). Becoming "black lambs" not "parrots": A poststructuralist orientation to intelligibility and identity. *TESOL Quarterly*, *39*, 513–533.

Granger, C. A. (2004). *Silence in second language learning*. Clevedon: Multilingual Matters.

Guilherme, M. (2007). English as a global language and education for cosmopolitan citizenship. *Language and Intercultural Communication*, *7*(1), 72–90.

Hafernick, J. J., Messerschmitt, D. S. & Vandrick, S. (2002). *Ethical issues for ESL faculty: Social justice in practice*. Mahwah, NJ: Lawrence Erlbaum Associates.

Hall, D. (2004). *Subjectivity*. New York: Routledge.

Hall, J. K., Vitanova, G. & Marchenkova, L. (Eds.) (2005). *Dialogue with Bakhtin on second and foreign language learning*. Mahwah, NJ: Lawrence Erlbaum Associates.

Haneda, M. (2006). Classrooms as communities of practice: A reevaluation. *TESOL Quarterly*, *40*, 807–817.

Haque, E., & Cray, E. (2007). Constraining teachers: Adult ESL settlement language training policy and implementation. *TESOL Quarterly*, *31*, 634–642.

Harklau, L. (2003). Representational practices and multi-modal communication in US high schools: Implications for adolescent immigrants. In R. Bayley & S. R. Schecter (Eds.), *Language socialization in bilingual and multilingual societies* (pp. 83–97). Clevedon: Multilingual Matters.

Harvey, S. (2006). Discourses of (non) western subjectivity and philosophical recovery. *Journal of Multicultural Discourses*, *1*(1), 27–34.

Holborow, M. (2007). Language, ideology and neoliberalism. *Journal of Language and Politics*, 6(1), 51–73.

Holliday, A. (2005). *The struggle to teach English as an international language*. Oxford: Oxford University Press.

Honig, B. (2001). *Democracy and the foreigner*. Princeton, NJ: Princeton University Press.

Hornberger, N. (2006). Voice and biliteracy in indigenous language revitalization: Contentious educational practices in Quechua, Guarani, and Maori contexts. *Journal of Language, Identity, & Education*, 5, 277–292.

House, J. (2003). English as a lingua franca: A threat to multilingualism? *Journal of Sociolinguistics*, 7(4), 556–578.

Ibrahim, A. (2003). Whassup, homeboy? Joining the African diaspora: Black English as a symbolic site of identification and language learning. In S. Makoni, G. Smitherman, A. F. Ball & A. K. Spears (Eds.), *Black linguistics: Language, society, and politics in Africa and the Americas* (pp. 169–185). New York: Routledge.

Johnson, K. (2006). The sociocultural turn and its challenges for second language teacher education. *TESOL Quarterly*, 40(1), 235–257.

Johnston, B. (2002). The rise and fall of a Dakota immersion pre-school. *Multilingual & Multicultural Development*, 23(3), 195–213.

Johnston, B. (2003). *Values in English language teaching*. Mahwah, NJ: Lawrence Erlbaum Associates.

Johnston, B., & Varghese, M. (2006). Neo-imperialism, evangelism, and ELT: Modernist missions and a postmodern profession. In J. Edge (Ed.), *(Re-)Locating TESOL in an Age of Empire* (pp. 195–207). Basingstoke: Palgrave Macmillan.

Jordao, C. (2009). English as a foreign language, globalization and conceptual questioning. *Globalization, Societies and Education*, 7(1), 95–107.

Kanno, Y. (2003). Imagined communities, school visions and the education of bilingual students in Japan. *Journal of Language, Identity, and Education*, 2, 285–300.

Kapra, R., & Vandrick, S. (2006). Silenced voices speak: Queer ESL students recount their experiences. *CATESOL Journal*, 18(1), 138–150.

Kay, S. (2003). *Zizek: A critical introduction*. Cambridge: Polity Press.

Kubota, R. (2004). The politics of cultural difference in second language education. *Critical Inquiry in Language Studies*, 1(1), 21–39.

Kubota, R., & Lin, A. (Eds.) (2009). *Race, culture, and identities in second language education: Exploring critically engaged practice*. New York: Routledge.

Kumaravadivelu, B. (2008). *Cultural globalization and language education*. New Haven: Yale University Press.

Ladson-Billings, G., & Tate IV, W. F. (2006). Toward a critical race theory of education. In A. D. Dixon & C. K. Rousseau (Eds.), *Critical race theory in education: All God's children got a song* (pp. 11–30). New York: Routledge.

Lantolf, J. L., & Thorne, S. L. (2006). *Sociocultural theory and the genesis of second language development*. Oxford: Oxford University Press.

Larsen-Freeman, D. (2003). *Teaching language: Fram grammar to grammaring*. Boston: Heinle.

Lesaux, N. K. (2006). Building consensus: Future directions for research on English language learners at risk for learning difficulties. *Teachers College Record*, 108(11), 2406–2438.

Lin, A. M. Y. (Ed.) (2008). *Problematizing identity: Everyday struggles in language, culture, and education*. New York: Taylor & Francis.

Lin, A. M. Y., & Luke, A. (Eds.) (2006). Special issue: Postcolonial approaches to TESOL. *Critical Inquiry in Language Studies*, 3(2&3).

Liddicoat, A. J. (2009). Sexual identity as linguistic failure: Trajectories of interaction in the heteronormative language classroom. *Journal of Language, Identity, and Education*, 8(2–3), 191–202.

Luke, A. (2004). Two takes on the critical. In B. Norton & K. Toohey (Eds.), *Critical pedagogies and language learning* (pp. 21–29). Cambridge: Cambridge University Press.

Luke, A. (2006). Teaching after the market. In L. Weis, C. McCarthy & G. Dimitriadis (Eds.), *Ideology, curriculum, and the new sociology of education: Revisiting the work of Michael Apple* (pp. 115–141). New York: Routledge.

Luke, A. (2009). Race and language as capital in school: A sociological template for languagee-education reform. In R. Kubota & A. M. Y. Lin (Eds.), *Race, culture, and identities in second language education* (pp. 286–308). New York: Routledge.

Luke, A., Luke, C. & Graham, P. (2007). Globalization, corporatism, and critical language education. *International Multilingual Research Journal*, 1(1), 1–13.

McGroarty, M. (2006). Neoliberal collusion or strategic simultaney? On multiple rationales for language-in-education policies. *Language Policy*, 5(1), 3–13.

McNamara, T. (2009). Identity? Paper presented at the second Discourse and Cultural Practices Conference, 7–9 July, University of Sydney, Australia.

Mahboob, A. (2009). English as an Islamic language: A case study of Pakistani English. *World Englishes*, 28(2), 175–189.

Makoni, S., & Pennycook, A. (2007). Disinventing and reconstituting languages. In S. Makoni & A. Pennycook (Eds.), *Disinventing and reconstituting languages* (pp. 1–41). Clevedon: Multilingual Matters.

Mansfield, N. (2000). *Subjectivity: Theories of the self from Freud to Haraway*. St Leonards: Allen & Unwin.

Mantero, M. (2004). Transcending tradition: Situated activity, discourse, and identity in language teacher education. *Critical Inquiry in Language Studies, 1*(3), 143–161.

Marginson, S. (2006). Engaging democratic education in the neoliberal age. *Educational Theory, 56*(2), 205–219.

Martin, I., & Tagalik, S. (2004). *Aajiiqatigiimgniq*: Lessons learned from Nunavut's language of instruction research project. In R. O. van Everdingen (Ed.), *Proceedings of the 14th Inuit Studies Conference, University of Calgary* (pp. 167–184). Retrieved October 10, 2009 from http://pubs.aina.ucalgary.ca/aina/14thISCProceedings.pdf.

Masny, D., & Cole, D. R. (2009). *Multiple literacies theory: A Deleuzian perspective.* Rotterdam: Sense Publishers.

Mayer, C. (2009). Issues in second language literacy education with learners who are deaf. *International Journal of Bilingual Education and Bilingualism, 12* (3), 325–334.

Menard-Warwick, J. (2005). Both a fiction and an existential fact: Theorizing identity in second language acquisition and literacy studies. *Linguistics and Education, 16*(3), 253–274.

Menard-Warwick, J. (2009). *Gendered identities and immigrant language learning.* Clevedon: Multilingual Matters.

Menezes de Souza, L. M. T. (2005). The ecology of writing among the Kashinawa: Indigenous multimodality in Brazil. In S. Canagarajah (Ed.), *Reclaiming the local in language policy and practice* (pp. 73–95). Mahwah, NJ: Lawrence Erlbaum Associates.

Menezes de Souza, L. M. T. (2007). Entering a culture quietly: Writing and cultural survival in indigenous education in Brazil. In S. Makoni & A. Pennycook (Eds.), *Disinventing and reconstituting languages* (pp. 135–169). Clevedon: Multilingual Matters.

Michael-Luna, S. (2009). Narratives in the wild: Unpacking critical race theory methodology for early childhood bilingual education. In R. Kubota & A. M. Y. Lin (Eds.), *Race, culture, and identities in second language education* (pp. 234–251). New York: Routledge.

Moffatt, L., & Norton, B. (2005). Popular culture and the reading teacher: A case for feminist pedagogy. *Critical Inquiry in Language Studies, 2*, 1–12.

Moita-Lopes, L. (2006) Queering literacy teaching: analyzing gay-themed discourses in a fifth-grade class in Brazil. *Journal of Language Identity, and Education, 5*(1), 31–50.

Morgan, B. (2003). Identity and L2 pronunciation: Towards an integrated practice in ELT. *The Journal of TESOL France, 10*, 49–64.

Morgan, B. (2004). Teacher identity as pedagogy: Towards a field-internal conceptualization in bilingual and second language education. *International Journal of Bilingual Education & Bilingualism, 7*(2–3), 172–188.

Morgan, B. (2007). Poststructuralism and applied linguistics: Complementary approaches to identity and culture in ELT. In J. Cummins & C. Davison (Eds.), *International handbook of English language teaching* (Vol. 2) (pp. 949–968). Norwell, MA: Springer Publishers.

Morgan, B., & Fleming, D. (2009). Critical citizenship practices in ESP and ESL programs: Canadian and global perspectives. In D. Belcher (Ed.), *English for specific purposes in theory and practice* (pp. 264–288). Ann Arbor: University of Michigan Press.

Morgan, B., & Ramanathan, V. (2005). Critical literacies and language education: Global and local perspectives. *Annual Review of Applied Linguistics, 25*, 151–169.

Nelson, C. D. (1999). Sexual identities in ESL: Queer theory and classroom inquiry. *TESOL Quarterly, 33*, 371–391.

Nelson, C. D. (2005). Transnational/Queer: Narratives from the contact zone. *Journal of Curriculum Theorizing, 21*, 109–117.

Norton, B. (2000). *Identity and language learning: Gender, ethnicity and educational change.* Singapore: Pearson Education.

Norton Peirce, B. (1995). Social identity, investment and language learning. *TESOL Quarterly, 29*(1), 9–32.

Norton, B., & Pavlenko, A. (Eds.) (2004). *Gender and English language learners.* Alexandria, VA: TESOL Publications.

Olssen, M. (2003). Structuralism, post-structuralism, neo-liberalism: Assessing Foucault's legacy. *Journal of Education Policy, 18*(2), 189–202.

Ó'Móchain, R. (2006). Discussing gender and sexuality in a context-appropriate way: Queer narratives in an EFL college classroom in Japan. *Journal of Language, Identity, and Education, 5*, 51–66.

Omoniyi, T., & White, G. (Eds.) (2006). *The sociolinguistics of identity.* London: Continuum.

Park, G. (2009). "I listened to Korean society. I always heard that women should be this way …": The negotiation and construction of gendered identities in claiming a dominant language and race in the United States. *Journal of Language, Identity & Education, 8*(2), 174–190.

Patrick, D. (2005). Language rights in Indigenous communities: The case of the Inuit of Arctic Québec. *Journal of Sociolinguistics, 9*(3), 369–389.

Pavlenko, A. (2006). Bilingual selves. In A. Pavlenko (Ed.), *Bilingual minds: Emotional experience, expression and representation* (pp. 1–33). Clevedon: Multilingual Matters.

Pavlenko, A., & Blackledge, A. (Eds.) (2004). *Negotiation of identities in multilingual contexts* (pp. 266–289). Clevedon: Multilingual Matters.

Pennycook, A. (2004). Performativity and language studies. *Critical Inquiry in Language Studies, 1*(1), 1–19.

Pennycook, A. (2007). *Global English and transcultural flows.* New York: Routledge.

Pennycook, A., & Coutand-Marin, S. (2003). Teaching English as a missionary language. *Discourse: Studies in the Cultural Politics of Education, 24,* 337–353.

Petrovic, J. (2005). The conservative restoration and neoliberal defenses of bilingual education. *Language Policy, 4*(4), 395–416.

Phan, L. H. (2008). *Teaching English as an international language: Identity, resistance and negotiation.* Clevedon: Multilingual Matters Ltd.

Phillipson, R. (2008). The linguistic imperialism of neoliberal empire. *Critical Inquiry in Language Studies, 5*(1), 1–43.

Porter, R. (2004). *Flesh in the age of reason: How the enlightenment transformed the way we see our bodies and souls.* London: Penguin.

Pratt, M. L. (1991). Arts of the contact zone. *Profession, 91,* 33–40.

Ramanathan, V. (2005). The *English-vernacular divide: postcolonial language politics and practice.* Clevedon: Multilingual Matters.

Ramanathan, V. (2006). Of texts AND translations AND rhizomes: Postcolonial anxieties AND deracinations AND knowledge constructions. *Critical Inquiry in Language Studies, 3*(4), 223–244.

Ramanathan, V. (2009a). Silencing and languaging in the assembling of the Indian nation-state: British public citizens, the epistolary form, and historiography. *Journal of Language, Identity, and Education, 8,* 203–219.

Ramanathan, V. (2009b). *Bodies and language: Health, ailments, disabilities.* Clevedon: Multilingual Matters.

Ramanathan, V., & Morgan, B. (2007). TESOL and policy enactments: Perspectives from practice. Introduction to the special issue on language policy. *TESOL Quarterly, 41*(3), 447–463.

Rampton, B. (1995). *Crossing: Language and ethnicity among adolescents.* London: Longman.

Rassool, N. (2007). *Global issues in language, education and development: Perspectives from postcolonial countries.* Clevedon: Multilingual Matters.

Reagan, T. (2004). Objectification, positivism and language studies: A reconsideration. *Critical Inquiry in Language Studies, 1*(1), 41–60.

Richards, K. (2006). "Being the teacher": Identity and classroom conversation. *Applied Linguistics, 27*(1), 51–77.

Roseboro, D. (2008). *Jacques Lacan and education.* Rotterdam: Sense Publishers.

Sarkar, M., & Allen, D. (2007). Hybrid identities in Quebec hip-hop: Language, territory, and ethnicity in the mix. *Journal of Language, Identity & Education, 6,* 117–130.

Scott, J. (2007). *The politics of the veil.* Princeton, NJ: Princeton University Press.

Sharkey, J. (2004). Lives stories don't tell: Exploring the untold in autobiographies. *Curriculum Inquiry, 34,* 495–512.

Shuck, G. (2006). Racializing the Nonnative English Speaker. *Journal of Language, Identity, and Education, 5,* 259–276.

Simon, R. (1992). *Teaching against the grain.* Toronto: OISE Press.

Singh, P., & Doherty, C. A. (2004). Global cultural flows and pedagogic dilemmas: Teaching in the global university contact zone. *TESOL Quarterly, 38*(1), 9–42.

Skeggs, B. (2008). The problem with identity. In A. M. Y. Lin (Ed.), *Problematizing identity: Everyday struggles in language, culture, and education* (pp. 11–34). New York: Taylor & Francis.

Sleeter, C. (Ed.) (2007). *Facing accountability in education: Democracy and equity at risk.* New York: Teachers College Press.

Smith, D. (2007). Spirituality and language pedagogy. In D. Smith & T. Osborn (Eds.), *Spirituality, social justice, and language learning* (pp. 13–29). Charlotte, NC: Information Age Publishing.

Starkey, H. (2007). Language education, identities and citizenship: Developing cosmopolitan perspectives. *Language and Intercultural Communication, 7*(1), 56–71.

Stritikus, T., & Varghese, M. (2005). "*Nadie me dijo* (Nobody told me)": Language policy negotiation and implications for teacher education. *Journal of Teacher Education, 56*(1), 73–87.

Swain, M. (2006). Languaging, agency and collaboration in advanced language proficiency. In H. Byrnes (Ed.), *Advanced language learning: The contribution of Halliday and Vygotsky* (pp. 95–108). London: Continuum.

Tan, P. K.W., & Rubdy, R. (Eds.) (2008). *Language as commodity: Global structures, local marketplaces.* London: Continuum.

Taylor, L. (2006). Wrestling with race: The implications of integrative antiracism education for immigrant ESL youth. *TESOL Quarterly, 40*(3), 519–544.

Thorne, S. L. (2005). Epistemology, politics, and ethics in sociocultural theory. *Modern Language Journal, 89*(3), 393–409.

Tsui, A. (2007). Complexities of identity formation: A narrative inquiry of an EFL teacher. *TESOL Quarterly, 41*(4), 657–680.

Unsworth, L. (Ed.) (2008). *Multimodal semiotics: Functional analysis in contexts of education.* London: Continuum.

Vandrick, S. (2009). *Interrogating privilege: Reflections of a second language educator.* Ann Arbor: University of Michigan Press.

van Lier, L. (2004). *The ecology and semiotics of language learning: A sociocultural perspective.* Dordrecht: Kluwer.

Varghese, M., Morgan, B., Johnston, B. & Johnson, K. A. (2005). Theorizing language teacher identity: Three perspectives and beyond. *Journal of Language Identity & Education, 4*(1), 21–44.

Warriner, D. S. (2007). Transnational literacies: Immigration, language learning, and identity. *Linguistics and Education, 18*, 201–214.

Waterstone, B. (2008). "I hate the ESL idea!": A case study in identity and academic literacy. *TESL Canada Journal, 26*(1), 52–67.

Wells, G. (2007). The mediating role of discoursing in activity. *Mind, Culture, and Activity, 14*(3), 160–177.

Wong, M., & Canagarajah, S. (Eds.) (2009). *Christian and critical English language educators in dialogue: Pedagogical and ethical dilemmas.* New York: Routledge.

50

Language Teaching and Learning from an Intercultural Perspective

Anthony J. Liddicoat

Introduction

An intercultural perspective in language learning teaching and learning has become prominent over the past two decades, and is variously known in English as Intercultural Language Teaching, or Intercultural Language Learning, or Intercultural Language Teaching and Learning.[1] It has at its basis the understanding that the role of language education is to prepare language learners for meaningful communication outside their own cultural environment and to develop in language learners a sense of themselves as mediators between languages and cultures (Buttjes & Byram, 1991; Zarate, Gohard-Radenkovic, Lussier & Penz, 2004). The development of intercultural language teaching and learning has involved a conceptual shift in the understanding of the nature and purpose of language teaching. Such a shift has necessitated considerable work in developing new ways of understanding the content and processes of language education. At the beginning of the development of intercultural language teaching and learning, Zarate (1986) argued that the teaching and learning of culture in language education has been problematic because sufficient attention has not been given to considering what is to be taught and how. The years since Zarate made this point have been a time of considerable work in this area, and while the intercultural project in language teaching and learning cannot be considered in any way complete, much progress has been made. This chapter aims to present some of the ways in which the field has begun to address these shortcomings. It will begin by outlining some of the basic assumptions about language, culture and learning that characterise an intercultural perspective in language education. It will then examine some aspects of the educational approaches developed within an intercultural framework—pedagogy, processes of learning and assessment.

The Intercultural in Language Learning

Intercultural language teaching and learning centres on the relationship between languages and culture—it is this relationship that is the starting point for the intercultural. It is possible to distinguish in language education two broad orientations to the teaching of culture that reflect views of the nature of the relationship between language and culture. The first of these can be termed a cultural orientation. A cultural orientation implies the development of knowledge about culture that remains external to the learner and is not intended to confront or transform the learner's existing identity, practices, values, attitudes, beliefs and worldview. It is about the acquisition of a body of knowledge about a culture (Kawakami, 2001; Liddicoat, 2005). Beacco (2000) finds this to be the dominant approach to culture in much language teaching material and remarks that the body of knowledge taught is often limited and overgeneralised and subordinated to the teaching of linguistic structures. Kawakami (2005) also argues that a focus on teaching the culture of the other as knowledge of differences risks entrenching stereotypical views of the other. This approach to culture is not strongly tied to language and culture is seen as existing independently of language and may be taught in isolation from the target language itself (Crozet & Liddicoat, 2000). The second is an intercultural orientation. This orientation implies a transformational engagement of the learner in the act of learning. Here learning involves the student in oppositional practice (Kramsch & Nolden, 1994) that seeks to decentre learners from their existing linguistic and cultural positionings and to develop an intercultural identity as a result of an engagement with another culture. Here the borders between self and other are explored, problematised and redrawn. Language is fundamental to this view of culture as language provides the point of engagement with a culture and it is thorough engagement with the language and culture as inter-related meaning-making systems that the desired learning is achieved. In teaching language from an intercultural perspective developing a static body of knowledge is not seen as the equivalent of developing an intercultural capability (Zarate, 1983). Rather, the learner needs to engage with language and culture and elements of a meaning-making system that influence and are influenced by each other. This means that language learning becomes a process of exploring the ways language and culture relate to lived realities—the learners' as well as that of the target community.

As a process of developing an intercultural capability, learners consider both their own "intracultural" positioning and how these are shaped by their own language and culture as part of the process of coming to understand the cultural situatedness of the other (Papademetre, 2000). This means that learners need to decentre from their own culture and to see their own positioning from the perspective of another (Byram, 1989a; Kramsch, 1993). This decentring is a process of varying the perspective one takes in understanding the world, not simply seeing the other as an object of study, but seeing his/her perspective as a valid understanding and exploring the consequences of diversity. This can only happen as the result of a deliberate process of teaching that brings to the students the kind of exposure they need to begin the decentring process and the development of skills and knowledge to understand and interpret these experiences. The study of language, therefore, has the potential to expose learners to other ways of viewing the world and develops flexibility and independence from a single linguistic and conceptual system through which to view the world (Byram, 1989a; Kramsch, 1993; Liddicoat, 2005). This can be characterised as a dynamic approach to culture (Liddicoat, 2002), which views culture as sets of variable practices in which people engage in order to live their lives and that are continually created and re-created by participants in interaction. Cultural practices represent a contextual framework that people use to structure and understand their social world and communicate with other people. Culture, then, is not about information and things; it is about actions and understanding. In order to learn about culture, it is necessary to engage with the linguistic and non-linguistic practices of the culture and to gain insights about the way of living in a particular cultural context (Kramsch, 1993; Liddicoat, 1997). Cultural knowledge is not a case of knowing information about the culture; it is about knowing how to engage with diverse others.

The intercultural, therefore, involves an awareness of the interrelationship between language and culture in the communication and interpretation of meanings. One's understanding is always informed by the past and present of a particular language and culture and, in intercultural contacts, it is necessary to recognise the same in others (Liddicoat & Scarino, 2010). This means understanding the impact of such situatedness on communication and relationships. The relationship between awareness and knowing is however not a unidirectional one in which awareness precedes knowledge, but a multidirectional one in which knowing contributes to expanded awareness and awareness contributes to expanded knowing. Through experiences of and engagement with languages and cultures, the intercultural learner develops an increasingly complex sense of self as a user of language and as a cultural being acting on and in the world. The intercultural in this sense involves not only awareness but also the ability to analyse, explain and elaborate this awareness; that is, it involves a meta-level of awareness (or meta-awareness) that needs to be captured in the elicitation of the intercultural. For the intercultural language learner, the development of awareness and knowing of language and culture is achieved through the experience of another language and through this language another culture. It is through exposure to and engagement with culturally situated text—whether spoken or written, intrapersonal or interpersonal—that the learner comes to appreciate the manifestation of diversity through language as a communicative process.

Interculturality is however not simply a manifestation of awareness and knowing, it also involves acting. The intercultural is manifested through language in use, through interpreting and expressing meaning across cultural boundaries in dialogue with self and others, drawing on awareness and knowledge gained through previous experience, recognising the possibility of multiple interpretations of messages and the culturally embedded nature of meaning (Liddicoat & Scarino, 2010). This conceptualisation of the intercultural involves understanding the learner as both participant and analyser in interaction; that is, as both learner and user of language and culture (Kern & Liddicoat, 2008; Liddicoat & Scarino, 2010). The intercultural communicator does not simply communicate in contexts of diversity but also monitors, reflects on and interprets what is occurring in communication. While it is not true that the participant and analyser roles are always present to the same degree in any act of communication, the capacity to draw on, combine and move between these interactional identities is however a fundamental element of the intercultural.

The interpersonal and interactional nature of the intercultural as it is conceived here requires that the language user is able to decentre form his/her own cultural and linguistic framework in order to see the world from alternative perspectives, or what (Byram, Gribkova & Starkey, 2002, p. 14) describe as the "ability to make the strange familiar and the familiar strange". Such decentring is a capacity to understand multiple perspectives and a willingness to search for and accept multiple possible interpretations of the same message. As an interpersonal phenomenon, interculturality is predicated on the development of reciprocity in interaction, which recognises one's own multiple roles and responsibilities and is sensitive to, and accommodating of, those of one's interlocutors. This means that, for us, to be intercultural involves continuous intercultural learning through experience and critical reflection. There can be no final end point at which the individual achieves the intercultural state, but rather to be intercultural is by its very nature an unfinishable work in progress of action in response to new experiences and reflection on the action.

One problem in intercultural language teaching and learning has been to articulate complex views of the nature of the intercultural as a construct that can be identified for teaching and assessment. The most elaborated model of intercultural competence is the model of *savoirs* developed by Byram and Zarate (1994): *savoir, savoir être, savoir comprendre* and *savoir apprendre. Savoir* refers to knowledge of self and others, of their products and practices and the general processes of interaction. This constitutes a body of knowledge on which other operations can be performed. These further operations are described as: *savoir être*, which involves an attitudinal disposition towards intercultural engagement manifested in approaching intercultural learning with curiosity, openness and reflexivity; *savoir comprendre*, which involves learning how to interpret and explain cultural practices or documents and to compare them with aspects of one's own culture; and *savoir apprendre*, which is the ability to make discoveries through personal involvement in social interaction. Byram (1997) adds a further dimension, *savoir s'engager*, which refers to the ability to make informed critical evaluations of aspects of one's own and other cultures. Sercu (2004, p. 76) has proposed that Byram's model of *savoirs* be extended to include "a meta-cognitive dimension"; that is, self-regulating mechanisms that enable learners to plan, monitor and evaluate their own learning processes. In addition to the limitation noted by Sercu, the model of *savoirs* does not elaborate on the important ways in which language affects culture and culture affects language and how this is understood by the learner. Moreover this model does not clarify how *savoirs* (knowledge) are understood. This is important, for example, because *savoir comprendre* (knowing that) and *savoir faire* (knowing how) do not represent knowing as embodied and embodiment of knowledge is an important aspect for understanding the intercultural person as social actor rather than just social analyser. One important dimension for future work in intercultural language teaching and learning is the need to articulate pedagogical models of the underlying construct that capture and reflect the complexity of the view of the intercultural.

Pedagogy

One important feature of intercultural language teaching and learning that needs to be considered before entering into further discussion is that it does not constitute a language teaching "method". There is no single set of pedagogical practices that can be considered to constitute intercultural language teaching and learning. It is more appropriate to consider what is happening in intercultural language teaching and learning as a "stance" as described by Cochran-Smith and Lytle (1999, p. 289)—that is, as "positions teachers and others … take toward knowledge and its relationship to practice". This means that intercultural language teaching and learning is best considered as a set of shared assumptions about the nature of language, culture and learning that shapes an overall understanding of what it means to teach language and to do this in an intercultural way. It is a perspective from which language educators construct practice rather than a set of practices to be adopted. In this way, intercultural language teaching may be considered as a "post-methods" pedagogy (Kumaravadivelu, 2006) in that it consists of a theoretical orientation that frames options and principles that are to be adapted by teachers in their own location specific practice.

An interculturally oriented pedagogy for language teaching and learning starts from the view that language, culture and learning are fundamentally integrated (Bolten, 1993; Byram & Feng, 2005; Byram & Zarate, 1994; Kramsch, 1995a, 1999; Liddicoat, Papademetre, Scarino & Kohler, 2003). This means that in developing a pedagogy of intercultural teaching and learning it is necessary to recognise the classroom as a cultural context in which teachers' and learners' experiences and expectations are shaped by the linguistic and cultural backgrounds that each brings to the classroom. Each participant in the class enacts through language his/her understanding and assumptions about fundamental aspects of practice such as what constitutes learning, what constitutes knowledge and how knowledge is to be displayed or used. This means that an important starting point for developing an intercultural pedagogy is for teachers individually to recognise the cultural locatedness of the ways they think about teaching and learning. Such recognition allows teachers to come to understand the motivation and conceptual underpinnings for their own action as teachers and how they themselves mediate between cultural assumptions in their work.

Liddicoat et al. (2003) propose a set of principles that provides a starting point for developing intercultural language teaching and learning. These principles are not strictly principles of the intercultural, but rather constitute principles of teaching and learning on which an intercultural pedagogy exists:

1. *Active construction*: Learning is understood as involving purposeful, active engagement in interpreting and creating meaning in interaction with others, and continuously reflecting on one's self and others in communication and meaning-making in variable contexts.
2. *Making connections*: Connections are made between existing conceptions and new understandings and between previous experiences and new experiences. Previous knowledge

is challenged and this creates new insights through which students connect, re-organise, elaborate and extend their understanding.

3. *Interaction*: Learning and communication are social and interactive; interacting and communicating interculturally means continuously developing one's own understanding of the relationship between one's own framework of language and culture and that of others.

4. *Reflection*: Learning involves becoming aware of how individuals think, know and learn about language, culture, knowing, understanding and the relationship between these, as well as concepts such as diversity, identity, experiences and one's own intercultural thoughts and feelings.

5. *Responsibility*: Learning depends on learner's attitudes, dispositions and values, developed over time.

These principles amount to constructivist theory of learning applied to the context of the intercultural as manifested through language. They are therefore starting points for an intercultural pedagogy not an intercultural pedagogy itself. They are intended as a framework that guides pedagogical options in developing locally situated practice.

This practice can be conceptualised as a series of four interrelated processes of noticing, comparing, reflecting and interacting (Figure 50.1). The process of noticing is fundamental to learning (Schmidt, 1993). In intercultural language teaching and learning, it is important for learners to notice cultural similarities and differences as they are made evident through language as this is a central element in intercultural learning beyond the classroom. When experiencing something new, learners need to examine the new information in their own terms and seek to understand what it is they are experiencing. Noticing, however, is not necessarily a naturally occurring activity for learners in the classroom. Rather noticing is an activity that occurs in a framework of understandings that regulate what can and should be noticed (Crozet & Liddicoat, 2000).

The most basic level of operations that students can perform on their experiences of language and culture is comparison in which students identify similarities and differences. The process of comparison is multilayered: it needs to allow space not only for comparisons between the learner's background culture and the target culture but also between what the learner already knows about the target language and culture and the new input s/he is noticing. Comparison of similarities and differences provide a resource for reflection and reflection as a classroom process is a core element

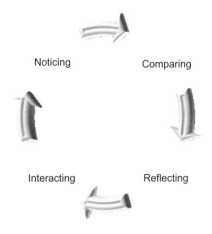

Noticing   Comparing

Interacting   Reflecting

Figure 50.1 Interacting processes of intercultural pedagogy
Source: Scarino and Liddicoat (2009).

of developing interculturality (Kohonen, 2000). Reflection involves several considerations. It is a process of interpretation of experience: this does not mean however that the learner is being required to draw "the right conclusion" or simply to explore his/her feelings about what has been discovered but rather that the learner makes personal sense of experiences. This involves the learner in reflecting on what one's experience of linguistic and cultural diversity means for oneself: how one reacts to diversity, how one thinks about diversity, how one feels about diversity and how one will find ways of engaging constructively with diversity. Finally, interculturality is not a passive knowing of aspects of diversity but rather an active engagement with diversity. This means that the intercultural learner needs to be engaged in interacting on the basis his/her learning and experiences of diversity in order to create personal meanings about one's experiences, to communicate those meanings, to explore those meanings and to reshape them in response to others.

Developing practice from principles such as those discussed above involves constructing learning opportunities in language learning programmes that engage learners with the intercultural. The principles and processes outlined above interact in the development of an overall pedagogy in which experiences of language become opportunities for experiences of culture. One way of engaging with the intercultural in language learning has been to identify the opportunities afforded by typical experiences of language learning and to integrate in them in interculturally focused learning activities. Such opportunities have typically been considered areas of culture learning, however, such learning has not necessarily been intercultural in its focus. For example, Liddicoat (2008) reports an instance of teaching practice used in late primary school-level Japanese class in which a small group of Japanese language texts about schooling were used as the basis for intercultural learning. The texts, which included illustrated stories written by Japanese children about their school day, timetables, etc., were used as the basis for a series of four focus activities. Focus one involved students thinking about their own knowledge of schooling in order to activate their understanding of schooling as a cultural practice. This focus involved students in descriptions of the environment and the organisation of the school day and in reflection on their own school in relation to other schools in their society. Focus two introduced students to the Japanese material and asked them to use one particular text as starting points for noticing aspects of Japanese schooling as a cultural phenomenon (*What do you notice about this school?*) as a prelude to a comparison between the Japanese schools and their own knowledge of schools (*How is it similar to your school? How is it different from your school?*) and a reflection in variability within another culture (*Do you think all Japanese schools are like this? What might be similar and what might be different?*). Focus two is therefore a progression from noticing through comparison to reflection in which learners actively construct an understanding of a new cultural context through target language texts. Each text is presented as an encounter with a new culture and is used as an opportunity for learning beyond the text itself. Focus three involved working through the questions used for focus two with a range of other input materials to create an incremental exploration of the new input, together with a reflection on how new information produced new understandings (*How has your view of Japanese schools changed after having looked at all the texts?*). Focus four was a reflection that used knowledge of two school systems to investigate personal reactions to the Japanese context (*What would you like about going to school in Japan? What wouldn't you like?*) together with a task which required students to adopt an external perspective on their own cultural context (*What do you think a Japanese person might like about your school? What do you think they wouldn't like?*). Focus four involves learners in a reflective task that includes a requirement to decentre from one's own culture and view it from an external perspective. At each point in the series of activities students are engaged in drawing connections, discussion and interaction as a way of engaging with culture through language.

The four focuses are attempts to construct a pathway by which students are encouraged to move from their own culture-internal views of familiar experience of life towards an understanding of another way of constructing the same experience. The stimulus for movement is not the delivery of new information but rather a question-led process of exploration that engages learners directly through target language texts as cultural artefacts. The pathway is designed not so much around the idea of acquiring knowledge but rather around developing the capacities for intercultural exploration. The key features of the activities discussed above are:

1. involving students in a process of noticing, comparing, reflecting and interacting;
2. constructing the background culture of the learner and the target culture as equally valid representations of human life;
3. viewing instances of language use as experiences of culture and opportunities for culture learning;
4. focusing on the capabilities required for on-going learning about cultures through experiences of language; and
5. encouraging the inclusion of multiple perspectives.

It is possible to identify two broad orientations to the use of experiences of language learning as opportunities for intercultural learning within views of intercultural language teaching and learning: a culture studies orientation, which focuses on the analysis of texts, and an ethnographic orientation, which focuses on the interpretation of direct experience. The culture studies orientation uses the language products of a community as an entry point for considering the culture of that community. Such products—texts in a wide sense of the word—are seen to represent meaningful instantiations of the culture that produced them. They can therefore be studied not as independent products in their own right but as culturally contexted discourses that enact aspects of cultures.

There has been a number of studies of the use of literature as a source of cultural learning and the emphasis on literature is unsurprising given the strong association between literature and culture in traditional approaches to language teaching and learning. Recent work on the use of literature has argued that the study of literature needs to move beyond literary criticism and textual study to begin to engage with context (for example Byram, 1988, 1989a; Kramsch, 1993). In intercultural approaches to the use of literature it is important that the literary text does not remain the object of study in itself, but rather becomes the vehicle for deeper reflection and for understanding of self and others. The reading of literary texts the becomes a case of developing oppositional practices through which the text can be used as an opportunity to explore the boundaries between one's own culture and the target culture (Kramsch & Nolden, 1994).

Kramsch (1993) approaches intercultural learning from the perspective of the interrelationships between texts people generate and contexts shaping them or shaped by them. In this work, Kramsch shows the power of textual analysis as a stimulus for intercultural learning by going beyond the text as artefact to explore possible meanings in the text. She identifies five significant elements of context—linguistic, situational, interactional, cultural and intertextual—and argues that language learning needs to provide opportunities to discover potential meanings through explorations of the context of the discourse under study. Meaning in a text produced in another culture needs to be made visible (Kramsch, 1995b) and learners need to explore the cues which signal meanings in the text. Through the investigation of culturally contexted meaning, the language learner comes to see language as culturally shaped and as culturally shaping rather than an unproblematised process of communication. In this way, texts open possibilities of new and hitherto undiscovered meanings that become possible for investigation (Kramsch, 2003).

In most work on the use of literature for culture learning, the emphasis has been on a two-way comparison between the culture of the learner and the target culture, however, some initial work has been done that uses a comparative literature perspective in which the same theme is examined through writings in different languages, written in different cultural contexts and that produce a richer, multilateral perspective on theme (Carroli, Hillman & Maurer, 1999, 2000).

The ethnographic orientation has sought to introduce direct experience of another culture into the formal language learning context. Ethnography involves a shift away from the interpretation of written and audio-visual texts provided by a cultural studies approach to a way of seeing direct experience of lived reality as a text for interpretation. Corbett (2003) argues that observing, interviewing, analysing and reporting are fundamental to encounters with another culture and argues that language learners need to learn these as an element of language curricula.

The fundamental pre-requisite for an ethnographic approach to intercultural language teaching is an experience, typically an out-of-class experience, of another culture. It has been particularly focused on experiences gained through study aboard programmes—a language learning context that is external to the delivery of language courses in educational institutions. Such experiences engage students in direct engagement with the everyday life of those whose language they are learning with an interpretative reflective component in which students situate their lived experience of the other within a broader socio-political context (Roberts, Byram, Barro, Jordan & Street, 2001). The study abroad experience is a direct experience of using an additional language in its own cultural context and as such is a process of communicative engagement with another community and its language and culture (Byram, 1989b; Byram & Feng, 2005; Coleman, 1997, 1998; Roberts et al., 2001). Study aboard is not in itself a form of intercultural learning, rather it provides the potential for such learning to occur. The realisation of this potential comes about as a result of the integration of study abroad into an adequately prepared learning program (Coleman, 1997; Schmidt & Jansen, 2004). It becomes intercultural when integrated into a process of teaching and learning that gives scope for sustained reflection on the experience.

Another way of including ethnography within language programmes has been through the use of ethnographic interviews. The depth to which this may go may be limited compared to the larger scale immersion of study abroad, but the essential aims of this more limited ethnographic approach remain similar to those of larger projects. The interviews are seen as a way of developing contact between the language learner and the target language community in a way that develops similar capabilities for reflection on language, culture and their relationship. Ethnographic interviews of native speakers make available to language learners a view of a culture from inside, that is, a description of a culture in its own terms (Damen, 1987), and allow for the discovery of similarities and shared values as well as differences between cultures. In particular, the ethnographic interview is seen as a way both of coming to understand another culture's perspective and of becoming aware of one's own cultural positioning (Bateman, 2002).

The use of ethnographic interviews in language education can be understood by practitioners in two ways—as a way of developing ethnographic skills that can be used for intercultural learning or as an intercultural engagement in their own right. Where ethnographic interviews are used to develop skills, intercultural learning may be considered as secondary to the development of the skills themselves. For example, Robinson-Stuart and Nocon (1996) used ethnographic interviews as a culture-learning tool with Spanish language learners. In this study, interviewing a speaker of the target language was integrated as an element of a regular language programme and students prepared a report based on the interview. They identify a number of changes in attitudes towards target language groups resulting from the process of interviewing, but the project they report seems to treat this as an outcome of the project rather than as the focus of the project itself. That is, the intercultural investigation was secondary to the doing ethnography. Bateman's (2002) use of ethnographic interviews similarly sees the development of the ability to conduct and report an ethnographic interview as the main gain from the process of interviewing and the affects on attitudes, etc. as resulting from having done the project rather than being the focus of the project.

Other language teachers use ethnographic interview specifically as a form of intercultural investigation. Sobolewski (2009) describes a language learning task in which investigation of some aspect of culture becomes the focus of the ethnographic interview. That is, the interviewees are positioned explicitly as a resource for promoting the students' own learning and ethnography as a mechanism for exploring an area of cultural interest. In this project, the interview is only a part of an overall research project in which culture is investigated through a range of complementary information sources to develop an enriched understanding of culture. In reporting on the project students were asked specifically to discuss their reactions to their learning and how the experience affected their views of both the target culture and their own. Sobolewski's work reveals an important dimension of the ethnographic interview for intercultural learning—that to be intercultural it needs to focus on the self and not just the other. An interview that gains insight into another culture without offering insight into one's own has not achieved the intercultural project, although it may have had such an outcome as a by-product of engagement with another culture. For this reason, Knutson (2006) proposes that ethnographic projects for intercultural learning should combine "home ethnographies" as well as ethnographies of the other and should be open to investigating outsiders' perceptions of one's own culture as well as one's own perceptions of the other.

The ethnographic interview presupposes that speakers of the target language are available in the learners' own community and so, like ethnography in study abroad, depend on a resource being available outside the learning context. There have been a number of attempts to introduce small-scale ethnographic projects in ways that are not dependent either on travel or on the local availability of language speakers.

Computer technology has been used as a way of bringing language learners and members of the target language communication into contact for the purpose of language and intercultural learning. Furstenberget, Levet, English and Maillet (2001) and Belz (Belz, 2003; Belz & Kinginger, 2002) report projects in which computer-mediated interactions became input for reflection on language and culture. The technology becomes a resource for collecting data about the target language community and their communicative practices, which then becomes available for comparison. Carel (2001) reports the use of an interactive computer courseware package to enable students to use ethnographic skills to observe and analyse cultural phenomena and to do virtual fieldwork. In this way, she overcame the separation of learner and target language community through technology and sought to replicate the learning possibilities of in-country experience in a classroom context. The computer courseware made it possible not only to observe difference but also for students to reflect on their own culture and their previous views of the target culture as a part of their virtual experience of the target culture and reflection about language and culture and the relationship between the two.

The approaches to integrating intercultural learning discussed so far take the form more of intercultural content to be included in language programs, with some additional teaching of skills to enable learners to work with that content. There are also a number of approaches that have been developed for teaching interculturally and an integrated part of all language teaching. These approaches seek to integrate intercultural learning as a basic element in the language teaching and learning process as a whole. They aim at an interculturally oriented pedagogy for language education rather than at the inclusion of interculturally oriented material in language programmes.

One proposal for integrating the intercultural into language learning as a coherent and consistent dimension of the language teaching process can be seen in work stemming from the pedagogical practices described by Crozet (Crozet, 1996, 1998; Crozet & Liddicoat, 1999; Liddicoat & Crozet, 2001). Crozet proposes a four-stage process of awareness raising, experimentation, production and feedback.

The awareness-raising stage is where the learners are introduced to new input about language and culture. This new input is introduced through participative tasks that encourage the learner to compare the new culture with their own practices and language use. Crozet uses a range of exemplifications of target culture ways of speaking as input at this point—video and audio texts, cartoons, written texts—each of which contributes an element of an overall representation of a culturally contexted communication practice. The learners are positioned at this point as observers of language and culture in use and are invited to notice differences between the new input and their own culture, with the teacher supporting them in noticing differences. Students' noticings are then followed up with an explanation of the function of particular actions in the target language to assist them in developing an explanatory framework for understanding what the speaker is doing. The sequence of noticing and then explanation is fundamental to Crozet's (1996, 1998) understanding of the process of learning in which learners have opportunities for active construction of meanings and understandings from experiences of language before explanations are offered. Here explanations are understood as ways of clarifying and organising learning not as the starting point for learning; the important element is the exploration of difference rather than teaching difference

The experimentation stage is designed to allow students to begin working with their new knowledge and trying out native-speaker-like ways of acting and speaking through short, supported communicative tasks that practice elements of the new knowledge and help to build towards overall learning for a new speech situation. This work involves picking apart some of the language and cultural needs of the students for focused practice and is aimed at consolidating new knowledge through experiential learning. Although the idea of stages indicates that students have moved into a new area of focus, noticing can still play a significant role here as students continue to work with culturally contexted language.

In the production stage, students put together the elements they have been trying out in the experimentation phase and integrate the information they have acquired in actual language use in a focused language task. Crozet (1996, 1998) sees this stage as an opportunity to try out native-speaker-like ways of interacting as an embodied experience of functioning outside one's own cultural frame. The idea here is not to assimilate students to native-speaker models but rather to experience the impact of using a different set of cultural assumptions on their identity and experiencing the comfort or discomfort this can bring. Crozet in her work used role-plays for this purpose which explicitly asked learners to try out culturally contexted ways of speaking and acting, which could then be used as a basis for reflection in the final, feedback stage. The feedback stage is an important part of the activity and involves reflecting on the experience of acting like a native speaker in the production phase. During this phase, students discuss with the teacher how they felt about speaking and acting in a particular way. This allows the teacher to comment on the language use of the student, but also allows the student to express how they felt. Some aspects of using a new language and culture are difficult or uncomfortable, others can be liberating. In the feedback, it is important to recognise the positives and negatives students express and to acknowledge the validity of these feelings. The feedback should allow the student to work towards discovering a "third place": a place of comfort between their first language and culture and their second (cf. Crozet & Liddicoat, 1999; Kramsch, 1993; Liddicoat, Crozet & Lo Bianco, 1999).

The pedagogies discussed here represent a diversity of ways in which language educators have sought to integrate an intercultural perspective into their teaching work. They represent a variety of ways of operationalising intercultural learning in language programmes, but a number of key themes can be indentified which connect these various ways of working. First, they all see an active engagement with the culture of the target language community as a form of lived experience, whether this is a direct experience of living in the country or a mediated experience achieved through interviewing or on-line interactions. Second, they all position the learners as mediators between cultures and recognise that there are multiple cultures involved in the learning context. Third, they engage the leaner is processes of reflection about language and culture and their relationship as a component of language learning. Different ways of working are responsive to different opportunities and different learning contexts and this reveals the situatedness of such pedagogical approaches as responses to a theoretical stance in relation to understandings of language and culture in language education.

Processes of Learning

The research on longer term processes of intercultural learning is relatively undeveloped. However, there are many reports of learning outcomes from particular instances of learning experiences (e.g. Kramsch, 2003; Kramsch & Nolden, 1994; Liddicoat & Crozet, 2001; McConachy, 2008; Zarate et al., 2004). Such studies have focused more on the nature of learning in intercultural engagement rather than only the developmental processes that characterise learning over time. There is however some work in the context of language learning that seeks to understand loner term processes of learning.

The most developed model of intercultural acquisition is Bennett, Bennett and Allen's (1999) Developmental Model of Intercultural Sensitivity (DMIS) that provides a basis for understanding the development of intercultural competence. This is not primarily a language-based model, but attempts have been made to integrate a linguistic component. The model seeks to explain how learners' abilities to operate in an intercultural context, to identify and appreciate cultural differences, and to develop strategies for dealing with cultural differences in communication evolve over time. The model is made up of two broad sets of stages: ethnocentrism and ethnorelativism. Ethnocentrism is defined by Bennett et al. as a disposition to view one's own cultural viewpoint as central to reality, while ethnorelativism is the conscious recognition that all behaviour exists within a cultural framework, including one's own. Bennett et al. argue that the starting point for all intercultural competence lies in ethnocentrism and that learners move towards progressively greater levels of ethnorelativism as the result of exposure to and reflection on cultural differences.

Both ethnocentrism and ethnorelativism are further divided into three stages that are developmentally ordered (see Figure 50.2). As the learner develops his/her intercultural competence s/he moves from a beginning point in the ethnocentric position of denial towards the ethnorelative position of integration, although Bennett et al. acknowledge that few learners actually reach the level

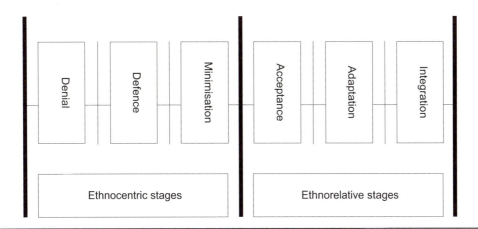

Figure 50.2 The developmental model of intercultural sensitivity
Source: Bennett et al. (1999).

of integration and for most learners, adaptation may be the most relevant outcome. The three stages of ethnocentrism are: denial, defence and minimization:

1. *Denial*: learners have not yet developed a conceptual category of cultural difference.
2. *Defence*: learners have gained some ability to notice cultural differences as the result of some form of exposure to other languages and/or cultures.
3. *Minimisation*: the problems confronted in the defence stage are resolved by assuming a basic similarity among all human beings either in terms of a *physical universalism* or a *transcendent universalism*.

The three stages of ethnorelativism are: acceptance, adaptation and integration:

1. *Acceptance*: learners develop an understanding of their own cultural context and so can accept the existence of different cultural contexts.
2. *Adaptation*: learners are able to shift their cultural frame of reference and consciously adopt perspectives of other cultural groups.
3. *Integration*: at the final stage of development, learners extend their ability to perceive events in a cultural context to their perceptions of their own identity.

The DMIS model is a linear model, which implies that the development of intercultural sensitivity is a progressive, scalar phenomenon. Bennett et al. (1999) propose a model of development that is presented at a very high level of abstraction and the linearity they present ranges across very high-level elements of intercultural competence developed over a quite extensive period of time. However, at a lower level of abstraction and over a shorter period of time, it appears unlikely that the development of intercultural competence is a linear, scalar phenomenon. Moreover, there is little overt linking between the interculturality and language in this model and the place of language and of language teaching in the model is not readily apparent. What is asserted is that particular levels of proficiency relate to particular dispositions, but there is no mechanism to indicate how such correlations can be established or on what basis the association between proficiency and worldview is hypothesised.

Liddicoat (2006) has proposed a progression in intercultural learning that sees the developmental points as embedded in earlier ways of engaging with the other cultures (see Figure 50.3).

The schematisation presented in Figure 50.3 maps a progression in intercultural learning from a point where cultural assumptions are based on first culture perspectives, which are then modified by input (especially textbooks and materials). When the input is appropriate, students then develop a more complex understanding of the phenomenon adding greater nuancing to their understandings of the phenomena being learnt. This complexification then appears to provide a basis on which the target culture and the first culture can be linked in constructive ways that increase understanding of each other. The process eventually leads to decentring from first culture perspectives so that the learner becomes able to use target culture perspectives to understand his/her own cultural nature. These stages do not appear to be linear in the sense that one replaces the other, but rather are nested, so that at each point in development, the prior perspectives remain available. Similar observations of non-linearity have been made in the work of Dewaele (Dewaele, 2002; Dewaele & Planchenault, 2006). However, such proposals remain limited in scope as they have been based only on the study of particular phenomena in learning rather than on intercultural learning as a holistic process within language learning more broadly.

The developmental nature of the intercultural in language learning is really something that has only recently come to be addressed in research. The ideas presented here are only indicative of the

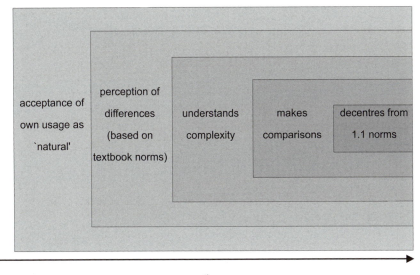

Figure 50.3 Progression in intercultural learning
Source: Liddicoat (2006).

nature of that process. What does come across from such studies is that the process of development is complex and non-linear and that progress needs to be seen in terms of developing complexity in ways of understanding and responding to linguistic and cultural differences rather than in developmental stages as they have been understood in second language acquisition. One of the factors that limits investigation into processes of acquisition in intercultural learning is the need to establish clear ways of assessing the intercultural that can be used as research tools for further developing research on learning processes.

Assessment

Intercultural competence in the context of language education imposes a number of challenges for assessment. In part, the difficulty lies in the diverse understandings of the construct to be assessed, but even then eliciting the performances of interculturality has proved to be problematic and assessment approaches may elicit only part of the overall construct, considering this to reflect the whole. Byram et al. (2002) argue that while assessing facts or decontextualised knowledge is relatively straightforward, such assessments will not capture what it means to be intercultural, in that they cannot capture the embodied framing of beliefs, attitudes and values that distinguishes intercultural engagement from cultural knowledge (Liddicoat, 2002, 2005; Liddicoat et al., 2003).

One approach to assessing interculturality is through the assessment of intercultural communicative behaviours. In this way, intercultural competence is treated as if it were a separable language skill, analogous to the conventional macro-skills of speaking, listening, reading and writing (Damen, 1987). The tasks used are forms of enactment tasks (Sercu, 2004) in which a learner is asked perform the role of a communicator in an intercultural situation. Common formats for such tasks include role-plays and simulations, which are used to test norms of interaction (Crozet, 1996), pragmatic norms (Hudson, Detmer & Brown, 1992; Kasper & Dahl, 1991) and some linguistic and paralinguistic phenomena (Liddicoat & Crozet, 2001); cross-cultural mediation tasks (Kordes, 1991; Meyer, 1991) and discourse completion tasks, which assess control of pragmatic norms and the accuracy of learners' understanding of native speakers' language use and the accuracy of their pragmatic choices (Kasper & Dahl, 1991). These enactment tasks elicit performance but it is often difficult to judge on the basis of such tasks whether or not the performance is in fact intercultural. If the task assesses conformity to a set of cultural norms of another group, this would show very little about the knowledge and dispositions that contribute to the performance. More critically, if conformity to native-speaker norms is rated highly, then the focus of the task is assimilation to a set of cultural norms, not the development of an intercultural stance.

The intercultural in communication is not a simple equation of performance with intercultural competence, but rather a reflective recognition of what is at play in a particular instance of communication (Liddicoat & Scarino, 2010). The surface manifestation of language use is not the only crucial dimension in assessment; the developing critical awareness that the learner brings to interaction as a language user is also central. The elicited behaviour is then not only the target language behaviour per se, but rather it includes an indication of the language user's critical awareness as participant and analyser of communication, with the potential to learn from and adjust to the intercultural realities that exist in communication.

A second tradition in assessing the intercultural is the elicitation of the learners' intercultural dispositions or understandings. Paige, Jorstad, Siaya, Klein and Colby (1999) examine three different types of such models as potential approaches for the assessment of intercultural skills: attitudinal tests; culture assimilator tests; and cultural awareness tests.

Attitudinal tests are designed to elicit people's reactions to a cultural group (e.g. Cadd, 1994). These tests are problematic for assessing intercultural understanding because they use binary oppositions, which run the risk of establishing stereotypes. More importantly for assessing language learning, they fail to engage with cultural variability, complexity, cultural knowledge or communicative and linguistic abilities, and as such are poor indicators of the ability to use a language in an intercultural context.

Culture assimilator tests (e.g. Brislin, Cushner, Cherrie & Yong, 1986) differ from attitudinal tests because they include in the eliciting contextual information in the form of short episodes of intercultural interaction or critical incidents of communication to which the respondent reacts. Such tests elicit the respondents' knowledge of cultural conventions, and their ability to interpret a situation from a different cultural perspective. However, they do not examine the productive use of this knowledge in communication, or their ability to modify their own patterns of cultural behaviour in order to achieve communicative goals.

Cultural awareness tests seek to elicit cultural knowledge as it is manifested in communicative tasks. What differs in these tests is the types of cultural knowledge being assessed. These can range from observation of controlled instances of specific cultural items (e.g. Baugh, 1994) to demonstrations of intangible learning such as empathy, and understanding of cultural relativity (e.g. Byram & Morgan, 1994). Cultural awareness tests cover a range of different approaches to questions of language and culture, moving from tests of integrated language and cultural knowledge to displays of meta-level cultural awareness, often with minimal connection to language.

What emerges from this survey of approaches to assessing the intercultural is that there is a great deal of complexity in the construct that is being assessed. In particular, the simultaneous positioning of learner as both performer and analyser in intercultural situations is very difficult to capture with any particular assessment approach. The types of tests discussed above tend to assess analysis (or awareness) of culture, but do not clearly connect to performance. Assessment tasks such as role-plays or discourse completion tasks evaluate performance but not the basis of the performance. This means that it is difficult to determine in what ways and to what extent the performance reflects interculturality. For example, the ability to produce native-like language behaviours does not necessarily demonstrate an underlying understanding of what constitutes such behaviour or an ability to interpret the meaning of such behaviours in context. It may only reflect accurate reproduction of a model. Similarly, behaviour that is not native-like may reflect a solid understanding of the meaning of a behaviour, but a reluctance to adopt practices that conflict with the performers sense of self.

Liddicoat and Scarino (2010) argue for a number of key considerations in assessment design for intercultural language teaching and learning:

- The elicitation procedure or task needs to involve interaction in the target language with other users of that language, which requires that learners decentre from their own language and culture.
- The task elicits learners' awareness of the language–culture nexus in such interactions and requires that for the purposes of assessment learners are able to analyse, explain and elaborate this awareness.
- The elicitation procedure positions the learner as both participant and analyser in interaction, though in any individual elicitation task one or the other role may be foregrounded, depending on purpose.
- Assessment procedures need to elicit learners' understanding of different perspectives in the interaction, as an ethical concern.
- The assessment process should not be episodic but consist of a connected scheme of a range of elicitation procedures be used to capture (1) the diverse and multi-dimensional nature of intercultural interaction and related awareness, and (2) the recognition of the need to manage the variability of context, given that each episode of intercultural interaction presents a new set of contextual considerations to be negotiated in communication.
- Elicitation procedures are considered within a long-term perspective that allows development and progress to be taken into account, for example, through the use of portfolios.
- The assessment includes self-assessment procedures that recognise learning as a personal process and a personally unique accomplishment.

It is unlikely that any single task can capture this diversity and that the sorts of tasks used to assess intercultural capabilities inevitably privilege one of the roles of performer or analyser. The assessment challenge then is to construct assessment schemes in which both roles are present and connected. Assessment of the intercultural, at least in languages education, needs to be based on demonstrations of both intercultural communication and the insights and dispositions towards diversity, with an orientation to assessing the individual's learning over time (Liddicoat & Scarino, 2010). What is needed is a combination of communicative and reflective tasks in the form of a portfolio collected over time. While the idea of a portfolio of tasks for assessing intercultural competence is not new, the ways in which portfolios are understood in language assessment vary. The arguments made so far indicate that a portfolio is not simply a collection of individual episodes, which may or may not have internal coherence and connectivity. In engaging and bringing into relation the roles of performer and analyser a portfolio would add to the collection of tasks commentaries on the tasks themselves in which the learner engages with and reflects on the task as an instance of intercultural experience. The reflective dimension of the portfolio is therefore central as it provides evidence of such on-going self-evaluation of perceptions of learners own progress towards an intercultural stance through the process of language learning. The aim of the reflection is to encourage the development of insight into oneself as an intercultural actor and ideally should be accompanied by a culminating commentary in which individual learners reflect on their own journey towards interculturality as an on-going and unfinished project.

The discussion here indicates that while some attention has been given to assessment within intercultural language teaching and learning, work on assessment remains currently an under-developed area. In part, this under-development derives from the complexity of the construct that needs to be assessed; however, there is a broader problem that needs to be addressed in assessment. The intercultural does not seem to be easily captured by the psychometric testing procedures that have predominated in language education. These procedures are not well adapted to the personalised and developmental nature of the intercultural or to the diversity of roles and positioning that constitute intercultural performance.

Conclusion

This overview of intercultural language teaching and learning has identified some key themes in work in this area in recent years. What emerges from the discussion is that there has been considerable developmental work that has attempted to address some of the difficulties indentified by Zarate (1986). Particular attention has been given to theorising the intercultural for language learning and this has led to a greater engagement with learning theory—explicitly or implicitly—as a result of emerging understandings of the role and nature of language learning. Much attention has also been given to pedagogy. There are at the same time some areas that remain under-developed and where further work is urgently needed. This is particularly the case in assessment, which remains the least developed area of pedagogical practice. The lack here is not simply a problem of developing assessment processes but relates also to problems of articulating the construct in a way that facilitates assessment and understanding the processes of development that would allow progress in intercultural learning to be identified and articulated. These issues have often had to be resolved at the local level for individual teachers teaching in an interculturally oriented way, but have not yet emerged as major research directions in the field. In returning to Zarate's (1986) observations, it seems that much attention has been given to aspects of what needs to be taught and how and, at a theoretical level, there is now a considerable body of work dealing with these issues. There is however a need to further investigate both the what and the how of intercultural language teaching and learning at the interface with practice.

Note

1. This chapter will hereafter use the form "intercultural language teaching and learning" without capitalisation to suggest a less formalised understanding of the nature of the field.

References

Bateman, B. E. (2002). Promoting openness toward culture learning: Ethnographic interviews for students of Spanish. *Modern Language Journal, 86*(3), 318–331.

Baugh, I. W. (1994). Hypermedia as performance-based assessment tool. *The Computing Teacher, 22,* 14–17.

Beacco, J.-C. (2000). *Les dimensions culturelles des enseignements de langue.* Hachette: Paris.

Belz, J. A. (2003). Linguistic perspectives on the development of intercultural competence in telecollaboration. *Language Learning and Technology, 7*(2), 68–99.

Belz, J. A., & Kinginger, C. (2002). Cross-linguistic development of address form use in telecollaborative language learning: Two case studies. *Revue Canadienne des Langues Vivantes, 59*(2), 189–214.

Bennett, J. M., Bennett, M. J., & Allen, W. (1999). Developing intercultural competence in the language classroom. In R. M. Paige, D. L. Lange & Y. A. Yershova (Eds.), *Culture as the core: Integrating culture into the language curriculum* (pp. 13–46). Minneapolis: CARLA, University of Minnesota.

Bolten, J. (1993). Interaktiv-interkulturelles Fremdsprach-lernen. In H. P. Kelz (Ed.), *Internationale Kommunikation und Sprachkomptenz* (pp. 99–139). Bonn: Dümmler.

Brislin, R., Cushner, K., Cherrie, C. & Yong, M. (1986). *Intercultural interactions: A practical guide.* New York: Sage

Buttjes, D., & Byram, M. (Eds.) (1991). *Mediating languages and cultures: Towards an intercultural theory of foreign language education.* Clevedon: Multingual Matters.

Byram, M. (1988). Foreign language education and cultural studies. *Language, Culture and Curriculum, 1*(1), 15–31.

Byram, M. (1989a). *Cultural studies in foreign language education.* Clevedon: Multilingual Matters.

Byram, M. (1989b). A school visit to France: Ethnographic explorations. *British Journal of Language Teaching, 27*(2), 99–103.

Byram, M. (1997). *Teaching and assessing intercultural communicative competence.* Clevedon: Multilingual Matters.

Byram, M., & Feng, A. (2005). Teaching and researching intercultural competence. In E. Hinkel (Ed.), *Handbook of research in second language teaching and learning* (pp. 911–930). Mahwah, NJ: Lawrence Erlbaum.

Byram, M., Gribkova, B. & Starkey, H. (2002). *Developing the intercultural dimension in language teaching. A practical introduction for teachers.* Strasbourg: Council of Europe.

Byram, M., & Morgan, C. (1994). *Teaching and learning language and culture.* Clevedon: Multilingual Matters

Byram, M., & Zarate, G. (1994). *Définitions, objectifs et évaluation de la compétence socio-culturelle.* Strasbourg: Report for the Council of Europe.

Cadd, M. (1994). An attempt to reduce ethnocentrism in the foreign language classroom. *Foreign Language Annals, 27*(2), 143–160.

Carel, S. (2001). Students as virtual ethnographers: Exploring the language culture connections. In M. Byram, A. Nichols & D. Stevens (Eds.), *Developing intercultural competence in practice* (pp. 146–161). Clevedon: Multilingual Matters.

Carroli, P., Hillman, R. & Maurer, L. (1999). Australian perspectives on (inter)national narratives. In J. Lo Bianco, A. J. Liddicoat & C. Crozet (Eds.), *Striving for the third place intercultural competence through language education* (pp. 155–166). Canberra: Language Australia.

Carroli, P., Hillman, R. & Maurer, L. (2000). Teaching literature across cultures and across artforms. In A. J. Liddicoat & C. Crozet (Eds.), *Teaching languages, teaching cultures* (pp. 89–104). Melbourne: Language Australia.

Cochran-Smith, M., & Little, S. (1999). Relationships of knowledge and practice: Teacher learning in communities. *Review of Research in Education, 24,* 249–306.

Coleman, J. A. (1997). Residence abroad within language study. *Language Teaching, 30*(1), 1–20.

Coleman, J. A. (1998). Language learning and study abroad: The European perspective. *Frontiers: The Interdisciplinary Journal of Study Abroad, 4*(1), 167–205.

Corbett, J. (2003). *An intercultural approach to english language teaching.* Clevedon: Multilingual Matters.

Crozet, C. (1996). Teaching verbal interaction and culture in the language classroom. *Australian Review of Applied Linguistics, 19*(2), 37–58.

Crozet, C. (1998). Teaching verbal interaction and culture. Unpublished Master of Arts thesis, Australian National University, Canberra.

Crozet, C., & Liddicoat, A. J. (1999). The challenge of intercultural language teaching: Engaging with culture in the classroom. In J. Lo Bianco, A. J. Liddicoat & C. Crozet (Eds.), *Striving for the third place: Intercultural Competence through language education* (pp. 113–126). Canberra: Language Australia.

Crozet, C., & Liddicoat, A. J. (2000). Teaching culture as an integrated part of language: Implications for the aims, approaches and pedagogies of language teaching. In A. J. Liddicoat & C. Crozet (Eds.), *Teaching languages, teaching cultures* (pp. 1–18). Melbourne: Language Australia.

Damen, L. (1987). *Culture learning: The fifth dimension in the language classroom.* Reading, MA: Addison-Wesley.

Dewaele, J.-M. (2002). Variation, chaos et système en interlangue française. *Acquisition et Interaction en Langue Étrangère, 17,* 143–167.

Dewaele, J.-M., & Planchenault, G. (2006). «Dites-moi *tu»* ? La perception de la difficulté du système des pronoms d'adresse en français. In M. Faraco (Ed.), *Regards croisés sur la classe de langue: Pratiques, méthodes et théories* (pp. 153–171). Aix-en-Provence: Publications de l'Université de Provence.

Furstenberg, G., Levet, S., English, K. & Maillet, K. (2001). Giving a virtual voice to the silent language of culture: The Culura project. *Language Learning and Technology, 5*(1), 55–102.

Hudson, T., Detmer, E. & Brown, J. D. (1992). *A framework for testing cross-cultural pragmatics.* Honolulu: University of Hawai'i Press

Kasper, G., & Dahl, M. (1991). *Research methods in interlanguage pragmatics.* Honolulu: University of Hawai'i Press

Kawakami, I. (2001). 新しい文化を創る言語教育. 国際文化フォーラム通信 (Language teaching that creates a "new culture"), *Communications of the International Cultural Forum, 52*(4–5).

Kawakami, I. (2005). "Children crossing borders" and their language education. Electronic version. *Perspectives on Language, Culture, and Society.* Retrieved 28 May, 2009 from http://www.gsjal.jp/kawakami/dat/litera_en.pdf.

Kern, R., & Liddicoat, A. J. (2008). De l'apprenant au locuteur/acteur. In C. Kramsch, D. Lévy & G. Zarate (Eds.), *Précis de plurilinguisme et du pluriculturalisme* (pp. 27–65). Paris: Éditions des archives contemporaines.

Knutson, E. M. (2006). Cross-cultural awareness for second/foreign language learners. *Canadian Modern Language Review*, 62(4), 591–610.

Kohonen, V. (2000). Student reflection in portfolio assessment: making language learning more visible. *Babylonia*, 1(13–16).

Kordes, H. (1991). Intercultural learning at school: Limits and possibilities. In D. Buttjes & M. Byram (Eds.), *Mediating languages and cultures: Towards an intercultural theory of foreign language education* (pp. 17–30). Clevedon: Multilingual Matters.

Kramsch, C. (1993). *Context and culture in language education*. Oxford: Oxford University Press.

Kramsch, C. (1995a). The cultural component of language teaching. *Language, Culture and Curriculum*, 8, 83–92.

Kramsch, C. (1995b). Introduction: Making meaning visible. In C. Kramsch (Ed.), *Redefining the boundaries of language study* (pp. ix–xxxiii). Boston: Heinle and Heinle.

Kramsch, C. (1999). Teaching along the cultural faultline. In R. M. Paige, D. L. Lange & Y. A. Yershova (Eds.), *Culture as the core: Interdisciplinary perspectives on culture teaching and learning in the second language curriculum* (pp. 15–32). Minneapolis: CARLA, University of Minnesota.

Kramsch, C. (2003). From practice to theory and back again. In M. Byram & P. Grundy (Eds.), *Context and culture in language teaching and learning* (pp. 4–17). Clevedon: Multilingual Matters.

Kramsch, C., & Nolden, T. (1994). Redefining literacy in a foreign language. *Die Unterrichtspraxis*, 27(1), 28–35.

Kumaravadivelu, B. (2006). *Understanding language teaching: From method to postmethod*. Mahwah, NJ: Lawrence Erlbaum.

Liddicoat, A. J. (1997). Everyday speech as culture: Implications for language teaching. In A. J. Liddicoat & C. Crozet (Eds.), *Teaching language, teaching culture* (pp. 55–70). Canberra: Applied Linguistics Association of Australia.

Liddicoat, A. J. (2002). Static and dynamic views of culture and intercultural language acquisition. *Babel*, 36(3), 4–11, 37.

Liddicoat, A. J. (2005). Culture for language learning in Australian language-in-education policy. *Australian Review of Applied Linguistics*, 28(2), 1–28.

Liddicoat, A. J. (2006). Learning the culture of interpersonal relationships: Students' understandings of person reference in French. *Intercultural Pragmatics*, 6(1), 55–80.

Liddicoat, A. J. (2008). Pedagogical practice for integrating the intercultural in language teaching and learning. *Japanese Studies*, 28(3), 277–290.

Liddicoat, A. J., & Crozet, C. (2001). Acquiring French interactional norms through instruction. In K. R. Rose & G. Kasper (Eds.), *Pragmatic development in instructional contexts* (pp. 125–144). Cambridge: Cambridge University Press.

Liddicoat, A. J., Crozet, C. & Lo Bianco, J. (1999). Striving for the third place: Consequences and implications. In J. Lo Bianco, A. J. Liddicoat & C. Crozet (Eds.), *Striving for the third place intercultural competence through language education* (pp. 1–20). Canberra: Language Australia.

Liddicoat, A. J., Papademetre, L., Scarino, A. & Kohler, M. (2003). *Report on intercultural language learning*. Canberra: DEST

Liddicoat, A. J., & Scarino, A. (2010). Eliciting the intercultural in foreign language education at school. In A. Paran & L. Sercu (Eds.), *Testing the untestable in language education* (pp. 52–74). London: Routledge.

McConachy, T. (2008). Teaching for intercultural awareness through a focus on conversational routines. *International Journal of Language, Society and Culture*, 24, 43–49.

Meyer, M. (1991). Developing transcultural competence: Case studies in advanced language learners. In D. Buttjes & M. Byram (Eds.), *Mediating languages and cultures: Towards an intercultural theory of foreign language education* (pp. 136–158). Clevedon: Multilingual Matters.

Paige, R. M., Jorstad, H., Siaya, L., Klein, F. & Colby, J. (1999). Culture learning in language education: A review of the literature. In R. M. Paige, D. L. Lange & Y. A. Yeshova (Eds.), *Culture as the core: Integrating culture into the language curriculum* (pp. 47–113). Minneapolis: University of Minnesota.

Papademetre, L. (2000). Developing pathways for conceptualising the integration of culture-and-language. In A. J. Liddicoat & C. Crozet (Eds.), *Teaching languages, teaching cultures* (pp. 141–149). Melbourne: Language Australia.

Roberts, C., Byram, M., Barro, A., Jordan, S. & Street, B. (2001). *Language learners as ethnographers*. Clevedon: Multilingual Matters.

Robinson-Stuart, G., & Nocon, H. (1996). Second culture acquisition: Ethnography in the foreign language classroom. *Modern Language Journal*, 80(4), 431–449.

Scarino, A., & Liddicoat, A. J. (2009). *Language teaching and learning: A guide*. Melbourne: Curriculum Corporation.

Schmidt, G., & Jansen, L. M. (2004). Enhancing overseas study. In A. J. Liddicoat, S. Eisenchlas & S. Trevaskes (Eds.), *Australian Perspectives on internationalising education* (pp. 129–139). Melbourne: Language Australia.

Schmidt, R. (1993). Consciousness, learning and interlanguage pragmatics. In G. Kasper & S. Blum-Kulka (Eds.), *Interlanguage pragmatics* (pp. 21–42). New York: Oxford University Press.

Sercu, L. (2004). Researching the acquisition of intercultural communicative competence in a foreign language: Setting the agenda for a research area. In O. St John, K. van Esch & E. Shalkwijk (Eds.), *New insights in foreign language teaching and learning* (pp. 131–156). Frankfurt: Peter Lang.

Sobolewski, P. (2009). Use of ethnographic interviews as a resource for developing intercultural understanding. *Babel, 43*(2), 28–33.

Zarate, G. (1983). Objectiver le rapport culture maternelle/culture étrangère. *Le français dans le monde, 181,* 34–39.

Zarate, G. (1986). *Enseigner une culture étrangère.* Paris: Hachette.

Zarate, G., Gohard-Radenkovic, A., Lussier, D. & Penz, H. (2004). *Médiation didactique et didactique des langues.* Kapfenberg: Council of Europe Publishing.

51

Critical Literacy and Second Language Learning

Allan Luke and Karen Dooley

Introduction

Critical literacy is the use of texts to analyse and transform relations of cultural, social and political power. It is part of a longstanding normative educational project to address social, economic and cultural injustice and inequality. It aims towards the equitable development and acquisition of language and literacy by historically marginalized communities and students, and towards the use of texts in a range of communications media to analyse, critique, represent and alter inequitable knowledge structures and social relations of school and society. Educators in the field for teaching English to speakers of other languages (TESOL) have adopted, used and developed different versions of critical literacy since the 1980s, leading to an array of pedagogic approaches. They derive a common principle from Paulo Freire (1972): that language teaching and learning is an act of political and cultural power with substantive material and social consequences and possibilities for learners and their communities. The normative premise of this work is that the *telos* of literacy as a human capacity is a will towards freedom, equality and emancipation.

The term "literacy" traditionally refers to mastery of capabilities in reading and writing print text. With the rapid expansion of new modes of information technology, definitions of literacy have pluralized, expanding to include engagement with a range of semiotic forms. Visual, aural and digital multimodal texts are now integral to language education, and to literacy education more generally. The cultural, linguistic and educational implications of digitalization are the focus of current research on cultural identity (e.g. Lam, 2004; Harklau, 2003) and on patterns of differential access and stratified educational outcomes along the fault lines of linguistic and cultural difference and social class (e.g. Warschauer & Matuchniak, 2010).

Critical literacy approaches view texts—print and multimodal, paper-based and digital—and their codes and discourses as human technologies for representing and reshaping possible worlds. Texts are not taken as part of a canonical curriculum tradition or received wisdom that is beyond criticism. Rather they are conceived of as malleable human designs and artefacts used in social fields. In this regard, critical approaches begin by culturally and historically situating languages and discourses, texts, their authors and readers—bracketing and disrupting their "natural", given or taken-for-granted authoritative status in institutional and everyday contexts. Texts, then, operate in identifiable social, cultural and political contexts. The aim is to develop learners capable of critiquing and making texts in their cultural and community interests. This involves an understanding of how texts and discourses can be constructed, deconstructed and reconstructed to represent, contest and, indeed, transform material, social and semiotic relations.

In TESOL, critical approaches have been informed by sociological, ethnographic and applied linguistics research on language policy and education for second language learners. This includes ongoing work on the international spread of English, research on the social and political implications of language education and on educational equity for linguistic and cultural minorities (Pennycook, 1999; Kubota & Lin, 2009). These foci mark a shift from the longstanding search for foundational cognitive and psycholinguistic theories of language acquisition and use, and a turn to a sociological, sociocultural and critical linguistic analysis of how language and texts figure in social power and inequality, agency and identity. Critical approaches to TESOL, then, are premised on upon contemporary analyses of linguistic and textual practice in state, media, corporation, school, religion, family and other institutions.

Current shifts in geopolitical power and the global economic crisis are reshaping the development and spread of English as both instrument and commodity, as a form of capital and as a complex sociolinguistic field in globalized cultural and economic exchange (Luke, 2004). Further, new international flows of workers and students, migrants and refugees to English-speaking Western societies are creating complex new demographic and cultural conditions for linguistic and socioeconomic inclusion and marginalization.

Here we ask: what counts as critical TESOL in *these* new complex, contradictory conditions of cultural and economic globalization? In what follows, we review research on language planning and ideologies and the educational status of linguistic and cultural minorities. These set the generative conditions and analytic grounds for two major approaches to critical TESOL: critical pedagogy and critical text analysis.

Language Policy and Ideologies

Freedom to use one's own language in everyday institutional, civic and cultural life is an inalienable human right (Hymes, 1995). Yet in its postwar genesis, the field of language planning was based on a technocratic approach to policy that treated language as a scientific, technical and ideologically neutral phenomenon (Luke, McHoul & Mey, 1990). The expansion of linguistic and literate competence in a dominant lingua franca was defined in terms of the causal development of human capital, the expansion of scientific/technical capacity, and social and economic advancement (Kaplan & Baldauf, 2003). Technocratic models of language policy did not adequately address complex local histories of colonialism and issues of neo-colonial economic and social conflict (Lin & Martin, 2005). Language ideologies are social class, locational and ethnocentric beliefs about the value and power of specific languages, deployed and shaped in everyday language use (Kumaravadivelu, 2006). While they may begin from scientific analyses of linguistic corpus and status, language policies are bids to reconcile and, in some instances, to suture ideological contestation between different social classes, cultural and linguistic communities (Tollefson, 2002a, 2002b). Hegemonic language policies set the conditions for "linguicism" (Skutnabb-Kangas, 2000), exclusionary discrimination on the basis of language in access to power and resources. Where the imposition of English (or other dominant languages) as a medium of instruction is tied to monolingual ideologies and policies, schooling can be a major contributor to first language, vernacular and regional minority language loss.

By this account, the international spread of English via Western curriculum and language teaching methods is a form of "linguistic imperialism" (Phillipson, 1992), generating inequality and benefiting core at the expense of peripheral communities and nations. Within culturally, racially and linguistically diverse English-speaking countries similar processes of "linguistic domination" (Lippi-Green, 1997) occur. "Audible difference" (Miller, 2003) is constructed in education and other social institutions through rejection of non-standard English dialects and "accents", and reluctance of first language speakers to shoulder responsibility for communicating effectively in interactions with language learners (Alim, 2009; Dooley, 2009b). Indeed, increased and diversified migration to English-speaking countries in recent decades has led to a reassertion of monolingualism in education. There is a renewed emphasis on standard English in UK education (Tollefson, 2002b), continued Official English and anti-bilingual activism in the US (Dicker, 2000; Tollefson, 2002b; Wiley, 2002; Alim, 2009) and a resurgence of English-only policies for Native North Americans, Aborigines and Torres Strait Islanders (Brayboy & Castagno, 2009). These are bids to establish a bias towards the mainstream standard of fluency with dominant lingua franca, dialect and accent.

Critics of exclusionary language policies have called for educational and civic policies promoting multilingualism, translation and exchange, while increasing non-elite access to English, languages, discourses and registers affiliated with mainstream social and economic power (Phillipson, 2003; Joseph & Ramani, 1998). Phillipson (2003) also argues that it would also include government regulation of market forces that favour English. Critical approaches to TESOL, then, are by definition responses to conflict over language ideology—with blended focus on issues of access to dominant languages, texts and discourses, on the recognition of students' voices and identities, first and vernacular language rights, and on the development of a critical stance towards linguistic and cultural hegemony in all of its historically pernicious forms.

Educational Equality for Linguistic and Cultural Minorities

A second driving force for critical approaches to TESOL has been inequitable schooling for migrants, refugees and other linguistic minorities. The underperformance of cultural and linguistic minority students is well documented in international comparative analyses (e.g. Organisation for Economic Co-operation and Development (OECD, 2000). TESOL developed as a field in the context of postwar immigration to the US, UK, Canada and other English-speaking countries. Its historical aims and functions have been ambiguous. It has contributed to the assimilation of minority speakers into mainstream cultures and economies. At the same time, it has been defined as a key educational strategy for equality of educational opportunity, access and participation for linguistic and cultural minorities.

Sociological analyses of educational inequality have focused on how schools and other institutions engage in the intergenerational social, cultural and economic reproduction of class and cultural status (Bourdieu & Passeron, 1990). Second language learners' "cultural capital" of linguistic and cultural resources can act as a disadvantage in mainstream lingua franca education. Structural discrimination in schools works through mechanisms such as streaming and tracking, labelling and self-fulfilling prophecies, linguistically and culturally-biased assessment (Wong, 2004) and homework assignments that assume access to material, discourse and social resources of mainstream and middle-class homes (Dooley, 2009a). When English as a second language (ESL) students do have access to intellectually substantive and critical education, issues can arise as to whether or not mainstream pedagogy is adequate to high-level attainment on the part of language learners (Dooley, 2009c). This set of challenges raises key questions about the definition and resourcing of TESOL in schools—whether it is viewed as a form of remediation for students who are construed as deficit (Toohey, 2000), and whether, where and how TESOL articulates into mainstream curriculum and instruction.

At the classroom level, a key mechanism of linguistic discrimination is the "misrecognition" (Bourdieu & Passeron, 1990) of students' linguistic competence and cultural resources (Orellana, Reynolds, Dorner & Meza, 2003). Working with Puerto Rican families, Compton-Lilly (2007) showed that children enjoyed abundant pro-school social capital with family adults including mothers, grandmothers, sisters and aunts. Teachers, however, did not recognize or value the cultural or linguistic capital that students brought to school. Stanton-Salazar, Dornbusch and Sanford (1995) describe a similar pattern of social distance and distrust between the students and institutional agents such as teachers, counsellors and high-status peers lead to a misrecognition of students' cultural, social and linguistic resources (cf. Valenzuela, 1999, 2008). Ethnographic and classroom discourse research in Hong Kong has shown that the attitudes and interests, linguistic skills and confidence that privileged students brought to English lessons in a Hong Kong school advantaged them over Cantonese-dominant working-class students. For these students, English lessons reproduced and reinforced the students' cultural capital, subjective anticipation and objective chances of success whereas for their less advantaged peers, English lessons created dilemmas of interest and understanding (Lin, 1999). A similar dynamic is evident in the high school experience of African students who arrived in Australia as refugees with little, no or severely interrupted schooling (Dooley, 2009b).

Yet even where mainstream schooling and English language teaching leads to inequitable educational outcomes for linguistic minorities—the actual imposition of English generates the conditions for what Erickson, Bargrodia, Cook-Sather, Espinoza & Jurrow et al. (2008) has termed a "paperthin hegemony". Canagarajah's (1993) ethnography of learning and teaching in a Sri Lankan classroom focuses on the complex classroom dynamics of cultural/linguistic power. Identities are "multiple, conflictual, negotiated, and evolving" involving the dynamics of resistance and contestation. These studies, and research on African American students learning academic English as a second dialect, Latino and Asian second language learners, suggest that resistance and hybrid identities can sometimes be found in "third spaces" in and outside the classroom—for example, in use of first language for peer relations (Goldstein, 2003), codeswitching, private asides, vernacular emails, and graffiti in textbooks (e.g. Gutiérrez, Baquedano-Lopez & Tejada, 1999; Rex, 2006).

Ethnographies of youth culture have documented how youth and adolescents play with diverse languages and language varieties in multiracial, multiracial and transcultural contexts (Alim, 2009). Outside of classrooms, youth appropriate and use English in often unpredictable, idiosyncratic ways to build identity, affiliation and cultural practice (Canagarajah, 1999; Pennycook, 2001; Pennycook & Mitchell, 2009). In spite of attempts by schools and other institutions to normalize language use, this leads to linguistic creolization, new uses of local vernaculars and the exploration of emergent genres and blended modalities of expression (Lam, 2004; Hull, Zacher & Hibbert, 2009). The emergence of a transnational, but highly localized hip hop culture documents the complex practices of blending and invention, fashioned around a non-standard countercultural dialect of English. Both in schools and broader community life, TESOL students develop resources and identities outside of the formal curriculum, with potential applications for critical literacy and language teaching.

Mainstream schooling, then, creates a site for contestation over language and cultural resources with tensions between mainstream second language and first language, institutional structure and learner agency, between linguistic/cultural reproduction and student resistance. In English-dominated educational systems, TESOL remains a key curriculum strategy for ameliorating educational disadvantage. Yet the evidence suggests that mainstream schools and classrooms continue to undervalue and misrecognize first language competence and cultural difference as deficit. At the same time, studies of linguistic and cultural minority learners also document the emergence of student and teacher agency, characterized by emergent forms of identity and blended expression (Kubota & Lin, 2009). Critical approaches to TESOL attempt to shift the balance of conventional TESOL, focusing on the enfranchisement of the lifeworlds and voices of students' communities and cultures and a direct engagement with codes and texts of power.

Critical Pedagogy Approaches

Paulo Freire's seminal work on critical education has been extended to the educational project of "critical pedagogy" (Lankshear & McLaren, 1993; Darder, 1991). Freire's work draws from Marx a classical view of ideology: that ruling-class ideology dominates what counts as school knowledge and ideology. By this view, approaches to literacy are expressions of dominant ideology, and succeed in creating a literacy that is principally receptive, involved in the passive transmission, decoding and reproduction of dominant and distorted views of the world. The alternative is to begin from learners' key problems, world views and "namings" of the phenomenal world, in effect turning them into teachers and inventors of the curriculum. This entails an agentive "renaming" of the world, a decoding and recoding of meaning. The focus is on ideology critique: exposing, second guessing and reconstructing dominant versions of the world provided in literature, textbooks and everyday texts and utterance. By degrees, this orientation runs through all approaches to critical literacy, but it features most strongly in explicitly political approaches to "critical pedagogy" (McLaren & Lankshear, 1994).

The explicit focus on critical analysis and normative transformation of dominant ideologies and material conditions is central to literacy campaigns initiated by Freire and colleagues in Brazil and Mozambique (e.g. Freire & Macedo, 1987) and it is the focus of current efforts at an explicitly political pedagogy in countries such as Venezuela, Brazil, Mexico, South Africa and elsewhere (e.g. Jennings & Da Matta, 2009). There the analysis of the effects of colonialism, imperialism, class division, multi-national corporatism and unequal economic relations is a principal theme of literacy instruction. In Freirian terms, this entails working with learners to use language to name and "problematicize" the world; that is, to take everyday ideological constructions of social relations, of class, race, gender relations, and to make them problematic through dialogue. In such a setting traditional authority and epistemic knowledge relations of teachers and student are shifted. Learners become teachers of their everyday understandings and experiences, and teachers becoming learners of these same contexts. In school classrooms, dialogic pedagogy might entail establishing student voice and democratic conditions for authentic exchange around issues of moral, social and cultural significance (Edelsky, 1992). In culturally diverse communities, dialogue might also be used as an approach to community–school relations, enabling immigrant parents and mainstream teachers to negotiate conflicting pedagogic beliefs, and teachers to reflect on their ideological stance and position of dominance in home–school relationships (Li, 2006). In adult migrant education, the approach encourages adults to investigate their own literacy practices, analyse how their capabilities and sense of possibilities have been shaped and constrained by cultural and linguistic ideologies, and decide on their own purposes in language and literacy studies (Auerbach, 2002; Boudin, 2002).

Practical critical approaches to TESOL advocated for English language learners in US schools and universities start from a focus on community relations or political events, moving towards agentive, alternative analyses (e.g. Vasquez, 2004; Hones, 1999). In schools and universities, these approaches also focus student reading and writing on community study, the analysis of social movements, and political activism (e.g. Kumishiro & Ngo, 2007). For high school-aged ESL students, skills development for activism might include training in public speaking and translation for public meetings, student journalism and participation in student government and clubs. Elementary ESL students might be involved in projects with investigative, advocacy and community service components on environmental and other local issues (Wong, 2004; Chang, 2009; Vasquez, 2004). These approaches have also extended to include a focus on critical "media literacy", the analysis of popular cultural texts including advertising, news, broadcast media and the internet. TESOL teacher education programmes have developed to engage teachers as community activists (Major & Celedon-Pattichis, 2001). Recently, similar principles have been proposed for promoting activism about local issues through English language studies in non-English-speaking countries (Akbari, 2008).

In the 1990s, feminist scholars argued that critical pedagogy did not adequately consider issues of epistemic and gendered standpoint. In everyday practice, there is a parallel risk of pedagogic imposition given the complex forms of gendered and raced voice and power, identity and subjectivity at work in the interactional contexts of classrooms and cultural circles (Luke & Gore, 1992). This analysis has been extended to the relations of gender and culture between critical pedagogy theorists, and TESOL academics and their students in East Asia—most of whom are female and second language speakers (Lin, 1999). These critiques have had a major impact on critical pedagogy. In Australia and Canada, approaches to school reading entail a critique of textual, visual and media representations of women and girls as ideological and patriarchal, that is, as projecting dominant constructions of gender and sexuality and inequitable patterns of face-to-face interaction (Ellsworth, 1992).

A parallel development drawing upon postcolonial and critical race theory has been a renewed stress on issues of "voice" in the classroom, an orientation towards recognitive justice and the representation of cultures, histories and identities (Moje & Luke, 2009). American approaches to critical literacy have developed a strong focus on the "politics of voice" (Kumishiro & Ngo, 2007; Nieto, Bode, Kang & Raible, 2008), on building interaction and textual focus around the distinctive cultural histories, identities and contexts faced by groups marginalized on the basis of difference of gender, language, culture and race, and sexual orientation. The aim is to give voice to ESL students who have been historically silenced, and to encourage the formation of new social identities, and the expression of alternative epistemologies (Wong, 2004; Norton & Toohey, 2004). The assumption is that these can be translated into forms of self-determination, agency and social movement (e.g. Darder, 2002).

Text Analytic Approaches

Research on the social contexts and practices of literacy demonstrates the cultural and social, cognitive and linguistic complexity in the development and acquisition of literacy (e.g. Pahl & Rowsell, 2005). This raises two substantive educational challenges for critical pedagogy. First, it is largely synchronic, without a broader template for developmental acquisition and use. Second, it lacks specificity in terms of how teachers and students can engage with the specialized and complex structures of texts. These are crucial issues in the development of critical approaches to TESOL. The acquisition of language, text and discourse requires the developmental engagement with levels of linguistic and discourse complexity (e.g. Lemke, 1995). Later models of critical literacy, particularly those developed in Australia and the UK, attempt to come to grips with these key theoretical and practical issues (Muspratt, Luke & Freebody, 1997).

An initial major critique of critical pedagogy was that it overlooked the pressing need for students to master a range of textual genres, including those scientific forms that constitute powerful understandings of the physical and material world (Halliday & Martin, 1993). This position was part of a more general recognition of the social class and culture-specific effects of progressive and student-centred language and literacy pedagogies (Delpit, 1995; Bernstein, 1990). The focus of this work is on explicit access to dominant language and discourse structures.

The mastery of genre entails a grasp of the social functions of lexical and syntactic functions, and an understanding of the relationships of these with affiliated discourses and ideologies (Hasan & Williams, 1996). Equitable access to how texts work, an essential component to redistributive justice, cannot be achieved through an exclusive focus on "voice" or ideology critique. Genre approaches, then, argue for explicit instruction, direct access and conscious control over "Secret English" and "genres of power" (Halliday & Martin, 1993).

Genre models have had a significant impact on TESOL in Australia and the UK. The emphasis on scaffolded, explicit instruction in dominant texts has been augmented with a focus on "critical language awareness" (Fairclough, 1989). While it is assumed that as control of genres is a necessary basis for analysis and critique of text, the lead time for critical engagement on the part of ESL students is necessarily long (Hammond & Macken-Horarik, 1999). Further there remain unresolved issues about what balance of direct access to canonical and culturally significant text forms and critique might constitute an enfranchising and activist approach to critical literacy (Luke, 1996). This is of particular importance given concerns about the privileging of elitist Western forms of expression over non-standard, non-Western forms (Gadd, 1998).

The melding of explicit instruction in genre and principles of ideology critique has been a crucial move in the development of models of critical TESOL. The adoption of critical discourse analysis (CDA) (Fairclough & Wodak, 1997/2004) for pedagogic purposes has been a central move in the development of text analytic approaches. CDA is committed to social change through human agency in the use of language (Janks, 1999, 2009). It begins from systemic functional linguistics (Halliday, 1994), making broad distinctions between ideological formations in texts (field: representational function), their social functions (tenor: relational functions), and their distinctive generic and modal features (mode: textual functions). The principal is that lexico-grammatical choices are socially and culturally shaped and ideologically implicated in the wider social order (Wallace, 2003).

The aim is detailed textual analyses that denaturalize ideologies in texts, showing how they are related to relations of power that systematically advantage some groups over others (Janks, 1999). Pedagogically, the focus is on making the ideological work of language an object of conscious awareness, bringing together ideology critique with an explicit instructional focus on teaching how texts work ideologically (Fairclough, 1989). This entails teaching students the analysis of a range of texts—functional, academic, literary—attending to their lexico-grammatical structure, their ideological contents and discourses and their identifiable conditions of production and use. The framework of field, tenor and mode enables teachers and students to focus on what texts say, that is, how words, grammar and discourse choices shape a representation or "version" of the material, natural and sociopolitical worlds. It also enables a focus on what texts "do", that is, how words and grammar attempt to establish relations of power between authors and readers, speakers and addressees. Finally, it enables a critical engagement with social fields where texts are used, by whom, in whose interests.

Critical literacy—by this account—entails the developmental engagement by learners with the major texts, discourses and modes of information in the culture. It attends to the ideological and hegemonic functions of texts, as in critical pedagogy models. But it augments this by providing students with categories and procedures for analysing how texts work, and how they might be manipulated otherwize by authors and readers. For example, this might entail the analysis of a textbook or media representation of political or economic life.

Wallace (2002, 2003) has developed the critical text analytic approach for UK university-level academic English studies. The object of this application is access to "literate" or "powerful" English in preparation for participation in the widest possible community of users of English. Distinguishing everyday conversational language from literate language and knowledge, the approach bridges local texts and practices with regional, national and global discourses and practices. In the first phase, students acquire critical awareness of literacies through ethnographies in their British homestays. In the second phase they build critical interpretations of particular texts through detailed textual analysis. Finally, they apply what has been learnt to practices and relations of the wider social context.

In South Africa and Australia, Janks and Comber (2006) have developed critical text analytic curriculum for children, many second language and dialect speakers, living in contexts of extreme, spatialized poverty. South African and Australian classes produced and exchanged picture alphabet books to "tell about here to others who are there". The project sought to make new resources available to students that would teach them about agency and transformative power. Informed by a focus on the transformative design of discourse (Kress, 2003), the project moved from critical analysis of texts produced by others to student redesign of texts to best represent their worlds (cf. Millard, 2006).

Other critical approaches have linked explicit study of language with issues of social identity and power relations (cf. Norton, 2000; Toohey, 2000; Ibrahim, 1999). Working with Chinese migrant students Morgan (1997, 2004) focused on issues of subjectivity through phonological patterns and modality. The project looked at how intonation and modality constituted particular gendered and cultured selves in texts and how this connected with student experience. Alim (2009) describes critical hip hop language pedagogies that build student metalinguistic awareness of sociolinguistic variation, patterns in their own use of language varieties, lexical innovations in hip hop culture, and the unique words of Black language. Students conduct fieldwork to learn about linguistic profiling, that is, linguistic discrimination based on inferences about race, geographic origin, gender, class and sexuality made from speech. The aim in these and other programmes is to move beyond a celebration of personal experience to critical engagement with students' knowledge, to both valorize and interrogate student voice (Ibrahim, 2009).

Towards Critical Literacies

The educational project of critical literacy is focused on the goal of social justice for marginalized and disenfranchised communities, in emergent, postcolonial settings and in postmodern, urbanized societies. This involves twin goals of redistributive and recognitive social justice (Fraser, 1997): that is, a focus on (1) the more equitable achievement of conventionally defined language and literacy acquisition and use and on (2) shifts in the dominant ideological contents, social and economic fields and uses of literacy under study. There is, then, a dual orientation towards a more equitable distribution of textual and discourse resources among learners and towards the critique of ideology, culture, political systems and inequitable material conditions. This tension runs across the approaches to TESOL we have described here, balancing a commitment to shared and equitable access to how high-stakes texts and discourses work with the project of critically unpacking and transforming material conditions and social relations of political economy, institutional and everyday life.

Models of critical literacy have followed diverse theoretical lines of development (e.g. feminism, critical race theory, postmodern cultural studies, postcolonialism, critical linguistics) moving well beyond dialectical materialist foundations in critical pedagogy. These developments have been in response to new social movements, profound shifts in the cultural and linguistic demographies of nations, new conditions of capitalism and political economy, and the emergence of new technological modes of information. They also are evidence of several decades of practical work at bringing critical literacy into schools and classrooms. But, as noted here, the focus necessarily has shifted from critical analysis of traditional texts and genres to encompass a broad array of texts from media, popular culture, and everyday consumption and work. At the same time, the purview of ideology critique has expanded beyond a focus on political structure, to include a more general critique of dominant institutions of language, media, corporation and economy (Luke, Luke & Graham, 2007).

Literacy is in transition—with the emergence of new technologies, modes of information and media of instruction presenting major challenges to print and oral traditions of schooling, the state, media and everyday life. The result has been a pluralization of "literacy" into multiple "literacies" (e.g. New London Group, 1996; Lankshear & Knobel, 2003). Accordingly, there are contending and multiple versions of "critical literacy" at play in the fields of second language education, and in the traditional curriculum fields of language education more generally: language arts, writing and composition, literature study, "other" language study (Larsen-Freeman & Freeman, 2008)—as well as in emergent curriculum fields: media study, cultural studies, design and the other areas of the digital/creative economies.

Is there a unified or singular approach to critical to TESOL education? To answer this question requires that we return to the foundational historical materialism of Freire's project. The approaches to critical TESOL and literacy that we have described here are themselves historically produced and culturally situated. That is, they are activist interventions by students and teachers, teacher educators, scholars and researchers to disrupt and redress specific conditions of educational inequality, political disenfranchisement, linguistic and cultural marginalization, social and economic injustice. Each is based on a situated "reading of the world" and a set of normative premises about what is to be done. It would be spurious to adjudge them on lofty theoretical and narrow empirical grounds. Each should be viewed in terms of transformative effects: whether and how they generated literacies that altered communities' critical analyses and action in the world and their material and social relations, individually and collectively, developmentally and longitudinally. The last three decades of work have demonstrated that TESOL teachers have the political commitment, professional expertize and institutional space to shift language curriculum and pedagogy in new normative directions. Whether and how critical approaches can make substantive differences in the cultural understandings, socioeconomic pathways and political engagement and agency of second language learners is the outstanding question.

References

Akbari, R. (2008). Transforming lives: Introducing critical pedagogy into ELT classrooms. *ELT Journal*, 62(3), 276–283.

Alim, H. S. (2009). Creating "an empire within an empire": Critical hip hop language pedagogies and the role of sociolinguistics. In H. S. Alim, A. Ibrahim & A. Pennycook (Eds.), *Global linguistic flows: Hip hop cultures, youth identities and the politics of language* (pp. 213–230). New York: Routledge.

Auerbach, E. R. (2002). What is a participatory approach to curriculum development? In V. Zamel & R. Spack (Eds.), *Enriching ESOL pedagogy: Readings and activities for engagement, reflection and inquiry* (pp. 269–293). Malwah, NJ: Erlbaum.

Bernstein, B. (1990). *The structuring of pedagogic discourse* (Class, codes and control, Vol. 4). London: Routledge.

Boudin, K. (2002). Participatory literacy education behind bars: AIDS opens the door. In V. Zamel & R. Spack (Eds.), *Enriching ESOL pedagogy: Readings and activities for engagement, reflection and inquiry* (pp. 341–369). Mahwah, NJ: Erlbaum.

Bourdieu, P., & Passeron, C. (1990). *Reproduction in education, culture and society* (2nd ed.). London: Sage.

Brayboy, B., & Castagno, A. (2009). Self-determination through self-education: Culturally responsive schooling for indigenous students in the USA. *Teaching Education*, 20(1), 31–53.

Canagarajah, S. (1993). Critical ethnography of a Sri Lankan classroom: Ambiguities in student opposition to reproduction through ESOL. *TESOL Quarterly*, 27(4), 601–626.

Canagarajah, S. (1999). On EFL teachers, awareness and agency. *ELT Journal*, 53(3), 207–214.

Chang, B. (2009). The platform: Liberator teaching, community organizing, and sustainability in inner-city Los Angeles. Unpublished PhD thesis, University of California, Los Angeles.

Compton-Lilly, C. (2007). The complexities of reading capital in two Puerto Rican families. *Reading Research Quarterly*, 42(1), 72–98.

Darder, A. (1991). *Culture and power in the classroom: A critical foundation for bicultural education*. New York: Bergin & Garvey.

Darder, A. (2002). *Re-inventing Paulo Freire: A pedagogy of love*. Boulder, CO: Westview Press.

Delpit, L. (1995). *Other people's children: Cultural conflict in the classroom*. New York: The New Press.

Dicker, S. J. (2000). Official English and bilingual education: The controversy over language pluralism in U.S. society. In J. Kelly Hall & W. G. Eggington (Eds.), *The sociopolitics of English language education* (pp. 45–66). Clevedon: Multilingual Matters.

Dooley, K. (2009a). Homework for refugee middle school students with backgrounds marked by low levels of engagement with English school literacy. *Literacy Learning: The Middle Years*, 17(3), 28–36.

Dooley, K. (2009b). Language and inclusion in mainstream classrooms. In J. Miller, A. Kostogriz & M. Gearon (Eds.), *Culturally and linguistically diverse classrooms: New dilemmas for teachers* (pp. 75–91). Clevedon: Multilingual Matters.

Dooley, K. (2009c). Re-thinking pedagogy for middle school students with little, no or severely interrupted schooling. *English Teaching: Practice and Critique*, 8(1), 5–22.

Edelsky, C. (1992). *With literacy and justice for all*. London: Falmer Press.

Ellsworth, E. (1992). Why doesn't this feel empowering? Working through the repressive myths of critical pedagogy. In C. Luke & J. Gore (Eds.), *Feminisms and critical pedagogy* (pp. 90–119). New York: Routledge.

Erickson, F., Bargrodia, R., Cook-Sather, A., Espinoza, M. & Jurrow, S. et al. (2008). Students' experience of school curriculum:

The everyday circumstances of granting and withholding assent to learn. In F. M. Connolly, M. F. He & J. Phillion (Eds.), *The Sage handbook of curriculum and instruction* (pp. 198–218). Thousand Oaks, CA: Sage.

Fairclough, N. (1989). *Language and power*. London: Longman.

Fairclough, N., & Wodak, R. (1997/2004). Critical discourse analysis. In C. Seale (Ed.), *Social research methods* (pp. 357–370). London and New York: Routledge.

Fraser, N. (1997). *Justice interruptus: Critical reflections on the "postsocialist" condition*. New York: Routledge.

Freire, P. (1972). *Pedagogy of the oppressed*. Harmondsworth: Penguin.

Freire, P., & Macedo, D. (1987). *The politics of education*. South Hadley, MA: Bergin and Garvey.

Gadd, N. (1998). Towards less humanistic English teaching. *ELT Journal, 52*(3), 223–234.

Goldstein, T. (2003). Contemporary bilingual life at a Canadian high school: Choices, risks, tensions and dilemmas. *Sociology of Education, 76*(3), 247–264.

Gutiérrez, K., Baquedano-Lopez, P. & Tejeda, C. (1999). Rethinking diversity: Hybridity and hybrid language practices in the third space. *Mind, Culture, & Activity, 6*(4), 286–303.

Halliday, M. A. K. (1994). *An introduction to functional grammar* (2nd ed.). London: Arnold.

Halliday, M. A. K., & Martin, J. (1993). *Writing science: Literacy and discursive power*. Pittsburgh: University of Pittsburgh Press.

Hammond, J., & Macken-Horarik, M. (1999). Critical literacy: Challenges and questions for ESL classrooms. *TESOL Quarterly, 33*(3), 528–544.

Harklau, L. (2003). Representational practices and multi-modal communication in US high schools: Implications for adolescent immigrants. In R. Bayley & S. R. Schecter (Eds.), *Language socialization in bilingual and multilingual societies* (pp. 83–97). Clevedon: Multilingual Matters.

Hasan, R., & Williams, G. (Eds.) (1996). *Literacy in society*. London and New York: Longman.

Hones, D. F. (1999). U.S. justice? Critical pedagogy and the case of Mumia Abu-Jamal. *TESOL Journal, 8*(4), 27–33.

Hull, G., Zacher, J., & Hibbert, L. (2009). Youth, risk, and equity in a global world. *Review of Research in Education, 33*(1), 117–159.

Hymes, D. (1995). *Ethnography, linguistics, narrative inequality*. London: Taylor & Francis.

Ibrahim, A. (1999). Becoming Black: Rap, hip hop, race, gender, identity, and the politics of ESL learning. *TESOL Quarterly, 33*(2), 349–369.

Ibrahim, A. (2009). Taking hip hop to a whole nother level: Metissage, affect, and pedagogy in a global hip hop nation. In H. S. Alim, A. Ibrahim & A. Pennycook (Eds.), *Global linguistic flows: Hip hop cultures, youth identities and the politics of language* (pp. 231–248). New York: Routledge.

Janks, H. (1999). Critical discourse analysis as a research tool. In J. Marshall & M. Peters (Eds.), *Education policy* (pp. 32–48). Cheltenham: Edward Elgar.

Jarks, H. (2009) *Literacy and power*. London: Routledge.

Janks, H., & Comber, B. (2006). Critical literacy across continents. In K. Pahl & J. Rowsell (Eds.), *Travel notes from the new literacy studies: Instances of practice* (pp. 95–117). Clevedon: Multilingual Matters.

Jennings, L. B., & Da Matta, G. B. (2009). Rooted in resistance: Women teachers constructing pedagogies in post-authoritarian Brazil. *Teaching Education, 20*(3), 215–228.

Joseph, M., & Ramani, E. (1998). The ELT specialist and linguistic hegemony: A response to Tully and Matthew. *ELT Journal, 52*(3), 214–222.

Kaplan, R., & Baldauf, R. (2003). *Language and language-in-education planning in the Pacific Basin*. Dordrecht: Kluwer.

Kress, G. (2003). *Literacy in the new media age*. London: RougledgeFalmer.

Kubota, R., & Lin, A. (Eds.) (2009). *Race, culture and identities in second language education*. London: Routledge.

Kumaravadivelu, B. (2006). *Understanding language teaching: From method to postmethod*. Mahwah, NJ: Lawrence Erlbaum Associates.

Kumishiro, K., & Ngo, B. (Eds.) (2007). *Six lenses for anti-oppressive education*. New York: Peter Lang.

Lam, W. S. E. (2004). Second language socialization in a bilingual chat room: Global and local considerations. *Language Learning and Technology, 8*(3), 44–65.

Lankshear, C., & Knobel, M. (2003). *New literacies: Changing knowledge and classroom learning*. Buckingham: Open University Press.

Lankshear, C., & McLaren, P. (Eds.) (1993). *Critical literacy*. Albany, NY: State University of New York Press.

Larsen-Freeman, D., & Freeman, D. (2008). Language moves: The place for "foreign" languages in classroom teaching and learning. *Review of Research in Education, 32*, 147–186.

Lemke, J. L. (1995). *Textual politics: Discourse and social dynamics*. London: Taylor & Francis.

Li, G. (2006). *Culturally contested pedagogy: Battles of literacy and schooling between mainstream teachers and Asian immigrant parents*. Albany, NY: State University of New York Press.

Lin, A. M. Y. (1999). Doing English—Lessons in the reproduction or transformation of social worlds? *TESOL Quarterly, 33*(3), 393–412.

Lin, A. M. Y., & Martin, P. (2005). *Decolonisation, globalisation: Language-in-education policy and practice.* Clevedon: Multilingual Matters.

Lippi-Green, R. (1997). *English with an accent: Language, ideology, and discrimination in the United States.* London: Routledge.

Luke, A. (1996). Genres of power: Literacy education and the production of capital. In R. Hasan & G. Williams (Eds.), *Literacy in society* (pp. 308–338). London: Longman.

Luke, A. (2004). At last: The trouble with English. *Research in the Teaching of English, 39*(1), 85–95.

Luke, A., Luke, C. & Graham, P. (2007). Globalization, corporatism, and critical language education. *International Multilingual Research Journal, 1*, 1–13.

Luke, A., McHoul, A. & Mey, J. L. (1990). On the limits of language planning: Class, state and power. In R. Baldauf & A. Luke (Eds.), *Language planning and education in Australasia and the South Pacific* (pp. 26–46). Clevedon: Multilingual Matters.

Luke, C., & Gore, J. (1992). *Feminisms and critical pedagogy.* New York: Routledge.

McLaren, P., & Lankshear, C. (1994). *Politics of liberation: Paths from Freire.* New York: State University of New York Press.

Major, E. M., & Celedon-Pattichis, C. (2001). Integrating socio-political awareness into a teacher education curriculum. *TESOL Journal, 10*(1), 21–26.

Millard, E. (2006). Transformative pedagogy: Teachers creating a literacy of fusion. In K. Pahl & J. Rowsell (Eds.), *Travel notes from the new literacy studies: Instances of practice* (pp. 234–253). Clevedon: Multilingual Matters.

Miller, J. (2003). *Audible difference: ESL and social identity in schools.* Clevedon: Multilingual Matters.

Moje, E. B., & Luke, A. (2009). Literacy and identity: Examining the metaphors in history and contemporary research. *Reading Research Quarterly, 44*(4), 415–437.

Morgan, B. (1997). Identity and intonation: Linking dynamic processes in an ESL classroom. *TESOL Quarterly, 31*(3), 431–450.

Morgan, B. (2004). Modals and memories: A grammar lesson on the Quebec referendum on sovereignty. In B. Norton & K. Toohey (Eds.), *Critical pedagogies and language learning* (pp. 158–178). Cambridge: Cambridge University Press.

Muspratt, S., Luke, A. & Freebody, P. (1997). *Constructing critical literacies: Teaching and learning textual practice.* St Leonards: Allen & Unwin.

New London Group. (1996). A pedagogy of multiliteracies: Designing social futures. *Harvard Educational Review, 66*(1), 60–93.

Nieto, S., Bode, P., Kang, E. & Raible, J. (2008). Identity, community, and diversity. In F. M. Connelly, M. F. He & J. I. Phillion (Eds.), *The Sage handbook of curriculum and instruction* (pp. 176–197). Los Angeles and London: Sage.

Norton, B. (2000). *Identity and language learning.* London: Longman.

Norton, B., & Toohey, K. (Eds.) (2004). *Critical pedagogies and language learning.* Cambridge: Cambridge University Press.

OECD (2000). *Factors related to equity and quality: PISA 2000.* Paris: OECD/CERI.

Orellana, M., Reynolds, J., Dorner, L. & Meza, M. (2003). In other words: Translating or "para-phrasing" as a family literacy practice in immigrant households. *Reading Research Quarterly, 38*(1), 12–34.

Pahl, K., & Rowsell, J. (2005). *Literacy and education.* London: Paul Chapman.

Pennycook, A. (1999). Introduction: Critical approaches to TESOL. *TESOL Quarterly, 33*(3), 329–348.

Pennycook, A. (2001). *Critical applied linguistics: A critical introduction.* Mahwah, NJ: Lawrence Erlbaum Associates.

Pennycook, A., & Mitchell, T. (2009). Hip Hop as dusty foot philosophy. In H. S. Alim, A. Ibrahim, and A. Pennycook (Eds.), *Global linguistic flows: Hip hop cultures, youth identities and the politics of language* (pp. 25–42). New York: Routledge.

Phillipson, R. (1992). *Linguistic imperialism.* Oxford: Oxford University Press.

Phillipson, R. (2003). *English-only Europe? Challenging language policy.* London: Routledge.

Rex, L. (2006). Acting "cool" and "appropriate": Toward a framework for considering literacy classroom interactions when race is a factor. *Journal of Literacy Research, 38*, 275–325.

Skutnabb-Kangas, T. (2000). Linguistic human rights and teachers of English. In J. Kelly Hall & W. G. Eggington (Eds.), *The sociopolitics of English language teaching* (pp. 22–44). Clevedon: Multilingual Matters.

Stanton-Salazar, R., Dornbusch, R. D. & Sanford, M. (1995). Social capital and the reproduction of inequality: Information networks among Mexican-origin high school students. *Sociology of Education, 68*(2), 116–135.

Tollefson, J. W. (2002a). Introduction: Critical issues in educational language policy. In J. W. Tollefson (Ed.), *Language policies in education: Critical issues* (pp. 3–15) Mahwah, NJ: Erlbaum.

Tollefson, J. W. (2002b). Limitations of language policy and planning. In R. B. Kaplan (Ed.), *The Oxford handbook of applied linguistics* (pp. 416–425). Oxford: Oxford University Press.

Toohey, K. (2000). *Learning English at school.* Clevedon: Multilingual Matters.

Valenzuela, A. (1999). *Subtractive schooling: U.S.–Mexican youth and the politics of caring.* Albany, NY: State University of New York Press.

Valenzuela, A. (2008). Ogbu's voluntary and involuntary minority hypothesis and the politics of caring. In J. U. Ogbu (Ed.), *Minority status, oppositional culture, and schooling* (pp. 496–530). New York: Routledge.

Vasquez, V. (2004). *Negotiating critical literacy with young children.* Mahwah, NJ: Erlbaum.

Wallace, C. (2002). Local literacies and global literacy. In D. Block & D. Cameron (Eds.), *Globalization and language teaching* (pp. 101–114). London: Routledge.

Wallace, C. (2003). *Critical reading in language education.* Basingstoke: Palgrave Macmillan.

Warschauer, M., & Matuchniak, T. (in press). New technologies and digital worlds: Analysing evidence in equity, access and outcomes. *Review of Research in Education, 34,* 179–22.

Wiley, T. G. (2002). Accessing language rights in education: A brief history of the U.S. context. In J. W. Tollefson (Ed.), *Language policies in education: Critical issues* (pp. 39–64). Mahwah, NJ: Lawrence Erlbaum.

Wong, S. (2004). *Dialogic approaches to TESOL.* Mahwah, NJ: Erlbaum.

VIII
Language Planning and Policy

Guest editor: Richard B. Baldauf Jr

52
The History and Theory of Language Planning

Jiří Nekvapil

Introductory Remarks

In language use, it is possible to differentiate between linguistic and metalinguistic activities—on the one hand, people produce utterances, while not devoting any attention to the language or the utterances, and on the other hand, people may orient their attention toward the language or the utterances, evaluate them, think about altering them and occasionally take action on those thoughts. Language planning can be primarily considered the second type of activity. The point of language planning is to bring about changes in language or in linguistic activities. These changes include, for example, the establishment of new terms, the standardization of thus far non-standard grammatical forms, the nomination of a certain variety of language as the official language, or the determination of which languages will be taught in schools. According to Kaplan and Baldauf (1997, p. 3) "language planning is a body of ideas, laws and regulations (language policy), change rules, beliefs, and practices intended to achieve a planned change (or to stop change from happening) in the language use in one or more communities."

Until the formation of sociolinguistics in the 1960s, linguists trained in structuralist procedures devoted themselves primarily to "non-planned" changes in language and they rejected interference into matters of language and communication with the slogan of *Leave Your Language Alone!* (Hall, 1950). This atmosphere is also reflected in the name of one of the first classical texts on language planning, *Can Language Be Planned?* (Rubin & Jernudd, 1971a) and even the recent title *Do Not Leave Your Language Alone* (Fishman, 2006), which, however, signaled an essential transformation in the attitudes toward language planning. The tension between positive and negative attitudes toward language planning can also be characterized as antagonism between the descriptive and prescriptive approaches to linguistic phenomena, emphasized by linguistic structuralism. The restrained attitude of linguists is due not only to the ideological foundations of structuralism, but also to the fact that language planning extends beyond the margin of linguistics even in a very broadly conceived sense; it is an interdisciplinary matter and, in its implementation, it is clearly a political matter. Language planning as an academic discipline, however, originally developed as a branch of sociolinguistics, that is, with ties to the development of various linguistic disciplines. The penultimate section of this chapter presents language planning in the framework of the broader concept of language management, which enables the integration of some interdisciplinary aspects of language planning, but also the "purely" linguistic aspects such as grammar or the production of utterances. Following Neustupný (1978) or Haarmann (1990), language planning is thus viewed against the background of a general theory of language.

Language planning as a specific discipline with this name has existed for less than fifty years, yet intervention in language and communication is an activity that dates back to antiquity. The following section briefly recalls four more recent language planning social systems that tend to be cited as the predecessors of modern language planning or as a significant source of inspiration for it. Note that some of them are based upon carefully formulated theories.

Examples from History

Neustupný (1993, 2006) attempted to describe the history of language planning as social practice using the concept of developmental types, which are determined by the specific order of a number of sociocultural phenomena (e.g., means of production, social equality level, dominant ideology or attitude toward language variation), and in this way he arrived at four historical types of language planning: Premodern, Early Modern, Modern and Postmodern. These types correspond to a certain degree with specific time periods, but in the language planning system of a specific country, several of these types or their features can be present at the same time. The first three of these historical types can be found in the following examples. The Postmodern type, which corresponds broadly with the current ecology of languages paradigm, will be presented in a subsequent section.

The French Academy

The first example, which can be categorized as a (late) Premodern type, is the initial activity of the *Académie française*, the language academy founded in 1634. This institution came into being due to the initiative of Cardinal Richelieu during a time when European elites began to use the local vernacular languages in functions that had up to that time been reserved for Latin, during the time when the French state was restabilizing, and when Richelieu wanted to strengthen the unity and order of this state through the unity and order of the language. The French academy's aim was "to give explicit rules to our language [i.e., French] and to render it pure, eloquent, and capable of treating the arts and sciences" (cited in Cooper, 1989, p. 10). This aim was to be achieved through the publication of grammars, dictionaries and manuals of rhetoric and poetics, though in the end only the dictionaries were written. The French academy became a model for the founding of similar institutions in Europe (e.g., in Sweden), but it was not the oldest institute of its kind in Europe, but rather it was continuing in the tradition of a similar "Italian" institution that was a half century older. The founding and activity of the *Académie française* is discussed in detail in Cooper (1989) as the primary part of the argument that the definitions of language planning must also incorporate language planning situations that are not connected to the breakdown of the colonial system that had occurred around 1960, i.e., not connected to the situations whose analysis led to the birth of language planning as an academic discipline (i.e., classic language planning).

European National Movements

A second example illustrating the Early Modern type is the language planning that was a part of the European national movements of the nineteenth century. These movements led to the formation of a number of modern nations in the Herderian sense (Slovak, Czech, Norwegian, Finnish and other nations). These were originally nations (ethnic groups) with less power, whose members were oppressed by more powerful nations within a single ethnically heterogeneous state unit. This was one of the reasons why these movements were originally oriented toward cultural and linguistic demands rather than social and political ones (see Hroch, 1998). If we add the influence of Romanticism, it becomes clear that questions of language and language planning itself held a significant position in these movements. Haugen (1969) analyzes an essay written by Norwegian language reformer Ivar Aasen (1813–1896) in 1836, and argues that this essay represents "a paradigm of a program of Language Planning." In it, Haugen essentially finds all the elements that should be considered in the analysis and evaluation of various language programs: background situation, program of action comprising a goal, policies leading to the goal, and procedures of implementing the policies, namely selection (of reference norms) and codification (in grammars and dictionaries) and/or elaboration (of functions) and propagation (of the proposed norms to new users).

Aasen targeted his program to oppose the use of Danish in Norway and proposed instead the postulation of a sort of generalized (i.e., not yet existent) norm of all Norwegian dialects as the starting point for Standard Norwegian. For Czech, the most significant representative of the first generation of the Czech national movement, Slavic Studies scholar Josef Dobrovský (1753–1829) codified the norm of Humanistic Czech (i.e., a variety of Czech that had not been used for a long period of time) as the standard language in a grammar in 1809 (2nd edition 1819). In both cases, this was a fundamental decision, the effects of which speakers and writers can still feel today.

Characteristic of language planning of the Early Modern type were large changes (reforms) concerning not only the selection of varieties to be standardized, but also orthography or lexicon (primarily for the purposes of science and art). In the Czech national movement, which was battling the more powerful German culture, the second generation of patriots led by Josef Jungmann (1773–1847) laid out the principles for enriching the Czech lexicon (they designated Old Czech, dialects and Slavic languages as the sources of the new lexicon, and the formation of new words was also considered acceptable), and they summarized the results of their work in the extensive five-volume Czech–German Dictionary (1834–1839).

Soviet Union of the 1920s and 1930s

The third case is the language planning in the Soviet Union that took place in the 1920s and 1930s. It can be categorized as belonging to the Early Modern type, yet with the presence of several features of the Premodern and Modern types. The formation of the Soviet Union meant that more than one hundred ethnic groups at very different levels of development found themselves together in one huge state, which for a limited period of time recognized and supported their languages. The language of most of these ethnic groups existed only in spoken form, and only a few of them had their own standard language, and these were also at various levels of development. During the early Soviet period (radical changes did not occur until the end of the 1930s), the Leninist doctrine of the Soviet state declared the right of self-determination for ethnic groups including schooling based on their languages. The promotion of the spread of Russian, including the Cyrillic alphabet, was associated with the previous oppressive regime of the Russian czars, and this is why it was rejected as the basis for the language planning at the beginning of the Soviet period. The basic task of language planning, called "language construction," thus consisted in the creation of tens of new alphabets, orthography systems, the modernization of most of the languages, above all in the area of terminology, but also in the production of textbooks, primers and the like. The work done was noteworthy: Alpatov (2000, p. 222), for example, claims that more than seventy alphabets were created for the languages of the Soviet Union during this period. A characteristic feature of Soviet language planning was the fact that its participants included the leading Soviet linguists, experts in the respective languages or language groups (e.g., E. D. Polivanov, N. F. Jakovlev et al.). They were advocates of the developing structuralist linguistics, and they combined their work on the graphization of languages with the development of phonological theory.[1] In other respects, these linguists framed language planning using Marxism, which led them to emphasize the social aspects of language and to the critique of structuralist linguistics for underestimating the value of the possibility of deliberate intervention into linguistic matters (for more details on this, see Alpatov, 2000). The scope, tasks and some of the approaches of the Soviet language planning of the 1920s and the first half of the 1930s are congruent with "classic language planning," which came into being thirty years later in an entirely different social context. This newer theory, however, developed without an intellectual relationship to the practical and theoretical experiences of language planning in the Soviet Union (but see Lewis, 1983). This was due to a number of causes: opposing ideologies, the Cold War since the 1950s, the language barrier and even the fact that the language planning in the Soviet Union itself developed in a considerably different manner following the end of the 1930s, and its new representatives made efforts to have the early Soviet language planning forgotten (see Alpatov, 2000; Kirkwood, 2000).

Czechoslovakia and the Prague Linguistic School

The fourth example is the language planning that occurred in Czechoslovakia in the 1920s and 1930s, the participants of which were the linguists of the Prague Linguistic School (above all B. Havránek and V. Mathesius, also in part R. O. Jakobson). This language planning embodies clear features of the Modern type—macro-social problems are more or less ignored, as large changes are not desired, attention is oriented above all toward microscopic problems and the goal is to modify details (see Neustupný, 2006). Czechoslovakia was formed in 1918 from the ruins of the Hapsburg Empire, and even though it was relatively ethnically diverse and the problems of inter-ethnic contact were significant, the Prague School's theory of language planning was devoted merely to the elaboration ("cultivation") of the majority Czech standard language. In this process, its protagonists continued with the work of some of their predecessors as well as such contemporaries as the Swedish linguist A. Noreen (see Noreen & Johannson, 1892) or the Russian linguist G. Vinokur (see Vinokur, 1925). The Prague School's theory of language cultivation achieved world renown and was, to a certain degree, acknowledged and accepted also in the later "classic language planning"—above all through B. H. Jernudd. Among the basic terms that marked this approach were norm, function, intellectualization and flexible stability of the standard language (see Daneš 1987a, 1987b; Garvin 1973, 1993; Havránek 1932a, 1932b; Kondrašov 1988; Mathesius 1932; Nekvapil, 2008; Neustupný & Nekvapil 2003; Scharnhorst & Ising 1976/1982). The cultivation approach is, in addition to the policy approach, one of the two basic approaches to language planning (Neustupný, 1970; Hornberger, 2006). It continues to be quite active in Europe and has also been applied to a number of minority languages (see Janich & Greule, 2002).

Haugen and Classic Language Planning

Language planning, i.e. the academic discipline with this name, was established at the end of the 1960s. It acquired individual features, which will be discussed in what follows, and existed in this form during the 1970s. In retrospect it is possible to call this era of language planning "classic language planning" (see, e.g., Ricento, 2000, p. 206). The fact that language planning was already a specific discipline during this period is evidenced not only by the fact that its subject of research was delimited, and that widely used research frameworks were developed and the respective research methods identified, but also that this research was institutionalized at a certain level (in the form of conferences, projects, representative publications and a newsletter) and it gained a new attractive name, i.e. "language planning." The main protagonists of classic language planning were associated with American academia (C. Ferguson and J. Fishman) and American funding sources enabled the development of extensive international research. This research was oriented above all toward the language situation in the "Third World," the multilingual developing nations that had gained independence following the collapse of the colonial system after Word War II (primarily after 1960) and were facing the necessity of quickly solving significant political, economic, social and also language problems—the general aim was their "modernization" and "development." Attention was concentrated above all on the linguistic aspects of the sociocultural unit ("nationalism") and political (administrative) integrity ("nationism") (Fishman, 1968) and the related programs of literacy, i.e., on "status planning." In addition, there was the development of planning oriented toward the form of the language itself, i.e., "corpus planning," the aim of which was above all the graphization, standardization and (lexical) modernization of language (Ferguson, 1968). Interest in language planning, however, was also conditioned by the situation in linguistics, in which matters of language and society moved into the forefront, and a specific, more general discipline—sociolinguistics—began to take form. Language planning was understood as a branch of sociolinguistics, and sociolinguists aimed to test their theories and approaches in the social "laboratory" of the Third World (see Fishman, 1968).

The term "language planning" was popularized in the linguistics literature by Haugen (1959) and it is in a certain sense paradoxical that classic language planning, oriented mainly toward the linguistic conditions in the Third World, found its guru in a specialist whose work had been devoted to the sociolinguistic situation above all in one European country—Norway, but also other Scandinavian countries. On the other hand, this fact supports the idea that the European tradition of language planning was to a certain degree also present in classic language planning. On language planning, Haugen writes:

> By language planning I understand the activity of preparing a normative orthography, grammar, and dictionary for the guidance of writers and speakers in a non-homogeneous speech community. In this practical application of linguistic knowledge we are proceeding beyond descriptive linguistics into an area where judgment must be exercised in the form of choices among available linguistic forms. Planning implies an attempt to guide the development of a language in a direction desired by the planners. It means not only predicting the future on the basis of available knowledge concerning the past, but a deliberate effort to influence it.
>
> (Haugen, 1959, p. 8)

It should be noted that this definition is still rather narrow, essentially covering only what was later conceptualized as "corpus planning." Fundamental for the formation of classic language planning was the introduction of the concept of "plan." This is how language planning became a branch of "social planning," which had begun to be elaborated on the theoretical level in the western social sciences of that time and was being applied in the policy and economies of a number of countries. Haugen also influenced the development of language planning by connecting the planning process to the "decision theory" of that time and formulating and describing in detail the "decision-making procedure" relevant for language planning. Its basic components were: problems that are to be solved, proposed alternative solutions including their limitations, principles of evaluating the alternatives, decision-makers and methods of implementation (see Haugen, 1966). Five years later, Rubin and Jernudd (1971b, p. xiii), in the introduction to the book that became a milestone in the theory of language planning, state simply that "the study of language planning describes decision-making about language"; in the same book, Jernudd and das Gupta (1971) build the theory of language planning and summarize their contribution thus:

> This paper outlines an approach to language planning as decision-making. We do not define planning as an idealistic and exclusively linguistic activity but as a political and administrative

activity for solving language problems in society. Public planning, that is, orderly decision-making about language on a national level, is motivated by public effects of some language problems and by the social context. We maintain that language is subject to planning because it is a resource that is and can be valued. Aspects of language code and language use can be changed to better correspond to the goals of society.

(Jernudd & das Gupta, 1971, p. 211)

As is apparent, it was economic thinking that was influential; after all, the solutions to language problems were to ultimately contribute to the economic prosperity of developing nations. Planning was conceived as a sequence of rational activities (fact-finding; planning goals, strategies and oucomes; implementation; and feedback), which take place in concrete social contexts, often in situations of limited material and human resources. For this reason, the criteria, values and type of information, on the basis of which a selection between alternative aims, strategies and predicted outcomes can be made, or the issue of "evaluation," attracted significant attention. Rubin (1971) in continuation of the literature in the area of business administration, economics and political planning of that time, identified formal evaluation techniques, which could improve the quality of language planning (the many examples she works with concern the teaching of languages, above all English and vernaculars, in developing nations).

Classic language planning is based on the premise that language planning takes place at the level of the state and the plans come into existence in the interest of the development of the *entire* society. The state (or government) is essentially the only actor determining the goals to be achieved. The political opinions that dominated the international group of theoreticians of language planning in the 1960s are commented on in retrospect by one of their protagonists thus: "we recognized and accepted the realities of political process and central state power; and we believed in the good of state action, that governments could act efficiently and satisfactorily" (Jernudd, 1997a, p. 132).

Language planning theory in the 1960s and 1970s was formed in a specific political and social context that left it with particular features. A number of them were criticized in the further development of the theory and practice of language planning (see the next section), yet language planning as a specific discipline did not lose its attractiveness, including the specialized literature produced during its beginnings (in addition to the literature already cited, this undoubtedly includes Rubin, Jernudd, das Gupta, Fishman & Ferguson, 1977). During this period, a number of variables relevant for language planning in general and the relationships between them were identified, and some basic terms such as corpus planning and status planning were introduced. Some continually relevant aspects of language planning, e.g., that planning must consider the "interests" of various social groups, or that the research on language planning cannot be only an issue for (socio)linguists, but rather, also for representatives from other specializations (multidisciplinary approach) were introduced as topics during this period, though not elaborated. To a certain degree, some aspects from this period remain relevant for the contemporary era, a dominant orientation that critics of language planning later reproached: the introduction and elaboration of formal procedures and concrete techniques of language planning. Not even the language planning of today could exist without them.

Critique of Classic Language Planning

During the 1980s and in the following years, there were many voices criticizing language planning theory of the previous period. There were several causes for this. The process of modernization of the developing nations, which language planning was meant to help, failed in many countries. The theory of classic language planning had only a small influence on the actual practice of language planning. The atmosphere in the social sciences was changing; the visible diversion from scientifically oriented structuralism was accompanied by the growing influence of critical theory. The economic planning model, the so-called "rational model," which was the basis for classic language planning theory, was criticized in general theories of social planning, and planning itself as a practical activity of the state gave way to the forces of the market economy.

Critical voices were heard even from the protagonists of classical language planning itself. Rubin (1986) joins the critique of the "rational model" and in addition to the simple "technical" problems admits the existence of numerous "wicked problems," which have no "stopping rules" evidently because there are other previously unconsidered or unknown factors at play. Further she argues that not just one actor, but rather, the greatest possible number of concerned parties including the "target population" should contribute to the formulation of goals to be achieved. This leads to the idea that became the central one on the later ecological approach in language planning: in a specific language planning social system, it is necessary to deal with all types of languages used and the relationships between them (Rubin, 1986, p. 119; on the ecological approach, see, e.g., Kaplan & Baldauf, 1997).

The book by Cooper (1989) is not only a well-considered synthesis and critique of the previous development of language planning, but it also introduces a number of innovations. Although he does not abandon the initial term "plan," he refuses to conceptualize language planning as problem-solving in his book (thereby abandoning the tradition of classic language planning) and he significantly expands the definition of language planning. According to Cooper (1989, p. 45), "language planning refers to deliberate efforts to influence the behaviour of others with respect to the acquisition, structure, or functional allocation of their language codes."

Thus, all of the cases cited in the section "Examples from History" can be characterized as language planning. Cooper's conceptualization of language planning became very influential in one additional respect. Cooper introduced the term "acquisition planning" as the third basic area of language planning (in addition to corpus and status planning), by which he made language planning explicitly relevant for applied linguistics dealing with the teaching of languages (first/second/foreign language teaching and learning).

More than twenty years after the publication of the volume *Can Language Be Planned?* (Rubin & Jernudd, 1971a), one of its main authors wrote about the book:

> Should the book be written today, it could not carry the subtitle "Sociolinguistic Theory and Practice for Developing Nations," but would have to take account of a broad range of different sociolinguistic situations at different levels of enlargement (from nation to firm), of a broad range of different interests and population groups (from women to refugees), under widely different communicative circumstances (of media, channels, information processing), and foremost, of the different ideological and real, global and local sociopolitical conditions.
>
> (Jernudd, 1997a, pp. 135, 136)

This formulation can also be read as an implicit critique of the early theory of language planning, further informed by the development of the whole discipline. Minimally, this raises the following issues: language planning is not specific to "developing nations," but rather, it also occurs in supposedly "developed" nations. It does not take place only on a state level, but also on lower levels, in other words, not only the macro, but also meso and micro planning (see Canagarajah, 2005; Liddicoat & Baldauf, 2008). It does not represent the interests of the socially non-differentiated societies (nation, state), but is the resultant force of the conflict between the interests of various groups. To put it another way, various interest groups plan language and communication on various levels of society in the context of the language planning of other interest groups of varying complexity. In the analysis of language planning, it is difficult to create abstractions from the social and political conditions, including the relevant ideologies.

A number of other authors have uncovered and criticized the "covert" ideational basis of classic language planning, thus problematizing its alleged ideological neutrality (in particular Williams, 1992; Tollefson, 1991, 2002; Blommaert, 1996). These authors argued that all language planning assumes a specific theory of social change (see also Cooper 1989) and as a political matter it cannot exist without political analysis. Furthermore, they argued that early language planning was closely connected to the evolutionary theory of modernization based on Parsons' structural functionalism, which was one of the reasons why, in spite of the intentions of the theoreticians of language planning, it did not contribute to change, but rather, to the solidification of the social and economic inequality in the developing nations. Symptomatic in this sense is the title of Tollefson's book *Planning Language, Planning Inequality* (Tollefson, 1991).

"Reversing Language Shift" and Its Critique

It is language "modernization" as an "(early) modernization" process that meant the unification of languages (with the help of standardization) and the suppression of linguistic diversity in Third World countries (among other reasons, due to the spread of European languages, in recent decades primarily English). Classic language planning brought concepts to the developing nations that were successful in the modernization of European countries ("one nation–one language"), even though as a discipline itself it had come into being in countries where post-modernization was beginning. The shift in attention from the "developing nations" to the "developed nations," however, led to the fact that the post-modern thinking was gradually being established in the considerations of language planning. The Postmodern language planning type supports variation and protects plurality (Neustupný, 2006 in theory and, e.g., Lo Bianco, 1987 in practice). Accordingly, new approaches inspired by ecology, that is, language ecology (see, e.g., Kaplan & Baldauf, 1997, pp. 311ff.) and human rights, that is, linguistic human rights (see, e.g., Skutnabb-Kangas & Phillipson, 1995) have been applied in theories of language planning. The protection of the plurality of languages has lead to the re-evaluation of the function of the spread of European languages (above all English) in the world. The linguistic imperialism framework that was developed by Phillipson (1992) emphasized the negative influences of these languages on the "ecosystem" of a number of countries as a part of globalization processes. Ricento (2000, p. 208) calls this new situation in the theory of language planning "the ecology of languages paradigm."

A significant place in this paradigm is occupied by the Reversing Language Shift model (Fishman, 1991, 2001), which achieved significant popularity and was applied to a number of language situations. Hornberger (2006, p. 35) considers it an example of a model that embodies three fundamental features of a newly emerging paradigm, these being ideology, ecology and agency. Even though this model has a narrower scope than the theory of classic language planning, Williams (2007, p. 162) considers it to be the height of language planning, and, pointing to its exceptional influence, argues that this model essentially replaced "language planning." The model of "Reversing Language Shift" reacts to the fact that in the contemporary globalizing world, a record number of languages are facing extinction, and the model should serve as a theoretical reflection as well as a practical guide to prevent this, or in some cases, for the revitalization of languages. The level of language endangerment is captured in the model through an eight-degree scale inspired by the Richter Scale, which measures the intensity of the disruption of the earth's surface. The "graded intergenerational disruption scale," the core of the entire model, then, is as follows (degree 1 means the *lowest*, degree 8 the *highest* extent of disruption):

Degree 1: (potentially) endangered language (still) used in the educational sphere, in the work sphere, in the mass media, and on higher levels, even on state level;

Degree 2: endangered language used on lower levels (local media and government offices);

Degree 3: endangered language used in the local work sphere, in which interaction between speakers of the minority and majority languages occurs;

Degree 4: endangered language used as the language of instruction in schools, in looser or tighter dependency on instruction in the majority language;

Degree 5: endangered language is used for instruction, but not in formal education;

Degree 6: endangered language used in family settings as a means of intergenerational handing down of traditions and is thus handed down in this way;

Degree 7: endangered language used by the older generation, which is already beyond the age of biological reproduction;

Degree 8: the endangered language used (known, remembered) only by several of its older speakers.

(Based on Fishman, 1991)

The scale has a (quasi) implicative character, in other words, the lower degrees (e.g., 6) in essence include the state of the language specified by the higher degrees (that is, 7, 8). The aim of this scale is to identify the level of disruption of a specific language, and in accordance with this to plan adequate measures, with the help of which the current state of disruption (e.g., 8) can be shifted to a lower one (e.g., 6), and in optimal cases to the full functioning of the language. A part of this model is also the component of "ideological clarification," the aim of which is to clarify the ideological conditions for potential revitalization.

The "Reversing Language Shift" model accents significantly different aspects than those on which classic language planning concentrated. In spite of this, it maintains some aspects of early language planning, such as evolutionism, the static concept of social change or the structural functionalist point of departure (Williams, 2007; Darquennes, 2007). A number of authors point to the fact that in a time when the role of the family in society has evidently decreased, the model places excessive weight on the role of handing over the language in the family and ignores the effects of socioeconomic processes in the revitalization of language. Williams (2007, p. 168) emphasizes that if the family were to be the only agent of passing down the language, revitalization today would essentially be impossible, as "dynamics of economic restructuring involve a degree of the circulation of capital which leads to migration, or the circulation of people," and thus to the disruption of linguistically homogeneous neighborhoods and families. Other authors argue that for successful revitalization it is necessary for potential users of the endangered language to begin to positively evaluate the economic benefits of the endangered language for their everyday life.

An alternative model that deals with some problems of Fishman's model is the circular model of language status change, the "Catherine Wheel" proposed by M. Strubell (see Strubell, 2001, pp. 279–280; in more detail Strubell, 1999). This model emphasizes the individual as a consumer and its point of departure is the fact that the following components are functionally interconnected: (1) the language competence of individuals, (2) the social use of language, (3) the existence of products and services in this language and the demand for them, (4) the motivation to learn and use this language. The relationship between these components can be captured in the following (simplified) manner: the language competence of individuals stimulates, or can stimulate the social use of language, which, in turn, stimulates or can stimulate the existence of products and services in this language and the demand for them and that, in turn, stimulates or can stimulate the motivation to learn and use the language, and thus the language competence of individuals is preserved, which, in turn, stimulates or can stimulate the social use of language, etc. The metaphor of the "Catherine Wheel" points to this very dynamic self-perpetuating process. This process, enriched by several other components, can be visualized through Figure 52.1.

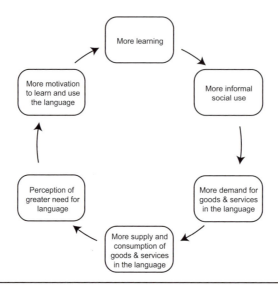

Figure 52.1 The "Catherine Wheel"
Based on Strubell (1999) and Darquennes (2007).

A specific language is endangered if this self-perpetuating process is disrupted. The aim of language planning and policy is then to identify in which component of the circular model the process was disrupted, and to renew its original dynamics through the appropriate measures.

Language Management Framework

While the models presented in the previous sections are rather narrow in scope and are models of some *specific* social reality, Language Management Theory (framework, model, LMT for short) has been constructed from the beginning as a broadly founded general theory, which on the one hand delimits its relationship to linguistics, but on the other hand considerably extends beyond its boundaries and even comprises the sociocultural (including the socioeconomic) dimension. While classic language planning, as well as the resulting approaches, emphasizes the role of the macrosocial level (the level of "social structures") and merely assumes the specific linguistic behavior of speakers in specific linguistic interactions, LMT reverses this perspective and emphasizes the practices of the speakers ("agency"). Because LMT provides extensive opportunities for practical applications, including in the area of the teaching and learning of foreign and second languages, let us now examine it in more detail.

Some basic features of LMT came into being almost in parallel with the classic theory of language planning (see Neustupný, 1978, Ch. XII), but the classic text is Jernudd and Neustupný (1987), who programmatically introduce the central concept of "language management."[2] The concept of "language management" has a clearly delimited theoretical content, which has little in common with the term "management" as it is currently used in applied linguistics or in Canadian language planning. LMT's point of departure is that in language use it is possible to differentiate between two processes: (1) the generation of utterances (communicative acts), and (2) management of utterances (communicative acts), in other words, linguistic and metalinguistic activities. With reference to Fishman (1971, p. 221), this distinction is often rendered as the difference between "linguistic behavior" and "behavior toward language." Theories of linguistic grammar (and "communicative grammar") deal with the process (1), while LMT deals with the process (2). The management takes place in the concrete interactions (conversations) of individuals or in institutions of varying complexity and in accordance with that it is possible to distinguish "simple management" (also known as discourse-based management, on-line management) and "organized management" (also known as directed management, off-line management). An example of simple management is when a teacher uses an unusual colloquial term during a foreign language lesson and immediately following its utterance adds the equivalent standard expression. An example of organized management is a language reform or the introduction of language X into a school system. Simple management takes place in several phases:

1. the speaker *notes* a deviation from the expected course ("norm") of communication (including linguistic form);
2. the speaker can (but need not) *evaluate* the deviation (if it is evaluated negatively, this is an "inadequacy" or "problem," and if positively, this is a "gratification");
3. as a reaction to this evaluation, the speaker can (but need not) create an "adjustment design";
4. the speaker can (but need not) *implement* this adjustment design.

As is evident, LMT does not limit itself to language *problems*, but its point of departure is the fact that efforts to influence the language behaviour of the self or others can also be motivated by positive feelings (e.g., that someone likes a language, its form, etc.). The phases of simple management listed above take place automatically in many cases, and the speaker is unaware of them, but in some genres (e.g., writing or training in school), it is possible to observe phase after phase. Noting, evaluation, adjustment design and implementation can also be identified in organized management. Organized management is characterized by the following features:

1. Management acts are trans-interactional.
2. A social network or even an institution is involved.
3. Communication about management takes place.
4. Theorizing and ideology intervene.
5. In addition to language as discourse, the object of management is language as a system.

While theories of language planning typically deal only with "organized" management, LMT's primary aim is to demonstrate the *connections* between "simple" and "organized" management (in the traditional terminology the connections between micro and macro language planning). In ideal cases, "organized" management is founded on instances of "simple" management, in other words, it is in harmony with the noting and evaluation of the speakers in specific interactions and with the help of adequate measures, it removes the speakers' problems or suits their needs in the cases of gratification, i.e., takes the form of a "language management cycle" (for more detail, see Nekvapil, 2009; Giger & Sloboda, 2008). Of course, LMT acknowledges the fact that this ideal is sometimes far from being the case in practice, as actors of "organized" management occasionally produce measures independently of concrete interactions, or do not orient toward contributing to "happy communication" (Jernudd, 1997b), in addition to "linguistic" interests they advocate "non-linguistic interests" (Jernudd & Neustupný, 1987), through which, conversely, they can cause further problems for speakers. Essential is the fact that LMT is a processual conceptual apparatus that can diagnose such a state, being as a whole "an academic response to people in power in reaction against central imposition" (Jernudd, 1993, p. 134). Accordingly, LMT offers a new view of the problem of "maintenance and shift" discussed earlier (see Sloboda, 2009).

What this suggests is that not only linguistic forms but also various aspects of the communicative act can be managed. In terms of the components of a Hymesian model of communication, these aspects are Variety, Situation, Function, Setting, Participant, Content, Form, Channel and Performance (Neustupný, 2004; Neustupný & Nekvapil, 2003). Because the communicative dimension is firmly embedded in the sociocultural dimension (including the socioeconomic dimension), it is only possible with great difficulty to perform successful *communicative* management, without the accompanying *socioeconomic* management. The following succession is an appropriate goal: socioeconomic management → communicative management → language (in a narrower sense) management (e.g., in the creation of specific jobs it is possible to encourage the development of specific communication networks, in which language X will be used, which can encourage the elaboration of such a language or the specific manners of communication; here the attention is thus oriented primarily toward the components Participant and Variety). Given the presence of the socioeconomic dimension in LMT, the theory cannot remain only in the hands of linguists.

Even though the discourse of LMT does not explicitly refer to the ecology metaphor, Kaplan and Baldauf (2005, p. 51) point out that LMT is ecologically informed in the sense that it deals with management, which takes place in a multiplicity of micro, meso and macro societal environments or levels: communicating individuals, families, associations, social organizations, media, economic bodies, educational institutions, local government, central government or international organizations.

In the context of this *Handbook of Research in Second Language Teaching and Learning* it is also appropriate to mention that LMT has been used, among other things, in the analysis of various aspects of foreign and second language acquisition and intercultural competence in general (Neustupný, 1995, 2008; Miyazaki & Marriott, 2003; Muraoka, 2009). In accordance with the basic principles of LMT, the point of departure in this area of study is the behavior of the speakers (both foreign language learners and natives) in an intercultural situation ("contact situation"), i.e., in a situation in which the norms of more than one linguistic/communicative/sociocultural system are applied. Researchers analyze which linguistic/communicative/sociocultural phenomena speakers note or, conversely, do not note in a given situation, what they experience as problems, and how they deal with the given problems in a specific interaction. From the perspective of methodology, this means capturing naturally occurring interaction with the help of audio or video recording devices and conducting follow-up interviews (a stimulated recall interview) with the participants of the interaction afterward. On the basis of the analysis of simple management, experts propose measures for the organization or improvement of the foreign or second language teaching ("organized management") (Fan, 2008, 2009). It is also worth mentioning that in connection with the increasing globalization of university life, research dealing with the acquisition of "academic competence" in academic contact situations has recently begun developing with the help of LMT (Marriott, 2004; Neustupný, 2004).

Summary and Concluding Remarks

This chapter has dealt with the development of language planning as a practice and its theory. It argues that language planning has been conducted in various countries for centuries and from the perspective of developmental types, it can be characterized as Premodern, Early Modern, Modern or Postmodern (Neustupný, 2006). These types are conceptualized on the basis of a number of sociocultural phenomena such as means of production, degree of social equality, dominant ideology or attitude toward language variation. These types correspond, to a certain degree, to specific time periods, yet what is essential is that several of these types or their features can be present at the same time in the language planning system of a specific country.

Although rather elaborated theories of language planning have existed minimally since the 1920s, the theory of language planning considered prototypical or classic in the Anglo-Saxon tradition, was formed in the 1960s and 1970s in connection with the collapse of the colonial system following World War II. Beginning in the 1980s, this field of study was strongly criticized for a number of reasons, and the ecological paradigm of language planning began to form, distinguishing itself from classic language planning through its emphasis on ideology, ecology and agency (Ricento, 2000). In this paradigm, a significant position has been occupied by the Reversing Language Shift model (Fishman, 1991). Although this model was broadly accepted, it was also criticized for under-estimating the value of socioeconomic factors. From this perspective, a more adequate model is the Catherine Wheel (Strubell, 1999). Language Management Theory, as indicated by Baldauf (2005), is an alternative conceptualization of the discipline of language planning (see also Blommaert, 1996 referring to Kuo & Jernudd, 1993). This theory has a very broad scope, includes both the *macro* dimension and the *micro* dimension ("agency"), examines language management as a *process*, views it in *communicative* and *sociocultural* terms (including socioeconomic ones), but at the same time is transparently compatible with *linguistics* and good for utilization on research on *second language* teaching and learning. It is thus possible to assume that its significance will grow (see also Lanstyák & Szabómihályová, 2009).

Even though the orientation of the theories, models and frameworks of language planning has changed since the 1960s, language planning as an academic discipline has developed in clear continuation. This is, on the one hand, due to the fact that classic language planning ultimately provided a number of valuable concepts, but also due to the fact that the dynamics of the development of the discipline was contributed to by some of its protagonists. This is most visible in the case of J. Fishman, who contributed greatly to the establishment of language planning as an academic discipline. He considerably influenced the research on language problems of developing nations (Fishman, 1968), but also contributed fundamentally to the formation of a new ecological paradigm (Fishman, 1991) and in his recent book (Fishman, 2006) analyzed the political and ideological aspects of corpus planning and thus significantly "de-technologized" one of the basic concepts of classic language planning, which was criticized precisely for its excessive emphasis on the technical aspects of planning activities.

The theories, models and frameworks of language planning will undoubtedly continue to develop based on the demand for language planning itself in contemporary society. It appears that this demand is growing rather than decreasing. The lion's share in this is held by three contemporary social processes: globalization, migration and the birth of new states and groupings of states (e.g., the European Union). These processes encourage language planning on the macro, meso and micro levels. It can be assumed that the newly forming planning situations will lead to the birth of new approaches and concepts or that it will be necessary to revise the old approaches and concepts. An example of this can be the language planning situations in some new post-Soviet countries, specifically the status of Russians and Russian in them—the question is, to what degree is it adequate to apply the traditional concepts of majority and minority and the related concept of "minority language rights" (Pavlenko, 2008) here? Even though the confrontation with new language planning situations can be a good inspiration for language planners to deconstruct established concepts, it is necessary to agree with Pennycook (2006), who calls for the deconstruction of *all* taken-for-granted categories upon which language planning theories are based, i.e., for the utilization of deconstruction as a permanent activity.

Acknowledgments

Thanks are due to (in alphabetical order) Richard B. Baldauf Jr, Miroslav Hroch, Roland Marti, Tamah Sherman and Marián Sloboda for their valuable comments on various versions of this chapter. While writing this chapter, I was supported by the Institutional Research Plan MSM 0021620825 awarded by the Czech Ministry of Education.

Notes

1. It is useful to recall that the most well known representatives of structuralist phonology, N. S. Trubetzkoy and R. O. Jakobson, also came from the Russian territory.
2. The most comprehensive work to use LMT is Neustupný and Nekvapil (2003); a theoretical systemization is Nekvapil (2006) or Nekvapil and Nekula (2006); further innovations can be found in Nekvapil and Sherman (2009a, 2009b).

References

Alpatov, V. M. (2000). *150 языков и политика 1917–2000. Социолингвистические проблемы СССР и постсоветского пространства* [150 languages and policy 1917–2000. Sociolinguistic problems in the Soviet Union and the Post-Soviet area]. Moskva: Kraft + IV RAN.

Baldauf, R. B., Jr (2005). Language planning and policy research: An overview. In E. Hinkel (Ed.), *Handbook of research in second language teaching and learning* (pp. 957–970). Mahwah, NJ: Lawrence Erlbaum.

Blommaert, J. (1996). Language planning as a discourse on language and society: The linguistic ideology of a scholarly tradition. *Language Problems & Language Planning, 20,* 199–222.

Canagarajah, A. S. (Ed.) (2005). *Reclaiming the local in language policy and practice.* Mahwah, NJ: Lawrence Erlbaum.

Cooper, R. L. (1989). *Language planning and social change.* Cambridge: Cambridge University Press.

Daneš, F. (1987a). Langue standard et culture de la langue. Élaboration et applications de l'approche praguoise [Standard language and the cultivation of language. The formation and uses of the Prague approach]. In J. Maurais (Ed.), *Politique et aménagement linguistique* (pp. 453–492). Québec and Paris: Conseil de la langue française, Le Robert.

Daneš, F. (1987b). Values and attitudes in language standardization. In J. Chloupek & J. Nekvapil (Eds.), *Reader in Czech sociolinguistics* (pp. 206–245). Amsterdam: John Benjamins.

Darquennes, J. (2007). Paths to language revitalization. In J. Darquennes (Ed.), *Contact linguistics and language minorities/ Kontaktlinguistik und sprachminderheiten/Linguistique de contact et minorités linguistiques* (*Plurilingua* 30) (pp. 61–76). St Augustin: Asgard.

Fan, S. K. (2008). Teaching Japanese interaction as a process of language management. In P. Heinrich & Y. Sugita (Eds.), *Japanese as foreign language in the age of globalization* (pp. 139–163). Munich: Iudicium.

Fan, S. K. (2009). Language planning or language management: Treatment of problems for the development of "Japanese in Context." *Intercultural Communication Studies, 21,* 7–35 (Kanda University of International Studies, Japan).

Ferguson, C. A. (1968). Language development. In J. A. Fishman, C. A. Ferguson, J. das Gupta (Eds.), *Language problems of developing nations* (pp. 27–35). New York: John Wiley & Sons,.

Fishman, J. A. (1968). Sociolinguistics and the language problems of the developing countries. In J. A. Fishman, C. A. Ferguson, J. das Gupta (Eds.), *Language problems of developing nations* (pp. 1–16). New York: John Wiley & Sons.

Fishman, J. A. (1971). The sociology of language: An interdisciplinary social science approach to language and society. In J. A. Fishman (Ed.), *Advances in the sociology of language* (pp. 217–404). The Hague: Mouton.

Fishman, J. A. (1991). *Reversing language shift. Theoretical and empircal foundations of assistance to threatened languages.* Clevedon: Multilingual Matters.

Fishman, J. A. (Ed.) (2001). *Can threatened languages be saved? Reversing language shift, revisited: A 21st century perspective.* Clevedon: Multilingual Matters.

Fishman, J. A. (2006). *Do not leave your language alone. The Hidden status agendas within corpus planning in language policy.* Mahwah, NJ: Lawrence Erlbaum.

Garvin, P. (1973). Some comments on language planning. In J. Rubin & R. Shuy (Eds.), *Language planning: Current issues and research* (pp. 24–33). Washington, DC: Georgetown University Press. Reprinted in J. A. Fishman (Ed.) (1974). *Advances in language planning* (pp. 69–78). The Hague: Mouton.

Garvin, P. (1993). A conceptual framework for the study of language standardization. *International Journal of the Sociology of Language, 100/101,* 37–54.

Giger, M., & Sloboda, M. (2008). Language management and language problems in Belarus: Education and beyond. *International Journal of Bilingual Education and Bilingualism, 11*(3–4), 314–338. Reprinted in A. Pavlenko (Ed.) (2008). *Multilingualism in post-soviet countries* (pp. 41–65). Bristol: Multilingual Matters.

Haarmann, H. (1990). Language planning in the light of a general theory of language: A methodological framework. *International Journal of the Sociology of Language, 86,* 103–126.

Hall, R. A. (1950). *Leave your language alone!* Ithaca, NY: Linguistica.

Haugen, E. (1959). Planning for a standard language in modern Norway. *Anthropological Linguistics, 1*(3), 8–21. Reprinted in a revised form (1961) as Language planning in modern Norway. *Scandinavian Studies, 33,* 68–81. This version was reprinted (1972) *The ecology of language. Essays by Einar Haugen* (pp. 133–147). Selected and introduced by Anwar S. Dil. Stanford, CA: Stanford University Press.

Haugen, E. (1966). Linguistics and language planning. In W. Bright (Ed.), *Sociolinguistics*. The Hague: Mouton. Reprinted (1972) *The ecology of language: Essays by Einar Haugen* (pp. 159–190). Selected and introduced by Anwar S. Dil. Stanford, CA: Stanford University Press.

Haugen, E. (1969). Language planning, theory and practice. In A. Graur (Ed.), *Actes du Xe Congrès International des Linguistes, Bucarest, 1967* (pp. 701–711). Bucharest: Éditions de L'Académie de la Republique Socialiste de Roumanie. Reprinted (1972) *The ecology of language. Essays by Einar Haugen* (pp. 287–298). Selected and introduced by Anwar S. Dil. Stanford, CA: Stanford University Press.

Havránek, B. (1932a). Úkoly spisovného jazyka a jeho kultura [The task of the standard language and its cultivation]. In B. Havránek & M. Weingart (Eds.), *Spisovnáčeština a jazyková kultura* [Standard Czech and the cultivation of language] (pp. 32–84). Prague: Melantrich. Partially translated into English in P. L. Garvin (Ed.) (1964). *A Prague School Reader on esthetics, literary structure and style* (pp. 3–16). Washington, DC: Georgetown University Press.

Havránek, B. (1932b). Obecné zásady pro kulturu jazyka [General principles for the cultivation of good language]. In B. Havránek & M. Weingart (Eds.), *Spisovná čeština a jazyková kultura* [Standard Czech and the cultivation of language] (pp. 245–258). Prague: Melantrich. English translation in J. Rubin & R. Shuy (Eds.) (1973). *Language planning: Current issues and research* (pp. 102–111). Washington, DC: Georgetown University Press. Reprinted in J. A. Fishman (Ed.) (1974) *Advances in language planning* (pp. 417–426). The Hague: Mouton.

Hornberger, N. H. (2006). Frameworks and models in language policy and planning. In T. Ricento (Ed.), *Language policy: Theory and method* (pp. 24–41). Malden, MA: Blackwell.

Hroch, M. (1998). Social interpretation of linguistic demands in European national movements. In H.-G. Haupt, M. G. Müller & S. Woolf (Eds.), *Regional and national identities in Europe in the XIXth and XXth centuries* (pp. 67–96). Alphen aan den Rijn: Kluwer Law International. Reprinted in M. Hroch (2007). *Comparative studies in modern European history: Nation, nationalism, social change* chapter V (pp. 67–96). Aldershot: Ashgate.

Janich, N., & Greule, A. (Eds.) (2002). *Sprachkulturen in Europa: Ein internationales Handbuch* [Language cultivation in European countries: An international handbook]. Tübingen: Gunter Narr.

Jernudd, B. H. (1993). Language planning from a management perspective: An interpretation of findings. In E. H. Jahr (Ed.), *Language conflict and language planning* (pp. 133–142). Berlin: Mouton de Gruyter.

Jernudd, B. H. (1997a). The [r]evolution of sociolinguistics. In C. B. Paulston & R. G. Tucker (Eds.), *The early days of sociolinguistics* (pp. 131–138). Dallas: Summer Institute of Linguistics.

Jernudd, B. H. (1997b). Theoretical and practical dimensions of language planning work. In Actes del Congrés Europeu sobre Planificació Lingüística [Proceedings of the European Conference on Language Planning] (pp. 9–19). Barcelona, 9–10 November 1995. Barcelona: Generalitat de Catalunya, Departament de Cultura.

Jernudd, B. H., & das Gupta, J. (1971). Towards a theory of language planning. In J. Rubin & B. H. Jernudd (Eds.) *Can language be planned?* (pp. 195–215). Honolulu: The University Press of Hawaii.

Jernudd, B. H., & Neustupný, J. V. (1987). Language plannning: for whom? In L. Laforge (Ed.), *Proceedings of the International Colloquium on Language Planning* (pp. 69–84). Québec: Les Presses de L'Université Laval.

Kaplan, R. B., & Baldauf, R. B., Jr (1997). *Language planning from practice to theory*. Clevedon: Multilingual Matters.

Kaplan, R. B., & Baldauf, R. B., Jr (2005). Editing contributed scholarly articles from a language management perspective. *Journal of Second Language Writing*, 14, 47–62.

Kirkwood, M. (2000). Language planning in the Soviet Union and in the post-Soviet period. In L. N. Zybatow (Ed.), *Sprachwandel in der Slavia* (pp. 701–724). Frankfurt am Main: Peter Lang.

Kondrašov, N. A. (Ed.) (1988). *Teorija literaturnogo jazyka v rabotax učěnyx ČSSR* [*Theory of the standard language in the scholarly works from the former Czechoslovakia*]. (Novoe v zarubežnoj lingvistike [New trends in linguistics abroad] series, XX). Moscow: Progress.

Kuo, E. C. Y., & Jernudd, B. H. (1993). Balancing macro- and micro-sociolinguistic perspectives in language management: The case of Singapore. *Language Problems & Language Planning*, 17, 1–21.

Lanstyák, I., & Szabómihályová, G. (2009). Hungarian in Slovakia: Language management in a bilingual minority community. In J. Nekvapil & T. Sherman (Eds.), *Language management in contact situations: Perspectives from three continents* (pp. 49–73). Frankfurt am Main: Peter Lang.

Lewis, G. (1983). Implementation of language planning in the Soviet Union. In J. Cobarrubias & J. A. Fishman (Eds.), *Progress in language planning. International perspectives* (pp. 309–326). Berlin: Mouton.

Liddicoat, A. J., & Baldauf, R. B., Jr (Eds.) (2008). *Language Planning in local contexts*. Clevedon: Multilingual Matters.

Lo Bianco, J. (1987). *National policy on languages*. Canberra: Australian Government Publishing Service.

Marriott, H. (Ed.) (2004). Academic interaction. Special issue of *Journal of Asian Pacific Communication*, 14(1).

Mathesius, V. (1932). O požadavku stability ve spisovném jazyce [On the requirement of stability for the standard language]. In B. Havránek & M. Weingart (eds.), *Spisovná čeština a jazyková kultura* [Standard Czech and the cultivation of language] (pp. 14–31). Prague: Melantrich. French translation in É. Bédard & J. Maurais (Eds.) (1983). *La norme linguistique* [The language norm] (pp. 809–813). Québec and Paris: Conseil de la langue française, Le Robert.

Miyazaki, S., & Marriott, H. (Eds.) (2003). *Sesshoku bamen to nihongo kyooiku: Neusutopunii no inpakuto* [Contact situation and Japanese as foreign language: The impact of Neustupný]. Tokyo: Meiji shoin.

Muraoka, H. (2009). A typology of problems in contact situations. In J. Nekvapil & T. Sherman (Eds.), *Language management in contact situations: Perspectives from three continents* (pp. 151–166). Frankfurt am Main: Peter Lang.

Nekvapil, J. (2006). From language planning to language management. *Sociolinguistica. International Yearbook of European Sociolinguistics, 20,* 92–104.

Nekvapil, J. (2008). Language cultivation in developed contexts. In B. Spolsky & F. M. Hult (Eds.), *The handbook of educational linguistics* (pp. 251–265). Malden, MA: Blackwell.

Nekvapil, J. (2009). The integrative potential of Language Management Theory. In J. Nekvapil & T. Sherman (Eds.), *Language management in contact situations: Perspectives from three continents* (pp. 1–11). Frankfurt am Main: Peter Lang.

Nekvapil, J., & Nekula, M. (2006). On language management in multinational companies in the Czech Republic. *Current Issues in Language Planning, 7,* 307–327. Reprinted in A. J. Liddicoat & R. B. Baldauf Jr. (Eds.) (2008). *Language planning in local contexts* (pp. 268–287). Clevedon: Multilingual Matters.

Nekvapil, J., & Sherman, T. (2009a). Pre-interaction management in multinational companies in Central Europe. *Current Issues in Language Planning, 10,* 181–198.

Nekvapil, J., & Sherman, T. (Eds.) (2009b). *Language management in contact situations: Perspectives from three continents.* Frankfurt am Main: Peter Lang.

Neustupný, J. V. (1970). Basic types of treatment of language problems. *Linguistic Communications, 1,* 77–98. Reprinted in J. A. Fishman (Ed.) (1974). *Advances in language planning* (pp. 37–48). The Hague: Mouton.

Neustupný, J. V. (1978). *Post-structural approaches to language.* Tokyo: University of Tokyo Press.

Neustupný, J. V. (1993). History of language planning: Retrospects and prospects. Paper presented at the 10th *International Congress of Applied Linguistics* (AILA '93). Amsterdam, August 13.

Neustupný, J. V. (1995). *Atarashii nihongo no tame ni* [Towards new perspectives in Japanese language teaching]. Tokyo: Taishuukan shoten. Partly translated in English and published as Neustupný (2008).

Neustupný, J. V. (2004). A theory of contact situations and the study of academic interaction. *Journal of Asian Pacific Communication, 14*(1), 3–31.

Neustupný, J. V. (2006). Sociolinguistic aspects of social modernization. In U. Ammon, N. Dittmar, K. J. Mattheier & P. Trudgill (Eds), *Sociolinguistics. An international handbook of the science of language and society* (pp. 2209–2223). Berlin: Walter de Gruyter.

Neustupný, J. V. (2008). On research on contact situations. In P. Heinrich & Y. Sugita (Eds.), *Japanese as foreign language in the age of globalization* (pp. 123–138). Munich: Iudicium.

Neustupný, J. V., & Nekvapil, J. (2003). Language management in the Czech Republic. *Current Issues in Language Planning, 4,* 181–366. Reprinted in R. B. Baldauf Jr & R. B. Kaplan (Eds.) (2006). *Language planning and policy in Europe, Vol. 2: The Czech Republic, the European Union and Northen Ireland* (pp. 16–201). Clevedon: Multilingual Matters.

Noreen, A., & Johannson, A. (1892). Über Sprachrichtigkeit [On linguistic correctness]. *Indogermanische Forschungen. Zeitschrift für indogermanische Sprach- und Altertumskunde* [*Journal of Indo-Germanic Studies*], *1,* 95–157.

Pavlenko, A. (2008). Multilingualism in post-Soviet countries: Language revival, language removal, and sociolinguistic theory. In A. Pavlenko (Ed.), *Multilingualism in post-Soviet countries* (pp. 1–40). Bristol: Multilingual Matters.

Pennycook, A. (2006). Postmodernism in language policy. In T. Ricento (Ed.), *Language policy: Theory and method* (pp. 60–76). Malden, MA: Blackwell.

Phillipson, R. (1992). *Linguistic imperialism.* Oxford: Oxford University Press.

Ricento, T. (2000). Historical and theoretical perspectives in language policy and planning. *Journal of Sociolinguistics, 4,* 196–213.

Rubin, J. (1971). Evaluation and language planning. In J. Rubin & B. H. Jernudd (Eds.), *Can language be planned?* (pp. 217–252). Honolulu: The University Press of Hawaii.

Rubin, J. (1986). City planning and language planning. In E. Annamalai, B. H. Jernudd & J. Rubin (Eds.), *Language planning. Proceedings of an institute* (pp. 105–122). Honolulu: Central Institute of Indian Languages, East–West Center.

Rubin, J., & Jernudd, B. H. (Eds.) (1971a). *Can language be planned?* Honolulu: The University Press of Hawaii.

Rubin, J., & Jernudd, B. H. (1971b). Introduction: Language planning as an element in modernization. In J. Rubin & B. H. Jernudd (Eds.) *Can language be planned?* (pp. xiii–xxiv). Honolulu: The University Press of Hawaii.

Rubin, J., Jernudd, B. H., das Gupta, J., Fishman, J. A. & Ferguson, C.A. (Eds.) (1977). *Language planning processes.* The Hague: Mouton.

Scharnhorst, J., & Ising, E. (Eds.) (1976/1982). *Grundlagen der Sprachkultur: Beiträge der Prager Linguistik zur Sprachtheorie und Sprachpflege* [*Fundamentals of the cultivation of language: Prague School contributions to the theory of language and language cultivation*] (Vols 1, 2). Berlin: Akademie-Verlag.

Skutnab-Kangas, T., & Phillipson, R. (Eds.) (1995). *Linguistic human rights: Overcoming linguistic discrimination.* Berlin: Mouton de Gruyter.

Sloboda, M. (2009). A language management approach to language maintenance and shift: A study from post-Soviet Belarus. In J. Nekvapil & T. Sherman (Eds.) *Language management in contact situations: Perspectives from three continents* (pp. 13–47). Frankfurt am Main: Peter Lang.

Strubell, M. (1999). From language planning to language policies and language politics. In P. J. Weber (Ed.), *Contact + confli(c)t. Language planning and minorities* (*Plurilingua* 21) (pp. 237–248). Bonn: Dümmler.

Strubell, M. (2001). Catalan a decade later. In J. A. Fishman (Ed.), *Can threatened languages be saved? Reversing language shift, revisited: A 21st century perspective* (pp. 260–283). Clevedon: Multilingual Matters.

Tollefson, J. W. (1991). *Planning language, planning inequality.* London, New York: Longman.

Tollefson, J. W. (2002). Limitations of language policy and planning. In R. B. Kaplan (Ed.), *Oxford handbook of applied linguistics.* Oxford: Oxford University Press.

Vinokur, G. (1925). *Kul'tura jazyka: Očerki lingvističeskoj texnologii* [*Language cultivation: An outline of linguistic techniques*]. Moscow: Rabotnik prosveščenija.

Williams, G. (1992). *Sociolinguistics. A sociological critique.* London: Routledge.

Williams, G. (2007). Reversing language shift—a sociological visit. In J. Darquennes (Ed.), *Contact linguistics and language minorities/Kontaktlinguistik und sprachminderheiten/Linguistique de contact et minorités linguistiques* (*Plurilingua* 30) (pp. 161–177). St Augustin: Asgard.

53
Language Planning
Approaches and Methods

Nkonko M. Kamwangamalu

Introduction

This chapter offers a survey of approaches and methods in language planning, a field of study whose mission is to find solutions to language problems (Fishman, 1987; Haugen, 1966; Rubin, 1983). A brief description of language planning is in order to provide the background against which the survey of approaches and methods is presented. Language planning has been described as a government authorized, long-term, sustained, and conscious effort to alter a language's function or form in society for the purpose of solving language problems (Fishman, 1987; Weinstein, 1980). It is a field of study where language is seen as a societal resource (Eastman, 1983, p. ix; Jernudd & Das Gupta, 1971, p. 196); that is, policy statements formulated against such a perspective are aimed to serve as guides by which language is preserved, managed, and developed (Ruiz, 1988, pp. 10–11).

As Spolsky (2004, p. 215) puts it, language planning is about choice—whether of a specific linguistic item, or expression, or of a specific variety or language—made by an individual, a group of individuals, or an authority. (See also Johnson & Johnson, 1998, p. 186; Haugen, 1972, p. 162.) Language planning, say Kaplan and Baldauf (1997, p. 303), is ultimately about human resource development; it is concerned with questions such as who has the right to do what to whom for what purpose. Along these same lines, Cooper (1989) remarks that language planning seeks to determine who defines the problem to be solved or the behavior to be changed, how decisions are reached with respect to goals and means, and the outcomes of implementation, and for each of these in the social context in which planning is embedded. For Haarmann (1990), an understanding of the overall effect of language planning cannot be attained by focusing solely on the aforementioned string of relations, namely, who does what to whom and for what purposes, but also one must take into consideration another set of relations including *who* accepts *what* planning provisions *from whom* and under *what* conditions (Haarmann, 1990, p. 123).

Taken together, these relations are captured in what Cooper (1989, pp. 97–98) calls an "accounting scheme for the study of language planning" that includes the following components: "(i) What *actors* (ii) attempt to influence what *behaviors*, (iii) of which *people*, (iv) for what *ends*, (v) under what *conditions*, (vi) by what *means*, (vii) through *what decision-making process*, (viii) with what *effect*." Cooper offers an elaborate description and illustration of the components of this theory (1989, pp. 88–98; see also Cooper, 1983, pp. 19–36), and a substantive discussion is also provided in Kaplan and

Baldauf (1997, pp. 52–58). It suffices to note, however, that Cooper's theory provides a broad picture of what a language planning exercise entails, bringing together the several variables that impact on language planning, such as those proposed in Haarmann (1990, p. 123), as highlighted previously, and other aspects that are subsequently developed by others in greater detail (see Spolsky, 2004, p. 5, 2009, p. 1; Paulston, 1983, pp. 57–65; Haugen, 1966, pp. 16–26, 1983, p. 275). However, Cooper's theory would benefit from an additional component, namely, historical and structural factors (see, e.g., Tollefson, 1991, pp. 31–38; Wiley, 2006, pp. 140, 142) that also tend to influence language planning outcomes.

In that regard, Tollefson contrasts two approaches to language planning, the neoclassical approach and the historical-structural approach. He criticizes the former for being ahistorical in that it does not, all else being equal, take into account the social forces that lead to the adoption of the planning approach, the historical and structural factors (e.g., a country's socio-economic development, the political organization of decision making, the role of language in social policy, the perceived status of and attitude toward various languages in a community, and so on) that determine the evaluative criteria by which plans are judged to be ineffective, or the political and economic interest that benefit from the perceived failure of planning (Tollefson, 1991, p. 28). In contrast, the historical-structural approach views language planning as a historical process inseparable from structural considerations, as previously highlighted, and as a mechanism by which the interests of dominant socio-political groups are maintained and the seeds of transformation are developed (p. 32). Accordingly, Tollefson argues that discussions of solutions to the language problems facing individuals must begin with a deep appreciation for the powerful historical and structural forces that pattern individual language behavior (p. 39). In other words, a polity's social history plays a central role in language planning, whether at the micro-level of interpersonal communication or the macro-level of state formation (Ricento, 2006a, p. 130). For instance, in South Africa the Black population prefers English-medium education over an education through the medium of an African language not solely because of the instrumental value with which English is associated, but also and more importantly because of past apartheid language policies such as the Bantu Education Act, which sought to deny the Black population access to English, the language needed for social mobility (Kamwangamalu, 1997, p. 237).

Traditionally and following Kloss (1969, pp. 81–83, 1977), efforts to address the questions raised in Cooper's framework have focused on either the status of a given language vis-à-vis other languages in a polity, hence *status planning*; or on its internal condition with a view to changing that condition, hence *corpus planning*; or on both of these since they are not mutually exclusive (Wardhaugh, 1987). More specifically, status planning regulates the power relationship between languages and their respective speakers in what Bourdieu (1991) has termed "the linguistic market place," that is, the social context in which language is used. It is often associated with the official recognition that national governments attach to various languages, and with authoritative attempts to restrict language use in various contexts (Wiley, 1996). *Corpus planning*, or what other scholars refer to as *language cultivation* (Paulston, 1983, p. 55) or *language development* (Jernudd, 1973), involves attempts to define or reform the standard language by changing or introducing forms of spelling, pronunciation, vocabulary, and grammar (Fishman, 1983).

In addition to the two categories of language planning mentioned, however, Cooper (1989, p. 33) and Haarmann (1990, p. 104) have each proposed an additional category, *acquisition planning* and *prestige planning*, respectively. With respect to the former, Cooper notes that language planning involves decisions concerning the teaching and use of language. Considerable planning energy is directed toward language spread, especially through education; and technically status planning relates to increasing or restricting the *uses* of a language but not to increasing the number of its *speakers*. Therefore, Cooper argues, when language planning is directed toward increasing the number of users, e.g., speakers, writers, listeners, or readers, then in addition to the status planning–corpus planning distinction, a separate category of language planning, *language acquisition planning*, is justified. With respect to the latter (prestige planning), Haarmann (1990) notes that whether a corpus- or status planning activity succeeds or fails depends on the positive values or prestige with which it is associated by the planners (i.e., *producers* of language planning) on the one hand, and the speech community (i.e., *receivers* of language planning) whose language is the target of planning, on the other. Accordingly, Haarmann argues, *prestige planning* must be recognized as a separate functional range of language planning because, in his view, it does not depend on activities in the ranges of corpus or status planning. It is debatable to what extent *prestige planning* can or cannot be treated as an aspect of *status planning* (see also Ager, 2005). However, there is overwhelming evidence from language planning in post-colonial polities in Africa and elsewhere that shows that giving official recognition to indigenous languages, for instance, does not necessarily translate, in practice, into prestige and status for those languages (e.g., Kamwendo, 1994; Kamwangamalu, 2004).

Regardless of the type of language planning being envisioned, whether status, corpus, acquisition, or prestige planning, essentially a language planning exercise can be understood in terms of the four-fold model of language planning proposed by Haugen (1983, pp. 270–276) that includes the following ordered stages, of which the first two deal with the norm and the next two with the function of language in society: (1) selection of *norm*; (2) codification of *norm*; (3) implementation of *function*; and (4) elaboration of *function*. Haugen says that (1) and (3) are primarily societal, hence external to the language, while (2) and (4) are primarily linguistic, hence internal to language. Thus, (1) and (3) on the one hand and (2) and (4) on the other represent what is traditionally called *status planning* and *corpus planning*, respectively.

The first stage in Haugen's framework, norm selection, is described as a socio-political act performed by society leaders of choosing a language or a variety that will have the most prestige and/or acceptance and enjoy a given status in society. The second stage, codification, is concerned with specifying the form of the chosen standard and designing strategies that would allow for the goals of norm selection (i.e., prestige, status) to be achieved. The third stage, implementation, or what Schiffman (1996, p. 119) understandably refers to as the "weakest link" in language policies, includes the activity of government agencies and non-governmental organizations geared toward promoting acceptance of and spreading the language form that has been selected. Acceptance has to do with the attitude of potential users of the chosen language or variety. It is fundamental to the formulation of language planning and a prerequisite for the success of its operation. As Baker (2006, p. 211) remarks, no language planning activity will succeed which does not conform to the expressed attitudes of those involved and persuade those who express negative attitudes about the rightness of the proposed planning. The last stage, elaboration, is seen as, in many ways, the continued implementation of the selected norm to ensure that it is developed enough to meet the needs of its users. Also, since language planning is a continuing activity that is shaped by the linguistic culture of the target community, it must be subject to evaluation, which Fishman (1983, p. 51) refers to as "the *bête noire* of all planning," to determine planning success or failure (Daoust, 1997, p. 450).

Furthermore, a language planning activity is context-bound, that is, it cannot be understood apart from its social context or apart from the history which produced that context (Cooper, 1989, p. 183). As Schiffman (1996, p. 22) notes,

> language policies do not evolve *ex nihilo*; they are not taken off a shelf, dusted off, and plugged into a particular polity; rather, they are *cultural constructs*, and are rooted in and evolve from historical elements of many kinds, some explicit and overt, some implicit and covert.

Anticipating Schiffman's and Cooper's points, Ferguson (1977, p. 9) noted that "all language planning activities take place in particular sociolinguistic settings, and the nature and scope of the planning can only be fully understood in relation to the settings." Finally, language planning is an interdisciplinary affair; in other words, language problems cannot be solved by attention to language alone; the social, economic, and political context in which a language functions must be taken into account as well (Fishman, 1987; Wardhaugh, 1987; Weinstein, 1980). As Grin (2006, p. 78) puts it, "no issue is, per se, sociological, linguistic, political, or economic; rather, almost every issue presents sociological, linguistic, political, and economic dimensions." Thus, it is not a coincidence that language planning has been of interest not only to linguists but also to researchers in cognate disciplines such as political sciences and economics in particular.

To summarize, in this section language planning and language planning type (corpus, status, acquisition, and prestige planning) are described, and some of the approaches that have informed language planning research over the years, such as Haugen's (1983) fourfold model of language planning, Cooper's (1989) accounting scheme for the study of language planning, Tollefson's (1991) historical-structural approach, and Haarmann's (1990) ideal typology of language planning have been highlighted. Additional approaches can be found in Rubin and Jernudd (1971), where Thorburn (1971) and Jernudd (1971) propose a "Cost-benefit analysis in language planning" and an "economic analysis for solving language problems," respectively. Kaplan and Baldauf (2003) have also suggested a framework that incorporates status, corpus, acquisition/language-in-education, and prestige planning.

Theoretical Approaches to Language Planning

The next section reviews some of the most recent or least explored approaches to language planning, with a focus on the following: critical language policy, game theory, language economics, and language management theory. The review is not exhaustive but it, nonetheless, covers most of the approaches found in the language planning literature to date.

Language Planning and Critical Theory

Tollefson (2006) describes critical language policy as an approach to language planning that investigates the processes by which systems of inequality are created and sustained through language. This it does by highlighting the concept of power in the reproduction of inequality. In critical language policy, power refers to the ability to control language for personal interest (Bourdieu, 1991; Fairclough, 1992; Foucault, 1979; Gramsci, 1988; Tollefson, 2006). Those who have power over language, says Edelman (1977, p. 31), use it to achieve political power. Those who have political power, the elites, use it to their advantage to formulate language policies that serve the best interest of the politically dominant social group. Against this background and unlike the neoclassical approach, a critical theory approach to language planning acknowledges that although language planning is about choice, individuals do not actually have freedom of language choice, be it in education or in social life (Paulston, 2003, p. 476). Accordingly, critical language policy researchers assume an adversarial model for social change, in which struggle is a prerequisite for social justice (Tollefson, 2006). Their goal is to describe and explain hegemonic practices, which Gramsci (1988) defines as institutional practices that ensure that power remains in the hands of the few. Linguists working in this field have the responsibility to not only understand how dominant social groups use language for establishing and maintaining social hierarchies, but also to investigate ways to alter those hierarchies (Tollefson, 2002).

There is ample evidence of hegemonic practices in language planning especially in multilingual polities around the world. Kamwangamalu (1997, 2004) reports that in Africa, efforts to replace former colonial languages with indigenous languages have generally failed because policy-makers privately subvert language policies they publicly profess to support. They do so by theoretically giving official status to the indigenous languages that is equal to that of former colonial languages, but not allowing indigenous languages access to important domains (e.g., extensive use in the educational system, socio-economic and political participation, or access to employment) that a former colonial language has for a minority of the population (the elite) that has access to it.

For instance, South Africa has 11 official languages and yet being egalitarian in official status has not resulted in equal outcomes for indigenous languages vis-à-vis English and Afrikaans. In contrast with the latter two languages, indigenous languages continue to be perceived as a barrier to social mobility, much as they were in the apartheid era (Kamwangamalu, 1997). In Tanzania, and despite the late President Julius Nyerere's effort to promote the use of Kiswahili in all the institutions of the state, Swahili lags behind English in terms of prestige and social outcomes. Tanzania's elites subvert the official policy by ensuring that they send their own children to private, English-medium schools either at home or abroad, so that they will not suffer the consequences (e.g., lack of access to high paying jobs) of an education through the medium of an indigenous language, Swahili (Mafu, 1999). Djite (1985, p. 76) makes a similar point concerning the population's attitude toward language policy in Ivory Coast:

> The dream of being able to speak Standard French one day and finally achieve higher social status is coupled with the suspicion that the officials are trying to rob them of that opportunity. They [i.e., the population] argue that while the officials are making promises about the new language policy, they are sending their own children abroad so that they do not have to suffer from the change. Thus, the national language is seen only as a lure to self-destruction.

Along these same lines, in his discussion of language policy in the Philippines Sibayan (1983) remarks that while Filipinos do not object entirely to having an education through the medium of Pilipino (since renamed Filipino), the language should allow individuals to have access to world knowledge and to achieve personal advancement. He admonishes policy-makers and language planners and implementers to interpret Filipino's reaction to language policy by saying "Do something to make Pilipino do many of the things that English is doing for the Filipino now" (Sibayan, 1983, p. 85). All these cases attest to hegemonic practices in language planning, practices that favor an exoglossic over an endoglossic approach to language planning especially in post-colonial settings.

Language Planning and Game Theory

Game theory has its foundation in mathematics. The theory emerged as a result of collaboration between the mathematician von Neumann and the economist Oskar Morgenstern in the early 1940s (Straffin, 1993). Described as the logical analysis of situations of conflict and cooperation, game theory deals with rational behavior in a social setting. In particular, the theory is concerned with explaining how participants or players in a game, be they individuals, groups, or organizations should act rather than with the question of how they will actually act in order to promote their interests (Harsanyi, 1977). Because playing the game is interest-driven, there is the potential for conflict and cooperation between the players. Conflict refers to the fact that the players will value the outcomes of a game differently. Cooperation refers to the fact that the players may coordinate their choices to achieve an outcome with better payoffs for everyone (Straffin, 1993).

In this theoretical framework, the term "game" is understood to mean any situation in which there are at least two players, each with a number of possible options or strategies to choose from in order to achieve desirable, payoffs-driven, outcomes (Laitin, 1992). It is noted that the outcome of a game is not determined by an individual player's choice alone, but also depends on the decisions taken by other players. Because of this consideration for other players, and if everyone does what is individually rational and has no incentive to change one's own behavior (Laitin, 1991), the outcome of a game is said to be in "*equilibrium*"; that is, "each player looks at the outcome and realizes that one could do not better by unilaterally changing one's strategy" (Laitin, 1992, p. 34). As Grin (1994, p. 29) puts it, players will compare the costs and benefits of several options available to them and select the option which yields the highest net payoffs.

The goal of game theory is to predict and explain real-life human behavior in various social situations. With respect to language planning, Harsanyi (1977) remarks that game theory has predictive power to determine whether a language policy will fail or succeed. In the language planning literature, there is a dearth of research based on game-theoretic ideas (Pool, 1993; Laitin, 1992, 1993). Drawing on game theory, Laitin (1992) conducted research on language policy outcomes in multilingual settings such as India and many African countries, with a view to predicting possible language policy scenarios. His findings, summarized in Kamwangamalu (1997, p. 80), made two predictions concerning language policy outcomes in post-colonial settings.

First, he predicted that market forces would force multilingual countries to formulate policies geared toward "a 3 ± 1 language outcome." By this formula, Laitin is referring to the number of languages citizens need to know if they are to have a wide set of mobility opportunities within their country. These languages would include an international language, a European language that is, which will be used in domains such as higher education, diplomacy, and international trade, and serve as a gateway to the outside world; a language for national integration, such as Swahili in Tanzania or Hindi in India, which will be the medium of instruction in later years of primary education and become a required subject for educational advancement throughout the country; and a national or regional language, which will be the medium of instruction in early years of primary education and serve as the language of government and administration in home regions. It is observed that those citizens whose mother tongue is the same as the national language will need to learn only two languages, hence the 3 − 1 outcome, while those whose vernacular is not will need to learn four, hence the 3 + 1 outcome.

Sibayan (1983) reached similar conclusions in a survey of language use and attitudes toward language in the Philippines. He notes, for instance, that Filipinos are confronted with the problem of reconciling the demands of ethnicity, nationalism, and modernization. He argues, however, that these demands can be harmonized by giving the competing languages—the vernaculars, Pilipino, and English—each their share in the advancement of Filipinos. It is interesting to note that the 3 ± 1 language outcome is consonant with Phillipson and Skutnabb-Kangas's (1995) view about language rights in multilingual contexts. In particular, the authors argue that everybody has the right to identify with, learn, and use their mother tongue in most official situations including schools. However, everybody whose mother tongue is not an official language in the country where they are resident can become bilingual, hence 3 − 1 language outcome, in the mother tongue and one of the official languages according to their own choice.

The second prediction that Laitin made about language planning outcomes in multilingual post-colonial societies is what he calls the *private subversion* of language planning, that is, the practice of agreeing with language policy publicly but subverting it privately (Laitin, 1993, p. 233, 1992, p. 43). Laitin gives two instructive examples of this phenomenon. The first example concerns Somalia, a country in which virtually all citizens speak Somali but where the elite Somalis feared that choosing Somali as the official language of the country (in lieu of the colonial languages—Arabic, English, and Italian) would work against their interests. Accordingly, although the elite agreed with the elevation of Somali to the status of official language, those with private resources found it individually beneficial to circumvent the policy by sending their own children to private schools within the country or abroad, where they would have an education through the medium of an international language. (See also Djite, 1985, cited earlier.) The second example concerns Catalan, the language of Catalonia in Spain. Laitin observes that in Catalonia, where he researched the language revival movement occurring there, private *subverters* would buy a local newspaper written in Catalan to cover the fact that they were reading *El Pais* or *La Vanguardia* (both prestigious Spanish language papers), which was hidden inside. He notes, pointedly, that the public face of Catalonia was masking the private reality of Spanish-language hegemony (Laitin, 1991, p. 134).

Almost two decades later, Laitin's findings have turned out to reflect the norm for language policy in most post-colonial polities including those in Africa and elsewhere, thus confirming the predictive power of game theory. In particular, the norm in these polities is that regional languages have become the normal language of primary education and local administration. At the same time, however, citizens have strong incentives to learn an international language such as English for its economic payoffs. It must be noted, however, that in post-colonial polities language policy outcomes are not always in equilibrium for everyone, nor do all the constituents in those polities participate in what may be called a "language-policy-making" game. The reality in post-colonial polities is rather starkly different. Language policies and their outcomes are designed by vested interests and ultimately benefit those who are in power, the elite. Nekvapil and Nekula (2006, p. 311) make a similar remark concerning power in their discussion of language management theory to be described later. In particular, they point out that the interests of different participants and social groups in language planning situations are not identical, and the distribution of power among them is uneven. It is not an accident that language policies in post-colonial states in Africa in particular and in some Asian countries are not any different than the inherited colonial language policies. Not only do the policies continue to ensure, through legislation, the hegemony of former colonial languages and concomitant marginalization of the indigenous languages, but they are also designed to advance the interest of one group, the elite, at the expense of another, the majority of a polity's population.

Commenting on Laitin's framework, Fardon and Furniss (1994) observe pointedly that the three-language formula comes close to stating the status quo in much of post-colonial Africa. They note that the originality of Laitin's interpretation of language policies in Africa lies in demonstrating that radical departure from this pattern is highly unlikely, unless there is a radical change that overthrows the inherited language policies and especially targets the social forces such as the elite who, understandably, have a vested interest in maintaining the status quo. Also, former colonial languages remain the language of government in most ex-colonies, and are accessible only to a minority of the elite class. In this regard, Pool (1993, p. 53) explains that rulers purposely make the language of rulers inaccessible to everyone since a larger ruling class would reduce the polity's total product and dilute the rulers' per-capita gains.

Language Planning and Language Economics

Like game theory, economic considerations in language planning constitute a relatively recent development. Traditionally, as Grin (2006, p. 77) remarks pointedly, policy discourses about language have tended to rely on one of three main perspectives: a legal one, in which language policy often takes the form of the enunciation of language rights in given contexts; a culturalist one, in which languages are mostly seen as manifestations of culture, confining policy to a set of measures affecting corpus or, at best, support for literary creation or publications; and an educational one, focusing on language teaching.

Language economics, also known as *the economics of language*, mainly focuses on the theoretical and empirical analysis of the ways in which linguistic and economic variables influence one another (Grin, 2001, p. 68; Vaillancourt, 1996). Some of the issues raised in "language economics" that are relevant to this chapter include the following:

- the relevance of language as a defining element of economic processes such as production, distribution, and consumption;
- the relevance of language as a commodity in the acquisition of which individual actors may have a good reason to invest;
- language teaching as a social investment, yielding net benefits (market-related or not);
- the economic implications (costs and benefits) of language policies, whether these costs and benefits are market-related or not.

(Grin, 2001, p. 66)

In addition, Grin (1994, p. 25) lists the following among the issues studied in language economics: the effect of language on income, language learning by immigrants, patterns of language maintenance and spread in multilingual societies, the selection and design of language policies, minority language protection and promotion, language use in the workplace, and market equilibrium for language-specific goods and services.

Within the framework of language economics, linguistic products such as language, language varieties, utterances, and accents are seen not only as goods or commodities to which the market assigns a value, but as signs of wealth or capital, which receive their value only in relation to a market, characterized by a particular law of price formation (Bourdieu, 1991, pp. 66–67). The term "market" refers to the social context in which linguistic products are used. In a given linguistic market, some products are valued more highly than others. This means, as Bourdieu puts it, that the market fixes the price for a linguistic product or capital, the nature, and therefore the objective value of which the practical anticipation of this price helped to determine (p. 77). The market value of a linguistic capital such as language or language variety is determined in relation to other linguistic products in the planetary economy (Coulmas, 1992, pp. 77–85). It is, as Gideon Strauss (1996, p. 9) notes, an index of the functional appreciation of the language by the relevant community. Bourdieu (1991, p. 18) argues that the more linguistic capital (i.e., perceptibly valuable linguistic capital) that speakers possess the more they are able to exploit the system of differences to their advantage and thereby secure a profit of distinction.

Under the framework of language economics, language planning issues are treated as a marketing problem (Kamwangamalu, 2004). Essentially, says Dominguez (1998, p. 4), all marketing action consists of placing the most ideal product (product policy) in the adequate place and moment (distribution policy), at the convenient price (price policy) causing consumer demand with the most efficacious means (promotion policy). Along these same lines, Cooper (1989, p. 72) remarks that viewing a language planning issue as a marketing problem entails "developing the right *product* backed by the right *promotion* and put in the right *place* at the right *price*." Concerning the *product*, Cooper says that language planners must recognize, identify, or design products which the potential consumer will find attractive. These products are to be defined and audiences targeted on the basis of (empirically determined) consumer needs. Dominguez (1998, p. 1) concurs, noting that the *product* is "the solution of a problem" or "what meets a conscious or unconscious need."

Promotion of a communicative innovation such as language refers to efforts to induce potential users to adopt it, whether adoption is viewed as awareness, positive evaluation, proficiency, or usage (Cooper, 1989, p. 74). Put differently, promotion deals with communicating the benefits that a product or service carries and persuading the market to buy it (Dominguez, 1998, p. 7). For instance, if a policy is designed to promote an indigenous language such as Zulu in South Africa, then the population needs to know what Zulu will do for them in terms of upward social mobility and access to resources. As Dominguez explains, the fact that access/promotion to certain jobs requires a language qualification creates a very visible economic component.

Place refers to the provision of adequate channels of distribution and response. That is, a person motivated to buy a product must know where to find it (Cooper, 1989, p. 78). And the *price* of a consumer product is viewed as the key to determining the product's appeal to the consumers (Cooper, 1989, p. 79). It is more so because, as Shabani (2004, p.195) remarks, the value of a language is tied to the value of the ends for which it is used.

The literature increasingly recognizes the importance of the relationship between language and the economy in the success or failure of language planning and policy (Canagarajah, 2006; Kamwangamalu, 2004; Le Page, 1997; Nettle, 2000; Paulston, 1988; Vaillancourt & Grin, 2000; Walsh, 2006). In particular, it provides ample evidence that language planning and policy activities succeed if they lead to desirable economic outcomes. Needless to say, these outcomes cannot be achieved unless language is seen as a commodity. To view language as a commodity, remarks Pennycook (2008, p. xii), "is to view language in instrumental, pragmatic and commercial terms, which is precisely the dominant discourse on language in many contemporary contexts."

For instance, Fishman (2006) refers to the success of the "Basquecization" activities in Spain, that is, activities intended to promote the Basque language in that country. He explains that *Basquecization* activities were successful because participation in these activities yielded certification at various levels of competence, entitling their bearers to qualify for promotions, raises, job tenure and other perquisites of success in the workplace (e.g., Fishman, 2006). Like Fishman, Vivian Edwards (2004) asserts that although language is part of our cultural capital, its market value is variable. She points to the case of Welsh and Māori, noting that official status of these languages has generated a range of employment prospects for minority language speakers in education, the media, and government. Likewise, Gibson Ferguson (2006) provides a comparative study of Welsh and Breton, showing that the revival of Welsh and the continuing decline of Breton are mostly due to different socio-political and economic factors. Clearly, all these cases point to the importance of economic considerations in language planning; ignoring them will not benefit policy implementation.

Language Planning and Language Management Theory

As already noted, language planning is a multidimensional discipline, encompassing as it does linguistic and sociolinguistic, economic and political aspects of the integration of language in society. Besides these aspects, some scholars have proposed that language planning can be approached from a management perspective (Jernudd, 1993; Jernudd & Neustupný, 1987; Neustupný, 2004; Spolsky, 2009; Webb, 2002; Nekvapil, Chapter 52, this volume). Generally, management is described as the set of activities undertaken to ensure that the goals of an organization are achieved in an effective and efficient way. In language planning terms, however, language management refers to the actions and strategies devised to achieve language policy objectives (Webb, 2002). From this perspective, a language management approach to language planning can be described as a top-down process, which is what it has been in most polities around the world. Other scholars, however, view language management differently (Jernudd, 1993; Jernudd & Neustupný, 1987; Nekvapil & Nekula, 2006; Spolsky, 2009). Jernudd (1993, 134, cited in Kaplan & Baldauf, 1997, p. 207) views language management approach to language planning as "a shift of focus from the concern of language planning concerned with finding optimal strategies for government-initiated action, to an interest in explaining how individuals manage language in communication, and uses this as the starting point for community-wide management."

As Jernudd and Neustupný (1987) put it, linguistics has moved toward a better understanding not merely of how people use language but also how they interact with it. It is this system of interaction that Jernudd and Neustupný (1987, p. 71) refer to as *language management*. As an object of linguistic inquiry, language management is viewed as a process in which (1) speaker/writer and hear/reader subconsciously not only monitor language use against the norms they possess but also *note* the deviations that occur, (2) *evaluate* the noted deviations and establish the inadequacies,

(3) *plan adjustments* to correct the deviations as needed according to the norms, and (4) complete the process when they *implement* the planned adjustments (Jernudd & Neustupný, 1987, pp. 75–76; Neustupný, 2004, p. 23). Nekvapil and Nekula (2006, p. 311) note that these four stages (noting, evaluation, planning of adjustments, implementation) constitute different stages of language management. The details of these stages and of language management theory as a whole are discussed in Jernudd and Neustupný (1987), Neustupný (2004), Neustupný and Nekvapil (2003) and so will not concern us here. It suffices to note briefly, however, that language management is said to operate at two levels, the micro- and macro-level. The former focuses on the discourse and is called "simple management," and the latter addresses language as a system and is called "organized management." The correction of an incorrect lexical selection, for instance, is an instance of simple management, whereas the introduction of a language into a school system, the choice of an official language, a systematic public language policy, etc., are examples of organized management. Unlike simple language management, organized language management is said to involve the use of theoretical components, a specific idiom for discussing language issues, extensive discussions between vested interests, and so on.

Spolsky (2009) also approaches language planning from a management perspective, but his theory of language management focuses on language choice rather than on how individuals interact with language. From this perspective, Sposky uses the term "language management" as synonymous with "language planning," which he says is about choice (Spolsky 2004, p. 215)—whether of a specific linguistic item, or expression, or of a specific variety or language—made by an individual, a group of individuals, or an authority. Accordingly, his theory of language management seeks to explain how in a speech community individuals choose what language to speak under what circumstances and for what purposes. For Spolsky, some of the language choices the members of a speech community make "are the result of management, reflecting conscious and explicit efforts by language managers to control the choices" (2009, p. 1). Language managers are understood to be either individuals, a special interest group, an institution or business, the government, schools, a legislative assembly, etc. At the heart of Spolsky's proposed language management theory is the argument that three conditions account for language choice in a speech community: practices, beliefs, and management. *Language practices* are determined by language proficiency and are defined as the observable behaviors and practices, what people actually do with language. They are a habitual pattern of selecting among the varieties that make up a community's linguistic repertoire (Spolsky, 2004, p. 5).

Beliefs about language, also known as ideology, are said to be values or statuses that the speech community associates with its language products, be they languages, language varieties, or language features such as accents. Like language economics, language management theory assumes that the value of a language product derives from the social and economic benefits a speaker can get by using it. But unlike language economics, language management theory does not delve into how linguistic and economic variables influence one another. Beliefs about language are part of what Harold Schiffman (1996) has termed "*linguistic culture*," which he defines as "the sum totality of ideas, values, beliefs, attitudes, prejudices, myths, religious strictures, and all other cultural 'baggage' that speakers bring to their dealings with language from their culture" (1996, p. 112).

The third condition that Spolsky says accounts for language choice in a speech community is *management*. This Spolsky describes as "the explicit and observable effort by someone or some group that has or claims authority over the participants in a domain (e.g., family, work, etc.) to modify their practices or beliefs" (2009, p. 1). It is said to refer to the formulation and proclamation of an explicit plan or policy, written or not, about language use. Taken together, language practices, beliefs, and management constitute what in an earlier study Spolsky (2004, p. 5) refers to as "the language policy of a speech community."

Language management adds to the theoretical apparatus in language planning research. It represents a bottom-up approach to language planning, for it is mainly concerned with how individuals interact with language (Jernudd & Neustupný, 1987) or with determining language choice in daily interactions among the members of a speech community (Spolsky, 2009). Data obtained from these interactions can serve as the basis on which language policies can be formulated that benefit not the select few but entire communities. As already noted, economic considerations are not a central tenant of a language management theory of language planning (however, cf. Neustupný & Nekvapil, 2003, p. 186, Nekvapil & Nekula, 2006, p. 312; Nekvapil, Chapter 52, this volume), suggesting that it must be augmented by other approaches such as those discussed previously (e.g., language economics, game theory) if it is to account for language choice and for simple and organized management (Neustupný, 2004, Nekvapil & Sherman, 2009) especially in multilingual societies.

Methods in Language Planning

The following section offers a review of some of the methods used in language planning studies, with a focus on language surveys, ethnographic methods, and geolinguistic analysis. Additional discussion of methods can be found in Baldauf (2010), Eastman (1983), Kaplan and Baldauf (1997), and Ricento (2006b).

Ethnographic Observations

Ethnography is a field of study which is concerned primarily and traditionally with the anthropological process of describing and analyzing a "whole" culture (Saville-Troike, 1982, p. 1; Green & Wallat, 1981, p. xi). Ethnographic work is said to be holistic not because of the size of the social unit under study, be it a community, an educational institution, a classroom or home, but because the units of analysis are considered analytically as wholes (Green & Wallat, 1981, p. xii). The emergence of ethnography from linguistics has its roots in Dell Hymes's (1964) paper entitled "Ethnography of communication," which was a response to a call by Hymes himself for an approach that would account for the relationship between language and culture. Ethnography has since served as a useful method for data collection on a wide range of issues, such as codeswitching, language attitudes, or language and identity. It includes a variety of data collection procedures, among them participant observation, interviews, mapping and charting patterns recorded in field notes, interaction analysis, study of historical records and current public documents, use of demographic data, case studies, case histories, or audio- and video-recording of communication patterns in the unit under study (Geertz, 1973; Green & Wallat, 1981; Lutz, 1981; Rudwick, 2005; Saville-Troike, 1982).

Although ethnography uses a bundle of methods, or what Geertz (1973) refers to as "a thick description," its central and defining feature is the participant observation of a society or a community through a complete cycle of events that regularly occur as that society interacts with its environment (Lutz, 1981, p. 52). The main goal of participant observation is to holistically understand a community in order to present a detailed description of a particular element, which for our purpose is language practice, in that community. For the ethnographer, then, doing ethnography involves first and foremost field work, including observing, asking questions, participating in group activities, and testing the validity of one's perceptions against the intuition of the members of the target community (Saville-Troike, 1982, p. 4).

In view of the data collection procedures it involves, ethnography can be described as a bottom-up method. As Ricento (2006b, p. 130) observes, ethnography can provide insights about life at the grass-roots level and lead to better understanding of the role of language in the lives of people directly affected by overt or covert language policies or regimes. These insights are vital for language planning decision-making, as they can help language planning producers, language planning receivers, and language planning professionals interpret lived experiences and local practices. In this regard,

Canagarajah (2006, pp. 157–158) remarks that ethnographic research can provide feedback on the diverse stages of language planning—before, during, and after implementation. Drawing on King (2001), Maddox (2001), and Schiffman (2003), Canagarajah (2006, p. 158) notes that before implementation, ethnography can provide crucial information on matters such as the target community's attitudes toward the languages for which planning is being made, or the significance of language for identity and community. During implementation, ethnography may explore how different agencies and institutions function in promoting the policy. After the implementation, ethnography may examine the consequences of language planning operation for the target community as well as the consistency with which the plan has been implemented in diverse localities.

The significance of ethnography to language planning lies in the fact that ethnography seeks to find answers to the questions of language choice that are also at the heart of language planning: who uses what (variety of) language, with whom, about what, in what setting, for what purposes? However, unlike language planning, which tends to be applied in a top-down fashion, the ultimate goal of an ethnographic description of language choice in a community is a conscious attempt to provide what Harris (1976) refers to as an *emic* account of the data; that is, a description and understanding of language behavior from the perspective and interests of the members of the community under study, *the insiders* (Hymes, 1974; Seviny, 1981).

Although ethnography helps collect first-hand data on language practices in a community, it has been criticized for being biased toward treating the views and interests of the community under study as always right (Canagarajah, 2006, p. 163). Lutz (1981, p. 51) puts the criticism bluntly, saying that "as educators twist the tool to fit their data (rather than shape their understanding of the data with the tool), ethnography, in particular, and sometimes ethnographic methods are often modified and occasionally bastardized." In addition, it could be argued that the very presence of the participant observer in a community, together with the tools (e.g., recording instruments) s/he uses for data collection, makes ethnographic observations somewhat intrusive. As such, ethnographic observations run into the problem that Labov (1978) refers to as the observer's paradox: to obtain the data most important for linguistic analysis, we have to observe how people speak when they are not being observed (1978, pp. 354, 356). On the other hand, the observer cannot make secret recordings of people's speech because such practice is unethical and often difficult. Furthermore, in interviews the participants may not feel comfortable expressing themselves freely especially if they are aware that their speech is being recorded. For this reason, Breitborde (1998, p. 15) observes that in order to be a successful participant observer, the researcher must be accepted by the community to be studied and must, in Saville-Troike's (1982, p. 122) view, have a high level of linguistic as well as cultural competence. Despite the criticism leveled against them, it must be said, however, that ethnographic observations can and generally do provide holistic insights into the ways in which a society interacts with and through language; and in doing so, help to find answers to the very questions with which language planning is concerned—who chooses what language, for what purposes, under what circumstances, and with what effect (Cooper, 1989; Haarmann, 1990; Haugen, 1983). Ethnographic observations can be augmented by other data collection procedures, such as language surveys, which are discussed in the next section.

Language Surveys

Generally speaking, language use surveys consist of questionnaires intended to determine, among other things, the speakers' attitudes toward the languages available to them, as well as the language the speaker uses when, where, with whom, and for what purpose (Fishman, 1972). Language surveys can be conducted to determine individual, family, community, organization, or national language practices. In this regard, Kaplan and Baldauf (1997, p. 104) note that a sociolinguistic survey may be intended to provide answers to questions such as the following: in what language does one read the newspapers, hear the news, address one's parents/peers/siblings/children/dependants/spouse, and so on? Reporting on his experience with a language survey in Kenya, Whiteley (1983) notes that social appropriateness determines language choice in this multilingual society, where Swahili, English, and the vernacular are in competition. Whether one or the other of these three languages is used in a given interaction depends upon what is at stake in the interaction. For instance,

> a man wishing to see a government officer about renewing a licence, may state his request to the girl typist in Swahili as a suitably neutral language if he does not know her. To start off in English would be unfortunate if she did not know it, as on her goodwill depends his gaining access to authority reasonably quickly. She may reply in Swahili, if she knows it as well as he does and wishes to be cooperative; or in English, if she is busy and not anxious to be disturbed; or in the local language, if she recognizes him and wishes to reduce the level of formality.
>
> (Whiteley, 1983, p. 74)

One of the most interesting aspects of language surveys, says Whiteley (1983) with respect to a survey of classroom language use in Kenya, is the light it throws on what languages are actually used in the domain under study. He observes, with a caveat, that the results of the survey are admittedly based on self-report rather than actual observation in the classroom. It is noted, however, that the results do indicate the importance of the teacher variable in language planning. The caveat in Whiteley's assessment of language surveys points to the relevance of the participant observation method for language planning, as discussed earlier.

Furthermore, as Sibayan (1983, p. 84) points out with respect to a survey of language use and attitudes toward language in the Philippines, it may be one thing to report what one prefers to read in what language; but what one actually reads may be a different story altogether, as was evident from Laitin's (1991) research into a language revival movement in Catalonia, as noted earlier. Some scholars have been very skeptical about the adequacy of language surveys to account for language use. Labov (1978), for instance, observes that language surveys generally represent the investigator's, rather than the user's, theory of speaking. In Labov's (1978, p. 354) view, with which I concur, any theory of language must be consistent with the language used by ordinary people in the course of their daily business. That is, a valid theory of language should fit the characteristics of the language that speakers actually use when the linguist is not present (Labov, 1978, p. 353). For instance, attempts to harmonize the Nguni languages (Zulu, Swati, Ndebele, Xhosa) in South Africa failed because they generated a Nguni hybrid variety with which none of the Nguni language groups could identify.

Geolinguistic Analysis

This section summarizes Cartwright's (2006) work on the relevance of geolinguistics to language planning. Geolinguistics is defined as a branch of human geography that is concerned with the socio-spatial context of language use and language choice, especially in ethnic minority communities. It is argued that these communities need protection, particularly when they are in contact with majority groups, to prevent language loss and erosion of the minority group's culture and identity. This protection can be secured through legislation, which Cartwright (2006, p. 197) says is a vital ingredient in the minority group's struggle to maintain its ethnolinguistic vitality.

The key questions to which geolinguistics seeks to find answers include the very questions that are also central to language planning, namely, who speaks what language, where, when and why. By investigating these questions, geolinguists aim to uncover the domains where minority languages are or are not used, and inform language policies geared towards the ratification of minority language rights and the expansion of domains for exclusive use of minority languages. Protecting minority language rights, says May (2001), necessitates a call for implementing national and international laws that secure the psychological development of individuals as well as their economic and social well-being (Pupavac, 2006). For immigrants, for instance, such laws would advocate what political scientists call the ideology of multiculturalism—the idea that public institutions should accommodate rather than require immigrants to abandon their ethnic identity in order to integrate (Kymlicka & Patten, 2003, pp. 6–7).

In an attempt to address both multiculturalism and the questions highlighted in the previous paragraph in particular, geolinguists look into the patterns of movement and contact of people as well as historical processes that have contributed to these patterns and the concomitant shifts in ethnic composition and language use. The shifts are evident especially in the present era of globalization, where "time/space convergence has intensified the processes that are perceived as culturally erosive" (Cartwright, 2006, p. 198) to minority groups, irrespective of their geographical location, peripheral or contiguous, to socio-economically hegemonic majority groups. Accordingly, Cartwright argues that to be effective, language planning must be functional rather than formal, and in concert with other reforms of the socio-economic conditions that sustain and structure language choice in minority communities (pp. 198, 205). In other words, language planning must be designed to make minority languages do for ethnic minorities many of the things that majority languages do for a polity's population as whole, such as facilitate political participation and access to employment and economic resources.

Summary

This chapter has offered a review of some of the approaches and methods used in language planning research. With respect to methods, the chapter has focused on ethnographic observation and language surveys, two of the methods that are known to generate a significant body of data for language planning activities. Additional methods, such as historical analysis, anthropological linguistics, and costs analysis are discussed in Kaplan and Baldauf (1997, pp. 88–100); while others, such as linguistic analysis and psycho-sociological analysis are described in Ricento (2006b, pp. 170–228). The methods reviewed in this chapter, just like those discussed elsewhere, each have their limitations and challenges, as noted with respect to the observer's paradox (Labov, 1978). A multi-method approach, one that uses a combination of methods for data collection and triangulation, might help counter these challenges and allow the investigator to gain greater insights into the language choices and decisions individuals make especially in multilingual societies. Concerning approaches, the review points clearly to the multidisciplinary nature of language planning. In other words, no single approach to language planning, whether the language management approach, critical language policy, game theory, language economics, or the classical approach, is enough to provide data to resolve the many problems—political, economic, socio-psychological, or historical—that arise from language planning activity.

References

Ager, E. D. (2005). Prestige and image planning. In E. Hinkel (Ed.), *Handbook of research in second language teaching and learning* (pp. 1035–1054). Mahwah, NJ: Lawrence Erlbaum Associates.

Baker, C. (2006). Psycho-sociological analysis in language policy. In T. Ricento (Ed.), *An introduction to language policy: Theory and method* (pp. 210–228). Malden, MA: Blackwell.

Baldauf, R. B., Jr (2010). Methodologies for policy and planning. In R. B. Kaplan (Ed.), *Oxford handbook of applied linguistics* (2nd ed.) (pp. 391–403). Oxford: Oxford University Press.

Bourdieu, P. (1991). *Language and symbolic power.* Cambridge: Polity Press.

Breitborde, L. B. (1998). *Speaking and social identity. English in the lives of urban Africans.* Berlin/New York: Mouton.

Canagarajah, S. (2006). Ethnographic methods in language policy. In T. Ricento (Ed.), *An introduction to language policy: Theory and method* (pp. 153–168). Malden, MA: Blackwell.

Cartwright, D. (2006). Geolinguistic analysis in language policy. In T. Ricento (Ed.), *An introduction to language policy: Theory and method* (pp. 194–209). Malden, MA: Blackwell.

Cooper, R. L. (1989). *Language planning and social change.* Cambridge: Cambridge University Press.

Cooper, R. L. (1983). Language planning, language spread and language change. In C. Kennedy (Ed.), *Language planning and language education* (pp. 17–36). London: George Allen & Unwin.

Coulmas, F. (1992). *Language and the economy.* Oxford: Blackwell.

Daoust, D. (1997). Language planning and language reform. In F. Coulmas (Ed.), *The handbook of sociolinguistics* (pp. 436–452). Malden, MA: Blackwell.

Djite, P. G. (1985). Language attitudes in Abidjan: Implications for language planning in the Ivory Coast. Doctoral dissertation, Georgetown University.

Dominguez, F. (1998). Toward a language-marketing model. *International Journal of the Sociology of Language, 134,* 1–13.

Eastman, C. M. (1983). *Language planning.* San Francisco: Chandler & Sharp.

Edelman, M. (1977). *Political language: Words that succeed and policies that fail.* New York: Academic Press.

Edwards, V. (2004) *Multilingualism in the English speaking world.* Malden, MA: Blackwell.

Fairclough, N. (1992). *Language and power.* London: Longman.

Fardon, R., & Furniss, G. (Eds.) (1994). *African languages, development and the state.* New York: Routledge.

Ferguson, C. A. (1977). Sociolinguistic settings of language planning. In J. Rubin, B. H. Jernudd, J. Das Gupta, J. A. Fishman, & C. A. Ferguson (Eds.), *Language planning processes* (pp. 9–30). The Hague: Mouton.

Ferguson, G. (2006). *Language planning in education.* Edinburgh: Edinburgh University Press.

Fishman, J. A. (1972). Domains and the relationship between micro and macro-sociolinguistics. In J. J. Gumperz & D. Hymes (Eds.), *Directions in sociolinguistics: The ethnographic of communication.* New York: Holt, Rinehart & Winston. (Revised version of 1971.)

Fishman, J. A. (1983). Language modernization and planning in comparison with other types of national modernization and planning. In C. Kennedy (Ed.), *Language planning and language education* (pp. 37–54). London: George Allen & Unwin.

Fishman, J. A. (1987). Conference comments: Reflections on the current status of language planning. In L. Laforge (Ed.), *Proceedings of the International Colloquium on Language Planning* (pp. 405–428). Quebec: Presses de l'Universite Laval.

Fishman, J. A. (2006). Language policy and language shift. In T. Ricento (Ed.), *An introduction to language policy: Theory and method* (pp. 311–328). Malden, MA: Blackwell.

Foucault, M. (1979). *Discipline and punish.* Harmondsworth: Penguin.

Geertz, C. (1973). *The interpretation of culture.* New York: Basic Books.

Gramsci, A. (1988). *A Gramsci reader: Selected writings* (D. Forgacs, Ed.). London: Lawrence & Wishart.

Green, J., & Wallat, C. (Eds.) (1981). *Ethnography and language in educational settings.* Norwood, NJ: Ablex.

Grin, F. (1994). The economics of language: Match or mismatch? *International Political Science Review, 15*(1), 25–42.

Grin, F. (2001). English as economic value. *World Englishes, 20*(1), 65–78.

Grin, F. (2006). Economic considerations in language policy. In T. Ricento (Ed.), *An introduction to language policy: Theory and method* (pp. 77–94). Malden, MA: Blackwell.

Haarmann, H. (1990). Language planning in the light of a general theory of language: A methodological framework. *International Journal of the Sociology of Language, 86,* 103–126.

Harris, M. (1976). History and significance of the emic/etic distinction. *Annual Review of Anthropology, 5,* 329–350.

Harsanyi, J. C. (1977). *Rational behavior and bargaining equilibrium in games and social situations.* New York: Cambridge University Press.

Haugen, E. (1966). *Language conflict and language planning: The case of modern Norwegian.* Cambridge, MA: Harvard University Press.

Haugen, E. (1972). *The ecology of language: Essays by Einar Haugen—selected and introduced by Anwar S. Dil.* Stanford, CA: Stanford University Press.

Haugen, E. (1983). The implementation of corpus planning: Theory and practice. In J. Cobarrubias & J. Fishman (Eds.), *Progress in language planning: International perspectives* (pp. 269–289). Berlin: Mouton.

Hymes, D. (Ed.) (1964). *Language in culture and society.* New York: Harper & Row.

Hymes, D. (1974). *Foundations in sociolinguistics: An ethnographic approach.* Philadelphia: University of Pennsylvania Press.

Jernudd, B. H. (1971). Notes on economic analysis for solving language problems. In J. Rubin & B. H. Jernudd (Eds.), *Can language be planned? Sociolinguistic theory and practice for developing nations* (pp. 263–276). Honolulu: University Press of Hawaii.

Jernudd, B. H. (1973). Language planning as a type of language treatment. In J. Rubin & R. Shuy (Eds.), *Language planning: Current issues and research* (pp. 11–23). Washington, DC: Georgetown University Press.

Jernudd, B. H. (1993). Language planning from a management perspective: An interpretation of findings. In E. H. Jahr (Ed.), *Language conflict and language planning* (pp. 133–142). Berlin: Mouton de Gruyter.

Jernudd, B., & Das Gupta, J. (1971). Toward a theory of language planning. In J. Rubin & B. H. Jernudd (Eds.), *Can language be planned? Sociolinguistic theory and practice for developing nations* (pp. 195–215). Honolulu: University Press of Hawaii.Jernudd, B. H., & Neustupný, J. V. (1987). Language planning: For whom? In L. LaForge (Ed.), *Proceedings of the International Colloquium on Language Planning* (pp. 69–84). May 25–29, Ottawa. Quebec: Les Presses Universitaires de L'Université Laval.

Johnson, K., & Johnson, H. (Eds.) (1998). *Encyclopedic dictionary of applied linguistics.* Oxford: Blackwell.

Kamwangamalu, N. M. (1997). Multilingualism and education policy in post-apartheid South Africa. *Language Problems & Language Planning, 21*(3), 234–253.

Kamwangamalu, N. M. (2004). Language policy/language economics interface and mother tongue education in post-apartheid South Africa. In N. M. Kamwangamalu (Ed.), *Language Problems & Language Planning, 28*(2), 131–146. (Special issue: South Africa.)

Kamwendo, G. (1994). Chichewa: A tool of national unity? Language ecology in Africa. *Logos, 14,* 90–95.

Kaplan, R. B., & Baldauf, R. B., Jr (1997). *Language planning: From practice to theory.* Clevedon: Multilingual Matters.

Kaplan, R. B., & Baldauf, R. B., Jr (2003). *Language and language-in-education planning in the Pacific Basin.* Dordrecht: Kluwer Academic.

King, K. A. (2001). *Language revitalization processes and practices: Quichua in the Ecuadorian Andes.* Clevedon: Multilingual Matters.

Kloss, H. (1969). *Research possibilities on group bilingualism: A report.* Quebec: International Center for Research on Bilingualism.

Kloss, H. (1977). *The American bilingual tradition.* Rowley, MA: Newbury House.

Kymlicka, W., & Patten, A. (2003). Language rights and political theory. In M. McGroarty et al. (Eds.) *Annual review of applied linguistics, Vol. 23* (pp. 3–21). Cambridge: Cambridge University Press.

Labov, W. (1978). Sociolinguistics. In W. O. Dingwall (Ed.), *A survey of linguistic science* (pp. 339–376). Stamford, CT: Greylock.

Laitin, D. D. (1991). Can language be planned? *Transition, 54,* 131–141.

Laitin, D. D. (1992). *Language repertoires and state construction in Africa.* Cambridge, MA: Cambridge University Press.

Laitin, D. D. (1993). The game theory of language regime. *International Political Science Review, 14*(3), 227–239.

Le Page, R. B. (1997). Political and economic aspects of vernacular literacy. In A. Tabouret-Keller, R. B. Le Page, P. Gardner-Chloros, & G. Varro, (Eds.), *Vernacular literacy: A re-evaluation* (pp. 23–81). Oxford: Clarendon Press.

Lutz, F. W. (1981). Ethnography—the holistic approach to understanding schooling. In J. Green & C. Wallat (Eds.), *Ethnography and language in educational settings* (pp. 51–63). Norwood, NJ: Ablex.

Mafu, S. T. A. (1999). The myth of English language vs knowledge in some former British colonies: The case of Tanzania. The Second International Conference on Major Varieties of English. University of Lincolnshire and Humberside, Lincoln, England, September 9–11.

Maddox, B. (2001). Literacy and the market: The economic uses of literacy among the peasantry in northwest Bangladesh. In B. Street (Ed.), *Literacy and development: Ethnographic perspectives* (pp. 137–151). London: Routledge.

May, S. (2001). *Language and minority rights: Ethnicity, nationalism and the politics of language.* London: Longman.

Nekvapil, J., & Nekula, M. (2006). On language management in multinational companies in the Czech Republic. *Current Issues in Language Planning, 7,* 307–327.

Nekvapil, J., & Sherman, T. (Eds.) (2009). *Language management in contact situations: Perspectives from three continents.* Frankfurt and Main: Peter Lang.

Nettle, D. (2000). Linguistic fragmentation and the wealth of nations: The Fishman–Pool hypothesis re-examined. *Economic Development and Cultural Change, 48*(2), 335–348.

Neustupný, J. V., & Nekvapil, J. (2003). Language management in the Czech Republic. *Current Issues in Language Planning, 4,* 186–366.

Neustupný, J. V. (2004). A theory of contact situations and the study of academic interaction. *Journal of Asian Pacific Communication, 14*(1), 3–31.

Paulston, C. B. (1983). Language planning. In C. Kennedy (Ed.), *Language planning and language education* (pp. 55–65). London: George Allen & Unwin.

Paulston, C. B. (Ed.) (1988). *International handbook of bilingualism and bilingual education.* New York: Greenwood Press.

Paulston, C. B. (2003). Language policies and language rights. In C. B. Paulston & R. G. Tucker (Eds.), *Sociolinguistics: The essential readings* (pp. 472–483). Malden, MA: Blackwell.

Pennycook, A. (2008). Praise for language as commodity: Global structures, local marketplaces. In P. Tan & R. Rubdy (Eds.), *Language as commodity* (p. xii). London: Continuum.

Phillipson, R., & Skutnabb-Kangas, T. (1995). Linguistic rights and wrongs. *Applied Linguistics, 16*, 483–504.

Pool, J. (1993). Linguistic exploitation. *International of the Sociology of Language, 103*, 31–55.

Pupaviac, V. (2006). Language rights in conflict and the denial of language as communication. *The International Journal of Human Rights, 10*(1), 61–78.

Ricento, T. (Ed.) (2006a). *An introduction to language policy: Theory and method.* Malden, MA: Blackwell.

Ricento, T. (2006b). Methodological perspectives in language policy: An overview. In T. Ricento (Ed.), *An introduction to language policy: Theory and method* (pp. 129–134). Malden, MA: Blackwell.

Rubin, J. (1983). Bilingual education and language planning. In C. Kennedy (Ed.), *Language planning and language education* (pp. 4–16). London: Allen & Unwin.

Rubin, J., & Jernudd, B. H. (Eds.) (1971). *Can language be planned?* Honolulu: University Press of Hawaii.

Rudwick, S. I. (2005). Language, identity and ethnicity in post-apartheid South Africa: The Umlazi Township Community. Doctoral dissertation, University of Natal, Durban, South Africa.

Ruiz, R. (1988). Orientations in language planning. In S. L. McKay & S.-L. Wong (Eds.), *Language diversity: Problem or resource?* (pp. 3–25). New York: Newbury House.

Saville-Troike, M. (1982). *The ethnography of communication.* Oxford: Basil Blackwell.

Schiffman, H. F. (1996). *Linguistic culture and language policy.* London: Routledge.

Schiffman, H. F. (2003). Tongue-tied in Singapore: A language policy for Tamil? *Journal of Language, Identity, and Education, 2*, 105–126.

Sevigny, M. J. (1981). Triangulated inquire—a methodology for analysis of classroom interaction. In J. Green & C. Wallat (Eds.), *Ethnography and language in educational settings* (pp. 65–85). Norwood, NJ: Ablex.

Shabani, O. A. P. (2004). Language policy and diverse societies: Constitutional patriotism and minority language rights. *Constellations, 11*(2), 193–216.

Sibayan, B. P. (1983). Survey of language use and attitudes towards language in the Philippines. In C. Kennedy (Ed.), *Language planning and language education* (pp. 80–95). London: George Allen & Unwin.

Spolsky, B. (2004). *Language policy—key topics in sociolinguistics.* Cambridge: Cambridge University Press.

Spolsky, B. (2009). *Language management.* Cambridge: Cambridge University Press.

Straffin, P. D. (1993). *Game theory and strategy.* New York: The Mathematical Association of America.

Strauss, G. (1996). The economics of language: Diversity and development in an information economy. *The Economics of Language. Language Report, 5*(2), 2–27.

Thorburn, T. (1971). Cost-benefit analysis in language planning. In J. Rubin & B. H. Jernudd (Eds.), *Can language be planned?* (pp. 253–262). Honolulu: University Press of Hawaii.

Tollefson, J. (1991). *Planning language, planning inequality.* London: Longman.

Tollefson, J. W. (2002). Language rights and the destruction of Yugoslavia. In J. W. Tollefson (Ed.), *Language policies in education: Critical issues* (pp. 179–199). Mahwah, NJ: Lawrence Erlbaum Associates.

Tollefson, J. (2006). Critical theory in language policy. In T. Ricento (Ed.), *An introduction to language policy: Theory and method* (pp. 42–59). Malden, MA: Blackwell.

Vaillancourt, F. (1996). Language and socioeconomic status in Quebec: Measurement, findings, determinants, and policy costs. *International Journal of the Sociology of Language, 121*, 69–92.

Vaillancourt, F., & Grin, F. (2000). *The choice of a language of instruction: The economic aspects. Distance learning course on language instruction in basic education.* Washington, DC: World Bank Institute.

Walsh, J. (2006). Language and socio-economic development: Towards a theoretical framework. *Language Problems & Language Planning, 30*(2), 127–148.

Wardhaugh, R. (1987). *Languages in competition: Dominance, diversity, and decline.* Oxford: Basil Blackwell.

Webb, V. (2002) *Language in South Africa: The role of language in national transformation, reconstruction and development.* Amsterdam: Benjamins.

Weinstein, B. (1980). Language planning in Francophone Africa. *Language Problems & Language Planning, 4*(1), 55–75.

Whiteley, W. H. (1983). Sociolinguistic survey at the national level. In C. Kennedy (Ed.), *Language planning and language education* (pp. 68–79). London: George Allen & Unwin.

Wiley, T. (2006). The lessons of historical investigations: Implications for the study of language policy and planning. In T. Ricento (Ed.), *An introduction to language policy: Theory and method* (pp. 135–152). Malden, MA: Blackwell.

Wiley, T. (1996). English-only and standard English ideologies in the US. *TESOL Quarterly, 30*, 511–535.

54
Actors in Language Planning

Shouhui Zhao

Introduction

The notion of "Actor" is a key issue in language planning and policy (henceforth LPP), and in recent years, an unavoidable focus in any literature discussing general issues in this domain. In Cooper's (1989) well-known accounting scheme for LPP, "who" is the first among the eight components that need to be considered in initiating any LPP program. This is quite a different understanding from the classical role of the actor in LPP that originates from Haugen's framework and is characterized by its two-dimensions-four-categories matrix model with its status versus corpus planning dichotomy. This model, which was originally developed in 1966 and revised in 1983, takes the technocratic view that language can be planned through state-mandated policies with a special focus on modifications of language form (e.g., codification such as graphization, grammatization and lexication) for corpus planning, and a focus on cultivation functions (e.g., terminological modernization, stylistic development) for status planning. The actors in LPP, within the purview of this framework, are largely confined to governmentally mandated organs or officially sanctioned institutional agencies, i.e., who the individuals are, is of little importance.

In the further development of the theorizing of LPP in the early 1990s, two new dimensions were added to the LPP framework. The first was Cooper's (1989) language acquisition or language-in-education planning dimension that expanded the focus of LPP to include language teaching and learning (see, Nekvapil, Chapter 52, this volume). This was followed by Haarmann's (1990) prestige planning, which is particularly significant in that he examines LPP implementation from the recipients' perspective and argues that the acceptance of the LPP products and the recipients' attitudes toward them are important considerations, giving rise to a more fundamental, but less overt factor in LPP—the human behavioral and psychological aspects needed to achieve the intended planning results. (For a critique of the logic of integrating Haarmann's prestige planning in an LPP framework as an independent dimension, see Bamgbose, 2004.) To build up the prestige of the planned language activities, Haarmann argues that LPP should occur at four different levels, namely, activities by individuals, groups, agencies and government bodies, each representing different prestige or efficiencies of both organizational and non-organizational impact, and that the success or failure of such planning affects overall language planning.

More recently, in formulating a comprehensive methodological framework for LPP, Kaplan and Baldauf (2003) have further expanded Haugen's theoretical framework by incorporating Haarmann's prestige planning and Cooper's language-in-education planning activities. In this expanded LPP framework, where corpus, status and acquisition planning are productive activities, prestige planning is a receptive or value function that influences how productive planning activities are acted upon by policy makers and received by the people. In terms of those involved in language planning activities, the introduction and subsequent integration of Haarmann's prestige planning, expands the notion of LPP actors from personnel with official authority in the areas of language management and education, to include wider professions related to the individual and group activities. (Also see, Nekvapil, Chapter 52, this volume, for the Language Management Theory view of individual agency, or Shohamy 2009, for LPP as individual experiences.)

Kaplan and Baldauf (2003) also suggested another two further dimensions that are needed to examine LPP approaches and goals, that is, planning activities can be overt or covert (explicit versus implicit) and can occur on a continuum marked by three levels: macro, meso and micro. These two dimensions are also important factors to be taken into consideration in any discussion of issues concerning actors in LPP. Working mainly within the Kaplan and Baldauf (2003) integrated framework, and arguing that individual agency might be a useful perspective for probing the impact of language planning actors on the effectiveness of LPP ventures, this chapter endeavors to provide a broad overview of the various issues concerning actors and their roles, and does so by addressing the following key questions:

- Who are and who can be actors in LPP processes? Alternatively, what kind of capacity and knowledge is required of them in order to be involved in LPP?
- What are the roles they can and should play in initiating and carrying out LPP programs in different phases of LPP implementation?
- How are actors limited by their inherent features from acting more effectively in LPP implementation?

In this chapter, having taken a postmodernist stance that emphasizes the actors' roles from the relevant micro level perspective, these concerns are addressed with the focus on individual agency in relation to the four components of the LPP framework just described (i.e., corpus planning, status planning, acquisition planning, and prestige planning). Examples of the conflict between the actors concerned are also addressed using historical experiences from different socio-cultural-political settings.

The Origin and Categorization of Actors: Toward an Individual Agency

Although it has been one of the major interests of LPP research for its key role in assuring success, actors only drew the sporadic attention of researchers in the early days, when the discipline was starting to take shape. One early serious effort that attempted to look at the issue was a series of articles published in a classical work *Language planning process* (Rubin, Jernudd, Das Gupta, Fishman & Ferguson, 1977). In this book, five articles were especially devoted to issues concerning actors, namely, the Hebrew Academy: Orientation and Operation (Fellman), Language Planning in India: Authority and Organization (Das Gupta), Agency Man (Jernudd), Three Language Planning Agencies and Three Swedish Newspapers (Jernudd) and Language Associations in India (Das Gupta). Based on empirical data, these articles discuss a range of issues, including the roles, manner of working and duties found in various LPP organizations under governmental auspices, and more interestingly, some articles also discuss the individual qualifications (education and background) of organization members.

These articles show that one striking feature of the early discussion about actors: actors were addressed in rather general terms. Researchers did not concern themselves with the individual exemplification of the actors in LPP organs or agencies. Instead of examining the individual role of actors, they impersonalized them and/or aggregated them, emphasizing their official features. Kaplan and Baldauf (1997, p. 55) note that in most cases, "exactly who these planners are is often left in general terms."

Baldauf (1982) was among the first LPP scholars to note the importance of actors. In his work on American Samoa, he called for the explicit description of who the planners were, pointing out that this is a potentially important variable in the language policy and planning situations. However, Cooper (1989) made the first serious attempt to look at actors from an individual perspective. Borrowing concepts from political science on policy makers, he distinguishes three categories of actors:

- formal elites: those who are officially empowered to make policy—presidents, governors, senators, congressional representatives, chief operating executives, school principals, teachers and so on;
- influentials: those who are "the privileged persons in the society, who usually have a vested interest in given policies and do their best to influence the emergence of such policies" (Bamgbose, 2004, p. 72)—e.g. writers, poets, missionaries, etc.
- authorities: those who actually make policy decisions.

Cooper's categorization, derived from political research, faces the difficulty of overlap between these three groups of people. He admits that "it is sometimes difficult to identify the authorities" and thus "the interested observer may find it difficult to assign roles to players" (1989, p. 89). They are sometimes formal elites, sometimes influentials and sometimes both. They can be the de facto policy makers if they are not the formal elite. Three other major researchers who have attempted to deal with actors in a somewhat systematic way are Haarmann (1990), Ricento and Hornberger (1996), and Kaplan and Baldauf (1997). These are succinctly summarized in what follows.

Haarmann did some pioneering work in building the theoretical foundations of prestige planning during the 1980s and 1990s (Baldauf, 2004). As the previous discussion indicates, prestige planning encourages changes in people's attitudes, something that cannot be mandated. Compared with Cooper's discussion about actors, Haarmann's expansion of the LPP focus to include group and individual activities is significant in two respects. First, his four categories of people's activities look far beyond the roles of the people who can influence LPP in the political and bureaucratic domain. Second, Haarmann's formal and explicit recognition of the crucial role (promoting or impeding) of the recipients of the planning marks a move away from the classical definition of the LPP as macro and top-down, suggesting a receptive perspective on LPP. However, Haarmann does not elaborate further on his four levels of activities occurring in LPP, or articulate clearly the rationale for individual promotion, albeit some names of historically influential figures are mentioned. We know only from Kaplan and Baldauf's (1997) exemplification of Haarmann's individual promotion that his individuals are largely equal to the influentials in Cooper's three categories.

Elaborating on the involvement of actors in the language planning process in connection with language education, Ricento and Hornberger (1996) compare LPP, as a whole, to an onion with three different layers—national, institutional and interpersonal—and discuss the degrees to which these layers engage in the development and implementation of LPP. Li (2008) summarizes and exemplifies the onion where the outer layer is the state, at the national/macro level, which plays a very important—although sometimes indirect—role in deciding which language(s) will receive support (usually through the education system), which will be repressed, and (often) which language(s) will be ignored. The next layer are the institutions (e.g., schools, organized religion, the media, civic and other private and publicly subsidized organizations and the business community) involved in meso level language planning, which often have a great impact on language policy development.

Finally, she questions whether teachers at the micro level have any influence on that language planning process.

In discussing how classical LPP is related to more general government planning, Kaplan and Baldauf (1997) see LPP as a subcategory of human resource development planning or practices derived from organization or corporation theories, where management has full control. They divide the actors into four categories: i.e. government agencies (various ministries), education agencies (at three levels), non/quasi government organizations and other organizations. The non/quasi government organizations are noteworthy among LPP organizations, and they include organizations such as banks, churches and hospitals (but it seems post offices, in "other organizations," should fall into this category as well). Also included are publicly funded agencies, aiming at international language promotion (see, Chua & Baldauf, Chapter 57, this volume). Typical among those are the Goethe Institute, the Alliance Française, the British Council, the Japan Foundation and a late-comer, the Confucian Institute. Kaplan and Baldauf's positivist view of language regulation categorization puts the emphasis on these organizations' official nature, i.e. their public mandate for language decisions at both a national and local level, thus limiting their categorization to the concept of actors in the traditional sense, i.e., those civil institutions that are top-down in nature.

The classical definitions of actors working within government-authorized agencies or other authoritative institutions have been criticized as being too restrictive. Cooper (1989) points out that orthodox understanding of LPP excludes two groups of actors: individuals, such as widely known Ben Yehuda in Palestine and Samuel Johnson in England; another group are those people who participate in LPP efforts more or less spontaneously at a grass-roots level. To address Cooper's critique of the restrictiveness of the traditional view of the actors, it is proposed that a concept of individual agency should be introduced to epitomize the people in the LPP process individually at the micro level, with an emphasis on receptive and acquisitive rather than productive ends.

A review of language planners involved in the definition of LPP shows that the classical definition of LPP refers to "the organized pursuit of solutions to language problems, typically at the national level" (Fishman, 1974, p. 79), signifying that any decision on language requires the sanction of an authority. Cooper (1989) has enumerated twelve definitions of LPP, and Grin (2003, p. 28) rearticulates them as

> systematic, rational, theory-based efforts at the societal level to modify the linguistic environment with a view to increasing aggregate welfare. It is typically conducted by official bodies or their surrogates and aimed at part or all of the population living under their jurisdiction.

Luke, McHoul and Mey (1990) point out that the technicist definitions that evolved for LPP, often mentioned actors as an amalgamation of a great variety of individuals aggregated in general terms in the plethora of literature on LPP. These actors come from such modern civil institutions as committees, boards, councils, agencies, organizations and associations, to individuals such as decision and policy makers, implementers, regulators and standard setters, actors, planners, controllers, LPP workers and professionals—all possessing a degree of judicial power in their official capacity to affect the decision-making. As a result, classical LPP research and practice have a narrow understanding of actors in LPP, focusing on the most explicit examples under these collective categories. In Baldauf and Kaplan's (2003, p. 33) words, "the actors are most likely to be (top-down) politicians, constrained by historical/constitutional circumstances, or else bureaucrats, those involved in education, or religious figures or groups."

Since the early 1990s, the dominant model in the LPP research literature has been challenged as more LPP researchers have begun to examine LPP implementation from the recipients' perspective. The changed perspective views the acceptance of the language products and the recipients' attitudes toward them as important. Cooper (1989, p. 183) defined language planning as "deliberate efforts to influence the behavior of others with respect to the acquisition, structure, or functional allocation of their language codes." Cooper's (1989) definition is noteworthy because of his emphasis on the perspective of the influenced, i.e., the recipients. His wording "to influence" should not be taken as a passing thought, but as a key element in his view about LPP, calling for the necessity of a bottom-up orientation. Situated against this background, the critical turn of the 1990s marked an important period of reorientation of the focus of LPP from an emphasis on imposition to reception.

Worthy of special attention is the recent trend to emphasize individuals' LPP agency and the need to study LPP operations at the micro level or in a localized context (see Chua & Baldauf, Chapter 56, this volume), which shows a growing awareness of a shift to the application of critical approaches in postmodernist theory to language policy study. Most critical theories of LPP researchers accept the political principle that people who experience the consequence of language policy should have a major role in making policy decisions (Tollefson, 2006).

While recognizing the complexities and subtleties of language matters, one of the core arguments of critical analysis is that the non-dominant ethno-linguistic groups can shape the language policies that affect them. Therefore, the renewed participation of informed and skeptical citizens in all forms of policy making should be encouraged. For instance, in a study dealing with the politics of Philippine English, Tupas (2004, cited in Baldauf, 2006) argues for the need to recognize the situated agency of speakers and their right to have their own variety recognized as legitimate way of speaking, free of neo-colonial constraints.

Ager (2001) identifies three categories of major actors in policy formation: individuals such as powerful rulers and opinion leaders, the ruling group or elite, and the state. Van Els (2005) observes that in formulating a national second language learning and teaching policy, rather than the school authorities, the local and/or regional authorities, the school inspectors, and the national government, the most obvious decision-making agents also include the pupils, their parents or caretakers and the teachers. Liddicoat and Baldauf (2008) emphasize the interaction between different language planning activities that begin at different levels. Language decisions are typically made at macro level institutions, but how these decisions are realized depends on decisions made at other levels: "No macro-level policy is transmitted directly and unmodified to a local context" (p. 11). Bamgbose (2004) notes when a decision on LPP programs made at the top trickles down to the bottom, "contradictory policies are adopted at different levels and what is implemented at a lower level is often different from what is prescribed at a higher level" (p. 61). Having reviewed a number of agents of LPP in local contexts, Liddicoat and Baldauf (2008) posit that people at the micro level of LPP encompass:

- individuals who work to revive or promote the use of a language;
- language organizations that play a significant role in the local LPP for small communities;
- official institutions, which are not necessarily language oriented; and
- community education groups, which may also play a significant role.

Therefore, understanding who the people with actual influence are and how these people act in actual discourse is consistent with the climate of the times and merits attention at the micro level in concrete contexts within complex discourse. Jernudd (1993, p. 134) considers the shift of focus from a holistic approach to individual perspective as "an academic response to people power in reaction against central imposition, and it recognizes the multitudes of competing group interests." The review of these studies indicates that the notion of actors has been conceptualized in a number of different ways. In the section that follows these insights, a possible framework is advanced for examining the role of actors in order to introduce a more fruitful model to account for the effectiveness of actors' participation in LPP activities.

Roles of Actors in Implementing Language Planning Goals

Drawing upon experiences of LPP in the modern Chinese history, with reference to a shift in both LPP definitions and the roles of actors' previously reviewed, Zhao and Baldauf (2008b) categorize individual actors' agency into the following four types:

1. *People with power.* These are the people holding public office, particularly national leaders and highly placed officials. Their influence on LPP stems from their judicial power, both officially and de facto. Of these four groups, the role of individuals with power in LPP has drawn the most attention from LPP scholars and is the most discussed in the LPP literature; their individual and often decisive role in status planning has been extensively evidenced.

2. *People with expertise.* These are linguists and applied linguists, as well as scientists and experts, highly professional people in their own fields, who occasionally get involved in LPP. In the Chinese context, for example, chemists are highly professional people with expertise in their own field, not relevant to LPP, but they play an important role in terminology development and new character creation (Zhao & Baldauf, 2008a). In the United States, when a heated debate about the adoption of the European metric system and its standard spelling occurred in the 1960s, members of professional bodies (e.g., physicians) were involved and took sides (Haugen, 1983). Most of them belonged to the higher stratum of the intellectual elite and were valued for their advisory roles in the initial phase. LPP professionals also fall in this group.

3. *People with influence.* These are traditionally the social elites, including a wide range of the people who have social influence because of their knowledge/skills, their contribution to society, their personality and high moral standard, or just the public nature of their careers. These people include, but are not limited to, scholars, scientists (whose field is not related to LPP), distinguished writers, priests, businessmen, artists (calligraphers in China), celebrities in the entertainment industry, civil rights lawyers, or ad hoc group lobbyists and so on. Their strong impact on LPP stems mainly from their position as language role models, influencing the linguistic behavior of the masses.

4. *People with interest.* In comparison with the three groups just described, this group of people possesses neither power nor the personal prestige bestowed on the former three groups. This group of actors was completely neglected in the initial phase of LPP development, but has drawn increasing attention over recent decades. These people are ordinary citizens at grassroots level, who passively or unconsciously get involved in making a decision on language use for themselves, often accidentally, partially because of their occupations, sometimes "bumping into" LPP. Their below-the-radar participation seems to be extremely intermittent and ad hoc, and is limited to rare occasions, but their individual attitudes toward language use taken as a collective can affect societal language behavior in a significant way.

One example of people with interest (point 4) is when a shopkeeper decides on what languages or language variety to use (e.g., Marriott, 1991), he or she acts in an individual way, but is implementing a policy and thus has a role in influencing policy. Many professions, such as a firm/bank/hospital manager, particularly those in international corporations, accountants or lawyers (when they set up their own practices, notably in polyglot cities and multicultural communities), often face a situation that requires adopting a particular language policy (e.g., Kaplan, Touchstone & Hagstrom, 1995). In a subsequent analysis, we will see that parents of preschool or school students, who are dubbed "invisible planners" by Pakir (1994), are important stakeholders in language-in-education planning and are a significant part of this group of people, although they may not have a continuous and sustaining role. Another important component of this group—occasionally enthusiastic amateurs who have a personal interest in language and the writing system—will be discussed in the case of the Chinese Romanization transliteration scheme design.

Zhao and Baldauf's (2008b) categorization is different from Cooper's in at least two respects. First, Cooper's categorization is taken directly from policy decision studies in political science research; clearly, all three categories he sketched (former elites, influentials and authorities) are top-down in nature, whereas Zhao and Baldauf's typology is broader in that it includes two grass-roots focused groups, i.e., people with expertise and people with interest. Second, Zhao and Baldauf have conceptualized the roles of actors from LPP practice (in China) instead of from textbook definitions, stipulating that each group should refer to its actual role in LPP activities, taking into account its disguised identity or power. Therefore, the multiple roles that the same individual can play in LPP situations are not ruled out. A well-known example occurs in India, where some political leaders (acting as people with power) reject English in public, yet in private life (acting as people with interest) send their children to English medium schools (Annamalai, 1994).

One good way to understand the nature of actors is through examining the role actors can play in LPP practice. Haarmann (1990), for example, differentiates four promotional impacts corresponding to the range of LPP contents and activities specified in Haugen's (1966, 1983) four matrix framework. Haarmann argues that LPP should be seen to occur at four different levels, which are affected by promotional activities that originate from the agency of governments, institutions, groups and individuals, representing differential prestige or efficiencies of organizational impact. Another effective way to underscore the definition of actors is to look at their roles in the stages of LPP implementation. Zhao and Baldauf (2008b) examine the respective roles played by the four aforementioned groups of individuals with agency. Working within Haugen's (1983) modified framework, they have tried to set out a typical step-by-step linear procedure for accomplishing planning goals, which they see as occurring in five stages, abbreviated as "I-5," namely, Initiation, Involvement, Influence, Intervention and Implementation. In their study, they postulate that different groups of individuals typically are related to each of these five developing stages because of the differentiated impact they can have when becoming involved in LPP. In what follows, Zhao and Baldauf's (2008b) discussion is briefly recapped, omitting the Chinese examples.

1. *Initiation.* At the initiation stage, problems need to be uncovered and politicians have to believe that a problem requires attention and is worth tackling. The key point in making the LPP programs happen is to align the language problem with political interests (see, e.g., Kaplan & Baldauf, 2007). In this stage, before the people with power make a formal decision at the official level, the people with influence play—and have always played—a key role (Fishman, 1993). It should be emphasized that the involvement of people with expertise is indispensable, as it will ensure the necessary technical quality and avoid obvious fatal flaws (Baldauf & Kaplan, 2003).

2. *Involvement.* Corresponding to Haugen's (1983) corpus planning, involvement means participation in codification and elaboration procedures. Following the decision for initiation, it is important to create active and extensive participation. Individuals with expertise are essential to carry out the corpus planning programs and should play a dominant role in this stage because of their linguistic knowledge and practical experience in the relevant areas.

3. *Influence.* The stage of influence is directly related to Haarmann's (1990) prestige planning. Prestige is a previously underemphasized stage, and is here posited as an independent stage from the other four stages because it "does not depend on activities in the ranges of corpus or status planning, and in the planning process, prestige is a force in its own right" (Haarmann, 1990, p. 105). As suggested by its appellation, this is the area where people with influence can play an important role, as their linguistic practices tend to persuade others to follow LPP

goals. Influence can be direct or indirect, covert or overt, passive or active, conscious and unconscious. Zhao and Baldauf (2008a) have presented some intriguing instances showing that the political leaders' (people with power) linguistic behavior and predilections can exercise enormous influence on public language use.

4. *Intervention*. Intervention is introduced when planning sometimes veers off course or is reversed during implementation, either as a necessary positive adjustment because emerging problems need to be mediated, or as a negative reversal which, in the Chinese case, has often been the result of political intervention (see Zhao, 2006). It appears that in most cases the intervention has negative connotations, often leading to the discontinuation or delay of the implementation because of undesirable external forces. Although the other three groups of people have the ability to impinge on the direction of a LPP program, it is people with power who are most relevant in an intervention.

5. *Implementation*. Implementation, which is the process where a decision is put into action, is labeled status planning and language cultivation in Haugen's (1983) framework. However, drawing upon Haarmann's (1990) and Ager's (2005) more recent theorization, in Zhao and Baldauf's (2008b) study the implementation of prestige and image planning is perceived as a bottom-up modus operandi, instead of seeing it as "the activities of a writer, an institution, a government, in adopting and attempting to spread the language form that has been selected and codified" (Haugen, 1983, p. 272). Therefore, implementation is a stage more concerned with processes—people with interest and influence—than with decision-making—people with power.

LPP can proceed by identifying the concrete areas of society that demand planned action regarding language resources and required expertise; values and ideas of technical experts will be ideally matched to the areas or stages of LPP implementation they are pertinent to and where they can best play their role. While the description of Zhao and Baldauf's I-5 stages run largely parallel to Haugen's (1983) four planning foci, the I-5 format is broader and more detailed insomuch as it accommodates a wider range of LPP participants. More importantly, Zhao and Baldauf's endeavor advances what they call an "ideal model," where LPP stages are differentiated to correspond to a particular group of actors in the Chinese context. Taking user acceptance as their point of departure, they place the people with influence and interest in the foreground. This contrasts with approaches under the classical definition of LPP, where the authoritative allocation of resources leads to the attainment of language status and corpus.

It should be said, however, that the distinctions between different stages are not clear-cut nor do they necessarily follow in a logical progression, as the actual situation is not that static or certain, but occurs on a continuum. In Haugen's (1983) model, which has been criticized by a number of researchers (e.g., Fishman, 1983), the status and corpus taxonomy per se is an artificial division. The differentiation of LPP procedures is also clearer in theory than in reality—it is often simultaneous and cyclical—and relations between different stages are porous and interact with each other. Cooper (1989, p. 85) aptly points out, "language planning is seldom a one-shot affair. Implementation of a decision may require repeated efforts by planners to cope with the resistance of those they seek to influence."

Actors in the Four Classical Components of LPP

The I-5 model described in the previous section introduces new categorizations for actors and for the LPP components, The following discussion that focuses on the actors element illustrating how these four groups of people identified in the I-5 model operate within each of four classical LPP components, namely, status planning, corpus planning, acquisition planning and prestige planning, the aim being to identify any patterns or tendencies specific to each of these groups of individuals. The use of the classical categories rather than the I-5 categories is to keep the focus of this chapter on "actors" rather than on a new system of categorization. This approach is appropriate given the use of historical examples that were framed within the classical model and because the new categories overlap to some extent with the classical ones. Debate about a new categorization system is best left to another discussion.

Actors in Status Planning

It is normally acknowledged that status planning (initiation) is a venue where the people with power should have a dominant influence. This is particularly true when it comes to newly independent countries, where the country's founders face the task of choosing a language for a centralized communication system. Experience shows that in many cases, language issues have been much discussed and debated by the people with influence and the people with expertise. However, what should be emphasized here is that despite the fact that there are cases where the individual with power can play a decisive role in language selection when a new nation state is founded (e.g., Mustafa Kemal Ataturk in Turkey), it may be questionable whether this is the best way for a language's ecological equilibrium to be reached or whether the status quo needs to be changed (see, e.g., Kaplan & Baldauf, 2010).

Baldauf and Kaplan's (2003) discussion of a Japanese case shows how risky change can be without sufficient consultation with people with expertise. In March 1999, seeking to build a political agenda, Japan's then Prime Minister, Keizo Obuchi, appointed a committee (with no connection with the extant Language Council) charged to project Japan's goals into the twenty-first century. In the language section of the Committee's report a rather controversial recommendation with respect to English was made, that English should be considered as Japan's official second language (reminiscent of a more radical but serious proposal made by the Meiji era politician Molialinoli (1847–1889) to replace Japanese with English (He, 2001). The proposal, not surprisingly, along with most other proposals, was forgotten with the death of Keizo Obuchi in 2000 (Butler & Iino, 2005; Kaplan & Baldauf, 2003). There are multiple reasons to account for this predicament, but from the perspective of actors, the policy was obviously made under the auspices of people with power in the absence of language-qualified specialists, and "the writers of the report overlooked some issues that would be obvious to any language-qualified specialists" (Baldauf & Kaplan, 2003, p. 23). This instance illustrates that leaders of a polity should use basic social and linguistic information about the language situation (people with expertise) in the polity to make language selection decisions, even though status planning is an area normally dominated by people with power.

Actors in Corpus Planning

Corpus planning (involvement) is defined as "those aspects of LPP, which are primarily linguistic and hence internal to language" (Kaplan & Baldauf, 1997, p. 38), which implies that it is a highly technical exercise, falling within the purview of inquiry dominated almost exclusively by linguists, applied linguists and LPP professionals. Haugen (1983) also points out that the major activities of corpus planning, such as selection and codification, are a "paper exercise" that "should in principle be done by a competent linguist" (p. 271).

While this type of agency may be generally most applicable, in the investigation of micro factors that impact upon LPP from the perspective of individual agency, it is also notable that there are instances where the efforts of the people with interest deserve to be mentioned (see, e.g. the various measures taken by the Wallisian community to strengthen their native language in Rensch, 1990).

The following two cases are frequently mentioned in discussions about the graphization of modern Chinese.

Before the first scheme of simplified Chinese characters (324 characters) was promulgated in 1935 by the then National Party government, the simplification movement was at its earliest stage a purely academic enterprise, initiated by a group of influential scholars. However, it became known later that Chen Guangyao, a solitary amateur enthusiast in character simplification, had played a crucially contributory role in collecting and verifying the short form characters in existence among public users. Despite the fact that most of Chen's work had been privately sponsored by politicians and important figures in various academic fields, Chen had neither formal status nor any official title, nor had he a formal occupation or membership of any civil institution until the People's Republic of China was established; then he was formally employed as a professional LPP worker. Nevertheless, Chen had devoted the whole of his life (and wealth) to the course of character simplification. His contribution has been long ignored and underestimated in the history of Chinese LPP, although Barnes' (1988) case study has revealed that Chen's contribution to the first scheme of character simplification played a formidable and irreplaceable role, which has yet to be fully evaluated and recognized.

Individual amateurs have shown great enthusiasm in devising an alphabetic scheme for Chinese character Romanization, another part of graphization during the early 1950s, when the Romanization movement reached its final stage in the official discourse and the Romanization scheme was at a stage of wanting input from the public. The official scheme, known as Pinyin, was formally promulgated in 1958 by the National People's Congress (China's Parliament). It is claimed (Zhou, 1979) that during the debate and discussion of that scheme, more than six hundred other schemes were received by the Scheme Committee and the devisers came from all walks of life, covering the entire literate populace (including overseas Chinese), with the majority being ordinary laymen (some of these schemes were subsequently compiled in a book). Presently, there are more than two thousand Romanization schemes, which range all the way from Romanizations to kana-like symbols, shorthand systems and picture scripts that have been devised and submitted (including those especially designed for computer input). Although the state LPP authorities long ago made it clear that they would not accept or consider any new unofficial scheme, the indomitable spirit and aspiration of maverick intellectual enthusiasts demonstrates how great an impact these individuals can potentially have in influencing LPP outcomes.

Actors in Language-in-Education Planning

Kaplan and Baldauf (2003) hold that eight policy processes are the key elements for successfully implementing a language program (intervention), ensuring that language-in-education planning meets societal, institutional or individual needs. These are: access policy, personnel policy, curriculum policy, methods and materials policy, resourcing policy, community policy, evaluation policy and teacher policy.

Largely reliant on the discourses of compulsory obligation, the site of language education is thought to be the domain that is most susceptible to planning (Rubin, 1983), where teachers as professional practitioners are the policy product implementers and the students the passive recipients of the package. Early researchers such as Haugen (1983, p. 272) thought that, "as long as a small, elite group has a monopoly on education, it is relatively simple to implement a given norm." The people involved in language-in-education planning are predominantly policy makers from educational authorities at various levels, including educational officials, expert curriculum developers and educational linguists. However, as Kaplan and Baldauf (1997, p. 303) pointed out, an "individual decision is the ultimate test for the language planner."

The new wave of pedagogical innovation and the diversification of language learning practices entail a second look at actors in language-in-education planning. On the one hand, teachers and local governance have been given more autonomy in order to enable them to become active participants in developing language education policies rather than simply being passive consumers of such policies (Butler & Iino, 2005; Ricento & Hornberger, 1996). On the other hand, a very important change coming to the fore is what Baldauf, Li and Zhao (2008) called non-mainstream language teaching, or other language teaching outside the school, which is composed of three categories: for communal, promotional and commercial purposes. The impact that these three non-mainstream types of language teaching can have on formal educational institutions should not be neglected, as they can have unexpected effects on the policy processes of language-in-education planning, notably and mostly in access policy, community policy and evaluation policy, but on other areas as well. The following two examples have been chosen because they show that, contrary to the prevailing belief, under certain circumstances, people with interest, although acting in an individual capacity, can affect other policy processes as well.

There is general agreement that the family and local community are the crucial arena for language maintenance and revitalization (Tollefson, 2006). Cooper's (1989) example of the public's response to the Israeli ministry's attempts to remove English from the curriculum of the first three grades of primary school illustrates that, because of the availability of language teaching resources in non-mainstream language teaching, official policy can be flouted by parents.

Straining an already inadequate budget, the Israeli ministry was reluctant to teach English at lower levels, in particular forbidding school principals from teaching English in the first three grades. However, given the usefulness of English in higher education and in the workplace, domains for which parents are eager to prepare their children, they demanded that school principals introduce English at lower grades. As a result of banning English in lower grades, the uncompromising policy by the highest educational authority, "parents banded together and hired English teachers to teach English in the schools, as an "extracurricular activity," although often during the regular school hours" (Cooper, 1989, p. 85). So widespread was this practice that at least one commercial agency exists to match the parents' committee with English teachers.

Access policy is usually made by the government or the education sectors of the government, in authoritarian polities in particular, to meet the societal, economic or political needs. However, under certain circumstances, the people with interest can impose their own policy and this kind of situation is becoming more common as aggressive non-mainstream language teaching is becoming such a ubiquitous phenomenon across the world. Perhaps the most powerful illustration of the effect of the people with interest on language-in-education is what Pakir (1994) calls the "invisible planners" in Singapore.

Historical documents show that the disappearance of Chinese medium schools in Singapore was virtually the result of the invisible planners' decisions. Although the gradual phasing out of Chinese medium schools was clearly inevitable, the announcement of the creation a national system of school education, where English was used as the only instruction medium, caused considerable anxiety among the Chinese-educated population. The government, stung by the furor and criticism over the announcement, responded by saying that if enough parents request Chinese-stream schools, the government would restart one or more of these schools, where English would be taught as a second language. However, as far as can be ascertained, there were few takers (Gopinathan, 1998). Then, at the end of 1983, noting that less than one percent of those eligible for starting primary schooling had enrolled in Chinese medium primary schools, the Ministry of Education announced that all pupils would be taught English as their first language by 1987, thus resulting in a national school system. Another implication of this case is that once again, as observed by LPP researchers (e.g., Annamalai, 1994), there is an interesting paradox between the parents as a collective group and as individuals.

Singapore is a typical case of a polity without an explicit official LPP agency. It has been dominated by a dynamic government's paternalistic and interventionist style of governance, where parents as invisible planners were not only able to play a decisive role in the successful implementation of the bilingual education policy, which is usually created top-down without the recipients' involvement, but they also have been a crucial factor in corpus planning. Pakir (1994, p. 166) argues that in the "norm-breaker of English usage" (not observing standards), a parent's informal colloquial English acts as a key cause in discouraging the spread of standard English, a phenomenon that also has been observed in an empirical study conducted by Zhao and Liu (2007).

Actors in Prestige Planning

As mentioned previously, prestige planning (influence) is a more recent construct that is increasingly being considered in LPP literature. Prestige planning work targets the recipient's psychological state. The use of coercive measures by governmental institutions is bound to have little efficacy, and they may trigger a negative reaction. That said, and supported by what follows, the language use of people with power, along with that of people with influence, has a unique persuasive influence in cultivating language prestige and can affect people's attitudes toward the targeted language. Action speaks for itself: no formal policy or any other kind of imposition is more effective than role model strategy is, as evidenced in a number of empirical studies (e.g., Winter & Pauwels, 2006). According to Bem's (1970) Modeling Theory, linguistic behavior represented by influential citizens and social elites serves as a reference point for the whole society. People are heavily influenced by the views of groups with which they identify, whose approval they want or that have authority. Language styles used by prestigious public figures provide the population with high-status models to follow, resulting in spontaneous imitation and rapid spread.

There is a plethora of cases, testifying that the language used by politicians (people with power) fosters language prestige. Kaplan and Baldauf (2003) note there are claims in Indonesia that the creative use of language of its charismatic former supreme ruler, Sukarno, set the norms of the acceptable use for the national language, and "this was more through usage and example rather than through direct involvement in LPP" (p. 90). In the Chinese context, numerous works (e.g., Ji, 2004) exist on the unique contribution of Mao's speeches and other pronouncements in shaping the creative language styles of modern Chinese.

As for the impact of high-status individuals not linked to government power (people with influence) in prestige planning, the Chinese case again serves as a good example. In the mid-1950s, during the national congress of language standardization, a consensus on the explicit criterion for the norms of the three major facets (pronunciation, vocabulary and grammar) of the modern Chinese language was reached. It was stipulated that the norm for modern Chinese grammar should be based on the styles prevalent in the seminal literature classics written by renowned writers. This provision is in contrast with the phonetic and lexical norms prescribed in the same codification documents, which were derived from regional dialectal standards, that is, Beijing phonology for pronunciation and "Northern Dialect" for vocabulary.

Key Issues of Actors: Conflict Between Actors and the Involved

As described previously, actors play multiple roles in different phases of LPP program implementation—they act in a different manner, depending on the concrete context. From the typology of actors and their roles in the four components of LPP, one can see that actors also can act at the macro, meso or micro level; their roles can be covert/invisible or overt/explicit; their actions can originate from both a productive and receptive direction, and their acts can manifest themselves as organizational and/or individual agency. In what fellows, the focus is on another important aspect of LPP actors—the often conflicting relationships among actors when they execute their roles.

In the literature dealing with language conflicts and LPP, LPP is often referred to—in a certain sense—as conflict management (e.g., Jahr, 1993). The conflict between actors and those involved stems from the very nature of the LPP activities. On the one hand, the venture of LPP quite often begins in situations where language conflict has been generated and planning is called for. Status planning deals with, or results in, external conflict between different languages, whereas corpus planning often leads to an internal conflict between different language varieties. Furthermore, LPP also is known as language politics: a human pursuit, subject to all the fallacies and viciousness of social ventures and political campaigns. Fishman (1973, p. 37) points out, "language planning is more difficult because it more centrally impinges upon human values, emotions and habits than does planning with respect to the production of tangible economic goods." As a result, the criticism of the fallacies and inefficiencies of LPP is often directed toward the actors. Therefore, it is not surprising that emotional attachment and irrational attitudes are a recurrent topic in the LPP literature. Tension and conflict occur both between actors themselves, between actors and the users of LPP products, and between actors and concerned governmental bureaucracies.

The Conflict Between Actors Themselves

One of the striking features of actors is that LPP agencies are intensely faction-ridden; personal ties and private interests make factionalism a concern in LPP literature (e.g., an Indian case in Das Gupta, 1977). Tense relations can sometimes develop into fierce internal conflict, even resulting in a physical violence (see what follows). Unprofessional incidents of this kind are rife among feuding camps of LPP professionals, but internal discontent or competing views are rarely made known to the public. This is partly so, because the agencies' activities are always examined from a collective point of view instead from the dimension of individual agency.

The conflict occurs not only between parallel LPP organs within the same polity, but more often than not, as there are many official or semi-official institutions under the same aegis, the conflict often develops within the same agency, or LPP congress. One major reason is that LPP is an interest-bonding enterprise and the members or representatives involved with the decision-making are invariably vested with various forms of regional and economic interest. In addition, there are also individual reasons, influenced by personal inclination or linguistic ideology.

There are many reasons for such conflicts and disagreements among actors; one example is regional feudalism, which can sometimes lead to exchanges of insults and even physical wrangling. A well-known case in Chinese LPP history happened in 1913 during the conference of National Language Unification. The heated discussion on common pronunciation was plagued by "incessant wrangling among the delegates" (DeFrancis, 1950, p. 56) from across the entire country for two months, without any hope of yielding a meaningful outcome. Then a scuffle between two key members, arguing respectively for southern sound and northern sound ensued, due to misunderstanding an innocuous Southern colloquial word being taken as an insulting Mandarin oath (DeFrancis, 1950, p. 58). The conference decided that the National Standard Pronunciation should be settled by allocating one vote to each province. Over a period lasting more than a month, phonology experts were engaged in recording pronunciation variants for 6,500 sounds (each associated with a particular character) provided by the provinces' representatives, and the so-called Old National Pronunciation was fixed by casting ballots for each one (Wang, 1995).

Decisions on national language policy are often based on the support or antipathy of an influential lobby group, but there are also cases in which language reform was sabotaged by a personal affront. These have been attested to in a number of polities, in which discussions about LPP issues have become unprofessional, and where "for some combatants it seems to be just an occasion to settle personal grudges" (Geerts, 1977, p. 233). In a Japanese case, the personal bickering among members was becoming so sour that it resulted in five members walking out from the last plenary session of the fifth Japanese Language Council in 1961. This was cited as the major reason that led to a significant reorganization of the Council, including a number of far-reaching changes, such as downgrading its brief to advisory role while the appointment of its members was also relinquished to the government bureaucracy (He, 2001). In discussing the cultivation of the national language of the Philippines, Gonzalez (2002, p. 10) has attributed the slow development of Filipino intellectualization to the "jejune debate of personal opinions of members" of the National Commission of the Filipino Language.

If the conflict results in politicization, the consequences can sometimes be grave. During the Cultural Revolution (1966–1976), the Committee of Chinese Language and Script Reform, the top language authority, was polarized by two feuding camps, one representing revolutionary ultra leftists and the other practical LPP professionals. The ascendance of leftist power seekers in the internal two-way struggle is considered the explanation for the sudden radical increase in the number of simplified Chinese characters put forward in the Second Scheme of Simplified Characters and its premature publication in 1977, leading to its abandonment in the following year (Zhao, 2005).

LPP issues are perhaps always a debatable and tangible part of the human condition, "generating more heat than light" (Gregersen, 1977, p. 421), and "often resemble a religious war more than a rational discourse" (Coulmas, 1989, p. 241). Haugen (1983, p. 290) lamented that the effort to alter some American spellings for words related to the metric system shows, "how much heat can be generated by even a minor change in our habits of English spelling."

Tense relations and conflicts put LPP affairs in a vulnerable position and compromised LPP effectiveness. Studying these relations reveals that the LPP agenda often is comprised of conflicting positions. While little has been done to evaluate how big the damage is that this kind of internal war of attrition can do to LPP implementation, it obviously creates a negative image of the actors and causes confusion among the public, which increases the difficulty of implementing LPP in practice. Fishman, Das Gupta, Jernudd and Rubin (1971, p. 296) argue that "[b]oth the composition of agency personnel and the nature of interpersonal ties (within and between the agencies) influence the goals and operations, thus justifying attempts to study the informal as well as formal operation of language agencies."

The examination of the occurrence of internal conflict—as a significant variable in the entire LPP context—adds an additional dimension to the understanding of the complexities and limitations of LPP, and should be seen as an important phenomenon worthy of serious study if the role of actors is to be examined from an individual perspective.

The Tension of the Relationship Between the Planners and the Users

The conflict between the planners and the consumers of the planned product, sometimes called the "target population," can be both communal and individual. For the former, that language decisions (status planning) trigger turmoil is well known. It even leads to social unrest and life loss when ethnic or religious issues are concerned. For example, the anti-Hindi movement in three southern Indian Tamil-speaking states in the mid-1960s (Annamalai, 2001) led to one of the bloodiest clashes in a language planning conflict. Perhaps the best known case is the imposition of Udu in Bengali-dominant East Pakistan in 1952, which eventually led to the separation of the country into Pakistan and Bangladesh, and for which the International Mother Language Day (February 21) was proclaimed by UNESCO's General Conference in November 1999.

Where individual conflicts are concerned, the dislike and aversion of corpus planners can be seen from the derogatory designations applied to them, such as "language police," a "self-claimed sage" or a "necessary evil." In Fishman's (1983, p. 116) words, "[n]arrow-gauged corpus planners often become the butts of humor, sarcasm, ridicule, unappreciated at best and vilified at worst." It is in this sense, Makoni, Makoni and Mashiri (2007) criticize the "common man—the consumer" of LP programs—as being present only by the proxy of the educated custodians of languages who carry the elite "cross" and decide what is "good" for the masses, through the virtue of their hold on the socio-political literary scene.

The conflict that occurs between actors and the targeted population in most instances is due to so-called linguistic purism. As pointed out by Fishman (1983), corpus planners attempt to predict and put into effect a "model of goodness" that the target population will like, learn and use. As a result, there is a substantial risk that corpus planners lose contact with the public and will not know how it is reacting to them. Fishman (1983) has cited some striking examples of the tension between the corpus planner and the user, due to the lack of sophisticated consideration of the socio-cultural-political sensitivities. Many instances show less tolerance toward language variation or the excessive pursuit of goodness in the delicate and complex social and cultural context that commonly surrounds corpus planning. In the worst case, corpus planners, as gatekeepers and custodians of the language, tend to become overzealous defenders of their models of the good language. As a result, some conflicts have to go to court, especially when disputes impinge on human/language rights.

In the early years of LPP practice in language-in-education planning, language suppression was widespread and professional ethical issues often became a concern. One extreme form of the conflict between the actors and the users was language prosecution through physical punishment and public humiliation. The worst cases in this kind of conflict use were a ban on local language use in schools. Three well-known cases (Kaplan & Baldauf, 1997) are the English "Welsh Not," the Chinese Mandarin "Dunce Board" and the Spanish "Basque Stick" (Luke, McHoul & Mey, 1990). In the "Basque Stick" example, pupils were required to carry a stick on outstretched arms, as punishment for using a Basque word or expression. In the "Welsh Not" and "Dunce Board" cases, children who spoke the forbidden languages were punished by having to wear a board suspended on a thong around their necks. In Wales, for example, during the late nineteenth and early twentieth centuries, offending children had to wear a board with the message "Welsh Not" on it, until another offender relieved him/her of the burden.

These cameos are often mentioned in relation to the suppression of a minority language. Some reflection on the negative incentives for making the required language change shows a failure to comprehend the delicacy and complexity of the relationship between the planners and those for whom language is being planned. For example, Jaspers and Meeuwis (2006) report that the Flemish Belgian public broadcasting corporation intensified debate around an already marked project of linguistic standardization, by explicitly identifying substandard language use as sloppy. While such practices may not be as prevalent as in the past, the confronting unproductive relationship between actors and users continues to manifest itself in other forms.

The Tension of the Relationship Between the Planners and the Clients

Apart from the instances previously mentioned, conflict also exists between actors and their clients. Client here is used by Fishman (1973) to refer to "the power authorities" such as the government, the party, the ministry, etc. The responsibility of any actor is to explain the best solution to achieve the planning goals, and the responsibility of the client, for whom the planner is working, is to implement this solution. However, this classical distinction between planners and clients, between solutions and implementations, is not always clearly defined. Consequently, as Fishman (p. 38) points out, "self-respecting planners are continually moved to set aside their roles as technocrats to assume political roles themselves on behalf of their plans." Thus, when selling, convincing and cajoling have been major components of the work undertaken, it is likely to lead to tension, if not conflict, in their relations with their clients.

Another form of tension in relationships can be seen in what Kaplan and Baldauf (1997) called "abuse of agency"—"agency" referring to the power authority, i.e. the clients. One of their examples cites the suppression or deletion of information (p. 215). For instance, "unfavorable" information is often suppressed because in many cases the authorities "do not actually want independent advice based on a careful analysis of the situation/data, unless the outcomes of those analyses confirm their preconceived notions about a language situation" (p. 210). The cover-up and suppression of information can legitimately—in political terms—be done by disguising it as a vague and unsubstantiated need for confidentiality. In such a situation, Kaplan and Baldauf (1997) observe that actors may find themselves under considerable pressure to produce LPP programs grounded not on the best available theoretical and practical knowledge about the issues, but based solely on preconceptions of what is politically or economically acceptable to their clients.

Summary and Conclusion

As initiator, an actor is a central player in LPP literature and can be a decisive factor in determining the extent to which the aims of a LPP program can be achieved. Das Gupta (1977) compares his or her importance to that of a player in a performance and a director to his film. Important though it is, this issue is only rarely touched on in the research literature. Moreover, this brief retrospective glance at the evolutionary trajectory of the relationship between LPP and actors clearly reveals that, previously, actors were depicted as policy imposers and their roles were usually discussed in abstract general terms. The necessity of stressing the importance of an individual's role lies in the inadequacy of existing paradigms to account for the thrust of LPP, and this situation obligates us to seek a breakthrough in research methodologies. (See, Kamwangamalu, Chapter 53, this volume.)

Baldauf (2006, p. 166) points out that the debate about the nature of agency "has broad philosophical underpinnings." To contextualize the developing notion of individual agency, it might be advantageous to elaborate briefly on the critical approach guided by postmodernist theories, and its application in LPP studies.

Using macro socio-political, the epistemological and strategic dimensions, Ricento (2000) proposes a three-period model of LPP, to account for the evolution of language policy and planning as an area of research. According to Ricento in the still developing third period from the 1980s until now, both LPP practices and research has been increasingly driven by postmodern theoretical approaches in terms of epistemological concepts, and "in this approach, individual agency—and not impersonal ideological forces—is the locus of analysis" (p. 205). Representative scholars such as Tollefson (e.g., 1991), Phillipson (e.g., 1992), Pennycook (e.g., 1994) and Canagarajah (e.g., 1999, 2005) have offered more nuanced contextualized and historical descriptions of events and practices, showing that the individual agency's covert role at the micro level receptive end is becoming the center of LPP research.

These two emerging tendencies (micro level and receptive direction) inevitably lead to actors' deregulation and diversification, resulting in the increasing importance of the implicit role of institutions and individuals; the idea of speech communities being important units of analysis is beginning to pervade the planning literature. As Tollefson (2006, p. 47) argues, the "critical approach in language planning research pays particular attention to such practices that have come to be invisible." Taking Israel as an example, Jernudd (1993) says that traditional LPP agencies, such as language academies, may well have had a role in a period of rhetorical enthusiasm and national-ideological fervor. However, "[a]s the society enters the postmodern period, the academy will, possibly inevitably, fossilize or fade out unless it can reorientate itself to deal with people's problems in people's actual use of the language" (p. 136).

Since the 1990s, based on the postmodernist view that has increasingly served as the epistemological light to guide the understanding modern social behavior, a number of authors (e.g., Luke, McHoul, & Mey, 1990) have questioned the role of traditional language planners or actors and have argued for the inclusion of a broader participation base. Pennycook (2002), for instance, using Foucault's notion of governmentality and expanding it to include "language governmentality," has argued for an emphasis on the strategies and techniques of the micro level operation "of diverse practices, rather than the macroregulations of the state" (p. 91).

It is in this epistemological light that this chapter concurs with researchers who are applying a critical approach to LPP studies, and for whom the postmodernist perspective offers great promise for extending the research on actors beyond the static concept of some LPP theories. Working from the perspective of an individual's role, this chapter expands the concept of actors to include a wider group of people through recategorizing actors into four broad groups, with each covering a range of personal capacities. The description of the respective roles of these four groups of individuals in the four LPP components places importance on the LPP participants without official status, i.e., people with expertise, influence and interest. It is argued that only viewing them as willing and passive recipients of the standard is not enough; they can be decisive in determining the success of a planned language outcome.

This proposal of individual agency provides an alternative way of looking at LPP that is congruent with the general epistemological trends in the social sciences. The theoretical usefulness of individual agency is its instrumentality in exploring the effectiveness and the limitations of LPP operations in context, and using individual agency as a departing point to investigate how LPP decisions are being arrived at and are accepted at the grass-roots level. In this chapter it only has been possible to give a brief outline of the functional areas of each group of actors, yet it is my hope that the ideas developed will be followed by future analysis into the overall nature of LPP, thus producing research toward more dynamic theories and complex models of language policy.

Acknowledgments

I wish to express my gratitude to Professor Richard B. Baldauf Jr and Professor Rita E. Silver for their most helpful inputs and comments on an earlier version of this chapter.

References

Ager, D. (2001). *Motivation in language planning and language policy*. Clevedon: Multilingual Matters.

Ager, D. (2005). Prestige and image planning. In E. Hinkel (Ed.), *Handbook of research in second language teaching and learning* (pp. 1035–1054). London: Lawrence Erlbaum Associates.

Annamalai, E. (1994). English in India: Unplanned development. In T. Kandiah & J. Kwan-Terry (Eds.), *English and language planning: A Southeast Asian contribution* (pp. 261–277). Singapore: Times Academic Press.

Annamalai, E. (2001). *Managing multilingualism in India*. New Delhi: Sage.

Baldauf, R. B., Jr (1982). The language situation in American Samoa: Planners, plans, and planning. *Language Planning Newsletter, 8*(1), 1–6.

Baldauf, R. B., Jr (2004). Issues of prestige and image in language-in-education planning in Australia. *Current Issues in Language Planning, 5*(4), 376–388.

Baldauf, R. B., Jr (2006). Rearticulating the case for micro language planning in a language ecology context. *Current Issues in Language Planning, 7*(2 & 3), 147–170.

Baldauf, R. B., Jr., & Kaplan, R. B. (2003). Language policy decision and power: Who are the actors? In P. M. Ryan & R. Terborg (Eds.), *Language: Issues of inequality* (pp. 19–39). Mexico City: Universidad Nacional Autónoma de México.

Baldauf, R. B. Jr, Li, M. L. & Zhao, S. H. (2008). Language acquisition management: Inside and outside the school. In B. Spolsky & F. M. Hult (Eds.), *Blackwell handbook of educational linguistics* (pp. 233–250). Malden, MA: Blackwell.

Bamgbose, A. (2004). Language planning and language policies: Issues and prospects. In P. G. J. van Sterkenburg (Ed.), *Linguistics today: Facing a greater challenge* (pp. 61–88). Amsterdam: John Benjamins.

Barnes, D. (1988). A continuity or constraints on orthographic change: Chen Guangyao and character simplification. *Journal of Oriental Studies* (Monumenta Serica, 1988–1989), *XXXVIII*, 135–166.

Bem, D. J. (1970). *Beliefs, attitudes, and human affairs.* Belmont, CA: Brooks Cole.

Butler, Y. G., & Iino, M. (2005). Current language reform in English language education: The 2003 "Action Plan." *Language Policy, 4*, 25–45.

Canagarajah, A. S. (1999). *Resisting English imperialism in English teaching.* Oxford: Oxford University Press.

Canagarajah, A. S. (Ed.) (2005). *Reclaiming the local in language policy and practice.* Mahwah, NJ: Lawrence Erlbaum.

Cooper, R. L. (1989). *Language planning and social change.* Cambridge: Cambridge University Press.

Coulmas, F. (1989). *The writing systems of the world.* Oxford: Blackwell.

Das Gupta, J. (1977). Language associations in India. In J. Rubin, B. H. Jernudd, J. Das Gupta, J. A. Fishman & C. A. Ferguson (Eds.), *Language planning process* (pp. 181–192). The Hague: Mouton.

DeFrancis, J. (1950). *Nationalism and language reform in China.* Princeton, NJ: Princeton University Press.

Fishman, J. A. (1973). *Language and nationalism: Two integrative essays.* Rowley, MA: Newbury House.

Fishman, J. A. (1974). Language modernization and planning in comparison with other types of national modernization and planning. In J. A. Fishman (Ed.), *Advances in language planning* (pp. 79–102). The Hague: Mouton.

Fishman, J. A. (1983). Modelling rationales in corpus planning. In J. Cobarrubias & J. A. Fishman (Eds.), *Progress in language planning* (pp. 107–118). Berlin: Mouton.

Fishman, J. A. (1993). *The earliest stage of language planning: The "First Congress" phenomenon.* New York: Mouton de Gruyter.

Fishman, J. A., Das Gupta, J., Jernudd, B. H. & Rubin, J. (1971). Research outline for comparative studies of language planning. In J. Rubin & B. H. Jernudd (Eds.), *Can language be planned?* (pp. 293–306). Honolulu: East West Center and University of Hawaii Press.

Geerts, G. (1977). Successes and failures in the Dutch spelling reform. In J. A. Fishman (Ed.), *Advances in the creation and revision of writing systems* (pp. 179–246). Paris/The Hague: Mouton.

Gonzalez, A. (2002). Language planning and intellectualization. *Current Issues in Language Planning, 3*(1), 5–27.

Gopinathan, B. (1998). Language policy changes 1979–1997: Politics and pedagogy. In S. Gopinathan, A. Pakir, W. K. Ho & V. Saravanan (Eds.), *Language, society and education in Singapore: Issues and trends* (pp. 19–42). Singapore: Times Academic Press.

Gregersen, E. A. (1977). Successes and failures in the modernization of Hausa spelling. In J. A. Fishman (Ed.), *Advances in the creation and revision of writing systems* (pp. 421–440). The Netherlands: Mouton.

Grin, F. (2003). Language planning and economics. *Current Issues in Language Planning, 4*(1), 1–66.

Haarmann, H. (1990). Language planning in the light of a general theory of language: A methodological framework. *International Journal of the Sociology of Language, 86*, 103–126.

Haugen, E. (1966). Dialect, language, nation. *American Anthropologist, 68*, 922–935.

Haugen, E. (1983). The implementation of corpus planning: Theory and practice. In J. Cobarrubias and J. A. Fishman (Eds.), *Progress in language planning* (pp. 269–290). Berlin: Mouton.

He, Q. X. (2001). *Hanzi zai Riben* [Chinese characters in Japan]. Hong Kong: Shangwu Yinshu Guan.

Jahr, E. H. (Ed.) (1993). *Language conflict and language planning.* Berlin/New York: Mouton de Gruyter.

Jaspers, J., & Meeuwis, M. (2006). Language choice and local identity construction. *Acta Academica Supplementum, 2*, 111–140.

Jernudd, J. H. (1993). Language planning from a management perspective. An interpretation of findings. In E. H. Jahr (Ed.), *Language conflict and language planning* (pp. 133–142). Berlin, New York: Mouton de Gruyter.

Ji, F. Y. (2004). *Linguistic engineering: Language and politics in Mao's China.* Honolulu: University of Hawai'i Press.

Kaplan, R. B., & Baldauf, R. B., Jr (1997). *Language planning: From practice to theory.* Clevedon: Multilingual Matters.

Kaplan, R. B., & Baldauf, R. B., Jr (2003). *Language and language-in-education planning in the Pacific Basin.* Dordrecht: Kluwer Academic.

Kaplan, R. B., & Baldauf, R. B., Jr (2007). Language spread policy: Learning from health and social policy models. *Language Problems & Language Planning, 31*(2), 107–129.

Kaplan, R. B., & Baldauf, R. B., Jr (2010). North Korea's language revision and some unforeseen consequences. In J. A. Fishman & O. Garcia (Eds.), *Handbook of language and ethnic identity: Vol. 2: Success and failure continuum.* Oxford: Oxford University Press (in press).

Kaplan, R. B., Touchstone, E. E. & Hagstrom, C. L. (1995). Image and reality: Banking in Los Angeles. *Text, 15*, 427–456.

Li, M. L. (2008). English language-in-education policy and planning in schools in the PRC: Teachers as actors or implementers. Thesis submitted for the degree of Doctor of Philosophy at the University of Queensland, Australia.

Liddicoat, A. J., & Baldauf, R. B., Jr (2008). Language planning in local contexts: Agents, contexts and interactions. In A. J. Liddicoat & R. B. Baldauf Jr (Eds.), *Language planning and policy: Language planning in local contexts* (pp. 3–17). Clevedon: Multilingual Matters.

Luke, A., McHoul, A. & Mey, J. L. (1990). On the limits of language planning: Class, state and power. In R. B. Baldauf Jr & A. Luke (Eds.), *Language planning and education* in *Australasia and the South Pacific* (pp. 25–44). Clevedon: Multilingual Matters.

Makoni, B., Makoni, S. & Mashiri, P. (2007). Naming practices and language planning in Zimbabwe. *Current Issues in Language Planning, 8*(3), 437–467.

Marriott, H. E. (1991). Language planning and language management for tourism shopping situations. In A. Liddicoat (Ed.), *Australian Review of Applied Linguistics (8)* (pp. 191–222). Australia: Applied Linguistics Association of Australia.

Pakir, A. (1994). Education and invisible language planning: The case of English in Singapore. T. Kandiah & J. Kwan-Terry (Eds.), *English and language planning: A Southeast Asian contribution* (pp. 158–181). Singapore: Times Academic Press.

Pennycook, A. (1994). *The cultural politics of English as an international language.* London: Longman.

Pennycook, A. (2002). Language policy and docile bodies: Hong Kong and governmentality. In J. W. Tollefson (Ed.), *Language policies in education: Critical issues* (pp. 91–110). Mahwah, NJ, London: Lawrence Erlbaum Associates.

Phillipson, R. (1992). *Linguistic imperialism.* Oxford: Oxford University Press.

Rensch, K. H. (1990). The delayed impact: Post-colonial language problems in the French overseas territory of Wallis and Futuna (Central Polynesia). *Language Problems & Language Planning, 14,* 224–236.

Ricento, T. K. (2000). Historical and theoretical perspectives in language policy and planning. *Journal of Sociolinguistics, 4*(2), 196–213.

Ricento, T. K., & Hornberger, N. H. (1996). Unpeeling the onion: Language planning and policy and the ELT professional. *TESOL Quarterly, 30*(3), 401–427.

Rubin, J. (1983). *Evaluating status planning: What has the past decade accomplished?* In J. Cobarrubias & J. A. Fishman (Eds.), *Progress in language planning* (pp. 329–343). Berlin: Mouton.

Rubin, J., Jernudd, B. H., Das Gupta, J., Fishman, J. A. & Ferguson, C. A. (Eds.) (1977). *Language planning process.* The Hague: Mouton.

Shohamy. E. (2009). Language policy as experiences. *Language Problems & Language Planning, 33*(2), 185–189.

Tollefson, J. W. (1991). *Planning language, planning inequality.* New York: Longman.

Tollefson, J. W. (2006). Critical theory in language policy. In T. Ricento (Ed.), *An introduction to language policy* (pp. 42–59). Malden, MA: Blackwell.

Tupas, T. R. F. (2004). The politics and Philippine English: Neocolonialism, global politics, and the problem of postcolonialism. *World Englishes, 23*(1), 47–58.

Van Els, T. (2005). Status planning for learning and teaching. In E. Hinkel (Ed.), *Handbook of research in second language teaching and learning* (pp. 971–991). Mahwah, NJ: Lawrence Erlbaum.

Wang, J. (1995). *Dangdai Zhongguo de Wenzi Gaige* [*Script reform in Modern China*]. Beijing: Dangdai Zhongguo Chubanshe.

Winter, J., & Pauwels, A. (2006). Trajectories of agency and discursive identities in education: A critical site in feminist language planning. *Current Issues in Language Planning, 7*(2 & 3), 171–188.

Zhao, S. H. (2005). Chinese character modernization in the digital era—a historical perspective. *Current Issues of Language Planning, 6*(3), 315–378.

Zhao, S. H. (2006). Chinese script reform: State intervention and individual influence. *Language Forum, 32*(1 & 2), 5–26.

Zhao, S. H., & Baldauf, R. B. Jr (2008a). *Planning Chinese characters: Evolution, revolution or reaction.* Dordrecht: Springer.

Zhao, S. H., & Baldauf, R. B. Jr (2008b). Prestige planning in Chinese script reform: Individual agency as a case. Paper presented to the American Association for Applied Linguistics (AAAL) 2008 Conference. Washington, DC, USA (March 29–April 1, 2008) (submitted to *Language Problem & Language Planning*).

Zhao, S. H., & Liu, Y. B. (2007). The home language shift and its implications for language planning in Singapore: From the perspective of prestige planning. *Asia-Pacific Education Researcher, 16*(2), 111–126.

Zhou, Y. G. (1979). *Wenzi Gaige Gailun* [*An introduction to Chinese script reform*]. Beijing: Wenzi Gaige Chubanshe.

55
Macro Language Planning

Robert B. Kaplan

Much of the work in language planning has been at the "macro-" (i.e., state) level. This is especially true for the early or classical period of language planning (Ricento, 2000). The field is a relatively new addition to the anatomy of the academy, having come into existence in the years immediately following World War II. That was a period marked by the beginning of the break-up of European colonial empires and the emergence of new nations, particularly in Africa and Asia. In the opening section of the second edition of the *Oxford Handbook of Applied Linguistics*, there is a chapter that attempts to trace the emergence of applied linguistics as a new discipline in the architecture of the university (Kaplan, in press). That chapter cites a great flurry of events occurring from the 1950s through the 1960s (Kaplan, 2003), and continuing through the 1970s and into the 1980s. (Also see, Nekvapil, Chapter 52, this volume.)

A number of those cardinal events was funded through the generous support of the Ford Foundation—a philanthropic organization that took it upon itself to act in lieu of the US federal government, which was preoccupied with other concerns and had essentially failed to recognize language activity as having significance both in the spread of the English language and in the building of the perception of the United States, as a friend to the newly emerging polities in the poorest parts of the world (Fox, 1975). The Ford Foundation also supported the creation of the Center for Applied Linguistics in Washington, DC. The British Council was similarly active on behalf of the United Kingdom.

The events of the 1950s and 1960s involved language planning activities in the newly emerging states. Those activities were heavily engaged in spreading the English language as a resource that would allow the citizens of such polities to have greater access to education and to solve social problems leading as a consequence to happier and more productive lives. In addition, there was an emphasis on the development of national languages in some polities. Subsequently, these efforts turned out to be disappointing.

The Purpose of Language Planning

Initially called *language engineering*, the discipline emerged as an approach to creating programs for solving "language problems" in newly independent "developing nations." Language planning was perceived as being done (note that the passive leaves the actors as an anonymous group) using a broadly based team approach (see, for example, Fox, 1975; Jernudd & Baldauf, 1987; Kaplan &

Baldauf, 1997, pp. 87ff.) from an objective, ideologically and politically neutral technological perspective in which the identity of the planners mattered little as long as they possessed the required range of technical skills. The historical link between language planning and *modernization/ development* insured that the implicit assumptions in language planning reflected assumptions in the social sciences that have subsequently been subject to re-evaluation and revision. Especially striking in hindsight is the optimism of early language planning that conveyed an underlying ideological faith in *development* and *modernization*. In early language planning research, practitioners were seen as having the expertise to specify ways in which changes in the linguistic situation would lead to desired social and political transformations (i.e., supporting the development of unity in the socio-cultural system, reducing economic inequalities, providing access to education). The belief in economic and social progress was perhaps best expressed in Eastman's introduction to language planning (1983) in which language planners are depicted as being at the forefront of fundamental shifts in the organization of global society: "Modernization and preservation efforts are seemingly happening everywhere, to provide all people with access to the modern world through technologically sophisticated languages and also to lend a sense of identity through encouraged use of their first languages" (p. 31).

Language Planning Differentiated from Language Policy

The terms *language planning* and *language policy* are frequently used, in both the technical and the popular literature, either interchangeably or in tandem. However, they actually represent two quite distinct aspects of the systemized language change process. *Language planning* is an activity, most visibly undertaken by government (simply because it potentially involves such massive changes in a society), intended to promote systematic linguistic change in some community of speakers. The reasons for such change lie in a reticulated pattern of structures developed by government and intended to maintain civil order and communication, and to move the entire society in some direction deemed "good" or "useful" by government.

The exercise of *language planning* leads to, or is directed by, the promulgation of a *language policy* by government (or other authoritative body or person). A *language policy* is a body of ideas, laws, regulations, rules and practices intended to achieve the planned language change in the society, group or system. Only when such policy exists can any sort of serious evaluation of planning occur (Rubin, 1971); i.e., in the absence of a policy there cannot be a plan to be adjusted. *Language policy* may be realized at a number of levels, from very formal language planning documents and pronouncements to informal statements of intent (i.e., the discourse of language, politics and society) that may not at first glance seem like language policies at all. Indeed, as Peddie (1991) points out, policy statements tend to fall into two types: *symbolic* and *substantive*. The first articulates good feelings toward change (or perhaps ends up being so nebulous that it is difficult to understand what language-specific concepts may be involved), while the latter articulates specific steps to be taken. This chapter concerns itself primarily with language planning. Complex motives and approaches, and large populations, are involved in modern states, and language policy-makers and planners have, up to the present time, most often worked in such *macro* situations.

Language Planning Linked to Modernization and Development

During the early or classical period of language planning development, emerging specialists believed that their new understanding of language in society could be implemented in practical programs of *modernization* and *development* having important benefits for *developing societies*.[1] This early period was characterized by an extensive growth in research by a limited number of authors (e.g., Fishman,

1968, 1971, 1972, 1974; Rubin & Jernudd, 1971; Rubin & Shuy, 1973) because the field was perceived to have practical significance for the newly independent post-colonial states (particularly in Africa) as well as theoretical value in providing "new opportunities to tackle a host of … novel theoretical concerns" (Fishman, Ferguson & Das Gupta, 1968, p. x) in sociology and political science since "few areas are more fruitful or urgent with respect to interdisciplinary attention" (pp. x–xi). Early practitioners believed that language planning could play a major role in achieving the goals of political/administrative integration and socio-cultural unity (Das Gupta, 1970, p. 3). Thus, a major focus of this early research involved analysis of the language planning needs specific to newly independent states, particularly language choice and literacy in processes of "nationism," and language maintenance, codification and elaboration in processes of "nationalism" (Fishman, 1968). This linkage of language planning with development and modernization—essential for the early emergence of the field—was influenced by modernization theory (e.g., Rostow, 1960); consequently, early research focused primarily on the role of language planning in developing societies. Consideration of the question of exactly who the planners were and what impact their views might have on the goals set to solve language problems has only been raised more recently (by, among others, Baldauf, 1982; Baldauf & Kaplan, 2003; Zhao, Chapter 54, this volume). By the 1970s, it had become apparent that language problems were not unique to developing nations, but also occurred as "macro" (i.e., state-level) language problems and situations in polities worldwide. Despite early optimism, in less than twenty years, by the mid-1980s, disillusionment with language planning—due to several factors—was widespread (Blommaert, 1996; Williams, 1992). Since the late 1990s, language policy and planning principles have also been increasingly applied in "micro" situations (for example, in relation to language problems in communities, organizations and companies; see, for instance, Canagarajah, 2005; Chua & Baldauf, Chapter 56, this volume).

In Hindsight, the Causes for Missed Opportunities

Ricento, in a review of the field (2000, p. 196), has suggested that research in language policy and planning can be divided into three historical phases:

- decolonization, structuralism and pragmatism (1950s, 1960s);
- the failure of modernization, critical sociolinguistics (1980s, 1990s);
- a new world order, postmodernism, linguistic human rights (twenty-first century).

An important change in language planning since the 1980s lies in the recognition that language planning is not necessarily an aspect of development but rather implicates a broad range of social processes including at least migration and the rise of nationalism in Europe and Central Asia. Migration constitutes a reason for the increases in the numbers of people worldwide that are learning languages and—consequently—for a significant increase in concern with language-in-education planning. With ten million refugees worldwide, more than twenty million people displaced within their own countries, and countless millions of economic migrants (e.g., Bosnians and Turks in Germany, Filipinos in Hong Kong, South Asians in the UK and Latinos in the US) language teaching programs have been dramatically affected throughout the world. In many countries, language-in-education planning has become central in efforts to deal with this massive movement of people (Tollefson, 1989), resulting in a range of new questions, which are in need of attention:

- What should be the role of migrants' languages in education and other official domains of use?
- How are local languages affected by migrants?
- What should be the status of new varieties of English and other lingua francas?

- How can acquisition planning be most effectively carried out?
- What factors constrain acquisition planning?

A second concern in language planning has emerged from the collapse of the Soviet Union and the realignment of political boundaries in Eastern Europe and Central Asia—a phenomenon giving rise to the emergence of new states in which language issues are intimately linked with ideological and political conflicts. Minority issues, including language planning are at the heart of conflicts between, for example, Armenia and Azerbaijan, Georgia and South Ossetia, Hungary and Slovakia (see BBC News, 2009), Russia and Chechnya, Russia and Ukraine, Slovenia and Austria, Turkey and its Kurdish minority, as well as elsewhere in the region. Also, these issues are central to the efforts of such new (or re-emerging) states to establish effective local institutions (e.g., Estonia, Latvia and Lithuania; see Hogan-Brun, Ozolins, Ramonienè & Rannut, 2007). In the Slovak Republic, for example, language policy has been a key issue for government leaders (see, e.g., Kaplan & Baldauf, 2001). Indeed, the emersion of the Slovak Republic has focused attention on a fundamental political problem of Europe and Central Asia—the relationship between minorities and nation-states. The language planning choices made by state planners, legislative bodies and citizens will probably play an important role in the management of political conflict in these new states for decades to come.

A third area of current research lies in the movement to deconstruct the ideology of monolingualism that has pervaded much language planning research (Williams, 1992), exactly because the focus has been on the monolingual state—one polity/one language/ one culture. Emerging research involves a re-examination of traditional assumptions about the costs of multilingualism and the benefits of monolingualism. Innovative language policies in post-apartheid South Africa (e.g., Webb & du Plessis, 2006)—based on an ideology of multilingualism as a symbol of national revival and asserted in a Constitution declaring eleven official languages to enhance the process of democratization (Blommaert, 1996)—serve as prologue to a wide range of new questions for language planning. The linking of multilingual policies and democratization (Deprez & du Plessis, 2000) has also become an important part of political debates elsewhere (e.g., in Guatemala, where official recognition of the country's indigenous languages constituted an important part of the peace accords ending the country's civil war).

Language Planning and Human Rights

The movement for linguistic human rights offers another significant point of view. While some language planning scholars have advocated mother tongue-promotion policies (e.g., Skutnabb-Kangas, 2000), others have linked language rights to political theory and to efforts to develop a theory of language planning (e.g., Cooper, 1989; Dua, 1994; May, 2001). Calls for expansion and implementation of language rights can be expected to continue, with language planning research heavily involved in the development of a better understanding of the role of language rights in state formation, in international organizations, in political conflict and in a variety of other social processes. Similarly, recent research on the links between language planning and social theory, long advocated by Fishman (1992) and Williams (1992), can contribute to deeper understandings of language rights and to new research methods (Ricento, 2006). Early language planning research had rarely considered the local legal framework of plans and policies; current research examines the ways in which language planning processes are constrained by constitutional and statutory law (Liddicoat, 2008).

Language Planning and Internal Inconsistencies

Even in limited situations, language planning exercises can be complex. The goals set to solve language planning problems may even be conflictive, especially when viewed alternately from dominant vs. minority language perspectives (Baldauf & Kaplan, 2003; Kaplan & Baldauf, 1997). For example, a fundamental tension may be said to occur between pluralism and democracy; i.e., the United States, ostensibly a democratic society, in principle sanctions the right of ethnic groups to maintain their separate languages, cultures and communities, but it simultaneously guarantees individual freedoms and specifically proscribes discrimination of various types. These two sets of rights, however, may be in conflict because the ethnic groups that are in positions of social and economic advantage, when exercising their prerogatives of associating with their own ethnic kind, may deprive outsiders of some rights and opportunities sanctioned by democratic norms. The conflict over language is particularly emblematic in such conflictive situations (Steinberg, 2001; Youmans, 2007).

Goals and Scope: The Sins of English

What is true for a polity as a whole may also be true for groups within that polity—i.e., groups may hold (and pursue) potentially conflicting goals without realizing that conflicts are occurring. For example, in the new nation of Timor Leste (East Timor), there is a need:

1. to learn the new national language (Portuguese—widely known by the older generations), which is also meant to become the universally spoken official language available to the entire population;
2. to learn the largest indigenous language—a lingua franca and a co-national language (Tetum, currently in the process of being standardized);
3. to learn a language of wider communication in order to interact with aid agencies and for trade (predominantly English); and
4. for the dozen or so ethnic groups, to maintain those languages and their own cultures;
5. for many younger individuals who were educated in Bahasa Indonesia, who may wish to use and develop their skills in that language, to learn the language of their nearest neighbor and their most recent colonial power. (See Taylor-Leech, 2009; see also Hajek, 2000, for further discussion of this language ecology.)

In such situations, goal conflicts—alternative perceptions of language as problem, language as right or language as resource (Ruiz, 1984) —occur because there are limits to the time and resources available to individuals, to groups and to the state: often there are difficult language policy choices to be made.

The existence of such conflicting goals and the feeling that choices of goals have often been made—(by planners) without consultation with those most immediately concerned and affected—has resulted in some serious critiques of language planning—particularly in the context of "linguistic imperialism," especially as the term *imperialism* relates to the seeming domination of English in a variety of situations. (See, e.g., Luke, McHoul & Mey, 1990; Pennycook, 1994; Phillipson, 1992; Skutnabb-Kangas, 2000; Tollefson, 1991.) Often critics have—perhaps unfairly—represented language planners to be self-interested, and language planning to be self-reproducing, inequitable, monocultural and colonialistic. However, as Fishman (1994), in the general context, and, more recently, van Els (2001, p. 26) with specific reference to English, have pointed out, the arguments about linguistic imperialism "are predominantly of a socioeconomic and political nature, and others have already conclusively invalidated the doom scenarios that were drawn up."

Some Assumptions

Fishman, Conrad and Rubal-Lopez (1996), in a collection of studies of nearly twenty former British colonies, come to the conclusion that the spread of English in these countries is related to the modern global economy and not necessarily to the interference of a former colonial master. (See also, Powell, 2002.) Kaplan (2001) argues that the seeming domination of English is in fact an accident resulting from the convergence of a number of forces in the period immediately following World War II. Brutt-Griffler (2002) argues further that the increasing dominance of English as a world language has only occurred since the end of the colonial period. More specifically, Chew (1999, pp. 39ff.), at least for the case of Singapore, suggests that a linguistic imperialist view "ascribes too much power to language, as opposed to the language policy-makers and the language users." Language choice, Chew adds, is a "conscious decision" on the part of "leaders and the populace, after careful consideration of world trends and local conditions." One might argue, for example, that any given language has *no* power at all; rather, that users of that language have and exert power. Finally, it has been suggested (Francis, 2005, p. 211) that these debates about language policy "suffer from a restricted perspective that elevates socio-political considerations above all others."

Thus, while planners are sometimes stereotyped in terms of "colonialism" or of "imperialism," or of some particular language (e.g., "English"), these classifications provide little advance over the traditional view of planners as being essentially anonymous. Furthermore, while English provides the most visible target, language-spread policy is clearly not unique to English or to English language institutions, since many polities have language-spread policies that may exist:

- at the national level (e.g., Ammon, 1992 for German; Dua, 1994 for Hindi);
- at the regional level (see Barrera i Vidal, 1994 for Catalan); or
- even cross polity boundaries (see von Gleich, 1994 for Quechua; see also the extensive literature on the spread of, among other languages, Arabic, Chinese, French and Spanish and the role of national language academies[2] and planning bodies).

Although a few scholars had noted the absence of any institution in the United States in which students can be adequately trained for either theoretical or applied involvement in the language problems of developing nations, a significant achievement of this early period of language planning was, on the one hand, permitting a better understanding of the relationship between linguistic structure and function and, on the other, a new comprehension of such forms of social organization as communities, ethnic groups or nations, linking language planning with important theoretical research in micro-sociolinguistic concerning, for example, code-switching, systematicity in style and register variation.

Some Further Assumptions

The failure of early or classical language planning activities to achieve their goals in many contexts and the intimate connection between early language planning and modernization theory meant that language planning was subject to the same criticisms as was modernization theory generally, including at least:

- the fact that economic models appropriate for one place may be ineffective in any other places;
- the fact that national economic development will not necessarily benefit all sectors of any given society, especially the poor (Steinberg, 2001);
- the fact that development generally fails to consider local contexts and the conflicting needs and desires of diverse communities; and
- the fact that development has a homogenizing effect on social and cultural diversity (Foster-Carter, 1985; Worsley, 1987).

A second assumption underlying the work in the early period of language planning was an emphasis on *cost-benefit analysis, efficiency* and *rationality* as criteria for evaluating plans and policies; i.e., Tauli (1968) proposed *clarity* and *economy*, while Haugen (1966) proposed *efficiency* as criteria for judging the effectiveness of language planning decisions. An emphasis on the technical aspect of language planning led Jernudd and Das Gupta (1971) to argue that planners may be better able than political authorities to apply rational decision-making in the solution of language problems. Such attempts to separate language planning from politics reflected not only a belief in the skills of technical specialists, but also a broader failure to link language planning with political analysis—the failure to acknowledge that language planning is fundamentally political is central to subsequent critiques of language planning.

A third assumption was that the nation-state is the appropriate focus for language planning research and practice, since language planning is a tool for political/administrative and socio-cultural integration of the nation-state, a view that had two important consequences:

1. the main actors in language planning were assumed to be government agencies, and thus most research examined the work of such agencies;
2. many researchers adopted a top-down perspective, limiting their interests to national plans and policies rather than to local language practices.

Language Planning and Politics

A problem in early language planning was its failure adequately to analyze the impact of local contexts on national policies, partially the consequence of an emphasis on technical rather than political evaluation of policies as well as a general separation of language planning from political analysis. As Blommaert argues, language planning "can no longer stand exclusively for practical issues of standardization, graphization, terminological elaboration, and so on. The link between language planning and sociopolitical developments is obviously of paramount importance" (1996, p. 217). Failing to link language planning to politics resulted in a situation in which planners could not predict the impact of their plans and policies. Language planning specialists in the early period believed that unexpected outcomes could be avoided as long as adequate information was available, but more recent scholarship assumes that unexpected outcomes are a normal feature of highly complex social systems:

- where linear cause–effect relationships between language and society do not apply; and
- where social groups may have covert goals for language planning (Ammon, 1997).

The more one examines the language planning situations with which one is familiar (or that one reads about in the literature), the more apparent it becomes that policy aspects of such planning (as opposed to the cultivation or the implementation aspect) are only secondarily a language planning activity; primarily, they are a political activity (Kaplan & Baldauf, 2007). Language planning is often perceived as some sort of monolithic activity, designed specifically to manage one particular kind of linguistic modification in a community at a particular moment in time. Language planning has tended to concern itself with the modification of one language only, having largely ignored the interaction of multiple languages in a community as well as multiple non-linguistic factors—that is, the total ecology of the linguistic environment. Language planning is really about power distribution and political expediency; it is about economic issues, and it is about the distribution of time and effort of administrators, scholars, teachers and students. Although a concern with *theory* suggests that such policy decisions should be based on data about learners and community language needs (see, e.g., Kaplan & Baldauf, 1997; van Els, 2005), in fact policy decisions are not about the needs of any given community, nor are they about the needs of learners. They are, rather, about the perceptions of language(s) held in the Ministry of Education[3] and to some extent in the generally perceptions of the society at large. Policy decisions rarely take into account such matters as learners' age, aptitude, attitude or motivation. They tend to be top-down in structure, reflecting the opinions and attitudes valued at the highest levels in the planning process; they are rarely about the linguistic needs or desires of any given society or community. Indeed, the least important factor in such planning decisions may well be the needs and desires of the target population (Kaplan, 2004).

Language planning has in fact not been limited to developing nations; on the contrary, it has been used by dominant groups in various nations to preserve their dominance. In the Soviet Union, for instance, the spread of Russian was selectively encouraged in regions where central planners sought to extend their authority (Kirkwood, 1990). In the United Kingdom, the renewed prominence of standard English in schools in the 1990s was linked to a wider effort to limit the role of immigrants' languages in education (Clark, 2001); and in the United States, federal policies suppressed indigenous languages (Shonerd, 1990) and, more recently, official English legislation in some states has become an effective tool for restricting the political power of Latinos (Donahue, 2001).

Even at the time when language planning was perceived as apolitical, governments were involved in supporting language planning activities. The Ford Foundation supported the development of language centers in Cairo, Hyderabad, Manila, Tunis, Washington, DC and the West Indies (Fox, 1975). Starting with the funding of the Central Institute of English in Hyderabad, the Ford Foundation began working closely with the British Council. However, as the Ford Foundation was a US-based charitable foundation headquartered in New York, the majority of the first directors of those various organizations, not surprisingly, either was North American or had been trained in North America. The Bureau of Educational and Cultural Affairs of the US Department of State substantially supported much of the work of English-language teachers and teacher-trainers abroad. As Fox observed retrospectively in 1975:

> Ford Foundation experience over the past two decades [i.e., 1952–1974] has shown that language projects that are designed to further national development cannot be limited to establishing resources to teach English … as a second language, or to creating linguistics and language scholars only at the university or to encouraging basic research about language use, or to training language specialists for work as educators or administrators, or to innovation in language curricula based on an appropriate experimentation.
>
> (Fox, 1975, p. 147)

Why Macro Language Planning

This chapter is not intended to bury macro language planning; rather, it is intended to look at the ways in which macro (state-level) language planning has changed over the half-century since it sprang into existence in the wake of the construction of new polities and a global process of decolonization. The early versions of state-level language planning failed, in part at least because:

- they were linked to faulty theory and social policy (i.e., modernization and development);
- they ignored political reality;
- they failed to understand that economic models appropriate for one place may be ineffective in any other places;
- they failed to involve the populations most centrally affected;
- they failed to recognize that the actors had intellectual histories that could affect outcomes;

- they failed to recognize that national economic development will not necessarily benefit all sectors of any given society, especially the poor;
- they failed to recognize that state-level development generally does not consider local contexts and the conflicting needs and desires of diverse communities;
- they failed to recognize that development has a homogenizing effect on social and cultural diversity;
- they defined the task in terms of the nineteenth-century European notion of one nation/one language/one culture; and
- they failed to recognize that language rights were implicated.

As the practice of language planning has evolved over time, most of the failures listed here have been recognized, and language planning activity has been modified on the basis of two major considerations:

1. A given language does not belong to a particular nation; rather, any given language exists in an ecology in relation to other languages (international or indigenous), their speakers (without reference to political boundaries) and their own history and development (whether creolization or decreolization; healthy or moribund);
2. Languages and the polities in which they reside are subject to political and legal constraints (on the local, nation and global levels; see, e.g., the language legislation developed by the Council of Europe; Charter of Regional or Minority Languages[4]).

It will remain necessary and desirable to undertake macro language planning—simply as a recognition that the scope of the activity is potentially great because language modification (for whatever reason) may be so vast an undertaking—far beyond alphabetization, standardization, graphization, terminological elaboration, acquisition and language-in-education functions—that no lesser social unit could possibly support it. Language planners will need to understand, however, that they bring to the activity their opinions and beliefs, that the communities of use have a great investment in the activity and that the object of planning is circumscribed by laws and regulations at the local, national and international level. The agents of state-level language planning will need to understand that the object of planning is not their property, but rather that it extends across political and ethnic boundaries and requires agreement from all communities of use wherever they happen to be located geographically and politically. Those agents will need to understand that the activity they wish to undertake cannot be invisible, but rather that open accreditation is necessary both for the activity itself and for the economic implications of the activity as well as for the actors.

Obviously, language planning specialists need to understand that unexpected outcomes cannot be avoided, but rather that unexpected outcomes are a normal feature of highly complex social systems. There are a number of contemporary examples of planning that has resulted in unexpected results—e.g., such examples as China, North Korea and the Soviet Union. Indeed, Joshua Fishman and Ofelia García are presently editing a volume dealing with language planning efforts judged to have been at least in large part unsuccessful by their participants entitled *The Success–Failure Continuum: Handbook of Language and Ethnic Identity, Volume II* to be published by Oxford University Press.

It is likely that state-level language planning efforts will not only continue to occur but are likely to increase as polities continue to recognize the importance of language in their existence, dealing with such issues as the role migrants' languages should play in education (e.g., Trim, 1999; see note 1 in Lo Bianco, 2008, p. 124) and other official domains of use and, reciprocally, the impact of migrant languages on local languages. There are literally dozens of new problems exploding into the twenty-first century and into the increasingly globalized world.

While state-level language planning persisted through the late 1990s, language planning principles are currently being applied in "micro" situations (see Chua & Baldauf, Chapter 56, this volume). Indeed, a whole distinct area of research known as *language-in-education planning* has come into being (e.g., Hornberger, 2004; Kaplan & Baldauf, 2003). As a result of the widespread recognition of minority languages (particularly within the European community—see Council of Europe, 1992), there has been an explosion of literature dealing with the special concerns around minority languages (Edwards, 2004; Gorter, 2008; May, 2001, 2003). These areas of language planning essentially fall outside the limits of macro language planning, but are mentioned here to demonstrate that language planning as an academic discipline continues to evolve and grow.

Notes

1. It is important to note the titles of some of the key works of the period:

    Fishman, J. A. (Ed.) (1971). *Advances in the sociology of language.* 2 vols. The Hague: Mouton.
    Fishman, J. A. (Ed.) (1974). *Advances in language planning.* The Hague: Mouton.
    Fishman, J. A., Ferguson, C. A. & Das Gupta, J. (Eds.) (1968). *Language problems of developing nations.* New York: Wiley.
    Rubin, J., & Jernudd, B. H. (Eds.) (1971). *Can language be planned? Sociolinguistic theory and practice for developing nations.* Honolulu: University Press of Hawai'i.

2. For the role of language academies in language policy and planning, see "The history and theory of language planning" by Jiří Nekvapil, Chapter 52, this volume. For the spread and scope of contemporary language academies, see the list of language regulators at http://en.wikipedia.org/wiki/List_of_language_regulators.

3. The label *Ministry of Education* is used here to designate any governmental agency charged with oversight of the educational system of a polity.

4. The European Charter for Regional or Minority Languages (ECRML) is a European treaty adopted in 1992 under the auspices of the Council of Europe to protect and promote historical regional and minority languages in Europe. It only applies to languages traditionally used by the nationals of the state parties (thus excluding languages used by recent immigrants from other states), which significantly differ from the majority or official language (thus excluding what the state party wishes to consider as local dialects of the official or majority language) and which either have a territorial basis (and are therefore traditionally spoken by populations of regions or areas within the state) or are used by linguistic minorities within the state as a whole (thereby including such languages as Yiddish and Romani, which are used over a wide geographic area). (See http://en.wikipedia.org/wiki/European_Charter_for_Regional_or_Minority_Languages.)

References

Ammon, U. (1992). The Federal Republic of Germany's policy of spreading German. *International Journal of the Sociology of Language, 95,* 33–50.

Ammon, U. (1997). Language spread policy. *Language Problems & Language Planning, 21,* 51–57.

Baldauf, R. B., Jr (1982). The language situation in American Samoa: Planners, plans and planning. *Language planning Newsletter, 8*(1), 1–6.

Baldauf, R. B., Jr, & Kaplan, R. B. (2003). Language policy decisions and power: Who are the actors? In P. M. Ryan & R. Terborg (Eds.), *Language: Issues of inequality* (pp. 19–40). Mexico City: Universidad National Autónoma de México [UNAM].

Barrera i Vidal, A. (1994). The politics of the language spread policy of Catalan [La Politique de diffusion du catalan]. *International Journal of the Sociology of Language, 107,* 41–65.

BBC News (2009). Protests over Slovak language law, September 2. Available at http://news.bbc.co.uk/go/pr/fr/-/2/hi/europe/8232878.stm (accessed September 24, 2010).

Blommaert, J. (1996). Language planning as a discourse on language and society: The linguistic ideology of a scholarly tradition. *Language Problems & Language Planning, 20,* 199–222.

Brutt-Griffler, J. (2002). Class, ethnicity and language rights: An analysis of British Colonial policy in Lesotho and Sri Lanka and some implications for language policy. *Journal of Language, Identity and Education, 1*(3), 207–234.

Canagarajah, A. S. (2005). *Reclaiming the local in language policy and practice.* Mahwah, NJ: Erlbaum.

Chew, P. G.-L. (1999). Linguistic imperialism, globalism and the English language. *AILA Review, 13,* 37–47.

Clark, U. (2001). *War words: Language, history and the disciplining of English.* Amsterdam: Elsevier.

Cooper, R. L. (1989). *Language planning and social change.* Cambridge: Cambridge University Press.

Council of Europe. (1992).—See the Charter for Regional and Minority Languages. Available at http://en.wikipedia.org/wiki/European_Charter_for_Regional_or_Minority_Languages (accessed September 24, 2010).

Das Gupta, J. (1970). *Language conflict and national development.* Berkeley, CA: University of California Press.

Deprez, K., & du Plessis, T. (Eds.) (2000). *Multilingualism and government: Belgium, Luxembourg, Switzerland, former Yugoslavia, South Africa.* Pretoria: Van Schaik.

Donahue, T. S. (2001). Language planning and the perils of ideological solipsism. In J. W. Tollefson (Ed.), *Language policies in education: Critical issues* (pp. 137–162). Mahwah, NJ: Lawrence Erlbaum.

Dua, H. R. (1994). Hindi language spread policy and its implementation: Achievements and prospects. *International Journal of the Sociology of Language, 107*, 115–143.

Eastman, C. A. (1983). *Language planning: An introduction.* San Francisco: Chandler and Sharp.

Edwards, V. (2004). *Multilingualism in the English speaking world.* Oxford: Blackwell.

Fishman, J. A. (1968). The sociology of language. In J. A. Fishman (Ed.), *Readings in the sociology of language* (Vol. 1) (pp. 5–13). The Hague: Mouton.

Fishman, J. A. (Ed.) (1971). *Advances in the sociology of language* (2 Vols). The Hague: Mouton.

Fishman, J. A. (1972). *The sociology of language.* Rowley, MA: Newbury House.

Fishman, J. A. (Ed.) (1974). *Advances in language planning.* The Hague: Mouton.

Fishman, J. A. (1992). Foreword: What can sociology contribute to the sociolinguistic enterprise? In G. Williams (Ed.), *Sociolinguistics: A sociological critique* (pp. vii–ix). London: Routledge.

Fishman, J. A. (1994). Critiques of language planning: A minority language perspective. *Journal of Multilingual and Multicultural Development, 15*, 91–99.

Fishman, J. A., Conrad, A. & Rubal-Lopez, A. (Eds.) (1996). *Post imperialist English.* Berlin: Mouton de Gruyter.

Fishman, J. A., Ferguson, C. A. & Das Gupta, J. (Eds.) (1968). *Language problems of developing nations.* New York: Wiley.

Foster-Carter, A. (1985). The sociology of development. In M. Haralambos (Ed.), *Sociology: New directions* (pp. 1–21). Ormskirk: Causeway Press.

Fox, M. J. (1975). *Language and development: A retrospective survey of Ford Foundation language projects 1952–1974.* New York: Ford Foundation.

Francis, N. (2005). Democratic language policy for multilingual educational systems. *Language Problems & Language Planning, 29*(3), 211–230.

Gorter, D. (2008). Developing a policy for teaching a minority language: The case of Frisian. *Current Issues in Language Planning, 9*(4), 510–520.

Hajek, J. (2000). Language planning and the sociolinguistic environment in East Timor: Colonial practice and changing language ecologies. *Current Issues in Language Planning, 1*(4), 400–414.

Haugen, E. (1966). *Language planning and language conflict: The case of modern Norwegian.* Cambridge, MA: Harvard University Press.

Hogan-Brun, G., Ozolins, U., Ramonienè, M. & Rannut, M. (2007). Language politics and practice in the Baltic States. In R. B. Kaplan & R. B. Baldauf Jr (Eds.), *Europe, Vol. 3: The Baltic States. Ireland and Italy* (pp. 31–192). Clevedon: Multilingual Matters.

Hornberger, N. (Ed.) (2004). Heritage/community language education: US and Australian perspectives. *International Journal of Bilingualism and Bilingual Education* (special issue).

Jernudd, B. H., & Baldauf, R. B. Jr (1987). Planning science communication for human resource development. In B. K. Das (Ed.), *Language Education in human resource development* (pp. 144–189). Singapore: Regional English Language Centre (RELC).

Jernudd, B. H., & Das Gupta, J. (1971). Towards a theory of language planning. In J. Rubin & B. H. Jernudd (Eds.), *Can language be planned? Sociolinguistic theory and practice for developing nations* (pp. 195–216). Honolulu: University Press of Hawai'i.

Kaplan, R. B. (2001). English—the Accidental Language of Science? In U. Ammon (Ed.), *The dominance of English as a language of science: Effects on other language communities* (pp. 3–26). Berlin: Mouton de Gruyter.

Kaplan, R. B. (2003). CATESOL, Yesterday and today—Tomorrow is left to younger hands. *The CATESOL Journal, 15*(1), 7–18.

Kaplan, R. B. (2004). Editorial: On a note of caution. *Current Issues in Language Planning, 5*(4), 243–350.

Kaplan, R. B. (in press). Whence applied linguistics? In R. B. Kaplan (Ed.), *The Oxford handbook of applied linguistics.* New York: Oxford University Press.

Kaplan, R. B., & Baldauf, R. B., Jr (1997). *Language planning from practice to theory.* Clevedon: Multilingual Matters.

Kaplan, R. B., & Baldauf, R. B., Jr (2001). Not only English: "English only" and the world. In R. D. Gonzalez & I. Melis

(Eds.), *Language ideologies: Critical perspectives on the official English movement. Vol. 2: History, theory and politics* (pp. 293–315). Urbana, IL: National Council of Teachers of English.

Kaplan, R. B., & Baldauf, R. B., Jr (2003). *Language and language-in-education planning in the Pacific Basin.* Dordrecht: Kluwer Academic.

Kaplan, R. B., & Baldauf, R. B., Jr (2007). Language policy spread: Learning from health and social policy models. *Language Problems & Language Planning, 31*(2), 107–129.

Kirkwood, M. (Ed.) (1990). *Language planning in the Soviet Union.* New York: St Martin's Press.

Liddicoat, A. J. (2008). Language planning and questions of national security: An overview of planning approaches. *Current Issues in Language Planning, 9*(2), 129–154.

Lo Bianco, J. (2008). Educational linguistics and education systems. In B. Spolsky & F. M. Holt (Eds.), *The handbook of educational linguistics* (pp. 113–126) Oxford: Blackwell.

Luke, A., McHoul, A. & Mey, J. L. (1990). On the limits of language planning: Class, state and power. In R. B. Baldauf Jr & A. Luke (Eds.), *Language planning and education in Australasia and the South Pacific* (pp. 25–44). Clevedon: Multilingual Matters.

May, S. (2001). *Language and minority rights: Ethnicity, Nationalism and the politics of language.* London: Longman.

May, S. (2003). Rearticulating the case for minority language rights. *Current Issues in Language Planning, 4*(2), 95–125.

Peddie, R. A. (1991). *One, two, or many? The Development and implementation of language policy in New Zealand.* Auckland: University of Auckland.

Pennycook, A. (1994). *The cultural politics of English as an international language.* Harlow: Longman.

Phillipson, R. (1992). *Linguistic imperialism.* Oxford: Oxford University Press.

Powell, R. (2002). Language planning in the British Empire: Comparing Pakistan, Malaysia and Kenya. *Current Issues in Language Planning, 3*(3), 205–279.

Ricento, T. (2000). Historical and theoretical perspectives in language policy and planning. *Journal of the Sociolinguistics, 4,* 196–213.

Ricento, T. (Ed.) (2006). *An introduction to language policy: Theory and method.* Oxford: Blackwell.

Rostow, W. W. (1960). *The stages of economic growth.* Cambridge: Cambridge University Press.

Rubin, J. (1971). Evaluation and language planning. In J. Rubin & B. H. Jernudd (Eds.), *Can language be planned? Sociolinguistic theory and practice for developing nations* (pp. 217–252). Honolulu: University of Hawai'i Press.

Rubin, J., & Jernudd, B. H. (Eds.) (1971). *Can language be planned? sociolinguistic theory and practice for developing nations.* Honolulu: University of Hawai'i Press.

Rubin, J., & Shuy, R. (Eds.) (1973). *Language planning: Current issues and research.* Washington, DC: Georgetown University School of Languages and Linguistics.

Ruiz, R. (1984). Orientations in language planning. *NABE Journal, 8*(2), 15–34.

Shonerd, H. G. (1990). Domesticating the barbarous tongue: Language policy for the Navajo in historical perspective. *Language Problems & Language Planning, 14,* 193–208.

Skutnabb-Kangas, T. (2000). *Linguistic genocide in education—or worldwide diversity and human rights?* Mahwah, NJ: Erlbaum.

Steinberg, S. (2001). *The ethnic myth: Race, ethnicity and class in America* (3rd ed.). Boston: Beacon Press.

Tauli, V. (1968). *Introduction to a theory of language planning.* Acta Universitatis Upsaliensis, Studia Philologiae Scandinavicae Upsaliensia, 6. Uppsala: University of Uppsala.

Taylor-Leech, K. (2009). The language situation in Timor-Leste. *Current Issues in Language Planning, 10*(1), 1–68.

Tollefson, J. W. (1989). *Alien winds: The reeducation of America's Indochinese Refugees.* New York: Praeger.

Tollefson, J. W. (1991). *Planning language, planning inequality. Language policy in the community.* London: Longman.

Trim, J. L. M. (1999). Language education policy—Europe. In B. Spolsky (Ed.), *Concise Encyclopedia of Educational Linguistics* (pp. 122–127). Amsterdam: Elsevier.

van Els, T. J. M. (2001). The European Union: Its institutions and its languages: Some language political observations. *Current Issues in Language Planning, 2*(4), 311–360.

van Els, T. J. M. (2005). Status planning for learning and teaching. In E. Hinkel (Ed.), *Handbook of research in second language teaching and learning* (pp. 971–992). Mahwah, NJ: Lawrence Erlbaum.

von Gleich, U. (1994). Language spread policy: The case of Quechua in the Andean Republics of Bolivia, Ecuador, and Peru. *International Journal of the Sociology of Language, 107,* 77–113.

Webb, V., & du Plessis, T. (Eds.) (2006). *The politics of language in South Africa.* Pretoria: Van Schaik.

Williams, G. (1992). *Sociolinguistics: A sociological critique.* London: Routledge.

Worsley, P. (1987). Development. In P. Worsley (Ed.), *Sociology* (pp. 48–83). Harmondsworth: Penguin Books.

Youmans, M. (2007). *Chicano-Anglo conversations: Truth, honesty and politeness.* Mahwah, NJ: Lawrence Erlbaum.

56
Micro Language Planning[1]

Catherine Chua Siew Kheng and Richard B. Baldauf Jr

Introduction

Micro or local language planning, which is a relatively new way of thinking about the field of language planning and policy (LPP), has come about as a realisation of two converging trends. First, classical or macro language planners have realised that for language planning to be effective, and to understand how those effects work, there is a need to examine activities at a local or micro level. Moreover, for some groups large scale language planning may not be possible. For example, sustaining small languages (or small groups of users of languages) requires hands on involvement at a local level that may not be practicable to orchestrate at a national level (Liddicoat & Baldauf, 2008). In addition, many language problems are of little consequence when seen as part of the macro scheme of things, i.e. what language provisions and support are available in a particular company (Nekvapil & Nekula, 2008), or how a language teacher implements a programme to ensure learning in a classroom (Martin, 2005). Such local or micro language problems may be of critical importance to a particular company, school, group or even to an individual, but they may not have any apparent wider significance. Second, there has been a critical turn in the language planning literature, evident in the work of Luke, McHoul and Mey (1990), where they have suggested that language planning should take a more critical ethnographic or discourse-oriented focus if it is to actually address language problems. One approach that explicitly does this has been Language Management Theory (Jernudd & Neustupný, 1987; Neustupný & Nekvapil, 2003; Nekvapil, Chapter 52, this volume), which provides an alternate LPP paradigm for examining language planning issues at the local or micro level through its notion of simple management.

In this chapter, the rise and development of micro or local language planning is examined, and a definition of this particular approach to language planning is discussed. The chapter then goes on to look at examples of micro language planning that have appeared in the literature and how those have begun to influence our understanding of what it means to be involved in language planning. In the final section, the relationships between macro and micro language planning are discussed.

Background

As the chapter on macro language planning indicated (Kaplan, Chapter 55, this volume), classical language planning began as an academic discipline in the 1960s with a focus on macro planning for decolonisation, i.e. planning at governmental and institutional levels with the main intention of bringing the peoples in these newly independent countries together to create a common national identity. However, this classical phase of language planning with its exclusive focus on the macro, while providing an important perspective, by itself, increasingly has proven to be inadequate to the task of bringing about desired changes in language behaviour in many language planning situations in which it has been used. By the 1980s, critics, and some classical language planners themselves, began to look more critically at their field in order to reassess the issues involved. The critical focus that was increasingly adopted suggested that the broader language ecology (e.g. Kaplan & Baldauf, 1997, 2008) and politics (e.g. Pennycook, 1998) of situations needed to be taken into account. These critical perspectives also have meant that the actors in language planning need to be considered, especially for their individual influence (see Zhao, Chapter 54, this volume) and that these issues in turn need to be related to the micro or local contexts that constitute the broader language ecology.

This change in perspective has led to a series of re-conceptualisations of classical language planning that have been discussed from various perspectives including language management theory (see Nekvapil, Chapter 52, this volume; Kamwangamalu, Chapter 53, this volume), language planning as it relates to agents and domains, such as international groupings, local governments, schools and the family, which ensure that planning occurs (Spolsky, 2004, 2009) or language planning at the micro or local level (Canagarajah, 2005; Liddicoat & Baldauf, 2008). All of these re-visitations of classical language planning theory recognise that despite the best efforts of planners at macro level planning, at the micro level, language planning occurs or does not occur when small groups or individuals support or oppose the use of that particular language chosen for a particular purpose (Liddicoat & Baldauf, 2008).

An Overview of Macro–Micro Language Planning Translation

Macro language planning is often large scale and systematic, involving specific actions that are planned and carried out in order to promulgate language policies and to obtain certain results (see Kaplan, Chapter 55, this volume). Since policies are most often deliberately planned, they exist in the form of text and action stipulating certain processes and expected outcomes. Policy-making is a continual cyclical process that implicates on-going modification to both text and action as part of a continuing implementation process (Taylor, Rizvi, Lingard & Henry, 2002). It includes processes that have taken place before the production of the texts, as well as processes that continue after these texts are produced and implemented (Ball, 1994). These policies are then translated into laws, regulations and/or rules and then are turned into practices undertaken by government, international bodies (see Chua & Baldauf, Chapter 57, this volume), companies and institutions.[2] Generally, macro policy and planning involves formal and overt planning with specific goals that are clearly stated.

According to Kaplan and Baldauf (2003; also see Baldauf, 2005a), such calculated planning is based on a goal-oriented framework that includes: status planning (about society), corpus planning (about language), language-in-education planning (about learning) and prestige planning (about image). These approaches are formulated to produce the processes that are required for transmitting different stages of the implementing process, and need to be read by the actors who are involved at different levels. Therefore, language policy is meant to work in a deliberate, systematic and predictable fashion with the aim of conveying the methods and purposes of the policy to other stakeholders (Stevens, 2004). From a policy planning approach, it is a deliberate alteration of a community's linguistic structure (Cooper, 1989). For example, under Singapore's bilingual policy, English and Mother Tongue[3] education have been implemented by the government, and it has become mandatory for students to be literate in English. As a consequence, Singaporean government bodies, its educational system, and the media have used English as the main medium of communication and instruction (Chua, 2004, 2006). This top-down approach was put in place to ensure that the bilingual policy was effectively carried out and was able to meet the stipulated goals. Its success as a literacy policy is reflected in the country's literacy rate which was reported to be 98 per cent in 2008, producing a clear affirmation that the policy has produced the desired results and has successfully changed the linguistic structure of Singapore (Chua, 2004, 2006; Statistics Singapore, 2009a).

Despite such controlled and deliberate interventions, these four stages of the language planning implementation process may not occur in a clear linear progression. This is because they are subject to multiple interpretations by different stakeholders and this produces different outcomes that can vary from the policy-makers' intentions (Trowler, 2003). In the case of a relatively small polity such as Singapore, even when the Singaporean government adopts a top-down approach in its policy-making, the process of the translation of that policy into practice is not without difficulty. Policy made at the state level needs to find resonance with the other stakeholders within the polity. Moreover, the translation process that occurs in language planning resembles an "evolutionary" process whereby certain aspects of the reforms are emphasised or de-emphasised depending on how they are interpreted in relation to the needs of that society. For example, although the Singaporean government holds the central responsibility to provide education for the country, it is the Ministry of Education's (MOE) responsibility to plan how the actual reforms will be carried out. The MOE has to decide exactly what is to be implemented and under what conditions the changes are to be carried out. In order for the reforms to become a reality, the MOE needs to translate these reforms into policies for different audiences—curriculum planners, educators, teachers and students. Furthermore, when it comes to implementing language policy inside the classroom, it is the teachers (on their own and in collaboration with pupils) who are the gatekeepers, not the language planners and policy-makers (Baldauf, Li & Zhao, 2008). Essentially, the teachers hold the power as they are placed in the position of mediator between the policy and the pupils, and they are in control of how their classes are to be engaged with the texts (Martin, 1999). Therefore, some argue that it is essential for the teachers to be equipped with the necessary skills and knowledge of the sociolinguistic and multilingual contexts in which they live and work (Martin, 2008) if teachers are to work for and not against the language policies.

This translation process may be problematic as Sommer (1991) has indicated since planning of policy reforms "can be effected—by both political representatives and by administration responsible for implementation" (pp. 129–130). The reality is policies will be negotiated and modified because of a range of contextual circumstances (Smith, 2003). In other words, policies and reforms made at the national level will generate different results at the operational level depending on a number of variable factors. In view of this, when doing macro language planning there is a need to look at the entire implementation structure to ensure that the systems required for this to occur are in place. Conversely, micro language planning focuses on the finer mechanisms of the implementation process. Thus, both macro and micro planning need to work together in order for effective planning to occur (Baldauf, 2008). However, as suggested in the introduction, not all micro language planning is related to macro policies. In many instances, macro or classical language planning may not be appropriate or possible in a particular situation, and the planning may only occur at the micro level. Thus, as Figure 56.1 indicates there are at least four broad categories of relationship or translation that exist when considering the macro–micro context.

Figure 56.1 shows that language policies made at the national level are subject to a number of contextual influences that will determine the effectiveness of reforms that start at the supra macro and macro levels. Furthermore, the success or failure of the policies is further dependent on a translation process that relates the macro to the micro and infra micro planning contexts that underlie macro planning. As reflected in Figure 56.1, supra macro and macro planning operate differently from micro and infra micro planning. At the supra macro and macro levels, plans are large scale

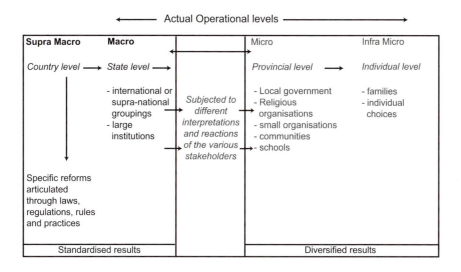

Figure 56.1 The relationships between macro and micro language planning

with specific rules and practices in principle leading to standardised results whereas micro planning involves a range of contextual factors and actors such as small organisations and schools with each interpreting and carrying out the policies in different ways. Inevitably, micro outcomes will not be standardised and the results will vary according to the various influences and interpretations found in the micro and infra micro environments.

In the sections that follow, micro and infra micro language planning are examined from the perspective of a number of different agents including: the community, the family and individual choice. While Figure 56.1 defines language planning on a continuum consisting of four main stages: supra macro, macro, micro and infra micro planning, within these four inter-related sets of processes, language planning goes through a number of different levels of translation. Figure 56.2 expands the four stages of language planning with each stage highlighting various levels of translating processes that involve a range of language planning actors (see Zhao, Chapter 54, this volume). The ten levels suggested are exemplary rather than definitive as which actors are involved in the translation process will depend on the particular context.[4]

Although language planning can start at different stages, Figure 56.2 indicates that some macro language planning may go through up to ten different levels of translation during the implementation process, i.e. that implementation may be undertaken by up to ten different participating groups of actors. As shown in Figure 56.2, in the supra macro planning level, level 1 (country) and level 3 (international institutions/bodies) are interchangeable in order, because some large international organisations can have a major informal impact on language planning in a country. For example, with the globalisation of the economy in recent years, many Swedish and Finnish companies have merged into large international Swedish–Finnish corporations, and this according to Winsa (2000) has affected the status of the Finnish language in Sweden. As these mergers have occurred, it has resulted in informal (covert) language planning that has strengthen the position of the Finnish language in Sweden, resulting in an increase in the number of novels published in Finnish. This example shows that language planning outcomes may be "unplanned", i.e. cannot necessarily be equated to formal planning (Baldauf, 1994).

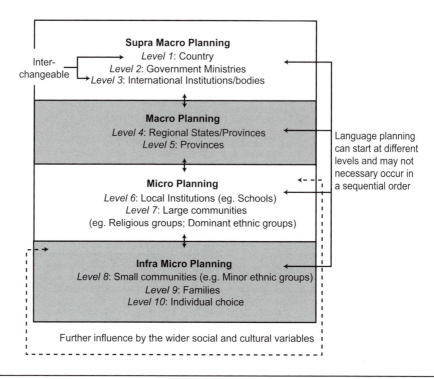

Figure 56.2 The four stages and ten levels of macro and micro policy planning

From a classical language planning perspective, the translation process should follow a linear pattern starting from the supra macro level to the infra micro level with each of the actors performing their role appropriately. The figure indicates that any top-down approaches that are the result of large scale planning processes need to be complemented with bottom-up processes. This is particularly important as the situational realities of the broader language ecology play a critical role in the success of language planning because they take into consideration the socio-political and educational contexts of the local communities where the policy is going to take place (Martin, 2005). Nevertheless in reality, the translation process does not always follow such a sequential order. For example in the United States, different states define the English language learner or limited English proficient student differently (Ferguson, 2006). Such inconsistency has created different expectations and interpretations of the language policy in different parts of United States making it inevitable that there will be different types of programmes and strategies that are designed and used, and hence variations in outcomes that will be produced. To further complicate the translation process, language planning can start at different levels and can bypass certain levels, thereby causing the translation process to occur in a non-sequential manner. Figure 56.2 therefore highlights the necessity for both top-down and bottom-up approaches to be congruent, and for language planning needs to take into account the various levels of the translating process, particularly at the micro and infra micro levels. This suggests that policies are not only subject to different interpretations, but that there are also a full range of variables at play in language planning (see, e.g., Ricento & Hornberger, 1996).

The First Step: The Power of Large Scale Macro Planning Processes

As in many other countries, in Sweden, language planning has typically begun at the macro level. For example, a parliamentary committee on the Swedish language was set up in 2000 to formulate action plans and strategies to promote the use of the language alongside with English (Winsa, 2000). The Committee on Cultural Affairs and the Swedish government proposed that the Swedish language should be regarded as the main language of the country and that it should be comprehensive and simple enough to use in the public domain. This qualification is important because in Sweden the population is not homogeneous with a variety of cultures and languages co-existing together including Finnish, varieties of Sami and Yiddish (*Regeringskansliet* Government Offices of Sweden, 2007). In 2006, the Swedish government further strengthened the position of the Swedish language when a new combined language planning organisation was recommended to improve language planning on the national level (*Sveriges Riksdag*, 2008). One of the proposals recommended was to use Swedish as the normal language in public administration, e.g. it was suggested that official government websites should be in Swedish with translation into English or other languages. The need to take this action occurred because since the Second World War English has been used in official matters particular in the area of international communication and the language has also been a mandatory subject in primary school (Winsa, 2000). In addition, English is fast becoming a much sought after language, and it is deemed to be the language of choice by Swedish educators and students in higher education (Marko, 1993). In order to ensure the use of the Swedish language, the government further advocated that it should be used to promote Swedish culture, and with the support of the local media and schools, the language should be used as the lingua franca in Sweden (Oakes, 2005). In this case, macro planning took on a holistic approach, and in a sequential manner the planning took into account the different possible avenues available to promote the use of the language at the government level, with government bodies, and in the state and the local schools. According to Oakes (2005), such macro planning has led to a renewed interest in the Swedish culture. Another study by Oakes (2001) found that Swedish students agreed that knowing Swedish is important as the language reflects its culture. This demonstrates that such formal and overt planning by government and macro level institutions can be successful in preserving and promoting certain languages through deliberate decisions about the use of the national or official language(s) in a society.

The Swedish example also shows that in order to ensure the success of large scale language planning, macro language planning needs to encompass the organisational and social structure of that society so that the policies are able to reach the target population more effectively. This means that there is a need to include the geographical and linguistic realities of that society so that appropriate promotion can be designed and carried out to ensure that the policy reaches a wide audience (Edwards & Newcombre, 2005). To take another example, upon independence in Singapore there were many dialect groups in the Chinese community—i.e. speakers of Hokkien, Teochew, Cantonese, Hakka, HockChia and others—all living in a tiny island state that had a total land area of 701.2 square kilometres (Statistics Singapore, 2009b). With such diversity, the government felt its survival depended upon a campaign to successfully unite the Chinese community through speaking a single common language (Chua, 2004). The early years of this campaign were aggressive and to a certain extent forceful because of the unique linguistic and geographical conditions in Singapore (Rubdy, 2005). Overt government intervention included such things as the use of numerous "Speak Mandarin" posters that were put up in many parts of the island and the dubbing of Hong Kong Cantonese movies that were shown in Singapore theatres and on television in Mandarin to ensure that only Mandarin was used—this practice continues even today. The Singapore government launched a campaign that took into account of the geographical and linguistic structures of the Chinese communities as well as the overall diversity of its population. An example of this strategy was to broadcast only Mandarin language movies on the only Chinese channel on the national television station. Even with the introduction of a new Chinese television channel, Channel U, only Mandarin-speaking programmes are shown. This continuing restriction clearly defines the objective of the campaign by exposing the selected group of people to that selected language at the national level.

Such large scale language planning can also be seen in the People's Republic of China's (PRC) national language policy. In 1956, the Chinese government chose the Han language, Mandarin, also known as Putonghua, to be the lingua franca for the Mainland Chinese regardless of dialect group. In 1986 the introduction of the PRC's Compulsory Education Act was instituted whereby schools were encouraged to promote the use of Mandarin and teachers were expected to use the language during school hours even if their native language was not Mandarin. Such large scale language planning has been successful as Mandarin is currently widely used in government agencies, in its mainstream media and among its people (Lin, 2004). Furthermore, in recent years, it has become an increasingly popular foreign language to learn in many countries (see Chua & Baldauf, Chapter 57, this volume).

The Next Step: Micro Language Planning—The Macro-Micro Translation

Such large scale planning is successful because the policies are explicitly stated and officially implemented, and thus they are able to cascade and be translated effectively to the micro level through supportive smaller policies and planning as in the cases of Singapore and China. However, this translation process does not always occur successfully in macro–micro language planning. According to Omar (2000), in Malaysia the act of allocating a functional role to the English language and endorsing it as a compulsory subject from primary school right through to university level does not naturally lead to community acceptance of it as a language for national use.

In Malaysia, the variations in power within groups within the society have created a conflicting situation in the macro–micro translation process that arises from Malaysia's top-down approach to language planning (Gill, 2005). The implementation of Bahasa Malayu as the national language of government and as the official medium of instruction in education has resulted in endorsing that language as both an indigenous language and at the same time as the lingua franca among the various races. As a result, Bahasa Malayu to Malaysians is not only the national language, it is the lingua franca that "bind[s] the ethnic groups into one, such that the national language becomes an embodiment of the sense of belonging that Malaysians should subscribe to" (Omar, 2000, p. 240). Thus, the implementation of a policy that called for a switch to English as a medium of instruction for science subjects at all levels[5] has resulted in outcomes that were conflicting. This is evident when based on public examinations and performance in jobs, the English standard is low, yet in government sections, schools, universities and in the private sector English is often a requirement (Omar, 2000). Thus, although both Bahasa Malayu and English have shared somewhat equal treatment in schooling, they have produced different outcomes.

To understand why this may be the case, there is a need for the language situation to be examined at the micro level. In Malaysia, the role the language is to play in society is ambiguous to many participants, and such imperfections in language planning translation can be attributed to the way the policy is perceived and carried out by the various actors. Hence, the Malaysian example shows that language planning needs to take into account the language ecology, and that the translation process from macro policy to micro usage may be imperfect as frequent exposure alone to the language through schooling does not produce an adequate basis for good English performance in schools and in society. According to Martin (2005), classroom language practices are the actual sites where language policies take place. As mentioned previously, teachers are the gatekeepers of the language policy, and they can either enhance or diminish the effectiveness of the policies. In his 2005 study, Martin found that code switching between English and native languages (Malay and Kelabit) by both the teachers and students, created tensions in a Malaysian classroom. He pointed out that such code switching practice in the classroom may be a "safe" way to ensure content is understood, but that it undermines policy and can hamper the learning of English. This practice also has been adopted in the Bruneian classroom. In Brunei, bilingualism means using Malay as the medium of instruction in the first three years of schooling but in the fourth year English is used instead to teach a number of subjects, and there is a move to use English language texts (Jones, 1996). Martin (1999) found that the teachers used the code switching technique (English, and both colloquial and standard Malay varieties) as a practical strategy to teach from the textbooks written in English, but that this had resulted in "major problems or 'lack of fit' between classroom practice and educational policy in Brunei" (Martin, 1999, p. 54).

When comparing Malaysia and Brunei to Singapore, which also adopts a top-down approach to language planning, a different outcome is produced. In Singapore, the government and schools strongly adhere to the bilingual policy of language separation and therefore the practice of code switching in the classroom is not encouraged either for teachers or students. In addition, unlike the Malaysian or Bruneian students who have to learn subjects such as history, geography, science and mathematics in Bahasa Malayu (Omar, 2000; Jones, 1996), in Singapore these subjects are conducted in English although Malay is Singapore's national language. Furthermore, a fail in English in Malaysia does not necessary deprive the students of certain certificates, and they still can be admitted to local university studies, creating problems for programmes such as engineering where English is used as the medium of instruction. In Singapore, a pass in English is mandatory if one desires to continue one's education in the local schools and tertiary institutions (Chua, 2004, 2006). Basically, English in Singapore is the lingua franca among the different races and it is regarded as the most important language to learn for all Singaporeans.

Another example of the importance of the micro context in the macro–micro transition process is related to the LOTE (Languages other than English) policy in Australia in the mid-1990s. Different states in Australia were given substantial Commonwealth funding for Asian language education in an attempt to strengthen the country's ties with the East Asia countries by learning their languages in schools. The four Asian languages chosen were: Indonesian, Japanese, Korean and Mandarin (Breen, 2002; NALSAS, 1994). This policy complemented the previously European language centred LOTE education where students were encouraged to study another language other than English. In order to enhance the probability of success of this programme, the ministerial working party proposed to have the primary school teachers trained as language specialists through an intensive training programme. In an evaluation of this programme in Western Australia, Breen (2002) found that the school in which the language specialist was located had a major impact on the success of the programme and stated that a negative environment, where there was insufficient support, limited resources and classroom facilities inevitably created restrictions for the teachers, which affected their performance. In addition, he also found that the wider social community, particularly the parents, play a critical role in the success of the language planning. Positive parental support tended to encourage the teachers to put more effort in language teaching, which according to Breen (2002) could even influence teaching pedagogies. This example affirms that supportive micro and infra micro level activities play a significant role in determining the outcome of the policies that are established at the supra or macro level.

The importance of micro planning is again highlighted in Māori language revival in New Zealand. The role of *kohanga reo* (language nests)—a community language initiative in schools by Māori elders—in support of Māori revitalisation in the 1970s and 1980s is well known (Benton, 1989). This revival of interest in Māori eventually led to the Māori Language Act of 1987 and to Māori gaining official language status. Formal language planning bodies, such as the Māori Language Commission were set up to consolidate Māori language rights, promote the language, foster research and publish Māori resources (Kaplan & Baldauf, 1997). Thus, extensive corpus planning initiatives were carried out to transform the Māori language into a modern language to ensure that the language was capable of serving a similar range of functions to those of any official language. This effort has paid off as now there are a wider range of Māori terms for use in the government departments and at the same time thousands of new terms have been developed so that the language can also be used in areas such as science, computing or economics (Māori Language Commission, 1996). Websites have also been set up to promote the language (*He Korero mo Te reo Māori*, 2009), and a special week has been set aside dedicated to learning Māori language and culture (Māori News, 2006). From a micro-driven revival, the language has undergone an extensive reformation process to extend its use so as to increase in the numbers of language users and subsequently to the development of language itself (Amery, 2001). Nevertheless, despite such significant increases in usage and gains in official language status, the Māori language still generates some opposition from the general public, businesses and institutions as a language to be learned (Amery, 2001). The language has now become symbolically powerful in New Zealand, but the specific choice to avoid learning Māori by the general public perhaps can be attributed to the speakers' decision to take up an alternative language that can provide them with greater perceived benefits (Edwards, 1995; Liddicoat & Bryant, 2001). Thus, even with a change in its status, the revival and spread of Māori still remains primarily, although importantly, symbolic at the macro level and continues to be a micro (individual and Māori community) language planning issue.

According to Haarmann (1990), such corpus planning and status planning activities that are directed at specific targets often have the ability to manipulate or change the linguistic structure of the society. However, the previous examples have highlighted the importance of the ecology that surrounds the community in which the LPP are to be implemented. They affirm that the accompanying policies and practices are equally important if macro language planning is to be translated effectively at the micro planning level thus determining the success of the LPP. Furthermore, despite the possibility of creating change through macro planning, the planning efforts still rely on issues of prestige or image (Ager, 2005)—the kind of psychological background that language planners may try to influence but that is beyond the direct control of the planner (or of supra macro and macro planning). Ultimately, the most crucial variable for any long-term planning lies with individuals' choice (at the infra micro level). Essentially, "the challenge of language revival efforts lies in the need for micro-planning: language planning which involves individual learners, small groups and small organisations" (Liddicoat & Bryant, 2001, p. 137).

Micro Language Planning: The Importance of the Individual (Micro–Infra Micro Translation)

A study done by Yoshimitsu (2000) shows that micro or local planning and language maintenance is a dynamic process as language planning is not just the designing of texts, actions and results. In her study, she explored a large number of possible variables that might influence the maintenance of the Japanese language by the Japanese children living outside Japan. She found that children who had succeeded in maintaining the language are those who were motivated and prepared to take the initiative to continue to use the Japanese language both in everyday and educational contexts. It was found that parental support or institutional support were insufficient to encourage them to use the language. Based on this finding, one can conclude that neither extrinsic motivation, large scale language planning nor even local planning may be successful if the individuals do not believe in the need for the language planning activity. Thus, language planning needs to take into consideration the positive effects that intrinsic motivation may have on individuals. Cheng (2004) also argues that individual choice can determine the level of success in a language planning situation. She cites the example of Hong Kong where although there is an awareness that English is important and a language used in education, government and international trade, many still choose to speak Cantonese with their families and friends. As a consequence, English is seldom used in Hong Kong and its standard remains low.

On the other hand, the positive power of individual choice is demonstrated in the successful revival of the New South Wales Australian indigenous language Gumbaynggir. According to Walsh

(2001), many attempts were made to revive the language but were unsuccessful. Revival only became successful through the work of individuals who has acted as the transmitters of the language by teaching the language to others thus affirming the importance of individuals and small communities in language planning. Likewise, in the twentieth century the Welsh language was under seriously threat due to English language hegemony in Wales. Although the passing of the Welsh Language Act in 1993 had a significant impact on the status of the language, it was the actions of English-speaking parents who had specifically chosen bilingual education that had helped to further strengthen the position of the language in the society (Edwards & Newcombe, 2005). Thus, according to Aitchison and Carter (2000), language planning has a higher rate of success if the home and community are proactive and use the language actively, which in turn encourages individuals to use that language actively. Similarly, when the Singapore government launched the Speak Mandarin Campaign in 1979 with the objective of eliminating the different dialects (i.e. Hokkien, Teochew, Cantonese, Hakka) to build a more unified community and to strengthen Mandarin learning in schools, the attempt could at one level be judged to be successful as the use of dialects declined among the Chinese community (Chua, 2004). However, although the government has put much effort into and provided many resources for promoting the use of Mandarin as a replacement for the dialects, it ultimately has been the individuals and community's choice to decide whether to make that switch. As the Singaporean context has provided English as an attractive alternative language choice, some individuals have decided to switch to it instead of to Mandarin, thereby failing to support the government's intent to bolster Mandarin in the community and its learning in schools. Thus, macro level language planning alone is often inadequate to understand or to bring about the changes desired at the macro level in a society, and micro level studies and planning are required to properly understand how local phenomena implicate language change. These infra–micro examples of individual and small group choices indicate the critical role local phenomena play in language planning.

Reversing the Order: Local Phenomena Implicate Change (Infra Micro–Micro–Macro Translation)

Micro planning also can be a local phenomenon with implications for creating macro level change and this increasingly has been realised by a number of language planners. Baron (2000) in his work on the Oakland Ebonics (Black English) resolution debate points out that the power of the community plays a critical role in determining the success of language planning. In 1996, the School Board of the Oakland Unified School District in California declared Ebonics to be an independent language and not a dialect of English for the African-American students in Oakland's schools. This sparked a huge reaction from the public (even among the Black community) claiming that this practice would further restrict Black students from attaining higher education. This was because Ebonics was perceived to be a mutated form of the English language, and it was argued its use would further lower the academic standards of the Black students. Because of this adverse reaction, the resolution was later withdrawn, and in 1998, the California voters went further by calling an end not just to Ebonics but also to bilingual education programmes. This occurred as a consequence of the passage of Proposition 227 that required English immersion programmes for all non-English speaking students or children of limited English proficiency. In this instance, language planning occurred at the micro level where a local board authority implemented a policy in which subsequently the local community and then higher state authorities were involved, i.e. the California state senator who banned the teaching of Ebonics in all the state's public school. In this example, the pattern of language planning was micro–micro–macro level.

In another case of micro language planning in Bolivia, a bottom-up approach played an important role in bringing back the Aymara language (Swinehart, 2009). In Bolivia, the radio is a very popular mode of communication. The Radio San Gabriel, the oldest Aymara language radio station in Bolivia has adopted a language policy that stresses the correct usage of the Aymara language by hiring staff who are competent in that language and through its educational programming. Such localised and personalised language planning has encouraged the use of the language within the community, which in return has strengthened the Bolivian 1994 National Education Reform that encouraged the teaching of all thirty Bolivia's indigenous languages alongside Spanish as subjects and as medium of instruction in all Bolivian schools (Hornberger, 1998, p. 443). Clearly, involvement at the local level and deliberate efforts to use a particular language in the public domain are essential if large scale language planning is to be successfully supported especially when there are multiple levels of translation processes.

In Spain, although the Catalan language was repressed and politically marginalised (and the users could be even persecuted if they are found to be using the language) since the eighteenth century, the language has been revived. This has occurred in particular since large scale government intervention was introduced in 1979 when the first Statute of Autonomy of Catalonia was declared which reaffirmed the status of the Catalan language. Moreover, in 1985 the Catalan government, together with the Institute of Catalan Studies took steps to develop, promote and regulate terminological activities for the language (Rodà-Bencells, 2009). Here, macro planning focused "on the 'normalisation' of the language … and its reintroduction into such public domains as education, the media and administration" (Ferguson, 2006, p. 77). Nevertheless, regardless of the different conceptions of the value of the language, the success of the revitalising of the Catalan language would not have been possible without participation of the public, i.e. it is the increased usage of the language by the people of Catalonia that has brought about its revival (Ferrer, 2000). The Catalan language may well have remained a symbolic language in Spain if not for the active participation and perhaps informal micro planning by the people of Catalonia.

These examples show that local phenomena or local communities (and individuals) can affect the type of language used independent of or in conjunction with more general language policy. Often such local policies can go unnoticed because seemingly unimportant variable factors can lead to a language change in a community (see Baldauf, 2005b; Liddicoat & Baldauf, 2008 for a range of additional examples). For example, Martin (2005) explained that besides education, migration and intermarriage are other factors that can cause a language shift. In his study, he found that a Belait community, which had relocated to Kuala Belait town, a relatively urban location, had managed to integrate effectively with the Malay-speaking people and this had led a change in status for their language. The Belait language was only used when communicating with the older generation, while for those under twenty-five, Malay was used instead. However, he found that in another Belait community, which had moved to Kuidang, a semi-rural location, both Belait and Malay were used by the younger generation. This highlights the importance of the local language ecology, which in the cases just cited resulted in the inter-action of two languages as a result of migration and a change in geographical area, but where the specific context produced two different linguistic outcomes, showing that such variation is a result of "the social, political and educational context in which it [language policy] takes place" (Ferguson, 2006, p. 37). These examples indicate the effect the local community can have in either encouraging or discouraging the use of a language.

Two-Layered Triangulated Approach to Macro and Micro Planning

Based on the previous discussion, this chapter suggests that for language planning to be effective it needs to adopt a two-layered triangulated approach since language planning is a complicated process that normally needs to include some degree of both macro and micro planning processes (see Figure 56.3).

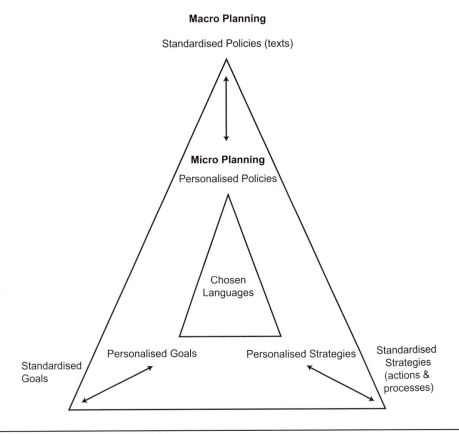

Figure 56.3 Two-layered triangulated approach to language planning

Figure 56.3 offers a framework that illustrates the unique relationships between macro–micro language planning. It shows that it consists of three central components: policies, goals and strategies. As indicated in Figure 56.1, for macro planning these components are standardised thereby providing an overall specific structure in which the policy can take place. As indicated in the cases of China, Singapore and Sweden, the governments' deliberate and calculated interventions in language planning in their polities have produced changes in desired language practices as evident in the official language in China and Singapore (Mandarin and English respectively), and in Sweden where the official government websites are available in Swedish alongside with English and other languages (*Regeringskansliet*, 2007). Likewise for micro planning, although on a smaller scale, the three components remain the same. In micro planning, instead of standardising these components, they are personalised since this level focuses on meeting the specific needs of particular communities and thus the policies, goals and strategies need to be customised and tailored to meet their needs. In the examples of learning the Japanese language outside of Japan and the Australian Gumbaynggir language, such localised micro language problems may seem to be of little significance to the wider Japanese and Australian communities. However, when looking at language problems, these local issues may be significant to individuals and local communities and can provide alternative ways to view or address overall language planning problems in that country (i.e. the need for migrant communities to learn their first languages, or for the revival of indigenous languages).

In retrospect, it is essential to look at both macro and micro planning processes when considering any language planning exercise. As the data that underlie the concepts that are discussed in this chapter and generalised in Figure 56.3 demonstrate, macro and micro planning are not normally independent processes. Instead, they are interdependent—although in some instances of micro planning, this may not always be obvious as micro planning is subsumed within the larger macro planning framework. Macro planning may remain only a symbolic set of standardised polices, goals and strategies if it fails to focus on the finer implementation processes and the different actors that are involved in the planning process (see Figure 56.2). As evident in the examples from Australia, Malaysia and New Zealand, top-down approaches to language planning have not always been very successful. This can be attributed, at least in some instances, to the failure to complement macro with micro planning.

Summary and Conclusions

Historically, language planning was associated with nation building and state formation, and thus policies were large scale as the main objective was to address certain language problems found in the countries. Based on this argument, LPP programmes are never neutral since they are designed to meet certain planned objectives. As illustrated in Figure 56.3, language planning needs to include macro and micro planning processes since micro planning is subsumed within the larger macro planning framework. Therefore, macro planning needs to be accompanied by personalised policies, goals and strategies by various actors found at the micro level. The example of Catalonia shows that language planning normally involves a two-layered triangulated approach—the macro level that implicates the government and the micro level that involves Catalan speakers from the various levels of the society. Nevertheless, although language planning appears to be a simple linear process or to adopt the two-layered triangulated framework, it is in reality more complicated since it exists in a language ecology where the effectiveness of language planning can be further affected by wider social and cultural factors that are beyond macro and micro planning. For example, it has been found that in Nepal, children without formal education can sometimes speak better English (though not grammatically correct) than the local graduates because of their exposure to tourists (Eagle, 2000). It is their need to earn a living that has compelled them to acquire a language through means other than formal education. Such informal planning affirms Kaplan and Baldauf's (1997) belief that the speakers will select the language that allows them the greatest flexibility in the society regardless of the educational interventions being made by the government. Besides overt and formal language planning from the supra macro to infra level, there also is a need to understand parallel issues of informal language planning as well since all language use ultimately will have a major effect on the social and economic structures of a polity.

Notes

1. Professor Peter W. Martin, who had agreed to write this chapter, died of a stroke at the age of 61 before he was able to contribute. His interest in language planning, multilingualism and language, culture and identity, and his experience in doing ethnographic language field work in a number of contexts, made him an ideal author for this chapter. While we don't know how he might have framed this important topic, we have cited some of his work that reflects his interest and expertise in the discipline and in doing so dedicate the chapter in memory of his scholarship and contribution to the field.
2. In classical language planning, this cycle was characterised by the collection of data through sociolinguistic surveys, the development of policy or plans and then the planning and implementation that followed (see, e.g., Kaplan & Baldauf, 1997; Jernudd & Baldauf, 1987). The language policy cycle (Canagarajah, 2006) also has been characterised in language management theory as moving from micro → macro → micro, i.e. ordinary language users bring problems they experience to linguists (planning experts) who create adjustments or solutions that language users implement (Nekvapil, 2009).

3. In this context mother-tongue refers to the use of the official mother-tongue languages in Singapore: Malay, Mandarin and Tamil.
4. Taking a language management theory perspective, Nekvapil (2009) suggests another way of viewing this continuum. He suggests that other cases exist beyond the typical language management cycle of micro → macro → micro where there are partial cycles, *micro* → *macro* or *macro* → *micro*, or fragments of the management cycle *micro only* or *macro only*.
5. Like many other post-colonial governments, Malaysia has tried to balance its commitment to Malay nationalism and Islamisation with the pragmatic realities of the need for English, the world lingua franca (Martin, 2005). In 2002 at the instigation of the outgoing Prime Minister Dr Mahathir, the Malaysian government changed school language policy for the subsequent year to one in which science and mathematics were taught in English. The government has reconsidered this policy and in 2010 appears to be reversing this process and reintroducing instruction in Bahasa Malayu.

References

Ager, D. E. (2005). Prestige and image planning. In E. Hinkel (Ed.), *Handbook of research in second language teaching and learning* (pp. 1034–1054). Mahwah, NJ: Lawrence Erlbaum Associates.

Aitchison, J. W., & Carter, H. (2000). *Language, economy and society: The changing fortunes of the Welsh language in the twentieth century.* Cardiff: University of Wales Press.

Amery, R. (2001). Language planning and language revival. *Current Issues in Language Planning, 2*(2&3), 141–221.

Baldauf, R. B., Jr (1994). "Unplanned" language policy and planning. In W. Grabe et al. (Eds.), *Annual review of applied linguistics 14* (pp. 82–89). Cambridge: Cambridge University Press.

Baldauf, R. B., Jr (2005a). Language planning and policy research: An overview. In E. Hinkel (Ed.), *Handbook of research in second language teaching and learning* (pp. 957–970). Mahwah, NJ: Lawrence Erlbaum Associates.

Baldauf, R. B., Jr (2005b). Micro language planning. In D. Atkinson, P. Bruthiaux, W. Grabe & V. Ramanathan (Eds.), *Directions in applied linguistics: Essays in honor of Robert B. Kaplan* (pp. 227–239). Clevedon: Multilingual Matters.

Baldauf, R. B., Jr (2008). Rearticulating the case for micro language planning in a language ecology context. In A. J. Liddicoat & R. B. Baldauf Jr (Eds.), *Language planning and policy: Language planning in local contexts* (pp. 18–41). Clevedon: Multilingual Matters.

Baldauf, R. B., Jr, Li, M.-L. & Zhao, S.-H. (2008). Language acquisition management inside and outside of school. In *Handbook of educational linguistics* (pp. 233–250). New York: Springer.

Ball, S. J. (1994). *Education reform: A critical and post-structural approach.* Buckingham: Open University Press.

Baron, D. (2000). Ebonics and the politics of English. *World Englishes, 19*(1), 5–19.

Benton, N. (1989). Education, language decline and language revitalisation: The case of Māori in New Zealand. *Language and Education, 3*(2), 65–82.

Breen, M. P. (2002). From a language policy to classroom practice: The intervention to identity and relationships. *Language and Education, 16*(4), 260–283.

Canagarajah, A. S. (Ed.) (2005). *Reclaiming the local in language policy and practice.* Mahwah, NJ: Lawrence Erlbaum Associates.

Canagarajah, A. S. (2006). Ethnographic methods in language policy. In T. Ricento (Ed.), *An introduction to language policy: Theory and method* (pp. 153–169). Oxford: Blackwell.

Cheng, N.-L. (2004). Hong Kong SAR. In W. K. Ho & R. Y. L. Wong (Eds.), *Language policies and language education: The impact in East Asian countries in the next decade* (pp. 100–114). Singapore: Eastern Universities Press.

Chua, S. K. C. (2004). Singapore's literacy policy and its conflicting ideologies. In A. J. Liddicoat (Ed.) (2007), *Language planning and policy: Issues in language planning and literacy* (pp. 76–88). Clevedon: Multilingual Matters.

Chua, S. K. C. (2006). Singaporean education planning: Moving from the macro to the micro. In A. J. Liddicoat & R. B. Baldauf Jr (Eds.) (2008), *Language planning and policy: Language planning in local contexts* (pp. 183–198). Clevedon: Multilingual Matters.

Cooper, R. L. (1989). *Language planning and social change.* Cambridge: Cambridge University Press.

Eagle, S. (2000). The language situation in Nepal. In R. B. Baldauf Jr & R. B. Kaplan (Eds.), *Language planning in Nepal, Taiwan and Sweden* (pp. 4–59). Clevedon: Multilingual Matters.

Edwards, J. (1995). *Multilingualism.* London: Penguin.

Edwards, V., & Newcombe, L. P (2005). Language transmission in the family in Wales: An example of innovative language planning. *Language Problems & language Planning, 29*(2), 135–150.

Ferguson, G. (2006). *Language planning and education.* Edinburgh: Edinburgh University Press.

Ferrer, F. (2000). Languages, minorities and education in Spain: The case of Catalonia. *Comparative Education, 36*(2), 187–197.

Gill, S. K. (2005). Language policy in Malaysia: Reversing direction. *Language Policy, 4,* 241–260.

Haarmann, H. (1990). Language planning in the light of a general theory of language: A methodological framework. *International Journal of Social Language, 86,* 103–126.

He Korero mo Te reo Māori. (2009). *Māori language information.* Retrieved 23 November 2009 from http://www.maorilanguage. info/.

Hornberger, N. H. (1998). Language policy, language education, language rights: Indigenous, immigration, and international perspectives. *Language in Society, 27,* 439–458.

Jernudd, B. H., & Baldauf, R. B., Jr (1987). Language education in human resource development. In B. K. Das (Ed.), *Human resource development* (pp. 144–189). Singapore: RELC Anthology Series No. 20.

Jernudd, B. H., & Neustupný, J. V. (1987). Language planning: for whom? In L. Laforge (Ed.), *Proceedings of the International Colloquium on Language Planning* (pp. 69–84). Québec: Les Presses de L'Université Laval.

Jones, G. (1996). The bilingual policy in Brunei Darussalam. In P. W. Martin, C. Ożóg & G. Poedjosoedarmo (Eds.), *Language use and change in Brunei Darussalam* (pp. 123–132). Athens, OH: Ohio University Center for International Studies.

Kaplan, R. B., & Baldauf, R. B., Jr (1997). *Language planning. From practice to theory.* Clevedon: Multilingual Matters.

Kaplan, R. B., & Baldauf, R. B., Jr (2003). *Language and language-in-educational planning in the Pacific Basin.* Dordrecht: Kluwer Academic.

Kaplan, R. B., & Baldauf, R. B., Jr (2008). An ecological perspective on language planning. In A. Creese, P. Martin & N. H. Hornberger (Eds.), *Encyclopedia of language and education (2nd Edn), Vol. 9 Ecology of language* (pp. 41–52). Heidelberg: Springer.

Liddicoat, A. J., & Bryant, P. (2001). Revival: A current issue in language planning. *Current Issues in Language Planning, 2*(2&3), 137–140.

Liddicoat, A. J., & Baldauf, R. B., Jr (2008). Language planning in local contexts: Agents, contexts and interactions. In A. J. Liddicoat & R. B. Baldauf Jr (Eds.), *Language planning and policy: Language planning in local contexts* (pp. 3–17). Clevedon: Multilingual Matters.

Lin, L. (2004). The People's Republic of China. In W. K. Ho & R. Y. L. Wong (Eds.), *Language policies and language education: The impact in East Asian countries in the next decade* (pp. 82–99). Singapore: Eastern Universities Press.

Luke, A., McHoul, A. & Mey, J. (1990). On the limits of language planning: Class, state and power. In R. B. Baldauf Jr & A. Luke (Eds.), *Language planning and education in Australasia and the South Pacific* (pp. 25–44). Clevedon: Multilingual Matters.

Māori Language Commission (*Te Taura Whiri i te Reo Māori*) (1996). *Te Matatiki: Contemporary Māori words.* Oxford: Oxford University Press.

Māori News. (2006). Māorilanguage.net: Māori language week. Retrieved 26 November 2009 from http://www.maorilan-guage.net/.

Marko, M. (1993). American English and higher education in Sweden. *American Studies in Scandinavia, 25,* 37–47. (Electronic source.)

Martin, P. (1999). Close encounters of a bilingual kind: Interactional practices in the primary classroom in Brunei. *International Journal of Educational Development, 19,* 127–140.

Martin, P. (2005). "Safe" language practices in two rural schools in Malaysia: Tensions between policy and practice. In A. M. Y. Lin & P. W. Martin (Eds.), *Decolonisation, globalisation: Language-in-education policy and practice* (pp. 74–97). Clevedon: Multilingual Matters.

Martin, P. (2008). Educational discourses and literacy in Brunei Darussalam. *The International Journal of Bilingual Education and Bilingualism, 11*(2), 206–225.

NALSAS (National Asian Languages/Studies Strategy for Australian Schools) (1994). *Asian languages and Australia's economic future: A report prepared for the Council of Australian Governments on a proposed National Asian Languages/Studies Strategy for Australian Schools.* Brisbane: Queensland Government Printer.

Nekvapil, J. (2009). The integrative potential of Language Management Theory. In J. Nekvapil & T. Sherman (Eds.), *Language management in contact situations: Perspectives from three continents* (pp. 1–11). Frankfurt am Main: Peter Lang.

Nekvapil, J., & Nekula, M. (2008). On language management in multinational companies in the Czech Republic. In A. J. Liddicoat & R. B. Baldauf Jr (Eds.), *Language planning and policy: Language planning in local contexts* (pp. 268–287). Clevedon: Multilingual Matters.

Neustupný, J. V., & Nekvapil, J. (2003). Language management in the Czech Republic. *Current Issues in Language Planning, 4,* 181–366.

Oakes, L. (2001). *Language and national identity: Comparing France and Sweden.* Amsterdam/Philadelphia: John Benjamins.

Oakes, L. (2005). From internationalisation to globalisation: Language and the nationalist revival in Sweden. *Language Problems & Language Planning, 29*(2), 151–176.

Omar, A. H. (2000). Managing languages in conflict situation: A specific reference to the implementation of the policy on Malay and English in Malaysia. *Journal of Asian Pacific Communication, 10*(2), 239–253.

Pennycook, A. (1998). *English and the discourses of colonialism.* London/New York: Routledge.

Regeringskansliet (2007). Retrieved 15 December 2009 from http://www.regeringen.se/.

Regeringskansliet Government Offices of Sweden. *(2007).* National minorities and minority languages: A summary of the government's minority policy. Retrieved 28 December 2009 from http://www.sweden.gov.se/content/1/c6/08/56/35/3b0f796c.pdf.

Ricento, T. K., & Hornberger, N. H. (1996). Unpeeling the onion: Language planning and policy and the ELT professional. *TESOL Quarterly, 30*(3), 401–427.

Rodà-Bencells, M. (2009). Language planning and policy and multilingual education in Catalonia. *Working Papers in Educational Linguistics, 24*(2), 57–78.

Rubdy, R. (2005). Remaking Singapore for the new age: Official ideology and the realities of practice in language-in-education. In A. M. Y. Lin & P. W. Martin (Eds.), *Decolonisation, globalisation: Language-in-education policy and practice* (pp. 55–73). Clevedon: Multilingual Matters.

Smith, D. L. (2003). Curriculum: Decisions, knowledge and ideology. In J. L. Terence & L. S. David (Eds.), *Curriculum: Action on reflection* (pp. 24–39). Tuggerah, NSW: Social Sciences Press.

Sommer, B. A. (1991). Yesterday's experts: The bureaucratic impact on language planning for Aboriginal bilingual education. *Australian Review of Applied Linguistics, S*(8), 109–134.

Spolsky, B. (2004). *Language policy.* Cambridge: Cambridge University Press.

Spolsky, B. (2009). *Language management.* Cambridge: Cambridge University Press.

Statistics Singapore. (2009a). Literacy & Education. Retrieved 10 November 2009 from http://www.singstat.gov.sg/stats/keyind.html#litedu.

Statistics Singapore. (2009b). Statistics. Retrieved 3 November 2009 from http://www.singstat.gov.sg/stats/keyind.html.

Stevens, L. P. (2004). Early literacy policy: National and local instantiations. *Current Issues in Language Planning, 5*(1), 18–33.

Sveriges Riksdag. (2008). New language policy for a multilingual Sweden 2005/2006. Retrieved 19 December 2009 from http://www.riksdagen.se/templates/R_PageExtended____7781.aspx.

Swinehart, K. E. (2009). Redemption radio: Aymara language planning at Radio San Gabriel. *Working Papers in Educational Linguistics, 24*(2), 79–98.

Taylor, S., Rizvi, F., Lingard, B. & Henry, M. (2002). *Educational policy and the politics of change.* London: Routledge.

Trowler, P. (2003). *Education policy* (2nd ed.). London: Routledge.

Walsh, M. (2001). A case of language revitalisation in "settled" Australia. *Current Issues in Language Planning, 2*(2&3), 251–258.

Winsa, B. (2000). Language planning in Sweden. In R. B. Baldauf Jr & R. B. Kaplan (Eds.), *Language planning in Nepal, Taiwan and Sweden* (pp. 107–203). Clevedon: Multilingual Matters.

Yoshimitsu, K. (2000). Japanese school children in Melbourne and their language maintenance efforts. *Journal of Asian Pacific Communication, 10*(2), 255–278.

57

Global Language
(De)Colonisation in the New Era

Catherine Chua Siew Kheng and Richard B. Baldauf Jr

Introduction

Globalisation is a much-used word symbolising a global reality that emphasises living in a new conceptual environment, one that is characterised by information technology. Globalisation can be understood as the forces that exercise pressure on standards and create demands in all societies (Javis, 2007). More than three-quarters of the people living in the world today are continuously shaped by this experience of global change, whether in the political, economic, social or environmental spheres. Thus, globalisation consists of multidimensional social processes that intensify worldwide social interdependencies, creating deeper connections between people from all over the world (Steger, 2003). The importance of these connections in the context of global change has affected the way languages are spread and used as it places greater emphasis on effective communicative situations at the individual, organisational, institutional and governmental level across the globe.

Global languages such as French, German, Japanese and, more recently, Mandarin, are popular languages to learn. However, English is by far the most frequently used language "for publishing, information gathering (reading), conferences or guest lectures, for informal written and oral correspondence and face-to-face communication (e.g. in networks, or for cooperation in labs)" (Ammon, 2006, p. 2). In addition, English is the first foreign language in many Asian countries and is seen as the key determinant of economic survival for countries in a changing socio-economic ecology (Mufwene, 2002). As the world has become more globalised, English has become the "world language" (Brutt-Griffler, 2002), but is being reconstructed by that process so that it no longer belongs to any country or culture, instead, belonging to anyone who speaks it (Herther, 2009).

Despite national macro influences on the international standards for languages, it is important to recognise that new variant standards have evolved. For example, currently, there are more than 75 countries that have English as their national or dominant language, and while 400 million people speak English as their first language, more than 750 million people speak it as their second language (Herther, 2009). Code-switching and localisation have created many varieties of Englishes, such as Spanglish (Spanish-speaking countries—a combination of Spanish and English), Manglish (Malaysia—a combination of English, Chinese and Malay) and Chinglish (China—a combination of Chinese and English). While there are common features in Asian varieties of Englishes that have led some to call for the creation of a standard Asian English, in many countries, the educational, political and business elites have viewed these varieties as inferior (Bolten, 2008) since they are often "restrictive" in use as they are only understood by people from the same country or culture. This analysis would also apply to a number of other internationalised languages including Arabic, Chinese, French, Portuguese and Spanish. This phenomenon is indicative of the death of language in a narrow sense (Reagan, 2005), as language and increasingly varieties of a language function as a means for societies to construct and express their moral, cultural and social developments, relationships and identities (Fairclough, 1992). Questions that arise in such globalised societies are: which languages are selected and used to aid communication in a variety of situations among the different people from different countries? With such a rich and versatile language ecology, how do global language policy and planning (LPP) decisions arise in response to the need to develop and maintain communicative standards and norms? In this chapter we look at this question from ten different "globalised" perspectives.

Globalised Language Planning

LPP for the globalisation of specific languages may occur at international or national levels, or in individual organisations. In the past, LPP was done mostly at the national level but today, LPP is increasingly being done at the global level. At the international level, organisations such as the Confucius Institutes are co-funded by the Chinese government to promote Chinese language and culture worldwide (Sim, 2009). In United States, there is a partnership between the College Board and the Chinese Language Council International, or *Hanban* for short, to work closely to introduce Chinese language and culture into the American schools (*Hanban*, 2001–2009b). Involvement in globalised planning of languages by governments also can occur at the state or district level. For example, as part of the national level LPP done in Singapore at independence in 1965, the Singaporean government decided that English was to be one of the country's official languages, and that simplified rather than traditional characters were to be used for Chinese mother-tongue instruction in Singaporean schools, although they could only be introduced subsequently. In Québec, the Charter of the French Language (*La charte de la langue française*), also known as Bill 101 (*Loi 101*), was passed making French the only official language of Québec. Under this legislation, children in Québec must be educated in French until they have completed their secondary education (*Éducation, Loisir et Sport, Québec*, 2007). In Mongolia, a country distant from most English-speaking nations, the government is determined to turn the country into a bilingual nation (Albey, 2008). At the local level, involvement in globalised LPP can occur in individual organisations such as the Woodstock Elementary School in Portland, Oregon, which has introduced a Mandarin-immersion programme in the school (Boufis, 2007).

External influences such as economic demands also play a significant role in promoting the types of languages learned and the standard that the users should attain. For example, although English has been a popular language to learn because of its economic, social, technological and educational advantages (Graddol, 2006), recently, China's influence and its emergence as an economic and diplomatic power have increased the number of people who want to learn to speak Mandarin (Boufis, 2007). The emergent popularity of Chinese has resulted in the formation of the *Hanban*, a non-governmental, non-profit organisation that strives to promote Chinese language internationally.[1] It sets the criteria for teaching Mandarin as a foreign language and, similar to the Cambridge International Examinations, it also undertakes the evaluation processes, and has put in place training programmes and certified standards for teachers of Chinese as a foreign language. Most importantly, it develops and promotes relevant teaching materials for those countries that are keen to implement Chinese programmes (*Hanban*, 2001–2009a). In a recent report in *The Straits Times* of Singapore, China is reported to be increasing the number of Confucius Institutes—which are equivalent to the British Council or the Goethe Institute—from 314 to 500 by 2010 in order to meet the growing demand, particularly in the European region, of people wanting to learn the Chinese language (Sim, 2009). In a similar manner, the French have the Superior Council of the French Language (*Conseil supérieur de la langue française*), an organisation that advises the government on issues that concern the usage of the French language. These organisations and others such as the British Council, the *Alliance Française*, the Goethe Institute and the Japanese *Monbusho* language education facilities (Gottlieb, 2009) help to maintain the norms and standards of different languages internationally.

Another interesting phenomenon that is increasingly being discussed—as more and more people communicate in different varieties of Englishes and with the changing landscape of English language use due to technology—is that a new form of English as a lingua franca (ELF) (Seidlhofer, 2005) or a "globalish" language is emerging and may subsequently gain widespread use (Ammon, 2006). It is suggested that this new variety would be "neither English nor by any compound of English, with its function fundamentally different from the English language, namely a lingua franca, whose norms were no longer under the control of native speakers of English" (Ammon, 2006, p. 25). Speakers would be bilingual in two native languages—e.g. English + Globalish, French + Globalish, or Japanese + Globalish. Perhaps this new language could become the international lingua franca among the different groups of people, however, setting and maintaining the norms and standards of this variety would be difficult or perhaps impossible without international language planning since it would not "belong" to any specific variety of the English language.

Globalised Languages

Imperial languages such as English, French, German, Japanese, Portuguese and Spanish were spread to various parts of the globe through colonisation. Thus, the type of language adopted in a polity or in a community has strong connections to its historical heritage. According to Ashcroft, Griffiths and Tiffin (2002), more than three-quarters of people in this world have had their lives shaped by the experience of colonialism. In view of this, the current linguistic make-up of a polity can be a result of colonialism; the very act of colonialism not only changes the culture, politics, economics and social aspects of the colonised countries in particular, it also changes how they communicate using the introduced coloniser's language. Varying degrees of linguistic hybridity have been introduced in polities such as Singapore (British English), Macau and Timor Leste (Portuguese), Canada (Québec-French) where a colonial foreign language has been adopted as one of the official languages.

An important question to ask in this context is who actually decides the norms and standards of these global languages? During the colonial period, one of the principal ways in which the norms and standards of the languages were maintained was through the types of texts and resources used in schools as well as the kinds of foreign teachers who were employed to teach in these schools. For example, Ashcroft et al. (2002) have argued that during the British colonial period, English literature was introduced through education in India for political reasons – to put in place the cultural enterprise of empire in India. Through acts of education such as this, the norms and standards of English (and elsewhere for other languages) have been introduced and reinforced as language provides the essential vehicle for education in its many forms (Matheson & Matheson, 2000). Currently, international examinations such as the Cambridge International Examinations and the International Baccalaureate (IB) act as the benchmark standard for the English language. For example, in the Singaporean education system, students are required to sit for the Cambridge Examinations after they have completed ten years of education (GCE O levels) and 12 years of education (GCE A Levels). The Singapore Ministry of Education (MOE) states that one of the main aims of the English Language in GCE O Level is to "speak, write and make presentations in internationally acceptable English that is grammatical, fluent and appropriate" (MOE, 2010). These arrangements mean that students have to prepare for the English language and English literature examinations according to the Cambridge standard. In Macau, students who are studying in Portuguese schools follow the Portuguese system with the main language being Portuguese.

School systems use a variety of resources to attain international language norms including dictionaries produced by Cambridge, Duden, Hachette, Oxford and Webster that reinforce the standard varieties. Furthermore, computer programs that are currently widely used in schools also play a significant role in putting in place standard varieties of languages through their spell check and grammar functions. Users have to choose between the standardised United States or United Kingdom English, or between Simplified/Traditional Mandarin, or Arabic, French or other languages' standard varieties. Thus, the globalised planning of languages is reinforced at the national level by governments and government bodies (e.g. MOEs) who play a critical role in choosing the type of language provided in education and by reinforcing particular standards and norms.

Globalised Institutions

What is a standard language? Why do some languages become internationally acceptable languages? Although multilingualism has been widespread, some languages are still considered more prestigious than others. Do large international bodies such as the Association of Southeast Asian Nations (ASEAN), the United Nations (UN), the European Union (EU), the World Bank, the United Nations Educational, Scientific and Cultural Organization (UNESCO) or the *Organisation Internationale de la Francophonie* (OIF) play a significant part in privileging certain languages over others?

The ASEAN is made up of Brunei, Cambodia, Indonesia, Laos, Malaysia, Myanmar, Philippines, Singapore, Thailand and Vietnam (ASEAN Foundation, 2008). Although each has its own national language(s), English was chosen as its official language for all communications within the organisation. In order to facilitate effective communication with the ASEAN countries, Laos and Vietnam, former French colonies, have opted to switch from French to English as their second language (Chalerm-palanupap, 1999). This favouring of English as the language of ASEAN communication has reinforced its status and stressed its importance. At the same time, it sets standards for the language since all documents and information are written in English.

Unlike the ASEAN, the UN, UNESCO and the World Bank have a large number of members. The UN's official website is available in six languages—Arabic, Chinese, English, French, Russian and Spanish. Although information is also available in non-official languages such as Thai and Japanese, more detailed information is only made available in the selected official languages. Although the UNESCO has 193 member states, it also uses these six languages as its official languages on its website (UNESCO, 1995–2009). However, certain specific information, such as information on communities, is only available in English, French and Spanish (UNESCO, 1995–2009). Similarly, the World Bank uses these six languages as its official languages, and websites, documents and publications are written in these languages.

On the other hand, the EU has 25 member states with 20 languages, and languages of lesser use such as Danish, Dutch, Finnish, Greek and Swedish are acknowledged as official and working languages, thereby in principle giving all languages the equal rights (Phillipson, 2003). However, van Els (2005, p. 269) has claimed that

> among the officials almost no languages other than English and French are used—and from time to time German ... [and] at the European Central Bank in Frankfurt ... all internal communication and all communication with the outside world happens only in English.

Some have argued that it is natural for there to be a reduction in the number of working languages to a single internal working language, English, since it is a logical and efficient solution to deal with linguistic diversity. In addition, as the EU and the United States have the biggest bilateral trading and investment relationship, this further implicates English as the language of choice. Thus, while all EU national languages are official EU languages, this status does not carry over into most of the realities of use. Similarly, the OIF adopts an open door policy whereby it welcomes a wide range of countries to join even though French may not be the language of the applicant country. It also works with other organisations to promote Spanish, Portuguese and Arabic at the international level (De Cock, 2006). Nevertheless, despite this apparent open door policy, the OIF still considers the position of the French language in the country as a key determinant of its eligibility when wanting to join the *Francophonie* (OIF, 2000–2009).

This raises the question of the extent to which the languages used by global institutions influence language teaching and learning in the member states? Van Els (2005) believed that it played a large role in the foreign teaching policy of the EU member states. For example, although Germany has been promoting its own language abroad, it has been upgrading English in the country. English has become a general subject in 16 German states in primary schools. At the tertiary level, English, together with German, are used as the medium of instruction for international programmes. In Finland, many schools are offering subjects through English language instruction. Thus, although the language choices made by these global bodies do not directly dictate language choice in the member countries, indirectly they help to strengthen the position of certain languages, in particular English. From a planning perspective then, these bodies act like a standardising force that privileges certain languages over others.

Globalised Agencies

Globalisation has enabled companies to expand internationally, and has increased collaboration between different countries. Inevitably, such contacts have resulted in the setting up of international agencies to facilitate international activities and communications. Examples of some of these agencies include the International Maritime Organisation (IMO), Air Traffic Control and *Médecins Sans Frontières* (MSF, Doctors Without Borders). To communicate and function effectively across a range of activities, there has been a need to create specialised languages, such as PoliceSpeak and TunnelSpeak, to facilitate effective communication between individuals from different nations. A number of these specialised agencies have developed specific protocols or subsets of language that are taught and used across national boundaries.

The IMO was established in 1958 and its main purpose is to "facilitate cooperation among governments in matter of international shipping, including: trade; maritime safety; marine pollution; and navigation" (McEntee-Atalianis, 2006, p. 345). Its language policy is similar to that of the UN; the IMO has adopted Arabic, Chinese, English, French, Russian and Spanish, with English, French and Spanish as the working languages. But, despite such a diverse membership, English is the primary language choice and is used as the lingua franca. The majority of its reports, electronic IMO documents and downloads are in English with only 3.35% in Spanish, 0.93% in Russian, 0.57% Chinese and 0.38% in Arabic (McEntee-Atalianis, 2006). A variety of English, Maritime English, is used to cover a wide range of inboard written and oral communication, ship to ship communication, ship to shore communication, including navigation, ship handling, medical, safety and other purposes. English is used as the language for pre-sea courses, and the content of these courses are written using agreed Standard Marine Navigational Vocabulary (Johnson, 1995). Clearly, the IMO is involved in and facilitates language planning by explicitly selecting English as the principal medium of instruction for all its communications. In a similar manner to the IMO, the International Civil Aviation Organization (ICAO) was officially established in 1947 in Montreal, Canada to facilitate air traffic navigation between different countries. Although its main office is based in Montreal, Québec, a French-speaking state, English was chosen as the language of communication in 1951 since the United States was dominant in aviation and world politics.

Another international agency, MSF, a medical humanitarian organisation was founded in 1971 by doctors and journalists in France with the aim of providing medical aid to countries in need. The two official languages for the MSF's website are English and French. There are also other MSF's international websites written in various languages, including Italian, Japanese and Spanish (MSF, Canada, n.d.). Despite having offices around the world and 19 associated organisations, in countries such as Australia, Denmark, Germany and Sweden, it is a recruitment requirement that when applying for a practical field job in MSF, French language skills are considered to be a major asset (MSF, 2009). Thus, although on its official website English is the most common language of communication, unlike IMO and ICAO, the role of French is privileged in practical domains. These examples suggest that globalised agencies play a major role in selecting languages to be used internationally and thus are involved in LPP.

An interesting effect of these close interactions between the different countries is that in some instances specialised languages, such as the PoliceSpeak and TunnelSpeak, have been created to facilitate communication between the parties involved. For example, the Channel Tunnel, the longest undersea tunnel in the world (EuroTunnel: The Channel Tunnel, 2009), provides rail infrastructure linking England and France. There are two centres that take it in turn to be the duty Control Centre, one on the English side and the other on the French side. Thus, instructions and maintenance procedures may involve the use of either language. As a result, pre-established standard messages in English and French (PoliceSpeak and TunnelSpeak) have been developed to ensure the safe operation of this facility. The PoliceSpeak lexicon is simple as its aim is to give maximum clarity between the English- and French-speaking police forces (Schaarschmidt, 1996). Likewise, TunnelSpeak is a specialised discourse that was invented using both English and French vocabulary that enables the British and French workers from both sides to communicate adequately with each other.

The need for different people to have close working relationships in globalised agencies has helped to reinforce the status of certain languages. The IMO and ICAO have clearly chosen English as their main language of interaction despite the problems this sometimes causes. On the other hand, the MSF stresses the importance of both English and French languages as reflected in its employment requirements. Interdependent working relationships have created several specific dialectal languages including PoliceSpeak and TunnelSpeak for the operation of the Channel Tunnel. These specific languages are different from the traditional understanding of languages as they are deliberately constructed, hybridised and simplified to facilitate accurate and effective communication between individuals from the countries involved.

Globalised Business

Big multinational companies and big business located in countries across the world, including China, Europe, Korea, Japan and United States have set up in countries such as India, Brazil and Mexico to source low-cost workers and manufacturing facilities for products and services and to access low-end markets to maximise their profits. They broaden their business empires either through collaboration with local partners or through wholly owned subsidiaries (Loos, 2007). Effective global communication, therefore, becomes essential as economic activity has moved from the local or national level to the global level creating physical distance and cultural differences between the parent and subsidiary operations (Spinks & Wells, 1997). What impact does such corporate globalisation have on languages?

Some argue in a globalised world where economics is pre-eminent, international businesses are influential in globalising languages because economic forces can act as an invisible power that strengthens preferences for certain languages. When conducting business abroad, foreign language skills are essential as they facilitate better access to the target market (Swift, 1991), and knowing the language of possible customers has the potential to help to open up markets for the producer and facilitate the worldwide distribution of goods and services (Ammon, 1995). For example, the parent website of the international Swedish home products retailer Ikea contains information in different languages about other sub branches of Ikea located in other parts of the world (Ikea, 1999–2009). In this instance Ikea introduces and globalises certain languages, such as English, German, Japanese, Mandarin and Spanish. To take another example, foreign companies that are located in Singapore are required to use English as the main mode of communication since English is the working language for all Singaporeans regardless of race. Singapore Food Regulations also require all food labels to be written in English (AVA, 2009), which means that food producers and importers have to ensure that all the necessary information is attached to their pre-packed products. In the commercial sector in Japan, although English is considered as a foreign language, it is used in hotels, restaurants and departmental stores (Kaplan & Baldauf, 2003). Learning to communicate in English in the business world has become essential and unavoidable ever since the rise of America in the 1950s (Chew, forthcoming).

Essentially, companies are expected to know how to "speak the language" of the country where they have businesses. This is known as the lingua franca model whereby subsidiary companies in general are run in the standard languages of the countries in which they are situated (Loos, 2007). For example, the Tata Technologies Limited, one of the oldest and largest businesses in India, has facilities in Canada, China, Germany, Ireland, France, Singapore, Thailand and United States (Tata Technologies, 2009). Eighty per cent of the employees the company hires are citizens from the countries in which the branch is located and only 20 per cent are Indians (Sirkin, Hemerling, Bhattacharya & Butman, 2008). These arrangements mean it is unavoidable that the main language of communication of the company will be that of the country where it is located. On the other hand, there are companies that prefer to employ expatriates from the parent country in important positions when the host country language differs from that of the parent company (Harzing, 1999). For example, leading Japanese multinationals are usually run by Japanese expatriates who communicate in Japanese between the host and parent companies although English may be widely used among their employees (Yoshihara, 1999). Some parent companies may choose to establish their subsidiary plants in countries where English, the dominant international language, is widely spoken (Welch, Welch & Marschan-Piekkari, 2001). For the non-English-speaking markets such as those in Asia, English is also used as it has become accepted in these countries as the universal language of business (Kirkpatrick, 2006).

More recently, Mandarin has become a language of choice in some international business situations because of the rising economic power of China. This increase in popularity is akin to the rise in the learning of Japanese in the 1960s (Chew, 2009b). This phenomenon suggests that the potential economic power of a nation can have an impact on language choice. Thus, foreigners are learning Mandarin so as to trade more successfully with China, and more Chinese are learning English in order to communicate effectively with their external counterparts. Nevertheless, it is important to note that economic influence may not necessary increase the popularity of a language. For example, although Korean products are popular, the demand for the Korean language is not as high and is more influenced by the media soap operas than by business.

As operations have globalised, it is critical for companies to have the ability to deal with multiple languages because in a globalised business world, effective communication between the parent and subsidiary company, as well as with its customers, is critical for business success. Although learning English is important, it is not enough because of the diversity in the customers' languages and cultures that are present in the global market. These examples show that language planning is more than a governmental or agency activity and is influenced by globalised businesses that through their internal language practices play an important part in strengthening or devaluing certain languages.

Globalised Higher Education

Education, particularly higher education, has been recognised as one of the fundamental driving forces for national development (UNESCO, 2004). Pressure on national public funding for higher education in countries such as Australia, New Zealand, the United Kingdom and the United States has forced many institutions to seek additional income from international students (Marginson, 2007). Furthermore, the increasing pressure to be more corporate and to find enough funds to run institutions has led to many becoming commercialised, with students increasingly being looked upon as customers. Hence, higher education programmes are becoming commoditised, particularly at the post-graduate education level (Steck, 2003). Thus, courses and programmes of study are increasingly being offered that not only cater for the local students but also for the international market place (Sidhu, 2009).

Traditionally, English-speaking nations, such as the United States and United Kingdom, have been academic superpowers with more than two-thirds of the best research universities located there (Marginson, 2007). The United States itself is home to a large proportion of top universities in the world and invests large amounts of money in research and development (Altbach, 2008). In addition, the stature of the global super league universities in the United States, such as Harvard University, Massachusetts Institute of Technology, Stanford University and University of California, Berkeley, (Marginson, 2006) appeals to a large number of international students. Consequently, these universities play a dominant role in the academic domain. For instance, the MBA degree, which was first developed in the United States, has since gained international popularity. MBA programmes that are offered in overseas universities often use English as the main medium of instruction and they adopt a largely US curriculum.

In recent years, countries such as Australia, Canada and New Zealand have placed greater importance on international education marketing initiatives (Alberta's international education strategy, 2001), and have been actively promoting their country's educational institutions and establishing branch campuses in other countries. For example, in Singapore, there are international institutions such as INSEAD from France, the University of Chicago Graduate School of Business, and the German Institute of Science and Technology. Other foreign universities operate in collaboration with the local Singaporean universities or institutions. For example, the National University of Singapore and Nanyang Technological University have joint programmes with institutions such as The Australian National University, the University of Basel (Switzerland), the Technical University of Denmark and King's College London (Chew, 2009a; Singapore Education, 2008). Although one may argue that in Singapore, where English is the official working language, the curriculum in these joint programmes would be in English, the curriculum is designed for a foreign market and English would have been chosen as the medium of communication even though the programmes originate in France or Germany. Another recent phenomenon is that European countries such as Holland and Germany are also increasingly adopting English as the medium of instruction in their institutions. In Holland, the Dutch Minister of Education suggested that the universities in Netherlands shift the language of instruction from Dutch to English in order to make Holland a more attractive education destination for international students (Altbach, 2008). This is but one of many instances of non-English-speaking countries considering or adopting aspects of English in their higher education system or for research in an attempt to go global as programmes that are conducted in English are attractive to many foreign students (Altbach, 2008; Marginson, 2007). However, offering programmes in English has substantial language planning consequences for providers that often are not well understood—success depends on good language support. In particular, programmes taught in English to second language speakers (e.g. in engineering in Malaysia) need to be properly supported and resourced if they are to successfully meet employer needs.

As more and more international academic programmes and courses are being designed and offered in English, the globalising impact of language planning decisions that arise from direct or indirect government decisions such as those taken in Holland, Malaysia or Singapore, can be felt. University governing bodies, through specific programmes and collaborative ventures, also contribute to this linguistic globalisation. Nevertheless, programme language choice is highly influenced by the societal, parental and student demand, and there is no certainty that this will favour English or English-speaking polities in all circumstances.

Globalised Science

In the global economy, countries that are strong in advanced technology, have high skills and have a well established science base, enhance their position in the international marketplace. As an example, in 2007 in the United States, at least 27 American universities earned "more than $10 million [each] from licensing the rights to vaccine, drugs, medical devices, and other intellectual property". The New University earned "nearly $800 million from technology transfer on 227 active licenses" while ten universities earned "more than $50 million each from license income" (Masterson, 2009, p. 14). What role have languages played in the globalisation of science and popularisation of it to the public, to education and to the science industry?

At the beginning of the twentieth century, English, French and German were considered to be of equal importance in the field of scientific communication. The more recent shift towards using English in scientific publication has largely been influenced by historical, socio-economic and political factors. The United States, whose economic infrastructure and educational institutions were left intact after World War II, was left as the dominant player in the world economy. Moreover, because of early US involvement in global education, more people from non-English-speaking countries were also learning, writing and publishing in English, and this in turn further strengthened the importance of English as the language of science (Grabe & Kaplan, 1986). The expanding power of the United States meant that the spread of English and its use in the scientific domain was unpreventable (Ammon, 2006; Cristina, Favilla & Calaresu, 2007). In today's world, English plays a dominant role in international (interlingual) scientific communication in all domains: publishing, information gathering, conferences, formal and informal writing, and oral communication (Ammon, 2006). The reason for this is that in the pure natural sciences discoveries often have universal relevance and attract a wider international readership that is more easily reached through English, as unlike other languages, such as French, German or Japanese, it is not restricted to culturally related domains or limited to countries speaking those languages. Finally, as the United States is the biggest player in research and development, and dominates scientific publication, English is often the preferred language as it ensures work is read and cited by a wider audience (Baldauf & Jernudd, 1986).

An example of the impact that the change to English can have can be seen from a German publisher, Fachverlag Chemie, whose journal *Angewandie Chemie* contained mainly German-language contributions. Because of declining subscription rates, it changed the journal title to *Applied Chemistry* and began publishing in English. The pay-off was impressive as the relaunched journal not only became profitable through an increase in sales, but it also ranked top in its field in terms of the Science Citation Index (SCI) impact factor (Ammon, 2006). This is not an isolated example; important scientific findings tend to be published in English since scientists and researchers understand that only by publishing in English will their discoveries reach an international audience and have a wider impact (Coulmas, 2007).

The founder of the SCI, Eugene Garfield, has further reinforced the status of English by making it clear that databases such as SCI favour documents written in English (Baldauf & Jernudd, 1983). The primary functions of the SCI are to provide a network of relationships among the articles published within a research field and to provide easy access to documents from a large collection of data (Mercer & Di Marco, 2003). Thomson Reuters, the publisher of the English language-based online academic citation service Web of Science, which includes the widely used SCI, Social Sciences Citation Index and Arts and Humanities Citation Index, is based in New York and generates 53 per cent of its revenue from the United States (Thomson Reuters, 2009). Furthermore, editors and board members of international recognised journals, such as the *International Journal of Social Inquiry* (IJSI) which publishes only in English, act as powerful gatekeepers—language planners—since they determine how science is to be reported and published (IJSI, 2007). Thus, globalised science as reflected in the major databases, international journals and academic publications is increasingly in English, while work in other languages is declining.

Globalised Religion

The relationship between globalisation and the spread of religion has its roots in the early years of colonialism. In Asia, Chinese characters were spread to Japan, Korea and Vietnam through religious practices dating back more than 1,000 years. The physical expansion of colonies meant that there was an increase in trade and the flow of people between the nations for both the colonisers and colonised. With this exchange of goods, services and people, there was a diffusion of cultures, values, beliefs and religions because when people moved to a new location, or came into contact, they brought their value systems with them (Park, 2004). For example, the Ottoman Empire (1520–1566) through conquest and trade with managed to spread its empire and Islam across Eastern Europe, North Africa and the Middle East. This spread of religion also implied the simultaneous spread of language since religion is acquired through the medium of language both in written and oral forms (Ahmad, 2007; Khaled, 2007). Language and religion are inter-related as the development of a religion is very much influenced by the growth of the teachings and philosophies of that religion that are embodied in linguistic culture (Schiffman, 1996).

A majority of religions have classical languages—Arabic, Hebrew, Greek, Latin and Pali—and sacred texts in those languages. More recently English and other languages have begun to be used as religious languages. By the early nineteenth century, during the peak of the global expansion by the European countries (i.e. England, France, the Netherlands, Portugal and Spain), Christian missionaries played an important part in spreading the gospel. In England leading nineteenth-century philologists such as Lepsius and Codrington were either missionaries or were heavily involved with missionary societies, and they were highly involved in language planning and policy making. For example, since linguistic diversity makes it difficult for missionaries to share the gospel with the non-believers, in the mid-1950s the first Bishop of Melanesia, Bishop Selwyn of the High Anglican Melanesian Mission, together with his fellow Anglican bishops, wanted to make English the lingua franca of the Pacific. The intention was to create an artificial world that would eliminate linguistic separation. By doing this, these missionaries were basically constructing a new linguistic ecology that promoted the use of English and diminished the importance of native languages (Mühlhäusler, 2000).

The spread of the English language through religion has been further enhanced by the adoption of high-speed information technology in society. For example, in Australia, Christian messages are aired on national television and radio stations (Australia Christian Channel, n.d.). The Internet has also become a popular platform for people of similar beliefs from around the world to come together to engage in religious discussions. The importance of tapping into modern technology in globalising Christianity was highlighted by the Archbishop Pietro Sambi who suggested that Catholic churches should find ways to more effectively make use of the media to spread the gospel to the techno-savvy younger generation (Zukowski, 2009). Even Pope Benedict XVI at the "2009 World Communication's Day confirm[ed] that catechists need to grasp the advantage of these new technologies" (Zukowski, 2009, p. 92). Technology and modern telecommunication have enabled biblical discussions, through international languages such as English, to reach a wider audience than was ever previously possible. Thus, religious organisations can be as dynamic as the religion itself—in this case Christianity—in transporting, planting and disseminating languages (Mühlhäusler & Mühlhäusler, 2005). However, while religions have been and continue to be powerful forces for globalising languages, there are cases, e.g. Guaraní in Paraguay (Gynan, 2007), the support for Hanguel writing in Korea (de Silva, 2008), or the work of the Summer Institute of Linguistics, where missionary work has supported the survival of local languages and writing systems.

Globalised Media

Over the years, the media has become an integral part of society and has provided de facto standards for languages and their use. Crystal (2003) notes that English has been used in the press for more than 340 years since the publication of early British newspapers such as the *London Gazette* (1666) and *Lloyd's News* (1696). Subsequently, in America the *Boston News-Letter* (1704) and the *New York City Daily Advertiser* (1785) were published mainly for the domestic market. The English and Americans had a head start on promulgating their language through the media as their European counterparts suffered from strict censorship and other restrictions. Other media-related inventions such as the telegraph and the radio were early adopters of English, and this is still is evident today as regional organisations such as the European Broadcasting Union and the Asia-Pacific Broadcasting Union use English as their official language (Crystal, 2003). International networks, such as the British Broadcasting Corporation (BBC), Columbia Broadcasting System (CBS) and the Cable News Network (CNN)—which still dominates the cable news on the television, radio and the Internet—also use English (Herman & McChesney, 1997).

The increase in the circulation of foreign made goods has made American products, such as Coca-Cola, Kodak, Disney and McDonald's popular international icons. This globalisation of products from many countries is based on the advertising of products through the media. According to Herman and McChesney (1997), it was American advertisement agencies that pioneered the global advertising movement, and have been a factor in the promotion of the English language through the media. Although advertisements are available in all languages, they often contain English words or phrases to add prestige or a positive emotional response (Martin, 2007). Japanese products that are exported overseas, including international brands such as National, Sony and Toshiba, come with English instructions to cater for the English-speaking countries to which they are exported. In the entertainment industry, blockbuster movies are often in English (e.g. Hollywood films such as *Titanic* and *Star Wars*) and attract an international audience (Crystal, 2003). The American-based global film industry, including firms such as Columbia, Paramount, United Artists and Warner Brothers, is still home to the world's major film producers (Herman & McChesney, 1997).

English songs tend to have an international appeal and artists such as Ricky Martin, a Puerto Rican who originally sang in Spanish, only became an international pop star after he started singing in English. In addition, the availability of Music Television (MTV), an American cable television service, iTunes and online music digital downloads through the computer or mobile phone have allowed English songs to reach a wider audience when compared to those of other languages that have a more restricted audience. The emergence of the Internet has further strengthened the status and importance of English language. America is currently the leading producer of computer hardware and software from technology giants, such as Microsoft and Apple. Furthermore, large amounts of information, data and computer software are written in English with more than 300 million users connected to English language resources (Bollag, 2000). The World Wide Web (WWW), the basic system of the Internet servers, was invented by Tim Berners-Lee, a British scientist living in the United States (BBC News, 2003). YouTube, a popular website that allows original videos to be uploaded and viewed by an international audience was also created by an American. Furthermore, well-known search engines Yahoo and Google were developed by the Americans (Google, 2009; Yahoo!, 2005). These globalised English language media ensure that English is promoted and used more widely than other languages.

Nevertheless, as the media becomes globalised and the technology is more readily available, other languages are also making their presence felt. For example, the rise of China has resulted in a growing demand for information about China and for Chinese language media. Presently, there are about 500 newspapers, 200 magazines, 70 radio stations and 50 television stations overseas (China Internet Information Center, 2004). It was estimated that the number of Chinese language users has had a greater proportional increase in the past seven years than English language users who only had 150 per cent growth (Virtual China, 2007). In addition, the Chinese also have created their own version of YouTube known as Tudou, currently the largest video sharing platform in China, and this website also is viewed by many overseas Chinese (Tudou.com, 2005–2009). Popular Chinese search engines including Baidu.com, QQ.com and sina.com.cn now attract a lot of Chinese users (Virtual China, 2007). In the entertainment industry, international programmes including those from Korea and Japan are slowly making inroads into world markets. For example, the Korean drama serials *Dae Jang Geum* and Japanese anime such as *Pokemon* are popular not only in Asian communities but also in Western countries.

The evidence outlined in this section suggests that the media is a major contributor to informal LPP as it caters for the demand for information. Although there are resources and information available in other languages, language use is related to power and English remains the dominant language and medium of communication on the Internet and in the media as America is still the strongest player in the market. However, as the media has become more globalised, it has also allowed other languages to flourish and find niche markets, particularly China, which looks like the next emerging giant in the globalised market. In the future, English may not be as dominant a language, but instead may be one of a group of major international languages. Thus, the globalised media can provide an alternative linguistic voice for minorities to present their views, cultures and values to the rest of the world.

Globalised Military

The military has always been a place where language training has occurred, and therefore a site for language planning. In Taiwan, for example, after its return to China in 1945, all young males were required to do military service, and were taught Mandarin as part of that training, effectively ensuring the re-spread of the language (Tsao, 2008). On the other hand, military forces have long used mercenaries (e.g. the Gurkha regiments from Nepal in the British army (Eagle, 2008)) so issues of language have frequently been an internal command problem. However, as the world has become increasingly globalised, language planning in the military has become more complicated as there are increasingly more cooperative military operations between the nations that require liaison and communication. This raises the question of what language(s) and strategies do they use to communicate with one another?

According to Spolsky (2009), in a multilingual military formation where a regiment is made up of different nationalities, commands and messages are often passed from the senior officers to the soldiers through a "middleman". These middlemen are usually the sergeants who are able to understand the languages from both sides. For example, during the colonial days in Singapore, the commanding officers were usually British while the regiment would be made up of the local Singaporeans (Ministry of Defence, Singapore, 2008). Effective communication across the different levels depended on the orders given by the commanding officers being translated from English to the vernacular languages by the sergeants as local soldiers were not able to understand English. In contrast, if the regiment consists of numerous units from different countries, such a UN Peacekeeping Force, the commanders of the each unit are expected to speak the common language, which in the case of the UN is at least in one of the six official languages. Alternatively, they have to ensure that qualified interpreters are available whenever the need arises (Spolsky, 2009).

By way of contrast, the British Council Peacekeeping English Project (PEP) takes a different approach to language planning with English playing an important part in peacekeeping efforts since the government of the United Kingdom funds most of the programmes, with contributions from the governments of Canada, Hungary, the Netherlands and Norway. The PEP helps to develop relevant expertise in some of the key areas to provide the personnel needed for peace support operations, and this is supported by the development of specialised English language courses for the peacekeepers (Crossey, 2008). In addition, Crossey (2008) believes that over the years, peacekeeping missions involving global participation have not only increased but are also better coordinated due to the increasing number of the English language training programmes that were made available to the non-native speakers' national contingents. Presently, the PEP's International Testers of English for the Military (ITEM) group is engaged in designing a proficiency test in an attempt to standardise the programme's test for use in worldwide military peacekeeping efforts. When the programme is completed and adopted, English is likely to become the dominant language used in global peacekeeping operations. In this situation, the decision to choose English as the target language of communication was very strongly influenced by the UK government's sponsorship of these programmes.

A recent phenomenon in international military operations is the increased participation of China in UN peacekeeping operations. However, it has been reported that China is experiencing difficulties in acquiring the necessary language skills (Crisis Group, 2009), as most of the Chinese military structure only knows how to communicate in Mandarin. Thus, in this situation of increasing participation, how do the Chinese communicate with the other participating states? Approaches to this problem would include establishing a common language, most likely English, through language training programmes, or the use of interpreters since the aim of language planning in this context is for the Chinese and other participating states to work more efficiently together. These examples from China and the UK suggest that language planning efforts in the globalised military operations are highly political and dependent on the power and degree of participation of particular countries in international military involvement.

Nevertheless, some have argued that knowing English is no longer enough to operate successfully in globalised military operations. In particular, Pratt (2004) has argued that in the United States, monolingualism needs to give way to bilingualism or even trilingualism if the US desires to maintain a close relationship with the rest of the world and have access to sources of military intelligence. She believes that national security activities in US require people who have an advanced knowledge of other languages and cultures. She argues that much effort is needed to change previous US monolingual policies, public attitudes and an education that trivialises language learning. Currently, funds are given to language schools to design programmes to train military personnel for defence-related work in strategic languages. Unlike the PEP project where English is strongly promoted and endorsed, in the US, there is a trend toward language learning. Professionals and service people of all kinds are encouraged to learn a different language. In the city of Oakland, Spanish and Chinese are recognised as the official second languages (Pratt, 2004). This suggests that in the future the status of English could be shared by other languages especially as the US spends far more in the defence sector than other countries (BBC News, 2008), and therefore it has the power to alter the current linguistic structure of the military operations. From this perspective, governments play an important role in determining the types of languages learned in the society, including the military, since they hold the power to provide the relevant funding and assistance.

Norms and Actors

When the global topics covered in this chapter are examined as a group, it is evident that there are various players and actors involved in language planning, and that they play a critical role in the initiation and implementation of language policies (see Figure 57.1; also see Zhao, Chapter 54, this volume). These planning and policy decisions subsequently set the norms and standards for the languages being planned, particularly and increasingly for the English language.

Figure 57.1 illustrates the fact that language policies and planning are largely directed by a number of actors in the market, which at the international level consists of the groups that have been the focus of this chapter. These actors wield massive power that influences and determines the types of languages used through specific school curriculum, government policies, programmes, sponsorships, funds, investments, specific rules and requirements or religious and ideological beliefs. At the national level, and sometimes at the state or district levels, the actors are bodies that carry out policies in response to requirements at least partially determined by international actors. While governments can reorder and reassemble language priorities to meet local needs, and individual actors have the

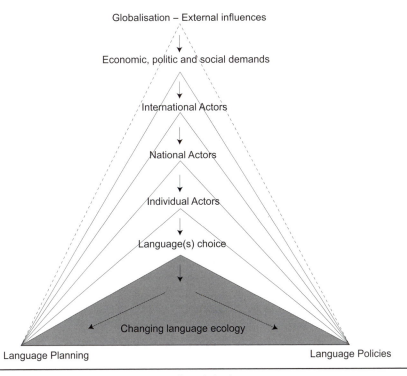

Figure 57.1 An overview of the players and actors in language policy and planning

power of individual choice—that is, the ability to decide which language(s) to use or to resist, as Figure 57.1 indicates, the language choices made by these actors are influenced by external forces. The context and impact of globalisation affects the economic, political and social needs of a country, and this effect cascades down to the various actors at increasingly local levels.

Summary and Conclusion

In this chapter we argue that globalisation has created a new powerful level of LPP that is carried out mainly indirectly through a range of high level and sometimes "colonial" activities. As our discussion has shown, LPP made at the international or national level is often tied to the external and wider demands of the society, and these demands are influenced by global needs. In this context, English has been regarded by many as the "ideal" globalised language due to early colonisation and the current position of the US, which has enabled English to spread and infiltrate into almost every aspect of societies—institutions, agencies, business, education, science, religion, the media and the military. Moreover, the actors in these various organisations have responded to these global needs and changes by setting up policies, rules and regulations, and by producing texts that further enhance the position of global languages, especially English as evidenced in its use by the EU, the UN, UNESCO, global news and international scientific journals. Furthermore, non-English-speaking countries are also learning English to equip themselves with the language skills needed to tap into the globalised network of predominately English language information.

Nevertheless, globalisation has also created other phenomenon. At the micro and local level, the process of globalisation has enabled the hybridisation of different languages thus creating new varieties of languages and possibilities for language use. Individual actors have the choice not only to decide which languages to use or resist, but how they are used in local contexts. For example, hybrid languages such as Singlish and Manglish can be seen as a natural response to the spread of English language and the need for local identity. These new varieties of languages allow countries to create their own linguistic identities through these new varieties, despite the intrusion of standard English in their societies. Another phenomenon that is occurring is that these new varieties not only have developed a diverse language ecology, but together with the advancement of technology are also creating a new form of language—which some have called ELF or Globalish. This new emergence complicates language planning and policy because it is a "shared" language, making the determination of shared norms and standards more complex. However, LPP is very much determined by the notion of "practically", as well as notions of power. Countries or groups that weld the most power will tend to have a stronger influence in the construction of this new language and how it should be used. This raises the question of whether there is a need (or even the possibility) for explicit planning at the global level or whether it is best left to be done on an ad hoc basis.

Note

1. While *Hanban* says on its English website that it is a non-governmental organisation, this term is ambiguous in the People's Republic of China context where most activities involve the state. "*Hanban*" probably stands for *Guowuyuan* (State Council) *Guojia* (State) *Duiwai Hanyu* (Teaching Chinese for Foreigners) *Jiaoxue* (Teaching and Learning) *Lingdao* (Lead) *Bangongshi* (Office).

References

Ahmad, I. (2007). The Muslim world: Its time, continuity and change. *Social Studies Review, 46*(2), 33–38.
Alberta's international education strategy. (2001). Retrieved 17 April 2009 from http://education.alberta.ca/media/316931/intledstrat.pdf.

Albey, M. (2008). *The prodigal tongue: Dispatches from the future of English*. London: William Heinemann.

Altbach, P. G. (2008). The imperial tongue: English as the dominating academic language. *International Educator, 17*(5), 56–59.

Ammon, U. (1995). To what extent is German an international language? In P. Stevenson (Ed.), *The German language and the real world: Sociolinguistic, cultural and pragmatic perspectives on contemporary German* (pp. 25–54). Oxford: Clarendon Press.

Ammon, U. (2006). Language planning for international scientific communication: An overview of questions and potential solutions. *Current Issues in Language Planning, 7*(1), 1–31. (Electronic version.)

ASEAN Foundation. (2008). Retrieved 18 March 2009 from http://www.aseanfoundation.org.

Ashcroft, B., Griffiths, G. & Tiffin, H. (2002). *The empire writes back: Theory and practice in post-colonial literatures* (2nd ed.).. London: Routledge.

Australia Christian Channel. (n.d.). Schedule. Retrieved 28 April 2009 from http://www.acctv.com.au/schedule.asp.

AVA (Agri-Food and Veterinary Authority of Singapore). (2009). Retrieved 16 April 2009 from http://www.ava.gov.sg/FoodSector/FoodLabelingAdvertisement/.

Baldauf, R. B., Jr, & Jernudd, B. H. (1983). Language of publication as a variable in scientific communication. *Australian Review of Applied Linguistics, 6*(1), 97–108.

Baldauf, R. B., Jr, & Jernudd, B. H. (1986). Aspects of language use in cross-cultural psychology. *Australian Journal of Psychology, 32*(3), 381–392.

BBC News. (2003). Web's inventor gets a knighthood. Retrieved 12 May 2009 from http://news.bbc.co.uk/1/hi/technology/3357073.stm.

BBC News. (2008). Q&A: China's military budget. Retrieved 12 May 2010 from http://news.bbc.co.uk/2/hi/asia-pacific/7277382.stm.

Bollag, B. (2000). The new Latin: English dominates in academe. *The Chronicle of Higher Education, 47*(2), A73.

Bolten, K. (2008). English in Asia, Asian Englishes, and the issue of proficiency. *English Today, 94*(24), 2 June, 3–12. (Electronic version.)

Boufis, C. (2007). The year of the Chinese language. *Scholastic Administr@tor, 7*(1), 23–26. (Electronic version.)

Brutt-Griffler, J. (2002). *World English: A study of its development*. Clevedon: Multilingual Matters.

Chalermpalanupap, T. (1999) ASEAN-10: Meeting the challenges. Retrieved 10 June 2009 from http://www.aseansec.org/2833.htm

Chew, P. G. L. (2009a). Addendum: Schools in the service of society. In I. C. Rotberg (Ed.), *Balancing change and tradition in global education reform* (2nd ed.) (pp. 226–283). Lanham, MD: Scarecrow Education.

Chew, P. G. L. (2009b). *Emergent lingua francas and world orders: The politics and place of English as a world language*. New York: Routledge.

China Internet Information Center. (2004). Chinese media spread global views. Retrieved 10 May 2009 from http://mdjnkj.china.com.cn/english/culture/114489.htm.

Coulmas, F. (2007). English monolingualism in scientific communication and progress in science, good or bad? *AILA Review, 20*, 5–13.

Crisis Group. (2009). China's growing role in UN peacekeeping. Retrieved 8 May 2009 from http://www.crisisgroup.org/en/regions/asia/north-east-asia/china/166-chinas-growing-role-in-un-peacekeeping.aspx.

Cristina, G., Favilla, M. E. & Calaresu, E. (2007). Stereotypes about English as the language of science. *AILA Review, 20*, 28–52.

Crossey, M. (2008). English for global peacekeeping. *Current Issues in Language Planning, 9*(2), 207–218.

Crystal, D. (2003). *English as a global language* (2nd ed.). Cambridge: Cambridge University Press.

De Cock, B. (2006). The European Union and the Organisation Internationale de la Francophonie. *Journal of Language and Politics, 5*(3), 385–413.

de Silva, J. (2008). Missionary contributions toward the revaluation of Hangeul in late nineteenth-century Korea. *International Journal of the Sociology of Language, 192*, 57–74.

Eagle, S. (2008). The language situation in Nepal. In R. B. Kaplan & R. B. Baldauf Jr (Eds.), *Language planning and policy: Asia, Vol 1: Japan, Nepal and Taiwan and Chinese Characters* (pp. 170–225). Bristol: Multilingual Matters.

Éducation, Loisir et Sport, Québec. (2007). Instruction in English in Québec. Retrieved 12 March 2009 from http://www.meq.gouv.qc.ca/daasa/rens/banque/Fiches/F95a.htm.

EuroTunnel: The Channel Tunnel. (2009). Retrieved 2 April 2009 from http://www.eurotunnel.com/ukcp3main.

Fairclough, N. (1992). *Discourse and social change*. Cambridge: Polity Press.

Google. (2009). Google corporate information: Google milestone. Retrieved 11 May 2009 from http://www.google.com/corporate/history.html.

Gottlieb, N. (2009). Japan: Language policy and planning in transition. In R. B. Kaplan and R. B. Baldauf Jr (Eds.), *Language planning and policy: Asia, Vol 1: Japan, Nepal and Taiwan and Chinese Characters* (pp. 102–169). Bristol: Multilingual Matters.

Grabe, W., & Kaplan, R. B. (1986). Science, technology, language and education: Implications for language- and language-in-education planning. *International Journal of the Sociology of Language, 59*, 47–71.

Graddol, D. (2006). *English next.* Plymouth: British Council.

Gynan, S. N. (2007). Language planning and policy in Paraguay. In R. B. Baldauf Jr & R. B. Kaplan (Eds.), *Language planning and policy: Latin America, Vol. 1: Ecuador, Mexico and Paraguay* (pp. 218–283). Bristol: Multilingual Matters.

Hanban. (2001–2009a). Functions of *Hanban.* Retrieved 13 March 2009 from http://english.hanban.edu.cn/hbzn.php (page no longer available).

Hanban. (2001–2009b). Major initiatives. Retrieved 14 March 2009 from http://english.hanban.edu.cn/zdxm.php (page no longer available).

Harzing, A. W. (1999). *Managing the multinationals.* Cheltenham: Edward Elgar.

Herman, E. S., & McChesney, R. W. (1997). *The global media: The new missionaries of corporate capitalism.* London: Cassell.

Herther, N. K. (2009). The changing language of search. *Searcher: The Magazine for Database Professionals,* February, 42–50.

Ikea. (1999–2009). Retrieved 16 April 2009 from http://www.ikea.com/.

IJSI. (2007). Retrieved 23 April 2009 from http://www.socialinquiry.org/.

Jarvis, P. (2007). *Globalisation, lifelong learning and the learning society: Sociological perspectives.* London: Routledge.

Johnson, B. (1995). Some features of maritime telex service communication. *English for Specific Purposes, 14*(2), 127–136.

Kaplan, R. B., & Baldauf, R. B., Jr (2003). *Language and language-in-education planning in the Pacific Basin.* Dordrecht: Kluwer Academic Publishers.

Khaled, M. (2007). Globalization and religion. Conference on Globalization, Conflict and the Experience of Localities, Rome, Italy 28–29 June. Retrieved 19 April 2009 from http://www.isarc47.org/Pages/ISA%20RC47%20Conference/Files/Papers/Khaled.pdf.

Kirkpatrick. A. (2006). Which model of English: Native-speaker, nativized or lingua franca? In R. Rubdy & M. Saraceni (Eds.), *English in the world: Global rules, global roles.* London: Continuum.

Loos, E. (2007). Language policy in an enacted world: The organization of linguistic diversity. *Language Problems & Language Planning, 31*(1), 37–60.

McEntee-Atalianis, L. J. (2006). Geostrategies of interlingualism: Language policy and practice in the International Maritime Organisation, London, UK. *Current Issues in Language Planning, 7*(2&3), 341–358.

Marginson, S. (2006). Notes on globalization and higher education: With some reference to the case of Australia. Retrieved 18 April 2009 from http://www.yorku.ca/yorkint/global/conference/canada/papers/simon-Marginson.pdf.

Marginson, S. (2007). Higher education in the global knowledge economy. Retrieved 18 April 2009 from http://www.cshe.unimelb.edu.au/people/staff_pages?Marginson/Beijing%20Forum%20November%202007.pdf.

Martin, E. (2007). "Frenglish" for sale: Multilingual discourses for addressing today's global consumer. *World Englishes, 26*(2), 170–190.

Masterson, K. (2009). Research and inventions earn big bucks for American Universities. *The Chronicle of Higher Education.* Retrieved 4 March 2009 from http://www.lsuhospitals.org/Media-Relations/InTheNews/01.27.09.pdf.

Matheson, C., & Matheson, D. (2000). Educational spaces and discourses. In C. Matheson & D. Matheson (Eds.), *Educational issues in the learning age* (pp. 1–12). London: Contiuum.

Mercer, R., & Di Marco, C. (2003). The importance of fine-grained cute phrases in scientific citations. *Proceedings of the Conference of the Canadian Society for the Computational Studies of Intelligence (CSCSI), 2003.* Retrieved 23 April 2009 from http://ai.uwaterloo.ca/cdimarco/pdf/publications/CSCSI2003.pdf.

Ministry of Defence, Singapore. (2008). 1957—Our first battalion. Retrieved 6 May 2009 from http://www.mindef.gov.sg/imindef/about_us/history/birth_of_saf/v02n11_history.html.

MOE. (2010). English language GCE Ordinary level (Syllabus 1127). Retrieved 28 September 2009 from http://www.seab.gov.sg/oLevel/syllabus/1127_2010.pdf.

MSF. (2009). Retrieved 3 April 2009 from http://www.doctorswithoutborders.org.

MSF, Canada. (n.d.). Retrieved 6 April 2009 from http://www.msf.ca.

Mufwene, S. S. (2002). Colonisation, globalisation, and the future of languages in the twenty-first century. *MOST Journal on Multicultural Societies, 4*(2). (Electronic version.)

Mühlhäusler, B. S., & Mühlhäusler, P. (2005). Simple English in the South Seas Evangelical mission: Social context and linguistic attributes. *Language Problems & Language Planning, 29*(1), 1–30.

Mühlhäusler, P. (2000). Language planning and language ecology. *Current Issues in Language Planning, 1*(3), 306–367.

OIF. (2000–2009). Membership—A proactive approach. Retrieved 3 March 2009 from http://translate.google.com/translate?hl=en&sl=fr&u=http://www.francophonie.org/&ei=nbQUSq7gCpeQ6AOnkeWsCg&sa=X&oi=translate&resnum=1&ct=result&prev=/search%3Fq%3Dorganisation%2Binternationale%2Bde%2Bla%2Bfrancophonie%26hl%3Den.

Park, C. (2004). Religion and geography. In J. R. Hinnells (Ed.), *Routledge companion to the study of religion* (pp. 439–455). London: Routledge.

Phillipson, R. (2003). *English-only Europe? Changing language policy.* London: Routledge.

Pratt, M. L. (2004). Language and national security: Making a new public commitment. *The Modern Language Journal, 88*(2), 289–291.

Reagan, T. (2005). Does language really exist? In *Critical questions, critical perspectives: Language and the second language educator* (pp. 1–16). Greenwich, CT: Information Age Publishing.

Schaarschmidt, G. (1996). Policespeak: Police communication and language and the Channel Tunnel; English-French Lexicon. *The Social Science Journal, 33*(3), 337. (Electronic source.)

Schiffman, H. F. (1996). Religion, myth and linguistic culture. In *Linguistic culture and language policy* (pp. 55–74). London and New York: Routledge.

Seidlhofer, B. (2005). Key concepts in ELT: English as a lingua franca. *ELT Journal, 59*(4), 339–341.

Sidhu, R. (2009). *Universities and globalization: To market, to market.* Mahwah, NJ; Lawrence Erlbaum Associates.

Sim. C. Y. (2009). China expands language network abroad. *The Straits Times*, 13 March, p. 6, Prime News.

Singapore Education. (2008). Universities. Retrieved 18 April 2009 from http://www.singaporeedu.gov.sg/htm/stu/stu0107.htm.

Sirkin, H. L., Hemerling, J. W., Bhattacharya, A. K. & Butman, J. (2008). *Globality: Competing with everyone from everywhere for everything.* New York: Business Plus.

Spinks, N., & Wells, B. (1997). Intercultural communication: A key element in global strategies. *Career Development International, 2*(6), 287–292.

Spolsky, B. (2009). *Language management.* Cambridge: Cambridge University Press.

Steck, H. (2003). Corporatization of the university: Seeking conceptual clarity. *Annals of the American Academy of Political and Social Science*, 585, *Higher Education in the Twenty-First Century*, 66–83. (Electronic source.)

Steger, M. (2003). *Globalization: A very short introduction.* New York: Oxford University Press.

Swift, J. S. (1991). Foreign language ability and international marketing. *European Journal of Marketing, 25*(12), 36–49.

Tata Technologies. (2009). Retrieved 16 April 2009 from http://www.tatatechnologies.com/global/news_view.aspx?NewsCode=6&MenuCode=2.

Thomson Reuters. (2009). Retrieved 21 April 2009 from http://www.thomsonreuters.com/about/.

Tsao, F.-f. (2008). The language planning situation in Taiwan. In R. B. Kaplan & R. B. Baldauf Jr (Eds.), *Language planning and policy: Asia, Vol 1: Japan, Nepal and Taiwan and Chinese Characters* (pp. 237–284). Bristol: Multilingual Matters.

Tudou.com. (2005–2009). About Tudou. Retrieved 11 May 2009 from http://www.tudou.com/aboutus/.

UNESCO. (1995–2009). Retrieved 20 March 2009 from http://portal.unesco.org/en/ev.php-URL_ID=29008&URL_DO=DO_TOPIC&URL_SECTION=201.html.

UNESCO. (2004). Higher education in a globalized society: UNESCO education position paper. Retrieved 19 April from http://unesdoc.unesco.org/images/0013/001362/136247e.pdf.

van Els, T. (2005). Multilingualism in the European Union. *International Journal of Applied Linguistics, 15*(3), 263–281.

Virtual China. (2007). The future of the Chinese language Internet. Retrieved 11 May 2009 from http://www.iftf.org/system/files/deliverables/SR-1129+virtual+china.pdf.

Welch, D. E., Welch, L. S. & Marschan-Piekkari, R. (2001). The persistent impact of language on global operations. *Prometheus, 19*(3), 194–209.

Yahoo! (2005). Yahoo! Media relations: The history of Yahoo!—How it all started. Retrieved 11 May 2009 from http://docs.yahoo.com/info/misc/history.html.

Yoshihara, H. (1999). Global operations managed by Japanese in Japanese. *TIEB Kobe Working Paper*, 108.

Zukowski, A. A. (2009). Digital catechesis: New thresholds into the future. *Momentum, 40*(1), 92. (Electronic version.)

List of Contributors

Richard B. Baldauf Jr
University of Queensland, Australia

Robert Bayley
University of California, Davis, USA

Barbara Birch
California State University, Fresno, USA

María Estela Brisk
Boston College, USA

James Dean Brown
University of Hawai'i at Mānoa, USA

Anne Burns
Aston University, UK/University of New South
    Wales, Australia

Carol Chapelle
Iowa State University, USA

Julie Choi
University of Technology, Sydney, Australia

Donna Christian
Center for Applied Linguistics, USA

Catherine Chua Siew Kheng
National Institute of Education, Nanyang
    Technological University, Singapore

Dorothy M. Chun
University of California, Santa Barbara, USA

Matthew Clarke
University of New South Wales, Australia

Andrew D. Cohen
University of Minnesota, USA

Vivian Cook
Newcastle University, UK

Martin Cortazzi
University of Warwick, UK

Robert DeKeyser
University of Maryland, USA

Reginald D'Silva
University of British Columbia, Canada

Karen Dooley
Queensland University of Technology, Australia

Rod Ellis
University of Auckland, New Zealand

Dana Ferris
University of California, Davis, USA

Lee Gunderson
University of British Columbia, Canada

Liz Hamp-Lyons
University of Nottingham, UK

Linda Harklau
University of Georgia, USA

Eli Hinkel
Seattle University, USA

Joan Jamieson
Northern Arizona University, USA

Lixian Jin
De Montfort University, UK

Yamuna Kachru
University of Illinois, Urbana-Champaign
(Emerita), USA

Nkonko M. Kamwangamalu
Howard University, USA

Robert B. Kaplan
University of Southern California (Emeritus),
USA

Joel Koeth
University of Maryland, USA

Juliet Langman
The University of Texas at San Antonio, USA

James P. Lantolf
Pennsylvania State University, USA

Anthony J. Liddicoat
University of South Australia, Australia

William Littlewood
Hong Kong Institute of Education, China

Virginia LoCastro
University of Florida, USA

Shawn Loewen
Michigan State University, USA

Allan Luke
Queensland University of Technology, Australia

Roy Lyster
McGill University, Canada

Tony McEnery
Lancaster University, UK

Sandra Lee McKay
San Francisco State University, USA

Bernard A. Mohan
University of British Columbia (Emeritus)/
Canada and King's College London, UK

Brian Morgan
Glendon College/York University, UK

Carmen Muñoz
University of Barcelona, Spain

Denise E. Murray
Macquarie University (Emerita), Australia

I. S. P. Nation
Victoria University of Wellington, New Zealand

Jiří Nekvapil
Charles University, Czech Republic

David Nunan
University of Hong Kong, China/Anaheim
University, USA

Dennis Murphy Odo
University of British Columbia, Canada

Brian Paltridge
University of Sydney, Australia

Teresa Pica
University of Pennsylvania, USA

James E. Purpura
Teachers College, Columbia University, USA

Keith Richards
University of Warwick, UK

Steven J. Ross
University of Maryland, College Park, USA

Rob Schoonen
University of Amsterdam, The Netherlands

Paul Seedhouse
Newcastle University, UK

Younghee Sheen
American University, USA

Sandra Silberstein
University of Washington, USA

David Singleton
Trinity College, Dublin, Ireland

Sue Starfield
University of New South Wales, Australia

James W. Tollefson
International Christian University, Japan

Amy B. M. Tsui
University of Hong Kong, China

Penny Ur
Oranim Academic College of Education, Israel

Leo van Lier
Monterey Institute of International Studies, USA

Larry Vandergrift
University of Ottawa, Canada

Stuart Webb
Victoria University of Wellington, New Zealand

Richard Xiao
Edge Hill University, UK

Richard F. Young
University of Wisconsin-Madison, USA

Shouhui Zhao
National Institute of Education, Nanyang Technological University, Singapore

Index